Dedicated To
BARRETT H. CLARK
in memory of his contribution
to the American drama and theater education

WORLD DRAMA

Ancient Greece, Rome, India, China,
Japan; Medieval Europe, and England

AN ANTHOLOGY EDITED BY
BARRETT H. CLARK

WITHDRAWN

DOVER PUBLICATIONS INC.

INTRODUCTION

The two volumes, *World Drama,* constitute a collection that is the first of its kind in English to offer a panoramic view of the dramatic achievement of the world from the earliest epoch of which any record exists to the beginning of the contemporary drama—which means the first of the modern plays of Ibsen. The modern period, from Ibsen to the present day, is well covered by fifty other collections. Aside from a very few dramatists who by universal consent could not be omitted from any such work as this, I have selected the plays of each country and epoch largely because they appeal to the mind of today, without attempting to exhibit in my table of contents a colorless reflection of the majority vote of the academic world. But in determining which nations and ages should be included I have been guided largely by historical considerations: in other words, ancient Greece could not possibly be left out, while the United States could not be admitted: our own country—until only a few years ago—had added nothing to the store of world drama. As for including a play of Shakespeare's, that would be a waste of good space: his presence may be taken for granted. I have included the living plays of the ages rather than their too glibly acknowledged masterpieces, preferring that students should read a few plays that may not take rank as supreme masterpieces to their praising the highest and being bored by them. I have tried my best not to include a single play in this book that has failed to move or delight me, in the hope that my pleasure may be shared by others; and in order to furnish historical data that has not before found its way into any anthology and to show that drama is not an exclusively literary affair, I have gone out of my way to print specimens of the informal folk drama that has undoubtedly exercised a far wider influence over the development of public taste (as well as the written drama) than we give it credit for. The Japanese farce *Abstraction,* the medieval French play of *The Wise Virgins and the Foolish Virgins,* the Italian Commedia dell'Arte *The Portrait,* and *The Play of St. George,* all belong in the picture I have tried to compose, because for every Euripides and every Shakespeare there existed a hundred humble playmakers whose very names are lost to us.

I hope therefore that the inclusion of such plays will give students the idea that drama at its best is a reflection of many phases of life; that the past as shown on the boards of the theater is not alone concerned with kings and great men, but with peasants and mechanics, saints and sinners; that it is not the exclusive province of fine writers but of inspired clowns, mountebanks and strolling mummers.

Of all the playwrights who have a place in this collection, Seneca alone is exceptional, in that it is not certain that his plays were actually written to be acted. But these have been so influential on the development of the drama of subsequent times that I have considered it wise to include one of the most brilliant examples of his extraordinary art.

To make my panorama as varied, as full and as colorful as the vast subject it aims to exhibit, I have gone to some trouble to have several plays translated that have never before been available to readers of English; others have been rescued from obscure or forgotten books or periodicals and restored to their proper places. With the assistance of generous and gifted scholars and able translators I am able to offer for the first time an authentic version of what is probably the greatest—certainly the most appealing— of Chinese plays, *The Chalk Circle*. The translator of that play has also provided me with a version of one of the most characteristic examples of the Italian improvised comedy, *The Portrait*. The Italian folk comedy *Bilora* and the French miracle play of *The Wise Virgins and the Foolish Virgins* are likewise for the first time made available in English translations. The *Adam* has not hitherto been accessible except in a back number of a scholarly university publication; *Abstraction* is reprinted from a collection that has for many years been out of print, and the same is true of several other items in the table of contents. The translations of *The Cave of Salamanca* and *Jeppe of the Hill* were made especially for these volumes; while the translations of *The King, the Greatest Alcalde, The Demi-Monde,* and *M. Poirier's Son-in-Law* were completely revised.

Taken as a whole, then, the plays in *World Drama* proclaim the never-ending stream of vital energy that underlies every form of artistic creation; they are a pageant of the life of man.

As such I am going to let them tell their own story, without comment. The student who wants to inquire into the background that produced these plays may refer to such books as Sheldon Cheney's *The Theater;* R. J. Taylor's *Story of the Drama;* and Thomas Wood Stevens' *The Theatre: From Athens to Broadway.*

B. H. C.

CONTENTS

PROMETHEUS BOUND

By ÆSCHYLUS

Produced at Athens, 468 or 466 B.C.

TRANSLATED BY J. S. BLACKIE

CHARACTERS

MIGHT and FORCE, *Ministers of Jove*
HEPHAESTUS or VULCAN, *the God of Fire*
PROMETHEUS, *Son of Iapetus, a Titan*
CHORUS OF OCEANIDES
OCEANUS
Io, *Daughter of* INACHUS, *King of Argos*
HERMES, *Messenger of the Gods*

SCENE—*A Rocky Desert in European Scythia.*

[*Enter* MIGHT *and* FORCE, *leading in* PRO-METHEUS; HEPHAESTUS, *with chains.*]
MIGHT. At length the utmost bound of Earth we've reached,
This Scythian soil, this wild untrodden waste.
Hephaestus now Jove's high behests demand
Thy care; to these steep cliffy rocks bind down
With close-linked chains of during adamant
This daring wretch. For he the bright-rayed fire,
Mother of arts, flower of thy potency,
Filched from the gods, and gave to mortals. Here,
Just guerdon of his sin shall find him; here
Let his pride learn to bow to Jove supreme,

And love men well, but love them not too much.
HEPHAESTUS. Ye twain, rude Might and Force, have done your work
To the perfect end; but I—my heart shrinks back
From the harsh task to nail a kindred god
To this storm-battered crag. Yet dare I must.
Where Jove commands, whoso neglects rebels,
And pays the traitor's fine. High-counselled son
Of right-decreeing Themis, I force myself
No less than thee, when to this friendless rock
With iron bonds I chain thee, where nor shape
Nor voice of wandering mortal shall relieve

1

Thy lonely watch; but the fierce-burning
sun
Shall parch and bleach thy fresh com-
plexion. Thou,
When motley-mantled Night hath hid the
day,
Shalt greet the darkness, with how short a
joy!
For the morn's sun the nightly dew shall
scatter,
And thou be pierced again with the same
pricks
Of endless woe—and saviour shall be none.
Such fruits thy forward love to men hath
wrought thee.
Thyself a god, the wrath of gods to thee
Seemed little, and to men thou didst dis-
pense
Forbidden gifts. For this thou shalt keep
watch
On this delightless rock, fixed and erect,
With lid unsleeping, and with knee un-
bent.
Alas! what groans and wails shalt thou
pour forth
Fruitless. Jove is not weak that he
should bend;
For young authority must ever be
Harsh and severe.

MIGHT.　　Enough of words and tears.
This god, whom all the gods detest, wilt
thou
Not hate, thou, whom his impious larceny
Did chiefly injure?

HEPHAESTUS.　　But, my friend, my
kinsman—

MIGHT. True, that respect; but the
dread father's word
Respect much more. Jove's word respect
and fear.

HEPHAESTUS. Harsh is thy nature, and
thy heart is full
Of pitiless daring.

MIGHT.　　　　Tears were wasted here,
And labour lost is all concern for him.

HEPHAESTUS. O thrice-cursed trade, that
e'er my hand should use it!

MIGHT. Curse not thy craft; the cun-
ning of thy hand
Makes not his woes; he made them for
himself.

HEPHAESTUS. Would that some other
hand had drawn the lot
To do this deed!

MIGHT.　　All things may be, but this
To dictate to the gods. There's one that's
free,
One only: Jove.

HEPHAESTUS. I know it, and am dumb.

MIGHT. Then gird thee to the work,
chain down the culprit,
Lest Jove thy laggard zeal behold, and
blame.

HEPHAESTUS. The irons here are ready.

MIGHT.　　　　　　Take them, and
strike
Stout blows with the hammer; nail him
to the rock.

HEPHAESTUS. The work speeds well, and
lingers not.

MIGHT.　　　　Strike! strike!
With ring, and clamp, and wedge make
sure the work.
He hath a subtle wit will find itself
A way where way is none.

HEPHAESTUS.　　　　This arm is fast.

MIGHT. Then clasp this other. Let the
sophist know,
Against great Jove how dull a thing is
wit.

HEPHAESTUS. None but the victim can
reprove my zeal.

MIGHT. Now take this adamantine bolt,
and force
Its point resistless through his rebel
breast.

HEPHAESTUS. Alas! alas! Prometheus,
but I pity thee!

MIGHT. Dost lag again, and for Jove's
enemies weep
Fond tears? Beware thou have no cause
to weep
Tears for thyself.

HEPHAESTUS.　　Thou see'st no sightly
sight
For eyes to look on.

MIGHT.　　　　I behold a sower
Reaping what thing he sow. But take
these thongs,
And bind his sides withal.

HEPHAESTUS.　　　　I must! I must!
Nor needs thy urging.

MIGHT.   Nay, but I will urge,
Command, and bellow in thine ear! Proceed,
Lower—yet lower—and with these iron rings
Enclasp his legs.
HEPHAESTUS.   'Tis done, and quickly done.
MIGHT. Now pierce his feet through with these nails. Strike hard!
There's one will sternly prove thy work, and thee.
HEPHAESTUS. Harsh is thy tongue, and, like thy nature, hard.
MIGHT. Art thou a weakling, do not therefore blame
The firm harsh-fronted will that suits my office.
HEPHAESTUS. Let us away. He's fettered limb and thew.
MIGHT. There lie, and feed thy pride on this bare rock,
Filching gods' gifts for mortal men. What man
Shall free thee from these woes? Thou hast been called
In vain the Provident: had thy soul possessed
The virtue of thy name, thou hadst foreseen
These cunning toils, and hadst unwound thee from them.
    [Exeunt all, except PROMETHEUS, who is left chained.]
PROMETHEUS. O divine ether, and swift-winged winds,
And river-fountains, and of ocean waves
The multitudinous laughter, and thou Earth,
Boon mother of us all, and thou bright round
Of the all-seeing Sun, you I invoke!
Behold what ignominy of causeless wrongs
I suffer from the gods, myself a god.
    See what piercing pains shall goad me
Through long ages myriad-numbered!
With such wrongful chains hath bound me
This new leader of the gods.
Ah me! present woes and future

I bemoan. O! when, O! when
Shall the just redemption dawn?
Yet why thus prate? I know what ills await me.
No unexpected torture can surprise
My soul prophetic; and with quiet mind
We all must bear our portioned fate, nor idly
Court battle with a strong necessity.
Alas! alas! 'tis hard to speak to the winds;
Still harder to be dumb! my well-deservings
To mortal men are all the offence that bowed me
Beneath this yoke. The secret fount of fire
I sought, and found, and in a reed concealed it;
Whence arts have sprung to man, and life hath drawn
Rich store of comforts. For such deed I suffer
These bonds, in the broad eye of gracious day,
Here crucified. Ah me! ah me! who comes?
What sound, what viewless breath, thus taints the air,
God sent, or mortal, or of mingled kind?
What errant traveller ill-sped comes to view
This naked ridge of extreme Earth, and me?
Whoe'er thou art, a hapless god thou see'st
Nailed to this crag; the foe of Jove thou see'st.
Him thou see'st, whom all the Immortals
Whoso tread the Olympian threshold,
Name with hatred; thou beholdest
Man's best friend, and, therefore, hated
    For excess of love.
Hark, again! I hear the whirring
As of winged birds approaching;
With the light strokes of their pinions
Ether pipes ill-boding whispers!—
Alas! alas! that I should fear
Each breath that nears me.
[The OCEANIDES approach, borne through the air in a winged car.]

STROPHE 1

CHORUS. Fear nothing; for a friendly
band approaches;
Fleet rivalry of wings
Oar'd us to this far height, with hard con-
sent
Wrung from our careful sire
The winds swift-sweeping bore me: for I
heard
The harsh hammer's note deep deep in
ocean caves,
And, throwing virgin shame aside, unshod
The winged car I mounted.
PROMETHEUS. Ah! ah!
Daughters of prolific Tethys,
And of ancient father Ocean,
With his sleepless current whirling
Round the firm ball of the globe.
Look! with rueful eyes behold me
Nailed by adamantine rivets,
Keeping weary watch unenvied
On this tempest-rifted rock!

ANTISTROPHE 1

CHORUS. I look, Prometheus; and a
tearful cloud
My woeful sight bedims,
To see thy goodliest form with insult
chained,
In adamantine bonds,
To this bare crag, where pinching airs
shall blast thee.
New gods now hold the helm of Heaven;
new laws
Mark Jove's unrighteous rule; the giant
trace
Of Titan times hath vanished.
PROMETHEUS. Deep in death-receiving
Hades
Had he bound me, had he whelmed me
In Tartarean pit, unfathomed,
Fettered with unyielding bonds!
Then nor god nor man had feasted
Eyes of triumph on my wrongs,
Nor I, thus swung in middle ether,
Moved the laughter of my foes.

STROPHE 2

CHORUS. Which of the gods hath heart
so hard

To mock thy woes? Who will withhold
The fellow-feeling and the tear,
Save only Jove. But he doth nurse
Strong wrath within his stubborn breast,
And holds all Heaven in awe.
Nor will he cease till his hot rage is
glutted,
Or some new venture shakes his stable
throne.
PROMETHEUS. By my Titan soul, I swear
it!
Though with harsh chains now he mocks
me,
Even now the hour is ripening,
When this haughty lord of Heaven
Shall embrace my knees, beseeching
Me to unveil the new-forged counsels
That shall hurl him from his throne.
But no honey-tongued persuasion,
No smooth words of artful charming,
No stout threats shall loose my tongue,
Till he loose these bonds of insult,
And himself make just atonement
For injustice done to me.

ANTISTROPHE 2

CHORUS. Thou art a bold man, and de-
fiest
The keenest pangs to force thy will.
With a most unreined tongue thou speak-
est;
But me—sharp fear hath pierced my
heart.
I fear for thee: and of thy woes
The distant, doubtful end
I see not. O, 'tis hard, most hard to reach
The heart of Jove! prayer beats his ear in
vain.
PROMETHEUS. Harsh is Jove, I know—
he frameth
Justice for himself; but soon,
When the destined arm o'ertakes him,
He shall tremble as a child.
He shall smooth his bristling anger,
Courting friendship shunned before,
More importunate to unbind me
Than impatient I of bonds.
CHORUS. Speak now, and let us know
the whole offence
Jove charges thee withal; for which he
seized,

And with dishonour and dire insult loads thee.
Unfold the tale; unless, perhaps, such sorrow
Irks thee to tell.
PROMETHEUS. To tell or not to tell
Irks me the same; which way I turn is pain.
When first the gods their fatal strife began,
And insurrection raged in Heaven—some striving
To cast old Kronos from his hoary throne,
That Jove might reign, and others to crush i' the bud
His swelling mastery—I wise counsel gave
To the Titans, sons of primal Heaven and Earth;
But gave in vain. Their dauntless stubborn souls
Spurned gentle ways, and patient-working wiles,
Weening swift triumph with a blow. But me,
My mother Themis, not once but oft, and Earth
(One shape of various names), prophetic told
That violence and rude strength in such a strife
Were vain—craft haply might prevail. This lesson
I taught the haughty Titans, but they deigned
Scarce with contempt to hear my prudent words.
Thus baffled in my plans, I deemed it best,
As things then were, leagued with my mother Themis,
To accept Jove's proffered friendship. By my counsels
From his primeval throne was Kronos hurled
Into the pit Tartarean, dark, profound,
With all his troop of friends. Such was the kindness
From me received by him who now doth hold
The masterdom of Heaven; these the rewards

Of my great zeal: for so it hath been ever.
Suspicion's a disease that cleaves to tyrants,
And they who love most are the first suspected.
As for your question, for what present fault
I bear the wrong that now afflicts me, hear.
Soon as he sat on his ancestral throne
He called the gods together, and assigned
To each his fair allotment, and his sphere
Of sway supreme; but, ah! for wretched man!
To him nor part nor portion fell: Jove vowed
To blot his memory from the Earth, and mould
The race anew. I only of the gods
Thwarted his will; and, but for my strong aid,
Hades had whelmed, and hopeless ruin swamped
All men that breathe. Such were my crimes: these pains
Grievous to suffer, pitiful to behold,
Were purchased thus; and mercy's now denied
To him whose crime was mercy to mankind:
And here I lie, in cunning torment stretched,
A spectacle inglorious to Jove.
CHORUS. An iron-heart were his, and flinty hard,
Who on thy woes could look without a tear,
Prometheus; I had liefer not so seen thee,
And seeing thee fain would call mine eyesight liar.
PROMETHEUS. Certes no sight am I for friends to look on.
CHORUS. Was this thy sole offence?
PROMETHEUS. I taught weak mortals
Not to foresee harm, and forestall the Fates.
CHORUS. A sore disease to anticipate mischance:
How didst thou cure it?
PROMETHEUS. Blind hopes of good I planted

In their dark breasts.

CHORUS.   That was a boon indeed,
To ephemeral man.

PROMETHEUS. Nay more, I gave them
fire.

CHORUS. And flame-faced fire is now
enjoyed by mortals?

PROMETHEUS. Enjoyed, and of all arts
the destined mother.

CHORUS. And is this all the roll of thy
offendings
That he should rage so fierce? Hath he
not set
Bounds to his vengeance?

PROMETHEUS. None, but his own pleasure.

CHORUS. And when shall he please?
Vain the hope; thou say'st
That thou hast erred; and that thou hast
to us
No pleasure brings, to thee excess of pain.
Of this enough. Seek now to cure the
evil.

PROMETHEUS. 'Tis a light thing for him
whose foot's unwarped
By misadventure's meshes to advise
And counsel the unfortunate. But I
Foreknew my fate, and if I erred, I erred
With conscious purpose, purchasing man's
weal
With mine own grief. I knew I should
offend
The Thunderer, though deeming not that
he
Would perch me thus to pine 'twixt Earth
and Sky,
Of this wild wintry waste sole habitant.
But cease to weep for ills that weeping
mends not;
Descend, and I'll discourse to thee at
length
Of chances yet to come. Nay, do not
doubt;
But leave thy car, nor be ashamed to
share
The afflictions of the afflicted; for Mishap,
Of things that lawless wander, wanders
most:
With me to-day it is with you to-morrow.

CHORUS. Not to sluggish ears, Prome-
theus,
Hast thou spoken thy desire;

From our breeze-borne car descending,
With light foot we greet the ground.
Leaving ether chaste, smooth pathway
Of the gently-winnowing wing,
On this craggy rock I stand,
To hear the tale, while thou mayst tell it,
Of thy sorrows to the end.

[*Enter* OCEAN.]

OCEAN. From my distant caves cerulean
This fleet-pinioned bird hath borne me;
Needed neither bit nor bridle,
Thought instinctive reined the creature;
Thus, to know thy griefs, Prometheus,
And to grieve with thee I come.
Soothly strong the tie of kindred
Binds the heart of man and god;
But, though no such tie had bound me,
I had wept for thee the same.
Well thou know'st not mine the cunning
To discourse with glozing phrase;
Tell me how I may relieve thee,
I am ready to relieve;
Friend thou boastest none than Ocean
Surer, in the hour of need.

PROMETHEUS. How now, old Ocean?
thou too come to view
My dire disasters?—how should'st thou
have dared,
Leaving the billowy stream whose name
thou bearest,
Thy rock-roofed halls, and self-built
palaces,
To visit this Scythian land, stern mother
of iron,
To know my sorrows, and to grieve with
me?
Look on this sight—thy friend, the friend
of Jove,
Who helped him to the sway which now
he bears,
Crushed by the self-same god himself
exalted.

OCEAN. I see, Prometheus; and I come
to speak
A wise word to the wise; receive it wisely.
Know what thou art, and make thy man-
ners new;
For a new king doth rule the subject gods.
Compose thy speech, nor cast such whetted
words

'Gainst Jove, who though he sits apart
sublime,
Hath ears, and with new pains may smite
his victim,
To which his present wrath shall seem a
toy.
Listen to me; slack thy fierce ire, and seek
Speedy deliverance from these woes. Trite
wisdom
Belike I speak, Prometheus; but thou
knowest
A lofty-sounding tongue with passionate
phrase
Buys its own ruin. Proud art thou, un-
yielding,
And heap'st new woes tenfold on thine
own head.
Why should'st thou kick against the
pricks? Jove reigns
A lord severe, and of his acts need give
Account to none. I go to plead for thee,
And, what I can, will try to save my kins-
man;
But be thou calm the while; curb thy
rash speech,
And let not fame report that one so wise
Fell by the forfeit of a foolish tongue.
    PROMETHEUS. Count thyself happy,
Ocean, being free
From blame, who shared and dared with
me. Be wise
And what thy meddling aids not, let alone.
In vain thou plead'st with him; his ears
are deaf.
Look to thyself: thy errand is not sate.
    OCEAN. Wise art thou, passing wise,
for others' weal,
For thine own good most foolish. Prithee
do not
So stretch thy stubborn whim to pull
against
The friends that pull for thee. 'Tis no
vain boast;
I know that Jove will hear me.
    PROMETHEUS. Thou art kind;
And for thy kind intent and friendly feel-
ing
Have my best thanks. But do not, I be-
seech thee,
Waste labour upon me. If thou wilt la-
bour,

Seek a more hopeful subject. Thou wert
wiser,
Being safe, to keep thee safe. I, when I
suffer,
Wish not that all my friends should suffer
with me.
Enough my brother Atlas' miseries grieve
me.
Who in the extreme West stands, stoutly
bearing
The pillars of Heaven and Earth upon his
shoulders,
No lightsome burden. Him too, I bewail,
That made his home in dark Cilician
caverns.
The hostile portent, Earth-born, hundred-
headed
Impetuous Typhon, quelled by force, who
stood
Alone, against the embattled host of
gods,
Hissing out murder from his monstrous
jaws;
And from his eyes there flashed a Gorgon
glare,
As he would smite the tyranny of great
Jove
Clean down; but he, with sleepless thun-
der watching,
Hurl'd headlong a flame-breathing bolt,
and laid
The big-mouthed vaunter low. Struck to
the heart
With blasted strength, and shrunk to
ashes, there
A huge and helpless hulk, outstretched he
lies,
Beside the salt sea's strait, pressed down
beneath
The roots of Ætna, on whose peaks
Hephaestus
Sits hammering the hot metal. Thence,
one day,
Shall streams of liquid fire, swift passage
forcing,
With savage jaws the wide-spread plains
devour
Of the fair-fruited Sicily. Such hot
shafts,
From the flame-breathing ferment of the
deep,

Shall Typhon cast with sateless wrath,
  though now
All scorched and cindered by the Thun-
  derer's stroke,
Moveless he lies.   But why should I teach
  thee?
Thou art a wise man, thine own wisdom
  use
To save thyself. For me, I'll even endure
These pains, till Jove shall please to slack
  his ire.
    OCEAN. Know'st thou not this, Prome-
      theus, that mild words
Are medicines of fierce wrath?
    PROMETHEUS.   They are, when
      spoken
In a mild hour; but the high-swelling
  heart
They do but fret the more.
    OCEAN.   But, in the attempt
To ward the threatened harm, what evil
  see'st thou?
    PROMETHEUS. Most bootless toil, and
      folly most inane.
    OCEAN. Be it so; but yet 'tis sometimes
      well, believe me,
That a wise man should seem to be a fool.
    PROMETHEUS. Seem fool, seem wise, I,
      in the end, am blamed.
    OCEAN. Thy reckless words reluctant
      send me home.
    PROMETHEUS. Beware, lest love for me
      make thyself hated.
    OCEAN. Of whom? Of him, who, on
      the all-powerful throne
Sits, a new lord?
    PROMETHEUS.   Even him. Beware
      thou vex not
Jove's jealous heart.
    OCEAN.   In this, thy fate
      shall warn me.
    PROMETHEUS. Away! farewell; and
      may the prudent thoughts,
That sway thy bosom now, direct thee
  ever.
    OCEAN. I go, and quickly. My four-
      footed bird
Brushes the broad path of the limpid air
With forward wing: right gladly will he
  bend
The wearied knee on his familiar stall.

CHORAL HYMN

STROPHE 1

Thy dire disasters, unexampled wrongs,
  I weep, Prometheus.
From its soft founts distilled the flowing
  tear
    My cheek bedashes.
'Tis hard, most hard! By self-made
  laws Jove rules,
And 'gainst the host of primal gods he
  points
    The lordly spear.

ANTISTROPHE 1

With echoing groans the ambient waste
  bewails
    Thy fate, Prometheus;
The neighbouring tribes of holy Asia
  weep
    For thee, Prometheus;
For thee and thine! names mighty and
  revered
Of yore, now shamed, dishonoured, and
  cast down,
    And chained with thee.

STROPHE 2

And Colchis, with her belted daughters,
  weeps
    For thee, Prometheus;
And Scythian tribes, on Earth's re-
  motest verge,
Where lone Mæotis spreads her wintry
  waters,
    Do weep for thee.

ANTISTROPHE 2

The flower of Araby's wandering war-
  riors weep
    For thee, Prometheus;
And they who high their airy holds
  have perched
On Caucasus' ridge, with pointed lances
  bristling,
    Do weep for thee.

EPODE

One only vexed like thee, and even as
  thou,
    In adamant bound,

A Titan, and a god scorned by the gods,
Atlas I knew.
He on his shoulders the surpassing
weight
Of the celestial pole stoutly upbore,
And groaned beneath.
Roars billowy Ocean, and the Deep sucks
back
Its waters when he sobs; from Earth's
dark caves
Deep hell resounds;
The fountains of the holy-streaming
rivers
Do moan with him.
PROMETHEUS. Deem me not self-willed,
nor with pride high-strung,
That I am dumb; my heart is gnawed
to see
Myself thus mocked and jeered. These
gods, to whom
Owe they their green advancement but to
me?
But this ye know; and, not to teach the
taught,
I'll speak of it no more. Of human kind,
My great offence in aiding them, in teach-
ing
The babe to speak, and rousing torpid
mind
To take the grasp of itself—of this I'll
talk;
Meaning to mortal men no blame, but
only
The true recital of mine own deserts.
For, soothly, having eyes to see they saw
not,
And hearing heard not; but like dreamy
phantoms,
A random life they led from year to year,
All blindly floundering on. No craft they
knew
With woven brick or jointed beam to pile
The sunward porch; but in the dark earth
burrowed
And housed, like tiny ants in sunless
caves.
No signs they knew to mark the wintry
year:
The flower-strewn Spring, and the fruit-
laden Summer,
Uncalendared, unregistered, returned—

Till I the difficult art of the stars re-
vealed,
Their risings and their settings. Num-
bers, too,
I taught them (a most choice device) and
how
By marshalled signs to fix their shifting
thoughts,
That Memory, mother of Muses, might
achieve
Her wondrous works. I first slaved to
the yoke
Both ox and ass. I, the rein-loving steeds
(Of wealth's gay-flaunting pomp the chief-
est pride)
Joined to the car; and bade them ease the
toils
Of labouring men vicarious. I the first
Upon the lint-winged car of mariner
Was launched, sea-wandering. Such wise
arts I found
To soothe the ills of man's ephemeral life;
But for myself, plunged in this depth of
woe,
No prop I find.
CHORUS. Sad chance! Thy wit
hath slipt
From its firm footing then when needed
most,
Like some unlearned leech who many
healed,
But being sick himself, from all his store,
Cannot cull out one medicinal drug.
PROMETHEUS. Hear me yet farther;
and in hearing marvel,
What arts and curious shifts my wit de-
vised.
Chiefest of all, the cure of dire disease
Men owe to me. Nor healing food, nor
drink,
Nor unguent knew they, but did slowly
wither
And waste away for lack of pharmacy,
Till taught by me to mix the soothing
drug,
And check corruption's march. I fixed the
art
Of divination with its various phase
Of dim revealings, making dreams speak
truth,
Stray voices, and encounters by the way

Significant; the flight of taloned birds
On right and left I marked—these fraught
    with ban,
With blissful augury those; their way of
    life,
Their mutual loves and enmities, their
    flocks,
And friendly gatherings; the entrails'
    smoothness,
The hue best liked by the gods, the gall,
    the liver
With all its just proportions. I first
    wrapped
In the smooth fat the thighs; first burnt
    the loins,
And from the flickering flame taught men
    to spell
No easy lore, and cleared the fire-faced
    signs
Obscure before. Yet more: I probed the
    Earth,
To yield its hidden wealth to help man's
    weakness—
Iron, copper, silver, gold. None but a
    fool,
A prating fool, will stint me of this praise.
And thus, with one short word to sum
    the tale,
Prometheus taught all arts to mortal
    men.
    CHORUS. Do good to men, but do it
    with discretion.
Why shouldst thou harm thyself? Good
    hope I nurse
To see thee soon from these harsh chains
    unbound,
As free, as mighty, as great Jove himself.
    PROMETHEUS. This may not be; the
    destined course of things
Fate must accomplish; I must bend me
    yet
'Neath wrongs on wrongs, ere I may 'scape
    these bonds.
Though Art be strong, Necessity is
    stronger.
    CHORUS. And who is lord of strong
    Necessity?
    PROMETHEUS. The triform Fates, and
    the sure-memoried Furies.
    CHORUS. And mighty Jove himself must
    yield to them?

PROMETHEUS. Nó more than others
    Jove can 'scape his doom.
    CHORUS. What doom?—No doom hath
    he but endless sway.
    PROMETHEUS. 'Tis not for thee to
    know: tempt not the question.
    CHORUS. There's some dread mystery
    in thy chary speech,
Close-veiled.
    PROMETHEUS. Urge this no more: the
    truth thou'lt know
In fitting season; now it lies concealed
In deepest darkness! for relenting Jove
Himself must woo this secret from my
    breast.

CHORAL HYMN

STROPHE 1

    Never, O never may Jove,
Who in Olympus reigns omnipotent lord,
Plant his high will against my weak
    opinion!
    Let me approach the gods
With blood of oxen and with holy feasts,
By Father Ocean's quenchless stream, and
    pay
    No backward vows:
Nor let my tongue offend; but in my heart
    Be lowly wisdom graven.

ANTISTROPHE 1

    For thus old Wisdom speaks:
Thy life 'tis sweet to cherish, and while
    the length
Of years is thine, thy heart with cheerful
    hopes
    And lightsome joys to feed.
But thee—ah me! my blood runs cold to
    see thee,
Pierced to the marrow with a thousand
    pains.
    Not fearing Jove,
Self-willed thou hast respect to man,
    Prometheus,
    Much more than man deserveth.

STROPHE 2

    For what is man? behold!
Can he requite thy love—child of a day—

Or help thy extreme need? Hast thou
  not seen
The blind and aimless strivings,
The barren blank endeavour,
The pithless deeds, of the fleeting dream-
  like race?
Never, O nevermore,
May mortal wit Jove's ordered plan de-
  ceive.

ANTISTROPHE 2

This lore my heart hath learned
From sight of thee, and thy sharp pains,
  Prometheus.
Alas! what diverse strain I sang thee
  then,
Around the bridal chamber,
And around the bridal bath,
When thou my sister fair, Hesione,
Won by rich gifts didst lead
From Ocean's caves thy spousal bed to
  share.
            [Enter Io.]
What land is this?—what race of mor-
  tals
Owns this desert? who art thou,
Rock-bound with these wintry fetters,
And for what crime tortured thus?
Worn and weary with far travel,
Tell me where my feet have borne me!
O pain! pain! pain! it stings and goads
  me again,
The fateful brize!—save me, O Earth!
  Avaunt
Thou horrible shadow of the Earth-born
  Argus!
Could not the grave close up thy hundred
  eyes,
  But thou must come,
Haunting my path with thy suspicious
  look,
  Unhoused from Hades?
Avaunt! avaunt!—why wilt thou hound
  my track,
The famished wanderer on the waste sea-
  shore?

STROPHE

Pipe not thy sounding wax-compacted reed
With drowsy drone at me! Ah wretched
  me!

Wandering, still wandering o'er wide
  Earth, and driven
Where, where? O tell me where?
O Son of Kronos, in what damned sin
Being caught hast thou to misery yoked
  me thus,
Pricked me to desperation, and my heart
  Pierced with thy furious goads?
Blast me with lightnings! bury me in
  Earth! To the gape
Of greedy sea-monsters give me! Hear,
  O hear
  My prayer, O King!
Enough, enough, these errant toils have
  tried me;
And yet no rest I find: nor when, nor
  where
These woes shall cease may know.
CHORUS. Dost hear the plaint of the
  ox-horned maid?
PROMETHEUS. How should I not? the
  Inachian maid who knows not,
Stung by the god-sent brize? the maid
  who smote
Jove's lustful heart with love: and his
  harsh spouse
Hounds her o'er Earth with chase in-
  terminable.

ANTISTROPHE

Io. My father's name thou know'st,
  and my descent!
Who art thou? god or mortal? Speak!
  what charm
Gives wretch like thee, the certain clue
  to know
  My lamentable fate?
Aye, and the god-sent plague thou know'st;
  the sting
That spurs me o'er the far-stretched
  Earth; the goad
That mads me sheer, wastes, withers, and
  consumes,
  A worn and famished maid,
Whipt by the scourge of jealous Hera's
  wrath!
Ah me! ah me! Misery has many
  shapes,
  But none like mine.
O thou, who named my Argive home, de-
  clare

What ills await me yet; what end; what
  hope?
If hope there be for Io.
CHORUS.   I pray thee speak to the
  weary way-worn maid.
PROMETHEUS.   I'll tell thee all thy wish,
  not in enigmas
Tangled and dark, but in plain phrase, as
  friend
Should speak to friend.   Thou see'st
  Prometheus, who
To mortal men gifted immortal fire.
  Io.   O thou, to man a common blessing
    given,
What crime hath bound thee to this
  wintry rock?
PROMETHEUS.   I have but ceased re-
  hearsing all my wrongs.
Io.   And dost thou then refuse the boon
  I ask?
PROMETHEUS.   What boon? ask what
  thou wilt, and I will answer.
Io.   Say, then, who bound thee to this
  ragged cliff?
PROMETHEUS.   Stern Jove's decree, and
  harsh Hephaestus' hand.
Io.   And for what crime?
PROMETHEUS.   Let what I've said
  suffice.
Io.   This, too, I ask—what bound hath
  fate appointed
To my far-wandering toils?
PROMETHEUS.   This not to know
Were better than to learn.
  Io.   Nay, do not hide
This thing from me!
PROMETHEUS.   If 'tis a boon, believe me,
I grudge it not.
  Io.   Then why so slow to answer?
PROMETHEUS.   I would not crush thee
  with the cruel truth.
Io.   Fear not; I choose to hear it.
PROMETHEUS.   Listen then.
CHORUS.   Nay, hear me rather.   With
  her own mouth this maid
Shall first her bygone woes rehearse; next
  thou
What yet remains shalt tell.
PROMETHEUS.   Even so.
  [To Io.] Speak thou;
They are the sisters of thy father, Io;

And to wail out our griefs, when they who
  listen
Our troubles with a willing tear requite,
Is not without its use.
  Io.   I will obey,
And in plain speech my chanceful story
  tell;
Though much it grieves me to retrace the
  source,
Whence sprung this god-sent pest, and of
  my shape
Disfigurement abhorred.   Night after night
Strange dreams around my maiden pillow
  hovering
Whispered soft temptings.   "O thrice-
  blessed maid,
Why pin'st thou thus in'virgin loneliness,
When   highest   wedlock   courts   thee?
  Struck by the shaft
Of fond desire for thee Jove burns, and
  pants
To twine his loves with thine.   Spurn not,
  O maid,
The proffered bed of Jove; but hie thee
  straight
To Lerne's bosomed mead, where are the
  sheep-folds
And ox-stalls of thy sire, that so the eye
Of Jove, being filled with thee, may cease
  from craving."
Such nightly dreams my restless couch
  possessed
Till I, all tears, did force me to unfold
The portent to my father.   He to Pytho
Sent frequent messengers, and to Dodona,
Searching the pleasure of the gods; but
  they
With various-woven phrase came back, and
  answers
More doubtful than the quest.   At length,
  a clear
And unambiguous voice came to my
  father,
Enjoining, with most strict command, to
  send me
Far from my home, and from my country
  far,
To the extreme bounds of Earth an out-
  cast wanderer,
Else that the fire-faced bolt of Jove should
  smite

Our universal race. By such responses,
Moved of oracular Loxias, my father
Reluctant me reluctant drove from home,
And shut the door against me. What he
    did
He did perforce; Jove's bit was in his
    mouth.
Forthwith my wit was frenzied, and my
    form
Assumed the brute. With maniac bound
    I rushed,
Horned as thou see'st, and with the sharp-
    mouthed sting
Of gad-fly pricked infuriate to the cliff
Of Lerne, and Cenchréa's limpid wave;
While Argus, Earth-born cow-herd, hun-
    dred-eyed,
Followed the winding traces of my path
With sharp observance. Him swift-swoop-
    ing Fate
Snatched unexpected from his sleepless
    guard;
But I from land to land still wander on,
Scourged by the wrath of Heaven's relent-
    less queen.
Thou hast my tale; the sequel, if thou
    know'st it,
Is thine to tell; but do not seek, I pray
    thee,
In pity for me, to drop soft lies; for
    nothing
Is worse than the smooth craft of prac-
    tised phrase.
    CHORUS. Enough, enough! Woe's me
        that ever
Such voices of strange grief should rend
    my ear!
    That such a tale of woe,
Insults, and wrongs, and horrors, should
    freeze me through,
    As with a two-edged sword!
O destiny! destiny! woes most hard to
    see,
More hard to bear! Alas! poor maid for
    thee!
    PROMETHEUS. Thy wails anticipate
        her woes; restrain
Thy trembling tears till thou hast heard
    the whole.
    CHORUS. Proceed: to know the worst
        some solace brings

To the vexed heart.
    PROMETHEUS.   Your first request
        I granted,
And lightly; from her own mouth, ye
    have heard
The spring of harm, the stream expect
    from me,
How Hera shall draw out her slow re-
    venge.
Meanwhile, thou seed of Inachus, lend an
    ear
And learn thy future travel. First to the
    east
Turn thee, and traverse the unploughed
    Scythian fields,
Whose wandering tribes their wattled
    homes transport
Aloft on well-wheeled wains, themselves
    well slung
With the far-darting bow. These pass,
    and, holding
Thy course by the salt sea's sounding
    surge, pass through
The land; next, on thy left, thou'lt reach
    the Chalybs,
Workers in iron. These too avoid—for
    they
Are savage, and harsh to strangers.
    Thence proceeding,
Thou to a stream shalt come, not falsely
    named
Hubristes: but the fierce ill-forded wave
Pass not till Caucasus, hugest hill, re-
    ceives thee,
There where the flood its gushing strength
    foams forth
Fresh from the rocky brow. Cross then
    the peaks
That neighbour with the stars, and thence
    direct
Southward thy path to where the Am-
    azons
Dwell, husband-hated, who shall one day
    people
Thermódon's bank, and Themiscyre, and
    where
Harsh Salmydessus whets his ravening
    jaws,
The sailor's foe, stepmother to the ships.
These maids shall give thee escort. Next
    thou'lt reach

The narrow Cimmerian isthmus, skirting
bleak
The waters of Mæotis. Here delay not,
But with bold breast cross thou the strait.
Thy passage
Linked with the storied name, of Bos-
phorus
Shall live through endless time. Here,
leaving Europe,
The Asian soil receives thee. Now, an-
swer me,
Daughters of Ocean, doth not Jove in all
things
Prove his despotic will?—In lawless love
Longing to mingle with this mortal maid,
He heaps her with these woes. A bitter
suitor,
Poor maid, was thine, and I have told
thee scarce
The prelude of thy griefs.

Io.   Ah! wretched me!
PROMETHEUS.   Alas, thy cries and
groans!—What wilt thou do,
When the full measure of thy woes is told
thee?

CHORUS. What! more? her cup of woes
not full?
PROMETHEUS.   'Twill flow
And overflow, a sea of whelming woes.

Io. Why do I live? Why not embrace
the gain
That, with one cast, this toppling cliff
secures,
And dash me headlong on the ground, to
end
Life and life's sorrows? Once to die is
better
Than thus to drag sick life.

PROMETHEUS.   Thou'rt happy, Io,
That death from all thy living wrongs
may free thee;
But I, whom Fate hath made immortal,
see
No end to my long-lingering pains ap-
pointed,
Till Jove from his usurping sway be
hurled.

Io. Jove from his tyranny hurled—can
such thing be?
PROMETHEUS. Doubtless 'twould feast
thine eyes to see't?

Io.   Ay, truly,
Wronged as I am by him.
PROMETHEUS.   Then, learn from me
That he is doomed to fall.
Io.   What hand shall wrest
Jove's sceptre?
PROMETHEUS.   Jove's own empty wit.
Io.   How so?
PROMETHEUS. From evil marriage reap-
ing evil fruit.
Io.   Marriage! of mortal lineage or
divine?
PROMETHEUS. Ask me no further. This
I may not answer.
Io. Shall his spouse thrust him from
his ancient throne?
PROMETHEUS. The son that she brings
forth shall wound his father.
Io. And hath he no redemption from
this doom?
PROMETHEUS. None, till he loose me
from these hated bonds.
Io. But who, in Jove's despite, shall
loose thee?
PROMETHEUS. One
From thine own womb descended.
Io.   How? My Son?
One born of me shall be thy Saviour!—
When?
PROMETHEUS. When generations ten
have passed, the third.
Io. Thou speak'st ambiguous oracles.
PROMETHEUS.   I have spoken
Enough for thee. Pry not into the Fates.
Io. Wilt thou hold forth a hope to
cheat my grasp?
PROMETHEUS. I give thee choice of two
things: choose thou one.
Io. What things? Speak, and I'll
choose.
PROMETHEUS.   Thou hast the choice
To hear thy toils to the end, or learn his
name
Who comes to save me.
CHORUS.   Nay, divide the choice;
One half to her concede, to me the other,
Thus doubly gracious: to the maid her
toils,
To me thy destined Saviour tell.
PROMETHEUS.   So be it!
Being thus whetted in desire, I would not

Oppose your wills. First Io, what remains
Of thy far-sweeping wanderings hear, and
  grave
My words on the sure tablets of thy mind.
When thou hast crossed the narrow stream
  that parts
The continents, to the far flame-faced East
Thou shalt proceed, the highway of the
  Sun;
Then cross the sounding Ocean, till thou
  reach
Cisthené and the Gorgon plains, where
  dwell
Phorcys' three daughters, maids with
  frosty eld
Hoar as the swan, with one eye and one
  tooth
Shared by the three; them Phœbus beamy-
  bright
Beholds not, nor the nightly Moon. Near
  them
Their winged sisters dwell, the Gorgons
  dire,
Man-hating monsters, snaky-locked, whom
  eye
Of mortal ne'er might look upon and live.
This for thy warning. One more sight
  remains,
That fills the eye with horror: mark me
  well;
The sharp-beaked Griffins, hounds of Jove,
  avoid.
Fell dogs that bark not; and the one-eyed
  host
Of Arimaspian horsemen with swift hoofs
Beating the banks of golden-rolling Pluto.
A distant land, a swarthy people next
Receives thee: near the fountains of the
  Sun
They dwell by Aethiops' wave. This river
  trace
Until thy weary feet shall reach the pass
Whence from the Bybline heights the sa-
  cred Nile
Pours his salubrious flood. The winding
  wave
Thence to triangled Egypt guides thee,
  where
A distant home awaits thee, fated mother
Of no unstoried race. And now, if aught
That I have spoken doubtful seem or dark,

Repeat the question, and in plainer speech
Expect reply. I feel no lack of leisure.
  CHORUS. If thou hast more to speak
    to her, speak on;
Or aught omitted to supply, supply it;
But if her tale is finished, as thou say'st,
Remember our request.
  PROMETHEUS. Her tale is told,
But for the more assurance of my words
The path of toils through which her feet
  had struggled
Before she reached this coast I will de-
  clare;
Lightly, and with no cumbrous comment,
  touching
Thy latest travel only, wandering Io.
When thou hadst trod the Molossian
  plains, and reached
Steep-ridged Dodona, where Thesprotian
  Jove
In council sits, and from the articulate
  oaks
(Strange wonder!) speaks prophetic, there
  thine ears
This salutation with no doubtful phrase
Received: *"All hail, great spouse of
  mighty Jove
That shall be!"*—say, was it a pleasing
  sound?
Thence by the sting of jealous Hera
  goaded,
Along the coast of Rhea's bosomed sea
Thy steps were driven: thence with mazy
  course
Tossed hither; gaining, if a gain, this
  solace,
That future times, by famous Io's name,
Shall know that sea. These things may
  be a sign
That I, beyond the outward show, can
  pierce
To the heart of truth. What yet remains,
  I tell
To thee and them in common, tracing
  back
My speech to whence it came. There is
  a city
In extreme Egypt, where with outspread
  loam
Nile breasts the sea, its name Canopus.
  There

Jove to thy sober sense shall bring thee
    back,
Soft with no fearful touch, and thou shalt
    bear
A son, dark Epaphus, whose name shall
    tell
The wonder of his birth; he shall possess
What fruitful fields fat Nile broad-stream-
    ing laves.
Four generations then shall pass; the
    fifth
In fifty daughters glorying shall return
To ancient Argos, fatal wedlock shunning
With fathers' brothers' sons; these, their
    wild hearts
Fooled with blind lust, as hawks the gen-
    tle doves,
Shall track the fugitive virgins; but a
    god
Shall disappoint their chase, and the fair
    prey
Save from their lawless touch; the Apian
    soil
Shall welcome them to death, and woman's
    hands
Shall dare the deed amid the nuptial
    watches.
Each bride shall rob her lord of life, and
    dip
The sharp steel in his throat. Such nup-
    tial bliss
May all my enemies know! Only one
    maid
Of all the fifty, with a blunted will,
Shall own the charm of love, and spare
    her mate,
And of two adverse reputations choose
The coward, not the murderess. She shall
    be
The mother of a royal race in Argos.
To tell what follows, with minute remark,
Were irksome; but from this same root
    shall spring
A hero, strong in the archer's craft,
    whose hand
Shall free me from these bonds. Such
    oracle spake
Titanian Themis, my time-honoured
    mother,
But how and why were a long tale to
    tell,

Nor being told would boot thine ear to
    hear it.
Io. Ah me! pain! pain! ah me!
Again the fevered spasm hath seized me,
And the stroke of madness smites!
Again that fiery sting torments me,
And my heart doth knock my ribs!
My aching eyes in dizziness roll,
And my helmless feet are driven
Whither gusty frenzy blows!
And my tongue with thick words strug-
    gling
Like a sinking swimmer plashes
'Gainst the whelming waves of woe!
                              [*Exit.*]

CHORAL HYMN

STROPHE

Wise was the man, most wise,
Who in deep-thoughted mood conceived,
    and first
In pictured speech and pregnant phrase
    declared
That marriage, if the Fates shall bless
    the bond,
    Must be of like with like;
And that the daughters of an humble
    house
Shun tempting union with the pomp of
    wealth
    And with the pride of birth.

ANTISTROPHE

Never, O! never may Fate,
All-powerful Fate which rules both gods
    and men,
See me approaching the dread Thun-
    derer's bed,
And sharing marriage with the Olym-
    pian king,
    An humble Ocean-maid!
May wretched Io, chased by Hera's
    wrath,
Unhusbanded, unfriended, fill my sense
    With profitable fear.

EPODE

Me may an equal bond
Bind with my equal: never may the eye
Of a celestial suitor fix the gaze
    Of forceful love on me.

This were against all odds of war to
war,
And in such strife entangled I were lost;
For how should humble maid resist the
embrace,
Against great Jove's decree?
PROMETHEUS. Nay, but this Jove,
though insolent now, shall soon
Be humbled low. Such wedlock even now
He blindly broods, as shall uptear his
kingdom,
And leave no trace behind; then shall the
curse,
Which Kronos heaped upon his ingrate
son,
When hurled unjustly from his hoary
throne,
Be all fulfilled. What remedy remains
For that dread ruin I alone can tell;
I only know. Then let him sit aloft,
Rolling his thunder, his fire-breathing bolt
Far-brandishing; his arts are vain; his
fall,
Unless my aid prevent, his shameful fall,
Is doomed. Against himself to life he
brings
A champion fierce, a portent of grim war,
Who shall invent a fiercer flame than
lightning,
And peals to outpeal the thunder, who
shall shiver
The trident mace that stirs the sea, and
shakes
The solid Earth, the spear of strong
Poseidon.
Thus shall the tyrant learn how much to
serve
Is different from to sway.
CHORUS. Thou dost but make
Thy wishes father to thy slanderous
phrase.
PROMETHEUS. I both speak truth and
wish the truth to be.
CHORUS. But who can think that Jove
shall find a master?
PROMETHEUS. He shall be mastered!
Ay, and worse endure.
CHORUS. Dost thou not blench to cast
such words about thee?
PROMETHEUS. How should I fear, being
a god and deathless?

CHORUS. But he can scourge with
something worse than death.
PROMETHEUS. Even let him scourge!
I'm armed for all conclusions.
CHORUS. Yet they are wise who wor-
ship Adrastéa.
PROMETHEUS. Worship, and pray;
fawn on the powers that be;
But Jove to me is less than very nothing.
Let him command, and rule his little hour
To please himself; long time he cannot
sway.
But lo! where comes the courier of this
Jove,
The obsequious minion of this upstart
King,
Doubtless the bearer of some weighty
news.
[*Enter* HERMES.]
HERMES. Thee, cunning sophist, dealing
bitter words
Most bitterly against the gods, the friend
Of ephemeral man, the thief of sacred
fire,
Thee, Father Jove commands to curb thy
boasts,
And say what marriage threats his stable
throne.
Answer this question in plain phrase, no
dark
Tangled enigmas; do not add, Prometheus,
A second journey to my first: and, mark
me!
Thy obduracy cannot soften Jove.
PROMETHEUS. This solemn mouthing,
this proud pomp of phrase
Beseems the lackey of the gods. New
gods
Ye are, and, being new, ye ween to hold
Unshaken citadels. Have I not seen
Two Monarchs ousted from that throne?
the third
I yet shall see precipitate hurled from
Heaven
With baser, speedier ruin. Do I seem
To quail before this new-forged dynasty?
Fear is my farthest thought. I pray
thee go
Turn up the dust again upon the road
Thou cam'st. Reply from me thou shalt
have none.

HERMES. This haughty tone hath been thy sin before:
Thy pride will strand thee on a worser woe.
PROMETHEUS. And were my woe tenfold what now it is,
I would not barter it for thy sweet chains;
For liefer would I lackey this bare rock
Than trip the messages of Father Jove.
The insolent thus with insolence I repay.
HERMES. Thou dost delight in miseries; thou art wanton.
PROMETHEUS. Wanton! delighted! would my worst enemies
Might wanton in these bonds, thyself the first!
HERMES. Must I, too, share the blame of thy distress?
PROMETHEUS. In one round sentence, every god I hate
That injures me who never injured him.
HERMES. Thou'rt mad, clean mad; thy wit's diseased, Prometheus.
PROMETHEUS. Most mad! if madness 'tis to hate our foes.
HERMES. Prosperity's too good for thee: thy temper
Could not endure't.
PROMETHEUS. Alas! this piercing pang!
HERMES. "Alas!"—this word Jove does not understand.
PROMETHEUS. As Time grows old he teaches many things.
HERMES. Yet Time that teaches all leaves thee untaught.
PROMETHEUS. Untaught in sooth, thus parleying with a slave!
HERMES. It seems thou wilt not grant great Jove's demand.
PROMETHEUS. Such love as his to me should be repaid
With like!
HERMES. Dost beard me like a boy? Beware.
PROMETHEUS. Art not a boy, and something yet more witless,
If thou expectest answer from my mouth?
Nor insult harsh, nor cunning craft of Jove
Shall force this tale from me, till he unloose

These bonds. Yea! let him dart his levin bolts,
With white-winged snows and subterranean thunders
Mix and confound the elements of things!
No threat, no fear, shall move me to reveal
The hand that hurls him from his tyrant's throne.
HERMES. Bethink thee well: thy vaunts can help thee nothing.
PROMETHEUS. I speak not rashly: what I said I said.
HERMES. If thou art not the bought and sold of folly,
Dare to learn wisdom from thy present ills.
PROMETHEUS. Speak to the waves: thou speak'st to me as vainly!
Deem not that I, to win a smile from Jove,
Will spread a maiden smoothness o'er my soul,
And importune the foe whom most I hate
With womanish upliftings of the hands.
Thou'lt see the deathless die first!
HERMES. I have said
Much, but that much is vain: thy rigid nature
To thaw with prayer is hopeless. A young colt
That frets the bit, and fights against the reins,
Art thou, fierce-champing with most impotent rage;
For wilful strength that hath no wisdom in it
Is less than nothing. But bethink thee well;
If thou despise my words of timely warning,
What wintry storm, what threefold surge of woes
Whelms thee inevitable. Jove shall split
These craggy cliffs with his cloud-bosomed bolt,
And sink thee deep: the cold rock shall embrace thee;
There thou shalt lie, till he shall please to bring thee
Back to the day, to find new pains prepared:

For he will send his Eagle-messenger,
His winged hound, in crimson food de-
    lighting,
To tear thy rags of flesh with bloody beak,
And daily come an uninvited guest
To banquet on thy gory liver. This,
And worse expect, unless some god endure
Vicarious thy tortures, and exchange
His sunny ether for the rayless homes
Of gloomy Hades, and deep Tartarus.
Consider well. No empty boast I speak,
But weighty words well weighed: the
    mouth of Jove
Hath never known a lie, and speech with
    him
Is prophet of its deed. Ponder and weigh,
Close not thy stubborn ears to good ad-
    vice.
    CHORUS. If we may speak, what Hermes
        says is wise,
And fitting the occasion. He advises
That stubborn will should yield to prudent
    counsel.
Obey: thy wisdom should not league with
    folly.
    PROMETHEUS. Nothing   new   this
        preacher preaches:
Seems it strange that foe should suffer
From the vengeance of his foe?
I am ready. Let him wreathe
Curls of scorching flame around me;
Let him fret the air with thunder,
And the savage-blustering winds!
Let the deep abysmal tempest
Wrench the firm roots of the Earth!
Let the sea upheave her billows,
Mingling the fierce rush of waters
With the pathway of the stars!
Let the harsh-winged hurricane sweep me
In its whirls, and fling me down
To black Tartarus: there to lie
Bound in the iron folds of Fate.
I will bear: but cannot die.
    HERMES. Whom the nymphs have struck
        with madness

Raves as this loud blusterer raves;
Seems he not a willing madman,
Let him reap the fruits he sowed!
But ye maids, who share his sorrows,
Not his crimes, with quick removal
Hie from this devoted spot,
Lest with idiocy the thunder
Harshly blast your maundering wits.
    CHORUS. Wouldst thou with thy words
        persuade me,
Use a more persuasive speech;
Urge no reasons to convince me
That an honest heart must hate.
With his sorrows I will sorrow:
I will hate a traitor's name;
Earth has plagues, but none more noisome
Than a faithless friend in need.
    HERMES. Ponder well my prudent coun-
        sel,
Nor, when evil hunts thee out,
Blame great Jove that he doth smite
    thee
With an unexpected stroke.
Not the gods; thy proper folly
Is the parent of thy woes.
Jove hath laid no trap to snare thee,
But the scapeless net of ruin
Thou hast woven for thyself.
    PROMETHEUS. Now his threats walk
        forth in action,
And the firm Earth quakes indeed.
Deep and loud the ambient Thunder
Bellows, and the flaring Lightning
Wreathes his fiery curls around me,
And the Whirlwind rolls his dust;
And the Winds from rival regions
Rush in elemental strife,
And the Ocean's storm-vexed billows
Mingle with the startled stars!
Doubtless now the tyrant gathers
All his hoarded wrath to whelm me.
Mighty Mother, worshipped Themis,
Circling Ether that diffusest
Light, a common joy to all,
Thou beholdest these my wrongs!

ANTIGONE

By SOPHOCLES

Produced at Athens, 442 or 440 B.C.

TRANSLATED BY SIR GEORGE YOUNG

CHARACTERS

ANTIGONE, } *daughters of Œdipus, late king of Thebes*
ISMENE,

CREON, *brother to Jocasta, late queen of Thebes, Captain-general of the army, and successor to the throne*

A Sentinel

HÆMON, *son to* CREON, *bethrothed to* ANTIGONE

TIRESIAS, *a seer.*

A Messenger in attendance on CREON

EURYDICE, *wife to* CREON

CHORUS *composed of Senators of Thebes*

GUARDS; ATTENDANTS; A BOY *leading Tiresias*

SCENE—*Before the Royal Palace at Thebes.*

TIME—*Early morning.*

[*Enter* ANTIGONE *and* ISMENE.]

ANTIGONE. Ismene, dear in very sister-hood,

Do you perceive how Heaven upon us two
Means to fulfil, before we come to die,
Out of all ills that grow from Œdipus—
What not, indeed? for there's no sorrow
    or harm,
No circumstance of scandal or of shame
I have not seen, among your griefs, and
    mine.
And now again, what is this word they
    say

Our Captain-general proclaimed but now
To the whole city? Did you hear and
    heed?
Or are you blind, while pains of enemies
Are passing on your friends?

ISMENE. Antigone,
To me no tidings about friends are come,
Pleasant or grievous, ever since we two
Of our two brothers were bereft, who died
Both in one day, each by the other's
    hand.
And since the Argive host in this same
    night

20

Took itself hence, I have heard nothing
  else,
To make me happier, or more miserable.
ANTIGONE. I knew as much; and for
  that reason made you
Go out of doors—to tell you privately.
ISMENE. What is it? I see you have
  some mystery.
ANTIGONE. What! has not Creon to
  the tomb preferred
One of our brothers, and with contumely
Withheld it from the other? Eteocles
Duly, they say, even as by law was due,
He hid beneath the earth, rendering him
  honour
Among the dead below; but the dead body
Of Polynices, miserably slain,
They say it has been given out publicly
None may bewail, none bury, all must
  leave
Unwept, unsepulchred, a dainty prize
For fowl that watch, gloating upon their
  prey!
This is the matter he has had proclaimed—
Excellent Creon! for your heed, they say,
And mine, I tell you—mine! and he moves
  hither,
Meaning to announce it plainly in the
  ears
Of such as do not know it, and to declare
It is no matter of small moment; he
Who does any of these things shall surely
  die;
The citizens shall stone him in the streets.
So stands the case. Now you will quickly
  show
If you are worthy of your birth or no.
ISMENE. But O rash heart, what good,
  if it be thus,
Could I effect, helping or hindering?
ANTIGONE. Look, will you join me?
  will you work with me?
ISMENE. In what attempt? What
  mean you?
ANTIGONE. Help me lift
The body up—
ISMENE. What, would you bury him?
Against the proclamation?
ANTIGONE. My own brother
And yours I will! If you will not, I
  will;

I shall not prove disloyal.
ISMENE. You are mad!
When Creon has forbidden it?
ANTIGONE. From mine own
He has no right to stay me.
ISMENE. Alas, O sister,
Think how our father perished! self-con-
  vict—
Abhorred—dishonoured—blind—his eyes
  put out
By his own hand! How she who was at
  once
His wife and mother with a knotted noose
Laid violent hands on her own life! And
  how
Our two unhappy brothers in one day
Each on his own head by the other's hand
Wrought common ruin! We now left
  alone—
Do but consider how most miserably
We too shall perish, if despite of law
We traverse the behest or power of kings.
We must remember we are women born,
Unapt to cope with men; and, being ruled
By mightier than ourselves, we have to
  bear
These things—and worse. For my part, I
  will ask
Pardon of those beneath, for what perforce
I needs must do, but yield obedience
To them that walk in power; to exceed
Is madness, and not wisdom.
ANTIGONE. Then in future
I will not bid you help me; nor hence-
  forth,
Though you desire, shall you, with my
  good will,
Share what I do. Be what seems right
  to you;
Him will I bury. Death, so met, were
  honour;
And for that capital crime of piety,
Loving and loved, I will lie by his side.
Far longer is there need I satisfy
Those nether Powers, than powers on
  earth; for there
For ever must I lie. You, if you will,
Hold up to scorn what is approved of
  Heaven!
ISMENE. I am not one to cover things
  with scorn;

But I was born too feeble to contend
Against the state.
ANTIGONE. Yes, you can put that for-
ward;
But I will go and heap a burial mound
Over my most dear brother.
ISMENE.   My poor sister,
How beyond measure do I fear for you!
ANTIGONE. Do not spend fear on me.
Shape your own course.
ISMENE. At least announce it, then, to
nobody,
But keep it close, as I will.
ANTIGONE.   Tell it, tell it!
You'll cross me worse, by far, if you keep
silence—
Not publish it to all.
ISMENE.   Your heart beats hotly
For chilling work!
ANTIGONE. I know that those approve
Whom I most need to please.
ISMENE.   If you could do it!
But you desire impossibilities.
ANTIGONE. Well, when I find I have
no power to stir,
I will cease trying.
ISMENE.   But things impossible
'Tis wrong to attempt at all.
ANTIGONE.   If you will say it,
I shall detest you soon; and you will
justly
Incur the dead man's hatred. Suffer me
And my unwisdom to endure the weight
Of what is threatened. I shall meet with
nothing
More grievous, at the worst, than death,
with honour.
ISMENE. Then go, if you will have it:
and take this with you,
You go on a fool's errand!
                    [Exit ANTIGONE.]
                    Lover true
To your beloved, none the less, are you!
                            [Exit.]
[Enter THEBAN SENATORS, as Chorus.]
                CHORUS.
                I. 1.
Sunbeam bright! Thou fairest ray
    That ever dawned on Theban eyes
        Over the portals seven!

O orb of aureate day,
    How glorious didst thou rise
        O'er Dirca's streams, shining from
        heaven,
Him, the man with shield of white
Who came from Argos in armour dight
Hurrying runagate o'er the plain,
Jerking harder his bridle rein;
Who by Polynices' quarrellous broil
Stirred up in arms to invade our soil
    With strident cries as an eagle flies
Swooped down on the fields before him,
'Neath cover of eagle pinion white
As drifted snow, a buckler bright
    On many a breast, and a horsetail
    crest
From each helm floating o'er him.

                I. 2.

Yawning with many a blood-stained
    spear
    Around our seven-gated town
        High o'er the roofs he stood;
Then, or ever a torch could sear
    With flames the rampart-crown—
        Or ever his jaws were filled with
        blood
Of us and ours, lo, he was fled!
Such clatter of war behind him spread,
Stress too sore for his utmost might
Matched with the Dragon in the fight;
For Zeus abhors tongue-glorious boasts;
And straightway as he beheld their hosts,
Where on they rolled, covered with gold,
    Streaming in mighty eddy,
Scornfully with a missile flame
He struck down Capaneus, as he came
Uplifting high his victory-cry
    At the topmost goal already.

                II. 1.

Tantalus-like aloft he hung, then fell;
    Earth at his fall resounded;
Even as, maddened by the Bacchic spell,
    On with torch in hand he bounded,
        Breathing blasts of hate.
So the stroke was turned aside,
    Mighty Ares rudely dealing
Others elsewhere, far and wide,
    Like a right-hand courser wheeling
Round the goals of fate.

For captains seven at portals seven
Found each his match in the combat even,
And left on the field both sword and
 shield
 As a trophy to Zeus, who o'erthrew
 them;
Save the wretched twain, who against
 each other
Though born of one father, and one
 mother,
Laid lances at aim—to their own death
 came,
And the common fate that slew them.

II. 2.

But now loud Victory returns at last
 On Theban chariots smiling,
Let us begin oblivion of the past,
 Memories of the late war beguiling
 Into slumber sound.
 Seek we every holy shrine;
 There begin the night-long chorus;
 Let the Theban Boy divine,
 Bacchus, lead the way before us,
 Shaking all the ground.

Leave we the song: the King is here;
Creon, Menœceus' son, draws near;
To the function strange—like the heaven-
 sent change
 Which has raised him newly to power:
What counsel urging—what ends of state,
That he summons us to deliberate,
The elders all, by his herald's call,
 At a strange unwonted hour?

[*Enter* CREON, *attended.*]
CREON. Sirs, for the ship of state—the
 Gods once more,
After much rocking on a stormy surge,
Set her on even keel. Now therefore you,
You of all others, by my summoners
I bade come hither; having found you first
Right loyal ever to the kingly power
In Laius' time; and next, while Œdipus
Ordered the commonwealth; and since his
 fall,
With steadfast purposes abiding still,
Circling their progeny. Now, since they
 perished,
Both on one day, slain by a two-edged
 fate,

Striking and stricken, sullied with a stain
Of mutual fratricide, I, as you know,
In right of kinship nearest to the dead,
Possess the throne and take the supreme
 power.
Howbeit it is impossible to know
The spirit of any man, purpose or will,
Before it be displayed by exercise
In government and laws. To me, I say,
Now as of old, that pilot of the state
Who sets no hand to the best policy,
But remains tongue-tied through some
 terror, seems
Vilest of men. Him too, who sets a friend
Before his native land, I prize at nothing.
God, who seest all things always, witness
 it!
If I perceive, where safety should have
 been,
Mischief advancing toward my citizens,
I will not sit in silence; nor account
As friend to me the country's enemy;
But thus I deem: she is our ark of safety;
And friends are made then only, when,
 embarked
Upon her deck, we ride the seas upright.
Such are the laws by which I mean to
 further
This city's welfare; and akin to these
I have given orders to the citizens
Touching the sons of Œdipus. Eteocles,
Who in this city's quarrel fought and fell,
The foremost of our champions in the
 fray,
They should entomb with the full sanctity
Of rites that solemnize the downward road
Of their dead greatest. Him the while,
 his brother,
That Polynices who, returning home
A banished man, sought to lay waste with
 fire
His household Gods, his native country—
 sought
To glut himself with his own kindred's
 blood,
Or carry them away to slavery,
It has been promulgated to the city
No man shall bury, none should wail for
 him;
Unsepulchred, shamed in the eyes of
 men,
His body shall be left to be devoured

By dogs and fowls of the air. Such is my
will.
Never with me shall wicked men usurp
The honours of the righteous; but whoe'er
Is friendly to this city shall, by me,
Living or dead, be honoured equally.
1ST SENATOR. Creon Menœceus' son, we
hear your pleasure
Both on this city's friend, and on her foe;
It is your sovereignty's prerogative
To pass with absolute freedom on the
dead,
And us, who have survived them.
CREON. Please to see
What has been said performed.
1ST SENATOR. That charge confer
On some one who is younger.
CREON. Of the body?
Sentries are set, already.
1ST SENATOR. Then what else
Is there, besides, which you would lay on
us?
CREON. Not to connive at disobedience.
1ST SENATOR. There's no such fool as
to embrace his death.
CREON. Death is the penalty. But men
right often
Are brought to ruin, through their dreams
of gain.
    [*Enter a* SENTINEL.]
SENTINEL. My lord, I will not say—
    "breathless with speed
I come, plying a nimble foot;" for truly
I had a many sticking-points of thought
Wheeling about to march upon my rear.
For my heart whispered me all sorts of
    counsel;
"Poor wretch, why go, to meet thy sen-
    tence?"—"Wretch,
Tarrying again? If Creon hear the news
From others' lips, how shalt thou then not
    rue it?"
Out of this whirligig it came to pass
I hastened—at my leisure; a short road,
Thus, becomes long. Nevertheless at last
It won the day to come hither, to your
    presence;
And speak I will, though nothing have to
    say;
For I come clinging to the hope that I
Can suffer nothing—save my destiny.

CREON. Well—and what caused you
    this disheartenment?
SENTINEL. First let me tell you what
    concerns myself.
I do protest, I neither did the deed,
Nor saw it done, whoever 'twas who did
    it;
Nor should I rightly come to any harm.
CREON. At all events you are a good
    tactician,
And fence the matter off all round. But
    clearly
You have some strange thing to tell?
SENTINEL. Yes. Serious tidings
Induce much hesitation.
CREON. Once for all
Please to speak out, and make an end,
    and go.
SENTINEL. Why, I am telling you. That
    body some one
Has just now buried—sprinkled thirsty
    dust
Over the form—added the proper rites,
And has gone off.
CREON. What say you? What man dared
To do it?
SENTINEL. I know not. There was no
    dint there
Of any mattock, not a sod was turned;
Merely hard ground and bare, without a
    break,
Without a rut from wheels; it was some
    workman
Who left no mark. When the first day-
    sentry
Shewed what had happened, we were all
    dismayed.
The body had vanished; not indeed in-
    terred,
But a light dust lay on it, as if poured
    out
By one who shunned the curse; and there
    appeared
No trace that a wild beast, or any hound,
Had come, or torn the carcase. Angry
    words
Were bandied up and down, guard blam-
    ing guard,
And blows had like to end it, none being
    by
To hinder; for each one of us in turn

Stood culprit, none convicted, but the plea
"I know not" passed. Ready were we to
take
Hot iron in hand, or pass through fire,
and call
The Gods to witness, that we neither did
it,
Nor were accessory to any man
Who compassed it, or did it. So at last,
When all our searching proved to be in
vain,
There speaks up one, who made us, every
man,
Hang down our heads for fear, knowing
no way
To say him nay, or without scathe comply,
His burden was, this business must be
carried
To you, without reserve. That voice pre-
vailed;
And me, poor wretch, the lot condemns to
get
This piece of luck. I come a post un-
willing,
I well believe it, to unwilling ears;
None loves the messenger who brings bad
news.
1ST SENATOR. My lord, my heart mis-
gave me from the first
This must be something more than natural.
CREON. Truce to your speech, before I
choke with rage,
Lest you be found at once grey-beard and
fool!
To say that guardian deities would care
For this dead body, is intolerable.
Could they, by way of supereminent
honour
Paid to a benefactor, give him burial,
Who came to fire their land, their pillared
fanes
And sacred treasures, and set laws at
nought?
Or do you see Gods honouring the bad?
'Tis false. These orders from the first
some people
Hardly accepted, murmuring at me,
Shaking their heads in secret, stiffening
Uneasy necks against this yoke of mine.
They have suborned these sentinels to do
it,

I know that well. No such ill currency
Ever appeared, as money to mankind:
This is it that sacks cities, this routs out
Men from their homes, and trains and
turns astray
The minds of honest mortals, setting them
Upon base actions; this made plain to men
Habits of all misdoing, and cognizance
Of every work of wickedness. Howbeit
Such hireling perpetrators, in the end,
Have wrought so far, that they shall pay
for it.
So surely as I live to worship Jove,
Know this for truth; I swear it in your
ears;
Except you find and bring before my face
The real actor in this funeral,
Death, by itself, shall not suffice for
you,
Before, hung up alive, you have revealed
The secret of this outrage; that henceforth
You may seek plunder—not without re-
spect
Of where your profit lies; and may be
taught
It is not good to covet all men's pay;
For mark you! by corruption few men
thrive,
And many come to mischief.
SENTINEL.   Have I leave
To say a word, or shall I turn and go?
CREON. Cannot you see your prating
tortures me?
SENTINEL. Pricks you how deep? In
the ears, or to the spleen?
CREON. Why do you gauge my chafing,
where it lies?
SENTINEL. Your heart-ache were the
doer's, your ear-ache mine.
CREON. Out, what a bare-faced babbler
born art thou!
SENTINEL. Never the actor in this busi-
ness, though!
CREON. Yes, and for money you would
sell your soul!
SENTINEL. Plague on it! 'tis hard, a
man should be suspicious,
And with a false suspicion!
CREON.   Yes, suspicion;
Mince it as best you may. Make me to
know

Whose are these doings, or you shall soon
  allow
Left-handed gains work their own punish-
  ment.   [*Exit.*]
SENTINEL. I wish he may be found.
  Chance must decide.
Whether or no, you will not, certainly,
See me returning hither.   Heaven be
  praised
I am in safety, past all thought or dream!
                              [*Exit.*]
          CHORUS

          I. 1.

Much is there passing strange;
  Nothing surpassing mankind.
He it is loves to range
Over the ocean hoar,
Thorough the surges' roar,
  South winds raging behind;

Earth, too, wears he away,
  The Mother of Gods on high,
Tireless, free from decay;
With team he furrows the ground,
And the ploughs go round and round,
  As year on year goes by.

          I. 2.

The bird-tribes, light of mind,
  The races of beasts of prey,
And sea-fish after their kind,
Man, abounding in wiles,
Entangles in his toils
  And carries captive away.

The roamers over the hill,
  The field-inhabiting deer,
By craft he conquers, at will;
He bends beneath his yoke
The neck of the steed unbroke,
  And pride of the upland steer.

          II. 1.

He has gotten him speech, and fancy
  breeze-betost,
  And for the state instinct of order
  meet;
He has found him shelter from the chill-
  ing frost

Of a clear sky, and from the arrowy
  sleet;
Illimitable in cunning, cunning-less
  He meets no change of fortune that can
  come;
He has found escape from pain and help-
  lessness;
  Only he knows no refuge from the tomb.

          II. 2.

Now bends he to the good, now to the ill,
  With craft of art, subtle past reach of
  sight;
Wresting his country's laws to his own
  will,
  Spurning the sanctions of celestial
  right;
High in the city, he is made city-less,
  Whoso is corrupt, for his impiety;
He that will work the works of wicked-
  ness,
  Let him not house, let him not hold,
  with me!

At this monstrous vision I stand in
  Doubt!   How dare I say, well knowing
  her,
That this maid is not—Antigone!
  Daughter of Œdipus!
Hapless child, of a hapless father!
Sure—ah surely they did not find thee
Madly defying our king's command-
  ments,
  And so prisoner bring thee here?

[*Enter* SENTINEL *with* ANTIGONE.]
SENTINEL. This is the woman who has
  done the deed.
We took her burying him.   Where's
  Creon?
1ST SENATOR. Here
Comes he again, out of the house, at need.

          [*Enter* CREON.]
CREON. What is it?   In what fit season
  come I forth?
SENTINEL. My lord, I see a man should
  never vow
He will not do a thing, for second thoughts
Bely the purpose.   Truly I could have
  sworn

It would be long indeed ere I came hither
Under that hail of threats you rained on
    me.
But since an unforeseen happy surprise
Passes all other pleasing out of measure,
I come, though I forswore it mightily,
Bringing this maiden, who was caught in
    act
To set that bier in order. Here, my lord,
No lot was cast; this windfall is to me,
And to no other. Take her, now, your-
    self;
Examine and convict her, as you please;
I wash my hands of it, and ought, of
    right,
To be clean quit of the scrape, for good
    and all.
  CREON. You seized—and bring—her?
    In what way, and whence?
  SENTINEL. Burying that man, herself!
    You know the whole.
  CREON. Are you in earnest? Do you
    understand
What you are saying?
  SENTINEL.   Yes, that I saw this girl
Burying that body you forbade to bury.
Do I speak clear and plain?
  CREON.   How might this be,
That she was seen, and taken in the act?
  SENTINEL. Why thus it happened.
    When we reached the place,
Wrought on by those dread menacings
    from you,
We swept away all dust that covered up
The body, and laid the clammy limbs quite
    bare,
And windward from the summit of the
    hill,
Out of the tainted air that spread from
    him,
We sat us down, each, as it might be,
    rousing
His neighbour with a clamour of abuse,
Wakening him up, whenever any one
Seemed to be slack in watching. This
    went on,
Till in mid air the luminous orb of day
Stood, and the heat grew sultry. Sud-
    denly
A violent eddy lifted from the ground
A hurricane, a trouble of the sky;

Ruffling all foliage of the woodland plain
It filled the horizon; the vast atmosphere
Thickened to meet it; we, closing our
    eyes,
Endured the Heaven-sent plague. After a
    while,
When it had ceased, there stands this
    maiden in sight,
And wails aloud, shrill as the bitter note
Of the sad bird, when as she finds the
    couch
Of her void nest robbed of her young; so
    she,
Soon as she sees the body stripped and
    bare,
Bursts out in shrieks, and calls down
    curses dire
On their heads who had done it. Straight-
    way then
She gathers handfuls of dry dust, and
    brings them,
And from a shapely brazen cruse held high
She crowns the body with drink-offerings,
Once, twice, and thrice. We at the sight
    rushed forward,
And trapped her, nothing daunted, on the
    spot;
And taxed her with the past offence, and
    this
The present. Not one whit did she deny;
A pleasant though a pitiful sight to me;
For nothing's sweeter than to have got off
In person; but to bring into mischance
Our friends is pitiful. And yet to pay
No more than this is cheap, to save one's
    life.
  CREON. Do you, I say—you, with your
    downcast brow—
Own or deny that you have done this
    deed?
  ANTIGONE. I say I did it; I deny it not.
  CREON. Take yourself hence, whither
    you will, sir knave;
You are acquitted of a heavy charge.
                    [Exit SENTINEL.]
Now tell me, not at length, but in brief
    space,
Knew you the order not to do it?
  ANTIGONE.   Yes,
I knew it; what should hinder? It was
    plain.

CREON. And you made free to overstep my law?

ANTIGONE. Because it was not Zeus who ordered it,
Nor Justice, dweller with the Nether Gods,
Gave such a law to men; nor did I deem
Your ordinance of so much binding force,
As that a mortal man could overbear
The unchangeable unwritten code of Heaven;
This is not of today and yesterday,
But lives for ever, having origin
Whence no man knows: whose sanctions I were loath
In Heaven's sight to provoke, fearing the will
Of any man. I knew that I should die—
How otherwise? even although your voice
Had never so prescribed. And that I die
Before my hour is due, that I count gain.
For one who lives in many ills, as I—
How should he fail to gain by dying? Thus
To me the pain is light, to meet this fate;
But had I borne to leave the body of him
My mother bare unburied, then, indeed,
I might feel pain; but as it is, I cannot;
And if my present action seems to you
Foolish—'tis like I am found guilty of folly
At a fool's mouth!

1ST SENATOR. Lo you, the spirit stout
Of her stout father's child—unapt to bend
Beneath misfortune!

CREON. But be well assured,
Tempers too stubborn are the first to fail;
The hardest iron from the furnace, forged
To stiffness, you may see most frequently
Shivered and broken; and the chafing steeds
I have known governed with a slender curb.
It is unseemly that a household drudge
Should be misproud; but she was conversant
With outrage, ever since she passed the bounds
Laid down by law; then hard upon that deed
Comes this, the second outrage, to exult
And triumph in her deed. Truly if here
She wield such powers uncensured, she is man,
I woman! Be she of my sister born,
Or nearer to myself than the whole band
Of our domestic tutelary Jove,
She, and the sister—for her equally
I charge with compassing this funeral—
Shall not escape a most tremendous doom.
And call her; for within the house but now
I saw her, frenzied and beside herself;
And it is common for the moody sprite
Of plotters in the dark to no good end
To have been caught, planning its knavery,
Before the deed is acted. None the less
I hate it, when one taken in misdoing
Straight seeks to gloss the facts!

ANTIGONE. Would you aught more
Than take my life, whom you did catch?

CREON. Not I;
Take that, take all.

ANTIGONE. Then why do you delay?
Since naught is pleasing of your words to me,
Or, as I trust, can ever please, so mine
Must needs be unacceptable to you.
And yet from whence could I have gathered praise
More worthily, than from depositing
My own brother in a tomb? These, all of them,
Would utter one approval, did not fear
Seal up their lips. 'Tis tyranny's privilege,
And not the least—power to declare and do
What it is minded.

CREON. You, of all this people,
Are singular in your discernment.

ANTIGONE. Nay,
They too discern; they but refrain their tongues
At your behest.

CREON. And you are not ashamed
That you deem otherwise?

ANTIGONE. It is no shame
To pay respect to our own flesh and blood.

CREON. And his dead foeman, was not he your brother
As well?

ANTIGONE. Yes, the same sire's and
mother's son.
CREON. Why pay, then, honours which
are wrongs to him?
ANTIGONE. The dead clay makes no
protest.
CREON. Not although
His with a villain's share your reverence?
ANTIGONE. It was no bondman perished,
but a brother.
CREON. Spoiling, I say, this country;
while his rival
Stood for it.
ANTIGONE. All the same, these rites are
due
To the underworld.
CREON. But not in equal measure
Both for the good man and the bad.
ANTIGONE. Who knows
This is not piety there?
CREON. The enemy
Can never be a friend, even in death.
ANTIGONE. Well, I was made for fel-
lowship in love,
Not fellowship in hate.
CREON. Then get you down
Thither, and love, if you must love, the
dead!
No woman, while I live, shall order me.

CHORUS

See where out by the doors Ismene
Weeping drops of sisterly grieving
Comes; and a cloud o'erhanging her eye-
brows
Mars her dark-flushed cheek, and moistens
Her fair face with pitiful tears.

[*Enter Attendants with* ISMENE.]
CREON. And you—who like a viper un-
awares
Have crept into my house, and sucked me
bloodless,
While I unknowingly was fostering you,
Twin furies, to the upsetting of my
throne—
Come, tell me, will you say you also
shared
This burying, or protest your innocence?
ISMENE. Yes,.I have done it—if Anti-
gone

Says so—I join with her to share the
blame.
ANTIGONE. That justice will not suffer;
you refused,
And I—I had no partner.
ISMENE. In your trouble
I do not blush to claim companionship
Of what you have to endure.
ANTIGONE. Whose was the deed
Death and the spirits of the dead can tell!
A friend in words is not a friend for me.
ISMENE. Shame me not, sister, by deny-
ing me
A death, for honouring the dead, with
you!
ANTIGONE. Mix not your death with
mine. Do not claim work
You did not touch. I shall suffice to die.
ISMENE. And what care I for life, if I
lost you?
ANTIGONE. Ask Creon; you are dutiful
to him.
ISMENE. Why do you cross me so, to no
good purpose?
ANTIGONE. Nay, I am sick at heart, if
I do make
My mock of you.
ISMENE. Nay, but what can I do,
Now, even yet, to help you?
ANTIGONE. Save yourself;
I do not grudge you your escape.
ISMENE. O me
Unhappy! And must I miss to share
your fate?
ANTIGONE. You made your choice, to
live; I mine, to die.
ISMENE. Not if you count my words
unsaid.
ANTIGONE. By some
Your judgment is approved; by others
mine.
ISMENE. Then our delinquency is equal,
too.
ANTIGONE. Take courage, you are liv-
ing; but my life
Long since has died, so I might serve the
dead.
CREON. Of these two girls I swear the
one even now
Has been proved witless; the other was so
born.

ISMENE. Ah sir, the wretched cannot
  keep the wit
That they were born with, but it flits
  away.
CREON. Yours did so, when you chose
  to join ill-doers
In their misdoing.
    ISMENE.   How could I live on
Alone, without my sister?
    CREON.   Do not say
"My sister"; for you have no sister more.
    ISMENE. What, will you put to death
  your own son's bride?
    CREON. He may go further afield—
    ISMENE.   Not as by troth
Plighted to her by him.
    CREON.   Unworthy wives
For sons of mine I hate.
    ANTIGONE.   O dearest Hæmon,
How are you slighted by your father!
    CREON.   I
Am weary of your marriage, and of you.
    ISMENE. Your own son! will you tear
  her from his arms?
    CREON. Death will prevent that bridal-
  rite, for me.
    1ST SENATOR. I see, the sentence of
  this maiden's death
Has been determined.
    CREON.   Then we see the same.
An end of trifling. Slaves, there, take
  them in!
As women, henceforth, must they live—
  not suffered
To gad abroad; for even bold men flinch,
When they view Death hard by the verge
  of Life.
[*Exeunt* ANTIGONE *and* ISMENE, *guarded.*]

CHORUS

I. 1.

Happy the man whose cup of life is free
  From taste of evil! If Heaven's influ-
    ence shake them,
No ill but follows, till it overtake them,
All generations of his family;
      Like as when before the sweep
      Of the sea-borne Thracian blast
      The surge of ocean coursing past
    Above the cavern of the deep

Rolls up from the region under
  All the blackness of the shore,
  And the beaten beaches thunder
  Answer to the roar.

I. 2.

Woes upon woes on Labdacus' race I see—
  Living or dead—inveterately descend;
  And son with sire entangled, without
    end,
And by some God smitten without remedy;
    For a light of late had spread
      O'er the last surviving root
    In the house of Œdipus;
      Now, the sickle murderous
      Of the Rulers of the dead,
      And wild words beyond control,
      And the frenzy of her own soul,
      Again mow down the shoot.

II. 1.

Thy power, O God, what pride of man
    constraineth,
Which neither sleep, that all things else
    enchaineth,
  Nor even the tireless moons of Heaven
    destroy?
      Thy throne is founded fast,
  High on Olympus, in great brilliancy,
      Far beyond Time's annoy.
  Through present and through future
    and through past
    Abideth one decree;
      Nought in excess
  Enters the life of man without unhappi-
    ness.

II. 2.

For wandering Hope to many among
    mankind
Seems pleasurable; but to many a mind
  Proves but a mockery of its wild desires.
      They know not aught, nor fear,
  Till their feet feel the pathway strewn
    with fires.
      "If evil good appear,
  That soul to his ruin is divinely led"—
      (Wisely the word was said!)
        And short the hour
  He spends unscathed by the avenging
    power.

Hæmon comes, thy last surviving
Child.   Is he here to bewail, in-
dignant,
His lost bride, Antigone? Grieves
he
For a vain promise—her
marriage-bed?

[*Enter* HÆMON.]

CREON.   We shall know soon, better
than seers can tell us.
Son, you are here in anger, are you not,
Against your sire, hearing his final doom
Upon your bride to be? Or are we friends,
Always, with you, whate'er our policy?
HÆMON.   Yours am I, father; and you
guide my steps
With your good counsels, which for my
part I
Will follow closely; for there is no mar-
riage
Shall occupy a larger place with me
Than your direction, in the path of
honour.
CREON.   So is it right, my son, to be
disposed—
In everything to back your father's
quarrel.
It is for this men pray to breed and rear
In their homes dutiful offspring—to re-
quite
The foe with evil, and their father's friend
Honour, as did their father. Whoso gets
Children unserviceable—what else could he
Be said to breed, but troubles for himself,
And store of laughter for his enemies?
Nay, never fling away your wits, my son,
Through liking for a woman; recollect,
Cold are embracings, where the wife is
naught,
Who shares your board and bed.   And
what worse sore
Can plague us, than a loved one's worth-
lessness?
Better to spurn this maiden as a foe!
Leave her to wed some bridegroom in the
grave!
For, having caught her in the act, alone
Of the whole city disobeying me,
I will not publicly bely myself,
But kill her. Now let her go glorify

Her God of kindred!   If I choose to
cherish
My own born kinsfolk in rebelliousness,
Then verily I must count on strangers too.
For he alone who is a man of worth
In his own household will appear upright
In the state also; and whoe'er offends
Against the laws by violence, or thinks
To give commands to rulers—I deny
Favour to such. Obedience is due
To the state's officer in small and great,
Just and unjust commandments; he who
pays it
I should be confident would govern well,
And cheerfully be governed, and abide
A true and trusty comrade at my back,
Firm in the ranks amid the storm of war.
There lives no greater fiend than Anarchy;
She ruins states, turns houses out of
doors,
Breaks up in rout the embattled soldiery;
While Discipline preserves the multitude
Of the ordered host alive. Therefore it is
We must assist the cause of order; this
Forbids concession to a feminine will;
Better be outcast, if we must, of men,
Than have it said a woman worsted us.
1ST SENATOR.   Unless old age have
robbed me of myself,
I think the tenor of your words is wise.
HÆMON.   Father, the Gods plant rea-
son in mankind,
Of all good gifts the highest; and to say
You speak not rightly in this, I lack the
power;
Nor do I crave it. Still, another's thought
Might be of service; and it is for me,
Being your son, to mark the words, the
deeds,
And the complaints of all. To a private
man
Your frown is dreadful, who has things to
say
That will offend you; but I secretly
Can gather this; how the folk mourn this
maid,
"Who of all women most unmeriting,
For noblest acts dies by the worst of
deaths,
Who her own brother battle-slain—un-
buried—

Would not allow to perish in the fangs
Of carrion hounds or any bird of prey;
And" (so the whisper darkling passes
    round)
"Is she not worthy to be carved in gold?"
Father, beside your welfare there is
    nothing
More prized by me; for what more glor-
    ious crown
Can be to children, than their father's
    honour?
Or to a father, from his sons, than theirs?
Do not persist, then, to retain at heart
One sole idea, that the thing is right
Which your mouth utters, and nought
    else beside.
For all men who believe themselves alone
Wise, or that they possess a soul or speech
Such as none other, turn them inside out,
They are found empty; and though a
    man be wise,
It is no shame for him to live and learn,
And not to stretch a course too far. You
    see
How all the trees on winter torrent banks,
Yielding, preserve their sprays; those that
    would stem it
Break, roots and all; the shipman too,
    who keeps
The vessel's main sheet taut, and will not
    slacken,
Goes cruising, in the end, keel uppermost:
Let thy wrath go! Be willing to relent!
For if some sense, even from a younger
    head,
Be mine to afford, I say it is far better
A man should be, for every accident,
Furnished with inbred skill; but what of
    that?
Since nature's bent will have it otherwise,
'Tis good to learn of those who counsel
    wisely.
    1st SENATOR.   Sir, you might learn,
        when he speaks seasonably;
And you, from him; for both have spoken
    well.
    CREON.   Men that we are, must we be
        sent to school
To learn discretion of a boy like this?
    HÆMON.   None that's dishonest; and if
        I am young,

It is not well to have regard to years
Rather than services.
    CREON.   Good service is it,
To pay respect to rebels?
    HÆMON.   To wrongdoers
I would not even ask for reverence.
    CREON.   Was it not some such taint
        infected her?
    HÆMON.   So say not all this populace
        of Thebes.
    CREON.   The city to prescribe me my
        decrees!
    HÆMON.   Look, say you so, you are too
        young in this!
    CREON.   Am I to rule this land after
        some will
Other than mine?
    HÆMON.   A city is no city
That is of one man only.
    CREON.   Is not the city
Held to be his who rules it?
    HÆMON.   That were brave—
You, a sole monarch of an empty land!
    CREON.   This fellow, it seems, fights on
        the woman's side.
    HÆMON.   An you be woman! My fore-
        thought is for you.
    CREON.   O villain—traversing thy
        father's rights!
    HÆMON.   Because I see you sinning
        against right.
    CREON.   Sin I, to cause my sway to be
        held sacred?
    HÆMON.   You desecrate, by trampling
        on Heaven's honour.
    CREON.   Foul spotted heart—a woman's
        follower!
    HÆMON.   You will not find me serving
        what is vile.
    CREON.   I say this talk of thine is all
        for her.
    HÆMON.   And you, and me, and for the
        Gods beneath!
    CREON.   Never shall she live on to
        marry thee!
    HÆMON.   Die as she may, she shall not
        die alone.
    CREON.   Art thou grown bold enough to
        threaten, too?
    HÆMON.   Where is the threat, to speak
        against vain counsel?

CREON. Vain boy, thyself shalt rue thy
counselling.
HÆMON. I had called you erring, were
you not my sire.
CREON. Thou woman's bondman, do not
spaniel me!
HÆMON. Do you expect to speak, and
not be answered?
CREON. Do I so? By Olympus over us,
If thou revile me, and find fault with
me,
Never believe but it shall cost thee dear!
Bring out the wretch, that in his sight, at
once,
Here, with her bridegroom by her, she
may die!
HÆMON. Not in my sight, at least—
not by my side,
Believe it, shall she perish! And for
thee—
Storm at the friends who choose thy com-
pany!
My face thou never shalt behold again.
[Exit.]
1ST SENATOR. The man is gone, my
lord, headlong with rage;
And wits so young, when galled, are full
of danger.
CREON. Let be, let him imagine more,
or do,
Than mortal may; yet he shall not redeem
From sentence those two maidens.
1ST SENATOR. Both of them?
Is it your will to slay them both alike?
CREON. That is well said; not her who
did not touch it.
1ST SENATOR. And by what death mean
you to kill the other?
CREON. Into some waste untrodden of
mankind
She shall be drawn, and, in some rock-
hewn cave,
With only food enough provided her
For expiation, so that all the city
Escape the guilt of blood, buried alive.
There, if she ask him, Hades, the one
God
Whom she regards, may grant her not to
perish;
Or there, at latest, she shall recognize
It is lost labour to revere the dead. [Exit.]

CHORUS

O Love, thou art victor in fight: thou
mak'st all things afraid;
Thou couchest thee softly at night on the
cheeks of a maid;
Thou passest the bounds of the sea, and
the folds of the fields;
To thee the immortal, to thee the
ephemeral yields;
Thou maddenest them that possess thee;
thou turnest astray
The souls of the just, to oppress them,
out of the way;
Thou hast kindled amongst us pride, and
the quarrel of kin;
Thou art lord, by the eyes of a bride, and
the love-light therein;
Thou sittest assessor with Right; her
kingdom is thine,
Who sports with invincible might, Aphro-
dite divine.

[Enter ANTIGONE, guarded.]
I too, myself, am carried as I look
Beyond the bounds of right;
Nor can I brook
The springing fountain of my tears, to see
My child, Antigone,
Pass to the chamber of universal night.

I. 1.

ANTIGONE. Behold me, people of my
native land:
I wend my latest way:
I gaze upon the latest light of day
That I shall ever see;
Death, who lays all to rest, is leading me
To Acheron's far strand
Alive; to me no bridal hymns belong,
For me no marriage song
Has yet been sung; but Acheron instead
Is it, whom I must wed.
CHORUS. Nay but with praise and voic-
ings of renown
Thou partest for that prison-house of the
dead;
Unsmitten by diseases that consume,
By sword unvisited,
Thou only of mortals freely shalt go down,
Alive, to the tomb.

I. 2.

ANTIGONE. I have heard tell the sorrowful end of her,
That Phrygian sojourner
On Sipylus' peak, offspring of Tantalus;
How stony shoots upgrown
Like ivy bands enclosed her in the stone;
With snows continuous
And ceaseless rain her body melts away;
Streams from her tear-flown head
Water her front; likest to hers the bed
My fate prepares today.
CHORUS. She was of godlike nature,
goddess-sprung,
And we are mortals, and of human race;
And it were glorious odds
For maiden slain, among
The equals of the Gods
In life—and then in death—to gain a
place.

II. 1.

ANTIGONE. They mock me. Gods of
Thebes! why scorn you me
Thus, to my face,
Alive, not death-stricken yet?
O city, and you the city's large-dowered
race,
Ye streams from Dirca's source,
Ye woods that shadow Theba's chariot-course,
Listen and see,
Let none of you forget,
How sacrificed, and for what laws
offended,
By no tears friended,
I to the prisoning mound
Of a strange grave am journeying under
ground.
Ah me unhappy! [home is none for
me;]
Alike in life or death an exile must I be.
CHORUS. Thou to the farthest verge
forth-faring,
O my child, of daring,
Against the lofty threshold of the laws
Didst stumble and fall. The cause
Is some ancestral load, which thou art
bearing.

II. 2.

ANTIGONE. There didst thou touch upon
my bitterest bale—
A threefold tale—
My father's piteous doom,
Doom of us all, scions of Labdacus.
Woe for my mother's bed!
Woe for the ill-starred spouse, from her
own womb
Untimely born!
O what a father's house
Was that from whence I drew my life
forlorn!
To whom, unwed,
Accursed, lo I come
To sojourn as a stranger in their home!
And thou too, ruined, my brother, in a
wife,
Didst by thy death bring death upon thy
sister's life!
CHORUS. To pay due reverence is a
duty, too:
And power—his power, whose empire is
confest,
May no wise be transgressed;
But thee thine own infatuate mood o'er-
threw.
ANTIGONE. Friendless, unwept, unwed,
I, sick at heart, am led
The way prepared for me;
Day's hallowed orb on high
I may no longer see;
For me no tears are spent,
Nor any friends lament
The death I die.

[*Enter* CREON.]

CREON. Think you that any one, if help
might be
In wailing and lament before he died,
Would ever make an end? Away with her!
Wall her up close in some deep catacomb,
As I have said; leave her alone, apart,
To perish, if she will; or if she live,
To make her tomb her tenement. For us,
We will be guiltless of this maiden's
blood;
But here on earth she shall abide no more.
ANTIGONE. Thou Grave, my bridal
chamber! dwelling-place

Hollowed in earth, the everlasting prison
Whither I bend my steps, to join the band
Of kindred, whose more numerous host
    already
Persephone hath counted with the dead;
Of whom I last and far most miserably
Descend, before my term of life is full;
I come, cherishing this hope especially,
To win approval in my father's sight,
Approval too, my mother, in thine, and
    thine
Dear brother! for that with these hands I
    paid
Unto you dead lavement and ordering
And sepulchre-libations; and that now,
Polynices, in the tendance of thy body
I meet with this reward. Yet to the wise
It was no crime, that I did honour thee.
For never had I, even had I been
Mother of children, or if spouse of mine
Lay dead and mouldering, in the state's
    despite
Taken this task upon me. Do you ask
What argument I follow here of law?
One husband dead, another might be mine;
Sons by another, did I lose the first;
But, sire and mother buried in the grave,
A brother is a branch that grows no more.
Yet I, preferring by this argument
To honour thee to the end, in Creon's
    sight
Appear in that I did so to offend,
And dare to do things heinous, O my
    brother!
And for this cause he hath bid lay hands
    on me,
And leads me, not as wives or brides are
    led,
Unblest with any marriage, any care
Of children; destitute of friends, forlorn,
Yet living, to the chambers of the dead
See me descend. Yet what celestial right
Did I transgress? How should I any more
Look up to heaven, in my adversity?
Whom should I call to aid? Am I not
    come
Through piety to be held impious? If
This is approved in Heaven, why let me
    suffer,
And own that I have sinned; but if the
    sin

Belong to these—O may their punishment
Be measured by the wrongfulness of mine!
1ST SENATOR.   Still the same storms
    possess her, with the same precipi-
    tance of spirit.
CREON.   Then for this
Her guards shall rue their slowness.
ANTIGONE.   Woe for me!
The word I hear comes hand in hand with
    death!
1ST SENATOR. I may not say Be com-
    forted, for this
Shall not be so; I have no words of cheer.
ANTIGONE. O City of Thebes! O my
    country! Gods,
The Fathers of my race! I am led hence—
I linger now no more. Behold me, lords,
The last of your kings' house—what doom
    is mine,
And at whose hands, and for what cause
    —that I
Duly performed the dues of piety!
        [*Exeunt* ANTIGONE *and guards.*]

CHORUS

I. 1.

For a dungeon brazen-barred
    The body of Danae endured
        To exchange Heaven's daylight of old,
    In a tomb-like chamber immured,
Hid beneath fetter and guard;
    And she was born, we are told,
    O child, my child, unto honour,
And a son was begotten upon her
To Zeus in a shower of gold.
But the stress of a Fate is hard;
    Nor wealth, nor warfare, nor ward,
    Nor black ships cleaving the sea
    Can resist her, or flee.

I. 2.

And the Thracians' king, Dryas' son,
    The hasty of wrath, was bound
        For his words of mocking and pride;
    Dionysus closing him round,
Pent in a prison of stone;
    Till, his madness casting aside
    Its flower and fury wild,
    He knew what God he reviled—
    Whose power he had defied;

Restraining the Mænad choir,
Quenching the Evian fire,
　Enraging the Muses' throng,
　The lovers of song.

II. 1.

And by the twofold main
　Of rocks Cyanean—there
　Lies the Bosporean strand,
And the lone Thracian plain
　Of Salmydessus, where
　Is Ares' border-land:
Who saw the stab of pain
Dealt on the Phineid pair
　At that fierce dame's command;
Blinding the orbits of their blasted sight,
Smitten, without spear to smite,
　By a spindle's point made bare,
　And by a bloody hand.

II. 2.

They mourned their mother dead,
　Their hearts with anguish wrung,
　Wasting away, poor seed
Of her deserted bed;
Who, Boreas' daughter, sprung
　From the old Erechtheid breed,
In remote caverns fed
　Her native gales among,
　Went swiftly as the steed,
Offspring of Heaven, over the steep-down
　wild;
Yet to her too, my child,
　The Destinies, that lead
　Lives of long ages, clung.

[*Enter* TIRESIAS *led by a boy.*]
TIRESIAS. Princes of Thebes, two fellow-
　travellers.
Debtors in common to the eyes of one,
We stand before you; for a blind man's
　path
Hangs on the guide who marshals him the
　way.
CREON. What would'st thou now, rev-
　erend Tiresias?
TIRESIAS. That will I tell. Do thou
　obey the seer.
CREON. I never have departed hitherto
From thy advice.

TIRESIAS.　　And therefore 'tis, thou
　steerest
The city's course straight forward.
　CREON.　　　　Thou hast done me
Good service, I can witness.
　TIRESIAS.　　　　　　Now again
Think, thou dost walk on fortune's razor-
　edge.
CREON. What is it? I tremble but to
　see thee speak.
TIRESIAS. Listen to what my art fore-
　shadoweth,
And thou shalt know. I lately, taking
　seat
On my accustomed bench of augury,
Whither all tribes of fowl after their
　kind
Alway resort, heard a strange noise of
　birds
Screaming with harsh and dissonant im-
　petus;
And was aware how each the other tore
With murderous talons; for the whirr of
　wings
Rose manifest. Then feared I, and straight
　made trial
Of sacrifices on the altar-hearths
All blazing; but, out of the offerings,
There sprang no flame; only upon embers
　charred
Thick droppings melted off the thigh-
　pieces,
And heaved and sputtered, and the gall-
　bladders
Burst, and were lost, while from the folds
　of fat
The loosened thigh-bones fell. Such augu-
　ries,
Failing of presage through the unseemli-
　ness
Of holy rites, I gather from this lad,
Who is to me, as I to others, guide.
And this state-sickness comes by thy self-
　will;
For all our hearths and altars are defiled
With prey of dogs and fowl, who have de-
　voured
The dead unhappy son of Œdipus.
Therefore the Gods accept not of us now
Solemn peace-offering or burnt sacrifice,
Nor bird trills out a happy-boding note,

Gorged with the fatness of a slain man's blood.
This, then, my son, consider; that to err
From the right path is common to mankind;
But having erred, that mortal is no more
Losel or fool, who medicines the ill
Wherein he fell, and stands not obstinate.
Conceit of will savours of emptiness.
Give place, then, in the presence of the dead.
Wound not the life that's perished. Where's thy valour
In slaying o'er the slain? Well I advise,
Meaning thee well; 'tis pleasantest to learn
Of good advisers, when their words bring gain.

CREON. Old man, ye all, like archers at a mark,
Are loosing shafts at me; I am not spared
Even your soothsayers' practice; by whose tribe
Long since have I been made as merchandize,
And bought, and sold. Gather your gains at will!
Market your Sardian silver, Indian gold!
That man ye shall not cover with a tomb;
Not though the eagle ministers of Jove
To Jove's own throne should bear their prey of him,
Not even for horror at such sacrilege
Will I permit his burial. This I know;
There is no power in any man to touch
The Gods with sacrilege; but foul the falls
Which men right cunning fall, Tiresias—
Old man, I say—when for the sake of gain
They speak foul treason with a fair outside.

TIRESIAS. Alas, does no man know, does no man think—
CREON. What should one think? What common saw is this?
TIRESIAS. How far good counsel passes all things good?
CREON. So far, I think, folly's the worst of harm!

TIRESIAS. That is the infirmity that fills thy nature.
CREON. I care not to retort upon thee, seer.
TIRESIAS. Thou dost, thou say'st my oracles are false.
CREON. All the prophetic tribe are covetous.
TIRESIAS. And that of kings fond of disgraceful gain.
CREON. Know'st thou of whom thou speak'st? I am thy lord.
TIRESIAS. Yea, thou hast saved the state; I gave it thee.
CREON. Thou art a wise seer, but in love with wrong.
TIRESIAS. Thou wilt impel me to give utterance
To my still dormant prescience.
CREON. Say on;
Only beware thou do not speak for gain.
TIRESIAS. For gain of thine, methinks, I do not speak.
CREON. Thou shalt not trade upon my wits, be sure.
TIRESIAS. And be thou sure of this; thou shalt not tell
Many more turns of the sun's chariotwheel,
Ere thou shalt render satisfaction, one
From thy own loins in payment, dead for dead,
For that thou hast made Life join hands with Death,
And sent a living soul unworthily
To dwell within a tomb, and keep'st a corpse
Here, from the presence of the Powers beneath,
Not for thy rights or any God's above,
But lawlessly in their despite usurped,
Unhallowed, disappointed, uninterred;
Wherefore the late-avenging punishers,
Furies, from Death and Heaven, lay wait for thee,
To take thee in the evil of thine own hands.
Look to it, whether I be bribed who speak;
For as to that, with no great wear of time,
Men's, women's wails to thine own house shall answer.

Also all cities rise in enmity,
To the strown relics of whose citizens
None pays due hallowing, save beasts of
prey,
Dogs, or some fowl, whose pinions to their
gates—
Yea, to each hearth—bear taint defiling
them.
Such bolts, in wrath, since thou dar'st
anger me,
I loosen at thy bosom, archer-like,
Sure-aimed, whose burning smart thou
shalt not shun.
Lead me away, boy, to my own home
again;
And let him vent his spleen on younger
men,
And learn to keep a tongue more gentle,
and
A brain more sober, than he carries now.
        [*Exeunt* TIRESIAS *and Boy.*]
  1ST SENATOR. The seer is gone, my lord,
denouncing woe;
And from the day my old hairs began to
indue
Their white for black, we have known him
for a watch
Who never barked to warn the state in
vain.
  CREON. I know it too; and I am ill at
ease;
'Tis bitter to submit; but Até's hand
Smites bitterly on the spirit that abides
her.
  1ST SENATOR. Creon, Menœceus' son, be
wise at need!
  CREON. What should I do? speak, I will
hearken.
  1ST SENATOR.   Go,
Set free the maiden from the vault, and
build
A tomb for that dead outcast.
  CREON.   You approve it?
You deem that I should yield?
  1ST SENATOR.   Sir, with all speed.
Swift-footed come calamities from Heaven
To cut off the perverse.
  CREON.   O God, 'tis hard!
But I quit heart, and yield; I cannot fight
At odds with destiny.
  1ST SENATOR.   Up then, to work!

Commit it not to others!
  CREON.   I am gone
Upon the instant. Quickly, quickly men,
You and your fellows, get you, axe in
hand,
Up to the place, there, yonder; and be-
cause
I am thus minded, other than before,
I who did bind her will be there to loose;
For it misgives me it is best to keep
The old appointed laws, all our life long.
        [*Exeunt* CREON *and Attendants.*]

CHORUS

I. 1.

Thou by many names addrest,
Child of Zeus loud-thundering,
Glory of a Theban maid,
Who unbidden wanderest
  Fair Italia's King,
And art lord in each deep glade
Whither all men seek to her,
Eleusinian Demeter;
Bacchus, who by soft-flowing waters
Of Ismenus habitest
Theba, mother of Bacchant daughters,
With the savage Dragon's stock,

I. 2.

Thee the lurid wild-fire meets
O'er the double-crested rock,
Where Corycian Nymphs arow
Bacchic-wise ascending go,
  Thee Castalia's rill;
Thee the ivy-covered capes
Usher forth of Nysa's hill,
And the shore with green of grapes
Clustering, where the hymn to thee
Rises up immortally,
Visitant in Theban Streets,
"Evoe, O Evoe!"

II. 1.

Wherefore, seeing thy City thus—
City far above all other
Dear to thee, and her, thy mother
Lightning-slain—by sickness grievous
Holden fast in all her gates,
Come with quickness to relieve us,
By the slopes of Parnassus,
  Or the roaring straits.

II. 2.

Hail to thee, the first advancing
In the stars' fire-breathing chorus!
Leader of the nightly strain,
Boy and son of Zeus and King!
Manifest thyself before us
With thy frenzied Thyiad train,
Who their lord Iacchus dancing
Praise, and all night sing.

[*Enter a* MESSENGER.]

MESSENGER. You citizens who dwell be-
side the roof
Of Cadmus and Amphion, there is no sort
Of human life that I could ever praise,
Or could dispraise, as constant; Fortune
still
Raising and Fortune overthrowing still
The happy and the unhappy; and none
can read
What is set down for mortals. Creon, me-
thought
Was enviable erewhile, when he preserved
This land of Cadmus from its enemies,
And took the country's absolute mon-
archy,
And ruled it, flourishing with a noble
growth
From his own seed; and now, he has
lost all.
For when men forfeit all their joys in life,
One in that case I do not count alive,
But deem of him as of some animate corse.
Pile now great riches, if thou wilt, at
home;
Wear thou the living semblance of a king;
An if delight be lacking, all the rest
I would not purchase, as compared with
joy,
From any, for the shadow of a shade.

1ST SENATOR. What new affliction to
the royal stock
Com'st thou to tell?

MESSENGER.   Death is upon them—
death
Caused by the living.

1ST SENATOR.   And who is the slayer?
Speak! who the victim?

MESSENGER.   Hæmon is no more;
His life-blood spilt, and by no stranger's
hand.

1ST SENATOR. What, by his father's, or
his own?

MESSENGER.   Self-slaughtered;
Wroth with his father for the maiden
slain.

1ST SENATOR. Prophet! how strictly is
thy word come true!

MESSENGER. Look to the future, for
these things are so.

1ST SENATOR. And I behold the poor
Eurydice
Come to us from the palace, Creon's wife;
Either of chance, or hearing her son's
name.

[*Enter* EURYDICE.]

EURYDICE. O all you citizens, I heard
the sound
Of your discourse, as I approached the
gates,
Meaning to bring my prayers before the
face
Of Pallas; even as I undid the bolts,
And set the door ajar, a voice of woe
To my own household pierces through my
ears;
And I sink backward on my handmaidens
Afaint for terror; but whate'er the tale,
Tell it again; I am no novice, I,
In misery, that hearken.

MESSENGER.   Dear my mistress,
I saw, and I will speak, and will let slip
No syllable of the truth. Why should we
soothe
Your ears with stories, only to appear
Liars thereafter? Truth is alway right.
—I followed in attendance on your lord,
To the flat hill-top, where despitefully
Was lying yet, harried by dogs, the body
Of Polynices. Pluto's name, and hers,
The wayside goddess, we invoked, to stay
Their anger and be favourable; and him
We washed with pure lustration, and con-
sumed
On fresh-lopped branches the remains of
him,
And piled a monument of natal earth
High over all; thence to the maiden's cell,
Chamber of death, with bridal couch of
stone,
We made as if to enter. But afar
One fellow hears a loud uplifted wail

Fill all the unhallowed precinct; comes,
and tells
His master, Creon; the uncertain sound
Of piteous crying, as he draws more nigh,
Comes round him, and he utters, groaning
loud
A lamentable plaint; "Me miserable!
Was I a prophet? Is this path I tread
The unhappiest of all ways I ever went?
My son's voice thrills my ear. What ho,
my guard!
Run quickly thither to the tomb where
stones
Have been dragged down to make an open-
ing,
Go in and look, whether I really hear
The voice of Hæmon, or am duped by
Heaven."
Quickly, at our distracted lord's command,
We looked: and in the tomb's inmost re-
cess
Found we her, as she had been hanged by
the neck,
Fast in a strip-like loop of linen; and him
Laid by her, clasping her about the waist,
Mourning his wedlock severed in the grave,
And his sire's deeds, and his ill-fated
bride.
He, when he sees them, with a terrible cry
Goes in towards him, calling out aloud
"Ah miserable, what hast thou done? what
mind
Hadst thou? by what misfortune art thou
crazed?
Come out, my son,—suppliant I ask of
thee!"
But with fierce aspect the youth glared
at him;
Spat in his face; answered him not a
word;
Grasped at the crossed hilts of his sword
and drew it,
And—for the father started forth in
flight—
Missed him! then, angered with himself,
poor fool,
There as he stood he flung himself along
Upon the sword-point firmly planted in
The middle of his breast, and, conscious
yet,
Clings to the maid, clasped in his failing
arms,

And gasping, sends forth on the pallid
cheek
Fast welling drops of blood: So lies he,
dead,
With his arms round the dead; there, in
the grave
His bridal rite is full; his misery
Is witness to mankind what worst of woe
The lack of counsel brings a man to
know!   [*Exit* EURYDICE.]
1ST SENATOR. What do you make of
this? The woman's gone
Back, and without one word, of good or
bad!
MESSENGER. I marvel too; and yet I
am in hope
She would not choose, hearing her son's
sad fate,
In public to begin her keening-cry;
But rather to her handmaids in the house
Dictate the mourning for a private pain.
She is not ignorant of self-control,
That she should err.
1ST SENATOR.   I know not; but on me
Weigh heavily both silence over-much,
And loud complaint in vain.
MESSENGER.   Well, we shall know it,
If she hide aught within a troubled heart
Even to suppression of its utterance,
If we approach the house. Yes, you say
truly,
It does weigh heavy, silence over-much.
                                    [*Exit.*]

CHORUS

Lo now, Creon himself draws near us,
Clasping a record
Manifest, if we sin not, saying it,
Of ruin unwrought by the hands of others,
    But fore-caused by his own self-will.

[*Enter* CREON, *attended, with the body of*
        HÆMON.]

I. 1.

CREON.   O sins of a mind
            That is minded to stray!
        Mighty to bind
            And almighty to slay!
Behold us, kin slayers and slain, O ye
    who stand by the way!
        Ah, newness of death!
            O my fruitless design!

New to life's breath,
O son that wert mine,
Ah, ah, thou art dead, thou art sped, for
a fault that was mine, not thine!
1ST SENATOR. Ah, how thou seem'st to
see the truth, too late!
CREON. Ah yes, I have learnt, I know
my wretchedness!

II. 1.

Heaviness hath o'ertaken me
And mine head the rod;
The roughness hath shaken me
Of the paths I trod;
Woe is me; my delight is brought low,
cast under the feet of a God!
Woe for man's labours that are profit-
less!

[*Reënter the* MESSENGER.]
MESSENGER. O master, now thou hast
and hast in store
Of sorrows; one thou bearest in thine
arms,
And one at home thou seemest to be come
Merely to witness.
CREON. And what more of sorrow,
Or what more sorrowful, is yet behind?
MESSENGER. Thy wife, the mother—
mother of the dead—
Is, by a blow just fallen, haplessly slain.

I. 2.

CREON. O hard to appease thee,
Haven of Death,
How should it please thee
To end this breath?
O herald of heavy news, what is this thy
mouth uttereth?

O man, why slayest thou
A man that is slain?
Alas, how sayest thou
Anew and again

That the slaying of a woman is added to
slaying—a pain to a pain?
MESSENGER. See for thyself; the palace
doors unclose.
[*The Altar is disclosed, with the
dead body of* EURYDICE.]

CREON. Woe is me again, for this new
sorrow I see.

II. 2.

What deed is not done?
What tale is not told?
Thy body, O son,
These arms enfold—
Dead—wretch that I am! Dead, too, is
the face these eyes behold.

Ah, child, for thy poor mother!
ah for thee!
MESSENGER. She with a sharp-edged
dagger in her heart
Lies at the altar; and her darkened lids
Close on her wailing for the glorious lot
Of Megareus, who died before, and next
For his, and last, upon her summoning
Evil to fall on thee, the child-slayer!

III. 1.

CREON. Alas, I faint for dread!
Is there none will deal
A thrust that shall lay me
dead
With the two-edged steel?
Ah woe is me!
I am all whelmed in utter misery!
MESSENGER. It may be so; thou art ar-
raigned of her
Who here lies dead, for the occasion thou
Hast wrought for Destiny on her, and him.
1ST SENATOR. In what way did she
slay herself and die?
MESSENGER. Soon as she heard the
raising of the wail
For her son's death, she stabbed herself
to the heart.

IV. 1.

CREON. Woe is me! to none else can
they lay it,
This guilt, but to me!
I, I was the slayer, I say it,
Unhappy, of thee!
O bear me, haste ye, spare not,
To the ends of earth,
More nothing than they who
were not
In the hour of birth!

1ST SENATOR. Thou counsellest well—
  if anything be well
To follow, in calamity; the ills
Lying in our path, soonest o'erpast, were
  best.

III. 2.

CREON. Come, thou most welcome Fate,
    Appear, O come;
    Bring my days' final date,
    Fill up their sum!
    Come quick, I pray;
    Let me not look upon another
    day!

1ST SENATOR. This for to-morrow; we
  must take some thought
On that which lies before us; for these
  griefs,
They are their care on whom the care has
  fallen.
CREON. I did but join your prayer for
  our desire.
1ST SENATOR. Pray thou for nothing
  more; there is no respite
To mortals from the ills of destiny.

IV. 2.

CREON. Lead me forth, cast me out, no
    other
    Than a man undone;
    Who did slay, unwitting, thy
    mother
    And thee, my son!
    I turn me I know not where
    For my plans ill-sped,
    And a doom that is heavy to
    bear
    Is come down on my head.
        [Exit CREON, *attended.]*

CHORUS

Wisdom first for a man's well-being
Maketh, of all things. Heaven's insistence
Nothing allows of man's irreverence;
And great blows great speeches aveng-
  ing,
  Dealt on a boaster,
Teach men wisdom in age, at last.
        [Exeunt omnes.]

ALCESTIS

By EURIPIDES

Produced at Athens, 438 B.C.

TRANSLATED BY R. POTTER

CHARACTERS

APOLLO
ORCUS
ALCESTIS
ADMETUS
EUMELUS
HERCULES
PHERES
ATTENDANTS
CHORUS OF PHERÆANS

APOLLO. Thy royal house, Admetus, yet again
I visit, where a slave among thy slaves
Thy table, though a god, I deigned to praise;
To this compelled by Jove, who slew my son,
The healing sage, launching against his breast
The flaming thunder; hence enraged I killed
The Cyclops, that prepared his fiery bolts.
For this a penal task my vengeful sire
Assigned me, to a mortal doomed a slave
Perforce; I hither came, and fed his herds,
Who friendly entertained me, guarding then,
And to this day, his hospitable house.
Holy the house, and holy is its lord,
The son of Pheres; him from death I saved
The Fates beguiling; for those ancient powers
Assented that Admetus should escape
Death then approaching, would some other go,
Exchanged for him, to the dark realms beneath.
His friends, his father, e'en the aged dame
That gave him birth, were asked in vain; not one
Was found, his wife except; for him she willed
To die, and view no more th' ethereal light.
She in the house, supported in their arms,
Now sighs out her last breath: for she must die.

And this the fate-appointed day: for this,
Dear as it is, I leave the friendly mansion,
Lest there pollution find me. But I see
Orcus advancing near, priest of the dead;
He to the house of Pluto will conduct
her;
Observant of the stated time he comes,
True to the day when she perforce must
die.

[ORCUS, APOLLO.]

ORCUS. Why art thou here? Why dost
thou make this house
Thy haunt, Apollo? Thou dost wrong,
again,
Th' infernal realms defrauding of their
honours,
Torn from them, or delayed. Sufficed it
not
T' have snatched Admetus from his doom,
the Fates
With fraudful arts deluding? Now again,
Armed with thy bow, why dost thou guard
his wife,
Daughter of Pelias, bound by solemn vow,
Saving her husband's life, to die for
him?
APOLLO. Fear not; thy right I rever-
ence and just claim.
ORCUS. What means thy bow, if thou
revere the right?
APOLLO. It ever is my wont to bear
these arms.
ORCUS. Ay, and unjustly to defend this
house.
APOLLO. I mourn th' afflictions of the
man I love.
ORCUS. Wouldst thou defraud me of
this second dead?
APOLLO. The first by violence I took not
from thee.
ORCUS. How on the earth then walks
he now alive?
APOLLO. Ransomed by her, for whom
thou now art come.
ORCUS. And I will lead her to the
realms below.
APOLLO. Take her: I know not if I
might persuade thee.
ORCUS. Him, whom I ought, to seize;
for that prepared.

APOLLO. No; but t' involve in death
ripe, lingering age.
ORCUS. Full well I understand thy
speech and zeal.
APOLLO. May then Alcestis to that age
be spared?
ORCUS. No: honour, be assured, de-
lights e'en me.
APOLLO. Thou canst but take a single
life, no more.
ORCUS. Greater my glory when the
youthful die.
APOLLO. More sumptuous obsequies
await her age.
ORCUS. This were a law in favour of
the rich.
APOLLO. What secret meaning hath thy
wisdom here?
ORCUS. They with their wealth would
purchase to die old.
APOLLO. Wilt thou not then indulge
me with this grace?
ORCUS. Not I indeed: go to: thou
knowest my manners.
APOLLO. Hostile to mortals, hateful to
the gods.
ORCUS. Thou canst not have all that
thou shouldst not have.
APOLLO. Yet, ruthless as thou art, soon
wilt thou cease
This contest; such a man to Pheres' house
Comes, to the frozen continent of Thrace
Sent by Eurystheus for the savage steeds
Yoked to the tyrant's car. He, in this
house
A welcome guest t' Admetus, will by force
Take his wife from thee; and no thanks
from me
Will be thy due; yet what I now entreat
Then thou wilt yield, and I shall hate thee
still.
ORCUS. Say what thou wilt, nothing
the more for that
Shalt thou from me obtain: this woman
goes,
Be sure of that, to Pluto's dark domain.
I go, and with this sword assert my claim,
For sacred to th' infernal gods that
head,
Whose hair is hallowed, by this charmèd
blade.

CHORUS

1ST SEMICHORUS. Before this royal mansion all is still:
What may this melancholy silence mean?
2ND SEMICHORUS. And not a friend is nigh, from whom to learn
Whether we ought to wail the queen now dead,
Or lives she yet, yet sees the light of heaven,
For conjugal affection justly deemed
By me, by all, the noblest of her sex.
1ST SEMICHORUS. Hear you a cry, hear you a clash of hands
Within, or lamentations for the dead?
2ND SEMICHORUS. Not e'en a servant holds his station here
Before the gates. O, 'midst this awful gloom
Appear, bright Pæan, and dispel the storm!
1ST SEMICHORUS. If she were dead, they would not be thus silent;
Nor could the body vanish from the house.
2ND SEMICHORUS. Whence is thy confidence? My fears o'ercome me.
1ST SEMICHORUS. A wife so honoured would Admetus bear
Without due pomp in silence to her tomb?
2ND SEMICHORUS. Nor vase of fountain water do I see
Before the doors, as custom claims, to bathe
The corse; and none hath on the portal placed
His locks, in solemn mourning for the dead
Usually shorn; nor does the younger train
Of females raise their sorrowing voices high.
1ST SEMICHORUS. Yet this the fatal day, when she must leave
The light of heaven.
2ND SEMICHORUS. Why dost thou mention this?
O, thou hast touched my heart, hast touched my soul.
1ST SEMICHORUS. When on the good afflictions fall, to grieve
Becomes the man that hath been prized as honest.

In vain, our pious vows are vain:
  Make we the flying sail our care,
The light bark bounding o'er the main,
  To what new realm shall we repair?
    To Lycia's hallowed strand?
Or where in solitary state,
'Midst thirsty deserts wild and wide
That close him round on ev'ry side,
Prophetic Ammon holds his awful seat?
  What charm, what potent hand
Shall save her from the realms beneath?
He comes, the ruthless tyrant Death:
  I have no priest, no altar more,
  Whose aid I may implore.

O that the son of Phœbus now
  Lived to behold th' ethereal light!
Then might she leave the seats below,
  Where Pluto reigns in cheerless night
    The Sage's potent art,
Till thund'ring Jove's avenging power
Hurled his red thunders at his breast,
Could from the yawning gulf releast
To the sweet light of life the dead restore.
    Who now shall aid impart?
To ev'ry god at ev'ry shrine
The king hath paid the rites divine:
  But vain his vows, his pious care;
  And ours is dark despair.

[CHORUS, FEMALE ATTENDANT.]

CHORUS. But of the female train one from the house
Comes bathed in tears: what tidings shall I hear?
To weep, if aught of ill befalls thy lords,
Becomes thee: I would know if yet she lives,
Or sinks beneath the ruthless power of death.
ATTENDANT. As living I may speak of her, and dead.
CHORUS. Living and dead at once, how may that be?
ATTENDANT. E'en now she sinks in death, and breathes her last.
CHORUS. Unhappy king, of what a wife bereft!

ATTENDANT. Nor knows our lord his suffering, ere it comes.

CHORUS. Is there no hope then yet to save her life?

ATTENDANT. Th' inevitable day of fate is come.

CHORUS. Have you prepared what the sad case requires?

ATTENDANT. Each honour that may grace her obsequies.

CHORUS. Illustrious in her death, the best of wives:

The sun in his wide course sees not her equal.

ATTENDANT. The best of wives indeed; who will gainsay it?

What could the brightest pattern of her sex

Do more? What greater proof give of the honour

She bears her husband, than a ready will

To die for him! This all the city knows.

How in the house she hath demeaned herself

Will claim thy admiration. When she knew

The destined day was come, in fountain water

She bathed her lily-tinctured limbs, then took

From her rich chests of odorous cedar formed

A splendid robe, and her most radiant dress;

Thus gorgeously arrayed she stood before

The hallowed flames, and thus addressed her prayer:

"O queen, I go to the infernal shades,

Yet, ere I go, with reverence let me breathe

My last request—Protect my orphan children,

Make my son happy with the wife he loves,

And wed my daughter to a noble husband:

Nor let them, like their mother, to the tomb

Untimely sink, but in their native land

Be blest through lengthened life to honoured age."

Then to each altar in the royal house

She went, and crowned it, and addressed her vows,

Plucking the myrtle bough: nor tear, nor sigh

Came from her, neither did th' approaching ill

Change the fresh beauties of her vermeil cheek.

Her chamber then she visits, and her bed;

There her tears flowed, and thus she spoke: "O bed,

To which my wedded lord, for whom I die,

Led me a virgin bride, farewell! To thee

No blame do I impute, for me alone

Hast thou destroyed. Disdaining to betray

Thee, and my lord, I die. To thee shall come

Some other woman, not more chaste, perchance

More happy." As she lay, she kissed the couch,

And bathed it with a flood of tears; that passed,

She left her chamber, then returned, and oft

She left it, oft returned, and on the couch

Fondly, each time she entered, cast herself.

Her children, as they hung upon her robes

Weeping, she raised, and clasped them to her breast

Each after each, as now about to die.

Each servant through the house burst into tears

In pity of their mistress; she to each

Stretched her right hand; nor was there one so mean

To whom she spoke not, and admitted him

To speak to her again. Within the house

These are our griefs. Admetus must have died,

Have perished; but escaping is immersed

In sorrows, which his heart shall ne'er forget.

CHORUS. Well may the groan burst from him, thus to lose

A wife with every excellence adorned.

ATTENDANT. He weeps indeed, and in his arm supports

His much-loved wife, entreats her not to leave him,
Asking impossibilities. She wastes
And fades with her disease; her languid limbs
Supporting on his hand, yet while some breath
Of life remains she wishes to behold
The radiance of the sun, 'tis her last view,
As never more to see his golden orb.
I go to tell them thou art here: not all
Bear to their lords that firm unshaken faith
T' attend them in their ills; but thou of old
Hast to this house approved thyself a friend.

CHORUS. Supreme of gods, is there no remedy
To these afflictions, from the storms of fate
No refuge to our lords? Some means of safety
Hast thou assigned? Or must these locks be shorn,
And sorrow robe me in her sable weeds?

ATTENDANT. Too plain, my friends, too plain: yet to the gods
Breathe we our vows, for great their power to save.
O royal Pæan, for Admetus' ills
Find some relief; assist him, O assist him!
As thou before didst save him, save him now
From death; repress the tyrant's murd'rous haste!

CHORUS. Alas, alas! Woe, woe is me!
Thou son
Of Pheres, wilt thou bear to live, deprived
Of such a wife? Will not despair unsheath
The self-destroying sword? Will it not find
Some means of violent death? This day thy wife—
Dear should I say? nay, dearest to thy soul—
Shalt thou see dead. But she comes forth, and with 'her
Her husband. Groan, thou land of Pheres, raise

The cry of mourning; for the best of women
Wastes with disease, and drooping to the earth
Sinks to th' infernal Pluto's dreary realms.
Never will I pronounce the nuptial state
To pleasure more allied than grief: of old
This often have I noted, chiefly now
Viewing my king's affliction, who, bereft
Of this sweet excellence, is doomed to pass
A solitary life estranged from joy.

[ALCESTIS, ADMETUS, EUMELUS, CHORUS.]

ALCESTIS. Thou sun, and thou fair light of day, ye clouds
That in quick eddies whirl along the sky!

ADMETUS. Sees thee and me most wretched, yet in nought
Offending 'gainst the gods that thou shouldst die.

ALCESTIS. O earth, ye tow'red roofs, thou bridal bed
Raised in Iolcos, my paternal seat!

ADMETUS. O thou poor sufferer, raise thee, leave me not;
Entreat the powerful gods to pity thee.

ALCESTIS. I see the two-oared boat, the Stygian barge;
And he, that wafts the dead, grasps in his hand
His pole, and calls me, "Why dost thou delay?
Haste thee; thou lingerest; all is ready here.
Charon impatient speeds me to be gone."

ADMETUS. A melancholy voyage this to me.
O thou unhappy, what a fate is ours!

ALCESTIS. He drags me, some one drags me to the gates
That close upon the dead; dost thou not see him,
How stern he frowns beneath his gloomy brows,
Th' impetuous Pluto? What wouldst thou with me?
Off, let me go! Ah, what a dreary path,
Wretched, most wretched, must I downwards tread!

ADMETUS. To thy friends mournful, most to me, and these

Thy children, who with me this sorrow
share.
ALCESTIS. No longer hold me up, hold
me no longer;
Here lay me down: I have not strength
to stand:
Death is hard by, dark night creeps o'er
my eyes.
My children, O my children, now no more,
Your mother is no more: farewell! May
you
More happy see the golden light of heaven!
ADMETUS. Ah, what a mournful word
is this! To me
Than any death more painful. By the
gods,
Forsake me not. Shouldst thou be taken
from me,
I were no more; in thee I live; thy love,
Thy sweet society my soul reveres.
ALCESTIS. Thou seest, Admetus, what
to me the Fates
Assign; yet, ere I die, I wish to tell thee
What lies most near my heart. I hon-
oured thee,
And in exchange for thine my forfeit life
Devoted; now I die for thee, though free
Not to have died, but from Thessalia's
chiefs
Preferring whom I pleased in royal state
To have lived happy here: I had no will
To live bereft of thee with these poor
orphans;
I die without reluctance, though the gifts
Of youth are mine to make life grateful
to me.
Yet he that gave thee birth, and she that
bore thee,
Deserted thee, though well it had beseemed
them
With honour to have died for thee, t' have
saved
Their son with honour, glorious in their
death.
They had no child but thee, they had no
hope
Of other offspring shouldst thou die; and I
Might thus have lived, thou mightst have
lived, till age
Crept slowly on, nor wouldst thou heave
the sigh

Thus of thy wife deprived, nor train alone
Thy orphan children. But some god ap-
pointed
It should be thus: thus be it. Thou to me
Requite this kindness; never shall I ask
An equal retribution, nothing bears
A value high as life: yet my request
Is just, thou wilt confess it; for thy love
To these our children equals mine, thy
soul
If wisdom tempers. In their mother's
house
Let them be lords: wed not again, to set
A stepdame o'er my children, some base
woman
That wants my virtues; she through jeal-
ousy
Will work against their lives, because to
thee
I bore them: do not this, I beg thee do
not;
For to the offspring of a former bed
A stepdame comes sharp as a serpent's
tooth.
My son, that holds endearing converse
with thee,
Hath in his father a secure protection.
But who, my daughter, shall with honour
guide
Thy virgin years? What woman shalt
thou find,
New-wedded to thy father, whose vile arts
Will not with slanderous falsehoods taint
thy name,
And blast thy nuptials in youth's freshest
bloom?
For never shall thy mother see thee led
A bride, nor at thy throes speak comfort
to thee,
Then present when a mother's tenderness
Is most alive: for I must die; the ill
Waits not a day, but quickly shall I be
Numbered amongst the dead. Farewell, be
happy
And thou, my husband, mayst with hon-
our boast
Thou hast been wedded to a virtuous wife;
And you, my children, glory in your
mother.
CHORUS. Fear not: I boldly pledge my
faith that this

He will perform, if reason holds her seat.

ADMETUS. This shall be done, let not
such fears disturb thee,
It shall be done; for living thou wast
mine,
And dead thou only shalt be called my
wife.
Never in thy dear place Thessalian bride
Shall call me husband: no, nor other
woman,
Though from a line of ancient kings she
draws
Her noble blood, and boasts each peerless
grace
Of native beauty. I am blest with chil-
dren,
Nor wish I more; in these I pray the gods
I may have joy, since all my joy in thee
Is lost. This mourning not one single
year,
But to my life's last period, shall be borne.
How hateful are my parents! for their
words
Alone were friendly, not their deeds;
whilst thou,
Paying the dearest forfeit for my life,
Hast saved me. Shall I ever cease to
mourn,
Deprived of such a wife? Hence I re-
nounce
The feast, the cheerful guest, the flow'ry
wreath
And song that used to echo through my
house.
For never will I touch the lyre again,
Nor to the Libyan flute's sweet measures
raise
My voice: with thee all my delights are
dead.
Thy beauteous figure, by the artist's hand
Skilfully wrought, shall in my bed be laid;
By that reclining, I will clasp it to me,
And call it by thy name, and think I hold
My dear wife in my arms, and have her
yet,
Though now no more I have her: cold de-
light
I ween; yet thus th' affliction of my soul
Shall I relieve, and visiting my dreams
Shalt thou delight me; for to see a friend
Is grateful to the soul, come when he will,

Though an unreal vision of the night.
Had I the voice of Orpheus, and his skill
Of power to soothe with my melodious
strains
The daughter of bright Ceres, or her hus-
band,
That from their realms I might receive
thee back,
I would go down; nor should th' infernal
dog,
Nor the stern Charon, sitting at his oar
To waft the dead, restrain me, till thy
life
I had restored to the fair light of day.
But there await me till I die; prepare
A mansion for me, as again with me
To dwell; for in thy tomb will I be laid
In the same cedar, by thy side composed;
For ev'n in death I will not be disjoined
From thee, who hast alone been faithful
to me.

CHORUS. For her dear sake thy sorrows
will I share
As friend with friend; and she is worthy
of it.

ALCESTIS. You hear, my children, what
your father's words
Have promised, not to wed another woman
To your discomfort, nor dishonour me.

ADMETUS. I now repeat it; firm shall
be my faith.

ALCESTIS. On this, receive thy children
from my hands.

ADMETUS. A much-loved gift, and from
a much-loved hand.

ALCESTIS. Be now, instead of me, a
mother to them.

ADMETUS. If they lose thee, it must in-
deed be so.

ALCESTIS. When I should live, I sink
among the dead.

ADMETUS. Ah me, what shall I do
bereft of thee!

ALCESTIS. Time will abate thy grief,
the dead is nothing.

ADMETUS. O lead me, by the gods, lead
me down with thee.

ALCESTIS. Enough, it is enough that
I die for thee.

ADMETUS. O fate, of what a wife dost
thou deprive me!

ALCESTIS. A heavy weight hangs on my darkened eye.

ADMETUS. If thou forsake me, I am lost indeed.

ALCESTIS. As one that is no more I now am nothing.

ADMETUS. Ah, raise thy face: do not forsake thy children.

ALCESTIS. It must be so perforce: farewell, my children!

ADMETUS. Look on them, but a look!

ALCESTIS. I am no more.

ADMETUS. How dost thou? Wilt thou leave us then?

ALCESTIS. Farewell!

ADMETUS. And what a wretch, what a lost wretch am I!

CHORUS. She's gone; thy wife, Admetus, is no more.

EUMELUS. O my unhappy fate!
My mother sinks to the dark realms of night,
Nor longer views this golden light;
But to the ills of life exposed
Leaves my poor orphan state.
Her eyes, my father, see, her eyes are closed,
And her hand nerveless falls.
Yet hear me, O my mother, hear my cries,
It is thy son that calls,
Who prostrate on the earth breathes on thy lips his sighs.

ADMETUS. On one that hears not, sees not: I and you
Must bend beneath affliction's heaviest load.

EUMELUS. Ah, she hath left my youth:
My mother, my dear mother, is no more,
Left me my sufferings to deplore;
Who shall my sorrows soothe?
Thou too, my sister, thy full share shalt know
Of grief, thy heart to rend.
Vain, O my father, vain thy nuptial vows,
Brought to this speedy end;
For, when my mother died, in ruin sunk thy house.

CHORUS. Admetus, thou perforce must bear these ills:
Thou'rt not the first, nor shalt thou be the last

Of mortal men, to lose a virtuous wife:
For know, death is a debt we all must pay.

ADMETUS. I know it well; not unawares this ill
Falls on me; I foresaw, and mourned it long.
But I will bear the body hence; attend:
And, whilst you wait, raise with alternate voice
The pæan to the ruthless god that rules
Below: and through my realms of Thessaly
I give command that all in solemn grief
For this dear woman shear their locks, and wear
The sable garb of mourning; from your steeds,
Whether in pairs they whirl the car, or bear
Single the rider's rein, their waving manes
Cut close; nor through the city be the sound
Of flute or lyre for twelve revolving moons.
Never shall I entomb one dearer to me,
Or one more kind: these honours from my hands
She merits, for she only died for me.

STROPHE 1

Immortal bliss be thine,
Daughter of Pelias in the realms below,
Immortal pleasures round thee flow,
Though never there the sun's bright beams shall shine.
Be the black-browed Pluto told,
And the Stygian boatman old,
Whose rude hands grasp the oar, the rudder guide,
The dead conveying o'er the tide,
Let him be told, so rich a freight before
His light skiff never bore;
Tell him that o'er the joyless lakes
The noblest of her sex her dreary passage takes.

STROPHE 2

Thy praise the bards shall tell,
When to their hymning voice the echo rings,
Or when they sweep the solemn strings,

And wake to rapture the seven-chorded
  shell,
Or in Sparta's jocund bowers,
Circling when the vernal hours
Bring the Carnean feast, whilst through
  the night
Full-orbed the high moon rolls her
  light;
Or where rich Athens proudly elevate
Shows her magnific state:
Their voice thy glorious death shall
  raise,
And swell th' enraptured strain to cele-
  brate thy praise.

ANTISTROPHE 1

O that I had the power,
Could I but bring thee from the shades of
  night
Again to view this golden light,
To leave that boat, to leave that dreary
  shore,
Where Cocytus deep and wide
Rolls along his sullen tide!
For thou, O best of women, thou alone
For thy lord's life daredst give thy
  own.
Light lie the earth upon that gentle
  breast,
And be thou ever blest!
But should he choose to wed again,
Mine and thy children's hearts would
  hold him in disdain.

ANTISTROPHE 2

When, to avert his doom,
His mother in the earth refused to lie;
Nor would his ancient father die
To save his son from an untimely tomb;
Though the hand of time had spread
Hoar hairs o'er each aged head;
In youth's fresh bloom, in beauty's radiant
  glow,
The darksome way thou daredst to go,
And for thy youthful lord's to give thy
  life.
Be mine so true a wife;
Though rare the lot: then should I
  prove
Th' indissoluble bond of faithfulness and
  love.

[HERCULES, CHORUS.]

HERCULES. Ye strangers, citizens of
  Pheræ, say
If I shall find Admetus in the house.
CHORUS. There is the son of Pheres,
  Hercules.
But what occasion, tell us, brought thee
  hither
To Thessaly; to Pheræ why this visit?
HERCULES. A toil imposed by the
  Tirynthian king.
CHORUS. And whither roving? On
  what journey bound?
HERCULES. For the four steeds that
  whirl the Thracian's car.
CHORUS. How to be won; art thou a
  stranger there?
HERCULES. A stranger, never on Bis-
  tonian ground.
CHORUS. These horses are not won with-
  out strong contest.
HERCULES. The toil, whate'er it be, I
  could not shun.
CHORUS. He must be slain, or death
  awaits thee there.
HERCULES. Not the first contest this
  I have essayed.
CHORUS. Shouldst thou o'ercome their
  lord, what is the prize?
HERCULES. His coursers to Eurystheus
  I shall lead.
CHORUS. No slight task in their mouths
  to place the curb.
HERCULES. I shall, though from their
  nostrils they breathe fire.
CHORUS. With their fierce jaws they
  rend the flesh of men.
HERCULES. So feeds the mountain sav-
  age, not the horse.
CHORUS. Their mangers shalt thou see
  all stained with blood.
HERCULES. From whom does he that
  bred them draw his race?
CHORUS. From Mars this king of
  golden-shielded Thrace.
HERCULES. How is this toil assigned
  me by my fate,
In enterprise so hazardous and high
Engaged, that always with the sons of
  Mars

I must join battle? With Lycaon first,
With Cygnus next; now with these furious steeds
And their proud lord another contest waits me:
But never shall Alcmena's son be seen
To tremble at the fierceness of a foe.
CHORUS. But, see, the sceptred ruler of this land,
Admetus, from his house advances to thee.

[ADMETUS, HERCULES, CHORUS.]

ADMETUS. Hail, son of Jove, of Perseus' noble blood.
HERCULES. Hail thou, Admetus, king of Thessaly.
ADMETUS. I am no stranger to thy friendly wishes.
HERCULES. Why are thy locks in sign of mourning shorn?
ADMETUS. 'Tis for one dead, whom I must this day bury.
HERCULES. The god avert thy mourning for a child!
ADMETUS. My children, what I had, live in my house.
HERCULES. Thy aged father, haply he is gone.
ADMETUS. My father lives, and she that bore me lives.
HERCULES. Lies then thy wife Alcestis 'mongst the dead?
ADMETUS. Of her I have in double wise to speak.
HERCULES. As of the living speakst thou, or the dead?
ADMETUS. She is, and is no more: this grief afflicts me.
HERCULES. This gives no information, dark thy words.
ADMETUS. Knowst thou not then the destiny assigned her?
HERCULES. I know that she submits to die for thee.
ADMETUS. To this assenting is she not no more?
HERCULES. Lament her not too soon; await the time.
ADMETUS. She's dead; one soon to die is now no more.

HERCULES. It differs wide to be, or not to be.
ADMETUS. Such are thy sentiments, far other mine.
HERCULES. But wherefore are thy tears? What friend is dead?
ADMETUS. A woman; of a woman made I mention.
HERCULES. Of foreign birth, or one allied to thee?
ADMETUS. Of foreign birth, but to my house most dear.
HERCULES. How in thy house then did she chance to die?
ADMETUS. Her father dead, she came an orphan hither.
HERCULES. Would I had found thee with no grief oppressed.
ADMETUS. With what intent dost thou express thee thus?
HERCULES. To seek some other hospitable hearth.
ADMETUS. Not so, O king; come not so great an ill.
HERCULES. To those that mourn a guest is troublesome.
ADMETUS. Dead are the dead: but enter thou my house.
HERCULES. Shame that with those who weep a guest should feast.
ADMETUS. We have apartments separate, to receive thee.
HERCULES. Permit me to depart, much will I thank thee.
ADMETUS. It must not be; no, to another house
Thou must not turn aside. Go thou before;
Ope those apartments of the house which bear
A different aspect; give command to those
Whose charge it is to spread the plenteous table,
And bar the doors between: the voice of woe
Unseemly heard afflicts the feasting guest.
CHORUS. What wouldst thou do, Admetus? Such a grief
Now lying heavy on thee, canst thou bear
T' admit a guest? Doth this bespeak thee wise?

ADMETUS. If from my house or city I
    should drive
A coming guest, wouldst thou commend
    me more?
Thou wouldst not: my affliction would not
    thus
Be less, but more unhospitable I;
And to my former ills this further ill
Be added, I should hear my mansion called
The stranger-hating house. Besides, to
    me
His hospitable doors are always open,
Whene'er I tread the thirsty soil of
    Argos.
CHORUS. Why didst thou then conceal
    thy present grief,
A stranger friend arriving, as thou sayst?
ADMETUS. My gate he would not enter,
    had he known
Of my affliction aught: yet acting thus
Some may perchance deem me unwise, nor
    hold me
Worthy of praise; yet never shall my
    house
Know to dishonour or reject a guest.

CHORUS

STROPHE 1

Yes, liberal house, with princely state
To many a stranger, many a guest
Oft hast thou oped thy friendly gate,
Oft spread the hospitable feast.
Beneath thy roof Apollo deigned to dwell,
Here strung his silver-sounding shell,
And mixing with thy menial train
Deigned to be called the shepherd of the
    plain:
And as he drove his flocks along,
Whether the winding vale they rove,
Or linger in the upland grove,
He tuned the pastoral pipe or rural song.

STROPHE 2

Delighted with thy tuneful lay
No more the savage thirsts for blood;
Amidst thy flocks in harmless play
Wantons the lynx's spotted brood;
Pleased from his lair on Othrys' rugged
    brow
The lion seeks the vale below;
Whilst to thy lyre's melodious sound

The dappled hinds in sportive measures
    bound;
And as the vocal echo rings,
Lightly their nimble feet they ply,
Leaving their pine-clad forests high,
Charmed with the sweet notes of thy
    gladdening strings.

ANTISTROPHE 1

Hence is thy house, Admetus, graced
    With all that Plenty's hand bestows,
Near the sweat-streaming current
    placed
    That from the lake of Bœbia flows.
Far to the west extends the wide domain,
Rich-pastured mead and cultured plain;
Its bound, the dark Molossian air,
Where the Sun stations his unharnessed
    car,
And stretching to his eastern ray,
Where Pelion rising in his pride
Frowns o'er th' Ægean's portless tide,
Reaches from sea to sea thy ample sway.

ANTISTROPHE 2

Yet wilt thou ope thy gate e'en now,
    E'en now wilt thou receive this guest:
Though from thine eye the warm tear
    flow,
    Though sorrow rend thy suffering
    breast:
Sad tribute to thy wife, who knew in
    death
    Lamented lies thy roof beneath,
But Nature thus her laws decreed,
The generous mind is prompt to generous
    deed;
For all the power of wisdom lies
Fixed in the righteous bosom: hence
My soul assumes this confidence,
Fair to the virtuous shall Success arise.

[ADMETUS, CHORUS.]

ADMETUS. Ye citizens of Pheræ, present
    here,
Benevolent to me, my dead adorned
With every honour, the attendant train
Are bearing to the tomb and funeral pyre.
Do you, for ancient usage so requires,
Address her as she takes her last sad way.

CHORUS. Thy father Pheres! See, his aged foot
Advances; his attendants in their hands
Bear gorgeous presents, honours to the dead.

[PHERES, ADMETUS, CHORUS.]

PHERES. I come, my son, joint sufferer in thy griefs;
For thou hast lost a good and virtuous wife,
None will gainsay it; but thou must perforce
Endure this, though severe. These ornaments
Receive, and let her go beneath the earth:
These honours are her due, since for thy life
She died, my son; nor would she I should be
Childless, nor suffered me bereft of thee
To waste in grief my sad remains of life.
The life of all her sex hath she adorned
With added lustre by this generous deed.
O thou, that hast preserved my son, and raised
Our sinking glories, hail! E'en in the house
Of Pluto be thou blest! Such marriages
Pronounce I good; others of little worth.
ADMETUS. Thou comest not to these obsequies by me
Invited, nor thy presence do I deem
Friendly. She never in thy ornaments
Shall be arrayed, nor wants she aught of thine
To grace her funeral rites. Then was the time
To show thy social sorrow, when my life
The Fates demanded: thou couldst stand aloof,
Old as thou art, and give a younger up
To die; and wouldst thou now bewail her death?
Art thou my father? No; nor she, who says
She brought me forth, my mother, though so called;
But the base offspring of some slave thy wife

Stole me, and put me to her breast. Thy deeds
Show what thou art by plain and evident proof:
And never can I deem myself thy son,
Who passest all in mean and abject spirit.
At such an age, just trembling on the verge
Of life, that wouldst not—nay, thou daredst not—die
For thine own son: but you could suffer her,
Though sprung from foreign blood. With justice then
Her only as my father must I deem,
Her only as my mother; yet this course
Mightst thou have run with glory, for thy son
Daring to die; brief was the space of life
That could remain to thee. I then had lived
My destined time; she too had lived, nor thus
Of her forsaken should I wail my loss.
Yet all that makes man happy hadst thou proved,
Blest through thy life: in royalty thy youth
Grew up; I was thy son t' inherit from thee
Thy treasures, that not childless hadst thou died,
Leaving thy desolated house a prey
To plundering strangers. Neither canst thou say
Thou gavest me up to death as one that held
Thy age in rude contempt: I honoured thee
With holy reverence, requited thus
By thee and her that bore me. Other sons
Wilt thou not therefore speed thee to beget.
To cherish thy old age, to grace thee dead
With sumptuous vest, and lay thee in the tomb?
That office never shall my hand perform,
For, far as in thee lay, I died; if yet
I view this light, fortune presenting me
Other deliverer, his son I am,
With pious fondness to support his age.

Unmeaning is the old man's wish to die,
Of age complaining and life's lengthened
course;
For, at th' advance of death, none has the
will
To die: old age is no more grievous to
them.
CHORUS. Forbear; enough the present
weight of woe.
My son, exasperate not a father's mind.
PHERES. Me as some worthless Lydian
dost thou rate,
My son, or Phrygian slave bought with
thy gold?
Dost thou not know I am Thessalian born,
Of a Thessalian father, truly free?
Opprobrious are thy words, reviling me
With youthful insolence, not quitted so.
I gave thee birth, thence lord of my fair
house;
I gave thee nurture, that indeed I owed
thee,
But not to die for thee: such law from
nature
Received I not, that fathers for their
sons
Should die, nor does Greece know it. For
thyself,
Whether misfortune press thee, or thy
state
Be happier, thou wast born: thou hast
from me
Whate'er behoves thee: o'er an ample
realm
Thou now art king, and I shall leave thee
more,
A large extent of lands; for from my
father
These I received. In what then have I
wronged thee?
Or what deprived thee? Die not thou for
me,
Nor I for thee. Is it to thee a joy
To view the light of heaven? and dost
thou think
Thy father joys not in it? Long I deem
The time below? But little is the space
Of life, yet pleasant. Thou, devoid of
shame,
Hast struggled not to die, and thou dost
live

Passing the bounds of life assigned by
fate,
By killing her. My mean and abject spirit
Thou dost rebuke, O thou most timid
wretch,
Vanquished e'en by a woman, who for
thee,
Her young and beauteous husband, freely
died.
A fine device that thou mightst never die,
Couldst thou persuade who at the time
might be
Thy wife to die for thee; yet canst thou
load
Thy friends with vile reproach, if they
decline
To do it, base and timid as thou art.
But hold thy peace; and think, if life be
dear
To thee, it must be dear to all. On us,
If thou wilt throw reproaches, thou shalt
hear
Enough of thy ill deeds, and nothing false.
CHORUS. Too much of ill already hath
been spoken:
Forbear, old man, nor thus revile thy son.
ADMETUS. Say what thou wilt, I have
declared my thoughts:
But if it gives thee pain to hear the truth,
Much it behoved thee not to wrong me
thus.
PHERES. Had I died for thee, greater
were the wrong.
ADMETUS. Is death alike then to the
young and old?
PHERES. With one life ought we live,
and not with two.
ADMETUS. Mayst thou then live a
greater age than Jove!
PHERES. And dost thou, nothing in-
jured, curse thy parents?
ADMETUS. I saw thee fondly coveting
long life.
PHERES. Her, that died for thee, wilt
thou not entomb?
ADMETUS. These are the tokens of thy
abject spirit.
PHERES. By us she died not, that thou
wilt not say.
ADMETUS. Ah, mayst thou some time
come to want my aid!

PHERES. Wed many wives, that more may die for thee.

ADMETUS. On thee be that reproach, thou wouldst not die.

PHERES. Sweet is this light of heaven, sweet is this light.

ADMETUS. Base is thy thought, unworthy of a man.

PHERES. Would it not joy thee to entomb my age?

ADMETUS. Die when thou wilt, inglorious wilt thou die.

PHERES. An ill report will not affect me dead.

ADMETUS. Alas, alas, how shameless is old age!

PHERES. She was not shameless, but thou foundst her mad.

ADMETUS. Begone, and suffer me t' entomb the dead.

PHERES. I go; thou shalt entomb her, as thyself
Her murderer. Look for vengeance from her friends.
Acastus is no man, if his hands fail
Dearly t' avenge on thee his sister's blood.

ADMETUS. Why get thee gone, thou and thy worthy wife;
Grow old together, as you well deserve,
Childless, your son yet living; never more
Meet me beneath this roof. Go! Were it decent
To interdict thee by the herald's voice,
I would forbid thee ever set thy foot
Within this mansion of thy ancestors.
But let us go, since we must bear our ill,
And place her body on the funeral pyre.

CHORUS. O thou unhappy, nobly daring woman,
Most generous, brightest excellence, farewell!
Courteous my Hermes and th' infernal king
Receive thee: in those realms if aught of grace
Awaits the virtuous, be those honours thine,
And be thy seat nigh Pluto's royal bride.

ATTENDANT. To many a guest ere now, from various realms
Arriving, in this mansion have I spread
The hospitable feast; but at this hearth
A viler than this stranger never shared
The bounty of Admetus: though he saw
My lord oppressed with grief, it checked him not,
He boldly entered; nor with sober cheer
Took the refreshment offered, though he knew
Th' affliction of the house. If what he would
We brought not on the instant, he enforced
His harsh commands; and, grasping in his hands
A goblet wreathed with ivy, filled it high
With the grape's purple juice, and quaffed it off
Untempered, till the glowing wine inflamed him;
Then, binding round his head a myrtle wreath,
Howls dismal discord; two unpleasing strains
We heard, his harsh notes, who in nought revered
Th' afflictions of Admetus, and the voice
Of sorrow through the family that wept
Our mistress; yet our tearful eyes we showed not,
Admetus so commanded, to the guest.
My office bids me wait, and in the house
Receive this stranger, some designing knave,
Or ruffian robber: she meantime is borne
Out of the house, nor did I follow her,
Nor stretched my hand lamenting my lost mistress:
She was a mother to me, and to all
My fellow-servants; from a thousand ills
She saved us, with her gentleness appeasing
Our lord when angry: justly do I hate
This stranger then, who came amidst our grief.

[HERCULES, ATTENDANT.]

HERCULES. You fellow, why that grave and thoughtful look?
Ill it becomes a servant's countenance
To frown on strangers, whom he should receive

With cheerfulness. A good friend of thy
    lord
Is present: all the welcome he can get
From thee, a sullen and contracted brow,
Mourning a loss that touches not this
    house.
Come hither, that thou mayst be wiser,
    friend;
Knowst thou the nature of all mortal
    things?
Not thou, I ween; how shouldst thou?
    Hear from me
By all of human race death is a debt
That must be paid, and none of mortal
    men
Knows whether till to-morrow life's short
    space
Shall be extended: such the dark events
Of fortune; never to be learned, nor traced
By any skill. Instructed thus by me
Bid pleasure welcome, drink, the life al-
    lowed
From day to day esteem thine own, all
    else
Fortune's. To Venus chief address thy
    vows—
Of all the heavenly powers she, gentle
    queen,
Kindest to man, and sweetest: all besides
Reckless let pass, and listen to my words,
If thou seest reason in them, as I think
Thou dost: then bid excessive grief fare-
    well,
And drink with us; master these present
    ills,
And bind thy brows with garlands; well
    I know
The circling bowl will waft thy spirits to
    bliss,
Now sunk in dark and sullen melancholy.
Since we are mortal, be our minds intent
On mortal things; to all the grave, whose
    brows
With cares are furrowed, let me judge for
    thee,
Life is no life, but a calamity.
  ATTENDANT. These things we know;
    but what becomes us now
Ill suits with festal revelry and mirth.
    HERCULES. O woman dies, one unre-
    lated; check

Thy grief: the lords of this fair mansion
    live.
  ATTENDANT. Live! Knowst thou not
    th' afflictions of this house?
  HERCULES. Unless thy lord in some-
    thing hath deceived me.
  ATTENDANT. Liberal his mind, too lib-
    eral to the guest.
  HERCULES. No: for a stranger dead
    he hath done well.
  ATTENDANT. No stranger, but a near
    domestic loss.
  HERCULES. Is it some sorrow which
    he told not me?
  ATTENDANT. Go thou with joy; ours
    are our lord's afflictions.
  HERCULES. These are not words that
    speak a foreign loss.
  ATTENDANT. If such, thy revelry had
    not displeased me.
  HERCULES. Then by my friendly host I
    much am wronged.
  ATTENDANT. Thy coming was unseason-
    able; this house
Wanted no guest: thou seest our locks all
    shorn,
Our grief and sable vests.
  HERCULES.   Who then is dead?
One of his children, or his aged father?
  ATTENDANT. His wife Alcestis, stran-
    ger, is no more.
  HERCULES. What sayst thou? And
    e'en so could you receive me?
  ATTENDANT. It shamed him to reject
    thee from his house.
  HERCULES. O wretch, of what a wife
    art thou bereft!
  ATTENDANT. Not she alone, we all are
    lost with her.
  HERCULES. I might have thought this
    when I saw his eye
Flowing with tears, his locks shorn off,
    and grief
Marked on his face: but he persuaded me,
Saying that one of foreign birth he
    mourned,
And bore her to the tomb: unwillingly
Ent'ring these gates I feasted in the house,
My hospitable friend with such a grief
Oppressed; nay more, I revelled, and my
    head

With garlands shaded: but the fault was
thine,
Who didst not tell me that a woe like this
Thy house afflicted. But inform me where
She is interred: where shall I find her
tomb?
ATTENDANT. Right in the way that to
Larissa leads
Without the city wilt thou find her tomb.
HERCULES. Now my firm heart, and
thou, my daring soul,
Show what a son the daughter of Elec-
tryon,
Alcmena of Tirynthia, bore to Jove.
This lady, new in death, behoves me save,
And, to Admetus rend'ring grateful ser-
vice,
Restore his lost Alcestis to his house.
This sable-vested tyrant of the dead
My eye shall watch, not without hope to
find him
Drinking th' oblations nigh the tomb. If
once
Seen from my secret stand I rush upon
him,
These arms shall grasp him till his pant-
ing sides
Labour for breath; and who shall force
him from me,
Till he gives back this woman? Should I
fail
To seize him there, as coming not to
taste
The spilt blood's thickening foam, I will
descend
To the drear house of Pluto and his queen,
Which the sun never cheers, and beg her
thence,
Assured that I shall lead her back, and
place her
In my friend's hands, whose hospitable
heart
Received me in his house, nor made excuse,
Though pierced with such a grief; this
he concealed
Through generous thought and reverence
to his friend.
Who in Thessalia bears a warmer love
To strangers? Who, through all the
realms of Greece?
It never shall be said this generous man

Received in me a base and worthless
wretch.

[ADMETUS, CHORUS]

ADMETUS. Ah me! Ah me! How
mournful this approach!
How hateful to my sight this widowed
house!
Ah, whither shall I go? where shall I
rest?
What shall I say? or what forbear to say?
How may I sink beneath this weight of
woe?
To misery was I born, wretch that I am;
I envy now the dead, I long for them,
Long to repose me in that house. No
more
With pleasure shall I view the sun's fair
beams,
No more with pleasure walk upon this
earth:
So dear an hostage death has rent from
me,
And yielded to th' infernal king his prey.
CHORUS. Go forward, yet go forward;
to thy house
Retire.
ADMETUS. Ah me!
CHORUS. Thy sufferings do indeed
Demand these groans.
ADMETUS. O miserable me!
CHORUS. Thy steps are set in sorrow,
well I know,
But all thy sorrow nought avails the dead.
ADMETUS. Wretch that I am!
CHORUS. To see thy wife no more,
No more to see her face, is grief indeed.
ADMETUS. O, thou hast touched on that
which deepest wounds
My mind: what greater ill can fall on
man
Than of a faithful wife to be deprived?
O that I ne'er had wedded, in the house
Had ne'er dwelt with her! The unmarried
state
I envy, and deem those supremely blest
Who have no children; in one single life
To mourn is pain that may be well en-
dured
To see our children wasting with disease,
To see death ravaging our nuptial bed,

This is not to be borne, when we might
pass
Our lives without a child, without a wife.
CHORUS. Fate comes, resistless Fate.
ADMETUS. Unhappy me!
CHORUS. But to thy sorrows wilt thou
put no bounds?
ADMETUS. Woe, woe, woe, woe!
CHORUS. A ponderous weight indeed
To bear, yet bear them. Thou art not the
first
That lost a wife: misery, in different
forms
To different men appearing, seizes all.
ADMETUS. Ye lasting griefs, ye sorrows
for our friends
Beneath the earth! Ah, why did ye re-
strain me?
I would have cast myself into the tomb,
The gaping tomb, and lain in death with
her,
The dearest, best of women; there for one
Pluto had coupled two most faithful souls,
Together passing o'er th' infernal lake.
CHORUS. I had a friend, by birth allied
to me,
Whose son, and such a son as claimed his
tears,
Died in the prime of youth, his only child;
Yet with the firmness of a man he bore
His grief, though childless, and declining
age
Led him with hasty steps to hoary hairs.
ADMETUS. Thou goodly mansion, how
shall I endure
To enter thee, how dwell beneath thy
roof,
My state thus sunk! Ah me, how changed
from that,
When 'midst the pines of Pelion blazing
round,
And hymeneal hymns, I held my way,
And led my loved Alcestis by her hand:
The festal train with many a cheerful
shout
Saluted her, now dead, and me, and hailed
Our union happy, as descended each
From generous blood and high-born an-
cestry.
Now for the nuptial song, the voice of
woe—

For gorgeous robes, this black and mourn-
ful garb—
Attends me to my halls, and to my couch,
Where solitary sorrow waits me now.
CHORUS. This sorrow came upon thee
'midst a state
Of happiness, a stranger thou to ills:
Yet is thy life preserved: thy wife is dead,
Leaving thy love; is there aught new in
this?
Many hath death reft of their wives be-
fore.
ADMETUS. My friends, I deem the for-
tune of my wife
Happier than mine, though otherwise it
seems;
For never more shall sorrow touch her
breast,
And she with glory rests from various ills.
But I, who ought not live, my destined
hour
O'erpassing, shall drag on a mournful life,
Late taught what sorrow is. How shall
I bear
To enter here? To whom shall I address
My speech? Whose greeting renders my
return
Delightful? Which way shall I turn?
Within
In lonely sorrow shall I waste away.
As widowed of my wife I see my couch,
The seats deserted where she sate, the
rooms
Wanting her elegance. Around my knees
My children hang, and weep their mother
lost:
These too lament their mistress now no
more.
This is the scene of misery in my house:
Abroad, the nuptials of Thessalia's youth
And the bright circles of assembled dames
Will but augment my grief: ne'er shall I
bear
To see the loved companions of my wife.
And if one hates me, he will say, "Behold
The man, who basely lives, who dared not
die,
But, giving through the meanness of his
soul
His wife, avoided death, yet would be
deemed

A man: he hates his parents, yet himself
Had not the spirit to die." These ill re-
    ports
Cleave to me: why then wish for longer
    life,
On evil tongues thus fallen, and evil days?

CHORUS

STROPHE 1

My venturous foot delights
To tread the Muses' arduous heights;
Their hallowed haunts I love t' explore,
And listen to their lore:
Yet never could my searching mind
Aught, like necessity, resistless find;
No herb of sovereign power to save,
Whose virtues Orpheus joyed to trace,
And wrote them in the rolls of Thrace;
Nor all that Phœbus gave,
Instructing the Asclepian train,
When various ills the human frame assail,
To heal the wound, to soothe the pain,
'Gainst her stern force avail.

ANTISTROPHE 1

Of all the powers divine
Alone none dares approach her shrine;
To her no hallowed image stands,
No altar she commands;
In vain the victim's blood would flow;
She never deigns to hear the suppliant
    vow.
Never to me mayst thou appear,
Dread goddess, with severer mien,
That oft in life's past tranquil scene
Thou hast been known to wear.
By thee Jove works his stern behest:
Thy force subdues e'en Scythia's stubborn
    steel
Nor ever does thy rugged breast
The touch of pity feel.

STROPHE 2

And now, with ruin pleased,
On thee, O king, her hands have seized,
And bound thee in her iron chain:
Yet her fell force sustain.
For from the gloomy realms of night
No tears recall the dead to life's sweet
    light;

No virtue, though to heaven allied,
Saves from th' inevitable doom:
Heroes and sons of gods have died,
And sunk into the tomb.
Dear, whilst our eyes her presence blest,
Dear, in the gloomy mansions of the dead;
Most generous she, the noblest, best
Who graced thy nuptial bed.

ANTISTROPHE 2

Thy wife's sepulchral mound
Deem not as common, worthless ground,
That swells their breathless bodies o'er
Who die, and are no more.
No: be it honoured as a shrine
Raised high, and hallowed to some power
    divine.
The traveller, as he passes by,
Shall thither bend his devious way,
With reverence gaze, and with a sigh
Smite on his breast, and say,
"She died of old to save her lord;
Now blest among the blest: Hail, power
    revered;
To us thy wonted grace afford!"
Such vows shall be preferred.
But see, Admetus, to thy house, I ween,
Alcmena's son bends his returning steps.

[HERCULES, ADMETUS, CHORUS]

HERCULES. I would speak freely to my
    friend, Admetus,
Nor what I blame keep secret in my breast.
I came to thee amidst thy ills, and
    thought
I had been worthy to be proved thy friend.
Thou toldst me not the obsequies pre-
    pared
Were for thy wife, but in thy house re-
    ceivdst me
As if thou grievdst for one of foreign
    birth.
I bound my head with garlands, to the
    gods
Pouring libations in thy house with grief
Oppressed. I blame this: yes, in such a
    state
I blame this: yet I come not in thine ills
To give thee pain; why I return in brief
Will I unfold. This woman from my hands
Receive to thy protection, till returned

I bring the Thracian steeds, having there
    slain
The proud Bistonian tyrant; should I fail,
Be that mischance not mine, for much I
    wish
Safe to revisit thee, yet should I fail,
I give her to the safeguard of thy house.
For with much toil she came into my
    hands.
To such as dare contend some public
    games,
Which well deserved my toil, I find pro-
    posed,
I bring her thence, she is the prize of
    conquest;
For slight assays each victor led away
A courser; but for those of harder proof
The conqueror was rewarded from the
    herd,
And with some female graced: victorious
    there,
A prize so noble it were base to slight.
Take her to thy protection, not by stealth
Obtained, but the reward of many toils;
The time perchance may come when thou
    wilt thank me.
    ADMETUS. Not that I slight thy friend-
        ship, or esteem thee
Other than noble, wished I to conceal
My wife's unhappy fate; but to my grief
It had been added grief, if thou hadst
    *sought
Elsewhere the rites of hospitality;
Suffice it that I mourn ills which are
    mine.
This woman, if it may be, give in charge,
I beg thee, king, to some Thessalian else,
That hath not cause like me to grieve;
    in Pheræ
Thou mayst find many friends; call not
    my woes
Fresh to my memory; never in my house
Could I behold her but my tears would
    flow;
To sorrow add not sorrow; now enough
I sink beneath its weight Where should
    her youth
With me be guarded? for her gorgeous
    vests
Proclaim her ·young; if mixing with the
    men

She dwell beneath my roof, how shall her
    fame,
Conversing with the youths, be kept un-
    sullied?
It is not easy to restrain the warmth
Of that intemperate age; my care for
    thee
Warns me of this. Or if from them re-
    moved
I hide her in th' apartments late my
    wife's,
How to my bed admit her? I should fear
A double blame; my citizens would scorn
    me
As light, and faithless to the kindest wife
That died for me, if to her bed I took
Another blooming bride; and to the
    dead
Behoves me pay the highest reverence
Due to her merit. And thou, lady, know,
Who'er thou art, that form, that shape,
    that air
Resembles my Alcestis. By the gods,
Remove her from my sight. It is too
    much,
I cannot bear it: when I look on her,
Methinks I see my wife; this wounds my
    heart,
And calls the tears fresh gushing from
    my eyes.
This is the bitterness of grief indeed.
    CHORUS. I cannot praise thy fortune;
        but behoves thee
To bear with firmness what the gods as-
    sign.
    HERCULES. O that from Jove I had the
        power to bring
Back from the mansions of the dead thy
    wife
To heaven's fair light, that grace achieving
    for thee!
    ADMETUS. I know thy friendly will.
        But how can this
Be done? The dead return not to this
    light.
    HERCULES. Check then thy swelling
        griefs; with reason rule them.
    ADMETUS. How easy to advise, but hard
        to bear!
    HERCULES. What would it profit
        shouldst thou always groan?

ADMETUS. I know it; but I am in love with grief.

HERCULES. Love to the dead calls forth the ceaseless tear.

ADMETUS. O, I am wretched more than words can speak.

HERCULES. A good wife hast thou lost, who can gainsay it?

ADMETUS. Never can life be pleasant to me more.

HERCULES. Thy sorrow now is new, time will abate it.

ADMETUS. Time, sayst thou? Yes, the time that brings me death.

HERCULES. Some young and lovely bride will bid it cease.

ADMETUS. No more: what sayst thou? Never could I think—

HERCULES. Wilt thou still lead a lonely, widowed life?

ADMETUS. Never shall other woman share my bed.

HERCULES. And think'st thou this will aught avail the dead?

ADMETUS. This honour is her due, where'er she be.

HERCULES. This hath my praise, though near allied to frenzy.

ADMETUS. Praise me, or not, I ne'er will wed again.

HERCULES. I praise thee that thou'rt faithful to thy wife.

ADMETUS. Though dead, if I betray her may I die!

HERCULES. Well, take this noble lady to thy house.

ADMETUS. No, by thy father Jove let me entreat thee.

HERCULES. Not to do this would be the greatest wrong.

ADMETUS. To do it would with anguish rend my heart.

HERCULES. Let me prevail; this grace may find its meed.

ADMETUS. O that thou never hadst received this prize!

HERCULES. Yet in my victory thou art victor with me.

ADMETUS. 'Tis nobly said: yet let this woman go.

HERCULES. If she must go, she shall: but must she go?

ADMETUS. She must, if I incur not thy displeasure.

HERCULES. There is a cause that prompts my earnestness.

ADMETUS. Thou hast prevailed, but much against my will.

HERCULES. The time will come when thou wilt thank me for it.

ADMETUS. Well, if I must receive her, lead her in.

HERCULES. Charge servants with her! No, that must not be.

ADMETUS. Lead her thyself then, if thy will incline thee.

HERCULES. No, to thy hand alone will I commit her.

ADMETUS. I touch her not; but she hath leave to enter.

HERCULES. I shall entrust her only to thy hand.

ADMETUS. Thou dost constrain me, king, against my will.

HERCULES. Venture to stretch thy hand, and touch the stranger's.

ADMETUS. I touch her, as I would the headless Gorgon.

HERCULES. Hast thou her hand?

ADMETUS. I have.

HERCULES. Then hold her safe. Hereafter thou wilt say the son of Jove Hath been a generous guest: view now her face,
See if she bears resemblance to thy wife,
And thus made happy bid farewell to grief.

ADMETUS. O gods, what shall I say? 'Tis marvellous,
Exceeding hope. See I my wife indeed?
Or doth some god distract me with false joy?

HERCULES. In very deed dost thou behold thy wife.

ADMETUS. See that it be no phantom from beneath.

HERCULES. Make not thy friend one that evokes the shades.

ADMETUS. And do I see my wife, whom I entombed?

HERCULES. I marvel not that thou art diffident.

ADMETUS. I touch her; may I speak to her as living?

HERCULES. Speak to her; thou hast all thy heart could wish.

ADMETUS. Dearest of women, do see I again

That face, that person? This exceeds all hope:

I never thought that I should see thee more.

HERCULES. Thou hast her; may no god be envious to thee.

ADMETUS. O, be thou blest, thou generous son of Jove!

Thy father's might protect thee! Thou alone

Hast raised her to me; from the realms below

How hast thou brought her to the light of life?

HERCULES. I fought with him that lords it o'er the shades.

ADMETUS. Where with the gloomy tyrant didst thou fight?

HERCULES. I lay in wait, and seized him at the tomb.

ADMETUS. But wherefore doth my wife thus speechless stand?

HERCULES. It is not yet permitted that thou hear

Her voice addressing thee, till from the gods

That rule beneath she be unsanctified

With hallowed rites, and the third morn return.

But lead her in: and as thou'rt just in all

Besides, Admetus, see thou reverence strangers.

Farewell: I go t' achieve the destined toil

For the imperial son of Sthenelus.

ADMETUS. Abide with us, and share my friendly hearth.

HERCULES. That time will come again; this demands speed.

ADMETUS. Success attend thee; safe mayst thou return.

Now to my citizens I give in charge,

And to each chief, that for this blest event

They institute the dance, let the steer bleed,

And the rich altars, as they pay their vows,

Breathe incense to the gods; for now I rise

To better life, and grateful own the blessing.

CHORUS. With various hand the gods dispense our fates:

Now showering various blessings, which our hopes

Dared not aspire to; now controlling ills

We deemed inevitable; thus the god

To these hath given an end exceeding thought.

Such is the fortune of this happy day.

THE CLOUDS

By ARISTOPHANES

Produced at Athens, 423 B.C.

TRANSLATED BY T. MITCHELL

CHARACTERS

STREPSIADES
PHEIDIPPIDES
SERVANT TO STREPSIADES
DISCIPLES OF SOCRATES
SOCRATES
CHORUS OF CLOUDS
DICÆOLOGOS
ADICÆOLOGOS
PASIAS
AMYNIAS
WITNESSES
CHÆREPHON

SCENE—*Athens.*

[STREPSIADES *is discovered in his chamber,* PHEIDIPPIDES *sleeping in his bed. Time, before break of day.*]

STREPSIADES [*stretching and yawning*].
Ah me, ah me! will this night never end?
Oh kingly Jove, shall there be no more day?
And yet the cock sung out long time ago;
I heard him—but my people lie and snore;
Snore in defiance, for the rascals know
It is their privilege in time of war,

Which with its other plagues brings this upon us,
That we mayn't rouse these vermin with a cudgel.
There's my young hopeful too, he sleeps it through,
Snug under five fat blankets at the least.
Would I could sleep so sound! but my poor eyes
Have no sleep in them; what with debts and duns
And stable-keepers' bills, which this fine spark

64

Heaps on my back, I lie awake the whilst:
And what cares he but to coil up his locks,
Ride, drive his horses, dream of them all night,
Whilst I, poor devil, may go hang—for now
The moon in her last quarter wains apace,
And my usurious creditors are gaping.
What hoa! a light! bring me my tablets, boy!
That I may set down all, and sum them up,
Debts, creditors, and interest upon interest— [*Boy enters with a light and tablets.*]
Let me see where I am and what the total—
Twelve pounds to Pasias—Hah! to Pasias twelve!
Out on it, and for what? A horse forsooth,
Right noble by the mark—Curse on such marks!
Would I had giv'n this eye from out this head,
Ere I had paid the purchase of this jennet!
PHEIDIPPIDES. Shame on you, Philo!—
Keep within your ring.
STREPSIADES. There 'tis! that's it! the bane of all my peace—
He's racing in his sleep.
PHEIDIPPIDES. A heat—a heat!
How many turns to a heat?
STREPSIADES. More than enough;
You've giv'n me turns in plenty—I am jaded.
But to my list—what name stands next to Pasias?
Amynias—three good pounds—still for the race—
A chariot mounted on its wheels complete.
PHEIDIPPIDES. Dismount! unharness and away!
STREPSIADES. I thank you;
You have unharness'd me: I am dismounted,
And with a vengeance—All my goods in pawn,
Fines, forfeiture, and penalties in plenty.

PHEIDIPPIDES [*wakes*]. My father! why so restless? who has vex'd you?
STREPSIADES. The sheriff vexes me; he breaks my rest.
PHEIDIPPIDES. Peace, self-tormentor, let me sleep!
STREPSIADES. Sleep on!
But take this with you; all these debts of mine
Will double on your head: a plague confound
That cursed match-maker, who drew me in
To wed, forsooth, that precious dam of thine.
I liv'd at ease in the country, coarsely clad,
Rough, free, and full withal as oil and honey
And store of stock could fill me, till I took,
Clown as I was, this limb of the Alcmæons,
This vain, extravagant, high-blooded dame:
Rare bed-fellows and dainty—were we not?
I, smelling of the wine-vat, figs and fleeces,
The produce of my farm, all essence she,
Saffron and harlot's kisses, paint and washes,
A pamper'd wanton—idle I'll not call her;
She took due pains in faith to work my ruin,
Which made me tell her, pointing to this cloak,
Now threadbare on my shoulders—see, goodwife,
This is your work—in troth you toil too hard. [*Boy reënters.*]
BOY. Master, the lamp has drunk up all its oil.
STREPSIADES. Aye, 'tis a drunken lamp; the more fault yours;
Whelp, you shall howl for this.
BOY. Why? for what fault?
STREPSIADES. For cramming such a greedy wick with oil. [*Exit boy.*]
Well! in good time this hopeful heir was born;
Then I and my beloved fell to wrangling
About the naming of the brat.—My wife

Would dub her colt Xanthippus or Char-
  ippus,
Or it might be Callipides, she car'd not
So 'twere equestrian the name—but I
Stuck for his grandfather Pheidonides;
At last when neither could prevail, the
  matter
Was compromis'd by calling him Pheidip-
  pides:
Then she began to fondle her sweet babe,
And taking him by th' hand—Lambkin,
  she cried,
When thou art some years older thou shalt
  drive,
Megacles-like, thy chariot to the city,
Rob'd in a saffron mantle.—No, quoth I,
Not so, my boy, but thou shalt drive thy
  goats,
When thou art able, from the fields of
  Phelle,
Clad in a woollen jacket like thy father:
But he is deaf to all these frugal rules,
And drives me on the gallop to my ruin;
Therefore all night I call my thoughts to
  council,
And after long debate find one chance
  left,
To which if I can lead him, all is safe,
If not—but soft: 'tis time that I should
  wake him.
But how to soothe him to the task—
    [speaking in a soft gentle tone.]
  Pheidippides!
Precious Pheidippides!
  PHEIDIPPIDES. What now, my father?
  STREPSIADES. Kiss me, my boy! reach
    me thine hand—
  PHEIDIPPIDES. Declare,
What would you?
  STREPSIADES.   Dost thou love me,
    sirrah? speak!
  PHEIDIPPIDES. Aye, by equestrian Nep-
    tune!
  STREPSIADES [angrily]. Name not him,
Name not that charioteer; he is my bane,
The source of all my sorrow—but, my
  son,
If thou dost love me, prove it by obedi-
  ence.
  PHEIDIPPIDES. In what must I obey?
  STREPSIADES. Reform your habits;

Quit them at once, and what I shall pre-
  scribe
That do!
  PHEIDIPPIDES. And what is it that you
    prescribe?
  STREPSIADES. But wilt thou do't?
  PHEIDIPPIDES. Yes, by Dionysus.
  STREPSIADES. 'Tis well: get up! come
    hither, boy! look out!
Yon little wicket and the hut hard by—
Dost see them?
  PHEIDIPPIDES. Clearly. What of that
    same hut?
  STREPSIADES. Why that's the council-
    chamber of all wisdom:
There the choice spirits dwell, who teach
  the world
That heav'n's great concave is one mighty
  oven,
And men its burning embers; these are
  they,
Who can show pleaders how to twist a
  cause,
So you'll but pay them for it, right or
  wrong.
  PHEIDIPPIDES. And how do you call
    them?
  STREPSIADES. Troth, I know not that,
But they are men, who take a world of
  pains;
Wondrous good men and able.
  PHEIDIPPIDES. Out upon 'em!
Poor rogues, I know them now; you mean
  those scabs,
Those squalid, barefoot, beggarly impos-
  tors,
The mighty cacodæmons of whose sect
Are Socrates and Chærephon. Away!
  STREPSIADES. Hush, hush! be still;
    don't vent such foolish prattle;
But if you'll take my counsel, join their
  college
And quit your riding-school.
  PHEIDIPPIDES. Not I, so help me
Dionysus our patron! though you brib'd
  me
With all the racers that Leogaras
Breeds from his Phasian stud.
  STREPSIADES. Dear, darling lad,
Prythee be rul'd, and learn.
  PHEIDIPPIDES. What shall I learn?

STREPSIADES. They have a choice of logic; this for justice,
That for injustice: learn that latter art,
And all these creditors, that now beset me,
Shall never touch a drachma that I owe them.
PHEIDIPPIDES. I'll learn of no such masters, nor be made
A scare-crow and a may-game to my comrades;
I have no zeal for starving.
STREPSIADES. No, nor I
For feasting you and your fine pamper'd cattle
At free cost any longer.—Horse and foot
To the crows I bequeath you. So begone!
PHEIDIPPIDES. Well, sir, I have an uncle rich and noble;
Megacles will not let me be unhors'd;
To him I go; I'll trouble you no longer.
[*Exit.*]
STREPSIADES [*alone*]. He has thrown me to the ground, but I'll not lie there;
I'll up, and, with permission of the gods,
Try if I cannot learn these arts myself:
But being old, sluggish, and dull of wit,
How am I sure these subtleties won't pose me?
Well! I'll attempt it: what avails complaint?
Why don't I knock and enter?—Hoa! within there!—
[*Knocks violently at the door.*]
DISCIPLE [*half opening the door*]. Go. hang yourself! and give the crows a dinner—
What noisy fellow art thou at the door?
STREPSIADES. Strepsiades of Cicynna, son of Pheidon.
DISCIPLE. Whoe'er thou art, 'fore Heaven, thou art a fool
Not to respect these doors; battering so loud,
And kicking with such vengeance, you have marr'd
The ripe conception of my pregnant brain,
And brought on a miscarriage.—
STREPSIADES. Oh! the pity!—
Pardon my ignorance: I'm country bred

And far a-field am come: I pray you tell me
What curious thought my luckless din has strangled,
Just as your brain was hatching.
DISCIPLE. These are things
We never speak of but amongst ourselves.
STREPSIADES. Speak boldly then to me, for I am come
To be amongst you, and partake the secrets
Of your profound academy.
DISCIPLE. Enough!
I will impart, but set it down in thought
Amongst our mysteries.—This is the question,
As it was put but now to Chærephon,
By our great master Socrates, to answer—
How many of his own lengths at one spring
A flea can hop—for we did see one vault
From Chærephon's black eye-brow to the head
Of the philosopher.
STREPSIADES. And how did t'other
Contrive to measure this?
DISCIPLE. Most accurately:
He dipt the insect's feet in melted wax,
Which, hard'ning into sandals as it cool'd,
Gave him the space by rule infallible.
STREPSIADES. Imperial Jove! what subtilty of thought!
DISCIPLE. But there's a deeper question yet behind;
What would you say to that?
STREPSIADES. I pray, impart it.
DISCIPLE. 'Twas put to Socrates, if he could say,
When a gnat humm'd, whether the sound did issue
From mouth or tail.
STREPSIADES. Aye; marry, what said he?
DISCIPLE. He said your gnat doth blow his trumpet backwards
From a sonorous cavity within him,
Which being filled with breath, and forc'd along
The narrow pipe or rectum of his body,
Doth vent itself in a loud hum behind.

STREPSIADES.   Hah! then I see the
    podex of your gnat
Is trumpet-fashion'd—Oh! the blessings
    on him
For this discovery; well may he escape
The law's strict scrutiny, who thus de-
    velops
The anatomy of a gnat.
    DISCIPLE.   Nor is this all;
Another grand experiment was blasted
By a curst cat.
    STREPSIADES.   As how, good sir; dis-
    cuss?
    DISCIPLE.   One night as he was gazing
    at the moon,
Curious and all intent upon her motions,
A cat on the house ridge was at her needs,
And squirted in his face.
    STREPSIADES.   Beshrew her for it!
Yet I must laugh no less to think a cat
Should so bespatter Socrates.
    DISCIPLE.   Last night
We were bilk'd of our supper.
    STREPSIADES.   Were you so?
What did your master substitute instead?
    DISCIPLE.   Why to say truth, he
    sprinkled a few ashes
Upon the board, then with a little broach,
Crook'd for the nonce, pretending to de-
    scribe
A circle, neatly filch'd away a cloak.
    STREPSIADES.   Why talk we then of
    Thales? Open to me,
Open the school, and let me see your
    master:
I am on fire to enter—Come, unbar!
        [*The door of the school is un-
        barred. The Socratic scholars
        are seen in various grotesque
        situations and positions.* STREP-
        SIADES, *with signs of astonish-
        ment, draws back a pace or
        two, then exclaims:*]
O Hercules, defend me! who are these?
What kind of cattle have we here in view?
    DISCIPLE.   Where is the wonder? What
    do they resemble?
    STREPSIADES.   Methinks they're like our
    Spartan prisoners,
Captur'd at Pylos. What are they in
    search of?

Why are their eyes so riveted to th' earth?
    DISCIPLE.   There their researches centre.
    STREPSIADES.   'Tis for onions
They are in quest—Come, lads, give o'er
    your search;
I'll show you what you want, a noble plat,
All round and sound—but soft! what
    mean those gentry,
Who dip their heads so low?
    DISCIPLE.   Marry, because
Their studies lead that way: They are
    now diving
To the dark realms of Tartarus and
    Night.
    STREPSIADES.   But why are all their
    cruppers mounted up?
    DISCIPLE.   To practise them in star-
    gazing, and teach them
Their proper elevations—but no more:
In, fellow-students, in: if chance the mas-
    ter come
And find us here—
        [*Addressing himself to some of
        his fellow students, who were
        crowding about the new-comer.*]
    STREPSIADES.   Nay, prythee let 'em stay,
And be of council with me in my business.
    DISCIPLE.   Impossible; they cannot give
    the time.
    STREPSIADES.   Now for the love of
    Heav'n, what have we here?
Explain their uses to me.   [*Observing the
                apparatus.*]
    DISCIPLE.   This machine
Is for astronomy—
    STREPSIADES.   And this?
    DISCIPLE.   For geometry.
    STREPSIADES.   As how?
    DISCIPLE.   For measuring the earth.
    STREPSIADES.   Indeed!
What, by the lot?
    DISCIPLE.   No, faith, sir, by the lump;
Ev'n the whole globe at once.
    STREPSIADES.   Well said, in troth.
A quaint device, and made for general use.
    DISCIPLE.   Look now, this line marks
    the circumference
Of the whole earth, d'ye see—This spot is
    Athens—
    STREPSIADES.   Athens! go to, I see no
    courts are sitting;

Therefore I can't believe you.
DISCIPLE. Nay, in truth,
This very tract is Attica.
STREPSIADES. And where,
Where is my own Cicynna?
DISCIPLE. Here it lies:
And here's Eubœa—Mark! how far it
runs—
STREPSIADES. How far it runs! Yes,
Pericles has made it
Run far enough from us—Where's Lace-
dæmon?
DISCIPLE. Here; close to Athens.
STREPSIADES. Ah! how much too close—
Prythee, good friends, take that bad neigh-
bour from us.
DISCIPLE. That's not for us to do.
STREPSIADES. The worse luck your's!
But look! [Casting up his eyes.] Who's
this suspended in a basket?
[SOCRATES is discovered.]
DISCIPLE [with solemnity]. HIMSELF.
The HE.
STREPSIADES. The HE? What HE?
DISCIPLE. Why, Socrates.
STREPSIADES. Hah! Socrates!—[To the
scholar.] Make up to him and roar,
Bid him come down! roar lustily.
DISCIPLE. Not I:
Do it yourself; I've other things to mind.
[Exit.]
STREPSIADES. Hoa! Socrates—What
hoa, my little Socrates!
SOCRATES. Mortal, how now! Thou in-
sect of a day,
What would'st thou?
STREPSIADES. I would know what thou
art doing.
SOCRATES. I tread in air, contemplating
the sun.
STREPSIADES. Ah! then I see you're
basketed so high,
That you look down upon the Gods—
Good hope,
You'll lower a peg on earth.
SOCRATES. Sublime in air,
Sublime in thought I carry my mind
with me,
Its cogitations all assimilated
To the pure atmosphere, in which I
float;

Lower me to earth, and my mind's subtle
powers,
Seiz'd by contagious dullness, lose their
spirit;
For the dry earth drinks up the generous
sap,
The vegetating vigour of philosophy,
And leaves it a mere husk.
STREPSIADES. What do you say?
Philosophy has sapt your vigour? Fie
upon it.
But come, my precious fellow, come down
quickly,
And teach me those fine things I'm here
in quest of.
SOCRATES. And what fine things are
they?
STREPSIADES. A new receipt
For sending off my creditors, and foiling
them
By the art logical; for you shall know
By debts, pawns, pledges, usuries, execu-
tions,
I am rackt and rent in tatters.
SOCRATES. Why permit it?
What strange infatuation seiz'd your
senses?
STREPSIADES. The horse-consumption, a
devouring plague;
But so you'll enter me amongst your
scholars,
And tutor me like them to bilk my cred-
itors,
Name your own price, and by the Gods I
swear
I'll pay you the last drachm.
SOCRATES. By what Gods?
Answer that first; for your Gods are not
mine.
STREPSIADES. How swear you then?
As the Byzantians swear
By their base iron coin?
SOCRATES. Art thou ambitious
To be instructed in celestial matters,
And taught to know them clearly?
STREPSIADES. Aye, aye, in faith,
So they be to my purpose, and celestial.
SOCRATES. What, if I bring you to a
conference
With my own proper Goddesses, the
Clouds?

STREPSIADES. 'Tis what I wish devoutly.

SOCRATES. Come, sit down;

Repose yourself upon this couch.

STREPSIADES. 'Tis done.

SOCRATES. Now take this chaplet—wear it.

STREPSIADES. Why this chaplet?

Would'st make of me another Athamas,

And sacrifice me to a cloud?

SOCRATES. Fear nothing;

It is a ceremony indispensable

At OUR initiations.

STREPSIADES. What to gain?

SOCRATES. [*Instead of the sacred meat, which was thrown on the sacrificed victim, a basket of stones is showered on the head of* STREPSIADES.]

'Twill sift your faculties as fine as powder,

Bolt 'em like meal, grind 'em as light as dust;

Only be patient.

STREPSIADES. Truly, you'll go near

To make your words good; an' you pound me thus,

You'll make me very dust and nothing else.

SOCRATES [*assuming all the magical solemnity and tone of voice of an adept*]. Keep silence, then, and listen to a prayer,

Which fits the gravity of age to hear—

Oh! Air, all powerful Air, which dost enfold

This pendant globe, thou vault of flaming gold.

Ye sacred Clouds, who bid the thunder roll,

Shine forth, approach, and cheer your suppliant's soul!

STREPSIADES. Hold, keep 'em off awhile, till I am ready.

Ah! luckless me, wou'd I had brought my bonnet,

And so escap'd a soaking.

SOCRATES. Come, come away!

Fly swift, ye Clouds, and give yourselves to view!

Whether on high Olympus' sacred top

Snow-crown'd ye sit, or in the azure vales

Of your own father Ocean sporting weave

Your misty dance, or dip your golden urns

In the seven mouths of Nile; whether ye dwell

On Thracian Mimas, or Mœotis' lake,

Hear me, yet hear, and thus invok'd approach!

[CHORUS OF CLOUDS. *The scene is at the remotest part of the stage. Thunder is heard. A large and shapeless Cloud is seen floating in the air; from which the following song is heard.*]

CHORUS OF CLOUDS. Ascend, ye watery Clouds, on high,

Daughters of Ocean, climb the sky,

And o'er the mountain's pine-capt brow

Towering your fleecy mantle throw:

Thence let us scan the wide-stretch'd scene,

Groves, lawns, and rilling streams between,

And stormy Neptune's vast expanse,

And grasp all nature at a glance.

Now the dark tempest flits away,

And lo! the glittering orb of day

Darts from his clear ethereal beam,

Come let us snatch the joyous gleam.

SOCRATES. Yes, ye Divinities, whom I adore,

I hail you now propitious to my prayer.

Didst thou not hear them speak in thunder to me?

STREPSIADES [*kneeling, and, with various acts of buffoonery, affecting terror and embarrassment.*]

And I too am your Cloudships' most obedient,

And under sufferance trump against your thunder:—

Nay [*turning to* SOCRATES], take it how you may, my frights and fears

Have pinch'd and cholic'd my poor bowels so,

That I can't choose but treat their holy nostrils

With an unsavoury sacrifice,

SOCRATES. Forbear

These gross scurrilities, for low buffoons

And mountebanks more fitting. Hush! be still,

List to the chorus of their heavenly voices,

For music is the language they delight in.

CHORUS OF CLOUDS [*approaching nearer*]. Ye Clouds replete with fruitful showers,
Here let us seek Minerva's towers,
The cradle of old Cecrops' race,
The world's chief ornament and grace;
Here mystic fanes and rites divine
And lamps in sacred splendour shine;
Here the Gods dwell in marble domes,
Feasted with costly hecatombs,
That round their votive statues blaze,
Whilst crowded temples ring with praise;
And pompous sacrifices here
Make holidays throughout the year,
And when gay spring-time comes again,
Bromius convokes his sportive train,
And pipe and song and choral dance
Hail the soft hours as they advance.

STREPSIADES. Now, in the name of Jove, I pray thee tell me
Who are these ranting dames, that talk in stilts?
Of the Amazonian cast no doubt.

SOCRATES. Not so,
No dames, but clouds celestial, friendly powers
To men of sluggish parts; from these we draw
Sense, apprehension, volubility,
Wit to confute, and cunning to ensnare.

STREPSIADES. Aye, therefore 'twas that my heart leapt within me
For very sympathy when first I heard 'em:
Now I could prattle shrewdly of first causes,
And spin out metaphysic cobwebs finely,
And dogmatise most rarely, and dispute
And paradox it with the best of you:
So, come what may, I must and will behold 'em;
Show me their faces, I conjure you.

SOCRATES. Look,
Look towards Mount Parnes as I point—
There, there!
Now they descend the hill; I see them plainly,
As plain as can be.

STREPSIADES. Where, where? I prythee, show me.

SOCRATES. Here! a whole troop of them thro' woods and hollows,

A byway of their own.

STREPSIADES. What ails my eyes,
That I can't catch a glimpse of them?

SOCRATES. Behold!
Here at the very entrance—

STREPSIADES. Never trust me,
If yet I see them clearly.

SOCRATES. Then you must be
Sand-blind or worse.

STREPSIADES. Nay, now by Father Jove,
I cannot choose but see them—precious creatures!
For in good faith here's plenty and to spare.

[CHORUS OF CLOUDS *enter*.]

SOCRATES. And didst thou doubt if they were goddesses?

STREPSIADES. Not I, so help me! only I'd a notion
That they were fog, and dew, and dusky vapour.

SOCRATES. For shame! Why, man, these are the nursing mothers
Of all our famous sophists, fortune-tellers,
Quacks, med'cine-mongers, bards bombastical,
Chorus projectors, and star interpreters,
And wonder-making cheats—the gang of idlers,
Who pay them for their feeding with good store
Of flattery and mouth-worship.

STREPSIADES. Now I see
Whom we may thank for driving them along
At such a furious dithyrambic rate,
Sun-shadowing clouds of many-colour'd hues,
Air-rending tempests, hundred-headed Typhons;
Now rousing, rattling them about our ears,
Now gently wafting them adown the sky,
Moist, airy, bending, bursting into showers;
For all which fine descriptions these poor knaves
Dine daintily on scraps.

SOCRATES. And proper fare;
What better do they merit?

STREPSIADES. Under favour,

If these be clouds (d'you mark me?)
very clouds,
How came they metamorphos'd into
women?
Clouds are not such as these.
SOCRATES. And what else are they?
STREPSIADES. Troth, I can't rightly tell,
but I should guess
Something like flakes of wool, not women,
sure;
And look! these dames have noses.
SOCRATES. Hark you, friend,
I'll put a question to you.
STREPSIADES. Out with it!
Be quick: let's have it.
SOCRATES. This it is, in short—
Hast thou ne'er seen a cloud, which thou
could'st fancy
Shap'd like a centaur, leopard, wolf, or
bull?
STREPSIADES. Yea, marry, have I, and
what then?
SOCRATES. Why then
Clouds can assume what shapes they will,
believe me;
For instance; should they spy some hairy
clown
Rugged and rough, and like the unlick't
cub
Of Xenophantes, straight they turn to
centaurs,
And kick at him for vengeance.
STREPSIADES. Well done, Clouds!
But should they spy that peculating
knave,
Simon, that public thief, how would they
treat him?
SOCRATES. As wolves—in character
most like his own.
STREPSIADES. Aye, there it is now;
when they saw Cleonymus,
That dastard runaway, they turn'd to
hinds
In honour of his cowardice.
SOCRATES. And now,
Having seen Cleisthenes, to mock his lewd-
ness
They change themselves to women.
STREPSIADES. Welcome, ladies!
Imperial ladies, welcome! An' it please
Your Highnesses so far to grace a mortal,

Give me a touch of your celestial voices.
CHORUS. Hail, grandsire! who at this
late hour of life
Would'st go to school for cunning; and
all hail,
Thou prince pontifical of quirks and quib-
bles,
Speak thy full mind, make known thy
wants and wishes!
Thee and our worthy Prodicus excepted,
Not one of all your sophists have our ear:
Him for his wit and learning we esteem,
Thee for thy proud deportment and high
looks,
In barefoot beggary strutting up and
down,
Content to suffer mockery for our sake,
And carry a grave face whilst others
laugh.
STREPSIADES. Oh! mother earth, was
ever voice like this,
So reverend, so portentous, so divine!
SOCRATES. These are your only deities,
all else
I flout at.
STREPSIADES. Hold! Olympian Jupi-
ter—
Is he no god?
SOCRATES. What Jupiter? what god?
Prythee no more—away with him at once!
STREPSIADES. Say'st thou? who gives
us rain? answer me that.
SOCRATES. These give us rain; as I will
straight demonstrate:
Come on now—When did you e'er see it
rain
Without a cloud? If Jupiter gives rain,
Let him rain down his favours in the
sunshine,
Nor ask the clouds to help him.
STREPSIADES. You have hit it,
'Tis so; heav'n help me! I did think till
now,
When 'twas his godship's pleasure, he
made water
Into a sieve and gave the earth a shower.
But, hark'ye me, who thunders? tell me
that;
For then it is I tremble.
SOCRATES. These, these thunder,
When they are tumbled.

STREPSIADES. How, blasphemer, how?

SOCRATES. When they are charg'd with vapours full to th' bursting,
And bandied to and fro against each other,
Then with the shock they burst and crack amain.

STREPSIADES. And who is he that jowls them thus together
But Jove himself?

SOCRATES. Jove! 'tis not Jove that does it,
But the ætherial vortex.

STREPSIADES. What is he?
I never heard of him; is he not Jove?
Or is Jove put aside, and Vortex crown'd
King of Olympus in his state and place?
But let me learn some more of this same thunder.

SOCRATES. Have you not learnt? I told you how the clouds,
Being surcharg'd with vapour, rush together,
And, in the conflict, shake the poles with thunder.

STREPSIADES. But who believes you?

SOCRATES. You, as I shall prove it:
Mark the Panathenæa, where you cram
Your belly full of pottage; if you shake
And stir it lustily about—what then?

STREPSIADES. Marry, why then it gives a desperate crack;
It bounces like a thunderbolt, the pottage
Keeps such a coil within me—At the first,
Pappax it cries—anon with double force,
Papappax!—when at length *Papappapax*
From forth my sounding entrails thund'ring bursts.

SOCRATES. Think then, if so your belly trumpets forth,
How must the vasty vault of heaven resound,
When the clouds crack with thunder!

STREPSIADES. Let that pass,
And tell me of the lightning, whose quick flash
Burns us to cinders; that, at least, great Jove
Keeps in reserve to launch at perjury?

SOCRATES. Dunce, dotard! were you born before the flood
To talk of perjury, whilst Simon breathes,

Theorus and Cleonymus, whilst they,
Thrice-perjur'd villains, brave the lightning's stroke,
And gaze the heav'ns unscorcht? Would these escape?
Why, man, Jove's random fires strike his own fane,
Strike Sunium's guiltless top, strike the dumb oak,
Who never yet broke faith or falsely swore.

STREPSIADES. It may be so, good sooth!
You talk this well:
But I would fain be taught the natural cause
Of these appearances.

SOCRATES. Mark when the winds,
In their free courses check'd, are pent and purs'd
As 'twere within a bladder, stretching then
And struggling for expansion, they burst forth
With crack so fierce as sets the air on fire.

STREPSIADES. The devil they do! why now the murder's out:
So was I serv'd with a damn'd paunch, I broil'd
On Jove's day last, just such a scurvy trick;
Because, forsooth, not dreaming of your thunder,
I never thought to give the rascal vent,
Bounce! goes the bag, and covers me all over
With filth and ordure till my eyes struck fire.

CHORUS. The envy of all Athens shalt thou be,
Happy old man, who from our lips dost suck
Into thy ears true wisdom, so thou art
But wise to learn, and studious to retain
What thou hast learnt; patient to bear the blows
And buffets of hard fortune; to persist,
Doing or suffering; firmly to abide
Hunger and cold, not craving where to dine,
To drink, to sport and trifle time away;

But holding that for best, which best be-
comes
A man who means to carry all things
through
Neatly, expertly, perfect at all points
With head, hands, tongue, to force his
way to fortune.
STREPSIADES. Be confident; I give my-
self for one
Of a tough heart, watchful as care can
make me,
A frugal, pinching fellow, that can sup
Upon a sprig of savory and to bed;
I am your man for this, hard as an anvil.
SOCRATES. 'Tis well, so you will ratify
your faith
In these our deities—CHAOS and CLOUDS
And SPELCH—to these and only these ad-
here.
STREPSIADES. If from this hour hence-
forth I ever waste
A single thought on any other gods,
Or give them sacrifice, libation, incense,
Nay, even common courtesy, renounce
me.
CHORUS. Speak your wish boldly then,
so shall you prosper
As you obey and worship us, and study
The wholesome art of thriving.
STREPSIADES. Gracious ladies,
I ask no mighty favour, simply this—
Let me but distance every tongue in
Greece,
And run 'em out of sight a hundred
lengths.
CHORUS. Is that all? There we are
your friends to serve you;
We will endow thee with such powers of
speech,
As henceforth not a demagogue in Athens
Shall spout such popular harangues as
thou shalt.
STREPSIADES. A fig for powers of spout-
ing! give me powers
Of nonsuiting my creditors.
CHORUS. A trifle—
Granted as soon as ask'd; only be bold,
And show yourself obedient to your
teachers.
STREPSIADES. With your help so I will,
being undone,

Stript of my pelf by these high-blooded
cattle,
And a fine dame, the torment of my life.
Now let them work their wicked will upon
me;
They're welcome to my carcass; let 'em
claw it,
Starve it with thirst and hunger, fry it,
freeze it,
Nay, flay the very skin off; 'tis their
own;
So that I may but fob my creditors,
Let the world talk; I care not though it
call me
A bold-faced, loud-tongued, overbearing
bully;
A shameless, vile, prevaricating cheat;
A tricking, quibbling, double-dealing
knave;
A prating, pettyfogging limb o' th' law;
A sly old fox, a perjurer, a hang-dog,
A raggamuffin made of shreds and patches,
The leavings of a dunghill—Let 'em rail,
Yea, marry, let 'em turn my guts to
fiddle-strings,
May my bread be my poison! if I care.
CHORUS. This fellow hath a prompt and
daring spirit—
Come hither, sir; do you perceive and
feel
What great and glorious fame you shall
acquire
By this our schooling of you?
STREPSIADES. What, I pray you!
CHORUS. What but to live the envy of
mankind
Under our patronage?
STREPSIADES. When shall I see
Those halcyon days?
CHORUS. Then shall your doors be
throng'd
With clients waiting for your coming
forth,
All eager to consult you, pressing all
To catch a word from you, with abstracts,
briefs,
And cases ready-drawn for your opinion.
But come, begin and lecture this old fel-
low;
Sift him, that we may see what meal he's
made of.

SOCRATES. Hark ye, let's hear what principles you hold,
That these being known, I may apply such tools
As tally with your stuff.

STREPSIADES. Tools! by the gods;
Are you about to spring a mine upon me?

SOCRATES. Not so, but simply in the way of practice
To try your memory.

STREPSIADES. Oh! as for that,
My memory is of two sorts, long and short:
With them who owe me aught, it never fails;
My creditors indeed complain of it,
As mainly apt to leak and lose its reck'-ning.

SOCRATES. But let us hear if nature hath endow'd you
With any grace of speaking.

STREPSIADES. None of speaking
But a most apt propensity to cheating.

SOCRATES. If this be all, how can you hope to learn?

STREPSIADES. Fear me not, never break your head for that.

SOCRATES. Well then be quick, and when I speak of things
Mysterious and profound, see that you make
No boggling, but—

STREPSIADES. I understand your meaning;
You'd have me bolt philosophy by mouthfuls,
Just like a hungry cur.

SOCRATES. Oh! brutal, gross
And barbarous ignorance! I must suspect,
Old as thou art, thou must be taught with stripes:
Tell me now, when thou art beaten, what dost feel?

STREPSIADES. The blows of him that beats me I do feel;
But having breath'd awhile I lay my action
And cite my witnesses; anon more cool,
I bring my cause into the court, and sue
For damages.

SOCRATES. Strip off your cloak! prepare.

STREPSIADES. Prepare for what? what crime have I committed?

SOCRATES. None; but the rule and custom is with us,
That all shall enter naked.

STREPSIADES. And why naked?
I come with no search-warrant; fear me not;
I'll carry nought away with me.

SOCRATES. No matter;
Conform yourself, and strip.

STREPSIADES. And if I do,
Tell me for my encouragement to which
Of all your scholars will you liken me.

SOCRATES. You shall be call'd a second Chærephon.

STREPSIADES. Ah! Chærephon is but another name
For a dead corpse—excuse me.

SOCRATES. No more words:
Pluck up your courage; answer not, but follow:
Haste and be perfected.

STREPSIADES. Give me my dole
Of honey-cake in hand, and pass me on;
Ne'er trust me if I do not quake and tremble
As if the cavern of Trophonius yawn'd,
And I were stepping in.

SOCRATES. What ails you? enter!
Why do you halt and loiter at the door?
[SOCRATES *and* STREPSIADES *enter the mansion of the former.*]

CHORUS. Go, brave adventurer, proceed!
May fortune crown the gallant deed;
Tho' far advanc'd in life's last stage,
Spurning the infirmities of age,
Thou canst to youthful labours rise,
And boldly struggle to be wise.

Ye, who are here spectators of our scene,
Give me your patience to a few plain words,
And by my patron Bacchus, whose I am,
I swear they shall be true ones.—Gentle friends,
So may I prosper in your fair esteem,
As I declare in truth that I was mov'd

To tender you my former comedy,
As deeming it the best of all my works,
And you its judges worthy of that work,
Which I had wrought with my best care
    and pains:
But fools were found to thrust me from
    the stage,
And you, whose better wisdom should have
    sav'd me
From that most vile cabal, permitted it;
For which I needs must chide, yet not so
    sharply
As to break off from such approv'd good
    friends:
No, you have been my patrons from all
    time,
Ev'n to my first-born issue: when I dropt
My bantling at your door to hide the
    shame
Of one, who call'd herself a maiden muse,
You charitably took the foundling in,
And gave it worthy training. Now, be-
    hold,
This sister comedy, Electra-like,
Comes on the search if she perchance may
    find
Some recognition of a brother lost,
Though but a relic of his well-known hair.
Seemly and modest she appears before
    you;
Not like our stage buffoons in shaggy hide
To set a mob a roaring; she will vent
No foolish jests at baldness, will not dance
Th' indecent cordax; we have no old
    man
Arm'd with a staff to practise manual
    jokes
On the by-standers' ribs, and keep the
    ring
For them who dance the chorus: you shall
    see
No howling furies burst upon the stage
Waving their torches; other weapons
Than the muse gives us we shall not em-
    ploy,
Nor let *ah me, ah me!* sigh in your ears.
Yet not of this I boast, nor that I scorn
To cater for your palates out of scraps
At second or third hand, but fresh and
    fair
And still original, as one, who knows,

When he has done a good deed, where to
    stop;
And, having levell'd Cleon to the ground,
Not to insult his carcass, like to those
Who, having once run down Hyperbolus,
Poor devil! mouth and mangle without
    mercy
Him and his mother too; foremost of these
Was Eupolis, who pilfer'd from my muse,
And pass'd it for his own with a new
    name,
Guilty the more for having dash'd his
    theft
With the obscene device of an old hag
Dancing the drunken cordax in her cups,
Like her Phrynichus feign'd to be de-
    vour'd
By the sea-monster.—Shame upon such
    scenes!
Hermippus next *Hyperbolis'd* amain,
And now the whole pack open in full
    cry,
Holding the game in chase, which I had
    rous'd.
If there be any here, who laugh with
    these,
Let such not smile with me; but if this
    night
Ye crown these scenes with merited ap-
    plause,
Posterity shall justify your taste.
    SEMICHORUS. Great Jove, supreme of
Gods, and heav'n's high king,
First I invoke; next him the Trident's
    lord,
Whose mighty stroke smites the wild
    waves asunder,
And makes the firm earth tremble; thee
    from whom
We draw our being, all-inspiring Air,
Parent of nature; and thee, radiant Sun,
Thron'd in thy flaming chariot, I invoke,
Dear to the gods and by the world ador'd.
    CHORUS OF CLOUDS. Most grave and
sapient judges, hear the charge,
Which we shall now prefer, of slights ill
    brook'd
By us your wrong'd appellants: for whilst
    we
The patronesses of your state, the Clouds,
Of all the powers celestial serve you most,

You graceless mortals serve us not at all;
Nor smoke, nor sacrifice ascends from
you,
But blank ingratitude and cold neglect.
If some rash enterprise you set on foot,
Some brainless project, straight with rain
or thunder,
Sure warnings, we apprise you of your
folly:
When late you made that offspring of a
tanner,
That Paphlagonian odious to the gods,
The general of your armies, mark how
fierce
We scowl'd upon you, and indignant roll'd
Our thunders intermixt with flashing
fires;
The Moon forsook her course, and the
vext Sun
Quench'd his bright torch, disdaining to
behold
Cleon your chief, yet chief that Cleon
was,
(For it should seem a proverb with your
people,
That measures badly taken best succeed):
But if you'll learn of us the ready mode
To cancel your past errors, and ensure
Fame and good-fortune for the public
weal,
You have nought else to do, but stop the
swallow
Of that wide-gaping cormorant, that thief
Convicted and avow'd, with a neat noose
Drawn tight and fitted to his scurvy
throat.
SEMICHORUS. Thou too, Apollo, of thy
native isle,
Upon the Cinthian mount high thron'd,
the king,
Hear and be present! thou, Ephesian god-
dess,
Whose golden shrine the Lydian damsels
serve
With rich and costly worship; thou,
Minerva,
Arm'd with the dreadful ægis, virgin
queen,
And patroness of Athens; thou, who
hold'st
Divided empire on Parnassus' heights,

Lead hither thy gay train of revellers,
Convivial god, and thus invok'd approach!
CHORUS. As we were hither journeying,
in midway
We crost upon the Moon, who for a
while
Held us in converse, and with courteous
greeting
To this assembly charg'd us.—This
premis'd,
The tenor of our next instruction points
To anger and complaint for ill returns
On your part to good offices on hers.
First for the loan of her bright silver
lamp
So long held out to you, by which you've
sav'd
Your torch and lacquey for this many a
night.
More she could name, if benefits avail'd;
But you have lost all reck'ning of your
feasts,
And turn'd your calendar quite topsy-
turvy;
So that the deities, who find themselves
Bilk'd of their dues, and supperless for
lack
Of their accustom'd sacrifices, rail
At her, poor Moon, and vent their hungry
spite,
As she were in the fault; whilst you, for-
sooth,
Maliciously select our gala days,
When feasting would be welcome, for your
suits
And criminal indictments; but when we
Keep fast and put on mourning for the
loss
Of Memnon or Sarpedon, sons of Heaven,
Then, then you mock us with the savoury
odour
Of smoking dainties, which we may not
taste:
Therefore it is, that when this year ye
sent
Your deputy Amphictyon to the diet,
(Hyperbolus forsooth) in just revenge
We tore away his crown, and drove him
back
To warn you how you slight the Moon
again.

[SOCRATES (*coming out of the house in violent indignation*), STREPSIADES, CHORUS.]

SOCRATES. O vivifying breath, æthereal air,
And thou profoundest chaos, witness for me
If ever wretch were seen so gross and dull,
So stupid and perplext as this old clown,
Whose shallow intellect can entertain
No image nor impression of a thought;
But ere you've told it, it is lost and gone!
'Tis time however he should now come forth
In the broad day—What hoa! Strepsiades—
Take up your pallet; bring yourself and it
Into the light.

STREPSIADES. Yes, if the bugs would let me.

SOCRATES. Quick, quick, I say; set down your load and listen!

STREPSIADES. Lo! here am I.

SOCRATES. Come, tell me what it is,
That you would learn besides what I have taught you;
Is it of measure, verse, or modulation?

STREPSIADES. Of measure by all means,
tor I was fobb'd
Of two days' dole i' th' measure of my meal
By a damn'd knavish huckster.

SOCRATES. Pish! who talks
Of meal? I ask which metre you prefer,
Tetrameter or trimeter.

STREPSIADES. I answer—
Give me a pint pot.

SOCRATES. Yes, but that's no answer.

STREPSIADES. No answer! stake your money, and I'll wager
That your tetrameter is half my pint pot.

SOCRATES. Go to the gallows, clodpate, with your pint pot!
Will nothing stick to you? But come, perhaps
We may try further and fare better with you—
Suppose I spoke to you of modulation;
Will you be taught of that?

STREPSIADES. Tell me first,

Will I be profited? will I be paid
The meal that I was chous'd of? tell me that.

SOCRATES. You will be profited by being taught
To bear your part at table in some sort
After a decent fashion; you will learn
Which verse is most commensurate and fit
To the arm'd chorus in the dance of war,
And which with most harmonious cadence guides
The dactyl in his course poetical.

STREPSIADES. The dactyl, quotha! Sure
I know that well.

SOCRATES. As how? discuss.

STREPSIADES. Here, at my fingers' end;
This is my dactyl, and has been my dactyl
Since I could count my fingers.

SOCRATES. Oh! the dolt.

STREPSIADES. I wish to be no wiser in these matters.

SOCRATES. What then?

STREPSIADES. Why then, teach me no other art
But the fine art of cozening.

SOCRATES. Granted; still
There is some previous matter, as for instance
The genders male and female.—Can you name them?

STREPSIADES. I were a fool else.—These are masculine:
Ram, bull, goat, dog, and pullet.

SOCRATES. There you're out:
Pullet is male and female.

STREPSIADES. Tell me how?

SOCRATES. Cock and hen pullet—so they should be nam'd.

STREPSIADES. And so they should, by the æthereal air!
You've hit it; for which rare discovery,
Take all the meal this cardopus contains.

SOCRATES. Why there again you sin against the genders.
To call your bolting-tub a cardopus,
Making that masculine which should be fem'nine.

STREPSIADES. How do I make my bolting-tub a male?

SOCRATES. Did you not call it cardopus? As well

You might have call'd Cleonymus a man;
He and your bolting-tub alike belong
To t'other sex, believe me.
STREPSIADES. Well, my trough
Shall be a cardopa and he Cleonyma;
Will that content you?
SOCRATES. Yes, and while you live
Learn to distinguish sex in proper names.
STREPSIADES. I do; the female I am
perfect in.
SOCRATES. Give me the proof.
STREPSIADES. Lysilla, she's a female;
Philinna, and Demetria, and Cleitagora.
SOCRATES. Now name your males.
STREPSIADES. A thousand—as for in-
stance,
Philoxenus, Melesias, and Amynias.
SOCRATES. Call you these masculine,
egregious dunce?
STREPSIADES. Are they not such with
you?
SOCRATES. No; put the case.
You and Amynias meet—how will you
greet him?
STREPSIADES. Why, thus for instance—
Hip! holla! Amynia!
SOCRATES. There, there! you make a
wench of him at once.
STREPSIADES. And fit it is for one who
shuns the field;
A coward ought not to be call'd a man;
Why teach me what is known to all the
world?
SOCRATES. Aye, why indeed?—but come,
repose yourself.
STREPSIADES. Why so?
SOCRATES. For meditation's sake: lie
down.
STREPSIADES. Not on this pallet I be-
seech you, sir;
But if I must lie down, let me repose
On the bare earth and meditate.
SOCRATES. Away!
There's nothing but this bed will cherish
thought.
STREPSIADES. It cherishes, alas! a host
of bugs,
That show no mercy on me.
SOCRATES. Come, begin,
Cudgel your brains and turn yourself
about;

Now ruminate awhile, and if you start
A thought that puzzles you, try t'other
side,
And turn to something else, but not to
sleep;
Suffer not sleep to close your eyes one mo-
ment.
STREPSIADES [after a considerable pause]
Ah! woe is me; ah, woeful, well-a-day!
SOCRATES. What ails you? why this
moaning?
STREPSIADES. I am lost;
I've rous'd the natives from their hiding
holes;
A colony of bugs in ambuscade
Have fall'n upon me: belly, back, and
ribs,
No part is free: I feed a commonwealth.
SOCRATES. Take not your sufferings
too much to heart.
STREPSIADES. How can I choose—a
wretch made up of wants!
Here am I penniless and spiritless,
Without a skin, Heav'n knows, without a
shoe;
And to complete my miseries here I lie,
Like a starv'd sentinel upon his post,
At watch and ward, till I am shrunk to
nothing.
[A pause of some duration.]
SOCRATES. How now; how fare you?
Have you sprung a thought?
STREPSIADES. Yes, yes, so help me Nep-
tune!
SOCRATES. Hah! what is it?
STREPSIADES. Why I am thinking if
these cursed vermin
Will leave one fragment of my carcass
free.
SOCRATES. A plague confound you!
STREPSIADES. Spare yourself that
prayer;
I'm plagued already to your heart's con-
tent.
SOCRATES. Prythee don't be so tender
of your skin;
Tuck yourself up and buff it like a man:
Keep your skull under cover, and depend
on't
'Twill make your brain bring forth some
precious project

For furthering your good-fortune at the
expense
Of little else but honesty and justice.
STREPSIADES. Ah! would to Heav'n
some friendly soul would help me
To a fine project how to cheat the bugs
With a sleek lambskin. [*A long pause.*]
SOCRATES. Whereabouts, I trow,
Sits the wind now? What ails you? are
you dozing?
STREPSIADES. Not I, by Heaven!
SOCRATES. Can you start nothing yet?
STREPSIADES. Nothing, so help me.
SOCRATES. Will your head breed no
project,
Tho' nurs'd so daintily?
STREPSIADES. What should it breed?
Tell me, sweet Socrates; give me some
hint.
SOCRATES. Say first what 'tis you wish.
STREPSIADES. A thousand times,
Ten thousand times I've said it o'er and
o'er—
My creditors, my creditors—'Tis them
I would fain bilk.
SOCRATES. Go to! get under cover,
Keep your head warm, and rarify your
wits
Till they shall sprout into some fine con-
ceit,
Some scheme of happy promise: sift it
well,
Divide, abstract, compound, and when 'tis
ready,
Out with it boldly.
STREPSIADES. Miserable me!
Would I were out!
SOCRATES. Lie still, and if you strike
Upon a thought that baffles you, break
off
From that entanglement and try another.
So shall your wits be fresh to start again.
STREPSIADES [*not attending to what
Socrates is saying*]. Hah! my dear
boy! My precious Socrates!
SOCRATES. What would'st thou, gaffer?
STREPSIADES. I have sprung a thought,
A plot upon my creditors.
SOCRATES. Discuss!
STREPSIADES. Answer me this—Suppose
that I should hire

A witch, who some fair night shall raise
a spell,
Whereby I'll snap the moon from out her
sphere
And bag her.
SOCRATES. What to do!
STREPSIADES. To hold her fast,
And never let her run her courses more;
So shall I 'scape my creditors.
SOCRATES. How so?
STREPSIADES. Because the calculations
of their usury
Are made from month to month.
SOCRATES. A gallant scheme;
And yet methinks I could suggest a hint
As practicable and no less ingenious—
Suppose you are arrested for a debt,
We'll say five talents, how will you con-
trive
To cancel at a stroke both debt and writ?
STREPSIADES. Gramercy! I can't tell
you how off hand;
It needs some cogitation.
SOCRATES. Were you apt,
Such cogitations would not be to seek;
They would be present at your fingers'
ends,
Buzzing alive, like chafers in a string,
Ready to slip and fly.
STREPSIADES. I've hit the nail
That does the deed, and so you will con-
fess.
SOCRATES. Out with it!
STREPSIADES. Good chance but you have
noted
A pretty toy, a trinket in the shops,
Which being rightly held produceth fire
From things combustible—
SOCRATES. A burning glass,
Vulgarly call'd—
STREPSIADES. You are right; 'tis so.
SOCRATES. Proceed!
STREPSIADES. Put the case now your
whoreson bailiff comes,
Shows me his writ—I, standing thus, d'ye
mark me,
In the sun's stream, measuring my dis-
tance, guide
My focus to a point upon his writ,
And off if goes in fumo!
SOCRATES. By the Graces!

'Tis wittingly devis'd.

STREPSIADES. The very thought
Of his five talents cancel'd at a stroke
Makes my heart dance for joy.

SOCRATES. But now again—

STREPSIADES. What next?

SOCRATES. Suppose yourself at bar,
surpris'd
Into a suit, no witnesses at hand,
The judge prepar'd to pass decree against
you—
How will you parry that?

STREPSIADES. As quick as thought—

SOCRATES. But how?

STREPSIADES. Incontinently hang my-
self,
And baulk the suitor—

SOCRATES. Come, you do but jest.

STREPSIADES. Serious, by all the gods!
A man that's dead
Is out of the law's reach.

SOCRATES. I've done with you—
Instruction's lost upon you; your vile
jests
Put me beyond all patience.

STREPSIADES. Nay, but tell me
What is it, my good fellow, that offends
thee?

SOCRATES. Your execrable lack of mem-
ory.
Why how now; what was the first rule I
taught you?

STREPSIADES. Say'st thou the first? the
very first—what was it?
Why, let me see; 'twas something, was it
not?
About the meal—Out on it! I have lost
it.

SOCRATES. Oh thou incorrigible, old
doating blockhead,
Can hanging be too bad for thee?

STREPSIADES. Why there now,
Was ever man so us'd? If I can't make
My tongue keep pace with yours, teach it
the quirks
And quibbles of your sophistry at once,
I may go hang—I am a fool forsooth—
Where shall I turn? Oh gracious Clouds,
befriend me,
Give me your counsel.

CHORUS. This it is, old man—

If that your son at home is apt and docile,
Depute him in your stead, and send him
hither.

STREPSIADES. My son is well endow'd
with nature's gifts,
But obstinately bent against instruction.

CHORUS. And do you suffer it?

STREPSIADES. What can I do?
He's a fine full-grown youth, a dashing
fellow,
And by the mother's side of noble blood:
I'll feel my way with him—but if he kicks,
Befall what may, nothing shall hinder me
But I will kick him headlong out of doors,
And let him graze ev'n where he will for
me—
Wait only my return; I'll soon dispatch.
[Exit.]

CHORUS. "Highly favour'd shalt thou
be,
With gifts and graces kept in store
For those who our divinities adore,
And to no other altars bend the knee:
And well we know th' obedience shown
   By this old clown deriv'd alone
   From lessons taught by thee.
Wherefore to swell thy lawful gains,
Thou soon shalt skin this silly cur,
Whom thou hast put in such a stir,
   And take his plunder for thy pains:
For mark how often dupes like him devise
Projects that only serve t' enrich the
wise."

[STREPSIADES (coming out of his house to
his Son, who stands at the door),
PHEIDIPPIDES.]

STREPSIADES. Out of my house! I call
the Clouds to witness
You shall not set a foot within my doors.
Go to your Lord Megacles! Get you
hence,
And gnaw his posts for hunger.

PHEIDIPPIDES. Ah, poor man!
I see how it is with you. You are mad,
Stark mad, by Jupiter!

STREPSIADES. You swear by Jupiter!
Why then, I swear by Jove there's no such
god—
Now who is mad but you?

PHEIDIPPIDES. Why do you turn

Such solemn truths to ridicule?

STREPSIADES. I laugh
To hear a child prate of such old men's
    fables;
But list to what I'll tell you, learn of
    me,
And from a child you shall become a
    man—
But keep the secret close, do you mark me,
    close;
Beware of babbling.

PHEIDIPPIDES. Heydey! what is com-
    ing?

STREPSIADES. You swore but now by
    Jupiter—

PHEIDIPPIDES. I did.

STREPSIADES. Mark now what 'tis to
    have a friend like me—
I tell you at a word there is no Jupiter.

PHEIDIPPIDES. How then?

STREPSIADES. He's off; I tell it you for
    truth;
He's out of place, and Vortex reigns in-
    stead.

PHEIDIPPIDES. Vortex indeed! What
    freak has caught you now?

STREPSIADES. No freak, 'tis fact.

PHEIDIPPIDES. Who tells you this?

STREPSIADES. E'en Socrates the Melian,
And Chærephon, the flea philosopher.

PHEIDIPPIDES. And are you so far gone
    in dotage, sir,
As to be dup'd by men like them, fellows
Whose bile has overflowed them?

STREPSIADES. Keep a good tongue;
Take heed you slander not such worthy
    men,
So wise withal and learned—men so pure
And cleanly in their morals, that no razor
Ever profan'd their beards; their un-
    wash'd hides
Ne'er dabbled in a bath, nor wafted scent
Of od'rous unguent as they pass'd along.
But you, a prodigal fine spark, make waste
And havoc of my means, as I were dead
And out of thought—but come, turn in
    and learn.

PHEIDIPPIDES. What can I learn or
    profit from such teachers?

STREPSIADES. Thou canst learn every-
    thing that turns to profit;

But first and foremost thou canst learn to
    know
Thyself how totally unlearn'd thou art;
How mere a blockhead, and how dull of
    brain—
But wait awhile with patience—
            [Enters the house hastily.]

PHEIDIPPIDES. Woe is me!
How shall I deal with this old crazy
    father?
What course pursue with one, whose rea-
    son wanders
Out of all course? Shall I take out the
    statute,
And cite him for a lunatic; or wait
Till nature and his phrenzy, with the help
Of the undertaker, shall provide a cure?
            [STREPSIADES returns, with a
            cock in one hand and a hen in
            the other.]

STREPSIADES. Now we shall see! Lo!
    what have I got here?

PHEIDIPPIDES. A chicken—

STREPSIADES. Well and this?

PHEIDIPPIDES. A chicken also.

STREPSIADES. Are they the same then?
    Have a care, good boy,
How you expose yourself, and for the fu-
    ture
Describe them cock and hen-chick sever-
    ally.

PHEIDIPPIDES. Ridiculous! Is this the
    grand discovery
You have just borrow'd from these sons
    o' th' dunghill?

STREPSIADES. This, and a thousand
    others—but being old
And lax of memory, I lose it all
As fast as it comes in.

PHEIDIPPIDES. Yes, and methinks
By the same token you have lost your
    cloak.

STREPSIADES. No, I've not lost it; I
    have laid it out
Upon the arts and sciences.

PHEIDIPPIDES. Your shoes—
They're vanish'd too. How have you laid
    them out?

STREPSIADES. Upon the commonwealth.
    —Like Pericles
I'm a barefooted patriot.—Now no more;

Do as thou wilt, so thou wilt but conform
And humour me this once, as in times past
I humour'd thee, and in thy playful age
Brought thee a penny go-cart from the fair,
Purchas'd with what my legal labours earn'd,
The fee for my attendance.
[*Going towards the house of* SOCRATES.]
PHEIDIPPIDES. You'll repent,
My life upon 't; you will repent of this.
[*Following reluctantly.*]
STREPSIADES. No matter, so you'll humour me—What, hoa!
Why Socrates, I say, come forth, behold,
Here is my son!
I've brought him, tho' in faith
Sorely against the grain.

[SOCRATES *enters.*]
SOCRATES. Aye, he's a novice,
And knows not where the panniers hang as yet.
PHEIDIPPIDES. I would you'd hang yourself there in their stead.
STREPSIADES. Oh monstrous impudence! this to your master!
SOCRATES. Mark how the idiot quibbles upon *hanging.*
Driv'ling and making mouths—Can he be taught
The loopholes of the law; whence to escape,
How to evade, and when to press a suit;—
Or tune his lips to that soft rhetoric,
Which steals upon the ear, and melts to pity
The heart of the stern judge?
STREPSIADES. Come, never doubt him;
He is a lad of parts, and from a child
Took wondrously to dabbling in the mud,
Whereof he'd build you up a house so natural
As would amaze you, trace you out a ship,
Make you a little cart out of the sole
Of an old shoe mayhap, and from the rind
Of a pomegranate cut you out a frog,
You'd swear it was alive. Now what do you think?
Hath he not wit enough to comprehend
Each rule both right and wrong? Or if not both,

The latter way at least—There he'll be perfect.
SOCRATES. Let him prepare: His lecturers are ready.
STREPSIADES. I will retire—When next we meet, remember
I look to find him able to contend
'Gainst right and reason, and outwit them both.   [*Exit.*]

[DICÆOLOGOS *and* ADICÆOLOGOS *enter.*]
DICÆOLOGOS. Come forth; turn out, thou bold audacious man,
And face this company.
ADICÆOLOGOS. Most willingly:
I do desire no better: take your ground
Before this audience, I am sure to triumph.
DICÆOLOGOS. And who are you that vapour in this fashion?
ADICÆOLOGOS. Fashion itself—the very style of the times.
DICÆOLOGOS. Aye, of the modern times, and them and you I set at naught.
ADICÆOLOGOS. I shall bring down your pride.
DICÆOLOGOS. By what most witty weapon?
ADICÆOLOGOS. By the gift
Of a most apt invention.
DICÆOLOGOS. Then I see
You have your fools to back you.
ADICÆOLOGOS. No,—the wise
Are those I deal with.
DICÆOLOGOS. I shall spoil your market.
ADICÆOLOGOS. As how, good sooth?
DICÆOLOGOS. By speaking such plain truths
As may appeal to justice.
ADICÆOLOGOS. What is justice?
There's no such thing—I traverse your appeal.
DICÆOLOGOS. How! No such thing as justice?
ADICÆOLOGOS. No; where is it?
DICÆOLOGOS. With the immortal gods.
ADICÆOLOGOS. If it be there,
How chanc'd it Jupiter himself escap'd
For his unnatural deeds to his own father?
DICÆOLOGOS. For shame, irreverent wretch, thus do you talk?
I sicken at impiety so gross,
My stomach kicks against it.

ADICÆOLOGOS. You are craz'd;
Your wits, old gentleman, are off the hinges.

DICÆOLOGOS. You are a vile blasphemer and buffoon.

ADICÆOLOGOS. Go on! you pelt me—
but it is with roses.

DICÆOLOGOS. A scoffer!

ADICÆOLOGOS. Every word your malice vents
Weaves a fresh wreath of triumph for my brows.

DICÆOLOGOS. A parricide!

ADICÆOLOGOS. Proceed, and spare me not—
You shower down gold upon me.

DICÆOLOGOS. Lead, not gold,
Had been your retribution in times past.

ADICÆOLOGOS. Aye, but times present cover me with glory.

DICÆOLOGOS. You are too wicked.

ADICÆOLOGOS. You are much too weak.

DICÆOLOGOS. Thank your own self, if our Athenian fathers
Coop up their sons at home, and fear to trust them
Within your schools, conscious that nothing else
But vice and folly can be learnt of you.

ADICÆOLOGOS. Methinks, friend, your's is but a ragged trade.

DICÆOLOGOS. And your's, oh shame! a thriving one, tho' late,
A perfect Telephus, you tramp'd the street
With beggar's wallet cramm'd with hungry scraps,
Choice gather'd from—Pandeletus' larder.

ADICÆOLOGOS. Oh! what rare wisdom you remind me of!

DICÆOLOGOS. Oh, what rank folly theirs, who rule this city,
And let it nourish such a pest as you,
To sap the morals of the rising age.

ADICÆOLOGOS. You'll not inspire your pupil with these notions,
Old hoary-headed time!

DICÆOLOGOS. I will inspire him,
If he has grace, to shun the malady
Of your eternal clack.

ADICÆOLOGOS. Turn to me, youth!

And let him rail at leisure.

DICÆOLOGOS. Keep your distance,
And lay your hands upon him at your peril.

CHORUS [interposing]. Come, no more wrangling.—Let us hear you both;
You of the former time produce your rules
Of ancient discipline—of modern, you—
That so, both weigh'd, the candidate may judge
Who offers fairest, and make choice between you.

DICÆOLOGOS. I close with the proposal.

ADICÆOLOGOS. 'Tis agreed.

CHORUS. But which of you shall open?

ADICÆOLOGOS. That shall he:
I yield him up that point; and in reply,
My words, like arrows levelled at a butt,
Shall pierce him through and through;
then, if he rallies,
If he comes on again with a rejoinder,
I'll launch a swarm of syllogisms at him,
That, like a nest of hornets, shall belabour him,
Till they have left him not an eye to see with.

CHORUS. "Now, sirs, exert your utmost care,
And gravely for the charge prepare;
The well-rang'd hoard of thought explore,
Where sage experience keeps her store;
All the resources of the mind
Employment in this cause will find,—
And he, who gives the best display
Of argument, shall win the day:
Wisdom this hour at issue stands,
And gives her fate into your hands;
Your's is a question that divides
And draws out friends on different sides:
Therefore on you, who, with such zealous praise,
Applaud the discipline of former days,
On you I call; now is your time to show
You merit no less praise than you bestow."

DICÆOLOGOS. Thus summon'd, I prepare myself to speak
Of manners primitive, and that good time,
Which I have seen, when discipline prevail'd,
And modesty was sanctioned by the laws,

No babbling then was suffer'd in our
    schools;—
The scholar's test was silence. The whole
    group
In orderly procession sallied forth
Right onwards, without straggling, to at-
    tend
Their teacher in harmonics; though the
    snow
Fell on them thick as meal, the hardy
    brood
Breasted the storm uncloak'd: their harps
    were strung
Not to ignoble strains, for they were
    taught
A loftier key, whether to chant the name
Of Pallas, terrible amidst the blaze
Of cities overthrown, or wide and far
To spread, as custom was, the echoing
    peal.
There let no low buffoon intrude his tricks,
Let no capricious quavering on a note,
No running of divisions high and low
Break the pure stream of harmony; no
    Phrynis
Practising wanton warblings out of place—
Woe to his back that so was found offend-
    ing!
Hard stripes and heavy would reform his
    taste.
Decent and chaste their postures in the
    school
Of their gymnastic exercises; none
Expos'd an attitude that might provoke
Irregular desire; their lips ne'er mov'd
In love-inspiring whispers, and their walks
From eyes obscene were sacred and secure,
Hot herbs, the old man's diet, were pro-
    scrib'd;
No radish, anise, parsley, deck'd their
    board;
No rioting, no revelling was there
At feast or frolic, no unseemly touch
Or signal, that inspires the hint impure.
    ADICÆOLOGOS. Why these are maxims
        obsolete and stale:
Worm-eaten rules, coeval with the hymns
Of old Ceceydas and Buphonian feasts.
    DICÆOLOGOS. Yet so were train'd the
        heroes, that imbru'd
The field of Marathon with hostile blood;

This discipline it was that braced their
    nerves
And fitted them for conquest. You, for-
    sooth,
At great Minerva's festival produce
Your martial dancers, not as they were
    wont,
But smother'd underneath the tawdry load
Of cumbrous armour, till I sweat to see
    them
Dangling their shields in such unseemly
    sort
As mars the sacred measure of the dance.
Be wise, therefore, young man, and turn
    to me.
Turn to the better guide, so shall you
    learn
To scorn the noisy forum, shun the bath,
And turn with blushes from the scene
    impure:
Then conscious innocence shall make you
    bold
To spurn the injurious, but to reverend
    age
Meek and submissive, rising from your
    seat
To pay the homage due, nor shall you
    ever
Or wring the parent's soul, or stain your
    own.
In purity of manners you shall live
A bright example; vain shall be the lures
Of the stage-wanton floating in the dance,
Vain all her arts to snare you in her arms,
And strip you of your virtue and good
    name.
No petulant reply shall you oppose
To fatherly commands, nor taunting vent
Irreverent mockery on his hoary head,
Crying—"Behold Iäpetus himself!"
Poor thanks for all his fond parental
    care.
    ADICÆOLOGOS. Aye, my brave youth, do,
        follow these fine rules,
And learn by them to be as mere a swine,
Driveller, and dolt, as any of the sons
Of our Hippocrates;—I swear by Bacchus,
Folly and foul contempt shall be your
    doom.
    DICÆOLOGOS. Not so, but fair and fresh
        in youthful bloom

Amongst our young athletics you shall
shine;
Not in the forum loit'ring time away
In gossip prattle, like our gang of idlers,
Nor yet in some vexatious paltry suit
Wrangling and quibbling in our petty
courts.
But in the solemn academic grove,
Crown'd with the modest reed, fit converse
hold
With your collegiate equals; there serene,
Calm as the scene around you, underneath
The fragrant foliage where the ilex
spreads,
Where the deciduous poplar strews her
leaves,
Where the tall elm-tree and wide-stretching plane
Sigh to the fanning breeze, you shall inhale
Sweet odours wafted in the breath of
spring.
This is the regimen that will insure
A healthful body and a vigorous mind,
A countenance serene, expanded chest,
Heroic stature and a temperate tongue;
But take these modern masters, and behold
These blessings all revers'd; a pallid cheek,
Shrunk shoulders, chest contracted, sapless limbs,
A tongue that never rests, and mind debas'd,
By their vile sophistry perversely taught
To call good evil, evil good, and be
That thing, which nature spurns at, that
disease,
A mere Antimachus, the sink of vice.
CHORUS.' "Oh sage instructor, how sublime
These maxims of the former time!
How sweet this unpolluted stream
Of eloquence, how pure the theme!
Thrice happy they, whose lot was cast
Amongst the generation past,
When virtuous morals were display'd
And these grave institutes obey'd.
Now you, that vaunt yourself so high,
Prepare; we wait for your reply,
And recollect, or ere you start,
You take in hand no easy part;

Well hath he spoke, and reasons good
By better only are withstood;
Sharpen your wits then, or you'll meet
Contempt as certain as defeat."
ADICÆOLOGOS. Doubt not I'm ready,
full up to the throat
And well nigh chok'd with plethory of
words,
Impatient to discharge them. I do know
The mighty masters of the modern school
Term me the Lower Logic, so distinguish'd
From the old practice of the upper time,
By him personified; which name of honour
I gain'd as the projector of that method,
Which can confute and puzzle all the
courts
Of law and justice—An invention worth
Thousands to them who practise it,
whereas
It nonsuits all opponents.—Let that pass.
Now take a sample of it in the ease,
With which I'll baffle this old vaunting
pedant
With his warm baths, that he forsooth
forbids.
Hark'ye, old man, discuss, if so it please
you,
Your excellent good reason for this rule,
That interdicts warm bathing.
DICÆOLOGOS. Simply this—
I hold it a relaxer, rendering men
Effeminate and feeble.
ADICÆOLOGOS. Hold awhile—
I have you on the hook. Answer me
this—
Of all the heroes Jupiter has father'd,
Which is for strength, for courage, and
a course
Of labours most renown'd?
DICÆOLOGOS. I know of none
Superior in those qualities to Hercules.
ADICÆOLOGOS. And who e'er heard Herculean baths were cold?
Yet Hercules himself you own was strong.
DICÆOLOGOS. Aye, this is in the very
style of the times;
These are the dialectics now in fashion
With our young sophists, who frequent
the baths

Whilst the palæstra starves.

ADICÆOLOGOS. I grant you this;
It is the style of the times, by you con-
demn'd,
By me approv'd, and not without good
cause;
For how but thus doth ancient Nestor
talk?
Can Homer err? Were all his wise men
fools?
They are my witnesses.—Now for this
tongue,
This member out of use by his decree,
Not so by mine.—His scholar must be
silent
And chaste withal—damping prescrip-
tions both—
For what good fortune ever did betide
The mute and modest? Instance me a
case.
DICÆOLOGOS. Many—Chaste Peleus so
obtained his sword.
ADICÆOLOGOS. His sword! and what
did Peleus gain by that?
Battle and blows this modest Peleus
gain'd;
Whilst mean Hyperbolus, whose wretched
craft
Was lamp-making, by craft of viler sort
Garbel'd his thousands, solid coin, not
swords.
DICÆOLOGOS. But continence befriended
Peleus so,
As won the goddess Thetis to his bed.
ADICÆOLOGOS. And drove her out of it
—for he was cold,
Languid and listless: she was brisk and
stirring,
And sought the sport elsewhere. Now are
you answered?
Good sooth you're in your dotage. Mark,
young sir.
These are the fruits of continence: you
see
What pleasure you must forfeit to pre-
serve it—
All the delights that woman can bestow;
No am'rous sports to catch the fair one's
smile,
No luscious dainties shall you then par-
take,

No gay convivial revels, where the glass
With peals of laughter circulates around;
These you must sacrifice, and without
these
What is your life?—So much for your de-
lights.—
Now let us see how stands your score
with nature—
You're in some scrape we'll say—intrigue
—adultery—
You're caught, convicted, crush'd—for
what can save you?
You have no powers of speech—but arm'd
by me,
You're up to all occasions: Nothing fear;
Ev'n give your genius scope; laugh, frolic,
sport,
And flout at shame; for should the wittol
spouse
Detect you in the fact, you shall so pose
him
In his appeal, that nothing shall stick to
you;
For Jove shall take the blame from off
your shoulders,
Being himself a cuckold-making god,
And you a poor frail mortal—Why should
you
Be wiser, stronger, purer than a god?
DICÆOLOGOS. But what if this your
scholar should incur
Th' adulterer's correction,—pill'd and
sanded,
And garnish'd with a radish in his crup-
per,
The scoff of all beholders—What fine
quirk
Will clear him at that pinch, but he must
pass
For a most perfect Ganimede?
ADICÆOLOGOS. What then?
Where is the harm?
DICÆOLOGOS. Can greater harm befall
him?
ADICÆOLOGOS. What will you say if
here I can confute you?
DICÆOLOGOS. Nothing—my silence shall
confess your triumph.
ADICÆOLOGOS. Come on then—answer
me to what I ask.
Our advocates—what are they?

DICÆOLOGOS. Catamites.

ADICÆOLOGOS. Our tragic poets—what are they?

DICÆOLOGOS. The same.

ADICÆOLOGOS. Good, very good!—our demagogues—

DICÆOLOGOS. No better.

ADICÆOLOGOS. See there! discern you not that you are foil'd?

Cast your eyes round this company!—

DICÆOLOGOS. I do.

ADICÆOLOGOS. And what do you discover?

DICÆOLOGOS. Numerous birds
Of the same filthy feather, so Heaven help me!
This man I mark; and this, and this fine fop
With his curl'd locks.—To all these I can swear.

ADICÆOLOGOS. What say you then?

DICÆOLOGOS. I say I am confuted—
Here, wagtails, catch my cloak—I'll be amongst you.

SOCRATES [to STREPSIADES, just returned]. Now, friend, what say you? who shall school your son?

STREPSIADES. School him and scourge him, take him to yourself.
And mind you whet him to an edge on both sides,
This for slight skirmish, that for stronger work.

SOCRATES. Doubt not, we'll finish him to your content
A perfect sophist.

PHEIDIPPIDES. Perfect skin and bone—
That I can well believe.

SOCRATES. No more.—Away!
[STREPSIADES retires.]

PHEIDIPPIDES. Trust me you've made a rod for your own back.
[Follows SOCRATES into the house.]
[CHORUS address the Spectators.]

CHORUS. Now to our candid judges we shall tell
What recompense they may expect from us,
If they indeed are studious to deserve it:
First, on your new-sown grounds in kindly showers,

Postponing other calls, we will descend.
The bearing branches of your vines shall sprout,
Nor scorch'd with summer heats nor chill'd with rain.
This to our friends who serve us,—but to him,
Who dares to slight us, let that mortal hear,
And tremble at the vengeance which awaits him:
Nor wine nor oil shall that man's farm produce;
For when his olive trees shall yield their fruit,
And his ripe vineyard tempts the gath'rer's hand,
We'll batter him to ruin, lay him bare;
And if we catch him with his roof untiled,
Heav'ns! how we'll drench him with a pelting storm
Of hail and rain incessant! above all,
Let him beware upon the wedding night;
When he brings home his own or kinsman's bride,
Let him look to't! Then we'll come down in torrents,
That he shall rather take his chance in Egypt,
Than stand the vengeful soaking we will give him.

[STREPSIADES with a sack of meal on his shoulder, and talking to himself.]

STREPSIADES. Lo! here's the fifth day gone—the fourth—the third—
The second too—day of all days to me
Most hateful and accurs'd—the dreadful eve,
Ushering the new moon, that lets in the tide
Of happy creditors, all sworn against me,
To rack and ruin me beyond redemption,
I, like a courteous debtor, who would fain
Soften their flinty bosoms, thus accost them—
"Ah, my good sir, this payment comes upon me

At a bad time, excuse me—That bill's due,
But you'll extend your grace—This you
    will cancel,
And totally acquit me."—By no means;
All with one voice cry out, they will be
    paid,
And I must be be-knav'd into the bargain,
And threaten'd with a writ to mend the
    matter—
Well, let it come!—They may ev'n do their
    worst;
I care not so my son hath learnt the
    trick
Of this new rhetoric, as will appear
When I have beat this door—[*Knocks at
    the door.*]—Boy, boy! come forth!

    [SOCRATES *comes forth.*]
SOCRATES. Hail to Strepsiades!
STREPSIADES. Thrice hail to Socrates!
But first I pray you [*Setting down the
    meal against the door.*] take this dole
    of meal.
In token of the reverence I bear you;
And now, so please you, tell me of my
    son,
Your late noviciate. Comes he on apace?
SOCRATES. He apprehends acutely.
STREPSIADES. Oh brave news!
Oh the transcendant excellence of fraud!
SOCRATES. Yes, you may set your cred-
    itors at naught—
STREPSIADES. And their avouchers
    too?—
SOCRATES. Had they a thousand.
STREPSIADES [*singing and dancing*].
    Then I'll sing out my song, and sing
    aloud,
And it shall be—Woe, woe to all your
    gang,
Ye money-jobbing caitiffs, usurers, sharks!
Hence with your registers, your cents-
    per-cent;
I fear you not; ye cannot hook me now.
Oh! such a son have I in training for
    you,
Arm'd with a two-edg'd tongue that cuts
    o' both sides,
The stay, support, and pillar of my house,
The scourge of my tormentors, the re-
    deemer

Of a most wretched father—Call him
    forth,
Call him, I say, and let my eyes feast on
    him—
What hoa! My son, my boy—your father
    calls;
Come forth and show yourself.

    [*To them* PHEIDIPPIDES.]
SOCRATES. Behold him present!
STREPSIADES. My dear—my darling—
SOCRATES. Lo! you have your darling.
STREPSIADES. Joy, joy, my son! all joy
    —for now you wear
A face of a right character and cast,
A wrangling, quibbling, contradicting
    face;
Now you have got it neatly on the
    tongue—
The very quirk o' th' time—"What's that
    you say?
What is it?"—Shifting from yourself the
    wrong
To him that suffers it—an arch conceit
To make a transfer of iniquity,
When it has serv'd your turn—Yes, you
    will pass;
You've the right Attic stamp upon your
    forehead.
Now let me see a sample of your service,
Forsooth to say you owe me a good turn.
PHEIDIPPIDES. What vexes you, my
    father?
STREPSIADES. What! the moon,
This day both new and old.
PHEIDIPPIDES. Both in one day?
Ridiculous!
STREPSIADES. No matter—'Tis the day
Will bring my creditors upon my back
All in a swarm together.
PHEIDIPPIDES. Let them swarm!
We'll smother 'em if they dare so to mis-
    call
One day as two days.
STREPSIADES. What should hinder them?
PHEIDIPPIDES. What, do you ask? Can
    the same woman be
Both young and old at once?
STREPSIADES. They speak by law:
The statute bears them out.
PHEIDIPPIDES. But they misconstrue

The spirit of the statute.

STREPSIADES. What's that?

PHEIDIPPIDES. Time-honour'd Solon was
the people's friend—

STREPSIADES. This makes not to the
case of new or old.

PHEIDIPPIDES. And he appointed two
days for the process,
The old and new day—for citation that,
This for discharge—

STREPSIADES. Why did he name two
days?

PHEIDIPPIDES. Why, but that one might
warn men of their debts,
The other serve them to escape the pay-
ment;
Else were they laid by th' heels, as sure
as fate,
On the new moon ensuing.

STREPSIADES. Wherefore then
Upon the former day do they commence
Their doles of first fruits at the Pry-
taneum,
And not at the new moon?

PHEIDIPPIDES. Because, forsooth,
They're hungry feeders, and make haste
to thrust
Their greedy fingers in the public dish.

STREPSIADES. Hence then, ye witless
creditors, begone!
We are the wise ones, we are the true
sort;
Ye are but blocks, mob, cattle, empty
casks—
"Therefore with ecstasy I'll raise
My jocund voice in fortune's praise,
And, oh rare son!—Oh happy me!
The burden of my song shall be;
For hark! each passing neighbour cries—
All hail, Strepsiades the wise!
Across the forum as I walk,
I and my son the public talk,
All striving which shall have to boast
He prais'd me first, or prais'd me most—
And now, my son, my welcome guest,
Enter my house and grace my feast."

[Exeunt.]

[PASIAS, and a Witness.]

PASIAS. Should this man be permitted
to go on
At such a desperate rate? It must not be.

Better for him to have brok'n up at once
Than to be thus beset. Therefore it is
That I am forc'd upon this hostile course,
Empowering you to summon this my
debtor
For the recovery of my own—Good sooth,
I will not put my country to the blush,
But I must rouse Strepsiades—

[STREPSIADES reënters.]

STREPSIADES. Who's this?

PASIAS. The old and new day call upon
you, sir.

STREPSIADES [to the spectators]. Bear
witness that this man has nam'd two
days—
And for what debt do you assail me thus?

PASIAS. For twelve good pounds that
you took up at interest
To pay for your son's racer.

STREPSIADES. I a racer?
Do you not hear him? Can you not all
witness
How mortally and from my soul I hate
All the whole racing calendar?

PASIAS. What then?
You took the gods to witness you would
pay me.

STREPSIADES. I grant you, in my folly
I did swear,
But then my son had not attain'd the art
Of the new logic unconfutable.

PASIAS. And have you now the face to
stand out
Against all evidence?

STREPSIADES. Assuredly—
Else how am I the better for my school-
ing?

PASIAS. And dare you, knowing it to
be a falsehood,
Take the great gods to witness to your
oath,
When I shall put it to you?

STREPSIADES. What great gods?

PASIAS [starting at the question]. Mer-
curius, Neptune, Jupiter himself—

STREPSIADES. Yes, and stake down
three-farthings as a handsel
That I will take the oath, so help me
Jove!

PASIAS. Insolent wretch, you'll perish
in your folly!

STREPSIADES. Oh! that this madman
was well scrubb'd with salt
To save his brains from addling!
PASIAS. Out upon't!
Do you make game of me?
STREPSIADES. I warrant me
He'll take at least six gallons for a
dressing.
PASIAS. So may great Jove and all the
gods deal with me
As I will handle you for this buffoonery!
STREPSIADES. I thank you for your
gods—They're pleasant fellows—
And for your Jupiter, the learn'd and wise
Hold him a very silly thing to swear by.
PASIAS. 'Tis well, rash man, 'tis well!
The time will come
When you shall wish these vaunting words
unsaid:
But will you pay the debt or will you not?
Say, and dismiss me.
STREPSIADES. Set your mind at rest;
You shall have satisfaction in a twin-
kling— [*Steps aside.*]
PASIAS. What think you of this chap?
WITNESS. That he will pay you.

[STREPSIADES *returns.*]
STREPSIADES. Where is this dun of
mine? Come hither, friend,
How do you call this thing?
PASIAS. A kneading-trough,
Or, as we say, a cardopus—
STREPSIADES. Go to!
Dost think I'll pay my money to a block-
head,
That calls this kneading-trough a *cardo-
pus?*
I tell you, man, it is a *cardopa*—
Go, go, you will not get a doit from me,
You and your *cardopus.*
PASIAS. Will you not pay me?
STREPSIADES. Assure yourself I will
not—Hence, begone!
Will you not beat your march, and quit
my doors?
PASIAS. I'm gone, but take this with
you, if I live
I'll sue you in the Prytaneum before
night.
STREPSIADES. You'll lose your suit, and
your twelve pounds besides.

I'm sorry for your loss, but who can help
it?
You may ev'n thank your cardopus for
that. [*Exit* PASIAS *and Witness.*]

[AMYNIAS *enters, followed by a
Witness.*]
AMYNIAS. Ah me, ah me!
STREPSIADES. Who's that with his—
Ah me?
Whom has *Carcinus* sent amongst us
now—
Which of his doleful deities?—
AMYNIAS. Alas!
Would you know who I am? Know then
I am
A wretch made up of woes—
STREPSIADES. A woeful wretch—
Granted! pass on.
AMYNIAS. Oh inauspicious chance!
Oh ye hard-hearted, chariot-breaking
fates!
Oh! Pallas my destroyer, what a crash
Is this that you have giv'n me!
STREPSIADES. Hah! what ails you?
Of what can you accuse Tlepolemus?
AMYNIAS. Mock not my miseries, but
bid your son
Repay what he has borrow'd.
STREPSIADES. Take me with you—
What should my son repay?
AMYNIAS. The sum I lent him.
STREPSIADES. Is that it? Then your
case is desperate;
Truly you're out of luck.
AMYNIAS. I'm out of everything—
I overthrew my chariot—By the gods
That's being *out*, I take it, with a ven-
geance.
STREPSIADES. Say rather you are kick'd
by an ass—a trifle!
AMYNIAS. But, sir, my lawful money is
no trifle;
I shall not choose to be kick'd out of
that.
STREPSIADES. I'll tell you what you are
—Out of your wits.
AMYNIAS. How so?
STREPSIADES. Because your brain seems
wondrous leaky.
AMYNIAS. Look to't! By Mercury, I'll
clap you up,

If you don't pay me.

STREPSIADES. Hark'ye, one short question—
When Jove rains on us does he rain fresh water,
Or only vapours that the sun exhales?
Answer me that.

AMYNIAS. I care not what he rains;
I trouble not my cap with such conceits.

STREPSIADES. And do you think a man, that has no wit
To argue upon these rare points, will argue me
Out of my money?

AMYNIAS. Let your debt go on,
And pay me up the interest.

STREPSIADES. What is that?
What kind of thing is that same interest?

AMYNIAS. A thing it is that grows from day to day,
And month to month, swelling as time rolls on
To a round sum of money.

STREPSIADES. Well defin'd!
One question more—What think you of the sea?
Is it not fuller now than heretofore?

AMYNIAS. No, by the Gods! not fuller, but as full:
That is my judgment of it.

STREPSIADES. Oh thou miser!
That so would'st stint the ocean, and yet cram
Thy swelling coffers till they overflow—
Fetch me a whip, that I may lash him hence:
Take to your heels—begone!

AMYNIAS. I will convoke
My witnesses against you.

STREPSIADES. Start! set off!—
Away! you jennet, you!

AMYNIAS [to the spectators]. Is not this outrage?

STREPSIADES [smacking his whip]. Will you not bolt? will you not buckle kindly
Into your geers, or must I mount and goad you
Under the crupper, till you kick and wince

For very madness? Oho! Are you off?
A welcome riddance—All the devils drive
You and your cursed chariot hence together!
[STREPSIADES goes into his house.]

MANET CHORUS. "Mark here how rarely it succeeds
To build our trust on guilty deeds:
Mark how this old cajoling elf,
Who sets a trap to catch himself,
Falsely believes he has found the way
To hold his creditors at bay.
Too late he'll curse the Sophists' school,
That taught his son to cheat by rule,
And train'd the modest lips of youth
In the vile art of torturing truth;
A modern logic much in use,
Invented for the law's abuse;
A subtle knack of spying flaws
To cast in doubt the clearest cause,
Whereby, in honesty's despite,
The wrong side triumphs o'er the right—
Alas! short triumph he must have,
Who glories that his son's a knave:
Ah foolish sire, the time will come
You'll wish that son of your's were dumb."

[STREPSIADES (rushing out of the house, in great confusion, followed by his Son)
PHEIDIPPIDES, CHORUS.]

STREPSIADES. Hoa there! What hoa! for pity's sake some help!
Friends, kinsmen, countrymen! turn out and help!
Oh! my poor head, my cheeks are bruis'd to jelly—
Help by all means!—Why, thou ungracious cub,
Thy father wouldst thou beat?

PHEIDIPPIDES. Assuredly.

STREPSIADES. There, there! he owns that he would beat his father.

PHEIDIPPIDES. I own it, good my father!

STREPSIADES. Parricide!
Impious assassin! Sacrilegious wretch!

PHEIDIPPIDES. All, all, and more—You cannot please me better;
I glory in these attributes. Go on!

STREPSIADES. Monster of turpitude!

PHEIDIPPIDES. Crown me with roses!

STREPSIADES. Wretch, will you strike your parent?
PHEIDIPPIDES. Piously,
And will maintain the right, by which I do it.
STREPSIADES. Oh shameless villain! can there be a right
Against all nature so to treat a father?
PHEIDIPPIDES. That I shall soon make clear to your conviction.
STREPSIADES. You, you convince me?
PHEIDIPPIDES. With the greatest ease:
And I can work the proof two several ways;
Therefore make choice between them.
STREPSIADES. What do you mean?
PHEIDIPPIDES. I mean to say we argue up or down—
Take which you like. It comes to the same end.
STREPSIADES. Aye, and a precious end you've brought it to,
If all my care of you must end in this,
That I have put you in the way to beat me,
(Which is a thing unnatural and profane)
And after justify it.
PHEIDIPPIDES. That I'll do.
By process clear and categorical,
That you shall fairly own yourself a convert
To a most wholesome cudgelling.
STREPSIADES. Come on!
Give me your arguments—but spare your blows.
CHORUS. How to restrain this headstrong son of yours
Behoves you now, old man, to find the means,
For sure he could not be thus confident
Without some cause; something there needs must be,
Some strong possession of himself within,
That buoys him up to this high pitch of daring,
This bold assumption; which that we may know,
Give us distinctively the whole detail
From first to last whence this contention sprang,

So shall we hear, and hearing judge betwixt you.
STREPSIADES. So please you then I will the cause unfold
Of this base treatment to your patient ears,
And thus it stands—When we had supp'd together,
As you all know, in friendly sort, I bade him
Take up his lute and give me the good song
Of old Simonides,—"the ram was shorn;"—
But he directly scouted my request—
It was a fashion out of date forsooth—
He would not sit twanging the lute, not he;
'Twas not for him to cackle o'er his wine,
As if he were some wench working the hand-mill—
'Twas vulgar and unseemly—
PHEIDIPPIDES. Grossly so;
And was it not high time that I should beat you,
Who had no better manners than to set
Your guest a chirping like a grasshopper?
STREPSIADES. These were his very words, and more than these;
For by and by he told me that Simonides
Was a most paltry poet. This you'll own
Was a tough morsel, yet I gulp'd it down,
And pass'd it off with bidding him recite
Some passage out of Æschylus, withal
Tendering a myrtle wreath, as custom is,
To grace the recitation.—He forsooth,
Flouting my tender, instantly replied—
"I hold your Æschylus, of all our poets,
First of the spouters, incoherent, harsh,
Precipitous and turgid."—Oh my friends,
Was not this more than flesh and blood should bear?
Yet, yet I smother'd rage within my heart,
And calmly said—"Call something else to mind
More to your taste and from some modern bard,
So it be good withal and worth the hearing—"
Whereat, would you believe it? he began
Repeating from Euripides—Great Jove,

Guard my chaste ears from such another
    dose!
A perilous long-winded tale of incest
'Twixt son and daughter of the same
    sad mother.
Sick to the soul I spurn'd at such declaim-
    ing,
Adding, as well I might, all that my scorn
Of such vile trash could add! till, to be
    short,
Words begat words, and blows too as it
    prov'd,
For leaping from his seat he sprung upon
    me,
Struck, buffeted, and bang'd me out of
    measure,
Throttled me, pounded me well nigh to
    dust—
PHEIDIPPIDES. And what less does that
    heretic deserve.
Who will not praise Euripides, the first
In wisdom of all poets?
STREPSIADES. He the first!
How my tongue itches!—but the rogue is
    ready;
He'll beat me if I answer.
PHEIDIPPIDES. And with reason.
STREPSIADES. What reason, graceless
    cub, will bear you out
For beating me, who in your baby age
Caress'd you, dandled you upon my knee,
Watch'd every motion, humour'd all your
    wants?
Then if you lisp'd a syllable I caught it—
Bryn cried the bantling—strait I gave
    you drink:
Mamman it mew'd—and that forsooth was
    bread:
Nay, I perform'd the nurse's dirtiest
    task,
And held you out before me at your needs;
And now in my necessity you show'd
No mercy to the pressing calls of nature,
But having pummel'd me till my poor
    bowels
Could hold no longer, kept me fast im-
    prison'd
To struggle with occasion as I could.
    CHORUS. Now every young man's heart
        beats an alarm,
Anxious to hear his advocate's appeal;

Which if he can establish, the same right
By him asserted will on all devolve,
And beating then will be so much in
    vogue
That old men's skins will be reduc'd to
    cobwebs.—
Now you, that hold up this new paradox,
Look well how you defend it, for it asks
No trivial reasons to enforce persuasion.
    PHEIDIPPIDES. Now gratefully the mind
        receives new lights,
Emerging from the shades of prejudice,
And casting old establishments aside!
Time was but now, when every thought of
    mine
Was centred in the stable; then I had
    not
Three words upon my tongue without a
    stumble;
But now, since I've been put into the way
Of knowing better things, and the fine
    art
Of subtle disputation, I am bold
To meet this question, and convince my
    hearers
How right it is to punish this old sinner.
    STREPSIADES. Mount, mount your
        chariot! Oh, that I could see you
Seated again behind your favourite horses,
Tho' 'twere with four in hand, so that
    you kept
From driving me at such a pelting rate.
    PHEIDIPPIDES. Now then I ask you,
        gathering up my thread
Where it was broken off, if you, my father,
When I was but a stripling, spar'd my
    back?
    STREPSIADES. No, for I studied all
        things for your good,
And therefore I corrected you.
    PHEIDIPPIDES. Agreed.
I also am like studious of your good,
And therefore I most lovingly correct
    you;
If beating be a proof of love, you have it
Plenteous in measure, for by what exemp-
    tion
Is your most sacred carcass freed from
    stripes
And mine made subject to them? Am
    not I

Free-born as you? Say, if the son's in
tears,
Should not the father weep?
STREPSIADES. By what one rule
Of equity?
PHEIDIPPIDES. What equity were that
If none but children are to be chastis'd?
And grant they were, the proverb's in
your teeth,
Which says old age is but a second child-
hood.
Again, if tears are seen to follow blows,
Ought not old men to expiate faults with
tears
Rather than children, who have more to
plead
In favour of their failings?
STREPSIADES. Where's the law
That warrants this proceeding? There's
none such.
PHEIDIPPIDES. And what was your law-
maker but a man,
Mortal as you and I are? And tho' time
Has sanctified his statutes, may not I
Take up the cause of youth, as he of age,
And publish a new ordinance for leave
By the right-filial to correct our fathers,
Remitting and consigning to oblivion
All *ex post facto* beating? Look at in-
stinct—
Inquire of nature how the brute creation
Kick at their parents, which does nothing
differ
From lordly man, except that they com-
pile
No laws, and hold their rights without a
statute.
STREPSIADES. If you are thus for peck-
ing at your father
Like a young fighting-cock, why don't you
peck
Your dinner from the dunghill, and at
night
Roost on a perch?
PHEIDIPPIDES. The cases do not tally.
Nor does my master Socrates prescribe
Rules so absurd.
STREPSIADES.. Cease then from beating
me;
Else you preclude yourself.
PHEIDIPPIDES. As how preclude?

STREPSIADES. Because the right I have
of beating you
Will be your right in time over your son,
When you shall have one.
PHEIDIPPIDES. But if I have none,
All my sad hours are lost, and you die
laughing.
STREPSIADES. There's no denying that.
—How say you, sirs?
Methinks there is good matter in his
plea;
And as for us old sinners, truth to say,
If we deserve a beating we must bear
it.
PHEIDIPPIDES. Hear me—there's more
to come—
STREPSIADES. Then I am lost,
For I can bear no more.
PHEIDIPPIDES. Oh fear it not,
Rather believe what I have now to tell
you
Will cause you to make light of what is
past,
'Twill bring such comfort to you.
STREPSIADES. Let me have it:
If it be comfort, give it me.
PHEIDIPPIDES. Then know,
Henceforth I am resolv'd to beat my
mother
As I have beaten you.
STREPSIADES. How say you? How?
Why this were to out-do all you have
done.
PHEIDIPPIDES. But what if I have not
a proof *in petto*,
To show the moral uses of this beating?
STREPSIADES. Show me a proof that
you have hang'd yourself,
And with your tutor Socrates beside you
Gone to the devil together in a string;
Those moral uses I will thank you for—
Oh inauspicious goddesses, O Clouds!
In you confiding, all these woes fall on
me.
CHORUS. Evil events from evil causes
spring,
And what you suffer flows from what
you've done.
STREPSIADES. Why was I not fore-
warn'd? You saw me old,
And practis'd on my weak simplicity.

CHORUS. 'Tis not for us to warn a wilful sinner;
We stay him not, but let him run his course,
Till by misfortunes rous'd, his conscience wakes,
And prompts him to appease th' offended gods.

STREPSIADES. I feel my sorrows, but I own them just:
Yes, ye reforming Clouds, I'm duly punish'd
For my intended fraud.—And now, my son,
Join hands with me and let us forth together
To wreak our vengeance on those base deceivers,
That Chærephon and Socrates the chief,
Who have cajol'd us both.

PHEIDIPPIDES. Grace forbid
I should lift up my hand against my masters!

STREPSIADES. Nay, nay, but rather dread avenging Jove,
God of your ancestors, and him revere.

PHEIDIPPIDES. You're mad, methinks, to talk to me of Jove—
Is there a god so call'd?

STREPSIADES. There is! there is!

PHEIDIPPIDES. There is no Jupiter, I tell you so;
Vortex has whirl'd him from his throne, and reigns
By right of conquest in the Thunderer's place.

STREPSIADES. 'Tis false, no Vortex reigns but in my brain.

PHEIDIPPIDES. Laugh at your own dull joke and be a fool! [Exit.]

STREPSIADES [striking his breast]. Insufferable blockhead that I was;
What ail'd me thus to court this Socrates,
Ev'n to the exclusion of the immortal gods?
O Mercury, forgive me; be not angry,
Dear tutelary god, but spare me still,
And cast a pitying eye upon my follies,
For I have been intemperate of tongue,
And dearly rue it.—Oh my better genius,
Inspire me with thy counsel how to act,
Whether by legal process to assail them,
Or by such apter means as thou may'st dictate,
I have it! Well hast thou inspir'd the thought;
Hence with the lazy law; thou art not for it.
With fire and faggot I will fall upon them,
And send their school in fumo to the Clouds.
Hoa, Xanthias [Calling to one of his slaves.] hoa! bring forth without delay
Your ladder and your mattock, mount the roof,
Break up the rafters, whelm the house upon them,
And bury the whole hive beneath the ruins.

[XANTHIAS mounts the roof and begins working with his mattock.]

Haste! if you love me, haste! Oh, for a torch,
A blazing torch new lighted, to set fire
To the infernal edifice.—I warrant me
I'll soon unhouse the rascals, that now carry
Their heads so high, and roll them in the dust.

[One of the scholars comes out.]

FIRST DISCIPLE. Woe! mischief! misery!

STREPSIADES [mounts the roof and fixes a torch to the joists].
Torch, play your part:
And we shall muster up a conflagration.

FIRST DISCIPLE. What are you doing, fellow?

STREPSIADES. Chopping logic;
Arguing a knotty point with your housebeams.

SECOND DISCIPLE. Oh horror! Who has set our house on fire?

STREPSIADES. The very man whose cloak you nabb'd so neatly.

SECOND DISCIPLE. Undone and ruin'd—!

STREPSIADES. Heartily I wish it—
And mean you should so be if this same mattock

Does not deceive my hopes, and I escape
With a whole neck.

[SOCRATES *comes forth.*]

SOCRATES. Hoa there! What man is that?
You there upon the roof—what are you doing?
STREPSIADES. Treading on air—contemplating the sun—
SOCRATES. Ah me! I'm suffocated, smother'd, lost—

[CHÆREPHON *appears.*]

CHÆREPHON. Wretch that I am, I'm melted, scorch'd, consum'd—
STREPSIADES. Blasphemers, why did you insult the gods?
Dash, drive, demolish them! Their crimes are many,
But their contemptuous treatment of the gods,
Their impious blasphemies, exceed them all.
CHORUS. Break up!—The Chorus have fulfill'd their part.

THE CAPTIVES

By PLAUTUS

(MARCUS ACCIUS PLAUTUS)

Produced at Rome, 200–190 B.C.

TRANSLATED BY E. H. SUGDEN

CHARACTERS

ERGASILUS, *a parasite*
HEGIO, *an old gentleman*
PHILOCRATES, *an Elian Knight,*⎫
TYNDARUS, *son of* HEGIO ⎬ *the prisoners*
ARISTOPHONTES, *a prisoner* ⎭
PHILOPOLEMUS, *a young man, son of* HEGIO
STALAGMUS, *a slave*
OVERSEERS OF SLAVES
A BOY

[*The Scene represents the house of* HEGIO *in Ætolia. Before the house are seen standing in chains the two prisoners,* PHILOCRATES *and* TYNDARUS.]

PROLOGUE. You all can see two prisoners standing here,
Standing in bonds; they stand, they do not sit;
In this you'll witness that I speak the truth.
Old Hegio, who lives here, is this one's father;
But how he's come to be his father's slave
My prologue shall inform you, if you'll listen.

This old man had two sons; the one of whom
Was stolen by a slave when four years old.
He ran away to Elis and there sold him
To this one's father.
—Do you see?—That's right?
Yon fellow in the gallery says he doesn't?
Let him come nearer, then! What, there's no room?
If there's no room to sit, there's room to walk!
You'd like to send me begging, would you, sir!
Pray, don't suppose I'll crack my lungs for *you!*
You gentlemen of means and noble rank
Receive the rest; I hate to be in debt.

That run-a-way, as I've already said,
When in his flight he'd stolen from his
home
His master's son, sold him to this man's
father,
Who, having bought him, gave him to his
son
To be his valet; for the two lads were
Much of an age. Now he's his father's
slave
In his own home, nor does his father know
it;
See how the gods play ball with us poor
men!
Now then, I've told you how he lost *one*
son.
The Ætolians and the Elians being at war,
His *other* son, a not uncommon thing
In war, was taken prisoner; and a doctor
At Elis, called Menarchus, bought him
there.
His father then began to buy up Elians,
To see if he could find one to exchange
Against his son,—the one that is a pris-
oner;
The other, who's at home, he doesn't know
Now, only yesterday he heard a rumor
How that an Elian knight of highest rank
And noblest family was taken prisoner;
He spared no cash if he might save his
son;
And so, to get him home more readily,
He bought these two from the commis-
sioners.
But they between themselves have laid a
plot,
So that the slave may get his lord sent
home.
Thus they've exchanged their clothing and
their names;
He's called Philocrates, *he* Tyndarus,
And either plays the other's part to-day.
The slave to-day will work this clever
dodge,
And get his master set at liberty.
By the same act he'll save his brother too,
And get him brought back free to home
and father,
Though all unwitting: oft we do more
good
In ignorance than by our best-laid plans.

Well, ignorantly, in their own deceit,
They've so arranged and worked their lit-
tle trick,
That he shall still remain his father's
slave.
For now, not knowing it, he serves his
father.
What things of naught are men, when one
reflects on 't!
This story's ours to act, and yours to see.
But let me give you one brief word of
warning:
It's well worth while to listen to this play.
It's not been treated in a hackneyed fash-
ion,
Nor like the rest of plays; here you'll not
find
Verses that are too nasty to be quoted.
Here is no perjured pimp, or crafty girl,
Or braggart captain.—Pray, don't be
afraid
Because I said a war was going on
Between the Ætolians and the Elians;
The battles won't take place upon the
stage.
We're dressed for comedy; you can't ex-
pect
That we should act a tragedy all at once.
If anybody's itching for a fight,
Just let him start a quarrel; if he gets
An opposite that's stronger, I dare bet
He'll quickly see more fighting than he
likes,
And never long to see a fight again.
I'm off. Farewell, ye most judicious
judges
At home, most valiant fighters in the
field! [*Exit* PROLOGUE.]

[*Enter* ERGASILUS *from the town.*]
ERGASILUS. *Grace* is the name the boys
have given me,
Because I'm always found *before the
meat!*
The wits, I know, say it's ridiculous;
But so don't I! For at the banquet-
table
Your gamester throws the dice and asks
for *grace.*
Then is *grace* there or not? Of course she
is!

But, more of course, we parasites are there,
Though no one ever asks or summons us!
Like mice we live on other people's food;
In holidays, when folks go out of town,
Our teeth enjoy a holiday as well.
As, when it's warm, the snails lie in their shells,
And, failing dew, live on their native juices;
So parasites lie hid in misery
All through the holidays, living on their juices,
Whilst those they feed on jaunt it in the country.
During the holidays, we parasites
Are greyhounds; when they're over, we are mastiffs,
Bred out of "Odious" by "Prince of Bores."
Now here, unless your parasite can stand
Hard fisticuffs, and has no strong objection
To have the crockery broken on his pate,
He'd better go and take a porter's billet
At the Trigeminal gate; which lot, I fear,
Is not at all unlikely to be mine.
My patron has been captured by the foe—
The Ætolians and the Elians are at war,
(This is Ætolia); Philopolemus,
The son of Hegio here, whose house this is,
In Elis lies a prisoner; so this house
A house of lamentation is to me;
As oft as I behold it, I must weep.
Now for his son's sake, he's begun a trade,
Dishonorable, hateful to himself;
He's buying prisoners, if perchance he may
Find any to exchange against his son.
O how I pray that he may gain his wish!
Till he's recovered, I am past recovery.
The other youths are selfish, hopelessly,
And only he keeps up the ancient style.
I've never flattered him without reward;
And the good father takes after his son!
Now I'll go see him. Ha! the door is opening,
Whence I have often come, just drunk with gorging.

[*Enter from the house* HEGIO *and an* OVERSEER.]

HEGIO. Attend to me; those prisoners that I bought
A day ago from the Commissioners
Out of the spoil, put lighter fetters on them;
Take off these heavier ones with which they're bound,
And let them walk indoors or out at will;
But watch them with the utmost carefulness.
For when a free man's taken prisoner,
He's just like a wild bird; if once he gets
A chance of running off, it's quite enough;
You needn't hope to catch your man again.
OVERSEER. Why, all of us would rather far be free
Than slaves.
HEGIO. Why not take steps, then, to be free?
OVERSEER. Shall I give *leg-bail?* I've naught else to give!
HEGIO. I fancy that in that case you would *catch it!*
OVERSEER. I'll be like that wild bird you spoke about.
HEGIO. All right; then I will clap you in a cage.
Enough of this; do what I said, and go.
[*Exit* OVERSEER *into the house.*]
I'll to my brother's, to my other captives,
To see how they've behaved themselves last night,
And then I'll come back home again straightway.
ERGASILUS [*aside*]. It grieves me that the poor old man should ply
This gaoler's trade to save his hapless son.
But if perchance the son can be brought back,
The father may turn hangman: what care I?
HEGIO. Who speaks there?
ERGASILUS. One who suffers in your grief.
I'm growing daily thinner, older, weaker!
See, I'm all skin and bones, as lean as lean!
All that I eat at home does me no good;
Only a bite at a friend's agrees with me.
HEGIO. Ergasilus! hail!
ERGASILUS. Heav'n bless you, Hegio!

HEGIO. Don't weep!

ERGASILUS. Not weep for him? What, not bewail
That excellent young man?

HEGIO.   I always knew
You and my son to be the best of friends.

ERGASILUS. Alas! we don't appreciate our blessings
Till we have lost the gifts we once enjoyed.
Now that your son is in the foeman's hands,
I realize how much he was to me!

HEGIO. Ah, if a stranger feels his loss so much,
What must *I* feel? He was my only joy.

ERGASILUS. A stranger? I a stranger? Hegio,
Never say that nor cherish such a thought!
Your only joy he was, but oh! to me
Far dearer than a thousand only joys.

HEGIO. You're right to make your friend's distress your own;
But come, cheer up!

ERGASILUS. Alas! it pains me here,
That now the feaster's army is discharged.

HEGIO. And can't you meantime find another general
To call to arms this army that's discharged?

ERGASILUS. No fear! since Philopolemus was taken,
Who filled that post, they all refuse to act.

HEGIO. And it's no wonder they refuse to act.
You need so many men of divers races
To work for you; first, those of Bakerton;
And several tribes inhabit Bakerton;
Then men of Breadport and of Biscuitville,
Of Thrushborough and Ortolania,
And all the various soldiers of the sea.

ERGASILUS. How oft the noblest talents lie concealed!
O what a splendid general you would make,
Though now you're serving as a private merely.

HEGIO. Be of good cheer; in a few days, I trust,

I shall receive my dear son home again.
I've got a youthful Elian prisoner,
Whom I am hoping to exchange for him,
One of the highest rank and greatest wealth.

ERGASILUS. May Heaven grant it!

HEGIO.   Where've you been invited
To dine to-day?

ERGASILUS. Why, nowhere that I know of.
Why do you ask?

HEGIO.   Because it is my birthday;
And so, I pray you, come and dine with me.

ERGASILUS. Well said indeed!

HEGIO.   That is if you're content
With frugal fare.

ERGASILUS. Well, if it's not *too* frugal;
I get enough of that, you know, at home.

HEGIO. Well, name your figure!

ERGASILUS.   Done! unless I get
A better offer, and on such conditions
As better suit my partners and myself.
As I am selling you my whole estate,
It's only fair that I should make my terms.

HEGIO. I fear that this estate you're selling me
Has got a bottomless abyss within't!
But if you come, come early.

ERGASILUS.   Now, if you like!

HEGIO. Go hunt a hare; you've only caught a weasel.
The path my guest must tread is full of stones.

ERGASILUS. You won't dissuade me, Hegio; don't think it!
I'll get my teeth well shod before I come.

HEGIO. My table's really coarse.

ERGASILUS.   Do you eat brambles?

HEGIO. My dinner's from the soil.

ERGASILUS.   So is good pork.

HEGIO. Plenty of cabbage!

ERGASILUS.   Food for invalids!
What more?

HEGIO. Be there in time.

ERGASILUS. I'll not forget. [*Exit*
ERGASILUS *to the marketplace.*]

HEGIO. Now I'll go in and look up my accounts,
To see what I have lying at my banker's;

Then to my brother's, as I said just now.
[*Exit* HEGIO *into the house.*]

[*Enter* OVERSEERS, PHILOCRATES *and* TYN-
DARUS, *each in the other's clothes, and
other slaves.*]

OVERSEER. Since Heaven has willed it
should be so,
That you must drink this cup of woe,
Why, bear it with a patient mind,
And so your pain you'll lighter find.
At home, I dare say, you were free;
Now that your lot is slavery,
Just take it as a thing of course,
Instead of making matters worse;
Behave yourselves and don't be queasy
About your lord's commands; 't is easy.

PRISONERS. Oh, oh!

OVERSEER. No need for howls and cries!
I see your sorrow in your eyes.
Be brave in your adversities.

TYNDARUS. But we're ashamed to wear
these chains.

OVERSEER. My lord would suffer far
worse pains,
Should he leave you to range at large out
of his custody,
Or set you at liberty whom he bought yes-
terday.

TYNDARUS. Oh, he needn't fear that
he'll lose his gains;
Should he release us, we know what's our
duty, sir.

OVERSEER. Yes, you'll run off; I know
that. You're a beauty, sir!

TYNDARUS. Run off? run off where?

OVERSEER. To the land of your birth.

TYNDARUS. Nay, truly, it never would
answer
To imitate runaway slaves.

OVERSEER. Well, by Jove!
I'd advise you, if you get a chance, sir.

TYNDARUS. One thing I beg of you.

OVERSEER. What's your petition, sir?

TYNDARUS. Give us a chance of ex-
changing a word,
Where there's no fear that we'll be over-
heard.

OVERSEER. Granted! Go, leave them.
We'll take our position there.
See that your talk doesn't last too long!

TYNDARUS. Oh, that's my intention.
So, now, come along!

OVERSEER. Go, leave them alone.

TYNDARUS. We ever shall own
We're in your debt for the kindness you've
shown to us;
You have the power, and you've proved
yourself bounteous.

PHILOCRATES. Come away farther, as
far as we can from them;
We must contrive to conceal our fine plan
from them,
Never disclose any trace of our trickery,
Else we shall find all our dodges a mock-
ery.
Once they get wind of it,
There'll be an end of it;
For if you are my master brave,
And I pretend to be your slave,
Then we must watch with greatest care;
Of eavesdroppers we must beware.
With caution and skill keep your senses
all waking;
There's no time to sleep; it's a big under-
taking.

TYNDARUS. So I'm to be master?

PHILOCRATES. Yes, that is the notion.

TYNDARUS. And so for your head (I
would pray you remark it),
You want me to carry my own head to
market!

PHILOCRATES. I know.

TYNDARUS. Well, when you've gained
your wish, remember my devotion.
This is the way that you'll find most men
treating you;
    Until they have
    The boon they crave,
They're kind as can be; but success makes
the knave!
When they have got it, they set to work
cheating you.
Now I have told you the treatment you
owe to me.
You I regard as a father, you know, to
me.

PHILOCRATES. Nay, let us say,—no con-
ventions shall hinder us,—
Next to my own, you're my father, dear
Tyndarus.

TYNDARUS. That will do!

PHILOCRATES. Now then, I warn you always to remember this;
I no longer am your master but your slave; don't be remiss.
Since kind Heav'n has shown us plainly that the way ourselves to save
Is for me, who was your master, now to turn into your slave,
Where before I gave you orders, now I beg of you in prayer,
By the changes in our fortune, by my father's kindly care,
By the common fetters fastened on us by the enemy,
Think of who you were and are, and pay no more respect to me
Than I used to pay to you, when you were slave and I was free.

TYNDARUS. Well, I know that I am you and you are me!

PHILOCRATES. Yes, stick to that!
Then I hope that by your shrewdness we shall gain what we are at.

[*Enter* HEGIO *from his house.*]

HEGIO [*addressing some one inside*]. I'll be back again directly when I've looked into the case:
Where are those whom I directed at the door to take their place?

PHILOCRATES. O by Pollux! you've been careful that we shouldn't be to seek;
Thus by bonds and guards surrounded we have had no chance to sneak!

HEGIO. Howsoever careful, none can be as careful as he ought;
When he thinks he's been most careful, oft your careful man is caught.
Don't you think that I've just cause to keep a careful watch on you,
When I've had to pay so large a sum of money for the two?

PHILOCRATES. Truly we've no right to blame you, that you watch and guard us ᵗhus;
And if we should get a chance and run away, you can't blame *us*.

HEGIO. Just like you, my son is held in slavery by your countrymen.

PHILOCRATES. Was he taken prisoner?

HEGIO.   Yes.

PHILOCRATES. We weren't the only cowards then.

HEGIO. Come aside here; there is something I would ask of you alone;
And I hope you'll not deceive me.

PHILOCRATES. Everything I know I'll own;
If in aught I'm ignorant, I'll tell you so, upon my life.

[HEGIO *and* PHILOCRATES *go aside;* TYNDARUS *standing where he can hear their conversation.*]

TYNDARUS [*aside*]. Now the old man's at the barber's; see my master whets his knife!
Why, he hasn't even put an apron on to shield his clothes!
Will he shave him close or only cut his hair?
                    Well, goodness knows!
But if he has any sense, he'll crop the old man properly!

HEGIO. Come now, tell me, would you rather be a slave or get set free?

PHILOCRATES. What I want is that which brings me most of good and least of ill.
Though I must confess my slavery wasn't very terrible;
Little difference was made between me and my master's son.

TYNDARUS [*aside*]. Bravo! I'd not give a cent for Thales, the Milesian!
For, compared with this man's cunning, he is but a trifling knave.
Mark how cleverly he talks, as if he'd always been a slave!

HEGIO. Tell me to what family Philocrates belongs?

PHILOCRATES. The Goldings;
That's a family most wealthy both in honors and in holdings.

HEGIO. Is your master there respected?

PHILOCRATES. Highly, by our foremost men.

HEGIO. If his influence amongst them is as great as you maintain,
                    Are his riches fat?

PHILOCRATES. I guess so! Fat as suet, one might say.

HEGIO. Is his father living?

PHILOCRATES. Well, he *was*, sir, when we came away;
Whether he still lives or not, you'll have to go to hell to see.

TYNDARUS [*aside*]. Saved again! for now he's adding to his lies philosophy!

HEGIO. What's his name, I pray?

PHILOCRATES. Thensaurocrœsonicochrysides.

HEGIO. I suppose a sort of nickname given to show how rich he is.

PHILOCRATES. Nay, by Pollux! it was given him for his avarice and greed.
Truth to tell you, Theodoromedes is his name indeed.

HEGIO. What is this? His father's grasping?

PHILOCRATES. Grasping? Ay, most covetous!
Just to show you, when he sacrifices to his Genius,
All the vessels that he uses are of Samian crockery,
Lest the Genius should steal them! There's his character, you see.

HEGIO. Come with me then.
Now I'll ask the other what I want to know.
[*To* TYNDARUS.] Now, Philocrates, your slave has acted as a man should do,
For from him I've learnt your birth; the whole he has confessed to me.
If you will admit the same, it shall to your advantage be;
For your slave has told me all.

TYNDARUS. It was his duty so to do.
All is true that he's confessed; although I must admit to you,
'T was my wish to hide from you my birth, and wealth, and family;
But now, Hegio, that I've lost my fatherland and liberty,
Naturally he should stand in awe of you much more than me,
Since by force of arms our fortunes stand on an equality.
I remember when he durst not speak a word to do me ill;

He may strike me now; so fortune plays with mortals as she will.
I, once free, am made a slave and brought from high to low degree,
And instead of giving orders must obey submissively.
But if I should have a master, such as *I* was when at home,
I've no fear that his commands will prove unjust or burdensome.
Hegio, will you bear from me a word of warning?

HEGIO. Yes, say on.

TYNDARUS. Once I was as free and happy as your own beloved son.
But the force of hostile arms has robbed him of his freedom, too;
He's a slave amongst our people, just as I am here with you.
Certainly there is a God who watches us where'er we be;
He will treat your son exactly as He finds that you treat me.
Virtue sure will be rewarded, vice will e'er bring sorrow on—
I've a father misses me, as much as you your absent son.

HEGIO. Yes, I know. Do you admit, then, what your slave confessed to me?

TYNDARUS. I admit, sir, that my father is a man of property,
And that I'm of noble birth. But I beseech you, Hegio,
Do not let my ample riches cause your avarice to grow,
Lest my father think it better, though I am his only son,
That I should continue serving you and keep your livery on,
Rather than come home a beggar to my infinite disgrace.

HEGIO. Thanks to Heav'n and my forefathers, I've been wealthy all my days;
Nor is wealth, in my opinion, always useful to obtain—
Many a man I've known degraded to a beast by too much gain;
There are times when loss is better far than gain, in every way.

Gold! I hate it! Oh, how many people has
it led astray!
Now, attend to me, and I my purpose
plainly will declare:
There in Elis, with your people, is my son
a prisoner.
If you'll bring him back to me, you shall
not pay a single cent:
I'll release you and your slave too; other-
wise I'll not relent.
TYNDARUS. That's the noblest, kindest
offer! All the world can't find your
mate!
But is he in slavery to a private man or
to the State?
HEGIO. To Menarchus, a physician.
TYNDARUS. Ah! my client! all is plain;
Everything will be as easy as the falling
of the rain.
HEGIO. Bring him home as soon as may
be.
TYNDARUS. Certainly; but, Hegio—
HEGIO. What's your wish? For I'll do
aught in reason.
TYNDARUS. Listen; you shall know.
I don't ask that I should be sent back
until your son has come.
Name the price you'll take for yonder
slave, to let me send him home,
That he may redeem your son.
HEGIO. Nay, some one else I should
prefer,
Whom I'll send when truce is made to go
and meet your father there.
He can take your father any message that
you like to send.
TYNDARUS. It's no use to send a
stranger; all your toil in smoke would
end.
Send my slave, he'll do the business just
as soon as he gets there;
You won't hit on anybody you can send
who's trustier,
Or more faithful; he's a man who does
his work with all his heart.
Boldly trust your son to him; and he will
truly play his part.
Don't you fear! at my own peril I'll make
trial of his truth;
For he knows my kindness to him; I can
safely trust the youth.

HEGIO. Well, I'll send him at your risk,
if you consent.
TYNDARUS. Oh, I agree.
HEGIO. Let him start as soon as may
be.
TYNDARUS. That will suit me perfectly.
HEGIO. Well, then, if he doesn't come
back here you'll pay me fifty pounds;
Are you willing?
TYNDARUS. Certainly.
HEGIO. Then go and loose him from
his bonds;
And the other too.
TYNDARUS. May Heaven ever treat you
graciously!
Since you've shown me so much kindness,
and from fetters set me free.
Ah, my neck's more comfortable, now I've
cast that iron ruff!
HEGIO. Gifts when given to good people
win their gratitude! Enough!
Now, if you are going to send him, teach
and tell him what to say,
When he gets home to your father. Shall
I call him?
TYNDARUS. Do so, pray!
[HEGIO crosses the stage to
PHILOCRATES and addresses
him.]
HEGIO. Heav'n bless this project to my
son and me,
And you as well! I, your new lord, desire
That you should give your true and faith-
ful service
To your old master. I have lent you to
him,
And set a price of fifty pounds upon
you.
He says he wants to send you to his
father
That he may ransom my dear son and
make
An interchange between us of our sons.
PHILOCRATES. Well, I'm prepared to
serve either one or t' other;
I'm like a wheel, just twist me as you
please!
I'll turn this way or that, as you com-
mand.
HEGIO. I'll see that you don't lose by
your compliance;

Since you are acting as a good slave
should.
Come on.

Now, here's your man.

TYNDARUS. I thank you, sir,
For giving me this opportunity
Of sending him to bring my father word
About my welfare and my purposes;
All which he'll tell my father as I bid
him.
Now, Tyndarus, we've come to an agree-
ment,
That you should go to Elis to my father;
And should you not come back, I've un-
dertaken
To pay the sum of fifty pounds for you.

PHILOCRATES. A fair agreement! for
your father looks
For me or for some other messenger
To come from hence to him.

TYNDARUS. Then, pray attend,
And I will tell you what to tell my father.

PHILOCRATES. I have always tried to
serve you hitherto, Philocrates,
As you wished me, to the utmost of my
poor abilities.
That I'll ever seek and aim at, heart and
soul and strength alway.

TYNDARUS. That is right: you know
your duty. Listen now to what I
say.
First of all, convey a greeting to my
parents dear from me,
And to other relatives and friends, if any
you should see.
Say I'm well, and held in bondage by this
worthy gentleman,
Who has shown and ever shows me all the
honor that he can.

PHILOCRATES. Oh, you needn't tell me
that, it's rooted in my memory.

TYNDARUS. If I didn't see my keeper,
I should think that I was free.
Tell my father of the bargain I have
made with Hegio,
For the ransom of his son.

PHILOCRATES. Don't stay to tell me
that. I know.

TYNDARUS. He must purchase and re-
store him, then we both shall be set
free.

PHILOCRATES. Good!

HEGIO. Bid him be quick, for your sake
and for mine in like degree.

PHILOCRATES. You don't long to see
your son more ardently than he does
his!

HEGIO. Why, each loves his own.

PHILOCRATES. Well, have you any other
messages?

TYNDARUS. Yes; don't hesitate to say
I'm well and happy, Tyndarus;
That no shade of disagreement ever sep-
arated us;
That you've never once deceived me nor
opposed your master's will,
And have stuck to me like wax in spite of
all this flood of ill.
By my side you've stood and helped me in
my sore adversities,
True and faithful to me ever. When my
father hears of this,
Tyndarus, and knows your noble conduct
towards himself and me,
He will never be so mean as to refuse to
set you free;
When I'm back I'll spare no effort that it
may be brought about.
To your toil, and skill, and courage, and
your wisdom, there's no doubt
That I owe my chance of getting to my
father's home again:
For 't was you confessed my birth and
riches to this best of men;
So you set your master free from fetters
by your ready wit.

PHILOCRATES. Yes, I did, sir, as you
say; I'm glad that you remember
it.
But indeed, you've well deserved it at my
hands, Philocrates;
For if I should try to utter all your many
kindnesses,
Night would fall before I'd finished; you
have done as much for me
As if you had been my slave.

HEGIO. Good heavens, what nobility
Shines in both their dispositions! I can
scarce refrain from tears
When I see their true affection, and the
way the slave reveres
And commends his master.

TYNDARUS. Truly he has not commended me
Even a hundredth part as much as he himself deserves to be.
HEGIO. Well, as you've behaved so nobly, now you have a splendid chance
Here to crown your services by doubly faithful vigilance.
PHILOCRATES. As I wish the thing accomplished, so I shall do all I know;
To assure you of it, I call Jove to witness, Hegio!
That I never will betray Philocrates, I'll take my oath!
HEGIO. Honest fellow!
PHILOCRATES. I will treat him as myself, upon my troth!
TYNDARUS. From these loving protestations, mind you never never swerve.
And if I've said less about you than your faithful deeds deserve,
Pray you, don't be angry with me on account of what I've said;
But remember you are going with a price upon your head;
And that both my life and honor I have staked on your return;
When you've left my sight, I pray you, don't forget what you have sworn,
Or when you have left me here in slavery instead of you,
Think that you are free, and so neglect what you are pledged to do,
And forget your solemn promise to redeem this good man's son.
Fifty pounds, remember, is the price that we've agreed upon.
Faithful to your faithful master, do not let your faith be bought;
And I'm well assured my father will do everything he ought.
Keep me as your friend forever, and this good old man as well.
Take my hand in yours, I pray you, swear an oath unbreakable,
That you'll always be as faithful as I've ever been to you.
Mind, you're now my master, aye protector, and my father too!
I commit to you my hopes and happiness.
PHILOCRATES. O that'll do!

Are you satisfied if I can carry this commission through?
TYNDARUS. Yes.
PHILOCRATES. Then I'll return in such a manner as shall please you both.
Is that all, sir?
HEGIO. Come back quickly.
PHILOCRATES. So I will, upon my troth.
HEGIO. Come along then to my banker's; I'll provide you for the way.
Also I will get a passport from the prætor.
TYNDARUS. Passport, eh?
HEGIO. Yes, to get him through the army so that they may let him go.
Step inside.
TYNDARUS. A pleasant journey!
PHILOCRATES. Fare-you-well!
HEGIO. By Pollux, though,
What a blessing that I bought these men from the Commissioners!
So, please Heav'n, I've saved my son from bondage to those foreigners.
Dear! How long I hesitated whether I should buy or not!
Please to take him in, good slaves, and do not let him leave the spot,
When there is no keeper with him; I shall soon be home again.
[Exeunt TYNDARUS and slaves into the house.]
Now I'll run down to my brother's and inspect my other men.
I'll inquire if any of them is acquainted with this youth.
[To PHILOCRATES.] Come along and I'll despatch you. That must be done first, in sooth. [Exeunt HEGIO and PHILOCRATES to the marketplace.]

[Enter ERGASILUS returning from the marketplace.]
ERGASILUS. Wretched he who seeks his dinner, and with trouble gets a haul;
Wretcheder who seeks with trouble, and can't find a meal at all;
Wretchedest who dies for food, and can't get any anyway.
If I could, I'd like to scratch the eyes out of this cursed day!
For it's filled all men with meanness towards me. Oh, I never saw

Day so hungry; why, it's stuffed with
famine in its greedy maw.
Never day pursued its purpose in so vacu-
ous a way;
For my gullet and my stomach have to
keep a holiday.
Out upon the parasite's profession: it's all
gone to pot!
For us impecunious wits the gilded youth
don't care a jot.
They no longer want us Spartans, owners
of a single chair,
Sons of Smacked-Face, whose whole stock-
in-trade is words, whose board is
bare.
Those that they invite are fellows who can
ask them back in turn.
Then they cater for themselves and us
poor parasites they spurn;
You will see them shopping in the market
with as little shame
As when, sitting on the bench, the culprit's
sentence they proclaim.
For us wits they don't care twopence;
keep entirely to their set.
When I went just now to market, there
a group of them I met;
"Hail!" says I; "where shall we go,"
says I, "to lunch?" They all were
mum.
"Who speaks first? Who volunteers?"
says I. And still the chaps were
dumb.
Not a smile! "Where shall we dine to-
gether? Answer." Not a word!
Then I flashed a jest upon them from my
very choicest hoard,
One that meant a month of dinners in the
old days, I declare.
No one smiled; and then I saw the whole
was a got-up affair.
Why, they wouldn't even do as much as
any angry cur;
If they couldn't smile, they might at least
have shown their teeth, I swear!
Well, I left the rascals when I saw that
they were making game;
Went to others; and to others; and to
others—still the same!
They had formed a ring together, just like
those who deal in oil

I' the Velabrum. So I left them when I
saw they mocked my toil.
In the Forum vainly prowling other para-
sites I saw.
I've resolved that I must try to get my
rights by Roman law.
As they've formed a plot to rob us of our
life and victuals too,
I shall summon them and fine them, as a
magistrate would do.
They shall give me ten good dinners, at a
time when food is dear!
So I'll do; now to the harbor; there I
may to dinner steer;
If that fails me, I'll return and try this
old man's wretched cheer. [*Exit*
ERGASILUS *to the harbor.*]

[*Enter* HEGIO *from his brother's with*
ARISTOPHONTES.]
HEGIO. How pleasant it is when you've
managed affairs
For the good of the public, as yesterday I
did,
When I bought those two fellows. Why,
every one stares
And congratulates me on the way I de-
cided.
To tell the plain truth, I am worried with
standing,
And weary with waiting;
From the flood of their words I could
scarce get a landing,
And even at the prætor's it showed no
abating.
I asked for a passport; and when it had
come,
I gave it to Tyndarus; *he* set off home.
When he had departed, for home off I
started;
Then went to my brother's, to question
the others,
Whether any among them Philocrates
knew.
Then one of them cries, "He's my friend,
good and true."
I told him I'd bought him;
He begged he might see him; and so I
have brought him.
I bade them loose him from his chains,
And came away. [*To* ARISTOPHONTES.]

Pray follow me;
Your earnest suit success obtains,
Your dear old friend you soon shall see.
[*Exeunt* HEGIO, ARISTOPHONTES *into
house;* TYNDARUS *rushes out.*]
TYNDARUS. Alas! the day has come on
which I wish I never had been born.
My hopes, resources, stratagems, have fled
and left me all forlorn.
On this sad day no hope remains of saving
my poor life, 't is clear;
No help or hope remains to me to drive
away my anxious fear.
No cloak I anywhere can find to cover up
my crafty lies,
No cloak, I say, comes in my way to hide
my tricks and rogueries.
There is no pardon for my fibs, and no
escape for my misdeeds;
My cheek can't find the shelter, nor my
craft the hiding-place it needs.
All that I hid has come to light; my plans
lie open to the day;
The whole thing's out,'and in this scrape
I fail to see a single ray
Of hope to shun the doom which I must
suffer for my master's sake.
This Aristophontes, who's just come, will
surely bring me to the stake;
He knows me, and he is the friend and
kinsman of Philocrates.
Salvation couldn't save me, if she would;
there is no way but this,
To plan some new and smarter trickeries.
Hang it, *what?* What shall I do? I *am*
just up a lofty tree,
If I can't contrive some new and quite
preposterous foolery.

[*Enter from the house* HEGIO *and*
ARISTOPHONTES.]
HEGIO. Where's the fellow gone whom
we saw rushing headlong from the
house?
TYNDARUS [*aside*]. Now the day of
doom has come; the foe's upon thee,
Tyndarus!
O, what story shall I tell them? What
deny and what confess?
My purposes are at all sea; O, ain't I in a
pretty mess?

O would that Heaven had blasted you
before you left your native land,
You wretch, Aristophontes, who have
ruined all that I had planned.
The game is up if I can't light on some
atrocious villainy!
HEGIO. Ah, there's your man: go speak
to him.
TYNDARUS [*aside*]. What man is
wretcheder than I?
ARISTOPHONTES. How is this that you
avoid my eyes and shun me, Tyn-
darus?
Why, you might have never known me,
fellow, that you treat me thus!
I'm a slave as much as you, although in
Elis I was free,
Whilst you from your earliest boyhood
were enthralled in slavery.
HEGIO. Well, by Jove! I'm not sur-
prised that he should shun you, when
he sees
That you call him Tyndarus, not, as you
should, Philocrates.
TYNDARUS. Hegio, this man in Elis was
considered raving mad.
Take no note of anything he tells you
either good or bad.
Why, he once attacked his father and his
mother with a spear;
And the epilepsy takes him in a form
that's most severe.
Don't go near him!
HEGIO. Keep your distance!
ARISTOPHONTES. Rascal! Did I rightly
hear,
That you say I'm mad, and once attacked
my father with a spear?
And that I have got the sickness for
which men are wont to spit?
HEGIO. Never mind! for many men be-
sides yourself have suffered it,
And the spitting was a means of healing
them, and they were glad.
ARISTOPHONTES. What, do you believe
the wretch?
HEGIO. In what respect?
ARISTOPHONTES. That I am mad!
TYNDARUS. Do you see him glaring
at you? Better leave him! O be-
ware!

Hegio, the fit is on him; he'll be raving soon! Take care!

HEGIO. Well, I thought he was a madman when he called you Tyndarus.

TYNDARUS. Why, he sometimes doesn't know his *own* name. Oh, he's often thus.

HEGIO. But he said you were his comrade.

TYNDARUS. Ah, no doubt! precisely so! And Alcmæon, and Orestes, and Lycurgus, don't you know,
Are my comrades quite as much as he is!

ARISTOPHONTES. Oh, you gallows bird, Dare you slander me? What, don't I know you?

HEGIO. Come, don't be absurd.
You don't know him, for you called him Tyndarus: that's very clear.
You don't know the man you see; you name the man who isn't here.

ARISTOPHONTES. Nay, he says he is the man he isn't, not the man he is.

TYNDARUS. O yes! Doubtless you know better whether I'm Philocrates
Than Philocrates himself does!

ARISTOPHONTES. You'd prove truth itself a liar,
As it strikes me. But, I pray you, look at me!

TYNDARUS. As you desire!

ARISTOPHONTES. Aren't you Tyndarus?

TYNDARUS. I'm not.

ARISTOPHONTES. You say you are Philocrates?

TYNDARUS. Certainly.

ARISTOPHONTES. Do you believe him?

HEGIO. Yes, and shall do, if I please.
For the other, who you say he is, went home from here to-day
To the father of this captive.

ARISTOPHONTES. Father? He's a slave.

TYNDARUS. And, pray!
Are you not a slave, though you were free once, as I hope to be,
When I have restored good Hegio's son to home and liberty?

ARISTOPHONTES. What's that, gaolbird? Do you tell me that you were a free-man born?

TYNDARUS. No! Philocrates, not Freeman, is my name.

ARISTOPHONTES. Pray, mark his scorn!
Hegio, I tell you, you're being mocked and swindled by this knave;
Why, he never had a slave except himself; for *he's* a slave.

TYNDARUS. Ah, because you're poor yourself, and have no means of livelihood,
You'd wish everybody else to be like you.
I know your mood;
All poor men like you are spiteful, envy those who're better off.

ARISTOPHONTES. Hegio, don't believe this fellow; for he's doing naught but scoff;
Sure I am, he'll play some scurvy trick on you before he's done;
I don't like this tale of his about the ransom of your son.

TYNDARUS. You don't like it, I dare say; but I'll accomplish it, you see!
I'll restore him to his father; he in turn releases me.
That's why I've sent Tyndarus to see my father.

ARISTOPHONTES. Come, that's lame!
You are Tyndarus yourself, the only slave who bears that name!

TYNDARUS. Why reproach me with my bondage? I was captured in the fray.

ARISTOPHONTES. Oh, I can't restrain my fury!

TYNDARUS. Don't you hear him? Run away!
He'll be hurling stones at us just now, if you don't have him bound.

ARISTOPHONTES. Oh, damnation!

TYNDARUS. How he glares at us! I hope your ropes are sound.
See, his body's covered over with bright spots of monstrous size!
It's the black bile that afflicts him.

ARISTOPHONTES. Pollux! if this old man's wise,
You will find black pitch afflict you, when it blazes round your breast.

TYNDARUS. Ah, he's wandering now, poor fellow! by foul spirits he's possessed!

HEGIO [to TYNDARUS]. What do you think? Would it be best to have him bound?

TYNDARUS. Yes, so I said.

ARISTOPHONTES. Oh, perdition take it! Would I had a stone to smash his head,
This whipped cur, who says I'm mad! By Jove, sir, I will make you smart!

TYNDARUS. Hear him calling out for stones!

ARISTOPHONTES. Pray, might we have a word apart, Hegio?

HEGIO. Yes, but keep your distance; there's no need to come so close!

TYNDARUS. If, by Pollux, you go any nearer, he'll bite off your nose.

ARISTOPHONTES. Hegio, I beg and pray you, don't believe that I am mad,
Or that I have epilepsy as this shameless fellow said.
But if you're afraid of me, then have me bound; I won't say no,
If you'll bind that rascal too.

TYNDARUS. O no, indeed, good Hegio! Bind the man who wishes it!

ARISTOPHONTES. Be quiet, you! The case stands thus;
I shall prove Philocrates the false to be true Tyndarus.
What are you winking for?

TYNDARUS. I wasn't.

ARISTOPHONTES. He winks before your very face!

HEGIO. What, if I approached this madman?

TYNDARUS. It would be a wild-goose chase.
He'll keep. chattering, till you can't make either head or tail of it.
Had they dressed him for the part, you'd say 't was Ajax in his fit.

HEGIO. Never mind, I *will* approach him.

TYNDARUS [aside]. Things are looking very blue.
I'm between the knife and altar, and I don't know what to do.

HEGIO. I attend, Aristophontes, if you've anything to say.

ARISTOPHONTES. You shall hear that that is true which you've been thinking false to-day.
First I wish to clear myself of all suspicion that I rave,
Or that I am subject to disease—except that I'm a slave.
So may He who's king of gods and men restore me home again:
He's no more Philocrates than you or I.

HEGIO. But tell me then, Who he is.

ARISTOPHONTES. The same that I have told you from the very first
If you find it otherwise, I pray that I may be accursed,
And may suffer forfeit of fatherland and freedom sweet.

HEGIO. What say *you?*

TYNDARUS. That I'm your slave, and you're my master.

HEGIO. That's not it.
Were you free?

TYNDARUS. I was.

ARISTOPHONTES. He wasn't. He's just lying worse and worse.

TYNDARUS. How do *you* know? Perhaps it happened that you were my mother's nurse,
That you dare to speak so boldly!

ARISTOPHONTES. Why, I saw you when a lad.

TYNDARUS. Well, I see you when a man to-day! So we are quits, by gad!
Did I meddle with your business? Just let mine alone then, please.

HEGIO. Was his father called Thensaurocrœsonicochrysides?

ARISTOPHONTES. No, he wasn't, and I never heard the name before to-day.
Theodoromedes was his master's father.

TYNDARUS [aside]. Deuce to pay!
O be quiet, or go straight and hang yourself, my beating heart!
You are dancing there, whilst I can hardly stand to play my part.

HEGIO. He in Elis was a slave then, if you are not telling lies,
And is not Philocrates?

ARISTOPHONTES. You'll never find it otherwise.

HEGIO. So I've been chopped into fragments and dissected, goodness knows, By the dodges of this scoundrel, who has led me by the nose.
Are you sure there's no mistake though?
ARISTOPHONTES. Yes, I speak of what I know.
HEGIO. Is it certain?
ARISTOPHONTES. Certain? Nothing could be more entirely so.
Why, Philocrates has been my friend from when he was a boy;
But where is he now?
HEGIO. Ah, that's what vexes me, but gives *him* joy.
Tell me though, what sort of looking man is this Philocrates?
ARISTOPHONTES. Thin i' the face, a sharpish nose, a fair complexion, coalblack eyes,
Reddish, crisp, and curly hair.
HEGIO. Yes, that's the fellow to a T.
TYNDARUS [*aside*]. Curse upon it, everything has gone all wrong to-day with me.
Woe unto those wretched rods that on my back to-day must die!
HEGIO. So I see that I've been cheated.
TYNDARUS [*aside*]. Come on, fetters, don't be shy!
Run to me and clasp my legs and I'll take care of you,.no fear!
HEGIO. Well, I've been sufficiently bamboozled by these villains here.
T' other said he was a slave, while this pretended to be free;
So I've gone and lost the kernel, and the husk is left to me.
Yes, they've corked my nose most finely! Don't I make a foolish show?
But this fellow here shan't mock me! Colaphus, Corax, Cordalio,
Come out here and bring your thongs.

[*Enter.* OVERSEERS.]
OVERSEER. To bind up faggots? Here's a go!
HEGIO. Come, bind your heaviest shackles on this wretch.
TYNDARUS. Why, what's the matter? what's my crime?

HEGIO. Your crime!
You've sowed and scattered ill, now you shall reap it.
TYNDARUS. Hadn't you better say I harrowed too?
For farmers always harrow first, then sow.
HEGIO. How boldly does he flout me to my face!
TYNDARUS. A harmless, guiltless man, although a slave,
Should boldly face his master, of all men.
HEGIO. Tie up his hands as tightly as you can.
TYNDARUS. You'd better cut them off; for I am yours.
But what's the matter? Why are you so angry?
HEGIO. Because my plans, as far as in you lay,
By your thrice-villainous and lying tricks
You've torn asunder, mangled limb from limb,
And ruined all my hopes and purposes.
Philocrates escaped me through your guile;
I thought he was the slave, and you the free;
For so you said, and interchanged your names
Between yourselves.
TYNDARUS. Yes, I admit all that.
'T is just as you have said, and cunningly
He's got away by means of my smart work;
But I beseech you, are you wroth at that?
HEGIO. You've brought the worst of torments on yourself.
TYNDARUS. If not for sin I perish, I don't care!
But though I perish, and he breaks his word,
And doesn't come back here, my joy is this:
My deed will be remembered when I'm dead,
How I redeemed my lord from slavery,
And rescued him and saved him from his foes,
To see once more his father and his home;
And how I rather chose to risk my life,

Than let my master perish in his bonds.
HEGIO. The only fame you'll get will be
in hell.
TYNDARUS. Nay, he who dies for virtue
doesn't perish.
HEGIO. When I've expended all my
torments on you,
And given you up to death for your de-
ceits,
People may call it death or perishing
Just as they like; so long as you are
dead,
I don't mind if they say that you're alive.
TYNDARUS. By Pollux! if you do so,
you'll repent,
When he comes back as I am sure he will.
ARISTOPHONTES. O Heavens! I see it
now! and understand
What it all means. My friend Philocrates
Is free at home, and in his native land.
I'm glad of that; nothing could please me
more.
But I am grieved I've got *him* into trouble,
Who stands here bound because of what
I said.
HEGIO. Did I forbid you to speak falsely
to me?
TYNDARUS. You did, sir.
HEGIO. Then how durst you tell me
lies?
TYNDARUS. Because to tell the truth
would have done hurt
To him I served; he profits by my lie.
HEGIO. But *you* shall smart for it!
TYNDARUS. O that's all right!
I've saved my master and am glad of that,
For I've been his companion from a boy;
His father, my old master, gave me to
him.
D' you now think this a crime?
HEGIO. A very vile one.
TYNDARUS. *I* say it's right; I don't
agree with you.
Consider, if a slave had done as much
For your own son, how grateful you would
be!
Wouldn't you give that slave his liberty?
Wouldn't that slave stand highest in your
favor?
Answer!
HEGIO. Well, yes.

TYNDARUS. Then why be wroth with
me?
HEGIO. Because you were more faithful
to your master
Than e'er to me.
TYNDARUS. What else could you expect?
Do you suppose that in one night and day
You could so train a man just taken cap-
tive,
A fresh newcomer, as to serve you better
Than him with whom he'd lived from
earliest childhood?
HEGIO. Then let him pay you for it.
Take him off,
And fit him with the heaviest, thickest
chains;
Thence to the quarries you shall go right
on.
And whilst the rest are hewing eight
stones each,
You shall each day do half as much again,
Or else be nicknamed the Six-hundred-
striper.
ARISTOPHONTES. By gods and men, I
pray you, Hegio,
Do not destroy him.
HEGIO. I'll take care of him!
For in the stocks all night he shall be
kept,
And quarry stones all day from out the
ground.
O, I'll prolong his torments day by day.
ARISTOPHONTES. Is this your purpose?
HEGIO. Death is not so sure.
Go take him to Hippolytus the smith;
Tell him to rivet heavy fetters on him.
Then cause him to be led out of the city
To Cordalus, my freedman at the quarries,
And tell him that I wish him to be treated
With greater harshness than the worst
slave there.
TYNDARUS. Why should I plead with
you when you're resolved?
The peril of my life is yours as well
When I am dead I have no ill to fear;
And if I live to an extreme old age,
My time of suffering will be but short.
Farewell! though you deserve a different
wish.
Aristophontes, as you've done to me,
So may you prosper; for it is through you

That this has come upon me.
HEGIO. Take him off.
TYNDARUS. But if Philocrates returns
to you,
Give me a chance of seeing him, I pray.
HEGIO. Come, take him from my sight
or I'll destroy you!
TYNDARUS. Nay, this is sheer assault
and battery! [*Exeunt* OVERSEERS *and*
TYNDARUS *to the quarries.*]
HEGIO. There, he has gone to prison as
he merits.
I'll give my other prisoners an example,
That none of them may dare repeat his
crime.
Had it not been for him, who laid it bare,
The rascals would have led me in a string.
Never again will I put trust in man.
Once cheated is enough. Alas! I hoped
That I had saved my son from slavery.
My hope has perished. One of my sons I
lost,
Stolen by a slave when he was four years
old;
Nor have I ever found the slave or him.
The elder's now a captive. What's my
crime,
That I beget my children but to lose
them?
Follow me, you! I'll take you where you
were.
Since no one pities me, I'll pity none.
ARISTOPHONTES. Under good auspices I
left my chain;
But I must take the auspices again.
[*Exeunt* ARISTOPHONTES *and*
HEGIO *to* HEGIO'S *brother's.*]

[*Enter* ERGASILUS *from the harbor.*]
ERGASILUS. Jove supreme, thou dost
protect me and increase my scanty
store,
Blessings lordly and magnific thou bestow-
est more and more;
Both thanks and gain, and sport and jest,
festivity and holidays,
Processions plenty, lots of drink and heaps
of meat and endless praise.
Ne'er again I'll play the beggar, every-
thing I want I've got;
I'm able now to bless my friends, and
send my enemies to pot.

With such joyful joyfulness this joyful
day has loaded me!
Though it hasn't been bequeathed me, I've
come into property!
So now I'll run and find the old man
Hegio. O what a store
Of good I bring to him, as much as ever
he could ask, and more.
I am resolved I'll do just what the slaves
do in a comedy;
I'll throw my cloak around my neck, that
he may hear it first from me.
For this good news I hope to get my board
in perpetuity.

[*Enter* HEGIO *from his brother's.*]
HEGIO. How sad the regrets in my heart
that are kindled,
As I think over all that has happened to
me.
O isn't it shameful the way I've been
swindled,
And yet couldn't see!
As soon as it's known, how they'll laugh
in the city!
When I come to the market they'll show
me no pity,
But chaffing say, "Wily old man up a
tree!"
But is this Ergasilus coming? Bless me!
His cloak's o'er his shoulder. Why, what
can it be?
ERGASILUS. Come, Ergasilus, act, and
act vigorously!
Hereby I denounce and threaten all who
shall obstruct my way;
Any man who dares to do so will have
seen his life's last day.
I will stand him on his head.
HEGIO. 'Fore me the man begins to
spar!
ERGASILUS. I shall do it. Wherefore
let all passers-by stand off afar;
Let none dare to stand conversing in this
street, till I've passed by;
For my fist's my catapult, my arm is my
artillery,
And my shoulder is my ram; who meets
my knee, to earth he goes.
Folk will have to pick their teeth up, if
with me they come to blows.
HEGIO. What's he mean by all this

threatening? I confess I'm puzzled quite.

ERGASILUS. I'll take care they don't forget this day, this place, my mickle might.

He who stops me in my course, will find he's stopped his life as well.

HEGIO. What he's after with these threats and menaces, I cannot tell.

ERGASILUS. I proclaim it first, that none may suffer inadvertently; Stay at home, good people all, and then you won't get hurt by me.

HEGIO. Oh, depend on't, it's a dinner that has stirred his valorous bile.

Woe to that poor wretch whose food has given him this lordly style!

ERGASILUS. First, for those pig-breeding millers, with their fat and bran-fed sows,

Stinking so that one is hardly able to get past the house;

If in any public place I catch their pigs outside their pen,

With my fists I'll hammer out the bran from those same filthy—men!

HEGIO. Here's pot-valour with a vengeance! He's as full as man could wish!

ERGASILUS. Then those fishmongers, who offer to the public stinking fish,

Riding to the market on a jumping, jolting, joggling cob,

Whose foul smell drives to the Forum every loafer in the mob;

With their fish baskets I'll deal them on their face a few smart blows,

Just to let them feel the nuisance that they cause the public nose.

HEGIO. Listen to his proclamations! What a royal style they keep!

ERGASILUS. Then the butchers, who arrange to steal the youngsters from the sheep,

Undertake to kill a lamb, but send you home right tough old mutton;

Nickname ancient ram as yearling, sweet enough for any glutton;

If in any public street or square that ram comes in my view,

I will make them sorry persons—ancient ram and butcher, too!

HEGIO. Bravo! he makes rules as if he were a mayor and corporation.

Surely he's been made the master of the market to our nation.

ERGASILUS. I'm no more a parasite, but kinglier than a king of kings.

Such a stock of belly-timber from the port my message brings.

Let me haste to heap on Hegio this good news of jollity.

Certainly there's no man living who's more fortunate than he.

HEGIO. What's this news of gladness which he gladly hastes on me to pour?

ERGASILUS. Ho! where are you? Who is there? Will some one open me this door?

HEGIO. Ah! the fellow's come to dinner.

ERGASILUS. Open me the door, I say;

Or I'll smash it into matchwood, if there's any more delay.

HEGIO. I'll speak to him. Ergasilus!

ERGASILUS. Who calls my name so lustily?

HEGIO. Pray, look my way!

ERGASILUS. You bid me do what Fortune never did to me! Who is it?

HEGIO. Why, just look at me. It's Hegio!

ERGASILUS. Ye gods! It's he.

Thou best of men, in nick of time we have each other greeted.

HEGIO. You've got a dinner at the port; that makes you so conceited.

ERGASILUS. Give me your hand.

HEGIO. My hand?

ERGASILUS. Your hand, I say, at once!

HEGIO. I give it. There!

ERGASILUS. Now rejoice!

HEGIO. Rejoice! but why?

ERGASILUS. 'T is my command. Begone dull care!

HEGIO. Nay, the sorrows of my household hinder me from feeling joy.

ERGASILUS. Ah, but I will wash you clean from every speck that can annoy.

Venture to rejoice!

HEGIO. All right, though I've no reason to be glad.

ERGASILUS. That's the way. Now order—

HEGIO. What?

ERGASILUS. To have a mighty fire made.

HEGIO. What, a mighty fire?

ERGASILUS. I said so; have it big enough.

HEGIO. What next?

Do you think I'll burn my house down at your asking?

ERGASILUS. Don't be vexed!

Have the pots and pans got ready. Is it to be done or not?

Put the ham and bacon in the oven, have it piping hot.

Send a man to buy the fish—

HEGIO. His eyes are open, but he dreams!

ERGASILUS. And another to buy pork, and lamb, and chickens—

HEGIO. Well, it seems

You could dine well, if you'd money.

ERGASILUS. —Perch and lamprey, if you please,

Pickled mackerel and sting-ray, then an eel and nice soft cheese.

HEGIO. Naming's easy, but for eating you won't find facilities

At my house, Ergasilus.

ERGASILUS. Why, do you think I'm ordering this

For myself?

HEGIO. Don't be deceived; for you'll eat neither much, nor little,

If you've brought no appetite for just your ordinary victual.

ERGASILUS. Nay, I'll make you eager for a feast though I should urge you not.

HEGIO. Me?

ERGASILUS. Yes, you.

HEGIO. Then you shall be my lord.

ERGASILUS. A kind one too, I wot!

Come, am I to make you happy?

HEGIO. Well, I'm not in love with woe.

ERGASILUS. Where's your hand?

HEGIO. There, take it.

ERGASILUS. Heaven's your friend!

HEGIO. But I don't mark it, though.

ERGASILUS. You're not in the *market*, that's why you don't *mark it:* come now, bid

That pure vessels be got ready for the offering, and a kid,

Fat and flourishing, be brought.

HEGIO. What for?

ERGASILUS. To make a sacrifice.

HEGIO. Why, to whom?

ERGASILUS. To me, of course!—I'm Jupiter in human guise!

Yes, to you I am Salvation, Fortune, Light, Delight, and Joy.

It's your business to placate my deity with food, dear boy!

HEGIO. Hunger seems to be your trouble.

ERGASILUS. Well, my hunger isn't yours.

HEGIO. As you say; so I can bear it.

ERGASILUS. Lifelong habit that ensures!

HEGIO. Jupiter and all the gods confound you!

ERGASILUS. Nothing of the sort!

Thanks I merit for re*port*ing such good tidings from the *port.*

Now I'll get a meal to suit me!

HEGIO. Idiot, go! you've come too late.

ERGASILUS. If I'd come before I did, your words would come with greater weight.

Now receive the joyful news I bring you. I have seen your son

Philopolemus in harbor safe; and he'll be here anon.

He was on a public vessel; with him was that Elian youth

And your slave Stalagmus, he who ran away—it's naught but truth—

He who stole your little boy when four years old so cruelly.

HEGIO. Curse you, cease your mocking!

ERGASILUS. So may holy Fulness smile on me,

Hegio, and make me ever worthy of her sacred name,

As I saw him.

HEGIO. Saw my son?

ERGASILUS. Your son, my patron: they're the same.

HEGIO. And the prisoner from Elis?

ERGASILUS. *Oui, parbleu!*

HEGIO. And that vile thief,
Him who stole my younger son, Stalagmus?

ERGASILUS. *Oui, monsieur, par Crieff!*

HEGIO. What, just now?

ERGASILUS. *Par Killiecrankie!*

HEGIO. Has he come?

ERGASILUS. *Oui, par Dundee!*

HEGIO. Are you sure?

ERGASILUS. *Par Auchtermuchtie!*

HEGIO. Certain?

ERGASILUS. *Oui, par Kirkcudbright!*

HEGIO. Why by these barbarian cities
do you swear?

ERGASILUS. Because they're rude,
As you said your dinner was.

HEGIO. That's just like your ingratitude!

ERGASILUS. Ah, I see you won't believe
me though it's simple truth I say.
But what countryman was this Stalagmus, when he went away?

HEGIO. A Sicilian.

ERGASILUS. Well, but he belongs to
*Colo*rado now;
For he's married to a *collar*, and she
squeezes him, I vow!

HEGIO. Tell me, is your story true?

ERGASILUS. It's really true—the very
truth.

HEGIO. O good Heav'ns! if you're not
mocking, I've indeed renewed my
youth.

ERGASILUS. What? Will you continue
doubting when I've pledged my sacred
troth?
As a last resource then, Hegio, if you can't
believe my oath,
Go and see.

HEGIO. Of course I will; go in, prepare
the feast at once;
Everything's at your disposal; you're my
steward for the nonce.

ERGASILUS. If my oracle's a false one,
with a cudgel comb my hide!

HEGIO. You shall have your board forever, if you've truly prophesied.

ERGASILUS. Who will pay?

HEGIO. My son and I.

ERGASILUS. You promise that?

HEGIO. I do indeed.

ERGASILUS. Then I promise you your
son has really come in very deed.

HEGIO. Take the best of everything!

ERGASILUS. May no delay your path
impede! [*Exit* HEGIO *to the harbor.*]

ERGASILUS. He has gone; and put his
kitchen absolutely in my hands!
Heav'ns! how necks and trunks will be
dissevered at my stern commands!
What a ban will fall on bacon, and what
harm on humble ham!
O what labor on the lard, and what calamity on lamb!
Butchers and pork dealers, you shall find
a deal to do to-day!
But to tell of all who deal in food would
cause too long delay.
Now, in virtue of my office, I'll give sentence on the lard,
Help those gammons, hung though uncondemned—a fate for them too hard.
[*Exit* ERGASILUS *into the house.*]
[*Enter a boy from the house of* HEGIO.]

BOY. May Jupiter and all the gods,
Ergasilus, confound you quite,
And all who ask you out to dine, and
every other parasite.
Destruction, ruin, dire distress, have come
upon our family.
I feared that, like a hungry wolf, he'd
make a fierce attack on me.
I cast an anxious look at him, he licked
his lips and glared around;
I shook with dread, by Hercules! he
gnashed his teeth with fearsome
sound.
When he'd got in, he made a raid upon the
meat-safe and the meats;
He seized a knife—from three fat sows he
cut away the dainty teats.
Save those which held at least a peck, he
shattered every pan and pot:
Then issued orders to the cook to get the
copper boiling hot.
He broke the cupboard doors and searched
the secrets of the storeroom's hoard.
So kindly watch him if you can, good
slaves, whilst I go seek my lord.
I'll tell him to lay in fresh stores, if he
wants any for himself,

For as this fellow's carrying on, there'll
soon be nothing on the shelf.
        [*Exit boy to the harbor.*]

[*Enter from the harbor* HEGIO, PHILOPOLE-
MUS, PHILOCRATES, *and* STALAGMUS.]
HEGIO. All praise and thanksgiving to
Jove I would render.
For bringing you back to your father
again;
For proving my staunch and successful
defender,
When, robbed of my son, I was tortured
with pain;
For restoring my runaway slave to my
hands;
For Philocrates' honor; unsullied it
stands.
PHILOPOLEMUS. Grieved I have enough
already, I don't want to grow still
thinner,
And you've told me all your sorrows at
the harbor, pending dinner.
Now to business!
PHILOCRATES. Tell me, Hegio, have I
kept my promises,
And restored your son to freedom?
HEGIO. Yes, you have, Philocrates.
I can never, never thank you for the serv-
ices you've done,
As you merit for the way you've dealt
with me and with my son.
PHILOPOLEMUS. Yes, you can, dear
father, and the gods will give us both
a chance,
Worthily to recompense the source of my
deliverance.
And I'm sure, my dearest father, it will
be a pleasing task.
HEGIO. Say no more. I have no tongue
that can deny you aught you ask.
PHILOCRATES. Then restore to me the
slave whom, as a pledge, I left behind.
He has always served me better than him-
self, with heart and mind.
To reward him for his kindness now shall
be my earnest care.
HEGIO. For your goodness he shall be
restored to you; 't is only fair.
That and aught beside you ask for, you
shall have. But don't, I pray,

Be enraged with me because in wrath I've
punished him to-day.
PHILOCRATES. Ah, what have you done?
HEGIO. I sent him to the quarries bound
with chains,
When I found how I'd been cheated.
PHILOCRATES. Woe is me! he bears
these pains,
Dear good fellow, for my sake, because he
gained me my release.
HEGIO. And on that account you shall
not pay for him a penny piece.
I will set him free for nothing.
PHILOCRATES. Well, by Pollux! Hegio,
That is kind. But send and fetch him
quickly, will you?
HEGIO. Be it so.
[*To a slave*]. Ho, where are you? Run
and quickly bid young Tyndarus re-
turn.
Now, go in; for from this slave, this whip-
ping-block, I fain would learn
What has happened to my younger son,
and if he's living still.
Meanwhile you can take a bath.
PHILOPOLEMUS. Come in, Philocrates.
PHILOCRATES. I will.
        [*Exeunt* PHILOPOLEMUS *and* PHI-
        LOCRATES *into the house.*]
HEGIO. Now stand forth, my worthy
sir, my slave so handsome, good, and
wise!
STALAGMUS. What can you expect from
me, when such a man as *you* tells
lies?
For I never was nor shall be fine or hand-
some, good or true;
If you're building on my goodness, it will
be the worse for you.
HEGIO. Well, it isn't hard for you to
see which way your interest lies;
If you tell the truth, 't will save you from
the harshest penalties.
Speak out, straight and true; although
you've not done right and true, I
guess.
STALAGMUS. Oh, you needn't think I
blush to hear you say what I con-
fess.
HEGIO. I will make you blush, you vil-
lain; for a bath of blood prepare!

STALAGMUS. That will be no novelty! you threaten one who's oft been there!
But no more of that; just tell me what you want to ask of me. Perhaps you'll get it.
HEGIO. You're too fluent; kindly speak with brevity.
STALAGMUS. As you please.
HEGIO. Ah, from a boy he was a supple, flattering knave.
But to business! Pray attend to me, and tell me what I crave.
If you speak the truth, you'll find your interest 't will best subserve.
STALAGMUS. Don't tell me! D' you think that I don't know full well what I deserve?
HEGIO. But you may escape a part if not the whole of your desert.
STALAGMUS. Oh, it's little I'll escape! and much will happen to my hurt:
For I ran away and stole your son from you, and him I sold.
HEGIO. Oh, to whom?
STALAGMUS. To Theodoromedes of the house of Gold.
For ten pounds.
HEGIO. Good Heav'ns! Why, that's the father of Philocrates.
STALAGMUS. Yes, I know that quite as well as you do—better, if you please.
HEGIO. Jupiter in Heaven, save me, and preserve my darling son!
On your soul, Philocrates, come out! I want you. Make haste, run!

[Enter PHILOCRATES from the house.]
PHILOCRATES. Hegio, I am at your service.
HEGIO. This man says he sold my son
To your father there in Elis for ten pounds.
PHILOCRATES. When was this done?
STALAGMUS. Twenty years ago.
PHILOCRATES. O, nonsense! Hegio, he's telling lies.
STALAGMUS. Either you or I am lying; for when you were little boys,
He was given you by your father to be trained along with you.
PHILOCRATES. Well, then, tell me what

his name was, if this tale of yours is true.
STALAGMUS. Pægnium at first; in after time you called him Tyndarus.
PHILOCRATES. How it is that I don't know you?
STALAGMUS. Men are oft oblivious,
And forget the names of those from whom they've nothing to expect.
PHILOCRATES. This child you sold my father, if your story is correct,
Was bestowed on me as valet. Who was he?
STALAGMUS. My master's son.
HEGIO. Is he living, fellow?
STALAGMUS. Nay, I got the money; then I'd done.
HEGIO. What say you?
PHILOCRATES. That Tyndarus is your lost son! I give you joy!
So at least this fellow's statements make me think; for he's the boy
Who received his education with myself all through our youth.
HEGIO. Well, I'm fortunate and wretched all at once, if you speak truth;
Wretched that I treated him so cruelly, if he's my son;
Oh, alas! I did both more and less than what I should have done!
How I'm vexed that I chastised him! Would that I could alter it!
See, he comes! and in a fashion that is anything but fit.

[Enter TYNDARUS from the quarries.]
TYNDARUS. Well, I've often seen in pictures all the torments of the damned;
But I'm certain that you couldn't find a hell that's stuffed and crammed
With such tortures as those quarries. There they've got a perfect cure
For all weariness; you simply drive it off by working more.
When I got there, just as wealthy fathers oft will give their boys
Starlings, goslings, quills to play with in the place of other toys,
So when I got there, a crow was given me as plaything pretty!
Ah, my lord is at the door; and my old lord from Elis city

Has returned!

HEGIO. O hail, my long lost son!

TYNDARUS. What means this talk of "sons"?

Oh, I see why you pretend to be my father; yes, for once
You have acted like a parent, for you've brought me to the light.

PHILOCRATES. Hail, good Tyndarus!

TYNDARUS. All hail! for you I'm in this pretty plight.

PHILOCRATES. Ah! but now you shall be free and wealthy; for you must be told,

Hegio's your father. That slave stole you hence when four years old;
And then sold you to my father for ten pounds, who gave you me,
When we both were little fellows, that my valet you might be.
This man whom we brought from Elis has most certain proofs supplied.

TYNDARUS. What, am I his son?

PHILOCRATES. You are; your brother too you'll find inside.

TYNDARUS. Then you have brought back with you his son who was a prisoner?

PHILOCRATES. Yes, and he is in the house.

TYNDARUS. You've done right well and nobly, sir.

PHILOCRATES. Now you have a father; here's the thief who stole you when a boy.

TYNDARUS. Now that I'm grown up, he'll find that theft will bring him little joy.

PHILOCRATES. He deserves your vengeance.

TYNDARUS. Oh, I'll have him paid for what he's done.
Tell me though, are you my father really?

HEGIO. Yes, I am, my son.

TYNDARUS. Now at length it dawns upon me, and I seem, when I reflect,
Yes, I seem to call to mind and somewhat vaguely recollect,
As if looking through a mist, my father's name was Hegio.

HEGIO. I am he!

PHILOCRATES. Then strike the fetters off your son and let him go!
And attach them to this villain.

HEGIO. Certainly, it shall be so.
Let's go in, and let the smith be summoned to strike off your chains,
And to put them on this fellow.

STALAGMUS. Right! For they're my only gains.

EPILOGUE. Gentlemen, this play's been written on the lines of modesty;
Here are found no wiles of women, no gay lovers' gallantry;
Here are no affiliations, and no tricks for getting gold;
No young lover buys his mistress whilst his father is cajoled.
It's not often nowadays that plays are written of this kind,
In which good folk are made better. Now then, if it be your mind,
And we've pleased you and not bored you, kindly undertake our cause,
And to modesty award the prize with heartiest applause.

PHORMIO

By TERENCE

(Publius Terentius Afer)

Produced at Rome, 161 B.C.

ANONYMOUS TRANSLATION, PUBLISHED AT LONDON, 1734

CHARACTERS

Chremes, } *brothers*
Demipho, }
Phædria, Chremes's *son*
Antipho, Demipho's *son*
Phormio, *a parasite*
Dorio, *a bawd*
Geta, Demipho's *servant*
Davus, *a crony of* Geta's
Hegio, }
Cratinus, } *lawyers*
Crito, }
Nausistrata, Chremes's *wife*
Sophrona, *a nurse*

Scene—*Athens*

PROLOGUE

Since the old bard can not provoke our
   poet
To leave the muse, and sit hereafter idle,
He new invectives now prepares, in hopes
To terrify him that he'll write no more:
His former plays, maliciously he crys,
Are lightly scribled, and the style is poor:
This he reports, because our poet never
Brought on the stage a frantic youth that
   saw
A hind in flight, and by the hounds pur-
   sued,
Her case lamenting, and imploring aid:
But was he conscious that his play's suc-
   cess
Was thro the actor's merit, not his own,

121

He wou'd not, as he now offends, offend,
And then his plays wou'd meet with
　greater favour.
If any now shall say, or can suppose,
That, had not the old poet first provok'd
The young one to abuse him in return,
This had not known what prologues to
　have wrote,
Our poet answers thus; the prize to all
The servants of the muses is propos'd.
He strove to drive our poet from his
　studies,
And to subject him to the hand of need:
This strives to answer him, not to pro-
　voke:
Had his contention been in gentle words,
He, in return, had gently been reprov'd:
But let him think that, which he brought,
　repay'd:
Henceforward I shall cease to speak of
　him,
Since he continues to expose himself.
　Now kindly to my humble suit attend:
I here present to ye a play that's new;
This comedy *Phormio* the Latins call,
And *Epidicazomenos* the Greeks:
Phormio 'tis call'd from the chief char-
　acter,
The parasite, who shall the bus'ness guide,
If in the poet's favour ye're inclin'd.
　Silent attend with an impartial ear,
That the same fortune now we may not
　meet,
Which we before had, when our company
Was by the tumult from their places
　drove;
Which, by the actor's excellence, have
　since,
Assisted by your goodness, been restor'd.

ACT I

SCENE I

DAVUS.　My good friend and country-
man Geta came to me yesterday: I had
a little money of his in my hands on an
old account; which he desir'd me to make
up; I have made it up, and am carrying
it to him. I hear that his master's son is
marry'd; I believe this is scrap'd together
for a present to his bride. How unjust it

is, that they who have but little shou'd
be always adding something to the wealth
of the rich! All that this poor fellow has
sav'd, by little and little, out of his wages,
cheating his belly at the same time for't,
must go at once to her, who does not think
with what difficulty 'twas got: besides
Geta will be struck for another sum when
his mistress is brought to bed, and for
another when the son's birthday comes
about next year, at which time he'll be
initiated: all this goes to the mother, tho
the boy's the pretence: but is n't that
Geta I see?

SCENE II

[GETA *and* DAVUS.]

GETA. If a red-hair'd man shou'd en-
quire for me——
DAVUS. Say no more, he's at your
elbow.
GETA. O! Davus, I was just coming
to you.
DAVUS. Here, take it; 'tis all good;
there's exactly what I owe you. [*He gives
the money to* GETA.]
GETA. I love you, and thank you for
not neglecting me.
DAVUS. Especially as times go now;
things are come to such a pass, that if a
man pays what he owes, his creditor's to
say he's much oblig'd to him: but why are
you melancholly?
GETA. I? You do n't know what tribu-
lation and danger I'm in.
DAVUS. What's the matter?
GETA. I'll tell you, if you can be secret.
DAVUS. Away, you fool: are you afraid
to trust him with words that you've found
faithful in money? What interest have I
in betraying you?
GETA. Well, hear me.
DAVUS. I'm attentive.
GETA. Do you know Chremes, Davus,
our old man's elder brother?
DAVUS. Know him? Yes.
GETA. Do you? And his son Phædria?
DAVUS. As well as I know you.
GETA. The old men both took a jour-
ney at one time, he that I've been speak-
ing of to Lemnos, our old gentleman to

Cilicia to an old acquaintance there: this same acquaintance tempted our old man over by letters, promising him mountains of gold, and what not?

DAVUS. To one so rich, and who has more than he knows what to do with?

GETA. Hold your tongue: 'tis his temper.

DAVUS. O! If I was what I ought to be, I shou'd be a king.

GETA. When the old men went from hence, they both left me as governor over their sons.

DAVUS. O! Geta, 'tis a hard task you've taken on yourself.

GETA. That I know by experience: I am sure my genius was angry, or I had not been left with such a charge. I began at first to oppose 'em: in short, while I was faithful to the old men, my shoulders smarted: I consider'd, that 'tis folly to kick against the pricks: I then devoted myself entirely to my young masters, and did ev'ry thing they'd have me.

DAVUS. You knew how to make you market.

GETA. Our spark did not fly into any mischief at first; but Phædria was not long before he got his music-girl; and he became desperately fond of her; she was in the hands of a sordid rascal of a cockbawd; and their fathers had taken care that they shou'd not have it in their pow'r to give anything: in the meanwhile he cou'd do nothing with her but feed his eyes, and dangle after her, and lead her to school and back again. We at our leisure gave Phædria our attendance: over against the school where this girl was educated was a barber's shop: there we usually waited till she came from school to go home: as we were sitting there, a young man came crying to us: we were surpris'd: we ask'd him what's the matter: "Poverty," says he, "never seem'd to me so sad and heavy a burden as it did just now. I have just seen a poor unhappy maid in the neighbourhood here, lamenting over her departed mother: she was plac'd just against her, without any kind friend, acquaintance, or relation, excepting one old woman, to assist her in the funeral: it griev'd my heart, to see such beauty in distress!" In short, he mov'd us all: then says Antipho immediately, "Shall we go and see her?" "Yes," says one, "let us go—pray shew us the way." We walk on, we come to the place, we behold her: fair she was indeed, and the more so, because she had no help from art to her beauty: loose was her hair, and bare her feet, she was dirty, ill dress'd, and all in tears, so that, had there not been a native force of beauty in her charms, they had been extinguish'd here. The spark that lov'd the music-girl only say'd, "She's pretty enough," but our——

DAVUS. I easily guess: he was wounded.

GETA. But can you guess how deeply? Observe the consequence. The next day he goes directly to the old woman; he intreats her to let him possess the girl: she refuses, and tells him 'tis unjust to do it, that she's a citizen of Athens, of a good character, and good parentage, if he has a mind to marry her, that he may lawfully do; he had a strong inclination to marry her, but was afraid of his father who's abroad.

DAVUS. Wou'd not his father give him leave, if he was come home?

GETA. He give him leave to marry a wench of no birth or fortune? Never.

DAVUS. What's come of it at last?

GETA. What's come of it? There's a certain parasite, one Phormio, a fellow of an undaunted assurance, who, the devil take him for it——

DAVUS. What has he done?

GETA. ——Gave him the following counsel: "'Tis a law," says he, "that young women, who are orphans, shall be marry'd to their nearest relations, and this same law obliges the men to marry them: I'll say you are her kinsman, and I'll be your prosecutor: I'll pretend to be her father's friend: we'll bring it before the judges: who her father was, who her mother, and how she's related to you, leave to my management, I'll have all ready, to carry it to my own advantage and in favor of me: when you disprove none of these articles, I shall gain my cause. Your father will come home: he'll have a pull with me: what then? We shall secure our woman."

DAVUS. A humourous piece of impudence!

GETA. He prevail'd on the young man: they set about it: they come into court: he marry'd her.

DAVUS. What's that you say?

GETA. 'Tis just as I tell you.

DAVUS. O! Geta, what will become of you?

GETA. I can't tell, by Hercules: this I know, whatever fortune lays upon me, I'll bear it patiently.

DAVUS. I'm glad to hear you say so: 'tis what we all ought to do.

GETA. All my hope is in myself.

DAVUS. I commend you.

GETA. Suppose I get one to intercede for me, this perhaps will be his speech—— "pray forgive him now, but if he does so again, I'll not speak a word for him." 'Tis well if he do n't add, "when I'm gone, e'en hang him."

DAVUS. What of the music-girl's hero? What exploit has he in hand?

GETA. Nothing worth speaking of.

DAVUS. Perhaps he has it not in his pow'r to give much.

GETA. He can give nothing but hope.

DAVUS. Is his father come home, or not?

GETA. Not yet.

DAVUS. Well, when d' y' expect your old man?

GETA. I do n't know certainly; but I hear'd just now that there's a letter come from him, and left at the port: I'll go for it.

DAVUS. Have you any more to say to me, Geta?

GETA. Nothing, but that I wish you well. [DAVUS goes.] Here boy. Will nobody come out? [A boy comes.] Take this, and give it to Dorcius.

[He gives the money to the boy and goes.]

SCENE III

[ANTIPHO and PHÆDRIA.]

ANTIPHO. That it shou'd come to this, Phædria, that I shou'd be afraid of my father when I do but think of his return, of a father who wishes me so well! Had I not been an inconsiderate fool, I might have expected him as I ought.

PHÆDRIA. What's the matter?

ANTIPHO. Is that a question for you to ask, who was my confidant in so bold an enterprise? O! that it had never enter'd into Phormio's head to persuade me to it, and that he had not drove me in my fit of love on what has prov'd the source of my misfortunes! If I had not obtain'd her, then I shou'd have been uneasy some few days; but I shou'd have escap'd this perplexity of mind, which ev'ry day torments me——

PHÆDRIA. I hear you.

ANTIPHO. ——While I'm ev'ry moment in expectation of his return, who will force me from the arms of my belov'd.

PHÆDRIA. 'Tis a grievance to some that they can't have what they love; satiety's the root of your complaint. Antipho, you're too rich in love; for such, by Hercules, is your situation, 'tis worth our warmest wishes and endeavours. By heav'n, cou'd I possess my love so long, I'd purchase it with death, nor think it dear: do but consider, what I endure amidst my present want, and what you gather from your plenteous store; not to mention your good fortune, in having gain'd, according to your will, an honest wellbred wife, whose character has never yet been stain'd: you're a happy man, if you had but this one thing, a mind to bear your fortune as you ought; you'd feel how 'tis, if you had to do with such a cock-bawd as I have: but 'tis in the nature of us all to murmur at our own condition.

ANTIPHO. But, on the contrary, Phædria, you are the fortunate man in my eye now; in whom is lodg'd the pow'r without constraint of consulting what pleases you best, to keep her, love her, or to leave her: I'm unhappily fall'n into such a strait, that I have no right to turn her off, nor pow'r to keep her:——but what's here? Is n't that Geta that comes running hither? 'Tis he himself: I'm afraid, lest he shou'd bring some news now that wo' n't please me.

SCENE IV

[GETA, ANTIPHO, and PHÆDRIA.]

GETA [*to himself, not seeing them*]. Thou'rt undone, Geta, unless thy invention can relieve thee soon, so many sudden misfortunes hang over thy head now when thou'rt ill prepar'd for 'em; which I know neither how to ward against, nor to get myself out of; for the boldness of our proceedings can't be a secret long; which, if not cunningly guarded against, will fall heavily on me or my master.

ANTIPHO. What's the meaning of his confusion here? [*To* PHÆDRIA.]

GETA. Then I've scarcely a minute to turn myself about in, my master's so near. [*To himself.*]

ANTIPHO. What mischief's forwards?

GETA. Which when he shall hear of, how shall I oppose his anger? Suppose I pretend to speak? I shall enrage him: what, if I say nothing? I shall provoke him: how if I attempt to clear myself? 'Twill be labour in vain. Alas! what an unhappy fellow I am! While I tremble for myself, I am as much on the rack for Antipho; I am concern'd for him; I fear on his account; 'tis he that detains me; for, was it not for him, I shou'd have taken care enough of myself, and have been reveng'd on the old man's anger; I shou'd have scrap'd up something for my journey, and have march'd off directly. [*To himself, not seeing them.*]

ANTIPHO. What journey is he making, or what is he scraping up? [*To* PHÆDRIA.]

GETA. But where shall I find Antipho? Or where shall I look for him? [*To himself, not seeing them.*]

PHÆDRIA. He names you. [*To* ANTIPHO.]

ANTIPHO. I'm afraid he's the messenger of some very ill news, tho I do n't know what. [*To* PHÆDRIA.]

PHÆDRIA. Ah! Have you loss'd your senses? [*To* ANTIPHO.]

GETA. I'll make the best of my way homewards: 'tis most likely he's there. [*To himself, not seeing them.*]

PHÆDRIA. Let's call the fellow back. [*To* ANTIPHO.]

ANTIPHO. Stop, you, immediately. [*To* GETA.]

GETA. Huy, huy! You speak with authority, whoever you are. [*Hearing, but not seeing him.*]

ANTIPHO. Geta. [*Aloud.*]

GETA. 'Tis the very person I wanted to meet. [*Seeing him.*]

ANTIPHO. Pray let us know what you're so full of; and tell us in a word, if you can. [*To* GETA.]

GETA. So I will.

ANTIPHO. Out with it.

GETA. There's now put into port——

ANTIPHO. Who, my father?

GETA. You're right.

ANTIPHO. I'm ruin'd.

PHÆDRIA. Pshaw!

ANTIPHO. What shall I do?

PHÆDRIA. What say you? [*To* GETA.]

GETA. That I saw his father your uncle.

ANTIPHO. Alas! what remedy shall I find now to this sudden evil? If such my fortune, my dear Phany, that I must be torn from you, let me part with life and you together.

GETA. Therefore as the affair stands, Antipho, you have the more need to look sharp about you: fortune helps the brave.

ANTIPHO. I'm quite confounded.

GETA. But now you've most occasion to exert yourself, Antipho; for if your father perceives you to be afraid, he'll conclude you're in fault.

PHÆDRIA. That's true.

ANTIPHO. I can't change my nature.

GETA. What wou'd you do if you had now a more difficult affair on your hands?

ANTIPHO. Since I can't go thro this, I shou'd be less able to bear that.

GETA. Here's nothing in this, Phædria;

let him go. Why do we labour in vain here? I'll be gone.

PHÆDRIA. So will I.

ANTIPHO. Pray now, suppose I put on a countenance, will it do?

GETA. You do but trifle.

ANTIPHO. Look in my face: hum! Will this do?

GETA. No.

ANTIPHO. What say you to this?

GETA. That will almost do.

ANTIPHO. What to this?

GETA. That will do: ay, keep that; and answer him word for word, and give him as good as he brings; and don't let him bluster you out of countenance in his passion.

ANTIPHO. Very well.

GETA. Say you was forc'd, against your will, by the law, and decree of the court: do you understand me? But what old man's that, which I see at the farther end of the street?

ANTIPHO. 'Tis he himself: I can't stand my ground.

GETA. Ah! what are you doing? Where are you going, Antipho? Stay I say.

ANTIPHO. I know myself and my offence: I leave my Phany and my life to your care. [ANTIPHO goes.]

SCENE V

[PHÆDRIA and GETA.]

PHÆDRIA. What's to be done now, Geta?

GETA. You'll have a chiding now; but hanging will be my lot, if I'm not mistaking: but what we just now here advis'd Antipho to do, we must do ourselves, Phædria.

PHÆDRIA. Leave out must; and command me what to do.

GETA. Do you remember what you say'd, at the beginning of this enterprise, as a defence necessary to be made, that their cause was just, plain, binding, and the fairest that could be?

PHÆDRIA. I remember.

GETA. Ah! now we have need of it in-

deed, or, if we cou'd have it, a better, and more subtle one.

PHÆDRIA. I'll take care about it.

GETA. Now go you up to him first: I'll lie ready to relieve you, if you shall happen to want auxiliaries.

PHÆDRIA. Come on.

SCENE VI

[DEMIPHO, GETA, and PHÆDRIA.]

DEMIPHO. Is it so, is Antipho marry'd without my consent? Shou'd not my authority—but I wave authority—shou'd not he have fear'd my displeasure at least? Is he not asham'd? Audacious act! O! Geta, thou tutor!
　　　　　[To himself, not seeing them.]

GETA. He's out at last.
　　　　　[Aside to PHÆDRIA.]

DEMIPHO. I wonder what they'll say to me, or what excuse they'll find.
　　　　　[To himself, not seeing them.]

GETA. I've found one already: look you for another.　　[Aside to PHÆDRIA.]

DEMIPHO. Will he excuse himself by saying, "I did it against my will, the law compell'd me?" I hear him, and allow it to be so.　[To himself, not seeing them.]

GETA. Well say'd.　　　　[Aside.]

DEMIPHO. But knowingly, without speaking a word, to give up his cause to his adversaries! Did the law compel him to that too?
　　　　　[To himself, not seeing them.]

PHÆDRIA. That strikes home.
　　　　　[Aside to GETA.]

GETA. I'll find an excuse for that: leave it to me:　[Aside to PHÆDRIA.]

DEMIPHO. I know not what to do, because this has happen'd beyond my expectation or belief: I'm so provok'd, that I am scarcely capable of thinking: ev'ry one therefore, in the heighth of his prosperity, should then think within himself how he cou'd bear adversity; let him always, as he returns home, consider thus, I may meet with dangers, losses, a disobedient son, a dead wife, or a sick daughter, and these are misfortunes common to all men, there's nothing new or strange in either of them, therefore whatever happens beyond his expectation he should account as gain.

[*To himself, not seeing them.*]

GETA. O! Phædria, 'tis scarcely to be believ'd how much wiser I am than my master: I have consider'd of all the inconveniences which can happen to me, if my master shou'd return, I concluded that I should be condemn'd to perpetual imprisonment to grind there, to be well drubbed, to be fettered, or sentenced to work in the fields; neither of which wou'd be new or strange to me; therefore whatever happens beyond my expectation I shall account as gain: but why do n't you go up to the old gentleman, and speak him fair? [*Aside to* PHÆDRIA.]

DEMIPHO. There's Phædria my brother's son, I see, coming this way. [*To himself.*]

PHÆDRIA. Uncle, your servant.

DEMIPHO. Your servant: but where's Antipho?

PHÆDRIA. I'm glad to see you safe return'd.

DEMIPHO. I believe you: but give me an answer to what I ask.

PHÆDRIA. He's very well; and he's not far off; but are all things as you'd have 'em?

DEMIPHO. I wish they were.

PHÆDRIA. What's the matter?

DEMIPHO. Do you ask, Phædria? Ye 've patch'd up a fine marriage here in my absence.

PHÆDRIA. O, what, are you angry with him for that?

GETA. He manages him dextrously!

[*To himself.*]

DEMIPHO. Ought I not to be angry with him? I wish he'd come into my presence, that he may see now how he has provok'd a good-natured father by his offence.

PHÆDRIA. But he has done nothing, uncle, to merit your displeasure.

DEMIPHO. See how they hang together; they're all alike; know one, you know all.

PHÆDRIA. Indeed you mistake us.

DEMIPHO. Let one commit a fault, and the other's ready to defend him; if one's

here, the other's not far off; so they help one another.

GETA. The old man has spoke the truth of them without knowing it.

[*To himself.*]

DEMIPHO. For if it was not so, you wou'd not stand up for him, Phædria.

PHÆDRIA. Uncle, if Antipho had been so much his own enemy as to have been guilty of any fault, contrary to his interest or honour, I would not open my lips in his behalf, but give him over to what he might deserve; but supposing any one, by his malicious stratagems, has lay'd a snare for us youth, and has caught us in it, are we to be blam'd or the judges, who often thro envy take from the rich, and as often thro pity add to the poor?

GETA. If I did not know the affair, I shou'd believe what he's saying to be true.

[*Aside.*]

DEMIPHO. How should any judge know your right, when you don't speak a word for yourself, as he did not?

PHÆDRIA. He behav'd like a gentleman; when he came before the judges, he was unable to utter what he had premeditated, his modesty and fear so confounded him.

GETA. Well defended: but why don't I go directly up to the old man? [*To himself.*] Your servant, Sir: I'm glad to see you safe return'd.

DEMIPHO. Oh! thou excellent guardian, your servant, thou prop of our family, to whose care I committed my son when I went from hence.

GETA. I hear you have been accusing us all undeservedly, and me most undeservedly of all; for what wou'd you have me do for you in this affair? The laws don't allow a servant to plead, nor is his evidence taken.

DEMIPHO. Well, be it so: grant besides that the young man was foolishly fearful, I allow it, you're but a servant; however, if she was ever so near related, there was no occasion for him to marry her; but, as the law requires, you shou'd have giv'n her a portion; and she might look out for another husband: what reason had he to take a beggar home?

GETA. We did not want reason, but money.

DEMIPHO. He shou'd have borrow'd it anywhere.

GETA. Anywhere? Nothing more easily said.

DEMIPHO. If he cou'd not borrow it on other terms, he shou'd have took it up on interest.

GETA. Huy! that's well said: as if any one would lend him money, while you are alive.

DEMIPHO. No, no, it must not be so, it never can: shall I suffer her to live with him one day? There's no temptation for it. I wish that fellow was brought before me, or that I knew where he lives.

GETA. You mean Phormio.

DEMIPHO. The woman's friend.

GETA. I'll bring him here presently.

DEMIPHO. Where's Antipho now?

GETA. Within.

DEMIPHO. Go, Phædria, look for him, and bring him hither.

PHÆDRIA. I'll go directly.

GETA. Yes to Pamphila. [*Aside.*]

[PHÆDRIA *and* GETA *go.*]

SCENE VII

[DEMIPHO.]

I'll go home and thank the Gods for my return; then I'll go to the market, and summons some of my friends to be present in this affair, that I may not be unprovided if Phormio comes.

ACT II

SCENE I

[PHORMIO *and* GETA.]

PHORMIO. Say you so, is he gone, and afraid to shew his face to his father?

GETA. 'Tis even so.

PHORMIO. And is Phanium left to herself, say you?

GETA. Neither better nor worse.

PHORMIO. And is the old man in a rage?

GETA. Yes, and in a great one.

PHORMIO. The burden, Phormio, must lie on your shoulders: you've a hard crust to mumble; you must down with it: set about it.

GETA. Pray do.

PHORMIO. Suppose he should question me about——

GETA. Our hope is in you.

PHORMIO. Ay, but consider, what if he replies?

GETA. You forced us.

PHORMIO. Well, I think that's right.

GETA. Come, give us your assistance.

PHORMIO. Let the old man come; I'll warrant you I am provided for him.

GETA. What do you intend?

PHORMIO. What, but secure Phanium's marriage, and free Antipho from what he's accused of, and take all the old man's anger on myself?

GETA. You've a stout heart of your own, and we are much oblig'd to you: but I'm very much afraid, Phormio, lest you draw the string till it breaks at last.

PHORMIO. Ah! there's no danger of that; I'm experienc'd in those things; I tread sure. How many men d' y' think I have worried to death, strangers and citizens? The oftener I've try'd, the more my hand's in. Tell me how, did you ever hear of an action of battery against me?

GETA. How have you escap'd?

PHORMIO. Because the net is never spread for such birds as the hawk or the kite, which are mischievous to us, but for such as do us no harm; because these are precious morsels, the other are not worth the labour: so they who have anything to lose are most in danger; they know I've nothing: but they'll commit you to prison, say you; to which I answer they do not chuse to maintain such a devouring fellow as I am; and, in my opinion, they'll shew their wisdom, in not doing me so good an office in return for a bad one.

GETA. He can never thank you enough for your favour.

PHORMIO. O! nobody can thank a prince

enough for his royal favour. Is it not pleasant for you to come at free cost, anointed, and fresh from the bath, with an easy mind, while another has the trouble and expense? While you have what you chuse, he's fretting himself, you laugh, drink the first cup, and take the first place, when the dubious entertainment is serv'd up.

GETA. Dubious, why dubious?

PHORMIO. Because you're doubtful what to eat of most:—when you consider how delicious and dear these things are, does not the master of the feast appear a very God to you?

GETA. Here comes the old man: be on your guard: the first onset's the fiercest; if you sustain that, you may wind him about as you will afterwards.

SCENE II

[DEMIPHO, GETA, PHORMIO, HEGIO, CRATINUS, *and* CRITO.]

DEMIPHO. Did ye ever hear of any one being more injuriously used than I am in this? Pray assist me.
[*To the Advocates.*]

GETA. He's in a passion.
[*Aside to* PHORMIO.]

PHORMIO. Do you but mind your cue; I'll rouse him presently. [*Aside to* GETA.] —Good Gods! does Demipho deny that Phanium's related to him? Does Demipho deny it? [*Aloud to* GETA.]

GETA. He does deny it. [*Aloud.*]

DEMIPHO. This is he, I think, that I've to do with. Keep close to me.
[*To the Advocates.*]

PHORMIO. And that he does not know who her father was? [*Aloud to* GETA.]

GETA. He denies it. [*Aloud.*]

PHORMIO. Nor who Stilpho was?
[*Aloud to* GETA.]

GETA. He knows nothing of him.
[*Aloud.*]

PHORMIO. Because she was left destitute, poor girl, her father's not known, and she's slighted: see, what avarice can make some people do! [*Aloud to* GETA.]

GETA. If you reflect upon my master for avarice, I'll give you your own.
[*Aloud to* PHORMIO.]

DEMIPHO. The impudence of the fellow! Does he come on purpose to accuse me? [*Aside to the Advocates.*]

PHORMIO. There's no reason to be angry with the young man, if he had no great knowledge of him; for the poor man was old, and liv'd by his labour, almost confining himself to the country: where he farm'd a piece of ground of my father: the old man has often told me that this kinsman of his slighted his; but what a man did he slight? The best 'man that I ever saw in my life. [*Aloud to* GETA.]

GETA. See that you say no more than you can prove of yourself and him.
[*Aloud to* PHORMIO.]

PHORMIO. Go hang yourself; if I did not think as well of him as I report him, I'd never get such ill will to our family as I do for her sake that he so ungenerously slights now. [*Aloud to* GETA.]

GETA. Do you still abuse my master in his absence, you villain?
[*Aloud to* PHORMIO.]

PHORMIO. 'Tis no more than he deserves. [*Aloud to* GETA.]

GETA. Say you so, you jailbird?
[*Aloud to* PHORMIO.]

DEMIPHO. Geta.

GETA. You're an invader of other people's rights, a perverter of the laws.
[*Aloud to* PHORMIO, *pretending not to hear* DEMIPHO.]

DEMIPHO. Geta.

PHORMIO. Answer him.
[*Aside to* GETA.]

GETA. Who's that? O! is't you, Sir?

DEMIPHO. Do n't talk to him.

GETA. He has been abusing you behind your back, without ceasing, in such a manner as you don't deserve, though he does.

DEMIPHO. Well, say no more. [*To* GETA.] ——First, young man, if you'll vouchsafe me an answer, I desire to know, with your good leave, who that friend of yours was, and how he claim'd relation to me. [*To* PHORMIO.]

PHORMIO. So you examine me, as if you did not know.

DEMIPHO. I know?

PHORMIO. Yes.

DEMIPHO. I deny it; you, who affirm it, rub up my memory.

PHORMIO. Huy, huy, as if you did not know your first cousin!

DEMIPHO. You kill me: tell me his name.

PHORMIO. His name?

DEMIPHO. To be sure. Why don't you tell it?

PHORMIO. I'm ruin'd, by Hercules, I've forgot his name. [*Aside.*]

DEMIPHO. Ha, what's that you say?

PHORMIO. Geta, if you remember the name I told you just now, tell it me. [*Aside to* GETA.]—I'll not tell you, as if you did not know! You come to try me. [*To* DEMIPHO.]

DEMIPHO. I try you?

GETA. Stilpho. [*Aside to* PHORMIO.]

PHORMIO. What is't to me? 'Tis Stilpho.

DEMIPHO. What's his name, say you?

PHORMIO. Stilpho, I say, you knew him.

DEMIPHO. I knew no such person, nor was any of that name related to me.

PHORMIO. Can you say so? Are n't you asham'd of this? But if he had left an estate of ten talents——

DEMIPHO. The Gods confound you.

PHORMIO. ——You'd have been the first to have trac'd your family from generation to generation.

DEMIPHO. It may be so; then, if I had gone about it, I could have told how she was related to me: now do you the same: tell me how she's my relation.

GETA. Well said, master. [*To* DEMIPHO.]—You, Sir, take care of yourself. [*To* PHORMIO.]

PHORMIO. I made it appear plain enough, where I ought, before the judges: if it was false, why did not your son then refute it?

DEMIPHO. What tell you me of my son, whose folly can't be sufficiently expressed?

PHORMIO. But do you, who are so very wise, make your appearance in court, and get the same cause tried over again, since you are sovereign here, and you only can obtain a second decree in the same cause.

DEMIPHO. Though I'm much injured, yet, rather than follow lawsuits, or hear you prate, I'll give you fifteen guineas with her, which is the portion that is requir'd by law supposing she was my relation.

PHORMIO. Ha, ha, ha, a pretty sort of a man.

DEMIPHO. What's the matter? Is there anything unreasonable in what I propose? Can't I obtain this, which is common justice?

PHORMIO. Is it come to that, pray, does the law require, after you have used a citizen like a whore, that you should pay her and turn her off? Is it not otherwise, is it not requir'd, to prevent her from bringing shame on herself through poverty, that she should be married to her next relation, that she may have to do only with him, which you are against?

DEMIPHO. Yes, to her next relation; but what have we to do with that? Why must we be concerned?

PHORMIO. O, O, 'tis all over, as they say, you can't try it again.

DEMIPHO. I'll not try it again: yet I'll not drop it till I have gone thro with it.

PHORMIO. Words, words.

DEMIPHO. See if I don't make 'em good.

PHORMIO. In short, Demipho, I've nothing to do with you; 'tis your son that's cast, not you; for you are a little too old for a young bride.

DEMIPHO. Imagine that 'tis he that says all which I now say to you, or I'll thrust him and his wife out of doors.

GETA. He's nettled. [*Aside to* PHORMIO.]

PHORMIO. You'll think better on't.

DEMIPHO. Are you so provided to do all you can against me, you unlucky knave?

PHORMIO. He's afraid of us, though he endeavours so earnestly to conceal it. [*Aside to* GETA.]

GETA. You have begun successfully. [*Aside to* PHORMIO.]

PHORMIO. Why don't you bear what can't be avoided like a man? 'Twill be more to your advantage, if you end it amicably with us.

DEMIPHO. Amicably with you? Why shou'd I see you, or hear your impertinence?

PHORMIO. If you and she can agree, you'll have a comfort to your old age: have some regard to your years.

DEMIPHO. Do you take her for a comfort.

PHORMIO. Be not in such a passion.

DEMIPHO. Observe me: we have had words enough; unless you take the wench away quickly, I'll turn her out: I have said it, Phormio.

PHORMIO. If you offer to handle her otherwise than becomes a gentlewoman, I'll bring a heavy action against you: I have said it, Demipho. [*Aloud to* DEMIPHO.]—If you want me, you'll find me at home. [*Aside to* GETA.]

GETA. I understand you.
[PHORMIO *goes.*]

SCENE III

[DEMIPHO, GETA, HEGIO, CRATINUS, *and* CRITO.]

DEMIPHO. What care and anxiety my son brings upon me, by intangling himself and me in this marriage! and he does not come near me, that I may know at least what he has to say for himself, or what his sentiments are now.—Go you, and see if he isn't come home yet. [*To* GETA.]

GETA. I will. [GETA *goes.*]

SCENE IV

[DEMIPHO, HEGIO, CRATINUS, *and* CRITO.]

DEMIPHO. Ye see how this affair stands: what must I do? Your opinion, Hegio.

HEGIO. Whose, mine? Let Cratinus speak first, if you think fit.

DEMIPHO. Your opinion, Cratinus.

CRATINUS. Mine?

DEMIPHO. Yes.

CRATINUS. I'd have you do what is most to your interest in this affair: I

think that what your son did in your absence ought in justice and equity to be made void; and that's what you'll obtain: I've given my opinion.

DEMIPHO. Now, Hegio, your opinion.

HEGIO. I believe he has spoke his best; but so it is, so many men so many minds; ev'ry one has his way: I think what the law has done can't be revoked; and 'tis scandalous to attempt it.

DEMIPHO. Crito, your opinion.

CRITO. I think it requires more time to consider of it: 'tis a weighty affair.

HEGIO. Do you want any more with us?

DEMIPHO. Ye 've done enough: [*The Advocates go.*]—I am now more at a loss than I was before.

SCENE V

[GETA *and* DEMIPHO.]

GETA. He's not come home, they say.

DEMIPHO. I wait for my brother, whose advice I'll follow in this affair: I'll go and enquire at the waterside, to learn what tidings I can of him.
[DEMIPHO *goes.*]

GETA. And I'll look out for Antipho, that I may inform him of what's done here: but here he comes just as I want him.

SCENE VI

[ANTIPHO *and* GETA.]

ANTIPHO. Indeed, Antipho, your want of courage is much to be blamed; could you go away, and leave your life and safety in the hands of other persons? Did you believe other people would be more careful of your affairs than yourself? However other things went, you ought certainly to consider her that you left at home, and not let her suffer any harm, and be deceived through her confidence in you, whose hope, poor creature, and all whose interest, now depend on you alone.
[*To himself, not seeing* GETA.]

GETA. And indeed, master, we did not spare you in your absence for going from us.

ANTIPHO. I was looking for you.

GETA. But we were never the more negligent for that.

ANTIPHO. Pray tell me how my interests and my fortunes stand: has my father any suspicion?

GETA. Not yet.

ANTIPHO. Is there any hope left?

GETA. I don't know.

ANTIPHO. How!

GETA. But Phædria did all he could for you.

ANTIPHO. There's nothing new in that.

GETA. Then Phormio has been as hearty and as active in this as in other affairs.

ANTIPHO. What has he done?

GETA. He was too hard for the old gentleman as angry as he was.

ANTIPHO. O! brave Phormio.

GETA. I did what I could too.

ANTIPHO. My Geta, I love ye all.

GETA. The first conference was as I tell you: the affair's in a good situation at present; and your father now waits for your uncle's arrival, before he proceeds any farther.

ANTIPHO. What does he wait for him for?

GETA. He said that he'd be directed by his advice in this affair.

ANTIPHO. How I dread my uncle's return now, Geta! For by his sentence only, as you tell me, I must live or die.

GETA. Here comes Phædria.

ANTIPHO. Where?

GETA. See, he's coming from his usual place of exercise.

SCENE VII

[PHÆDRIA, DORIO, ANTIPHO, and GETA.]

PHÆDRIA. Prithee hear me, Dorio.
          [Not seeing ANTIPHO and GETA.]

DORIO. Not I.

PHÆDRIA. A little.

DORIO. Don't trouble me.

PHÆDRIA. Hear what I have to say.

DORIO. But 'tis tiresome to hear the same a thousand times over and over.

PHÆDRIA. But you'll be pleas'd with what I'm going to say now.

DORIO. Well, let's hear.

PHÆDRIA. Can't I prevail on you to stay three days longer? Where are you going?

DORIO. I should wonder if you had offered anything new to me.

ANTIPHO. The bawd, I fear, is drawing an old house over his head.
          [Aside to GETA.]

GETA. I fear so too.
          [Aside to ANTIPHO.]

PHÆDRIA. You do not believe me.

DORIO. There you're right.

PHÆDRIA. Upon my credit.

DORIO. Mere flams.

PHÆDRIA. You'll have no reason to repent, you'll confess so afterwards.

DORIO. Words, words.

PHÆDRIA. Believe me, you'll be glad of it; 'tis true, by Hercules.

DORIO. 'Tis all a dream.

PHÆDRIA. Do but try, 'tis not long.

DORIO. The same story over again.

PHÆDRIA. I'll acknowledge you for a kinsman, a father, a friend, a——

DORIO. 'Tis all but talk.

PHÆDRIA. That you can be so hardened and inexorable, to be moved neither by pity nor entreaty!

DORIO. That you can be so inconsiderate and ignorant, Phædria, to think by your fine speeches to wheedle me out of what's my own for nothing!

ANTIPHO. I pity him. [Aside to GETA.]

PHÆDRIA. Ah! what he says is too true.   [To himself.]

GETA. How they both keep to their characters!   [Aside to ANTIPHO.]

PHÆDRIA. When Antipho is in full possession of his love, that I should have this plague!

ANTIPHO. Ah! Phædria, what's the matter?

PHÆDRIA. O! fortunate Antipho!

ANTIPHO. I fortunate?

PHÆDRIA. Yes, in having what you love at home, and in not having to do with such a villain as this.

ANTIPHO. What I love at home? Yes, as the saying is, I have a wolf by the ears; for I know not how to let her go, nor how to keep her.

DORIO. That's my case with this spark.

ANTIPHO. O! brave bawd, don't depart from your character. [*To the bawd.*]— What has he done at last?

[*To* PHÆDRIA.]

PHÆDRIA. Done? Like an inhuman fellow, he has sold my Pamphila.

GETA. What? Sold her?

ANTIPHO. Sold her, say you?

PHÆDRIA. He has sold her.

DORIO. A horrid crime, to sell a wench that I paid for!

PHÆDRIA. I can't persuade him to break off with the other, and stay three days, till I get the money which my friends promis'd: [*To* ANTIPHO.]——if I don't give it you then, don't stay an hour longer. [*To the bawd.*]

DORIO. You stun me.

ANTIPHO. 'Tis but a little time that he requires, Dorio: be prevail'd upon: he'll make it doubly up to you, and you'll deserve it.

DORIO. These are but words.

ANTIPHO. Will you endure that Pamphila should be carried from this town? [*To* PHÆDRIA.]——Can you be so hardhearted as to tear these lovers from one another? [*To the bawd.*]

DORIO. 'Tis neither I, nor you, that do it.

GETA. May the Gods deny you nothing that you deserve.

DORIO. I have, contrary to my disposition, indulged you many months, you've promised, and whimpered, but never performed anything; now I have found one that proceeds in quite a different strain, who can pay without sniveling; give place to your betters.

ANTIPHO. Certainly, if I remember rightly, there was a day fixed formerly, in which you was to let him have her. [*To the bawd.*]

PHÆDRIA. There was so.

DORIO. Do I deny it?

ANTIPHO. Is that day pass'd?

DORIO. No, but this is come before it.

ANTIPHO. Aren't you ashamed of your roguery?

DORIO. Not when 'tis to my advantage.

GETA. Dirty rascal!

PHÆDRIA. Dorio, d'y' think you do as you ought?

DORIO. 'Tis my custom, if you like me, use me.

ANTIPHO. Do you impose upon him thus?

DORIO. Rather, Antipho, he imposes upon me; for he knew me to be such a person; I thought him another sort of a man; he has deceived me; I am just the same with him that I always was: but yet, however the affair stands, I'll do this; the captain promised to bring me the money early to-morrow; if you bring it before he does, Phædria, I'll keep up my custom, and prefer the first comer: so adieu.

[DORIO *goes.*]

SCENE VIII

[PHÆDRIA, ANTIPHO, *and* GETA.]

PHÆDRIA. What shall I do? How shall I now, that am not worth a straw, raise the money for him so suddenly? If he could but have been prevailed upon to stay three days, I was promised it then.

ANTIPHO. Shall we forsake him, Geta, in his distress, that, according to your own report, assisted me so friendly just now? Rather let us try to return the favor, now there's occasion.

GETA. I know it is but just that we should.

ANTIPHO. Set about it therefore, you are the only man that can save him.

GETA. What can I do?

ANTIPHO. Raise the money.

GETA. With all my heart; but tell me how.

ANTIPHO. My father's at hand.

GETA. I know that; but what then?

ANTIPHO. Pshaw, a word to the wise is enough.

GETA. Say you so?

ANTIPHO. Yes.

GETA. Very fine advice, by Hercules! Why don't you go about it? Shan't I have reason to triumph, if I escape on the account of your marriage, but you must now insist on my bringing one misfortune on the back of another over my head, for his sake too?

ANTIPHO. What he says is true.

PHÆDRIA. What? Do you look upon me as a stranger, Geta?

GETA. By no means; but is it of no consideration, now we have enraged the old man against us all, whether we provoke him so that no room can be left for entreaty?

PHÆDRIA. Shall another man bear her from my eyes to an unknown land? Alas! Speak to me, Antipho, and consider me, while you may, and while I'm with ye.

ANTIPHO. Why? What are you about now? Tell me.

PHÆDRIA. Whatever part of the world she's carried to, I'm resolved to follow her, or to perish.

GETA. Good luck go with you; yet I'd advise you not to be in a hurry.

ANTIPHO. See if you can assist him, do.

GETA. Assist him? How?

ANTIPHO. Pray try, lest he should do more or less, Geta, than we'd wish, and which we shou'd be sorry for afterwards.

GETA. I'm trying.—— He's secure, I believe; but I'm afraid that I shall suffer for't.

ANTIPHO. Don't be afraid: we'll share your fortune with you, be it good or bad.

GETA. How much money d'y' want? Tell me. [*To* PHÆDRIA.]

PHÆDRIA. But little more than ninety guineas.

GETA. Ninety guineas? Ah! she's very dear, Phædria.

PHÆDRIA. She's very cheap at that price.

GETA. Well, well, I'll get 'em.

PHÆDRIA. There's a good fellow! [*Hugging* GETA.]

GETA. Let me go, hands off.

PHÆDRIA. I want the money now.

GETA. You shall have it presently; but I must have Phormio's assistance.

ANTIPHO. He's ready; lay what burden on him you will, and he'll bear it: he's of all men truest to his friend.

GETA. Therefore let us hasten to him.

ANTIPHO. Have ye any farther occasion for me?

GETA. No; but go home, and comfort that poor creature, who is now, I know, quite dispirited with fear. Why d'y' stay?

ANTIPHO. There's nothing that I can do with so good a will.

PHÆDRIA. How do you propose doing that?

GETA. I'll tell you as we go; but make haste from hence.

ACT III

SCENE I

[DEMIPHO *and* CHREMES.]

DEMIPHO. Why, what did you go to Lemnos for, Chremes? Have you brought your daughter with you?

CHREMES. No.

DEMIPHO. How so?

CHREMES. Her mother, seeing that I stayed here longer than ordinary, and that the girl was of an age that required a husband, is reported to have come here with all her family in search of me.

DEMIPHO. Pray what detained you so long there then, after you had heard it?

CHREMES. A disease.

DEMIPHO. How did you get it? Or what was it?

CHREMES. There's a question! Old age itself is a disease: but the captain who brought them over told me that they arrived safe.

DEMIPHO. Have you heard what has happened to my son in my absence, Chremes?

CHREMES. 'Tis that which now makes me uncertain what to do; for if I should marry her to a stranger, I must tell him how she's my daughter, and who's her mother: I know that you wish me as well as I do myself; but if one who was no relation before should marry her, he'll be silent as long as there's a good understanding betwixt us; but if he begins to have no value for me, I shall wish he did not know so much of me: and I'm afraid it should come to my wife's knowledge; and should it, I've nothing to do but to brush off, and leave my house; for I'm the only friend I have at home.

DEMIPHO. I know it; and that's what troubles me; nor will I desist, till I have performed all that I've promised you.

SCENE II

[GETA, CHREMES, and DEMIPHO.]

GETA [to himself, not seeing CHREMES and DEMIPHO]. Surely there never was a cunninger fellow than Phormio: I went to him, to inform him that money must be had, and how it might be got: he understood me before I had spoke half what I had to say: he rejoiced, commended me, enquired after the old man, and thanked the Gods that he had an opportunity to shew himself as much Phædria's friend as Antipho's: I bade him wait for me at the market, where I would bring the old man to him: but here he is: who is that behind him? Egad, 'tis Phædria's father: but why, like a beast, should I be afraid? Because I have two in my power now to choose instead of one? 'Tis better, I think, to have two strings to a bow: I'll set upon him that I first proposed; if I get it from him, 'tis well; if I make nothing of him, then I must attack this newcomer.

SCENE III

[ANTIPHO, GETA, CHREMES, and DEMIPHO.]

ANTIPHO. I expect Geta here:—but surely that's my uncle standing with my father there: Death! I'm in pain to know what effect his arrival will have on my father in my affair! [To himself.]

GETA. I'll go up to 'em: [To himself.] —welcome home, Master Chremes.

CHREMES. How is't, Geta?

GETA. I'm glad to see you safe returned.

CHREMES. I believe you.

GETA. How go affairs?

CHREMES. I meet with many alterations here, according to custom.

GETA. True: have you heard what has happened to Antipho?

CHREMES. Yes, all.

GETA. Have you informed him. [To DEMIPHO.]—What a shameful thing 'tis, Chremes, to be so imposed upon!

DEMIPHO. That's what I was talking to him about now.

GETA. By Hercules, as I was thinking seriously of it with myself, I believe I found a remedy to this evil.

CHREMES. What is it, Geta?

DEMIPHO. What remedy?

GETA. As I went from you, I happened to meet Phormio.

CHREMES. Who, Phormio?

GETA. The same that took the young woman's part.

CHREMES. I know whom you mean.

GETA. I thought it proper to pump him first. I take him aside: "Phormio," quoth I, "why don't we see and make an end of this business by fair means rather than by foul? My master's a generous man, and hates strife; I can assure you that all his friends have unanimously advised him to turn her out."

ANTIPHO. What is the fellow about, or what will this come to at last?
[To himself.]

GETA. Do you think he's in any danger from the laws, if he should turn her out? He has had counsel about that; pshaw, you'll have enough to do, if you go to law with him, he does not want words: but suppose you should cast him, he won't lose his life, a little money will bring him off." When I perceived that what I had said had took down his courage, "We are now alone here, continued I; hark y', what would you expect down to drop this suit, to have her sent back, and to let us be no more troubled with you?—"

ANTIPHO. Is the devil in him?
[To himself.]

GETA. "—I very well know, if you should make a proposal any way just and reasonable, that he's so good a man, you will not have three words to a bargain."

DEMIPHO. By what authority did you say so?

CHREMES. He could not bring about what we want better.

ANTIPHO. I'm ruined! [*To himself.*]

CHREMES. Go on.

GETA. At first the fellow raved.

DEMIPHO. Why, what does he ask?

GETA. Ask? Too much.

CHREMES. Tell what he demands.

GETA. He talked of no less than a great talent.

DEMIPHO. Hang the rascal: isn't he ashamed?

GETA. I said as much to him. What, continued I, could he do more, if he was going to portion out an only daughter of his own? At that rate he has not gain'd much by not bringing one up, if another is found that he must give a fortune to: to be short, and passing over his impertinences, this was his final answer; I would, says he, at first have marry'd my friend's daughter, as 'twas reasonable I should; for I considered what inconveniences she would be subjected to, poor creature, by marrying into a rich family to be made a slave of: but, to be plain with you now, I wanted one that could bring in something to pay the little that I owe; therefore now, if Demipho will give as much with her, as I am to have with this that I'm engag'd to, I don't know one in the world that I would sooner choose for a wife than her.

ANTIPHO. I can't tell whether 'tis folly or malice that makes him talk thus, whether he does it designedly or not. [*To himself.*]

DEMIPHO. What is't to us if he owes his soul to any one?

GETA. He mortgaged a piece of ground, he says, for thirty guineas.

DEMIPHO. Well, well, let him marry her; I'll give him as much.

GETA. And a house for thirty more.

DEMIPHO. Huy, huy! that's too much.

CHREMES. Silence: you shall have these thirty from me.

GETA. A maid must be bought for his wife; then some more furniture is wanted; and the expense of the wedding is to be defrayed: these, says he, will require thirty more.

DEMIPHO. I'll sooner bear six hundred actions against me; I'll give nothing; shall I make myself a laughingstock to the rogue?

CHREMES. Pray be quiet, I'll pay the money; only do you prevail on your son to marry the woman we'd have him.

ANTIPHO. Ah! Geta, thou hast ruined me by thy treachery. [*To himself.*]

CHREMES. 'Tis on my account she's turned off; 'tis but just therefore that I should defray the expense.

GETA. Let me know as soon as you can, says he, that if they think fit to let me marry her, I may rid myself of the other, and not remain in an uncertainty; for they've appointed to pay me the fortune directly.

CHREMES. He shall have the money immediately; let him break off with the other, and marry this.

DEMIPHO. And ill luck go with him.

CHREMES. I have very seasonably brought money with me now, the rents of my wife's farms at Lemnos; I'll make use of part of that; and I'll tell my wife that you wanted it.

[CHREMES *and* DEMIPHO *go.*]

SCENE IV

[ANTIPHO *and* GETA.]

ANTIPHO. Geta.

GETA. Ha!

ANTIPHO. What have you done?

GETA. I have cleanly chus'd the old men of the money.

ANTIPHO. Is that sufficient?

GETA. That I can't tell, but I've done no more than I was ordered.

ANTIPHO. I'll drub you; won't you answer me to the purpose?

GETA. What d'y' mean?

ANTIPHO. What can I mean? You might as well have giv'n me a halter as have done what you have. Heav'n and hell confound you for an example to such rascals! If any one wants to be brought out of a calm into a storm, I'd recommend him to you. What could you have done worse than have touched on this sore, or named my wife? You have giv'n my father hopes of his being able to turn her away. Prithee tell me now, if Phormio accepts the portion, he must marry her, what must be done then?

GETA. But he'll not marry her.

ANTIPHO. I grant it: but when they demand the money of him back, our cause will be much the better I suppose.

GETA. There's nothing, Antipho, but may be spoiled in the telling: the good you omit here; but you mention the bad: now hear me; if he takes the money, he must marry her, as you say; I admit it; but there must be a little time allow'd to prepare for the wedding, to invite friends, and to sacrifice: in the meanwhile the other will get the money which his friends promised him, and he may return it out of that.

ANTIPHO. How can that be? Or what excuse will he make?

GETA. Would you know? What strange prodigies, he may say, have happened to me since the agreement! A strange black dog came into my house, a snake fell off the tiles through the spout into my yard, my hen crowed, the soothsayer warned me, the fortune-teller forbad me to enter on any new business before winter; there can't be better excuses: these will do.

ANTIPHO. Would they may.

GETA. They will; depend on me. Your father's coming. Go, tell Phædria he shall have the money.   [ANTIPHO goes.]

SCENE V

[DEMIPHO, GETA, and CHREMES.]

DEMIPHO. Be easy, I say; I'll take care that he sha' n't impose upon us: I'll never part with this rashly, but I'll have witnesses present, when I give it; and I'll have a memorandum taken of the occasion of my giving it.

GETA. How wary he is, where there is no reason!   [To himself.]

CHREMES. 'Tis necessary you should do so; and make haste, while he is in this same humor; for if that other woman insists on the contract, he may leave us perhaps in the lurch.

GETA. Well thought of.

DEMIPHO. Therefore show me to him.

GETA. As soon as you will.

CHREMES. When you have done this, go to my wife, that she may talk to her before she goes away: let her tell her that, to prevent any resentment on her side, we have agreed to marry her to Phormio, he being a proper match for her, being more intimate with her, that we have done our duty, having consented to give him as large a portion as he desired.

DEMIPHO. What have you to do with that?

CHREMES. A great deal, Demipho.

DEMIPHO. Is it not enough for you to do your duty, without being publicly applauded for it?

CHREMES. I'd have her consent to what we do, that she mayn't say we force her away.

DEMIPHO. I can manage that myself.

CHREMES. Not so well as one woman can with another.

DEMIPHO. I'll ask your wife to do it.

CHREMES. I am considering where I shall find those women now. [To himself.]
    [They go.]

ACT IV

SCENE I

[SOPHRONA and CHREMES.]

SOPHRONA. What shall I do? Where shall I find a friend in my distress? Or to whom can I relate my tale? Or where apply for aid? I'm afraid my mistress will suffer undeservedly for following my advice, I hear the young gentleman's father is so enraged at what is done.
    [To herself, not seeing CHREMES.]

CHREMES. What old woman's this, that comes panting from my brother's?
    [To himself.]

SOPHRONA. Necessity compelled me to what I did (though I knew the match was not good), that I might contrive how to preserve her from want.

[*To herself, not seeing* CHREMES.]

CHREMES. Certainly, if I don't mistake, or if I'm not blind, that's my daughter's nurse I see there. [*To himself.*]

SOPHRONA. And her father——

[*To herself, not seeing* CHREMES.]

CHREMES. What's to done?

[*To himself.*]

SOPHRONA. ——is not to be found:——

[*To herself, not seeing* CHREMES.]

CHREMES. Shall I go to her, or wait and hear what more she has to say?

[*To himself.*]

SOPHRONA. ——but if I can find him now, I shall not have any occasion to fear.

[*To herself, not seeing* CHREMES.]

CHREMES. 'Tis she: I'll speak to her.

[*To himself.*]

SOPHRONA. Whose voice is that?

[*To herself, hearing* CHREMES.]

CHREMES. Sophrona.

SOPHRONA. And he names me!

[*To herself.*]

CHREMES. Look this way.

SOPHRONA. Good Gods, is not this Stilpho? [*Aloud.*]

CHREMES. No.

SOPHRONA. Do you deny your name?

CHREMES. Pray come a little this way from that door, Sophrona: and don't call me by that name any more.

SOPHRONA. How? Are not you the person you always said you was?

CHREMES. St.

SOPHRONA. Why are you afraid of this door?

CHREMES. I have a shrew of a wife shut up here: therefore I gave myself that wrong name formerly, lest any of ye should unadvisedly blab out my right name, and be the occasion of my wife's knowing the affair.

SOPHRONA. That's the reason we poor wretches could never find you out here.

CHREMES. Hark y', tell me what business you have with that family from whence you came now? And where are your mistresses?

SOPHRONA. Alas! alas!

CHREMES. Ah! What's the matter? Are they alive?

SOPHRONA. Your daughter is: but her poor mother died with grief.

CHREMES. O! sad!

SOPHRONA. I, who am a forsaken, poor, ignorant, old woman, did all I could to marry your daughter to the young gentleman of this house.

CHREMES. To whom? To Antipho?

SOPHRONA. To the very same I assure you.

CHREMES. What? Has he two wives?

SOPHRONA. No, I beseech you; he has none but her.

CHREMES. What's the other that they said was his kinswoman?

SOPHRONA. This is she.

CHREMES. What say you?

SOPHRONA. 'Twas done with a design, that, as he was in love with her, he might marry her without a portion.

CHREMES. Good Gods, how things often happen accidentally which we have not courage to wish for! I have found, upon my arrival, my daughter married to the person I would have had her married to, and all as I could have wished: what we both took the greatest pains to bring about, this old woman has alone accomplished by her own great care, without any help from us.

SOPHRONA. Consider now what is necessary to be done: here comes the young gentleman's father; and they say he's very angry at this marriage.

CHREMES. There's no danger: but in the names of Heaven and Earth, don't let any one know she's mine.

SOPHRONA. Nobody shall know from me.

CHREMES. Follow me: you shall hear the rest within. [*They go.*]

SCENE II

[DEMIPHO *and* GETA.]

DEMIPHO. 'Tis our own fault that people get by being dishonest, while we study to be thought over punctual and generous: never run into extremes, as the saying is:

PHORMIO

was it not enough to bear his imposition, but we must give him more than was expected, to put it in his power to support himself, till he can contrive some other mischief?

GETA. You're very right.

DEMIPHO. They are rewarded now, who turn right into wrong.

GETA. 'Tis too true.

DEMIPHO. How foolishly we managed the affair with him!

GETA. If he performs his agreement, and marries her, 'tis well enough.

DEMIPHO. Is that to be doubted?

GETA. Considering what sort of a man he is, I don't know, by Hercules, but he may change his mind.

DEMIPHO. How! change his mind?

GETA. I don't know; but, if it should be so, I say.

DEMIPHO. I'll follow my brother's advice; I'll bring his wife hither to talk with her: go you, Geta, and give her notice of her coming. [DEMIPHO *goes.*]

SCENE III

[GETA.]

The money's procured for Phædria; and no words are made about it: and care's taken that she mayn't stir from hence at present: what more now? What's to be done? You're as deep in the mire as before, you'll pay all with interest, Geta, you only put off a beating to another day, you'll have the more lashes, if you don't look about you: now I'll go home, and instruct Phanium, that she mayn't be afraid of marrying Phormio, nor frighted at what Nausistrata will say to her.

[*He goes.*]

SCENE IV

[DEMIPHO *and* NAUSISTRATA.]

DEMIPHO. Come, Nausistrata, use some of your art now; and manage her so that she may do as we would have her, and at the same time let it be with her own consent.

NAUSISTRATA. I'll do my best.

DEMIPHO. Assist me now with your labour, as you've done before with your money.

NAUSISTRATA. 'Tis in my inclination; but 'tis less in my power than it ought to be, through my husband's mismanagement.

DEMIPHO. How so?

NAUSISTRATA. Because the estate which came by my father is very ill looked after; he made two talents a year with ease of those farms: ah! what a difference there is betwixt man and man!

DEMIPHO. Two talents, say you?

NAUSISTRATA. Yes, two talents, and in much worse seasons.

DEMIPHO. Indeed!

NAUSISTRATA. What, does this seem strange?

DEMIPHO. Yes, truly.

NAUSISTRATA. I wish I'd been born a man, I'd show him——

DEMIPHO. That you would.

NAUSISTRATA. ——How——

DEMIPHO. Don't heat yourself, that you may be able to engage the young woman, and she mayn't run you down.

NAUSISTRATA. I'll do as you direct me: but my husband, I see, is coming from your house.

SCENE V

[CHREMES, DEMIPHO, *and* NAUSISTRATA.]

CHREMES. O! Demipho, has he had the money yet?

DEMIPHO. I paid it him directly.

CHREMES. I wish you had not. [*To* DEMIPHO.]—Ah! here's my wife: I'd almost blabbed too much. [*Aside.*]

DEMIPHO. Why d'y' wish I had not, Chremes?

CHREMES. 'Tis very well.

DEMIPHO. What have you done? Have you told her the occasion of your wife's coming to her?

CHREMES. I went through it.

DEMIPHO. What says she to it?

CHREMES. She can't go.

DEMIPHO. How can't?

CHREMES. Because their affection is mutual.

DEMIPHO. What have we to do with that?

CHREMES. A great deal: besides, I've discovered her to be related to us.

DEMIPHO. What, are you mad?

CHREMES. So it is; I don't speak without foundation; I have recollected myself.

DEMIPHO. Are you in your senses?

NAUSISTRATA. Ah! pray see you don't injure a kinswoman.

DEMIPHO. She's no kinswoman.

CHREMES. Don't deny her; her father went by another name, 'tis that breeds this mistake in you.

DEMIPHO. Did not she know her father?

CHREMES. Yes, yes.

DEMIPHO. Why did he go by another name?

CHREMES. Will you never yield to what I say, nor understand me?
[Aside to DEMIPHO.]

DEMIPHO. I don't know what you talk of; how should I understand you?

CHREMES. You ruin all.
[Aside to DEMIPHO.]

NAUSISTRATA. I wonder what's the meaning of all this.

DEMIPHO. By Hercules, I don't know.

CHREMES. Shall I tell you? As I hope to be saved, she has not a nearer relation in the world than you and I are.

DEMIPHO. Good Gods! Let us all go together to her; I'll know whether 'tis so or not.

CHREMES. Ah!

DEMIPHO. What's the matter?

CHREMES. Is my credit so little with you?

DEMIPHO. Would you have me take what you've said for granted? Would you have me seek no farther into it? Well, be it so: but consider, what's to be done with our friend's daughter?

CHREMES. She'll do very well.

DEMIPHO. Must we dismiss her at last?

CHREMES. Why not?

DEMIPHO. And let her stay that is here?

CHREMES. Yes.

DEMIPHO. Then you may go home again, Nausistrata.

NAUSISTRATA. By Pollux, I think your last resolution best, that she should stay here; for she seemed, when I saw her, to be very much of a gentlewoman.
[NAUSISTRATA goes.]

SCENE VI

[DEMIPHO and CHREMES.]

DEMIPHO. What is this business?

CHREMES. Has she shut the door yet?

DEMIPHO. Yes.

CHREMES. O! Jupiter! the Gods are certainly our friends; 'tis my daughter, I find, that is married to your son.

DEMIPHO. Ah! how came that to pass?

CHREMES. 'Tis not safe to tell you here.

DEMIPHO. Go in then.

CHREMES. Hark y', I would not have our sons know of this.
[They go.]

ACT V

SCENE I

[ANTIPHO.]

ANTIPHO. I am glad, however my own affairs go, that my brother's succeed to his desire. How prudent it is for a man to entertain such appetites as he may easily satisfy when things run cross! As soon as he received the money, he rid himself of his care; but I can find no remedy to my troubles; for if this business continues a secret, I shall be in fear, and, if 'tis discovered, I shall be disgraced: and I should have no heart to go home now, unless I'd some hope of keeping her: but where can I find Geta, that I may consult him about a proper time to meet my father?

SCENE II

[PHORMIO and ANTIPHO.]

PHORMIO. I've received the money, given it to the bawd, brought away the woman, and put Phædria in possession of her; for she's no longer a slave: now one thing still remains, which I must bring about, that is to get leave of the old men to go and tipple a little; for I'm resolved to enjoy myself these few days.

[*To himself, not seeing* ANTIPHO.]

ANTIPHO. But here's Phormio: [*To himself.*] ——Well, what say you?

PHORMIO. Of what?

ANTIPHO. What's Phædria about now? How does he propose to have his fill of love?

PHORMIO. He's going, in his turn, to act your part.

ANTIPHO. What part?

PHORMIO. To avoid his father: he entreats you again to appear for him, and plead his cause; for he's going to take a glass at my house. I'll tell the old men that I'm going to Sunium to the fair, to buy a girl that Geta spoke of a little while ago, lest, when they miss me here, they should believe that I'm consuming their money: but your door creaks.

ANTIPHO. See who's coming out.

PHORMIO. 'Tis Geta.

SCENE III

[GETA, ANTIPHO, *and* PHORMIO.]

GETA. O! fortune! O! propitious fortune, what unexpected favors have you this day heap'd on my Master Antipho!

[*To himself, not seeing them.*]

ANTIPHO. What is he talking of to himself? [*To* PHORMIO.]

GETA. And how have you freed us his friends from fear! But this is no time to loiter, I should throw my cloak cross my shoulder, and run to find him, that I may tell him what has happened.

[*To himself, not seeing them.*]

ANTIPHO. Do you understand what he says? [*To* PHORMIO.]

PHORMIO. Do you?

ANTIPHO. Not a word.

PHORMIO. Nor I.

GETA. I'll go directly to the bawd's; they are there now.

[*To himself, not seeing them.*]

ANTIPHO. Soho, Geta.

GETA. See there! Is there anything wonderful or new in being called back, when a man's going forwards?

[*Hearing, but not seeing, him.*]

ANTIPHO. Geta.

GETA. Again? By Hercules, you may bawl as long as you will, but you shall never bring me back.

[*Hearing, but not seeing, him.*]

ANTIPHO. Won't you stay?

GETA. Go on and be drubbed.

[*Hearing, but not seeing, him.*]

ANTIPHO. That's what you shall be soon, if you don't stay, you Bridewell-cur.

GETA. This should be one that's very well acquainted with me, he is so free with his threats: but is it he that I'm in search of, or not?—The very man.

[*Aside.*]

PHORMIO. Go up to him immediately.

[*To* ANTIPHO.]

ANTIPHO. Well, how go our affairs?

[*To* GETA.]

GETA. O! 'tis impossible there can be a more fortunate man living than yourself, for, without dispute, you're the only favorite of Heaven, Antipho.

ANTIPHO. I should be glad of that; but I wish you would give me some reason to believe it.

GETA. Is it not sufficient if I plunge you all over in joy?

ANTIPHO. You kill me.

PHORMIO. Don't keep us in suspence, but out with what you have to tell.

GETA. Oh! are you here too, Phormio?

PHORMIO. Yes; but why are you so tedious?

GETA. Well, I'll tell you. As soon as we gave you the money at the marketplace, we went directly home; [*To* PHORMIO.]—then my master sends me to your wife. [*To* ANTIPHO.]

ANTIPHO. For what?

GETA. I'll omit that; because it signifys nothing to this affair, Antipho. As I was going to her apartment, her boy Mida runs to me; he takes hold on my cloak behind, and pulls me back; I turn my head, and ask him why he stops me; there are orders, says he, that nobody should go in to my mistress; Sophrona, continues he, carried our old gentleman's brother, Chremes, in just now, and he's with 'em there at this time; as soon as I heard this, I crept on tiptoe softly to the door; I went to it, and there I stood; I held my breath, put my ear close to the door, and fixed myself in this manner to hear.

ANTIPHO. Well done, Geta.

GETA. There I heard the finest story, that made me almost cry out for joy, by Hercules.

ANTIPHO. What was it?

GETA. What d'y' think?

ANTIPHO. I don't know.

GETA. The most surprising! Your uncle is discovered to be your wife's, your Phany's, father.

ANTIPHO. How! What say you?

GETA. He had formerly a private correspondence with her mother at Lemnos.

PHORMIO. He dreams: how could she be ignorant of her own father?

GETA. Depend upon it Phormio, there's some reason for it: but do you imagine that I, who was without, could understand all that was doing among themselves within?

ANTIPHO. By Hercules, I've heard the same too.

GETA. I'll give you farther reasons to believe it: in the meanwhile your uncle goes out; and not long after he returns with your father and goes in with him; and they both said you're at liberty to keep your wife: at last I was sent to find you and bring you thither.

ANTIPHO. Carry me to them immediately: why d'y' loiter?

GETA. I'll go with you.

ANTIPHO. Adieu, my Phormio.

PHORMIO. Antipho, adieu: 'tis very lucky, as I hope for happiness.

[ANTIPHO and GETA go.]

SCENE IV

[PHORMIO.]

PHORMIO. I'm rejoiced at the good fortune that has happened to them so unexpectedly. Here's a fine occasion offered to me now to choose the old men, and to rid Phædria of the care that he's under for money, that he mayn't lay himself under an obligation to any of his friends for it; for this same money, however 'tis given, will be given with an ill will to him: I have found out a way how I shall surely get it. I must now put on a new face, and a new behavior: but I'll retire into the next alley; and when they come out, I'll shew myself to 'em. I shall not go to the fair as I pretended I should.

SCENE V

[DEMIPHO, PHORMIO, and CHREMES.]

DEMIPHO. The Gods deserve my thanks, and they have 'em, since these things have proved so fortunate to us, brother. Let us find Phormio as soon as we can, that we may get our ninety pieces from him before he has consumed 'em.

[To CHREMES, not seeing PHORMIO.]

PHORMIO. I'll go and see if Demipho's at home, that I may——

[To himself, pretending not to see them.]

DEMIPHO. We were coming to you, Phormio.

PHORMIO. On this same affair perhaps.

DEMIPHO. On the very same, by Hercules.

PHORMIO. So I thought: but why did you give yourselves the trouble? What a jest that is! Are ye afraid that I should not be so good as my word? Notwithstanding I'm so very poor, I have hitherto taken care of one thing, I've preserved my credit.

CHREMES. Isn't she a genteel girl?

[To DEMIPHO.]

DEMIPHO. Indeed she is.

PHORMIO. Therefore I was coming to ye, Demipho, to tell ye I'm ready: I'll marry her when ye will; for I've laid aside all other business, as I ought, since I saw ye were so earnest for my having her.

DEMIPHO. But my brother here has advised me not to let you have her: "For what will the people say, if you should do so," says he? "When you could have disposed of her before with honor, then you neglected it; it would be base now to make a widow of her, and turn her out." He made all the same objections which you did to me before.

PHORMIO. You insult me at your pleasure.

DEMIPHO. How so?

PHORMIO. Is that a question? Because I can't marry the other now; for with what face can I go back to her that I've cast off?

CHREMES. Besides, I see that Antipho's unwilling to part with her, say.

[Aside to DEMIPHO.]

DEMIPHO. Besides I see that my son is unwilling to part with her: therefore go to the market, Phormio, and order that money to be paid me back.

PHORMIO. How can that be, when I've paid it to my creditors?

DEMIPHO. What's to be done now?

[Aside to CHREMES.]

PHORMIO. If you'll give me the wife you promised, I'll marry her; but if you'd rather keep her to yourselves, let me keep the portion, Demipho; for 'tis unjust that I should be disappointed on your account, when for your honor I broke off from the other, who had as good a portion.

DEMIPHO. Go and be hanged you blust'ring vagabond; d'y' think now we don't know you or your pranks?

PHORMIO. This is provoking.

DEMIPHO. Would you marry her, if you might?

PHORMIO. Try me.

DEMIPHO. Your scheme then was that my son should have her at your house.

PHORMIO. What's that you say, pray?

DEMIPHO. Give me back the money.

PHORMIO. Do you give me my wife.

DEMIPHO. Come before a judge.

PHORMIO. Before a judge? Really if you continue being so troublesome——

DEMIPHO. What will you do?

PHORMIO. Do? Perhaps ye think that I've only beggars under my protection, but you'll find I've others.

CHREMES. What's that to us?

PHORMIO. Nothing: but I know a certain gentlewoman here, whose husband had——

CHREMES. Ah! [Aside.]

DEMIPHO. What's the matter?

[Aside to CHREMES.]

PHORMIO. ——another wife at Lemnos;——

CHREMES. I'm a dead man. [Aside.]

PHORMIO. ——by whom he had a daughter; which he brings up privately.

CHREMES. I'm buried. [Aside.]

PHORMIO. I'll go this instant and tell the gentlewoman this.

CHREMES. Pray don't.

PHORMIO. Why, was you the man?

DEMIPHO. What a jest he makes of us!

CHREMES. We'll let you go.

PHORMIO. That's all pretence.

CHREMES. What would you have? We give you leave to keep the money that you have.

PHORMIO. I hear you: but why do ye trifle thus shamefully with me, with your foolish childish speeches? I won't, I will, I will, I won't again, take it, give it back; said, and unsaid; a bargain and no bargain.

CHREMES. How or where did he come to the knowledge of this?

[To DEMIPHO.]

DEMIPHO. I can't tell; but I'm sure I told nobody of it. [To CHREMES.]

CHREMES. As I hoped to be saved, 'tis next to a miracle. [Aside to DEMIPHO.]

PHORMIO. I've graveled them.

[To himself.]

DEMIPHO. Zooks, shall he carry off such a sum from us, and laugh at us so openly too? By Hercules I'd sooner lose my life: bear up, man, with courage. You see that this slip of thine is no secret abroad, therefore it can't be long concealed from your wife: now 'tis better for ourselves to tell her what she'll soon hear from other persons, we shall more easily make our peace if we do: then we may revenge ourselves at our pleasure on this villain.

[Aside to CHREMES.]

PHORMIO. Body o' me! If I don't look

out sharp, I shall be filed, they make towards me with such terrible looks.
[*To himself.*]
CHREMES. But I'm afraid she will not be easily reconciled. [*Aside to* DEMIPHO.]
DEMIPHO. Have a good heart: I'll bring you into favor again, depend upon it, Chremes, since she's dead by whom you had this daughter. [*Aside to* CHREMES.]
PHORMIO. Do ye deal thus with me? Ye set upon me very cunningly [*To both.*] —By Hercules, Demipho, you don't consult his good in provoking me. [*To* DEMIPHO.]—Do you think, when you've been following your pleasures abroad, without paying any regard to this worthy gentlewoman here, but offering a strange indignity to her, to come now and wash away your offence by entreatys? I'll so fire her for you by a relation of these pranks, that you shan't be able to quench her, though you melt into tears.
[*To* CHREMES.]
DEMIPHO. May all the Gods and Goddesses confound him: that any man should be possessed of so much impudence! Don't this villain deserve to be transported by the public into some desert?
CHREMES. He has reduced me to such a situation, that I don't know what to do with him.
DEMIPHO. I know; let us go before a judge.
PHORMIO. Before a judge? Yes, in here, if you will.
DEMIPHO. Follow him, and hold him, till I call the servants hither.
CHREMES. I can't alone; come and help me.
PHORMIO. I've an action against you.
[*To* DEMIPHO.]
CHREMES. Do your worst then.
PHORMIO. And another against you, Chremes.
DEMIPHO. Away with him.
[*To the servants.*]
PHORMIO. Are ye at that sport? Then I must use my voice: Nausistrata, come hither.
CHREMES. Stop his mouth.
[*To the servants.*]

DEMIPHO. See how strong the villain is.
PHORMIO. Nausistrata, I say.
CHREMES. Won't you hold your tongue?
PHORMIO. Hold my tongue?
DEMIPHO. If he won't follow, punch your fist in his belly.
PHORMIO. If you tear my eyes out, I shall find a time to be sufficiently revenged on ye.

SCENE VI

[NAUSISTRATA, CHREMES, PHORMIO, *and* DEMIPHO.]

NAUSISTRATA. Who calls me?
CHREMES. Ah!   [*Aside.*]
NAUSISTRATA. Pray, husband, what's this disturbance here?
PHORMIO. Ah! what, are you thunderstruck now?   [*To* CHREMES.]
NAUSISTRATA. Who is this fellow? Don't you answer me?   [*To* CHREMES.]
PHORMIO. How should he answer you, who don't know where himself is?
CHREMES. Take care how you believe him.   [*To* NAUSISTRATA.]
PHORMIO. Go and feel him, if he is not all over in a cold fit, kill me.
CHREMES. That's nothing.
NAUSISTRATA. Then let me know what it is he has to say?
PHORMIO. That you shall; do but hear me.
CHREMES. Do you resolve to believe him?
NAUSISTRATA. How should I believe one that has said nothing?
PHORMIO. Fear has took the poor man's senses away.
NAUSISTRATA. By Pollux, you are not thus fearful for nothing? [*To* CHREMES.]
CHREMES. I fearful?
PHORMIO. Very well truly; since you're afraid of nothing, and what I have to say signifys nothing, do you tell it.
DEMIPHO. Must he tell at your bidding, rascal?
PHORMIO. Well said, you do well to stand up for your brother.
NAUSISTRATA. Won't you tell me, husband?

CHREMES. Why——
NAUSISTRATA. What—why?
CHREMES. 'Tis of no consequence to tell you.
PHORMIO. You think so; but 'tis of great consequence to this lady. [*To* CHREMES.] ——In Lemnos——
[*To* NAUSISTRATA.]
CHREMES. Ah? What are you about?
DEMIPHO. Will you not hold your tongue?
PHORMIO. Unknown to you——
[*To* NAUSISTRATA.]
CHREMES. I'm ruined! [*Aside.*]
PHORMIO. ——he married another woman:——
NAUSISTRATA. Husband, Heaven forbid.
PHORMIO. 'Tis even so.
NAUSISTRATA. What an unhappy undone woman am I!
PHORMIO. ——And he had a daughter by her, while you dreamed nothing of it.
CHREMES. What must we do now?
[*To* DEMIPHO.]
NAUSISTRATA. Immortal Gods, what an unworthy and injurious act is this!
DEMIPHO. 'Tis done and can't be recalled.
NAUSISTRATA. Was there ever so unworthy an act? When they come to their wives, then they are old.—Demipho, I apply myself to you, for it's irksome to me to speak to him: were these his frequent journies, and long continuance at Lemnos? Was this the cheapness of provisions that lowered our rents?
DEMIPHO. Nausistrata, I don't deny that he deserves blame in this affair, but 'tis such as may be pardon'd;——
PHORMIO. She's deaf to what he says.
[*Aside.*]
DEMIPHO. ——for it was not through any neglect or hatred of you he did it; but, being in liquor about fifteen years since, he happened to have an intrigue with the woman by whom he had this daughter; and he never touched her afterwards; she's dead now; the objection in this affair is now removed: therefore, pray, exert your usual good nature, and bear it patiently.
NAUSISTRATA. What should I bear pa-

tiently? I wish I was rid of this troublesome affair; but what can I hope? Have I any reason to think age will make him better? He was old enough then, if age would have preserved his modesty: have my years and beauty more temptations in 'em now than before, Demipho? What can you advance to make me expect or hope that 'twill be no more so?
PHORMIO. They who have a mind to be at Chremes's funeral come now, now is the time; I'll give it him home: come on now, and provoke Phormio who dares; he shall meet with the same fate.—He may get into favor again; I've had revenge enough; she has something to ring in his ear as long as he lives.
NAUSISTRATA. Can I believe that I've deserved such usage? Why, Demipho, should I repeat how faithful I have been to him in every particular?
DEMIPHO. I know all that as well as yourself.
NAUSISTRATA. Do you think I've deserved this?
DEMIPHO. Nobody less; but, since your reproaches can't undo what is done, forgive him: he asks your pardon, acknowledges his fault, and excuses himself; what would you have more?
PHORMIO. But before she pronounces his pardon, I must take care of myself and Phædria. ([*Aside.*]—Hark y', Nausistrata, hear me before you answer him without consideration.
NAUSISTRATA. What have you to say?
PHORMIO. I chous'd him of ninety pieces by a stratagem; which I gave to your son; which he gave to the bawd for his mistress.
CHREMES. Ah! what's that you say?
NAUSISTRATA. Do you think it such a crime, that your son, who is a young man, should have one mistress, while you have two wives? Aren't you ashamed? With what face can you reprove him? answer me.
DEMIPHO. He'll do what you will.
NAUSISTRATA. Well, that you may know my resolution now, I'll neither for-

give, nor promise anything, nor answer, till I see my son; I'll be determined by his judgement; I'll do what he desires.

PHORMIO. You are a woman of judgement, Nausistrata.

NAUSISTRATA. Do you approve of it?

PHORMIO. Yes indeed, I'm come well off, and beyond my expectation.

NAUSISTRATA. Tell me your name.

PHORMIO. My name? Phormio, a friend to your family, but more especially to Phædria.

NAUSISTRAT. By Castor, Phormio, from this time forwards I'll serve you in whatever you ask of me, to the utmost of my power, in word and deed.

PHORMIO. You're very good.

NAUSISTRATA. By Pollux, you deserve it.

PHORMIO. First now will you do that, Nausistrata, which will please me, and make your husband's eyes ache?

NAUSISTRATA. With all my heart.

PHORMIO. Invite me to supper.

NAUSISTRATA. By Pollux, I do invite you.

DEMIPHO. Now let us go in.

NAUSISTRATA. We will; but where's Phædria our judge?

PHORMIO. I'll bring him immediately. [To NAUSISTRATA.]—Farewell, and give us your applause. [To the Spectators.]

MEDEA

By SENECA

(L. Annæus Seneca)

Written probably 1st century A.D., *but no record of performance exists.*

TRANSLATED BY FRANK JUSTUS MILLER *

CHARACTERS

MEDEA, *daughter of* AEËTES, *King of Colchis, and wife of*
JASON

JASON, *son of* AESON, *and nephew of* PELIAS, *the usurp-
ing king of Thessaly; organizer and leader of the
Argonautic expedition to Colchis in quest of the
golden fleece.*

CREON, *King of Corinth, who had received into his hos-
pitable kingdom* MEDEA *and* JASON, *fugitives from
Thessaly, after* MEDEA *had plotted the death of*
PELIAS

NURSE, *of Medea*

MESSENGER

TWO SONS, *of* MEDEA *and* JASON (*personæ mutæ*)

CHORUS OF CORINTHIANS. *Friendly to* JASON *and hos-
tile to* MEDEA

*The time of the play is confined to the single day of
the culmination of the tragedy, the_ day proposed by*
CREON *for the banishment of* MEDEA *and marriage of*
JASON *to* CREÜSA, *daughter of* CREON.

The scene is in Corinth, in the court of the house of
JASON.

ACT I

MEDEA. Ye gods of wedlock, thou the
nuptial couch's guard,
Lucina, thou from whom that tamer of the
deep,

The Argo's pilot, learned to guide his
pristine bark,
And Neptune, thou stern ruler of the
ocean's depths,
And Titan, by whose rays the shining day
is born,

---

* Reprinted from *The Tragedies of Seneca*, University of Chicago Press, copyright
1907, by permission of the translator and publisher.

Thou triformed maiden Hecate, whose con-
scious beams
With splendor shine upon the mystic wor-
shipers—
Upon ye all I call, the powers of heaven,
the gods
By whose divinity false Jason swore; and
ye
Whose aid Medea may more boldly claim,
thou world
Of endless night, th' antipodes of heavenly
realms,
Ye damnèd ghosts, thou lord of hades'
dark domain,
Whose mistress was with trustier pledge
won to thy side—
Before ye all this baleful prayer I bring:
Be near!
Be near! Ye crime-avenging furies, come
and loose
Your horrid locks with serpent coils en-
twined, and grasp
With bloody hands the smoking torch; be
near as once
Ye stood in dread array beside my wedding
couch.
Upon this new-made bride destruction
send, and death
Upon the king and all the royal line!
But he,
My husband, may he live to meet some
heavier doom;
This curse I imprecate upon his head;
may he,
Through distant lands, in want, in exile
wander, scorned
And houseless. Nay, may he once more
my favor woo;
A stranger's threshold may he seek where
now he walks
A well-known guest; and—this the black-
est curse I know—
May children rise to him to emulate their
sire,
Their mother's image bear.—Now won is
vengeance, won!
For I have children borne.—Nay, nay, 'tis
empty plaints
And useless words I frame. Shall I not
rather rush

Against the foe and dash the torches from
their hands,
The light from heaven? Does Father
Phoebus suffer this?
Do men behold his face, as, seated in his
car,
He rolls along th' accustomed track of
sky serene?
Why does he not return to morning's
gates, the law
Of heaven reversing? Grant that I be
borne aloft
In my ancestral car! Give me the reins,
O sire,
Thy fiery team grant me to guide with
lines of flame.
Then Corinth, though with double shore
delaying fate,
Herself consumed with fire, shall light
two seas with flame.
But no, this course alone remains, that
I myself
Should bear the wedding torch, with ac-
quiescent prayers,
And slay the victims on the altars con-
secrate.
Thyself inspect the entrails, and seek there
the way
By prayer, if still, O soul, thou livest, if
there still
Remaineth aught of old-time strength in
thee! Away
With woman's fears! Put on thy heart
a breast-plate hard
And chill as Caucasus! Then all the
wizard arts
That Phasis knew, or Pontus, shall be
seen again
In Corinth. Now with mad, unheard of,
dreadful deeds,
Whereat high heaven and earth below
shall pale and quake,
My pregnant soul is teeming; and my
heart is full
Of pictured wounds and death and slaugh-
ter.—Ah, too long
On trifling ills I dwell. These were my
virgin deeds.
Now that a mother's pains I've felt, my
larger heart

Must larger crimes conceive. Then passion, gird thyself,
Put on thy strength, and for the issue now prepare!
Let my rejection pay as dread a fee as when,
Of old, through impious deeds of blood, I came to him.
Come, break through slow delay, and let the home once won
By crime, by equal deeds of crime be done away!

CHORUS [*chanting the epithalamium for the nuptials of* JASON *and* CREÜSA].
Now on our royal nuptials graciously smiling,
Here may the lords of heaven and the deeps of the ocean
Come while the people feast in pious rejoicing!

First to the gods who sway the scepter of heaven,
Pealing forth their will in the voice of thunder,
Let the white bull his proud head bow in tribute.

Then to the fair Lucina, her gift we offer,
White as the driven snow, this beautiful heifer,
Still with her neck untouched by the yoke of bondage.
Thou who alone canst rule the heart of the war-god,
Thou who linkest in peace the opposing nations,
Out of thy generous hand abundance pouring—
Thee we offer a daintier gift, O Concord!

Thou who, on the marriage torches attending,
Night's dark gloom with favoring hand dispellest,
Hither come with languishing footstep drunken,
Binding thy temples fair with garlands of roses!

Star of the evening, thou who to twilight leadest

The day, and hailest again the dawn of the morning,
All too slowly thou com'st for lovers impatient,
Eager to see thy sign in the glow of the sunset.

The fairest of girls is she,
The Athenian maids outshining,
Or the Spartan maiden with armor laden,
No burden of war declining.

Not by Alpheus' sacred stream,
Nor Boeotia's musical water,
Is there any fair who can compare
With our lovely Corinthian daughter.

Our Thessalian prince excels,
In beauty of form and face,
Even Bacchus, the son of the fierce-flaming one,
Who yokes the wild tigers in place.

The murmuring tripod's lord,
Though the fairest in heavenly story,
The twins with their star bright gleaming afar—
All yield to our Jason in glory.

When in her train of courtly maidens she mingles—
Like the bright sunshine paling the starry splendor,
Or the full* moonlight quenching the Pleiads' brilliance,
So does she shine, all peerless, of fair ones the fairest.

Now, O Jason, freed from the hateful wedlock
That held thee bound to the barbarous Colchian woman,
Joyfully wed the fair Corinthian maiden,
While at last her parents' blessings attend thee.

Ho then, youths, with licensed jest and rejoicing,
Loud let the songs of gladness ring through the city;
Rarely against our lords such freedom is given.

Fair and noble band of Bacchus, the thyrsus-bearer,

Now is the time to light the glittering
torches of pinewood.
Shake on high the festal fire with lan-
guishing fingers;

Now let the bold and merry Fescennine
laughter and jesting
Sound through our ranks.   Let Medea
fare in silence and darkness,
If perchance another lord she shall wed
in her exile.

ACT II

MEDEA.   We are undone!   How harsh
upon mine ears doth grate
The song! and even now I cannot com-
prehend
The vast extent of woe that hath befallen
me.
Could Jason prove so false?   Bereft of
native land,
And home, and kingdom, could he leave
me here alone
On foreign shores?   Oh, cruel, could he
quite reject
My sum of service, he who saw the fire
and sea
With crime o'ercome for his dear sake?
And does he think
That thus the fatal chapter can be ended?
Wild,
Devoid of reason, sick of soul, my swift
mind darts
In all directions seeking whence revenge
may come!
I would he had a brother!   But his
wife—'gainst her
Be aimed the blow!   Can thus my wrongs
be satisfied?
Nay, nay—to meet my sum of woe must
be heaped high
The crimes of Greece, of strange barbaric
lands, and those
Which even thy hands have not known.
Now lash thy soul
With memory's scourge, and call thy dark
deeds in review:
The glory of thy father's kingdom reft
away;

Thy brother, guiltless comrade of thy
guilty flight,
All hewn in pieces and his corpse strewn
on the deep,
To break his royal father's heart; and,
last of crimes,
Old Pelias by his daughters slain at thy
command.
O impious one, what streams of blood
have flowed to work
Thy ends!   And yet, not one of all my
crimes by wrath
Was prompted.   Love, ill-omened love,
suggested all.
Yet, what could Jason else have done,
compelled to serve
Another's will, another's law?   He should
have died
Before he yielded to the tyrant's will.
Nay, nay,
Thou raging passion, speak not so!   For,
if he may,
I would that Jason still may live and
still be mine,
As once he was; if not, yet may he still
live on,
And, mindful of my merits, live without
my aid.
The guilt is Creon's all, who with un-
bridled power
Dissolves the marriage bond, my children
separates
From me who bore them, yea, and makes
the strongest pledge,
Though ratified with straightest oath, of
none effect.
Let him alone sustain my wrath; let
Creon pay
The debt of guilt he owes!   His palace
will I bring
To utter desolation; and the whirling fire
To far-off Malea's crags shall send its
lurid glare.
NURSE.   Be silent now, I pray thee, and
thy plaints confine
To secret woe!   The man who heavy blows
can bear
In silence, biding still his time with pa-
tient soul,
Full oft his vengeance gains.   'Tis hidden
wrath that harms;

But hate proclaimed oft loses half its power to harm.

MEDEA. But small the grief is that can counsel take and hide
Its head; great ills lie not in hiding, but must rush
Abroad and work their will.

NURSE. Oh, cease this mad complaint,
My mistress; scarce can friendly silence help thee now.

MEDEA. But fortune fears the brave, the faint of heart o'erwhelms.

NURSE. Then valor be approved, if for it still there's room.

MEDEA. But it must always be that valor finds its place.

NURSE. No star of hope points out the way from these our woes.

MEDEA. The man who hopes for naught at least has naught to fear.

NURSE. The Colchians are thy foes; thy husband's vows have failed;
Of all thy vast possessions not a jot is left.

MEDEA. Yet I am left. There's left both sea and land and fire
And sword and gods and hurtling thunderbolts.

NURSE. The king must be revered.

MEDEA. My father was a king.

NURSE. Dost thou not fear?

MEDEA. Not though the earth produced the foe.

NURSE. Thou'lt perish.

MEDEA. So I wish it.

NURSE. Flee!

MEDEA. I'm done with flight.
Why should Medea flee?

NURSE. Thy children!

MEDEA. Whose, thou know'st.

NURSE. And dost thou still delay?

MEDEA. I go, but vengeance first.

NURSE. Th' avenger will pursue.

MEDEA. Perchance I'll stop his course.

NURSE. Nay, hold thy words, and cease thy threats, O foolish one.
Thy temper curb; 'tis well to yield to fate's decrees.

MEDEA. Though fate may strip me of my all, myself am left.

But who flings wide the royal palace doors? Behold,
'Tis Creon's self, exalted high in Grecian sway. [MEDEA retires to back of stage; exit NURSE; enter CREON.]

CREON. Medea, baleful daughter of the Colchian king,
Has not yet taken her hateful presence from our realm.
On mischief is she bent. Well known her treach'rous power.
For who escapes her? Who may pass his days in peace?
This cursèd pestilence at once would I have stayed
By force of arms; but Jason's prayers prevailed. She still
May live, but let her free my borders from the fear
Her presence genders, and her safety gain by flight.
[He sees MEDEA approaching.]
But lo, she comes, with fierce and threatening mien, to seek
An audience with us. [To attendants.]
Slaves defend us from her touch
And pestilential presence! Bid her silence keep,
And learn to yield obedience to the king's commands. [To MEDEA.]
Go, speed thy flight, thou thing of evil, fell, and monstrous!

MEDEA. But tell me what the crime, my lord, or what the guilt
That merits exile?

CREON. Let the guiltless question thus.

MEDEA. If now thou judgest, hear me; if thou reign'st, command.

CREON. The king's command thou must abide, nor question aught.

MEDEA. Unrighteous sovereignty has never long endured.

CREON. Go hence, and to the Colchians complain.

MEDEA. I go,
But let him take me hence who brought me to thy shores.

CREON. Thy prayer has come too late, for fixed is my decree.

MEDEA. Who judges, and denies his ear to either side,

Though right his judgment, still is he
    himself unjust.
CREON. Didst lend thine ear to Pelias,
    ere thou judgedst him?
But come, I'll give thee grace to plead
    thy goodly cause.
MEDEA. How hard the task to turn the
    soul from wrath, when once
To wrath inclined; how 'tis the creed of
    sceptered kings
To swerve not from the purposed course
    they once have taken,
Full well I know, for I have tasted roy-
    alty.
For, though by present storms of ill I'm
    overwhelmed,
An exile, suppliant, lone, forsaken, all
    forlorn,
I once in happier times a royal princess
    shone,
And traced my proud descent from heav-
    enly Phoebus' self.
My father's realm extended wide o'er all
    the land
Where Phasis' gentle waters flow, o'er
    Scythia's plains
Whose rivers sweeten Pontus' briny
    waves; where, too,
Thermodon's banks inclose the race of
    warlike maids,
Whose gleaming shields strike terror to
    their foes. All this
My father held in sway. And I, of noble
    birth,
And blessed of heaven, in royal state was
    high upraised.
Then princes humbly sought my hand in
    wedlock, mine,
Who now must sue. O changeful fortune,
    thou my throne
Hast reft away, and given me exile in
    its stead.
Trust not in kingly realms, since fickle
    chance may strew
Their treasures to the winds. Lo, this is
    regal, this
The work of kings, which time nor change
    cannot undo:
To succor the afflicted, to provide at need
A trusty refuge for the suppliant. This
    alone

I brought of all my Colchian treasure, this
    renown,
This very flower of fame, that by my arts
    I saved
The bulwark of the Greeks, the offspring
    of the gods.
My princely gift to Greece is Orpheus,
    that sweet bard
Who can the trees in willing bondage
    draw, and melt
The crag's hard heart. Mine too are
    Boreas' wingèd sons,
And Leda's heaven-born progeny, and Lyn-
    ceus, he
Whose glance can pierce the distant view
    —yea, all the Greeks,
Save Jason; for I mention not the king
    of kings,
The leader of the leaders; he is mine
    alone,
My labor's recompense; the rest I give to
    you.
Nay, come, O king, arraign me, and re-
    hearse my crimes.
But stay! for I'll confess them all. The
    only crime
Of which I stand accused is this—the
    Argo saved.
Suppose my maiden scruples had opposed
    the deed;
Suppose my filial piety had stayed my
    hand:
Then had the mighty chieftains fall'n, and
    in their fate
All Greece had been o'erwhelmed; then
    this, thy son-in-law,
Had felt the bull's consuming breath, and
    perished there.
Nay, nay, let fortune, when she will, my
    doom decree;
I glory still that kings have owed their
    lives to me.
But what reward I reap for all my glori-
    ous deeds
Is in thy hands. Convict me, if thou wilt,
    of sin,
But give him back for whom I sinned. O
    Creon, see,
I own that I am guilty. This much thou
    didst know,

When first I clasped thy knees, a humble
　　suppliant,
And sought the shelter of thy royal
　　clemency.
Some little corner of thy kingdom now I
　　ask,
In which to hide my grief.　If I must
　　flee again,
Oh, let some nook remote within thy broad
　　domain
Be found for me!
　　CREON.　That I my power in mercy wield,
And spurn not those who seek my aid let
　　Jason's self
My witness be, who, exiled, overwhelmed
　　by fate,
And smitten sore with fear, a refuge found
　　with me.
For lo, Thessalia's monarch, bent on ven-
　　geance dire,
Seeks Jason at my hand.　The cause, in-
　　deed, is just:
For that his sire, o'erburdened with the
　　weight of years,
Was foully taken off, while by thy wicked
　　guile
His guileless sisters' hands were nerved
　　to do the deed.
If now our Jason can unlink his cause
　　from thine,
'Tis easy his defense to make, for on his
　　hands
No stain of blood is found.　His arm no
　　sword upraised,
And he has had no part nor lot in this
　　thy crime.
No, thou and thou alone the arch contriver
　　art,
Uniting in thy person woman's fertile wit
And man's effective strength; while in
　　thy reckless heart
No thought of reputation dwells to check
　　thy hand.
Then go thou hence and purge our king-
　　dom of its stain;
Bear hence thy deadly poisons; free the
　　citizens
From fear; abiding in some other land
　　than this,
Outwear the patience of the gods.
　　MEDEA.　　　　　Thou bid'st me flee?

Then give me back my bark wherein to
　　flee.　Restore
The partner of my flight!　Why should
　　I flee alone?
I came not thus.　Or if avenging war
　　thou fear'st,
Then banish both the culprits; why dis-
　　tinguish me
From Jason?　'Twas for him old Pelias
　　was o'ercome;
For him the flight, the plunder of my
　　father's realm,
My sire forsaken and my infant brother
　　slain,
And all the guilt that love suggests; 'twas
　　all for him.
Deep dyed in sin am I, but on my guilty
　　soul
The sin of profit lieth not.
　　CREON.　　　　　Why seek delay
By speech?　Too long thou tarriest.
　　MEDEA.　　　　　I go, but grant
This last request: let not the mother's fall
　　o'erwhelm
Her hapless babes.
　　CREON.　Then go in peace.　For I to
　　them
A father's place will fill, and take them
　　to my heart.
　　MEDEA.　Now by the fair hopes born
　　upon this wedding day,
And by thy hopes of lasting sovereignty
　　secure
From changeful fate's assault, I pray thee
　　grant from flight
A respite brief, while I upon my children's
　　lips
A mother's kiss imprint, perchance the
　　last.
　　CREON.　A time
Thou seek'st for treachery.
　　MEDEA.　　　　　What fraud can be devised
In one short hour?
　　CREON.　To those on mischief bent, be
　　sure,
The briefest time is fraught with mis-
　　chief's fatal power.
　　MEDEA.　Dost thou refuse me, then, one
　　little space for tears?
　　CREON.　Though deep-ingrafted fear
　　would fain resist thy plea,

A single day I'll give thee ere my sentence holds.

MEDEA. Too gracious thou. But let my respite further shrink,
And I'll depart content.

CREON. Thy life shall surely pay
The forfeit if tomorrow's sun beholds thee still
In Corinth. But the voice of Hymen calls away
To solemnize the rites of this his festal day. [*Exeunt.*]

CHORUS. Too bold the man who first upon the seas,
The treacherous seas, his fragile bark confided;
Who, as the well-known shore behind him glided,
His life intrusted to the fickle breeze;

And, as his unknown seaward course he sped
Within his slender craft with foolish daring,
Midway 'twixt life and death went onward faring,
Along the perilous narrow margin led.

Not yet were sparkling constellations known,
Or sky, all spangled with the starry glory;
Not yet could sailors read the warning story
By stormy Hyades upon the heavens thrown.

Not yet was Zeus's foster-mother famed,
Nor slow Boötes round the north star wheeling;
Nor Boreas nor Zephyr gently stealing,
Each feared or welcomed, though as yet unnamed.

First Tiphys dared to spread his venturous sail,
The hidden lesson of the breezes learning,
Now all his canvas to the Zephyrs turning,
Now shifting all to catch the changing gale.

Now midway on the mast the yard remains,
Now at the head with all its canvas drawing,
While eager sailors lure the breezes blowing,
And over all the gleaming topsail strains.

The guiltless golden age our fathers saw,
When youth and age the same horizon bounded;
No greed of gain their simple hearts confounded;
Their native wealth enough, 'twas all they knew.

But lo, the severed worlds have been brought near
And linked in one by Argo's hand uniting;
While seas endure the oar's unwonted smiting,
And add their fury to the primal fear.

This impious bark its guilt in dread atoned
When clashing mountains were together driven,
And sea, from sea in mighty conflict riven,
The stars besprinkled with the leaping foam.

Amid these perils sturdy Tiphys paled,
And from his nerveless hand the vessel bounded;
While stricken Orpheus' lyre no more resounded,
And tuneful Argo's warning message failed.

What sinking terror filled each quaking breast,
When near the borders of sea-girt Pelorus,
There smote upon their ears the horrid chorus
Of Scylla's baying wolves around them pressed.

What terror when they neared the
  Sirens' lair,
Who soothe the troubled waves with
  witching measures!
But Orpheus filled their souls with nobler
  pleasures,
And left the foe in impotent despair.

And of this wild adventure what the
  prize,
That lured the daring bark with heroes
  laden?
The fleece of gold, and this mad Colchian
  maiden,
Well fit to be the first ship's mer-
  chandize.

The sea, subdued, the victor's law
  obeys;
No vessel needs a goddess' art in framing,
Nor oars in heroes' hands, the ocean tam-
  ing:
The frailest craft now dares the
  roughest waves.

Now, every bound removed, new cities
  rise
In lands remote, their ancient walls re-
  moving;
While men of Ind by Caspian shores are
  roving,
And Persia's face now greets the
  western skies.

The time will come, as lapsing ages
  flee,
When every land shall yield its hidden
  treasure;
When men no more shall unknown courses
  measure,
For round the world no "farthest
  land" shall be.

ACT III

[MEDEA *is rushing out to seek vengeance,
while the* NURSE *tries in vain to restrain
her.*]
NURSE. My foster-daughter, whither
speedest thou abroad?

Oh, stay, I pray thee, and restrain thy
  passion's force.
  [MEDEA *hastens by without an-
    swering. The* NURSE *solilo-
    quizes.*]
As some wild Bacchanal, whose fury's
  raging fire
The god inflames, now roams distraught
  on Pindus' snows,
And now on lofty Nysa's rugged slopes;
  so she,
Now here, now there, with frenzied step
  is hurried on,
Her face revealing every mark of stricken
  woe,
With flushing cheek and sighs deep drawn,
  wild cries, and tears,
And laughter worse than tears. In her a
  medley strange
Of every passion may be seen: o'ertopping
  wrath,
Bewailings, bitter groans of anguish.
  Whither tends
This overburdened soul? What mean her
  frenzied threats?
When will the foaming wave of fury spend
  itself?
No common crime, I fear, no easy deed of
  ill
She meditates. Herself she will outvie.
  For well
I recognize the wonted marks of rage.
  Some deed
Is threatening, wild, profane, and hideous.
  [*Reënter* MEDEA.]   Behold
Her face betrays her madness. O ye gods,
  may these
Our fears prove vain forebodings!
MEDEA [*not noticing the* NURSE'S *pres-
  ence*]. For thy hate, poor soul,
Dost thou a measure seek? Let it be deep
  as love.
And shall I tamely view the wedding
  torches' glare?
And shall all this day go uneventful by, this
  day,
So hardly won, so grudgingly bestowed?
  Nay, nay,
While, poised upon her heights, the central
  earth shall bear

The heavens up; while seasons run their
  endless round,
And sands unnumbered lie; while days,
  and nights, and sun,
And stars in due procession pass; while
  round the pole
The ocean-fearing bears revolve, and
  tumbling streams
Flow downward to the sea; my grief shall
  never cease
To seek revenge, and shall forever grow.
  What rage
Of savage beast can equal mine? What
  Scylla famed?
What sea-engulfing pool? What burning
  Aetna placed
On impious Titan's heaving breast? No
  torrent stream,
Nor storm-tossed sea, nor breath of flame
  fanned by the gale,
Can check or equal my wild storm of rage.
  My will
Is set on limitless revenge!
                    Will Jason say
He feared the power of Creon and Acastus'
  threats?
True love is proof against the fear of
  man. But grant
He was compelled to yield, and pledged
  his hand in fear:
He might at least have sought his wife
  with one last word
Of comfort and farewell. But this, though
  brave in heart,
He feared to do. The cruel terms of ban-
  ishment
Could Creon's son-in-law not soften? No.
  One day
Alone was giv'n for last farewell to both
  my babes.
But time's short space I'll not bewail;
  though brief in hours,
In consequence it stretches out eternally.
This day shall see a deed that ne'er shall
  be forgot.
But now I'll go and pray the gods, and
  move high heaven
But I shall work my will!
  NURSE. Thy heart all passion-tossed,
I pray thee, mistress, soothe, and calm
  thy troubled soul.

MEDEA. My troubled soul can never
  know a time of rest
Until it sees all things o'erwhelmed in
  common doom.
All must go down with me! 'Tis sweet
  such death to die.
                    [Exit MEDEA.]
  NURSE [calling after her]. Oh, think
  what perils thou must meet if thou
  persist!
No one with safety may defy a sceptered
  king.
              [Enter JASON.]
  JASON. O heartless fate, if frowns or
  smiles bedeck thy brow,
How often are thy cures far worse than
  the disease
They seek to cure! If, now, I wish to
  keep the troth
I plighted to my lawful bride, my life
  must pay
The forfeit; if I shrink from death, my
  guilty soul
Must perjured be. I fear no power that
  man can wield;
But in my heart paternal love unmans
  me quite;
For well I know that in my death my
  children's fate
Is sealed. O sacred Justice, if in heaven
  thou dwell'st,
Be witness now, that for my children's
  sake I act.
Nay, sure am I that even she, Medea's
  self,
Though fierce she is of soul and brooking
  no restraint,
Will see her children's good outweighing
  all her wrongs.
With this good argument my purpose now
  is fixed,
In humble wise to brave her wrath.

              [Enter MEDEA.]
                    At sight of me
Her raging fury flames anew! Hate, like
  a shield,
She bears, and in her face is pictured all
  her woe.
  MEDEA. Thou see'st, Jason, that we flee.
  'Tis no new thing

To suffer exile, but the cause of flight is
  strange;
For with thee I was wont to flee, not from
  thee. Yes,
I go. But whither dost thou send me
  whom thou driv'st
From out thy home? Shall I the Colchians
  seek again,
My royal father's realm, whose soil is
  steeped in blood
My brother shed? What country dost
  thou bid me seek?
What way by sea is open? Shall I fare
  again
Where once I saved the noble kings of
  Greece, and thee,
Thou wanton, through the threatening
  jaws of Pontus' strait,
The blue Symplegades? Or shall I hie me
  back
To fair Thessalia's realms? Lo, all the
  doors which I,
For thee, have opened wide, I've closed
  upon myself.
But whither dost thou send me now?
  Thou bid'st me flee,
But show'st no way or means of flight.
  But 'tis enough:
The king's own son-in-law commands and
  I obey.
Come, heap thy torments on me; I deserve
  them all.
Let royal wrath oppress me, wanton that
  I am,
With cruel hand, and load my guilty limbs
  with chains;
And let me be immured in dungeons black
  as night:
Still will my punishment be less than my
  offense.
O ingrate! hast thou then forgot the
  brazen bull,
And his consuming breath? the fear that
  smote thee, when,
Upon the field of Mars, the earth-born
  brood stood forth
To meet thy single sword? 'Twas by my
  arts that they,
The monsters, fell by mutual blows. Re-
  member, too,

The long-sought fleece of gold I won for
  thee, whose guard,
The dragon huge, was lulled to rest at my
  command;
My brother slain for thee. For thee old
  Pelias fell,
When, taken by my guile, his daughters
  slew their sire,
Whose life could not return. All this I
  did for thee.
In quest of thine advantage have I quite
  forgot
Mine own.

     And now, by all thy fond
  paternal hopes,
By thine established house, by all the
  monsters slain
For thee, by these my hands which I have
  ever held
To work thy will, by all the perils past, by
  heaven
And sea that witnessed at my wedlock,
  pity me!
Since thou art blessed, restore me what I
  lost for thee:
That countless treasure plundered from
  the swarthy tribes
Of India, which filled our goodly vaults
  with wealth,
And decked our very trees with gold. This
  costly store
I left for thee, my native land, my brother,
  sire,
My reputation—all; and with this dower
  I came.
If now to homeless exile thou dost send
  me forth,
Give back the countless treasures which
  I left for thee.
JASON. Though Creon in a vengeful
  mood would have thy life,
I moved him by my tears to grant thee
  flight instead.
MEDEA. I thought my exile punish-
  ment; 'tis now, I see,
A gracious boon!
JASON. Oh, flee while still the respite
  holds;
Provoke him not, for deadly is the wrath
  of kings.

MEDEA. Not so. 'Tis for Creüsa's love
thou sayest this;
Thou wouldst remove the hated wanton
once thy wife.
JASON. Dost thou reproach me with a
guilty love?
MEDEA.   Yea, that,
And murder too, and treachery.
JASON.   But name me now,
If so thou canst, the crimes that I have
done.
MEDEA. Thy crimes—
Whatever I have done.
JASON. Why then, in truth, thy guilt
Must all be mine, if all thy crimes are
mine.
MEDEA.   They are,
They are all thine; for who by sin ad-
vantage gains,
Commits the sin. All men proclaim thy
wife defiled.
Do thou thyself protect her, and condone
her sin.
Let her be guiltless in thine eyes who for
thy gain
Has sinned.
JASON. But gifts which sin has bought
'twere shame to take.
MEDEA. Why keep'st thou then the
gifts which it were shame to take?
JASON. Nay, curb thy fiery soul! Thy
children—for their sake
Be calm.
MEDEA. My children! Them I do refuse,
reject,
Renounce! Shall then Creüsa brothers
bear to these
My children?
JASON. But the queen can aid thy
wretched sons.
MEDEA. May that day never dawn, that
day of shame and woe,
When in one house are joined the low born
and the high,
The sons of that foul robber Sisyphus, and
these,
The sons of Phoebus.
JASON. Wretched one, and wilt thou
then
Involve me also in thy fall? Begone, I
pray.
MEDEA. Creon hath heard my prayer.

JASON. What wouldst thou have me do?
MEDEA. For me? I'd have thee dare the
law.
JASON.   The royal power
Doth compass me.
MEDEA. A greater than the king is
here:
Medea. Set us front to front and let us
strive;
And of this royal strife let Jason be the
prize.
JASON. O'erwearied by my woes I yield.
But be thou ware,
Medea, lest too often thou shouldst tempt
thy fate.
MEDEA. Yet fortune's mistress have I
ever been.
JASON.   But see,
With hostile front Acastus comes, on
vengeance bent,
While Creon threatens instant death.
MEDEA.   Then flee them both.
I ask thee not to draw thy sword against
the king
Nor yet to stain thy pious hands with
kindred blood.
Come, flee with me.
JASON.   But what resistance can we
make,
If war with double visage rear his horrid
front,
If Creon and Acastus join in common
cause?
MEDEA. Add, too, the Colchian armies
with my father's self
To lead them; join the Scythian and
Pelasgian hordes:
In one deep gulf of ruin will I whelm them
all.
JASON. Yet on the scepter do I look
with fear.
MEDEA.   Beware,
Lest not the fear, but lust of power pre-
vail with thee.
JASON. Too long we strive: have done,
lest we suspicion breed.
MEDEA. Now Jove, throughout thy
heavens let the thunders roll!
Thy mighty arm in wrath make bare!
Thy darting flames
Of vengeance loose, and shake the lofty
firmament

With rending storms! At random hurl
thy vengeful bolts,
Selecting neither me nor Jason with thy
aim;
That thus whoever falls may perish with
the brand
Of guilt upon him; for thy hurtling darts
can take
No erring flight.
JASON. Recall thee and in calmness
speak
With words of peace and reason. Then if
any gift
From Creon's royal house can compensate
thy woes,
Take that as solace of thy flight.
MEDEA. My soul doth scorn
The wealth of kings. But let me have my
little ones
As comrades of my flight, that in their
childish breasts
Their mother's tears may flow. New sons
await thy home.
JASON. My heart inclines to yield to
thee, but love forbids.
For these my sons shall never from my
arms be reft,
Though Creon's self demand. My very
spring of life,
My sore heart's comfort, and my joy are
these my sons;
And sooner could I part with limbs or
vital breath,
Or light of life.
MEDEA [aside]. Doth he thus love his
sons? 'Tis well;
Then is he bound, and in his armored
strength this flaw
Reveals the place to strike. [To JASON.]
At least, ere I depart,
Grant me this last request: let me once
more embrace
My sons. E'en that small boon will com-
fort my sad heart.
And this my latest prayer to thee: if, in
my grief,
My tongue was over bold, let not my words
remain
To rankle in thy heart. Remember hap-
pier things

Of me, and let my bitter words be straight
forgot.
JASON. Not one shall linger in my soul;
and curb, I pray,
Thy too impetuous heart, and gently yield
to fate.
For resignation ever soothes the woeful
soul. [Exit JASON.]
MEDEA. He's gone! And can it be?
And shall he thus depart,
Forgetting me and all my service? Must
I drop,
Like some discarded toy, out of his faith-
less heart?
It shall not be. Up then, and summon all
thy strength
And all thy skill! And, this the fruit of
former crime,
Count nothing criminal that works thy
will. But lo,
We're hedged about; scant room is left for
our designs.
Now must the attack be made where least
suspicion wakes
The least resistance. Now Medea, on!
and do
And dare thine utmost, yea, beyond thine
utmost power! [To the NURSE.]
Do thou, my faithful nurse, the comrade
of my grief,
And all the devious wanderings of my
checkered course,
Assist me now in these my plans. There
is a robe,
The glory of our Colchian realm, the
precious gift
Of Phoebus' self to king Aeëtes as a proof
Of fatherhood; a gleaming circlet, too, all
wrought
With threads of gold, the yellow gold be-
spangled o'er
With gems, a fitting crown to deck a
princess' head.
These treasures let Medea's children bear
as gifts
To Jason's bride. But first infuse them
with the power
Of magic, and invoke the aid of Hecate;
The woe-producing sacrifices then prepare,
And let the sacred flames through all our
courts resound.

CHORUS. No force of name or raging
          gale,
Or whizzing bolt so fearful is,
As when a wife, by her lord betrayed,
    Burns hot with hate.

Not such a force is Auster's blast,
When he marshals forth the wintry
          storms;
Nor Hister's headlong rushing stream,
Which, wrecking bridges in its course,
    Pours reckless on;

Nor yet the Rhone, whose current strong
Beats back the sea; nor when the snows,
Beneath the lengthening days of spring
And the sun's warm rays, melt down in
          streams
    From Haemus' top.

Blind is the rage of passion's fire,
Will not be governed, brooks no reins,
And scoffs at death; nay, hostile swords
    It gladly courts.

Spare, O ye gods, be merciful,
That he who tamed the sea may live.
But much we fear, for the lord of the deep
Is wroth that his realm of the second lot
    Should be subdued.

The thoughtless youth who dared to drive
His father's sacred chariot,
Was by those fires, which o'er the heavens
He scattered in his mad career,
    Himself consumed.

The beaten path has never proved
The way of danger. Walk ye then
Where your forefathers safely trod,
And keep great nature's holy laws
    Inviolate.

Whoever dipped the famous oars
Of that bold bark in the rushing sea;
Whoe'er despoiled old Pelion
Of the thick, dark shade of his sacred
          groves;
Whoever dared the clashing rocks,
And, after countless perils passed,
His vessel moored on a barbarous shore,
Hoping to fare on his homeward way
The master of the golden fleece,
All by a fearful end appeased
    The offended sea.

First Tiphys, tamer of the deep,
Abandoned to an untrained hand
His vessel's helm. On a foreign shore,
Far from his native land he died;
And now within a common tomb,
'Midst unknown ghosts, he lies at rest.
In wrathful memory of her king
Lost on the sea, did Aulis then
Within her sluggish harbor hold
    The impatient ships

Then he, the tuneful Muse's son,
At whose sweet strains the streams stood
          still,
The winds were silent, and the birds,
Their songs forgotten, flocked to him,
The whole wood following after—he,
Over the Thracian fields was hurled
In scattered fragments; but his head
Down Hebrus' grieving stream was borne.
The well-remembered Styx he reached,
And Tartarus, whence ne'er again
    Would he return.

The wingèd sons of Boreas
Alcides slew, and Neptune's son
Who in a thousand changing forms
Could clothe himself. But after peace
On land and sea had been proclaimed,
And after savage Pluto's realm
Had been revealed to mortal eyes,
Then did Alcides' self, alive,
On burning Oeta's top lie down,
And give his body to the flames;
For sore distressed was he, consumed
By Deianira's deadly gift,
    The double blood.

A savage boar Ancaeus slew;
Thou, Meleager, impiously
Thy mother's brother in wrath didst slay,
And by that angry mother's hand
Didst die. All these deserved their death.
But for what crime did Hylas die,
A tender lad whom Hercules
Long time but vainly sought? For he,
'Mid waters safe was done to death.
Go then, and fearlessly the deep
Plow with your daring ships; but fear
    The peaceful pools.

Idmon, though well he knew the fates,
A serpent slew on Afric sands;

And Mopsus, to all others true,
False to himself, died far from Thebes.
If he with truth the future sang,
Then Nauplius, who strove to wreck
The Argive ships by lying fires,
Shall headlong fall into the sea.
And for his father's daring crime
Shall Ajax, that Oïleus' son,
Make full atonement, perishing
'Midst flame and flood.

And thou, Admetus' faithful mate,
Shalt for thy husband pay thy life,
Redeeming his from death. But he,
Who bade the first ship sail in quest
Of the golden spoil, King Pelias,
Seethed in a boiling cauldron, swam
'Mid those restricted waves. Enough,
O gods, have ye avenged the sea:
Spare him, we pray, who did but go
On ordered ways.

ACT IV

NURSE [alone]. My spirit trembles, for
I feel the near approach
Of some unseen disaster. Swiftly grows
her grief,
Its own fires kindling; and again her pas-
sion's force
Hath leaped to life. I oft have seen her,
with the fit
Of inspiration in her soul, confront the
gods
And force the very heavens to her will.
But now,
A monstrous deed, of greater moment far
than these,
Medea is preparing. For, but now, did
she
With step of frenzy hurry off until she
reached
Her stricken home. There, in her cham-
ber, all her stores
Of magic wonders are revealed; once more
she views
The things herself hath held in fear these
many years,
Unloosing one by one her ministers of ill,
Occult, unspeakable, and wrapt in mys-
tery;

And, grasping with her hand the sacred
altar-horn,
With prayers, she straightly summons all
destructive powers,
The creatures bred in Libya's sands, and
on the peaks
Of frigid Taurus, clad in everlasting
snows.
Obedient to her potent charms, the scaly
brood
Of serpents leave their darksome lairs and
swarm to her;
One savage creature rolls his monstrous
length along,
And darts his forkèd tongue with its en-
venomed sting,
Death-dealing; at the charming sound he
stops amazed,
And fold on fold his body writhes in nerve-
less coils.
"But these are petty ills; unworthy of
my hand,"
She cries, "are such weak, earth-born
weapons. Potent charms
Are bred in heaven. Now, now 'tis time
to summon powers
Transcending common magic. Down I'll
draw from heaven
That serpent huge whose body lies athwart
the sky
Like some great ocean stream, in whose
constricting folds
The greater and the lesser Bears are held
enthralled,
The greater set as guide for Grecian
ships, the less
For Sidon's mariners! Let Ophiuchus
loose
His hand and pour forth venom from his
captive thrall!
And let the Python huge, that dared to
rear its head
Against the heavenly twins, be present
at my prayer!
Let Hydra's writhing heads, which by
Alcides' hand
Were severed, all return to life and give
me aid!
Thou too be near and leave thy ancient
Colchian home,

Thou watchful dragon, to whose eyes the
first sleep came
In answer to my incantations."
      When she thus
Had summoned all the serpent brood, she
cast her store
Of baleful herbs together; all the poisons
brewed
Amid the rocky caves of trackless Eryx;
plants
That flourish on the snowy peaks of Cau-
casus,
Whose crags were spattered with Prome-
theus' gore; the herbs
Within whose deadly juice the Arab dips
his darts,
And the quiver-bearing Mede and fleeing
Parthian;
Those potent juices, too, which, near the
shivering pole,
The Suabian chieftains gather in Hyr-
canian groves.
The seasons, too, have paid their tribute
to her stores:
Whatever earth produces in the nesting
time,
And when the stiff'ning hand of winter's
frost has stripped
The glory from the trees and fettered all
the land
With icy bonds; whatever flow'ring plant
conceals
Destruction in its bloom, or in its twisted
roots
Distils the juice of death, she gathers to
her use.
These pestilential herbs Haemonian Athos
gave;
And these on lofty Pindus grew; a bloody
knife
Clipped off these slender leaves on Mace-
donia's heights;
Still others grew beside the Tigris, whirl-
ing on
His flood to meet the sea; the Danube
nourished some;
These grew on bright gem-starred
Hydaspes' tepid stream;
And these the Baetis bore, which gave the
land its name,

Displacing with its languorous tide, the
western sea.
These felt the knife when early dawn be-
gins to break;
The fruit of these was cut in midnight's
gloomy hour;
This fatal crop was reaped with sickle
magic-edged.
These deadly, potent herbs she takes and
sprinkles o'er
With serpent venom, mixing all; and in
the broth
She mingles unclean birds: a wailing
screech owl's heart,
A ghastly vampire's vitals torn from liv-
ing flesh.
Her magic poisons all she ranges for her
use.
The ravening power of hidden fire is held
in these,
While deep in others lurks the numbing
chill of frost.
Now magic runes she adds more potent
far. But lo!
Her voice resounds! and, as with mad-
dened step she comes,
She chants her charms, while heaven and
earth convulsive rock.

[*Enter* MEDEA, *chanting her incantations.*]
  MEDEA. I supplicate the silent throng,
    and you, the gods
Of death's sad rites, and groping chaos,
    and the home
Of gloomy Pluto, and the black abyss of
    death
Girt by the banks of Tartarus! Ye storied
    shades,
Your torments leave and haste to grace
    the festival
At Hymen's call! Let stop the whirling
    wheel that holds
Ixion's limbs and let him tread Corinthian
    ground;
Let Tantalus unfrighted drink Pirene's
    stream.
On Creon's stock alone let heavier tor-
    ments fall,
And backward o'er the rocks let Sisyphus
    be hurled.

You too, the seed of Danaüs, whose fruitless toil
The ever-empty urns deride, I summon you;
This day requires your helping hands.
Thou radiant moon,
Night's glorious orb, my supplications hear and come
To aid; put on thy sternest guise, thou goddess dread
Of triple form! Full oft have I with flowing locks,
And feet unsandaled, wandered through thy darkling groves
And by thy inspiration summoned forth the rain
From cloudless skies; the heaving seas have I subdued,
And sent the vanquished waves to ocean's lowest depths.
At my command the sun and stars together shine,
The heavenly law reversed; while in the Arctic sea
The Bears have plunged. The seasons, too, obey my will:
I've made the burning summer blossom as the spring,
And hoary winter autumn's golden harvests bear.
The Phasis sends his swirling waves to seek their source,
And Ister, flowing to the sea with many mouths,
His eager water checks and sluggish rolls along.
The billows roar, the mad sea rages, though the winds
All silent lie. At my command primeval groves
Have lost their shade; the sun, abandoning the day,
Has stood in middle heaven; while falling Hyades
Attest my charms.
　　But now thy sacred hour is come,
O Phoebe. Thine these bonds with bloody hand entwined
With ninefold serpent coils; these cords I offer thee,

Which on his hybrid limbs Typhoeus bore, who shook
The throne of Jove. This vessel holds the dying blood
Of Nessus, faithless porter of Alcides' bride.
Here are the ashes of the pyre on Oeta's top
Which drank the poisoned blood of dying Hercules;
And here the fatal billet that Althaea burned
In vengeance on her son. These plumes the Harpies left
Within their caverned lair when Zetes drove them forth;
And these the feathers of that vile Stymphalian bird
Which arrows, dipped in Lerna's deadly poison, pierced.
But lo! mine altar fires resound!
While in the tripod's answering voice
Behold the present deity!
I see the car of Trivia,
Not full and clear as when she drives
The livelong night to meet the dawn;
But with a baleful, lurid glare,
As, harried by Thessalian cries,
She holds a more restricted course.
Send such uncanny light abroad!
Fill mortals with a dread unknown;
And let our Corinth's priceless bronze
Resound, Dictynna, for thy aid!
To thee a solemn sacrifice
On bloody altar do we pay!
To thee, snatched from the mournful tomb,
The blazing torch nocturnal burns;
On thee I call with tossing head,
And many a frantic gesture make;
Corpselike upon the bier I lie,
My hair with priestly fillet bound;
Before thy awful shrine is waved
The branch in Stygian waters dipped.
And, calling on thy name, with gleaming shoulders bared,
Like Bacchus' mad adorers, will I lash my arms
With sacrificial knife. Now let my lifeblood flow!

And let my hands be used to draw the
  deadly sword,
And learn to shed belovèd blood!
  [*She cuts her arm and lets the
  blood flow upon the altar.*]
Behold, self-stricken have I poured the
  sacrifice!
But if too oft upon thy name I call,
I pray forgive this importunity!
The cause, O Hecate, of all my prayers
Is ever Jason; this my constant care.
  [*To attendants.*]
Take now Creüsa's bridal robe, and steep
  in these,
My potent drugs; and when she dons the
  clinging folds,
Let subtle flames go stealing through her
  inmost heart.
The fire that in this tawny golden circlet
  lurks
Prometheus gave, who, for his daring
  heavenly theft
In human aid, endured an ever-living
  death.
'Twas Vulcan showed the fires concealed
  in sulphur's veins;
While from my brother Phaëthon I gained
  a flame
That never dies; I have preserved Chi-
  mera's breath,
And that fierce heat that parched the
  fiery, brazen bull
Of Colchis. These dread fires commingled
  with the gall
Of dire Medusa have I bidden keep the
  power
Of lurking evil. Now, O Hecate,
Give added force to these my deadly
  gifts.
And strictly guard the hidden seeds
  of flame.
Let them deceive the sight, endure the
  touch;
But through her veins let burning
  fever run;
In fervent heat consume her very
  bones,
And let her fiercely blazing locks out-
  shine
Her marriage torches! Lo, my prayer
  is heard:

Thrice have replied the hounds of
  Hecate,
And she has shown her baleful, gleam-
  ing fires.
Now all is ready: hither call my sons,
And let them bear these presents to
  the bride.

  [*Enter sons.*]
Go, go, my sons, of hapless mother
  born,
And win with costly gifts and many
  prayers
The favor of the queen, your father's
  wife.
Begone, but quick your homeward
  way retrace,
That I may fold you in a last em-
  brace.
  [*Exeunt sons toward the palace,*
  MEDEA *in opposite direction.*]
CHORUS.   Where hastes this Bacchic
  fury now,
All passion-swept? what evil deed
Does her unbridled rage prepare?
Her features are congealed with rage,
And with a queenly bearing, grand
But terrible, she sets herself
Against e'en Creon's royal power.
An exile who would deem her now?
Her cheeks anon with anger flush,
And now a deadly pallor show;
Each feeling quick succeeds to each,
While all the passions of her heart
Her changing aspect testifies.
She wanders restless here and there,
As a tigress, of her young bereft,
In frantic grief the jungle scours.
Medea knows not how in check
To hold her wrath nor yet her love;
If love and wrath make common
  cause,
What dire results will come?
When will this scourge of Corinth
  leave
Our Grecian shores for Colchis' strand,
And free our kingdom from its fear?
Now, Phoebus, hasten on thy course
With no retarding rein.
Let friendly darkness quickly veil the
  light,

And this dread day be buried deep in night.

ACT V

MESSENGER [*comes running in from the direction of the palace*]. Lo, all is lost! the kingdom totters from its base!
The daughter and the father lie in common dust!
CHORUS. By what snare taken?
MESSENGER. By gifts, the common snare of kings.
CHORUS. What harm could lurk in them?
MESSENGER. In equal doubt I stand; And, though my eyes proclaim the dreadful deed is done,
I scarce can trust their witness.
CHORUS. What the mode of death?
MESSENGER. Devouring flames consume the palace at the will
Of her who sent them; there complete destruction reigns,
While men do tremble for the very city's doom.
CHORUS. Let water quench the fire.
MESSENGER. Nay here is added wonder:
The copious streams of water feed the deadly flames;
And opposition only fans their fiery rage
To whiter heat. The very bulwarks feel their power.

[MEDEA *enters in time to hear that her magic has been successful.*]
NURSE [*to* MEDEA]. Oh, haste thee, leave this land of Greece, in headlong flight!
MEDEA. Thou bid'st me speed my flight? Nay rather, had I fled,
I should return for this. Strange bridal rites I see!
[*Absorbed in her own reflections.*]
Why dost thou falter, O my soul? 'Tis well begun;
But still how small a portion of thy just revenge

Is that which gives thee present joy?
Not yet has love
Been banished from thy maddened heart if 'tis enough
That Jason widowed be. Pursue thy vengeful quest
To acts as yet unknown, and steel thyself for these.
Away with every thought and fear of God and man;
Too lightly falls the rod that pious hands upbear.
Give passion fullest sway; exhaust thy ancient powers;
And let the worst thou yet hast done be innocent
Beside thy present deeds. Come, let them know how slight
Were those thy crimes already done;
mere training they
For greater deeds. For what could hands untrained in crime
Accomplish? Or what mattered maiden rage? But now,
I am Medea; in the bitter school of woe
My powers have ripened.
[*In an ecstasy of madness.*]
Oh, the bliss of memory!
My infant brother slain, his limbs asunder rent,
My royal father spoiled of his ancestral realm,
And Pelias' guiltless daughters lured to slay their sire!
But here I must not rest; no untrained hand I bring
To execute my deeds. But now, by what approach
Or by what weapon wilt thou threat the treacherous foe?
Deep hidden in my secret heart have I conceived
A purpose which I dare not utter. Oh, I fear
That in my foolish madness I have gone too far—
I would that children had been born to him of this
My hated rival. Still, since she hath gained his heart,

His children too are hers—
That punishment would be most fitting
and deserved.
Yes, now I see the final deed of crime,
and thou,
My soul, must face it. You, who once
were called my sons,
Must pay the penalty of these your
father's crimes—
My heart with horror melts, a numbing
chill pervades
My limbs, and all my soul is filled with
sinking fear.
Now wrath gives place, and, heedless of
my husband's sins,
The tender mother-instinct quite possesses
me.
And could I shed my helpless children's
blood? Not so,
Oh, say not so, my maddened heart! Far
from my hand
And thought be that unnameable and
hideous deed!
What sin have they that shedding of their
wretched blood
Would wash away?
          Their sin—that Jason is their sire,
And, deeper guilt, that I have borne them.
Let them die;
They are not mine. Nay, nay! they are
my own, my sons,
And with no spot of guilt. Full innocent
they are,
'Tis true—my brother, too, was innocent.
O soul,
Why dost thou hesitate? Why flow these
streaming tears,
While with contending thoughts my waver-
ing heart is torn?
As when conflicting winds contend in
stubborn strife,
And waves, to stormy waves opposed, the
sea invade,
And to their lowest sands the briny waters
boil;
With such a storm my heart is tossed.
Hate conquers love,
And love puts impious hate to flight. Oh,
yield thee, grief,
To love! Then come, my sons, sole com-
fort of my heart,

Come, cling within your mother's close
embrace. Unharmed
Your sire may keep you, while your
mother holds you too.
          [*Embraces her sons.*]
But flight and exile drive me forth! And
even now
My children must be torn away with tears
and cries.
Then let them die to Jason since they're
lost to me.
Once more has hate resumed her sway,
and passion's fire
Is hot within my soul. Now fury, as of
yore,
Reseeks her own. Lead on, I follow to the
end!
I would that I had borne twice seven
sons, the boast
Of Niobe! But all too barren have I been.
Still will my two sufficient be to satisfy
My brother and my sire.
          [*Sees a vision of the furies and
          her brother's ghost.*]
          But whither hastes that throng
Of furies? What their quest? What
mean their brandished fires?
Whom threats this hellish host with hor-
rid, bloody brands?
I hear the writhing lash resound of ser-
pents huge.
Whom seeks Megaera with her deadly
torch? Whose shade
Comes gibbering there with scattered
limbs? It is my brother!
Revenge he seeks, and we will grant his
quest. Then come,
Within my heart plunge all your torches,
rend me, burn;
For lo, my bosom open to your fury's
stroke.
O brother, bid these vengeful goddesses
depart
And go in peace down to the lowest shades
of hell.
And do thou leave me to myself, and let
this hand
That slew thee with the sword now offer
sacrifice
Unto thy shade.   [*Slays her first son.*]
          What sudden uproar meets my ear?

'Tis Corinth's citizens on my destruction
bent.
Unto the palace roof I'll mount and there
complete
This bloody sacrifice.
[*To her remaining son.*]
Do thou come hence with me.
But thee, poor senseless corse, within
mine arms I'll bear.
Now gird thyself, my heart, with strength.
Nor must this deed
Lose all its just renown because in secret
done;
But to the public eye my hand must be
approved.
JASON [*in the street below shouting to
citizens*]. Ho, all ye loyal sons, who
mourn the death of kings!
Come, let us seize the worker of this
hideous crime.
Now ply your arms and raze her palace
to the ground.
MEDEA [*appearing on the housetop with
her two sons.*] Now, now have I
regained my regal state, my sire,
My brother! Once again the Colchians
hold the spoil
Of precious gold! And by the magic of
this hour
I am a maid once more. O heavenly pow-
ers, appeased
At length! O festal hour! O nuptial
day! On, on!
Accomplished is the guilt, but not the
recompense.
Complete the task while yet thy hands
are strong to act!
Why dost thou linger still? why dost thou
hesitate
Upon the threshold of the deed? Thou
canst perform it.
Now wrath has died within me, and my
soul is filled
With shame and deep remorse. Ah me,
what have I done,
Wretch that I am? Wretch that thou
art, well mayst thou mourn,
For thou hast done it!
At that thought delirious joy
O'ermasters me and fills my heart which
fain would grieve.

And yet, methinks, the act was almost
meaningless,
Since Jason saw it not; for naught has
been performed
If to his grief be added not the woe of
sight.
JASON [*discovering her*]. Lo, there she
stands upon the lofty battlements!
Bring torches! fire the house, that she
may fall ensnared
By those devices she herself hath planned.
MEDEA (*derisively*). Not so,
But rather build a lofty pyre for these
thy sons;
Their funeral rites prepare. Already for
thy bride
And father have I done the service due
the dead;
For in their ruined palace have I buried
them.
One son of thine has met his doom; and
this shall die
Before his father's face.
JASON. By all the gods, and by the
perils of our flight,
And by our marriage bond which I have
ne'er betrayed,
I pray thee spare the boy, for he is inno-
cent.
If aught of sin there be. 'tis mine. My-
self I give
To be the victim. Take my guilty soul
for his.
MEDEA. 'Tis for thy prayers and tears
I draw, not sheathe the sword.
Go now, and take thee maids for wives,
thou faithless one;
Abandon and betray the mother of thy
sons.
JASON. And yet, I pray thee, let one
sacrifice atone.
MEDEA. If in the blood of one my pas-
sion could be quenched,
No vengeance had it sought. Though both
my sons I slay,
The number still is all too small to satisfy
My boundless grief.
JASON. Then finish what thou hast
begun—
I ask no more—and grant at least that
no delay

Prolong my helpless agony.

MEDEA.   Now hasten not,
Relentless passion, but enjoy a slow revenge.
This day is in thy hands; its fertile hours
    employ.

JASON.   Oh, take my life, thou heartless
    one.

MEDEA.   Thou bid'st me pity—
Well! [*Slays the second child.*]—'Tis
    done!
No more atonement, passion, can I offer
    thee.
Now hither lift thy tearful eyes ungrateful one.
Dost recognize thy wife? 'Twas thus of
    old I fled.

The heavens themselves provide me with
    a safe retreat.
    [*A chariot drawn by dragons appears in the air.*]
Twin serpents bow their necks submissive
    to the yoke.
Now, father, take thy sons; while I, upon
    my car,
With wingèd speed am borne aloft through
    realms of air.
    [*Mounts her car and is borne away.*]

JASON [*calling after her*]. Speed on
    through realms of air that mortals
    never see:
But, witness heaven, where thou art gone
    no gods can be!

ŚAKOONTALÁ

By KÁLIDÁSA

Written and produced probably in the 5th century, A.D.

TRANSLATED BY SIR MONIER MONIER-WILLIAMS

PERSONS REPRESENTED

DUSHYANTA, *King of India*
MÁṬHAVYA, *the jester, friend, and companion of the King*
KANWA, *chief of the hermits, foster-father of* ŚAKOONTALÁ
ŚÁRNGARAVA,} *two Bráhmans, belonging to the hermitage of* KANWA
ŚÁRADWATA, }
MITRÁVASU, *brother-in-law of the King, and superintendent of the city police*
JÁNUKA *and* SÚCHAKA, *two constables*
VÁTÁYANA, *the chamberlain or attendant on the women's apartments*
SOMARÁTA, *the domestic priest*
KARABHAKA, *a messenger of the queen-mother*
RAIVATIKA, *the warder or doorkeeper*
MÁTALI, *charioteer of Indra*
SARVA-DAMANA, *afterwards* BHARATA, *a little boy, son of* DUSHYANTA *by* ŚAKOONTALÁ
KAŚYAPA, *a divine sage, progenitor of men and gods, son of* MARÍCHI, *and grandson of* BRAHMÁ
ŚAKOONTALÁ, *daughter of the sage* VIŚWÁMITRA *and the nymph* MENAKÁ, *foster-child of the hermit* KANWA
PRIYAMVADÁ *and* ANASÚYÁ, *female attendants, companions of* ŚAKOONTALÁ
GAUTAMÍ, *a holy matron, Superior of the female inhabitants of the hermitage*
VASUMATÍ, *the Queen of* DUSHYANTA
SÁNUMATÍ, *a nymph, friend of* ŚAKOONTALÁ
TARALIKÁ, *personal attendant of the Queen*
CHATURIKÁ, *personal attendant of the King*
VETRAVATÍ, *female warder or doorkeeper*
PARABHRITIKÁ *and* MADHUKARIKÁ, *maidens in charge of royal gardens*
SUVRATÁ, *a nurse*
ADITI, *wife of* KAŚYAPA; *granddaughter of* BRAHMÁ *through her father* DAKSHA
Charioteer, Fisherman, Officers, and Hermits

PROLOGUE

BENEDICTION

Íśa preserve you! he who is revealed
In these eight forms by man perceptible—
Water, of all creation's works the first;
The Fire that bears on high the sacrifice
Presented with solemnity to heaven;
The Priest, the holy offerer of gifts;
The Sun and Moon, those two majestic
    orbs,
Eternal marshallers of day and night;
The subtle Ether, vehicle of sound,
Diffused throughout the boundless uni-
    verse;
The Earth, by sages called 'The place of
    birth
Of all material essences and things';
And Air, which giveth life to all that
    breathe.

STAGE-MANAGER [*after the recitation of
the benediction, looking toward the tiring-
room*]. Lady, when you have finished
attiring yourself, come this way.

ACTRESS [*entering*]. Here I am, Sir;
what are your commands?

STAGE-MANAGER. We are here before
the eyes of an audience of educated and
discerning men; and have to represent in
their presence a new drama composed by
Kâlidâsa, called 'Śakoontalâ; or, the Lost
Ring.' Let the whole company exert
themselves to do justice to their several
parts.

ACTRESS. You, Sir, have so judiciously
managed the cast of the characters, that
nothing will be defective in the acting.

STAGE-MANAGER. Lady, I will tell you
the exact state of the case.
No skill in acting can I deem complete,
Till from the wise the actor gain ap-
    plause;
Know that the heart e'en of the truly
    skilful,
Shrinks from too boastful confidence in
    self.

ACTRESS [*modestly*]. You judge cor-
rectly. And now, what are your com-
mands?

STAGE-MANAGER. What can you do bet-
ter than engage the attention of the
audience by some captivating melody?

ACTRESS. Which among the seasons
shall I select as the subject of my song?

STAGE-MANAGER. You surely ought to
give the preference to the present summer
season that has but recently commenced,
a season so rich in enjoyment. For now
Unceasing are the charms of halcyon days,
When the cool bath exhilarates the frame;
When sylvan gales are laden with the
    scent
Of fragrant Pâtalas; when soothing sleep
Creeps softly on beneath the deepening
    shade;
And when, at last, the dulcet calm of eve
Entrancing steals o'er every yielding sense.

ACTRESS. I will:—   [*Sings.*]
Fond maids, the chosen of their hearts to
    please,
Entwine their ears with sweet Śirisha
    flowers,
Whose fragrant lips attract the kiss of
    bees
That softly murmur through the sum-
    mer hours.

STAGE-MANAGER. Charmingly sung!
The audience are motionless as statues,
their souls riveted by the enchanting
strain. What subject shall we select for
representation, that we may ensure a
continuance of their favour?

ACTRESS. Why not the same, Sir, an-
nounced by you at first? Let the drama
called 'Śakoontalâ; or, the Lost Ring,' be
the subject of our dramatic performance.

STAGE-MANAGER. Rightly reminded!
For the moment I had forgotten it.
Your song's transporting melody decoyed
My thoughts, and rapt with ecstasy my
    soul;
As now the bounding antelope allures
The King Dushyanta on the chase intent.
                                [*Exeunt.*]

ACT I

SCENE—*A Forest.*

[*Enter* KING DUSHYANTA, *armed with a
bow and arrow, in a chariot, chasing an
antelope, attended by his* CHARIOTEER.]

CHARIOTEER [*looking at the deer, and then at the* KING]. Great Prince.

When on the antelope I bend my gaze,
And on your Majesty, whose mighty bow
Has its string firmly braced; before my eyes
The god that wields the trident seems revealed,
Chasing the deer that flies from him in vain.

KING. Charioteer, this fleet antelope has drawn us far from my attendants.

See! there he runs:
Aye and anon his graceful neck he bends
To cast a glance at the pursuing car;
And dreading now the swift-descending shaft,
Contracts into itself his slender frame;
About his path, in scattered fragments strewn,
The half-chewed grass falls from his panting mouth;
See! in his airy bounds he seems to fly,
And leaves no trace upon th' elastic turf.
[*With astonishment.*]
How now! swift as is our pursuit, I scarce can see him.

CHARIOTEER. Sire, the ground here is full of hollows; I have therefore drawn in the reins and checked the speed of the chariot. Hence the deer has somewhat gained upon us. Now that we are passing over level ground, we shall have no difficulty in overtaking him.

KING. Loosen the reins, then.

CHARIOTEER. The King is obeyed.
[*Drives the chariot at full speed.*]

Great Prince, see! see!
Responsive to the slackened rein, the steeds,
Chafing with eager rivalry, career
With emulative fleetness o'er the plain;
Their necks outstretched, their waving plumes, that late
Fluttered above their brows, are motionless;

Their sprightly ears, but now erect, bent low;
Themselves unsullied by the circling dust
That vainly follows on their rapid course.

KING [*joyously*]. In good sooth, the horses seem as if they would outstrip the steeds of Indra and the Sun.

That which but now showed to my view minute
Quickly assumes dimension; that which seemed
A moment since disjoined in diverse parts,
Looks suddenly like one compacted whole;
That which is really crooked in its shape
In the far distance left, grows regular;
Wondrous the chariot's speed, that in a breath,
Makes the near distant and the distant near.

Now, Charioteer, see me kill the deer.
[*Takes aim.*]
A VOICE [*behind the scenes*]. Hold, O King! this deer belongs to our hermitage. Kill it not! kill it not!

CHARIOTEER [*listening and looking*]. Great King, some hermits have stationed themselves so as to screen the antelope at the very moment of its coming within range of your arrow.

KING [*hastily*]. Then stop the horses.

CHARIOTEER. I obey. [*Stops the chariot.*]

[*Enter a* HERMIT, *and two others with him.*]

HERMIT [*raising his hand*]. This deer, O King, belongs to our hermitage. Kill it not! kill it not!

Now heaven forbid this barbèd shaft descend
Upon the fragile body of a fawn,
Like fire upon a heap of tender flowers!
Can thy steel bolts no meeter quarry find
Than the warm life-blood of a harmless deer?
Restore, great Prince, thy weapon to its quiver.

More it becomes thy arms to shield the
    weak,
Than to bring anguish on the innocent.
KING. 'Tis done. [*Replaces the arrow
                        in its quiver.*]
HERMIT. Worthy is this action of a
Prince, the light of Puru's race.
Well does this act befit a Prince like thee,
Right worthy is it of thine ancestry.
Thy guerdon be a son of peerless worth,
Whose wide dominion shall embrace the
    earth.

BOTH THE OTHER HERMITS [*raising
their hands*]. May heaven indeed grant
thee a son, a sovereign of the earth from
sea to sea!
KING [*bowing*]. I accept with gratitude
a Bráhman's [benediction].
HERMIT. We came hither, mighty
Prince, to collect sacrificial wood. Here
on the banks of the Málini you may per-
ceive the hermitage of the great sage
Kanwa. If other duties require not your
presence, deign to enter and accept our
hospitality.

When you behold our penitential rites
Performed without impediment by saints
Rich only in devotion, then with pride
Will you reflect:—Such are the holy men
Who call me Guardian; such the men for
    whom
To wield the bow I bare my nervous arm,
Scarred by the motion of the glancing
    string.

KING. Is the Chief of your Society now
at home?
HERMIT. No; he has gone to Soma-
tírtha to propitiate Destiny, which
threatens his daughter Śakoontalá with
some calamity; but he has commissioned
her in his absence to entertain all guests
with hospitality.
KING. Good! I will pay her a visit.
She will make me acquainted with the
mighty sage's acts of penance and devo-
tion.
HERMIT. And we will depart on our
errand.   [*Exit with his companions.*]

KING. Charioteer, urge on the horses.
We will at least purify our souls by a
sight of this hallowed retreat.
CHARIOTEER. Your Majesty is obeyed.
[*Drives the chariot with great velocity.*]
KING [*looking all about him*]. Chariot-
eer, even without being told, I should
have known that these were the precincts
of a grove consecrated to penitential rites.
CHARIOTEER. How so?
KING. Do not you observe?

Beneath the trees, whose hollow trunks
    afford
Secure retreat to many a nestling brood
Of parrots, scattered grains of rice lie
    strewn.
Lo! here and there are seen the polished
    slabs
That serve to bruise the fruit of Ingudí.
The gentle roe-deer, taught to trust in
    man,
Unstartled hear our voices. On the paths
Appear the traces of bark-woven vests
Borne dripping from the limpid fount of
    waters.
And mark!
Laved are the roots of trees by deep
    canals,
Whose glassy waters tremble in the
    breeze;
The sprouting verdure of the leaves is
    dimmed
By dusky wreaths of upward curling
    smoke
From burnt oblations; and on new-mown
    lawns
Around our car graze leisurely the fawns.

CHARIOTEER. I observe it all.
KING [*advancing a little further*]. The
inhabitants of this sacred retreat must
not be disturbed. Stay the chariot, that
I may alight.
CHARIOTEER. The reins are held in.
Your Majesty may descend.
KING [*alighting*]. Charioteer, groves
devoted to penance must be entered in
humble attire. Take these ornaments.
[*Delivers his ornaments and bow to the
CHARIOTEER.*] Charioteer, see that the

horses are watered, and attend to them until I return from visiting the inhabitants of the hermitage.

CHARIOTEER. I will. [*Exit.*]

KING [*walking and looking about*]. Here is the entrance to the hermitage. I will now go in.

[*Entering and feeling a throbbing sensation in his arm.*]

Serenest peace is in this calm retreat, By passion's breath unruffled; what portends My throbbing arm? Why should it whisper here Of happy love? Yet everywhere around us Stand the closed portals of events unknown.

A VOICE [*behind the scenes*]. This way, my dear companions; this way.

KING [*listening*]. Hark! I hear voices to the right of yonder grove of trees. I will walk in that direction. [*Walking and looking about.*] Ah! here are the maidens of the hermitage coming this way to·water the shrubs, carrying water-pots proportioned to their strength. [*Gazing at them.*] How graceful they look!

In palaces such charms are rarely ours; The woodland plants outshine the garden flowers.

I will conceal myself in this shade and watch them. [*Stands gazing at them.*]

[*Enter ŚAKOONTALÁ, with her two female companions, employed in the manner described.*]

ŚAKOONTALÁ. This way, my dear companions; this way.

ANASÚYÁ. Dear Śakoontalá, one would think that father Kanwa had more affection for the shrubs of the hermitage even than for you, seeing he assigns to you, who are yourself as delicate as the fresh-blown jasmine, the task of filling with water the trenches which encircle their roots.

ŚAKOONTALÁ. Dear Anasúyá, although I am charged by my good father with this duty, yet I cannot regard it as a task. I really feel a sisterly love for these plants. [*Continues watering the shrubs.*]

KING. Can this be the daughter of Kanwa? The saintly man, though descended from the great Kaśyapa, must be very deficient in judgment to habituate such a maiden to the life of the recluse.

The sage who would this form of artless grace Inure to penance, thoughtlessly attempts To cleave in twain the hard acacia's stem With the soft edge of a blue lotus-leaf.

Well! concealed behind this tree, I will watch her without raising her suspicions. [*Conceals himself.*]

ŚAKOONTALÁ. Good Anasúyá, Priyamvadá has drawn this bark-dress too tightly about my chest. I pray thee, loosen it a little.

ANASÚYÁ. I will. [*Loosens it.*]

PRIYAMVADÁ [*smiling*]. Why do you lay the blame on me? Blame rather your own blooming youthfulness which imparts fulness to your bosom.

KING. A most just observation!

This youthful form, whose bosom's swelling charms By the bark's knotted tissue are concealed, Like some fair bud close folded in its sheath, Gives not to view the blooming of its beauty. But what am I saying? In real truth this bark-dress, though ill-suited to her figure, sets it off like an ornament. The lotus with the Śaivala entwined Is not a whit less brilliant; dusky spots Heighten the lustre of the cold-rayed moon; This lovely maiden in her dress of bark Seems all the lovelier. E'en the meanest garb Gives to true beauty fresh attractiveness.

ŚAKOONTALÁ [*looking before her*]. Yon Keśara-tree beckons to me with its young shoots, which, as the breeze waves them to and fro, appear like slender fingers. I will go and attend to it. [*Walks towards it.*]

PRIYAMVADA. Dear Śakoontalá, prithee, rest in that attitude one moment.

ŚAKOONTALÁ. Why so?

PRIYAMVADÁ. The Keśara-tree, whilst your graceful form bends about its stem, appears as if it were wedded to some lovely twining creeper.

ŚAKOONTALÁ. Ah! saucy girl, you are most appropriately named Priyam-vadá ['Speaker of flattering things'].

KING. What Priyamvadá says, though complimentary, is nevertheless true. Verily,

Her ruddy lip vies with the opening bud;
Her graceful arms are as the twining stalks;
And her whole form is radiant with the glow
Of youthful beauty, as the tree with bloom.

ANASÚYÁ. See, dear Śakoontalá, here is the young jasmine, which you named 'the Moonlight of the Grove,' the self-elected wife of the mango-tree. Have you forgotten it?

ŚAKOONTALÁ. Rather will I forget myself. [Approaching the plant and looking at it.] How delightful is the season when the jasmine-creeper and the mango-tree seem thus to unite in mutual embraces! The fresh blossoms of the jasmine resemble the bloom of a young bride, and the newly-formed shoots of the mango appear to make it her natural protector.
[Continues gazing at it.]

PRIYAMVADÁ. Do you know, my Anasúyá, why Śakoontalá gazes so intently at the jasmine?

ANASÚYÁ. No, indeed, I cannot imagine. I pray thee tell me.

PRIYAMVADÁ. She is wishing that as the jasmine is united to a suitable tree, so, in like manner, she may obtain a husband worthy of her.

ŚAKOONTALÁ. Speak for yourself, girl; this is the thought in your own mind.
[Continues watering the flowers.]

KING. Would that my union with her were permissible! and yet I hardly dare hope that the maiden is sprung from a caste different from that of the Head of the hermitage. But away with doubt:

That she is free to wed a warrior-king
My heart attests. For, in conflicting doubts,
The secret promptings of the good man's soul
Are an unerring index of the truth.

However, come what may, I will ascertain the fact.

ŚAKOONTALÁ [in a flurry]. Ah! a bee, disturbed by the sprinkling of the water, has left the young jasmine, and is trying to settle on my face.
[Attempts to drive it away.]

KING [gazing at her ardently]. Beautiful! there is something charming even in her repulse.

Where'er the bee his eager onset plies,
Now here, now there, she darts her kindling eyes;
What love hath yet to teach, fear teaches now,
The furtive glances and the frowning brow. [In a tone of envy.]
Ah, happy bee! how boldly dost thou try
To steal the lustre from her sparkling eye;
And in thy circling movements hover near,
To murmur tender secrets in her ear;
Or, as she coyly waves her hand, to sip
Voluptuous nectar from her lower lip!
While rising doubts my heart's fond hopes destroy,
Thou dost the fulness of her charms enjoy.

ŚAKOONTALÁ. This impertinent bee will not rest quiet. I must move elsewhere. [Moving a few steps off, and casting a glance around.] How now! he is following me here. Help! my dear friends, help! deliver me from the attacks of this troublesome insect.

PRIYAMVADÁ and ANASÚYÁ. How can we deliver you? Call Dushyanta to your aid. The sacred groves are under the King's special protection.

KING. An excellent opportunity for me to show myself. Fear not—[checks himself when the words are half-uttered.

Aside.] But stay, if I introduce myself in this manner, they will know me to be the King. Be it so, I will accost them, nevertheless.

ŚAKOONTALÁ [*moving a step or two further off*]. What! it still persists in following me.

KING [*advancing hastily*]. When mighty Puru's offspring sways the earth,
And o'er the wayward holds his threatening rod,
Who dares molest the gentle maids that keep
Their holy vigils here in Kanwa's grove?

[*All look at the* KING, *and all are embarrassed.*]

ANASÚYÁ. Kind Sir, no outrage has been committed; only our dear friend here was teased by the attacks of a troublesome bee. [*Points to* ŚAKOONTALÁ.]

KING [*turning to* ŚAKOONTALÁ]. I trust all is well with your devotional rites?

[ŚAKOONTALÁ *stands confused and silent.*]

ANASÚYÁ. All is well indeed, now that we are honoured by the reception of a distinguished guest. Dear Śakoontalá, go, bring from the hermitage an offering of flowers, rice, and fruit. This water that we have brought with us will serve to bathe our guest's feet.

KING. The rites of hospitality are already performed; your truly kind words are the best offering I can receive.

PRIYAMVADÁ. At least be good enough, gentle Sir, to sit down awhile, and rest yourself on this seat shaded by the leaves of the Sapta-parṇa tree.

KING. You, too, must all be fatigued by your employment.

ANASÚYÁ. Dear Śakoontalá, there is no impropriety in our sitting by the side of our guest; come, let us sit down here.

[*All sit down together.*]

ŚAKOONTALÁ [*aside*]. How is it that the sight of this man has made me sensible of emotions inconsistent with religious vows?

KING [*gazing at them all by turns*]. How charmingly your friendship is in keeping with the equality of your ages and appearance!

PRIYAMVADÁ [*aside to* ANASÚYÁ]. Who can this person be, whose lively yet dignified manner, and polite conversation, bespeak him a man of high rank?

ANASÚYÁ. I, too, my dear, am very curious to know. I will ask him myself. [*Aloud.*] Your kind words, noble Sir, fill me with confidence, and prompt me to inquire of what regal family our noble guest is the ornament? what country is now mourning his absence? and what induced a person so delicately nurtured to expose himself to the fatigue of visiting this grove of penance?

ŚAKOONTALÁ [*aside*]. Be not troubled, O my heart, Anasúyá is giving utterance to thy thoughts.

KING [*aside*]. How now shall I reply? shall I make myself known, or shall I still disguise my real rank? I have it; I will answer her thus. [*Aloud.*] I am the person charged by his Majesty, the descendant of Puru, with the administration of justice and religion; and am come to this sacred grove to satisfy myself that the rites of the hermits are free from obstruction.

ANASÚYÁ. The hermits, then, and all the members of our religious society, have now a guardian.

[ŚAKOONTALÁ *gazes bashfully at the* KING.]

PRIYAMVADÁ *and* ANASÚYÁ [*perceiving the state of her feelings, and of the* KING'S. *Aside to* ŚAKOONTALÁ]. Dear Śakoontalá, if father Kanwa were but at home to-day——

ŚAKOONTALÁ [*angrily*]. What if he were?

PRIYAMVADÁ *and* ANASÚYÁ. He would honour this our distinguished guest with an offering of the most precious of his possessions.

ŚAKOONTALÁ. Go to! you have some silly idea in your minds. I will not listen to such remarks.

KING. May I be allowed, in my turn, to

ask you maidens a few particulars respecting your friend?

PRIYAMVADÁ and ANASÚYÁ. Your request, Sir, is an honour.

KING. The sage Kanwa lives in the constant practice of austerities. How, then, can this friend of yours be called his daughter?

ANASÚYÁ. I will explain to you, Sir. You have heard of an illustrious sage of regal caste, Viswámitra, whose family name is Kausika.

KING. I have.

ANASÚYÁ. Know that he is the real father of our friend. The venerable Kanwa is only her reputed father. He it was who brought her up, when she was deserted by her mother.

KING. 'Deserted by her mother!' My curiosity is excited; pray let me hear the story from the beginning.

ANASÚYÁ. You shall hear it, Sir. Some time since, this sage of regal caste, while performing a most severe penance on the banks of the river Godávarí, excited the jealousy and alarm of the gods; insomuch that they despatched a lovely nymph named Menaká to interrupt his devotions.

KING. The inferior gods, I am aware, are jealous of the power which the practice of excessive devotion confers on mortals.

ANASÚYÁ. Well, then, it happened that Viswámitra, gazing on the bewitching beauty of that nymph at a season when, spring being in its glory—[*Stops short, and appears confused.*]

KING. The rest may be easily divined. Sakoontalá, then, is the offspring of the nymph.

ANASÚYÁ. Just so.

KING. It is quite intelligible.

How could a mortal to such charms give birth?
The lightning's radiance flashes not from earth. [*SAKOONTALÁ remains modestly seated with downcast eyes.*]

[*Aside.*] And so my desire has really scope for its indulgence. Yet I am still distracted by doubts, remembering the

pleasantry of her female companions respecting her wish for a husband.

PRIYAMVADÁ [*looking with a smile at SAKOONTALÁ, and then turning towards the KING*]. You seem desirous, Sir, of asking something further.

[*SAKOONTALÁ makes a chiding gesture with her finger.*]

KING. You conjecture truly. I am so eager to hear the particulars of your friend's history, that I have still another question to ask.

PRIYAMVADÁ. Scruple not to do so. Persons who lead the life of hermits may be questioned unreservedly.

KING. I wish to ascertain one point respecting your friend.

Will she be bound by solitary vows
Opposed to love, till her espousals only?
Or ever dwell with these her cherished fawns,
Whose eyes, in lustre vying with her own,
Return her gaze of sisterly affection?

PRIYAMVADÁ. Hitherto, Sir, she has been engaged in the practice of religious duties, and has lived in subjection to her foster-father; but it is now his fixed intention to give her away in marriage to a husband worthy of her.

KING [*aside*]. His intention may be easily carried into effect.

Be hopeful, O my heart, thy harrowing doubts
Are past and gone; that which thou didst believe
To be as unapproachable as fire,
Is found a glittering gem that may be touched.

SAKOONTALÁ [*pretending anger*]. Anasúyá, I shall leave you.

ANASÚYÁ. Why so?

SAKOONTALÁ. That I may go and report this impertinent Priyamvadá to the venerable matron, Gautamí.

ANASÚYÁ. Surely, dear friend, it would not be right to leave a distinguished guest before he has received the rites of hospitality, and quit his presence in this wilful manner.

[ŚAKOONTALÁ, *without answering a word, moves away.*]

KING [*making a movement to arrest her departure, but checking himself. Aside*].

Ah! a lover's feelings betray themselves by his gestures.

When I would fain have stayed the maid, a sense
Of due decorum checked my bold design;
Though I have stirred not, yet my mien betrays
My eagerness to follow on her steps.

PRIYAMVADÁ [*holding* ŚAKOONTALÁ *back*]. Dear Śakoontalá, it does not become you to go away in this manner.

ŚAKOONTALÁ [*frowning*]. Why not, pray?

PRIYAMVADÁ. You are under a promise to water two more shrubs for me. When you have paid your debt, you shall go, and not before. [*Forces her to turn back.*]

KING. Spare her this trouble, gentle maiden. The exertion of watering the shrubs has already fatigued her.

The water-jar has overtasked the strength
Of her slim arms; her shoulders droop, her hands
Are ruddy with the glow of quickened pulses;
E'en now her agitated breath imparts
Unwonted tremor to her heaving breast;
The pearly drops that mar the recent bloom
Of the Śirísha pendent in her ear,
Gather in clustering circles on her cheek;
Loosed is the fillet of her hair; her hand
Restrains the locks that struggle to be free.

Suffer me, then, thus to discharge the debt for you.
[*Offers a ring to* PRIYAMVADÁ. *Both the maidens, reading the name* DUSHYANTA *on the seal, look at each other with surprise.*]

KING. Nay, think not that I am King Dushyanta. I am only the King's officer, and this is the ring which I have received from him as my credentials.

PRIYAMVADÁ. The greater the reason you ought not to part with the ring from your finger. I am content to release her from her obligation at your simple request. [*With a smile.*] Now, Śakoontalá, my love, you are at liberty to retire, thanks to the intercession of this noble stranger, or rather of this mighty prince.

ŚAKOONTALÁ [*aside*]. My movements are no longer under my own control. [*Aloud.*] Pray, what authority have you over me, either to send me away or keep me back?

KING [*gazing at* ŚAKOONTALÁ. *Aside*]. Would I could ascertain whether she is affected towards me as I am towards her! At any rate, my hopes are free to indulge themselves. Because,

Although she mingles not her words with mine,
Yet doth her listening ear drink in my speech;
Although her eye shrinks from my ardent gaze,
No form but mine attracts its timid glances.

A VOICE [*behind the scenes*]. O hermits, be ready to protect the animals belonging to our hermitage. King Dushyanta, amusing himself with hunting, is near at hand.

Lo! by the feet of prancing horses raised,
Thick clouds of moving dust, like glittering swarms
Of locusts, in the glow of eventide,
Fall on the branches of our sacred trees;
Where hang the dripping vests of woven bark,
Bleached by the waters of the cleansing fountain.

And see!

Scared by the royal chariot in its course,
With headlong haste an elephant invades
The hallowed precincts of our sacred grove;

Himself the terror of the startled deer,
And an embodied hindrance to our rites.
The hedge of creepers clinging to his
  feet,
Feeble obstruction to his mad career,
Is dragged behind him in a tangled chain;
And with terrific shock one tusk he
  drives
Into the riven body of a tree,
Sweeping before him all impediments.

KING [aside]. Out upon it! my retinue
are looking for me, and are disturbing
this holy retreat. Well! there is no help
for it; I must go and meet them.
PRIYAMVADÁ and ANASÚYÁ. Noble Sir,
we are terrified by the accidental dis-
turbance caused by the wild elephant.
Permit us to return to the cottage.
KING [hastily]. Go, gentle maidens.
It shall be our care that no injury hap-
pen to the hermitage. [All rise up.]
PRIYAMVADÁ and ANASÚYÁ. After such
poor hospitality, we are ashamed to re-
quest the honour of a second visit from
you.
KING. Say not so. The mere sight of
you, sweet maidens, has been to me the
best entertainment.
ŚAKOONTALÁ. Anasúyá, a pointed blade
of Kuśa-grass has pricked my foot; and
my bark-mantle is caught in the branch
of a Kuruvaka-bush. Be so good as to
wait for me until I have disentangled it.
  [Exit with her two companions,
  after making pretexts for de-
  lay, that she may steal glances
  at the KING.]
KING. I have no longer any desire to
return to the city. I will therefore re-
join my attendants, and make them en-
camp somewhere in the vicinity of this
sacred grove. In good truth, Śakoontalá
has taken such possession of my thoughts,
that I cannot turn myself in any other
direction.

My limbs drawn onward leave my heart
  behind,
Like silken pennon borne against the
  wind.

ACT II

SCENE—A plain on the skirts of the forest

[Enter the Jester MÁṬHAVYA, in a
melancholy mood.]

MÁṬHAVYA [sighing]. Heigh-ho! what
an unlucky fellow I am! worn to a
shadow by my royal friend's sporting
propensities. 'Here's a deer!' 'There
goes a boar!' 'Yonder's a tiger!' This
is the only burden of our talk, while in
the heat of the meridian sun we toil on
from jungle to jungle, wandering about
in the paths of the woods, where the trees
afford us no shelter. Are we thirsty?
We have nothing to drink but the dirty
water of some mountain stream mixed
with dry leaves, which give it a most
pungent flavour. Are we hungry? We
have nothing to eat but roast game, which
we must swallow down at odd times, as
best we can. Even at night there is no
peace to be had. Sleeping is out of the
question, with joints all strained by
dancing attendance upon my sporting
friend; or if I do happen to doze, I am
awakened at the very earliest dawn by
the horrible din of a lot of rascally beaters
and huntsmen, who must needs surround
the wood before sunrise, and deafen me
with their clatter. Nor are these my only
troubles. Here's a fresh grievance, like
a new boil rising upon an old one! Yes-
terday, while we were lagging behind, my
royal friend entered yonder hermitage
after a deer; and there, as ill-luck would
have it, caught sight of a beautiful girl,
called Śakoontalá, the hermit's daughter.
From that moment, not another thought
about returning to the city! and all last
night not a wink of sleep did he get for
thinking of the damsel. What is to be
done? At any rate I will be on the
watch for him as soon as he has finished
his toilet. [Walking and looking about.]
Oh! here he comes, attended by the Yavana
women, with bows in their hands, and
wearing garlands of wild flowers. What
shall I do? I have it. I will pretend to
stand in the easiest attitude for resting

my bruised and crippled limbs. [*Stands leaning on a staff.*]

[*Enter* KING DUSHYANTA, *followed by a retinue, in the manner described.*]

KING. True, by no easy conquest may I win her,
Yet are my hopes encouraged by her mien.
Love is not yet triumphant; but, methinks,
The hearts of both are ripe for his delights.

[*Smiling.*] Ah! thus does the lover delude himself; judging of the state of his loved one's feelings by his own desires.

But yet,
The stolen glance with half-averted eye,
The hesitating gait, the quick rebuke
Addressed to her companion, who would fain
Have stayed her counterfeit departure; these
Are signs not unpropitious to my suit.
So eagerly the lover feeds his hopes,
Claiming each trivial gesture for his own.

MÁṬHAVYA [*still in the same attitude*]. Ah, friends, my hands cannot move to greet you with the usual salutation. I can only just command my lips to wish your Majesty victory.

KING. Why, what has paralysed your limbs?

MÁṬHAVYA. You might as well ask me how my eye comes to water after you have poked your finger into it.

KING. I don't understand you; speak more intelligibly.

MÁṬHAVYA. Ah, my dear friend, is yonder upright reed transformed into a crooked plant by its own act, or by the force of the current?

KING. The current of the river causes it, I suppose.

MÁṬHAVYA. Ay; just as you are the cause of my crippled limbs.

KING. How so?

MÁṬHAVYA. Here are you living the life of a wild man of the woods in a savage unfrequented region, while your State-affairs are left to shift for themselves; and as for poor me, I am no longer master of my own limbs, but have to follow you about day after day in your chases after wild animals, till my bones are all crippled and out of joint. Do, my dear friend, let me have one day's rest.

KING [*aside*]. This fellow little knows, while he talks in this manner, that my mind is wholly engrossed by recollections of the hermit's daughter, and quite as disinclined to the chase as his own.

No longer can I bend my well-braced bow
Against the timid deer; nor e'er again
With well-aimed arrows can I think to harm
These her beloved associates, who enjoy
The privilege of her companionship;
Teaching her tender glances in return.

MÁṬHAVYA [*looking in the* KING's *face*]. I may as well speak to the winds, for any attention you pay to my requests. I suppose you have something on your mind, and are talking it over to yourself.

KING [*smiling*]. I was only thinking that I ought not to disregard a friend's request.

MÁṬHAVYA. Then may the King live for ever! [*Moves off.*]

KING. Stay a moment, my dear friend. I have something else to say to you.

MÁṬHAVYA. Say on, then.

KING. When you have rested, you must assist me in another business which will give you no fatigue.

MÁṬHAVYA. Ah! In eating something nice, I hope.

KING. You shall know at some future time.

MÁṬHAVYA. No time better than the present.

KING. What ho, there!

WARDER [*entering*]. What are your Majesty's commands?

KING. O Raivatika, bid the General of the forces attend.

WARDER. I will, Sire. [*Exit and re-enters with the* GENERAL.] Come forward, General; his Majesty is looking towards you, and has some order to give you.

GENERAL [*looking at the* KING].

Though hunting is known to produce ill effects, my royal master has derived only benefit from it. For
Like the majestic elephant that roams
O'er mountain wilds, so does the King display
A stalwart frame, instinct with vigorous life.
His brawny arms and manly chest are scored
By frequent passage of the sounding string;
Unharmed he bears the midday sun; no toil
His mighty spirit daunts; his sturdy limbs,
Stripped of redundant flesh, relinquish nought
Of their robust proportions, but appear
In muscle, nerve, and sinewy fibre cased.

[*Approaching the* KING.] Victory to the King! We have tracked the wild beasts to their lairs in the forest. Why delay, when everything is ready?

KING My friend Máthavya here has been disparaging the chase, till he has taken away all my relish for it.

GENERAL [*aside to* MÁTHAVYA]. Persevere in your opposition, my good fellow; I will sound the King's real feelings, and humour him accordingly. [*Aloud.*] The blockhead talks nonsense, and your Majesty in your own person furnishes the best proof of it. Observe, Sire, the advantage and pleasure the hunter derives from the chase.

Freed from all grosser influences his frame
Loses its sluggish humours, and becomes
Buoyant, compact, and fit for bold encounter.
'Tis his to mark with joy the varied passions,
Fierce heats of anger, terror, blank dismay,
Of forest animals that cross his path.
Then what a thrill transports the hunter's soul

When, with unerring course, his driven shaft
Pierces the moving mark! Oh! 'tis conceit
In moralists to call the chase a vice;
What recreation can compare with this?

MÁTHAVYA [*angrily*]. Away! tempter, away! The King has recovered his senses, and is himself again. As for you, you may, if you choose, wander about from forest to forest, till some old bear seizes you by the nose, and makes a mouthful of you.

KING. My good General, as we are just now in the neighbourhood of a consecrated grove, your panegyric upon hunting is somewhat ill-timed, and I cannot assent to all you have said. For the present,

All undisturbed the buffaloes shall sport
In yonder pool, and with their ponderous horns
Scatter its tranquil waters, while the deer,
Couched here and there in groups beneath the shade
Of spreading branches, ruminate in peace.
And all securely shall the herd of boars
Feed on the marshy sedge; and thou, my bow,
With slackened string, enjoy a long repose.

GENERAL. So please your Majesty, it shall be as you desire.

KING. Recall, then, the beaters who were sent in advance to surround the forest. My troops must not be allowed to disturb this sacred retreat, and irritate its pious inhabitants.

Know that within the calm and cold recluse
Lurks unperceived a germ of smothered flame,
All-potent to destroy; a latent fire
That rashly kindled bursts with fury forth;
As in the disc of crystal that remains
Cool to the touch, until the solar ray

Falls on its polished surface, and excites
The burning heat that lies within concealed.

GENERAL. Your Majesty's commands shall be obeyed.

MÁṬHAVYA. Off with you, you son of a slave! Your nonsense won't go down here, my fine fellow. [*Exit* GENERAL.]

KING [*looking at his attendants*]. Here, women, take my hunting-dress; and you, Raivatika, keep guard carefully outside.

ATTENDANTS. We will, Sire. [*Exeunt.*]

MÁṬHAVYA. Now that you have got rid of these plagues, who have been buzzing about us like so many flies, sit down, do, on that stone slab, with the shade of the tree as your canopy, and I will seat myself by you quite comfortably.

KING. Go you, and sit down first.

MÁṬHAVYA. Come along, then. [*Both walk on a little way, and seat themselves.*]

KING. Máṭhavya, it may be said of you that you have never beheld anything worth seeing; for your eyes have not yet looked upon the loveliest object in creation.

MÁṬHAVYA. How can you say so, when I see your Majesty before me at this moment?

KING. It is very natural that every one should consider his own friend perfect; but I was alluding to Śakoontalá, the brightest ornament of these hallowed groves.

MÁṬHAVYA [*aside*]. I understand well enough, but I am not going to humour him. [*Aloud.*] If, as you intimate, she is a hermit's daughter, you cannot lawfully ask her in marriage. You may as well then dismiss her from your mind, for any good the mere sight of her can do.

KING. Think you that a descendant of the mighty Puru could fix his affections on an unlawful object?

Though, as men say, the offspring of the sage,
The maiden to a nymph celestial owes
Her being, and by her mother left on earth,

Was found and nurtured by the holy man
As his own daughter, in this hermitage.
So, when dissevered from its parent stalk,
Some falling blossom of the jasmine, wafted
Upon the sturdy sun-flower, is preserved
By its support from premature decay.

MÁṬHAVYA [*smiling*]. This passion of yours for a rustic maiden, when you have so many gems of women at home in your palace, seems to me very like the fancy of a man who is tired of sweet dates, and longs for sour tamarinds as a variety.

KING. You have not seen her, or you would not talk in this fashion.

MÁṬHAVYA. I can quite understand it must require something surpassingly attractive to excite the admiration of such a great man as you.

KING. I will describe her, my dear friend, in a few words.

Man's all-wise Maker, wishing to create
A faultless form, whose matchless symmetry
Should far transcend Creation's choicest works,
Did call together by his mighty will,
And garner up in his eternal mind,
A bright assemblage of all lovely things;
And then, as in a picture, fashion them
Into one perfect and ideal form—
Such the divine, the wondrous prototype,
Whence her fair shape was moulded into being.

MÁṬHAVYA. If that's the case, she must indeed throw all other beauties into the shade.

KING. To my mind she really does.

This peerless maid is like a fragrant flower,
Whose perfumed breath has never been diffused;
A tender bud, that no profaning hand
Has dared to sever from its parent stalk;
A gem of priceless water, just released
Pure and unblemished from its glittering bed.
Or may the maiden haply be compared
To sweetest honey, that no mortal lip

Has sipped; or, rather, to the mellowed
    fruit
Of virtuous actions in some former birth,
Now brought to full perfection! Lives
    the man
Whom bounteous heaven has destined to
    espouse her?

MÁTHAVYA. Make haste, then, to her
aid; you have no time to lose, if you
don't wish this fruit of all the virtues to
drop into the mouth of some greasy-
headed rustic of devout habits.

KING. The lady is not her own mis-
tress, and her foster-father is not at home.

MÁTHAVYA. Well, but tell me, did she
look at all kindly upon you?

KING. Maidens brought up in a hermi-
tage are naturally shy and reserved; but
for all that

She did look towards me, though she quick
    withdrew
Her stealthy glances when she met my
    gaze;
She smiled upon me sweetly, but dis-
    guised
With maiden grace the secret of her
    smiles.
Coy love was half unveiled; then, sudden
    checked
By modesty, left half to be divined.

MÁTHAVYA. Why, of course, my dear
friend, you never could seriously expect
that at the very first sight she would
fall over head and ears in love with you,
and without more ado come and sit in
your lap.

KING. When we parted from each other,
she betrayed her liking for me by clearer
indications, but still with the utmost
modesty.

Scarce had the fair one from my presence
    passed,
When, suddenly, without apparent cause,
She stopped, and, counterfeiting pain, ex-
    claimed,
'My foot is wounded by this prickly
    grass.'
Then, glancing at me tenderly, she feigned
Another charming pretext for delay,

Pretending that a bush had caught her
    robe
And turned as if to disentangle it.

MÁTHAVYA. I trust you have laid in
a good stock of provisions, for I see you
intend making this consecrated grove your
game-preserve, and will be roaming here
in quest of sport for some time to come.

KING. You must know, my good fel-
low, that I have been recognised by some
of the inmates of the hermitage. Now
I want the assistance of your fertile in-
vention, in devising some excuse for going
there again.

MÁTHAVYA. There is but one expedient
that I can suggest. You are the King,
are you not?

KING. What then?

MÁTHAVYA. Say you have come for the
sixth part of their grain, which they owe
you for tribute.

KING. No, no, foolish man; those
hermits pay me a very different kind of
tribute, which I value more than heaps of
gold or jewels; observe,
The tribute which my other subjects bring
Must moulder into dust, but holy men
Present me with a portion of the fruits
Of penitential services and prayers—
A precious and imperishable gift.

A VOICE [behind the scenes]. We are
fortunate; here is the object of our
search.

KING [listening]. Surely those must be
the voices of hermits, to judge by their
deep tones.

WARDER [entering]. Victory to the
King! two young hermits are in waiting
outside, and solicit an audience of your
Majesty.

KING. Introduce them immediately.

WARDER. I will, my liege. [Goes out,
and reënters with Two YOUNG HERMITS.]
This way, Sirs, this way. [Both the
    HERMITS look at the KING.]

FIRST HERMIT. How majestic is his
mien, and yet what confidence it inspires!
But this might be expected in a king,
whose character and habits have earned
for him a title only one degree removed
from that* of a Sage.

In this secluded grove, whose sacred
joys
All may participate, he deigns to dwell
Like one of us; and daily treasures up
A store of purest merit for himself,
By the protection of our holy rites.
In his own person wondrously are joined
Both majesty and saintlike holiness;
And often chanted by inspirèd bards,
His hallowed title of 'Imperial Sage'
Ascends in joyous accents to the skies.

SECOND HERMIT. Bear in mind, Gau-
tama, that this is the great Dushyanta,
the friend of Indra.

FIRST HERMIT. What of that?

SECOND HERMIT. Where is the wonder
if his nervous arm,
Puissant and massive as the iron bar
That binds a castle gateway, singly sways
The sceptre of the universal earth,
E'en to its dark-green boundary of waters?
Or if the gods, beholden to his aid
In their fierce warfare with the powers
of hell,
Should blend his name with Indra's in
their songs
Of victory, and gratefully accord
No lower meed of praise to his braced
bow,
Than to the thunders of the god of
heaven?

BOTH THE HERMITS [approaching]. Vic-
tory to the King!

KING [.ising from his seat]. Hail to
you both!

BOTH THE HERMITS. Heaven bless your
Majesty! [They offer fruits.]

KING [respectfully receiving the offer-
ing]. Tell me, I pray you, the object
of your visit.

BOTH THE HERMITS. The inhabitants
of the hermitage, having heard of your
Majesty's sojourn in our neighbourhood,
make this humble petition:—

KING. What are their commands?

BOTH THE HERMITS. In the absence of
our Superior, the great sage Kanwa, evil
demons are disturbing our sacrificial rites.
Deign, therefore, accompanied by your

charioteer, to take up your abode in our
hermitage for a few days.

KING. I am honoured by your invita-
tion.

MÁTHAVYA [aside]. Most opportune
and convenient, certainly!

KING [smiling]. Ho, there, Raivatika!
Tell the charioteer from me to bring
round the chariot with my bow.

WARDER. I will, Sire. [Exit.]

BOTH THE HERMITS [joyfully]. Well
it becomes the King by acts of grace
To emulate the virtues of his race.
Such acts thy lofty destiny attest;
Thy mission is to succour the distressed.

KING [bowing to the HERMITS]. Go
first, reverend Sirs, I will follow you
immediately.

BOTH THE HERMITS. May victory at-
tend you! [Exeunt.]

KING. My dear Máthavya, are not you
full of longing to see Sakoontalá?

MÁTHAVYA. To tell you the truth,
though I was just now brimful of desire
to see her, I have not a drop left since
this piece of news about the demons.

KING. Never fear; you shall keep close
to me for protection.

MÁTHAVYA. Well, you must be my
guardian-angel, and act the part of a
very Vishṇu to me.

WARDER [entering]. Sire, the chariot
is ready, and only waits to conduct you to
victory. But here is a messenger named
Karabhaka, just arrived from your capi-
tal, with a message from the Queen, your
mother.

KING [respectfully]. How say you? a
messenger from the venerable Queen?

WARDER. Even so.

KING. Introduce him at once.

WARDER. I will, Sire. [Goes out and
reënters with KARABHAKA.] Behold the
King. Approach.

KARABHAKA. Victory to the King!
The Queen-mother bids me say that in
four days from the present time she in-
tends celebrating a solemn ceremony for
the advancement and preservation of her
son. She expects that your Majesty will

honour her with your presence on that occasion.

KING. This places me in a dilemma. Here, on the one hand, is the commission of these holy men to be executed; and, on the other, the command of my revered parent to be obeyed. Both duties are too sacred to be neglected. What is to be done?

MÁṬHAVYA. You will have to take up an intermediate position between the two, like King Triśanku, who was suspended between heaven and earth, because the sage Viśwámitra commanded him to mount up to heaven, and the gods ordered him down again.

KING. I am certainly very much perplexed. For here,

Two different duties are required of me
In widely distant places; how can I
In my own person satisfy them both?
Thus is my mind distracted, and impelled
In opposite directions like a stream
That, driven back by rocks, still rushes on,
Forming two currents in its eddying course.

[Reflecting.] Friend Máṭhavya, as you were my play-fellow in childhood, the Queen has already received you like a second son; go you, then, back to her, and tell her of my solemn engagement to assist these holy men. You can supply my place in the ceremony, and act the part of a son to the Queen.

MÁṬHAVYA. With the greatest pleasure in the world; but don't suppose that I am really coward enough to have the slightest fear of those trumpery demons.

KING [smiling]. Oh! of course not; a great Bráhman like you could not possibly give way to such weakness.

MÁṬHAVYA. You must let me travel in a manner suitable to the King's younger brother.

KING. Yes, I shall send my retinue with you, that there may be no further disturbance in this sacred forest.

MÁṬHAVYA [with a strut]. Already I feel quite like a young prince.

KING [aside]. This is a giddy fellow, and in all probability he will let out the truth about my present pursuit to the women of the palace. What is to be done? I must say something to deceive him. [Aloud to MÁṬHAVYA, taking him by the hand.] Dear friend, I am going to the hermitage wholly and solely out of respect for its pious inhabitants, and not because I have really any liking for Śakoontalá, the hermit's daughter. Observe:—

What suitable communion could there be
Between a monarch and a rustic girl?
I did but feign an idle passion, friend,
Take not in earnest what was said in jest.

MÁṬHAVYA. Don't distress yourself; I quite understand. [Exeunt.]

PRELUDE TO ACT III

SCENE—The Hermitage

[Enter a YOUNG BRÁHMAN carrying bundles of Kuśa-grass for the use of the sacrificing priest.]

YOUNG BRÁHMAN. How wonderful is the power of King Dushyanta! No sooner did he enter our hermitage, than we were able to proceed with our sacrificial rites, unmolested by the evil demons.

No need to fix the arrow to the bow;
The mighty monarch sounds the quivering string,
And, by the thunder of his arms dismayed,
Our demon foes are scattered to the wind.

I must now, therefore, make haste and deliver to the sacrificing priests these bundles of Kuśa-grass, to be strewn round the altar. [Walking and looking about; then addressing some one off the stage.] Why, Priyamvadá, for whose use are you carrying that ointment of Usíra-root and those lotus-leaves with fibres attached to them? [Listening for her answer.] What say you?—that Śakoontalá is suffering from fever produced by exposure to the sun, and that this ointment is to cool her burning frame? Nurse her with care, then, Priyamvadá, for she is cherished by our reverend Superior as the very breath of his nostrils. I, for my part, will contrive that soothing waters, hallowed in the sacrifice, be administered to her by the hands of Gautamí. [*Exit.*]

ACT III

SCENE—*The Sacred Grove*

[*Enter* KING DUSHYANTA, *with the air of one in love.*]

KING [*sighing thoughtfully*]. The holy sage possesses magic power In virtue of his penance; she, his ward, Under the shadow of his tutelage, Rests in security. I know it well; Yet sooner shall the rushing cataract In foaming eddies re-ascend the steep, Than my fond heart turn back from its pursuit.

God of love! God of the flowery shafts! we lovers are cruelly deceived by thee, and by the Moon, however deserving of confidence you may both appear.

For not to us do these thine arrows seem Pointed with tender flowerets; not to us Doth the pale Moon irradiate the earth With beams of silver fraught with cooling dews; But on our fevered frames the moon-beams fall Like darts of fire, and every flower-tipt shaft Of Káma, as it probes our throbbing hearts, Seems to be barbed with hardest adamant.

Adorable god of love! hast thou no pity for me? [*In a tone of anguish.*] How can thy arrows be so sharp when they are pointed with flowers? Ah! I know the reason:

É'en now in thine unbodied essence lurks The fire of Śiva's anger, like the flame That ever hidden in the secret depths Of ocean, smoulders there unseen. How else Could'st thou, all immaterial as thou art, Inflame our hearts thus fiercely?—thou, whose form Was scorched to ashes by a sudden flash From the offended god's terrific eye. Yet, methinks, Welcome this anguish, welcome to my heart These rankling wounds inflicted by the god, Who on his scutcheon bears the monster-fish Slain by his prowess; welcome death itself, So that, commissioned by the lord of love, This fair one be my executioner.

Adorable divinity! Can I by no reproaches excite your commiseration? Have I not daily offered at thy shrine Innumerable vows, the only food Of thine ethereal essence? Are my prayers Thus to be slighted? Is it meet that thou Should'st aim thy shafts at thy true votary's heart, Drawing thy bow-string even to thy ear? [*Pacing up and down in a melancholy manner.*] Now that the holy men have completed their rites, and have no more need of my services, how shall I dispel my melancholy? [*Sighing.*] I have but one resource. Oh for another sight of the idol of my soul! I will seek her. [*Glancing at the sun.*] In all probability, as the sun's heat is now at its height, Śakoontalá is passing her time under the shade of the bowers on the banks of the Málini, attended by her maidens. I will go and look for her there. [*Walking and looking about.*] I suspect the fair one has but just passed by this avenue of young trees.

Here, as she tripped along, her fingers plucked The opening buds: these lacerated plants, Shorn of their fairest blossoms by her hand,

Seem like dismembered trunks, whose recent wounds
Are still unclosed; while from the bleeding socket
Of many a severed stalk, the milky juice
Still slowly trickles, and betrays her path.
[*Feeling a breeze.*]
What a delicious breeze meets me in this spot!
Here may the zephyr, fragrant with the scent
Of lotuses, and laden with the spray
Caught from the waters of the rippling stream,
Fold in its close embrace my fevered limbs.

[*Walking and looking about.*] She must be somewhere in the neighbourhood of this arbour of overhanging creepers enclosed by plantations of cane; [*Looking down.*] For at the entrance here I plainly see
A line of footsteps printed in the sand.
Here are the fresh impressions of her feet;
Their well-known outline faintly marked in front,
More deeply towards the heel; betokening
The graceful undulation of her gait.
I will peep through those branches.

[*Walking and looking. With transport.*] Ah! now my eyes are gratified by an entrancing sight. Yonder is the beloved of my heart reclining on a rock strewn with flowers, and attended by her two friends. How fortunate! Concealed behind the leaves, I will listen to their conversation, without raising their suspicions. [*Stands concealed, and gazes at them.*]

[ŚAKOONTALÁ *and her two attendants, holding fans in their hands, are discovered as described.*]

PRIYAMVADÁ *and* ANASÚYÁ [*fanning her. In a tone of affection*]. Dearest Śakoontalá, is the breeze raised by these broad lotus-leaves refreshing to you?

ŚAKOONTALÁ. Dear friends, why should you trouble yourselves to fan me?

[PRIYAMVADÁ *and* ANASÚYÁ *look sorrowfully at one another.*]

KING. Śakoontalá seems indeed to be seriously ill. [*Thoughtfully.*] Can it be the intensity of the heat that has affected her? or does my heart suggest the true cause of her malady? [*Gazing at her passionately.*] Why should I doubt it?
The maiden's spotless bosom is o'erspread
With cooling balsam; on her slender arm
Her only bracelet, twined with lotus-stalks,
Hangs loose and withered; her recumbent form
Betokens languor. Ne'er could noon-day sun
Inflict such fair disorder on a maid—
No, love, and love alone, is here to blame.

PRIYAMVADÁ [*aside to* ANASÚYÁ]. I have observed, Anasúyá, that Śakoontalá has been indisposed ever since her first interview with King Dushyanta. Depend upon it, her ailment is to be traced to that source.

ANASÚYÁ. The same suspicion, dear, has crossed my mind. But I will at once ask her and ascertain the truth. [*Aloud.*] Dear Śakoontalá, I am about to put a question to you. Your indisposition is really very serious.

ŚAKOONTALÁ [*half rising from her couch*]. What were you going to ask?

ANASÚYÁ. We know very little about love-matters, dear Śakoontalá; but for all that, I cannot help suspecting your present state to be something similar to that of the lovers we have heard about in romances. Tell us frankly what is the cause of your disorder. It is useless to apply a remedy, until the disease be understood.

KING Anasúyá bears me out in my suspicion.

ŚAKOONTALÁ [*aside*]. I am, indeed, deeply in love; but cannot rashly disclose my passion to these young girls.

PRIYAMVADÁ. What Anasúyá says, dear Śakoontalá, is very just. Why give so little heed to your ailment? Every day you are becoming thinner; though I must confess your complexion is still as beautiful as ever.

KING. Priyamvadá speaks most truly. Sunk is her velvet cheek; her wasted bosom
Loses its fulness; e'en her slender waist
Grows more attenuate; her face is wan,
Her shoulders droop;—as when the vernal blasts
Sear the young blossoms of the Mádhaví,
Blighting their bloom; so mournful is the change,
Yet in its sadness, fascinating still,
Inflicted by the mighty lord of love
On the fair figure of the hermit's daughter.

ŚAKOONTALÁ. Dear friends, to no one would I rather reveal the nature of my malady than to you; but I should only be troubling you.

PRIYAMVADÁ and ANASÚYÁ. Nay, this is the very point about which we are so solicitous. Sorrow shared with affectionate friends is relieved of half its poignancy.

KING. Pressed by the partners of her joys and griefs,
Her much beloved companions, to reveal
The cherished secret locked within her breast,
She needs must utter it; although her looks
Encourage me to hope, my bosom throbs
As anxiously I listen for her answer.

ŚAKOONTALÁ. Know then, dear friends, that from the first moment the illustrious Prince who is the guardian of our sacred grove presented himself to my sight— [Stops short, and appears confused.]

PRIYAMVADÁ and ANASÚYÁ. Say on, dear Śakoontalá, say on.

ŚAKOONTALÁ. Ever since that happy moment, my heart's affections have been fixed upon him, and my energies of mind and body have all deserted me, as you see.

KING [with rapture]. Her own lips have uttered the words I most longed to hear.

Love lit the flame, and Love himself allays
My burning fever, as when gathering clouds

Rise o'er the earth in summer's dazzling noon,
And grateful showers dispel the morning heat.

ŚAKOONTALÁ. You must consent, then, dear friends, to contrive some means by which I may find favour with the King, or you will have ere long to assist at my funeral.

KING. Enough! These words remove all my doubts.

PRIYAMVADÁ [aside to ANASÚYÁ]. She is far gone in love, dear Anasúyá, and no time ought to be lost. Since she has fixed her affections on a monarch who is the ornament of Puru's line, we need not hesitate for a moment to express our approval.

ANASÚYÁ. I quite agree with you.

PRIYAMVADÁ [aloud]. We wish you joy, dear Śakoontalá. Your affections are fixed on an object in every respect worthy of you. The noblest river will unite itself to the ocean, and the lovely Mádhavi-creeper clings naturally to the mango, the only tree capable of supporting it.

KING. Why need we wonder if the beautiful constellation Viśákhá pines to be united with the Moon?

ANASÚYÁ. By what stratagem can we best secure to our friend the accomplishment of her heart's desire both speedily and secretly?

PRIYAMVADÁ. The latter point is all we have to think about. As to 'speedily,' I look upon the whole affair as already settled.

ANASÚYÁ. How so?

PRIYAMVADÁ. Did you not observe how the King betrayed his liking by the tender manner in which he gazed upon her, and how thin he has become the last few days, as if he had been lying awake thinking of her?

KING [looking at himself]. Quite true! I certainly am becoming thin from want of sleep:

As night by night in anxious thought I raise
This wasted arm to rest my sleepless head,

My jewelled bracelet, sullied by the tears
That trickle from my eyes in scalding
    streams,
Slips towards my elbow from my shriv-
    elled wrist.
Oft I replace the bauble, but in vain;
So easily it spans the fleshless limb
That e'en the rough and corrugated skin,
Scarred by the bow-string, will not check
    its fall.

PRIYAMVADÁ [thoughtfully]. An idea
strikes me, Anasúyá. Let Śakoontalá
write a love-letter; I will conceal it in a
flower, and contrive to drop it in the
King's path. He will surely mistake it
for the remains of some sacred offering,
and will, in all probability, pick it up.

ANASÚYÁ. A very ingenious device! It
has my entire approval; but what says
Śakoontalá?

ŚAKOONTALÁ. I must consider before I
can consent to it.

PRIYAMVADÁ. Could you not, dear
Śakoontalá, think of some pretty composi-
tion in verse, containing a delicate decla-
ration of your love?

ŚAKOONTALÁ. Well, I will do my best;
but my heart trembles when I think of the
chances of a refusal.

KING [with rapture]. Too timid maid,
    here stands the man from whom
Thou fearest a repulse; supremely blessed
To call thee all his own. Well might he
    doubt
His title to thy love; but how could'st
    thou
Believe thy beauty powerless to subdue
    him?

PRIYAMVADÁ and ANASÚYÁ. You un-
dervalue your own merits, dear Śakoon-
talá. What man in his senses would inter-
cept with the skirt of his robe the bright
rays of the autumnal moon, which alone
can allay the fever of his body?

ŚAKOONTALÁ [smiling]. Then it seems
I must do as I am bid.
    [Sits down and appears to be
    thinking.]

KING. How charming she looks! My

very eyes forget to wink, jealous of losing
even for an instant a sight so enchanting.
How beautiful the movement of her brow,
As through her mind love's tender fancies
    flow!
And, as she weighs her thoughts, how
    sweet to trace
The ardent passion mantling in her face!

ŚAKOONTALÁ. Dear girls, I have thought
of a verse, but I have no writing-materials
at hand.

PRIYAMVADÁ. Write the letters with
your nail on this lotus-leaf, which is
smooth as a parrot's breast.

ŚAKOONTALÁ [after writing the verse].
Listen, dear friends, and tell me whether
the ideas are appropriately expressed.

PRIYAMVADÁ and ANASÚYÁ. We are all
attention.

ŚAKOONTALÁ [reads]. I know not the
    secret thy bosom conceals,
Thy form is not near me to gladden my
    sight;
But sad is the tale that my fever reveals,
Of the love that consumes me by day
    and by night.

KING [advancing hastily towards her].
Nay, Love does but warm thee, fair
    maiden,—thy frame
Only droops like the bud in the glare of
    the noon;
But me he consumes with a pitiless flame,
As the beams of the day-star destroy
    the pale moon.

PRIYAMVADÁ and ANASÚYÁ [looking at
him joyfully and rising to salute him].
Welcome, the desire of our hearts, that so
speedily presents itself!
    [ŚAKOONTALÁ makes an effort to
    rise.]

KING. Nay, trouble not thyself, dear
    maiden.
Move not to do me homage; let thy limbs
Still softly rest upon their flowery couch,
And gather fragrance from the lotus-
    stalks,
Bruised by the fevered contact of thy
    frame.

ANASÚYÁ. Deign, gentle Sir, to seat yourself on the rock on which our friend is reposing.

[*The* KING *sits down.* ŚAKOON-TALÁ *is confused.*]

PRIYAMVADÁ. Any one may see at a glance that you are deeply attached to each other. But the affection I have for my friend prompts me to say something of which you hardly require to be informed.

KING. Do not hesitate to speak out, my good girl. If you omit to say what is in your mind, you may be sorry for it afterwards.

PRIYAMVADÁ. Is it not your special office as a King to remove the suffering of your subjects who are in trouble?

KING. Such is my duty, most assuredly.

PRIYAMVADÁ. Know, then, that our dear friend has been brought to her present state of suffering entirely through love for you. Her life is in your hands; take pity on her and restore her to health.

KING. Excellent maiden, our attachment is mutual. It is I who am the most honoured by it.

ŚAKOONTALÁ [*looking at* PRIYAMVADÁ]. What do you mean by detaining the King, who must be anxious to return to his royal consorts after so long a separation?

KING. Sweet maiden, banish from thy mind the thought
That I could love another. Thou dost reign
Supreme, without a rival, in my heart,
And I am thine alone; disown me not,
Else must I die a second deadlier death,
Killed by thy words, as erst by Káma's shafts.

ANASÚYÁ. Kind Sir, we have heard it said that kings have many favourite consorts. You must not, then, by your behaviour towards our dear friend, give her relations cause to sorrow for her.

KING. Listen, gentle maiden, while in a few words I quiet your anxiety.

Though many beauteous forms my palace grace,
Henceforth two things alone will I esteem

The glory of my royal dynasty—
My sea-girt realm, and this most lovely maid.

PRIYAMVADÁ *and* ANASÚYÁ. We are satisfied by your assurances.

PRIYAMVADÁ [*glancing on one side*]. See, Anasúyá, there is our favourite little fawn running about in great distress, and turning its eyes in every direction as if looking for its mother; come, let us help the little thing to find her.

[*Both move away.*]

ŚAKOONTALÁ. Dear friends, dear friends, leave me not alone and unprotected. Why need you both go?

PRIYAMVADÁ *and* ANASÚYÁ. Unprotected! when the Protector of the world is at your side. [*Exeunt.*]

ŚAKOONTALÁ. What! have they both really left me?

KING. Distress not thyself, sweet maiden. Thy adorer is at hand to wait upon thee.

Oh let me tend thee, fair one, in the place
Of thy dear friends; and with broad lotus fans
Raise cooling breezes to refresh thy frame;
Or shall I rather, with caressing touch,
Allay the fever of thy limbs, and soothe
Thy aching feet, beauteous as blushing lilies?

ŚAKOONTALÁ. Nay, touch me not. I will not incur the censure of those whom I am bound to respect.

[*Rises and attempts to go.*]

KING. Fair one, the heat of noon has not yet subsided, and thy body is still feeble.

How canst thou quit thy fragrant couch of flowers,
And from thy throbbing bosom cast aside
Its covering of lotus-leaves, to brave
With weak and fainting limbs the noonday heat? [*Forces her to turn back.*]

ŚAKOONTALÁ. Infringe not the rules of decorum, mighty descendant of Puru. Remember, though I love you, I have no power to dispose of myself.

KING. Why this fear of offending your relations, timid maid? When your venerable foster-father hears of it, he will not find fault with you. He knows that the law permits us to be united without consulting him.

In Indra's heaven, so at least 'tis said,
No nuptial rites prevail, nor is the bride
Led to the altar by her future lord;
But all in secret does the bridegroom plight
His troth, and each unto the other vow
Mutual allegiance. Such espousals, too,
Are authorised on earth, and many daughters
Of royal saints thus wedded to their lords
Have still received their father's benison.

ŚAKOONTALÁ. Leave me, leave me; I must take counsel with my female friends.
KING. I will leave thee when—
ŚAKOONTALÁ. When?

KING. When I have gently stolen from thy lips
Their yet untasted nectar, to allay
The raging of my thirst, e'en as the bee
Sips the fresh honey from the opening bud. [Attempts to raise her face. ŚAKOONTALÁ tries to prevent him.]

A VOICE [behind the scenes]. The loving birds, doomed by fate to nightly separation, must bid farewell to each other, for evening is at hand.
ŚAKOONTALÁ [in confusion]. Great Prince, I hear the voice of the matron Gautamí. She is coming this way to inquire after my health. Hasten and conceal yourself behind the branches.
KING. I will. [Conceals himself.]

[Enter GAUTAMÍ with a vase in her hand, preceded by two attendants.]
ATTENDANTS. This way, most venerable Gautamí.
GAUTAMÍ [approaching ŚAKOONTALÁ]. My child, is the fever of thy limbs allayed?
ŚAKOONTALÁ. Venerable mother, there is certainly a change for the better.

GAUTAMÍ. Let me sprinkle you with this holy water, and all your ailments will depart. [Sprinkling ŚAKOONTALÁ's head.] The day is closing, my child; come, let us go to the cottage. [They all move away.]
ŚAKOONTALÁ [aside]. Oh, my heart! thou didst fear to taste of happiness when it was within thy reach. Now that the object of thy desires is torn from thee, how bitter will be thy remorse, how distracting thine anguish! [Moving on a few steps and stopping. Aloud.] Farewell! bower of creepers, sweet soother of my sufferings, farewell! may I soon again be happy under thy shade.
[Exit reluctantly with the others.]
KING [returning to his former seat in the arbour. Sighing]. Alas! how many are the obstacles to the accomplishment of our wishes!

Albeit she did coyly turn away
Her glowing cheek, and with her fingers guard
Her pouting lips, that murmured a denial
In faltering accents, she did yield herself
A sweet reluctant captive to my will,
As eagerly I raised her lovely face;
But ere with gentle force I stole the kiss,
Too envious Fate did mar my daring purpose.

Whither now shall I betake myself? I will tarry for a brief space in this bower of creepers, so endeared to me by the presence of my beloved Śakoontalá.
[Looking round.]

Here printed on the flowery couch I see
The fair impression of her slender limbs;
Here is the sweet confession of her love,
Traced with her nail upon the lotus-leaf;
And yonder are the withered lily-stalks
That graced her wrist. While all around I view
Things that recall her image, can I quit
This bower, e'en though its living charm be fled?

A VOICE [in the air]. Great King.

Scarce is our evening sacrifice begun,
When evil demons, lurid as the clouds
That gather round the dying orb of day,

Cluster in hideous troops, obscene and
dread,
About our altars, casting far and near
Terrific shadows, while the sacred fire
Sheds a pale lustre o'er their ghostly
shapes.

KING. I come to the rescue, I come.
[*Exit.*]

PRELUDE TO ACT IV

SCENE—*The Garden of the Hermitage.*

[*Enter* PRIYAMVADÁ *and* ANASÚYÁ *in the
act of gathering flowers.*]

ANASÚYÁ. Although, dear Priyamvadá,
it rejoices my heart to think that Śakoon-
talá has been happily united to a husband
in every respect worthy of her, by the
form of marriage prevalent among Indra's
celestial musicians, nevertheless, I cannot
help feeling somewhat uneasy in my mind.

PRIYAMVADÁ. How so?

ANASÚYÁ. You know that the pious
King was gratefully dismissed by the her-
mits on the successful termination of their
sacrificial rites. He has now returned to
his capital, leaving Śakoontalá under our
care; and it may be doubted whether, in
the society of his royal consorts, he will
not forget all that has taken place in this
hermitage of ours.

PRIYAMVADÁ. On that score be at ease.
Persons of his noble nature are not so
destitute of all honourable feeling. I
confess, however, that there is one point
about which I am rather anxious. What,
think you, will Father Kanwa say when
he hears what has occurred?

ANASÚYÁ. In my opinion, he will ap-
prove the marriage.

PRIYAMVADÁ. What makes you think
so?

ANASÚYÁ. From the first, it was al-
ways his fixed purpose to bestow the
maiden on a husband worthy of her; and
since heaven has given her such a hus-
band, his wishes have been realised with-
out any trouble to himself.

PRIYAMVADÁ [*looking at the flower-
basket*]. We have gathered flowers enough
for the sacred offering, dear Anasúyá.

ANASÚYÁ. Well, then, let us now gather
more, that we may have wherewith to
propitiate the guardian-deity of our dear
Śakoontalá.

PRIYAMVADÁ. By all means.
[*They continue gathering.*]

A VOICE [*behind the scenes*]. Ho there!
See you not that I am here!

ANASÚYÁ [*listening*]. That must be
the voice of a guest announcing his ar-
rival.

PRIYAMVADÁ. Surely, Śakoontalá is not
absent from the cottage. [*Aside.*] Her
heart at least is absent, I fear.

ANASÚYÁ. Come along, come along; we
have gathered flowers enough.
[*They move away.*]

THE SAME VOICE [*behind the scenes*].

Woe to thee, maiden, for daring to slight
a guest like me!
Shall I stand here unwelcomed—even I,
A very mine of penitential merit,
Worthy of all respect?   Shalt thou, rash
maid,
Thus set at nought the ever sacred ties
Of hospitality? and fix thy thoughts
Upon the cherished object of thy love,
While I am present?   Thus I curse thee,
then—
He, even he of whom thou thinkest, he
Shall think no more of thee; nor in his
heart
Retain thine image.   Vainly shalt thou
strive
To waken his remembrance of the past;
He shall disown thee, even as the sot,
Roused from his midnight drunkenness,
denies
The words he uttered in his revellings.

PRIYAMVADÁ. Alas! alas!   I fear a
terrible misfortune has occurred. Śakoon-
talá, from absence of mind, must have
offended some guest whom she was bound
to treat with respect. [*Looking behind
the scenes.*] Ah! yes; I see; and not less
a person than the great sage Durvásas,
who is known to be most irascible. He it
is that has just cursed her, and is now
retiring with hasty strides, trembling with
passion, and looking as if nothing could

turn him. His wrath is like a consuming fire.

ANASÚYÁ. Go quickly, dear Priyamvadá, throw yourself at his feet, and persuade him to come back, while I prepare a propitiatory offering for him, with water and refreshments.

PRIYAMVADÁ. I will. [*Exit.*]

ANASÚYÁ [*advancing hastily a few steps and stumbling*]. Alas! alas! this comes of being in a hurry. My foot has slipped, and my basket of flowers has fallen from my hand.

[*Stays to gather them up.*]

PRIYAMVADÁ [*reëntering*]. Well, dear Anasúyá, I have done my best; but what living being could succeed in pacifying such a cross-grained, ill-tempered old fellow? However, I managed to mollify him a little.

ANASÚYÁ [*smiling*]. Even a little was much for him. Say on.

PRIYAMVADÁ. When he refused to turn back, I implored his forgiveness in these words: 'Most venerable sage, pardon, I beseech you, this first offence of a young and inexperienced girl, who was ignorant of the respect due to your saintly character and exalted rank.'

ANASÚYÁ. And what did he reply?

PRIYAMVADÁ. 'My word must not be falsified; but at the sight of the ring of recognition the spell shall cease.' So saying, he disappeared.

ANASÚYÁ. Oh! then we may breathe again; for, now I think of it, the King himself, at his departure, fastened on Śakoontalá's finger, as a token of remembrance, a ring on which his own name was engraved. She has, therefore, a remedy for her misfortune at her own command.

PRIYAMVADÁ. Come, dear Anasúyá, let us proceed with our religious duties.

[*They walk round.*]

PRIYAMVADÁ [*looking off the stage*]. See, Anasúyá, there sits our dear friend, motionless as a statue, resting her face on her left hand, her whole mind absorbed in thinking of her absent husband. She can pay no attention to herself, much less to a stranger.

ANASÚYÁ. Priyamvadá, let this affair never pass our lips. We must spare our dear friend's feelings. Her constitution is too delicate to bear much emotion.

PRIYAMVADÁ. I agree with you. Who would think of watering a tender jasmine with hot water?

ACT IV

SCENE—*The Neighbourhood of the Hermitage.*

[*Enter one of* KANWA'S *pupils just arisen from his couch at the dawn of day.*]

PUPIL. My master, the venerable Kanwa, who is but lately returned from his pilgrimage, has ordered me to ascertain how the time goes. I have therefore come into the open air to see if it be still dark. [*Walking and looking about.*] Oh! the dawn has already broken.

Lo! in one quarter of the sky, the Moon,
Lord of the herbs and night-expanding flowers,
Sinks towards his bed behind the western hills;
While in the east, preceded by the Dawn,
His blushing charioteer, the glorious Sun
Begins his course, and far into the gloom
Casts the first radiance of his orient beams.
Hail; co-eternal orbs, that rise to set,
And set to rise again; symbols divine
Of man's reverses, life's vicissitudes.

And now,
While the round Moon withdraws his looming disc
Beneath the western sky, the full-blown flower
Of the night-loving lotus sheds her leaves
In sorrow for his loss, bequeathing nought
But the sweet memory of her loveliness
To my bereavèd sight; e'en as the bride
Disconsolately mourns her absent lord,
And yields her heart a prey to anxious grief.

ANASÚYÁ [*entering abruptly*]. Little as I know of the ways of the world, I cannot help thinking that King Dushyanta is treating Śakoontalá very improperly.

PUPIL. Well, I must let my revered preceptor know that it is time to offer the burnt oblation. [Exit.]

ANASÚYÁ. I am broad awake, but what shall I do? I have no energy to go about my usual occupations. My hands and feet seem to have lost their power. Well, Love has gained his object; and Love only is to blame for having induced our dear friend, in the innocence of her heart, to confide in such a perfidious man. Possibly, however, the imprecation of Durvásas may be already taking effect. Indeed, I cannot otherwise account for the King's strange conduct, in allowing so long a time to elapse without even a letter; and that, too, after so many promises and protestations. I cannot think what to do unless we send him the ring which was to be the token of recognition. But which of these austere hermits could we ask to be the bearer of it? Then, again, Father Kanwa has just returned from his pilgrimage; and how am I to inform him of Śakoontalá's marriage to King Dushyanta, and her expectation of becoming soon a mother? I never could bring myself to tell him, even if I felt that Śakoontalá had been in fault, which she certainly has not. What is to be done?

PRIYAMVADÁ [entering joyfully]. Quick! quick! Anasúyá! come and assist in the joyful preparations for Śakoontalá's departure to her husband's palace.

ANASÚYÁ. My dear girl, what can you mean?

PRIYAMVADÁ. Listen, now, and I will tell you all about it. I went just now to Śakoontalá, to inquire whether she had slept comfortably—

ANASÚYÁ. Well, well; go on.

PRIYAMVADÁ. She was sitting with her face bowed down to the very ground with shame, when Father Kanwa entered, and, embracing her, of his own accord offered her his congratulations. 'I give thee joy, my child,' he said, 'we have had an auspicious omen. The priest who offered the oblation dropped it into the very centre of the sacred fire, though thick smoke obstructed his vision. Henceforth thou wilt

cease to be an object of compassion. This very day I purpose sending thee, under the charge of certain trusty hermits, to the King's palace; and shall deliver thee into the hands of thy husband, as I would commit knowledge to the keeping of a wise and faithful student.'

ANASÚYÁ. Who, then, informed the holy father of what passed in his absence?

PRIYAMVADÁ. As he was entering the sanctuary of the consecrated fire, an invisible being chanted a verse in celestial strains.

ANASÚYÁ [with astonishment]. Indeed! pray repeat it.

PRIYAMVADÁ [repeating the verse].

Glows in thy daughter King Dushyanta's glory,
As in the sacred tree the mystic fire;
Let worlds rejoice to hear the welcome story,
And may the son immortalize the sire.

ANASÚYÁ [embracing PRIYAMVADÁ]. Oh, my dear Priyamvadá, what delightful news! I am pleased beyond measure; yet when I think that we are to lose our dear Śakoontalá this very day, a feeling of melancholy mingles with my joy.

PRIYAMVADÁ. We shall find means of consoling ourselves after her departure. Let the dear creature only be made happy at any cost.

ANASÚYÁ. Yes, yes, Priyamvadá, it shall be so; and now to prepare the bridal array. I have always looked forward to this occasion, and some time since, I deposited a beautiful garland of Keśara flowers in a cocoa-nut box, and suspended it on a bough of yonder mango-tree. Be good enough to stretch out your hand and take it down, while I compound unguents and perfumes with this consecrated paste and these blades of sacred grass.

PRIYAMVADÁ. Very well.

[Exit ANASÚYÁ. PRIYAMVADÁ takes down the flowers.]

A VOICE [behind the scenes]. Gautamí bid Śárngarava and the others hold themselves in readiness to escort Śakoontalá.

PRIYAMVADÁ [*listening*]. Quick, quick, Anasúyá! They are calling the hermits who are to go with Śakoontalá to Hastinapur.

ANASÚYÁ [*reëntering with the perfumed unguents in her hand*]. Come along then, Priyamvadá; I am ready to go with you. [*They walk away.*]

PRIYAMVADÁ [*looking*]. See! there sits Śakoontalá, her locks arranged even at this early hour of the morning. The holy women of the hermitage are congratulating her, and invoking blessings on her head, while they present her with wedding-gifts and offerings of consecrated wild-rice. Let us join them. [*They approach.*]

[ŚAKOONTALÁ *is seen seated, with women surrounding her, occupied in the manner described.*]

FIRST WOMAN [*to* ŚAKOONTALÁ]. My child, may'st thou receive the title of 'Chief-queen,' and may thy husband delight to honour thee above all others!

SECOND WOMAN. My child, may'st thou be the mother of a hero!

THIRD WOMAN. My child, may'st thou be highly honoured by thy lord!

[*Exeunt all the women, excepting* GAUTAMÍ, *after blessing* ŚAKOONTALÁ.]

PRIYAMVADÁ *and* ANASÚYÁ [*approaching*]. Dear Śakoontalá, we are come to assist you at your toilet, and may a blessing attend it!

ŚAKOONTALÁ. Welcome, dear friends, welcome. Sit down here.

PRIYAMVADÁ *and* ANASÚYÁ [*taking the baskets containing the bridal decorations, and sitting down*]. Now, then, dearest, prepare to let us dress you. We must first rub your limbs with these perfumed unguents.

ŚAKOONTALÁ. I ought indeed to be grateful for your kind offices, now that I am so soon to be deprived of them. Dear, dear friends, perhaps I shall never be dressed by you again. [*Bursts into tears.*]

PRIYAMVADÁ *and* ANASÚYÁ. Weep not, dearest; tears are out of season on such a happy occasion. [*They wipe away her tears and begin to dress her.*]

PRIYAMVADÁ. Alas! these simple flowers and rude ornaments, which our hermitage offers in abundance, do not set off your beauty as it deserves.

[*Enter* TWO YOUNG HERMITS, *bearing costly presents.*]

BOTH HERMITS. Here are ornaments suitable for a queen.

[*The women look at them in astonishment.*]

GAUTAMÍ. Why, Nárada, my son, whence came these?

FIRST HERMIT. You owe them to the devotion of Father Kanwa.

GAUTAMÍ. Did he create them by the power of his own mind?

SECOND HERMIT. Certainly not; but you shall hear. The venerable sage ordered us to collect flowers for Śakoontalá from the forest-trees; and we went to the wood for that purpose, when

Straightway depending from a neighbouring tree

Appeared a robe of linen tissue, pure

And spotless as a moonbeam—mystic pledge

Of bridal happiness; another tree

Distilled a roseate dye wherewith to stain

The lady's feet; and other branches near

Glistened with rare and costly ornaments.

While, 'mid the leaves, the hands of forest-nymphs,

Vying in beauty with the opening buds,

Presented us with sylvan offerings.

PRIYAMVADÁ [*looking at* ŚAKOONTALÁ]. The wood-nymphs have done you honour, indeed. This favour doubtless signifies that you are soon to be received as a happy wife into your husband's house, and are from this time forward to become the partner of his royal fortunes.

[ŚAKOONTALÁ *appears abashed.*]

FIRST HERMIT. Come, Gautamí; Father Kanwa has finished his ablutions. Let us go and inform him of the favour we have received from the deities who preside over our trees.

SECOND HERMIT. By all means.

[Exeunt.]

PRIYAMVADÁ and ANASÚYÁ. Alas! what are we to do? We are unused to such splendid decorations, and are at a loss how to arrange them. Our knowledge of painting must be our guide. We will dispose the ornaments as we have seen them in pictures.

ŚAKOONTALÁ. Whatever pleases you, dear girls, will please me. I have perfect confidence in your taste.

[They commence dressing her.]

[Enter KANWA, having just finished his ablutions.]

KANWA. This day my loved one leaves me, and my heart
Is heavy with its grief; the streams of sorrow,
Choked at the source, repress my faltering voice.
I have no words to speak; mine eyes are dimmed
By the dark shadows of the thoughts that rise
Within my soul. If such the force of grief
In an old hermit parted from his nursling,
What anguish must the stricken parent feel—
Bereft for ever of an only daughter.

[Advances towards ŚAKOONTALÁ.]

PRIYAMVADÁ and ANASÚYÁ. Now, dearest Śakoontalá, we have finished decorating you. You have only to put on the two linen mantles.

[ŚAKOONTALÁ rises and puts them on.]

GAUTAMÍ. Daughter, see, here comes thy foster-father; he is eager to fold thee in his arms; his eyes swim with tears of joy. Hasten to do him reverence.

ŚAKOONTALÁ [reverently]. My father, I salute you.

KANWA. My daughter,
May'st thou be highly honoured by thy lord,
E'en as Yayáti Śarmishṭhá adored!

And, as she bore him Puru, so may'st thou
Bring forth a son to whom the world shall bow!

GAUTAMÍ. Most venerable father, she accepts your benediction as if she already possessed the boon it confers.

KANWA. Now come this way, my child, and walk reverently round these sacrificial fires. [They all walk round.]

KANWA [repeats a prayer in the metre
of the Rig-veda].

Holy flames, that gleam around
Every altar's hallowed ground;
Holy flames, whose frequent food
Is the consecrated wood,
And for whose encircling bed,
Sacred Kuśa-grass is spread;
Holy flames, that waft to heaven
Sweet oblations daily given,
Mortal guilt to purge away,
Hear, oh hear me, when I pray—
Purify my child this day!

Now then, my daughter, set out on thy journey. [Looking on one side.] Where are thy attendants, Śárngarava and the others?

YOUNG HERMIT [entering]. Here we are, most venerable father.

KANWA. Lead the way for thy sister.

ŚÁRNGARAVA. Come, Śakoontalá, let us proceed. [All move away.]

KANWA. Hear me, ye trees that surround our hermitage!
Śakoontalá ne'er moistened in the stream
Her own parched lips, till she had fondly poured
Its purest water on your thirsty roots;
And oft, when she would fain have decked her hair
With your thick-clustering blossoms, in her love
She robbed you not e'en of a single flower.
Her highest joy was ever to behold
The early glory of your opening buds;
Oh, then, dismiss her with a kind farewell.
This very day she quits her father's home,
To seek the palace of her wedded lord.

[The note of a Koïl is heard.]

Hark! heard'st thou not the answer of the trees,
Our sylvan sisters, warbled in the note
Of the melodious Koïl? they dismiss
Their dear Śakoontalá with loving wishes.

VOICES IN THE AIR. Fare thee well,
  journey pleasantly on amid streams
Where the lotuses bloom, and the sun's
  glowing beams
Never pierce the deep shade of the wide-
  spreading trees,
While gently around thee shall sport the
  cool breeze;
Then light be thy footsteps and easy thy
  tread,
Beneath thee shall carpets of lilies be
  spread;
Journey on to thy lord, let thy spirit be
  gay,
For the smiles of all Nature shall gladden
  thy way.

[*All listen with astonishment.*]
GAUTAMÍ. Daughter! the nymphs of the wood, who love thee with the affection of a sister, dismiss thee with kind wishes for thy happiness. Take thou leave of them reverentially.

ŚAKOONTALÁ [*bowing respectfully and walking on. Aside to her friend*]. Eager as I am, dear Priyamvadá, to see my husband once more, yet my feet refuse to move, now that I am quitting forever the home of my girlhood.

PRIYAMVADÁ. You are not the only one, dearest, to feel the bitterness of parting. As the time of separation approaches, the whole grove seems to share your anguish.

In sorrow for thy loss, the herd of deer
Forget to browse; the peacock on the
  lawn
Ceases its dance; the very trees around
Shed their pale leaves, like tears, upon
  the ground.

ŚAKOONTALÁ [*recollecting herself*]. My father, let me, before I go, bid adieu to my pet jasmine, the Moonlight of the Grove. I love the plant almost as a sister.

KANWA. Yes, yes, my child, I remem-ber thy sisterly affection for the creeper. Here it is on the right.

ŚAKOONTALÁ [*approaching the jasmine*]. My beloved jasmine! most brilliant of climbing plants, how sweet it is to see thee cling thus fondly to thy husband, the mango-tree; yet, prithee, turn thy twining arms for a moment in this direction to embrace thy sister; she is going far away, and may never see thee again.

KANWA. Daughter, the cherished pur-
  pose of my heart
Has ever been to wed thee to a man
That should be worthy of thee; such a
  spouse
Hast thou thyself, by thine own merits,
  won.
To him thou goest, and about his neck
Soon shalt thou cling confidingly, as now
Thy favourite Jasmine twines its loving
  arms
Around the sturdy mango. Leave thou it
To its protector—e'en as I consign
Thee to thy lord, and henceforth from
  my mind
Banish all anxious thought on thy behalf.

Proceed on thy journey, my child.

ŚAKOONTALÁ [*to PRIYAMVADÁ and ANA-SÚYÁ*]. To you, my sweet companions, I leave it as a keepsake. Take charge of it when I am gone.

PRIYAMVADÁ and ANASÚYÁ [*bursting into tears*]. And to whose charge do you leave us, dearest? Who will care for us when you are gone?

KANWA. For shame, Anasúyá! dry your tears. Is this the way to cheer your friend at a time when she needs your support and consolation? [*All move on.*]

ŚAKOONTALÁ. My father, see you there my pet deer, grazing close to the hermi-tage? She expects soon to fawn, and even now the weight of the little one she carries hinders her movements. Do not forget to send me word when she becomes a mother.

KANWA. I will not forget it.

ŚAKOONTALÁ [*feeling herself drawn back*]. What can this be, fastened to my dress?   [*Turns round.*]

KANWA. My daughter,
It is the little fawn, thy foster-child.
Poor helpless orphan! it remembers well
How with a mother's tenderness and love
Thou didst protect it, and with grains of
    rice
From thine own hand didst daily nourish
    it;
And, ever and anon, when some sharp
    thorn
Had pierced its mouth, how gently thou
    didst tend
The bleeding wound, and pour in healing
    balm.
The grateful nursling clings to its pro-
    tectress,
Mutely imploring leave to follow her.

ŚAKOONTALÁ. My poor little fawn! dost
thou ask to follow an ungrateful wretch
who hesitates not to desert her com-
panions! When thy mother died, soon
after thy birth, I supplied her place, and
reared thee with my own hand; and now
that thy second mother is about to leave
thee, who will care for thee? My father,
be thou a mother to her. My child, go
back, and be a daughter to my father.
    [*Moves on, weeping.*]

KANWA. Weep not, my daughter,
    check the gathering tear
That lurks beneath thine eyelid, ere it
    flow
And weaken thy resolve; be firm and
    true—
True to thyself and me; the path of life
Will lead o'er hill and plain, o'er rough
    and smooth,
And all must feel the steepness of the
    way;
Though rugged be thy course, press boldly
    on.

ŚÁRNGARAVA. Venerable Sire! the sa-
cred precept is:—"Accompany thy friend
as far as the margin of the first stream."
Here, then, we are arrived at the border
of a lake. It is time for you to give us
your final instructions and return.

KANWA. Be it so; let us tarry for a
moment under the shade of this fig-tree.

[*They do so. Aside.*] I must think of
some appropriate message to send to his
Majesty King Dushyanta.   [*Reflects.*]
ŚAKOONTALÁ [*aside to* ANASÚYÁ]. See,
see, dear Anasúyá, the poor female Chak-
raváka-bird, whom cruel fate dooms to
nightly separation from her mate, calls
to him in mournful notes from the other
side of the stream, though he is only hid-
den from her view by the spreading leaves
of the water-lily. Her cry is so piteous
that I could almost fancy she was lament-
ing her hard lot in intelligible words.
ANASÚYÁ. Say not so, dearest:
Fond bird! though sorrow lengthen out
    her night
Of widowhood, yet with a cry of joy
She hails the morning light that brings
    her mate
Back to her side. The agony of parting
Would wound us like a sword, but that
    its edge
Is blunted by the hope of future meeting.

KANWA. Śárngarava! when you have
introduced Śakoontalá into the presence
of the King, you must give him this mes-
sage from me:—
ŚÁRNGARAVA. Let me hear it, venerable
father.
KANWA. This is it:—
Most puissant prince! we here present be-
    fore thee
One thou art bound to cherish and receive
As thine own wife; yea, even to enthrone
As thine own queen—worthy of equal
    love
With thine imperial consorts. So much,
    Sire,
We claim of thee as justice due to us,
In virtue of our holy character,
In virtue of thine honourable rank,
In virtue of the pure spontaneous love
That secretly grew up 'twixt thee and
    her,
Without consent or privity of us.
We ask no more—the rest we freely leave
To thy just feeling and to destiny.

ŚÁRNGARAVA. A most suitable message!
I will take care to deliver it correctly.
KANWA. And, now, my child, a few

words of advice for thee. We hermits, though we live secluded from the world are not ignorant of worldly matters.

ŚÁRNGARAVA. No, indeed. Wise men are conversant with all subjects.

KANWA. Listen, then, my daughter. When thou reachest thy husband's palace, and art admitted into his family,

Honour thy betters; ever be respectful
To those above thee; and, should others
  share
Thy husband's love, ne'er yield thyself a
  prey
To jealousy; but ever be a friend,
A loving friend, to those who rival thee
In his affections. Should thy wedded lord
Treat thee with harshness, thou must
  never be
Harsh in return, but patient and sub-
  missive.
Be to thy menials courteous, and to all
Placed under thee, considerate and kind;
Be never self-indulgent, but avoid
Excess in pleasure; and, when fortune
  smiles,
Be not puffed up. Thus to thy husband's
  house
Wilt thou a blessing prove, and not a
  curse.

What thinks Gautamí of this advice?

GAUTAMÍ. An excellent compendium, truly, of every wife's duties! Lay it well to heart, my daughter.

KANWA. Come, my beloved child, one parting embrace for me and for thy companions, and then we leave thee.

ŚAKOONTALÁ. My father, must Priyamvadá and Anasúyá really return with you? They are very dear to me.

KANWA. Yes, my child; they, too, in good time, will be given in marriage to suitable husbands. It would not be proper for them to accompany thee to such a public place. But Gautamí shall be thy companion.

ŚAKOONTALÁ [embracing him]. Removed from thy bosom, my beloved father, like a young tendril of the sandal-tree torn from its home in the western moun-

tains, how shall I be able to support life in a foreign soil?

KANWA. Daughter, thy fears are groundless.

Soon shall thy lord prefer thee to the rank
Of his own consort; and unnumbered
  cares
Befitting his imperial dignity
Shall constantly engross thee. Then the
  bliss
Of bearing him a son—a noble boy,
Bright as the day-star, shall transport thy
  soul
With new delights, and little shalt thou
  reck
Of the light sorrow that afflicts thee now
At parting from thy father and thy
  friends.

[ŚAKOONTALÁ throws herself at
her foster-father's feet.]

KANWA. Blessings on thee, my child! May all my hopes of thee be realized!

ŚAKOONTALÁ [approaching her friends]. Come, my two loved companions, embrace me, both of you together.

PRIYAMVADÁ and ANASÚYÁ [embracing her]. Dear Śakoontalá, remember, if the King should by any chance be slow in recognizing you, you have only to show him this ring, on which his own name is engraved.

ŚAKOONTALÁ. The bare thought of it puts me in a tremor.

PRIYAMVADÁ and ANASÚYÁ. There is no real cause for fear, dearest. Excessive affection is too apt to suspect evil where none exists.

ŚÁRNGARAVA. Come, lady, we must hasten on. The sun is rising in the heavens.

ŚAKOONTALÁ [looking towards the hermitage]. Dear father, when shall I ever see this hallowed grove again?

KANWA. I will tell thee; listen:—

When thou hast passed a long and blissful
  life
As King Dushyanta's queen, and jointly
  shared
With all the earth his ever-watchful care;

And hast beheld thine own heroic son,
Matchless in arms, united to a bride
In happy wedlock; when his aged sire,
Thy faithful husband, hath to him re-
signed
The helm of state; then, weary of the
world,
Together with Dushyanta thou shalt seek
The calm seclusion of thy former home;
There amid holy scenes to be at peace,
Till thy pure spirit gain its last release.

GAUTAMÍ. Come, my child, the favour-
able time for our journey is fast passing.
Let thy father return. Venerable Sire,
be thou the first to move homewards, or
these last words will never end.

KANWA. Daughter, detain me no
longer. My religious duties must not be
interrupted.

ŚAKOONTALÁ [again embracing her fos-
ter-father]. Beloved father, thy frame is
much enfeebled by penitential exercises.
Do not, oh! do not, allow thyself to sor-
row too much on my account.

KANWA [sighing]. How, O my child,
shall my bereavèd heart
Forget its bitterness, when, day by day,
Full in my sight shall grow the tender
plants
Reared by thy care, or sprung from hal-
lowed grain
Which thy loved hands have strewn around
the door—
A frequent offering to our household gods?

Go, my daughter, and may thy journey
be prosperous. [Exit ŚAKOONTALÁ with
her escort.]

PRIYAMVADÁ and ANASÚYÁ [gazing
after ŚAKOONTALÁ]. Alas! alas! she is
gone, and now the trees hide our darling
from our view.

KANWA [sighing]. Well, Anasúyá, your
sister has departed. Moderate your grief,
both of you, and follow me. I go back
to the hermitage.

PRIYAMVADÁ and ANASÚYÁ. Holy
father, the sacred grove will be a desert
without Śakoontalá. How can we ever
return to it?

KANWA. It is natural enough that your
affection should make you view it in this
light. [Walking pensively on.] As for
me, I am quite surprised at myself. Now
that I have fairly dismissed her to her
husband's house, my mind is easy; for,
indeed,

A daughter is a loan—a precious jewel
Lent to a parent till her husband claim
her.
And now that to her rightful lord and
master
I have delivered her, my burdened soul
Is lightened, and I seem to breathe more
freely. [Exeunt.]

ACT V

SCENE—A Room in the Palace

[The King DUSHYANTA and the Jester
MÁTHAVYA are discovered seated.]

MÁTHAVYA [listening]. Hark! my dear
friend, listen a minute, and you will hear
sweet sounds proceeding from the music-
room. Some one is singing a charming
air. Who can it be? Oh! I know. The
queen Hansapadiká is practising her notes,
that she may greet you with a new song.

KING. Hush! Let me listen.

A VOICE [sings behind the scenes]. How
often hither didst thou rove,
Sweet bee, to kiss the mango's cheek;
Oh! leave not, then, thy early love,
The lily's honeyed lip to seek.

KING. A most impassioned strain,
truly!

MÁTHAVYA. Do you understand the
meaning of the words?

KING [smiling]. She means to reprove
me, because I once paid her great atten-
tion, and have lately deserted her for the
queen Vasumatí. Go, my dear fellow,
and tell Hansapadiká from me that I
take her delicate reproof as it is in-
tended.

MÁTHAVYA. Very well. [Rising from
his seat]. But stay—I don't much relish
being sent to bear the brunt of her jeal-
ousy. The chances are that she will have

me seized by the hair of the head and beaten to a jelly. I would as soon expose myself, after a vow of celibacy, to the seductions of a lovely nymph, as encounter the fury of a jealous woman.

KING. Go, go; you can disarm her wrath by a civil speech; but give her my message.

MÁṬHAVYA. What must be must be, I suppose.   [*Exit.*]

KING [*aside*]. Strange! that song has filled me with a most peculiar sensation. A melancholy feeling has come over me, and I seem to yearn after some long-forgotten object of affection. Singular, indeed! but

Not seldom in our happy hours of ease,
When thought is still, the sight of some fair form,
Or mournful fall of music breathing low,
Will stir strange fancies, thrilling all the soul
With a mysterious sadness, and a sense
Of vague yet earnest longing. Can it be
That the dim memory of events long past,
Or friendships formed in other states of being,
Flits like a passing shadow o'er the spirit?   [*Remains pensive and sad.*]

[*Enter the* CHAMBERLAIN, *named* VÁTÁYANA.]

CHAMBERLAIN. Alas! to what an advanced period of life have I attained!

Even this wand betrays the lapse of years;
In youthful days 'twas but a useless badge
And symbol of my office; now it serves
As a support to prop my tottering steps.

Ah me! I feel very unwilling to announce to the King that a deputation of young hermits from the sage Kanwa has arrived, and craves an immediate audience. Certainly, his Majesty ought not to neglect a matter of sacred duty, yet I hardly like to trouble him when he has just risen from the judgment-seat. Well, well; a monarch's business is to sustain the world, and he must not expect much repose; because—

Onward, for ever onward, in his car
The unwearied Sun pursues his daily course,
Nor tarries to unyoke his glittering steeds.
And, ever moving, speeds the rushing Wind
Through boundless space, filling the universe
With his life-giving breezes. Day and night,
The King of Serpents on his thousand heads
Upholds the incumbent earth; and even so,
Unceasing toil is aye the lot of kings,
Who, in return, draw nurture from their subjects.

I will therefore deliver my message.

[*Walking on and looking about.*]   Ah! here comes the King.

His subjects are his children; through the day,
Like a fond father, to supply their wants,
Incessantly he labours; wearied now,
The monarch seeks seclusion and repose;
E'en as the prince of elephants defies
The sun's fierce heat, and leads the fainting herd
To verdant pastures, ere his wayworn limbs
He yields to rest beneath the cooling shade.

[*Approaching.*]   Victory to the King! So please your Majesty, some hermits who live in a forest near the Snowy Mountains have arrived here, bringing certain women with them. They have a message to deliver from the sage Kanwa, and desire an audience. I await your Majesty's commands.

KING [*respectfully*]. A message from the sage Kanwa, did you say?

CHAMBERLAIN. Even so, my liege.

KING. Tell my domestic priest Somaráta to receive the hermits with due honour, according to the prescribed form. He may then himself introduce them into my presence. I will await them in a place suitable for the reception of such holy guests.

CHAMBERLAIN. Your Majesty's commands shall be obeyed.   [*Exit.*]
KING [*rising and addressing the WARDER*]. Vetravatí, lead the way to the chamber of the consecrated fire.
WARDER. This way, Sire.
KING [*walking on, with the air of one oppressed by the cares of Government.*]

People are generally contented and happy when they have gained their desires; but kings have no sooner attained the object of their aspirations than all their troubles begin.
'Tis a fond thought that to attain the end
And object of ambition is to rest;
Success doth only mitigate the fever
Of anxious expectation; soon the fear
Of losing what we have, the constant care
Of guarding it, doth weary. Ceaseless toil
Must be the lot of him who with his hands
Supports the canopy that shields his subjects.

TWO HERALDS [*behind the scenes*]. May the King be victorious!
FIRST HERALD. Honour to him who labours day by day
For the world's weal, forgetful of his own;
Like some tall tree that with its stately head
Endures the solar beam, while underneath
It yields refreshing shelter to the weary.
SECOND HERALD. Let but the monarch wield his threatening rod
And e'en the guilty tremble; at his voice
The rebel spirit cowers; his grateful subjects
Acknowledge him their guardian; rich and poor
Hail him a faithful friend—a loving kinsman.

KING. Weary as I was before, this complimentary address has refreshed me.
                    [*Walks on.*]
WARDER. Here is the terrace of the hallowed fire-chamber, and yonder stands the cow that yields the milk for the oblations. The sacred enclosure has been recently purified, and looks clean and beautiful. Ascend, Sire.

KING [*leans on the shoulders of his attendants, and ascends*]. Vetravatí, what can possibly be the message that the venerable Kanwa has sent me by these hermits?

Perchance their sacred rites have been disturbed
By demons, or some evil has befallen
The innocent herds, their favourites, that graze
Within the precincts of the hermitage;
Or haply, through my sins, some withering blight
Has nipped the creeping plants that spread their arms
Around the hallowed grove. Such troubled thoughts
Crowd through my mind, and fill me with misgiving.

WARDER. If you ask my opinion, Sire, I think the hermits merely wish to take an opportunity to testifying their loyalty, and are therefore come to offer homage to your Majesty.

[*Enter the HERMITS leading ŚAKOONTALÁ, attended by GAUTAMÍ; and in advance of them, the CHAMBERLAIN and the DOMESTIC PRIEST.*]

CHAMBERLAIN. This way, reverend Sirs, this way.
ŚÁRNGARAVA. O Śáradwata,

'Tis true the monarch lacks no royal grace,
Nor ever swerves from justice; true, his people,
Yea such as in life's humblest walks are found,
Refrain from evil courses; still to me,
A lonely hermit reared in solitude,
This throng appears bewildering, and I seem
To look upon a burning house, whose inmates
Are running to and fro in wild dismay.

ŚÁRADWATA. It is natural that the first sight of the King's capital should affect you in this manner; my own sensations are very similar.

As one just bathed beholds the man polluted;
As one late purified, the yet impure;
As one awake looks on the yet unawakened;
Or as the freeman gazes on the thrall,
So I regard this crowd of pleasureseekers.

SAKOONTALÁ [feeling a quivering sensation in her right eyelid, and suspecting a bad omen]. Alas! what means this throbbing of my right eyelid?

GAUTAMÍ. Heaven avert the evil omen, my child! May the guardian deities of thy husband's family convert it into a sign of good fortune! [Walks on.]

PRIEST [pointing to the KING]. Most reverend Sirs, there stands the protector of the four classes of the people; the guardian of the four conditions of the priesthood. He has just left the judgment-seat, and is waiting for you. Behold him!

SÁRNGARAVA. Great Bráhman, we are happy in thinking that the King's power is exerted for the protection of all classes of his subjects. We have not come as petitioners—we have the fullest confidence in the generosity of his nature.

The loftiest trees bend humbly to the ground
Beneath the teeming burden of their fruit;
High in the vernal sky the pregnant clouds
Suspend their stately course, and, hanging low,
Scatter their sparkling treasures o'er the earth;
And such is true benevolence; the good
Are never rendered arrogant by riches.

WARDER. So please your Majesty, I judge from the placid countenance of the hermits that they have no alarming message to deliver.

KING [looking at SAKOONTALÁ]. But the lady there—

Who can she be, whose form of matchless grace
Is half concealed beneath her flowing veil?
Among the sombre hermits she appears
Like a fresh bud 'mid sear and yellow leaves.

WARDER. So please your Majesty, my curiosity is also roused, but no conjecture occurs to my mind. This at least is certain, that she deserves to be looked at more closely.

KING. True; but it is not right to gaze at another man's wife.

SAKOONTALÁ [placing her hand on her bosom. Aside]. O my heart, why this throbbing? Remember thy lord's affection, and take courage.

PRIEST [advancing]. These holy men have been received with all due honour. One of them has now a message to deliver from his spiritual superior. Will your Majesty deign to hear it?

KING. I am all attention.

HERMITS [extending their hands]. Victory to the King!

KING. Accept my respectful greeting.

HERMITS. May the desires of your soul be accomplished!

KING. I trust no one is molesting you in the prosecution of your religious rites.

HERMITS. Who dares disturb our penitential rites
When thou art our protector? Can the night
Prevail to cast her shadows o'er the earth
While the sun's beams irradiate the sky?

KING. Such, indeed, is the very meaning of my title—'Defender of the Just.' I trust the venerable Kanwa is in good health. The world is interested in his well-being.

HERMITS. Holy men have health and prosperity in their own power. He bade us greet your Majesty, and, after kind inquiries, deliver this message.

KING. Let me hear his commands.

SÁRNGARAVA. He bade us say that he feels happy in giving his sanction to the marriage which your Majesty contracted with this lady, his daughter, privately and by mutual agreement. Because,

By us thou art esteemed the most illustrious
Of noble husbands; and Śakoontalá,
Virtue herself in human form revealed.
Great Brahmá hath in equal yoke united
A bride unto a husband worthy of her;
Henceforth let none make blasphemous complaint
That he is pleased with ill-assorted unions.

Since, therefore, she expects soon to be the mother of thy child, receive her into thy palace, that she may perform, in conjunction with thee, the ceremonies prescribed by religion on such an occasion.

GAUTAMÍ. So please your Majesty, I would add a few words; but why should I intrude my sentiments when an opportunity of speaking my mind has never been allowed me?

She took no counsel with her kindred; thou
Didst not confer with thine, but all alone
Didst solemnize thy nuptials with thy wife.
Together, then, hold converse; let us leave you.

ŚAKOONTALÁ [aside]. Ah! how I tremble for my lord's reply.

KING. What strange proposal is this?

ŚAKOONTALÁ [aside]. His words are like fire to me.

ŚÁRNGARAVA. What do I hear? Dost thou, then, hesitate? Monarch, thou art well acquainted with the ways of the world, and knowest that

A wife, however virtuous and discreet,
If she live separate from her wedded lord,
Though under shelter of her parent's roof,
Is mark for vile suspicion. Let her dwell
Beside her husband, though he hold her not
In his affection. So her kinsmen will it.

KING. Do you really mean to assert that I ever married this lady?

ŚAKOONTALÁ [despondingly. Aside]. O my heart, thy worst misgivings are confirmed.

ŚÁRNGARAVA. Is it becoming in a monarch to depart from the rules of justice, because he repents of his engagements?

KING. I cannot answer a question which is based on a mere fabrication.

ŚÁRNGARAVA. Such inconstancy is fortunately not common, except in men intoxicated by power.

KING. Is that remark aimed at me?

GAUTAMÍ. Be not ashamed, my daughter. Let me remove thy veil for a little space. Thy husband will then recognize thee. [Removes her veil.]

KING [gazing at ŚAKOONTALÁ. Aside].

What charms are here revealed before mine eyes!
Truly no blemish mars the symmetry
Of that fair form; yet can I ne'er believe
She is my wedded wife; and like a bee
That circles round the flower whose nectared cup
Teems with the dew of morning, I must pause
Ere eagerly I taste the proffered sweetness. [Remains wrapped in thought.]

WARDER. How admirably does our royal master's behaviour prove his regard for justice! Who else would hesitate for a moment when good fortune offered for his acceptance a form of such rare beauty?

ŚÁRNGARAVA. Great King, why art thou silent?

KING. Holy men, I have revolved the matter in my mind; but the more I think of it, the less able am I to recollect that I ever contracted an alliance with this lady. What answer, then, can I possibly give you when I do not believe myself to be her husband, and I plainly see that she is soon to become a mother?

ŚAKOONTALÁ [aside]. Woe! woe! Is our very marriage to be called in question by my own husband? Ah me! is this to be the end of all my bright visions of wedded happiness?

ŚÁRNGARAVA. Beware!
Beware how thou insult the holy Sage!

Remember how he generously allowed
Thy secret union with his foster-child;
And how, when thou didst rob him of his
treasure,
He sought to furnish thee excuse, when
rather
He should have cursed thee for a ravisher.

ŚÁRADWATA. Śárngarava, speak to him
no more. Śakoontalá, our part is per-
formed; we have said all we have to say,
and the King has replied in the manner
thou hast heard. It is now thy turn to
give him convincing evidence of thy mar-
riage.

ŚAKOONTALÁ [aside]. Since his feeling
towards me has undergone a complete
revolution, what will it avail to revive
old recollections? One thing is clear—I
shall soon have to mourn my own widow-
hood. [Aloud.] My revered husband—
[Stops short.] But no—I dare not ad-
dress thee by this title, since thou hast
refused to acknowledge our union. Noble
descendant of Puru! It is not worthy of
thee to betray an innocent-minded girl,
and disown her in such terms, after hav-
ing so lately and so solemnly plighted
thy vows to her in the hermitage.

KING [stopping his ears]. I will hear
no more. Be such a crime far from my
thoughts!

What evil spirit can possess thee, lady,
That thou dost seek to sully my good
name
By base aspersions, like a swollen torrent,
That, leaping from its narrow bed, o'er-
throws
The tree upon its bank, and strives to
blend
Its turbid waters with the crystal stream?

ŚAKOONTALÁ. If, then, thou really be-
lievest me to be the wife of another, and
thy present conduct proceeds from some
cloud that obscures thy recollection, I will
easily convince thee by this token.

KING. An excellent idea!

ŚAKOONTALÁ [feeling for the ring].
Alas! alas! woe is me! There is no ring
on my finger!

[Looks with anguish at GAUTAMÍ.]

GAUTAMÍ. The ring must have slipped
off when thou wast in the act of offering
homage to the holy water of Śachí's sacred
pool, near Śakrávatára.

KING [smiling]. People may well talk
of the readiness of woman's invention!
Here is an instance of it.

ŚAKOONTALÁ. Say, rather, of the om-
nipotence of fate. I will mention another
circumstance, which may yet convince
thee.

KING. By all means let me hear it at
once.

ŚAKOONTALÁ. One day, while we were
seated in a jasmine-bower, thou didst pour
into the hollow of thine hand some water,
sprinkled by a recent shower in the cup
of a lotus-blossom—

KING. I am listening; proceed.

ŚAKOONTALÁ. At that instant, my
adopted child, the little fawn, with soft,
long eyes, came running towards us.
Upon which, before tasting the water thy-
self, thou didst kindly offer some to the
little creature, saying fondly:—'Drink
first, gentle fawn.' But she could not be
induced to drink from the hand of a
stranger; though immediately afterwards,
when I took the water in my own hand,
she drank with perfect confidence. Then,
with a smile, thou didst say:—'Every
creature confides naturally in its own
kind. You are both inhabitants of the
same forest, and have learnt to trust
each other.'

KING. Voluptuaries may allow them-
selves to be seduced from the path of
duty by falsehoods such as these, ex-
pressed in honeyed words.

GAUTAMÍ. Speak not thus, illustrious
Prince. This lady was brought up in a
hermitage, and has never learnt deceit.

KING. Holy matron,

E'en in untutored brutes, the female sex
Is marked by inborn subtlety—much
more
In beings gifted with intelligence.
The wily Koïl, ere towards the sky
She wings her sportive flight, commits her
eggs

To other nests, and artfully consigns
The rearing of her little ones to strangers.

ŚAKOONTALÁ [*angrily*]. Dishonourable man, thou judgest of others by thine own evil heart. Thou, at least, art unrivalled in perfidy, and standest alone—a base deceiver in the garb of virtue and religion—like a deep pit whose yawning mouth is concealed by smiling flowers.

KING [*aside*]. Her anger, at any rate, appears genuine, and makes me almost doubt whether I am in the right. For indeed,

When I had vainly searched my memory,
And so with stern severity denied
The fabled story of our secret loves,
Her brows, that met before in graceful curves,
Like the arched weapon of the god of love,
Seemed by her frown dissevered; while the fire
Of sudden anger kindled in her eyes.

[*Aloud.*] My good lady, Dushyanta's character is well known to all. I comprehend not your meaning.

ŚAKOONTALÁ. Well do I deserve to be thought a harlot for having in the innocence of my heart, and out of the confidence I reposed in a Prince of Puru's race, entrusted my honour to a man whose mouth distils honey, while his heart is full of poison. [*Covers her face with her mantle, and bursts into tears.*]

ŚÁRNGARAVA. Thus it is that burning remorse must ever follow rash actions which might have been avoided, and for which one has only one's self to blame.

Not hastily should marriage be contracted,
And specially in secret. Many a time,
In hearts that know not each the other's fancies,
Fond love is changed into most bitter hate. .

KING. How now! Do you give credence to this woman rather than to me, that you heap such accusations on me?

ŚÁRNGARAVA [*sarcastically*]. That would be too absurd, certainly. You have heard the proverb:—

Hold in contempt the innocent words of those
Who from their infancy have known no guile;
But trust the treacherous counsels of the man
Who makes a very science of deceit.

KING. Most veracious Bráhman, grant that you are in the right, what end would be gained by betraying this lady?

ŚÁRNGARAVA. Ruin.

KING. No one will believe that a Prince of Puru's race would seek to ruin others or himself.

ŚÁRADWATA. This altercation is idle, Śárngarava. We have executed the commission of our preceptor; come, let us return. [*To the* KING.]

Śakoontalá is certainly thy bride;
Receive her or reject her, she is thine.
Do with her, King, according to thy pleasure—
The husband o'er the wife is absolute.
Go on before us, Gautamí.

[*They move away.*]

ŚAKOONTALÁ. What! is it not enough to have been betrayed by this perfidious man? Must you also forsake me, regardless of my tears and lamentations? [*Attempts to follow them.*]

GAUTAMÍ [*stopping*]. My son Śárngarava, see! Śakoontalá is following us, and with tears implores us not to leave her. Alas! poor child, what will she do here with a cruel husband who casts her from him?

ŚÁRNGARAVA [*turning angrily towards her*]. Wilful woman, dost thou seek to be independent of thy lord?

[ŚAKOONTALÁ *trembles with fear.*]

Śakoontalá!
If thou art really what the King proclaims thee,
How can thy father e'er receive thee back
Into his house and home? but if thy conscience

Be witness to thy purity of soul,
E'en should thy husband to a handmaid's
lot
Condemn thee, thou may'st cheerfully en-
dure it,
When ranked among the number of his
household.
The duty therefore is to stay. As for us,
we must return immediately.

KING. Deceive not the lady, my good
hermit, by any such expectations.

The moon expands the lotus of the night,
The rising sun awakens the lily; each
Is with his own contented. Even so
The virtuous man is master of his pas-
sions,
And from another's wife averts his gaze.

ŚÁRNGARAVA. Since thy union with an-
other woman has rendered thee oblivious
of thy marriage with Śakoontalá, whence
this fear of losing thy character for con-
stancy and virtue?

KING [to his domestic PRIEST]. You
must counsel me, revered Sir, as to my
course of action. Which of the two evils
involves the greater or less sin?

Whether by some dark veil my mind be
clouded,
Or this designing woman speak untruly,
I know not. Tell me, must I rather be
The base disowner of my wedded wife,
Or the defiling and defiled adulterer?

PRIEST [after deliberation]. You must
take an intermediate course.
KING. What course, revered Sir? Tell
me at once.
PRIEST. I will provide an asylum for
the lady in my own house until the birth
of her child; and my reason, if you ask
me, is this: Soothsayers have predicted
that your first-born will have universal
dominion. Now, if the hermit's daughter
bring forth a son with the discus or mark
of empire in the lines of his hand, you
must admit her immediately into your
royal apartments with great rejoicings; if
not, then determine to send her back as
soon as possible to her father.

KING. I bow to the decision of my
spiritual adviser.
PRIEST. Daughter, follow me.
ŚAKOONTALÁ. O divine earth, open and
receive me into thy bosom!
[Exit ŚAKOONTALÁ weeping, with
the PRIEST and the HERMITS.
The KING remains absorbed in
thinking of her, though the
curse still clouds his recollec-
tion.]
A VOICE [behind the scenes]. A mira-
cle! a miracle!
KING [listening]. What has happened
now?
PRIEST [entering with an air of aston-
ishment]. Great Prince, a stupendous
prodigy has just occurred.
KING. What is it?
PRIEST. May it please your Majesty,
so soon as Kanwa's pupils had departed,
Śakoontalá, her eyes all bathed in tears,
With outstretched arms, bewailed her
cruel fate—
KING. Well, well, what happened then?
PRIEST. When suddenly a shining ap-
parition,
In female shape, descended from the skies,
Near the nymph's pool, and bore her up
to heaven.
[All remain motionless with as-
tonishment.]
KING. My good priest, from the very
first I declined having anything to do
with this matter. It is now all over,
and we can never, by our conjectures,
unravel the mystery; let it rest; go, seek
repose.
PRIEST [looking at the KING]. Be it
so. Victory to the King! [Exit.
KING. Vetravatí, I am tired out; lead
the way to the bedchamber.
WARDER. This way, Sire.
[They move away.]

KING. Do what I will, I cannot call to
mind
That I did e'er espouse the sage's daugh-
ter;
Therefore I have disowned her; yet 'tis
strange

How painfully my agitated heart
Bears witness to the truth of her asser-
tion,
And makes me credit her against my
judgment. [*Exeunt.*]

PRELUDE TO ACT VI

SCENE—*A Street*

[*Enter the King's brother-in-law as* SU-
PERINTENDENT *of the city police; and with
him* TWO CONSTABLES, *dragging a poor*
FISHERMAN, *who has his hands tied be-
hind his back.*]

BOTH THE CONSTABLES [*striking the
prisoner*]. Take that for a rascally thief
that you are; and now tell us, sirrah,
where you found this ring—aye, the King's
own signet-ring. See, here is the royal
name engraved on the setting of the
jewel.

FISHERMAN [*with a gesture of alarm*].
Mercy! kind sirs, mercy! I did not steal
it; indeed I did not.

FIRST CONSTABLE. Oh! then I suppose
the King took you for some fine Bráhman,
and made you a present of it?

FISHERMAN. Only hear me. I am but
a poor fisherman, living at Śakrávatára—

SECOND CONSTABLE. Scoundrel, who
ever asked you, pray, for a history of
your birth and parentage?

SUPERINTENDENT [*to one of the* CON-
STABLES]. Súchaka, let the fellow tell his
own story from the beginning. Don't in-
terrupt him.

BOTH CONSTABLES. As you please,
master. Go on, then, sirrah, and say
what you've got to say.

FISHERMAN. You see in me a poor
man, who supports his family by catching
fish with nets, hooks, and the like.

SUPERINTENDENT [*laughing*]. A most
refined occupation, certainly!

FISHERMAN. Blame me not for it, mas-
ter.
The father's occupation, though despised
By others, casts no shame upon the son,

And he should not forsake it. Is the
priest
Who kills the animal for sacrifice
Therefore deemed cruel? Sure a low-born
man
May, though a fisherman, be tender-
hearted.

SUPERINTENDENT. Well, well; go on
with your story.

FISHERMAN. One day I was cutting
open a large carp I had just hooked, when
the sparkle of a jewel caught my eye,
and what should I find in the fish's maw
but that ring! Soon afterwards, when I
was offering it for sale, I was seized by
your honours. Now you know everything.
Whether you kill me, or whether you let
me go, this is the true account of how
the ring came into my possession.

SUPERINTENDENT [*to one of the* CON-
STABLES]. Well, Jánuka, the rascal emits
such a fishy odour that I have no doubt
of his being a fisherman; but we must
inquire a little more closely into this
queer story about the finding of the ring.
Come, we'll take him before the King's
household.

BOTH CONSTABLES. Very good, master.
Get on with you, you cutpurse.
[*All move on.*]

SUPERINTENDENT. Now attend, Súch-
aka; keep your guard here at the gate;
and hark ye, sirrahs, take good care your
prisoner does not escape, while I go in
and lay the whole story of the discovery
of this ring before the King in person.
I will soon return and let you know his
commands.

BOTH CONSTABLES. Go in, master, by
all means; and may you find favour in the
King's sight. [*Exit* SUPERINTENDENT.]

FIRST CONSTABLE [*after an interval*].
I say, Jánuka, the Superintendent is a
long time away.

SECOND CONSTABLE. Aye, aye; kings are
not to be got at so easily. Folks must
bide the proper opportunity.

FIRST CONSTABLE. Jánuka, my fingers
itch to strike the first blow at this royal
victim here. We must kill him with all

the honours, you know. I long to begin binding the flowers round his head. [*Pretends to strike a blow at the* FISHERMAN.]
FISHERMAN. Your Honour sur2ly will not put an innocent man to a cruel death.
SECOND CONSTABLE [*looking*]. There's our Superintendent at last, I declare. See! he is coming towards us with a paper in his hand. We shall soon know the King's command; so prepare, my fine fellow, either to become food for the vultures, or to make acquaintance with some hungry cur.
SUPERINTENDENT [*entering*]. Ho, there, Súchaka! set the fisherman at liberty, I tell you. His story about the ring is all correct.
SÚCHAKA. Oh! very good, Sir; as you please.
SECOND CONSTABLE. The fellow had one foot in hell, and now here he is in the land of the living. [*Releases him.*]
FISHERMAN [*bowing to the* SUPERINTENDENT]. Now, master, what think you of my way of getting a livelihood?
SUPERINTENDENT. Here, my good man, the King desired me to present you with this purse. It contains a sum of money equal to the full value of the ring.
[*Gives him the money.*]
FISHERMAN [*taking it and bowing*]. His Majesty does me too great honour.
SÚCHAKA. You may well say so. He might as well have taken you from the gallows to seat you on his state elephant.
JÁNUKA. Master, the King must value the ring very highly, or he would never have sent such a sum of money to this ragamuffin.
SUPERINTENDENT. I don't think he prizes it as a costly jewel so much as a memorial of some person he tenderly loves. The moment it was shown to him he became much agitated, though in general he conceals his feelings.
SÚCHAKA. Then you must have done a great service—
JÁNUKA. Yes, to this husband of a fish-wife.
[*Looks enviously at the* FISHERMAN.]

FISHERMAN. Here's half the money for you, my masters. It will serve to purchase the flowers you spoke of, if not to buy me your good-will.
JÁNUKA. Well, now, that's just as it should be.
SUPERINTENDENT. My good fisherman, you are an excellent fellow, and I begin to feel quite a regard for you. Let us seal our first friendship over a glass of good liquor. Come along to the next wine-shop, and we'll drink your health.
ALL. By all means. [*Exeunt.*]

ACT VI

SCENE—*The Garden of a Palace*

[*The nymph* SÁNUMATÍ *is seen descending in a celestial car.*]

SÁNUMATÍ. Behold me just arrived from attending in my proper turn at the nymphs' pool, where I have left the other nymphs to perform their ablutions, whilst I seek to ascertain, with my own eyes, how it fares with King Dushyanta. My connexion with the nymph Menaká has made her daughter Śakoontalá dearer to me than my own flesh and blood; and Menaká it was who charged me with this errand on her daughter's behalf. [*Looking round in all directions.*] How is it that I see no preparations in the King's household for celebrating the great vernal festival? I could easily discover the reason by my divine faculty of meditation; but respect must be shown to the wishes of my friend. How then shall I arrive at the truth? I know what I will do. I will become invisible, and place myself near those two maidens who are tending the plants in the garden.
[*Descends and takes her station.*]

[*Enter a* MAIDEN, *who stops in front of a mango-tree, and gazes at the blossom. Another* MAIDEN *is seen behind her.*]
FIRST MAIDEN. Hail to thee, lovely harbinger of spring!
The varied radiance of thy opening flowers

Is welcome to my sight. I bid thee hail,
Sweet mango, soul of this enchanting season.

SECOND MAIDEN. Parabhṛitiká, what are you saying there to yourself?

FIRST MAIDEN. Dear Madhukariká, am I not named after the Koïl? and does not the Koïl sing for joy at the first appearance of the mango-blossom?

SECOND MAIDEN [approaching hastily, with transport]. What! is spring really come?

FIRST MAIDEN. Yes, indeed, Madhukariká, and with it the season of joy, love, and song.

SECOND MAIDEN. Let me lean upon you, dear, while I stand on tip-toe and pluck a blossom of the mango, that I may present it as an offering to the god of love.

FIRST MAIDEN. Provided you let me have half the reward which the god will bestow in return.

SECOND MAIDEN. To be sure you shall, and that without asking. Are we not one in heart and soul, though divided in body? [Leans on her friend and plucks a mango-blossom.] Ah! here is a bud just bursting into flower. It diffuses a delicious perfume, though not yet quite expanded. [Joining her hands reverentially.] God of the bow, who with spring's choicest flowers
Dost point thy five unerring shafts; to thee
I dedicate this blossom; let it serve
To barb thy truest arrow; be its mark
Some youthful heart that pines to be beloved. [Throws down a mango-blossom.]

CHAMBERLAIN [entering in a hurried manner, angrily]. Hold there, thoughtless woman. What are you about, breaking off those mango-blossoms, when the King has forbidden the celebration of the spring festival?

BOTH MAIDENS [alarmed]. Pardon us, kind Sir, we have heard nothing of it.

CHAMBERLAIN. You have heard nothing of it? Why, all the vernal plants and shrubs, and the very birds that lodge in their branches, show more respect to the King's order than you do.

Yon mango-blossoms, though long since expanded,
Gather no down upon their tender crests;
The flower still lingers in the amaranth,
Imprisoned in its bud; the tuneful Koïl,
Though winter's chilly dews be overpast,
Suspends the liquid volume of his song
Scarce uttered in his throat; e'en Love,
    dismayed,
Restores the half-drawn arrow to his
    quiver.

BOTH MAIDENS. The mighty power of King Dushyanta is not to be disputed.

FIRST MAIDEN. It is but a few days since Mitrávasu, the King's brother-in-law, sent us to wait upon his Majesty; and, during the whole of our sojourn here, we have been entrusted with the charge of the royal pleasure-grounds. We are therefore strangers in this place, and heard nothing of the order till you informed us of it.

CHAMBERLAIN. Well then, now you know it, take care you don't continue your preparations.

BOTH MAIDENS. But tell us, kind Sir, why has the King prohibited the usual festivities? We are curious to hear, if we may.

SÁNUMATÍ [aside]. Men are naturally fond of festive entertainments. There must be some good reason for the prohibition.

CHAMBERLAIN. The whole affair is now public; why should I not speak of it? Has not the gossip about the King's rejection of Śakoontalá reached your ears yet?

BOTH MAIDENS. Oh yes, we heard the story from the King's brother-in-law, as far, at least, as the discovery of the ring.

CHAMBERLAIN. Then there is little more to tell you. As soon as the King's memory was restored by the sight of his own ring, he exclaimed: 'Yes, it is all true. I remember now my secret marriage with Śakoontalá. When I repudiated her, I had lost my recollection!' Ever since that moment, he has yielded himself a prey to the bitterest remorse.

He loathes his former pleasures; he rejects
The daily homage of his ministers;
On his lone couch he tosses to and fro,
Courting repose in vain. Whene'er he meets
The ladies of his palace, and would fain
Address them with politeness, he confounds
Their names; or, calling them 'Śakoontalá,'
Is straightway silent and abashed with shame.

SÁNUMATÍ [aside]. To me this account is delightful.

CHAMBERLAIN. In short, the King is so completely out of his mind that the festival has been prohibited.

BOTH MAIDENS. Perfectly right.

A VOICE [behind the scenes]. The King! the King! This way, Sire, this way.

CHAMBERLAIN [listening]. Oh! here comes his Majesty in this direction. Pass on, maidens; attend to your duties.

BOTH MAIDENS. We will, sir.
[Exeunt.]

[Enter King DUSHYANTA, dressed in deep mourning, attended by his Jester, MÁ-ṬHAVYA, and preceded by VETRAVATÍ.]

CHAMBERLAIN [gazing at the KING]. Well, noble forms are certainly pleasing, under all varieties of outward circumstances. The King's person is as charming as ever, notwithstanding his sorrow of mind.

Though but a single golden bracelet spans
His wasted arm; though costly ornaments
Have given place to penitential weeds;
Though oft-repeated sighs have blanched his lips,
And robbed them of their bloom; though sleepless care
And carking thought have dimmed his beaming eye;
Yet does his form, by its inherent lustre,
Dazzle the gaze; and, like a priceless gem

Committed to some cunning polisher,
Grow more effulgent by the loss of substance.

SÁNUMATÍ [aside. Looking at the KING]. Now that I have seen him, I can well understand why Śakoontalá should pine after such a man, in spite of his disdainful rejection of her.

KING [walking slowly up and down in deep thought]. When fatal lethargy o'erwhelmed my soul,
My loved one strove to rouse me, but in vain;
And now, when I would fain in slumber deep
Forget myself, full soon remorse doth wake me.

SÁNUMATÍ [aside]. My poor Śakoontalá's sufferings are very similar.

MÁṬHAVYA [aside]. He is taken with another attack of this odious Śakoontalá-fever. How shall we ever cure him?

CHAMBERLAIN [approaching]. Victory to the King! Great Prince, the royal pleasure-grounds have been put in order. Your Majesty can resort to them for exercise and amusement whenever you think proper.

KING. Vetravatí, tell the worthy Piśuna, my prime minister, from me, that I am so exhausted by want of sleep that I cannot sit on the judgment-seat to-day. If any case of importance be brought before the tribunal, he must give it his best attention, and inform me of the circumstances by letter.

VETRAVATÍ. Your Majesty's commands shall be obeyed. [Exit.]

KING [to the CHAMBERLAIN]. And you, Vátáyana, may go about your own affairs.

CHAMBERLAIN. I will, Sire. [Exit.]

MÁṬHAVYA. Now that you have rid yourself of these troublesome fellows, you can enjoy the delightful coolness of your pleasure-grounds without interruption.

KING. Ah! my dear friend, there is an old adage:—'When affliction has a mind to enter, she will find a crevice somewhere'; and it is verified in me.

Scarce is my soul delivered from the cloud
That darkened its remembrance of the
past,
When lo! the heart-born deity of love
With yonder blossom of the mango barbs
His keenest shaft, and aims it at my
breast.

MÁṬHAVYA. Well, then, wait a moment; I will soon demolish Master Káma's arrow with a cut of my cane. [*Raises his stick and strikes off the mango-blossom.*]

KING [*smiling*]. That will do. I see very well the god of love is not a match for a Bráhman. And now, my dear friend, where shall I sit down, that I may enchant my sight by gazing on the twining plants, which seem to remind me of the graceful shape of my beloved?

MÁṬHAVYA. Don't you remember? you told your personal attendant, Chaturiká, that you would pass the heat of the day in the jasmine-bower; and commanded her to bring the likeness of your queen Śakoontalá, sketched with your own hand.

KING. True. The sight of her picture will refresh my soul. Lead the way to the arbour.

MÁṬHAVYA. This way, Sire. [*Both move on, followed by* SÁNUMATÍ.]

MÁṬHAVYA. Here we are at the jasmine-bower. Look, it has a marble seat, and seems to bid us welcome with its offerings of delicious flowers. You have only to enter and sit down. [*Both enter and seat themselves.*]

SÁNUMATÍ [*aside*]. I will lean against these young jasmines. I can easily, from behind them, glance at my friend's picture, and will then hasten to inform her of her husband's ardent affection. [*Stands leaning against the creepers.*]

KING. Oh! my dear friend, how vividly all the circumstances of my union with Śakoontalá present themselves to my recollection at this moment! But tell me now how it was that, between the time of my leaving her in the hermitage and my subsequent rejection of her, you never breathed her name to me? True, you

were not by my side when I disowned her; but I had confided to you the story of my love, and you were acquainted with every particular. Did it pass out of your mind as it did out of mine?

MÁṬHAVYA. No, no; trust me for that. But, if you remember, when you had finished telling me about it, you added that I was not to take the story in earnest, for that you were not really in love with a country girl, but were only jesting; and I was dull and thick-headed enough to believe you. But so fate decreed, and there is no help for it.

SÁNUMATÍ [*aside*]. Exactly.

KING [*after deep thought*]. My dear friend, suggest some relief for my misery.

MÁṬHAVYA. Come, come, cheer up; why do you give way? Such weakness is unworthy of you. Great men never surrender themselves to uncontrolled grief. Do not mountains remain unshaken even in a gale of wind?

KING. How can I be otherwise than inconsolable, when I call to mind the agonized demeanour of the dear one on the occasion of my disowning her?

When cruelly I spurned her from my presence,
She fain had left me; but the young recluse,
Stern as the Sage, and with authority
As from his saintly master, in a voice
That brooked not contradiction, bade her stay.
Then through her pleading eyes, bedimmed with tears,
She cast on me one long reproachful look,
Which like a poisoned shaft torments me still.

SÁNUMATÍ [*aside*]. Alas! such is the force of self-reproach following a rash action. But his anguish only rejoices me.

MÁṬHAVYA. An idea has just struck me. I should not wonder if some celestial being had carried her off to heaven.

KING Very likely. Who else would have dared to lay a finger on a wife, the idol of her husband? It is said that Menaká, the nymph of heaven, gave her birth.

The suspicion has certainly crossed my mind that some of her celestial companions may have taken her to their own abode.

SÁNUMATÍ [aside]. His present recollection of every circumstance of her history does not surprise me so much as his former forgetfulness.

MÁṬHAVYA. If that's the case, you will be certain to meet her before long.

KING. Why?

MÁṬHAVYA. No father and mother can endure to see a daughter suffering the pain of separation from her husband.

KING. Oh! my dear Máṭhavya,
Was it a dream? or did some magic dire,
Dulling my senses with a strange delusion,
O'ercome my spirit? or did destiny,
Jealous of my good actions, mar their fruit,
And rob me of their guerdon? It is past,
Whate'er the spell that bound me. Once again
Am I awake, but only to behold
The precipice o'er which my hopes have fallen.

MÁṬHAVYA. Do not despair in this manner. Is not this very ring a proof that what has been lost may be unexpectedly found?

KING [gazing at the ring]. Ah! this ring, too, has fallen from a station not easily regained, and I offer it my sympathy.
O gem,
The punishment we suffer is deserved,
And equal is the merit of our works,
When such our common doom. Thou didst enjoy
The thrilling contact of those slender fingers,
Bright as the dawn; and now how changed thy lot!

SÁNUMATÍ [aside]. Had it found its way to the hand of any other person, then indeed its fate would have been deplorable.

MÁṬHAVYA. Pray, how did the ring ever come upon her hand at all?

SÁNUMATÍ [aside]. I myself am curious to know.

KING. You shall hear. When I was leaving my beloved Śakoontalá that I might return to my own capital, she said to me, with tears in her eyes: 'How long will it be ere my lord send for me to his palace and make me his queen?'

MÁṬHAVYA. Well, what was your reply?

KING. Then I placed the ring on her finger, and thus addressed her:—

Repeat each day one letter of the name
Engraven on this gem; ere thou hast reckoned
The tale of syllables, my minister
Shall come to lead thee to thy husband's palace.

But, hard-hearted man that I was, I forgot to fulfil my promise, owing to the infatuation that took possession of me.

SÁNUMATÍ [aside]. A pleasant arrangement! Fate, however, ordained that the appointment should not be kept.

MÁṬHAVYA. But how did the ring contrive to pass into the stomach of that carp which the fisherman caught and was cutting up?

KING. It must have slipped from my Śakoontalá's hand, and fallen into the stream of the Ganges, while she was offering homage to the water of Śachí's holy pool.

MÁṬHAVYA. Very likely.

SÁNUMATÍ [aside]. Hence it happened I suppose, that the King, always fearful of committing the least injustice, came to doubt his marriage with my poor Śakoontalá. But why should affection so strong as his stand in need of any token of recognition?

KING. Let me now address a few words of reproof to this ring.

MÁṬHAVYA [aside]. He is going stark mad, I verily believe.

KING. Hear me, thou dull and undiscerning bauble!
For so it argues thee, that thou could'st leave
The slender fingers of her hand, to sink
Beneath the waters. Yet what marvel is it

That thou should'st lack discernment? let me rather
Heap curses on myself, who, though endowed
With reason, yet rejected her I loved.

MÁTHAVYA [aside]. And so, I suppose, I must stand here to be devoured by hunger, whilst he goes on in this sentimental strain.

KING. O forsaken one, unjustly banished from my presence, take pity on thy slave, whose heart is consumed by the fire of remorse, and return to my sight.

[Enter CHATURIKÁ hurriedly, with a picture in her hand.]

CHATURIKÁ. Here is the Queen's portrait. [Shows the picture.]

MÁTHAVYA. Excellent, my dear friend, excellent! The imitation of nature is perfect, and the attitude of the figures is really charming. They stand out in such bold relief that the eye is quite deceived.

SÁNUMATÍ [aside]. A most artistic performance! I admire the King's skill, and could almost believe that Śakoontalá herself was before me.

KING. I own 'tis not amiss, though it portrays
But feebly her angelic loveliness.
Aught less than perfect is depicted falsely,
And fancy must supply the imperfection.

SÁNUMATÍ [aside]. A very just remark from a modest man, whose affection is exaggerated by the keenness of his remorse.

MÁTHAVYA. Tell me:—I see three female figures drawn on the canvas, and all of them beautiful; which of the three is her Majesty Śakoontalá?

SÁNUMATÍ [aside]. If he cannot distinguish her from the others, the simpleton might as well have no eyes in his head.

KING. Which should you imagine to be intended for her?

MÁTHAVYA. She who is leaning, apparently a little tired, against the stem of that mango-tree, the tender leaves of which glitter with the water she has poured upon them. Her arms are grace-

fully extended; her face is somewhat flushed with the heat; and a few flowers have escaped from her hair, which has become unfastened, and hangs in loose tresses about her neck. That must be the queen Śakoontalá, and the others, I presume, are her two attendants.

KING. I congratulate you on your discernment. Behold the proof of my passion;

My finger, burning with the glow of love,
Has left its impress on the painted tablet;
While here and there, alas! a scalding tear
Has fallen on the cheek and dimmed its brightness.

Chaturiká, the garden in the background of the picture is only half-painted. Go, fetch the brush that I may finish it.

CHATURIKÁ. Worthy Máthavya, have the kindness to hold the picture until I return.

KING. Nay, I will hold it myself.
[Takes the picture.]
[Exit CHATURIKÁ.]

My loved one came but lately to my presence
And offered me herself, but in my folly
I spurned the gift, and now I fondly cling
To her mere image; even as a madman
Would pass the waters of the gushing stream,
And thirst for airy vapours of the desert.

MÁTHAVYA [aside]. He has been fool enough to forego the reality for the semblance, the substance for the shadow. [Aloud.] Tell us, I pray, what else remains to be painted.

SÁNUMATÍ [aside]. He longs, no doubt, to delineate some favourite spot where my Śakoontalá delighted to ramble.

KING. You shall hear:—

I wish to see the Máliní portrayed,
Its tranquil course by banks of sand impeded;
Upon the brink a pair of swans; beyond,
The hills adjacent to Himálaya,

Studded with deer; and, near the spreading shade
Of some large tree, where 'mid the branches hang
The hermits' vests of bark, a tender doe,
Rubbing its downy forehead on the horn
Of a black antelope, should be depicted.

MÁṬHAVYA [aside]. Pooh! if I were he, I would fill up the vacant spaces with a lot of grizzly-bearded old hermits.

KING My dear Máṭhavya, there is still a part of Śakoontalá's dress which I purposed to draw, but find I have omitted.

MÁṬHAVYA. What is that?

SÁNUMATÍ [aside]. Something suitable, I suppose, to the simple attire of a young and beautiful girl dwelling in a forest.

KING. A sweet Śirísha blossom should be twined
Behind her ear, its perfumed crest depending
Towards her cheek; and, resting on her bosom,
A lotus-fibre necklace, soft and bright
As an autumnal moonbeam, should be traced.

MÁṬHAVYA. Pray, why does the Queen cover her lips with the tips of her fingers, bright as the blossom of a lily, as if she were afraid of something? [Looking more closely.] Oh! I see; a vagabond bee, intent on thieving honey from the flowers, has mistaken her mouth for a rosebud, and is trying to settle upon it.

KING. A bee! drive off the impudent insect, will you?

MÁṬHAVYA. That's your business. Your royal prerogative gives you power over all offenders.

KING. Very true. Listen to me, thou favourite guest of flowering plants; why give thyself the trouble of hovering here?

See where thy partner sits on yonder flower,
And waits for thee ere she will sip its dew.

SÁNUMATÍ [aside]. A most polite way of warning him off!

MÁṬHAVYA. You'll find the obstinate

creature is not to be sent about his business so easily as you think.

KING. Dost thou presume to disobey? Now hear me:—
An thou but touch the lips of my beloved,
Sweet as the opening blossom, whence I quaffed
In happier days love's nectar, I will place thee
Within the hollow of yon lotus cup,
And there imprison thee for thy presumption.

MÁṬHAVYA. He must be bold indeed not to show any fear when you threaten him with such an awful punishment. [Smiling, aside.] He is stark mad, that's clear; and I believe, by keeping him company, I am beginning to talk almost as wildly. [Aloud.] Look, it is only a painted bee.

KING. Painted? impossible!

SÁNUMATÍ [aside]. Even I did not perceive it; how much less should he!

KING. Oh! my dear friend, why were you so ill-natured as to tell me the truth?

While all entranced, I gazed upon her picture,
My loved one seemed to live before my eyes
Till every fibre of my being thrilled
With rapturous emotion. Oh! 'twas cruel
To dissipate the day-dream, and transform
The blissful vision to a lifeless image.
[Sheds tears.]

SÁNUMATÍ [aside]. Separated lovers are very difficult to please; but he seems more difficult than usual.

KING Alas! my dear Máṭhavya, why am I doomed to be the victim of perpetual disappointment?

Vain is the hope of meeting her in dreams,
For slumber night by night forsakes my couch;
And now that I would fain assuage my grief
By gazing on her portrait here before me,
Tears of despairing love obscure my sight.

SÁNUMATÍ [aside]. You have made ample amends for the wrong you did Śakoontalá in disowning her.

CHATURIKÁ [entering]. Victory to the King! I was coming along with the box of colours in my hand—

KING. What now?

CHATURIKÁ. When I met the queen Vasumatí, attended by Taraliká. She insisted on taking it from me, and declared she would herself deliver it into your Majesty's hands.

MÁTHAVYA. By what luck did you contrive to escape her?

CHATURIKÁ. While her maid was disengaging her mantle, which had caught in the branch of a shrub, I ran away.

KING. Here, my good friend, take the picture and conceal it. My attentions to the Queen have made her presumptuous. She will be here in a minute.

MÁTHAVYA. Conceal the picture! conceal myself, you mean. [Getting up and taking the picture.] The Queen has a bitter draught in store for you, which you will have to swallow, as Śiva did the poison at the Deluge. When you are well quit of her, you may send and call me from the Palace of Clouds, where I shall take refuge. [Exit, running.]

SÁNUMATÍ [aside]. Although the King's affections are transferred to another object, yet he respects his previous attachments. I fear his love must be somewhat fickle.

VETRAVATÍ [entering with a despatch in her hand]. Victory to the King!

KING. Vetravatí, did you observe the queen Vasumatí coming in this direction?

VETRAVATÍ. I did; but when she saw that I had a despatch in my hand for your Majesty, she turned back.

KING. The Queen has too much regard for propriety to interrupt me when I am engaged with State-affairs.

VETRAVATÍ. So please your Majesty, your prime minister begs respectfully to inform you that he has devoted much time to the settlement of financial calculations, and only one case of importance has been submitted by the citizens for his consideration. He has made a written report of the facts, and requests your Majesty to cast your eyes over it.

KING. Hand me the paper.

[VETRAVATÍ delivers it.]

[Reading.]

What have we here? ' A merchant named Dhanamitra, trading by sea, was lost in a late shipwreck. Though a wealthy trader, he was childless; and the whole of his immense property becomes by law forfeited to the king.' So writes the minister. Alas! alas! for his childlessness! But surely, if he was wealthy, he must have had many wives. Let an inquiry be made whether any one of them is expecting to give birth to a child.

VETRAVATÍ. They say that his wife, the daughter of the foreman of a guild belonging to Ayodhyá, has just completed the ceremonies usual upon such expectations.

KING. The unborn child has a title to its father's property. Such is my decree. Go, bid my minister proclaim it so.

VETRAVATÍ [going]. I will, my liege.

KING. Stay a moment.

VETRAVATÍ. I am at your Majesty's service.

KING. Let there be no question whether he may or may not have left offspring;

Rather be it proclaimed that whosoe'er
Of King Dushyanta's subjects be bereaved
Of any loved relation, an it be not
That his estates are forfeited for crimes,
Dushyanta will himself to them supply
That kinsman's place in tenderest affection.

VETRAVATÍ. It shall be so proclaimed.

[Exit VETRAVATÍ, and reënters after an interval.]

VETRAVATÍ. Your Majesty's proclamation was received with acclamations of joy, like grateful rain at the right season.

KING [drawing a deep sigh]. So, then, the property of rich men, who have no lineal descendants, passes over to a stranger at their decease. And such, alas! must be the fate of the fortunes of the race of Puru at my death; even as when fertile soil is sown with seed at the wrong season.

VETRAVATÍ. Heaven forbid!

KING. Fool that I was to reject such happiness when it offered itself for my acceptance!

SÁNUMATÍ [aside]. He may well blame his own folly when he calls to mind his treatment of my beloved Śakoontalá.

KING. Ah! woe is me! when I forsook my wife—
My lawful wife—concealed within her breast
There lay my second self, a child unborn,
Hope of my race, e'en as the choicest fruit
Lies hidden in the bosom of the earth.

SÁNUMATÍ [aside]. There is no fear of your race being cut off for want of a son.

CHATURIKÁ [aside to VETRAVATÍ]. The affair of the merchant's death has quite upset our royal master, and caused him sad distress. Would it not be better to fetch the worthy Máthavya from the Palace of Clouds to comfort him?

VETRAVATÍ. A very good idea. [Exit.]

KING. Alas! the shades of my forefathers are even now beginning to be alarmed, lest at my death they may be deprived of their funeral libations.
No son remains in King Dushyanta's place
To offer sacred homage to the dead
Of Puru's noble line; my ancestors
Must drink these glistening tears, the last libation
A childless man can ever hope to make them. [Falls down in an agony of grief.]

CHATURIKÁ [looking at him in consternation]. Great King, compose yourself.

SÁNUMATÍ [aside]. Alas! alas! though a bright light is shining near him, he is involved in the blackest darkness, by reason of the veil that obscures his sight. I will now reveal all, and put an end to his misery. But no; I heard the mother of the great Indra, when she was consoling Śakoontalá, say that the gods will soon bring about a joyful union between

husband and wife, being eager for the sacrifice which will be celebrated in their honour on the occasion. I must not anticipate the happy moment, but will return at once to my dear friend and cheer her with an account of what I have seen and heard. [Rises aloft and disappears.]

A VOICE [behind the scenes]. Help! help! to the rescue!

KING [recovering himself. Listening]. Ha! I heard a cry of distress, and in Máthavya's voice too. What ho, there!

VETRAVATÍ [entering]. Your friend is in danger; save him, great King.

KING. Who dares insult the worthy Máthavya?

VETRAVATÍ. Some evil demon, invisible to human eyes, has seized him, and carried him to one of the turrets of the Palace of Clouds.

KING [rising]. Impossible! Have evil spirits power over my subjects, even in my private apartments? Well, well:—
Daily I seem less able to avert
Misfortune from myself, and o'er my actions
Less competent to exercise control;
How can I then direct my subjects' ways,
Or shelter them from tyranny and wrong?

A VOICE [behind the scenes]. Halloo there! my dear friend; help! help!

KING [advancing with rapid strides]. Fear nothing——

THE SAME VOICE [behind the scenes]. Fear nothing, indeed! How can I help fearing when some monster is twisting back my neck, and is about to snap it as he would a sugar-cane?

KING [looking round]. What ho, there! my bow!

SLAVE [entering with a bow]. Behold your bow, Sire, and your arm-guard.
[The KING snatches up the bow and arrows.]

ANOTHER VOICE [behind the scenes.]
Here, thirsting for thy life-blood, will I slay thee,
As a fierce tiger rends his struggling prey.
Call now thy friend Dushyanta to thy aid;

His bow is mighty to defend the weak;
Yet all its vaunted power shall be as
nought.

KING [with fury]. What! dares he
defy me to my face? Hold there, monster! Prepare to die, for your time is
come. [Stringing his bow.] Vetravatí,
lead the way to the terrace.

VETRAVATÍ. This way, Sire. [They
advance in haste.]

KING [looking on every side]. How's
this? there is nothing to be seen.
A VOICE [behind the scenes]. Help!
Save me! I can see you, though you cannot see me. I am like a mouse in the
claws of a cat; my life is not worth a
minute's purchase.

KING. Avaunt, monster! You may
pride yourself on the magic that renders
you invisible, but my arrow shall find
you out. Thus do I fix a shaft
That shall discern between an impious
demon,
And a good Bráhman; bearing death to
thee,
To him deliverance—even as the swan
Distinguishes the milk from worthless
water. [Takes aim.]

[Enter MÁTALI holding MÁṬHAVYA, whom
he releases.]

MÁTALI. Turn thou thy deadly arrows
on the demons;
Such is the will of Indra; let thy bow
Be drawn against the enemies of the
gods;
But on thy friends cast only looks of
favour.

KING [putting back his arrow]. What,
Mátali! Welcome, most noble charioteer
of the mighty Indra.

MÁṬHAVYA. So, here is a monster who
thought as little about slaughtering me
as if I had been a bullock for sacrifice,
and you must e'en greet him with a welcome.

MÁTALI [smiling]. Great Prince, hear
on what errand Indra sent me into your
presence.

KING. I am all attention.

MÁTALI. There is a race of giants, the
descendants of Kálanemi, whom the gods
find it difficult to subdue.

KING. So I have already heard from
Nárada.

MÁTALI. Heaven's mighty lord, who
deigns to call thee 'friend,'
Appoints thee to the post of highest
honour,
As leader of his armies; and commits
The subjugation of this giant brood
To thy resistless arms, e'en as the sun
Leaves the pale moon to dissipate the
darkness.

Let your Majesty, therefore, ascend at
once the celestial car of Indra; and, grasping your arms, advance to victory.

KING. The mighty Indra honours me
too highly by such a mark of distinction.
But tell me, what made you act thus
towards my poor friend Máṭhavya?

MÁTALI. I will tell you. Perceiving
that your Majesty's spirit was completely
broken by some distress of mind under
which you were labouring, I determined
to rouse your energies by moving you to
anger. Because
To light a flame, we need but stir the
embers;
The cobra, when incensed, extends his
head
And springs upon his foe; the bravest
men
Display their courage only when provoked.

KING [aside to MÁṬHAVYA]. My dear
Máṭhavya, the commands of the great
Indra must not be left unfulfilled. Go
you and acquaint my minister, Piśuna,
with what has happened, and say to him
from me:—

Dushyanta to thy care confides his realm—
Protect with all the vigour of thy mind
The interests of his people; while his
bow
Is braced against the enemies of heaven.

MÁṬHAVYA. I obey. [Exit.]
MÁTALI. Ascend, illustrious Prince.
[The KING ascends the car.]
[Exeunt.]

ACT VII

SCENE—*The Sky*

[*Enter* KING DUSHYANTA *and* MATALI *in the car of Indra, moving in the air.*]

KING. My good Mátali, it appears to me incredible that I can merit such a mark of distinction for having simply fulfilled the behests of the great Indra.

MÁTALI [*smiling*]. Great Prince, it seems to me that neither of you is satisfied with himself.

You underrate the services you have rendered,
And think too highly of the god's reward;
He deems it scarce sufficient recompense
For your heroic deeds on his behalf.

KING. Nay, Mátali, say not so. My most ambitious expectations were more than realised by the honour conferred on me at the moment when I took my leave.
For,
Tinged with celestial sandal, from the breast
Of the great Indra, where before it hung,
A garland of the ever-blooming tree
Of Nandana was cast about my neck
By his own hand; while, in the very presence
Of the assembled gods, I was enthroned
Beside their mighty lord, who smiled to see
His son Jayanta envious of the honour.

MÁTALI. There is no mark of distinction which your Majesty does not deserve at the hands of the immortals. See,
Heaven's hosts acknowledge thee their second saviour;
For now thy bow's unerring shafts (as erst
The Lion-man's terrific claws) have purged
The empyreal sphere from taint of demons foul.

KING. The praise of my victory must be ascribed to the majesty of Indra.
When mighty gods make men their delegates
In martial enterprise, to them belongs
The palm of victory; and not to mortals.

Could the pale Dawn dispel the shades of night,
Did not the god of day, whose diadem
Is jewelled with a thousand beams of light,
Place him in front of his effulgent car?

MÁTALI. A very just comparison!
[*Driving on.*] Great King behold! the glory of thy fame has reached even to the vault of heaven.
Hark! yonder inmates of the starry sphere
Sing anthems worthy of thy martial deeds,
While with celestial colours they depict
The story of thy victories on scrolls
Formed of the leaves of heaven's immortal trees.

KING. My good Mátali, yesterday, when I ascended the sky, I was so eager to do battle with the demons, that the road by which we were travelling towards Indra's heaven escaped my observation. Tell me, in which path of the seven winds are we now moving?

MÁTALI. We journey in the path of Parivaha—
The wind that bears along the triple Ganges
And causes Ursa's seven stars to roll
In their appointed orbits, scattering
Their several rays with equal distribution.
'Tis the same path that once was sanctified
By the divine impression of the foot
Of Vishṇu, when, to conquer haughty Bali,
He spanned the heavens in his second stride.

KING. This is the reason, I suppose, that a sensation of calm repose pervades all my senses. [*Looking down at the wheels.*] Ah! Mátali, we are descending towards the earth's atmosphere.

MÁTALI. What makes you think so?

KING. The car itself instructs me; we are moving
O'er pregnant clouds, surcharged with rain; below us
I see the moisture-loving Chátakas
In sportive flight dart through the spokes; the steeds

Of Indra glisten with the lightning's flash;
And a thick mist bedews the circling wheels.

MÁTALI. You are right; in a little while the chariot will touch the ground, and you will be in your own dominions.

KING [looking down]. How wonderful the appearance of the earth as we rapidly descend!

Stupendous prospect! yonder lofty hills
Do suddenly uprear their towering heads
Amid the plain, while from beneath their crests
The ground receding sinks; the trees, whose stem
Seemed lately hid within their leafy tresses,
Rise into elevation, and display
Their branching shoulders; yonder streams, whose waters,
Like silver threads, were scarce, but now, discerned,
Grow into mighty rivers; lo! the earth
Seems upward hurled by some gigantic power.

MÁTALI. Well described! [Looking with awe.] Grand, indeed, and lovely is the spectacle presented by the earth.

KING. Tell me, Mátali, what is the range of mountains which, like a bank of clouds illumined by the setting sun, pours down a stream of gold? On one side its base dips into the eastern ocean, and on the other side into the western.

MÁTALI. Great Prince, it is called 'Golden-peak,' and is the abode of the attendants of the god of wealth. In this spot the highest forms of penance are wrought out.

There Kaśyapa, the great progenitor
Of demons and of gods, himself the off-spring
Of the divine Maríchi, Brahmá's son,
With Aditi, his wife, in calm seclusion,
Does holy penance for the good of mortals.

KING. Then I must not neglect so good an opportunity of obtaining his blessing. I should much like to visit this venerable personage and offer him my homage.

MÁTALI. By all means. An excellent idea! [Guides the car to the earth.]

KING [in a tone of wonder]. How's this?
Our chariot wheels move noiselessly. Around
No clouds of dust arise; no shock betokened
Our contact with the earth; we seem to glide
Above the ground, so lightly do we touch it.

MÁTALI. Such is the difference between the car of Indra and that of your Majesty.

KING. In which direction, Mátali, is Kaśyapa's sacred retreat?

MÁTALI [pointing]. Where stands yon anchorite, towards the orb
Of the meridian sun, immovable
As a tree's stem, his body half-concealed
By a huge ant-hill. Round about his breast
No sacred cord is twined, but in its stead
A hideous serpent's skin. In place of necklace,
The tendrils of a withered creeper chafe
His wasted neck. His matted hair depends
In thick entanglement about his shoulders,
And birds construct their nests within its folds.

KING. I salute thee, thou man of austere devotion.

MÁTALI [holding in the reins of the car]. Great Prince, we are now in the sacred grove of the holy Kaśyapa—the grove that boasts as its ornament one of the five trees of Indra's heaven, reared by Aditi.

KING. This sacred retreat is more delightful than heaven itself. I could almost fancy myself bathing in a pool of nectar.

MÁTALI [stopping the chariot]. Descend, mighty Prince.

KING [descending]. And what will you do, Mátali?

MÁTALI. The chariot will remain where I have stopped it. We may both descend.

[*Doing so.*] This way, great King. [*Walking on.*] You see around you the celebrated region where the holiest sages devote themselves to penitential rites.

KING. I am filled with awe and wonder as I gaze.

In such a place as this do saints of earth
Long to complete their acts of penance; here,
Beneath the shade of everlasting trees,
Transplanted from the groves of Paradise,
May they inhale the balmy air, and need
No other nourishment; here may they bathe
In fountains sparkling with the golden dust
Of lilies; here, on jewelled slabs of marble,
In meditation rapt, may they recline;
Here, in the presence of celestial nymphs,
E'en passion's voice is powerless to move them.

MÁTALI. So true is it that the aspirations of the good and great are ever soaring upwards. [*Turning round and speaking off the stage.*] Tell me, Vṛiddha-śákalya, how is the divine son of Maríchi now engaged? What sayest thou? that he is conversing with Aditi and some of the wives of the great sages, and that they are questioning him respecting the duties of a faithful wife?

KING [*listening*]. Then we must await the holy father's leisure.

MÁTALI [*looking at the* KING]. If your Majesty will rest under the shade, at the foot of this Aśoka-tree, I will seek an opportunity of announcing your arrival to Indra's reputed father.

KING [*remains under the tree*]. As you think proper.

MÁTALI. Great King, I go. [*Exit.*]

KING [*feeling his arm throb*]. Wherefore this causeless throbbing, O mine arm?

All hope has fled for ever; mock me not
With presages of good, when happiness
Is lost, and nought but misery remains.

A VOICE [*behind the scenes*]. Be not

so naughty. Do you begin already to show a refractory spirit?

KING [*listening*]. This is no place for petulance. Who can it be whose behaviour calls for such a rebuke? [*Looking in the direction of the sound and smiling.*] A child, is it? closely attended by two holy women. His disposition seems anything but child-like. See!

He braves the fury of yon lioness
Suckling its savage offspring, and compels
The angry whelp to leave the half-sucked dug,
Tearing its tender mane in boisterous sport.

[*Enter a* CHILD, *attended by* TWO WOMEN *of the hermitage, in manner described.*]

CHILD. Open your mouth, my young lion, I want to count your teeth.

FIRST ATTENDANT. You naughty child, why do you tease the animals? Know you not that we cherish them in this hermitage as if they were our own children? In good sooth, you have a high spirit of your own, and are beginning already to do justice to the name Sarva-damana ('All-taming'), given you by the hermits.

KING. Strange! My heart inclines towards the boy with almost as much affection as if he were my own child. What can be the reason? I suppose my own childlessness makes me yearn towards the sons of others.

SECOND ATTENDANT. This lioness will certainly attack you if you do not release her whelp.

CHILD [*laughing*]. Oh! indeed! let her come. Much I fear her, to be sure! [*Pouts his under-lip in defiance.*]

KING. The germ of mighty courage lies concealed
Within this noble infant, like a spark
Beneath the fuel, waiting but a breath
To fan the flame and raise a conflagration.

FIRST ATTENDANT. Let the young lion go, like a dear child, and I will give you something else to play with.

CHILD. Where is it? Give it me first.
[*Stretches out his hand.*]

KING [*looking at his hand*]. How's that? His hand exhibits one of those mystic marks which are the sure prognostic of universal empire. See!
His fingers stretched in eager expectation
To grasp the wished-for toy, and knit together
By a close-woven web, in shape resemble
A lotus blossom, whose expanding petals
The early dawn has only half unfolded.

SECOND ATTENDANT. We shall never pacify him by mere words, dear Suvratá. Be kind enough to go to my cottage, and you will find there a plaything belonging to Márkaṇḍeya, one of the hermit's children. It is a peacock made of chinaware, painted in many colours. Bring it here for the child.

FIRST ATTENDANT. Very well. [*Exit.*]

CHILD. No, no; I shall go on playing with the young lion. [*Looks at the FEMALE ATTENDANT and laughs.*]

KING. I feel an unaccountable affection for this wayward child.
How blessed the virtuous parents whose attire
Is soiled with dust, by raising from the ground
The child that asks a refuge in their arms!
And happy are they while with lisping prattle,
In accents sweetly inarticulate,
He charms their ears; and with his artless smiles
Gladdens their hearts, revealing to their gaze
His pearly teeth just budding into view.

ATTENDANT. I see how it is. He pays me no manner of attention. [*Looking off the stage.*] I wonder whether any of the hermits are about here. [*Seeing the KING.*] Kind Sir, could you come hither a moment and help me to release the young lion from the clutch of this child who is teasing him in boyish play?

KING [*approaching and smiling*]. Listen to me, thou child of a mighty saint! Dost thou dare show a wayward spirit here?

Here, in this hallowea region? Take thou heed
Lest, as the serpent's young defiles the sandal,
Thou bring dishonour on the holy Sage
Thy tender-hearted parent, who delights
To shield from harm the tenants of the wood.

ATTENDANT. Gentle Sir, I thank you; but he is not the Saint's son.

KING. His behaviour and whole bearing would have led me to doubt it, had not the place of his abode encouraged the idea. [*Follows the CHILD, and takes him by the hand, according to the request of the attendant. Aside.*]
I marvel that the touch of this strange child
Should thrill me with delight; if so it be,
How must the fond caresses of a son
Transport the father's soul who gave him being!

ATTENDANT [*looking at them both*]. Wonderful! Prodigious!

KING. What excites your surprise, my good woman?

ATTENDANT. I am astonished at the striking resemblance between the child and yourself; and, what is still more extraordinary, he seems to have taken to you kindly and submissively, though you are a stranger to him.

KING [*fondling the CHILD*]. If he be not the son of the great Sage, of what family does he come, may I ask?

ATTENDANT. Of the race of Puru.

KING [*aside*]. What! are we, then, descended from the same ancestry? This, no doubt, accounts · for the resemblance she traces between the child and me. Certainly it has always been an established usage among the princes of Puru's race,
To dedicate the morning of their days
To the world's weal, in palaces and halls,
'Mid luxury and regal pomp abiding;
Then, in the wane of life, to seek release
From kingly cares, and make the hallowed shade
Of sacred trees their last asylum, where
As hermits they may practise self-abasement,

And bind themselves by rigid vows of penance.

[*Aloud.*] But how could mortals by their own power gain admission to this sacred region?

ATTENDANT. Your remark is just; but your wonder will cease when I tell you that his mother is the offspring of a celestial nymph, and gave him birth in the hallowed grove of Kaśyapa.

KING [*aside*]. Strange that my hopes should be again excited! [*Aloud.*] But what, let me ask, was the name of the prince whom she deigned to honour with her hand?

ATTENDANT. How could I think of polluting my lips by the mention of a wretch who had the cruelty to desert his lawful wife?

KING [*aside*]. Ha! the description suits me exactly. Would I could bring myself to inquire the name of the child's mother! [*Reflecting.*] But it is against propriety to make too minute inquiries about the wife of another man.

FIRST ATTENDANT [*entering with the china peacock in her hand*]. Sarva-damana, Sarva-damana, see, see, what a beautiful Śakoonta [bird].

CHILD [*looking round*]. My mother! Where? Let me go to her.

BOTH ATTENDANTS. He mistook the word Śakoonta for Śakoontalá. The boy dotes upon his mother, and she is ever uppermost in his thoughts.

SECOND ATTENDANT. Nay, my dear child, I said: Look at the beauty of this Śakoonta.

KING [*aside*]. What! is his mother's name Śakoontalá? But the name is not uncommon among women. Alas! I fear the mere similarity of a name, like the deceitful vapour of the desert, has once more raised my hopes only to dash them to the ground.

CHILD. Dear nurse, what a beautiful peacock! [*Takes the toy.*]

FIRST ATTENDANT [*looking at the CHILD. In great distress*]. Alas! alas! I do not see the amulet on his wrist.

KING. Don't distress yourself. Here it is. It fell off while he was struggling with the young lion. [*Stoops to pick it up.*]

BOTH ATTENDANTS. Hold! hold! Touch it not, for your life. How marvellous! He has actually taken it up without the slightest hesitation. [*Both raise their hands to their breasts and look at each ther in astonishment.*]

KING. Why did you try to prevent my touching it?

FIRST ATTENDANT. Listen, great Monarch. This amulet, known as 'The Invincible,' was given to the boy by the divine son of Maríchi, soon after his birth, when the natal ceremony was performed. Its peculiar virtue is, that when it falls on the ground, no one except the father or mother of the child can touch it unhurt.

KING. And suppose another person touches it?

FIRST ATTENDANT. Then it instantly becomes a serpent, and bites him.

KING. Have you ever witnessed the transformation with your own eyes?

BOTH ATTENDANTS. Over and over again.

KING [*with rapture. Aside*]. Joy! joy! Are then my dearest hopes to be fulfilled? [*Embraces the CHILD.*]

SECOND ATTENDANT. Come, my dear Suvratá, we must inform Śakoontalá immediately of this wonderful event, though we have to interrupt her in the performance of her religious vows. [*Exeunt.*]

CHILD [*to the KING*]. Don't hold me. I want to go to my mother.

KING. We will go to her together, and give her joy, my son.

CHILD. Dushyanta is my father, not you.

KING [*smiling*]. His contradiction only convinces me the more.

[*Enter ŚAKOONTALÁ, in widow's apparel, with her long hair twisted into a single braid.*]

ŚAKOONTALÁ [*aside*]. I have just heard that Sarva-damana's amulet has retained its form, though a stranger raised it from the ground. I can hardly believe in my good fortune. Yet why should not Sánumatí's prediction be verified?

KING [*gazing at* ŚAKOONTALÁ]. Alas! can this indeed be my Śakoontalá?

Clad in the weeds of widowhood, her face
Emaciate with fasting, her long hair
Twined in a single braid, her whole demeanour
Expressive of her purity of soul;
With patient constancy she thus prolongs
The vow to which my cruelty condemned her.

ŚAKOONTALÁ [*gazing at the* KING, *who is pale with remorse*]. Surely this is not like my husband; yet who can it be that dares pollute by the pressure of his hand my child, whose amulet should protect him from a stranger's touch?

CHILD [*going to his mother*]. Mother, who is this man that has been kissing me and calling me his son?

KING. My best beloved, I have indeed treated thee most cruelly, but am now once more thy fond and affectionate lover. Refuse not to acknowledge me as thy husband.

ŚAKOONTALÁ [*aside*]. Be of good cheer, my heart. The anger of Destiny is at last appeased. Heaven regards thee with compassion. But is he in very truth my husband?

KING. Behold me, best and loveliest of women,
Delivered from the cloud of fatal darkness
That erst oppressed my memory. Again
Behold us brought together by the grace
Of the great lord of Heaven. So the moon
Shines forth from dim eclipse, to blend his rays
With the soft lustre of his Rohiṇí.

ŚAKOONTALÁ. May my husband be victorious— [*She stops short, her voice choked with tears.*]

KING. O.fair one, though the utterance of thy prayer
Be lost amid the torrent of thy tears,
Yet does the sight of thy fair countenance
And of thy pallid lips, all unadorned

And colourless in sorrow for my absence,
Make me already more than conqueror.

CHILD. Mother, who is this man?

ŚAKOONTALÁ. My child, ask the deity that presides over thy destiny.

KING [*falling at* ŚAKOONTALÁ'S *feet*].
Fairest of women, banish from thy mind
The memory of my cruelty; reproach
The fell delusion that o'erpowered my soul,
And blame not me, thy husband; 'tis the curse
Of him in whom the power of darkness reigns,
That he mistakes the gifts of those he loves
For deadly evils. Even though a friend
Should wreathe a garland on a blind man's brow,
Will he not cast it from him as a serpent?

ŚAKOONTALÁ. Rise, my own husband, rise. Thou wast not to blame. My own evil deeds, committed in a former state of being, brought down this judgment upon me. How else could my husband, who was ever of a compassionate disposition, have acted so unfeelingly? [*The* KING *rises.*] But tell me, my husband, how did the remembrance of thine unfortunate wife return to thy mind?

KING. As soon as my heart's anguish is removed, and its wounds are healed, I will tell thee all.
Oh! let me, fair one, chase away the drop
That still bedews the fringes of thine eye;
And let me thus efface the memory
Of every tear that · stained thy velvet cheek,
Unnoticed and unheeded by thy lord,
When in his madness he rejected thee.
[*Wipes away the tear.*]

ŚAKOONTALÁ [*seeing the signet-ring on his finger*]. Ah! my dear husband, is that the Lost Ring?

KING. Yes; the moment I recovered it my memory was restored.

ŚAKOONTALÁ. The ring was to blame in allowing itself to be lost at the very time when I was anxious to convince my noble husband of the reality of my marriage.

KING. Receive it back, as the beautiful twining-plant receives again its blossom in token of its reunion with the spring.

ŚAKOONTALÁ. Nay; I can never more place confidence in it. Let my husband retain it.

[Enter MÁTALI.]

MÁTALI. I congratulate your Majesty. Happy are you in your reunion with your wife; happy are you in beholding the face of your own son.

KING. Yes, indeed. My heart's dearest wish has borne sweet fruit. But tell me, Mátali, is this joyful event known to the great Indra?

MÁTALI [smiling]. What is unknown to the gods? But come with me, noble Prince, the divine Kaśyapa graciously permits thee to be presented to him.

KING. Śakoontalá, take our child and lead the way. We will together go into the presence of the holy Sage.

ŚAKOONTALÁ. I shrink from entering the august presence of the great Saint, even with my husband at my side.

KING. Nay; on such a joyous occasion it is highly proper. Come, come; I entreat thee. [All advance.]

[KAŚYAPA is discovered seated on a throne with his wife ADITI.]

KAŚYAPA [gazing at DUSHYANTA. To his wife]. O Aditi,
This is the mighty hero, King Dushyanta,
Protector of the earth, who, at the head
Of the celestial armies of thy son,
Does battle with the enemies of heaven.
Thanks to his bow, the thunderbolt of Indra
Rests from its work, no more the minister
Of death and desolation to the world,
But a mere symbol of divinity.

ADITI. He bears in his noble form all the marks of dignity.

MÁTALI [to DUSHYANTA]. Sire, the venerable progenitors of the celestials are gazing at your Majesty with as much affection as if you were their son. You may advance towards them.

KING. Are these, O Mátali, the holy pair,
Offspring of Daksha and divine Maríchi,
Children of Brahmá's sons, by sages deemed
Sole fountain of celestial light, diffused
Through twelve effulgent orbs? Are these the pair
From whom the ruler of the triple world,
Sovereign of gods and lord of sacrifice,
Sprang into being? That immortal pair
Whom Vishnu, greater than the Self-existent,
Chose for his parents, when, to save mankind,
He took upon himself the shape of mortals?

MÁTALI. Even so.

KING [prostrating himself]. Most august of beings! Dushyanta, content to have fulfilled the commands of your son Indra, offers you his adoration.

KAŚYAPA. My son, long may'st thou live, and happily may'st thou reign over the earth!

ADITI. My son, may'st thou ever be invincible in the field of battle!

ŚAKOONTALÁ. I also prostrate myself before you, most adorable Beings, and my child with me.

KAŚYAPA. My daughter,
Thy lord resembles Indra, and thy child
Is noble as Jayanta, Indra's son;
I have no worthier blessing left for thee,
May'st thou be faithful as the god's own wife!

ADITI. My daughter, may'st thou be always the object of thy husband's fondest love; and may thy son live long to be the joy of both his parents! Be seated. [All sit down in the presence of KAŚYAPA.]

KAŚYAPA [regarding each of them by turns]. Hail to the beautiful Śakoontalá,
Hail to her noble son, and hail to thee,
Illustrious Prince—rare triple combination
Of virtue, wealth, and energy united.

KING. Most venerable Kaśyapa, by your favour all my desires were accomplished even before I was admitted to your presence. Never was mortal so honoured that his boon should be granted ere it was solicited. Because—
Bloom before fruit, the clouds before the rain,
Cause first and then effect, in endless sequence,
Is the unchanging law of constant nature;
But, ere the blessing issued from thy lips,
The wishes of my heart were all fulfilled.

MÁTALI. It is thus that the great progenitors of the world confer favours.

KING. Most reverend Sage, this thy handmaid was married to me by the Gándharva ceremony, and after a time was conducted to my palace by her relations. Meanwhile a fatal delusion seized me; I lost my memory and rejected her, thus committing a grievous offence against the venerable Kanwa, who is of thy divine race. Afterwards the sight of this ring restored my faculties, and brought back to my mind all the circumstances of my union with his daughter. But my conduct still seems to me incomprehensible;
As foolish as the fancies of a man
Who, when he sees an elephant, denies
That 'tis an elephant; then afterwards,
When its huge bulk moves onward, hesitates;
Yet will not be convinced till it has passed
For ever from his sight, and left behind
No vestige of its presence save his footsteps.

KAŚYAPA. My son, cease to think thyself in fault. Even the delusion that possessed thy mind was not brought about by any act of thine. Listen to me.

KING. I am attentive.

KAŚYAPA. Know that when the nymph Menaká, the mother of Śakoontalá, became aware of her daughter's anguish in consequence of the loss of the ring at the nymph's pool, and of thy subsequent rejection of her, she brought her and confided her to the care of Aditi. And I no sooner saw her than I ascertained by my divine faculty of meditation, that thy repudiation of thy poor faithful wife had been caused entirely by the curse of Durvásas—not by thine own fault—and that the spell would terminate on the discovery of the ring.

KING [drawing a deep breath]. Oh! what a weight is taken off my mind, now that my character is cleared of reproach.

ŚAKOONTALÁ [aside]. Joy! Joy! My revered husband did not, then, reject me without good reason, though I have no recollection of the curse pronounced upon me. But, in all probability, I unconsciously brought it upon myself, when I was so distracted on being separated from my husband soon after our marriage. For I now remember that my two friends advised me not to fail to show the ring in case he should have forgotten me.

KAŚYAPA. At last, my daughter, thou art happy, and hast gained thy heart's desire. Indulge, then, no feeling of resentment against thy consort. See, now, Though he repulsed thee, 'twas the sage's curse
That clouded his remembrance; 'twas the curse
That made thy tender husband harsh towards thee.
Soon as the spell was broken, and his soul
Delivered from its darkness, in a moment
Thou didst regain thine empire o'er his heart.
So on the tarnished surface of a mirror
No image is reflected, till the dust,
That dimmed its wonted lustre, is removed.

KING. Holy father, see here the hope of my royal race. [Takes his CHILD by the hand.]

KAŚYAPA. Know that he, too, will become the monarch of the whole earth. Observe,
Soon, a resistless hero, shall he cross
The trackless ocean, borne above the waves
In an aërial car; and shall subdue
The earth's seven sea-girt isles. Now has he gained,
As the brave tamer of the forest-beasts,
The title Sarva-damana; but then

Mankind shall hail him as King Bharata,
And call him the supporter of the world.

KING. We cannot but entertain the highest hopes of a child for whom your Highness performed the natal rites.

ADITI. My revered husband, should not the intelligence be conveyed to Kanwa, that his daughter's wishes are fulfilled, and her happiness complete? He is Śakoontalá's foster-father. Menaká, who is one of my attendants, is her mother, and dearly does she love her daughter.

ŚAKOONTALÁ [aside]. The venerable matron has given utterance to the very wish that was in my mind.

KAŚYAPA. His penances have gained for him the faculty of omniscience, and the whole scene is already present to his mind's eye.

KING. Then most assuredly he cannot be very angry with me.

KAŚYAPA. Nevertheless, it becomes us to send him intelligence of this happy event, and hear his reply. What ho, there!

PUPIL [entering]. Holy father, what are your commands?

KAŚYAPA. My good Gálava, delay not an instant, but hasten through the air and convey to the venerable Kanwa, from me, the happy news that the fatal spell has ceased, that Dushyanta's memory is restored, that his daughter Śakoontalá has a son, and that she is once more tenderly acknowledged by her husband.

PUPIL. Your Highness' commands shall be obeyed. [Exit.]

KAŚYAPA. And now, my dear son, take thy consort and thy child, re-ascend the car of Indra, and return to thy imperial capital.

KING. Most holy father, I obey.

KAŚYAPA. And accept this blessing—

For countless ages may the god of gods,
Lord of the atmosphere, by copious
    showers
Secure abundant harvests to thy sub-
    jects;
And thou by frequent offerings preserve
The Thunderer's friendship. Thus, by in-
    terchange
Of kindly actions may you both confer
Unnumbered benefits on earth and heaven.

KING. Holy father, I will strive, as far as I am able, to attain this happiness.

KAŚYAPA. What other favour can I bestow on thee, my son?

KING. What other can I desire? If, however, you permit me to form another wish, I would humbly beg that the saying of the sage Bharata be fulfilled:

May kings reign only for their subjects'
    weal;
May the divine Saraswatí, the source
Of speech, and goddess of dramatic art,
Be ever honoured by the great and wise;
And may the purple self-existent god,
Whose vital Energy pervades all space,
From future transmigrations save my
    soul.   [Exeunt omnes.]

THE CHALK CIRCLE

ANONYMOUS

Written and produced probably in the 13th or the 14th century

TRANSLATED BY ETHEL VAN DER VEER

CHARACTERS

MRS. CH'ANG

MA CHUN-SHING, *the lord* MA

MRS. MA, *his First Wife*

HAI-T'ANG, *daughter of* MRS. CH'ANG, *and Second Wife of* MA CHUN-SHING

SHIU-LANG, *the young child of* HAI-T'ANG *and the lord* MA

CH'ANG-LIN, *son of* MRS. CH'ANG

CH'AO, *clerk of the Court, lover of* MRS. MA

SU-SHUN, *governor and judge of* Ch'ing-ch-iu

Many Officers, Sergeants and Guards in the suite of SU-SHUN

Two Neighbors of MRS. MA

MRS. LIU SSU-SHIN } *midwives*
MRS. WEI-WU   }

A Wine-seller and Innkeeper

T'ANG-SHAO } *police officers or guards*
HSIEH-PA   }

PAO-CH'ING, *governor and supreme judge at* Kai Fang-Fu

Many Officers of the suite of PAO-CH'ING

A Sergeant, under-officer of justice, occupying the office of Lictor

PROLOGUE

[*The scene is the house of* MRS. CH'ANG.]

MRS. CH'ANG. I am a native of Ch'ing-ch'ao. My family name is Liu; that of my husband was Ch'ang. He died very young, a long time ago, and left me two children, a boy and a girl. My son's name is Ch'ang-Lin. I taught him to read and write. My daughter's name is Ch'ang Hai-t'ang. I have no need to say much of one so distinguished for her beauty and

227

fineness and greatness of soul. She knows the arts of writing and drawing, can play the flute most delicately and dance like the spirit of a white butterfly flitting amongst the ethereal flowers of heaven. She can sing like a nightingale and accompany herself most ravishingly upon the guitar. In a word, there is not a talent she does not possess to perfection. For seven generations my ancestors held high positions and achieved literary success. But alas! the wheel of fortune turned and in the wink of an eye I had lost all that I had. And now, pressed by necessity, I have had to force my daughter to make traffic of her beauty in order that she may continue to live and be charming. In this neighborhood dwells a rich man named Ma Chun-shing, a frequent caller at our house. He has seen my daughter and has made persistent proposals, offering her the rank of Second Wife. My daughter asks nothing better than to have him for a husband, but I could not give up the fine raiment and manner of living procured for me by her trade. I shall wait until she comes and then talk over with her the subject which now engrosses me.

[*Enter* CH'ANG-LIN.]

CH'ANG-LIN. I am called Ch'ang-lin. . . . Well, my Honorable Mother, you know that my father and my ancestors held high places in the literary world and positions of eminence. If you are pleased to allow that miserable little wretch to continue to practice an infamous trade which dishonors her family, what kind of a figure do you think I can make in the world?

MRS. CH'ANG. What is the meaning of this idle talk? If you fear that the conduct of your sister dishonors your family, would it not be better for you to seek some means of gaining silver yourself for the support of your aged mother?

[*Enter* HAI-T'ANG.]

HAI-T'ANG. My brother, if you would be a gallant youth, take upon yourself the maintenance of our venerable mother.

CH'ANG-LIN. Most degraded of sisters, how is it that you can practice this ignoble profession? If you do not fear the contempt of society, I do. And for that reason, vile creature, I would that you were broken into bits. [*He strikes her.*]

MRS. CH'ANG [*arresting his hand*]. Do not strike her. [*And as he withdraws.*] It is more fitting that I should be the one to strike her.

CH'ANG-LIN. My Honorable Mother, I am weary of these domestic wrangles and beg that you will cease them immediately. Let her receive her punishment through the maledictions and railleries of good people. I am leaving for P'ien-ching, the city where my uncle lives. I shall endeavor to find there some means of gaining a livelihood. It is commonly said that first of all a young man must look out for himself. Big and strong as I am, do you believe that I shall perish of hunger after I have quit this house?

[*To* HAI-T'ANG.]

And thou, vile creature, after I have departed, see that you take good care of your mother. Should any misfortune befall her, I warn you that you may hope for no pardon.

Inflamed with rage,
This house I quit in haste
To find elsewhere some means
Of sustenance.
So vigorous am I,
I cannot think
The heavens have decreed
I spend my days
In penury.

[*Bows to* MRS. CH'ANG.]

I go.

[*He goes, running as from the
seven devils.*]

HAI-T'ANG. How often, Respected Mother, am I to suffer such aspersions upon my character? How much better should you graciously permit me to wed the Honorable Ma Chun-shing.

MRS. CH'ANG. You are right, O Daughter of Wisdom. But wait until the Honorable Ma Chun-shing arrives and you shall see that I am augustly disposed to consent to your marriage.

[MA CHUN-SHING *enters and stands apart from the others.*]

MA CHUN-SHING. My family name is Ma and my surname Chun-shing. My ancestors settled in Ch'ing-ch'iu. In my youth I followed the career of letters and acquired a profound knowledge of the classics and of history. As I enjoy a considerable fortune, every one gives me the title of Yuan-wei. I constantly seek pleasure and am passionately drawn toward what is known as the primrose path. Near by lives a most alluring little beauty who exercises the sweetest of all arts and has for some time past maintained with me the most agreeable of relations. Her name is Ch'ang Hai-t'ang. I have no need to describe the perfect accord of her sentiments with mine, for I have the intention of taking her to wife. She has conveyed to me her desire to become united with me, but her old mother has twenty obstacles to offer to our happiness. I suspect her object is to obtain from me rich presents. I have heard that during the last few days Ch'ang Hai-t'ang has had some lively altercations with her brother, Ch'ang-Lin, and that he precipitately left the maternal mansion to find his uncle in P'ien-ching. I imagine that he will not return for some time, or at least not before the happy day. It is best that I prepare the wedding gifts and renew my demands for the marriage. How fortunate that the heavens favor me and that I am about to realize so delightful a project. But what do I perceive? The Honorable Ch'ang Hai-t'ang stands within the entrance of her house, and as usual is most brilliantly arrayed. Her beauty lights the morn with Celestial radiance and her smile is lovelier than the rarest jade. But softly—let us speak with her a while.

[*He regards* HAI-T'ANG *and bows to her.*]

HAI-T'ANG. My lord, since you are here, let us profit by the absence of my brother. It should be the easier to bring my mother around to our project and make her augustly consent. She is in the best of humors and has graciously suffered me to converse with her upon the subject. Let us both go to her.

MA CHUN-SHING. Since she is so well disposed, I see that the moment of my happiness has arrived.

[*He perceives* MRS. CH'ANG.]

MRS. CH'ANG. My lord, to-day my son, Ch'ang-Lin, has failed in obedience and filial piety. Without respect for my old age, he has conducted himself with violence toward me. I pray you, I pray you to bring the smelling salts.

MA CHUN-SHING. And what was the altercation you had with your son? I came this morning to offer you one hundred pieces of silver, ten rolls of silk and two porcelain cuspidors of refined shape, of the Sung dynasty. Also when Hai-t'ang shall have become my wife, should you be in need of wood or rice, I shall hasten to procure them for you. Be assured, O Venerable Mother, that you will want for nothing. Give yourself over to a day of happiness. Accept my unworthy and insignificant offerings, and augustly give your consent to our marriage.

MRS. CH'ANG. I cannot think very highly of a daughter who daily involves me in quarrels. But after she is married I can live free from disquietude. But, my lord, you have already a wife of first rank. Therefore I must make sure that my daughter will not be subjected to insults and maltreatment, before I allow her to set foot in the bridal chamber. Otherwise, I should prefer to have her remain with me. But once my doubts are set at rest, I shall, my lord, be happy to give my consent to your marriage.

MA CHUN-SHING. Have no fears. My First Wife is as incapable as myself of ill-bred conduct. Your honorable daughter will no sooner take up her residence with me than Mrs. Ma will regard her as a beloved sister. As for myself, notwithstanding her secondary rank, she shall have the same privileges as the other. But if Hai-t'ang shall augustly give to the world a man-child, from that moment she shall be in charge of all the affairs of my house. Thus, Respected Mother, you need give yourself no further uneasiness concerning your exalted and sublimely beautiful daughter.

MRS. CH'ANG. My lord, the matter is concluded. Since I have your magnificent gifts, my inferior and ill-favored offspring is yours. You may this instant take her. . . . And thou, my child, my Golden Lotus, know that it was not I who removed you from the shelter of my arms. You are now elevated to the rank of wife. I hope that from now on you will not again take up your former profession.

HAI-T'ANG. My lord, since your First Wife directs all the affairs of your household, I trust you will not fail ever to stand as my protector and support.

My aged mother hopes
That all my days
I shall remain
Quite faithful to my husband.
She also hopes
To rest on me her head—
Her venerable head—
White with the years.

My master, I love you better than all the world.

MA CHUN-SHING. That is too much, my betrothed.

HAI-T'ANG. The sweetness of your character
Is what I most adore;
Your noble sentiments,
Sincerity and loftiness.
And so I give to you to-day
My heart;
But giving it, take to myself the joys
Of which I long have dreamed.

I go to announce to my friends that Ch'ang Hai-t'ang is to wed the illustrious Yuan-wei, Ma Chun-shing. And henceforth I hope that no one will again cast aspersions upon me.

From all aspersions now
I shall be free;
No more can it be said
I smirch the honor of the family.
[*She goes out with* MA CHUN-SHING.]

MRS. CH'ANG. I go to-day to marry my daughter to the noble Ma Chun-shing, who presented me with one hundred pieces of silver and other valuable gifts. This means that I shall pass the rest of my days in joy and abundance. As this affair occupies me much, I shall first go in search of my aunt and my sisters, whom I have not seen for some time. We will then have tea together and regale ourselves in a neighboring tavern.

END OF THE PROLOGUE

ACT I

[*The scene is in the house of* MA CHUN-SHING.]

MRS. MA. The men do not cease
To eulogize my charms,
And because I desire their pleasure
There is vermillion upon my lips
And bright colors glorify my cheeks.
Yet in the twinkling of an eye
The rouge and white paint may disappear;
It takes only a basin
Of pure water.

I occupy the important position of First Wife to Ma Chun-shing. He has a Second Wife by the name of Hai-t'ang, a daughter of some person named Ch'ang. She has given our husband a son who is already five years of age. . . . For me, I have succeeded in imposing upon the confidence of my lord Ma. Near here dwells a clerk named Ch'ao, who is as handsome as a spring morning and who passionately adores the gentler sex. I maintain with him certain relations and appreciate his rare qualities. Also, my particular wish, my most ardent desire is to undo this Ma Chun-shing, in order to live always with Ch'ao as a wife with her husband. To-day, seeing that the excellent lord Ma is from home, I have sent some one to Ch'ao with a request that he pass by here. I hope that at any moment he may arrive.

CH'AO. My station in life
Is that of a clerk.
But privately
There are two things I love
Surpassingly:
Good wine
And the women
Of other men.

What is the present object of my affections? A lady whose cheeks rival the most beautiful flowers. . . . My name is Ch'ao. I hold the position of clerk at the court of Ch'ing-ch'iu. Near here lives the First Wife of the Yuan-wei, Ma Chunshing. One day when he invited me to dine with him, I saw by chance this Wife who is endowed with a most seductive face, the equal of which it may be doubted if heaven or earth has ever produced. The sight of this charming beauty struck deep into my heart. Night and day she is present in my thoughts, before the eyes of my mind. I imagine that she also had fixed her regard upon me because, imposing upon the confidence of her husband, she would hold with me certain relations not entirely in accord with morality. She has begged me to come to see her to-day. Let us go and find her. We do not yet know what is the motive of the message. . . . I now have arrived at the house where she lives. I shall enter without being announced. . . . Madam, you have commanded my presence. May I learn what you desire of me?

MRS. MA. It is a most simple matter. I am troubled over the mystery with which we have need to cover our furtive amours. We have not yet come to the point of fixing the date for our union. What happiness will be ours when we live together as husband and wife.

For man achieves
Not by himself alone,
Nor woman, either;
But like the fabled
One-winged birds, they two
Must rise together.

And to this end I desire but one thing now, to discover with you the most felicitous method of poisoning my lord Ma.

CH'AO. Need we mention this matter? Is it possible that she whom I regard already as my wife should form such a project without its having also presented itself to my own thoughts? Is this not poison? For some time I have been ready to execute this plan.

[*He hands the poison to* MRS. MA.]

Here, I shall confide it to you. I am obliged to return to the court to fulfill my duties there. [*He goes out.*]

MRS. MA. Ch'ao is gone. Let us take this poison and put it in some safe hiding place. I shall not rest until I have discovered a favorable moment to strike the blow I meditate. But I am thoughtless. I had forgotten that to-day is the anniversary of the birth of the young child. I go to pray with my lord Ma in all the temples, to burn perfume and gild the figure of Fu.*

HAI-T'ANG. I am named Hai-t'ang. It is five years since I was married to my lord Ma. My Venerable Mother has long ago departed to the Land of the Gods. I do not know the whereabouts of my brother, as since his departure I have received no news of him. The child which I had from my marriage is called Shiulang. Since he was three years of age he has stayed by the side of Mrs. Ma, who took him to bring up. As to-day is the anniversary of his birth, my lord and Mrs. Ma have taken him to all the temples in the city to burn sweet perfumes and to gild the image of Fu. I go now to prepare rice and tea to receive them as soon as they shall have returned. . . . Hai-t'ang, since you have espoused the lord Ma, nothing has interfered with your happiness.

Through the silken curtains
At my window
I contemplate the moon
And its cold shadows.

---

* Buddha.

It shines alike without reproach or pas-
sion
Upon my richly embroidered curtains
And upon that street which is the abode
of vice.
Could I ever have hoped one day
To abandon that degrading profession,
The companionship of rakes and their mis-
tresses,
With their orgies and licentious songs?
Yet I have forever said farewell
To that theatre of pleasure.
Let them follow me if they will
With railleries and aspersions.
Never again will I make advances for gain
Nor stretch forth a seducing hand to no-
blemen.
No more will I make traffic with my
beauty
Nor return to the follies of the gay life.
They shall see me no more
In the abode of the Flowers of the Weep-
ing Willow Tree,
Seeking new paramours
And inviting the return of old ones.
No longer do I fear that officers of the
law
Will remove me violently from the Palace
of Pleasure.
Nor shall I ever again be the slave
Of the go-between.
I shall suffer no more the amorous callers
Who succeeded one another without cessa-
tion.
Nor will my door be broken down
And my house invaded by insolent neigh-
bors.
No longer must I vex myself
About the slenderness of my resources
And the boredom of my profession.
Untroubled by the wickedness of the world
outside,
I live the long hours through in tranquil
peace.
Even as the wild duck seeks its mate in
the grass,
I have found a husband
Whose heart accords happily with mine,
And who each day begs me
To recompense his tenderness.
And so, that I may taste with him

The sweetness of slumber,
Ere the moon silvers the edges
Of my window curtains,
I send back to her own apartment
That woman so jealous of my serenity.

I await the return of my lord and Mrs.
Ma. . . . But they do not come. . . . Let
us go out for a moment and look for them
in the distance.

[*She steps outside and with a
hand shading her eyes, peers
off.*]

[*Enter* CH'ANG-LIN.]

CH'ANG-LIN.   From the bounty of my
fellow mortals
I have acquired sad experience.
I see now that it is much better
To place one's trust in the High Gods.
I am Ch'ang-Lin. After having had, in
the past, a lively altercation with my sis-
ter, I quitted the maternal house to go in
search of my uncle. Who would have
dreamed that I would find him departed
for Ch'ong Hse-tao accompanied by some
individual named Yen P'ing-fu? Having
discovered no one who would tender me
hospitality, I have returned benumbed by
cold and weighed down by fatigue. I fell
down ill in the middle of the road. I
have no need to tell how soon my money
and my provisions for the journey were
used up. In order to exist, I was forced
first to pawn, then to sell the clothing off
my back. I returned to my family, but
my Venerable Mother has long since been
enjoying herself in the Celestial Rice
Fields. In our ancestral dwelling there
is now no place where I can lay my head.
I have learned that my sister is married
to the great Ma Chun-shing. He is a man
of wealth. Without doubt he will deign
to regard with compassion his unfortunate
brother-in-law and accord him the means
of reclaiming his position. Who could
blame me for seeking him out? I shall
implore his assistance and ask of him re-
lief for my most pressing needs. In a
moment I shall arrive at the house of
Ma Chun-shing. . . . Why, if I'm not mis-

taken, there stands my sister just within the doorway!

HAI-T'ANG. I say to myself, who is it that arrives below? Well, if it isn't my brother! . . . Fat and plump as you are, you have nothing to ask here. Get you gone.

CH'ANG-LIN. Most Honored Sister, grant me, I pray you, but two words with you.

HAI-T'ANG. I think, my worthy brother, it must be that you have come to erect a tombstone over the hallowed spot where reposes the body of our Honored Mother, and duly to console me in my grief.

CH'ANG-LIN. Respected Sister, I beg of you do not look at my face but rather at the way I am clothed. I am in penury and tormented by the pangs of hunger. How then can you possibly believe that I have come for the purpose of erecting a tombstone over the grave of our lamented mother?

HAI-T'ANG. When death took my mother, I furnished the shroud and winding sheet and also the camphor wood for the double coffin. I saw to it that with her were buried replicas of all the articles necessary for her comfort while upon this earth, and the spirit money with which to pay her way to the First Heaven. I supported all these expenses without having recourse to my lord Ma Chun-shing.

CH'ANG-LIN. As it was your husband who defrayed the cost of the obsequies, I know that you are under immense obligation to him.

HAI-T'ANG. Having lost my August Father,
Without resources
I was left the care of my mother.
How could you suffer your own sister
To exercise a profession which tarnished
The honor of the house?
I see now that in the depths of your heart
You do not belong to the family of Ch'ang.
[She strikes him.]

CH'ANG-LIN. Why do you strike me, Most Marvelous of Sisters? I realize that I am greatly indebted to you. Be assured

that I have only the highest admiration for your extreme filial piety.

HAI-T'ANG. Sweet morsels fall from your lips
Like cherries dipped in honey.
I see that you have learned that flattery
Is the password to a warm welcome.

CH'ANG-LIN. I came to-day, my sister, to ask your assistance. How is it you receive me with such coldness?

HAI-T'ANG. It is not for you to reproach me with the coldness you observe upon my countenance. Do you recall, my brother, the day when, burning with anger, you addressed frightful threats to me, after which you fled as if you wanted to run to the end of the world?

CH'ANG-LIN. My sister, that is ancient history. What pleasure can it give you to bring up the past?

HAI-T'ANG. Since you set forth
Upon the shining road
To cover yourself with glory,
I ask you how
Do you now return
Clad in rags and tatters?

CH'ANG-LIN. You know, my Excellent Sister, that we are the children of one father and of one mother. Therefore if your brother has done you wrong, you should forget it and cool your wrath in the beneficent waters of forgiveness.

HAI-T'ANG. My brother, how could you have the face to seek me out to-day? You will hear to the very end what I have in my heart.

CH'ANG-LIN. Honorable Sister, it was necessity that forced me to appeal to you. Pressed by extremity as I am, I shall not question the amount of the help you accord me and shall leave immediately after receiving it.

HAI-T'ANG. My brother, of silver I have none. It is foolish to demand it of me. You must understand that even the robes and head-ornaments I am wearing are the property of Ma Chun-shing and Mrs. Ma. How could I dispose of them for your benefit? I myself possess nothing to offer as a sacrifice to your needs. Go. It is useless for you to remain.

CH'ANG-LIN. My sister, you are hard and unrelenting. It pierces my marrow that not only have you denied me succor, but you have overwhelmed me with abuse and ill-treatment. However, I shall not take myself off. I shall rest here upon the doorstep until the arrival of the Honorable Ma Chun-shing. Perhaps he will deign to augustly extend to me some bounty.

[*Enter* MRS. MA.]

MRS. MA. I am the First Wife of Ma Chun-shing. I have raised the young child and I have prayed and burned incense for him upon the altars of all the temples.

[*Approaching.*]

But what do I perceive? A mendicant upon the portal? Ho there, what evil purpose brings you hither?

CH'ANG-LIN [*rising*]. Madam, I do not merit such language. I am the brother of Ch'ang Hai-t'ang. I have come to call upon my sister.

MRS. MA. Ah! Ah! You are the brother of Hai-t'ang. That makes you my brother-in-law. You know me?

CH'ANG-LIN. Your unworthy servant is unacquainted with the illustrious lady with whom he speaks.

MRS. MA. I am the First Wife of Ma Chun-shing.

CH'ANG-LIN. Gracious Madam, I dare hope that you have not taken offense because I failed to know you.

[*He bows to her.*]

MRS. MA. My brother-in-law, what was your purpose in looking up your sister?

CH'ANG-LIN. Though the truth is painful I shall not dissimulate. Pressed by necessity and having nothing upon which to subsist, I came to ask my sister for something with which to assuage my urgent need.

MRS. MA. How much did she give you?

CH'ANG-LIN. She replied that all the articles in this house belonged to you and that she therefore had no right to dispose of anything, and that she herself had nothing.

MRS. MA. My brother-in-law, you are no doubt ignorant of the fact that since her marriage with Ma Chun-shing your sister has given him a son who is already five years of age. He is your nephew. Ever since his birth your sister has held the keys of the rice-bin and the entire compound is under her direction. That is because I have no son.

[*She beats her breast.*]

I have not even the shadow of a son! . . . Since you are the brother of Hai-t'ang, I regard you as my brother. I shall go to her and demand assistance for you. Should you obtain it, do not be too joyful. On your discretion will depend your good or your bad fortune.

CH'ANG-LIN. Your inferior servant realizes that you are a lady of fine spirit and much wisdom.

HAI-T'ANG [*perceiving* MRS. MA]. Madam, you are the first to return. You have had a tedious pilgrimage. I am sorry to have caused you so much fatigue.

MRS. MA. Hai-t'ang, who is the man seated upon the doorstep?

HAI-T'ANG. It is my brother, Ch'ang-Lin.

MRS. MA. Ah! It is your brother? Why has he come here?

HAI-T'ANG. He came to ask of his sister something to supply his needs.

MRS. MA. And is it possible that you have given him nothing?

HAI-T'ANG. It was Ma Chun-shing and his First Wife who presented me with these robes and head-ornaments. Tell me if it would be augustly right of me to give them away.

MRS. MA. Since the articles were given to you, what is to prevent your giving them, in turn, to your brother?

HAI-T'ANG. Madam, I believe that to be far from my duty. What should I say if Ma Chun-shing were to inquire what I had done with them?

MRS. MA. If Ma Chun-shing questions you, I shall be there to justify you, and he will present you with new ones. Run along and make haste to take them off and give them to your brother.

HAI-T'ANG [*obediently*]. Since you permit me, I shall at once remove these robes and ornaments and give them to my brother. [She strips them off.]

MRS. MA. Since he believes they are not your own, give me the things and I will offer them to him myself.

[She takes them and approaches CH'ANG-LIN.]

My brother-in-law, to obtain help for you, I have aroused the anger of Ch'ang Hai-t'ang. I would never have thought that your own sister could be so unkind to you. Who would have imagined that she, who possesses so rich a wardrobe, would not have deigned to present you with so small a part of it? Or that she would refuse so slight a sacrifice with as much fury as if I were wanting to take away some pieces of her flesh. These robes and ornaments were given to me a long time ago as marriage gifts by my Esteemed Mother and Father. I give them to my brother-in-law in order that they may be sold at once to relieve for the moment his most pressing needs. I trust he will not despise them because of their smallness.

CH'ANG-LIN [taking the things which she offers]. Receive, O Most Noble and Generous Lady, my sincerest thanks. Like the little bird whose life was saved by Yang-pao and who returned later in the form of a young man, bearing gifts of four white jade bracelets to his benefactor, I shall place all my efforts into testifying to you worthily of my grateful memory of this august day.

[He bows low to thank her.]

MRS. MA [returning his bow]. My brother-in-law, as Ma Chun-shing is from home, I dare not invite you to dine. I trust you will not be offended.

[He bows and goes.]

CH'ANG-LIN. I believed at first that the robes and the head ornaments were the property of my sister. Who would have supposed they belonged to the honorable Mrs. Ma. . . . Oh well, you are my sister. We had the same father and the same mother. Yet not only have you failed to give me a mite to relieve my distress, but also you have repulsed me in a manner most hard and brutal. On the other hand, this estimable lady to whom I am an entire stranger, most graciously gives me of her clothing and head ornaments. Inasmuch as the written symbol for the word trouble is two women under one roof-tree, I imagine the First Wife and the Second Wife, in the seclusion of the within apartments, have many differences. It is not unlikely that they frequently need the intervention of the police. . . . For the moment, I shall sell only the head ornaments to buy myself some clothing. Afterwards, I shall endeavor to obtain employment as an official in the law-court of Kai Fang-fu. My sister, look well to your conduct, that we may not meet face to face, should any accusation bring you before the tribunal; because I wish to take the skin from off your shoulders with the blows of a stick.

[He goes.]

[Enter MRS. MA.]

MRS. MA [perceiving HAI-T'ANG]. Hai-t'ang, I have just come from presenting the robes and head ornaments which you handed over to me.

HAI-T'ANG. Madam, you give me my life. But I fear one thing, and that is when my lord Ma Chun-shing demands of me what I have done with the things. When this occurs, I hope you will defend me.

MRS. MA. Without any doubt. Put all your trust in me.

[HAI-T'ANG goes out.]

MRS. MA [alone]. Hai-t'ang, thy brother has parted with the robes and head ornaments. I think you will not have any occasion to enjoy yourself about it, because if Ma Chun-shing asks what you have done, I am sorry for you! . . .

[Enter MA CHUN-SHING and his son, SHIU-LANG.]

MA CHUN-SHING [holding his son by the hand]. I am Ma, surnamed Chun-shing. As soon as I had married Ch'ang Hai-t'ang, I had by her this young child, whose name is Shiu-lang. He is five years of age. As to-day is the anniversary of his birth, I have gone with him to all the temples to burn perfumes in honor of Fu. Observing that the temple of the goddess who presides over the birth of boys is crumbling in many places, I have given silver with which to make the repairs. That is the reason for my prolonged absence. But in one instant I shall arrive at my house.

HAI-T'ANG. There comes my lord Ma. He is weary and fatigued. I must go quickly for tea. [*She goes.*]

MA CHUN-SHING. Madam, how is it that I do not see the customary robes and ornaments upon Ch'ang Hai-t'ang?

MRS. MA. My lord, had you not questioned me, I should have kept my lips sealed. Because she has given you a son, you have heaped good things upon her and you have toward her a tolerance past bearing. Who would have thought that in your absence she would have taken a lover? To-day, while we were away burning perfume in all the temples, she gave her robes and head ornaments to her paramour. At the moment when she was going in search of other garments and ornaments, I surprised her and uncovered her intrigue. It was I who prevented her from concealing the situation and repairing the disorder of her appearance. I have been awaiting your arrival in order that you may reward the traitress according to her merits. It is not that I am jealous of her; even she does not impute that to me.

MA CHUNG-SHING [*snorting*]. So then, Hai-t'ang has given her robes and her ornaments to a lover. I see clearly that she is a person naturally depraved. Such conduct makes me die of grief and indignation.

[*He calls* HAI-T'ANG *and strikes her.*] I will annihilate you, vile creature, for violating the most sacred of all bonds.

MRS. MA [*egging on her husband*]. Beat her, beat her! That is fine! What will you do with a strumpet who has dishonored your house? Augustly kill her with blows.

HAI-T'ANG. The robes, the head ornaments, I would not at first give to my brother, but she forced me to by her insistence. Who would have thought that in the presence of My Lord she would say that I had given them to a lover? In all this there is nothing for which Hai-t'ang should be reproached.

I used to ponder secretly
But not to vex myself;
Mistrusting none of her designs,
Nor yet suspecting this abyss
She's dug to plunge me in
With malice that is past belief.
I tremble now no less from fear
Than from the blows.

MA CHUNG-SHIN [*transported with rage*]. Wrah! To think that you, who have given me a son, should so strip yourself also of honor and decency. You'll make me die of anger.

MRS. MA. Why do you thus excite yourself? You should rather be thankful that you have at least one woman of unquestioned virtue in your household, and annihilate the other with blows.

HAI-T'ANG. All the time, he has had in his house
A First Wife.
All the time, sole dominion she's had,
She alone.
Who would think she could steal from the fox
His cunning,
Or from the wolf
His ferocity?

It is you who have taken to yourself a lover. How dare you hang upon me this outrageous calumny?

Because in my youth
I was a sing-song girl,
I have no wish to emulate her;
All that is past.

It will not be astonishing if she involves me in a crime.

Dare you cast upon me
The shame of your own debauches?

MRS. MA. Vile creature, I see well that your natural depravity is reawakened. You have given your robes and head ornaments to a lover, while deceiving your husband.

HAI-T'ANG. Surely the young wife named Sang was less cruel than you. You who glory in belonging to an ancient family, dare you say to me, whose heart is true and constant, that I have deceived the head of the house?

MRS. MA. With whom have you carried on this liaison?

HAI-T'ANG. She says that, disrobed,
I received a lover.
I might as well assist her
To cover me with mud
As to suffer without a word
This aspersion she casts upon me.

MA CHUNG-SHING [appearing indisposed]. This wretch of a woman will make me die of indignation. Madam, I am faint. Fetch quickly some broth to restore me.

MRS. MA. It is Hai-t'ang the good-for-nothing who has caused the wrath that suffocates the august one. Hai-t'ang, go at once and heat some broth for the Honorable Lord Ma.

HAI-T'ANG. I obey.

Within the hour
There has rained upon my shoulders
A shower of blows.
And now behold!
I am sent to the kitchen
To heat some broth.
Without ceasing
This First Wife irritates lord Ma,
And angers him;
While making me
The victim of his anger
And suspicion. [She brings in the broth.]
Here, madam, is the broth.

MRS. MA. Bring it to me that I may taste of it. [She tastes the broth.] It needs a little more salt. Run and get it. [Exit HAI-T'ANG.]

MRS. MA. Let us procure quickly the poison prepared some days ago for the August Lord Ma, and put it in the broth. [She pours in the poison.] Hai-t'ang, make haste!

[HAI-T'ANG enters.]

HAI-T'ANG. What troubles now my lady Ma,
What makes her shake and tremble?
How could a little lack of salt
Produce such agitation?

Madam, here is the salt.
[MRS. MA sprinkles salt in the broth and stirs it, then holds out the cup to her.]

MRS. MA. Here, Hai-t'ang, run and take it to him.

HAI-T'ANG. Madam, present it to him yourself. I fear to approach the Excellent One, as he augustly permits himself to be in a new fit of rage.

MRS. MA. If you yourself do not take it to him, he will infer that you are displeased with him.

HAI-T'ANG [bowing]. I obey. [She goes to MA CHUN-SHING with the broth.]

HAI-T'ANG. My lord, take a sip of this. [MA CHUN-SHING takes the cup and drinks.]

HAI-T'ANG. Alas! What's this I see!
He sinks beneath the weight of pain,
His mouth convulsed with bitterness—
And yet the broth was sweet.
[MA CHUN-SHING expires.]

HAI-T'ANG [terrified]. My lord, my lord, deign to open your eyes!

Behold now this sudden pallor
Replacing the warm yellow hue.
What can, in one little instant,
Have taken the light from his eyes?
Frozen with terror, my courage is gone;
My own eyes but rivers of tears.
This spectacle chills while it palsies,
Can nothing prevent this untimely end?

He leaves his two wives and his five-year-old son without protection. . . . Poor mother! I alone remain with my young son and must finish my days in desolate widowhood. And thou, my child, what protector will now sustain thy frail existence? [*She goes to* MRS. MA.] Madam, my lord Ma is no more.

MRS. MA. This same lord Ma Chunshing had the ungraciousness to neglect me and take to himself a Second Wife. . . . Hai-t'ang, wretch that thou art, but a moment ago the excellent lord Ma was in the best of health. Is it possible that the cup of broth you gave him could bring all of a sudden the coldness of death? It is because you put poison in it. Is it not?

HAI-T'ANG. Madam, you tasted the broth yourself. Therefore, if it had been poisoned, it would have killed you first. But in any case, he is dead. And bitter will be my bowls of rice from this time on. [*She weeps and rends her garments.*] Oh heaven! I shall die of grief and despair.

MRS. MA [*calls off*]. My good servants, where are you?

[SERVANTS *enter.*]

Go and choose, upon a bit of high ground, a fitting place to dig a grave. Fell the wood for a coffin and inter for me the honorable lord Ma.

[*The* SERVANTS *make haste to bear away on their shoulders the body of the honorable lord* MA CHUN-SHING.]

MRS. MA. Hai-t'ang, you little wretch, wait a bit until we have disposed of the honorable body of Ma Chun-shing, and I shall make suitable arrangements for you, as surely you will not dare venture to continue your residence here.

HAI-T'ANG [*weeping*]. Madam, since the illustrious Ma Chun-shing is no more, I have no right to remain. Permit me only to take my son with me and I shall immediately take my leave.

MRS. MA. The young child whom he gave to us both?

HAI-T'ANG. It was me to whom he gave the child.

MRS. MA. If it was to you he gave the little Shiu-lang, why did you not nurse and care for him yourself? Ever since his birth he has been close to my side, close in my arms. It was I who fed him and chafed his cold limbs. It was to me that he brought each day his little troubles to be cared for with the tenderness of a mother. Soothing a thousand vexations, to what pains have I been to bring him up properly? And now you have the effrontery to demand that I hand over to you the child I so patiently raised. You have had a secret lover and you have murdered your husband. Therefore the best thing you can do is to renounce your claim upon the child. Will you do so voluntarily, or be compelled under the authority of the law?

HAI-T'ANG. What do you mean by that?

MRS. MA. If you give him up voluntarily, leaving the young child with me, the entire fortune of Ma Chun-shing—his houses, his lands, everything that he possessed, shall be yours. I shall leave, taking Shiu-lang with me. But if you do not withdraw except under legal pressure, I shall bring to mind the fact that you poisoned your husband. As you must know, that is no trifle, and I shall take you before the magistrate.

HAI-T'ANG. As it was not I who poisoned Ma Chun-shing, what fear have I of the magistrate? I am perfectly willing that we should go to him together.

MRS. MA. The magistrate is discriminating and will soon discover the truth. He will not fail to punish the guilty one. Very well then, since you fear nothing in appearing before the judge, I shall conduct you to the court.

HAI-T'ANG. I indeed fear nothing. By all means let us go to the court.

I shall see that the truth is known
And no credence given her mendacity.
I shall call in as witnesses
The two women
Who assisted him into the world.
They shall say which is the mother
And which the stepmother.

MRS. MA [*embarrassed*]. I am the true . . . true mother of the child. . . . That boy is my . . . my . . . real . . . real child. [*Passionately.*] He is my heart, my blood, my life, the child of my womb. How could I let go of him?

HAI-T'ANG. How impose upon all the inhabitants
Of this quarter;
They who know of his birth
And have watched him grow
From infancy
Into a little lad?

MRS. MA. You have poisoned my lord Ma. It is within my power to hush up that fact.

HAI-T'ANG. For a long time you had the poison in readiness and you secretly put it into his broth.

MRS. MA. There is plain evidence that you poisoned the broth. All that I fear is that you may not suffer sufficient retribution.

HAI-T'ANG. Who is it that poisoned her husband?
You wish beyond doubt
That in expiation of your crime
I should sacrifice my life,
There is nothing to incriminate others,
Therefore you calumniate innocence.
No, surely among all the wives
Of first rank,
There is not another on earth
So corrupt and so barbarous as you.

MRS. MA [*alone*]. How is it that she has divined my strategy? . . . If only I can keep the child, the entire fortune of the honorable lord Ma will become my property. Clearly, this is a matter requiring due consideration. Everything must be carefully thought out if I am to spare myself the bitter food of painful regrets in. the future. Let us reflect a little. . . . It is certainly a fact that the child is not my own. If Hai-t'ang invokes the testimony of her midwives and of the neighbors who knew of his birth, all these witnesses will testify before the magistrate in her favor. The whole project will be ruined. But when their black eyes perceive this shining metal— [*She displays silver.*] they will undoubtedly burn to possess it. Therefore let us gain in advance their honorable interest, and in payment present each of them with a piece of silver. Then, at least a number of them will speak in my favor. But that is not all. I must also graciously win over the magistrate. What luck that Ch'ao is connected with the Courthouse and that I can send for him to talk the matter over. I must at once consult him as to the course of action I am to follow.

[*Enter* CH'AO.]

CH'AO. Some one has just been here asking for Ch'ao. Well, here I am. It is some days since I have called upon the honorable Mrs. Ma. I have had in the depths of my heart a most lively desire to see her. Without her, my spirit becomes downcast. . . . But I am now arriving at the door of her house. If her husband is absent, nothing will prevent my seeing her.

[*Perceiving* MRS. MA.]
Honorable Madam, I have been burning with thoughts of you. My longing has been augustly unutterable.

MRS. MA. Ch'ao, you are not aware that I have administered the poison you brought to the honorable lord Ma. Presently I go to take Hai-t'ang before the magistrate to lodge a complaint against her. I would take unto myself not only the inheritance of the lord Ma, but his son as well. Manage to win over the magistrate. Use all your wits, all your influence to arrange the case according to my wishes. Then we can entwine our lives together in lasting connubial bliss.

CH'AO. Nothing will be easier. I foresee but one difficulty; that the child is not your own. What good will it do you to remain guardian to him? It were the part of great wisdom to let go of him and be free of encumbrance.

Mrs. Ma. Is it possible to hold the post of clerk of the court and yet be so stupid? If I give up the child to Hait'ang, as he is the heir of the Excellent Lord Ma, he will come and despoil me of his fortune. He will not permit me to keep so much as a stick of incense. As to Hai-t'ang, she plans to call as witnesses the midwives who attended her at the birth and many of the people who live near by. But I intend to make things easy for myself by means of this.

[*Indicating silver.*] And if you can attend to the details at your end, recourse to the law will avail her nothing. I ask of you but one thing, to go and promptly make the necessary preparations.

Ch'ao. Very well, Madam, but make haste to present your accusations. I go to the tribunal to prepare for everything. [*He goes out.*]

Mrs. Ma. Ch'ao has gone. I go to bind the arms of Hai-t'ang. The proverb says:

"Man dreams not of injuring the tiger; It is the tiger who dreams Of devouring man."

But I say:

What man dare attack a tiger Without getting his flesh torn To shreds?

END OF ACT I

ACT II

[*The scene is the Court of* Ch'ing-ch'iu *and there are present* Su-shun *and his suite.*]

Su-shun. I am the governor of the Court of Ch'ing-ch'iu. My name is Su-shun.

Although I perform the functions of judge, I am unacquainted With a single article of the code. I love but one thing

With his death it has flown The clink of silver; Graced with this beauteous White metal, The pleader is sure to win his case.

I detest this county of Ch'ing-ch'iu, which ridicules my extreme indulgence toward the guilty. They have given me the nickname of Su Mo-lun. These words have a double meaning. The character of Mo signifies "to take with the hand," and lun means a square piece of wood. The idea is that whether one receives it with the right hand or the left, it is all the same. It is by that absurd name that I am familiarly known. . . . In my opinion there are many magistrates whose rigid inflexibility has caused the downfall of an infinitude of people. But as for Su Mo-lun, one may try in vain to count the number of persons he has covertly saved. . . . This morning I am opening court unusually early. Ho! officers, bring me the tablets of cases scheduled for to-day.

An Officer [*bowing*]. I obey.

[*Enter* Mrs. Ma, *dragging after her* Hai-t'ang *and her young son,* Shiu-lang.]

Mrs. Ma. I am taking you before the magistrate, to ask for vengeance.

Hai-t'ang [*struggling*]. Let go of me! Let go of me!

She envelops me Like a devouring flame. She bound me with hemp And dragged me hither.

Mrs. Ma. You have poisoned your husband, and the penalty is death.

Hai-t'ang. You claim I have committed a crime, The penalty for which Is death. If that were so, How could I escape? Alas, Hai-t'ang! In espousing the noble lord Ma, I attained the pinnacle of happiness. Of that happiness there remains not a trace.

Like red leaves
Before the Autumn wind.
Oppressed by calumny,
I cannot open my mouth to prove my
innocence;
But the heavens know the falseness
Of her accusations.

MRS. MA. It is perfectly evident that
you poisoned our husband. The heavens
themselves were witness to your crime.

HAI-T'ANG. I attest my innocence
Before all space.
Though truth be hid from mortal sight,
The gods look down on all
The whole day through
And nothing can escape their eyes.

MRS. MA. Vile creature! . . . Here is
the entrance to the Courthouse of Kai
Fang-fu. Should you dare to falsify be-
fore the judge, you will be forced to
undergo, one after another, all of the
many tortures. It were far better to
acknowledge your misdeed. And now,
consider well: will you renounce your
claim, or undergo the hideous suffering?

HAI-T'ANG. Though they beat me to a
pulp, I shall never do as you demand.
All I ask is that you unbind me and right
willingly will I go with you before the
judge.

You say that I shall suffer
In the hands of the Honorable Judge;
That one by one I shall be subjected
To all the tortures.
But to convict me,
He must find a motive for the deed.
So kind, so good, so deeply loved,
How could I have murdered my husband?
Having persevered most diligently in wis-
dom,
Having spent my years
In contemplating the shadows
Of the Six Virtues,
Why should I fear this ordeal
Or the threatened tortures? Alas!
Despite my innocence,
I have fallen into the most odious of
traps.

MRS. MA [taking firmer grip on HAI-
T'ANG; crying loudly]. Justice! . . . Jus-
tice!

SU-SHUN. I would see the person who
cries outside the door. Officers, go
quickly and bring her before me.

AN OFFICER. She is here.

[Enter MRS. MA, followed by HAI-T'ANG
and her son. Perceiving the judge, they
sink to their knees.]

SU-SHUN. Who is the plaintiff?

MRS. MA. It is your unworthy servant.

SU-SHUN. In that case, let the plain-
tiff kneel on that side and the defendant
kneel on the opposite side.

[They kneel in places indicated.]

SU-SHUN. I now order that the plain-
tiff lay before me the reasons for her
accusation. Speak: you can count on me
for justice.

MRS. MA. Your unworthy servant was
the First Wife and now the widow of the
illustrious Ma Chun-shing, with title of
Yuan-wei.

SU-SHUN [rising from his chair]. In
that case, Madam, you may stand up.

AN OFFICER. Your Excellency, this
woman is a suppliant. How can she sup-
plicate standing up?

SU-SHUN. She came here to inform us
that she was the wife and now the widow
of Ma Chun-shing, with the title of Yuan-
wei.

AN OFFICER. The title of Yuan-wei,
being honorary, means nothing. It is
given to all men who possess fortunes,
but carries no rank or public office.

SU-SHUN [reseating himself]. In that
case, kneel down again. . . . Now let us
have your accusation.

MRS. MA. Her name is Ch'ang Hai-
t'ang. She is the Second Wife of Ma
Chun-shing. I accuse her of having a
secret paramour and of having, together
with him, poisoned her husband. Also
of having appropriated my son and of
having stolen my property. Deign, hon-
ored sir, to render me prompt justice.

SU-SHUN. With what fluency, with
what facility this woman speaks. But I

confess I have failed to comprehend a word of her complaint. . . . Let some one call quickly the Clerk of the Court.

[CH'AO *enters.*]

CH'AO. I am Ch'ao, the Clerk of the Court. I was in my office copying judicial documents when His Excellency had me summoned. Undoubtedly that means he is occupied in conducting a trial and, confronted with some difficulty, has need of me to throw light upon it.

[*Perceiving* SU-SHUN.]

Sir, what is perplexing you and retarding your decision?

SU-SHUN. Honorable Clerk, here is a person presenting an accusation.

CH'AO. Let me interrogate her. Ho woman! against whom are you making your complaint?

MRS. MA. I accuse Hai-t'ang there of having poisoned her husband, of having appropriated my son, and of having stolen my property. Have pity on me and deign to render me justice.

CH'AO. So! they have brought before me Hai-t'ang. . . . Why have you poisoned your husband? Come, out with the truth. If you do not confess, you must take the consequences. Officers, were it my choice it would be the biggest stick for her.

HAI-T'ANG. Prostrate upon her knees, Your servant entreats you
To uncover the origin
Of her misfortunes.

CH'AO. Speak plainly! Defend yourself.

HAI-T'ANG. The guards surround me
Like so many wolves;
The six officials are ranged against me
Like a troup of malignant spirits.

CH'AO. You have poisoned your husband. That is one of the six crimes which are punishable by death.

HAI-T'ANG. If the burden of guilt
Rests upon me
By so much as the weight
Of a grain of rice,
I hope to expire
Amid the cruelest of tortures.

CH'AO. What was your origin? What kind of people were your parents? By what means were you enabled to marry the honorable lord Ma? Go on, speak— I am listening.

HAI-T'ANG. I am of an ancient and distinguished family.
But having lost, little by little,
Our fortune,
My August Mother and I
Were finally without resources.
Would you have dreamed that your servant
Had then lived by her beauty?
Happily I had the good fortune
To please my lord Ma,
Who made rich wedding presents
To my Honorable Mother,
And married me—as Second Wife.

CH'AO. Ah! ah! you began as a Singsong girl, a Flower of the Weeping Willow. That profession does not speak much in your favor. Well, when the lord Ma took you into his establishment, what did you give him—a boy or a girl?

HAI-T'ANG. I gave him both
A boy and a girl,*
And shall spare no pains
In bringing them up.

CH'AO. There was a man who called upon you at your house?

HAI-T'ANG. My brother, pressed by hunger, clad in rags,
Came to ask me for aid.
I spoke with him upon the step,
Then returned into the house,
Having given him nothing.
We were both observed by Mrs. Ma.

CHA'O. If it was your brother, there was no harm in her seeing you together.

HAI-T'ANG. Mrs. Ma said to me: Hai-t'ang, since your brother is in need of assistance and you have no silver, why not give him the robes and the head ornaments you have on? He can then sell them and procure what he needs.

CH'AO. What you tell of her proves her benevolence.

---

* Note: The above is the only reference to the girl-child, throughout the play.

HAI-T'ANG. Obeying her counsel, I took off my robes and head ornaments, and she gave them to my brother. But when the lord Ma returned, he wanted to know why I was no longer wearing them and declared I must have given them to a lover.

Who would have thought that this woman,
Professing charity,
Would be double-faced,
Double-tongued—
And would turn my husband
Against me?

MRS. MA. Such falsehood! In the town of Ch'ing-ch'iu I pass for a model of wisdom and virtue. How dare you say I have two tongues and two faces?

CH'AO. That is a trifle and is not a part of the evidence. . . . I am asking you why you poisoned your husband, why you appropriated the son of this woman and why you stole her property? Come, answer these accusations and confess to all the crimes of which you are guilty.

HAI-T'ANG. In a fit of anger
My husband fell to the ground;
Lacking power to move,
He remained there.
But when he had recovered his senses,
Mrs. Ma helped me to lift him up.

Then she said to me: Hai-t'ang, the lord Ma desires some broth. Go quickly and heat a cupful for him.

When I brought the cup
Of hot broth,
She tasted it and said
There was not enough salt.

She profited by the moment I was gone in search of the salt.

Who would have thought
That she would furtively
Pour poison
Into the cup?

My lord Ma then took the broth, but the moment he tasted of it he expired.

Honored Sir, examine well the facts and weigh them carefully.

The servants then burned
The body
And disposed of the ashes
In a desert-place beyond the town.

CH'AO. I see clearly that you administered the poison. But why did you appropriate this woman's son and steal her property? What answers have you to these indictments?

HAI-T'ANG. It is I who am the true mother of the child. Honored Sir, if you will but call before you Mrs. Liu Ssu-shin and Mrs. Wei-Wu, who assisted at his birth, and the people of the quarter where I lived, their testimony will verify my claim.

CH'AO. Your demand is a reasonable one. Officers, fetch the two women and some of the people of the quarter.
[SU-SHUN makes a gesture. AN OFFICER
[goes out.]
OFFICER [calling outside]. Ho ye! men and respectable ladies of the quarter, you are called before the tribunal.

[Enter MRS. LIU SSU-SHIN, MRS. WEI-WU and NEIGHBORS.]
A MAN. The proverb is right: When one has received silver from another, one is disposed to help him out of his troubles. . . . To-day the First Wife of the August Lord Ma has brought an accusation before the Court. We are desired to depose in her favor. The fact is that the First Wife is not the mother of the child. But, graced with the silver with which she gratified us, we shall affirm that it was she who gave him birth. Have no misgivings, you others; do not be troubled in mind.

TWO NEIGHBORS. We know what we have to testify. [They follow the OFFICER and fall upon their knees.] We are here.

CH'AO. It is true that you are inhabitants of the quarter wherein these two wives of Ma Chun-shing reside? . . . Well then, who is the mother of the child?

A NEIGHBOR. The lord Ma was a rich personage and our obscurity prevented close association with him. But when five years ago his wife gave him a son, he distributed to each of the inhabitants of the quarter a piece of silver, in order that we might share in his joy. After one moon, the lord Ma invited us to come and drink and regale ourselves with him. We saw the beautiful child in whose honor the feast was given. In the years following, on each birthday of his son, the Yuan-wei and his Lady took him themselves to all the pagodas and burned perfumes in honor of Fu. All of the other people of the quarter saw them, the same as we did, and could testify to it.

CH'AO. After these depositions it is quite evident that Mrs. Ma is the mother of the child.

HAI-T'ANG. Excellency, these neighbors have been bribed by Mrs. Ma. Their testimony is worth nothing.

THE NEIGHBORS. No, we have not been given so much as a grain of silver. What we are advancing is the purest truth. There is not a false syllable in our depositions. [To HAI-T'ANG.] I hope you get a fever-blister on your lip as big as a tea-cup!

HAI-T'ANG. Now I invoke the testimony Of Mrs. Liu Ssu-shin and Mrs. Ch'ang, Who aided in bringing my son Into the world.
During the first moon of his life They came more than ten times To visit me.
Now I am in great trouble, Calumny having pursued me To the very feet of Justice.
It hurts me to see my neighbors Thus perjure themselves And outrage truth and honor.
It is silver That has caused them to persist In their mendacity.

Respected Sir, kindly interrogate these estimable women. No one can be better informed than they.

CH'AO. Who is the mother of the child?

MRS. LIU SSU-SHIN. We midwives attend at least seven or eight cases every day. How then can we recall those which occurred years ago.

CH'AO. The child is not over five years old. Consequently it is not such a very long time since he was born. Make haste now and tell me which of these two women is his mother.

MRS. LIU SSU-SHIN. Wait a bit while I try to draw together the scattered threads of memory. On that day the room in which the mother lay was carefully closed for the most part. The semi-darkness did not permit me to see her features clearly.

CH'AO. It is your turn, Mrs. Wei-Wu. Make your depositions.

MRS. WEI-WU. On that day when I came to deliver the woman, it was the First Wife who was great with child. Thus there is no doubt but that Mrs. Ma is the true mother.

HAI-T'ANG. Is it possible that you both testify so unfairly?

Mrs. Liu, when you came
To receive the newly-born,
I spoke to you gently.
You carried me in your arms
From the couch where I lay
To my bed.
And you, Mrs. Wei-Wu,
After you had placed the child
On my breast,
Who lighted for me
The fragrant candles
Before the shrine of Kuang-yün?
You are neither of you
So greatly advanced in age
As to cause impairment
Of your memory.
I ask you how it is
That you could say what you did
With such unbelievable assurance!
Is it possible,
With all this false testimony,
That the judge will be able to distinguish
Right from wrong,
Virtue from crime?

The truth is as tangled as water-weeds
In the dark sea of falsehood.

CH'AO. You see how it is. These re-
spectable women both swear that Mrs. Ma
is the true mother. Also it is known that
you made no objection to her raising the
child.

HAI-T'ANG. Respected Sir, the neigh-
bors and these women were bribed with
silver by Mrs. Ma. Allow my son to be
called as witness. Although he is but
five years old, he is endowed with marked
intelligence. Will you question him?

MRS. MA [holding the child in her
arms]. Say that I am your true mother
and that it was I who nursed you.

THE CHILD. There is my own mother.
[To HAI-T'ANG.]
It was you who nursed me.

HAI-T'ANG. Behold another proof of his
rare intelligence!

Dear child, dream in the depths
Of thy little heart;
Dream, alas! of the many times
That cruel woman
Bruised thy tender skin
With blows.
Thou dost remember well
That it was she
Whom you call mother,
Who nourished you with her milk
And cradled you
On her breast.
But how could she always
Preserve thee from the fury
Of that vixen?

CH'AO. The words of the child count
for nothing. It is upon the weight of the
testimony of the many that the judge
makes his decisions. For the rest, since
it is known that you appropriated to
yourself the child of the other woman, it
is not important to prove that you stole
goods from her. Come, admit at once
that you poisoned your husband.

HAI-T'ANG. I had nothing whatsoever
to do with the poisoning.

CH'AO. Perhaps a good beating will
hasten your confession. Ho! Officers, take
this hardened wretch and give her a good
chastening.
[They beat her until she sinks
weakly to the floor.]

MRS. MA. Beat her! Beat her! That's
right, that's good. Kill her with blows,
it's all the same to me, [HAI-T'ANG faints.]

CH'AO. She is shamming death. Of-
ficers, lift her up. [They do so.]

HAI-T'ANG [regaining her senses].
When the blows hailed their fire upon my
shoulders,
Hissing like the wind,
A mortal agony shook my spirit;
My trembling soul was nigh unto escape.
The pitiless ones!
They will tear out my hair. . . .

AN OFFICER. Come on now, confess. It
is better than to undergo torture.

HAI-T'ANG. Confusion is ringing in my
ears.
Alas! this perverse clerk
Accords grace to the culprit
And betrays innocence
Into the hands of his ferocious minions.

CH'AO. Confess who was your paramour.

SU-SHUN. If she continues her obstin-
acy, I will talk to her myself and then
she will admit everything.

HAI-T'ANG. With violence the magis-
trate would force me
To confess to an imaginary lover
Who does not exist.
Thrice have I tried to escape
By the door in the wall,
But in vain.
What reward will you have
For the blood which streams
From my body?
Alas! did I but possess some silver,
It would be easy to obtain
My deliverance;
But lacking silver as I do,
How can I bring myself to endure
These frightful tortures?

CH'AO. Officers, give her another taste
of the rod.

HAI-T'ANG. I come of a good family. How can I submit to these indignities?

SH-SHUN. Let us waste no more of our valuable time.

[*He makes a sign and* TWO SER- GEANTS *put on ghastly, fiend- ish masks and approach her with knives.*]

HAI-T'ANG [*groans*]. They beat me until I fell unconscious. They cut me with knives and I groaned in my anguish. The fiends tear at my flesh, and my body is writhing with exquisite pain. Van- quished by suffering, I see myself forced to admit crimes of which I am innocent.

[*She comes forward and sinks on her knees before* SU-SHUN.]

Honored Sir, your servant recollects that she poisoned her husband, that she ab- ducted the child and stole property. Oh heaven! this injustice is killing me.

CH'AO [*apart*]. Though it be a thou- sand times an injustice, what is that to me? And happily the injustice works well for her who would be awarded the boy. . . . Officers, since the woman has admitted her crimes, have her sign her declaration. Then place a large cangue about her neck, after which conduct her to Kai Fang-fu where she will receive her final sentence.

SU-SHUN. Officers, use that brand-new heavy cangue. It weighs nine and a half pounds.

AN OFFICER. You are obeyed. . . . Vile woman, put your neck in this cangue.

[OFFICERS *fasten the wooden yoke about her neck.*]

HAI-T'ANG. Oh heaven!

The cruel magistrate ceases not his tyr- anny.

Without regard for justice,

He records on paper imaginary crimes.

No longer am I to remain here

To invoke, with groaning voice,

The brassy heavens.

The ears of the gods are turned to stone

And the world swarms with infamous ac- cusers.

Ah, where can I find a judge of integrity

Who will recognize my innocence?

CH'AO. Brazen-face! the August Head of this Court is a magistrate of the ut- most fairness and incorruptible integrity. His decisions are ever based upon the law. Nowhere in the world will you find a judge so equitable, so superbly impartial as His Excellency.

HAI-T'ANG [*sobbing*]. Feeble and dying as I am,

How can I endure the rigors

Of the dungeon

Where I am to await

The crowning agony?

[*She goes out with the guards.*]

CH'AO. Behold! the matter is at an end. The witnesses may return tranquilly to their homes. As to the Honorable Plaintiff, I promise to acquaint her with the decision of the Supreme Court as soon as it is reported to me. . . . For me, con- sider that I have been occupied an entire day in judging. Hunger presses me. It is necessary that I return home for din- ner.

[*The Neighbors and Witnesses prostrate themselves and then retire. Exit* CH'AO.]

SU-SHUN [*alone*]. The case is at last settled. Though I am a magistrate, I need never exert myself to pass sentence. When it is a question of whether to flog some one or to set him at liberty, I leave it to the pleasure of the clerk Ch'ao, even at the risk of having it said that I am a downright rogue.

Now that he has rendered his decision,

I need trouble my head no further.

Whether the accusation be true or false,

Whether the sentence be a cudgeling,

Deportation or exile,

He is at perfect liberty to choose.

I demand but one thing,

Silver.

Always I divide the silver

Into two portions;

One for me

And one for my clever clerk.

[*He goes out.*]

END OF ACT II

ACT III

[The scene is a wine-shop and vicinity.]

A WINE-SELLER. I am a seller of wines. My business is situated ten *lis* * from the town of Ch'ing-ch'iu. The merchants and the travelers on their way north and south never fail to stop at my place for refreshment. I go now to open the door of my shop and to heat this kettle of wine over my brazier. Soon some customers will appear and I must be ready for them.

[He goes out.]

[Enter HAI-T'ANG, *led in by two guards,* T'ANG-SHAO, *and* HSIEH-PA. *She falls down, rises again and seats herself.]*

T'ANG-SHAO. I am a guard employed by the Court of Ch'ing-ch'iu. My name is T'ang-shao. This is my companion, Hsieh-pa. We are conducting the woman named Ch'ang Hai-t'ang to the Supreme Court of Kai Fang-fu, where she will receive her final sentence. . . . Ho, woman, hurry a bit! Don't you hear the roar of the wind? Can't you see the whirling eddies of snow? I suppose you are hungry. Well, take this food. We go to purchase a cup of wine. As soon as you have eaten you will have to go on. *[She falls weakly.]* Hey! None of that! *[Strikes her.]*

HAI-T'ANG *[rising]*. I pray you, my friend, not to strike. I am unjustly condemned and have not long to live. I ask but one thing: that you pity my condition.

T'ANG-SHAO. Woman, why did you poison your husband? Why did you abduct the son of the First Wife? Why did you steal from her? Come, tell me quietly and I will listen.

HAI-T'ANG. How shall I clear myself of the crimes they impute to me! To whom can I recount the injustice that has been done me? How shall I denounce that woman who, after robbing me of my child, accused me of having poisoned my husband? Where shall I find a disinterested judge, one of integrity?

* 10 *lis* equal about 2.7 miles.

HSIEH-PA. If you give something to me and my comrade no one will bother you further. You'll have no need to concern yourself with the iniquity of judges.

HAI-T'ANG. Every friend of justice should pity me. Covered with blood from the wounds of the torture, a prey to unheard-of miseries, how can I suppress the sighs that issue from me and the cries that rend the air? How can I eat anything? Alas, my clothing is in tatters, the iron padlock of my chains, this heavy cangue, I bow beneath their weight. Hard and cruel as you are, what do you care that I am the victim of a foul plot?

T'ANG-SHAO. Whoever is responsible for your situation, it is not right for you to accuse us. We are not responsible for your train of misfortunes. What would you have us do? But hasten your steps. The snow is coming down with new force. Come along!

HAI-T'ANG. The goddess of the snow is without pity.
The snow is blinding my tear-swollen eyes.
The wind pushes me back with its powerful arms,
Howling like a wild thing
In the trees of the forest.
Alas! I am desolate
And am suffering cruel anguish.
Though strength has abandoned me,
Yet must I go on.
My clothing is in tatters
And my knees are bared to the elements.
The wounds from the torture are bleeding anew.

HSIEH-PA. We are having a hard enough time ourselves, and she will not go on. *[Strikes her.]*

HAI-T'ANG. Why are you vexed at the sight of my condition?
I am walking as fast as I can.
If you continue to hit me,
I shall die under the blows.

T'ANG-SHAO. I should be inclined to liberate you, if you had not confessed to the murder. What impelled you to do so?

HAI-T'ANG. My friend, do not weary me with importunate questions. I wish only that you would listen.

When the merciless judge employed
against me
All the severity of the law,
I went through the torments of the Seven
Hells.
Vanquished by suffering,
My endurance at an end,
I surrendered at last to their wishes
And signed my declaration.
There was no one to intercede for me.
Victim alas, of a false accusation,
I was yet put through every degree of
torture.
T'ANG-SHAO. Rise, woman!
[*Meaningly.*]
After we have rounded the next hill, I
can promise you the pleasure of a very
long rest.
HAI-T'ANG. Would I had turned that
hill.
Alack! numbed by the cold,
Weakened by suffering,
I cannot so much as stand.
[*Takes a few steps and falls.*]
When I lifted my feet
I felt as if all the Shui-mang devils
Were penetrating my flesh.
T'ANG-SHAO [*angrily*]. Get up!
HAI-T'ANG. Aïe! your temper
Is as impetuous as a flame.
See, my friend,
The ground is hard-frozen and glassy.
How can I keep myself
From slipping?
HSIEH-PA. A thousand people, yes ten
thousand have passed this way without
falling. Wait while I precede you. If
I keep my balance, I shall not fail to
bruise your legs with my stick.
[*He walks on the ice and falls down.*]
As a matter of fact, the road is a bit
slippery.
[CH'ANG-LIN *enters.*]
CH'ANG-LIN. I am called Ch'ang-Lin. I
am the First Clerk of the Court of Kai
Fang-fu. This morning the governor, Pao-
ch'ing, sent me on a military commission
to the frontier of Si-yen. On my return
I was surprised by this blinding snow-
storm. Oh heaven, if only it would cease
for an instant!

HAI-T'ANG [*perceiving him*]. That man
over there resembles my brother, Ch'ang-
Lin.

I have observed his features,
Surely it must be my brother.
But my eyes, swollen with over-weeping
And blinded by the sleet,
May be deceiving me. . . .
Let me look again. . . .
Aïe! I am not mistaken;
It is he and none other.
I straighten with an effort my trembling
shoulders;
I hold with my hands my fluttering
bosom. . . .
Alas! How can I catch up with him,
Impeded by this iron chain and heavy
cangue?
CH'ANG-LIN [*to the guards*]. Where
are you taking that woman with the iron
chain and the heavy cangue?
HAI-T'ANG. My brother!
O my Honorable Brother!
Stop and deliver your sister.

My brother!

Hi-yah! you appear in my sight
As a living image of Kuang-yün the
Merciful,
Come down from the Mountain of Lo-chia-
shan
To preserve me.
Why do you wait to manifest
The goodness and compassion that you
feel?

O Honorable Brother, deliver me, your
sister.
CH'ANG-LIN. Who are you?
HAI-T'ANG. I am your sister Hai-t'ang,
and sorrow is eating my heart.
[*She approaches him.*]
CH'ANG-LIN [*repulses and strikes her*].
Vile prostitute! Do you recall how you
helped *me* on that day I implored you
for assistance? [*Turns away.*]
HAI-T'ANG [*weeping and running
toward him*]. I ask why you speak thus
to me!

Yet I am aware that it is difficult
To suppress a fire
That has long burned secretly.
The sight of me has revived
An old enmity.
It is seeing me
That has revived his burning wrath.
[*Brokenly.*]
My brother!
[CH'ANG-LIN *continues on his
way.*]
He does not deign to recognize me.
As I am in fear of my life,
I shall run after him
And catch him by his garments.
[*Dragging her chain, she runs
after him and clutches him.
T'ANG-SHAO follows.*]
CH'ANG-LIN. Vile prostitute! Let go
of me! Let go of me!
T'ANG-SHAO [*seizing her by the hair*].
This woman is molesting passers-by and
wearying them with her importunities.
HAI-T'ANG. Swifter than I,
He has seized me by the hair.

I supplicate you, cruel man, to give
me an instant's respite. And thou, my
brother, I pray you to listen to the true
story of my misfortunes.
CH'ANG-LIN. Wretch! Could you have
foreseen this day you would not have re-
fused me those robes and head ornaments.

HAI-T'ANG. She! She! She!
Loves to bring death and destruction
To others.
All of her projects were born of craft
And perfidy.
Thou didst take the robes
And the golden spire
Which ornamented my hair;
And me, me, me!
For having given them,
I am plunged into the abyss
In which you find me.

My brother, the frightful misfortunes
which have overwhelmed your sister all
sprang from those same robes and head
ornaments. At first, believing it would

not meet with her approval, I dared not
turn them over to you to supply your
needs. Could I ever have believed that
she would herself have taken them off me
and given them to you herself? . . . On
the return of the lord Ma Chun-shing,
she told him that, in his absence, I had
been entertaining a lover to whom I had
given the robes and ornaments. Trans-
ported with rage, the Honorable Lord Ma
fainted and fell ill. But that is far from
all. She gave him a poisoned beverage
which swiftly carried him to the Vale of
Longevity. Then she dragged thine hon-
orable sister before the judge and con-
demned me for having poisoned my hus-
band and appropriated her son. O
Heaven! Have pity on me! I succumb
under the weight of unjust accusations.
CH'ANG-LIN. To whom belonged these
robes and head ornaments?
HAI-T'ANG. To me! To thy sister.
CH'ANG-LIN. What! They were yours?
And to think that that wicked woman as-
sured me the things had come from the
trousseau given her by her parents. I
was wrong to have so misjudged you. . . .
We are before the entrance to an inn.
Come inside with me and we will together
have some cups of warm reviving wine.
[*He leads her to the wine-shop,
the two guards following.*]
Hey waiter! Fetch us some wine.
THE WINE-SELLER. Right here! Right
here! Come in and find seats.
CH'ANG-LIN [*to the guards*]. Officers
of the police, I am the chief clerk of the
Court of Kai Fang-fu. My name is
Ch'ang-Lin. This woman is my sister. I
was sent on a mission by the illustrious
governor Pao, from which I am now re-
turning. I pledge myself to look after her
and to relieve you of responsibility.
T'ANG-SHAO. My friend, you have no
need to give us that assurance. All we
ask is that as soon as you arrive in the
city, you despatch to us the official answer
we are to bring back.
CH'ANG-LIN. That is easy. . . . And
now, my sister, I said a while back that
that woman was a model of wisdom and

prudence. But now that I have learned of the cruelty of her nature, I am wondering how you can escape from the net she has thrown around you.

HAI-T'ANG. That woman, whose visage is bright
With artificial splendor,
Appeared to you to be prudent and wise.
When my husband questioned her, she used against me
All the venom of her long serpent's tongue,
Heaping falsehood upon falsehood.
Later she declared I had poisoned my husband,
Stolen her property and appropriated her child.
On top of that she dragged me
To the Court of Ch'ing-ch'iu
And stood by indifferently
While they put me through the tortures.
Oy-ah! despite my innocence
I am bruised by blows, bleeding from wounds
And doomed to fall under the glittering blade
Of the executioner,
To whom shall I impute the death that menaces me,
If not to that inhuman monster?

My brother, let us rest here a moment in this secluded corner.

[*Enter* CH'AO, *followed by* MRS. MA.]
CH'AO. I am Ch'ao the clerk. I come in search of Ch'ang Hai-t'ang. I am quite sure that she has not a near relative who would interest himself in her affairs and demand a reversal of the judgment given at the Court of Ch'ing-ch'iu. However, to be on the safe side, I felt it advisable to have her killed along the way. I chose two guards who do not spare the stick. These are T'ang-shao and Hsieh-pa. According to my instructions, it was not necessary to wait until they had gone any great distance. They were to stop at the first deserted place they came to and there despatch her. But as they had not returned to render an account of their commission, I began to have misgivings. It is necessary that Mrs. Ma and I make this journey in order to clear up our doubts.

MRS. MA. In making my way through this blinding snowstorm I am benumbed by the cold. Let us go into this inn where we may obtain some warm wine before continuing our journey.

CH'AO. Madam, that is an excellent suggestion. [*They enter the inn.* HAI-T'ANG *perceives them.*]

HAI-T'ANG. What a fortunate encounter. She herself has happened in here with the companion of her debauches. Let us inform my brother.

This woman is cruel and brazen.
Since providentially they are both present,
Here is my opportunity
To arrest the course
Of their iniquity.
But by what means?

My brother, this debauched woman is here in this very inn, accompanied by her accomplice. Let us seize and hold her.

CH'ANG-LIN [*to the guards*]. My friends, arrest that adultress and her paramour.

HAI-T'ANG. Make haste to seize them swiftly,
Lest they become frightened and make their escape.
Now we shall see which of us is innocent
And which shall receive the penalty for crime. [*To* CH'ANG-LIN.]
Let us not wait for the guards,
But go and capture them ourselves.

[CH'ANG-LIN *and* HAI-T'ANG *go to lay hold of them, but the two guards make signs to them to flee.* HAI-T'ANG *grabs at* MRS. MA, *who disengages her hands and escapes with* CH'AO.]

HAI-T'ANG. I seized her clothing
And through the fault of these men
She fled under my hands.
Above all it distresses me
That when we so nearly had them,
The guards gave them warning

And caused the flight
Of those illicit lovers.

CH'ANG-LIN [to T'ANG-SHAO]. Imbecile that you are! The sign that you and your comrade made, warned them and gave them a chance to escape. Are you aware that I am the Chief Clerk at the Court of Kai Fang-fu, and that, if I chastise you, I need fear no consequences?
                    [Strikes T'ANG-SHAO.]
T'ANG-SHAO. Since your rank is higher than that of the master I serve, you have the right to strike me. But I, in turn, have the right to strike my prisoner. Therefore, for every blow I receive from your stick, she shall receive one from mine.   [Strikes HAI-T'ANG.]

HAI-T'ANG. These men conduct me
By order of the magistrate.
Of what use to strike them
When they pass along each blow?
          [CH'ANG-LIN seizes T'ANG-SHAO
            by the hair, and T'ANG-SHAO
            promptly seizes HAI-T'ANG in
            the same manner.]
HAI-T'ANG. He grasps tightly his poor prisoner.
Without pity for my sufferings
He overwhelms me with blows.
He bruises, he kills me . . . !

THE WINE-SELLER [laying hold of them]. Here!—pay me for the wine you have drunk and get out.
HSIEH-PA. Take this for payment!
          [He sends him up upside down
            with a kick, and goes out
            with the others.]
THE WINE-SELLER. See how unfortunate I am. I wasted a good part of the day on my doorstep, waiting for customers. At length came three or four persons asking for wine. I served them and got a shower of blows in exchange. As for money, I have received not so much as a piece of brass. I have decided to close my shop and, from this day on, to go into some more remunerative business. This trade is far from a flourishing one. Every day the folk to whom I sell

wine, make me lose instead of gaining. I shall draw the bolts and close my shop. I had better go into the business of selling water-fowl, which pays in cash instead of in kicks.   [He goes out.]

END OF ACT III

ACT IV

[The scene is in the Court of KAI FANG-FU.]

[The governor, PAO-CH'ING, enters, followed by the FIRST OFFICER of the COURT and several guards.]'

FIRST OFFICER [imperiously]. Order in the Court! Attendants, bring the writing-desk of His Excellency the Governor.
PAO-CH'ING. I preside over this Court
By decree of the Emperor,
The Son of Heaven.
          [With a reverential bow.]
I hold at the same time,
The imperial Golden Token
And the Sword, symbol of power.

My family name is Pao, my surname Ch'ing and my honorary name is Hi-wen. I am a native of the village of Lao-eul in the district of Ssu-hiang, a principality of Chin-tiu in the province of Liu-ch'iu. All the public functionaries are aware of the unshakability of my moral fibre and my inflexibility in upholding the mandates of the law. They now consecrate themselves with zeal to the service of the State and fear to permit themselves to be swayed by self-interest and cupidity. They choose as their officers only those men who are renowned for their probity and their filial piety, and spurn the company of slanderers and flatterers. The Emperor has bestowed many honors upon me. I have lately received the title of Member of the Cabinet of Antiquaries, whose duty it is to preserve the ancient chronicles of the archives. In conferring upon me the dignity of Governor, the Son of Heaven [He bows low.] bestowed on me the Golden Token, and the Sword, the symbol of

power. He charged me not only to scru-
tinize the conduct of magistrates and em-
ployees unfaithful to their duties, but
also to avenge the wrongs of the people
and render justice to the oppressed. He
permits me to order the decapitation of
the guilty and to see that their sentence is
carried out. Thus my name alone suffices
to arrest the arms of those inclined to
abuse their authority. Even my shadow
is enough to petrify with fear the cruel
and the debauched. Past the balustrade
of knotted ropes and near to the walls of
this enclosure, I have caused a prison to
be built. In it rest those functionaries
who have imposed upon their public office
and those who have failed in their duty.
On the stone tablet which flanks the en-
trance I have had engraved the words
IU-TCHI, meaning By Order of the Em-
peror, so that all may see it and be filled
with awe. At the foot of the Blue Stair-
case which leads to this, my courtroom,
I have placed a sign which reads TI-
CHING, or Speak Softly. Under the
acacias, which cast their weaving shadows
upon the stone flagging of the pathway, I
have displayed twenty-four cangues of the
largest size, and before the doors to this
hall where I deliver my judgments and
pass sentences, there are stacked many
hundreds of clubs, all studded with the
fangs of wolves. At the very entrance
stands a bamboo cage containing the head
of a robber, "for the punishment must
match the deed and frighten evil-doers."

Through all the days there comes no dust
To soil the mind of the governor.
The acacias alone cast shade
Upon the path whereon he walks.
In passing him,
The men of evil still their tongues,
And birds of prey
Suspend their raucous cries.

I saw yesterday a report sent me by the
governor of Ch'ing-ch'iu. It states that a
Second Wife, named Ch'ang Hai-t'ang, has
poisoned her husband in order to satisfy
an illicit passion. Also, that she abducted
by force a child belonging to the First
Wife and likewise stole goods from her.
Such crimes are numbered among those
punishable by immediate death, without
waiting for the more formal regular Au-
tumnal executions. In my opinion, one
frequently finds women sufficiently de-
praved to murder their husbands. But
what good did it do this one to abduct the
child of the First Wife? I fear this affair
may be the result of a calumnious imputa-
tion. Therefore I have secretly given
orders to arrest and bring before me the
accuser and her witnesses. Their presence
is necessary if I am to pass correct judg-
ment. This procedure proves my justice
and impartiality. . . . Officer, bring me
the tablet of cases submitted to me for
final judgment. After which, bring before
me the plaintiffs in the order of their
arrival, that I may condemn the guilty
and redeem the innocent.

[*The scene changes for a moment to the
road outside the courthouse. Enter* HAI-
T'ANG *with* GUARDS *and* CH'ANG-LIN.]

CH'ANG-LIN.   Honorable Sister, when
you are brought before the magistrate, he
will not fail to interrogate you. He must
be informed of the injustice of which you
are a victim. This supreme judge will
examine anew the evidence and end by
annulling your sentence. If you do not
wish to make your own explanations, keep
silent and I will undertake to speak in
your place.

HAI-T'ANG.   How can I denounce this
infamous calumny if I fail to make the
most of this day's opportunity?

CH'ANG-LIN.   It behooves us to present
our case promptly. Let us hurry.

HAI-T'ANG.   Who knows the injustice
    that weighs
So heavily upon my heart?
Alas! what can I do but groan;
Let flow these rivulets of tears?
Not having foreseen in the beginning
The misfortunes which have come upon me,
I am eating the bitter fruits
Of useless regret.

These cruel men drag me hither and
  thither
And allow me no repose.

CH'ANG-LIN. My sister, we have arrived
before the entrance of the Court of Kai
Fang-fu. Allow me to precede you, as you
will enter in the custody of the police.
Take courage. The judge is like a shining
mirror which reflects in its crystal purity
all the objects placed before it. The mo-
ment a matter is brought to his attention
he sees it as clearly as if he were familiar
with all the details. Make an effort to
regain your poise and explain your situa-
tion to him in your own words.

HAI-T'ANG. Thou sayest the judge,
Like a mirror of finest glass,
Placed in the highest position
In the tribunal of the South,
Reflects all that is below
With crystalline purity.
Then what am I to fear?
But alas! weighed down by this cangue
  and iron chain,
I feel that I may lack the strength
To adequately express myself.
If I am unable to send conviction to his
  soul,
I ask you, my brother, to aid me in my
  defense.
[CH'ANG-LIN goes into the courthouse.
HAI-T'ANG follows with the GUARDS.]

[The scene changes back to the courtroom.]
T'ANG-SHAO. We bring before Your Ex-
cellency our prisoner, Ch'ang Hai-t'ang.
FIRST OFFICER. Honored Sir, deliver to
these guards their official report, that they
may return to render an account of their
mission.
PAO-CH'ING. Let them remain here.
You may furnish them with their report
after I have judged the case.
FIRST OFFICER [bowing]. You are
obeyed.
PAO-CH'ING. Ch'ang Hai-t'ang, is it true
that you poisoned your husband in order
to live with a paramour, that you ab-
ducted the son of the First Wife and stole

her property? Reply to these questions in
the sequence in which they were given.
Speak, I am listening.
    [HAI-T'ANG looks mutely at her
        brother.]
CH'ANG-LIN. You cannot? Ah well, I
shall speak for you.   [He kneels.]
Honored Sir, Ch'ang Hai-t'ang has not
maintained criminal relations with a lover,
she has not poisoned her husband, she did
not abduct the child, she has not stolen
property. It is the First Wife herself
who maintained guilty relations with a
clerk named Ch'ao. When she accused my
sister before the judge, it was that same
Ch'ao who influenced the decision against
her. I adjure you, Honored Sir, that if
she admitted the crimes with which she
was charged, it was under the intolerable
anguish of torture.
PAO-CH'ING. How droll you are! Who
requested you to answer for her? Officer,
take this man and give him twenty blows
with a stick. [OFFICER grabs CH'ANG-LIN
and begins beating him.]
CH'ANG-LIN [prostrating himself]. This
woman is my Honorable Sister. She has
never come into the presence of a magis-
trate so imposing as Your Excellency, and
is therefore bashful and timid. She has
not the forcefulness necessary to make the
truth known to you. That is why I pre-
sumed to talk for her.
PAO-CH'ING. If you are indeed her bro-
ther, I shall permit you to answer in her
stead. But if you are not he, I shall slice
your head with this large knife. . . .
Come, woman, speak with all the sincerity
and exactitude of which you are capable.
You may count on my fairness.

HAI-T'ANG [clasping her hands]. Hon-
  ored Sir!
Trembling, distracted,
I kneel at your imposing feet.
Your Excellency has bidden me unfold
The circumstances
Which have led to my present situation.
How alas! can I endure the fury
Of the merciless guards
Who press and harass me

Like tigers and devouring wolves?
Will you, Honored Sir,
Listen attentively while I detail to you
The facts appertaining to my case?

PAO-CH'ING. Very well, Ch'ang Hai-t'ang. Who were you as a girl? What was your estate when you were married to Ma Chun-shing in the rank of Second Wife?

HAI-T'ANG. I was a Flower of the Weeping Willow Tree. I entertained one man after another and my occupation was singing and dancing.

PAO-CH'ING. Ah! ah! you were a sing-song girl! And this Ma Chun-shing, he treated you well?

HAI-T'ANG. We lived as two doves Most tenderly united.

PAO-CH'ING. Is it true that Ch'ang-Lin is your brother?

CH'ANG-LIN. Ch'ang Hai-t'ang is the sister of your unworthy servant.

HAI-T'ANG. It came to pass, one day, That my brother, Raggedly clad and dilapidated in fortune, Came to seek my aid.

PAO-CH'ING. And you helped him?

HAI-T'ANG. Yes, Honored Sir, I gave him some robes And head-ornaments.

CH'ANG-LIN. The money with which I purchased new clothing was obtained from the sale of part of these effects.

PAO-CH'ING [to HAI-T'ANG]. Your husband did not inquire what had become of the robes and ornaments?

HAI-T'ANG. He did indeed. But this woman, who had herself advised me to give the things to my brother, accused me before the lord Ma of having secretly given them to a lover. Was not that enough to make him expire with wrath?

Transported with ire,
My husband
Addressed violent reproaches to me
And fell ill.

PAO-CH'ING. Since it was that which killed your husband, why the accusation that you had poisoned him?

HAI-T'ANG. Dragged, despite my inno-cence,
Before the tribunal,
I was subjected
To all of the tortures.

PAO-CH'ING. Your husband being dead, what was your idea in abducting the child?

HAI-T'ANG. Death having taken my spouse,
That woman would now separate me
From my son.

PAO-CH'ING. They say she is the mother of the child.

HAI-T'ANG. Driven by natural perversity and the basest jealousy. . . .

PAO-CH'ING. The neighbors affirmed that she was the mother.

HAI-T'ANG. She bought the testimony
Of the witnesses,
Both men and women,
With silver,
And involved them in her scheme.

PAO-CH'ING. Can it be that the magis-trate did not verify their depositions?

HAI-T'ANG. Not every magistrate
Takes the pains
To sift out the truth
From falsehood,
Crime from innocence.

PAO-CH'ING. Is it possible that the magistrate of Ch'ing-ch'iu could compel you to undergo the severities of the tor-ture?

HAI-T'ANG. How could I resist?
What chance had I against a magistrate
Who tortures the accused
Without investigating
On which side is the crime
Or which the innocence!
And that is not all.
I found in that same tribunal
A most implacable enemy
Who seconded the cruel officers
And I was left before them
Without defense and without support.

Oy-ah!
I heard a sudden scream like a burst of
  thunder.
A shower of blows rained on my back and
  bared it.
On the one side,
They afflicted me with wounds
Which caused intolerable distress.
On the other side, the witnesses,
Bought with silver,
Received no chastisement whatsoever.
My teeth chattering,
My movements stiff with agony,
My bones breaking under the blows
Of my tormentors,
Their sinewy arms rest not until I fall
Unconscious and motionless.

AN OFFICER [heard outside]. People of
Ch'ing-ch'iu, you who are about to be
judged, assemble in the court.
PAO-CH'ING. Have them come in.

[MRS. MA, with the young child SHIU-
LANG, the NEIGHBORS and the TWO MID-
WIVES enter and fall on their knees.]
OFFICER [to PAO-CH'ING]. They are be-
fore you.
PAO-CH'ING [to MRS. MA]. Woman, who
is the mother of that child?
MRS. MA. It is I who am the mother.
PAO-CH'ING. And you, neighbors, tell
me who is the mother of that child.
ALL [together]. We swear that the
First Wife is his mother.
PAO-CH'ING. Very good. . . . Ch'ang-
Lin, there is some one yet to come. [He
makes a gesture and CH'ANG-LIN goes
out.]
PAO-CH'ING. Officer, fetch a piece of
chalk. You will trace below the bench a
circle, in the center of which you will
place the young child. Then you will
order the two women to wait, each of them
at opposite sides of the circle. When the
real mother takes hold of him, it will be
easy for. the child to come outside the
circle. But the pretended mother cannot
lead him out.
OFFICER. You are obeyed.

[He traces a circle with the chalk
and motions the boy to stand
in the center of it. MRS. MA
takes the child's hand and
leads him out of the circle.
HAI-T'ANG fails to contend
with her.]
PAO-CH'ING. It is evident that this
woman is not the mother of the child,
since she did not come forward to draw
him out of the circle. Officer, bring
Ch'ang Hai-t'ang hither and beat her.
          [The OFFICER does so.]
PAO-CH'ING. Have the two women try
once more to lead the child outside the
circle.
[Again MRS. MA leads him out,
while HAI-T'ANG again fails
to contend.]
PAO-CH'ING. I have the proof twice
over. I saw that neither time did you
make the slightest effort to draw the child
outside the circle. Officer, fetch your
largest stick and flog her vigorously.
HAI-T'ANG. I supplicate you, Honored
Sir, to calm your wrath which frightens
me like a roll of thunder. Soften this
menacing aspect, which is like that of the
wolf or the tiger. . . . Very soon after
your unworthy servant was married to the
August Lord Ma, she presented him with
a child. After giving him the great gift
of life, I nourished him with milk from
my breast and cared for him with ma-
ternal love for the period of three years.
When he was cold I would gently chafe
his jade-like limbs. Delicate and fragile
as the first young shoots of the bamboo
tree, one could not, without wounding him
grievously, take him to opposite sides of
the circle. If I cannot, Honored Sir, ob-
tain my son without dislocating his arm
or bruising his baby flesh, I would rather
perish under the blows than make the
least effort to take him out of the circle.

How could a tender mother
Decide otherwise?

Honored Sir, see for yourself.

The child's arms are fragile
As the first tender stalks of the bamboo
tree
In the flush of springtide.
How could this cruel and inhuman woman
understand my fears?
And you, Honored Sir,
How is it that for all your sagacity,
You have not been able to discover the
truth?
Alack! how different our positions!
She has a reputation and a fortune,
While I am humiliated and an object of
scorn.
Yes, if between us
We would tear apart this tender child,
You would not hesitate to see him
Torn limb from limb.
You were ready to break his bones
And you would have seen his flesh torn to
shreds.

PAO-CH'ING. Although the articles of
the code are often difficult to interpret, it
is possible to penetrate the sentiments of
the human heart. A sage of old once said:
What man can hide that which he really
is, once you have observed his actions,
found the motive for his conduct and
recognized the intent of his purpose? . . .
Behold the power of the chalk circle! In
the depths of her heart, this woman de-
sired to seize the fortune of Ma Chun-
shing, and with that end in view, took the
child to bring up. How could she have
doubted that the hidden truth would re-
veal itself?

For the purpose of gaining the inheritance,
She raised the young child.
But the chalk circle augustly brought out
The truth and the falsity.
She has an engaging exterior,
But her heart is corrupt.
The true mother
Is at last recognized.

I have instructed Ch'ang-Lin to fetch
here the adulterous lover, and shall be
surprised if he does not appear.

[*Enter* CH'ANG-LIN, *conducting the clerk*
CH'AO.]
CH'ANG-LIN [*kneeling*]. Here, Honored
Sir, is the clerk Ch'ao whom I have
brought before you.
PAO-CH'ING. So, my friend Ch'ao, you've
got yourself into a pretty mess. Come,
confess point by point that in order to
satisfy an illicit passion, you poisoned Ma
Chun-shing. You assisted in the retention
of the child in order to profit by his for-
tune, and bribed these men and women to
render false testimony in your interests.
CH'AO. Your servant is employed at the
court in the capacity of clerk. All that
occurred is to be imputed to the governor
of Ch'ing-ch'iu, who is nicknamed Su Mo-
lun. When the court is in session I am
only an instrument in his hands. I hold
the ink-brush and write down the replies
of the accused. If there has been a slip
or an error in the verbal process, it is not
the poor clerk who should be blamed.
PAO-CH'ING. I am not inquiring if there
was any verbal slip or error. Tell me
only that in order to satisfy an illicit
passion you poisoned Ma Chun-shing.
CH'AO [*indicating* MRS. MA]. Excel-
lency, do you not see that this woman's
face is a mask of paint and powder? If
one were to remove with water the artifi-
cial coloring, one would no doubt find
beneath it a most hideous visage. How
could she have been able to seduce your
servant and entangle him in an illicit
love-affair?
MRS. MA. Oy-ay! And in private you
used to tell me that I was more beautiful
than Kuang-yün! Now you treat me in
this insulting fashion. Perfidious as thou
art, you are not worthy of being called a
man.
CH'ANG-LIN. Yesterday, when the snow
was falling in great flakes, Ch'ao, with
Mrs. Ma, took the road in pursuit of the
police-guards, in order to come to an un-
derstanding with them. Is it not evident
that he was her lover? For the rest, Hon-
ored Sir, if you will question the two
guards, it will then be easy to recognize
the truth.

T'ANG-SHAO. This morning we ourselves took them into custody.

PAO-CH'ING. Officer, seize the clerk Ch'ao and let some one beat him vigorously with the biggest stick.

OFFICER. You are obeyed.

[*He beats* CH'AO.]

HAI-T'ANG. You hoped to dwell forever
With Mrs. Ma.
You hoped that I should never
Return from whence you sent me.
With what intention
Did you both follow me
On the way here?
Answer me that
The pair of you. [CH'AO *assumes death.*]

PAO-CH'ING. The rascal is feigning death. Officer, restore him to life with a jug of cold water.

[*The* OFFICER *throws water in his face and* CH'AO *revives.*]

PAO-CH'ING. Come, confess at once.

CH'AO. For a long time your servant has been having an affair with this woman. According to the law I am guilty of nothing more than adultery. My crime is not among those punishable by death. Regarding the poisoning of Ma Chun-shing, I purchased the poison. That part is true enough. But it was not I who conceived the idea. It was this woman who took the poison and put it in her husband's broth. I had nothing whatever to do with the retention of the child. In fact I said to Mrs. Ma, "Since you are not his mother, why not give him up?" She replied that if she could keep the child she would become mistress of the entire fortune left by the lord Ma. I am only a poor employee and I never could have found the money with which to buy the testimony of the neighbors and these old women. She alone bribed them in order that she might, on the way here, get Hai-t'ang into her clutches. Yes, it was she, yes, it was she.

MRS. MA. Coward that you are! Make haste with your confession. Go on! What do you expect *me* to say? It was I, it was I who did everything. After all, is it such a misfortune to die? After we have lost our honorable lives, shall we not be reunited forever in the other world, like two turtle-doves?

[*A gong sounds and all are silent.*]

PAO-CH'ING. You who are here present, listen to my final sentence: Su-shun, the governor of Ch'ing-ch'iu, for having transgressed the law, will be despoiled of his bonnet and his sword-belt. He will return to the rank of the people and, to the end of his days, he shall never obtain employment. The Neighbors and the two old Midwives will never more receive bribes for rendering false testimony. Each of them shall be given twenty-four strokes with a stick and then be banished to a place three hundred *li*s distant. T'ang-shao and Hsieh-pa, in their positions as guards, will never again accept presents. They will be punished with great severity. Each will receive one hundred strokes of the stick, besides being banished to the frontier, in an arid and uninhabitable country. The adulterous woman and her infamous accomplice, for having killed Ma Chun-shing with poison, for having appropriated the young child that they might fraudulently obtain his inheritance, will be dragged to a public place where they will suffer a slow and ignominious death. Each of them will be cut into twenty-four pieces. Everything that they possess will be awarded to Ch'ang Hai-t'ang and her son Shiu-lang, in order that she may continue her tender care of him. As for Ch'ang-Lin, he may now quit his profession and go to live with his honorable sister.

Because the clerk Ch'ao
Would indulge a criminal passion,
Ch'ang Hai-t'ang was calumniated
In a manner most odious,
And unjustly accused.
But with the aid of the chalk circle,
The truth has this day been brought to light.
Those who permitted themselves
To be bribed with money

Will be sent into exile.
The two principals in the crime
Will be decapitated in a public place.
Ch'ang-Lin himself will take the sword
And execute the sentence.
And the little boy and his honorable
    mother
Will henceforth augustly remain reunited.

[CH'ANG-LIN *and* HAI-T'ANG *prostrate themselves before him.*]

HAI-T'ANG. Old women! did I hear you
    swear
That after the long years
You found you could not gather up
The scattered threads of memory?
Clerk Ch'ao, did you assure me
That your magistrate

Observed the law?
Dame Ma! did you say that you occupied
The place of First Wife
With prudence and sagacity?
But in the end
The Augustly Supreme Judge
Uncovered the odious plot.
These men are exiled
To an arid and uninhabitable land
And the two chief culprits
Are publicly to receive their just chastisement.
Honored Sir, this history
Of the Chalk Circle
Is worthy of being spread
Over the four seas
And over all the kingdoms
Of the Celestial Empire.

ABSTRACTION

ANONYMOUS

Written and produced probably in the 14th or 15th century

TRANSLATED BY B. H. CHAMBERLIN

CHARACTERS

A HUSBAND

HIS WIFE

THEIR SERVANT TARAUKUWAZHIYA

SCENE—*A room in a private house in Kiyauto.*

HUSBAND. I am a resident in the suburbs of the metropolis. On the occasion of a recent journey down East, I was served [at a tea-house] in the post-town of Nogami, in the province of Mino, by a girl called Hana, who, having since then heard of my return to the capital, has followed me up here, and settled down at Kita-Shirakaha, where she expects me this evening according to a promise made by letter. But my vixen of a wife has got scent of the affair, and thus made it difficult for me to go. So what I mean to do is to call her, and tell her some pretty fable that may set me free. Halloo! halloo! are you there, pray? are you there?

WIFE. So it seems you are pleased to call me. What may it be that makes you thus call me?

HUSBAND. Well, please to come in.

WIFE. Your commands are obeyed.

HUSBAND. My reason for calling you is just simply this: I want to tell you how much my spirits have been affected lately by continual dreams that I have had. That is why I have called you.

WIFE. You are talking rubbish. Dreams proceed from organic disturbance, and do not come true; so pray don't trouble your head about them.

HUSBAND. What you say is quite correct. Dreams, proceeding as they do from organic disturbance, do not come true nine times out of ten. Still, mine have affected my spirits to such an extent, that I think of making some pilgrimage or other to offer up prayers both on your behalf and on my own.

WIFE. Then where shall you go?

HUSBAND. I mean (to say nothing of those in the metropolis and in the suburbs) to worship at every Shiñtau shrine and every Buddhist temple [throughout the land].

WIFE. No, no! I won't allow you to go out of the house for a single hour. If you are so completely bent upon it, choose some devotion that can be performed at home.

HUSBAND. Some devotion to be performed at home? What devotion could it be?

259

WIFE. Burning incense on your arm or on your head.

HUSBAND. How thoughtlessly you do talk! What! is a devotion like that to suit *me*—a layman if ever there was one?

WIFE. I won't tolerate any devotion that cannot be performed at home.

HUSBAND. Well, I never! You *are* one for talking at random. Hang it! what devotion shall it be? [*He reflects a few moments.*] Ah! I have it! I will perform the devotion of abstraction.

WIFE. Abstraction? What is that?

HUSBAND. Your want of familiarity [with the term] is but natural. It is a devotion that was practised in days of old by Saint Daruma: (blessings on him!) you put your head under what is called the "abstraction blanket," and obtain salvation by forgetting all things past and to come—a most difficult form of devotion.

WIFE. About how long does it take?

HUSBAND. Well, I should say about a week or two.

WIFE. That won't do either, if it is to last so many days.

HUSBAND. Then for how long would my own darling consent to it without complaining?

WIFE. About one hour is what I should suggest; but, however, if you can do it in a day, you are welcome to try.

HUSBAND. Never, never! This important devotion is not a thing to be so easily performed within the limits of a single day. Please, won't you grant me leave for at least a day and a night?

WIFE. A day and a night?

HUSBAND. Yes.

WIFE. I don't much relish the idea; but if you are so completely bent upon it, take a day and a night for your devotion.

HUSBAND. Really and truly?

WIFE. Yes, really and truly.

HUSBAND. Oh! that is indeed too delightful! But I have something to tell you: know then that if a woman so much as peep through a chink, to say nothing of

her coming into the actual room where the devotee is sitting, the spell of the devotion is instantly broken. So be sure not to come to where I am.

WIFE. All right. I will not come to you. So perform away.

HUSBAND. Well, then, we will meet again after it shall have been happily accomplished.

WIFE. I shall have the pleasure of seeing you when it is over.

HUSBAND.⎱Good-by! good-by!
WIFE.　⎰

[*She moves away.*]

HUSBAND. I say!

WIFE. What is it?

HUSBAND. As I mentioned before, mind you don't come to me. We have the Buddhist's warning words: "When there is a row in the kitchen, to be rapt in abstraction is an impossibility." So, whatever you do, do not come to me.

WIFE. Please feel no uneasiness. I shall not think of intruding.

HUSBAND. Well, then, we shall meet again when the devotion is over.

WIFE. When it is done, I shall have the pleasure of seeing you.

HUSBAND.⎱Good-by! good-by!
WIFE.　⎰

HUSBAND [*laughing*]. What fools women are, to be sure! To think of the delight of her taking it all for truth, when I tell her that I am going to perform the religious devotion of abstraction for one whole day and night! Taraukuwazhiya, are you there? halloo?

SERVANT. Yes, sir!

HUSBAND. Are you there?

SERVANT. At your service.

HUSBAND. Oh! you have been quick in coming.

SERVANT. You seem, master, to be in good spirits.

HUSBAND. For my good spirits there is a good reason. I had made, as you know, an engagement to go and visit Hana this evening. But as my old woman has got scent of the affair, thus making it difficult for me to go, I have told her that I mean to perform the religious devotion of abstraction for a whole day and night—a good device, is it not? for carrying out my plan of going to see Hana!

SERVANT. A very good device indeed, sir.

HUSBAND. But in connection with it, I want to ask you to do me a good turn. Will you?

SERVANT. Pray, what may it be?

HUSBAND. Why, just simply this: it is that I have told my old woman not to intrude on my devotions; but, being the vixen that she is, who knows but what she may not peep and look in? in which case she would make a fine noise if there were no semblance [of a religious practice to be seen]; and so, though it is giving you a great deal of trouble, I wish you would oblige me by taking my place until my return.

SERVANT. Oh! it would be no trouble; but I shall get such a scolding if found out, that I would rather ask you to excuse me.

HUSBAND. What nonsense you talk! Do oblige me by taking my place; for I will not allow her to scold you.

SERVANT. Oh, sir! that is all very well; but pray excuse me for this time.

HUSBAND. No, no! you must please do this for me; for I will not so much as let her point a finger at you.

SERVANT. Please, please let me off!

HUSBAND. Gracious goodness! The fellow heeds what my wife says, and won't heed what I say myself! Do you mean that you have made up your mind to brave me?

[Threatening to beat him.]

SERVANT. Oh! I will obey.

HUSBAND. No, no! you mean to brave me?

SERVANT. Oh no, sir! surely I have no help but to obey.

HUSBAND. Really and truly?

SERVANT. Yes, really and truly.

HUSBAND. [My anger] was only a feint. Well, then, take my place, please.

SERVANT. Yes, to be sure; if it is your desire, I will do so.

HUSBAND. That is really too delightful. Just stop quiet while I set things to rights for you to sit in abstraction.

SERVANT. Your commands are laid to heart.

HUSBAND. Sit down here.

SERVANT. Oh! what an unexpected [honour]!

HUSBAND. Now, then; I fear it will be uncomfortable, but oblige me by putting your head under this "abstraction blanket."

SERVANT. Your commands are laid to heart.

HUSBAND. Well, it is scarcely necessary to say so; but even if my old woman should tell you to take off the "abstraction blanket," be sure not to do so until my return.

SERVANT. Of course not. I should not think of taking it off. Pray don't be alarmed.

HUSBAND. I will be back soon.

SERVANT. Please be good enough to return quickly.

HUSBAND. Ah! that is well over! No doubt Hana is waiting impatiently for me. I will make haste and go.

WIFE. I am mistress of this house. I perfectly understood my partner the first time he asked me not to come to him on account of the religious devotion which he was going to perform. But there is something suspicious in his insisting on it a second time with a "Don't come to look at me! don't come to look at me!" So I will just peep through some hidden corner, and see what the thing looks like. [Peeping.] What's this? Why, it seems much more uncomfortable than I had supposed! [Coming in and drawing near.] Please,

please; you told me not to come to you, and therefore I had intended not to do so; but I felt anxious, and so I have come. Won't you lift off that "abstraction blanket," and take something, if only a cup of tea, to unbend your mind a little? [*The figure under the blanket shakes its head.*] You are quite right. The thought of my being so disobedient and coming to you after the care you took to tell me not to intrude may justly rouse your anger; but please forgive my rudeness, and do please take that blanket off and repose yourself, do! [*The figure shakes its head again.*] You may say no again and again, but I *will* have it off. You *must* take it off. Do you hear? [*She pulls it off, and* TARAUHUWAZHIYA *stands exposed.*] What! you, you rascal? Where has my old man gone? Won't you speak? won't you speak?

SERVANT. Oh! I know nothing.

WIFE. Oh! how furious I am! Oh! how furious I am! Of course he must have gone to that woman's house. Won't you speak? won't you speak? I shall tear you in pieces!

SERVANT. In that case, how can I keep anything from you? Master has walked out to see Miss Hana.

WIFE. What! *Miss* Hana, do you say? Say *Minx*, say *Minx*. Gracious me, what a rage I am in! Then he really has gone to Hana's house, has he?

SERVANT. Yes, he really has gone there.

WIFE. Oh! when I hear he has gone to Hana's house, I feel all ablaze, and oh! in such a passion! oh! in such a passion!

[*She bursts out crying.*]

SERVANT. [Your tears] are but natural.

WIFE. Ah! I had meant not to let you go unhurt if you had kept it from me. But as you have told the truth, I forgive you. So get up.

SERVANT. I am extremely grateful for your kindness.

WIFE. Now tell me, how came you to be sitting there?

SERVANT. It was master's order that I should take his place; and so, although it was most repugnant to me, there was no alternative but for me to sit down, and I did so.

WIFE. Naturally. Now I want to ask you to do me a good turn. Will you?

SERVANT. Pray, what may it be?

WIFE. Why, just simply this: you will arrange the blanket on the top of me just as it was arranged on the top of you; won't you?

SERVANT. Oh! your commands ought of course to be laid to heart; but I shall get such a scolding if the thing becomes known, that I would rather ask you to excuse me.

WIFE. No, no! I will not allow him to scold you; so you must really please arrange me.

SERVANT. Please, please, let me off this time.

WIFE. No, no! you must arrange me, as I will not so much as let him point a finger at you.

SERVANT. Well, then, if it comes to my getting a scolding, I count on you, ma'am, as an intercessor.

WIFE. Of course. I will intercede for you; so do you please arrange me.

SERVANT. In that case, be so good as to sit down here.

WIFE. All right.

SERVANT. I fear it will be uncomfortable, but I must ask you to put your head under this.

WIFE. Please arrange me so that he cannot possibly know the difference [between us].

SERVANT. He will never know. It will do very nicely like this.

WIFE. Will it?

SERVANT. Yes.

WIFE. Well then! do you go and rest.

SERVANT. Your commands are laid to heart. [*He moves away.*]

WIFE. Wait a moment, Taraukuwazhiya!

SERVANT. Yes, ma'am.

WIFE. It is scarcely necessary to say so, but be sure not to tell him that it is I..

SERVANT. Of course not. I should not think of telling him.

WIFE. It has come to my ears that you have been secretly wishing for a purse and a silk wrapper. I will give you one of each which I have worked myself.

SERVANT. I am extremely grateful for your kindness.

WIFE. Now be off and rest.

SERVANT. Yes, ma'am.

[*Enter* HUSBAND *singing as he walks along the road.*]

HUSBAND. Why should the lonely sleeper heed
The midnight bell, the bird of dawn?
But ah! they're sorrowful indeed
When loosen'd was the damask zone.

Her image still, with locks that sleep
Had tangled, haunts me, and for aye;
Like willow-sprays where winds do sweep,
All tangled, too, my feelings lie.

As the world goes, it rarely happens even with the most ardent secret love; but in my case I never see her but what I care for her more and more:

'Twas in the spring-tide that we first did meet,
Nor e'en can I forget my flow'ret sweet.

Ah well! ah well! I keep talking like one in a dream, and meantime Taraukuwazhiya is sure to be impatiently awaiting me. I must get home. How will he have been keeping my place for me? I feel a bit uneasy.   [*He arrives at his house.*] Halloo! halloo! Taraukuwazhiya! I'm back! I'm back!   [*He enters the room.*] I'm just back. Poor fellow! the time must have seemed long to you. There now! [*Seating himself.*]   Well, I should like to tell you to take off the "abstraction blanket"; but you would probably feel ashamed at being exposed. Anyhow, I will relate to you what Hana said last night, if you care to listen. Do you? [*The figure nods acquiescence.*]   So you would like to? Well, then, I'll tell you all about it:
I made all the haste I could, but yet it

was nearly dark before I arrived; and I was just going to ask admittance, my thoughts full of how anxiously Hana must be waiting for me in her loneliness, saying, perhaps, with the Chinese poet:

"He promised, but he comes not, and I lie
on my pillow in the fifth watch of the night:
The wind shakes the pine-trees and the bamboos; can it be my beloved?"

when there comes borne to me the sound of her voice, humming as she sat alone:

"The breezes through the pine-trees moan,
The dying torch burns low;
Ah me! 'tis eerie all alone!
Say, will he come or no?"

So I gave a gentle rap on the back-door, on hearing which she cried out: "Who's there? who's there?" Well, a shower was falling at the time. So I answered by singing:

"Who comes to see you, Hana dear,
Regardless of the soaking rain?
And do your words, 'Who's there, who's there?'
Mean that you wait for lovers twain?"

to which Hana replied:

"What a fine joke! well, who can tell?
On such a dark and rainy night
Who ventures out must love me well,
And I, of course, must be polite,

and say: Pray, sir, pass this way!" and, with these words, she loosened the ring and staple with a cling-a-ring, and pushed open the door with a crick-a-tick; and, while the breeze from the bamboo-blind poured towards me laden with the scent of flowers, out she comes to me, and, "At your service, sir," says she, "though I am but a poor country maid." So in we went hand in hand to the parlour. But yet her first question, "Who's there?" had left me so doubtful as to whether she might not be playing a double game, that I turned my back on her, and said crossly that I supposed she had been expecting a number of lovers, and that the thought quite spoilt my pleasure. But oh! what a darling Hana is! Coming to my side and clasping tight my hand, she whispered, saying:

"If I do please you not, then from the first Better have said that I do please you not; But wherefore pledge your troth, and after turn
Against me? alas! alas!

Why be so angry? I am playing no double game." Then she asked why I had not brought you, Taraukuwazhiya, with me; and on my telling her the reason why you had remained at home, "Poor fellow!" said she, "how lonely he must be all by himself! Never was there a handier lad at everything than he, though doubtless it is a case of the mugwort planted among the hemp, which grows straight without need of twisting, and of the sand mixed with the mud, which gets black without need of dyeing, and it is his having been bound to you from a boy that has made him so genteel and so clever. Please always be a kind master to him." Yes, those are the things you have said of you when Hana is the speaker. As for my old vixen, she wouldn't let as much fall from her mug in the course of a century, I'll warrant! [Violent shaking under the blanket.] Then she asked me to pass into the inner room to rest awhile. So in we went to the inner room, hand in hand. And then she brought out wine and food, and pressed me to drink, so that what with drinking oneself, and passing the cup to her, and pressing each other to drink, we kept feasting until quite far into the night, when at her suggestion another room was sought, and a little repose taken. But soon day began to break, and I said I would go home. Then Hana exclaimed:

"Methought that when I met thee, dearest heart!
I'd tell thee all that swells within my breast:

But now already 'tis the hour to part,
And oh! how much still lingers un-express'd!

Please stay and rest a little longer!" "But no!" said I, "I must get home. All the temple-bells are a-ringing." "And heartless priests they are," cried she, "that ring them! Horrid wretches to begin their ding-dong, ding-dong, ding-dong, when it is still the middle of the night!" But for all her entreaties, and for all my own regrets, I remembered that "meeting is but parting," and,

Tearing me loose, I made to go; farewell! Farewell a thousand times, like ocean sands
Untold! and follow'd by her distant gaze I went; but as I turn'd me round, the moon,
A slender rim, sparkling remain'd behind, And oh! what pain it was to me to part!

[He shed tears.] And so I came home. Oh! isn't it a pity? [Weeping again.] Ah well! out of my heart's joy has flowed all this long history, and meanwhile you must be very uncomfortable. Take off that "abstraction blanket." Take it off, for I have nothing more to tell you. Gracious goodness! what a stickler you are! Well then! I must pull it off myself. I will have it off, man! do you hear me?

[He pulls off the blanket, and up jumps his wife.]

WIFE. Oh! how furious I am! Oh! how furious I am! To hoax me and go off to Hana in that manner!

HUSBAND. Oh! not at all, not at all! I never went to Hana. I have been performing my devotions, indeed I have.

WIFE. What! so he means to come and tell me that he has been performing his devotions? and then into the bargain to talk about "things the old vixen would never have let drop"! Oh! I'm all ablaze with rage! Hoaxing me and going off,— where? going off where? [Pursuing her husband round the stage.]

HUSBAND. Not at all, not at all! I never said anything of the kind. Do, do forgive me! do forgive me!

WIFE. Oh! how furious I am! Oh! how furious I am! Where have you been, sir? where have you been?

HUSBAND. Well then! why should I conceal it from you? I have been to pray both for your welfare and for my own at the Temple of the Five Hundred Disciples in Tsukushi.

WIFE. Oh! how furious I am! Oh! how furious I am! as if you could have got as far as the Five Hundred Disciples!

HUSBAND. Do, do forgive me! Do forgive me!

WIFE. Oh! how furious I am! Oh! how furious I am! [*The husband runs away.*]

Where's the unprincipled wretch off to? Is there nobody there? Please catch him! I won't let him escape! I won't let him escape!

NAKAMITSU

[MANJU]

By SEAMI

Written and produced probably in the early 15th century

TRANSLATED BY B. H. CHAMBERLIN

CHARACTERS

MITSUNAKA, *Lord of the Horse to the Emperor Mura-kami*

BIJIYAU, *son of* MITSUNAKA, *and still a boy*

NAKAMITSU, *retainer of* MITSUNAKA

KAUZHIYU, *son of* NAKAMITSU, *and foster-brother of* BIJIYAU

WESHIÑ, *Abbot of the great monastery on Mount Hiyei, near Kiyauto (Miaco)*

The Chorus

SCENE—*The Temple of Chiynuzañzhi, and my Lord* MITSUNAKA'S *palace in Kiyauto.*

TIME—*Early in the tenth century.*

PART I

NAKAMITSU. I am Nakamitsu, a man of the Fujihara clan, and retainer of Mitsunaka, Lord of Tada in the land of Setsushiu. Now you must know that my lord hath an only son, and him hath he sent to a certain monastery amid the mountains named Chiynuzañzhi, while I, too, have a son called Kauzhiyu, who is gone as page to young my lord. But young my lord doth not condescend to apply his mind unto study, loving rather nothing so well as to spend from morn to night in quar-relling and disturbance. Wherefore, thinking doubtless to disinherit young my lord, my lord already this many a time, hath sent his messengers to the temple with summons to return home to Kiyauto. Nevertheless as he cometh not, me hath he now sent on the same errand.

[*The above words are supposed to be spoken during the journey, and* NAKAMITSU *now arrives at the monastery.*]

Prithee! is any within?

KAUZHIYU. Who is it that deigneth to ask admittance?

NAKAMITSU. What! is that Kauzhiyu? Tell young my lord that I have come to fetch him home.

KAUZHIYU. Your commands shall be obeyed. [*He goes to his youthful master's apartment.*]

How shall I dare to address my lord? Nakamitsu is come to fetch my lord.

BIJIYAU. Call him hither.

KAUZHIYU. Your commands shall be obeyed. [*He returns to the outer hall and addresses his father.*]

Condescend to come this way.

[*They go to* BIJIYAU'S *apartment.*]

NAKAMITSU. It is long since I was last here.

BIJIYAU. And what is it that hath now brought thee?

NAKAMITSU. 'Tis that my lord your father hath sent me to bid your lordship follow me home without delay.

BIJIYAU. Shall I, then, go without saying anything to the priests my preceptors?

NAKAMITSU. Yes; if the priests be told, they will surely wish to see your lordship on the way, whereas my lord your father's commands were, that I alone was to escort you.

BIJIYAU. Then we will away.

NAKAMITSU. Kauzhiyu! thou, too, shalt accompany thy master.

KAUZHIYU. Your commands shall be obeyed.

[*They depart from the temple, and arrive at* MITSUNAKA'S *palace.*]

NAKAMITSU. How shall I dare to address my lord? I have brought hither his lordship Bijiyau.

MITSUNAKA. Well, Bijiyau! my only reason for sending thee up to the monastery was to help thy learning; and I would fain begin, by hearing thee read aloud from the Scriptures.

MITSUNAKA. And with these words, and bidding him read on,
He lays on ebon desk before his son
The sacred text in golden letters writ.

BIJIYAU. But how may he who never bent his wit
To make the pencil trace Asáka's line

Spell out one letter of the book divine?
In vain, in vain his sire's behest he hears:
Nought may he do but choke with idle tears.

MITSUNAKA. Ah! surely 'tis that, being my child, he respecteth the Scriptures too deeply, and chooseth not to read them except for purposes of devotion. What of verse-making, then?

BIJIYAU. I cannot make any.

MITSUNAKA. And music?

[BIJIYAU *makes no answer.*]

MITSUNAKA. What! no reply? Hast lost thy tongue, young fool?

CHORUS. Whom, then, to profit wentest thou to school?
And can it be that e'en a father's word,
Like snow that falling melts, is scarcely heard,
But 'tis unheeded? Ah! 'twill drive me wild
To point thee out to strangers as my child!
No sooner said, than out the scabbard flies
His trusty sword, and with fierce flashing eyes
Forward he darts; but, rushing in between,
Good Nakamitsu checks the bloody scene—
Firm though respectful, stays his master's arm,
And saves the lad from perilous alarm.

NAKAMITSU. Good my lord, deign to be merciful this once!

MITSUNAKA. Why stayedst thou my hand? Haste thou now and slay Bijiyau with this my sword.

NAKAMITSU. Your commands shall be obeyed.

[*He retires into another apartment.*]

What is this horror unutterable? 'Tis no mere passing fit of anger. What shall I do?—Ah! I have it! I have it! I will take upon myself to contrive some plan for his escape. Kauzhiyu, Kauzhiyu, art thou there?

KAUZHIYU. Behold me at thy service.

NAKAMITSU. Where is my lord Bijiyau?

KAUZHIYU. All my prayers have been unavailing to make him leave this spot.

NAKAMITSU. But why will he not seek refuge somewhere? Here am I come from my lord his father as a messenger of death!

[BIJIYAU *shows himself.*]

BIJIYAU. That I am alive here at this moment is thy doing. But through the lattice I heard my father's words to thee just now.

Little imports it an' I die or live,
But 'tis for thee I cannot choose but grieve
If thou do vex thy lord: to avert his ire
Strike off my head, and show it to my sire!

NAKAMITSU. My lord, deign to be calm! I will take upon myself to contrive some plan for your escape.—What! say you a messenger hath come? My heart sinks within me.—What! another messenger?

[*These are messengers from* MIT-SUNAKA *to ask whether his orders be not yet carried into execution.*]

NAKAMITSU. Alas! each joy, each grief we see unfurl'd
Rewards some action in a former world.

KAUZHIYU. In ages past thou sinnedst;

BIJIYAU. And to-day

CHORUS. Comes retribution: think not then to say
'Tis others' fault, nor foolishly upbraid
The lot thyself for thine own self hast made.
Say not the world's askew! with idle prate
Of never-ending grief the hour grows late.
Strike off my head! with many a tear he cries,
And might, in sooth, draw tears from any eyes.

NAKAMITSU. Ah! young my lord, were I but of like age with thee, how readily would I not redeem thy life at the cost of mine own! Alas! that so easy a sacrifice should not be possible!

KAUZHIYU. Father, I would make bold to speak a word unto thee.

NAKAMITSU. What may it be?

KAUZHIYU. 'Tis, father, that the words thou hast just spoken have found a lodgement in mine ears. Thy charge, truly, is Mitsunaka; but Mitsunaka's son is mine. This, if any, is a great occasion, and my years point to me as of right the chief actor in it. Be quick! be quick! strike off my head, and show it to Mitsunaka as the head of my lord Bijiyau!

NAKAMITSU. Thou'st spoken truly, Nakamitsu cries,
And the long sword from out his scabbard flies,
What time he strides behind his boy.

BIJIYAU. But no!
The youthful lord on such stupendous woe
May never gaze unmov'd; with bitter wail
The father's sleeve he clasps. Nought may't avail,
He weeping cries, e'en should the deed be done,
For I will slay myself if falls thy son.

KAUZHIYU. But 'tis the rule—a rule of good renown—
That for his lord a warrior must lay down
His lesser life.

BIJIYAU. But e'en if lesser, yet
He, too, is human; neither shouldst forget
What shame will e'er be mine if I survive.

NAKAMITSU. Alas! alas! and 'tis for death they strive!

KAUZHIYU. Me deign to hear.

BIJIYAU. No! mine the truer word!

NAKAMITSU. Ah! this my child!

KAUZHIYU. And there behold thy lord!

NAKAMITSU. Betwixt the two see Nakamitsu stand:

CHORUS. His own brave life, an' 'twere his lord's command,
Were freely giv'n; but now, in sore dismay,
E'en his fierce courage fades and droops away.

BIJIYAU. Why heed a life my sire himself holds cheap?
Nought may thy pity do but sink more deep
My soul in wretchedness.

KAUZHIYU. Mistake me not!
Think not 'tis pity moves me; but a blot

The martial honour of our house will
stain,
If, when I might have bled, my lord be
slain.
CHORUS. On either side 'tis infancy
that pleads.
NAKAMITSU. And yet how well they've
learnt where duty leads!
CHORUS. Dear is thy lord!
NAKAMITSU. And mine own child how
dear!
CHORUS. But Nakamitsu knows full
well that ne'er,
To save the child his craven heart ador'd,
Warrior yet dar'd lay hands upon his
lord.
He to the left, the trembling father cries,
Was sure my boy, nor lifts his tear-
stain'd eyes:
A flash, a moment, the fell sabre gleams,
And sends his infant to the land of
dreams.

NAKAMITSU. Oh, horror unutterable!
to think that I should have slain mine
own innocent child! But I must go and
inform my lord.
[He goes to MITSUNAKA'S apartment.]
How shall I dare to address my lord?
I have slain my lord Bijiyau according
to your commands.
MITSUNAKA. So thou has killed the
fellow? I trow his last moments were
those of a coward. Is it not true?
NAKAMITSU. Not so, my lord. As I
stood there aghast, holding in my hand
the sword your lordship gave me, your son
called out, "Why doth Nakamitsu thus de-
lay?" and those were the last words he
was pleased to utter.
MITSUNAKA. As thou well knowest,
Bijiyau was mine only child. Go and
call thy son Kauzhiyu, and I will adopt
him as mine heir.
NAKAMITSU. Kauzhiyu, my lord, in de-
spair at being separated from young my
lord, hath cut off his locks, and vanished
none knows whither.

NAKAMITSU. I, too, thy gracious li-
cense would obtain
Hence to depart, and in some holy fane
To join the priesthood.

MITSUNAKA. Harsh was my decree,
Yet can I think what thy heart's grief
must be
That as its own my recreant child re-
ceiv'd,
And now of both its children is bereav'd.
But 'tis a rule of universal sway
That a retainer ever must obey.
CHORUS. Thus would his lord, with
many a suasion fond,
Have rais'd poor Nakamitsu from despond.
Nor eke himself, with heart all stony
hard,
Mote, as a father, ev'ry pang discard:
Behold him now, oh! lamentable sight!
O'er his own son perform the fun'ral rite.

PART II

[Some time is supposed to have elapsed,
and WESHIÑ, abbot of the monastery
on Mount Hiyei, comes down from
that retreat to MITSUNAKA'S palace
in the capital, bringing with him
BIJIYAU, who had been persuaded by
NAKAMITSU to take refuge with the
holy man.]

WESHIÑ. I am the priest Weshiñ, and
am hastening on my way to my lord Mit-
sunaka's palace, whither certain motives
guide me. [They arrive at the gate, and
he cries out:] I would fain crave admit-
tance.
NAKAMITSU. Who is it that asks to be
admitted? Ah! 'tis his reverence Weshiñ.
WESHIÑ. Alas for poor Kauzhiyu!
NAKAMITSU. Yes; but prithee speak
not of this before his lordship.
WESHIÑ. I understand. Pray tell my
lord that I am come.
NAKAMITSU. Wait here, I pray thee,
while I go and inform his lordship.
[He goes to MITSUNAKA'S apartment.]
How shall I venture to address my lord?
His reverence Weshiñ hath arrived from
Mount Hiyei.
MITSUNAKA. Call him hither.
NAKAMITSU. Your commands shall be
obeyed. [He goes to the room where
WESHIÑ is waiting, and says:] Be pleased
to pass this way.
[They enter MITSUNAKA'S apartment.]

MITSUNAKA. What may it be that has brought your reverence here to-day?

WESHIN. 'Tis this, and this only. I come desiring to speak to your lordship anent my lord Bijiyau.

MITSUNAKA. Respecting him I gave orders to Nakamitsu, which orders have been carried out.

WESHIN. Ah! my lord, 'tis that, 'tis that I would discourse of. Be not agitated, but graciously deign to give me thine attention while I speak. Thou didst indeed command that my lord Bijiyau's head should be struck off. But never might Nakamitsu prevail upon himself to lay hands on one to whom, as his lord, he knew himself bound in reverence through all the changing scenes of the Three Worlds. Wherefore he slew his own son, Kauzhiyu, to save my lord Bijiyau's life. And now here I come bringing Bijiyau with me, and would humbly supplicate thee to forgive one who was so loved that a man hath given his own son in exchange for him.

MITSUNAKA. Then he *was* a coward, as I thought. Wherefore, if Kauzhiyu was sacrificed, did he, too, not slay himself?

WESHIN. My lord, put all other thoughts aside, and, if it be only as an act of piety towards Kauzhiyu's soul— Curse not thy son!

CHORUS. As thus the good man speaks, Tears of entreaty pour adown his cheeks. The father hears, and e'en his ruthless breast, Soft'ning at last, admits the fond request, While Nakamitsu, crowning their delight, The flow'ry wine brings forth, and cups that might Have serv'd the fays: but who would choose to set Their fav'rite's bliss that, home returning, met His grandsons' grandsons' still remoter line, Beside the joy that doth itself entwine Round the fond hearts of father and of son, Parted and now in the same life made one?

WESHIN. Prithee, Nakamitsu, wilt thou not dance and sing to us a while in honour of this halcyon hour?

[*During the following song* NAKAMITSU *dances.*]

NAKAMITSU. Water-bird, left all alone Now thy little mate hath flown, On the billows to and fro Flutter, flutter, full of woe!

CHORUS. Full of woe, so full of woe, Flutter, flutter, full of woe!

NAKAMITSU. Ah! if my darling were but here to-day I'd make the two together dance and play While I beat time, and, gazing on my boy, Instead of tears of grief, shed tears of joy!

CHORUS. Behold him weep!

NAKAMITSU. But the gay throng perceive Nought but the rhythmic waving of my sleeve,

CHORUS. Hither and thither flutt'ring in the wind,

NAKAMITSU. Above, beneath, with many a dewdrop lin'd!

CHORUS. Ah, dewy tears! in this our world of woe If any stay, the friends he loves must go: Thus 'tis ordain'd, and he that smiles to-day To-morrow owns blank desolation's sway. But now 'tis time to part, the good priest cries. Him his disciple follows, and they rise; While Nakamitsu, walking in their train, The palanquin escorts; for he would fain Last counsel give: "Beware, young lord, beware! Nor cease from toilsome study; for if e'er Thy sire again be anger'd, all is lost!" Then takes his leave, low bending to the dust. Forward they're borne; but Nakamitsu stays, [gaze, Watching and watching with heart-broken And, mutely weeping, thinks how ne'er again He'll see his child borne homeward o'er the plain.

FAIR LADIES AT A GAME OF POEM-CARDS

By CHIKAMATSU MONZAEMON

Produced in the early 18th century

TRANSLATED BY ASATARO MIYAMORA AND ROBERT NICHOLS *

I

During the reign of the Emperor Taka-kura, eighty-eighth emperor, it was Kiyo-mori, the Prime Minister, and his clan the Taira who in reality steered the ship of state and achieved the zenith of their prosperity. His son and heir, Shigémori, Lord Keeper of the Privy Seal, celebrated throughout Japan for his wisdom and virtue, for literary accomplishments and military proficiency, was an object of love and veneration among the warriors of the two greatest military houses, the Taira and the Minamoto. Among courtiers and court nobles he was also held in esteem, inasmuch as he was elder brother of the merciful and sagacious Empress Kenrei-Mon-in, mother of the Crown Prince shortly destined to become the Emperor Antoku.

On September the ninth, the Feast of the Chrysanthemum, of the first year of Yōwa, Lady Tonasé, chief lady-in-waiting, was despatched by the Empress as messenger to Shigémori. The warrior nobleman, having accorded her a hearty welcome, requested her to reveal her message.

"Permit me to congratulate your lord-ship upon this happy occasion," began Lady Tonasé. "Since the chrysanthemums are now in full bloom, Her Imperial Majesty graciously deems that the maple leaves upon the mountains must be at their best and accordingly desires to view them. It is therefore her Imperial pleasure that your lordship should order a mushroom picking party to be held upon Mount Kita according to annual custom."

"Your message delights me, my lady," replied Shigémori. "I had intended to transmit precisely this suggestion to Her Majesty. Pray tell Her Majesty that the mushroom picking party will take place on the twelfth and the moon viewing party on the thirteenth, and that I beg Her Majesty to prolong her visit upon the mountain for two or three days after the parties are over."

"The invitation gives me pleasure," returned the Imperial messenger. "I can well imagine what delight that will cause Her Majesty. The younger ladies-in-waiting, nay, even the more elderly, such as myself, always look forward with great pleasure to the two annual Imperial pic-nics, the flower viewing in spring and the maple-leaf viewing in autumn. Now I must hasten to return and report your lordship's kindly answer to my Imperial mistress. Well can I imagine the scarlet brocade upon the trees and the sweet music of the field insects. Since we have had fine weather for several days now the moon is sure to be bright and beautiful. We should all enjoy ourselves exceedingly.

* Reprinted from *Masterpieces of Chikamatsu*, published by E. P. Dutton & Co., by permission of the publishers.

I heartily thank your lordship's samurai in advance for the trouble they will be at in making the appropriate arrangements. I beg to take leave of your lordship." Her ceremonial speech ended, she returned to the Imperial palace.

Shigémori summoned his retainers, Morihisa, Moritsugu and Takiguchi and thus addressed them:—"The Imperial mushroom picking party is to be given on the twelfth. You must do your utmost, as is your wont each year, in the matter of escorting Her Imperial Majesty, in sweeping the mountain, and in building the temporary Imperial pavilion. Furthermore, Her Majesty being a great lover of song-birds, you are to place in front of the pavilion for her entertainment a large and beautiful cage containing many song-birds of the four seasons. I hear that the titmouse recently presented to me by Lord Kadowaki can perform several feats at suggestions of the hand, such for instance as passing through rings and drawing water. It were a somewhat childish thing in me to make much ado about such a bird; I therefore wish to make a present of it to Her Majesty. Takiguchi, this errand shall be yours. Make ready." With these words Shigémori entered the inner apartment.

Takiguchi was an extremely handsome youth of barely nineteen, a fitting envoy for such a task. He promptly trimmed himself up and set out for the Imperial palace accompanied by a henchman who carried the precious bird in a cage.

Now that the date for the mushroom picking party had been announced, the maids-of-honour impatiently awaited the day, not so much for the pleasure of the picnic as for the opportunities afforded of seeing young samurai. For the samurai and men-servants in the palace of the Empress were all men above sixty.

There were to be found among these court ladies two damsels in particular, exceedingly beautiful, named Yokobué and Karumo, both great favourites with the Empress on account of their personal grace, intelligence and sweetness of dis-

position. Their comrades too felt for them real affection. This day it was Yokobué's turn to serve as usher. She was on duty in the chamber. The other young ladies were gathered in the same chamber and were chattering merrily.

"Yokobué Dono," said one of them, "let us hope that on the occasion of the mushroom picking party we get plenty of chances to see handsome young samurai. I can't help wondering who will accompany Lord Shigémori on that day. What young men of the Taira clan will there be? What fun it will be if there are handsome young men among the attendants! But if it unfortunately turns out that only such warriors as the ferocious, woman-hating Lord of Noto should appear, a very poor time of it we shall get."

"Have no fear on that score," Karumo took up the tale. "Tastes differ. Lord Tsunémasa is commonly held to be the most handsome of the clan of Taira, but he is such a precocious boy that his voice broke at fourteen. Such a trifler too! I don't fancy him. Lord Atsumori is a simple-minded, lovable creature, but I fear he is already engaged to a certain lady. Master Moritsugu's younger brother, Yoshitsugu Dono, is a kind-hearted, lovable man I've no doubt, but that scorpion of a brother of his is so strict about his behaviour that not a girl can get near him. How can a woman choose her comrade for life when this is the case? We can but leave the matter to providence."

"I don't agree with you," said Yakumo and O-Hana simultaneously. "If we leave the matter entirely to providence it is probable that she will provide us with such boorish warriors as Kagékiyo or Gorōbyōé. How could one live a happy life with such a person as that? Master Morihisa certainly played a very pretty tune on the lute at last year's mushroom picnic on Mount Kita, but what an effeminate fellow he is! The gallant who suits the taste of everybody, high and low alike, the paragon of men, he is surely Master Saitō Takiguchi Yorikata. Don't you agree with me, Yokobué Dono?"

Yokobué met this banter with, "I don't share the opinion of any of you, my friends. You talk as if Master Takiguchi were the only handsome man in existence. He's handsome enough in all faith; nobody can call him ill-favoured; but such a person is always too conceited about his own good looks and usually spoilt and ill-natured into the bargain. I tell you I positively dislike him."

But this assertion only provoked an immediate burst of laughter.

"What a liar!" everyone cried. "The hypocrite! Nobody blames Karumo Dono who frankly states she thinks Master Yoshitsugu is the sort of man one could love. We hate such dishonesty in Yokobué Dono. You are loud in your protestations of dislike for Master Yorikata, but your tenderness of heart did not escape us when you were good enough to mend a burst seam of his *hakama* and we all know how you kissed its gusset at the football match at Lord Shigémori's house the other day. What's more you carried to your lips with obvious pleasure a towel with which he had wiped his mouth. And yet you dare to declare that you positively dislike him! What a little liar! Make a clean breast of it, Yokobué Dono! Confess! If you don't we'll untie your *obi* as a punishment and strip you to the skin. Come, girls, let's do it now!"

"Please forgive me!"

"Tickle her!" cried the girls, laughing. "Pinch her!"

It was at this moment that Takiguchi arrived before the porch and announced, "Saitō Takiguchi, a messenger from Lord Shigémori, desires to see the lady usher."

At this announcement the girls were overcome with merriment and excitement.

"Speak of angels——" one of them whispered, laughing. "Your beloved's come, Yokobué Dono!"

"Dear Yokobué," said another, "you're in luck to-day, being usher."

"I can never hope to be a *yokobué*, but I desire to be a *shakuhachi* and to be set to the mouth of that *takiguchi*."

"I should like to bring him tea."

They stole toward the paper doors of the porch and peeped through.

"I'd like to bite those lovely cheeks," one whispered.

"I'd like to be held so hard in his arms that I'd die."

The chatterboxes were startled to hear the voice of the chief lady of the court crying, not without asperity, "Girls, Her Majesty summons you! Her Majesty has clapped her hands several times. It's very thoughtless of you that not one of you is in attendance on Her Majesty."

"Gracious me! That old thunderstorm of a hag is blowing up again.' Hurry, lest the lightning strike you!"

The girls precipitated themselves into the inner apartments.

Yokobué, who had longed for Takiguchi, opened the doors. Her heart was violently beating. The words she pronounced were tremulous.

"Welcome, sir messenger."

Takiguchi, who had pined for the girl, was transported to see her before him. For a moment he was struck speechless. It was with an effort that he controlled himself sufficiently to say a moment later, "I beg to declare to you my errand. My Lord Shigémori orders me to announce that Her Imperial Majesty be requested to set out early in the morning of the day after to-morrow that she may visit Mount Kita."

His attitude underwent an abrupt change.

"I think and think of you till dawn breaks. All night I am awake thinking of you, so that I never meet you in dreams. By daylight your figure floats continually before me and comes before me and my duties. Passionately I long for you and most of all toward evening. A warrior ought never to shed tears, no, not even once between birth and the grave. Little befits it him to do so. And yet from morn to evening I find tears in my eyes. Can you guess who makes me weep? What nonsense I have been talking! Please forgive me! Well, as I was saying, this titmouse performs several tricks at suggestions made by the hand. She can pass through rings and draw water. Her name therefore is 'The Wonder of the Capital.' Lord Shigémori begs respectfuly to present this bird to Her Majesty since he knows her to be a great lover of songbirds. Now, my pretty"—he addressed the bird—"do some tricks for the entertainment of the lady usher."

So saying, Takiguchi made some passes with his hand, whereupon the little bird threw several somersaults round and round the perch—*hira-hira-hira, kuru-kuru-kuru.* Next the bird nimbly threaded the first, second, third, fourth and fifth rings. Now she hopped to the well and, seizing the rope with her beak, lifted the bucket and drew the water. This operation she repeated again and again—*shiton, shiton, shiton.*

"Oh, Yokobué Dono," said Takiguchi, not without significant glances, "I have improvised an ode on this dear little creature. Please listen:—

'The very titmouse hops through rings,
Draws water if my will so be;
I would that you would draw my heart
And through great trials come to me.'

If it's not asking you too much, would you be kind enough to make an ode in reply?"

Yokobué, so much entranced that she had noticed neither the bird nor Takiguchi's message, drew close to him, murmuring, "A delightful verse, dear Takiguchi";—she fell into a brown study, then her face brightened as if with a happy thought—"here is my reply," she said.

"The walnut which the titmouse loves
Lies fallen in the dingle, where
Scarlet the autumn maples burn
And you, my love, may find it there."

"You suggest that we meet secretly in the glen on Mount Kita at the mushroom hunting?"

"Exactly."

"I thank you. I shall not fail."

They drew nearer and embraced so passionately that they tilted the cage, which fell on its side. The bird's food and water rolled out, the rings lost their form. Panic-stricken, Takiguchi hurriedly opened the door of the cage, inserted both his hands and endeavoured to right the damage. But as fast as he pulled one piece straight another would go out of shape. Now he turned the cage upside down, now he laid it on its side, while the frightened bird struggled, flutter-flutter. In his confusion Takiguchi ignored for a moment or two the fact that the cage door was open. With a glad twitter the little prisoner escaped. Frantic with despair, the pair pursued the bird hither and thither around the garden. Takiguchi waved his hand, crying, "Come, my pretty!"—at which the titmouse somersaulted in the air two or three times, then, rejoicing in her freedom, sped away across the sky. Takiguchi and Yokobué stood watching the bird with a vacant stare. They were at their wits' end. They followed the bird with their eyes.

Kaga-no-Gunji Morotaka, police superintendent of the Empress' palace, younger brother to Lady Tonasé and a haughty, heartless old samurai who tyrannized over his subordinates, hearing of the occurrence, rushed out. To Takiguchi he did not vouchsafe a single word of greeting; Yokobué he seized by the arm. "Hussy!" he roared, bending upon her a withering glance. "Do you think this palace is a tea-house or a brothel? Even in the Emperor's palace certain rules of etiquette are observed in the conduct of messenger and usher. How much more then are they and must they be observed here, where almost every office, high and low, is occupied by a woman. Despite the eye I have been keeping on you, you have managed to behave with indecency, nay, the word indecent does not adequately describe your conduct. What is more, you have been so careless as to cause the escape of this precious bird. With these misdeeds to answer for how can you live on shamelessly and dare to show your face before people? Were you a samurai I could apportion you a certain heavy punishment for these serious offences. Since, however, you are a woman, I sentence you to imprisonment. Now, my men, bind Yokobué and be quick about it."

Takiguchi stepped forward and excitedly intervened.

"No, no, Morotaka Dono, Yokobué is not to blame. I am entirely responsible for this mishap. I am resolved to commit *seppuku* as apology. I cannot however allow what you said just now to pass unchallenged. What was your meaning when you said, 'Were you a samurai I could assign to you a certain heavy punishment'? I am a samurai; tell me what punishment you propose for me."

"You are overexcited. I never meant such punishment for you. Don't take what I said amiss. If any samurai under my command were guilty of such impropriety I could forthwith order him to be bound, decapitated and his head to be exposed. You, however, are a retainer of Lord Shigémori; therefore, though you should flirt with a maid-of-honour, pluck the titmouse's feathers, roast and eat it, whatever you might do would be of no consequence to me. If you care to commit *seppuku*, however, you are perfectly at liberty to do so. It would make no difference to the fate of Yokobué. Now, my men, why delay? Bind her at once and cast her into prison."

The desperate girl defied him.

"Morotaka Dono, blame yourself before you blame others. There is not one of us to whom you, superintendent as you are, have not written notes. What explanation have you for this foulness?"

Takiguchi laid his hand upon his sword.

"Morotaka," he cried, "I have no option but to believe Yokobué's charge. If it be indeed the law to bind a samurai and behead him for such offences, I, retainer of Lord Shigémori, will begin with you. Prepare yourself, you old fool!"

He rushed upon Morotaka, but the latter leapt back.

"Bind me if you can!" he replied.

None could tell what the outcome might be. Maids and henchmen, struck with terror, could but look at them with anxiety and fear.

At this juncture a voice was heard saying, "See that the quarrel is stopped." It was none other than the Empress, who had been informed of the incident and now stepped out on to the verandah. Upon which the maids cried all together, "It is Her Majesty's pleasure that you stop quarrelling!"

Both samurai instantaneously stopped and bowed their heads in respect.

"I cannot but consider," said the Empress, "that the report is false which accuses Yokobué of impropriety. If any of my maids were guilty of impropriety the blame would be upon Morotaka who is their superintendent. That Takiguchi has let the titmouse escape is no offence at all. Every time he gave the bird food and water he had to open the door of the cage. Is it to be wondered at that the caged bird longs for the blue sky and hungers for an opportunity to escape? Luckily enough the titmouse alighted in the inner garden and I myself have caught her and put her in the *fusege*. I learn that a large cage containing song-birds is to be ready for my diversion on Mount Kita. Takiguchi, tell Lord Shigémori that I will place the titmouse among the other birds and display her to his lordship. Yokobué and Takiguchi, be of good cheer about that bird. Girls, entertain Takiguchi with *saké* and give him refreshment. Be of good courage, Takiguchi, and present Lord Shigémori with my hearty thanks for his precious gift."

At these kindly words Takiguchi and Yokobué reverentially bowed their heads and gave way to tears of gratitude. Morotaka made a wry face and ground his teeth in mortification.

"And Morotaka," continued the Empress, turning her eyes upon him, "you are most strictly to command all under your authority never to say a word of what has happened to-day. Should they, in spite of your injunctions, mention this matter, it is you who will be held answerable for it."

Having thus spoken to the relief and satisfaction of all present save the old samurai, the Empress withdrew. The day of the picnic at last arrived. Shigémori, as host, had done all in his power to make the Imperial visit a success. On Mount Kita had been built a temporary pavilion beautifully thatched with scarlet maple leaves. In front of this was set a large cage containing hundreds of pretty birds, such as nightingales, wagtails, robins, parrots, tits and ducks. Their fine plumage shone brilliantly in the gold of the afternoon sun. They flitted hither and thither uttering sweet notes. The Empress and her retinue had that morning been escorted thither by a large number of Shigémori's retainers.

The Empress stepped down, advanced to the cage and contemplated the birds with seeming interest. Need attention be drawn to the fact that the titmouse presented by Shigémori was not to be found among them? The Empress had pretended that she had caught the bird in order to cover the fault of Takiguchi and his sweetheart.

"My Lord," said the Empress after a while, "I thank you for your kindness in diverting me with the sight of these beautiful birds. True, I enjoy the sight of them exceedingly, but even more joy will be mine at setting these birds free. It is said that even such little birds as these have the same Buddhist nature as ourselves. Permit me to set them at liberty."

So saying she opened the doors of the cage and let the birds escape. The little creatures, uttering cries of happiness, flew out and soared far away into the blue sky. Shigémori who, like his sister, was of a compassionate nature, was struck with admiration.

"This is a real *Hōjōé!*" he exclaimed. "I cannot but admire Your Majesty's benevolence. Your Majesty would do well to view the maple leaves and search for mushrooms to-morrow. Let us retire early this evening in order to enjoy the sound of the deer's cries in the stillness of the night."

So saying, both retired into the pavilion.

The night was far advanced; all was still. The mountain sides were obscure, for the thickets obstructed the brightness of the moonlight.

Yoshitsugu, a retainer of Shigémori and younger brother of Moritsugu, referred to above, had stolen from his post and was now standing, head and face swathed in a kerchief, by the hedge of the Imperial pavilion, the place of the assignation made between himself and his sweetheart Karumo, maid-of-honour. There was a love of long standing between them. Passionately had they desired to meet in secret; they had sworn to avail themselves of to-night's opportunity. Yokobué, who likewise had promised to meet her lover by stealth this night, arose when all her companions had fallen asleep. Now wearing a *katsugi* she stepped down to the hedge. She beckoned to the man in disguise. He advanced toward her readily enough. They conversed in nods and gestures and were in such a state of joyful excitement that they did not trouble to verify each other's identity. The young samurai lifted the damsel on to his back. In this manner their faces remained undisclosed to one another. The young samurai set out with a light heart toward the glen.

As for Karumo, intending to keep her word with Yoshitsugu, she stole out, also wearing a *katsugi*, at a moment when the position of the moon in the sky declared that midnight had passed. Now she awaited her lover's arrival. Takiguchi, with a kerchief about his head and face, emerged from the darkness intending to meet Yokobué. The expectant Karumo, as was only natural, mistook him for her sweetheart. She beckoned to him. Nor did Takiguchi harbour any doubts as to her identity. Hurriedly he hoisted her on to his back and hastened toward the glen. Presently the passionate lover found himself on the bank of a rivulet, along which he walked awhile, when, to his surprise, he overtook another man also with a woman on his back, toiling upstream. Each was equally scared and tried to avoid being seen by the other, but since they were colleagues by daylight it was not long before they recognized each other.

"Is it Takiguchi?"

"Yoshitsugu, is it?"

"You're in for luck, I too am enjoying myself. Ha! Ha!"

"Let us keep our sweet secrets to ourselves."

With that they parted and each hurried on his particular way. But the girls on their backs remarked to each other, "It would seem we have got mixed up. Are you not Yokobué Dono?"

"Is it Karumo Dono?"

"Eh? Have we got the wrong girls?" said one of the samurai. "We are a couple of fools!"

The two samurai lowered their lovely burdens. Each man removed his kerchief and each girl her veil. The four, to their vast surprise, realized the mistake that had been made. All burst out laughing.

"It would appear we have been overhasty! Had we not realized our mistake until a little later there is no knowing what might not have happened. We're lucky! Let each return his charge to the other none the worse."

They wandered no further. Each pair settled down in a chosen spot and enjoyed moments of supreme happiness.

At this moment a considerable body of men carrying sticks and paper lanterns appeared upon the further hillside. These lanterns bore upon them a crest which turned out to be none other than the butterfly of Morotaka, police superintendent of the Empress' court.

"Heaven defend us!" cried the samurai. "If our secret is detected by that fellow it will prove our ruin. Sweet ladies, do you think you could climb up the valley and find your way safely to the pavilion?"

"Of course. For love's sake we would be ready to tread upon sword-blades. As

for you, samurai, make haste and save yourselves."

Hastily bidding their lovers farewell the girls summoned up courage and hand in hand made their way up the glen. A happy thought came to Takiguchi in the shape of a plan to detain Morotaka in the wood sufficiently long to give the girls time to make good their return in his absence. He assumed Yokobué's katsugi that he might appear like a woman. So disguised, he waited near Yoshitsugu for Morotaka's coming.

Having searched here and there and all to no purpose, Morotaka cried, "No wonder Karumo and Yokobué are missing! I know who their seducers are! See, over there are some figures, down by the rivulet. Don't let them escape."

No sooner had he spoken than Morotaka and his followers swooped upon the erstwhile lovers and surrounded Yoshitsugu.

"Aha!" cried Morotaka in triumph. "So Yoshitsugu is the man, is he? Arrest him."

"An unjust charge!" cried Yoshitsugu, as if in confusion. "I came here but a few minutes ago to view the maple leaves by moonlight. That's the exact truth; I am not guilty of any such crime as seduction."

Hardly had he spoken when the superintendent roared, "No further lies, you rogue! That figure over there is Karumo, I'll be bound. It's two years now since my heart was set on her. Had she yielded to my wishes I intended to ask Her Majesty to bestow her on me as wife. It appears that I have wooed her day and night to no purpose, because of her attachment to you. I have long suspected the cause. You are a criminal who corrupts the morals of court ladies. Why, you're as good as the lover of my would-be wife! That woman standing there is an adulteress."

Morotaka rushed upon the supposed Karumo and snatched away the veil. What was his astonishment and fear to behold himself confronted by Takiguchi who glowered upon him, hand laid upon sword-hilt. But he recovered his presence of mind.

"If you're here," he said brusquely, "Yokobué must be hereabouts. You must have scented the danger and concealed her. Well, I shall inquire into this matter later. Let us return, my men."

Morotaka beat a retreat; but Yoshitsugu and Takiguchi made haste to intercept him in a threatening fashion.

"There's no 'later on' about it, you old fool," they said. "We want justice here and now. Do you think you can make off with impunity, after snatching a veil from one samurai and seeing fit to call the other a seducer of women? You can't behave with us as you behave when you lord it over the Empress's court and thunder at the maids-of-honour. Just you try to return to the pavilion without first explaining those insults and you'll find, if these swords can speak, that you'll have no legs to walk on!"

"Calm yourselves, sirs," replied Morotaka, not without trepidation. "It is Yokobué and Karumo whom I call corrupters of morals. As their superintendent it is my duty to inquire into every particular of these happenings, but with you I have nothing to do. If my words offend you I pray your forgiveness and throw myself upon your generosity."

"Sir Superintendent," returned Takiguchi provocatively, "but a few minutes ago you confessed that during the last few years your heart has been set upon Karumo and that you have wooed her day and night. Who then is her seducer if it isn't you? As you yourself were good enough to remark at court the other day, such an offender as yourself richly deserves to be bound and decapitated. Now, Yoshitsugu, bind this fellow! I'll behead him. His retainers too we will chasten. See that they don't escape."

At this threat Morotaka's henchmen threw down their sticks and lanterns and ran for their lives.

"How mercilessly you have argued me down!" cried the deserted Morotaka.

"But you wait! I'll show you how I'll be revenged on Yokobué and Karumo!" So saying, he precipitantly took to his heels.

The two samurai burst into uproarious laughter; then they made their way back to the pavilion at their leisure.

II

Takiguchi's father, Katsuyori, was an old samurai with a record of long service under Shigémori and Shigémori's father, Kiyomori. He had abandoned the profession of arms, had shaved his head, hoary with the snows of seventy winters, and, having assumed the sacerdotal name of Sairai and having donned a *henzan* (clerical robe), now led a life of abstinence and devotion and made it his daily task to visit the family temple that he might worship Buddha.

One day Sairai, producing an *eboshi* and a beautiful *kariginu*, summoned his son Takiguchi and spoke as follows: "These articles were the gift of Lord Shigémori to me many years ago on the occasion of a grand banquet to the ministers of state. I wore them and, in company with my colleagues, received the guests. I make them yours. As heir of our house, you are to wear them on public occasions. Up to now I have not heard any reports, favourable or unfavourable, concerning the manner in which you discharge your duties. Tell me how you stand in the graces of your lord?"

"My dear father," respectfully returned Takiguchi, "albeit my ability is small, I stand, thanks to your influence, higher in his lordship's favour than any of my comrades. Such pleasure does this give me that I serve his lordship with all the loyalty of which I am capable and attend to my duties with the utmost diligence. Furthermore, Her Imperial Majesty is pleased to regard me with a special favour, so that I am entrusted with all messages to Her Majesty's court. Thus, upon the occasion of the recent picnic upon Mount Kita, I often had the honour of being summoned to Her Imperial presence for this purpose or that. Also I was made much of by the maids-of-honour and my colleagues. Under these circumstances I am not without hopes that, thanks to his lordship's authority and your influence, I may shortly receive promotion."

Hardly had he uttered these words when Sairai glowered upon him and roared, "Silence, silence! Listen to me, you brazen-faced boy! In your foolishness you are bold enough to suppose that I have no knowledge of your behaviour. Forasmuch as I have retired from the world I have no particular business with it, but waking or dreaming I never cease to consider your well-being. Indeed, I give more thought to that than to my future happiness. I am ever all ears to pick up any rumour, good or bad, concerning you. You need not therefore presume to suppose that your movements escape me. I know very well how infatuated you are with a maid-of-honour named Yokobué. You made such a fool of yourself flirting with her that you let the titmouse, intended for the Empress, escape. For that you were severely reprimanded by the superintendent Morotaka, who sentenced you to a heavy punishment from which Her Majesty's mercy alone released you. That ignominious news came to my ears the very day of the incident itself. As if this mishap were not sufficient warning, you shamelessly misconducted yourself, as I hear, under cover of night with Yokobué on the occasion of the Imperial picnic on Mount Kita. Caught in the act by Morotaka, notwithstanding the multitude of your shortcomings, you yet managed to turn the tables upon your accuser. What behaviour! What audacity! Even I in my retirement have heard the circumstances. That it should have reached my ears is a sure sign that the story is common property, and what the general public knows must of course have reached the ears of the mighty Lord Shigémori. You must know that Lord Shigémori is the wisest man alive and, albeit his lordship does not let his feelings show in his countenance, yet one can hardly doubt but that his lordship has given you up as a good-for-nothing. Without the protection of his lordship our house is bound sooner or later to come to ruin. I grieve for this. You must know how true the story is better than any one else. The report goes abroad that your boon companion, Yoshitsugu, like you was carrying on an affair with a maid-of-honour. Her name is Karumo and she is pregnant by him. It is further asserted that his brother, Moritsugu, keeps him confined to his house on the score of pretended sickness. If I follow his example and confine or disown you, our house, since I have no other son, will become extinct. How can I on your account suffer our house to come to extinction? Our house which, for generation after generation, has served in vassalage the great family of Taira. It had been my hope to continue my life in comfortable seclusion on the pension graciously bestowed upon me by my lord and to have devoted my remaining years to the attainment of spiritual enlightenment and to prayer, that I may live happily in the Pure Land with your dear mother. Alas! Your behaviour has entirely undone my hopes; nay, your sins will bring us to hell. Undutiful wretch!" —he burst into warm tears—"but what good can come of reviling a devil? From to-day on I return to my secular life and once again serve Lord Shigémori as warrior. I am no longer Sairai but Katsuyori! My seven long years of abstinence and devotion are now at an end!"

With these words he slipped from off him the clerical robe and assumed the *eboshi* and the *kariginu*. Takiguchi, overwhelmed by tears, clung to him exclaiming, "Not so, father! I declare to you that I will once for all give up my love. I will start a new life and serve my lord to the best of my ability. Pray forgive my errors, father."

The old man pushed him aside.

"A father may well forgive you, but

how can we apologize to my lord and to the world at large? I hardly see how you can remain in your present position." He rose to his feet and took both his swords in his hand.

"Listen, my men," he cried with an air of determination, "make yourselves ready to follow me! Saitō Katsuyori is once again about to serve Lord Shigémori as a warrior!"

With that he entered the inner chamber. Takiguchi was at his wits' end. His sobbing was followed by a melancholy reverie. At length he roused himself, slapped his thigh and thus communed with his spirit: "That's how it stands, is it? My tears are vain. The reproaches of my father are reasonable, but what is done is done. Nothing will be gained by weeping over a past error. I must do something to atone for my fault. Should I attain to spiritual rebirth my wise and compassionate lord would pardon me and my past would be wiped out. But ah, what shame it is to think how I have stood in the way of my father's spiritual enlightenment and of the peace of my mother's soul! That is indeed a greater sin than the Eight Crimes, the Five Crimes and the Ten Evils rolled in one. Well, let me follow the example of Mongaku, who took to the priesthood in consequence of the great love he bore a lady and in time was enabled to lead all his relations to the Pure Land. Life is after all but a dream; reputation and infamy illusions; hatred and compassion but reflections quivering upon the water. Let me hope that my mistake in love will prove but a first step upon the path of spiritual enlightenment. Yokobué will doubtless grieve at my resolution. But she will offer up prayers to meet me and I too will pray for future happiness until such a time as we two are again joined together in the Pure Land. Now is the time for me to make my resolution"— he drew his dirk, cut off his queue and, reverently taking up his father's clerical robe, slipped it over his clothes—"I thank you, father, for your kindly hint. My living father, my dead mother, my sweetheart and I—do we not all aim at attaining a new life in the lotus flower! Namu Amida Buddha." He prepared himself for a journey, then stole out to find his way to some Buddhist temple.

Karumo, having repeatedly met her lover in secret, now found herself, to her great mortification, pregnant. The scandal had spread beyond court circles. Very much ashamed of herself, she again and again begged dismissal, but Morotaka prevented her discharge. She remained in her chamber; her comrades were strictly forbidden to pay her visits of sympathy; two or three maids were permitted to serve her. Under such circumstances the girl's heart was heavy with shame and grief; her tears fell without ceasing.

One day Morotaka, followed by his retainer Iwamura Gengo and by servants bearing a palanquin, intruded upon her in her room.

"Karumo," said he, assuming a severe air, "this is indeed licentious conduct of yours, that you, a woman in the Imperial service, should over and over again have stolen out of the strictly guarded palace gate to a clandestine meeting until at last you have become great with child. You presume too much in begging for your mere dismissal after the committal of such grave offences. You will have heard, I am sure, that your lover Yoshitsugu is confined to his room by his brother's command. As to your own offence, forasmuch as you are in the Imperial service, the laws require that you be heavily punished. But for all that, my heart, which has been set on you all these years, remains the same toward you as before the event. Come, will you not change your mind and, mindful of all my notes to you, tell me in one word that you are mine? Pronounce the word and I will at once take you to my residence. You shall become my wife and be honoured as such, and this palanquin shall be your bridal palanquin. If, however, you answer 'no,' this palanquin shall be a prisoner's palanquin. Answer 'yes' or 'no' promptly. Remember that this pressure I put upon you is entirely because I am enamoured of you."

The old satyr, who had spoken in a coaxing tone, now concluded and cast sheep's eyes toward the lady.

"It is very kind of you," answered Karumo with a forced smile, "not only not to hate me, though my offence is heavy, but to offer to take me to yourself as your lady. Many thanks for your attentions; I am minded to become your wife, but I very much fear me that Yoshitsugu will hardly give his consent. What would you do should he refuse?"

"Have no fears on that score. No difficulty would be experienced in disposing of that fellow on the pretext of an Imperial order. Well then, we may consider the bargain struck. Be happy my girl."

"Shall I arrange for a discreet abortion or may I give birth to my child, sir?"

"An arrangement of that sort is apt to be dangerous to the mother, so I won't have it. A child is indeed a somewhat unacceptable remembrance of an unfortunate episode; but for my sweet girl's sake I would have it enjoy an easy and natural birth. And if it be a boy I will adopt it as my son and heir."

"There's the rub, sir. This child is Yoshitsugu's son. When he grows up and discovers you are his father's murderer I hardly see how he can fail to plan your death. What would you do then?"

"Oh, kill the young devil. Don't worry about that!"

He had hardly answered when Karumo angrily broke in.

"Do you indeed deem me such a nerveless kind of woman as would be contented to remain the wife of the murderer of her sweetheart and child? The devil take you! Love is everything with a real man or woman. For its sweet sake one takes no care for one's life. It was not because I wished to escape death or preserve my name untarnished that I sought dismissal. My object was, the displeasure of Yoshitsugu's brother being known to me, to visit Yoshitsugu and share his fate. Were I a woman forsaken by all the Gods and by Buddha, were I, I say, such a woman, I might consent to be your wife. Nothing however is further from my present intentions. Most willingly would I forfeit my life for my sweet love's sake. Wreak your vengeance on me, you rascal! Take your fill of it! My only grief is to imagine with what severity you may visit yourself upon Yoshitsugu, doing so under the pretence of an Imperial order. Mean and merciless man that you are! Do you think you can live for ever? Everyone is doomed to die once. Do you imagine there is no future world? That divine justice knows no way to retribution? If you think so, you are but a thoughtless shallow-pate."

With such reproaches the luckless girl sought to overwhelm him until at last she sank to the floor, weeping the bitterest tears. These many insults had their effect upon Morotaka, who flew into a tremendous passion.

"Iwamura Gengo!" he cried. "This wench's reckoning is made up. Away with her to Funaoka-Yama and do with her as I bade you!"

"I will, my lord."

Gengo gripped the damsel by one arm and by the hair, forced her face down toward the floor and thrust her into the palanquin. Her maids, in tears, did their best to prevent this, but Gengo, either pushing them aside or kicking them down, motioned to the servants to carry the palanquin away to Funaoka-Yama. He himself headed the little procession.

Takiguchi had sought refuge in the Ōjōin, a Buddhist temple in the farthest corner of the lonely country district of Saga, which lies many miles west of the capital. He entered the priesthood, assumed the sacerdotal name of Saishun, but soon found the temple was too near the capital for him to be able to apply himself wholly to the life of devotion. Tidings of what passed in the capital occasionally reached his ear and disturbed his quiet study of the scriptures. He therefore resolved to go to the great monastery of Kōyasan, one of the holiest spots in Japan, and which is at a great distance from the capital; but though he had resolved upon this change, he still lingered in the Ōjōin and nightly visited cemeteries in the neighbourhood of the capital. In these cemeteries it was his practice loudly to chant prayers, striking with a stick at the same time upon a small bell that hung about his neck. This he did by way of bidding an eternal farewell to his birthplace and by way of praying for the peace of his dead mother's spirit and his father's future bliss.

One evening Takiguchi found himself in such a cemetery at Funaoka-Yama. He prayed at all the new made graves in succession. Here the smoke from one cremation died away; yonder arose the smoke from another—both smokes symbolizing the uncertainty of human life. He who had been left behind by one who had already taken the journey of the spirit, now, in his turn, left behind another fellow-traveller who would follow him the next day. Takiguchi found himself pleased in reflecting that he had become a priest praying for the departed. Again he sounded his bell, fervently praying the while, "Namu Amida! Namu Amida! Namu Amida Buddha! Show thy mercy upon all creatures. May all aspire to Buddhahood. Amen."

At that moment a warrior appeared accompanied by some soldiers who bore a palanquin. The warrior glanced hither and thither about the burial-ground, then, selecting a spot overshadowed by a tall pine-tree, ordered the palanquin to be set down.

"Another dead person," Takiguchi thought to himself. "Poor soul—already hastening on the journey to Hades. But sooner or later one and all are bound to follow him." And, unnoticed, he murmured a prayer for the supposed deceased.

The soldiers dragged the occupant forth from the palanquin. To Takiguchi's great astonishment it proved not a corpse but a damsel of noble appearance.

All agog to know what was about to happen, our hero hid himself behind a tombstone. Iwamura Gengo, for it was none but he, cried, "Now, Karumo, face your last moment! Once your head falls all is over. It is my master Lord Morotaka's pleasure that you be beheaded at once, but it seems to me a distinct pity that this should occur. Come, can't you see how cruel it is to let the child now in your womb be slain along with you, thus suffering it not to see the light? Neither living nor dead can you expect to meet your sweetheart again, so as far as that matter is concerned there is nothing to choose between them. But if you consent to become Lord Morotaka's lady there is not one of us who will not regard you with the respect due to you as our mistress. Ponder the question well before you answer."

"A saucy fellow! You will remember I refused to answer even your master— why should I change my mind? Don't disturb my preparations for the future life by provoking me at the last moment, but cut off my head and be quick about it."

"A stiff-necked woman! Die then!"

Gengo drew his sword and took station behind her, but, before his blade could flash down, Takiguchi rushed forward and shielded Karumo.

"One moment, sir!"

"Out, fool of a priest! Do you dare plead for this girl's life? No, that's impossible."

"That is not my meaning, sir. I am a priest who nightly visits these cemeteries to pray for the dead. You are, it would appear, about to kill this woman for some grave offence. 'Sin reaps its reward'; that is inevitable. But you have said the woman is pregnant. Are you going to slay the guiltless with the guilty? What do you think can be your reward for such a deed? We do not know the child's age, but as many months as it has lived will it have patron Gods and

Buddhas. Queen Maya's Scripture runs, that the wrath of such patrons and Gods descends upon the infanticide, who will presently be seized with an incurable disease or perish by the sword, cut off before a year is out. Nevertheless it is sometimes necessary for a warrior to kill a pregnant woman. In such a case he can divert the divine wrath from his head by the triple repetition of a mystic formula before he commits the deed. There's nothing for it apparently but to slay this poor girl; but, inasmuch as I am acquainted with the formula, it would be wanton cruelty on my part not to try and save you from such punishment. Of a truth I feel very sorry for you and that is the reason why I have momentarily stayed your hand."

"Are these things true?" exclaimed Gengo, overcome by surprise and fear. "I never dreamed of such things. A thousand thanks to you, kind and reverend sir. If it's not asking too much of you, would you please be so good as to teach me the formula?"

"I learned this formula after three weeks' practice of religious austerities and it is one of my greatest secrets; but I can hardly refuse to instruct you in it when it is a case of sudden death for you if I do not. Be sure, however, never to teach it to others."

Having thus cautioned him, Takiguchi whispered in the warrior's ear, "*Riken sokuzé Mida-gō* (The title of Amida is a sharp sword to cut off thy sins with) *Isshō shōnen zaikaijo* (If thou once sayest 'Namu Amida' thou shalt be absolved from all thy sins). Repeat this formula thrice before you kill this woman and no evil shall come to you after the deed. Should evil fall on you, however small, I will make atonement for it."

"Dear me! How hard the formula is! I shall never be able to learn it. Isn't there a shorter form?—one easier to learn?"

"Hand me your sword. I'll enchant its blade by repeating the formula over it.

And that will be as good as if you repeated the formula itself."

"Excellent! Please be so good as to enchant my sword for me."

So saying, Gengo, without the least misgiving, handed the delighted Takiguchi the drawn sword.

"Well, sir," said Takiguchi sarcastically, "I observe that after all you won't need the formula or any other thing of that kind; for since the girl is now not going to be killed neither retribution nor curse will fall upon you."

"Impostor of a priest!" roared Gengo, flying into a great rage. "Was this all a trick to rob me of my sword? How can I suffer you to remain in possession of that sword? What a fool you are to lose your life in the senseless attempt to save the life of a sinner! Prepare to die!"

He sprang at Takiguchi. Takiguchi dodged.

"Come, come," he cried, "it's unreasonable of you, a mere layman, to try and recover what has come into a priest's possession. I will now proceed to take this girl too"—he placed his hand upon Karumo's—"Taste the sharpness of Amida's sword!"

With these words he lifted the sword.

"Insolent priest!" cried Gengo and the soldiers and precipitated themselves upon him. Hither and thither Takiguchi whirled the blade. His adversaries, finding themselves no match for him, were not long in taking to their heels. Gengo, however, eager to recover his sword, ambushed himself behind a large tombstone. Presently the soldiers returned and attacked Takiguchi from right and left simultaneously. Again Takiguchi whirled the blade with such dexterity that, as he advanced upon them, they were at last reduced to standing at bay against the tombstone. Takiguchi pressed them and suddenly the tombstone, heavy as it was, toppled over upon the hidden Gengo and crushed him to death. The panic-stricken soldiers sought safety in flight. Takiguchi returned to the girl.

"Can you recognize me, Karumo Dono?"

"Can I believe that you are Master Takiguchi? A thousand thanks to you. But for your assistance I should by now be dead; but I cannot suppress my surprise at finding you a priest."

"We will speak of such things at leisure. Here we should linger no further." Takiguchi hoisted the girl on his back and hurried away.

III

Shigémori, Lord Keeper of the Privy Seal, who was Leniency and Sympathy incarnate, not only refused to sit in judgment upon the misbehaviour of Yoshitsugu and Takiguchi, but even went so far as to feign perfect ignorance of the scandal. Among his retainers, and among his younger warriors in particular, the affair was a subject of frequent gossip. "Poor soul!" Takiguchi's friends whispered, "Takiguchi, led astray by the wanton Yoshitsugu, has come to ruin. Yoshitsugu is the cause of all his troubles." While those who sympathized with Yoshitsugu murmured, "Yoshitsugu, through keeping company with the lecherous Takiguchi, has earned a bad name for himself. A man is known by the company he keeps, good or bad. Yoshitsugu's brother, Moritsugu, has also lost in reputation on account of Takiguchi. Moritsugu's anguish is sure sooner or later to give rise to a quarrel between him and Takiguchi's father, Katsuyori."

Subject to this tittle-tattle, which rose whenever and wherever Shigémori's retainers were gathered together, Katsuyori and Moritsugu became little by little estranged, to such an extent that at last a hidden feud arose between them. One day Moritsugu came to duty in the drawing-room of Shigémori's palace and was there greeted by those young samurai who sympathized with his brother. They saluted him with enthusiasm.

"Master Moritsugu, we are delighted to see you. It grieves us to hear of your brother's lot. We young men are apt to be led into youthful follies by bad companions. We wish to say how deeply we sympathize with you and your brother."

"Many thanks for your sympathy, my friends, but you are misinformed. The truth is, Yoshitsugu is seriously ill."

Hardly had Moritsugu seated himself when Katsuyori, who as ill luck would have it happened to be his appointed comrade on duty for this day, appeared. He wore an *eboshi* (official head-gear) pressed down to the eyes to conceal his shaven head. Takiguchi's friends gave him a hearty welcome.

"We hear your son, Takiguchi Dono, has forsaken the world. What a pity! But it is always one's friends who lead one to fame or to ruin and, as the Chinese proverb runs, 'To such as possesses three good friends, three bad Dame Fortune also sends.' He's a lucky man who never meets either a bad friend or a whirlwind. We can well imagine how you feel towards your former friend."

Katsuyori made his salute to Moritsugu, then, like the haughty old samurai he was, took a seat higher than Moritsugu's.

"How now! Priest Sairai!" exclaimed the indignant Moritsugu, "I can't but think your aged eyes fail to recognize me. Know then that I am Moritsugu. You have taken the wrong seat. Take a lower."

"Eh?" replied Katsuyori in scorn. "Believe me, my aged eyes don't fail to recognize my colleague's face. Albeit you are not yet well on in years, your memory seems to fail you with regrettable ease. Kindly recall to yourself that you are of the Fifth Grade in court rank, while I am of the Fourth. There is therefore nothing incorrect in my sitting above you. A very forgetful person evidently! A few drops of medicine might indeed be efficacious in restoring your health and memory."

"Insolent dotard! Take a lower seat and be quick about it, or I will pull you down to a lower. And if I resort to force your hat may slip off and your shiny pate appear, to your shame and humiliation. Perhaps you would prefer that, eh?"

So saying, Moritsugu pressed against the old warrior.

"So you despise me because of my old age? Seize me by the arm if you choose. What new-fangled notion of etiquette is it that requires a samurai of the Fourth Grade to sit below another of the Fifth? Where is the authority enables you to insist upon it? Come, give me a reason, you green boy!"

"You're in your dotage all right," returned Moritsugu, in no whit discomposed. "Fourth Grade, Coarse Grade! True you are of the Fourth Grade, but aren't you also a lay-brother and consequently out of office and service? In point of fact it's your son Takiguchi's turn to be on duty, but there are those that say that, ashamed of his past bad behaviour and consequent ill reputation, he has seen fit to forsake the ways of the wicked world. It is as well that he has done so. Had he remained in office, any young samurai who might have continued as his friends and colleagues could only have followed his bad example and shared his degradation. Takiguchi's punishment, however, depends upon the pleasure of our lord, and whether he will be ordered to commit suicide or will be beheaded none can tell. I understand that, acting on the supposition that your son's forsaking of the world saved him from punishment, you have returned to secular life and are once more in his lordship's service. To-day I meet you in your second service for the first time. You see there has been no change in our turns of service for some considerable time and to-day Takiguchi and I are to be on duty together. You appear then to-day as Takiguchi's substitute. Now I, Moritsugu, am of the Fifth Grade, while Takiguchi is of the Sixth; and I have never sat below your son. Accordingly you, as his substitute, should sit below me. If I am wrong pray correct me at once."

"So!" sneered Katsuyori. "No more cavilling, please, about the ordering of our seats. You would seem to blame me for having permitted Takiguchi to forsake the world sooner than await our lord's punishment, but, if it be our lord's pleasure to have him recalled for self-slaughter or for decapitation, I can so call him back. Since when has it become impossible to punish one who has forsaken the world? As for your brother, Yoshitsugu, is it not everyone's secret that you have confined him to your house, alleging illness, the better in your cowardice to cover up the ill name his bad behaviour has earned him? It is as well that you have done so. Were such a man as he allowed to remain in office, the young samurai, his friends and colleagues, would be bound to follow his bad example and this would lead to their utter degradation. But were our lord, out of his great mercy, to employ him again without first punishing him, you would, I suppose, have the unblushing impudence to permit him to return to service among the other samurai. No man of honour of course could do such a thing, but we all know that, as the saying goes, the scarlet-faced ape laughs at the golden face of the Lord Buddha when he marks the difference in their complexions!"

"Well, well. And another saying goes, the crab who walks sideways laughs at the man who walks forward."

"And the green persimmon, so they say, laughs at the sweet persimmon in the beak of the crow."

"And the man crucified head downward, so I've heard, dies of laughing at an exposed head because it's set forsooth below his feet."

"You seem to speak from experience."

"You perhaps have never seen steel? Shall I let you have a taste of it?"

"Do you think you can do that?"

"Why not? I will oblige you this minute if you wish it."

The excited couple prepared to draw their swords and forthwith all the other samurai, taking sides, assumed defiant attitudes. A period of breathless suspense followed. It was broken by the startling announcement that a messenger from the Empress had this moment arrived. A moment later Shigémori made his appearance and seated himself on the dais. All kneeled reverently. Morotaka, for it was he, addressed Lord Shigémori.

"I beg to deliver my message to your lordship. Recently two court ladies, named respectively Yokobué and Karumo, indulged themselves with Takiguchi and Yoshitsugu. This has occasioned great scandal and disaffection at court. Furthermore, Karumo became pregnant and could no longer remain in service. Her Imperial Majesty, grievously offended with her, ordered me to put a period to her existence. Finding it impossible to disobey the Imperial command, I ordered the damsel to be taken to Funaoka-Yama for execution. Her decapitation was imminent when an unknown stranger, suddenly falling upon my retainer, Iwamura Gengo the executioner, murdered him and carried the prisoner whither none knows. It can hardly be doubted that the rogue in question is Karumo's lover Yoshitsugu. This heinous crime, by which the law has been set at naught and the Imperial will flouted, has much incensed Her Majesty. She requires that Yoshitsugu be instantly executed. Yokobué is to be beheaded at court. Her Majesty will let your lordship know later on the arrangements made for this ceremony. Allow me to repeat once more that it is Her Majesty's pleasure that Yoshitsugu be forthwith beheaded."

"An infamous order!" exclaimed Shigémori after a brief silence. "The like of which has never been heard of before. Izumi Shikibu indulged herself with Hirai-no-Yasumasa and later with Tachibana-no-Michisada, by whom she became the mother of Koshikibu, the poetess. There are the cases too of Akazomé Emon and Nakano Kwampaku; also of Murasaki Shikibu with Nishinomiya-no-Sadaijin. All the above affairs took place while the ladies were in the Imperial service and yet Jōtō-Mon-in, the Empress then reigning, inflicted upon them no punishment

whatever. Thus, not only were these ladies spared any disgrace, but have left behind them undying names as authoresses. With these precedents before my eyes, I cannot but deem the present Imperial order of an excessive severity. Surely, Morotaka, you and your sister Lady Tonasé must have joined in remonstrating with Her Majesty?"

"Yes, my lord, my sister and I again and again importuned our Imperial mistress, but with no result. Since Her Majesty is your lordship's sister and comes of a military family she ordains everything according to the manners and customs of the military classes."

"There you err. The Imperial order is contrary to the rules of the military class. I would draw your attention to the fact that the executioner Gengo, in having Karumo carried off, did not act according to the manners that obtain among warriors. Do you suppose that the strict guard kept over a criminal with drawn spears and naked halberds is merely an arrangement made for the safety of the condemned? Is it not also to fend off any violence that may be indulged in by his comrades and relatives? It appears to me to have been an uncommon piece of carelessness on his part that Gengo should not only have permitted his prisoner to be snatched from him, but also to have suffered the loss of his own life. The corpse of so foolish a warrior should undoubtedly be crucified; his relatives should be punished; and you, his lord, required to commit suicide. Such is the rule of the military classes. The Imperial order is against the law inasmuch as it is neither in accordance with the rule of the military class nor with that of the court. To me it appears quite unreasonable; but Her Majesty's pleasure is no less binding than His Majesty's order. Yoshitsugu shall therefore be beheaded during the course of the day. Moritsugu, order your brother to come here! Now, Morotaka, so Yokobué is to be executed at court, eh? Who is to be her executioner? I feel nervous about the matter. Should she be carried off, even as Karumo was, I can well imagine what a scandal would arise at court. You will return therefore to Her Majesty and inform her that I shall send an inspector and an executioner. Such is Shigémori's reply to the Imperial order. And by the way, now I'm on the subject of love affairs, I hear there is a samurai—his name escapes me at this moment—who has written notes to a court lady and who now, out of jealousy caused by her rejection of his suit, is attempting to avenge himself upon her and her lover. There is a villain if you like! If he does not submit himself to punishment by you let me know, Morotaka, for I would have you know that it is my intention to have him heavily punished."

Cowed by these words, Morotaka could but murmur, "Yes, yes, my lord." A cold perspiration bathed his body. He made a bewildered bow, then, stumbling over the skirt of his *hakama* and slipping on the mats, precipitantly withdrew.

Luckless Yoshitsugu! Promptly obeying his brother's urgent summons, never dreaming of the doom in store for him, he dressed himself completely albeit his hair remained in an unpresentable condition. He hastened to Shigémori's mansion and presented himself at the hall of reception. Moritsugu said to him, "His lordship's order is that you leave your two swords here and go round to the *shirasu.*"

Instantly the frightful truth flashed upon the mind of the young samurai, but he smiled as he answered, "Certainly, sir." His composed air as he removed his swords showed that he was prepared for the worst.

"A pattern of knighthood," murmured all the samurai present. Their eyes glistened with tears of admiration.

Shigémori bent his gaze upon the young man and said kindly enough, "I am delighted to see you, Yoshitsugu, but I greatly regret that I must tell you that Her Imperial Majesty, in her displeasure at your misbehaviour, has ordered that

you be at once beheaded. Know therefore that there is no hope of reprieve. Alas, my poor friend! Since you have served me from your childhood with all possible faithfulness I very much wish that I could at least permit you to commit self-dispatch, but I cannot act in a manner contrary to Her Majesty's pleasure. By reason however of the sympathy and love that a lord feels toward his retainer, I will slay you with my own hands. Therefore bid farewell to your brother and your colleagues and quickly make your way round to the inner courtyard."

So saying Shigémori rose and went within.

Yoshitsugu looked round the company and thus addressed them: "My brother and my friends, pray listen to me a moment. I wish to record the shame my misbehaviour causes me and for which I richly deserve capital punishment. Yet, shamed though I am, I deem myself fortunate in that I am to be slain by His Excellency Lord Shigémori, who is at once my own liege lord and the wisest personage in all Japan. Moreover his lordship saw fit to address some words of gracious consolation and compassion to me, which are indeed of more comfort to me than the ministrations of a holy priest. Dearly do I wish to live on in this world that, if the need arose, I might fight to the death in defence of his lordship, so to requite his favours toward me. It is the consideration of such an interest that alone worries me on the eve of my death. Farewell, farewell, my dearest brother and my most honourable friends."

Having spoken these few words he made his way toward the inner courtyard. Every warrior present, both his friends and those who had aforetime entertained no feeling for him—and his brother who was already completely resigned to his condemnation—everyone of them was moved to silent tears.

After a brief space Moritsugu exclaimed, casting the while a scornful glance at Katsuyori, "I am a glad man! Had Yoshitsugu forsaken the world, not only would he have missed being favoured with his lordship's comfort and the privilege of dying at his honourable hands, but he would have suffered the humiliation of having his shaven head cut from his body by a nameless soldier. My brother's manner of death is truly worthy of a warrior."

At this moment Morihisa, the chief retainer of Shigémori, emerged from the inner apartments carrying two headboxes in his hand.

"Here, Katsuyori," he said with an air of authority, "his lordship has slain Yoshitsugu and has placed his head in this box, which has been sealed. Your orders are to take this box to the court, to break the seal, to examine the head and to display it to Her Imperial Majesty. When you have done this, you are to decapitate Yokobué, place her head in this box and bring it back. You, Moritsugu, are ordered to act as inspector at her execution. You are both to proceed at once upon your errand."

"His lordship shall be promptly obeyed," answered Katsuyori respectfully.

He took up the two boxes and rose to his feet. Moritsugu also rose.

"Katsuyori," said he, "dare you accept the order? Can you really be going to examine my brother's head and decapitate Yokobué?"

"Why not? Dare you not act as inspector?"

"Of course, I certainly intend to. And I would have you know that if your manner of head examination and of decapitation is in any way faulty I shall not fail to report it to his lordship. You understand?"

"I do indeed. And if you are at fault as sheriff, I in my turn will not fail to take notice of it. You understand?"

"Yes. We have given each other our words. Don't forget that. Come with me."

"Go before me."

The two samurai, glaring upon each other, proceeded on their way. They resembled two hardy pine-trees growing on a rugged rock, the one old and the other young, which struggle with one another in the storm.

Under the early winter twilight, rain mixed with hail was falling. From the boughs of the trees in the gardens of the Empress' palace the scarlet embroidery of the leaves had been loosened; already the chrysanthemums had faded; the crickets shrilled sadly. That the tedium caused by the weary atmosphere might be shaken off, the Empress thus addressed her maids-of-honour: "Backgammon does not hold my interest since the die does not fall as I wish. *Hentsugi* is so difficult; *kaiawasé* chills our hands; what do you say to a game of poem-cards, my girls?"

"A merry game, Your Majesty. Quick, let's play it!"

The young girls promptly seated themselves, produced the cards and spread them on the mats. So engaged, they chattered blithely and glanced about in all directions. Not so Yokobué—who, all melancholy, pined for her lover—for she had continued in service despite the fact that her sleeves were forever wet with her tears. The Empress, in her mercy, had extended her sympathy and tenderness to the damsel and had even comforted her with kind words. Observing Yokobué's mood and touched by it, the Empress had a happy idea. "Somehow," she said to the party, "I feel that I would prefer not to take part in the game, but to be merely the reader. I think you will find an increased interest in the game if you practise a sort of divination by the poems you pick up, a divination to inform you whether your wishes are to become facts or no. If I were you I would put up an inward petition to the gods of poetry to grant that you have your favourite cards in your hand. Well, are you ready? I am going to read the first lines. This is Semi Maru's poem:

" 'The stranger who has travelled far,
The friend with welcome smile,
All sorts of men who come and go'

"I would have Yokobué get the last half of this. Don't let the others pick up this card, my dear. Look sharp!"

"I must get it, I must get it," Yokobué thought to herself. "It runs:

" 'Meet at this mountain stile,—
They meet and rest awhile.'

"And it seems to suggest our happy reunion."

Eagerly she sought the card, her heart beating violently with hope and fear. But Kozakura, another girl, too quick for her, picked it up to the disappointment of both the Empress and Yokobué.

"Come, this is the Minister Fujiwara-no-Sanékata's poem:

" 'Though love, like blisters made from leaves
Grown on Mount Ibuki
Torments me more than I can say.' "

Hardly had the Empress read when Izayoi picked up the card and read:

" 'My lady shall not see
How she is paining me.'

"This poem does not apply to my case. I'm certain nobody pines for me."

"But we are not so sure!" cried the other girls, laughing.

"Now Lady Isé's poem:

" 'The double cherry-trees which grew
At Nara in past days
Now beautify this palace, and'

"The last lines symbolize good fortune and happiness. Now Yokobué!"

"Thank you, Your Majesty," responded Yokobué. But Ukon, flurrying her, picked the card up and read:

" 'Their blossoms all ablaze
Perfume the royal ways.'

"That's lucky!" she exclaimed. "The poem must mean that the clothes I am going to receive at the year-end will be as beautiful as these cherry-blossoms."

"The next is the poem by the Mother of the Minister of State:

" 'How difficult it is for men
Not to forget the past!' "

"At least I can't fail to pick one up!" cried Yokobué excitedly. She took up the card and read mechanically:

" 'I fear my husband's love for me
Is disappearing fast;
This day must be my last.'

"Oh, I hate this!" she exclaimed regretfully. "What a luckless omen!"

"Here, girls, is the poem by the Mother of Udaishō Michitsuna:

"Throughout the long and dreary night
I lie awake and moan; ' "

The bewildered Yokobué again picked up the correct card. It read:

" 'How desolate my chamber feels,
How weary I have grown
Of being left alone.' "

The exactness of this description was too much for her; she burst into sobs.

"The High Priest Gyōson sings:

" 'In lonely solitude I dwell,
No human face I see;'

"I myself will take up this one." With this the Empress took up the card and read:

" 'And so we two must sympathize,
O, mountain cherry-tree;
I have no friend but thee.'

"Don't say 'I have no friend but thee,' Yokobué," continued the Empress, gazing with kindness into the girl's face, "for you see you have a sympathetic friend in me."

Yokobué wept in joy and gratitude. "Come, girls, be quick. Kakinomoto-no-Hitomaru's poem:

" 'Long is the mountain pheasant's tail
That curves down in its flight;' "

Another girl picked up the card which read:

" 'But longer still it seems to me,
Left in my lonely plight,
Is this unending night.' "

"Don't be despondent, girl," said the Empress in a soothing tone. "I will not long permit you to be left in solitude. Now, girls, Prince Kentoku's poem:

" 'I dare not hope my lady-love
Will smile on me again;'

It's Kohagi, I'll be bound, who has picked up the last half:

" 'She knows no pity and my life
I care not to retain
Since all my prayers are vain.'

"You are still only fourteen. Never put yourself in such a position as may cause you to exclaim, 'My life I care not to retain.' The Imperial adviser Yakamochi's poem:

" 'When on the Magpies' Bridge I see
The Hoar-frost King has cast
His sparkling mantle, well I know.' "

"Heaven!" said Kojijū, smiling, as she took up the latter lines:

" 'The night is nearly past,
Daylight approaches fast.'

"Even now I feel drowsy enough over my nightly vigil. How much more drowsy I should feel if I had to watch till daylight came!"
"The retired Emperor Sutoku's poem:

" 'The rock divides the flood in two,
Both streams with might and main
Go tumbling down the waterfall,'

"How interesting this poem is! The second half reads:

" 'But well I know the twain
Will soon unite again.'

"Suggestive surely of the successful attainment of every desire. Can't you see it? Look, look, it's there!"
So saying the Empress glanced at Yokobué. The grateful girl, pushing some of her comrades aside, picked up the card. "I have it!"
Overjoyed at this happy omen, she pressed the card to her breast, and the Empress showed the delight with which she read the girl's feelings.
At this moment an aged lady of the court entered and announced that Superintendent Morotaka would shortly be present, having come on some urgent matter which required a personal interview with the Empress.
"Indeed?" said the Empress, amazed. "Why doesn't he speak through Lady Tonasé? What can be the matter, I wonder. Now, Yokobué, hide yourself under this awhile"—she bade the girl lie down and concealed her under the *fuségo* —"don't speak, not a sound."
Then she spread a silk garment over the *fuségo*, drew it close to her back and was sitting at her ease when, a little later, Morotaka presented himself wearing an 'assumed air of dejection.
"I regret to have to inform Your Majesty that a melancholy message has arrived from His Excellency Lord Shigémori. His Excellency, having heard that Karumo has been discharged on account of her pregnancy caused by a love affair with Yoshitsugu, has seen fit to slay Yoshitsugu with his own hands and has ordered Katsuyori to bring Yoshitsugu's head hither to display it to Your Majesty. The old messenger is now waiting with it. Furthermore, His Excellency wishes to de-

clare that he is of the opinion that Taki-guchi deserves the same fate, yet, inasmuch as he has forsaken the world and his present whereabouts are unknown, His Excellency considers that Yokobué should be decapitated in his stead. 'If Her Majesty refuses to deliver Yokobué'—such were the words His Excellency spoke to Katsuyori—'it will be your duty to hunt out and behead Takiguchi, but do your utmost to prevail upon Her Majesty to deliver up Yokobué, then decapitate her and bring her head to me.' Acting on these orders, Katsuyori and Moritsugu are at hand in respective capacities of executioner and sheriff; they await Your Majesty's pleasure at the middle gate. This is indeed in my opinion a cruel punishment and one unworthy of His Excellency, but against it there is no remedy. I venture to assert that Your Majesty had better yield to His Excellency's wish and permit them to behead Yokobué. Poor girl! She has served Your Majesty so faithfully; I am saddened at the thought."

He let fall a few crocodile tears. For a while the Empress was speechless with astonishment. Yokobué, struck with terror and grief, closed her mouth with her sleeve lest she should utter a cry. The tears ran down her face. "It grieves me to have to say such a thing of my brother," exclaimed the Empress, "but verily I believe Lord Shigémori must be out of his senses. To indulge the passion of love with a married person is extremely wicked and Sakya Muni counsels us against it. Sincere love, however, is the root of faithfulness and in the sacred art of poesy love is considered as the most important of themes. In days of old the court noble Ariwara-no-Narihira carried on an intrigue with a virgin princess who was at that time purifying herself for the priesthood at the great Isé Shrine; and albeit his conduct was brought to light, yet was he acquitted because of his fame as a poet. This precedent clearly displays to us that the punishment meted out by Lord Shigémori is not in accordance with the rules that regulate the

lives of court nobles. The celebrated authoresses Izumi Shikibu, Koshikibu, Murasaki Shikibu and Akazomé Emon again took lovers to themselves while in the Imperial service; yet Generals Yorimitsu and Yorinobu, the actual rulers in those days, did not punish them. The proposed execution of Yokobué therefore cannot be in accordance with the rules regulating the life of the military classes. Whatever her misbehaviour, how is it possible for me to suffer Yokobué to be killed, who has served me with all diligence and loyalty? I and Yokobué, as mistress and maid, are tied with the Karma relations of the three existences. On no account will I consent to her execution, nay, even though I run the risk of losing my rank as Empress and my very life by so doing."—She put her hand behind her back and took a firm hold of Yokobué's fingers —"Morotaka, from to-day henceforth you would do well to consider me as Yokobué's sister or her mother. Never will I permit my daughter to be slain or my sister to be beheaded. Sympathize with me and be so good as to plead with Lord Shigémori on her behalf."

Overwhelmed with gratitude and writhing with anxiety, Yokobué reverently pressed the Empress' hand to her forehead. Morotaka, however, remained unmoved.

"I fear, Your Majesty," he returned, "that the executioner and the sheriff, who have come hither for a definite purpose, will not be readily persuaded to depart. Shall I tell them that, as Yokobué's death is against the will of Your Majesty, they are to hunt out Takiguchi and decapitate him?"

'Twas with difficulty that Yokobué restrained herself. She made as if to emerge from her hiding-place, but the Empress, covering her face with her flowing sleeve, looked back and signed to the girl to do no such thing. The girl drew herself up on her knees and whispered in the Empress' ear between her sobs, "I beg Your Majesty's pardon for seeming to reject your mercy, but Morotaka Dono says that if my life is spared my sweetheart's will be taken. May I ask Your Majesty to deliver me up and thus save Takiguchi from death?"

A brief silence ensued; then the Empress said to Morotaka, "I understand that it is Lord Shigémori's will that either Yokobué or Takiguchi shall be slain; very well. You tell me that two warriors have come, one as executioner and one as sheriff. Now, girls, bid the two warriors enter the neighbouring chamber, as I have something to impart to them from behind the lowered blind. You, too, Morotaka, are to listen to me."

The Empress wiped away her tears, then took her position on a low seat and in a posture full of dignity behind a bamboo blind. Beauty, awe and majesty emanated from her countenance and bearing. Presently the warriors were announced. The Empress' voice was clearly heard.

"Welcome, both of you. Albeit Lord Shigémori is my elder brother, yet he is now my subject. Despite the fact that he occupies the exalted position of Lord Keeper of the Privy Seal, he has with his own hands beheaded Yoshitsugu. I cannot but think he is bereft of his senses. I count it an outrageous thing moreover that he should have dispatched persons of brutal office to the court. Is it nothing to him that he should desecrate the Imperial Palace with bloodshed? How can I suffer that poor girl Yokobué, who has tended me from her youth up, cruelly to perish by the executioner's sword? Albeit a woman, I was born of a 'family of bow and arrow' and am the daughter of Lord Kiyomori, a Prime Minister. I have not learnt how to deal death in battle, but there is no reason why I should not be able to perform the office of beheading another person. I will myself behead Yokobué and display her head to the sheriff. Moritsugu—that is your name, isn't it?—if you are proficient in the duties proper to a sheriff you will carefully examine the head and report on it to Lord Shigémori. When I have performed the

deed I, in my turn, will inspect Yoshitsugu's head. Yokobué, I would do everything and anything in my power, but it is evident that my efforts are unavailing. Step forth therefore and prepare for death."

The bright, keen eyes of the Empress glistened with tears. Yokobué revealed herself and prostrated herself before her Imperial mistress.

"Most gracious Majesty," she sobbed, "your benevolence is higher than Mount Shumi and deeper than the ocean, but to pollute your honourable hands with my blood, that is impossible! Divine punishment would visit itself upon me; I should bring disgrace on myself in the next world. I beg one more boon of Your Majesty—let me die by the executioner's sword. I will not complain of the mode of execution, however severe. It is my hope that I shall be able to meet my sweetheart in the life to come. I grieve to part from Your Majesty, whose benevolence is so overwhelming that, were I to be reborn seven times into this world, I could scarcely hope to find another mistress of a like benevolence. Permit me to die at the hands of the executioner."

"No, I cannot permit the maid who is dearest to me to be slain by a warrior. Reconcile yourself to dying by the edge of my sword."

The Empress tucked up her skirts and, taking her sword from the sword-rack, tucked it under her left arm, saying, "Come with me, my girl, you shall meet your death in one of the inner chambers."

She departed quietly and composedly. Yokobué followed her. All those present, and particularly Katsuyori and Moritsugu, were smitten by awe and pain at what seemed her wrath and at the melancholy they read upon her countenance.

"Katsuyori Dono," remarked Moritsugu in tones of reconciliation, "have you noticed that the views of Her Majesty upon the subject of Yokobué and my brother would seem entirely contrary to what was asserted to be her first command? Have you observed how Her Majesty and Lord

Shigémori seem to find fault with each other? Does not this seem strange? I am certain that some wicked wretch is deceiving both of them. Our mutual hostility is a private matter and the affairs of Takiguchi and Yoshitsugu are matters of but small public importance. An estrangement, nay, a discord between Her Majesty and Lord Shigémori, however, were an affair of grave concern which might lead to public disturbance. Let us therefore make our peace and bend our joint powers to inquiring into the matter."

"Certainly," nodded Katsuyori, "that is precisely my thought too. First of all let us consider our friendship restored, then let us take note of everybody and keep a sharp lookout."

The two warriors exchanged significant glances, then sternly looked about them. Morotaka, who all this while had been ill at ease, could no longer contain himself.

"Ugh! I have a fit of lumbago, my loins ache; I can bear the pain no longer. Pray excuse me, sirs. Be so good as to apologize to Her Majesty for my taking my leave now. Ugh! There again! Good-bye, sirs."

With a wry face and holding his sides, Morotaka took himself off. The eyes of the two warriors followed his retreating figure not without wonder.

"I consider it very suspicious," both exclaimed, "that this fellow, who is the superintendent of this palace, should remove himself on an occasion like this which is one of greatest importance, merely offering a pretext of sudden illness."

Hardly had they spoken when Lady Tonasé appeared, head-box in hand.

"Good-evening, sirs," said she as she sat herself down. "Her Majesty has beheaded Yokobué and has placed her head in this box which, as you see, she has sealed. Her Majesty orders me to receive Yoshitsugu's head from you and, when I have done so, to deliver Yokobué's head to you."

Katsuyori bowed his head respectfully and, unsealing the box he had brought, removed its lid. With what wonder did not all three behold within, not Yoshitsugu's head, but a queue and a stone as make-weight. Then Lady Tonasé, in her turn, cut the seal from her box with her dagger and so disclosed the contents. Lo and behold! these consisted merely of a bamboo flute cut in two at the mouthpiece and, as make-weight, some earth! All three were dumbfounded. After some rumination Katsuyori exclaimed, "It is above the privilege accorded a man of my rank and station to remark it, but what wise persons Her Majesty and Lord Shigémori are! I am filled with awe and reverence at the boundless benevolence displayed and at the precisely same measure each has taken without pre-arrangement between them. Had his lordship slain Yoshitsugu he could not have spared Karumo's life; it has therefore pleased his lordship graciously to spare Yoshitsugu by cutting off this queue of his and so making a priest of him. By entering the priesthood a man disconnects himself with the secular world, for he who has taken to himself a Buddhist name is, after a manner of speaking, a dead man. This make-weight of a stone is a symbol of the tomb; thus one may say his lordship has slain Yoshitsugu. This is a merciful measure and in accordance with the Buddhist doctrine that 'the bad shall be saved in the same hour as the good.' Her Majesty is apparently of the same mind. Had Her Majesty beheaded Yokobué, how could Takiguchi have survived? The yokobué or flute is a wonderful instrument, possessing miraculous notes and a soul of its own. By cutting this flute in twain and covering it with earth Her Majesty signifies that Yokobué, being dismissed, is as it were no more in this world. Thus, two of them being saved from death, it follows that the four of them are saved and how great will be the joy and gratitude of their parents, brothers, sisters, other relatives and friends. It would appear that a life-granting measure, such as has here been taken by Lord Shigémori and Her Majesty, is a more pious deed than prayers offered by a million priests for æons. Boundless is their benevolence! Oh, Moritsugu, how can we repay this great favour shown us in sparing the lives of your brother and his would-be wife and of my son and his would-be wife? The mercy, the benevolence of it!"

The lion-hearted heroes grasped each other's hands and were speechless, choked by tears of gratitude. Lady Tonasé was also moved to tears.

"I am ashamed, sirs," she said, "for at the bottom of this affair there is a great knave. I need not specify his name. Now that my parents are no more, the love I bear my brother is like the love of a mother for her son. Alas, to know him for the man he is! How can his wickedness fail to attract the notice of Her Majesty and of Lord Shigémori, both being so wise and sagacious? I cannot but think that they will judge me his accomplice. I am prepared for that, though by the Gods and Buddha I have had no hand in the matter. I fear however that their suspicions will not be allayed, even after I am dead. Pray sympathize with me, sirs."

A melancholy silence ensued. At length Katsuyori spoke softly.

"You have our hearty sympathy, lady. Everyone has a mind of his own. A parent cannot know what is in a child's mind and the mind of a brother is unknown to his sister. We can very well understand that you are a perfect stranger to your brother's intentions. A mirror reflects an object exactly as an object appears. Gaze in a mirror with distorted features and a distorted face will look back at you; gaze at it with a placid face and a placid face will greet you. The same is true of Her Majesty: behave innocently and sincerely toward Her Majesty and your reflection will be the same in Her Majesty's mental mirror."

They exchanged head-boxes. The warriors bade her a polite farewell and went their way.

IV

Luckless Yokobué! For a considerable period she had led a sequestered life at Kwazan, nigh the capital, though not a day passed without her pining for Takiguchi. At length her passionate longing induced her to undertake a journey in quest of her sweetheart. Having assumed travelling garb and veiled her face with a sedge hat, she set out one morning before daybreak. She bade a sad farewell to her hermitage and wearily trudged the narrow roads through the rice-fields.

As she plodded on she beheld, far away to the south, the scarlet maple leaves upon Mount Inari, which the poetess Izumi Shikibu immortalized in a love-poem. Her fancy wandered to the village of Fukakusa, situated below the mountain famous for its connection with the court noble Fukakusa-no-Shōshō, who died a tragic death because of the power of his love for the beautiful poetess Komachi. As, crossing the Kamo River, she came to the street of Gojō, she beheld pass by many flower-sellers' carts on which reposed mountains of flowers sparkling with morning dew. At sight of them the love-sick maiden could not but associate them with the ox-cart in which the hero of *The Story of Genji* visits the daughter of a peasant living in this neighbourhood. Before she reached the village of Saga, the retreat of numerous recluses, she had to pass through many villages and forests and cross certain streams. Their very names were significant to her, either of hope or fear.

At Saga she found so many hermitages in the glens and on the hill-tops that she knew not at which to call in inquiry after her sweetheart. In this quandary she addressed a peasant girl who was going home from the garden where she had been gathering vegetables.

"Somewhere hereabouts lives a young samurai of the capital who has turned priest. Pray tell me which is his hut?"

"Hm! A young samurai is it, who's a priest? Let me see, which can it be? Father Nensai was a huntsman.

Father Dōkin was a—shall I say a Dorking cock? Father Dōsai it cannot be, for he has removed to Nara. I have it!—some time ago a young samurai of the Taira family shaved his head at the Ōjōin Temple yonder. Follow this lane and you will find his hermitage easily enough. Listen, you can hear the sound of prayers in his cell."

Having said this the girl made off. The joy of Yokobué knew no bounds. Beyond doubt the young priest must be her Takiguchi. She ran along the lane and soon reached the cottage, from within which sounded the bell accompanying prayers. It was with a beating heart that she lifted her hand and knocked upon the garden gate and fence.

"I want to speak to you, sir! Please unlock the door; please open the gate."

"As you will," replied a gruff voice.

The next moment there appeared within the fence a shabbily attired man with a shaven head, of about forty years of age.

"My mistake," he said, leering, "I thought it was the woman bringing rice for to-morrow. Here comes an excellent meal for the night-time; I'd have you know, my pretty girl, that the priest here is a young man, but he was a samurai once and behaves himself very strictly. However skittishly forward you may be with him, let me warn you he will in nowise do even so much as to uncover your dish. No, not he, never! As for me, I too abstain from flesh to-day and to-morrow, but if it's only a matter of a small consideration, call again the day after to-morrow."

"Nonsense! What do you mean? I know very well he is a man of strong will; but if we meet he will recognize me. Pray be so good as just to tell him, sir."

"You're his friend then? You might have told me so earlier. Wait a moment." So saying he ran into the cell. Yokobué, following him with her eyes, said to herself, "Takiguchi Sama was wont to say that he had a favourite sandal-carrier; this fellow should be he. What a loyal servant to have entered the priesthood with his master! How admirable!"

The shaven henchman ran out crying, "Oh, terrible, terrible! Are you waiting still, girl? What a fright I got! When I told my master of your coming he glared at me with eyes like saucers and roared at me, 'Have I ever invited in a girl or woman since I retired here? In the first place I am short of money. You lecher! Whenever you come across a woman you dilly-dally with her. I am tired of such an idiot! Never come on such an errand again!' And when he had said this he beat me again and again about the head with a bell hammer. Be off, girl!"

"Indeed, he did right in taking amiss what I said. I am sorry to put you to further trouble, but be so kind as to inform him that I come from Her Majesty's court. Your master will then understand."

"No, no," he said sourly, shaking his head with vehemence, "let there be no tattle about Her Majesty's court. He never will give ear to any mention of silk coat or petticoat. If I go and speak to him I shall get another knock. Terrible, terrible!"

"You seem to have recently shaved your head. I expect you feel cold about the head? I should like to present you with a hood, but I haven't got one, so allow me to offer you this."

Yokobué proffered him a cloth wrapper, then threw it over the fence. The fellow seized it joyfully enough.

"Thank you, girl. This is expensive crêpe I see, and the lining red silk. I can use it as a hood. Wasn't there something wrapped up in it?"

"Yes, it contained money which I gave to beggars on my way here, but next time I come I will bring you anything you want. I suppose you have nose-paper?"

"Yes, I have such things. What would do better—you understand?"

"I understand. I shan't fail to bring it. Will you please grant my request?"

"Very well then."

Once more he rushed into the hermitage.

"None are so frank and simple-minded as people of the lower classes," she said. "He is indeed love's messenger on my behalf. I think I will stay at this hut to-night and talk with my sweetheart all night long."

An ecstasy possessed her. She trembled on tiptoe. But it was a crestfallen messenger of love who returned a moment or two later.

"Well, what did he say? Quick!"

"All for nothing. He refuses to see you. He merely rapped out with an oath, 'A friend, eh! No friend if it's a female. I wouldn't cross the road to speak with a bitch or a hen, much less with a woman.' I'm sorry, my girl. I fear you've given me a crêpe wrapper in vain."

He disappeared into the hut again. Yokobué's disappointment was so deep that she was quite confounded. She sank to the ground and wept bitterly. "What change in him! Three years we pined for each other. Three years may seem a short space of time, but when told day by day they amount to more than a thousand days and nights. For so many days and nights did he and I pine for each other. Once we had achieved intimacy, what trouble and difficulty was ours, managing to meet in secret! We vowed to each other that we would become husband and wife through seven existences to come and now he even refuses to see me."

She clung to the gate-post and cried bitterly, but no one came to comfort her. "It is an idle complaint that I make. Now that I am forsaken by my belovèd, to what purpose do I live on? What are the bright moon and the beautiful flowers to me? I will drown myself in yonder stream and in Hades enjoy gazing at the reflection of my lover as it comes and goes upon the river." Having come to this melancholy resolve, the girl hurried toward the "Plover's Pool."

The serving-man turned priest caught sight of her and was astonished.

"Master! The girl is going to drown herself. See, see! She is running toward the river."

The startled priest rushed out, wrenched open the outer gate and, running to the girl, seized her in his arms.

"Takiguchi Sama, is it?" she exclaimed as she embraced him.

"No, I am not Takiguchi."

"Don't lie to me, dear."

She clung to him but he gently freed himself.

"Is it Yokobué Dono?"

"Are you Yoshitsugu Sama? I feel sad. My life was spared through Her Majesty's mercy; since when I have lived on in hopes of meeting Takiguchi Dono. Alas, my hope is frustrated. Pray kill me, Yoshitsugu Sama."

She seized Yoshitsugu's sleeve and wept bitterly.

"Don't be so cast down," said Yoshitsugu, himself almost in tears. "I too was graciously pardoned by my liege lord, since when I have become a priest. I have not been able, however, to free myself from worldly passions, so that I never cease from remembering my belovèd Karumo. Beholding your grief, I can well imagine how passionately she is longing after me. Even in this life we four are separated by fate from one another, so that there seems even less hope that we may be able to 'live together in one lotus blossom in the Pure Land.' But since Takiguchi and Karumo, both of whom are pining for us, cannot have gone to the furthest provinces, let us set out in quest of them. The proverb says, 'Desire finds its way even through a rock'; sooner or later what we wish will be accomplished. Be of good heart, Yokobué Dono. In this world a priest has no fixed place of stay; I can therefore start at any moment. Buddha is one and the same all over the world. Everywhere and anywhere Buddha can be found. I therefore need not take leave of the Buddha in my shrine. Hold yourself ready to depart, Yokobué Dono."

On that Yoshitsugu made over the hermitage to his serving-man turned priest, bade the fellow farewell and departed with the girl.

Like a mandarin duck separated from

its drake and a cock pheasant parted from its hen, the pair wandered hither and thither, weeping inwardly, but comforting each other as week after week went by without the achievement of any special destination.

Late one winter's afternoon they found themselves trudging along a mountain path in the district of Shiga. Snow was falling thick and fast. A freezing wind from Mount Hiei howled through the snow-crusted trees. The sufferings she had endured upon the long journey had told upon Yokobué. Recently she had grown weaker and now the bitter weather tried her so hard that she seemed scarcely able to take another step.

"Take heart of grace, Yokobué. Have no fears on account of your weakness. I am sure you will soon be able to meet Takiguchi."

"Thank you—for—your—kind—words." So benumbed were her lips that these words proceeded from them but brokenly.

"Naturally you are tired," returned Yoshitsugu. "It was very much my idea to beg two or three nights' lodging for your health's good, but unfortunately it is near the year's end and every house consequently is busy, and in any event nobody would give lodging to a priest and a young woman. We have slept in the open air now no less than a hundred nights—a hard time this must have been for you who have led an easy and comfortable life at court from your childhood up. You have my sympathy. About a mile further on lies the village of Shiga. I will certainly ask them, at the very first house we come on, to give us lodging for the night. Please try to walk on."

Thus urged, Yokobué did her best to obey, but so weak and benumbed were her legs that she tottered and fell down in the snow.

"What a helpless creature I am!" she exclaimed. "Indeed your kindness overwhelms me. You are searching for your love, yet, despite your sufferings, you have fended every care from me for a long while. You have kindly tended a dying woman without any sign of impatience, despite the heavy snow-storm sweeping this strange country-side and without taking thought to your own discomfort at all. Surely you must have been my father or brother in a former existence; in nowise can I consider you a mere friend. I was lucky in coming across you, but I begin to wonder why I have been so long unable to meet Takiguchi with whom I exchanged vows of fidelity. I fear my hapless lot may be a divine counterpoise to the undeserved benevolence Her Majesty showed towards me. By my own anguish I can well imagine Karumo Dono's pain. Five long years have passed since she was with child and yet you have not met each other. A hard lot hers! I heartily sympathize with you in your agony. It grieves me much to have put you to such trouble when you are already weighed down by your own troubles, but there is no help for it. My anguish and this snow-storm seem to rob me of my breath; I feel dizzy; I think I shall scarcely live until the morrow. My hours are numbered. I have not even strength enough to pray to Buddha. Aid me to pray, that I be suffered to be re-born in the lotus flower in the Pure Land with Takiguchi." She found difficulty in breathing and seemed on the point of death. Yoshitsugu, himself grief-stricken and much fatigued, spoke somewhat sternly to encourage his sick companion.

"This is spiritless of you, Yokobué. If your sympathy really extends even to Karumo, why do you not take part and venture not only through the snow but also through fire to find Takiguchi and then to search for Karumo in his company and mine? You appear a somewhat helpless woman."

He aided her to her feet.

The exhausted Yokobué exclaimed, "I am ashamed of my helplessness and selfishness; I ask pardon of you."

She leaned upon Yoshitsugu's arm. They continued on through the dusk by the light of the snow itself. When they had toiled a little further through the falling snow they were overjoyed to descry, far ahead, a cottage lit by a hearth fire. They stumbled to it and, peeping through the chinks of the paper door, caught sight of a flame drowsily wavering before the images of the "Three Deities of Welcome." They saw too an intelligent-looking boy of five to six summers feeding with firewood the hearth, whereon a kettle was boiling. Hope brightened in them. Yoshitsugu slightly opened the door.

"I say, little sir?"

"Who is it?" said the child on tiptoe. "What do you want?"

"We are travellers who have lost our way in the snow; there are but two of us. Please allow us to rest in that corner till day breaks."

"I'm sorry," replied the boy, with an innocent but firm air, "but the priest of this house has given me orders never to open the door in his absence. I therefore can't allow you in."

"You are right to refuse, as 'tis the time of the year when every house must be guarded against thieves. But see—my companion is a woman who is sick. We are neither of us such as steal. I beg your pardon for using such phrases as are used to grown-ups, but it would be a work of great mercy to give us a lodging. We will apologize to your master. Again I say, do be so good as to grant our request."

"No, I can't."

"Then will you permit us a drink of the water that is boiling there?"

"That is not water but medicine. The first infusion is not yet made."

"There's somebody sick here then? Who is it?"

"My mother. She's long been ill. She lies abed behind that screen day and night. The priest cooks the morning and evening meals. This evening he has gone down to the village hard by, to get mother's medicine."

"In that case, though the priest be absent, you will still be able to ask your mother to give us a night's lodging. Please be so kind, little sir."

"No, no. The priest takes every care of my mother. He says I am never to let in anybody, whomsoever they may be, in his absence, for fear mother should be carried away. I can't allow you in."

"Kaméwaka," called a woman's thin voice from behind the screen, "there are travellers asking for lodging, aren't there? They must be cold in this weather. The priest will soon be back, so call them in quick."

"No, mother," said the boy stubbornly, "the priest told me never to open the door, even to our friends. I'll just go down and fetch him."

So saying, he took from the wall a large hat of bamboo sheaths, placed it on his head and set out through the heavy snow.

"Well," Yoshitsugu said to himself, "it's only natural a priest should hide his wife. I suppose he calls this son of his a pupil. While the boy's away let me steal in with Yokobué and let us warm ourselves by the fire. Ah, no. If the priest is offended we shall get no lodging to-night; let us be patient a little longer."

He laid his hat and the girl's on Yokobué where she lay in the snow and, shivering with cold himself, endeavoured to warm her in his arms. Thickly fell the snow upon their hats. Night wore on. When he shook himself the snowflakes fell off him like goose feathers; the icicles hanging from the sleeves of both of them tinkled like tiny bells.

"Hey, travellers!" cried a youthful voice. "The priest is back."

Priest and child appeared out of the darkness.

"Are you the folk asking for lodging?"

"I am, sir. What, you're Takiguchi, aren't you?"

"Yoshitsugu! A strange reunion indeed! Before anything else let me return to you my precious charges. This is your son from whom you parted when he was yet in his mother's womb. Karumo Dono!"

Karumo made her appearance. She was overjoyed.

"My dear Yoshitsugu, this is our son."

"My dear father!"

The three embraced each other, gazing happily from face to face. All were speechless with joy.

After a brief pause Yoshitsugu said to his friend, "As for me, I have brought you a splendid present; here is your Yokobué Dono."

"I thank you for your friendship."

Takiguchi shook his sweetheart, crying, "Yokobué! My dear Yokobué!" But answer came there none.

He shook the snow from the girl. He clasped her in his arms. In vain! To their consternation she showed no sign of life. He forced open her clenched teeth and blew a restorative into her mouth, but to no purpose. Pulse and life had completely fled. Takiguchi, grief-stricken, held her on his knees and warmed her body by pressing her to his naked breast.

"Oh, Yokobué, how unlucky our love is!" he exclaimed with sobs. "These five long years have we pined for each other and suffered hardships indescribable for each other's sake. And now you have died without enjoying a single day of complete wifehood. How sad it is that you came all unwittingly to your own beloved's door and were frozen to death in the snow when all the while a cheerful fire was burning within! Oh, Yokobué, if you really love me, let me hear the single word 'My dear' from your lips!"

Yoshitsugu and Karumo, also in tears, assisted in lifting Yokobué's body up to the hearth, where they warmed it with great care and tenderness. No signs of revival appeared. Karumo, between her sobs, opened her amulet case, saying, "Here I have a precious incense named 'The King of Medicines' and it is said to be possessed of miraculous powers. It is a portion of a present from the Chinese Emperor to the Emperor Goshirakawa, who gave it to Her Majesty. Her Majesty graciously bestowed it on Yokobué Dono and myself as a token of the relationship between mistress and servant extending to the next world. It is my trust that the odour of this incense will restore Yokobué to life. I will therefore burn it."

No sooner did she begin to burn the incense than a sweet odour filled the air and, wonder of wonders, Yokobué's body instantly recovered its warmth and pulse and her face its colour. She gave a sigh and opened her eyes. Then she cried, "Is it Takiguchi Sama? I am overjoyed to see you!" She was again a beautiful woman in sound health. The others were filled with amaze and joy.

"When my spirit had all but fled and I seemed to be half in a dream, I smelled the sweet odour of precious incense and heard Her Majesty's voice crying, 'Yokobué! Yokobué!' The next instant my dream dissolved and I came to my senses. Great is Her Majesty's goodness!"

All of them spent a happy night, merrily talking of what each had experienced during those five weary years.

V

When the full extent of Morotaka's roguery and calumny became known, it was evident that he deserved death, but for the sake of his sister Lady Tonasé and because the quality of mercy is the foundational principle of government, his punishment was reduced to banishment from the Imperial city. He found it difficult to keep body and soul together and so formed a gang with the villains Genkurō and Muzō, relatives of his retainer Iwamura Gengo, slain at Funaoka-Yama. They roamed the neighbourhood of Karasaki, on Lake Biwa, eking out a living by swindling, highway robbery, burglary, blackmail and the like, as chance and opportunity served.

One day Morotaka whispered to his subordinates, "To-day there should be many visitors to the Shrine of the God Sannō in this place. See, there is a boat adrift yonder! Genkurō will pretend to be her boatman, will give passage to some of the worshippers and rob them when you have rowed out some distance. In the Hall of

Worship in the Myōjin Shrine the priest leaves his hat and robe. Muzō will wear them, pretend to be the priest and appropriate the offertory and the money paid for the 'Twelve Lights.' I, for my part, will prowl the highway and pick the pockets of absent-minded travellers. Come, let us set about our jobs."

They parted on their respective enterprises.

Presently Lady Tonasé, in a palanquin, accompanied by a few attendants, arrived under the Giant Pine-Tree at Karasaki. She had come to the town of Ōtsu, as proxy for the Empress, for a week's worship at the Shrine of Sannō and of Myōjin. She alighted from her carriage, glanced about and said to her attendants, "See whether the priest Sandayū is now in the shrine."

Muzō, having donned the priest's robe, made his appearance.

"Honoured lady," said he, "I am Sandayū's father. I may take orders for the Sacred Dance or the Twelve Lights as well as he."

"Are you Sandayū's father? Sandaū must be sixty and you look younger."

Muzō was confused. "No, no. I said Sandayū was my father. My name is Nidayū."

"So you are his son? Come nearer."

The rogue perforce advanced.

"I have the honour," continued the lady, "of doing proxy to Her Imperial Majesty. Sandayū may have told you that the young court ladies, Yokobué and Karumo, were discharged some years ago on account of their love affairs. Her Majesty has taken pity on them and, a report having come to her ears that they are living a miserable life hereabouts with their lovers, Takiguchi and Yoshitsugu, Her Majesty has commanded me to find them and bring them back to the capital. With this purpose in my mind I have journeyed hither and am now putting up in Ōtsu in order to pray here to the Gods Sannō and Myōjin for guidance as to their whereabouts. I intended worship of a week and have already spent five days

in prayer. I beg you to pray to the God to let me have news of their whereabouts."

So saying, she worshipped the deity with her whole heart and soul.

Morotaka who, unnoticed, had played the eavesdropper, suddenly rushed upon her, seized her by the nape and drew her down on her back.

"What villainy!" the frightened woman cried. "Who does this deed?"

"Let not the villain escape!"

So cried her henchmen; and the palanquin bearers instantly hemmed him in.

"Maggots! Touch me if you dare! Hi! Comrades! Knock the old woman down and strip her of her garments."

Genkurō jumped from the boat and cut at the servants. Muzō, who had also rushed to the scene, drew and flourished his weapon. The terrified, cowardly servants precipitantly took to their heels, crying, "Robbery in broad daylight! Highwaymen! Help! Help!"

"So it is you, wild beast and brother!" exclaimed Lady Tonasé. "You who gave so much trouble to Her Majesty, you who wronged so many, you who, for these crimes, were about to be put to death! To whom do you think you owe it that your head still remains upon your shoulders? Partly it is due to me, but also largely to the benevolence of Her Majesty. You ought immediately to have become a priest, that you might atone for your crime. A cursèd wretch, reduced to such a condition, do you not even yet repent of your crime? What shame this is!"

"Pah! If I had repented I should not have come to this pass. Since we are relations I spare your life. I know your purse is full; you have, I am sure, three or four *ryō* about you. Come, hand it to me at once. If you don't I will kill you."

He forced her head to the ground as he spoke.

"A base villain!" said the lady. "You say you mean to kill me if I don't give you my money! Naturally I would not grudge even thousands of *ryō* as the price of the redemption of my life. What should a chief court lady have money about her for? Kill me if you choose."

"Aha! I see you have no money on you. Your money must be in your inn at Ōtsu. You are not to stir till I fetch it."

He produced a cord, bound her cruelly and thrust her into the palanquin. "Come along with me and be quick about it, comrades. Since she says she's to stop here for a week she must have brought plenty of gold and silver coins with her. Think of the special booty there will be—her chests, her fine clothes, her bed-trappings!"

They ran off highly pleased.

They had scarcely taken themselves off when Yoshitsugu with his wife and son appeared. They had spent many days at the temple praying the God Myōjin to restore Yoshitsugu to his former situation as a retainer to Shigémori. They now proceeded to the shrine and, bowing their heads and clapping their hands, prayed with great fervour. While they were absorbed in their devotions a voice was heard insistently crying, "Karumo Dono! Yoshitsugu Sama!" The surprised couple glanced backward.

"The cry comes from that palanquin, I believe."

"Yes, you're right. It is from the palanquin. Dear Karumo Dono, please come to me!"

Karumo rushed to the palanquin and slid open the door.

"Is it Lady Tonasé? Why, how's this! How did you get into such a state?"

She lifted the old woman out and loosened the cord. Tonasé thanked her and, restraining her tears, said, "Where are Takiguchi and Yokobué? I have come here as Her Majesty's proxy to pray for guidance as to your whereabouts. In point of fact Her Majesty orders me to find you and bring you and your friends back to the capital. A few minutes ago, as I was worshipping the God, that villainous brother of mine, who had been banished and who appears to have turned robber, seized and bound me in the fashion you found me in just now. He will shortly return. Before he returns, let us set out together to the capital."

"Have no fear," laughed Yoshitsugu, "nothing will happen to you now that I am with you. Takiguchi and Yokobué will presently be here to worship. Abide here a while. Karumo, you will hide in this palanquin and when Morotaka returns you will say to him, 'I am forsaken by that heartless monster Yoshitsugu.' Appeal to his sympathy and coax him into going aboard that boat. I will pretend to be the boatman. I have a plan for his chastisement."

"Certainly," returned Karumo, entering the palanquin. "I will do my best, dear husband. But be careful of yourself."

"Have no fears for me."

Yoshitsugu took his child in his arms and embarked with Tonasé. He hid them both in the bottom of the boat and, assuming a straw rain-coat and a sedge hat, sat down and feigned a doze. Morotaka presently returned, exuding perspiration.

"Sister," cried he, striking the palanquin, "they would deliver us nothing at your inn without a note from you. We cannot break into your rooms in broad daylight. You will please write a note demanding the delivery of your money and clothes. Be quick about it!"

No response.

"What next!" he cried, and, tearing the blind from the carriage, was amazed to find Karumo within.

"Oh!" said she, assuming a bashful air. "I am ashamed to meet you in this plight, Morotaka Sama. I regret to have to tell you that I have been unkindly forsaken, as a just punishment for my flat refusal of your kind proposal, by that brute Yoshitsugu. Enraged by his jealousy, he swears that he will drown me in this lake. I have managed with great difficulty to escape and have hidden in this unoccupied palanquin. I trust that, though it he but half of what formerly obtained, your affection for me still exists?"

"Has my sister fled then? But I wouldn't exchange you for a thousand sisters. How unkind of you to say 'half my former affection'! Truly my love has grown an hundredfold since then. Make your mind easy; under my protection you are now in no danger. You're even handsomer than when I last saw you. I am madly in love with you! I would die for you, my dearest girl!"

So saying, he embraced her.

"Don't! People might see us. What do you say to hiring yonder boat and spending cosy and pleasant hours in the offing, away from the eyes of common folk?"

"Aha! You've improved in wits as well as looks. Hello, my man! I thought it was merely a boat adrift, but it's yours, boatman, is it? Row us over to Ishiyama, will you?"

"With pleasure, sir. I saw in a glance you were lovers. I shan't be wanting any fare. Come, get aboard."

"Thank you. This really is, as the saying goes, a boat that arrives just when one wants to cross over."

The old rascal was making as if to embark with Karumo, when Yoshitsugu exclaimed, "It's dangerous for two to try and get on board simultaneously; one at a time, please; the girl first."

He took Karumo in his arms and placed her in the boat, then, seizing the oar, to Morotaka's vast surprise and anger, rowed out into the lake. A moment later the boat was a hundred yards from the shore.

"Slave-trader! Robber!" roared the villain. Frantic with despair he waded into the shallows. Yoshitsugu, doffing his coat of straw and his sedge hat, disclosed himself to the astonished Morotaka.

"Has divine punishment sealed your eyes, you villain?" he cried. "Know then that I am Yoshitsugu! It is I have sheltered Lady Tonasé. My advice to you is that you kill yourself instead of continuing to lead a dishonourable life."

Lady Tonasé and Yoshitsugu's son appeared.

"Ah! That I should have been duped! Were this water a hundred or a thousand fathoms deep, yet would I wade out to your boat and capsize it!"

With these words Morotaka tucked up his skirt and rolled up his sleeves for action; but at this moment Takiguchi and Yokobué came on the scene. Takiguchi rushed at him, knocked him down on to the beach and kneeled upon him, while Yokobué beat his head and pinched his legs. The villain writhed. "A shame it is," he cried, "to have been brought down by a greenhorn of a boy!"

"Don't kill him!" Yoshitsugu shouted. "It would be wrong for us to kill one whose life Their Imperial Majesties have graciously seen fit to spare. Let us lie in wait for his comrades and kill them."

He rowed to the beach, jumped ashore, trussed the old knave up hand and foot, thrust a handful of straw into his mouth, wound a kerchief round his face and threw him into the palanquin. The party then hid behind the shrine.

Presently Muzō and Genkurō, both out of breath, returned at a run.

"Can't find our boss anywhere! And a pretty poor time we've been having! We owe it all to this old hag too; let us finish her."

They approached the palanquin on both sides and thrust their swords again and again through the blinds.

"She mayn't have any money, but I daresay we can find something or other hidden in her bosom."

They dragged the corpse out. Great was their consternation to find themselves gazing upon the bloody body of their chief.

"Muzō, beware!" exclaimed Genkurō, alarmed. "Takiguchi or Yoshitsugu must be about."

"A good guess, villains!" cried the two heroes, rushing from hiding. "You see Yoshitsugu *and* Takiguchi before you!"

Mighty strokes fell upon the frightened

rascals. The villains were held down, stabbed to death.

At this moment Saitō Katsuyori and Etchū Moritsugu appeared.

"Listen, Takiguchi and Yoshitsugu!" they cried. "We bring you a written order from Lord Shigémori, restoring you to your former situations and fiefs."

The joy and gratitude of both couples knew no bounds and the whole company wept for delight over their happy reunion after five years of weary separation.

ADAM

[THE MYSTERY OF ADAM]

ANONYMOUS

Written and produced probably about the middle of the 12th century

TRANSLATED FROM THE FRENCH AND LATIN BY EDWARD NOBLE STONE *

ORDER OF THE PRESENTATION OF ADAM

Let Paradise be set up in a somewhat lofty place; let there be put about it curtains and silken hangings, at such an height that those persons who shall be in Paradise can be seen from the shoulders upward; let there be planted there sweet-smelling flowers and foliage; let divers trees be therein, and fruits hanging upon them, so that it may seem a most delectable place.

Then let the Saviour come, clothed in a dalmatic, and let ADAM and EVE be set before him. Let ADAM be clothed in a red tunic; EVE, however, in a woman's garment of white, and a white silken wimple; and let them both stand before the FIGURE; but ADAM a little nearer, with composed countenance; EVE, however, with countenance a little more subdued.

And let ADAM himself be well instructed when he shall make his answers, lest in answering he be either too swift or too slow. Let not only ADAM, but all the persons, be so instructed that they shall speak composedly and shall use such gestures as become the matter whereof they are speaking; and in uttering the verses, let them neither add a syllable nor take away, but let them pronounce all clearly; and let those things that are to be said be said in their due order.

Whoever shall speak the name of Paradise, let him look back at it and point it out with his hand.

Then let the Lesson begin: "In the beginning God created the heaven and the earth."

And after this is ended let the choir sing: "And the Lord God formed man."

And when this is ended, let the FIGURE say: Adam! *And let him answer:* Lord!

FIGURE. Out of earthy clay
I fashioned thee.

ADAM. I know it, yea!

FIGURE. A living soul to thee I gave,
In thee my likeness did I grave,
Mine earthly image making thee.
Never must thou rebellious be.

---

* Reprinted from the *University of Washington Publications in Language and Literature,* University of Washington Press, copyright, 1926, by permission of the translator and publisher.

ADAM. Not I! but I will trust thee aye,
And my Creator I'll obey.
FIGURE. A fitting fere I've given thee
(Eve is she hight) thy wife to be—
Thy wife to be and partner,
And thou must ever cleave to her,
Do thou love her, let her love thee;
So shall ye both be blest of me.
Let her thine own commands obey,
And both be subject to my sway.
From thy rib-bone her form I wrought;
No stranger she, but from thee brought.
Out of thy body I shaped her frame;
From thee, not from without, she came.
Govern her, then, with counsel wise,
Nor let dissent betwixt you rise,
But love and mutual service great.
Such is the law of wedlock's state.
FIGURE [to EVE]. Now will I speak to
thee, O Eve.
Take heed, nor lightly this receive:
If thou to do my will art fain,
Thy heart its goodness will retain;
Honor and love to me accord,
Thy Maker and acknowledged Lord;
To serve me be thy heart inclined
With all thy might and all thy mind.
Love Adam, hold him dear as life;
He is thy husband, thou his wife;
Ever to him submit thy heart
And from his teaching ne'er depart;
Serve him and love, with willing mind;
Therein is wedlock's law defined.
If thou art proved a helper meet,
I'll set you both in glory's seat.
EVE. Lord, I will do what pleaseth
thee,
In nothing will neglectful be;
To thee, as sovereign, I will bow,
And him my fere and liege avow.
To him I will at all times cleave,
From me good counsel he'll receive;
Thy pleasure and his service aye
Will I perform, in every way.
[Then let the FIGURE call ADAM
nearer, and ·more particularly
addressing him, say:]
Listen! O Adam. Hearken unto me.
I formed thee; now this gift I add in fee;
Thou mayest live alway—if you loyal
be—

And hale and sound, from every sickness
free.
Thou'lt hunger not, nor thirst shall thee
annoy,
Neither shall heat nor cold thine ease
destroy,
Nor weariness thy perfect bliss alloy,
Nor any suffering abate thy joy.
All of thy life in pleasance thou shalt
spend;
'T will not be short—a life withouten
end!
I tell thee this, and will that Eve attend;
Unless she heed, to folly she will bend.
Dominion over all the earth ye'll
hold;
Birds, beasts—all creatures—be by you
controlled;
Who grudgeth this, his worth is lightly
told,
For your demesne shall the whole world
enfold.
Of good and ill I grant you choice to
make;
(Who hath such choice is tethered to no
stake;)
Weigh all in the balance fairly, nor mis-
take;
Be true to me, my counsel ne'er forsake.
Leave thou the evil, choose the good as
guide;
Love thou thy Lord, and keep thee at his
side;
None other counsel e'er for mine be tried:
Do this, so shalt thou without sin abide.
ADAM. Great thanks I give thee for
thy kindness, Lord,
Who madest me and dost such grace ac-
cord,
To place both good and evil in my ward.
Thy service shall my fullest joy afford.
Thou art my Lord, and in myself I see
Thy handiwork, for thou didst fashion
me;
Nor ever shall my will so stubborn be,
But that my chiefest care be serving thee.
[Then let the FIGURE with its
hand point out Paradise to
ADAM, saying:]
Adam!
ADAM. Lord!

FIGURE. Hear my plan; lift up thine eyes;
This garden see.
ADAM. Its name?
FIGURE. 'Tis Paradise.
ADAM. A place most fair!
FIGURE. Myself did it devise
And plant. Who here shall dwell as friend
I'll prize.
I place it in thy trust, to keep for aye.
  [*Then shall he send them into
  Paradise, saying:*]
I set you both herein.
ADAM. And shall we stay?
FIGURE. Through all your life. Nothing
  shall you affray;
Now ye can neither die nor waste away.
  [*Let the choir sing:* "And the
  Lord took the man."
  Then shall the FIGURE *stretch
  forth his hand toward Paradise,
  saying:*]
The nature of this garden I'll recite:
Here shalt thou feel the lack of no delight;
No earthly good, desired of any wight,
But each may here be found in measure
  right.
Here wife from man shall no harsh
  word obtain,
Nor man from wife have shame or cause
  to plain;
Begetting, man shall sinless still remain,
And woman bear her children without pain.
For aye thou'lt live; so blest is this
  sojourn,
With passing years thine age no change
  shall learn;
Nor dread of death shall bring to thee
  concern;
I will thy dwelling here to be eterne.
  [*Let the choir sing:* "And the
  Lord said unto ADAM."
  Then let the FIGURE *with his
  hand point out unto* ADAM *the
  trees of Paradise, saying:*]
Of all these fruits thou mayest eat each
  day.
  [*And let him shew him the forbidden
  tree, and its fruits, saying:*]

This I forbid thee, here make no essay;
If thou dost eat thereof thou'rt dead
  straightway;
My love thou'lt lose, thy weal with woe
  repay.
ADAM. All thy commandments will I
  keep in mind,
Nor I nor Eve to break them be inclined;
If for one fruit such dwelling were resigned,
Rightly should I be outcast to the wind.
If for an apple I thy love gainsay,
Ne'er in my life can I my folly pay;
A traitor should judgèd be for aye,
Who doth himself forswear, his lord betray.
  [*Then let the* FIGURE *go to the
  church, and let* ADAM *and* EVE
  *walk about, innocently delighting
  themselves in Paradise. In
  the mean time, let the demons
  run to and fro through the
  square, making fitting gestures;
  and let them come, one after
  mother, alongside of Paradise,
  shewing* EVE *the forbidden
  fruit, as if entreating her to
  eat thereof. Then let the* DEVIL
  come unto ADAM; *and he shall
  say unto him:*]
DEVIL. How liv'st thou, Adam?
ADAM. In felicity.
DEVIL. Is it well with thee?
ADAM. There's nothing vexeth me.
DEVIL. It can be better.
ADAM. Nay—I know not how.
DEVIL. Then, wouldst thou know?
ADAM. It recks me little now.
DEVIL. I know, forsooth!
ADAM. What boots it me to learn?
DEVIL. And why not, pray?
ADAM. Naught doth it me concern.
DEVIL. Concern thee 't will!
ADAM. I know not when.
DEVIL. I'll not make haste to tell thee,
  then.
ADAM. Nay, tell me!
DEVIL. No! I'll keep thee waiting
Till thou art sick of supplicating.
ADAM. To know this thing I have no
  need.

DEVIL. Thou dost deserve no boon, indeed!
The boon thou hast thou canst not use.
ADAM. Prithee, how's that?
DEVIL. Thou'lt not refuse
To hear? Well, then,—'twixt thee and me,—
ADAM. I'll listen, most assuredly!
DEVIL. Now mark me, Adam. I tell thee it
For thine own good.
ADAM. That I'll admit.
DEVIL. Thou'lt trust me, then?
ADAM. Full trust I bring!
DEVIL. In every point?
ADAM. All—save one thing.
DEVIL. What thing is that?
ADAM. This: I'll do naught
Offensive to my Maker's thought.
DEVIL. Dost fear him so?
ADAM. I fear him; yes—
Both love and fear.
DEVIL. That's foolishness!
What can he do thee?
ADAM. Good and bale.
DEVIL. Thou'st listened to an idle tale!
An evil thing befall thee? Why,
In glory born, thou canst not die!
ADAM. God saith I'll die, without redress,
Whene'er his precepts I transgress.
DEVIL. What is this great transgression, pray?
I fain would learn without delay.
ADAM. I'll tell thee all in perfect truth.
This the command he gave, forsooth:
Of all the fruits of Paradise
I've leave to eat (such his advice)—
—All, save one only, which is banned;
That I'll not touch, e'en with my hand.
DEVIL. Which fruit is that?
[*Then let* ADAM *stretch forth his hand and shew him the forbidden fruit, saying:*]
ADAM. See'st yonder tree?
That fruit hath he forbidden me.
DEVIL. Dost know the reason?
ADAM. Certes, no!
DEVIL. The occasion of this thing I'll show:
No whit cares he for all the rest;

But yon, that hangeth loftiest,
—The fruit of Knowledge—can bestow
The gift all mysteries to know.
If thou eat'st that, 't will profit thee.
ADAM. In what way, pray?
DEVIL. That thou shalt see:
Thine eyes will straightway be unsealed,
All future things to thee revealed;
All that thou will'st thou canst perform;
'T will bring thee blessings in a swarm.
Eat, and thou shalt repent it not;
Then thou'lt not fear thy God in aught;
Instead, thou'lt be in all his peer;
For this, he filled thy soul with fear.
Wilt trust me? Then to taste proceed.
ADAM. That will I not!
DEVIL. Fine words, indeed!
Thou wilt not?
ADAM. No!
DEVIL. A fool art thou!
Thou'lt yet mind what I tell thee now.
[*Then let the* DEVIL *depart; and he shall go to the other demons, and he shall make an excursion through the square; and after some little interval, cheerful and rejoicing, he shall return to his tempting of* ADAM, *and he shall say unto him:*]
How farest thou, Adam? Wilt change thy mind?
Or still to stubbornness inclined?
I meant to tell thee recently
God as his almsman keepeth thee.
He put thee here the fruit to eat;
Hast other recreation sweet?
ADAM. Here nothing lacks I could desire.
DEVIL. Dost to naught loftier aspire?
Canst boast thyself a man of price!
—God's gardener of Paradise!
He made thee keeper of his park;
Wilt thou not seek a higher mark?
Filling thy belly!—Surely, he
Had nobler aims in mind for thee!
Listen now, Adam, and attend
The honest counsel that I lend:
Thou couldest from thy Lord be free,
And thy Creator's equal be.
In brief, I'll this assurance make:

If of this apple thou partake, [*Then shall
   he lift his hand toward Paradise.*]
Then thou shalt reign in majesty!
In power, God's partner thou canst be!
ADAM. Go! Get thee hence!
DEVIL.   What! Adam. —How!
ADAM. Go! Get thee hence! Satan
   art thou!
Ill counsel giv'st thou.
DEVIL.   How, pray tell!
ADAM. Thou would'st deliver me to
   hell!
Thou would'st me with my Lord embroil,
Move me from bliss to bale and moil.
I will not trust thee! Get thee hence!
Nor ever have the impudence
Again to come before my face!
Traitor forsworn, withouten grace!

   [*Then shall the* DEVIL, *sadly and
   with downcast countenance, de-
   part from* ADAM *and he shall
   go even unto the gates of Hell,
   and he shall hold converse
   there with the other demons.
   Thereafter, he shall make an
   excursion among the people;
   but presently he shall draw
   near to Paradise, on the side
   where* EVE *is, and approaching*
   EVE *with a cheerful counte-
   nance and much blandishment,
   he thus accosteth her:*]

DEVIL. Eve, hither am I come, to thee.
EVE. And prithee, Satan, why to me?
DEVIL. Seeking thy weal, thine honour,
   too.
EVE. God grant it!
DEVIL.   Then, thy fears eschew.
Long since, I've mastered by my pains
Each secret Paradise contains;
A part of them to thee I'll tell.
EVE. Begin, then, and I'll listen well.
DEVIL. Thou'lt hearken to me?
EVE.   Hearken?—yea,
Nor vex thy soul in any way.
DEVIL. Thou'lt keep it hidden?
EVE.   Yea, in truth.
DEVIL. Nor publish it?
EVE.   Not I! forsooth.
DEVIL. Then, to this contract I'll agree,
Nor further pledge require of thee.

EVE. Might'st safely trust my promise,
   though.
DEVIL. Thou'st been to a good school,
   I trow!
Adam I've seen—a fool is he.
EVE. A little hard.
DEVIL.   He'll softer be;
But harder now than iron is.
EVE. A noble man!
DEVIL.   A churl! I wis.
Thought for himself he will not take;
Let him have care, e'en for thy sake.
Thou art a delicate, tender thing,
Thou'rt fresher than the rose in spring;
Thou'rt whiter than the crystal pale,
Than snow that falls in the icy vale.
An ill-matched pair did God create!
Too tender thou, too hard thy mate.
But thou'rt the wiser, I confess;
Thy heart is full of cleverness;
Therefore 't is good to treat with thee.
To thee I'd speak; have faith in me.
Let none know of it.
EVE.   Who should know?
DEVIL. Not Adam even.
EVE.   Be it so.
DEVIL. Now will I speak; do thou give
   ear.
None, save us twain, is present here,
(And Adam yon, who hath not heard.)
EVE. Speak up! He'll not perceive a
   word.
DEVIL. I'll shew thee, then, what crafty
   plot
Was 'gainst you in this garden wrought:
The fruit God gave you to possess
Hath in it little goodliness,
But in the fruit to you forbidden
Exceeding virtue lieth hidden;
Therein is found of life the dower,
Dominion, mastery, and power,
Knowledge of evil and of good.
EVE. What savour hath 't?
DEVIL.   'T is heavenly food!
To thy fair body, to thy face,
Most meet it were to add this grace:
That thou be queen of the world—of this,
Of the firmament, and of the abyss—
And know all things that shall befall,
And be the mistress of them all.
EVE. Is such the fruit?

DEVIL. Truly, it is.
[*Then shall* EVE *carefully con-
sider the forbidden fruit, and
after she hath considered it for
a season, she shall say:*]
EVE. Only to see it brings me bliss!
DEVIL. But what, if thou shalt eat it,
Eve?
EVE. How should I know?
DEVIL. Wilt not believe?
First take it, and to Adam bear;
Heaven's crown will then be yours to
wear;
Ye shall be like your Maker then,
He'll hide no secrets from your ken.
Soon as ye've eaten of the fruit,
Your hearts it straightway will trans-
mute;
With God ye'll be—free from all blight—
Of equal goodness, equal might.
Come taste it!
EVE. That I'm thinking on.
DEVIL. Trust Adam not!
EVE. I'll taste anon.
DEVIL. But when?
EVE. Let me deferment make
Till Adam his repose shall take.
DEVIL. But eat it. Put thy fears away.
'Twere childish greatly to delay.
[*Then shall the* DEVIL *depart
from* EVE *and shall go unto
Hell; but* ADAM *shall come
unto* EVE, *being sore displeased
because the* DEVIL *hath spoken
with her, and he shall say unto
her:*]
ADAM. Say, wife, what thing of thee
inquired
That evil Satan?—what desired?
EVE. 'T was of our honour he con-
versed.
ADAM. Believe him not—the traitor
curs'd!
That he's a traitor, I've no doubt.
EVE. And wherefore, pray?
ADAM. I've found him out.
EVE. What boots it? See him once—
thou'lt find
Eftsoons he'll make thee change thy mind!
ADAM. Not he! I'll trust him not at
all

Till I've made trial of him withal.
Let him no more come near to thee;
He's full of foulest perfidy,
His sovereign Lord he sought to cheat
And set himself in the highest seat.
A knave that's done such wickedness
To thee shall never have access.
[*Then a serpent, cunningly put
together, shall ascend along the
trunk of the forbidden tree,
unto which* EVE *shall approach
her ear, as if hearkening unto
its counsel. Thereafter,* EVE
*shall take the apple, and shall
offer it unto* ADAM. *But he
shall not yet receive it, and*
EVE *shall say unto him:*]
EVE. Eat! Adam; thou know'st not
what is offered!
Let's take the gift thus freely proffered.
ADAM. Is it so good?
EVE. That thou shalt see;
But canst not, till it tasted be.
ADAM. I fear!
EVE. Then, leave it!
ADAM. Nay, I'll taste.
EVE. Faint-heart! so long thy time to
waste!
ADAM. I'll take the fruit.
EVE. Here, eat it! So
Thou shalt both good and evil know.
But, first, myself I'll taste it now.
ADAM. And I next?
EVE. Marry! Next shalt thou.
[*Then shall* EVE *eat a part of the
apple, and she shall say unto*
ADAM:]
I've tasted! Pardi! What a savour!
I've never known so sweet a flavour!
With such a savour 't is endued—
ADAM. What savour?
EVE. —as no mortal food!
Now do mine eyes so clearly see
I seem Almighty God to be!
All that has been or shall befall
I know—am mistress of it all!
Eat! Adam, eat! No more abstain;
Thou'lt do it to thy lasting gain.
[*Then shall* ADAM *receive the ap-
ple from the hand of* EVE, *say-
ing:*]

ADAM. I'll trust thy word, thou art my peer.

EVE. Take, eat; thou hast no cause to fear.

[*Then shall* ADAM *eat a part of the apple; and having eaten it, he shall straightway take knowledge of his sin; and he shall bow himself down so that he cannot be seen of the people, and shall put off his goodly garments, and shall put on poor garments of fig-leaves sewn together; and manifesting exceeding great sorrow, he shall begin his lamentation:*]

ADAM. O! sinful wretch! What have I done?

Now my avoidless death 's begun!
Now, without rescue, am I dead;
My fortune fair is evil sped;
My lot, a little time ago
So happy, now is turned to woe;
I my Creator did forsake
Through counsel of my evil make.
O! sinner lost! What shall I do?
How can I now my Maker view?
Upon my Maker can I look,
Whom through my folly I forsook?
Ne'er such ill bargain did I strike!
Now do I know what sin is like!
O Death! Why dost thou let me live,
Nor to the earth clean riddance give?
Why, cumbering earth, do I yet stay?
The depths of hell must I essay;
In hell my dwelling aye shall be
Until one come to succour me.
In hell henceforward I shall fare,
And whence shall help come to me there?
Whence shall aid thither come to me?
Who from such pains shall set me free?
Why did I thus my Lord offend?
Now there is none can be my friend;
None will there be can me avail;
Lost am I now, withouten fail!
Against my Lord I've done such sin,
No suit with him can I begin,
For right is he, and wrong am I.
O God! 'Neath what a curse I lie!
Who, henceforth, will take thought of me,
Who've wronged the King of Majesty?

'Gainst Heaven's own king such wrong I've done
That claim upon him have I none.
No friend I have, no neighbour near,
Who as my surety might appear;
And whom shall I beseech for aid,
When mine own wife hath me betrayed,
Whom God gave me my fere to be?
An evil counsel gave she me!
Alas! O Eve!   [*Then shall he look upon* EVE, *his wife, and shall say:*]
                        Insensate wife!
In an ill hour I gave thee life!
O had that rib been burned, alas!
That brought me to this evil pass!
Had but the fire that rib consumed,
That me to such confusion doomed!
Why, when from me the rib he drew,
Burned he it not, nor me then slew?
The rib the body hath betrayed,
Ill-treated, and all useless made.
I know not what to say or try;
Unless grace reach me from on high,
From pain I cannot be released,
Such malady on me hath seized.
Alas! O Eve! Woe worth the day—
Such torment holdeth me in sway—
Thou e'er becamest wife to me!
Now I am lost through heeding thee;
Through heeding thee I'm in this plight,
Brought down most low from a great height.
Thence will no mortal rescue me—
None, save the God of majesty.
What say I? Wretch! Why named I him?
He help? I've gained his anger grim!
None will e'er bring me succour—none
Save him who'll come as Mary's son.
From none can I henceforth get aid
Since we our trust with God betrayed.
Then, let all be as God ordains;
No course, except to die, remains.

[*Then let the choir begin:* "The voice of the Lord God walking in the garden."
After this hath been sung, the FIGURE *shall come, wearing a stole, and looking about him, as if seeking to know where* ADAM *is. But* ADAM *and* EVE

shall be hidden in a corner of Paradise, as if conscious of their wretchedness; and the FIGURE *shall say:* Adam, where art thou?
Then shall they both arise and stand before the FIGURE, *yet not fully upright, but through shame for their sin, bending forward a little, and exceeding sad; and let* ADAM *make answer:*]

ADAM. Lord, I'm here.
I hid; thine anger did I fear;
I saw my nakedness revealed,
Therefore myself have I concealed.
FIGURE. What hast thou done? How gone astray?
Who thee from goodness drew away?
What hast thou done? Why blushest thou?
How shall I reckon with thee now?
Thou hadst, a little while ago,
No reason any shame to show;
Now see I thee downcast, distraught;
Small joy thy dwelling here hath brought!
ADAM. So great is my confusion, I
Do hide me from thee, Lord.
FIGURE. And why?
ADAM. Such shame my body doth enlace,
I dare not look thee in the face.
FIGURE. Why overstept'st thou my decree?
Hath this brought any gain to thee?
My servant thou, thy Lord am I.
ADAM. This can I in no wise deny.
FIGURE. In mine own likeness thee I wrought;
Why set'st thou my command at naught?
After mine image formed I thee;
Why hast thou thus affronted me?
Thou didst in no wise heed my hest;
Deliberately thou hast transgressed!
That fruit thou atest which I said
I had for thee prohibited.
Didst reckon thus my peer to be?
I do not think thou'lt jest with me!
[Then shall ADAM *stretch forth his hand toward the* FIGURE, *and thereafter toward* EVE, *saying:*]

ADAM. The woman that thou gavest me,
She first did this iniquity;
She gave me it, and I did eat;
Now is my life with woe replete.
Most rashly meddled I therein;
'T was through my wife that I did sin.
FIGURE. Thy wife thou trustedst more than me,
Didst eat without my warranty;
This recompense to thee I'll make:
Curs'd shall the ground be for thy sake,
Where thou shalt wish thy grain to sow,
Nor shall it any fruit bestow;
Curs'd shall it 'neath thy hand remain,
And all thy tillage be in vain.
Its fruit to thee it shall not yield,
But thorns and thistles fill thy field;
'T will change whate'er is sown by thee;
Its curse shall be thy penalty.
With grievous toil and bitter pain
To eat thy bread shalt thou be fain;
In sweat, in great affliction, aye
Thou'lt live hereafter, night and day.
[Then shall the FIGURE *turn toward* EVE, *and with a threatening countenance shall say unto her:*]

FIGURE. Thou, too, O Eve, a woman of sin,
Didst thy rebellion soon begin
And briefly heededest my decree.
EVE. The wicked serpent tempted me.
FIGURE. Didst think through him to be my peer?
Hast learned to make things hidden clear?
Erstwhile thou heldest sovereignty
Over all living things that be;
How quickly hast thou lost thy crown!
Now see I thee sad and cast down.
Hast thou thereby got gain or hurt?
I'll render thee thy just desert;
Thy service I will thus repay:
Woe thee shall find in every way;
In sorrow thou'lt thy children bear,
In pain throughout their life they'll fare;
In sorrow they'll be born of thee,
And end their days in misery.
To such distress and direful need
Thou'st brought thyself and all thy seed;
All thy descendants ever more

Thy sin shall bitterly deplore.
[*And* EVE *shall make answer,
saying:*]
EVE. Yea, I have sinned—'t was
through my folly vain;
For one sole apple I have got such bane
As doometh me and mine to bitter pain—
Great toll of wretchedness, with little
gain!
If I have sinned, 't was nothing
strange, I fear,
Whenas the serpent charmed my silly ear;
Much guile he hath, no lamb doth he ap-
pear;
Unhappy he who would his counsel hear!
I took the fruit—'t was folly, now
I see;
This wickedness I wrought 'gainst thy
decree;
I tasted it, and won thine enmity.
For a little fruit, my life must forfeit be!
[*Then shall the* FIGURE *threaten
the serpent, saying:*]
FIGURE. Thou, too, O Serpent, curs'd
shalt be;
I will exact my due of thee:
Upon thy belly shalt thou go
Through all the days thy life shall know;
The dust shall be thy daily food,
On moor or heath, or in the wood;
Woman shall bear thee enmity,
An evil neighbour ever be;
To strike her heel thou'lt lie in wait,
But she herself shall bruise thy pate;
Thy head with such a Hammer smite
'T will put thee in a sorry plight;
Therefrom shall she such aidance get,
She'll be avengèd of thee yet!
Thou sought'st her acquaintance to thy
woe;
She yet shall bring thy head full low;
There yet shall spring from her a Root
That all thy cunning shall confute.
[*Then shall the* FIGURE *drive
them forth out of Paradise,
saying:*]
FIGURE. From Paradise, go! get you
hence!
Ye've made ill change of residence.
On earth shall ye your dwelling make;
In Paradise ye have no stake,

No title there, and no concern;
Forth shall ye go, without return.
Through judgment ye can claim naught
there;
Now find you lodgement otherwhere.
Go! From felicity depart!
Hunger shall fail you not, nor smart,
But pain and weariness abound
Day after day, the whole week round.
On earth a weary term ye'll spend,
And die thereafter, in the end;
After ye've tasted death, straightway
To hell ye'll come without delay.
Here exile shall your bodies quell,
And danger daunt your souls in hell.
Satan shall hold your souls in thrall;
There'll be no helper ye can call,
None by whom rescue can be sent,
Unless I pity and relent.
[*Let the choir sing:* "In the
sweat of thy face."
*In the mean time there shall
come an angel, clad in white
garments, and bearing a shin-
ing sword in his hand, whom
the* FIGURE *shall set over
against the gate of Paradise,
and he shall say unto him:*]
FIGURE. Guard well my Paradise, that
ne'er
Again this outlaw enter there—
That him no leave or chance befall
To touch the fruit of Life at all;
With this thy sword that flameth aye,
Forever bar for him the way.
[*When they shall be clean outside
of Paradise, sad and con-
founded in appearance, they
shall bow themselves to the
ground, even unto their feet,
and the* FIGURE *shall point to
them with his hand, his face
being turned toward Paradise;
and the choir shall begin:*
"Behold Adam is become as one
(of us)."
And when this is ended, the FIG-
URE *shall go back unto the
church.
Then shall* ADAM *have a spade,
and* EVE *a mattock, and they*

shall begin to till the ground, and they shall sow wheat therein. After they shall have finished their sowing, they shall go and sit for a season in a certain place, as if wearied with their toil, and with tearful eyes shall they look back ofttimes at Paradise, beating their breasts. Meanwhile shall the DEVIL come and plant thorns and thistles in their tillage, and then he shall depart. When ADAM and EVE shall come to their tillage, and when they shall have beheld the thorns and thistles that have sprung up, stricken with grievous sorrow, they shall cast themselves down upon the ground; and remaining there, they shall beat their breasts and their thighs, manifesting their grief by their gestures; and ADAM shall then begin his lamentation:]

ADAM. Woe worth the hour—hateful for ever more—
That e'er my sinfulness so whelmed me o'er!
That I forsook the Lord whom all adore!
To succour me, whom shall I now implore?
    [Here let ADAM look back at Paradise; and he shall lift up both hands toward it; and devoutly bowing his head, he shall say:]
O Paradise! How sweet to dwell in thee!
Garden of glory! Oh how fair to see!
Thence, for my sin, must I an outcast be;
Hope of return is ever lost to me!
    I was therein; but little joy I got;
Through heeding counsel false I thence was brought.
Now I repent; scorn earn I, as I ought.
'T is all too late, my sighing boots me naught.
    Where was my memory? whither fled my wit?
That I, for Satan, glory's King should quit!

Now, sore my grief—no help is there in it;
My sin on history's pages shall be writ.
    [Then shall ADAM lift up his hand against EVE, who shall have been set some little distance away, on higher ground, and moving his head with great indignation, he shall say unto her:]
O evil woman, full of perfidy!
How quickly to perdition brought'st thou me,
When thou mad'st sense and reason both to flee!
Now I repent, but can no pardon see.
    To evil how inclined wert thou to cleave!
How quick the serpent's counsel to receive!
Through thee I die, through thee my life I leave.
Writ in the book thy sin shall be, O Eve!
    Seest thou these tokens of confusion dread?
Earth doth perceive what curse o'erhangs our head;
'T was corn we sowed—thistles spring up instead.
Greatly we've sweat, ill have we profited!
    Thou seest the outset of our evil state;
Great sorrow 't is, but greater doth await;
To hell shall we be brought, without rebate;
Pain shall not fail us, neither torment great.
    O wretched Eve! How seemeth it to thee?
This hast thou gained thee as thy dowery:
Ne'er more canst thou bring man felicity,
But aye opposed to reason thou wilt be.
    All they who come hereafter, of our seed,
Shall feel the punishment of thy misdeed;
Thou sinnedst; all must bear the doom decreed.
Late will he come who shall relieve their need.
    [Then let EVE make answer unto ADAM:]

Eve. Adam, dear lord, much hast thou
chidden me,
And much reviled and blamed my vil-
lainy;
If I have sinned, my punishment I dree;
Guilty I am, of God I'll judgèd be.
Toward God and thee much evil have
I wrought;
'Gainst my offence long shall reproach be
brought;
My fault is great, my sin torments my
thought!
O wretched me! Of good in me is naught!
No ground have I wherewith to make
my plea,
That God's just doom be not pronounced
on me;
Forgive me!—no atonement can I see,
Else would my sacrifice be offered free.
A miserable sinner, vile within,
Hiding my face from God for my great
sin—
Oh, take me. Death! Now let my death
begin!
Shipwrecked and lost, the shore I cannot
win.
The serpent fell, the snake of evil
fame,
Caused me to eat the apple, to my shame;
I gave it thee—to serve thee was mine
aim;
For this thy sin thyself I may not blame.
Oh, why did I my Maker's will defy?
Wherefore, dear lord, thy teachings thus
deny?
Thou sinnedst, but the root thereof am I!
Our sickness doth a long, long cure imply.
For my great error, my adventure
vain,
Our seed, henceforth, will dearly pay
again;
The fruit was sweet, bitter will be the
pain!
In sin we ate, ours will the guilt remain.
Yet, none the less, my hope in God
I base:
Sometime atonement will our guilt efface,
And I shall know God's favour and his
grace;
His power will bring us from that evil
place.

[*Then shall the* Devil *come, and
three or four other devils with
him, bearing in their hands
chains and iron shackles, which
they shall place on the necks
of* Adam *and* Eve.

*And certain ones shall push
them on, others shall drag
them toward hell; other devils,
however, shall be close beside
hell, waiting for them as they
come, and these shall make a
great dancing and jubilation
over their destruction; and
other devils shall, one after
another, point to them as they
come; and they shall take
them up and thrust them into
hell; and thereupon they shall
cause a great smoke to arise,
and they shall shout one to
another in hell, greatly rejoic-
ing; and they shall dash to-
gether their pots and kettles,
so that they may be heard
without. And after some little
interval, the devils shall go
forth, and shall run to and fro
in the square; certain of them,
however, shall remain behind in
hell.*]

[*Then shall come* Cain *and* Abel.
Let Cain *be clad in red gar-
ments, but* Abel *in garments
of white; and they shall till
the ground that hath been
made ready; and after* Abel
*shall have rested a little from
his labor, let him address his
brother* Cain *in a fond and
friendly fashion, saying unto
him:*]

Abel. O Cain, my brother, of one blood
are we;
Both Adam's sons—the first of men was
he—
And of one mother, also,—Eve hight
she;
In serving God, let us no niggards be.

To do our Maker's hests let us be
fain;
So serve him that we shall his love re-
gain,
Which our poor parents lost through folly
vain.
Let steadfast love abide betwixt us twain.
  So serve we God that we may please
him aye,
Pay him his dues in full, keep naught
away;
If we with cheerful hearts his word obey,
No dread of death our souls shall e'er
affray.
  Pay we his tithes, his tributes justly
tell,
First-fruits and offerings, sacrifice as
well;
If ever greed do us to fraud impel,
Without remission we'll be lost in hell.
  Betwixt us twain let great affection
be,
Let never envy come, nor enmity;
For why should strife arise 'twixt thee
and me,
When all the earth to us hath been made
free?
  [*Then shall* CAIN *look at his
brother* ABEL, *as if mocking
him; and he shall say unto
him:*]
CAIN. Good brother Abel, featly canst
thou preach!
Canst order well thy points, and stablish
each;
But should one practice that which thou
dost teach,
In a few days, his gifts their end would
reach!
  This giving tithes ne'er suited me one
whit.
Thou, with thy stuff, thy pious vows ac-
quit,
And I, with mine, will do what seems me
fit;
If I do wrong, thou'lt not be damned for
it!
  To love each other, Nature taught us
twain;
Let neither, then, dissemble aught, or
feign;

Whiche'er of us shall raise contention vain,
Let him pay dear and have good cause to
plain.
  [*Let* ABEL *again address his
brother* CAIN; *since* CAIN *hath
answered him more mildly than
is his wont, he shall say:*]
ABEL. Good brother Cain, now list to
me.
CAIN. Gladly! Pray tell what moveth
thee.
ABEL. Thine own advantage.
CAIN.   Better still!
ABEL. Rebel no more against God's
will,
Nor flaunt thy froward hardihood:
This I adjure thee.
CAIN.   Well and good!
ABEL. Then let us sacrifice, that thus
The Lord may be well pleased with us;
If his forgiveness thus we win,
He will no more regard our sin,
Nor heaviness our souls shall touch;
To gain his love doth profit much.
Come, let us on his altar set
Such gifts as shall his favour get;
Let us his love beseech, and pray
That he defend us night and day.
  [*Then shall* CAIN *make answer,
as if* ABEL'S *counsel were ac-
ceptable to him, saying:*]
CAIN. Good brother, thou hast said
aright!
This sermon didst thou well indite,
And I will pay good heed to it;
Let's make our offerings, as is fit.
What offerest thou?
ABEL.   A lamb I'll bring,
The fairest and the choicest thing
That I can find in all the fold;
That one I'll offer, nor withhold;
And incense, also, will I bring.
Now I have told thee everything;
What offerest thou?
CAIN.   Wheat from my field,
Such as God suffereth it to yield.
ABEL. The choicest?
CAIN.   God forbid! Instead,
From that, tonight I'll make my bread.
ABEL. Such sacrifice will not avail
To please him.

CAIN.   Pish! a silly tale!
ABEL. Thou'rt a rich man, much cattle
   hast—
CAIN. That have I!
ABEL.   Count them, to the last,
And give to him a tenth of all;
This part shalt thou God's portion call.
Offer him this whole-heartedly,
And rich reward shall come to thee.
Wilt do this?
CAIN.   Fie! Thou'rt mad, I guess!
To give a tenth were foolishness;
Of ten, there'd then be left but nine!
A fig for all thy counsel fine!
Come, let each offer severally
What seems him good.
ABEL.   So let it be.
   [*Then shall they go unto two
   great stones, which shall have
   been made ready for this pur-
   pose. The one stone shall be
   set at such a distance from the
   other that, when the* FIGURE
   appeareth, ABEL'S *stone shall
   be on his right hand, but the
   stone of* CAIN *on his left.*
   ABEL *shall offer up a lamb, and
   incense, whence he shall cause
   smoke to arise.* CAIN *shall
   offer a handful of corn. Then
   the* FIGURE *shall appear, and
   he shall bless* ABEL'S *offering,
   but the offering of* CAIN *shall
   he regard with scorn. Where-
   fore, after the oblation,* CAIN
   shall set his face against ABEL;
   *and when their sacrifices are
   ended, they shall go again unto
   their own places.*
   Then shall CAIN *come unto* ABEL,
   *seeking craftily to lead him
   forth, that he may slay him;
   and he shall say unto him:*]
CAIN. Good brother, let us hence!
   Arise!
ABEL. Wherefore?
CAIN.   Ourselves to exercise,
To view the tillage of our fields,
What growth, what flowering it yields;
Then, to the meadows we will go,
Thereby we'll be refreshed, I know.

ABEL. I'll go with thee, where thou
   shalt say.
CAIN. Come then; it will thy pains re-
   pay.
ABEL. Thou art my elder brother, thou,
And to thy wishes I will bow.
CAIN. Do thou go first, I'll follow thee
With loitering steps and leisurely.
   [*Then shall they both go to a
   place apart, and secret, as it
   were, where* CAIN *shall rush
   upon* ABEL, *like unto a mad
   man, desiring to slay him; and
   he shall say unto him:*]
CAIN. Abel, thou diest!
ABEL.   Wherefore? Speak!
CAIN. I will my vengeance on thee
   wreak!
ABEL. Have I thee wronged?
CAIN.   Aye, wronged enow!
A traitor fully proved art thou.
ABEL. Surely I'm not!
CAIN.   Dost thou deny?
ABEL. I'd ne'er do treachery—not I!
CAIN. Thou hast already!
ABEL.   How? I'd know.
CAIN. Thou'lt know full soon.
ABEL.   Can this be so!
CAIN. I'll set thee right full speedily.
ABEL. But thou canst nothing prove
   'gainst me.
CAIN. The proof 's here!
ABEL.   God will overthrow it.
CAIN. I'll slay thee!
ABEL.   God will surely know it.
   [*Then shall* CAIN *lift up his right
   hand threateningly against him,
   saying:*]
CAIN. Lo, this is what will prove the
   case!
ABEL. In God alone my trust I place.
CAIN. 'Gainst me, small aid from him
   thou'lt get.
ABEL. Haply, he'll thwart thy purpose
   yet.
CAIN. He cannot turn thy death aside.
ABEL. By his good pleasure I abide.
CAIN. Would'st hear wherefore I will
   thee kill?
ABEL. O tell me it!
CAIN.   Tell thee I will.

Too long hast thou usurped God's ear!
Through thee, my prayers he would not
 hear,
Through thee, he spurned the gifts I bore;
Dost think I'll not pay off this score?
Certes, I'll render thee thy pay!
Dead on this sand thou'lt lie today!
ABEL. If thou slay me, great wrong 't
 will be;
God will avenge my death on thee.
God wot I thee have harmèd not,
Nor slandered thee to him in aught;
But bade thee so thy acts employ
That thou his favor might'st enjoy,
Bade thee grant all his claims—such
 things
As tithes, firstfruits, and offerings;
Thereby hadst thou his love obtained;
Through failing this, his wrath thou'st
 gained.
God keepeth faith; who serves him fain,
Shall nothing lose, but greatly gain.
CAIN. Thou'st talked too long; thou
 diest now!
ABEL. Brother! what say'st? My guide
 wert thou;
Hither I came in perfect trust.
CAIN. Trust cannot save thee; die thou
 must!
I'll slay thee now! I challenge thee!
ABEL. May God be merciful to me!

[*Then shall* ABEL *kneel down,
facing the East; and he shall
have a pot hidden underneath
his garments, which* CAIN *shall
strike violently, as if he were
slaying* ABEL *himself.* ABEL,
*however, shall lie stretched out,
as if he were dead.
The choir shall sing:* "Where is
Abel, thy brother?"
Meanwhile, the FIGURE *shall
come forth from the church and
go toward* CAIN, *and after the
choir shall have ended the re-
sponsorium, he shall say unto*
CAIN, *as if very wroth with
him:*]
FIGURE. Where is thy brother Abel,
 Cain?
To make rebellion art thou fain?

'Gainst me hast thou begun to strive?
Show me thy brother now, alive!
CAIN. How should I know where he
 may be?
—At home, or with his husbandry?
And why should I be forced to find him?
I was not set to keep and mind him!
FIGURE. What hast thou done with him,
 O Cain?
Right well I know! Him thou hast slain!
Thy brother's blood to me doth cry;
Its voice hath come to me on high.
Great wickedness didst thou commit,
Thy life long thou'lt be curs'd for it;
This malison thou'lt bear for aye;
As was the deed, so be the pay!
Yet I will not that thou be slain,
But pass thy life in dole and pain;
Whoever, therefore, Cain shall slay,
A sevenfold penalty shall pay.
Thou slewest him who trusted me;
Most heavy shall thy penance be.

[*Then shall the* FIGURE *return
unto the church; but the devils
shall come forth and lead* CAIN
*away to hell, beating him again
and again.* ABEL, *also, shall
they lead away, albeit in a
more gentle fashion.*]

[*Then shall the Prophets be made
ready, one by one, in a secret
place, as their order is.
Let the Lesson be read in the
choir.* "You, I say, do I chal-
lenge, O Jews."
*And let the Prophets be sum-
moned by name; and when they
shall come forward, let them
advance with dignity and utter
their prophecies loudly and
distinctly. So shall* ABRAHAM
*come first, an old man with an
exceeding long beard, arrayed
in ample robes; and when he
shall have sat for a brief sea-
son upon the bench, let him be-
gin his prophecy in a loud
voice:*]
ABRAHAM. Thy seed shall possess the

gates of their enemies, and in thy seed
shall all the nations of the earth be blessed.
Abraham, I; such is my name.
Hear, now, the message I proclaim:
Whose hope is on God's promise stayed,
Let him keep faith and trust unswayed;
Whose faith is fixed in God, for aye
Will God be with him. This I say
Through knowledge; God my faith did
    test;
I did his will, obeyed his hest;
For him, mine own son had I slain,
But God's hand did my hand restrain.
The unfinished offering did he bless,
'T was counted me for righteousness.
God promised me—'t is truth, indeed,—
An heir shall issue from my seed
Who shall subdue his every foe,
And strong and mighty shall he grow;
Their gates possessing, ne'er shall he
A menial in their castles be.
E'en such an one, sprung from my root,
Shall all our punishment commute;
By him the world shall ransomed be,
And Adam from his pain set free;
And men, of every race and kind
On earth, through him shall blessing find.
  [*After these words have been
  said, and a little time hath in-
  tervened, the devils shall lead*
  ABRAHAM *to hell.*
  Then shall come MOSES, *bearing
  in his right hand a rod, and in
  his left the tables (of stone).
  After he hath seated himself,
  let him utter his prophecy:*]
MOSES. God shall raise up a prophet
from among your brethren; to him shall
ye hearken as to me.
That which I speak, through God I
    saw;
From our own brethren, from our law,
God shall raise up a man who'll be
Prophet and sum of prophecy.
Heaven's secrets all shall he receive;
Him, more than me, shall ye believe.
  [*Thereafter shall he be led away
  by the* DEVIL *into hell. In like
  manner shall it be done with
  all the prophets.
  Then shall come* AARON, *in the*

*vestments of a bishop, bearing
in his hand a rod having flow-
ers and fruit; and being seated,
let him say:*]
AARON. From this rod the flower that
    springeth
Perfume of salvation bringeth;
Sweet its fruit, 't will end all crying
And all sorrow for our dying.
This rod—unplanted, without root,—
Can bud, and blossom, and bear fruit;
Such Rod from mine own line shall spring
And deadly hurt to Satan bring.
No taint of fleshly birth he'll bear,
Yet man's own nature shall he wear.
This is salvation's fruit, 't will free
Adam from his captivity.
  [*After him, let* DAVID *draw nigh,
  arrayed in royal robes and
  wearing a crown; and let him
  say:*]
DAVID. Truth is sprung out of the
earth; and justice hath looked down from
heaven. For the Lord will give goodness;
and our earth shall yield her fruit.
Out of the earth shall truth arise,
And justice watch us from the skies;
Yea, God shall give us all things good;
Our land shall richly bring us food,
Her increase yield that saving Bread
Whereby Eve's sons shall all be fed;
O'er all the earth shall he hold sway,
Shall stablish peace, drive war away.
  [*Thereafter let* SOLOMON *come
  forth, with the same adorn-
  ments as* DAVID, *yet in such a
  manner that he shall seem to
  be younger; and sitting down,
  let him say:*]
SOLOMON. Being ministers of God's
kingdom, you have not judged rightly,
nor kept the law of justice, nor walked
according to the will of God; horribly and
speedily will he appear to you; for a most
severe judgment shall be for them that
bear rule. For to him that is little, mercy
is granted.
God gave to you his law, O Jews,
But faith with him ye would not use;
Wardens of his domain were ye,
He stablished you right royally;

Ye would not render judgment right,
Your verdicts were in God's despite;
His will ye would perform no more,
And your iniquity waxed sore.
Your deeds shall all to light be brought;
Most grievous vengeance shall be wrought
On those that highest sat of all.
And they shall suffer fearful fall.
But God shall set the lowly free
And raise him to felicity.
This saying shall be verified
When God's own Son for us hath died.
The masters of the law 't will be
That slay him, most unlawfully;
Against all justice, all belief,
They'll crucify him, like a thief.
But they shall lose their lordly seat,
Who envy him, and ill entreat.
Low down they'll come, from a great
    height,
Well may they mourn their woeful plight.
Howbeit, poor Adam shall he see
And pity, and from sin set free.
    [*After him shall come* BALAAM,
    *an old man arrayed in ample
    robes, sitting upon an ass; and
    he shall come into the midst,
    and still sitting upon his beast,
    he shall speak his prophecy:*]
BALAAM. A Star shall rise out of Jacob,
and a Sceptre shall spring up from Israel,
and shall strike the chiefs of Moab, and
shall waste all the children of Seth.
From Jacob shall a Star arise,
Reddening with heaven's own fire the skies,
A Sceptre spring from Israel
That shall 'gainst Moab's rule rebel,
Their haughtiness diminishing;
For out of Israel Christ shall spring,
And he shall be that glorious Star
Whereby all things illumined are.
His faithful ones he'll lead to joy,
But all his enemies destroy.
    [*Thereafter shall* DANIEL *draw
    nigh, in years a youth, but in
    his demeanour like unto an old
    man; and when he shall have
    seated himself, let him speak
    his prophecy, stretching forth
    his hand against those whom
    he addresseth:*]

DANIEL. When the Most Holy One shall
    have come, your anointing shall cease.
You, O ye Jews, do I address,
Who use toward God great wickedness.
When he, the Chief of Saints, draws
    near,
Then your confusion shall appear,
For then shall your anointing cease;
All claim thereto must ye release.
This Holy One is Christ, 't is plain;
Through him the faithful life shall gain.
To earth come, for his people's sake,
On him your race great war shall make,
Shall drive him to his Passion; so
Shall they their unction's grace forego,
Thenceforth nor priest nor king shall own,
Their Law lost through themselves alone.
    [*After him shall come* HABAK-
    KUK, *an old man; and sitting
    down, when he beginneth his
    prophecy, he shall lift up his
    hands toward the church, mani-
    festing wonder and fear. Let
    him say:*]
HABAKKUK. O Lord, I have heard thy
    speech and was afraid. In the midst
    of the two beasts shalt thou be recog-
    nized.
From God strange tidings have I heard,
Whereby my mind is greatly stirred;
So long did I this sign explore
My heart thereat is troubled sore:
Between two beasts shall he be shown,
By all the world he shall be known.
To him of whom this thing I say,
Behold, a star shall point the way;
Shepherds shall find him, thither brought,
Within a crib in dry stone wrought
Wherefrom the beasts shall eat their hay;
To kings he'll be declared straightway;
Thither the star shall lead the kings,
All three shall bring their offerings.
    [*Then shall* JEREMIAH *enter,
    bearing a scroll in his hand;
    and let him say:*]
JEREMIAH. Hear ye the word of the
Lord, all ye men of Judah, that enter in
at these gates to adore the Lord. Thus
saith the Lord of Hosts, the God of Israel:
Make your ways and your doings good,
and I will dwell with you in this place.

The holy word of God now hear,
All who are of his school, give ear,
All righteous Judah's mighty race,
Who in his household have a place:
Ye all shall enter by this door,
Our Lord to worship, evermore;
The Lord of Hosts to you doth cry,
The God of Israel, from on high:
Make good your ways, amend each one,
Let them be straight as furrows run,
And let your hearts be clean, withal,
Lest any evil you befall;
Let all your thoughts in good abound,
Nor wickedness therein be found.
If thus ye do, then God will come.
And in your dwellings make his home,
The Son of God, the glorious,
For you come down to earth, and thus,
As mortal man, with you shall be—
The Lord of heavenly majesty!
Adam he shall from prison bring,
Himself as ransom offering.

[*After him shall come* ISAIAS, *bearing a book in his hand, and wrapped in a large mantle; and let him speak his prophecy:*]

ISAIAS. And there shall come forth a rod out of the root of Jesse, and a flower shall rise up out of his root, and the Spirit of the Lord shall rest upon it. Now will I tell a wondrous thing:
From Jesse's root a Rod shall spring,
Shall burgeon and bear flower withal,
Whereto great honor shall befall;
The Holy Spirit shall enclose
This flower, and shall thereon repose.

[*Then shall there stand up a certain one of the synagogue, disputing with* ISAIAS; *and he shall say unto him:*]

JEW. Now, Sir Isaias, answer me:
Is this a tale, or prophecy?
This thing thou'st told—pray, what is it?
Didst it invent, or is it writ?
Thou'st been asleep—didst dream the rest?
Speak'st thou in earnest, or in jest?

ISAIAS. This is no tale, 't is very truth!

JEW. Then, let's know all of it, forsooth!

ISAIAS. What I have spoke is prophecy.

JEW. Writ in a book?

ISAIAS. Yea, verily,
—In Life's! I've dreamed it not, but seen!

JEW. And how?

ISAIAS. Through grace of God, I ween.

JEW. Thou seem'st to me a dotard grey,
Thy mind and sense all gone astray!
A soothsayer thou seem'st, indeed,
Skilled in the glass, perchance, to read;
Come, read me now this hand, and tell

[*Then shall he shew him his hand:*]

Whether my heart be sick or well.

ISAIAS. Thou hast sin's murrain in thy soul,
Ne'er in thy life shalt thou be whole!

JEW. Am I, then, sick?

ISAIAS. With error sore.

JEW. When shall I mend me?

ISAIAS. Never more!

JEW. Begin thy soothsaying, I pray.

ISAIAS. There'll be no lie in what I say.

JEW. Come now, re-tell thy vision, quick!
If 't was a rod, or but a stick,
And what its blossom shall engender;
Then due respect to thee we'll render,
And all the present generation
Will listen to thy dissertation.

ISAIAS. Then, this great marvel shall ye hear,
—Such ne'er was told to mortal ear,
To such a marvel never man
Hath listened since the world began:
"Behold, a virgin shall conceive and bear a son, and his name shall be called Immanuel."
The time is near, within your ken,
Not tarrying or distant, when
A virgin shall conceive, most fair,
And, virgin still, a son shall bear;
His name shall be Emmanuel.
Saint Gabriel shall the message tell;
The maid shall Virgin Mary be,
She'll bear the fruit of Life's own tree,
Jesus, our Saviour, who shall bring
Adam from dole and suffering,
And him to Paradise return.
That which I speak from God I learn;

All this shall surely be fulfilled,
And ye thereon your hope shall build.

[*Then shall come* NEBUCHAD-
NEZZAR, *adorned as befitteth a
king. And he shall say:*]

NEBUCHADNEZZAR. Did we not cast
three youths, bound, into the fire?

HIS MINISTERS. True, O King.

NEBUCHADNEZZAR. Lo, I see four men
loose, walking in the midst of the fire,
and they have no hurt, and the form of
the fourth is like the Son of God.
Hear now a wondrous prodigy,
Unheard-of by all men that be!

This saw I with the children three
Cast in the blazing fire by me:
The fire was hot and fierce to dree,
The bright flame glowed exceedingly;
The three rejoiced and made great glee,
Within the furnace walking free.
But when I came the fourth to see,
(Great comfort to the rest gave he,)
His face shone, full of majesty,
The Son of God he seemed to be! *

---

* The ms. breaks off at this point, prob-
ably very near the end of the play.—ED.

THE WISE VIRGINS AND THE FOOLISH VIRGINS

ANONYMOUS

Written and produced probably about the middle of the 12th century

TRANSLATED ESPECIALLY FOR THIS WORK BY BABETTE AND GLENN HUGHES

THUS SAY THE WOMEN. Where is the Christ, my Lord and exalted Son? Let us hasten to the sepulchre.

THE GUARDIAN ANGEL OF THE SEPULCHRE. He whom you seek in the sepulchre, O Christians, is no longer here. He has arisen, as he prophesied. Go, and announce to his disciples that he has gone before you into Galilee. Verily, the Lord has arisen from the tomb in glory. Hallelujah!

THE BRIDEGROOM. Behold the Bridegroom who is the Christ! Be watchful, virgins! Men now rejoice at his coming, and will further rejoice, for he has come to deliver the cradle of nations from the strong hand of the oppressor, from the forces of evil whose power sprang from the sin of the first mother. It is he whom the prophet calls the second Adam, and through whom the sin of the first Adam is destroyed in us. It is he who suffered on the cross that our blessed homeland should be restored to us, and that we should be saved from the powers of evil. He comes, the Bridegroom who, by his death, has expiated and washed away our sins, and has suffered the agony of the cross.

THE WISE VIRGINS. Hearken, ye virgins, where ye stand,
Give ear unto our wise command:
Jesus, the Bridegroom, is at hand.

Scarce hath he slept,
This Bridegroom ye attend.

For thy sins came he to earth,
In Bethlehem was his virgin birth,
In Jordan's waters was he cleansed,
Scarce hath he slept,
This Bridegroom ye attend.

Rejected was he, mocked, and flailed,
High on the cross beaten and nailed:
The tomb stood ready for the end.
Scarce hath he slept,
This Bridegroom ye attend.

Now he is arisen, as the Scripture said.
Gabriel am I, and this my stead.
Await him here whom ye shall wed.
Scarce hath he slept,
This Bridegroom ye attend.

THE FOOLISH VIRGINS. We virgins who come seeking you, we have carelessly spilled our oil. We pray to you as sisters in whom we put all our trust.

Sorrowful ones! Frail ones! Too long
have we slept!

We are all fellow travellers; you are our sisters. Whatever the cause of our misfortunes, you can help us enter heaven.

Sorrowful ones! Frail ones! Too long
have we slept!

Light then our lamps; have pity on our ignorance, so that we shall not be shut without the door when the Bridegroom calleth you to enter his dwelling.

Sorrowful ones! Frail ones! Too long have we slept!

THE WISE VIRGINS. Cease, we implore you, sisters. Supplicate us no further, for in this matter your supplication is in vain.

Sorrowful ones! Frail ones! Too long have we slept!

Haste ye now; go quickly and ask of the merchants that they furnish you, the careless ones, with oil for your lamps.

Sorrowful ones! Frail ones! Too long have we slept!

THE FOOLISH VIRGINS. Ah, luckless ones that we are! What can we do here? Can we not keep watch? We have brought this trouble upon our own heads.

Sorrowful ones! Frail ones! Too long have we slept!

Oh, that the merchant may give us oil quickly! Either the merchant or his helper. Let us go now to find oil, for we have thoughtlessly spilled ours.

Sorrowful ones! Frail ones! Too long have we slept!

THE WISE VIRGINS. Of our oil ye shall have none, though ye ask us for it. Go and buy it from the merchant whom you see yonder.

Sorrowful ones! Frail ones! Too long have we slept!

THE MERCHANTS. Gentle ladies, go away!
This is no fit place to stay.
Seek help elsewhere—not from us;
Seek help from the generous.

Sorrowful ones! Frail ones! Too long have we slept!
Back to your wise sisters wend;
Ask in God's name that they lend
Oil for your lamps—do not delay,
Soon comes the Bridegroom on his way.

Sorrowful ones! Frail ones! Too long have we slept!

THE FOOLISH VIRGINS. Ah, luckless ones that we are! What will now befall us? Truly, we have found nothing of that we sought. It was prophesied and soon it shall come to pass. . . . Never shall we celebrate our marriage.

Sorrowful ones! Frail ones! Too long have we slept!

Hearken, Bridegroom, to the voices of thy supplicants. Open the door to us, even as to our sisters. Pity our distress.
[*Now the* BRIDEGROOM *appears.*]
THE CHRIST. Verily I say unto you, I know you not, for your lamps are unlighted. The way is long, and those who walk with me have need of light.

Go, ye frail ones! Go, unfortunates!
Forever are ye damned to pain.
To Hades go and there remain.

[*Immediately they are seized by demons and hurried off to Hades.*]
Ye Jews, who deny the word of God, hearken now as man after man of your race bears witness for the King. And you, gentlemen, who doubted the Virgin birth, expiate your error by teaching the truth among your fellows.
ISRAEL. Israel, thou gentle man, tell us: what dost thou know for certain of the Christ?
RESPONSE. There was no king in Judea before the coming of Him who was known by all. The peoples of the earth await, as I do, the cleansing Word of God.
MOSES. Lawgiver, approach and speak worthily of the Christ.
RESPONSE. God will give you a prophet. Hearken unto him as ye hearken unto me.

He who hearkens not shall be driven forth from his people.

ISAIAH. Isaiah, who knowest the truth, why speakest thou it not?

RESPONSE. From the seed of Jesse shall spring a flower, and that flower shall be the spirit of God.

JEREMIAH. Come near, Jeremiah. Speak some prophecies concerning the Christ.

RESPONSE. So be it. This one is our God. There shall be no other.

DANIEL. Daniel, lift thy prophetic voice and specify the facts concerning our Lord.

RESPONSE. The Saint of Saints shall come, and sacraments shall cease.

HABAKKUK. Habakkuk, show us now what kind of witness thou art on behalf of the King of Heaven.

RESPONSE. I awaited, and lo! straightway I was seized with terror in the presence of Thy miracles. At the sight of Thy handiwork I hid myself among the beasts of the field.

DAVID. Speak, O thou David, concerning thy grandson, whose works thou well knowest.

RESPONSE. All the faithful adored the Lord; he whom all future peoples shall serve. The Lord God hath said unto my Lord: thy seat is at my right hand.

SIMEON. Now let Simeon come near; he of whom it was said that he should not die without seeing the Lord.

RESPONSE. And now, O Lord, Thou hast permitted me to finish my life in peace, for I have looked upon Him whom Thou has sent into the world for the salvation of the people.

ELIZABETH. Concerning the Lord, thus speaketh Elizabeth to the multitude.

RESPONSE. Why should my master's mother come to visit me? Because of him, a joyous child is stirring in my womb.

JOHN THE BAPTIST. Say why it is, thou Baptist, that even in thy mother's womb thou hast praised the Christ. Bring forth thy testimony in favor of Him whom thou hast praised so joyously.

RESPONSE. There is one that cometh after me, the latchet of whose shoe I am not worthy to unloose.

VIRGIL. Virgil, thou prophet of the Gentiles, give testimony of the Christ.

RESPONSE. Behold a new day dawns! A new race of men has appeared upon the earth.

NEBUCHADNEZZAR. Come! With thy mouth to the bottle, speak the truth that thou knowest of Christ.

RESPONSE. Nebuchadnezzar, by means of a prophecy, give authority to the author of all things.

RESPONSE. When I had a vision of the three men whom I condemned to die by fire, I saw also the Son of God sharing their fate in the flames. Three men only did I condemn to the fire. The fourth was the Son of God.

SIBYL. Speak truly, Sibyl. What do you presage of the Christ?

RESPONSE. There will come a sign of judgment. The earth shall sweat. From heaven a king shall come. All this at a later day. Here in the flesh he will sit in judgment on the world. Incredulous Judea, why art thou still without fear?

[Here commences the Benedicamus.]

Filled with gladness, let us rejoice. Gather round; let us celebrate with great joy the birth of Christ. He has come bringing grace and has shed His light upon the faithful.

THE SECOND SHEPHERDS' PLAY

[FROM THE *Townely,* OR *Wakefield* CYCLE]

ANONYMOUS *

Written and produced probably between 1360–1410

CHARACTERS

1ST SHEPHERD
2ND SHEPHERD
3RD SHEPHERD
MAK, *the Sheep-stealer*
MAK'S WIFE
MARY
THE CHILD CHRIST
AN ANGEL

1ST SHEPHERD. Lord! What, these weathers are cold, and I am ill-happed;
I am near numb of hand, so long have I napped;
My legs bend and fold, my fingers are chapped;
It is not as I would, for I am all lapped
In sorrow.
In storms and tempest,
Now in the east, now in the west,
Woe is him has never rest,
Mid-day nor morrow!
But we poor shepherds, that walk on the moor,
In faith, we are near-hands out of the door;
No wonder, as it stands, if we be poor,
For the tilth of our lands lies fallow as the floor,
As ye ken.
We are so lamed,
Over-taxed and shamed,
We are made hand-tamed,
With these gentlery-men.
Thus they rob us our rest, Our Lady them wary!
These men that are tied fast, they cause the plow tarry.
Which men say is for the best, we find it contrary,
Thus are husband-men oppressed, in point to miscarry
In life.
Thus hold they us under,
Thus they bring us in blunder,

* The present version is modernized by the editor, and based to a certain extent upon earlier versions.

It were great wonder,
    If ever should we thrive.
For may he get a painted sleeve, or a
        brooch nowadays,
Woe is him that shall grieve, or once
        againsays,
Dare no man him reprove, what mast'ry
    he has,
And yet may no man believe one word
        that he says—
    No letter.
He can make purveyance,
With boast and bragging,
And all is through maintenance,
    Of men that are greater.
There shall come a swain, as proud as a
        peacock,
He must borrow my wain, my plow also,
Then I am full fain to grant ere he go.
Thus live we in pain, anger, and woe,
    By night and day;
He must have if he longed
If I should forego it,
I were better be hanged
    Than once say him nay.
It does me good, as I walk thus by mine
        own,
Of this world for to talk in manner of
        moan—
To my sheep will I stalk and hearken
        anon,
There abide on a balk, or sit on a stone
    Full soon.
For I trow, pardie!
True men if they be,
We get more company
    Ere it be noon.
    2ND SHEPHERD. *Benedicite* and *Domi-nus!* what may this mean?
Why fares this world thus? Oft have
        we not seen!
Lord, these weathers are spiteful, and the
        weather full keen;
And the frost so hideous they water mine
        e'en,
    No lie!
Now in dry, now in wet,
Now in snow, now in sleet,
When my shoon freeze to my feet,
    It is not all easy.
But as far as I ken, or yet as I go,

We poor husbands suffer much—
We have sorrow then and then, it falls
        often so,
Poor Capel, our hen, both to and fro
    She cackles,
But begin she to croak,
To groan or to cluck,
Woe is him, our cock,
    For he is in the shackles.
These men that are wed have not all
        their will,
When they are full hard put, they sigh
        full still;
God wot they are led full hard and full
        ill,
In bower nor in bed they say nought
        theretill,
    This tide.
My part have I found,
My lesson is learned,
Woe is him that is bound,
    For he must abide.
But now late in our lives,—a marvel to
        me,
That I think my heart breaks such won-
        ders to see,
What that destiny drives, it should so
        be!
Some men will have two wives, and some
        men three,
    In store.
Some are woe that have any;
But so far ken I,
Woe is him that has many,
    For he feels sore.
But young men of wooing, for God that
        you bought,
Be full 'ware of wedding, and think in
        your thought
"Had I wist" is a thing it serves of
        nought;
Mickle still mourning has wedding home
        brought,
    And griefs,
With many a sharp shower,
For thou may catch in an hour
That shall savor full sour
    As long as thou liv'st.
For as read I epistle, I have one to my
        mate
As sharp as a thistle, as rough as a briar.

She is browed like a bristle with a sour-
    looking cheer;
Had she once wet her whistle she could
    sing full clear
      Her Pater-Noster.
She is as great as a whale,
She has a gallon of gall;
By Him that died for us all!
      I would I had run till I'd lost her.
    1ST SHEPHERD. God look over the row,
      fully deafly ye stand.
    2ND SHEPHERD. Yea, the devil in thy
      maw!—so tarrying,
Saw'st thou anywhere Daw?
    1ST SHEPHERD. Yea, on a fallow land
Heard I him blow. He comes here at
    hand.
    Not far; stand still.
    2ND SHEPHERD. Why?
    1ST SHEPHERD. For he comes, hope
    I.
    2ND SHEPHERD. He will make us both
    a lie,
    Unless we beware.
    3RD SHEPHERD. Christ's Cross me speed,
      and Saint Nicholas!
Thereof had I need, it is worse than it
    was.
Whoso could, take heed, and let the world
    pass,
It is ever in dread and brittle as glass,
    And slippery.
This world fared never so,
With marvels more and more—
Now in weal, now in woe,
    And all-thing'awry.
Was never since Noah's flood such floods
    seen,
Winds and rains so rude, and storms so
    keen,
Some stammered, some stood in doubt, as
    I ween,
Now God turn all to good! I say as I
    mean,
    For ponder:
These floods so they drown
Both in fields and in town,
And bear all down,
    And that is a wonder.
We that walk in the nights, our cattle
    to keep,

We see sudden sights, when other men
    sleep:
Yet methinks my heart lights, I see knaves
    peep,
Ye are two tall wights, I will give my
    sheep
    A turn.
But full ill have I meant,
As I walk on this bent,
I may lightly repent,
    My toes if I spurn.
Ah, sir, God you save, and master mine!
A drink fain would I have and somewhat
    to dine.
    1ST SHEPHERD. Christ's curse, my
      knave, thou art a lazy hind!
    2ND SHEPHERD. What, the boy pleases
      to rave. Abide until later,
    We have made it.
I'll thrift on thy pate!
Though the knave came late
Yet is he in state
    To dine, if he had it.
    3RD SHEPHERD. Such servants as I, that
      sweats and swinks,
Eats our bread full dry, and that me for-
    thinks;
We are oft wet and weary when master-
    men winks,
Yet comes full lately both dinners and
    drinks,
    But thoroughly.
Both our dame and our sire,
When we have run in the mire,
They can nip at our hire,
    And pay us full lately.
But hear my truth, master, for the fare
    that ye make,
I shall do thereafter work, as I take;
I shall do a little, sir, now and then,
For yet lay my supper never on my
    stomach
    In fields.
Whereto should I argue?
With my staff can I leap,
And men say "a cheap bargain yields
    poorly."
    1ST SHEPHERD. Thou wert an ill lad
      to ride a-wooing
With a man that had but little of spend-
    ing.

2ND SHEPHERD. Peace, boy, I bade: no
      more jangling,
Or I shall make thee afraid, by the
      heaven's king!
   With thy gauds;
Where are our sheep, boy, we scorn?
3RD SHEPHERD. Sir, this same day at
      morn
I them left in the corn,
   When they rang Lauds;
They have pasture good, they cannot go
      wrong.
1ST SHEPHERD. That is right. By the
      rood, these nights are long!
Yet I would, or we went, one gave us a
      song.
2ND SHEPHERD. So I thought as I stood,
      to mirth us among.
3RD SHEPHERD. I grant.
1ST SHEPHERD. Let me sing the tenory.
2ND SHEPHERD. And I the treble so
      high.
3RD SHEPHERD. Then the mean falls to
      me;
   Let see how ye chant.

[MAK enters, with a cloak thrown over his
      smock.]
MAK. Now, Lord, for thy names seven,
      that made both moon and stars
Well more than I can name: thy will,
Lord, leaves something lacking;
I am all upset, that moves oft my brains,
Now would God I were in heaven, for
      there weep no bairns,
   So still.
1ST SHEP. Who is that pipes so poor?
MAK. Would God ye wist how I fare!
Lo, a man that walks on the moor,
   And has not all his will.
2ND SHEPHERD. Mak, where hast thou
      gone? Tell us tidings.
3RD SHEPHERD. Is he come? Then each
      one take heed to this thing.
      [Takes his cloak from him.]
MAK. What, I be a yeoman, I tell you,
      of the king;
The self and the same, sent from a great
      lording,
   And such.
Fie on you; go hence,

Out of my presence!
I must have reverence,
   Why, who be I?
1ST SHEPHERD. Why make ye it so
      quaint? Mak, ye do wrong.
2ND SHEPHERD. But, Mak, play ye
      saint? I trow that ye sang.
3RD SHEPHERD. I trow the knave can
      paint, the devil might him hang!
MAK. I shall make complaint, and
      make you all be flogged.
   At a word,
And tell even how ye doth.
1ST SHEPHERD. But, Mak, is that
      sooth?
Now take out that southern tooth,
   And set in a turd.
2ND SHEPHERD. Mak, the devil in your
      eye, a stroke would I lend you.
3RD SHEPHERD. Mak, know ye not me?
   By God, I could beat you.
MAK. God look you all three! Me-
      thought I had seen you.
Ye are a fair company.
1ST SHEPHERD. Can ye now remember
      you?
2ND SHEPHERD. Joke on, knave!
Thus late as thou goes,
What will men suppose?
And thou hast an ill name
   Of stealing of sheep.
MAK. And I am true as steel, all men
      wot,
But a sickness I feel, that holds me full
      hot,
My belly fares not well, it is out of estate.
3RD SHEPHERD. Seldom lies the devil
      dead by the gate.
MAK.   Therefore
Full sore am I and ill,
If I stand stock-still;
I eat not a tittle
   This month and more.
1ST SHEPHERD. How fares thy wife?
      By my hood, how fares she?
MAK. Lies weltering by the road! by
      the fire, lo!
And a house full of brew she drinks well
      too,
Ill speed other good that she will do
   But so.

Eats as fast as she can,
And each year that comes to man,
She brings forth a child,
    And some years two.
But were I not more gracious, and richer
    by far,
I were eaten out of house and of harbor,
Yet is she a foul dear, if ye come near.
There is none that trows, nor knows,
        worse
    Than ken I.
Now will ye see what I proffer,
To give all in my coffer
To-morrow next to offer,
    Her head mass-penny.
    2ND SHEPHERD. I wot so tired watch-
        ing is none in this shire:
I would sleep if I took less to my hire.
    3RD SHEPHERD. I am cold and naked,
        and would have a fire.
    1ST SHEPHERD. I am weary of walking,
        and run in the mire.
    Wake thou!
    2ND SHEPHERD. Nay, I will lie down by,
For I must sleep truly.
    3RD SHEPHERD. As good a man's son
        was I
    As any of you.
But, Mak, come hither, between shalt thou
    lie down.
    MAK. Then might I prevent you forth-
        with: of that ye would say,
    No dread.
From my head to my toe
Manus tuas commendo,
Pontio Pilato.
        Christ's cross me speed,   [*He rises,*
        while the shepherds sleep, and says:]
Now were time for a man that lacks what
    he would,
To stalk privily then into a fold,
And nimbly to work then, and be not too
    bold,
He might regret the bargain, if it were
    told
    At the ending.
Now were time for to begin;
But he needs good counsel
That fain would fare well,
    And has but little spending.   [MAK
        works a spell on them.]

But about you a circle as round as a
    moon,
Till I have done that I will, till that it
    be noon,
That ye lie stone-still, till that I have
    done,
And I shall say theretill of good words a
    few
    Aloud.
Over your heads my hand I lift,
Out go your eyes, ford your sight!
But yet I must make better shift,
    And it be right.
Lord, what? they sleep hard! that may
    ye all hear;
Was I never a shepherd, but now will I
    learn
If the flock be scared, yet shall I nip near.
How, draw hitherward! now mends our
    cheer,
    From sorrow:
A fat sheep, I daresay,
A good fleece dare I lay,
Repay when I may,
    But this will I borrow.   [*He steals
        a sheep and goes home.*]
    MAK [*at his own door*]. How, Gill,
        art thou in? Get us some light.
    HIS WIFE. Who makes such din this
        time of the night?
I am set for to spin: I hope not I might
Rise a penny to win: I shrew them on
    height.
    So fares
A housewife that has been
To be raced thus between:
There may no jobs be seen
    For such small chores.
    MAK. Good wife, open the door. See'st
        thou not what I bring?
    WIFE. I may let thee draw the latch.
        Ah! come in, my sweeting.
    MAK. Yea, thou dost not reck of my
        long standing.
    WIFE. By thy naked neck, thou art like
        for to hang.
    MAK.   Go away:
I am worthy my meat,
For in a strait can I get
More than they that swink and sweat
    All the long day.

Thus it fell to my lot, Gill, I had such
        grace.
WIFE. It were a foul blot to be hanged
        for the case.
MAK. I have scaped, Gillot, oft as hard
        a blow.
WIFE. But so long goes the pot to the
        water, men says,
At last comes it home broken.
MAK. Well know I the token,
But let it never be spoken;
        But come and help fast.
I would he were slain; I list well eat:
This twelvemonth was I not so fain of one
        sheep-meat.
WIFE. Come they ere he be slain, and
        hear the sheep bleat!
MAK. Then might I be ta'en: that were
        a cold sweat.
Go bar
        The gate door.
WIFE.   Yes, Mak,
For and they come at thy back.
MAK. Then might I pay for all the
        pack:
The devil of them give warning!
WIFE. A good trick have I spied, since
        thou can none:
Here shall we him hide, till they be gone;
In my cradle abide. Let me alone,
And I shall lie beside in childbed and
        groan.
MAK.   Thou advise well.
And I shall say thou wast delivered
Of a knave child this night.
WIFE. Now well is me! Day bright,
        That ever I was bred!
This is a good guise and a far cast;
Yet a woman's advice helps at the last.
I care never who spies: again go thou
        fast.
MAK. But I come ere they rise; else
        blows a cold blast.
I will go sleep.   [MAK *goes back to*
                                the field.]
Yet sleep all this company.
And I shall go stalk privily,
As it had never been I
        That carried their sheep.
1ST SHEPHERD. *Resurrex a mortruis:*
        have hold my hand.

Judas carnas dominus! I may not well
        stand:
My foot sleeps, by Jesus, and I water
        fasting!
I thought that we laid us full near Eng-
        land.
2ND SHEPHERD.   Ah ya!
Lord, I have slept well!
As fresh as an eel,
        As light I me feel
        As leaf on a tree.
3RD SHEPHERD. *Benedicite!* be herein!
        So my body quakes,
My heart is out of skin, what-so it makes.
Who makes all this din? So my brow
        aches,
To the door will I win. Hark fellows,
        wake!
        We were four.
See ye anywhere Mak now?
1ST SHEPHERD. We were up ere thou.
2ND SHEPHERD. Man, I give God a
        vow,
        Yet went he nowhere.
3RD SHEPHERD. Methought he was
        wrapped in a wolf-skin.
1ST SHEPHERD. So are many happed
        now, namely within.
2ND SHEPHERD. When we had long
        napped; methought with a gin
A fat sheep he trapped, but he made no
        din.
3RD SHEPHERD.   Be still:
Thy dream makes thee mad.
It is but phantom, by the rood.
1ST SHEPHERD. Now God turn all to
        good,
        If it be his will.
2ND SHEPHERD. Rise, Mak, for shame!
        thou liest right long.
MAK. Now Christ's holy name be us
        among,
What is this? For Saint James!—I may
        not well go.
I trow I be the same. Ah! my neck has
        lain wrong
        Enough
Mickle thank, since yester-even.
Now, by Saint Stephen!
I was frightened by a dream;
        My heart jumped out of my breast

I thought Gill began to croak, and travail
    full sad,
Well nigh at the first cock,—of a young
    lad,
For to mend our flock: then be I never
    glad.
To have two to provide for,—more than
    ever I had.
    Ah, my head!
A house full of young mouths,
The devil knock out their brains!
Woe is he has many bairns,
    And thereto little bread.
I must go home, by your leave, to Gill,
    as I thought.
I pray you look my sleeve, that I steal
    nought:
I am loth you to grieve, or from you take
    aught.
    3RD SHEPHERD. Go forth, ill might thou
      thrive, now would I we sought,
    This morn,
That we had all our store.
    1ST SHEPHERD. But I will go before,
Let us meet.
    2ND SHEPHERD. Where?
    3RD SHEPHERD. At the crooked thorn.
    MAK [*at his own door again*]. Undo
      this door! Who is here?
    How long shall I stand?
    WIFE. Who makes such a stir? Now
      walk in the waning of the moon.
    MAK. Ah, Gill, what cheer? It is I,
      Mak, your husband.
    HIS WIFE. Then may we see here the
      devil in a band,
    Sir Guile.
Lo, he comes with noise,
As he were holden in the throat.
I may not sit at my work
    A hand-long while.
    MAK. Will ye hear what fare she
      makes—to get her an excuse?
And do naught but plays—and claws her
    toes.
    WIFE. Why, who wanders, who wakes,
      who comes, who goes?
Who brews, who bakes? Who makes for
    me this hose?
    And then
It is pity to behold,

Now in hot, now in cold,
Full woful is the household
    That wants a woman.
But what end hast thou made with the
    shepherds, Mak?
    MAK. The last word that they said,
      when I turned my back,
They would look that they had their sheep,
    all the pack.
I hope they will not be well paid, when
    they their sheep lack.
    Pardie!
But howso the game goes,
To me they will suspect,
And make a foul noise,
    And cry out upon me.
But thou must do as thou promised.
    WIFE.   I accord me
    thereto.
I shall swaddle him right in my cradle.
If it were a greater sleight, yet could I
    help our ends.
I will lie down straight. Come wrap me
    up.
    MAK.   I will
    WIFE.   Behind!
Come Coll and his mate,
They will nip us full narrow.
    MAK. But I may cry out "Harrow!"
    The sheep if they find.
    WIFE. Hearken aye when they call:
      they will come anon.
Come and make ready all, and sing by
    thine own,
Sing "Lullay!" thou shall, for I must
    groan,
And cry out by the wall on Mary and
    John,
    Full sore.
Sing "Lullay" full fast
When thou hears at the last;
And but I play a false cast
    Trust me no more.

    [*Reënter the Three Shepherds.*]
    3RD SHEPHERD. Ah, Coll! good morn:
      why sleep'st thou not?
    1ST SHEPHERD. Alas, that ever was I
      born! We have a foul blot.
A fat wether have we lorn.
    3RD SHEPHERD.   Marry, Gods forbid!

2ND SHEPHERD. Who should do us that
　　scorn? That were a foul spot.
1ST SHEPHERD. Some knave.
I have sought with my dogs,
All Horbury thickets,
And of fifteen hogs
　　Found I but one ewe.
3RD SHEPHERD. Now trust me if you
　　will, by Saint Thomas of Kent!
Either Mak or Gill—was at that assent.
1ST SHEPHERD. Peace, man, be still; I
　　saw when he went.
Thou slander'st him ill; thou ought to
　　repent.
　　Good speed.
2ND SHEPHERD. Now as ever might I
　　thrive,
If I should even here die,
I would say it were he,
　　That did that same deed.
3RD SHEPHERD. Go we thither I advise,
　　and run on our feet.
May I never eat bread, the truth till I
　　wit.
1ST SHEPHERD. Nor drink in my head,
　　with him till I meet.
2ND SHEPHERD. I will rest in no stead,
　　till that I him greet,
　　My brother.
One thing I will promise:
Till I see him in sight
Shall I never sleep one night
　　Where I do another.
3RD SHEPHERD. Will ye hear how they
　　sing! Our Sire! list, how they
　　croon!
1ST SHEPHERD. Heard I never none
　　crack so clear out of tune.
Call on him.
2ND SHEPHERD. Mak! Undo your door
　　soon.
MAK. Who is it that spoke as it were
　　noon?
　　Loudly?
Who is that I say?
3RD SHEPHERD. Good fellows! were it
　　day?
MAK. As far as ye may,
　　Good, speak soft!
Over a sick woman's head,—that is at mal-
　　ease,

I had liefer be dead, or she had any
　　disease.
WIFE. Go to another stead; I may not
　　well breathe;
Each foot that ye tread, goes near make
　　me sneeze
　　So he!
1ST SHEPHERD. Tell us, Mak, if ye
　　may,
How fare ye, I say?
MAK. But are ye in this town to-
　　day?
　　Now how fare ye?
Ye have run in the mire, and are yet
　　wet.
I shall make you a fire, if ye will sit.
A horse would I hire; think ye of it.
Well quit is my hire, my dream, this is
　　it:
　　A season.
I have bairns if ye knew,
Well more than enough,
But we must drink as we brew,
　　And that is but reason.
I would ye dined e'er ye went: methink
　　that ye sweat.
2ND SHEPHERD. Nay, neither mends our
　　mode, drink nor meat.
MAK. Why, sir, ails you aught but
　　good?
3RD SHEPHERD. Yes, our sheep that we
　　gat,
Are stolen as they went. Our loss is
　　great.
MAK. Sirs, drink!
Had I been there,
Some should have bought it full dear.
1ST SHEPHERD. Marry, some men trow
　　that ye were,
　　And that makes us repent.
2ND SHEPHERD. Mak, some men trow
　　that it should be ye.
3RD SHEPHERD. Either ye or your
　　spouse; so say we.
MAK. Now if ye have suspicion to
　　Gill or to me,
Come and rip our house, and then may
　　ye see
　　Who had her.
If I any sheep got,
Either cow or stot,

And Gill, my wife rose not
  Here since she laid her.
As I am both true and leal, to God here
  I pray,
That this be the first meal, I shall eat
  this day.
    1ST SHEPHERD. Mak, as I have weal,
    arise thee, I say!
"He learned timely to steal, that could not
  say nay."
    WIFE.   I swelter.
Out, thieves, from my house!
  Ye come to rob us for the nonce.
    MAK. Hear ye not how she groans?
    Your heart should melt.
    WIFE. Out thieves, from my bairn!
    Nigh him not there.
    MAK. Knew ye how she had fared,
    your hearts would be sore.
Ye do wrong, I you warn, that thus comes
  before
To a woman that has fared, but I say
  no more.
    WIFE.   Ah, my middle!
I pray to God so mild,
If ever I you beguiled,
That I eat this child,
  That lies in this cradle.
    MAK. Peace, woman, for God's pain,
    and cry not so:
Thou spill'st thy brain, and mak'st me
  full woe.
    2ND SHEPHERD. I know our sheep be
    slain, what find ye two?
    3RD SHEPHERD. All work we in vain:
    as well may we go.
  But, hatters!
I can find no flesh,
Hard nor soft,
Salt nor fresh,
  But two bare platters:
Live cattle but this, tame nor wild,
None, as have I bliss; as loud as he
  smiled.
    WIFE. No, so God me bless, and give
    me joy of my child.
    1ST SHEPHERD. We have marked amiss:
    I hold us beguiled.
    2ND SHEPHERD.   Sir, done!
Sir, our lady him save,
  Is your child a boy?

    MAK. Any lord might him have
    This child to his son.
When he wakens he snatches, that joy is
  to see.
    3RD SHEPHERD. In good time, be his
    steps, and happy be they!
But who were his good parents, tell now
  to me!
    MAK. So fair fall their lips!
    1ST SHEPHERD.   Hark now, a lie!
    MAK.   So God them thank,
Parkin, and Gibbon Waller, I say,
And gentle John Horne, in good faith,
He made all the noise,
  With the great shank.
    2ND SHEPHERD. Mak, friends will we
    be, for we are all one.
    MAK. Why! now I hold for me, for
    help get I none.
Farewell all three: all glad were ye
  gone.
    3RD SHEPHERD. Fair words may there
    be, but love there is none.
    1ST SHEPHERD. Gave ye the child any-
    thing?
    2ND SHEPHERD. I trust not one
    farthing.
    3RD SHEPHERD. Fast again will I fling,
    Abide ye me there.   [*He returns to*
                MAK'S cot.]
Mak, take it to no grief, if I come to thy
  bairn.
    MAK. Nay, thou dost me great reprieve,
    and foul hast thou fared.
    3RD SHEPHERD. The child will it not
    grieve, that little day-star.
Mak, with your leave, let me give your
  bairn
  But sixpence.
    MAK. Nay, go 'way: he sleeps.
    3RD SHEPHERD. Methink he peeps.
    MAK. When he wakens he weeps.
I pray you go hence.
    3RD SHEPHERD. Give me leave him to
    kiss, and lift up the clout.
What the devil is this? He has a long
  snout.
    1ST SHEPHERD. He is marked amiss. We
    wait ill about.
    2ND SHEPHERD. Ill-spun weft, I-wis, aye
    cometh foul out;

Aye so!
He is like to our sheep.
3RD SHEPHERD.   How, Gib, may I
    peep?
1ST SHEPHERD.   I trow, nature will
    creep,
  Where it may not go.
2ND SHEPHERD.   This was a quaint
    trick, and a far cast;
It was a high fraud.
3RD SHEPHERD.   Yea, sirs, was't.
Let burn this bawd and bind her fast.
A false scold hangs at the last;
  So shall thou.
Will ye see how they swaddle
His four feet in the middle?
Saw I never in a cradle
  A hornèd lad ere now.
MAK.   Peace, bid I!   What! let be
    your fare;
I am he that him gat, and yon woman
    him bare.
  1ST SHEPHERD.   What devil shall he be
    called?   Lo, God, Mak's heir.
  2ND SHEPHERD.   Let be all that.   Now
    God give him care!   I say.
WIFE.   A pretty child is he,
As sits on a woman's knee;
A dilly-down, perdie!
  To make a man laugh.
3RD SHEPHERD.   I know him by the ear-
    mark—that is a good token.
MAK.   I tell you, sirs, hark: his nose
    was broken.
Since then, told me a clerk, that he was
    bewitched.
  1ST SHEPHERD.   This is a false work.—
    I would fain be avenged.
  Get a weapon!
WIFE.   He was taken by an elf;
I saw it myself.
When the clock struck twelve,
  Was he mis-shapen.
2ND SHEPHERD.   Ye two are right deft,
    —same in a stead.
3RD SHEPHERD.   Since they maintain
    their theft,—let's do them to
    dead.
MAK.   If I trespass eft, gird off my
    head.
With you will I be left.

1ST SHEPHERD.   Sirs, do my advice
  For this trespass,
We will neither curse nor flout,
Fight, nor chide,
But seize him tight,
  And cast him in canvas.   [They toss
                    MAK in a sheet.]

.   .   .   .

1ST SHEPHERD [as the three return to
    the fold].   Lord, how I am sore,
    in point for to burst.
In faith I may no more, therefore will I
    rest.
2ND SHEPHERD.   As a sheep of seven
    score, he weighed in my fist.
For to sleep anywhere, methink that I
    list.
3RD SHEPHERD.   Now I pray you,
Lie down on this green.
  1ST SHEPHERD.   On these thefts yet I
    consider.
  3RD SHEPHERD.   Whereto should ye
    worry?
  Do as I say you.

[Enter an ANGEL above, who sings "Gloria
    in Excelsis," then says:]
ANGEL.   Rise, herd-men, gracious, for
    now is he born
That shall take from the fiend, what
    Adam had lorn:
That fiend to overthrow, this night is he
    born.
God is made your friend: now at this
    morn,
  He behests;
To Bedlem go see,
There lies that Divine One,
In a crib full poorly,
  Betwixt two beasts.
1ST SHEPHERD.   This was a quaint voice
    that ever yet I heard.
It is a marvel to relate thus to be scared.
2ND SHEPHERD.   Of God's son of heaven,
    he spoke up word.
All the wood like the lightning, methought
    that he made
  Appear.
3RD SHEPHERD.   He spake of a bairn
In Bedlem, I you warn.

1ST SHEPHERD. That betokens yonder
    star.
  Let us seek him there.
2ND SHEPHERD. Say, what was his
    song? Heard ye not how he
    cracked it?
Three breves to a long.
3RD SHEPHERD. Yea, marry, he shouted
    it.
Was no crochet wrong, nor no thing that
    lacked it.
  1ST SHEPHERD. For to sing us among,
    right as he trilled it,
  I can.
2ND SHEPHERD. Let us see how ye
    croon
Can ye bark at the moon?
  3RD SHEPHERD. Hold your tongues, have
    done.
1ST SHEPHERD. Hark after, then.
2ND SHEPHERD. To Bedlem he bade that
    we should go.
I am full feared that we tarry too long.
  3RD SHEPHERD. Be merry and not sad:
    of mirth is our song,
Everlasting glad, our road may we take,
    Without noise.
1ST SHEPHERD. Hie we thither quickly;
If we be wet and weary,
To that child and that lady
  We have it not to delay.
2ND SHEPHERD. We find by the prophecy
    —let be your din—
Of David and Isaiah, and more than I
    can mind,
They prophesied by clergy, that on a
    virgin
Should he light and lie, to pardon our sin
  And slake it,
Our kind from woe;
For Isaiah said so,
    Cite virgo
    Concipiet a child that is naked.
  3RD SHEPHERD. Full glad may we be,
    and abide that day
That lovely to see, that shall have all
    power.
Lord, well for me for once and for aye,
Might I kneel on my knee some word for
    to say
    To that child.

But the angel said
In a crib was he laid;
He was poorly arrayed,
  Both meek and mild.
  1ST SHEPHERD. Patriarchs that have
    been, and prophets beforn,
They desired to have seen this child that
    is born.
They are gone full clean, that have they
    lorn.
We shall see him, I ween, ere it be morn
  By token.
When I see him and feel,
Then know I full weel
It is true as steel
    That prophets have spoken.
To so poor as we are, that he would ap-
    pear,
First find, and declare by his messenger.
  2ND SHEPHERD. Go we now, let us
    fare: the place is us near.
  3RD SHEPHERD. I am ready and eager:
    go we in fear
  To that light!
Lord! if thy wills be,
We are rude all three,
Thou grant us of thy glee,
  To comfort thy wight.

.   .   .   .

[*The* SHEPHERDS *arrive at Bethlehem.*]

  1ST SHEPHERD. Hail, comely and clean;
    hail, young child!
Hail, maker, as I mean, of a maiden so
    mild!
Thou hast banned, I ween, the devil so
    wild,
The false guiler of woe, now goes he
    beguiled.
  Lo, he merry is!
Lo, he laughs, my sweeting,
A welcome meeting!
I have given my greeting
  Have a bob of cherries?
  2ND SHEPHERD. Hail, sovereign Savior,
    for thou hast us sought!
Hail freely, leaf and flow'r, that all thing
    has wrought!
Hail full of favor, that made all of
    nought!

Hail! I kneel and I cower. A bird have
I brought
To my bairn!
Hail, little tiny darling,
Of our creed thou art crop!
I would drink in thy cup,
Little day-star.
3RD SHEPHERD. Hail, darling dear, full
of godhead!
I pray thee be near, when that I have
need.
Hail! sweet is thy cheer: my heart would
bleed
To see thee sit here in so poor weed,
With no pennies.
Hail! put forth thy hand.
I bring thee but a ball
Have and play thee with all,
And go to the tennis.
MARY. The Father of Heaven, God
omnipotent,
That set all aright, his son has he sent.
My name could he say, and laugh as if
he knew.

I conceived him full even, through might,
as God meant;
And new is he born.
He keep you from woe:
I shall pray him so;
Tell forth as ye go,
And mind on this morn.
1ST SHEPHERD. Farewell, lady, so fair
to behold,
With thy child on thy knee.
2ND SHEPHERD. But he lies full
cold,
Lord, well is me: now we go forth, be-
hold!
3RD SHEPHERD. Forsooth, already it
seems to be told
Full oft.
1ST SHEPHERD. What grace we have
found.
2ND SHEPHERD. Come forth, now are
we won.
3RD SHEPHERD. To sing are we bound.
Let us sing it aloud!

THE FARCE OF THE WORTHY MASTER PIERRE PATELIN

ANONYMOUS

Printed probably about 1469

TRANSLATED BY M. JAGENDORF *

CHARACTERS

THE JUDGE, *whom no man dare judge*

PATELIN, *the Lawyer, a counselor indeed, possessing all those virtues which a good counselor should possess*

GUILLEMETTE, *his wife, a fit wife for a lawyer*

GUILLAUME JOCEAULME, *the draper, a successful merchant who has been cheating his customers from the day he began selling*

TIBALD LAMBKIN, *a shepherd, a fellow who, if his lot in life had been better, might have become a lawyer like* PATELIN, *or a merchant like* JOCEAULME

This happened in a little town in France in the Year of Our Lord, 1400

SCENE I—*On either side of the stage is a street scene. In back, a curtain is partly drawn to each side showing the interior of* PATELIN'S *house.* PATELIN *sits in bed reading a large folio; on a chair next to the bed* GUILLEMETTE *sits mending an old dress. On a bench a little to the side are kitchen utensils: a frying pan, a broom, etc. On the bed lies a nightgown and a cap.*

GUILLEMETTE. You have nothing to say now, I suppose, have you? . . . While I needs must mend rags a beggar would be ashamed to wear—and you, a member of the learned profession . . . a lawyer . . . !

PATELIN [*in bed*]. There was a time when my door was crowded with clients . . . when I had plenty of work . . . and fine clothes to wear, too.

GUILLEMETTE. Of what good is that to-day—eh?

PATELIN. Wife, I was too shrewd for them. Men don't like people wiser than themselves.

GUILLEMETTE. Aye, you could always

* Reprinted from the edition published by D. Appleton & Co., copyright 1925, by permission of the translator and publisher.

beat them at law. . . . But that was long ago.

PATELIN. It hurts me truly to see you mending rags . . . and wives of men who are thick-skulled asses wearing golden-threaded cloth and fine wool. There is that draper's wife across the way. . . .

GUILLEMETTE. Cease the cackling. [*Silently working for a while.*] I'd give something rare and costly for a new gown on St. Mary's day. Heaven knows I need it.

PATELIN. So you do and so do I as well. It is not fit to see one of the learned profession walking about like a beggar on the highway. Ah! If I could only get some clients! I know my law well enough yet. There is not many a one can beat me at the finer points.

GUILLEMETTE. A fig for it all. Of what good is it? We are all but starved . . . and as for clothes—look. [*Holds up the dress she is mending.*]

PATELIN. Silence, good wife! Could I but have some business and put my head with seriousness to it. . . . Who knows but the days of plenty would soon enough return!

GUILLEMETTE. There is not a soul in town but a fool would trust himself to you. They know too well your way of handling cases. They say you are a master . . . at cheating.

[PATELIN *rises indignant.*]

PATELIN. They mean at law . . . at law, good wife. Ha, I should like to see a lawyer beat me at it . . . and . . . [*Suddenly stops, thinks for a moment, then his whole face lights up.*] I am going to market. I have just thought of a little business I have there. [*Gets out of bed.*]

GUILLEMETTE. Going to market? What for? You have no money.

PATELIN. I am going to market . . . on business . . . to the long-nosed donkey, our neighbor . . . the Draper.

GUILLEMETTE. What for?

PATELIN. To buy some cloth. . . .

GUILLEMETTE. Holy Saints! You know well he is more close-fisted than any other merchant in town. He'll never trust you.

PATELIN. Ah, that's just why I am going. The more miserly, the easier to gull; and . . . I have thought of something fine . . . that will get us enough cloth . . . both for you and me.

GUILLEMETTE. You must be mad.

PATELIN [*not heeding her*]. Let me see. . . . [*Measuring her with his arm's length.*] Two and one-half for you. . . . [*Measuring himself in the same way.*] Three for me . . . and . . . What color would you want it? Green or red?

GUILLEMETTE. I'll be pleased with any kind. Beggars can't be choosers. But don't think I believe what you say. I am not a fool. You'll never get any from Master Joceaulme. He'll never trust you, I am certain.

PATELIN. Who knows? Who knows? He might . . . and then really get paid . . . on Doom's-day. . . . Ho, ho. . . .

GUILLEMETTE. Don't you think you had better make haste, lest all the cloth be sold?

PATELIN [*offended, walking off*]. Wife, I forgive you. You are only a woman. I'll teach you a fine lesson now. If I don't bring home a fine piece of cloth—dark green or blue, such as wives of great lords wear, then never believe another word I say.

GUILLEMETTE. But how will you do it? You haven't a copper in your pocket.

PATELIN. Ah! That's a secret. Just wait and see. So . . . [*to himself as he walks slowly away*] two and one-half for her and three for me. . . . Look well to the house while I am away, wife.

GUILLEMETTE. What fool of a merchant'll trust him! . . . unless he is blind and deaf!

[*The back curtains are closed and now only the street scene is visible.*]

SCENE II—PATELIN *comes from his door and walks across to* THE DRAPER'S *table.* THE DRAPER *is just coming out with a pack of cloth and wools which he throws on the table. He busies himself arranging his goods.* PATELIN *looks on for a while, then goes right up to him.*

PATELIN. Ho, there, worthy Master Guillaume Joceaulme, permit me the pleasure of shaking your hand. How do you feel?

THE DRAPER. Very fine, the Saints be thanked.

PATELIN. I am truly happy to hear that. And business?

THE DRAPER. You know how . . . one day one way, the other, altogether different. You can never tell when ill luck may blow your way.

PATELIN. May the Saints keep it from your doors! It's the very phrase I often heard your father use. God rest his soul among the Martyrs! What a man he was! Wise! There was not an event in Church, State, or market he did not foretell. No other was more esteemed. And you—they say that you are more and more like him each day.

THE DRAPER. Do seat yourself, good Master Patelin.

PATELIN. Oh, I can well stand.

THE DRAPER. Oh, but you must.

[*Forcing him to sit on the bench.*]

PATELIN. Ah! I knew him well, your father. You resemble him as one drop of milk another. Lord, what a man he was! Wise! We, among the learned, called him the weather-cock. Well-nigh every piece of clothing I wore came from his shop.

THE DRAPER. He was an honest man, and people liked to buy from him.

PATELIN. A more honest soul there never was. And I have heard often said the apple has fallen nigh the tree.

THE DRAPER. Of a truth, good Master . . .

PATELIN. It's not flattery, either. [*Looking intently at him.*] Lord, but you do resemble him! No child was ever so like his father. Each marked like the other. This is just his nose, his ears, nay, the very dimple on his chin.

THE DRAPER. Yes, they do say I look much like him.

PATELIN. Like one drop of water another. . . . And kind-hearted! He was ever ready to trust and help, no matter who came along. The Lord knows he was ever the gainer by it. Even the worst scoundrels thought twice before cheating him.

THE DRAPER. A merchant must always take heed, good Master Patelin. You can never know whether a man is honest or not.

PATELIN. Aye, that's true. But he had a way of guessing whether it was an honest man he was dealing with that was a marvel to behold. Many a funny tale he told of it—when we sat over a bottle of wine. [*Feeling the cloth on the table.*] What a fine piece of cloth! Did you make it from your own wool? Your father always used to weave his cloths from the wool of his own sheep.

THE DRAPER. So do I, Sir. From the wool of my own sheep.

PATELIN. You don't say so! This is business in a manner I like to see it done. The father all over again.

THE DRAPER [*seeing the possibility of a sale*]. Ah, worthy Master Patelin, it is a great hardship indeed, to which I put myself because of this. And the loss and cost! Here a shepherd kills your sheep, I have a case against one of those scoundrels right now. The weavers ask pay like goldsmiths. But to me this is all of little account. . . . I'd attend to the making of each piece myself were it to cost ten times as much as I get in return. . . . So long as I please those who buy.

PATELIN. I can see this. It would make a fine gown.

THE DRAPER. You could not get a finer piece even in the city of Paris.

PATELIN. I am sorry I am not out to do any buying just now, though I am tempted to.

THE DRAPER. Business bad? Money scarce?

PATELIN. No, indeed not. I have a nice little sum of gold crowns even now, but I am about to invest them in something profitable. . . . It's as strong as iron, this cloth here. [*Examining it.*]

THE DRAPER. You may take my word for it, Master, there is not a finer or stronger in town. What's more, it can be bought cheap just now. It's a fine investment. Wool is certain to go up.

PATELIN. Aye, it's a fine piece of cloth, Master Joceaulme. . . . But then I shouldn't . . . yet . . .

THE DRAPER. Come, Master Patelin, come. You need the cloth and have the money to buy. Then you'll invest a few crowns less. A man should always have a gown tucked away in the coffer. What would you say if some fine day, comes along the town crier shouting: there has been a new judge appointed and it is Master Pa . . .

PATELIN. You must have your little joke, worthy Sir. Just like your father. I would pass his shop, a friendly chat . . . and then my purse was much the lighter for it. But I never regretted it, never.

THE DRAPER. You wouldn't now, either. It's well worth buying.

PATELIN. It tempts me. . . . It would look well on my good wife, and I could use it well for myself.

THE DRAPER. It needs but your saying. Come, what's the word, Master?

PATELIN. Well. . . .

THE DRAPER. It's yours even though you hadn't a copper.

PATELIN [*somewhat absent-minded*]. Oh, I know that.

THE DRAPER. What?

PATELIN. I'll take it.

THE DRAPER. That's talking. How much do you want?

PATELIN. How much is it per yard?

THE DRAPER. Which do you like best? The blue?

PATELIN. Yes, that is the one.

THE DRAPER. You want a rock bottom price, no haggling. This is the finest piece in my shop. For you I'll make it twenty-one sous per yard.

PATELIN. Holy Saints! Master! What do you take me for? A fool? It isn't the first time I am buying cloth.

THE DRAPER. It's the price it cost me myself; by all the Saints in Heaven.

PATELIN. That's too much—entirely too much.

THE DRAPER. Wool costs like holy oil now, and these shepherds are forever robbing me.

PATELIN. Well, there is truth in what you say. I'll take it at the price. I like to see every man make his honest penny. Measure it.

THE DRAPER. How much do you want?

PATELIN. Let me see. Two and a half for her, three for me, that makes five and a half.

THE DRAPER. Take hold there, Master, here they are. [*Measuring out.*] One . . . two . . . three . . . four . . . five. I'll make it six. You'll not mind the few coppers more.

PATELIN. Not when I get something fine in return. Then I need a cap, too.

THE DRAPER. Would you like me to measure it backwards?

PATELIN. Oh, no, I trust your honesty. How much is it?

THE DRAPER. Six yards at twenty-one sous the yard—that's exactly nine francs.

PATELIN. Nine francs . . . [*Under his breath.*] Here it goes. Nine francs.

THE DRAPER. Yes, and a good bargain you got.

PATELIN [*searching his pockets*]. No . . . I have but little with me, and I must buy some small things. You'll get your money to-morrow.

THE DRAPER. What!!! . . . No . . . No . . .

PATELIN. Well, good Master Joceaulme, you don't think I carry gold coin with me, do you? You'd have me give thieves a good chance to steal it? Your father trusted me many a time. And you, Master Guillaume, should take after your father.

THE DRAPER. I like my money cash.

PATELIN. It's there waiting for you, good Master Draper. You can come for it, I hope.

THE DRAPER. It's bad custom to sell on credit.

PATELIN. Did I ask you for credit: for

a month, a week, a day? Come to my house at noon, and you will find your money ready. Does that satisfy you?

THE DRAPER. I prefer my money cash, right on the purchase. . . .

PATELIN. And then, Master Guillaume, you have not been to my house for I don't know how long. Your father was there many a time—but you don't seem to care for poor folk like myself.

THE DRAPER. It's we merchants who are poor. We have no bags of gold lying idle for investments.

PATELIN. They are there, Master, waiting for you. And my good wife put a fine goose on the spit just when I left. You can have a tender wing. Your father always liked it.

THE DRAPER. Perhaps. . . . It's true. I haven't been to your house for a long time. I'll come at noon, Master Patelin, and bring the cloth with me.

PATELIN [snatching the cloth from him]. Oh, I would never trouble you. I can carry it.

THE DRAPER. But . . .

PATELIN. No, good Sir, not for the wealth of the East. I would not think of asking you to carry it for me.

THE DRAPER. I'd rather . . . well . . . I'll soon be there, Master. I'll come before the noon meal. Don't forget the nine francs.

PATELIN. Aye, I'll not. And there'll be a bottle of red wine . . . and a fine fat goose. Be certain to come. [Exit PATELIN.]

THE DRAPER. That I will right soon. Ho, ho, ho—ha, ha, ha—the fool! A good bargain he got! Twenty-one sous the yard. It isn't worth one-half that. And on top of it a fine dinner . . . Burgundy wine and a roasted goose! For a customer like that every day! Now I'll take in my cloth. I'll soon to his house. [Takes up the cloth and leaves.]

SCENE III—The back curtains are drawn aside showing PATELIN's chamber.

PATELIN [running in]. Wife, wife . . . [GUILLEMETTE enters, the old gown in her hand.] Well, Madam . . . now . . . I've got it . . . right here I have it. What did I tell you?

GUILLEMETTE. What have you?

PATELIN. Something you desire greatly. But what are you doing with this old rag? I think it will do well for a bed for your cat. I did promise you a new gown and get you one I did.

GUILLEMETTE. What's gotten into your head? Did you drink anything on the way?

PATELIN. And it's paid for, Madam. It's paid for, I tell you.

GUILLEMETTE. Are you making sport of me? What are you plappering?

PATELIN. I have it right here.

GUILLEMETTE. What have you?

PATELIN. Cloth fit for the Queen of Sheba. [Displaying the cloth.] Here it is!

GUILLEMETTE. Holy Virgin! Where did you steal it? Who'll pay for it? What kind of a scrape have you gotten into now?

PATELIN. You need not worry, good Dame. It's paid for . . . and a good price at that.

GUILLEMETTE. Why, how much did it cost? You did not have a copper when you left.

PATELIN. It cost nine francs, fair Lady . . . a bottle of red wine . . . and the wing of a roasted goose.

GUILLEMETTE. Are you crazy? You had no money, no goose!!!

PATELIN. Aye, aye, that I did. I paid for it as it behooves one of the learned profession of law; in promissory statements. And the merchant who took them is no fool either, oh, no; not a fool at all; but a very wise man and a shrewd. . . .

GUILLEMETTE. Who was he? How . . .

PATELIN. He is the king of asses, the Pope of Idiots, the chancellor of baboons . . . our worthy neighbor, the long-nosed draper, Master Joceaulme.

GUILLEMETTE. Will you cease this jabbering and tell me how it happened? How did he come to trust you? There is no worse skinflint in town than he.

PATELIN. Ah, wife! My head! My knowledge of the law! I turned him into a noble and fine lord. I told him what a jewel his father was; I laid on him all the nine virtues thick as wax, and . . . in the end he trusted me most willingly with six yards of his fine cloth.

GUILLEMETTE. Ho, ho, ho, you are a marvel! And when does he expect to get paid?

PATELIN. By noon.

GUILLEMETTE. Holy Lord, what will we do when he comes for the money?

PATELIN. He'll be here for it and soon to boot. He must be dreaming even now of his nine francs, and his wine, and the goose. Oh, we'll give him a goose! Now you get the bed ready and I'll get in.

GUILLEMETTE. What for?

PATELIN. As soon as he comes and asks for me, swear by all the Saints that I've been in bed here for the last two months. Tell it in a sad voice and with tears in your eyes. And if he says anything, shout at him to speak lower. If he cries: "My cloth, my money," tell him he is crazy, that I haven't been in bed for weeks. And if he doesn't go with that, I'll dance him a little tune that'll make him wonder whether he is on earth or in hell.

[PATELIN *puts on his nightgown and cap.* GUILLEMETTE *goes to the door and returns quickly.*]

GUILLEMETTE. He is coming, he is coming; what if he arrests you?

PATELIN. Don't worry; just do what I tell you. Quick, hide the cloth under the bedclothes., Don't forget. I've been sick for two months.

GUILLEMETTE. Quick, quick, here he is.

[PATELIN *gets into bed and draws the curtains.* GUILLEMETTE *sits down and begins to mend the old dress.* THE DRAPER *enters.*]

THE DRAPER. Good day, fair Dame.

GUILLEMETTE. Sh . . . for the Saints' sake. Speak lower.

THE DRAPER. Why? What's the matter?

GUILLEMETTE. You don't know!

THE DRAPER. Where is he?

GUILLEMETTE. Alas! Nearer to Paradise than to Earth. [*Begins to cry.*]

THE DRAPER. Who?

GUILLEMETTE. How can you be so heartless and ask me that, when you know he has been in bed for the last eleven weeks?

THE DRAPER. Who?

GUILLEMETTE. My husband.

THE DRAPER. Who?

GUILLEMETTE. My husband—Master Pierre, once a lawyer . . . and now a sick man . . . on his death-bed.

THE DRAPER. What!!!!!

GUILLEMETTE [*crying*]. You have not heard of it? Alas! And . . .

THE DRAPER. And who was it just took six yards of cloth from my shop?

GUILLEMETTE. Alas! How am I to know? It was surely not he.

THE DRAPER. You must be dreaming, good woman. Are you his wife? The wife of Pierre Patelin, the lawyer?

GUILLEMETTE. That I am, good Sir.

THE DRAPER. Then it was your husband, who was such a good friend of my father, who came to my shop a quarter of an hour ago and bought six yards of cloth for nine francs. And now I am here for my money. Where is he?

GUILLEMETTE. This is no time for jesting, good Sir.

THE DRAPER. Are you crazy? I want my money, that's all.

GUILLEMETTE. Don't scream. It's little sleep he gets as it is, and here you come squealing like a dying pig. He has been in bed for nigh twelve weeks and hardly slept three nights.

THE DRAPER. Who? What are you talking about?

GUILLEMETTE. Who! My poor sick husband. [*Weeps.*]

THE DRAPER. Come! What's this? Stop that fooling. I want my money, my nine francs.

GUILLEMETTE [*screaming*]. Don't scream so loud. He is dying.

THE DRAPER. But that's a black lie.

He was at my shop, but a quarter of an hour ago.

PATELIN [*groaning from behind the curtain*]. Au, au, au . . .

GUILLEMETTE. Ah, there he is on his deathbed. He has been there for thirteen weeks yesterday without eating as much as a fly.

THE DRAPER. What are you talking about? He was at my shop just now and bought six yards of cloth . . . blue cloth.

GUILLEMETTE. How can you make sport of me? Good Master Guillaume, don't you see how he is! Do speak lower. Noise puts him in agony.

THE DRAPER. The devil speak lower! It's you who are howling. Give me my money, and I'll not speak at all.

GUILLEMETTE [*screaming*]. He is deadly sick. This is no time for fooling. Stop screaming. What is it you want?

THE DRAPER. I want my money, or the cloth . . . the cloth he bought from me only a little while ago.

GUILLEMETTE. What are you talking about, my good man? There is something strange in your voice.

THE DRAPER. You see, good lady, your husband, Pierre Patelin, the learned counselor, who was such a good friend of my father, came to my shop but a quarter of an hour ago and chose six yards of blue cloth . . . and then told me to come to his house to get the money and . . .

GUILLEMETTE. Ha, ha, ha, what a fine joke. You seem to be in good humor today, Master Draper! To-day? . . . When he has been in bed for fourteen weeks . . . on the point of death! [*She screams louder and louder all the time.*] To-day, hey! Why do you come to make sport of me? Get out, get out!

THE DRAPER. I will. Give me my money first . . . or give me my cloth. Where is he with it?

GUILLEMETTE. Ah me! He is very sick and refuses to eat a bite.

THE DRAPER. I am speaking about my cloth. If he does not want it, or hasn't the money, I'll gladly take it back. He took it this morning. I'll swear to it.

Ask him yourself. I saw him and spoke to him. A piece of blue cloth.

GUILLEMETTE. Are you cracked or have you been drinking?

THE DRAPER [*becoming frantic*]. He took six yards of cloth, blue cloth.

GUILLEMETTE. What do I care whether it is green or blue? My husband has not left the house for the last fifteen weeks.

THE DRAPER. May the Lord bless me! But I am sure I saw him. It was he I am' sure.

GUILLEMETTE. Have you no heart? I have had enough of your fooling.

THE DRAPER. Damn it all! If you think I am a fool . . .

PATELIN [*behind the curtain*]. Au, au, au, come and raise my pillow. Stop the braying of that ass! Everything is black and yellow! Drive these black beasts away! *Marmara carimari, carimara!*

THE DRAPER. It's he!

GUILLEMETTE. Yes, it is; alas!

THE DRAPER. Good Master Patelin, I've come for my nine francs, . . . which you promised me . . .

PATELIN [*sitting up and sticks his head out between the curtains*]. Ha, you dog . . . come here. Shut the door. Rub the soles of my feet . . . tickle my toes. . . . Drive these devils away It's a monk; there, up he goes . . .

THE DRAPER. What's this? Are you crazy?

PATELIN [*getting out of bed*]. Ha . . . do you see him? A black monk flying in the air with the draper hanging on his nose. Catch him . . . quick. [*Speaking right in* THE DRAPER'S *face, who retreats.*] The cat! The monk! Up he flies, and there are ten little devils tweaking your long nose! Heigh, ho!

[*Goes back to bed, falling on it seemingly exhausted.*]

GUILLEMETTE [*in loud lamentations*]. Now see what you have done.

THE DRAPER. But what does this mean? . . . I don't understand it.

GUILLEMETTE. Don't you see, don't you see!

THE DRAPER. It serves me right; why

did I ever sell on credit? But I sold it, I am certain of that, and I would swear 'twas to him this morning. Did he become sick since he returned?

GUILLEMETTE. Are you beginning that joke all over again?

THE DRAPER. I am sure I sold it to him. Ah, but this may be just a cooked up story. By God! ... tell me, have you a goose on the spit?

GUILLEMETTE. A goose on the spit! No-o-o-o, not on the spit! You are the nearest.... But I've had enough of this. Get out and leave me in peace.

THE DRAPER. Maybe you are right. I am commencing to doubt it all. Don't cry. I must think this over for a while. But ... the devil. I am sure I had six yards of cloth ... and he chose the blue. I gave it to him with my own hands. Yet ... here he is in bed sick ... fifteen weeks. But he was at my shop a little while ago. "Come to my house and eat some goose," he said. Never, never, holy Lord, will I trust any one again.

GUILLEMETTE. Perhaps your memory is getting wobbly with age. I think you had better go and look before you talk. Maybe the cloth is still there.

[Exit THE DRAPER, across the front stage and into his shop.]

PATELIN [getting up cautiously and speaking low]. Is he gone?

GUILLEMETTE. Take care, he may come back.

PATELIN. I can't stand this any longer. [Jumps out.] We put it to him heavy, didn't we, my pretty one, eh? Ho, ho, ho. [Laughs uproariously.]

THE DRAPER [coming from his shop, looking under the table]. The thief, the liar, the damned liar, he did buy ... steal it? It isn't there. This was all sham. Ha, I'll get it, though. [Runs toward PATELIN's house.] What's this I hear ... laughing! ... The robbers. [Rushes in.] You thieves. ... I want my cloth. ...

[PATELIN finding no time to get back into bed, gets hold of the broom, puts the frying pan on

his head and begins to jump around, straddling the broom stick. GUILLEMETTE can't stop laughing.]

THE DRAPER. Laughing in my very nose, eh! Ah, my money, pay. ...

GUILLEMETTE. I am laughing for unhappiness. Look, how the poor man is, it is you who have done this, with your bellowing.

PATELIN. Ha. ... Where is the Guitar? ... The lady Guitar I married. ... She gave birth to twenty little Guitars yesterday. Ho, ho. Come, my children. ... Light the lanterns. Ho, ho, ha. ...

[Stops, looking intently into the air.]

THE DRAPER. Damn your jabbering. My money! Please, my money ... for the cloth. ...

GUILLEMETTE. Again. ... Didn't you have enough before? But. ... Oh. ... [Looking intently at him.] Now I understand!!! Why, I am sure of it. You are mad ... else you wouldn't talk this way.

THE DRAPER. Oh, Holy Lord ... perhaps I am.

PATELIN [begins to jump around as if possessed, playing a thousand and one crazy antics.] Mère de dieu, la coronade ... que de l'argent il ne me sonne. Hast understood me, gentle Sir?

THE DRAPER. What's this? I want my money. ...

GUILLEMETTE. He is speaking in delirium; he once had an uncle in Limoges and it's the language of that country.

[PATELIN gives THE DRAPER a kick and falls down as if exhausted.]

THE DRAPER. Oh! Oh! Where am I? This is the strangest sickness I ever saw.

GUILLEMETTE [who has run to her husband]. Do you see what you have done?

PATELIN [jumps up and acts still wilder]. Ha! The devil ... the green cat ... with the draper. I am happy. ...

[Chases THE DRAPER and his wife around the room. GUILLEMETTE seeks protection, clinging to THE DRAPER.]

GUILLEMETTE. Oh, I am afraid, I am afraid. Help me, kind Sir, he may do me some harm.

THE DRAPER [*running around the room with* GUILLEMETTE *clinging to him*]. Holy Ghost, what's this? He is bewitching me. PATELIN [*tries to talk in signs to* THE DRAPER, *who retreats.* PATELIN *follows him, whacking the floor and furniture and occasionally getting in one on* THE DRAPER. *Finally* THE DRAPER *gets on one side of the bed, and* PATELIN *on the other. In that position he addresses him in a preachy, serious voice*]. *Et bona dies sit vobis, magister amantissime, pater reverendissime, quomodo brulis?* [*Falls on the floor near the bed as if dead.*]

GUILLEMETTE. Oh, kind Sir. Help me. He is dead. Help me put him to bed. . . . [*They both drag him into bed.*]

THE DRAPER. It were well for me to go, I think. He might die and I might be blamed for it. It must have been some imps or some devils who took my cloth . . . and I came here for the money, led by an evil spirit. It's passing strange . . . but I think I had better go. [*Exit.* THE DRAPER *goes to his shop.* GUILLEMETTE *watches, turning every moment to* PATELIN *who has sat up in bed, warning him not to get out. When* THE DRAPER *disappears, she turns around and bursts out laughing.*]

PATELIN [*jumping out*]. Now, wife, what do you think of me, eh? [*Takes the cloth.*] Oh! Didn't we play a clever game? By Saint Peter, I did not think I could do it so well. He got a hot goose, didn't he? [*Spreading the cloth.*] This'll do for both and there'll be a goodly piece left.

GUILLEMETTE. You are an angel. Oh, ho! And now let us go and begin to cut it up.

[*Both exit, and the curtain is drawn.*]

SCENE IV—*The street scene.* JO-CEAULME *comes from the shop with a piece of cloth under his arm. He is much upset.*

Looks once more under the table for the cloth which PATELIN *took.*

THE DRAPER. The Devil! These hounds. . . . I'll get them yet. Here's a fine piece of cloth! Only the fiend himself knows who took it—and then that shepherd. To think of it . . . robbing me for years. But him I'll get surely. I'll see him hanged, yet. By the holy Lord I will. [TIBALD LAMBKIN *appears from the other side.*] Ah, here he comes. . . .

THE SHEPHERD [*stutters, thick voice; a typical yokel*]. God give you a good day, sweet Sir. I greet you, good Sir. . . . I was not sure it was you, good Sir. . . .

THE DRAPER. You were not, eh? You knave; but you will soon know for certain . . . when your head is on the gallows . . . high up. . . .

THE SHEPHERD. Yes, good Sir . . . no . . . I saw the constable . . . and he spoke to me that you want to see me. . . .

THE DRAPER. Oh, no! Not I, my fine thief . . . but the judge.

THE SHEPHERD. Oh, Lord! Why did you summon me? I don't know why. I never killed your sheep.

THE DRAPER. Oh, no, you are a Saint. It's you, you mangy dog . . . all the while you were robbing me of my sheep. But now you'll pay for it with your head. I'll see you hanged.

THE SHEPHERD. Hang by the neck! Oh, Lord! Good Master, have pity.

THE DRAPER. Pity, eh? And you had pity when you were robbing me of my cloth. . . . I mean my sheep. Thief, scoundrel, you robber . . . where is my cloth . . . my sheep?

THE SHEPHERD. They died of sickness, Sir . . .

THE DRAPER. You lie, you caitiff, you stole them and now . . .

THE SHEPHERD. It is not so, good Master. I swear. On my soul. . . .

THE DRAPER. You have no soul, you thief. By all the Saints, I'll see you dangling this Saturday. . . .

THE SHEPHERD. Good and sweet Master, won't you please make a settlement . . . and not bring me to court.

THE DRAPER. Away, you thief. I'll make you pay for those six yards . . . I mean those sheep. You just wait.

[*Walks off in a fury.*]

THE SHEPHERD. Oh, Lord! I must quickly find a lawyer. . . . I've heard of Master Patelin . . . they say no man is better at gulling. It's here he lives. [PATELIN *comes just then from his house. When he sees* LAMBKIN *he tries to get back, fearing it may be* THE DRAPER, *but on hearing his voice he stops.*] Ho, there, Master! Is it you who are Master Patelin the lawyer?

PATELIN. What is it you want of him?

THE SHEPHERD. I have a little business for him.

PATELIN. Oh! is it that! Well, I am Master Patelin. Good man, tell me the nature of your business. Is it anything pertaining to the law?

THE SHEPHERD. I'll pay well. . . . I am a shepherd, good Master. A poor man, but I can pay well. I need a lawyer for a little case I have.

PATELIN. Come this way, where we can talk lower. Some one might overhear us . . . I mean disturb us. Now good man, what may your business be?

THE SHEPHERD. Good Master Lawyer, teach me what to say to the judge.

PATELIN. What is it you have done, or has some one done you an injustice?

THE SHEPHERD. Must I tell you everything . . . exactly as it happened?

PATELIN. You can tell me the truth, I am your lawyer. . . . But, good friend, counsel is costly.

THE SHEPHERD. I'll pay all right. It's my Master whose sheep I stole who summoned me to the Judge. He is going to have me hanged because I stole his sheep. You see. . . . He paid like a miser. . . . Must I tell you the truth?

PATELIN. I have told you once. You must tell me how everything really happened.

THE SHEPHERD. Well . . . he paid like a miser . . . so I told him some sheep

had the hoof sickness and died from it . . . and I buried them far . . . far . . . away, so that the others shouldn't get it. But I really killed them and ate the meat and used the wool for myself,—and he caught me right so that I cannot deny it. Now I beseech you. . . I can pay well— though he has the law on his side . . . tell me . . . whether you cannot beat him. If you can, I'll pay you in fine, gold crowns, sweet Master.

PATELIN. Gold crowns!!! H'm, what's your name?

THE SHEPHERD. Tibald Lambkin, a poor shepherd, but I have a few crowns put aside. You just . . .

PATELIN. What do you intend to pay for this case?

THE SHEPHERD. Will five . . . four crowns be enough, sweet Sir?

PATELIN [*hardly able to contain himself for excitement*]. Ah! . . . Hm . . . well . . . that will be plenty, seeing that you are a poor man. But I get much greater sums, friend, I do. . . . Did you say . . . five?

THE SHEPHERD. Yes, sweet Sir.

PATELIN. You'll have to make it six. I may tell you, though, that your case is a good one, and I am sure to win it. But now tell me, are there any witnesses the plaintiff can produce? Those who saw you killing the sheep?

THE SHEPHERD. Not one. . . .

PATELIN. That's fine.

THE SHEPHERD. . . . But more'n a dozen.

PATELIN. That's bad. Hm, let me see now . . . no. . . . [*He seems to hold a deep and learned debate with himself.*] No . . . but. . . . The book says otherwise. [*Suddenly his face lights up.*] By all the Saints, and the nine hundred and ninety-nine Virgins! I've got it . . . aye, what a wonderful idea! Two ideas in one day! You can understand a sly trick, can't you, fellow?

THE SHEPHERD. Can I? Ho, ho, ho, ho. . . .

PATELIN. But you'll pay as you promised.

THE SHEPHERD. Hang me if I don't. But I can't pay if I hang, ho, ho, ho. . . .

PATELIN [*gleefully*]. Now, first, you have never seen me; nor heard of me. . . .

THE SHEPHERD. Oh, no, not that. . . .

PATELIN. Silent until I have finished. Second, you mustn't talk a single word but "Ba." . . . [*Imitating the bleating of a sheep.*] Only bleat like your sheep. No matter what they talk to you. Just say Ba. . . . Even if they call you an ass, or an idiot, or villain, or fool, don't answer anything but Ba. . . . Just as if you were a sheep.

THE SHEPHERD. Oh, I can do that.

PATELIN. Even if I talk to you, say nothing but Ba. . . . And if they split roaring at you, just say Ba. . . . The rest you leave to me. I'll get you out for certain.

THE SHEPHERD. I'll surely not say another word. And I will do it right proper.

PATELIN. Your case is as good as won. But don't forget the six gold crowns.

THE SHEPHERD. I'll sure not, wise and sweet Master Patelin.

CRIER [*is heard from afar*]. "The court, make room." . . .

PATELIN. Ah, here they come. Don't forget Ba. . . . I'll be there to help you. And . . . the money . . . don't forget that.

[*Attendants, constables, town clerks and villagers enter. Two clerks carry a seat for* THE JUDGE *which is placed in the center of the stage.* THE JUDGE, *fat and grouchy, comes to the front, looks about for a moment, then goes to his seat and sits down.*]

THE JUDGE. If there is any business to be done, come to it; the court wants to adjourn.

PATELIN. May heaven bless you and grant you all you desire.

THE JUDGE. Welcome, Sir. May the Saints give you plenty of clients.

[THE DRAPER *now comes running in.* PATELIN *suddenly realizes that it is against him that* THE SHEPHERD *must be defended and expresses uneasiness. He hides himself behind the crowd.*]

THE DRAPER. My lawyer is soon coming, your worship. He has a little business elsewhere which is detaining him.

THE JUDGE. You must think I have nothing to do but to wait for your lawyer. You are the plaintiff, aren't you? Bring your complaint. Where is the defendant?

THE DRAPER. Right there, your worship; that lummox shepherd, who has been hiding behind that good citizen there as if he couldn't say Ba. . . . But your honor, it's in fear of justice.

THE JUDGE. Both being present, I will examine you. [*To* THE DRAPER.] Tell me all the facts of your case. Was he in your hire?

THE DRAPER. Yes, your lordship. He killed my sheep and after I treated him like a father. . . .

THE JUDGE. Did you pay him a good wage?

PATELIN [*edging up sideways, and covering his face with his hand*]. Your lordship, I have heard it said that he never paid him a copper for his work.

THE DRAPER [*recognizing* PATELIN]. By all that's holy. . . . You. . . . !!!!??? 'Tis he and no other.

THE JUDGE. Why do you cover your face, Master Patelin?

PATELIN. Oh, your lordship, I have a terrible toothache.

THE JUDGE. I am sorry for you, for I had one myself the other day. I'll tell you a fine cure, Master. Hold your feet in cold water wherein are three hoofs of a red cow from Gascogne. This'll draw the ache into the nails of your toes and you can then rid yourself of it with great ease by cutting them. 'Tis a sovereign remedy. Try it and see, Master. But let us go on. Come, Master Draper, I am in a hurry.

THE DRAPER [*not heeding* THE JUDGE *but still staring at* PATELIN]. It's you, isn't it? It's to you I sold six yards of cloth. Where is my money?

THE JUDGE. What is that you are talking about?

PATELIN. His mind is clouded, your lordship. He is not accustomed to speaking clearly. Perhaps the defendant will enlighten us. You . . .

THE DRAPER. I am not speaking clearly!! You thief . . . liar. . . .

PATELIN. Your worship, I think I understand him now. It's strange how incoherently those who have no legal training speak. I think he means he could have made six yards of cloth from the sheep the shepherd is supposed to have stolen or killed.

THE JUDGE. Aye, so it would seem. Come, Master Guillaume, finish your tale.

PATELIN. Get to the facts as the judge directs you.

THE DRAPER. And you dare talk to me like that!

THE JUDGE. Master Guillaume, come to your sheep.

[During the rest of the court scene PATELIN works always so as to attract the attention of THE DRAPER every time he tries to talk of his sheep, and so diverts his attention from that and leads him to talk of the cloth. Whenever THE DRAPER talks of his case, PATELIN either sticks his face up to him or places himself in such a position that THE DRAPER must see him.]

THE DRAPER. You see, your lordship . . . he took my six yards of cloth this morning . . . the thief. . . .

THE JUDGE. Do you think I am a fool or an ass? Either you come to the point or I'll dismiss the case.

PATELIN. Your worship, let us call the defendant. He, I am sure, will speak clearer than this draper.

THE JUDGE. Yes, that will be wise. Step forward, Shepherd.

THE SHEPHERD. Ba . . . a . . .

THE JUDGE. What's this, am I a goat?

THE SHEPHERD. Ba . . . a . . .

PATELIN. Your lordship, it seems this man is half-witted and thinks himself among his sheep.

THE DRAPER. Damn you! He can talk, and he is not half-witted, either . . . but a thief like you. It was you who took my cloth!

THE JUDGE. Cloth! What are you talking about, anyhow? Now, you either get back to your sheep or I'll dismiss the case.

THE DRAPER. I will, your lordship, though the other lies as near to my heart, but I'll leave it for another time. That shepherd there . . . he took six yards of cloth . . . I mean, sheep. Your honor must forgive me. This thief . . . my shepherd, he told me I would get my money . . . for the cloth as soon . . . I mean this shepherd was to watch over my flocks and he played sick when I came to his house. Ah, Master Pierre. . . . He killed my sheep and told me they died from hoof-sickness . . . and I saw him take the cloth . . . I mean he swore he never killed them. And his wife swore he was sick and said he never took the cloth. . . . No, that shepherd there. . . . He took the sheep and made out that he was crazy. . . . Oh, my Lord! I don't know what . . .

THE JUDGE [leaping up]. Keep quiet, you don't know what you are talking about. You are crazy. I have listened to your idiotic talk about sheep, and cloth, and wool, and money. What is it you want here? Either you answer sensibly, or . . . this is your last chance.

PATELIN. There is surely something strange about this poor man's talk, and I would advise that a physician be consulted. At times, though, it seems as if he were talking about some money he owes this poor shepherd.

THE DRAPER. You thief! You robber! You might at least keep quiet. Where is my cloth? You have it. . . . You are not sick.

THE JUDGE. What has he? Who isn't

sick? Are you going to talk of your business or not?

THE DRAPER. He has it as certain as there is a God in heaven. But I'll speak of this later. Now, I'll attend to this thief, this shepherd.

PATELIN. This shepherd cannot answer the charges himself, Your Lordship. I will gladly give my services to defend him.

THE JUDGE. You won't get much for your pains.

PATELIN. Ah, but the knowledge that I am doing a kind and honest deed, and then, I may be able to stop this haggling which annoys your lordship so much.

THE JUDGE. I'd be greatly thankful.

THE DRAPER. You'll defend him . . . you thief . . . you . . .

THE JUDGE. Now Master Guillaume, you keep quiet or I'll have you put in the stocks. I have listened long enough to your idiotic gab. Proceed, Master Patelin.

PATELIN. I thank your lordship. Now, come on, my good fellow. It's for your own good · I am working as you heard me say. Just because I would do you a kind deed. Answer everything well and direct.

THE SHEPHERD. Ba . . . a . . .

PATELIN. Come, I am your lawyer, not a lamb.

THE SHEPHERD. Ba . . .

PATELIN. What's Ba . . . ? Are you crazy? Tell me, did this man pay you money for your work?

THE SHEPHERD. Ba . . .

PATELIN [seemingly losing his temper]. You idiot, answer, it's I, your lawyer, who is talking to you. Answer.

THE SHEPHERD. Ba . . .

THE DRAPER [who has listened open-mouthed and bewildered]. But, your lordship, he can talk when he wants to. He spoke to me this morning.

PATELIN [severely]. Everything happened to ·you this morning, Master Joceaulme. Now it seems to me, it would be far wiser for you to send this shepherd back to his sheep, he is used to their company ·far more than to that of men.

It does not look as if this fool had sense enough to kill a fly, let alone a sheep.

THE DRAPER. You . . . you . . . robber . . . liar!!!

THE JUDGE. I honestly think they are both crazy.

PATELIN. It seems as if your lordship is right.

THE DRAPER. I am crazy! You scoundrel! You robber! Where is my cloth? They are both thieves. . . .

THE JUDGE. Keep quiet, I say.

THE DRAPER. But, your lordship!

THE JUDGE. All you get is vexation, in dealing with dolts and idiots, be they male or female, so says the law. To finish this wrangling the court is adjourned.

THE DRAPER. And my cloth . . . my money . . . I mean my sheep! Is there no justice? Will you not listen to me?

THE JUDGE. Eh, listen to you, you miser? You dare scoff at justice? You hire half crazy people; and then you don't pay them, then you bellow something about cloth which has nothing to do with the case and expect me to listen to you?

THE DRAPER. But he took my cloth . . . and he killed my sheep. I swear to to you. There he stands, the thief.
[Pointing to PATELIN.]

THE JUDGE. Stop your bellowing. I discharge this half-witted shepherd. Get home and don't ever come in my sight again no matter how many bailiffs summon you.

PATELIN [to THE SHEPHERD]. Say thanks to his lordship.

THE SHEPHERD. Ba . . .

THE JUDGE. By all the Saints, never have I come upon such a nest of idiots!

THE DRAPER. My cloth gone . . . my sheep. . . .

THE JUDGE. Huh! You. . . . Well, I have business elsewhere. May I never see your like again. The court is adjourned. Good day, Master Patelin.

PATELIN. A joyous day to you.
[All leave except PATELIN, THE DRAPER, and THE SHEPHERD.]

THE DRAPER. You thieves . . . you scoundrels! You. . . . You. . . .

PATELIN. Don't shout yourself hoarse, good Master Joceaulme.

THE DRAPER. You stole my cloth and played crazy . . . and now it was because of you, that I lost my sheep. . . .

PATELIN. A fine tale! Do you think any one will believe you?

THE DRAPER. I am not blind. Didn't I see you dancing this morning? I saw you. . . .

PATELIN. Are you so certain? Good Sir, it may have been Jean de Noyon. He resembles me very much.

THE DRAPER. But I know you when I see you. You screamed and acted mad, shouting a tale of dogs and . . .

PATELIN. Perhaps you imagined it all. Go back to my house and see if I am not *still* there.

THE DRAPER [*looks much puzzled*]. May the Lord. . . . Perhaps. . . . But I'll go to your house and if I don't find you there, I'll go to the Judge and see to it that he listens to my story. I'll get a lawyer from Paris. [*To* THE SHEPHERD, *who has been standing at a safe distance.*] You thief! I'll get you yet. [*To* PATELIN.] I'll go to your house now.

PATELIN. That's a wise action.

[*Exit* THE DRAPER.]

PATELIN. Now Tibald, my fellow. What do you think of me? Didn't we do a fine piece of work?

THE SHEPHERD. Ba . . .

PATELIN. Yes. Ho, ho—wasn't it great!

THE SHEPHERD. Ba . . .

PATELIN. No one is near now; your Master is gone. It was a great idea, wasn't it? This legal stroke. You may speak now without fear. . . . I said you could speak without fear, no one is near. Where is the money?

THE SHEPHERD. Ba . . .

PATELIN. I can't stay with you all day. What is this game?

THE SHEPHERD. Ba . . .

PATELIN. How now? Come, I have business elsewhere.

THE SHEPHERD. Ba . . .

PATELIN. What do you mean? You are are not going to pay?

THE SHEPHERD [*with a grin*]. Ba . . .

PATELIN. Yes, you played your rôle well, good Lambkin. But now it's over. Next time you may count on me again. Now my money; the six crowns.

THE SHEPHERD. Ba . . .

PATELIN [*sees the game now, stops. In a somewhat pathetic voice*]. Is that all I am going to get for my work?

THE SHEPHERD. Ba . . .

PATELIN [*getting furious*]. By the Holy Lord, I'll have a bailiff after you, you thief . . . you scoundrel . . . you robber. . . .

THE SHEPHERD. Ho, ho, ho. . . . Ba . . .! The Judge said I need never come back. And—ho, ho, ho, I never knew you. . . . Ba . . . a . . .! [*Runs out.*]

PATELIN [*silent for a time, then grinning pathetically*]. Alas! 'Tis only paying me in my own coin. . . . Nevertheless 'twas a fine idea. . . .   [*Exit.*]

EVERYMAN

ANONYMOUS

Written and produced during the 16th century

CHARACTERS

MESSENGER
EVERYMAN
GOD *(Adonai)*
DEATH
FELLOWSHIP
COUSIN
KINDRED *(woman)*
GOODS
GOOD-DEEDS *(woman)*
STRENGTH *(woman)*
DISCRETION
FIVE-WITS
BEAUTY *(woman)*
KNOWLEDGE *(woman)*
CONFESSION *(woman)*
ANGEL
DOCTOR

Here beginneth a treatise how the high father of Heaven sendeth death to summon every creature to come and give account of their lives in this world and is in manner of a moral play.

MESSENGER. I pray you all give your audience,
And hear this matter with reverence,
By figure a moral play—
The *Summoning of Everyman* called it is,
That of our lives and ending shows
How transitory we be all day.
This matter is wondrous precious,
But the intent of it is more gracious,
And sweet to bear away.
The story saith,—Man, in the beginning,
Look well, and take good heed to the ending,
Be you never so gay!
Ye think sin in the beginning full sweet,
Which in the end causeth thy soul to weep,

351

When the body lieth in clay.
Here shall you see how Fellowship and
    Jollity,
Both Strength, Pleasure, and Beauty,
Will fade from thee as flower in May.
For ye shall hear, how our heaven king
Calleth Everyman to a general reckoning:
Give audience, and hear what he doth say.
    GOD. I perceive here in my majesty,
How that all creatures be to me unkind,
Living without dread in worldly prosper-
    ity:
Of ghostly sight the people be so blind,
Drowned in sin, they know me not for
    their God;
In worldly riches is all their mind,
They fear not my rightwiseness, the sharp
    rod;
My law that I shewed, when I for them
    died,
They forget clean, and shedding of my
    blood red;
I hanged between two, it cannot be de-
    nied;
To get them life I suffered to be dead;
I healed their feet, with thorns hurt was
    my head:
I could do no more than I did truly,
And now I see the people do clean forsake
    me.
They use the seven deadly sins damnable;
As pride, covetise, wrath, and lechery,
Now in the world be made commendable;
And thus they leave of angels the heavenly
    company;
Everyman liveth so after his own pleas-
    ure,
And yet of their life they be nothing sure:
I see the more that I them forbear
The worse they be from year to year;
All that liveth appaireth fast,
Therefore I will in all the haste
Have a reckoning of Everyman's person
For and I leave the people thus alone
In their life and wicked tempests,
Verily they will become much worse than
    beasts;
For now one would by envy another up
    eat;
Charity they all do clean forget.
I hoped well that Everyman

In my glory should make his mansion,
And thereto I had them all elect;
But now I see, like traitors deject,
They thank me not for the pleasure that
    I to them meant,
Nor yet for their being that I them have
    lent;
I proffered the people great multitude of
    mercy,
And few there be that asketh it heartily;
They be so cumbered with worldly riches,
That needs on them I must do justice,
On Everyman living without fear.
Where art thou, Death, thou mighty mes-
    senger?
    DEATH. Almighty God, I am here at
    your will,
Your commandment to fulfil.
    GOD. Go thou to Everyman,
And show him in my name
A pilgrimage he must on him take,
Which he in no wise may escape;
And that he bring with him a sure reckon-
    ing
Without delay or any tarrying.
    DEATH. Lord, I will in the world go
    run over all,
And cruelly outsearch both great and
    small;
Every man will I beset that liveth beastly
Out of God's laws, and dreadeth not folly:
He that loveth riches I will strike with
    my dart,
His sight to blind, and from heaven to
    depart,
Except that alms be his good friend,
In hell for to dwell, world without end.
Lo, yonder I see Everyman walking;
Full little he thinketh on my coming;
His mind is on fleshly lusts and his treas-
    ure,
And great pain it shall cause him to en-
    dure
Before the Lord Heaven King.
Everyman, stand still; whither art thou
    going
Thus gaily? Hast thou thy Maker forgot?
    EVERYMAN. Why askst thou?
Wouldest thou wete?
    DEATH. Yea, sir, I will show you;
In great haste I am sent to thee

From God out of his majesty.

EVERYMAN. What, sent to me?

DEATH. Yea, certainly.

Though thou have forget him here,

He thinketh on thee in the heavenly sphere,

As, or we depart, thou shalt know.

EVERYMAN. What desireth God of me?

DEATH. That shall I show thee;

A reckoning he will needs have

Without any longer respite.

EVERYMAN. To give a reckoning longer leisure I crave;

This blind matter troubleth my wit.

DEATH. On thee thou must take a long journey:

Therefore thy book of count with thee thou bring;

For turn again thou can not by no way,

And look thou be sure of thy reckoning:

For before God thou shalt answer, and show

Thy many bad deeds and good but a few;

How thou hast spent thy life, and in what wise,

Before the chief lord of paradise.

Have ado that we were in that way,

For, wete thou well, thou shalt make none attournay.

EVERYMAN. Full unready I am such reckoning to give.

I know thee not: what messenger art thou?

DEATH. I am Death, that no man dreadeth.

For every man I rest and no man spareth;

For it is God's commandment

That all to me should be obedient.

EVERYMAN. O Death, thou comest when I had thee least in mind;

In thy power it lieth me to save,

Yet of my good will I give thee, if ye will be kind,

Yea, a thousand pound shalt thou have,

And defer this matter till another day.

DEATH. Everyman, it may not be by no way;

I set not by gold, silver, nor riches,

Ne by pope, emperor, king, duke, ne princes.

For and I would receive gifts great,

All the world I might get;

But my custom is clean contrary.

I give thee no respite: come hence, and not tarry.

EVERYMAN. Alas, shall I have no longer respite?

I may say Death giveth no warning:

To think on thee, it maketh my heart sick,

For all unready is my book of reckoning.

But twelve year and I might have abiding,

My counting book I would make so clear,

That my reckoning I should not need to fear.

Wherefore, *Death*, I pray thee, for God's mercy,

Spare me till I be provided of remedy.

DEATH. Thee availeth not to cry, weep, and pray:

But haste thee lightly that you were gone the journey,

And prove thy friends if thou can.

For, wete thou well, the tide abideth no man,

And in the world each living creature

For *Adam's* sin must die of nature.

EVERYMAN. *Death*, if I should this pilgrimage take,

And my reckoning surely make,

Show me, for Saint Charity,

Should I not come again shortly?

DEATH. No, Everyman; and thou be once there,

Thou mayst never come here,

Trust me verily.

EVERYMAN. O gracious God, in the high seat celestial,

Have mercy on me in this most need;

Shall I have no company from this vale terrestrial

Of mine acquaintance that way me to lead?

DEATH. Yea, if any be so hardy,

That would go with thee and bear thee company.

Hie thee that you were gone to God's magnificence,

Thy reckoning to give before his presence.

What, weenest thou thy life is given
thee,
And thy world goods also?
EVERYMAN. I had wend so, verily.
DEATH. Nay, nay; it was but lent
thee;
For as soon as thou art go,
Another awhile shall have it, and then go
therefro
Even as thou hast done.
Everyman, thou art mad; thou hast thy
wits five,
And here on earth will not amend thy
life,
For suddenly I do come.
EVERYMAN. O wretched caitiff, whither
shall I flee,
That I might scape this endless sorrow!
Now, gentle Death, spare me till tomor-
row,
That I may amend me
With good advisement.
DEATH. Nay, thereto I will not con-
sent,
Nor no man will I respite,
But to the heart suddenly I shall smite
Without any advisement.
And now out of thy sight I will me hie;
See thou make thee ready shortly,
For thou mayst say this is the day
That no man living may scape away.
EVERYMAN. Alas, I may well weep with
sighs deep;
Now have I no manner of company
To help me in my journey, and me to
keep;
And also my writing is full unready.
How shall I do now for to excuse me?
I would to God I had never be gete!
To my soul a full great profit it had be;
For now I fear pains huge and great.
Time passeth; Lord, help that all
wrought;
For though I mourn it availeth nought.
The day passeth, and is almost a-go;
I wot not well what for to do.
To whom were I best my complaint to
make?
What, and I to Fellowship thereof spake,
And showed him of this sudden chance?
For in him is all mine affiance;

We have in the world so many a day
Be on good friends in sport and play.
I see him yonder, certainly;
I trust that he will bear me company;
Therefore to him will I speak to ease my
sorrow.
Well met, good Fellowship, and good mor-
row!
FELLOWSHIP [speaketh]. Everyman,
good morrow by this day.
Sir, why lookest thou so piteously?
If any thing be amiss, I pray thee, me say,
That I may help to remedy.
EVERYMAN. Yea, good Fellowship, yea.
I am in great jeopardy.
FELLOWSHIP. My true friend, show to
me your mind;
I will not forsake thee, unto my life's end,
In the way of good company.
EVERYMAN. That was well spoken, and
lovingly.
FELLOWSHIP. Sir, I must needs know
your heaviness;
I have pity to see you in any distress;
If any have you wronged ye shall re-
venged be,
Though I on the ground be slain for
thee,—
Though that I know before that I should
die.
EVERYMAN. Verily, Fellowship, gra-
mercy.
FELLOWSHIP. Tush! by thy thanks I
set not a straw.
Show me your grief, and say no more.
EVERYMAN. If my heart should to you
break,
And then you to turn your mind from
me,
And would not me comfort, when you hear
me speak,
Then should I ten times sorrier be.
FELLOWSHIP. Sir, I say as I will do in
deed.
EVERYMAN. Then be you a good friend
in need;
I have found you true here before.
FELLOWSHIP. And so ye shall ever-
more;
For, in faith, and thou go to Hell,
I will not forsake thee by the way!

EVERYMAN. Ye speak like a good friend; I believe you well;
I shall deserve it, and I may.
FELLOWSHIP. I speak of no deserving, by this day.
For he that will say and nothing do
Is not worthy with good company to go;
Therefore show me the grief of your mind,
As to your friend most loving and kind.
EVERYMAN. I shall show you how it is;
Commanded I am to go a journey,
A long way, hard and dangerous,
And give a strait count without delay
Before the high judge Adonai.
Wherefore I pray you, bear me company,
As ye have promised, in this journey.
FELLOWSHIP. That is matter indeed! Promise is duty,
But, and I should take such a voyage on me,
I know it well, it should be to my pain:
Also it make me afeard, certain.
But let us take counsel here as well as we can,
For your words would fear a strong man.
EVERYMAN. Why, ye said, if I had need,
Ye would me never forsake, quick nor dead,
Though it were to hell truly.
FELLOWSHIP.   So I said, certainly,
But such pleasures be set aside, thee sooth to say:
And also, if we took such a journey,
When should we come again?
EVERYMAN. Nay, never again till the day of doom.
FELLOWSHIP. In faith, then will not I come there!
Who hath you these tidings brought?
EVERYMAN. Indeed, Death was with me here.
FELLOWSHIP. Now, by God that all hath brought,
If Death were the messenger,
For no man that is living to-day
I will not go that loath journey—
Not for the father that begat me!
EVERYMAN. Ye promised other wise, pardie.
FELLOWSHIP. I wot well I say so truly;

And yet if thou wilt eat, and drink, and make good cheer,
Or haunt to women, the lusty company,
I would not forsake you, while the day is clear,
Trust me verily!
EVERYMAN. Yea, thereto ye would be ready;
To go to mirth, solace, and play,
Your mind will sooner apply
Than to bear me company in my long journey.
FELLOWSHIP. Now, in good faith, I will not that way.
But and thou wilt murder, or any man kill,
In that I will help thee with a good will!
EVERYMAN. O that is a simple advice indeed!
Gentle *fellow*, help me in my necessity;
We have loved long, and now I need,
And now, gentle Fellowship, remember me.
FELLOWSHIP. Whether ye have loved me or no,
By Saint John, I will not with thee go.
EVERYMAN. Yet I pray thee, take the labour, and do so much for me
To bring me forward, for saint charity,
And comfort me till I come without the town.
FELLOWSHIP. Nay, and thou would give me a new gown,
I will not a foot with thee go;
But and you had tarried I would not have left thee so.
And as now, God speed thee in thy journey,
For from thee I will depart as fast as I may.
EVERYMAN. Whither away, Fellowship? will you forsake me?
FELLOWSHIP. Yea, by my fay, to God I betake thee.
EVERYMAN. Farewell, good Fellowship; for this my heart is sore;
Adieu for ever, I shall see thee no more.
FELLOWSHIP. In faith, Everyman, farewell now at the end;
For you I will remember that parting is mourning.

EVERYMAN. Alack! shall we thus depart indeed?

Our Lady, help, without any more comfort,

Lo, Fellowship forsaketh me in my most need:

For help in this world whither shall I resort?

Fellowship herebefore with me would merry make;

And now little sorrow for me doth he take.

It is said, in prosperity men friends may find,

Which in adversity be full unkind.

Now whither for succour shall I flee,

Sith that Fellowship hath forsaken me?

To my kinsmen I will truly,

Praying them to help me in my necessity;

I believe that they will do so,

For kind will creep where it may not go.

I will go say, for yonder I see them go.

Where be ye now, my friends and kinsmen?

KINDRED. Here be we now at your commandment.

Cousin, I pray you show us your intent

In any wise, and not spare.

COUSIN. Yea, Everyman, and to us declare

If ye be disposed to go any whither,

For wete you well, we will live and die together.

KINDRED. In wealth and woe we will with you hold,

For over his kin a man may be bold.

EVERYMAN. Gramercy, my friends and kinsmen kind.

Now shall I show you the grief of my mind:

I was commanded by a messenger,

That is an high king's chief officer;

He bade me go a pilgrimage to my pain,

And I know well I shall never come again;

Also I must give a reckoning straight,

For I have a great enemy, that hath me in wait,

Which intendeth me for to hinder.

KINDRED. What account is that which ye must render?

That would I know.

EVERYMAN. Of all my works I must show

How I have lived and my days spent;

Also of ill deeds, that I have used

In my time, sith life was me lent;

And of all virtues that I have refused.

Therefore I pray you go thither with me,

To help to make mine account, for Saint Charity.

COUSIN. What, to go thither? Is that the matter?

Nay, Everyman, I had liefer fast bread and water

All this five year and more.

EVERYMAN. Alas, that ever I was bore!

For now shall I never be merry

If that you forsake me.

KINDRED. Ah, sir; what, ye be a merry man!

Take good heart to you, and make no moan.

But one thing I warn you, by Saint Anne,

As for me, ye shall go alone.

EVERYMAN. My Cousin, will you not with me go?

COUSIN. No, by our Lady; I have the cramp in my toe.

Trust not to me, for, so God me speed,

I will deceive you in your most need.

KINDRED. It availeth not us to tice.

Ye shall have my maid with all my heart;

She loveth to go to feasts, there to be nice,

And to dance, and abroad to start:

I will give her leave to help you in that journey,

If that you and she may agree.

EVERYMAN. Now show me the very effect of your mind.

Will you go with me, or abide behind?

KINDRED. Abide behind? yea, that I will and I may!

Therefore farewell until another day.

EVERYMAN. How should I be merry or glad?

For fair promises to me make,

But when I have most need, they me forsake.

I am deceived; that maketh me sad.

COUSIN. Cousin Everyman, farewell now,

For verily I will not go with you;
Also of mine own an unready reckoning
I have to account; therefore I make tarry-
ing.
Now, God keep thee, for now I go.
  EVERYMAN. Ah Jesus, is all come
    hereto?
Lo, fair words maketh fools feign;
They promise and nothing will do certain.
My kinsmen promised me faithfully
For to abide with me steadfastly,
And now fast away do they flee.
Even so Fellowship promised me.
What friend were best me of to provide?
I lose my time here longer to abide.
Yet in my mind a thing there is;—
All my life I have loved riches;
If that my good now help me might,
He would make my heart full light.
I will speak to him in this distress.—
Where art thou, my Goods and riches?
  GOODS. Who calleth me? Everyman?
    what haste thou hast!
I lie here in corners, trussed and piled so
    high,
And in chests I am locked so fast,
Also sacked in bags, thou mayst see with
    thine eye,
I cannot stir; in packs low I lie.
What would ye have, lightly me say.
  EVERYMAN. Come hither, Goods, in all
    the haste thou may,
For of counsel I must desire thee.
  GOODS. Sir, and ye in the world have
    trouble or adversity,
That can I help you to remedy shortly.
  EVERYMAN. It is another disease that
    grieveth me;
In this world it is not, I tell thee so.
I am sent for another way to go,
To give a straight account general
Before the highest Jupiter of all;
And all my life I have had joy and pleas-
    ure in thee.
Therefore I pray thee go with me,
For, peradventure, thou mayst before God
    Almighty
My reckoning help to clean and purify;
For it is said ever among,
That money maketh all right that is
    wrong.

  GOODS. Nay, Everyman, I sing another
    song,
I follow no man in such voyages;
For and I went with thee
Thou shouldst fare much the worse for
    me;
For because on me thou did set thy mind,
Thy reckoning I have made blotted and
    blind,
That thine account thou can not make
    truly;
And that hast thou for the love of me.
  EVERYMAN. That would grieve me full
    sore,
When I should come to that fearful an-
    swer.
Up, let us go thither together.
  GOODS. Nay, not so, I am too brittle,
    I may not endure;
I will follow no man one foot, be ye sure.
  EVERYMAN. Alas, I have thee loved,
    and had great pleasure
All my life-days on good and treasure.
  GOODS. That is to thy damnation with-
    out lesing,
For my love is contrary to the love ever-
    lasting.
But if thou had me loved moderately dur-
    ing,
As, to the poor give part of me,
Then shouldst thou not in this dolour
    be,
Nor in this great sorrow and care.
  EVERYMAN. Lo, now was I deceived or
    I was ware,
And all I may wyte my spending of time.
  GOODS. What, weenest thou that I am
    thine?
  EVERYMAN. I had wend so.
  GOODS. Nay, Everyman, I say no;
As for a while I was lent thee,
A season thou hast had me in prosperity;
My condition is man's soul to kill;
If I save one, a thousand I do spill;
Weenest thou that I will follow thee?
Nay, from this world, not verily.
  EVERYMAN. I had wend otherwise.
  GOODS. Therefore to thy soul Goods is
    a thief;
For when thou art dead, this is my guise
Another to deceive in the same wise

As I have done thee, and all to his soul's
  reprief.
EVERYMAN. O false Goods, cursed thou
  be!
Thou traitor to God, that hast deceived
  me,
And caught me in thy snare.
GOODS. Marry, thou brought thyself in
  care,
Whereof I am glad,
I must needs laugh, I cannot be sad.
EVERYMAN. Ah Goods, thou hast had
  long my heartly love;
I gave thee that which should be the
  Lord's above.
But wilt thou not go with me in deed?
I pray thee truth to say.
GOODS. No, so God me speed,
Therefore farewell, and have good day.
EVERYMAN. O, to whom shall I make
  my moan
For to go with me in that heavy journey?
First Fellowship said he would with me
  gone;
His words were very pleasant and gay,
But afterward he left me alone.
Then spake I to my kinsmen all in de-
  spair,
And also they gave me words fair,
They lacked no fair speaking,
But all forsake me in the ending.
Then went I to my Goods that I loved
  best,
In hope to have comfort, but there had I
  least;
For my Goods sharply did me tell
That he bringeth many into hell.
Then of myself I was ashamed,
And so I am worthy to be blamed;
Thus may I well myself hate.
Of whom shall I now counsel take?
I think that I shall never speed
Till that I got to my Good-Deeds,
But alas, she is so weak,
That she can neither go nor speak;
Yet will I venture on her now.—
My Good-Deeds, where be you?
GOOD-DEEDS. Here I lie cold in the
  ground;
Thy sins hath me sore bound,
That I cannot stir.

EVERYMAN. O, Good-Deeds, I stand in
  fear;
I must you pray of counsel,
For help now should come right well.
GOOD-DEEDS. Everyman, I have under-
  standing
That ye be summoned account to make
Before Messias, of Jerusalem King;
And you do by me that journey what you
  will I take.
EVERYMAN. Therefore I come to you,
  my moan to make;
I pray you, that ye will go with me.
GOOD-DEEDS. I would full fain, but I
  cannot stand verily.
EVERYMAN. Why, is there anything on
  you fall?
GOOD-DEEDS. Yea, sir, I may thank you
  of all;
If ye had perfectly cheered me,
Your book of account now full ready had
  be.
Look, the books of your works and deeds
  eke;
Oh, see how they lie under the feet,
To your soul's heaviness.
EVERYMAN. Our Lord Jesus, help me!
For one letter here I can not see.
GOOD-DEEDS. There is a blind reckoning
  in time of distress!
EVERYMAN. Good-Deeds, I pray you,
  help me in this need,
Or else I am for ever damned indeed;
Therefore help me to make reckoning
Before the redeemer of all thing,
That king is, and was, and ever shall.
GOOD-DEEDS. Everyman, I am sorry of
  your fall,
And fain would I help you, and I were
  able.
EVERYMAN. Good-Deeds, your counsel I
  pray you give me.
GOOD-DEEDS. That shall I do verily;
Though that on my feet I may not go,
I have a sister, that shall with you also,
Called Knowledge, which shall with you
  abide,
To help you to make that dreadful reckon-
  ing.
KNOWLEDGE. Everyman, I will go with
  thee, and be thy guide,

In thy most need to go by thy side.

EVERYMAN. In good condition I am
now in everything,
And am wholly content with this good
thing;
Thanked be God my Creator.

GOOD-DEEDS. And when he hath brought
thee there,
Where thou shalt heal thee of thy smart,
Then go you with your reckoning and
your Good-Deeds together.
For to make you joyful at heart
Before the blessed Trinity.

EVERYMAN. My Good-Deeds, gramercy;
I am well content, certainly,
With your words sweet.

KNOWLEDGE. Now go we together lov-
ingly,
To Confession, that cleansing river.

EVERYMAN. For joy I weep; I would
we were there;
But, I pray you, give me cognition
Where dwelleth that holy man, Confes-
sion.

KNOWLEDGE. In the house of salvation:
We shall find him in that place,
That shall us comfort by God's grace.
Lo, this is Confession; kneel down and
ask mercy,
For he is in good conceit with God al-
mighty.

EVERYMAN. O glorious fountain that
all uncleanness doth clarify,
Wash from me the spots of vices unclean,
That on me no sin may be seen;
I come with Knowledge for my redemp-
tion,
Repent with hearty and full contrition;
For I am commanded a pilgrimage to take,
And great accounts before God to make.
Now, I pray you, Shrift, mother of salva-
tion,
Help my good deeds for my piteous ex-
clamation

CONFESSION. I know your sorrow well,
Everyman;
Because with Knowledge ye come to me,
I will you comfort as well as I can,
And a precious jewel I will give thee,
Called penance, wise voider of adversity;
Therewith shall your body chastised be,

With abstinence and perseverance in God's
service:
Here shall you receive that scourge of me,
Which is penance strong, that ye must
endure,
To remember thy Saviour was scourged
for thee
With sharp scourges, and suffered it pa-
tiently;
So must thou, or thou scape that painful
pilgrimage;
Knowledge, keep him in this voyage,
And by that time Good-Deeds will be with
thee.
But in any wise, be sure of mercy,
For your time draweth fast, and ye will
saved be;
Ask God mercy, and He will grant truly,
When with the scourge of penance man
doth him bind,
The oil of forgiveness then shall he find.

EVERYMAN. Thanked be God for his
gracious work!
For now I will my penance begin;
This hath rejoiced and lighted my heart,
Though the knots be painful and hard
within.

KNOWLEDGE. Everyman, look your pen-
ance that ye fulfil,
What pain that ever it to you be,
And Knowledge shall give you counsel
at will,
How your accounts ye shall make clearly.

EVERYMAN. O eternal God, O heavenly
figure,
O way of rightwiseness, O goodly vision,
Which descended down in a virgin pure
Because he would Everyman redeem,
Which Adam forfeited by his disobedi-
ence:
O blessed Godhead, elect and high-divine,
Forgive my grievous offence;
Here I cry thee mercy in this presence.
O ghostly treasure, O ransomer and re-
deemer
Of all the world, hope and conductor,
Mirror of joy, and founder of mercy,
Which illumineth heaven and earth
thereby,
Hear my clamorous complaint, though it
late be;

Receive my prayers; unworthy in this heavy life,
Though I be, a sinner most abominable,
Yet let my name be written in Moses' table;
O Mary, pray to the Maker of all thing,
Me for to help at my ending,
And save me from the power of my enemy,
For Death assaileth me strongly;
And, Lady, that I may by means of thy prayer
Of your Son's glory to be partaker,
By the means of his passion I it crave,
I beseech you, help my soul to save.—
Knowledge, give me the scourge of penance;
My flesh therewith shall give a quittance:
I will now begin, if God give me grace.

KNOWLEDGE. Everyman, God give you time and space:
Thus I bequeath you in the hands of our Saviour,
Thus may you make your reckoning sure.

EVERYMAN. In the name of the Holy Trinity,
My body sore punished shall be:
Take this body for the sin of the flesh;
Also thou delightest to go gay and fresh,
And in the way of damnation thou did me bring;
Therefore suffer now strokes and punishing.
Now of penance I will wade the water clear,
To save me from purgatory, that sharp fire.

GOOD-DEEDS. I thank God, now I can walk and go;
And am delivered of my sickness and woe.
Therefore with Everyman I will go, and not spare;
His good works I will help him to declare.

KNOWLEDGE. Now, Everyman, be merry and glad;
Your Good-Deeds cometh now; ye may not be sad;
Now is your Good-Deeds whole and sound,
Going upright upon the ground.

EVERYMAN. My heart is light, and shall be evermore;
Now will I smite faster than I did before.

GOOD-DEEDS. Everyman, pilgrim, my special friend,
Blessed be thou without end;
For thee is prepared the eternal glory.
Ye have me made whole and sound,
Therefore I will bide by thee in every stound.

EVERYMAN. Welcome, my Good-Deeds; now I hear thy voice,
I weep for very sweetness of love.

KNOWLEDGE. Be no more sad, but ever rejoice,
God seeth thy living in his throne above;
Put on this garment to thy behove,
Which is wet with your tears,
Or else before God you may it miss,
When you to your journey's end come shall.

EVERYMAN. Gentle Knowledge, what do you it call?

KNOWLEDGE. It is a garment of sorrow:
From pain it will you borrow;
Contrition it is,
That getteth forgiveness;
It pleaseth God passing well.

GOOD-DEEDS. Everyman, will you wear it for your heal?

EVERYMAN. Now blessed be Jesu, Mary's Son!
For now have I on true contrition.
And let us go now without tarrying;
Good-Deeds, have we clear our reckoning?

GOOD-DEEDS. Yea, indeed I have it here.

EVERYMAN. Then I trust we need not fear;
Now, friends, let us not part in twain.

KNOWLEDGE. Nay, Everyman, that will we not, certain.

GOOD-DEEDS. Yet must thou lead with thee
Three persons of great might.

EVERYMAN. Who should they be?

GOOD-DEEDS. Discretion and Strength they hight,
And thy Beauty may not abide behind.

KNOWLEDGE. Also ye must call to mind
Your Five-Wits as for your counsellors.

GOOD-DEEDS. You must have them ready at all hours.

EVERYMAN. How shall I get them hither?

KNOWLEDGE. You must call them all together,
And they will hear you incontinent.

EVERYMAN. My friends, come hither and be present,
Discretion, Strength, my Five-Wits, and Beauty.

BEAUTY. Here at your will we be already.
What will ye that we should do?

GOOD-DEEDS. That ye would with Everyman go,
And help him in his pilgrimage,
Advise you, will ye with him or not in that voyage?

STRENGTH. We will bring him all thither,
To his help and comfort, ye may believe me.

DISCRETION. So will we go with him all together.

EVERYMAN. Almighty God, loved thou be,
I give thee laud that I have hither brought
Strength, Discretion, Beauty, and Five-Wits; lack I nought;
And my Good-Deeds, with Knowledge clear,
All be in my company at my will here;
I desire no more to my business.

STRENGTH. And I, Strength, will by you stand in distress,
Though thou would in battle fight on the ground.

FIVE-WITS. And though it were through the world round,
We will not depart for sweet nor sour.

BEAUTY. No more will I undo death's hour,
Whatsoever thereof befall.

DISCRETION. Everyman, advise you first of all;
Go with a good advisement and deliberation;
We all give you virtuous monition
That all shall be well.

EVERYMAN. My friends, hearken what I will tell:
I pray God reward you in his heavenly sphere.
Now hearken, all that be here.
For I will make my testament
Here before you all present.
In alms half my good I will give with my hands twain
In the way of charity, with good intent,
And the other half still shall remain
In quiet to be returned there it ought to be.
This I do in despite of the fiend of hell
To go quite out of his peril
Ever after and this day.

KNOWLEDGE. Everyman, hearken what I say;
Go to priesthood, I you advise,
And receive of him in any wise
The holy sacrament and ointment together;
Then shortly see ye turn again hither;
We will all abide you here.

FIVE-WITS. Yea, Everyman, hie you that ye ready were,
There is no emperor, king, duke, ne baron,
That of God hath commission,
As hath the least priest in the world being;
For of the blessed sacraments pure and benign,
He bearth the keys and thereof hath the cure
For man's redemption, it is ever sure;
Which God for our soul's medicine
Gave us out of his heart with great pine;
Here in this transitory life, for thee and me
The blessed sacraments seven there be,
Baptism, confirmation, with priesthood good,
And the sacrament of God's precious flesh and blood,
Marriage, the holy extreme unction, and penance;
These seven be good to have in remembrance,
Gracious sacraments of high divinity.

EVERYMAN. Fain would I receive that holy body
And meekly to my ghostly father I will go.

FIVE-WITS. Everyman, that is the best that ye can do:
God will you to salvation bring,
For priesthood exceedeth all other thing;
To us Holy Scripture they do teach,
And converteth man from sin heaven to reach;
God hath to them more power given,
Than to any angel that is in heaven;
With five words he may consecrate
God's body in flesh and blood to make,
And handleth his maker between his hands;
The priest bindeth and unbindeth all bands,
Both in earth and in heaven;
Thou ministers all the sacraments seven;
Though we kissed thy feet thou wert worthy;
Thou art surgeon that cureth sin deadly:
No remedy we find under God
But all only priesthood.
Everyman, God gave priests that dignity,
And setteth them in his stead among us to be;
Thus be they above angels in degree.
KNOWLEDGE. If priests be good it is so surely;
But when Jesus hanged on the cross with great smart
There he gave, out of his blessed heart,
The same sacrament in great torment:
He sold them not to us, that Lord Omnipotent.
Therefore Saint Peter the apostle doth say
That Jesu's curse hath all they
Which God their Saviour do buy or sell,
Or they for any money do take or tell.
Sinful priests giveth the sinners example bad;
Their children sitteth by other men's fires, I have heard;
And some haunteth women's company,
With unclean life, as lusts of lechery
These be with sin made blind.
FIVE-WITS. I trust to God no such may we find;
Therefore let us priesthood honour,
And follow their doctrine for our soul's succour;

We be their sheep, and they shepherds be
By whom we all be kept in surety.
Peace, for yonder I see Everyman come,
Which hath made true satisfaction.
GOOD-DEEDS. Methinketh it is he indeed.
EVERYMAN. Now Jesu be our alder speed.
I have received the sacrament for my redemption,
And then mine extreme unction:
Blessed be all they that counselled me to take it!
And now, friends, let us go without longer respite;
I thank God that ye have tarried so long.
Now set each of you on this rod your hand,
And shortly follow me:
I go before, there I would be; God be our guide.
STRENGTH. Everyman, we will not from you go,
Till ye have gone this voyage long.
DISCRETION. I, Discretion, will bide by you also.
KNOWLEDGE. And though this pilgrimage be never so strong,
I will never part you fro:
Everyman, I will be as sure by thee
As ever I did by Judas Maccabee.
EVERYMAN. Alas, I am so faint I may not stand.
My limbs under me do fold;
Friends, let us not turn again to this land,
Not for all the world's gold.
For into this cave must I creep
And turn to the earth and there to sleep.
BEAUTY. What, into this grave? alas!
EVERYMAN. Yea, there shall you consume more and less.
BEAUTY. And what, should I smother here?
EVERYMAN. Yea, by my faith, and never more appear.
In this world live no more we shall,
But in heaven before the highest Lord of all.
BEAUTY. I cross out all this; adieu by Saint John;

I take my cap in my lap and am gone.

EVERYMAN. What, Beauty, whither will ye?

BEAUTY. Peace, I am deaf; I look not behind me,

Not and thou would give me all the gold in thy chest.

EVERYMAN. Alas, whereto may I trust?

Beauty goeth fast away hie;

She promised with me to live and die.

STRENGTH. Everyman, I will thee also forsake and deny;

Thy game liketh me not at all.

EVERYMAN. Why, then ye will forsake me all.

Sweet Strength, tarry a little space.

STRENGTH. Nay, sir, by the rood of grace

I will hie me from thee fast,

Though thou weep till thy heart brast.

EVERYMAN. Ye would ever bide by me, ye said.

STRENGTH. Yea, I have you far enough conveyed;

Ye be old enough, I understand,

Your pilgrimage to take on hand;

I repent me that I hither came.

EVERYMAN. Strength, you to displease I am to blame;

Will you break promise that is debt?

STRENGTH. In faith, I care not;

Thou art but a fool to complain,

You spend your speech and waste your brain;

Go thrust thee into the ground.

EVERYMAN. I had wend surer I should you have found.

He that trusteth in his Strength

She him deceiveth at the length.

Both Strength and Beauty forsaketh me,

Yet they promised me fair and lovingly.

DISCRETION. Everyman, I will after Strength be gone,

As for me, I will leave you alone.

EVERYMAN. Why, Discretion, will ye forsake me?

DISCRETION. Yea, in faith, I will go from thee,

For when Strength goeth before

I follow after evermore.

EVERYMAN. Yet, I pray thee, for the love of the Trinity,

Look in my grave once piteously.

DISCRETION. Nay, so nigh will I not come.

Farewell, every one!

EVERYMAN. O all thing faileth, save God alone;

Beauty, Strength, and Discretion;

For when Death bloweth his blast,

They all run from me full fast.

FIVE-WITS. Everyman, my leave now of thee I take;

I will follow the other, for here I thee forsake.

EVERYMAN. Alas! then may I wail and weep,

For I took you for my best friend.

FIVE-WITS. I will no longer thee keep;

Now farewell, and there an end.

EVERYMAN. O Jesu, help, all hath forsaken me!

GOOD-DEEDS. Nay, Everyman, I will bide with thee,

I will not forsake thee indeed;

Thou shalt find me a good friend at need.

EVERYMAN. Gramercy, Good-Deeds; now may I true friends see;

They have forsaken me every one;

I loved them better than my Good-Deeds alone.

Knowledge, will ye forsake me also?

KNOWLEDGE. Yea, Everyman, when ye to death do go:

But not yet for no manner of danger.

EVERYMAN. Gramercy, Knowledge, with all my heart.

KNOWLEDGE. Nay, yet I will not from hence depart,

Till I see where ye shall be come.

EVERYMAN. Methinketh, alas, that I must be gone,

To make my reckoning and my debts pay,

For I see my time is nigh spent away.

Take example, all ye that this do hear or see,

How they that I loved best do forsake me,

Except my Good-Deeds that bideth truly.

GOOD-DEEDS. All earthly things is but vanity:

Beauty, Strength, and Discretion, do man
forsake,
Foolish friends and kinsmen, that fair
spake,
All fleeth save Good-Deeds, and that am I.
  EVERYMAN. Have mercy on me, God
  most mighty;
And stand by me, thou Mother and Maid,
holy Mary.
  GOOD-DEEDS. Fear not, I will speak for
  thee.
  EVERYMAN. Here I cry God mercy.
  GOOD-DEEDS. Short our end, and minish
  our pain;
Let us go and never come again.
  EVERYMAN. Into thy hands, Lord, my
  soul I commend;
Receive it, Lord, that it be not lost;
As thou me boughtest, so me defend,
And save me from the fiend's boast,
That I may appear with that blessed host
That shall be saved at the day of doom.
In manus tuas—of might's most
For ever—*commendo spiritum meum.*
  KNOWLEDGE. Now hath he suffered
  that we all shall endure;
The Good-Deeds shall make all sure.
Now hath he made ending;
Methinketh that I hear angels sing
And make great joy and melody,
Where Everyman's soul received shall be.
  ANGEL. Come, excellent elect spouse to
  Jesu:
Hereabove thou shalt go
Because of thy singular virtue:

Now the soul is taken the body fro;
Thy reckoning is crystal-clear.
Now shalt thou into the heavenly sphere,
Unto the which all ye shall come
That liveth well before the day of doom.
  DOCTOR. This moral men may have in
  mind;
Ye hearers, take it of worth, old and
young,
And forsake pride, for he deceiveth you
in the end,
And remember Beauty, Five-Wits, Strength
and Discretion,
They all at the last do Everyman forsake,
Save his Good-Deeds, there doth he take.
But beware, and they be small
Before God, he hath no help at all.
None excuse may be there for Everyman:
Alas, how shall he do then?
For after death amends may no man
make,
For then mercy and pity do him forsake.
If his reckoning be not clear when he do
come,
God will say—*ite maledicti in ignem
aeternum.*
And he that hath his account whole and
sound,
High in heaven he shall be crowned;
Unto which place God bring us all thither
That we may live body and soul together.
Thereto help the Trinity,
Amen, say ye, for Saint Charity.
  THUS ENDETH THIS MORALL PLAY OF
    EVERYMAN.

THE WANDERING SCHOLAR
FROM PARADISE

By HANS SACHS

Published 1550 and probably produced about that time

TRANSLATED FROM THE GERMAN BY SAMUEL A. ELIOT, JR.*

[*Before and during the slow rise of the curtain, the voice of the* WIFE *is heard in simple song.*]

THE WIFE [*tearfully, with ludicrous breaks and intervals*].
Peasant maiden, love is bright:
He may come to thee to-night!
Peasant maiden, love is sweet:
He may kneel before thy feet!
Peasant wife, put love away!
He cares not for thee to-day.
[*The song stops with the suggestion of a sob.* THE WIFE *appears in the doorway, back center, wipes her eyes, sobs again, leans against the jamb, and sighs deeply, her gaze far away.*]
Heigho, how many sighs do I heave,
When-as over times long past I grieve!
Then my first man was still alive.
[*Sniffing.*]
Our love so strove, nothing else could thrive!
He was a simple and pious wight.
With him died all my sweet delight,
However another man won me o'er!

He is far from like my first: so dour,
So bent on wealth, so scrimping and mean,
By him my mirth and good cheer are but teen!
God bless the old man who was so friendly!
Could I but return it him now—
[*Starting a little and crossing herself.*]
—reverently!

[THE WANDERING STUDENT *comes in from the right, sees her, doffs his cap and bows low.*]
THE STUDENT. Ah, kind dame! Prithee, let me commend
Myself to your alms, and for no by-end:
For many an art have I conned in books,
And [*with an intimate wink*] in Venusberg I have hugged the books
And watched thence many a lusty wooing!
[*She smiles down at him. He strikes a pose for her.*]
A scholar am I, the wide world viewing;
A stroller—left Paris but three days since—

---

* Reprinted from *Little Theater Classics*, IV, copyright, 1922, by Little, Brown & Co., by permission of the translator.

365

THE WIFE [*starting, and stepping down to him excitedly*].
What, what? Left Paradise?—Come you thence?
Dear sir! One thing I must ask you at once:
Lately—[*wiping her eyes again, and sniffing*] within the last twelve months—
My husband died. Did you see *him* there?
So honest and good he was, I could ne'er
Misdoubt but *he* went to Paradise!

THE STUDENT [*striking a thoughtful attitude, finger to forehead, and eyeing her under his brows*]. I can tell you forthright all he possessed:
A blue hat on, and a winding sheet
Not quite of the best—the grave to cheat—
Nought else, if I must admit the truth.

THE STUDENT [*having abashed her by showing surprise at such a niggardly costume, follows up his idea*]. Ah, my good dame! *He* was uncouth!
He goes about there without boots,
Breeches, or smock—or substitutes!
As queer as he was laid in earth!
Cock his hat as he may, or girth
[*With a graphic gesture.*]
His shroud around him,—when others feast
He stays outside, penniless, fleeced,
Lingering there with longing eyes,
Living on alms the rest despise—
Dirty and wretched beyond expression!

THE WIFE [*moved to tears*]. Ah, husband! Art in such depression?
Hast not a penny for a bath?
Now, woe is me for thy stony path!
Alas! Good sir!—But [*getting an idea*], oblige me twice:
Wend you *again* to Paradise?

THE STUDENT [*nodding reassuringly*]. To-morrow I start, and if nought delays
Thither I win in thirteen days.

THE WIFE [*beseechingly*]. Oh, *would* you carry me something to him?
My new man's wealth is not so slim.

THE STUDENT [*starting and glancing about for the new husband*]. Gladly, Good wife; but haste! make it trim!

THE WIFE. Pardon me, just a minute, while
I bundle up my little pile!
[*She disappears into the cottage.*]

THE STUDENT. Good, simple soul! Just right for me!
[*Rubbing his hands.*]
Money and clothes for the legatee!
[*Glancing about again apprehensively.*]
But I must toddle before he comes:
He might bequeath me scantier sums!
It's best to be heir to a *dead* man's crumbs!
[THE WIFE *reappears with a bundle in one hand and a moldy leather wallet in the other. She has difficulty telling which is which as she talks.*]

THE WIFE. Now be a good messenger, kind sir!
These twelve red goldens I transfer
To him, that I've long kept buried away
In my cowshed against a troublous day;
[THE STUDENT *transfers the coins to his own purse and gives back the old wallet.*]
And take this bundle to him too:
Therein are hosen, shirt and shoe,
And a coat of stuff that will suffice
For that far land of Paradise!
His purse I send [*giving back the same wallet*] and his long knife,
[THE STUDENT *cautiously, for fear of the knife, arranges the pack on his shoulder.*]
And tell him that next time his fond wife
Will have laid up more goods and gold
To keep him clear of hunger and cold—
[*Wiping her eyes again.*]
For he's still the dearest of the twain!

THE STUDENT [*cheering her up*]. Oh, how will I gladden him—full fain!—
That now on a holiday he too
May drink and game as the others do!

THE WIFE. How long, Good Sir, must you be away
Before you can bring me word of him, pray?

THE STUDENT [*hastily*]. Oh, I can't
come this way again soon!
            [*Explaining.*]
'Tis a hard road—seldom opportune!
THE WIFE [*tearful again*]. Alas! then
his money may shortly fail!
No bath, no sport, no meat nor ale!
He'll have to beg for it all again!
      [*Brightening up as she thinks of
        something.*]
But when we are done with threshing,
      then
I can soon hoard up a little more
And hide it under the cowshed floor
From my near husband, as before.
      [*To the* STUDENT, *contentedly,
        putting a coin in his hand.*]
Look: take this taler for your pay,
And greet my husband lovingly, pray!
      [*Without more delay* THE STU-
        DENT *bows to her and makes
        off, left. She sings happily the
        same song as at the beginning.
        THE FARMER, her husband, en-
        ters right, stooped and intent,
        goes into the house and returns
        with a stocking heavy with
        small coins.*]
THE FARMER [*noticing her, pausing in
the door*]. Dame, thou art merry.
      Prithee tell
What hath so pleased thee. What befell?
THE WIFE [*affectionately in her pleas-
ure*]. Ah, husband dear, rejoice
      with me!
Good hap have I to tell to thee!
THE FARMER [*with surly kindliness*].
      Who hit the bull's eye this time, eh?
THE WIFE [*beginning to realize the
miraculous nature of her news*]. Oh,
      how shall I the marvel say?
A strolling scholar, to still my sighs,
Came by here out of Paradise!
There he had seen my former man—
And swears that he is poorer than
The meanest, without shirt or shoes
Or money—nothing he can use
But hat and sheet! Think!—nothing
      save
What we thrust with him in the grave!
THE FARMER [*with a grim smile*].

Wouldst thou not send him something
      fit?
THE WIFE [*surprised at the suggestion
from him, accepting it eagerly*]. Oh,
      husband dear, I did!
      [*Her husband starts violently,
        clutching the stocking like a
        bludgeon, but controls himself:
        and she goes on quite un-
        aware.*]
To wit,
The old coat, hosen, shirt and shoon,
And a bit of money, as a boon,
I gave the student to take him soon.
THE FARMER [*crisply, losing no time
in passion*]. Right well bethought;
      but whither went
The man by whom thy gifts were sent?
THE WIFE [*pointing left, but also to-
ward the nether regions*]. He took
      the downward road. He hies
With speed thereby to Paradise.
THE FARMER [*biting his words out*].
      Not with so marked a speed, I trust,
But I can catch him, as I must!
      [*Checking any possible protest on
        her part with sarcasm she can-
        not perceive.*]
Thou gav'st him far too little money
For thy dead husband's alimony!
He cannot well live long therewith!
Go, have the fast horse saddled forthwith.
      [*She starts lumberingly off left.*]
And I will gallop after him
And give him ten more groschen grim!
      [*She does not notice the last
        word, or see the ominous swing
        of the stocking which accom-
        panies its utterance.*]
THE WIFE [*turning back to him, vacu-
ously grateful*]. Dear husband, thanks
      that thou tak'st not ill
My love for my former husband still!
For thy goodness to him will I pay *thee*
      back:
After thy soul too will I send a pack—
THE FARMER [*almost exploding*].
      Enough of babble and prattle for
      now!
The stranger may be lost in the slough!
Go get some fellow to saddle my horse!

[THE WIFE *scurries out, left.*
THE FARMER *runs in and out
of the house, getting his spurs,
putting them on, looking for
his horse, etc., talking bitterly
all the while.*]

Ach, Lieber Gott, what a wife I cherish!
Her like is not in all our parish!
In soul, in sense—in body perforce—
Innocent! Idiot!—drinks discourse
From any smart stroller and gives him
     things
To take to her husband, dead two springs!
I'll ride till I catch him, and beat him
     well,
And flat to the ground I will him fell,
And get back from him both garb and
     gold!
Once home again with them, I'll not with-
     hold
Two fists from her face, but blacken her
     eyes
Till to her folly she testifies!
Else verily she'll be my undoing!
Whatever possessed me to her wooing?
Now I must curse what I then did beg.
I would she had gotten St. Urban's
     plague!
     THE WIFE [*returning from left, in high
          spirits*]. The horse is ready! Mount!
          Away!
And God bestead thee through the day!
     [*He runs off. She resumes her
          happy ditty, and goes into the
          house. The curtain with the
          slough painted on it closes be-
          fore her.*]
     THE STUDENT [*entering from right*].
          I' faith, my luck is kind to-day!
Upon good booty still I stray.
     [*He takes the heavy pack from
          his shoulder and weighs it in
          his hand.*]
This will last me the winter through
These simple goodies are all too few
     [*With an appreciative backward
          glance.*]
Who commission a man to Paradise!
     [*Looking off right, he starts,
          drops the bundle, and peers off
          under his hand.*]

But 'ware the steed that yonder flies
After me fast o'er swamp and slough!
If it be not *he*, 'tis a fiend, I vow,
He has sent to harry me! Pack, lie
     there!
     [*He tucks the pack under the
          bottom of the curtain.*]
He shall not know me by what I *bear*!
     [*Peering off again.*]
Ah—ha! He is bogged! He must needs
     dismount.
Now, Mum! and oafish! and he'll account.
Me a poor boor hunting a silly duck.
     [*He stands staring clownishly
          all around.* THE FARMER, *an-
          grier than ever, enters, right,
          peering intently off left.*]
     THE FARMER [*offhand*]. How now, lit-
          tle fellow?
     THE STUDENT [*stupidly*]. Luck!
     THE FARMER.   Good luck!
Hast thou seen one hereabouts run full
     tilt
With back bowed under a pack of guilt?
     THE STUDENT [*vaguely*]. Ya—just
          now—over yonder,—Ran—
               [*Very graphically, though
                    stupidly.*]
Puff, pant, sweat, snort!—like under a
     ban!   [*Nodding.*]
You'll catch him in the furze
               [*Waving vaguely left.*]
                    Over there.
     THE FARMER [*savagely*]. Now on mine
          oath, it was he for fair! [*He crosses
                         and turns.*]
Good little fellow, look to my horse.
I must go on foot through yonder gorse.
I'll find the rogue, and give him one
He'll rue as far as he can run—
And he'll never get to confess it either.
     THE STUDENT. I have to wait—no short
          time neither—
For a holy man to pass by here.
I'll watch your mount till you come—no
     fear!
     THE FARMER. I'll give you a kreutzer
          in return.
Be careful now. [*Without a backward
          glance he goes, stepping warily
          in the bog.*]

THE STUDENT. I'll gladly earn—
        [*Seeing* THE FARMER *is out of
        earshot.*]
                A horse from thee!
        [*With a snap of the fingers and
        a cut up.*]
Fair fortune, thanks!
And ease to ye, my weary shanks!
She [*Thumb to the right.*] let me have
        warm goods and gold.
He [*Thumb to the left.*] leaves tired me
        his horse—to hold!
Seeing that I'm a little man
And fain to help me all he can.
Good sooth, they're a kind-hearted couple!
And faith [*peering after him, left*], he
        had best be quick and supple
Now, for he treads a treacherous bog!
The fellow he hunts for, all agog,
May follow *him* to Paradise
And take a bundle thither twice! [*He
        pulls out the bundle again.*]
Well, I must hence. Should he come
        back,
He'd thwack me black, and sack my pack!
Now on my Pegasus I'll rise
Till I reach the Inn that is Paradise
Where fat roast fowls in the firelight
        glow—
And [*with a jaunty farewell wave to the
        left*] leave him to moil in the muck
        below!
                [*He goes off, right. The curtain
                is drawn again, revealing* THE
                WIFE *in the cottage door, per-
                haps with the yoke on her back
                for her milk pails.*]
THE WIFE [*peering off left*]. Ach!
        How long my husband has been gone!
I fear he lost his way upon
The moor, and my first dear must go
Without the coins he would bestow.
The mist is thick upon the slough.
'Tis time I went to milk my cow.
                [*She disappears into the house.
                THE FARMER enters slowly and
                wearily, left, looking about for
                his horse.*]
THE FARMER [*giving up his last hope—
        that it had run away home*]. Ods-
        bodykins! It didn't come home.

He rode it away! [*Beating his head.*]
        O silly coxcomb!
The earth ne'er saw such a simple dunce!
The rogue got money and clothing once
But the second time my fastest horse!
My wife, whom I'd meant without remorse
To beat for her gullibility
Is proved a lesser fool than me!
What shall I say to her now? What
        can—?
THE WIFE [*reappearing*]. How? On
        foot? Didst thou find the man?
Gav'st him the money?
        THE FARMER [*stumblingly*]. He was
        tired;
The way was long, he said, and mired;
So, that he bring thy husband quick,
In Paradise, what thou didst pick,
I added on the horse thereto,
And he will give that to him too.
Was it well done?
        THE WIFE [*throwing her arms around
        his neck*].   Oh, treasure mine!
I never guessed thee so benign!
If God should summon thee to-night
Soon wouldst thou see how I'll requite
Thy generous help! I'll send thee there
Whatever thou might'st wish to wear
And keep back nought of all I own—
Cow, goose, or sow! Thou'dst well be
        shown
What faith was mine, both fore and aft!
        THE FARMER [*disengaging himself;
        drily*]. Wife, say no more, and
        watch for craft.
Keep close such sacred things as these.
        THE WIFE [*jubilantly*]. Nay, the
        whole parish knows and agrees!
        THE FARMER [*much startled*]. Eh?
        Who told them of it so quick?
        THE WIFE. Why, before thou hadst
        reached yon rick   [*pointing left*]
I had told them all from beginning to
        end:
What to my husband I would send,
With all respect, to Paradise.
And everybody was so nice—
Laughed aloud and made sport with
        me!
        THE FARMER [*out of temper*]. Of thee,
        thou devil's devotee!

Dear God, what a wench it is to bilk!

[*Recovering himself: kindly.*]

Go in and set me a sup of milk

THE WIFE [*still gay and affectionate*]. Straightway! Come soon, dear husband mine!

[*She bounces into the house. Her husband clasps his head.*]

THE FARMER. Well can that man at his luck repine

Who is yoked to such a wife!—'Tis for me

To keep her in harness, to oversee

And set her right when her fool feet trip.

Mine, too, out of the stirrup may slip!

He who lets fall the shuttlecock

May find *himself* a laughing stock.

[*Gradually losing his character and speaking directly to the audience for the author.*]

Folly in folly must find excuse

If married folks are to live in truce

And the bonds of wedlock not how cracks—

Which is the warning, and wish, of Hans Sachs.

THE PLAY OF ST. GEORGE

Traditional Folk Play *

ANONYMOUS

Probably 13th–15th century

CHARACTERS

FATHER CHRISTMAS
SAINT GEORGE
VALIANT SOLDIER
TURKISH KNIGHT
DOCTOR
THE SARACEN

[*Enter* FATHER CHRISTMAS. *He walks round swinging his club and clearing the room.*]
FATHER CHRISTMAS. Here come I, old
    Father Christmas;
  Welcome or welcome not,
I hope old Father Christmas
Will never be forgot:—
Although it's Father Christmas I've a
    short time to stay,
But I've come to show you pleasure be-
    fore I pass away!
  Make room, make room, my gallants,
    room,
    And give us space to rhyme;
  We've come to show Saint George's
    play
    Upon this Christmas time.

And if you don't believe my words, I
    straight call out, Walk in,
Walk in, O Valiant Soldier, and boldly
    now begin!

    [*Enter the* VALIANT SOLDIER.]
  VALIANT SOLDIER. Here come I, the
    Valiant Soldier,
  Slasher is my name,
With sword and buckler by my side
  I hope to win the game.
One of my brethren I've seen wounded,
  Another I've seen slain,
So I will fight with any foe
  Upon this British plain.
Yes, with my sword and with my
    spear
  To 'fend the right, I'll battle here!

---

* This version of a traditional folk play was reconstructed from memory by Thomas Hardy, and is reprinted from the text published by Samuel French and copyright, 1928, by Roger S. Loomis, the editor, and Mrs. Thomas Hardy.

[*Enter the* TURKISH KNIGHT.]

TURKISH KNIGHT.   Here come I, the
  Turkish Knight,
Come from Turkish land to fight;
I'll fight Saint George and all his crew,
Aye, countryfolk and warriors too.
Who is this man with courage bold?
If his blood's hot, I'll make it cold!

VALIANT SOLDIER [*coming forward*]. If
  thou art called the Turkish Knight,
Draw out thy sword, and let us fight!
I am the friend of good Saint George,
I've fought men o'er and o'er,
And for the sake of good Saint George
I'd fight a hundred more.

      [*They fight. The* VALIANT SOL-
          DIER *falls.*]

To slay this false Knight did I try—
'Tis for the right I have to die! [*Dies.*]

TURKISH KNIGHT [*marching round*]. If
  Saint George but meet me here,
I'll try his mettle without fear!

[*Enter* SAINT GEORGE.]

SAINT GEORGE.   Here come I, Saint
  George, the Valiant man,
With glittering sword and spear in
  hand,
Who fought the Dragon boldly, and
  brought him to the slaughter,
By which I won fair Sabra, the King of
  Egypt's daughter.
  So haste away, make no delay,
  For I can give some lusty thumps,
And, like a true born Englishman,
Fight on my legs or on my stumps!
What mortal man would dare to stand
Before me with my sword in hand?

TURKISH KNIGHT [*advancing*]. Make
  not so bold, Saint George, I pray;
Though thou'rt all this, thou'rt one I'll
  slay!

SAINT GEORGE. My blood is hot as any
  fire,
So I must say thee Nay,
For with my trusty sword and spear
I'll take *thy* life away!

TURKISH KNIGHT.   Then thou and I
  will battle try.

SAINT GEORGE. And if I conquer thou
  shalt die!

So give me leave, I'll give thee battle,
And quickly make thy bones to rattle!

      [*They fight.   The* TURKISH
          KNIGHT *is wounded and falls
          upon one knee.*]

TURKISH KNIGHT. Can there a doctor
  come to me
From anywhere in this countree?

FATHER CHRISTMAS [*looking about*]. Is
  there a doctor to be found
To cure this man of his deadly wound?
For whatsoever wrath you feel
Toward your foeman, we must heal.

[*Enter the* DOCTOR, *a bottle strapped
      under his arm.*]

DOCTOR.   Yes, there's a doctor to be
  found
To cure this man of his deadly wound.
With this small bottle that you see
I cure all evils there can be;
The phthisic, the palsy and the gout,
If the devil's in I'll blow him out.

FATHER CHRISTMAS.   Doctor then, O
  what's thy fee,
For doing of this great merc-y?

DOCTOR. Fifty pound is my fee,
But ten pound less I'll take of thee.

FATHER CHRISTMAS.   What dost say,
  eh? Half a crown?

DOCTOR. No. I tell thee forty poun'—
A small sum that to save a man,
And you've the money in your han'.

FATHER CHRISTMAS.   Try thy skill; it
  must be so,
Whe'r I pay thy fee or no.
Small money have I, but do thy best,
And trust the victors for the rest.

      [*The* DOCTOR *restores the* KNIGHT
          *by giving him a draught from
          the bottle he carries.   Exit*
          DOCTOR.   *The fight is resumed.
          But the* TURKISH KNIGHT *sinks
          by degrees, and is at last killed
          by* SAINT GEORGE.]

SAINT GEORGE. The first one, Father,
  now is dead:
Call in the second, that Champion whom
  I dread.

      [FATHER CHRISTMAS *looks about,
          but nobody appears. Pause.*]

Where is the Saracen? He doth so long delay,
That hero of renown, I long to show him play!

[*Enter the* SARACEN *with a loud strut.*]
SARACEN. The Saracen behold in me:
I am the man who'll conquer thee!
My head is cased in iron, my body in steel;
I'll fight with thee, Saint George, and make thee feel! [*Looks at the dead bodies.*]
O see what blood Saint George has spilled in fight;
I'll vanquish him before I sleep this night.
SAINT GEORGE. Since then 'tis not against thy will,
Nor yet against thy might,
If thou canst battle with Saint George
Draw out thy sword and smite.
[*They fight. The* SARACEN *falls wounded.*]
Tremble, thou tyrant, for thy sin that's past,
Tremble to think to-night shall be thy last;
My conquering arm shall send thy fire and fume
By one more stroke to thy eternal doom;
Aye, I, despite the steel thou boastest so,
Dispatch thee now to where the wicked go.
SARACEN. O pardon me, Saint George.
Thy pardon now I crave,
O pardon me this night, and I will be thy slave!
SAINT GEORGE. I never will pardon thee, thou Saracen,
But rise, and draw, and we will fight again!
[*The* SARACEN *rises. They fight. The* SARACEN *is killed and his head cut off.*]
FATHER CHRISTMAS [*advances*]. To greet our ears, O what wild moans
Throughout this fight, and what deep groans!
Is there a doctor to be found
That can raise dead men from the ground,
So as to have them for to stand

And walk again upon this land?
I've heard of a mill that grinds old people young,
But not of a leech to give these dead men tongue!
SAINT GEORGE. Yes, that same doctor can be found
To raise these dead men from the ground,
So as to have them for to stand
And walk again upon the land.
FATHER CHRISTMAS. Then, Doctor, Doctor, prithee come,
And raise these men now dead and dumb:
Saint George, thyself hadst better call him here,
To save these corpses from the dreadful bier.
SAINT GEORGE. I warrant he'll answer to my call;
[*Calls.*] Doctor, haste here and save them all!

[*Enter* DOCTOR *slowly.*]
FATHER CHRISTMAS. Ha, Doctor, is it in thy skill
To cure dead men as if but ill?
DOCTOR. Being a doctor of great fame
Who from the ancient countries came,
And knowing Asia, Afric-ay,
And every mystery out that way,
I've learned to do the best of cures
For all the human frame endures.
I can restore a leg or arm
From mortification or from harm,
I can repair a sword-slit pate,
A leg cut off—if not too late.
FATHER CHRISTMAS. But, Doctor——
DOCTOR. Yea, more; this little bottle of alicumpane [*Touches the bottle.*]
Will raise dead men to walk the earth again!
FATHER CHRISTMAS. That is, forsooth, a strange refrain!
Try thy skill on these men slain.
DOCTOR. A hundred guineas is my fee
And nothing less I'll take of thee.
[FATHER CHRISTMAS *starts astonished.*]
SAINT GEORGE. Such money I will freely give

If that thou mak'st these men to live.

DOCTOR [*advancing to the fallen men*].
I put a drop to each soldier's heart. [*He
holds his bottle to the lips and to the
heart of each, adding slowly.*]

Rise — Champions — and — all — play
— your — part!

> [*They rise inch by inch,* FATHER
> CHRISTMAS, SAINT GEORGE *and
> the* DOCTOR *singing a slow song
> or chant as they rise. A lively
> song follows from the whole
> company, walking round. Ex-
> eunt omnes, except* FATHER
> CHRISTMAS.]

FATHER CHRISTMAS. You needs will
have confest
That our calling is the best,
But now we won't delay, lest tediousness
befall,
And I wish you a Merry Christmas, and
God bless you all!

> [*Exit* FATHER CHRISTMAS.]

THE TRAGICAL HISTORY OF
DR. FAUSTUS

By CHRISTOPHER MARLOWE

Produced at London probably 1588–89

CHARACTERS

THE POPE

CARDINAL OF LORRAIN

THE EMPEROR OF GERMANY

DUKE OF VANHOLT

FAUSTUS

VALDES,
CORNELIUS, } *friends to* FAUSTUS

WAGNER, *servant to* FAUSTUS

CLOWN

ROBIN

RALPH

VINTNER

HORSE-COURSER

A KNIGHT

AN OLD MAN

SCHOLARS, FRIARS, *and* ATTENDANTS

DUCHESS OF VANHOLT

LUCIFER

BELZEBUB

MEPHISTOPHILIS

GOOD ANGEL

EVIL ANGEL

THE SEVEN DEADLY SINS

DEVILS

SPIRITS *in the shapes of* ALEXANDER THE GREAT, *of his* PARAMOUR *and of* HELEN

CHORUS

[*Enter* CHORUS.]

CHORUS. Not marching now in fields of Thrasymene,
Where Mars did mate the Carthaginians;
Nor sporting in the dalliance of love,
In courts of kings where state is overturn'd;
Nor in the pomp of proud audacious deeds,
Intends our Muse to vaunt her heavenly verse:
Only this, gentlemen,—we must perform
The form of Faustus' fortunes, good or bad:
To patient judgments we appeal our plaud,
And speak for Faustus in his infancy.
Now is he born, his parents base of stock,
In Germany, within a town call'd Rhodes:
Of riper years, to Wertenberg he went,
Whereas his kinsmen chiefly brought him up.
So soon he profits in divinity,
The fruitful plot of scholarism grac'd,
That shortly he was grac'd with doctor's name,
Excelling all whose sweet delight disputes
In heavenly matters of theology;
Till swoln with cunning, of a self-conceit,
His waxen wings did mount above his reach,
And, melting, heavens conspir'd his overthrow;
For, falling to a devilish exercise,
And glutted now with learning's golden gifts,
He surfeits upon cursed necromancy;
Nothing so sweet as magic is to him,
Which he prefers before his chiefest bliss:
And this the man that in his study sits.
[*Exit.*]

SCENE I

[FAUSTUS *discovered in his study.*]

FAUSTUS. Settle thy studies, Faustus, and begin
To sound the depth of that thou wilt profess:
Having commenc'd, be a divine in show,
Yet level at the end of every art,
And live and die in Aristotle's works.
Sweet Analytics, 'tis thou hast ravish'd me!
Bene disserere est finis logices.
Is, to dispute well, logic's chiefest end?
Affords this art no greater miracle?
Then read no more; thou hast attain'd that end:
A greater subject fitteth Faustus' wit:
Bid Economy farewell, and Galen come,
Seeing, *Ubi desinit philosophus, ibi incipit medicus:*
Be a physician, Faustus; heap up gold,
And be eternis'd for some wondrous cure:
Summum bonum medicinæ sanitas,
The end of physic is our body's health.
Why, Faustus, hast thou not attain'd that end?
Is not thy common talk found aphorisms?
Are not thy bills hung up as monuments,
Whereby whole cities have escap'd the plague,
And thousand desperate maladies been eas'd?
Yet art thou still but Faustus, and a man.
Couldst thou make men to live eternally,
Or, being dead, raise them to life again,
Then this profession were to be esteem'd.
Physic, farewell! Where is Justinian?
[*Reads.*]
Si una eademque res legatur duobus, alter rem, alter valorem, rei, etc.
A pretty case of paltry legacies! [*Reads.*]
Exhæreditare filium non potest pater nisi, etc.
Such is the subject of the institute,
And universal body of the law:
This study fits a mercenary drudge,
Who aims at nothing but external trash;
Too servile and illiberal for me.
When all is done, divinity is best:
Jerome's Bible, Faustus; view it well.
[*Reads.*]
Stipendium peccati mors est. Ha! *Stipendium, etc.*
The reward of sin is death: that's hard.
[*Reads.*]
Si peccasse negamus, fallimur, et nulia est in nobis veritas;
If we say that we have no sin, we deceive ourselves, and there's no truth in us.

Why, then, belike we must sin, and so
consequently die:
Ay, we must die an everlasting death.
What doctrine call you this, *Che sera,
sera,*
What will be, shall be? Divinity, adieu!
These metaphysics of magicians,
And necromantic books are heavenly;
Lines, circles, scenes, letters, and charac-
ters;
Ay, these are those that Faustus most
desires.
O, what a world of profit and delight,
Of power, of honour, of omnipotence,
Is promis'd to the studious artisan!
All things that move between the quiet
poles
Shall be at my command: emperors and
kings
Are but obeyed in their several provinces,
Nor can they raise the wind, or rend the
clouds;
But his dominion that exceeds in this,
Stretcheth as far as doth the mind of
man;
A sound magician is a mighty god:
Here, Faustus, tire thy brains to gain
a deity.

[*Enter* WAGNER.]
Wagner, commend me to my dearest
friends,
The German Valdes and Cornelius;
Request them earnestly to visit me.
WAGNER. I will, sir.   [*Exit.*]
FAUSTUS. Their conference will be a
greater help to me
Than all my labours, plod I ne'er so fast.

[*Enter* GOOD ANGEL *and* EVIL ANGEL.]
GOOD ANGEL. O, Faustus, lay thy
damned book aside,
And gaze not on it, lest it tempt thy soul,
And heap God's heavy wrath upon thy
head!
Read, read the Scriptures:—that is
blasphemy.
EVIL ANGEL. Go forward, Faustus, in
that famous art
Wherein all Nature's treasure is con-
tain'd:

Be thou on earth as Jove is in the sky,
Lord and commander of these elements.
               [*Exeunt* ANGELS.]
FAUSTUS. How am I glutted with con-
ceit of this!
Shall I make spirits fetch me what I
please,
Resolve me of all ambiguities,
Perform what desperate enterprise I will?
I'll have them fly to India for gold,
Ransack the ocean for orient pearl,
And search all corners of the new-found
world
For pleasant fruits and princely delicates;
I'll have them read me strange philoso-
phy.
And tell the secrets of all foreign kings;
I'll have them wall all Germany with
brass,
And make swift Rhine circle fair Werten-
berg;
I'll have them fill the public schools with
silk,
Wherewith the students shall be bravely
clad;
I'll levy soldiers with the coin they bring,
And chase the Prince of Parma from our
land,
And reign sole king of all the provinces;
Yea, stranger engines for the brunt of
war,
Than was the fiery keel at Antwerp's
bridge,
I'll make my servile spirits to invent.

[*Enter* VALDES *and* CORNELIUS.]
Come, German Valdes and Cornelius,
And make me blest with your sage con-
ference.
Valdes, sweet Valdes, and Cornelius,
Know that your words have won me at
the last
To practise magic and concealed arts:
Yet not your words only, but mine own
fantasy,
That will receive no object; for my head
But ruminates on necromantic skill.
Philosophy is odious and obscure;
Both law and physic are for petty wits;
Divinity is basest of the three,
Unpleasant, harsh, contemptible, and vile:

'Tis magic, magic, that hath ravish'd me.
Then, gentle friends, aid me in this at-
    tempt;
And I, that have with concise syllogisms
Gravell'd the pastors of the German
    church,
And made the flowering pride of Werten-
    berg
Swarm to my problems, as the infernal
    spirits
On sweet Musæus when he came to hell,
Will be as cunning as Agrippa was,
Whose shadow made all Europe honour
    him.
    VALDES. Faustus, these books, thy wit,
    and our experience,
Shall make all nations to canonise us.
As Indian Moors obey their Spanish lords,
So shall the spirits of every element
Be always serviceable to us three;
Like lions shall they guard us when we
    please;
Like Almain rutters with their horsemen's
    staves;
Or Lapland giants, trotting by our sides;
Sometimes like women, or unwedded
    maids,
Shadowing more beauty in their airy
    brows
Than have the white breasts of the queen
    of love:
From Venice shall they drag huge argo-
    sies,
And from America the golden fleece
That yearly stuffs old Philip's treasury;
If learned Faustus will be resolute.
    FAUSTUS. Valdes, as resolute am I in
    this
As thou to live: therefore object it not.
    CORNELIUS. The miracles that magic
    will perform
Will make thee vow to study nothing
    else.
He that is grounded in astrology,
Enrich'd with tongues, well seen in min-
    erals,
Hath all the principles magic doth re-
    quire:
Then doubt not, Faustus, but to be re-
    nown'd,
And more frequented for this mystery

Than heretofore the Delphian oracle.
The spirits tell me they can dry the sea,
And fetch the treasure of all foreign
    wrecks,
Ay, all the wealth that our forefathers
    hid
Within the massy entrails of the earth:
Then tell me, Faustus, what shall we
    three want?
    FAUSTUS. Nothing, Cornelius. O, this
    cheers my soul!
Come, show me some demonstrations magi-
    cal,
That I may conjure in some lusty grove,
And have these joys in full possession.
    VALDES. Then haste thee to some soli-
    tary grove,
And bear wise Bacon's and Albertus'
    works,
The Hebrew Psalter, and New Testament;
And whatsoever else is requisite
We will inform thee ere our conference
    cease.
    CORNELIUS. Valdes, first let him know
    the words of art;
And then, all other ceremonies learn'd,
Faustus may try his cunning by himself.
    VALDES. First I'll instruct thee in the
    rudiments,
And then wilt thou be perfecter than I.
    FAUSTUS. Then come and dine with
    me, and, after meat,
We'll canvass every quiddity thereof;
For, ere I sleep, I'll try what I can do:
This night I'll conjure, though I die there-
    fore.   [*Exeunt.*]

SCENE II—*Before* FAUSTUS'S *house.*

    [*Enter two* SCHOLARS.]
    1ST SCHOLAR. I wonder what's become
of Faustus, that was wont to make our
schools ring with *sic probo.*
    2ND SCHOLAR. That shall we know, for
see, here comes his boy.

    [*Enter* WAGNER.]
    1ST SCHOLAR. How now, sirrah! where's
thy master?
    WAGNER. God in heaven knows.

2ND SCHOLAR. Why, dost not thou know?

WAGNER. Yes, I know; but that follows not.

1ST SCHOLAR. Go to, sirrah! leave your jesting, and tell us where he is.

WAGNER. That follows not necessary by force of argument, that you, being licentiates, should stand upon: therefore acknowledge your error, and be attentive.

2ND SCHOLAR. Well, you will not tell thou knewest?

WAGNER. Have you any witness on't?

1ST SCHOLAR. Yes, sirrah, I heard you.

WAGNER. Ask my fellow if I be a thief.

2ND SCHOLAR. Well, you will not tell us?

WAGNER. Yes, sir, I will tell you; yet, if you were not dunces, you would never ask me such a question, for is not he *corpus naturale?* and is not that *mobile?* then wherefore should you ask me such a question? But that I am by nature phlegmatic, slow to wrath, and prone to lechery (to love, I would say), it were not for you to come within forty foot of the place of execution, although I do not doubt to see you both hanged the next sessions. Thus having triumphed over you, I will set my countenance like a precisian, and begin to speak thus:— Truly, my dear brethren, my master is within at dinner, with Valdes and Cornelius, as this wine, if it could speak, would inform your worships: and so, the Lord bless you, preserve you, and keep you, my dear brethren, my dear brethren!
                                                   [*Exit.*]

1ST SCHOLAR. Nay, then, I fear he has fallen into that damned art for which they two are infamous through the world.

2ND. SCHOLAR. Were he a stranger, and not allied to me, yet should I grieve for him. But, come, let us go and inform the Rector, and see if he by his grave counsel can reclaim him.

1ST SCHOLAR. O, but I fear me nothing can reclaim him!

2ND SCHOLAR. You let us try what we can do.   [*Exeunt.*]

SCENE III—*A grove.*

[*Enter* FAUSTUS *to conjure.*]

FAUSTUS. Now that the gloomy shadow of the earth,
Longing to view Orion's drizzling look,
Leaps from th' antarctic world unto the sky,
And dims the welkin with her pitchy breath,
Faustus, begin thine incantations,
And try if devils will obey thy hest,
Seeing thou hast pray'd and sacrific'd to them.
Within this circle is Jehovah's name,
Forward and backward anagrammatis'd,
Th' abbreviated names of holy saints,
Figures of every adjunct to the heavens,
And characters of signs and erring stars,
By which the spirits are enforc'd to rise:
Then fear not, Faustus, but be resolute,
And try the uttermost magic can perform.—
Sint mihi dei Acherontis propitii!
Valeat numen triplex Jehovæ! Ignei,
aërii, aquatani spiritus, salvete! Orientis
princeps Belzebub, inferni ardentis mon-
archa, et Demogorgon, propitiamus vos, ut
appareat et surgat Mephistophilis, quod
tumeraris: per Jehovam, Gehennam, et
consecratam aquam quam nunc spargo,
signumque crucis quod nunc facio, et per
vota nostra, ipse nunc surgat nobis dicatus
Mephistophilis!

[*Enter* MEPHISTOPHILIS.]

I charge thee to return, and change thy shape;
Thou art too ugly to attend on me:
Go, and return an old Franciscan friar;
That holy shape becomes a devil best.
                              [*Exit* MEPHISTOPHILIS.]
I see there's virtue in my heavenly words:
Who would not be proficient in this art?
How pliant is this Mephistophilis,
Full of obedience and humility!
Such is the force of magic and my spells:
No, Faustus, thou art conjuror laureat,
That canst command great Mephistophilis.

[*Reënter* MEPHISTOPHILIS *like a Francis-
can friar.*]

MEPHISTOPHILIS. Now, Faustus, what
wouldst thou have me do?

FAUSTUS. I charge thee wait upon me
whilst I live,
To do whatever Faustus shall command,
Be it to make the moon drop from her
sphere,
Or the ocean to overwhelm the world.

MEPHISTOPHILIS. I am a servant to
great Lucifer,
And may not follow thee without his
leave;
No more than he commands must we per-
form.

FAUSTUS. Did not he charge thee to
appear to me?

MEPHISTOPHILIS. No, I came hither
of mine own accord.

FAUSTUS. Did not my conjuring
speeches raise thee? speak.

MEPHISTOPHILIS. That was the cause,
but yet *per accidens;*
For, when we hear one rack the name of
God,
Abjure the Scriptures and his Saviour
Christ,
We fly, in hope, to get his glorious soul;
Nor will we come, unless he use such
means
Whereby he is in danger to be damn'd.
Therefore the shortest cut for conjuring
Is stoutly to abjure the Trinity,
And pray devoutly to the prince of hell.

FAUSTUS. So Faustus hath
Already done; and holds this principle,
There is no chief but only Belzebub;
To whom Faustus doth dedicate himself.
This word "damnation" terrifies not him,
For he confounds hell in Elysium:
His ghost be with the old philosophers!
But, leaving these vain trifles of men's
souls,
Tell me what is that Lucifer thy lord?

MEPHISTOPHILIS. Arch-regent and com-
mander of all spirits.

FAUSTUS. Was not that Lucifer an
angel once?

MEPHISTOPHILIS. Yes, Faustus, and
most dearly lov'd of God.

FAUSTUS. How comes it, then, that he
is prince of devils?

MEPHISTOPHILIS. O, by aspiring pride
and insolence;
For which God threw him from the face
of heaven.

FAUSTUS. And what are you that live
with Lucifer?

MEPHISTOPHILIS. Unhappy spirits that
fell with Lucifer?
Conspir'd against our God with Lucifer,
And are for ever damn'd with Lucifer.

FAUSTUS. Where are you damn'd?

MEPHISTOPHILIS. In hell.

FAUSTUS. How comes it, then, that
thou art out of hell?

MEPHISTOPHILIS. Why, this is hell, nor
am I out of it.
Think'st thou that I, who saw the face
of God,
And tasted the eternal joys of heaven,
Am not tormented with ten thousand
hells,
In being depriv'd of everlasting bliss?
O, Faustus, leave these frivolous demands,
Which strike a terror to my fainting
soul!

FAUSTUS. What, is great Mephistophi-
lis so passionate
For being deprived of the joys of heaven?
Learn thou of Faustus manly fortitude
And scorn those joys thou never shalt
possess.
Go bear these tidings to great Lucifer:
Seeing Faustus hath incurr'd eternal
death
By desperate thoughts against Jove's
deity,
Say, he surrenders up to him his soul,
So he will spare him four-and-twenty
years,
Letting him live in all voluptuousness;
Having thee ever to attend on me,
To give me whatsoever I shall ask,
To tell me whatsoever I demand,
To slay mine enemies, and aid my friends,
And always be obedient to my will.
Go and return to mighty Lucifer,
And meet me in my study at midnight,
And then resolve me of thy master's
mind.

MEPHISTOPHILIS.   I will, Faustus.
[*Exit.*]

FAUSTUS.   Had I as many souls as
there be stars,
I'd give them all for Mephistophilis.
By him I'll be great emperor of the
world,
And make a bridge through the moving
air,
To pass the ocean with a band of men;
I'll join the hills that bind the Afric
shore,
And make that country continent to Spain,
And both contributory to my crown:
The Emperor shall not live but by my
leave,
Nor any potentate of Germany.
Now that I have obtained what I de-
sir'd,
I'll live in speculation of this art,
Till Mephistophilis return again. [*Exit.*]

SCENE IV—*A street.*

[*Enter* WAGNER *and* CLOWN.]

WAGNER.   Sirrah boy, come hither.

CLOWN.   How, boy! swowns, boy! I
hope you have seen many boys with such
pickadevaunts as I have: boy, quotha!

WAGNER.   Tell me, sirrah, hast thou any
comings in?

CLOWN.   Ay, and goings out too; you
may see else.

WAGNER.   Alas, poor slave! see how
poverty jesteth in his nakedness! the vil-
lain is bare and out of service, and so
hungry, that I know he would give his
soul to the devil for a shoulder of mut-
ton, though it were blood-raw.

CLOWN.   How! my soul to the devil for
a shoulder of mutton, though 'twere
blood-raw! not so, good friend: by'r lady,
I had need have it well roasted, and good
sauce to it, if I pay so dear.

WAGNER.   Well, wilt thou serve me, and
I'll make thee go like *Qui mihi discipulus.*

CLOWN.   How, in verse?

WAGNER.   No, sirrah; in beaten silk and
staves-acre.

CLOWN.   How, how, knaves-acre! ay, I
thought that was all the land his father

left him. Do you hear? I would be sorry
to rob you of your living.

WAGNER.   Sirrah, I say in staves-acre.

CLOWN.   Oho, oho, staves-acre! why,
then, belike, if I were your man, I should
be full of vermin.

WAGNER.   So thou shalt, whether thou
beest with me or no. But, sirrah, leave
your jesting, and bind yourself presently
unto me for seven years, or I'll turn all
the lice about thee into familiars, and
they shall tear thee in pieces.

CLOWN.   Do you hear, sir? you may
save that labour; they are too familiar
with me already: swowns, they are as
bold with my flesh as if they had paid
for their meat and drink.

WAGNER.   Well, do you hear, sirrah?
hold, take these guilders. [*Gives money.*]

CLOWN.   Gridirons! what be they?

WAGNER.   Why, French crowns.

CLOWN.   Mass, but for the name of
French crowns, a man were as good have
as many English counters. And what
should I do with these?

WAGNER.   Why, now, sirrah, thou art
at an hour's warning, whensoever and
wheresoever the devil shall fetch thee.

CLOWN.   No, no; here, take your grid-
irons again.

WAGNER.   Truly, I'll none of them.

CLOWN.   Truly, but you shall.

WAGNER.   Bear witness I gave them him.

CLOWN.   Bear witness I give them you
again.

WAGNER.   Well, I will cause two devils
presently to fetch thee away—Baliol and
Belcher!

CLOWN.   Let your Baliol and your
Belcher come here, and I'll knock them,
they were never so knocked since they
were devils: say I should kill one of
them, what would folks say? "Do ye
see yonder tall fellow in the round slop?
he has killed the devil." So I should be
called Kill-devil all the parish over.

[*Enter two* DEVILS; *and the* CLOWN *runs
up and down crying.*]

WAGNER.   Baliol and Belcher,—spirits,
away!   [*Exeunt* DEVILS.]

CLOWN. What, are they gone? a vengeance on them! they have vile long nails. There was a he-devil and a she-devil: I'll tell you how you shall know them; all he-devils has horns, and all she-devils has cloven feet.

WAGNER. Well, sirrah, follow me.

CLOWN. But, do you hear? if I should serve you, would you teach me to raise up Banios and Belcheos?

WAGNER. I will teach thee to turn thyself to anything, to a dog, or a cat, or a mouse, or a rat, or anything.

CLOWN. How! a Christian fellow to a dog, or a cat, a mouse, or a rat! no, no, sir; if you turn me into anything, let it be in the likeness of a little pretty frisking flea, that I may be here and there and everywhere.

WAGNER. Well, sirrah, come.

CLOWN. But, do you hear, Wagner?

WAGNER. How!—Baliol and Belcher!

CLOWN. O Lord! I pray, sir, let Banio and Belcher go sleep.

WAGNER. Villain, call me Master Wagner, and let thy left eye be diametarily fixed upon my right heel, with *quasi vestigiis nostris insistere.* [*Exit.*]

CLOWN. God forgive me, he speaks Dutch fustian.

Well, I'll follow him; I'll serve him, that's flat. [*Exit.*]

SCENE V

[FAUSTUS *discovered in his study.*]

FAUSTUS. Now, Faustus, must
Thou needs be damn'd and canst thou not be sav'd:
What boots it, then, to think of God or heaven?
Away with such vain fancies, and despair;
Despair in God, and trust in Belzebub:
Now go not backward; no, Faustus, be resolute:
Why waver'st thou? O, something soundeth in mine ears,
"Abjure this magic, turn to God again!"
Ay, and Faustus will turn to God again.
To God? he loves thee not;

The god thou serv'st is thine own appetite,
Wherein is fix'd the love of Belzebub:
To him I'll build an altar and a church,
And offer lukewarm blood of new-born babes.

[*Enter* GOOD ANGEL *and* EVIL ANGEL.]

GOOD ANGEL. Sweet Faustus, leave that execrable art.

FAUSTUS. Contrition, prayer, repentance—what of them?

GOOD ANGEL. O, they are means to bring thee unto heaven!

EVIL ANGEL. Rather illusions, fruits of lunacy,
That make men foolish that do trust them most.

GOOD ANGEL. Sweet Faustus, think of heaven and heavenly things.

EVIL ANGEL. No, Faustus; think of honour and of wealth. [*Exeunt* ANGELS.]

FAUSTUS. Of wealth!
Why, the signiory of Embden shall be mine.
When Mephistophilis shall stand by me,
What god can hurt thee, Faustus? thou art safe:
Cast no more doubts.—Come, Mephistophilis,
And bring glad tidings from great Lucifer;—
Is't not midnight?—come, Mephistophilis,
Veni, veni Mephistophile!

[*Enter* MEPHISTOPHILIS.]

Now tell me what says Lucifer, thy lord?

MEPHISTOPHILIS. That I shall wait on Faustus whilst he lives,
So he will buy my service with his soul.

FAUSTUS. Already Faustus hath hazarded that for thee.

MEPHISTOPHILIS. But, Faustus, thou must bequeath it solemnly,
And write a deed of gift with thine own blood;
For that security craves great Lucifer.
If thou deny it, I will back to hell.

FAUSTUS. Stay, Mephistophilis, and

tell me, what good will my soul do thy lord?

MEPHISTOPHILIS. Enlarge his kingdom.

FAUSTUS. Is that the reason why he tempts us thus?

MEPHISTOPHILIS. *Solamen miseris socios habuisse doloris.*

FAUSTUS. Why, have you any pain that torture others!

MEPHISTOPHILIS. As great as have the human souls of men.

But, tell me, Faustus, shall I have thy soul?

And I will be thy slave, and wait on thee,

And give thee more than thou hast wit to ask.

FAUSTUS. Ay, Mephistophilis, I give it thee.

MEPHISTOPHILIS. Then, Faustus, stab thy arm courageously,

And bind thy soul, that at some certain day

Great Lucifer may claim it as his own;

And then be thou as great as Lucifer.

FAUSTUS [*stabbing his arm*]. Lo, Mephistophilis, for love of thee

I cut mine arm, and with my proper blood

Assure my soul to be great Lucifer's,

Chief lord and regent of perpetual night!

View here the blood that trickles from mine arm,

And let it be propitious for my wish.

MEPHISTOPHILIS. But, Faustus, thou must

Write it in manner of a deed of gift.

FAUSTUS. Ay, so I will.   [*Writes.*]

But, Mephistophilis,

My blood congeals, and I can write no more.

MEPHISTOPHILIS. I'll fetch thee fire to dissolve it straight.   [*Exit.*]

FAUSTUS. Why might the staying of my blood portend?

Is it unwilling I should write this bill?

Why streams it not, that I may write afresh?

Faustus gives to thee his soul: ah, there it stay'd!

Why shouldst thou not? is not thy soul thine own?

Then write again, *Faustus gives to thee his soul.*

[*Reënter* MEPHISTOPHILIS *with a chafer of coals.*]

MEPHISTOPHILIS. Here's fire; come, Faustus, set it on.

FAUSTUS. So, now the blood begins to clear again;

Now will I make an end immediately.

[*Writes.*]

MEPHISTOPHILIS [*aside*]. O, what will not I do to obtain his soul!

FAUSTUS. *Consummatum est;* this bill is ended,

And Faustus hath bequeathed his soul to Lucifer.

But what is this inscription on mine arm?

Homo, fuge: whither should I fly?

If unto God, he'll throw me down to hell.

My senses are deceiv'd; here's nothing writ:—

I see it plain; here in this place is writ,

Homo, fuge: yet shall not Faustus fly.

MEPHISTOPHILIS [*aside*]. I'll fetch him somewhat to delight his mind. [*Exit.*]

[*Reënter* MEPHISTOPHILIS *with* DEVILS, *who give crowns and rich apparel to* FAUSTUS, *dance, and then depart.*]

FAUSTUS. Speak, Mephistophilis, what means this show?

MEPHISTOPHILIS. Nothing, Faustus, but to delight thy mind withal,

And to show thee what magic can perform.

FAUSTUS. But may I raise up spirits when I please?

MEPHISTOPHILIS. Ay, Faustus, and do greater things than these.

FAUSTUS. Then there's enough for a thousand souls.

Here, Mephistophilis, receive this scroll,

A deed of gift of body and of soul:

But yet conditionally that thou perform

All articles prescrib'd between us both.

MEPHISTOPHILIS. Faustus, I swear by hell and Lucifer

To effect all promises between us made!

FAUSTUS. Then hear me read them.

[*Reads.*] On these conditions following.

First, that Faustus may be a spirit in

form and substance. Secondly, that Mephistophilis shall be his servant, and at his command. Thirdly, that Mephistophilis shall do for him, and bring him whatsoever he desires. Fourthly, that he shall be in his chamber or house invisible. Lastly, that he shall appear to the said John Faustus, at all times, in what form or shape soever he please. I, John Faustus, of Wertenberg, Doctor, by these presents, do give both body and soul to Lucifer prince of the east, and his minister Mephistophilis; and furthermore grant unto them, that, twenty-four years being expired, the articles above-written inviolate, full power to fetch or carry the said John Faustus, body and soul, flesh, blood, or goods, into their habitation wheresoever. By me, John Faustus.

MEPHISTOPHILIS. Speak, Faustus, do you deliver this as your deed?

FAUSTUS. Ay, take it, and the devil give thee good on't!

MEPHISTOPHILIS. Now, Faustus, ask what thou wilt.

FAUSTUS. First will I question with thee about hell.

Tell me, where is the place that men call hell?

MEPHISTOPHILIS. Under the heavens.

FAUSTUS. Ay, but whereabout?

MEPHISTOPHILIS. Within the bowels of these elements,

Where we are tortur'd and remain for ever:

Hell hath no limits, nor is circumscrib'd

In one self place; for where we are is hell,

And where hell is, there must we ever be:

And, to conclude, when all the world dissolves,

And every creature shall be purified,

All places shall be hell that are not heaven.

FAUSTUS. Come, I think hell's a fable.

MEPHISTOPHILIS. Ay, think so still, till experience change thy mind.

FAUSTUS. Why, think'st thou, then, that Faustus shall be damn'd?

MEPHISTOPHILIS. Ay, of necessity, for here's the scroll

Wherein thou hast given thy soul to Lucifer.

FAUSTUS. Ay, and body too: but what of that?

Think'st thou that Faustus is so fond to imagine

That, after this life, there is any pain?

Tush, these are trifles and mere old wives' tales.

MEPHISTOPHILIS. But, Faustus, I am an instance to prove the contrary

For I am damn'd, and am now in hell.

FAUSTUS. How! now in hell!

Nay, an this be hell, I'll willingly be damn'd here:

What! walking, disputing, etc.

But, leaving off this, let me have a wife,

The fairest maid in Germany.

MEPHISTOPHILIS. How! a wife!

I prithee, Faustus, talk not of a wife.

FAUSTUS. Nay, sweet Mephistophilis, fetch me one, for I will have one.

MEPHISTOPHILIS. Well, thou wilt have one? Sit there till I come: I'll fetch thee a wife in the devil's name.   [Exit.]

[Reënter MEPHISTOPHILIS with a DEVIL drest like a Woman, with fireworks.]

MEPHISTOPHILIS. Tell me, Faustus, how dost thou like thy wife:

FAUSTUS. A plague on her!

MEPHISTOPHILIS. Tut, Faustus,

Marriage is but a ceremonial toy;

If thou lovest me, think no more of it.

She whom thine eye shall like, thy heart shall have,

Be she as chaste as was Penelope,

As wise as Saba, or as beautiful

As was bright Lucifer before his fall.

Hold, take this book, peruse it thoroughly: [Gives book.]

The iterating of these lines brings gold;

The framing of this circle on the ground

Brings whirlwinds, tempests, thunder, and lightning;

Pronounce this thrice devoutly to thyself,

And men in armour shall appear to thee,

Ready to execute what thou desir'st.

FAUSTUS. Thanks, Mephistophilis: yet fain would I have a book wherein I might behold all spells and incantations, that I might raise up spirits when I please.

MEPHISTOPHILIS. Here they are in this book. [*Turns to them.*]

FAUSTUS. Now would I have a book where I might see all characters and planets of the heavens, that I might know their motions and dispositions.

MEPHISTOPHILIS. Here they are too. [*Turns to them.*]

FAUSTUS. Nay, let me have one book more,—and then I have done,—wherein I might see all plants, herbs and trees, that grow upon the earth.

MEPHISTOPHILIS. Here they be.

FAUSTUS. O, thou art deceived.

MEPHISTOPHILIS. Tut, I warrant thee. [*Turns to them. Exeunt.*]

SCENE VI—*A room in* FAUSTUS'S *house.*

FAUSTUS. When I behold the heavens, then I repent,
And curse thee, wicked Mephistophilis,
Because thou hast depriv'd me of those joys.

MEPHISTOPHILIS. Why, Faustus,
Thinkest thou heaven is such a glorious thing?
I tell thee, 'tis not half so fair as thou,
Or any man that breathes on earth.

FAUSTUS. How prov'st thou that?

MEPHISTOPHILIS. 'Twas made for man, therefore is man more excellent.

FAUSTUS. If it were made for man, 'twas made for me:
I will renounce this magic and repent.

[*Enter* GOOD ANGEL *and* EVIL ANGEL.]

GOOD ANGEL. Faustus, repent; yet God will pity thee.

EVIL ANGEL. Thou art a spirit; God cannot pity thee.

FAUSTUS. Who buzzeth in mine ears I am a spirit?
Be I a devil, yet God may pity me;
Ay, God will pity me, if I repent.

EVIL ANGEL. Ay, but Faustus never shall repent. [*Exeunt* ANGELS.]

FAUSTUS. My heart's so harden'd, I cannot repent:

Scarce can I name salvation, faith, or heaven,
But fearful echoes thunder in mine ears,
"Faustus, thou art damn'd!" then swords, and knives,
Poison, guns, halters, and envenom'd steel
Are laid before me to despatch myself;
And long ere this I should have slain myself,
Had not sweet pleasure conquer'd deep despair.
Have not I made blind Homer sing to me
Of Alexander's love and Œnon's death?
And hath not he, that built the walls of Thebes
With ravishing sound of his melodious harp,
Made music with my Mephistophilis?
Why should I die, then, or basely despair!
I am resolv'd; Faustus shall ne'er repent.—
Come, Mephistophilis, let us dispute again,
And argue of divine astrology.
Tell me, are there many heavens above the moon?
Are all celestial bodies but one globe,
As is the substance of this centric earth?

MEPHISTOPHILIS. As are the elements, such are the spheres,
Mutually folded in each other's orb,
And, Faustus,
All jointly move upon one axletree,
Whose terminus is term'd the world's wide pole;
Nor are the names of Saturn, Mars, or Jupiter
Feign'd, but are erring stars.

FAUSTUS. But, tell me, have they all one motion, both *situ et tempore?*

MEPHISTOPHILIS. All jointly move from east to west in twenty-four hours upon the poles of the world; but differ in their motion upon the poles of the zodiac.

FAUSTUS. Tush,
These slender trifles Wagner can decide:
Hath Mephistophilis no greater skill?
Who knows not the double motion of the planets?
The first is finish'd in a natural day;
The second thus; as Saturn in thirty

years; Jupiter in twelve; Mars in four;
the Sun, Venus, and Mercury in a year;
the Moon in twenty-eight days.   Tush,
these are freshmen's suppositions.   But,
tell me, hath every sphere a dominion or
intelligentia?

MEPHISTOPHILIS. Ay.

FAUSTUS. How many heavens or spheres
are there?

MEPHISTOPHILIS. Nine; the seven plan-
ets, the firmament, and the empyreal
heaven.

FAUSTUS. Well resolve me in this ques-
tion; why have we not conjunctions, oppo-
sitions, aspects, eclipses, all at one time,
but in some years we have more, in some
less?

MEPHISTOPHILIS. *Per inœqualem motum
respectu totius.*

FAUSTUS. Well, I am answered.   Tell
me who made the world?

MEPHISTOPHILIS. I will not.

FAUSTUS.   Sweet Mephistophilis, tell
me.

MEPHISTOPHILIS.   Move me not, for I
will not tell thee.

FAUSTUS.   Villain, have I not bound
thee to tell me anything?

MEPHISTOPHILIS.   Ay, that is not
against our kingdom; but this is.
Think thou on hell, Faustus, for thou art
damned.

FAUSTUS.   Think, Faustus, upon God
that made the world.

MEPHISTOPHILIS.   Remember this.
                                   [*Exit.*]

FAUSTUS.   Ay, go, accursed spirit, to
ugly hell!
'Tis thou hast damn'd distressed Faustus's
soul.
Is't not too late?

[*Reënter* GOOD ANGEL *and* EVIL ANGEL.]

EVIL ANGEL.   Too late.

GOOD ANGEL.   Never too late, if Faustus
can repent.

EVIL ANGEL.   If thou repent, devils
shall tear thee in pieces.

GOOD ANGEL.   Repent, and they shall
never raze thy skin.
                        [*Exeunt* ANGELS.]

FAUSTUS.   Ah, Christ, my Saviour,
Seek to save distressed Faustus' soul!

[*Enter* LUCIFER, BELZEBUB, *and* MEPHIS-
TOPHILIS.]

LUCIFER.   Christ cannot save thy soul,
for he is just:
There's none but I have interest in the
same.

FAUSTUS.   O, who art thou that look'st
so terrible?

LUCIFER.   I am Lucifer.
And this is my companion-prince in hell.

FAUSTUS.   O, Faustus, they are come to
fetch away thy soul!

LUCIFER.   We come to tell thee thou
dost injure us;
Thou talk'st of Christ, contrary to thy
promise:
Thou shouldst not think of God: think of
the devil,
And of his dam too.

FAUSTUS.   Nor will I henceforth: par-
don me in this,
And Faustus vows never to look to
heaven,
Never to name God, or to pray to Him,
To burn his Scriptures, slay his ministers,
And make my spirits pull his churches
down.

LUCIFER.   Do so, and we will highly
gratify thee.
Faustus, we are come from hell to show
thee some pastime: sit down, and thou
shalt see all the Seven Deadly Sins appear
in their proper shapes.

FAUSTUS.   That sight will be as pleasing
unto me,
As Paradise was to Adam, the first day
Of his creation.

LUCIFER.   Talk not of Paradise nor crea-
tion; but mark this show: talk of the
devil, and nothing else.—Come away!

[*Enter the* SEVEN DEADLY SINS.]

Now, Faustus, examine them of their sev-
eral names and dispositions.

FAUSTUS.   What art thou, the first?

PRIDE.   I am Pride.   I disdain to have
any parents.   But, fie, what a scent is
here!   I'll not speak another word, except

the ground were perfumed, and covered with cloth of arras.

FAUSTUS. What art thou, the second?

COVETOUSNESS. I am Covetousness, begotten of an old churl, in an old leathern bag: and, might I have my wish, I would desire that this house and all the people in it were turned to gold, that I might lock you up in my good chest: O, my sweet gold!

FAUSTUS. What art thou, the third?

WRATH. I am Wrath. I had neither father nor mother: I leapt out of a lion's mouth when I was scarce half an hour old; and ever since I have run up and down the world with this case of rapiers, wounding myself when I had nobody to fight withal. I was born in hell; and look to it, for some of you shall be my father.

FAUSTUS. What art thou, the fourth?

ENVY. I am Envy, begotten of a chimney-sweeper and an oyster-wife. I cannot read, and therefore wish all books were burnt. I am lean with seeing others eat. O, that there would come a famine through all the world, that all might die, and I live alone! then thou shouldst see how fat I would be. But must thou sit, and I stand? come down, with a vengeance!

FAUSTUS. Away, envious rascal!—What art thou, the fifth?

GLUTTONY. Who, I, sir? I am Gluttony. My parents are all dead, and the devil a penny they have left me, but a bare pension, and that is thirty meals a day, and ten bevers,—a small trifle to suffice nature. O, I come of a royal parentage! my grandfather was a Gammon of Bacon, my grandmother a Hogshead of Claret-wine; my godfathers were these, Peter Pickle-herring and Martin Martlemas-beef; O, but my godmother, she was a jolly gentlewoman, and well-beloved in every good town and city; her name was Mistress Margery March-beer. Now, Faustus, thou hast heard all my progeny; wilt thou bid me to supper?

FAUSTUS. No, I'll see thee hanged: thou wilt eat up all my victuals.

GLUTTONY. Then the devil choke thee!

FAUSTUS. Choke thyself, glutton!—What art thou, the sixth?

SLOTH. I am Sloth. I was begotten on a sunny bank, where I have lain ever since; and you have done me great injury to bring me from thence: let me be carried thither again by Gluttony and Lechery. I'll not speak another word for a king's ransom.

FAUSTUS. What are you, Mistress Minx, the seventh and last?

LECHERY. Who, I, sir? I am one that loves an inch of raw mutton better than an ell of fried stock-fish; and the first letter of my name begins with L.

FAUSTUS. Away, to hell, to hell!

[Exeunt the SINS.]

LUCIFER. Now, Faustus, how dost thou like this?

FAUSTUS. O, this feeds my soul!

LUCIFER. Tut, Faustus, in hell is all manner of delight.

FAUSTUS. O, might I see hell, and return again,
How happy were I then!

LUCIFER. Thou shalt; I will send for thee at midnight.
In meantime take this book; peruse it thoroughly,
And thou shalt turn thyself into what shape thou wilt.

FAUSTUS. Great thanks, mighty Lucifer!
This will I keep as chary as my life.

LUCIFER. Farewell, Faustus, and think on the devil.

FAUSTUS. Farewell, great Lucifer.

[Exeunt LUCIFER and BELZEBUB.]
Come, Mephistophilis.   [Exeunt.]

[Enter CHORUS.]

CHORUS. Learned Faustus,
To know the secrets of astronomy
Graven in the book of Jove's high firmament,
Did mount himself to scale Olympus' top,
Being seated in a chariot burning bright,
Drawn by the strength of yoky dragons' necks
He now is gone to prove cosmography,
And, as I guess, will first arrive in Rome,

To see the Pope and manner of his court,
And take some part of holy Peter's feast,
That to this day is highly solemnis'd.

[Exit.]

SCENE VII—The POPE'S privy-chamber.

[Enter FAUSTUS and MEPHISTOPHILIS.]
FAUSTUS. Having now, my good Meph-
istophilis,
Pass'd with delight the stately town of
Trier,
Environ'd round with airy mountain-
tops,
With walls of flint, and deep-entrenched
lakes,
Not to be won by any conquering prince;
From Paris next, coasting the realm of
France,
We saw the river Maine fall into Rhine,
Whose banks are set with groves of fruit-
ful vines;
Then up to Naples, rich Campania,
Whose buildings fair and gorgeous to the
eye,
The streets straight forth, and pav'd with
finest brick,
Quarter the town in four equivalents:
There saw we learned Maro's golden tomb,
The way he cut, an English mile in length,
Through a rock of stone, in one night's
space;
From thence to Venice, Padua, and the
rest,
In one of which a sumptuous temple
stands,
That threats the stars with her aspiring
top.
Thus hitherto hath Faustus spent his
time:
But tell me now what resting-place is
this?
Hast thou, as erst I did command,
Conducted me within the walls of Rome?
MEPHISTOPHILIS. Faustus, I have; and,
because we will not be unprovided, I have
taken up his Holiness' privy-chamber for
our use.
FAUSTUS. I hope his Holiness will bid
us welcome.

MEPHISTOPHILIS. Tut, 'tis no matter,
man; we'll be bold with his good cheer.
And now, my Faustus, that thou mayst
perceive
What Rome containeth to delight thee
with,
Know that this city stands upon seven
hills
That underprop the groundwork of the
same:
Just through the midst runs flowing
Tiber's stream
With winding banks that cut it in two
parts;
Over the which four stately bridges lean,
That make safe passage to each part of
Rome:
Upon the bridge call'd Ponte Angelo
Erected is a castle passing strong,
Within whose walls such store of ordnance
are,
And double cannons fram'd of carved
brass,
As match the days within one complete
year;
Besides the gates, and high pyramides,
Which Julius Caesar brought from Africa.
FAUSTUS. Now, by the kingdoms of
infernal rule,
Of Styx, of Acheron, and the fiery lake
Of ever-burning Phlegethon, I swear
That I do long to see the monuments
And situation of bright-splendent Rome:
Come, therefore, let's away.
MEPHISTOPHILIS. Nay, Faustus, stay: I
know you'd fain see the Pope
And take some part of holy Peter's
feast,
Where thou shalt see a troop of bald-pate
friars,
Whose summum bonum is in belly-cheer.
FAUSTUS. Well, I'm content to compass
then some sport,
And by their folly make us merriment.
Then charm me, that I
May be invisible, to do what I please,
Unseen of any whilst I stay in Rome.

[MEPHISTOPHILIS charms him.]

MEPHISTOPHILIS. So, Faustus; now
Do what thou wilt, thou shalt not be
discern'd.

[*Sound a Sonnet. Enter the* POPE *and the* CARDINAL OF LORRAIN *to the banquet, with* FRIARS *attending.*]

POPE. My lord of Lorrain, will't please you draw near?

FAUSTUS. Fall to, and the devil choke you, an you spare!

POPE. How now! who's that which spake?—Friars, look about.

1ST FRIAR. Here's nobody, if it like your Holiness.

POPE. My lord, here is a dainty dish was sent me from the Bishop of Milan.

FAUSTUS. I thank you, sir.

[*Snatches the dish.*]

POPE. How now! who's that which snatched the meat from me? will no man look?—My lord, this dish was sent me from the Cardinal of Florence.

FAUSTUS. You say true: I'll ha't.

[*Snatches the dish.*]

POPE. What, again!—My lord, I'll drink to your grace.

FAUSTUS. I'll pledge your grace.

[*Snatches the cup.*]

CARDINAL OF LORRAIN. My lord, it may be some ghost, newly crept out of Purgatory, come to beg a pardon of your Holiness.

POPE. It may be so.—Friars, prepare a dirge to lay the fury of this ghost.—Once again, my lord, fall to.

[*The* POPE *crosses himself.*]

FAUSTUS. What, are you crossing of yourself?

Well, use that trick no more, I would advise you.

[*The* POPE *crosses himself again.*]

Well, there's the second time. Aware the third;

I give you fair warning.

[*The* POPE *crosses himself again, and* FAUSTUS *hits him a box on the ear, and they all run away.*]

Come on, Mephistophilis; what shall we do?

MEPHISTOPHILIS. Nay, I know not: we shall be cursed with bell, book, and candle.

FAUSTUS. How! bell, book, and candle, —candle, book, and bell,—

Forward and backward, to curse Faustus to hell!

Anon you shall hear a hog grunt, a calf bleat, and an ass bray,

Because it is Saint Peter's holiday.

[*Reënter all the* FRIARS *to sing the Dirge.*]

1ST FRIAR. Come, brethren, let's about our business with good devotion.

[*They sing.*]

Cursed be he that stole away his Holiness' meat from the table! *maledicat Dominus!*

Cursed be he that struck his Holiness a blow on the face! *maledicat Dominus!*

Cursed be he that took Friar Sandelo a blow on the pate! *maledicat Dominus!*

Cursed be he that disturbeth our holy dirge! *maledicat Dominus!*

Cursed be he that took away his Holiness' wine! *maledicat Dominus!*

Et omnes Sancti! Amen!

[MEPHISTOPHILIS *and* FAUSTUS *beat the* FRIARS, *and fling fireworks among them; and so exeunt.*]

[*Enter* CHORUS.]

CHORUS. When Faustus had with pleasure ta'en the view

Of rarest things, and royal courts of kings,

He stay'd his course, and so returned home;

Where such as bear his absence but with grief,

I mean his friends and near'st companions,

Did gratulate his safety with kind words,

And in their conference of what befell,

Touching his journey through the world and air,

They put forth questions of astrology,

Which Faustus answer'd with such learned skill

As they admir'd and wonder'd at his wit.

Now is his fame spread forth in every land:

Amongst the rest the Emperor is one,

Carolus the Fifth, at whose palace now
Faustus is feasted 'mongst his noblemen.
What there he did, in trial of his art,
I leave untold; your eyes shall see ['t]
perform'd.   [*Exit.*]

SCENE VIII—*An Inn-Yard.*

[*Enter* ROBIN *the Ostler, with a book in
his hand.*]

ROBIN.   O, this is admirable! here I
ha' stolen one of Doctor Faustus' conjur-
ing books, and i'faith, I mean to search
some circles for my own use. Now will I
make all the maidens in our parish dance
at my pleasure.

[*Enter* RALPH, *calling* ROBIN.]

RALPH.   Robin, prithee, come away;
there's a gentleman tarries to have his
horse, and he would have his things
rubbed and made clean: he keeps such a
chafing with my mistress about it; and
she has set me to look thee out; prithee,
come away.

ROBIN.   Keep out, keep out, or else you
are blown up, you are dismembered,
Ralph: keep out, for I am about a roaring
piece of work.

RALPH.   Come, what doest thou with
that same book? thou canst not read?

ROBIN.   Yes, my master and mistress
shall find that I can read, or else my art
fails.

RALPH.   Why, Robin, what book is that?

ROBIN.   What book! why, the most in-
tolerable book for conjuring that e'er was
invented by any brimstone devil.

RALPH.   Canst thou conjure with it?

ROBIN.   I can do all these things easily
with it; first, I can make thee drunk with
ippocras at any tavern in Europe for
nothing; that's one of my conjuring
works.

RALPH.   Our Master Parson says that's
nothing.

ROBIN.   No more, sweet Ralph: let's go
and make clean our boots, which lie foul
upon our hands, and then to our conjur-
ing in the devil's name.   [*Exeunt.*]

SCENE IX

[*Enter* ROBIN *and* RALPH *with a silver
goblet.*]

ROBIN.   Come, Ralph: did not I tell
thee, we were for ever made by this Doctor
Faustus' book? *ecce, signum!* here's a
simple purchase for horse-keepers: our
horses shall eat no hay as long as this
lasts.

RALPH.   But, Robin, here comes the
Vintner.

ROBIN.   Hush! I'll gull him super-
naturally.

[*Enter* VINTNER.]

Drawer, I hope all is paid; God be with
you!—Come, Ralph.

VINTNER.   Soft, sir; a word with you.
I must yet have a goblet paid from you,
ere you go.

ROBIN.   I a goblet, Ralph, I a goblet!—
I scorn you; and you are but a—, etc. I a
goblet! search me.

VINTNER.   I mean so, sir, with your
favour.   [*Searches* ROBIN.]

ROBIN.   How say you now?

VINTNER.   I must say somewhat to your
fellow. You, sir!

ROBIN.   Me, sir! me, sir! search your
fill. [VINTNER *searches him.*] Now, sir,
you may be ashamed to burden honest
men with a matter of truth.

VINTNER.   Well, one of you hath this
goblet about you.

ROBIN.   You lie, drawer, 'tis afore me.
[*Aside.*]—Sirrah you, I'll teach you to
impeach honest men;—stand by;—I'll
scour you for a goblet;—stand aside you
had best, I charge you in the name of
Belzebub. [*Aside to* RALPH.]—Look to
the goblet, Ralph.

VINTNER.   What mean you, sirrah?

ROBIN.   I'll tell you what I mean.
[*Reads from a book.*] *Sanctobulorum
Periphrasticon*—nay, I'll tickle you, Vint-
ner. [*Aside to* RALPH.]—Look to the
goblet, Ralph.—[*Reads.*] *Polypragmos
Belseborams framanto pacostiphos tostu,
Mephistophilis, etc.*

[*Enter* MEPHISTOPHILIS, *sets squibs at their backs, and then exit. They run about.*]

VINTNER. *O, nomine Domini!* what meanest thou, Robin! thou hast no goblet.

RALPH. *Peccatum peccatorum!* Here's thy goblet, good Vintner.
[*Gives the goblet to* VINTNER, *who exit.*]

ROBIN. *Misericordia pro nobis!* what shall I do? Good devil, forgive me now, and I'll never rob thy library more.

[*Reënter* MEPHISTOPHILIS.]

MEPHISTOPHILIS. Monarch of hell, under whose black survey
Great potentates do kneel with awful fear,
Upon whose altars thousand souls do lie,
How am I vexed with these villains' charms?
From Constantinople am I hither come,
Only for pleasure of these damned slaves.

ROBIN. How, from Constantinople! you have had a great journey: will you take sixpence in your purse to pay for your supper, and be gone?

MEPHISTOPHILIS. Well, villains, for your presumption, I transform thee into an ape, and thee into a dog; and so be gone!   [*Exit.*]

ROBIN. How, into an ape! that's brave: I'll have fine sport with the boys; I'll get nuts and apples enow.

RALPH. And I must be a dog.

ROBIN. I'faith, thy head will never be out of the pottage-pot.   [*Exeunt.*]

SCENE X—*An apartment in the* EMPEROR'S *palace.*

[*Enter* EMPEROR, FAUSTUS, *and a* KNIGHT, *with* ATTENDANTS.]

EMPEROR. Master Doctor Faustus, I have heard strange report of thy knowledge in the black art, how that none in my empire nor in the whole world can compare with thee for the rare effects of magic: they say thou hast a familiar spirit, by whom thou canst accomplish what thou list. This, therefore, is my request, that thou let me see some proof of thy skill, that mine eyes may be witnesses to confirm what mine ears have heard reported: and here I swear to thee, by the honour of mine imperial crown, that, whatever thou doest, thou shalt be no ways prejudiced or endamaged.

KNIGHT [*aside*]. I'faith, he looks much like a conjurer.

FAUSTUS. My gracious sovereign, though I must confess myself far inferior to the report men have published, and nothing answerable to the honour of your imperial majesty, yet, for that love and duty binds me thereunto, I am content to do whatsoever your majesty shall command me.

EMPEROR. Then, Doctor Faustus, mark what I shall say.
As I was sometime solitary set
Within my closet, sundry thoughts arose
About the honour of mine ancestors,
How they had won by prowess such exploits,
Got such riches, subdu'd so many kingdoms,
As we that do succeed, or they that shall
Hereafter possess our throne, shall
(I fear me) ne'er attain to that degree
Of high renown and great authority:
Amongst which kings is Alexander the Great,
Chief spectacle of the world's pre-eminence,
The bright shining of whose glorious acts
Lightens the world with his reflecting beams,
As when I hear but motion made of him,
It grieves my soul I never saw the man:
If, therefore, thou, by cunning of thine art,
Canst raise this man from hollow vaults below,
Where lies entomb'd this famous conqueror,
And bring with him his beauteous paramour,
Both in their right shapes, gesture, and attire
They us'd to wear during their time of life,

Thou shalt both satisfy my just desire,
And give me cause to praise thee whilst I live.

FAUSTUS. My gracious lord, I am ready to accomplish your request, so far forth as my art and power of my spirit I am able to perform.

KNIGHT [aside]. I'faith, that's just nothing at all.

FAUSTUS. But, if it like your grace, it is not in my ability to present before your eyes the true substantial bodies of those two deceased princes, which long since are consumed to dust.

KNIGHT [aside]. Ay, marry, Master Doctor, now there's a sign of grace in you, when you will confess the truth.

FAUSTUS. But such spirits as can lively resemble Alexander and his paramour shall appear before your grace, in that manner that they both lived in, in their most flourishing estate; which I doubt not shall sufficiently content your imperial majesty.

EMPEROR. Go to, Master Doctor; let me see them presently.

KNIGHT. Do you hear, Master Doctor? you bring Alexander and his paramour before the Emperor!

FAUSTUS. How then, sir?

KNIGHT. I'faith, that's as true as Diana turned me to a stag.

FAUSTUS. Mephistophilis, be gone.

[Exit MEPHISTOPHILIS.]

KNIGHT. Nay, an you go to conjuring, I'll be gone. [Exit.]

FAUSTUS. I'll meet with you anon for interrupting me so.—Here they are, my gracious lord.

[Reënter MEPHISTOPHILIS with SPIRITS in the shapes of ALEXANDER and his PARAMOUR.]

EMPEROR. Master Doctor, I heard this lady, while she lived, had a wart or mole in her neck: how shall I know whether it be so or no?

FAUSTUS. Your highness may boldly go and see.

EMPEROR. Sure, these are no spirits, but the true substantial bodies of those two deceased princes. [Exeunt SPIRITS.]

FAUSTUS. Wilt please your highness now to send for the knight that was so pleasant with me here of late?

EMPEROR. One of you call him forth.

[Exit ATTENDANT.]

[Reënter the KNIGHT with a pair of horns on his head.]

How now, sir knight! Feel on thy head.

KNIGHT. Thou damned wretch and execrable dog,
Bred in the concave of some monstrous rock,
How dar'st thou thus abuse a gentleman?
Villain, I say, undo what thou hast done!

FAUSTUS. O, not so fast, sir! there's no haste: but, good, are you remembered how you crossed me in my conference with the Emperor? I think I have met with you for it.

EMPEROR. Good Master Doctor, at my entreaty release him: he hath done penance sufficient.

FAUSTUS. My gracious lord, not so much for the injury he offereth me here in your presence, as to delight you with some mirth, hath Faustus worthily requited this injurious knight; which being all I desire, I am content to release him of his horns:—and, sir knight, hereafter speak well of scholars.—Mephistophilis, transform him straight. [MEPHISTOPHILIS removes the horns.]—Now, my good lord, having done my duty, I humbly take my leave.

EMPEROR. Farewell, Master Doctor: yet, ere you go,
Expect from me a bounteous reward.

[Exeunt EMPEROR, KNIGHT, and ATTENDANTS.]

SCENE XI—A fair and pleasant green.

FAUSTUS. Now, Mephistophilis, the restless course
That time doth run with calm and silent foot,
Shortening my days and thread of vital life,

Calls for the payment of my latest years:
Therefore, sweet Mephistophilis, let us
Make haste to Wertenberg.

MEPHISTOPHILIS. What, will you go on
horseback or on foot?

FAUSTUS. Nay, till I'm past this fair
and pleasant green, I'll walk on foot.

SCENE XII—*In or near the home of*
FAUSTUS.

[*Enter a* HORSE-COURSER.]

HORSE-COURSER. I have been all this
day seeking one Master Fustian: mass, see
where he is!—God save you, Master Doctor!

FAUSTUS. What, Horse-Courser! you
are well met.

HORSE-COURSER. Do you hear, sir? I
have brought you forty dollars for your
horse.

FAUSTUS. I cannot sell him so: if thou
likest him for fifty, take him.

HORSE-COURSER. Alas, sir, I have no
more!—I pray you, speak for me.

MEPHISTOPHILIS. I pray you, let him
have him: he is an honest fellow, and he
has a great charge, neither wife nor
child.

FAUSTUS. Well, come, give me your
money [HORSE-COURSER *gives* FAUSTUS *the
money.*]: my boy will deliver him to you.
But I must tell you one thing before you
have him; ride him not into the water, at
any hand.

HORSE-COURSER. Why, sir, will he not
drink of all waters?

FAUSTUS. O, yes, he will drink of all
waters; but ride him not into the water;
ride him over hedge or ditch, or where
thou wilt, but not into the water.

HORSE-COURSER. Well, sir.—Now am I
made man for ever: I'll not leave my horse
for forty: if he had but the quality of
hey-ding-ding, hey-ding-ding, I'd make a
brave living on him: he has a buttock as
slick as an eel. [*Aside.*]—Well, God
b'wi'ye, sir: your boy will deliver him me:
but, hark you, sir; if my horse be sick or
ill at ease, you'll tell me what it is?

FAUSTUS. Away, you villain! what,
dost think I am a horse-doctor?

[*Exit* HORSE-COURSER.]

What art thou, Faustus, but a man condemn'd to die?
Thy fatal time doth draw to final end;
Despair doth drive distrust into my
thoughts:
Confound these passions with a quiet
sleep:
Tush, Christ did call the thief upon the
Cross;
Then rest thee, Faustus, quiet in conceit.

[*Sleeps in his chair.*]

[*Reënter* HORSE-COURSER, *all wet, crying.*]

HORSE-COURSER. Alas, alas! Doctor
Fustian, quotha? mass, Doctor Lopus was
never such a doctor: has given me a purgation, has purged me of forty dollars; I
shall never see them more. But yet, like
an ass as I was, I would not be ruled by
him, for he bade me I should ride him
into no water: now I, thinking my horse
had had some rare quality that he would
not have had me know of, I, like a venturous youth, rid him into the deep pond at
the town's end. I was no sooner in the
middle of the pond, but my horse vanished
away, and I sat upon a bottle of hay,
never so near drowning in my life. But
I'll seek out my doctor, and have my forty
dollars again, or I'll make it the dearest
horse!—O, yonder is his snipper-snapper.
Do you hear? you, hey-pass, where's your
master?

MEPHISTOPHILIS. Why, sir, what would
you? you cannot speak with him.

HORSE-COURSER. But I will speak with
him.

MEPHISTOPHILIS. Why, he's fast asleep:
come some other time.

HORSE-COURSER. I'll speak with him
now, or I'll break his glass-windows about
his ears.

MEPHISTOPHILIS. I tell thee, he has not
slept this eight nights.

HORSE-COURSER. An he have not slept
this eight weeks, I'll speak with him.

MEPHISTOPHILIS. See, where he is, fast
asleep.

HORSE-COURSER. Ay, this is he—God save you, Master Doctor, Master Doctor, Master Doctor Fustian! forty dollars, forty dollars for a bottle of hay!

MEPHISTOPHILIS. Why, thou seest he hears thee not.

HORSE-COURSER. So-ho, ho! So-ho, ho! [*In his ear.*] No, will you not wake? I'll make you wake ere I go. [*Pulls* FAUSTUS *by the leg, and pulls it away.*] Alas, I am undone! what shall I do?

FAUSTUS. O, my leg, my leg!—Help, Mephistophilis! call the officers.—My leg, my leg!

MEPHISTOPHILIS. Come, villain, to the constable.

HORSE-COURSER. O Lord, sir, let me go, and I'll give you forty dollars more!

MEPHISTOPHILIS. Where be they?

HORSE-COURSER. I have none about me: come to my ostry, and I'll give them you.

MEPHISTOPHILIS. Be gone quickly.

[HORSE-COURSER *runs away.*]

FAUSTUS. What, is he gone? farewell he! Faustus has his leg again, and the Horse-Courser, I take it, a bottle of hay for his labour: well, this trick shall cost him forty dollars more.

[*Enter* WAGNER.]

How now, Wagner! what's the news with thee?

WAGNER. Sir, the Duke of Vanholt doth earnestly entreat your company.

FAUSTUS. The Duke of Vanholt! an honourable gentleman, to whom I must be no niggard of my cunning.—Come, Mephistophilis, let's away to him. [*Exeunt.*]

SCENE XIII—*The court of the* DUKE OF VANHOLT.

[*Enter the* DUKE OF VANHOLT, *the* DUCHESS, *and* FAUSTUS.]

DUKE. Believe me, Master Doctor, this merriment hath much pleased me.

FAUSTUS. My gracious lord, I am glad it contents you so well.—But it may be, madam, you take no delight in this. I have heard that women do long for some dainties or other: what is it, madam? tell me, and you shall have it.

DUCHESS. Thanks, good Master Doctor: and, for I see your courteous intent to pleasure me, I will not hide from you the thing my heart desires; and, were it now summer, as it is January and the dead time of the winter, I would desire no better meat than a dish of ripe grapes.

FAUSTUS. Alas, madam, that's nothing!—Mephistophilis, be gone. [*Exit* MEPHISTOPHILIS.] Were it a greater thing than this, so it would content you, you should have it.

[*Reënter* MEPHISTOPHILIS *with grapes.*]

Here they be, madam: wilt please you taste on them?

DUKE. Believe me, Master Doctor, this makes me wonder above the rest, that being in the dead time of winter and in the month of January, how you should come by these grapes.

FAUSTUS. If it like your grace, the year is divided into two circles over the whole world, that, when it is here winter with us, in the contrary circle it is summer with them, as in India, Saba, and farther countries in the east; and by means of a swift spirit that I have, I had them brought hither, as you see.—How do you like them, madam? be they good?

DUCHESS. Believe me, Master Doctor, they be the best grapes that e'er I tasted in my life before.

FAUSTUS. I am glad they content you so, madam.

DUKE. Come, madam, let us in, where you must well reward this learned man for the great kindness he hath showed to you.

DUCHESS. And so I will, my lord; and, whilst I live, rest beholding for this courtesy.

FAUSTUS. I humbly thank your grace.

DUKE. Come, Master Doctor, follow us, and receive your reward. [*Exeunt.*]

Scene XIV—*A room in the house of* Faustus.

[*Enter* Wagner.]

Wagner. I think my master means to die shortly,

For he hath given to me all his goods:

And yet, methinks, if that death were near,

He would not banquet, and carouse, and swill

Amongst the students, as even now he doth,

Who are at supper with such belly-cheer

As Wagner ne'er beheld in all his life.

See, where they come! belike the feast is ended.   [*Exit.*]

[*Enter* Faustus *with two or three* Scholars, *and* Mephistophilis.]

1st Scholar. Master Doctor Faustus, since our conference about fair ladies, which was the beautifulest in all the world, we have determined with ourselves that Helen of Greece was the admirablest lady that ever lived: therefore, Master Doctor, if you will do us that favour, as to let us see that peerless dame of Greece, whom all the world admires for majesty, we should think ourselves much beholding unto you.

Faustus. Gentlemen,

For that I know your friendship is unfeign'd,

And Faustus' custom is not to deny

The just requests of those that wish him well,

You shall behold that peerless dame of Greece,

No otherways for pomp and majesty

Than when Sir Paris cross'd the seas with her,

And brought the spoils to rich Dardania.

Be silent, then, for danger is in words.

[*Music sounds, and* Helen *passeth over the stage.*]

2nd Scholar. Too simple is my wit to tell her praise,

Whom all the world admires for majesty.

3rd Scholar. No marvel though the angry Greeks pursu'd

With ten years' war the rape of such a queen,

Whose heavenly beauty passeth all compare.

1st Scholar. Since we have seen the pride of Nature's works,

And only paragon of excellence,

Let us depart; and for this glorious deed

Happy and blest be Faustus evermore!

Faustus. Gentlemen, farewell: the same I wish to you.

[*Exeunt* Scholars.]

[*Enter an* Old Man.]

Old Man. Ah, Doctor Faustus, that I might prevail

To guide thy steps unto the way of life,

By which sweet path thou mayst attain the goal

That shall conduct thee to celestial rest!

Break heart, drop blood, and mingle it with tears,

Tears falling from repentant heaviness

Of thy most vile and loathsome filthiness,

The stench whereof corrupts the inward soul

With such flagitious crimes of heinous sin

As no commiseration may expel,

But mercy, Faustus, of thy Saviour sweet,

Whose blood alone must wash away thy guilt.

Faustus. Where art thou, Faustus? wretch, what hast thou done?

Damn'd art thou, Faustus, damn'd; despair and die!

Hell calls for right, and with a roaring voice

Says, "Faustus, come; thine hour is almost come;"

And Faustus now will come to do thee right.

[Mephistophilis *gives him a dagger.*]

Old Man. Ah, stay, good Faustus, stay thy desperate steps!

I see an angel hovers o'er thy head,

And, with a vial full of precious grace,

Offers to pour the same into thy soul:

Then call for mercy, and avoid despair.

Faustus. Ah, my sweet friend, I feel

Thy words to comfort my distressed soul!
Leave me a while to ponder on my sins.
OLD MAN. I go, sweet Faustus; but
    with heavy cheer,
Fearing the ruin of thy hopeless soul.
                                    [*Exit.*]
FAUSTUS. Accursed Faustus, where is
    mercy now?
I do repent, and yet I do despair:
Hell strives with grace for conquest in
    my breast:
What shall I do to shun the snares of
    death?
MEPHISTOPHILIS. Thou traitor, Faus-
    tus, I arrest thy soul
For disobedience to my sovereign lord:
Revolt, or I'll in piece-meal tear thy flesh.
FAUSTUS. Sweet Mephistophilis, en-
    treat thy lord
To pardon my unjust presumption,
And with my blood again I will confirm
My former vow I made to Lucifer.
MEPHISTOPHILIS. Do it, then, quickly,
    with unfeigned heart,
Lest greater danger do attend thy drift.
FAUSTUS. Torment, sweet friend, that
    base and crooked age,
That durst dissuade me from thy Lucifer,
With greatest torments that our hell
    affords.
MEPHISTOPHILIS. His faith is great; I
    cannot touch his soul;
But what I may afflict his body with
I will attempt, which is but little worth.
FAUSTUS. One thing, good servant, let
    me crave of thee,
To glut the longing of my heart's desire,
That I might have unto my paramour
That heavenly Helen which I saw of late,
Whose sweet embracings may extinguish
    clean
Those thoughts that do dissuade me from
    my vow,
And keep mine oath I made to Lucifer.
MEPHISTOPHILIS. Faustus, this, or
    what else thou shalt desire,
Shall be perform'd in twinkling of an eye.

[*Reënter* HELEN.]
FAUSTUS. Was this the face that
    launch'd a thousand ships,

And burnt the topless towers of Ilium?—
Sweet Helen, make me immortal with a
    kiss.—   [*Kisses her.*]
Her lips suck forth my soul: see, where
    it flies!—
Come, Helen, come, give me my soul again.
Here will I dwell, for heaven is in these
    lips,
And all is dross that is not Helena.
I will be Paris, and for love of thee,
Instead of Troy, shall Wertenberg be
    sack'd;
And I will combat with weak Menelaus,
And wear thy colours on my plumed
    crest;
Yes, I will wound Achilles in the heel,
And then return to Helen for a kiss.
O, thou art fairer than the evening air
Clad in the beauty of a thousand stars;
Brighter art thou than flaming Jupiter
When he appear'd to hapless Semele;
More lovely than the monarch of the sky
In wanton Arethusa's azur'd arms;
And none but thou shalt be my paramour!
                                    [*Exeunt.*]

SCENE XV—*A room in the* OLD MAN'S
                house.

[*Enter the* OLD MAN.]
OLD MAN. Accursed Faustus, miserable
    man,
That from thy soul exclud'st the grace of
    heaven,
And fly'st the throne of his tribunal-seat!

[*Enter* DEVILS.]
Satan begins to sift me with his pride:
As in this furnace God shall try my
    faith,
My faith, vile hell, shall triumph over
    thee,
Ambitious fiends, see how the heavens
    smile
At your repulse, and laugh your state to
    scorn!
Hence, hell! for hence I fly unto my God.
        [*Exeunt—on one side*, DEVILS, *on
                the other*, OLD MAN.]

SCENE XVI—*A room in the house of* FAUSTUS.

[*Enter* FAUSTUS, *with* SCHOLARS.]

FAUSTUS. Ah, gentlemen!

1ST SCHOLAR. What ails Faustus?

FAUSTUS. Ah, my sweet chamber-fellow, had I lived with thee, then had I lived still! but now I die eternally. Look, comes he not? comes he not?

2ND SCHOLAR. What means Faustus?

3RD SCHOLAR. Belike he is grown into some sickness by being over-solitary.

1ST SCHOLAR. If it be so, we'll have physicians to cure him.—'Tis but a surfeit; never fear, man.

FAUSTUS. A surfeit of deadly sin, that hath damned both body and soul.

2ND SCHOLAR. Yet, Faustus, look up to heaven; remember God's mercies are infinite.

FAUSTUS. But Faustus' offence can ne'er be pardoned: the serpent that tempted Eve may be saved, but not Faustus. Ah, gentlemen, hear me with patience, and tremble not at my speeches! Though my heart pants and quivers to remember that I have been a student here these thirty years, O, would I had never seen Wertenberg, never read book! and what wonders I have done, all Germany can witness, yea, all the world; for which Faustus hath lost both Germany and the world, yea, heaven itself, heaven, the seat of God, the throne of the blessed, the kingdom of joy; and must remain in hell for ever, hell, ah, hell, for ever! Sweet friends, what shall become of Faustus, being in hell for ever?

3RD SCHOLAR. Yet, Faustus, call on God.

FAUSTUS. On God, whom Faustus hath abjured! on God, whom Faustus hath blasphemed! Ah, my God, I would weep! but the devil draws in my tears. Gush forth blood, instead of tears! yea, life and soul! O, he stays my tongue! I would lift up my hands; but see, they hold them, they hold them!

ALL. Who, Faustus?

FAUSTUS. Lucifer and Mephistophilis.

Ah, gentlemen, I gave them my soul for my cunning!

ALL. God forbid!

FAUSTUS. God forbade it, indeed; but Faustus hath done it: for vain pleasure of twenty-four years hath Faustus lost eternal joy and felicity. I writ them a bill with mine own blood: the date is expired; the time will come, and he will fetch me.

1ST SCHOLAR. Why did not Faustus tell us of this before, that divines might have prayed for thee?

FAUSTUS. Oft have I thought to have done so; but the devil threatened to tear me in pieces, if I named God, to fetch both body and soul, if I once gave ear to divinity: and now 'tis too late. Gentlemen, away, lest you perish with me.

2ND SCHOLAR. O, what shall we do to save Faustus?

FAUSTUS. Talk not of me, but save yourselves, and depart.

3RD SCHOLAR. God will strengthen me; I will stay with Faustus.

1ST SCHOLAR. Tempt not God, sweet friend; but let us into the next room, and there pray for him.

FAUSTUS. Ay, pray for me, pray for me; and what noise soever ye hear, come not unto me, for nothing can rescue me.

2ND SCHOLAR. Pray thou, and we will pray that God may have mercy upon thee.

FAUSTUS. Gentlemen, farewell: if I live till morning, I'll visit you; if not, Faustus is gone to hell.

ALL. Faustus, farewell.

[*Exeunt* SCHOLARS.—*The clock strikes eleven.*]

FAUSTUS. Ah, Faustus,

Now hast thou but one bare hour to live,
And then thou must be damn'd perpetually!

Stand still, you ever-moving spheres of heaven,

That time may cease, and midnight never come;

Fair Nature's eye, rise, rise again, and make

Perpetual day; or let this hour be but

A year, a month, a week, a natural day,

That Faustus may repent and save his
soul!
O lente, lente currite, noctis equi!
The stars move still, time runs, the clock
will strike,
The devil will come, and Faustus must be
damn'd.
O, I'll leap up to my God!—Who pulls me
down?—
See, see, where Christ's blood streams in
the firmament!
One drop would save my soul, half a drop:
ah, my Christ!—
Ah, rend not my heart for naming of my
Christ!
Yet will I call on him: O, spare me,
Lucifer!—
Where is it now? 'tis gone: and see,
where God
Stretcheth out his arm, and bends his
ireful brows!
Mountains and hills, come, come, and fall
on me,
And hide me from the heavy wrath of
God!
No, no!
Then will I headlong run into the earth:
Earth, gape! O, no, it will not harbour
me!
You stars that reign'd at my nativity,
Whose influence hath allotted death and
hell,
Now draw up Faustus, like a foggy mist,
Into the entrails of yon labouring clouds,
That, when you vomit forth into the
air,
My limbs may issue from your smoky
mouths,
So that my soul may but ascend to
heaven!
     [*The clock strikes the half-hour.*]
Ah, half the hour is past! 'twill all be
past anon.
O God,
If thou wilt not have mercy on my soul,
Yet for Christ's sake, whose blood hath
ransom'd me,
Impose some end to my incessant pain;
Let Faustus live in hell a thousand years,

A hundred thousand, and at last be sav'd!
O, no end is limited to damned souls!
Why wert thou not a creature wanting
soul?
Or why is this immortal that thou hast?
Ah, Pythagoras' metempsychosis, were
that true,
This soul should fly from me, and I be
chang'd
Unto some brutish beast! all beasts are
happy,
For, when they die,
Their souls are soon dissolv'd in elements;
But mine must live still to be plagu'd in
hell.
Curs'd be the parents that engender'd me!
No, Faustus, curse thyself, curse Lucifer
That hath depriv'd thee of the joys of
heaven.
     [*The clock strikes twelve.*]
O, it strikes, it strikes! Now, body, turn
to air,
Or Lucifer will bear thee quick to hell!
     [*Thunder and lightning.*]
O soul, be chang'd into little water-drops,
And fall into the ocean, ne'er be found!
     [*Enter* DEVILS.]
My God, my God, look not so fierce on
me!
Adders and serpents, let me breathe a
while!
Ugly hell, gape not! come not, Lucifer!
I'll burn my books!—Ah, Mephistophilis!
     [*Exeunt* DEVILS *with* FAUSTUS.]
     [*Enter* CHORUS.]
  CHORUS. Cut is the branch that might
have grown full straight,
And burnèd is Apollo's laurel-bough,
That sometime grew within this learnèd
man.
Faustus is gone: regard his hellish fall,
Whose fiendful fortune may exhort the
wise,
Only to wonder at unlawful things,
Whose deepness doth entice such forward
wits
To practise more than heavenly power
permits.   [*Exit.*]
Terminat hora diem; terminat auctor opus.

EVERY MAN IN HIS HUMOUR

By BEN JONSON

Produced at London, 1598

CHARACTERS

KNOWELL, *an old gentleman*
EDWARD KNOWELL, *his son*
BRAINWORM, *the father's man*
GEORGE DOWNRIGHT, *a plain squire*
WELLBRED, *his half-brother*
KITELY, *a merchant*
CAPTAIN BOBADILL, *a Paul's man*
MASTER STEPHEN, *a country gull*
MASTER MATHEW, *the town gull*
THOMAS CASH, KITELY'S *cashier*
OLIVER COB, *a water-bearer*
JUSTICE CLEMENT, *an old merry magistrate*
ROGER FORMAL, *his clerk*
WELLBRED'S SERVANT
DAME KITELY, KITELY'S *wife*
MRS. BRIDGET, *his sister*
TIB, COB'S *wife*
SERVANTS, *etc.*

SCENE—*London.*

PROLOGUE

Though need make many poets, and some
  such
As art and nature have not better'd much;
Yet ours for want hath not so loved the
  stage,
As he dare serve the ill customs of the
  age,

Or purchase your delight at such a rate,
As, for it, he himself must justly hate:
To make a child now swaddled, to proceed
Man, and then shoot up, in one beard and
  weed,
Past threescore years; or, with three
  rusty swords,
And help of some few foot and half-foot
  words,

Fight over York and Lancaster's long jars,
And in the tyring-house bring wounds to
  scars.
He rather prays you will be pleas'd to see
One such to-day, as other plays should be;
Where neither chorus wafts you o'er the
  seas,
Nor creaking throne comes down the boys
  to please;
Nor nimble squib is seen to make afeard
The gentlewomen; nor roll'd bullet heard
To say, it thunders; nor tempestuous
  drum
Rumbles, to tell you when the storm doth
  come;
But deeds, and language, such as men do
  use,
And persons, such as comedy would choose,
When she would shew an image of the
  times,
And sport with human follies, not with
  crimes.
Except we make them such, by loving still
Our popular errors, when we know they're
  ill.
I mean such errors as you'll all confess,
By laughing at them, they deserve no
  less:
Which when you heartily do, there's hope
  left then,
You, that have so grac'd monsters, may
  like men.

ACT I

Scene I—*A street.*

[*Enter* Knowell, *at the door of his house.*]
KNOWELL. A goodly day toward, and a
fresh morning.—Brainworm!

[*Enter* Brainworm.]
Call up your young master: bid him rise,
  sir.
Tell him, I have some business to employ
  him.
  BRAINWORM. I will, sir, presently.
  KNOWELL.   But hear you, sirrah,
If he be at his book, disturb him not.
  BRAINWORM. Very good, sir.   [*Exit.*]

KNOWELL. How happy yet should I es-
  teem myself,
Could I, by any practice, wean the boy
From one vain course of study he affects.
He is a scholar, if a man may trust
The liberal voice of fame in her report,
Of good account in both our Universities,
Either of which hath favoured him with
  graces:
But their indulgence must not spring in
  me
A fond opinion that he cannot err.
Myself was once a student, and indeed,
Fed with the self-same humour he is now,
Dreaming on nought but idle poetry,
That fruitless and unprofitable art,
Good unto none, but least to the profes-
  sors;
Which then I thought the mistress of all
  knowledge:
But since, time and the truth have waked
  my judgment,
And reason taught me better to distin-
  guish
The vain from the useful learnings.

[*Enter* Master Stephen.]
              Cousin Stephen,
What news with you, that you are here
  so early?
  STEPHEN. Nothing, but e'en come to
see how you do, uncle.
  KNOWELL. That's kindly done; you are
welcome, coz.
  STEPHEN. Ay, I know that, sir; I
would not have come else. How does my
cousin Edward, uncle?
  KNOWELL. O, well, coz; go in and see;
I doubt he be scarce stirring yet.
  STEPHEN. Uncle, afore I go in, can you
tell me, an he have e'er a book of the
science of hawking and hunting; I would
fain borrow it.
  KNOWELL. Why, I hope you will not a
hawking now, will you?
  STEPHEN. No, wusse; but I'll practise
against next year, uncle. I have bought
me a hawk, and a hood, and bells, and all;
I lack nothing but a book to keep it by.
  KNOWELL. Oh, most ridiculous!
  STEPHEN. Nay, look you now, you are

angry, uncle:—Why, you know an a man have not skill in the hawking and hunting languages now-a-days, I'll not give a rush for him: they are more studied than the Greek, or the Latin. He is for no gallant's company without them; and by gadslid I scorn it, I, so I do, to be a consort for every humdrum: hang them, scroyles! there's nothing in them i' the world. What do you talk on it? Because I dwell at Hogsden, I shall keep company with none but the archers of Finsbury, or the citizens that come a ducking to Islington ponds! A fine jest, i' faith! 'Slid, a gentleman mun shew himself like a gentleman. Uncle, I pray you be not angry; I know what I have to do, I trow, I am no novice.

KNOWELL. You are a prodigal, absurd coxcomb, go to!

Nay, never look at me, 'tis I that speak;
Take't as you will, sir, I'll not flatter you.
Have you not yet found means enow to waste
That which your friends have left you, but you must
Go cast away your money on a buzzard,
And know not how to keep it, when you have done?
O, it is comely! this will make you a gentleman!
Well, cousin, well, I see you are e'en past hope
Of all reclaim:—ay, so; now you are told on't,
You look another way.

STEPHEN. What would you ha' me do?

KNOWELL. What would I have you do?
I'll tell you, kinsman;
Learn to be wise, and practise how to thrive;
That would I have you do: and not to spend
Your coin on every bauble that you fancy,
Or every foolish brain that humours you.
I would not have you to invade each place,
Nor thrust yourself on all societies,
Till men's affections, or your own desert,
Should worthily invite you to your rank.
He that is so respectless in his courses,

Oft sells his reputation at cheap market.
Nor would I, you should melt away yourself
In flashing bravery, lest, while you affect
To make a blaze of gentry to the world,
A little puff of scorn extinguish it;
And you be left like an unsavoury snuff,
Whose property is only to offend.
I'd have you sober, and contain yourself,
Not that your sail be bigger than your boat;
But moderate your expenses now, at first,
As you may keep the same proportion still:
Nor stand so much on your gentility,
Which is an airy and mere borrow'd thing,
From dead men's dust and bones; and none of yours,
Except you make, or hold it.

[*Enter a* SERVANT.]
                Who comes here?

SERVANT. Save you, gentlemen!

STEPHEN. Nay, we do not stand much on our gentility, friend; yet you are welcome: and I assure you mine uncle here is a man of a thousand a year, Middlesex land. He has but one son in all the world, I am his next heir, at the common law, master Stephen, as simple as I stand here, if my cousin die, as there's hope he will: I have a pretty living o' mine own too, beside, hard by here.

SERVANT. In good time, sir.

STEPHEN. In good time, sir! why, and in very good time, sir! You do not flout, friend, do you?

SERVANT. Not I, sir.

STEPHEN. Not you, sir! you were best not, sir; an you should, here be them can perceive it, and that quickly too; go to: and they can give it again soundly too, an need be.

SERVANT. Why, sir, let this satisfy you; good faith, I had no such intent.

STEPHEN. Sir, an I thought you had, I would talk with you, and that presently.

SERVANT. Good master Stephen, so you may, sir, at your pleasure.

STEPHEN. And so I would, sir, good

my saucy companion! an you were out
o' mine uncle's ground, I can tell you;
though I do not stand upon my gentility
neither, in't.

KNOWELL. Cousin, cousin, will this
ne'er be left?

STEPHEN. Whoreson, base fellow! a
mechanical serving-man! By this cudgel,
an 'twere not for shame, I would—

KNOWELL. What would you do, you
peremptory gull?
If you cannot be quiet, get you hence.
You see the honest man demeans himself
Modestly tow'rds you, giving no reply
To your unseason'd, quarrelling, rude
fashion;
And still you huff it, with a kind of car-
riage
As void of wit, as of humanity.
Go, get you in; 'fore heaven, I am
ashamed
Thou hast a kinsman's interest in me.

[Exit MASTER STEPHEN.]

SERVANT. I pray, sir, is this master
Knowell's house?

KNOWELL. Yes, marry is it, sir.

SERVANT. I should inquire for a gen-
tleman here, one master Edward Know-
ell; do you know any such, sir, I pray
you?

KNOWELL. I should forget myself else,
sir.

SERVANT. Are you the gentleman? cry
you mercy, sir: I was required by a gen-
tleman in the city, as I rode out at this
end o' the town, to deliver you this letter,
sir.

KNOWELL. To me, sir! What do you
mean? pray you remember your court'sy.
[Reads.] *To his most selected friend,
master Edward Knowell.* What might the
gentleman's name be, sir, that sent it?
Nay, pray you be covered.

SERVANT. One master Wellbred, sir.

KNOWELL. Master Wellbred! a young
gentleman, is he not?

SERVANT. The same, sir; master Kitely
married his sister; the rich merchant in
the Old Jewry.

KNOWELL. You say very true.—Brain-
worm!

[Enter BRAINWORM.]

BRAINWORM. Sir.

KNOWELL. Make this honest friend
drink here: pray you, go in.

[Exeunt BRAINWORM and SERVANT.]

This letter is directed to my son;
Yet I am Edward Knowell too, and
may,
With the safe conscience of good manners,
use
The fellow's error to my satisfaction.
Well, I will break it ope (old men are
curious),
Be it but for the style's sake and the
phrase;
To see if both do answer my son's praises,
Who is almost grown the idolater
Of this young Wellbred. What have we
here? What's this?

[Reads] Why, Ned, I beseech thee, hast
thou forsworn all thy friends in the Old
Jewry? or dost thou think us all Jews
that inhabit there? yet, if thou dost,
come over, and but see our frippery;
change an old shirt for a whole smock
with us: do not conceive that antipathy
between us and Hogsden, as was between
Jews and hogs-flesh. Leave thy vigilant
father alone, to number over his green
apricots, evening and morning, on the
north-west wall: an I had been his son,
I had saved him the labour long since,
if taking in all the young wenches that
pass by at the backdoor, and codling
every kernel of the fruit for them, would
have served. But, pr'ythee, come over to
me quickly this morning; I have such a
present for thee!—our Turkey company
never sent the like to the Grand Signior.
One is a rhymer, sir, of your own batch,
your own leaven; but doth think himself
poet-major of the town, willing to be
shewn, and worthy to be seen. The other
—I will not venture his description with
you, till you come, because I would have
you make hither with an appetite. If
the worst of 'em be not worth your jour-
ney, draw your bill of charges, as un-
conscionable as any Guildhall verdict
will give it you, and you shall be allowed
your viaticum. [*From the Windmill.*]

From the Bordello it might come as well,
The Spittle, or Pict-hatch. Is this the
    man
My son hath sung so, for the happiest
    wit,
The choicest brain, the times have sent
    us forth!
I know not what he may be in the arts,
Nor what in schools; but, surely, for his
    manners,
I judge him a profane and dissolute
    wretch;
Worse by possession of such great good
    gifts,
Being the master of so loose a spirit.
Why, what unhallowed ruffian would have
    writ
In such scurrilous manner to a friend!
Why should he think I tell my apricots,
Or play the Hesperian dragon with my
    fruit,
To watch it? Well, my son, I had thought
    you
Had had more judgment to have made
    election
Of your companions, than t' have ta'en
    on trust
Such petulant, jeering gamesters, that
    can spare
No argument or subject from their jest.
But I perceive affection makes a fool
Of any man too much the father.—Brain-
    worm!

[*Enter* BRAINWORM.]

BRAINWORM. Sir.
KNOWELL. Is the fellow gone that
brought this letter?
BRAINWORM. Yes, sir, a pretty while
since.
KNOWELL. And where is your young
master?
BRAINWORM. In his chamber, sir.
KNOWELL. He spake not with the fel-
low, did he?
BRAINWORM. No, sir, he saw him not.
KNOWELL. Take you this letter, and
deliver it my son; but with no notice
that I have opened it, on your life.
BRAINWORM. O Lord, sir! that were a
jest indeed.   [*Exit.*]

KNOWELL. I am resolved I will not
    stop his journey,
Nor practise any violent means to stay
The unbridled course of youth in him; for
    that
Restrain'd, grows more impatient; and in
    kind
Like to the eager, but the generous grey-
    hound,
Who ne'er so little from his game with-
    held,
Turns head, and leaps up at his holder's
    throat.
There is a way of winning more by
    love,
And urging of the modesty, than fear:
Force works on servile natures, not the
    free.
He that's compell'd to goodness, may be
    good,
But 'tis but for that fit; where others,
    drawn
By softness and example, get a habit.
Then, if they stray, but warn them, and
    the same
They should for virtue have done, they'll
    do for shame.   [*Exit.*]

SCENE II—*A room in* KNOWELL'S *house.*

[*Enter* EDWARD KNOWELL, *with a letter
in his hand, followed by* BRAINWORM.]
EDWARD KNOWELL. Did he open it,
say'st thou?
BRAINWORM. Yes, o' my word, sir, and
read the contents.
EDWARD KNOWELL. That scarce con-
tents me. What countenance, prithee,
made he in the reading of it? was he
angry, or pleased?
BRAINWORM. Nay, sir, I saw him not
read it, nor open it, I assure your wor-
ship.
EDWARD KNOWELL. No! how know'st
thou then that he did either?
BRAINWORM. Marry, sir, because he
charged me, on my life, to tell nobody
that he open'd it; which, unless he had
done, he would never fear to have it re-
vealed.

EDWARD KNOWELL. That's true: well, I thank thee, Brainworm.

[*Enter* STEPHEN.]

STEPHEN. O, Brainworm, didst thou not see a fellow here in what-sha-call-him doublet? he brought mine uncle a letter e'en now.

BRAINWORM. Yes, master Stephen; what of him?

STEPHEN. O, I have such a mind to beat him——where is he, canst thou tell?

BRAINWORM. Faith, he is not of that mind: he is gone, master Stephen.

STEPHEN. Gone! which way? when went he? how long since?

BRAINWORM. He is rid hence; he took horse at the street-door.

STEPHEN. And I staid in the fields! Whoreson scanderbag rogue! O that I had but a horse to fetch him back again!

BRAINWORM. Why, you may have my master's gelding, to save your longing, sir.

STEPHEN. But I have no boots, that's the spite on't.

BRAINWORM. Why, a fine wisp of hay, roll'd hard, master Stephen.

STEPHEN. No, faith, it's no boot to follow him now: let him e'en go and hang. Prithee, help to truss me a little: he does so vex me——

BRAINWORM. You'll be worse vexed when you are trussed, master Stephen. Best keep unbraced, and walk yourself till you be cold; your choler may founder you else.

STEPHEN. By my faith, and so I will, now thou tell'st me on't: how dost thou like my leg, Brainworm?

BRAINWORM. A very good leg, master Stephen; but the woollen stocking does not commend it so well.

STEPHEN. Foh! the stockings be good enough, now summer is coming on, for the dust: I'll have a pair of silk against winter, that I go to dwell in the town. I think my leg would shew in a silk hose——

BRAINWORM. Believe me, master Stephen, rarely well.

STEPHEN. In sadness, I think it would: I have a reasonable good leg.

BRAINWORM. You have an excellent good leg, master Stephen; but I cannot stay to praise it longer now, and I am very sorry for it.   [*Exit.*]

STEPHEN. Another time will serve, Brainworm. Gramercy for this.

EDWARD KNOWELL. Ha, ha, ha!

STEPHEN. Slid, I hope he laughs not at me; an he do——

EDWARD KNOWELL. Here was a letter indeed, to be intercepted by a man's father, and do him good with him! He cannot but think most virtuously, both of me, and the sender, sure, that make the careful costermonger of him in our familiar epistles. Well, if he read this with patience I'll be gelt, and troll ballads for master John Trundle yonder, the rest of my mortality. It is true, and likely, my father may have as much patience as another man, for he takes much physic; and oft taking physic makes a man very patient. But would your packet, master Wellbred, had arrived at him in such a minute of his patience! then we had known the end of it, which now is doubtful, and threatens——[*Sees* MASTER STEPHEN.] What, my wise cousin! nay, then I'll furnish our feast with one gull more toward the mess. He writes to me of a brace, and here's one, that's three: oh, for a fourth, Fortune, if ever thou'lt use thine eyes, I entreat thee——

STEPHEN. Oh, now I see who he laughed at: he laughed at somebody in that letter. By this good light, an he had laughed at me——

EDWARD KNOWELL. How now, cousin Stephen, melancholy?

STEPHEN. Yes, a little: I thought you had laughed at me, cousin.

EDWARD KNOWELL. Why, what an I had, coz? what would you have done?

STEPHEN. By this light, I would have told mine uncle.

EDWARD KNOWELL. Nay, if you would have told your uncle, I did laugh at you, coz.

STEPHEN. Did you, indeed?

EDWARD KNOWELL. Yes, indeed.

STEPHEN. Why then—

EDWARD KNOWELL. What then?

STEPHEN. I am satisfied; it is sufficient.

EDWARD KNOWELL. Why, be so, gentle coz: and, I pray you, let me entreat a courtesy of you. I am sent for this morning by a friend in the Old Jewry, to come to him; it is but crossing over the fields to Moorgate: Will you bear me company? I protest it is not to draw you into bond or any plot against the state, coz.

STEPHEN. Sir, that's all one an it were; you shall command me twice so far as Moorgate, to do you good in such a matter. Do you think I would leave you? I protest—

EDWARD KNOWELL. No, no, you shall not protest, coz.

STEPHEN. By my fackings, but I will, by your leave:—I'll protest more to my friend, than I'll speak of at this time.

EDWARD KNOWELL. You speak very well, coz.

STEPHEN. Nay, not so neither, you shall pardon me: but I speak to serve my turn.

EDWARD KNOWELL. Your turn, coz! do you know what you say? A gentleman of your sorts, parts, carriage, and estimation, to talk of your turn in this company, and to me alone, like a tankard-bearer at a conduit! fie! A wight that, hitherto, his every step hath left the stamp of a great foot behind him, as every word the savour of a strong spirit, and he! this man! so graced, gilded, or, to use a more fit metaphor, so tinfoiled by nature, as not ten housewives' pewter, again a good time, shews more bright to the world than he! and he! (as I said last, so I say again, and still shall say it) this man! to conceal such real ornaments as these, and shadow their glory, as a milliner's wife does her wrought stomacher, with a smoky lawn, or a black cyprus! O, coz! it cannot be answered; go not about it: Drake's old ship at Deptford may sooner circle the world

again. Come, wrong not the quality of your desert, with looking downward, coz; but hold up your head, so; and let the idea of what you are be portrayed in your face, that men may read in your physnomy, *here within this place is to be seen the true, rare, and accomplished monster, or miracle of nature,* which is all one. What think you of this, coz?

STEPHEN. Why, I do think of it: and I will be more proud, and melancholy, and gentlemanlike, than I have been, I'll insure you.

EDWARD KNOWELL. Why, that's resolute, master Stephen!—Now, if I can but hold him up to his height, as it is happily begun, it will do well for a suburb humour: we may hap have a match with the city, and play him for forty pound.— Come, coz.

STEPHEN. I'll follow you.

EDWARD KNOWELL. Follow me! you must go before.

STEPHEN. Nay, an I must, I will. Pray you shew me, good cousin.   [*Exeunt.*]

SCENE III—*The lane before* COB'S *house.*

[*Enter* MASTER MATHEW.]

MATHEW. I think this be the house: what ho!

[*Enter* COB.]

COB. Who's there? O, master Mathew! give your worship good morrow.

MATHEW. What, Cob! how dost thou, good Cob? dost thou inhabit here, Cob?

COB. Ay, sir, I and my lineage have kept a poor house here, in our days.

MATHEW. Thy lineage, monsieur Cob! what lineage, what lineage?

COB. Why, sir, an ancient lineage, and a princely. Mine ance'try came from a king's belly, no worse man; and yet no man either, by your worship's leave, I did lie in that, but herring, the king of fish (from his belly I proceed), one of the monarchs of the world, I assure you. The first red herring that was broiled in Adam and Eve's kitchen, do I fetch my pedigree from, by the harrot's book. His cob was my great, great, mighty great grandfather.

MATHEW. Why mighty, why mighty, I pray thee?

COB. O, it was a mighty while ago, sir, and a mighty great cob.

MATHEW. How know'st thou that?

COB. How know I! why, I smell his ghost ever and anon.

MATHEW. Smell a ghost! O unsavoury jest! and the ghost of a herring cob?

COB. Ay, sir: With favour of your worship's nose, master Mathew, why not the ghost of a herring cob, as well as the ghost of Rasher Bacon?

MATHEW. Roger Bacon, thou would'st say.

COB. I say Rasher Bacon. They were both broiled on the coals; and a man may smell broiled meat, I hope! you are a scholar, upsolve me that now.

MATHEW. O raw ignorance!—Cob, canst thou shew me of a gentleman, one captain Bobadill, where his lodging is?

COB. O, my guest, sir, you mean.

MATHEW. Thy guest! alas, ha, ha, ha!

COB. Why do you laugh, sir? do you not mean captain Bobadill?

MATHEW. Cob, pray thee advise thyself well; do not wrong the gentleman, and thyself too. I dare be sworn, he scorns thy house; he! he lodge in such a base obscure place as thy house! Tut, I know his disposition so well, he would not lie in thy bed if thou'dst give it him.

COB. I will not give it him though, sir. Mass, I thought somewhat was in it, we could not get him to bed all night: Well, sir, though he lie not on my bed, he lies on my bench: an't please you to go up, sir, you shall find him with two cushions under his head, and his cloak wrapped about him, as though he had neither won nor lost, and yet, I warrant, he ne'er cast better in his life, than he has done to-night.

MATHEW. Why, was he drunk?

COB. Drunk, sir! you hear not me say so: perhaps he swallowed a tavern-token, or some such device, sir, I have nothing to do withal. I deal with water and not with wine—Give me my tankard there, ho!—God be wi' you, sir. It's six o'clock: I should have carried two turns by this. What ho! my stopple! come.

[*Enter* TIB *with a water-tankard.*]

MATHEW. Lie in a water-bearer's house! a gentleman of his havings! Well, I'll tell him my mind.

COB. What, Tib; shew this gentleman up to the captain. [*Exit* TIB *with* MASTER MATHEW.] Oh, an my house were the Brazen-head now! faith it would e'en speak *Moe fools yet.* You should have some now would take this master Mathew to be a gentleman, at the least. His father's an honest man, a worshipful fishmonger, and so forth; and now does he creep and wriggle into acquaintance with all the brave gallants about the town, such as my guest is (O, my guest is a fine man!), and they flout him invincibly. He useth every day to a merchant's house where I serve water, one master Kitely's, in the Old Jewry; and here's the jest, he is in love with my master's sister, Mrs. Bridget, and calls her mistress; and there he will sit you a whole afternoon sometimes, reading of these same abominable, vile (a pox on 'em! I cannot abide them), rascally verses, poetrie, poetrie, and speaking of interludes; 'twill make a man burst to hear him. And the wenches, they do so jeer, and ti-he at him—Well, should they do so much to me, I'd forswear them all, by the foot of Pharaoh! There's an oath! How many water-bearers shall you hear swear such an oath? O, I have a guest—he teaches me—he does swear the legiblest of any man christened: *By St. George! the foot of Pharaoh! the body of me! as I am a gentleman and a soldier!* such dainty oaths! and withal he does take this same filthy roguish tobacco, the finest and cleanliest! it would do a man good to see the fumes come forth at's tonnels.—Well, he owes me forty shillings, my wife lent him out of her purse, by sixpence at a time, besides his lodging: I would I had it! I shall have it, he says, the next action. Helter skelter, hang sorrow, care'll kill a cat, up-tails all, and a louse for the hangman.

[*Exit.*]

SCENE IV—*A room in* COB'S *house.*

[BOBADILL *discovered lying on a bench.*]
BOBADILL. Hostess, hostess!

[*Enter* TIB.]
TIB. What say you, sir?
BOBADILL. A cup of thy small beer, sweet hostess.
TIB. Sir, there's a gentleman below would speak with you.
BOBADILL. A gentleman! 'odso, I am not within.
TIB. My husband told him you were, sir.
BOBADILL. What a plague—what meant he?
MATHEW [*below*]. Captain Bobadill!
BOBADILL. Who's there!—Take away the bason, good hostess;—Come up, sir.
TIB. He would desire you to come up, sir. You come into a cleanly house, here.

[*Enter* MATHEW.]
MATHEW. Save you, sir; save you, captain!
BOBADILL. Gentle master Mathew! Is it you, sir? please you to sit down.
MATHEW. Thank you, good captain; you may see I am somewhat audacious.
BOBADILL. Not so, sir. I was requested to supper last night by a sort of gallants, where you were wished for, and drunk to, I assure you.
MATHEW. Vouchsafe me, by whom, good captain?
BOBADILL. Marry, by young Wellbred, and others.—Why, hostess, a stool here for this gentleman.
MATHEW. No haste, sir, 'tis very well.
BOBADILL. Body o' me! it was so late ere we parted last night, I can scarce open my eyes yet; I was but new risen, as you came; how passes the day abroad, sir? you can tell.

MATHEW. Faith, some half hour to seven; now, trust me, you have an exceeding fine lodging here, very neat, and private.
BOBADILL. Ay, sir: sit down, I pray you. Master Mathew, in any case possess no gentlemen of our acquaintance with notice of my lodging.
MATHEW. Who? I, sir; no.
BOBADILL. Not that I need to care who know it, for the cabin is convenient; but in regard I would not be too popular, and generally visited, as some are.
MATHEW. True, captain, I conceive you.
BOBADILL. For, do you see, sir, by the heart of valour in me, except it be to some peculiar and choice spirits, to whom I am extraordinarily engaged, as yourself, or so, I could not extend thus far.
MATHEW. O Lord, sir! I resolve so.
BOBADILL. I confess I love a cleanly and quiet privacy, above all the tumult and roar of fortune. What new book have you there? What! Go by, Hieronymo?
MATHEW. Ay: did you ever see it acted? Is't not well penned?
BOBADILL. Well penned! I would fain see all the poets of these times pen such another play as that was: they'll prate and swagger, and keep a stir of art and devices, when, as I am a gentleman, read 'em, they are the most shallow, pitiful, barren fellows, that live upon the face of the earth again.

[*While* MASTER MATHEW *reads*, BOBADILL *makes himself ready.*]

MATHEW. Indeed here are a number of fine speeches in this book. *O eyes, no eyes, but fountains fraught with tears!* there's a conceit! *fountains fraught with tears! O life, no life, but lively form of death!* another. *O world, no world, but mass of public wrongs!* a third. *Confused and fill'd with murder and misdeeds!* a fourth. O, the muses! Is't not excellent? Is't not simply the best that ever you heard, captain? Ha! how do you like it?
BOBADILL. 'Tis good.

MATHEW. To thee, the purest object to my sense,

The most refined essence heaven covers,
Send I these lines, wherein I do commence
The happy state of turtle-billing lovers.
If they prove rough, unpolish'd, harsh, and rude,
Haste made the waste: thus mildly I conclude.

BOBADILL. Nay, proceed, proceed. Where's this?

MATHEW. This, sir! a toy of mine own, in my non-age; the infancy of my muses. But when will you come and see my study? good faith, I can shew you some very good things I have done of late.— That boot becomes your leg passing well, captain, methinks.

BOBADILL. So, so; it's the fashion gentlemen now use.

MATHEW. Troth, captain, and now you speak of the fashion, master Wellbred's elder brother and I are fallen out exceedingly: This other day, I happened to enter into some discourse of a hanger, which, I assure you, both for fashion and workmanship, was most peremptory beautiful and gentlemanlike: yet he condemned, and cried it down for the most pied and ridiculous that ever he saw.

BOBADILL. Squire Downright, the half-brother, was't not?

MATHEW. Ay, sir, he.

BOBADILL. Hang him, rook! he! why he has no more judgment than a malt-horse: By St. George, I wonder you'd lose a thought upon such an animal; the most peremptory absurd clown of Christendom, this day, he is holden. I protest to you, as I am a gentleman and a soldier, I ne'er changed with his like. By his discourse, he should eat nothing but hay; he was born for the manger, pannier, or pack-saddle. He has not so much as a good phrase in his belly, but all old iron and rusty proverbs: a good commodity for some smith to make hob-nails of.

MATHEW. Ay, and he thinks to carry it away with his manhood still, where he comes; he brags he will give me the bastinado, as I hear.

BOBADILL. How! he the bastinado! how came he by that word, trow?

MATHEW. Nay, indeed, he said cudgel me; I termed it so, for my more grace.

BOBADILL. That may be: for I was sure it was none of his word; but when, when said he so?

MATHEW. Faith, yesterday, they say; a young gallant, a friend of mine, told me so.

BOBADILL. By the foot of Pharaoh, an 'twere my case now, I should send him a chartel presently. The bastinado! a most proper and sufficient dependence, warranted by the great Caranza. Come hither, you shall chartel him; I'll shew you a trick or two you shall kill him with at pleasure; the first stoccata, if you will, by this air.

MATHEW. Indeed, you have absolute knowledge in the mystery, I have heard, sir.

BOBADILL. Of whom, of whom, have you heard it, I beseech you?

MATHEW. Troth, I have heard it spoken of divers, that you have very rare, and un-in-one-breath-utterable skill, sir.

BOBADILL. By heaven, no, not I; no skill in the earth; some small rudiments in the science, as to know my time, distance, or so. I have professed it more for noblemen and gentlemen's use, than mine own practice, I assure you.—Hostess, accommodate us with another bed-staff here quickly. Lend us another bed-staff—the woman does not understand the words of action.—Look you, sir: exalt not your point above this state, at any hand, and let your poniard maintain your defence, thus:—give it the gentleman, and leave us. [Exit TIB.] So, sir. Come on: O, twine your body more about, that you may fall to a more sweet, comely, gentlemanlike guard; so! indifferent: hollow your body more, sir, thus: now, stand fast o' your left leg, note your distance, keep your due proportion of time—oh, you disorder your point most irregularly.

MATHEW. How is the bearing of it now, sir?

BOBADILL. O, out of measure ill: a well-experienced hand would pass upon you at pleasure.

MATHEW. How mean you, sir, pass upon me?

BOBADILL. Why, thus, sir,—make a thrust at me—[MASTER MATHEW *pushes at* BOBADILL.] come in upon the answer, control your point, and make a full career at the body: The best-practised gallants of the time name it the passado; a most desperate thrust, believe it.

MATHEW. Well, come, sir.

BOBADILL. Why, you do not manage your weapon with any facility or grace to invite me. I have no spirit to play with you; your dearth of judgment renders you tedious.

MATHEW. But one venue, sir.

BOBADILL. Venue! fie; the most gross denomination as ever I heard: O, the stoccata, while you live, sir; note that.— Come, put on your cloke, and we'll go to some private place where you are acquainted; some tavern, or so—and have a bit. I'll send for one of these fencers, and he shall breathe you, by my direction; and then I will teach you your trick: you shall kill him with it at the first, if you please. Why, I will learn you, by the true judgment of the eye, hand, and foot, to control any enemy's point in the world. Should your adversary confront you with a pistol, 'twere nothing, by this hand! you should, by the same rule, control his bullet, in a line, except it were hail shot, and spread. What money have you about you, master Mathew?

MATHEW. Faith, I have not past a two shilling or so.

BOBADILL. 'Tis somewhat with the least; but come; we will have a bunch of radish and salt to taste our wine, and a pipe of tobacco to close the orifice of the stomach: and then we'll call upon young Wellbred: perhaps we shall meet the Corydon his brother there, and put him to the question.

ACT II

SCENE I—*The Old Jewry. A hall in* KITELY'S *house.*

[*Enter* KITELY, CASH, *and* DOWNRIGHT.]

KITELY. Thomas, come hither.
There lies a note within upon my desk;
Here take my key: it is no matter neither.—
Where is the boy?

CASH. Within, sir, in the warehouse.

KITELY. Let him tell over straight
that Spanish gold,
And weigh it, with the pieces of eight. Do you
See the delivery of those silver stuffs
To Master Lucar: tell him, if he will,
He shall have the grograns, at the rate I told him,
And I will meet him on the Exchange anon.

CASH. Good sir. [*Exit.*]

KITELY. Do you see that fellow, brother Downright?

DOWNRIGHT. Ay, what of him?

KITELY. He is a jewel, brother.
I took him of a child up at my door,
And christen'd him, gave him mine own name, Thomas:
Since bred him at the Hospital; where proving
A toward imp, I call'd him home, and taught him
So much, as I have made him my cashier,
And giv'n him, who had none, a surname, Cash:
And find him in his place so full of faith,
That I durst trust my life into his hands.

DOWNRIGHT. So would not I in any bastard's, brother,
As it is like he is, although I knew
Myself his father. But you said you had somewhat
To tell me, gentle brother: what is't, what is't?

KITELY. Faith, I am very loath to utter it,
As fearing it may hurt your patience:
But that I know your judgment is of strength,
Against the nearness of affection—

DOWNRIGHT. What need this circumstance? pray you, be direct.

KITELY. I will not say how much I do ascribe
Unto your friendship, nor in what regard
I hold your love; but let my past behaviour,
And usage of your sister, [both] confirm
How well I have been affected to your—

DOWNRIGHT. You are too tedious; come to the matter, the matter.

KITELY. Then, without further ceremony, thus.
My brother Wellbred, sir, I know not how,
Of late is much declined in what he was,
And greatly alter'd in his disposition.
When he came first to lodge here in my house,
Ne'er trust me if I were not proud of him:
Methought he bare himself in such a fashion,
So full of man, and sweetness in his carriage,
And what was chief, it shew'd not borrow'd in him,
But all he did became him as his own,
And seem'd as perfect, proper, and possest,
As breath with life, or colour with the blood.
But now, his course is so irregular,
So loose, affected, and deprived of grace,
And he himself withal so far fallen off
From that first place, as scarce no note remains,
To tell men's judgments where he lately stood.
He's grown a stranger to all due respect,
Forgetful of his friends; and not content
To stale himself in all societies,
He makes my house here common as a mart,
A theatre, a public receptacle
For giddy humour, and deceased riot;
And here, as in a tavern or a stews,
He and his wild associates spend their hours,
In repetition of lascivious jests,
Swear, leap, drink, dance, and revel night by night,
Control my servants; and, indeed, what not?

DOWNRIGHT. 'Sdeins, I know not what I should say to him, in the whole world!
He values me at a crack'd three-farthings, for aught I see. It will never out of the flesh that's bred in the bone. I have told him enough, one would think, if that would serve; but counsel to him is as good as a shoulder of mutton to a sick horse. Well! he knows what to trust to, for George: let him spend, and spend, and domineer, till his heart ake; and he think to be relieved by me, when he is got into one o' your city pounds, the counters, he has the wrong sow by the ear, i'faith; and claps his dish at the wrong man's door: I'll lay my hand on my halfpenny, ere I part with it to fetch him out, I'll assure him.

KITELY. Nay, good brother, let it not trouble you thus.

DOWNRIGHT. 'Sdeath! he mads me; I could eat my very spur-leathers for anger! But, why are you so tame? why do you not speak to him, and tell him how he disquiets your house?

KITELY. O, there are divers reasons to dissuade me.
But, would yourself vouchsafe to travail in it
(Though but with plain and easy circumstance),
It would both come much better to his sense,
And savour less of stomach, or of passion.
You are his elder brother, and that title
Both gives and warrants your authority,
Which, by your presence seconded, must breed
A kind of duty in him, and regard:
Whereas, if I should intimate the least,
It would but add contempt to his neglect,
Heap worse on ill, make up a pile of hatred,
That in the rearing would come tottering down,
And in the ruin bury all our love.
Nay, more than this, brother; if I should speak,

He would be ready, from his heat of humour,
And overflowing of the vapour in him,
To blow the ears of his familiars
With the false breath of telling what disgraces,
And low disparagements, I had put upon him.
Whilst they, sir, to relieve him in the fable,
Make their loose comments upon every word,
Gesture, or look, I use; mock me all over,
From my flat cap unto my shining shoes;
And, out of their impetuous rioting phant'sies,
Beget some slander that shall dwell with me.
And what would that be, think you? marry, this:
They would give out, because my wife is fair,
Myself but lately married, and my sister
Here sojourning a virgin in my house,
That I were jealous!—nay, as sure as death,
That they would say: and, how that I had quarrell'd
My brother purposely, thereby to find
An apt pretext to banish them my house.
DOWNRIGHT. Mass, perhaps so; they're like enough to do it.
KITELY. Brother, they would, believe it; so should I,
Like one of these penurious quack-salvers,
But set the bills up to mine own disgrace,
And try experiments upon myself;
Lend scorn and envy opportunity
To stab my reputation and good name—

[*Enter* MASTER MATHEW *struggling with* BOBADILL.]

MATHEW. I will speak to him.
BOBADILL. Speak to him! away! By the foot of Pharaoh, you shall not! you shall not do him that grace.—The time of day to you, gentleman o' the house. Is master Wellbred stirring?

DOWNRIGHT. How then? what should he do?
BOBADILL. Gentleman of the house, it is to you: is he within, sir?
KITELY. He came not to his lodging to-night, sir, I assure you.
DOWNRIGHT. Why, do you hear? you!
BOBADILL. The gentleman citizen hath satisfied me;
I'll talk to no scavenger. [*Exeunt* BOBADILL *and* MATHEW.]
DOWNRIGHT. How! scavenger! stay, sir, stay!
KITELY. Nay, brother Downright.
DOWNRIGHT. 'Heart! stand you away, an you love me.
KITELY. You shall not follow him now, I pray you, brother, good faith you shall not; I will overrule you.
DOWNRIGHT. Ha! scavenger! well, go to, I say little: but, by this good day (God forgive me I should swear), if I put it up so, say I am the rankest cow that ever pist. 'Sdeins, an I swallow this, I'll ne'er draw my sword in the sight of Fleet-street again while I live; I'll sit in a barn with madge-howlet, and catch mice first. Scavenger! heart!—and I'll go near to fill that huge tumbrel-slop of yours with somewhat, an I have good luck: your Garagantua breech cannot carry it away so.
KITELY. Oh, do not fret yourself thus: never think on't.
DOWNRIGHT. These are my brother's consorts, these! these are his camerades, his walking mates! he's a gallant, a cavaliero too, right hangman cut! Let me not live, an I could not find in my heart to swinge the whole gang of 'em, one after another, and begin with him first. I am grieved it should be said he is my brother, and take these courses: Well, as he brews, so shall he drink, for George, again. Yet he shall hear on't, and that tightly too, an I live, i'faith.
KITELY. But, brother, let your reprehension, then,
Run in an easy current, not o'er high
Carried with rashness, or devouring choler;

But rather use the soft persuading way,
Whose powers will work more gently, and
    compose
The imperfect thoughts you labour to re-
    claim;
More winning, than enforcing the consent.
DOWNRIGHT. Ay, ay, let me alone for
that, I warrant you.
KITELY. How now! [*Bell rings.*] Oh,
    the bell rings to breakfast.
Brother, I pray you go in, and bear my
    wife company till I come;
I'll but give order for some despatch of
    business to my servants.
                [*Exit* DOWNRIGHT.]

[*Enter* COB, *with his tankard.*]
KITELY. What, Cob! our maids will
have you by the back, i'faith, for coming
so late this morning.
COB. Perhaps so, sir; take heed some-
body have not them by the belly, for
walking so late in the evening.   [*Exit.*]
KITELY. Well; yet my troubled spirit's
    somewhat eased,
Though not reposed in that security
As I could wish: but I must be content,
Howe'er I set a face on't to the world.
Would I had lost this finger at a venture,
So Wellbred had ne'er lodged within my
    house.
Why't cannot be, where there is such
    resort
Of wanton gallants, and young revellers,
That any woman should be honest long.
Is't like, that factious beauty will pre-
    serve
The public weal of chastity unshaken,
When such strong motives muster, and
    make head
Against her single peace? No, no: beware.
When mutual appetite doth meet to treat,
And spirits of one kind and quality
Come once to parley in the pride of blood,
It is no slow conspiracy that follows.
Well, to be plain, if I but thought the
    time
Had answer'd their affections, all the
    world
Should not persuade me but I were a
    cuckold.

Marry, I hope they have not got that
    start;
For opportunity hath balk'd them yet,
And shall do still, while I have eyes and
    ears
To attend the impositions of my heart.
My presence shall be as an iron bar,
'Twixt the conspiring motions of de-
    sire:
Yea, every look or glance mine eye ejects
Shall check occasion, as one doth his
    slave,
When he forgets the limits of prescription.

[*Enter* DAME KITELY *and* BRIDGET.]
DAME KITELY. Sister Bridget, pray you
fetch down the rose-water, above in the
closet.   [*Exit* BRIDGET.]
—Sweet-heart, will you come in to break-
fast?
KITELY. An she have overheard me
now!—
DAME KITELY. I pray thee, good muss,
we stay for you.
KITELY. By heaven, I would not for a
thousand angels.
DAME KITELY. What ail you, sweet-
heart? are you not well? speak, good
muss.
KITELY. Troth my head akes extremely
on a sudden.
DAME KITELY [*putting her hand to his
forehead*]. O, the Lord!
KITELY. How now! What?
DAME KITELY. Alas, how it burns!
Muss, keep you warm; good truth it is
this new disease, there's a number are
troubled withal. For love's sake, sweet-
heart, come in, out of the air.
KITELY. How simple, and how subtle
    are her answers!
A new disease, and many troubled with
    it?
Why true; she heard me, all the world to
    nothing.
DAME KITELY. I pray thee, good sweet-
heart, come in; the air will do you harm,
in troth.
KITELY. The air! she has me in the
wind.—Sweet-heart, I'll come to you pres-
ently; 'twill away, I hope.

DAME KITELY. Pray Heaven it do.
[*Exit.*]
KITELY. A new disease! I know not, new or old,
But it may well be call'd poor mortals' plague;
For, like a pestilence, it doth infect
The houses of the brain. First it begins
Solely to work upon the phantasy,
Filling her seat with such pestiferous air,
As soon corrupts the judgment; and from thence,
Sends like contagion to the memory:
Still each to other giving the infection.
Which as a subtle vapour spreads itself
Confusedly through every sensive part,
Till not a thought or motion in the mind
Be free from the black poison of suspect.
Ah! but what misery is it to know this?
Or, knowing it, to want the mind's erection
In such extremes? Well, I will once more strive,
In spite of this black cloud, myself to be,
And shake the fever off that thus shakes me. [*Exit.*]

SCENE II—*Moorfields.*

[*Enter* BRAINWORM *disguised like a maimed Soldier.*]

BRAINWORM. 'Slid, I cannot choose but laugh to see myself translated thus, from a poor creature to a creator; for now must I create an intolerable sort of lies, or my present profession loses the grace: and yet the lie, to a man of my coat, is as ominous a fruit as the fico. O, sir, it holds for good polity ever, to have that outwardly in vilest estimation, that inwardly is most dear to us: so much for my borrowed shape. Well, the troth is, my old master intends to follow my young master, dry-foot, over Moorfields to London, this morning; now, I knowing of this hunting-match, or rather conspiracy, and to insinuate with my young master (for so must we that are blue waiters, and men of hope and service do, or perhaps we may wear motley at the year's end, and who wears motley, you know),

have got me afore in this disguise, determining here to lie in ambuscado, and intercept him in the mid-way. If I can but get his cloke, his purse, and his hat, nay, any thing to cut him off, that is, to stay his journey, *Veni, vidi, vici,* I may say with captain Cæsar, I am made for ever, i'faith. Well, now I must practise to get the true garb of one of these lance-knights, my arm here, and my——Odso! my young master, and his cousin, master Stephen, as I am true counterfeit man of war, and no soldier!

[*Enter* EDWARD KNOWELL *and* STEPHEN.]

EDWARD KNOWELL. So, sir! and how then, coz?
STEPHEN. 'Sfoot! I have lost my purse, I think.
EDWARD KNOWELL. How! lost your purse? where? when had you it?
STEPHEN. I cannot tell; stay.
BRAINWORM. 'Slid, I am afraid they will know me: would I could get by them!
EDWARD KNOWELL. What, have you it?
STEPHEN. No; I think I was bewitched, I— [*Cries.*]
EDWARD KNOWELL. Nay, do not weep the loss: hang it, let it go.
STEPHEN. Oh, it's here: No, an it had been lost, I had not cared, but for a jet ring mistress Mary sent me.
EDWARD KNOWELL. A jet ring! O the poesie, the poesie?
STEPHEN. Fine, i'faith.—
Though Fancy sleep,
My love is deep.
Meaning, that though I did not fancy her, yet she loved me dearly.
EDWARD KNOWELL. Most excellent!
STEPHEN. And then I sent her another, and my poesie was,
The deeper the sweeter,
I'll be judg'd by St. Peter.
EDWARD KNOWELL. How, by St. Peter? I do not conceive that.
STEPHEN. Marry, St. Peter, to make up the metre.
EDWARD KNOWELL. Well, there the saint was your good patron, he help'd you at your need; thank him, thank him.

BRAINWORM. I cannot take leave on 'em so; I will venture, come what will. [*Comes forward.*] Gentlemen, please you change a few crowns for a very excellent blade here? I am a poor gentleman, a soldier, one that, in the better state of my fortunes, scorned so mean a refuge; but now it is the humour of necessity to have it so. You seem to be gentlemen well affected to martial men, else I should rather die with silence, than live with shame: however, vouchsafe to remember it is my want speaks, not myself; this condition agrees not with my spirit—

EDWARD KNOWELL. Where hast thou served?

BRAINWORM. May it please you, sir, in all the late wars of Bohemia, Hungary, Dalmatia, Poland, where not, sir? I have been a poor servitor by sea and land any time this fourteen years, and followed the fortunes of the best commanders in Christendom. I was twice shot at the taking of Aleppo, once at the relief of Vienna; I have been at Marseilles, Naples, and the Adriatic gulf, a gentleman-slave in the gallies, thrice; where I was most dangerously shot in the head, through both the thighs; and yet, being thus maimed, I am void of maintenance, nothing left me but my scars, the noted marks of my resolution.

STEPHEN. How will you sell this rapier, friend?

BRAINWORM. Generous sir, I refer it to your own judgment; you are a gentleman, give me what you please.

STEPHEN. True, I am a gentleman, I know that, friend; but what though! I pray you say, what would you ask?

BRAINWORM. I assure you, the blade may become the side or thigh of the best prince in Europe.

EDWARD KNOWELL. Ay, with a velvet scabbard, I think.

STEPHEN. Nay, an't be mine, it shall have a velvet scabbard, coz, that's flat; I'd not wear it, as it is, an you would give me an angel.

BRAINWORM. At your worship's pleasure, sir; nay, 'tis a most pure Toledo.

STEPHEN. I had rather it were a Spaniard. But tell me, what shall I give you for it? An it had a silver hilt—

EDWARD KNOWELL. Come, come, you shall not buy it: hold, there's a shilling, fellow; take thy rapier.

STEPHEN. Why, but I will buy it now, because you say so; and there's another shilling, fellow; I scorn to be out-bidden. What, shall I walk with a cudgel, like Higginbottom, and may have a rapier for money?

EDWARD KNOWELL. You may buy one in the city.

STEPHEN. Tut! I'll buy this i' the field, so I will: I have a mind to't, because 'tis a field rapier. Tell me your lowest price.

EDWARD KNOWELL. You shall not buy it, I say.

STEPHEN. By this money, but I will, though I give more than 'tis worth.

EDWARD KNOWELL. Come away, you are a fool.

STEPHEN. Friend, I am a fool, that's granted; but I'll have it, for that word's sake. Follow me for your money.

BRAINWORM. At your service, sir.

[*Exeunt.*]

SCENE III—*Another part of Moorfields.*

[*Enter* KNOWELL.]

KNOWELL. I cannot lose the thought yet of this letter,
Sent to my son; nor leave t' admire the change
Of manners, and the breeding of our youth
Within the kingdom, since myself was one.—
When I was young, he lived not in the stews
Durst have conceived a scorn, and utter'd it,
On a gray head; age was authority
Against a buffoon, and a man had then
A certain reverence paid unto his years,
That had none due unto his life: so much
The sanctity of some prevail'd for others.

But now we all are fallen; youth, from
    their fear,
And age, from that which bred it, good
    example.
Nay, would ourselves were not the first,
    even parents,
That did destroy the hopes in our own
    children;
Or they not learn'd our vices in their
    cradles,
And suck'd in our ill customs with their
    milk;
Ere all their teeth be born, or they can
    speak,
We make their palates cunning; the first
    words
We form their tongues with, are licentious
    jests:
Can it call whore? cry bastard? O, then,
    kiss it!
A witty child! can't swear? the father's
    darling!
Give it two plums. Nay, rather than't
    shall learn
No bawdy song, the mother herself will
    teach it!—
But this is in the infancy, the days
Of the long coat; when it puts on the
    breeches,
It will put off all this: Ay, it is like,
When it is gone into the bone already!
No, no; this dye goes deeper than the
    coat,
Or shirt, or skin; it stains into the
    liver,
And heart, in some: and, rather than it
    should not,
Note what we fathers do! look how we
    live!
What mistresses we keep! at what ex-
    pense,
In our sons' eyes! where they may handle
    our gifts,
Hear our lascivious courtships, see our
    dalliance,
Taste of the same provoking meats with
    us,
To ruin of our states! Nay, when our
    own
Portion is fled, to prey on the remainder,
We call them into fellowship of vice;

Bait 'em with the young chamber-maid, to
    seal,
And teach 'em all bad ways to buy afflic-
    tion.
This is one path: but there are millions
    more,
In which we spoil our own, with leading
    them.
Well, I thank heaven, I never yet was he
That travell'd with my son, before sixteen,
To shew him the Venetian courtezans;
Nor read the grammar of cheating I had
    made,
To my sharp boy, at twelve; repeating
    still
The rule, *Get money; still, get money,
    boy;*
*No matter by what means; money will do
More, boy, than my lord's letter.* Neither
    have I
Drest snails or mushrooms curiously be-
    fore him,
Perfumed my sauces, and taught him how
    to make them;
Preceding still, with my gray gluttony,
At all the ord'naries, and only fear'd
His palate should degenerate, not his man-
    ners.
These are the trade of fathers now; how-
    ever,
My son, I hope, hath met within my
    threshold
None of these household precedents,
    which are strong,
And swift, to rape youth to their precipice.
But let the house at home be ne'er so
    clean
Swept, or kept sweet from filth, nay dust
    and cobwebs,
If he will live abroad with his companions,
In dung and leystals, it is worth a fear;
Nor is the danger of conversing less
Than all that I have mention'd of 'exam-
    ple.

[*Enter* BRAINWORM, *disguised as before.*]
    BRAINWORM. My master! nay, faith,
have at you; I am flesh'd now, I have
sped so well. [*Aside.*] Worshipful sir,
I beseech you, respect the estate of a poor
soldier; I am ashamed of this base course

of life,—God's my comfort—but extremity provokes me to't: what remedy?

KNOWELL. I have not for you, now.

BRAINWORM. By the faith I bear unto truth, gentleman, it is no ordinary custom in me, but only to preserve manhood. I protest to you, a man I have been: a man I may be, by your sweet bounty.

KNOWELL. Pray thee, good friend, be satisfied.

BRAINWORM. Good sir, by that hand, you may do the part of a kind gentleman, in lending a poor soldier the price of two cans of beer, a matter of small value: the king of heaven shall pay you, and I shall rest thankful: Sweet worship—

KNOWELL. Nay, an you be so importunate—

BRAINWORM. Oh, tender sir! need will have its course: I was not made to this vile use. Well, the edge of the enemy could not have abated me so much: it's hard when a man hath served in his prince's cause, and be thus. [*Weeps.*] Honourable worship, let me derive a small piece of silver from you, it shall not be given in the course of time. By this good ground, I was fain to pawn my rapier last night for a poor supper; I had suck'd the hilts long before, I am a pagan else: Sweet honour—

KNOWELL. Believe me, I am taken with some wonder,
To think a fellow of thy outward presence,
Should, in the frame and fashion of his mind,
Be so degenerate, and sordid-base.
Art thou a man? and sham'st thou not to beg,
To practise such a servile kind of life?
Why, were thy education ne'er so mean,
Having thy limbs, a thousand fairer courses
Offer themselves to thy election.
Either the wars might still supply thy wants,
Or service of some virtuous gentleman,
Or honest labour; nay, what can I name,
But would become thee better than to beg:
But men of thy condition feed on sloth,

As doth the beetle on the dung she breeds in;
Nor caring how the metal of your minds
Is eaten with the rust of idleness.
Now, afore me, whate'er he be, that should
Relieve a person of thy quality,
While thou insist'st in this loose desperate course,
I would esteem the sin not thine, but his.

BRAINWORM. Faith, sir, I would gladly find some other course, if so—

KNOWELL. Ay,
You'd gladly find it, but you will not seek it.

BRAINWORM. Alas, sir, where should a man seek? in the wars, there's no ascent by desert in these days; but—and for service, would it were as soon purchased, as wished for! the air's my comfort.— [*Sighs.*]—I know what I would say.

KNOWELL. What's thy name?

BRAINWORM. Please you, Fitz-Sword, sir.

KNOWELL. Fitz-Sword!
Say that a man should entertain thee now,
Wouldst thou be honest, humble, just, and true?

BRAINWORM. Sir, by the place and honour of a soldier—

KNOWELL. Nay, nay, I like not these affected oaths; speak plainly, man, what think'st thou of my words?

BRAINWORM. Nothing, sir, but wish my fortunes were as happy as my service should be honest.

KNOWELL. Well, follow me; I'll prove thee, if thy deeds
Will carry a proportion to thy words.
[*Exit.*]

BRAINWORM. Yes, sir, straight; I'll but garter my hose. O that my belly were hoop'd now, for I am ready to burst with laughing! never was bottle or bagpipe fuller. 'Slid, was there ever seen a fox in years to betray himself thus! now shall I be possest of all his counsels; and, by that conduit, my young master. Well, he is resolved to prove my honesty; faith, and I'm resolved to prove his patience: Oh, I shall abuse him intolerably. This small piece of service will bring him clean out of love with the soldier for ever. He will never come within the sign of it, the sight of a cassock, or a musket-rest again. He will hate the musters at Mileend for it, to his dying day. It's no matter, let the world think me a bad counterfeit, if I cannot give him the slip at an instant: why, this is better than to have staid his journey: well, I'll follow him. Oh, how I long to be employed!

[*Exit* BRAINWORM.]

ACT III

SCENE I—*The Old Jewry. A room in the Windmill Tavern.*

[*Enter* MASTER MATHEW, WELLBRED, *and* BOBADILL.]

MATHEW. Yes, faith, sir, we were at your lodging to seek you too.

WELLBRED. Oh, I came not there tonight.

BOBADILL. Your brother delivered us as much.

WELLBRED. Who, my brother Downright?

BOBADILL. He. Mr. Wellbred, I know not in what kind you hold me; but let me say to you this: as sure as honour, I esteem it so much out of the sunshine of reputation, to throw the least beam of regard upon such a—

WELLBRED. Sir, I must hear no ill words of my brother.

BOBADILL. I protest to you, as I have a thing to be saved about me, I never saw any gentlemanlike part—

WELLBRED. Good captain, faces about to some other discourse.

BOBADILL. With your leave, sir, an there were no more men living upon the face of the earth, I should not fancy him, by St. George!

MATHEW. Troth, nor I; he is of a rustical cut, I know not how: he doth not carry himself like a gentleman of fashion.

WELLBRED. Oh, master Mathew, that's

a grace peculiar but to a few, *quos æquus amavit Jupiter.*

MATHEW. I understand you, sir.

WELLBRED. No question, you do,—or do you not, sir.

[*Enter* EDWARD KNOWELL *and* MASTER STEPHEN.]

Ned Knowell! by my soul, welcome: how dost thou, sweet spirit, my genius? 'Slid, I shall love Apollo and the mad Thespian girls the better, while I live, for this, my dear Fury; now, I see there's some love in thee. Sirrah, these be the two I writ to thee of: nay, what a drowsy humour in this now! why dost thou not speak?

EDWARD KNOWELL. Oh, you are a fine gallant; you sent me a rare letter.

WELLBRED. Why, was't not rare?

EDWARD KNOWELL. Yes, I'll be sworn, I was ne'er guilty of reading the like: match it in all Pliny, or Symmachus's epistles, and I'll have my judgment burn'd in the ear for a rogue: make much of thy vein, for it is inimitable. But I marle what camel it was, that had the carriage of it; for, doubtless, he was no ordinary beast that brought it.

WELLBRED. Why?

EDWARD KNOWELL. Why, say'st thou! why, dost thou think that any reasonable creature, especially in the morning, the sober time of the day too, could have mistaken my father for me?

WELLBRED. 'Slid, you jest, I hope.

EDWARD KNOWELL. Indeed, the best use we can turn it to, is to make a jest on't, now: but I'll assure you, my father had the full view of your flourishing style some hour before I saw it.

WELLBRED. What a dull slave was this! but, sirrah, what said he to it, i'faith?

EDWARD KNOWELL. Nay, I know not what he said; but I have a shrewd guess what he thought.

WELLBRED. What, what?

EDWARD KNOWELL. Marry, that thou art some strange, dissolute young fellow, and I—a grain or two better, for keeping thee company.

WELLBRED. Tut! that thought is like the moon in her last quarter, 'twill change shortly: but, sirrah, I pray thee be acquainted with my two hang-by's here; thou wilt take exceeding pleasure in them if thou hear'st 'em once go; my wind-instruments; I'll wind them up——But what strange piece of silence is this, the sign of the Dumb Man?

EDWARD KNOWELL. Oh, sir, a kinsman of mine, one that may make your music the fuller, an he please; he has his humour, sir.

WELLBRED. Oh, what is't, what is't?

EDWARD KNOWELL. Nay, I'll neither do your judgment nor his folly that wrong, as to prepare your apprehension: I'll leave him to the mercy of your search; if you can take him, so!

WELLBRED. Well, captain Bobadill, master Mathew, pray you know this gentleman here; he is a friend of mine, and one that will deserve your affection. I know not your name, sir, [to STEPHEN.] but I shall be glad of any occasion to render me more familiar to you.

STEPHEN. My name is master Stephen, sir; I am this gentleman's own cousin, sir; his father is mine uncle, sir: I am somewhat melancholy, but you shall command me, sir, in whatsoever is incident to a gentleman.

BOBADILL. Sir, I must tell you this, I am no general man; but for master Wellbred's sake, (you may embrace it at what height of favour you please,) I do communicate with you, and conceive you to be a gentleman of some parts; I love few words.

EDWARD KNOWELL. And I fewer, sir; I have scarce enough to thank you.

MATHEW. But are you, indeed, sir, so given to it?

STEPHEN. Ay, truly, sir, I am mightily given to melancholy.

MATHEW. Oh, it's your only fine humour, sir: your true melancholy breeds your perfect fine wit, sir. I am melancholy myself, diver times, sir, and then do I no more but take pen and paper, presently, and overflow you half a score, or a dozen of sonnets at a sitting.

EDWARD KNOWELL. Sure he utters them then by the gross. [Aside.]

STEPHEN. Truly, sir, and I love such things out of measure.

EDWARD KNOWELL. I'faith, better than in measure, I'll undertake.

MATHEW. Why, I pray you, sir, make use of my study, it's at your service.

STEPHEN. I thank you, sir, I shall be bold I warrant you; have you a stool there to be melancholy upon?

MATHEW. That I have, sir, and some papers there of mine own doing, at idle hours, that you'll say there's some sparks of wit in 'em, when you see them.

WELLBRED. Would the sparks would kindle once, and become a fire amongst them! I might see self-love burnt for her heresy. [Aside.]

STEPHEN. Cousin, is it well? am I melancholy enough?

EDWARD KNOWELL. Oh ay, excellent.

WELLBRED. Captain Bobadill, why muse you so?

EDWARD KNOWELL. He is melancholy too.

BOBADILL. Faith, sir, I was thinking of a most honourable piece of service, was performed to-morrow, being St. Mark's day, shall be some ten years now.

EDWARD KNOWELL. In what place, captain?

BOBADILL. Why, at the beleaguering of Strigonium, where, in less than two hours, seven hundred resolute gentlemen, as any were in Europe, lost their lives upon the breach. I'll tell you, gentlemen, it was the first, but the best leaguer that ever I beheld with these eyes, except the taking in of—what do you call it? last year, by the Genoways; but that, of all other, was the most fatal and dangerous exploit that ever I was ranged in, since I first bore arms before the face of the enemy, as I am a gentleman and a soldier!

STEPHEN. So! I had as lief as an angel I could swear as well as that gentleman.

EDWARD KNOWELL. Then, you were a

servitor at both, it seems; at Strigonium, and what do you call't?

BOBADILL. O lord, sir! By St. George, I was the first man that entered the breach; and had I not effected it with resolution, I had been slain if I had had a million of lives.

EDWARD KNOWELL. 'Twas pity you had not ten; a cat's and your own, i'faith. But, was it possible?

MATHEW. Pray you mark this discourse, sir.

STEPHEN. So I do.

BOBADILL. I assure you, upon my reputation, 'tis true, and yourself shall confess.

EDWARD KNOWELL. You must bring me to the rack, first.   [*Aside.*]

BOBADILL. Observe me judicially, sweet sir; they had planted me three demiculverins just in the mouth of the breach; now, sir, as we were to give on, their master-gunner [a man of no mean skill and mark, you must think,) confronts me with his linstock, ready to give fire; I, spying his intendment, discharged my petronel in his bosom, and with these single arms, my poor rapier, ran violently upon the Moors that guarded the ordnance, and put them pell-mell to the sword.

WELLBRED. To the sword! To the rapier, captain.

EDWARD KNOWELL. Oh, it was a good figure observed, sir: but did you all this, captain, without hurting your blade?

BOBADILL. Without any impeach o' the earth: you shall perceive, sir. [*Shews his rapier.*] It is the most fortunate weapon that ever rid on poor gentleman's thigh. Shall I tell you, sir? You talk of Morglay, Excalibur, Durindana, or so; tut! I lend no credit to that is fabled of 'em: I know the virtue of mine own, and therefore I dare the boldlier maintain it.

STEPHEN. I marle whether it be a Toledo or no.

BOBADILL. A most perfect Toledo, I assure you, sir.

STEPHEN. I have a countryman of his here.

MATHEW. Pray you, let's see, sir; yes, faith, it is.

BOBADILL. This a Toledo! Pish!

STEPHEN. Why do you pish, captain?

BOBADILL. A Fleming, by heaven! I'll buy them for a guilder a-piece, an I would have a thousand of them.

EDWARD KNOWELL. How say you, cousin? I told you thus much.

WELLBRED. Where bought you it, master Stephen?

STEPHEN. Of a scurvy rogue soldier: a hundred of lice go with him! He swore it was a Toledo.

BOBADILL. A poor provant rapier, no better.

MATHEW. Mass, I think it be indeed, now I look on't better.

EDWARD KNOWELL. Nay, the longer you look on't, the worse. Put it up, put it up.

STEPHEN. Well, I will put it up; but by—I have forgot the captain's oath, I thought to have sworn by it—an e'er I meet him—

WELLBRED. O, it is past help now, sir; you must have patience.

STEPHEN. Whoreson, coney-hatching rascal! I could eat the very hilts for anger.

EDWARD KNOWELL. A sign of good digestion; you have an ostrich stomach, cousin.

STEPHEN. A stomach! would I had him here, you should see an I had a stomach.

WELLBRED. It's better as it is.—Come, gentlemen, shall we go?

[*Enter* BRAINWORM, *disguised as before.*]

EDWARD KNOWELL. A miracle, cousin; look here, look here!

STEPHEN. Oh—'Od's lid. By your leave, do you know me, sir?

BRAINWORM. Ay, sir, I know you by sight.

STEPHEN. You sold me a rapier, did you not?

BRAINWORM. Yes, marry did I, sir.

STEPHEN. You said it was a Toledo, ha?

BRAINWORM. True, I did so.

STEPHEN. But it is none.

BRAINWORM. No, sir, I confess it; it is none.

STEPHEN. Do you confess it? Gentlemen, bear witness, he has confest it:— 'Od's will, an you had not confest it—

EDWARD KNOWELL. Oh, cousin, forbear, forbear!

STEPHEN. Nay, I have done, cousin.

WELLBRED. Why, you have done like a gentleman; he has confest it, what would you more?

STEPHEN. Yet, by his leave, he is a rascal, under his favour, do you see.

EDWARD KNOWELL. Ay, by his leave, he is, and under favour: a pretty piece of civility! Sirrah, how dost thou like him?

WELLBRED. Oh, it's a most precious fool, make much on him: I can compare him to nothing more happily than a drum; for every one may play upon him.

EDWARD KNOWELL. No, no, a child's whistle were far the fitter.

BRAINWORM. Shall I intreat a word with you?

EDWARD KNOWELL. With me, sir? you have not another Toledo to sell, have you?

BRAINWORM. You are conceited, sir: Your name is Master Knowell, as I take it?

EDWARD KNOWELL. You are in the right; you mean not to proceed in the catechism, do you?

BRAINWORM. No, sir; I am none of that coat.

EDWARD KNOWELL. Of as bare a coat, though: well, say, sir.

BRAINWORM [taking EDWARD KNOWELL aside]. Faith, sir, I am but servant to the drum extraordinary, and indeed, this smoky varnish being washed off, and three or four patches removed, I appear your worship's in reversion, after the decease of your good father, Brainworm.

EDWARD KNOWELL. Brainworm! 'Slight, what breath of a conjurer hath blown thee hither in this shape?

BRAINWORM. The breath of your letter, sir, this morning; the same that blew you to the Windmill, and your father after you.

EDWARD KNOWELL. My father!

BRAINWORM. Nay, never start, 'tis true; he has followed you over the fields by the foot, as you would do a hare in the snow.

EDWARD KNOWELL. Sirrah Wellbred, what shall we do, sirrah? my father is come over after me.

WELLBRED. Thy father! Where is he?

BRAINWORM. At justice Clement's house, in Coleman-street, where he but stays my return; and then—

WELLBRED. Who's this? Brainworm!

BRAINWORM. The same, sir.

WELLBRED. Why how, in the name of wit, com'st thou transmuted thus?

BRAINWORM. Faith, a device, a device; nay, for the love of reason, gentlemen, and avoiding the danger, stand not here; withdraw, and I'll tell you all.

WELLBRED. But art thou sure he will stay thy return?

BRAINWORM. Do I live, sir? what a question is that!

WELLBRED. We'll prorogue his expectation, then, a little: Brainworm, thou shalt go with us.—Come on, gentlemen.—Nay, I pray thee, sweet Ned, droop not; 'heart, an our wits be so wretchedly dull, that one old plodding brain can outstrip us all, would we were e'en prest to make porters of, and serve out the remnant of our days in Thames-street, or at Custom-house key, in a civil war against the carmen!

BRAINWORM. Amen, amen, amen, say I. [Exeunt.]

SCENE II—The Old Jewry. KITELY'S warehouse.

[Enter KITELY and CASH.]

KITELY. What says he, Thomas? did you speak with him?

CASH. He will expect you, sir, within this half hour.

KITELY. Has he the money ready, can you tell?

CASH. Yes, sir, the money was brought in last night.

KITELY. O, that is well; fetch me my cloak, my cloak!— [*Exit* CASH.]
Stay, let me see, an hour to go and come;
Ay, that will be the least; and then 'twill be
An hour before I can dispatch with him,
Or very near; well, I will say two hours.
Two hours! ha! things never dreamt of yet,
May be contrived, ay, and effected too,
In two hours' absence; well, I will not go.
Two hours! No, fleering Opportunity,
I will not give your subtilty that scope.
Who will not judge him worthy to be robb'd,
That sets his doors wide open to a thief,
And shews the felon where his treasure lies?
Again, what earthly spirit but will attempt
To taste the fruit of beauty's golden tree,
When leaden sleep seals up the dragon's eyes?
I will not go. Business, *go by* for once.
No, beauty, no; you are of too good caract,
To be left so, without a guard, or open.
Your lustre, too, 'll inflame at any distance,
Draw courtship to you, as a jet doth straws;
Put motion in a stone, strike fire from ice,
Nay, make a porter leap you with his burden.
You must be then kept up, close, and well watch'd,
For, give you opportunity, no quick-sand
Devours or swallows swifter! He that lends
His wife, if she be fair, or time or place,
Compels her to be false. I will not go!
The dangers are too many;—and then the dressing
Is a most main attractive! Our great heads
Within this city never were in safety
Since our wives wore these little caps:
I'll change 'em;

I'll change 'em straight in mine: mine shall no more
Wear three-piled acorns, to make my horns ake.
Nor will I go; I am resolved for that.

[*Reënter* CASH *with a cloak.*]

Carry in my cloak again. Yet stay. Yet do, too:
I will defer going, on all occasions.
   CASH. Sir, Snare, your scrivener, will be there with the bonds.
   KITELY. That's true: fool on me! I had clean forgot it;
I must go. What's a clock?
   CASH.   Exchange-time, sir.
   KITELY. 'Heart, then will Wellbred presently be here too,
With one or other of his loose consorts.
I am a knave, if I know what to say,
What course to take, or which way to resolve.
My brain, methinks, is like an hour-glass,
Wherein my imaginations run like sands,
Filling up time; but then are turn'd and turn'd:
So that I know not what to stay upon,
And less, to put in act.—It shall be so.
Nay, I dare build upon his secrecy,
He knows not to deceive me.—Thomas!
   CASH.   Sir.
   KITELY. Yet now I have bethought me too, I will not.—
Thomas, is Cob within?
   CASH.   I think he be, sir.
   KITELY. But he'll prate too, there is no speech of him.
No, there were no man on the earth to Thomas,
If I durst trust him; there is all the doubt.
But should he have a clink in him, I were gone.
Lost in my fame for ever, talk for th' Exchange!
The manner he hath stood with, till this present,
Doth promise no such change: what should I fear then?
Well, come what will, I'll tempt my fortune once.

Thomas—you may deceive me, but, I hope—
Your love to me is more—

CASH. Sir, if a servant's
Duty, with faith, may be call'd love, you are
More than in hope, you are possess'd of it.

KITELY. I thank you heartily, Thomas: give me your hand:
With all my heart, good Thomas. I have, Thomas,
A secret to impart unto you—but,
When once you have it, I must seal your lips up;
So far I tell you, Thomas.

CASH. Sir, for that—

KITELY. Nay, hear me out. Think I esteem you, Thomas,
When I will let you in thus to my private.
It is a thing sits nearer to my crest,
Than thou art 'ware of, Thomas; if thou should'st
Reveal it, but—

CASH. How, I reveal it?

KITELY. Nay,
I do not think thou would'st; but if thou should'st,
'Twere a great weakness.

CASH. A great treachery:
Give it no other name.

KITELY. Thou wilt not do't, then?

CASH. Sir, if I do, mankind disclaim me ever!

KITELY. He will not swear, he has some reservation,
Some conceal'd purpose, and close meaning sure;
Else, being urg'd so much, how should he choose
But lend an oath to all this protestation?
He's no precisian, that I'm certain of,
Nor rigid Roman Catholic: he'll play
At fayles, and tick-tack; I have heard him swear.
What should I think of it? urge him again,
And by some other way! I will do so.
Well, Thomas, thou hast sworn not to disclose:—
Yes, you did swear?

CASH. Not yet, sir, but I will,
Please you—

KITELY. No, Thomas, I dare take thy word,
But, if thou wilt swear, do as thou think'st good;
I am resolv'd without it; at thy pleasure.

CASH. By my soul's safety then, sir, I protest,
My tongue shall ne'er take knowledge of a word
Deliver'd me in nature of your trust.

KITELY. It is too much; these ceremonies need not:
I know thy faith to be as firm as rock.
Thomas, come hither, near; we cannot be
Too private in this business. So it is,—
Now he has sworn, I dare the safelier venture. [Aside.]
I have of late, by divers observations—
But whether his oath can bind him, yea, or no,
Being not taken lawfully? ha! say you?
I will ask council ere I do proceed:— [Aside.]
Thomas, it will be now too long to stay,
I'll spy some fitter time soon, or to-morrow.

CASH. Sir, at your pleasure.

KITELY. I will think:—and, Thomas,
I pray you search the books 'gainst my return,
For the receipts 'twixt me and Traps.

CASH. I will, sir.

KITELY. And hear you, if your mistress's brother, Wellbred,
Chance to bring hither any gentleman,
Ere I come back, let one straight bring me word.

CASH. Very well, sir.

KITELY. To the Exchange, do you hear?
Or here in Coleman-street, to justice Clement's.
Forget it not, nor be not out of the way.

CASH. I will not, sir.

KITELY. I pray you have a care on't.
Or, whether he come or no, if any other,
Stranger, or else; fail not to send me word.

CASH. I shall not, sir.

KITELY.   Be it your special business
Now to remember it.

CASH.   Sir, I warrant you.

KITELY. But, Thomas, this is not the
    secret, Thomas,

I told you of.

CASH.   No, sir: I do suppose it.

KITELY. Believe me, it is not.

CASH.   Sir, I do believe you.

KITELY. By heaven it is not, that's
    enough; but, Thomas,

I would not you should utter it, do you
    see,

To any creature living; yet I care not.

Well, I must hence. Thomas, conceive
    thus much;

It was a trial of you, when I meant

So deep a secret to you, I mean not this,

But that I have to tell you; this is noth-
    ing, this.

But, Thomas, keep this from my wife, I
    charge you,

Lock'd up in silence, midnight, buried
    here.—

No greater hell than to be slave to fear.

                                    [*Exit.*]

CASH. *Lock'd up in silence, midnight,
    buried here!*

Whence should this flood of passion, trow,
    take head? ha!

Best dream no longer of this running
    humour,

For fear I sink; the violence of the stream

Already hath transported me so far,

That I can feel no ground at all: but
    soft—

Oh, 'tis our water-bearer: somewhat has
    crost him now.

[*Enter* COB, *hastily.*]

COB. Fasting-days! what tell you me of
fasting-days? 'Slid, would they were all
on a light fire for me! they say the whole
world shall be consumed with fire one day,
but would I had these Ember-weeks and
villanous Fridays burnt in the mean time,
and then—

CASH. Why, how now, Cob? what moves
thee to this choler, ha?

COB. Collar, master Thomas! I scorn
your collar, I, sir; I am none o' your

cart-horse, though I carry and draw water.
An you offer to ride me with your collar
or halter either, I may hap shew you a
jade's trick, sir.

CASH. O, you'll slip your head out of
the collar? why, goodman Cob, you mis-
take me.

COB. Nay, I have my rheum, and I can
be angry as well as another, sir.

CASH. Thy rheum, Cob! thy humour,
thy humour—thou mistak'st.

COB. Humour! mack, I think it be so
indeed; what is that humour? some rare
thing, I warrant.

CASH. Marry I'll tell thee, Cob: it is a
gentlemanlike monster, bred in the special
gallantry of our time, by affectation; and
fed by folly.

COB. How! must it be fed?

CASH. Oh ay, humour is nothing if it
be not fed: didst thou never hear that?
it's a common phrase, *feed my humour.*

COB. I'll none on it: humour, avaunt!
I know you not, be gone! let who will
make hungry meals for your monstership,
it shall not be I. Feed you, quoth he!
'slid, I have much ado to feed myself;
especially on these lean rascally days too;
an't had been any other day but a fasting-
day—a plague on them all for me! By
this light, one might have done the com-
monwealth good service, and have drown'd
them all in the flood, two or three hundred
thousand years ago. O, I do stomach them
hugely. I have a maw now, and 'twere for
sir Bevis his horse, against them.

CASH. I pray thee, good Cob, what
makes thee so out of love with fasting
days?

COB. Marry, that which will make any
man out of love with 'em, I think; their
bad conditions, an you will needs know.
First, they are of a Flemish breed, I am
sure on't, for they raven up more butter
than all the days of the week beside; next,
they stink of fish and leek-porridge miser-
ably; thirdly, they'll keep a man devoutly
hungry all day, and at night send him
supperless to bed.

CASH. Indeed, these are faults, Cob.

COB. Nay, an this were all, 'twere

something; but they are the only known enemies to my generation. A fasting-day no sooner comes, but my lineage goes to wrack; poor cobs! they smoak for it, they are made martyrs o' the gridiron, they melt in passion: and your maids to know this, and yet would have me turn Hannibal, and eat my own flesh and blood. My princely coz, [*Pulls out a red herring.*] fear nothing; I have not the heart to devour you, an I might be made as rich as king Cophetua. O that I had room for my tears, I could weep salt-water enough now to preserve the lives of ten thousand thousand of my kin! But I may curse none but these filthy almanacks; for an't were not for them, these days of persecution would never be known. I'll be hang'd an some fishmonger's son do not make of 'em, and puts in more fasting-days than he should do, because he would utter his father's dried stock-fish and stinking conger.

CASH. 'Slight peace! thou'lt be beaten like a stock-fish else: here's master Mathew.

[*Enter* WELLBRED, EDWARD KNOWELL, BRAINWORM, MATHEW, BOBADILL, *and* STEPHEN.]
Now must I look out for a messenger to my master. [*Exit with* COB.]

WELLBRED. Beshrew me, but it was an absolute good jest, and exceedingly well carried!

EDWARD KNOWELL. Ay, and our ignorance maintain'd it as well, did it not?

WELLBRED. Yes, faith; but was it possible thou shouldst not know him? I forgive master, Stephen, for he is stupidity itself.

EDWARD KNOWELL. 'Fore God, not I, an I might have been join'd patten with one of the seven wise masters for knowing him. He had so writhen himself into the habit of one of your poor infantry, your decayed, ruinous, worm-eaten gentlemen of the round; such as have vowed to sit on the skirts of the city, let your provost and his half-dozen of halberdiers do what they can; and have translated begging out of

the old hackney-pace to a fine easy amble, and made it run as smooth off the tongue as a shove-groat shilling. Into the likeness of one of these reformados had he moulded himself so perfectly, observing every trick of their action, as, varying the accent, swearing with an emphasis, indeed, all with so special and exquisite a grace, that, hadst thou seen him, thou wouldst have sworn he might have been sergeant-major, if not lieutenant-colonel to the regiment.

WELLBRED. Why, Brainworm, who would have thought thou hadst been such an artificer?

EDWARD KNOWELL. An artificer! an architect. Except a man had studied begging all his life time, and been a weaver of language from his infancy for the cloathing of it, I never saw his rival.

WELLBRED. Where got'st thou this coat, I marle?

BRAINWORM. Of a Hounsditch man, sir, one of the devil's near kinsmen, a broker.

WELLBRED. That cannot be, if the proverb hold; for *A crafty knave needs no broker.*

BRAINWORM. True, sir; but I did *need a broker, ergo—*

WELLBRED. Well put off:—*no crafty knave,* you'll say.

EDWARD KNOWELL. Tut, he has more of these shifts.

BRAINWORM. And yet, where I have one the broker has ten, sir.

[*Reënter* CASH.]
CASH. Francis! Martin! ne'er a one to be found now? what a spite's this!

WELLBRED. How now, Thomas? Is my brother Kitely within?

CASH. No, sir, my master went forth e'en now; but master Downright is within. —Cob! what, Cob! Is he gone too?

WELLBRED. Whither went your master, Thomas, canst thou tell?

CASH. I know not: to justice Clement's, I think, sir—Cob! [*Exit.*]

EDWARD KNOWELL. Justice Clement! what's he?

WELLBRED. Why, dost thou not know

him? He is a city-magistrate, a justice here, an excellent good lawyer, and a great scholar; but the only mad, merry old fellow in Europe. I shewed him you the other day.

EDWARD KNOWELL. Oh, is that he? I remember him now. Good faith, and he is a very strange presence methinks; it shews as if he stood out of the rank from other men: I have heard many of his jests in the University. They say he will commit a man for taking the wall of his horse.

WELLBRED. Ay, or wearing his cloak on one shoulder, or serving of God; any thing, indeed, if it come in the way of his humour.

[*Reënter* CASH.]

CASH. Gasper! Martin! Cob! 'Heart, where should they be, trow?

BOBADILL. Master Kitely's man, pray thee vouchsafe us the lighting of this match.

CASH. Fire on your match! no time but now to *vouchsafe?*—Francis! Cob! [*Exit.*]

BOBADILL. Body o' me! here's the remainder of seven pound since yesterday was seven-night. 'Tis your right Trinidado: did you never take any, master Stephen?

STEPHEN. No, truly, sir; but I'll learn to take it now, since you commend it so.

BOBADILL. Sir, believe me, upon my relation for what I tell you, the world shall not reprove. I have been in the Indies, where this herb grows, where neither myself, nor a dozen gentlemen more of my knowledge, have received the taste of any other nutriment in the world, for the space of one and twenty weeks, but the fume of this simple only: therefore, it cannot be, but 'tis most divine. Further, take it in the nature, in the true kind; so, it makes an antidote, that, had you taken the most deadly poisonous plant in all Italy, it should expel it, and clarify you, with as much ease as I speak. And for your green wound,—your Balsamum and your St. John's wort, are all mere gulleries and trash to it, especially your Trinidado: your Nicotian is good too. I

could say what I know of the virtue of it, for the expulsion of rheums, raw humours, crudities, obstructions, with a thousand of this kind; but I profess myself no quacksalver. Only thus much; by Hercules, I do hold it, and will affirm it before any prince in Europe, to be the most sovereign and precious weed that ever the earth tendered to the use of man.

EDWARD KNOWELL. This speech would have done decently in a tobacco-trader's mouth.

[*Reënter* CASH *with* COB.]

CASH. At justice Clement's he is, in the middle of Coleman-street.

COB. Oh, oh!

BOBADILL. Where's the match I gave thee, master Kitely's man?

CASH. Would his match and he, and pipe and all, were at Sancto Domingo! I had forgot it.   [*Exit.*]

COB. 'Od's me, I marle what pleasure or felicity they have in taking this roguish tobacco. It's good for nothing but to choke a man, and fill him full of smoke and embers: there were four died out of one house last week with taking of it, and two more the bell went for yesternight; one of them, they say, will never scape it; he voided a bushel of soot yesterday, upward and downward. By the stocks, an there were no wiser men than I, I'd have it present whipping, man or woman, that should but deal with a tobacco pipe: why, it will stifle them all in the end, as many as use it; it's little better than ratsbane or rosaker.   [BOBADILL *beats him.*]

ALL. Oh, good captain, hold, hold!

BOBADILL. You base cullion, you!

[*Reënter* CASH.]

CASH. Sir, here's your match. Come, thou must needs be talking too, thou'rt well enough served.

COB. Nay, he will not meddle with his match, I warrant you: well, it shall be a dear beating, an I live.

BOBADILL. Do you prate, do you murmur?

EDWARD KNOWELL. Nay, good captain,

will you regard the humour of a fool?
Away, knave.

WELLBRED. Thomas, get him away.

[*Exit* CASH *with* COB.]

BOBADILL. A whoreson filthy slave, a
dung-worm, an excrement! Body o' Cæsar,
but that I scorn to let forth so mean
a spirit, I'd have stabb'd him to the
earth.

WELLBRED. Marry, the law forbid, sir!

BOBADILL. By Pharaoh's foot, I would
have done it.

STEPHEN. Oh, he swears most admir-
ably! By Pharaoh's foot! Body o' Cæsar!
—I shall never do it, sure. Upon mine
honour, and by St. George!—No, I have
not the right grace.

MATHEW. Master Stephen, will you
any? By this air, the most divine tobacco
that ever I drunk.

STEPHEN. None, I thank you, sir. O,
this gentleman does it rarely too: but
nothing like the other. By this air!
[*Practises at the post.*] As I am a gen-
tleman! By—

[*Exeunt* BOBADILL *and* MATHEW.]

BRAINWORM [*pointing to* MASTER
STEPHEN]. Master, glance, glance! master
Wellbred!

STEPHEN. As I have somewhat to be
saved, I protest—

WELLBRED. You are a fool; it needs no
affidavit.

EDWARD KNOWELL. Cousin, will you
any tobacco?

STEPHEN. I, sir! Upon my reputa-
tion—

EDWARD KNOWELL. How now, cousin!

STEPHEN. I protest, as I am a gentle-
man, but no soldier, indeed—

WELLBRED. No, master Stephen! As I
remember, your name is entered in the
artillery-garden.

STEPHEN. Ay, sir, that's true. Cousin,
may I swear, as I am a soldier, by that?

EDWARD KNOWELL. O yes, that you
may; it is all you have for your money.

STEPHEN. Then, as I am a gentleman,
and a soldier, it is "divine tobacco!"

WELLBRED. But soft, where's master
Mathew? Gone?

BRAINWORM. No, sir; they went in
here.

WELLBRED. O let's follow them: master
Mathew is gone to salute his mistress in
verse; we shall have the happiness to hear
some of his poetry now; he never comes
unfinished.—Brainworm!

STEPHEN. Brainworm! Where? Is this
Brainworm?

EDWARD KNOWELL. Ay, cousin; no
words of it, upon your gentility.

STEPHEN. Not I, body of me! By this
air! St. George! and the foot of Pharaoh!

WELLBRED. Rare! Your cousin's dis-
course is simply drawn out with oaths.

EDWARD KNOWELL. 'Tis larded with
them; a kind of French dressing, if you
love it. [*Exeunt.*]

SCENE III—*Coleman-street. A room in*
JUSTICE CLEMENT'S *house.*

[*Enter* KITELY *and* COB.]

KITELY. Ha! how many are there, say'st
thou?

COB. Marry, sir, your brother, master
Wellbred—

KITELY. Tut, beside him: what strang-
ers are there, man?

COB. Strangers? let me see, one, two;
mass, I know not well, there are so many.

KITELY. How! so many?

COB. Ay, there's some five or six of
them at the most.

KITELY. A swarm, a swarm!
Spite of the devil, how they sting my
head
With forked stings, thus wide and large!
But, Cob,
How long hast thou been coming hither,
Cob?

COB. A little while, sir.

KITELY. Didst thou come running?

COB. No, sir.

KITELY. Nay, then I am familiar with
thy haste.
Bane to my fortunes! what meant I to
marry?
I, that before was rank'd in such content,
My mind at rest too, in so soft a peace,

Being free master of mine own free
    thoughts,
And now become a slave? What! never
    sigh;
Be of good cheer, man; for thou art a
    cuckold:
'Tis done, 'tis done! Nay, when such
    flowing-store,
Plenty itself, falls into my wife's lap,
The cornucopiæ will be mine, I know.—
But, Cob,
What entertainment had they? I am sure
My sister and my wife would bid them
    welcome: ha?

COB. Like enough, sir; yet I heard not
a word of it.

KITELY. No;
Their lips were seal'd with kisses, and the
    voice,
Drown'd in a flood of joy at their arrival,
Had lost her motion, state and faculty.—
Cob,
Which of them was it that first kiss'd my
    wife,
My sister, I should say?—My wife, alas!
I fear not her: ha! who was it say'st
    thou?

COB. By my troth, sir, will you have
the truth of it?

KITELY. Oh, ay, good Cob, I pray thee
heartily.

COB. Then I am a vagabond, and fitter
for Bridewell than your worship's com-
pany, if I saw any body to be kiss'd, un-
less they would have kiss'd the post in
the middle of the warehouse; for there I
left them all at their tobacco, with a pox!

KITELY. How! were they not gone in
then ere thou cam'st?

COB. O no, sir.

KITELY. Spite of the devil! what do I
stay here then? Cob, follow me. [Exit.]

COB. Nay, soft and fair; I have eggs
on the spit; I cannot go yet, sir. Now am
I, for some five and fifty reasons, hammer-
ing, hammering revenge; O for three or
four gallons of vinegar, to sharpen my
wits! Revenge, vinegar revenge, vinegar
and mustard revenge! Nay, an he had
not lien in my house, 'twould never have
grieved me; but being my guest, one that,

I'll be sworn, my wife has lent him her
smock off her back, while his own shirt
has been at washing; pawned her neck-
kerchers for clean bands for him; sold
almost all my platters, to buy him to-
bacco; and he to turn monster of ingrati-
tude, and strike his lawful host! Well, I
hope to raise up an host of fury for't:
here comes justice Clement.

[*Enter* JUSTICE CLEMENT, KNOWELL, *and*
    FORMAL.]

CLEMENT. What's master Kitely gone,
Roger?

FORMAL. Ay, sir.

CLEMENT. Heart o' me! what made him
leave us so abruptly?—How now, sirrah!
what make you here? what would you
have, ha?

COB. An't please your worship, I am a
poor neighbour of your worship's—

CLEMENT. A poor neighbour of mine!
Why, speak, poor neighbour.

COB. I dwell, sir, at the sign of the
Water-tankard, hard by the Green Lat-
tice: I have paid scot and lot there any
time this eighteen years.

CLEMENT. To the Green Lattice?

COB. No, sir, to the parish: Marry, I
have seldom scaped scot-free at the Lat-
tice.

CLEMENT. O, well; what business has
my poor neighbour with me?

COB. An't like your worship, I am come
to crave the peace of your worship.

CLEMENT. Of me, knave! Peace of me,
knave! Did I ever hurt thee, or threaten
thee, or wrong thee, ha?

COB. No, sir; but your worship's war-
rant for one that has wrong'd me, sir: his
arms are at too much liberty, I would fain
have them bound to a treaty of peace, an
my credit could compass it with your
worship.

CLEMENT. Thou goest far enough about
for't, I am sure.

KNOWELL. Why, dost thou go in danger
of thy life for him, friend?

COB. No, sir; but I go in danger of my
death every hour, by his means; an I die
within a twelve-month and a day, I may

swear by the law of the land that he killed me.

CLEMENT. How, how, knave, swear he killed thee, and by the law? What pretence, what colour hast thou for that?

COB. Marry, an't please your worship, both black and blue; colour enough, I warrant you. I have it here to shew your worship.

CLEMENT. What is he that gave you this, sirrah?

COB. A gentleman and a soldier, he says, he is, of the city here.

CLEMENT. A soldier of the city! What call you him?

COB. Captain Bobadill.

CLEMENT. Bobadill! and why did he bob and beat you, sirrah? How began the quarrel betwixt you, ha? speak truly, knave, I advise you.

COB. Marry, indeed, an't please your worship, only because I spake against their vagrant tobacco, as I came by them when they were taking on't; for nothing else.

CLEMENT. Ha! you speak against tobacco? Formal, his name.

FORMAL. What's your name, sirrah?

COB. Oliver, sir, Oliver Cob, sir.

CLEMENT. Tell Oliver Cob he shall go to the jail, Formal.

FORMAL. Oliver Cobb, my master, justice Clement, says you shall go to the jail.

COB. O, I beseech your worship, for God's sake, dear master justice!

CLEMENT. 'Sprecious! an such drunkards and tankards as you are, come to dispute of tobacco once, I have done: away with him!

COB. O, good master justice! Sweet old gentleman! [To KNOWELL.]

KNOWELL. "Sweet Oliver," would I could do thee any good!—justice Clement, let me intreat you, sir.

CLEMENT. What! a thread-bare rascal, a beggar, a slave that never drunk out of better than piss-pot metal in his life! and he to deprave and abuse the virtue of an herb so generally received in the courts of princes, the chambers of nobles, the bowers of sweet ladies, the cabins of soldiers!—

Roger, away with him! 'Od's precious— I say, go to.

COB. Dear master justice, let me be beaten again, I have deserved it: but not the prison, I beseech you.

KNOWELL. Alas, poor Oliver!

CLEMENT. Roger, make him a warrant: —he shall not go, I but fear the knave.

FORMAL. Do not stink, sweet Oliver, you shall not go; my master will give you a warrant.

COB. O, the Lord maintain his worship, his worthy worship!

CLEMENT. Away, dispatch him. [Exeunt FORMAL and COB.] How now, master Knowell, in dumps, in dumps! Come, this becomes not.

KNOWELL. Sir, would I could not feel my cares.

CLEMENT. Your cares are nothing: they are like my cap, soon put on, and as soon put off. What! your son is old enough to govern himself: let him run his course, it's the only way to make him a staid man. If he were an unthrift, a ruffian, a drunkard, or a licentious liver, then you had reason; you had reason to take care: but, being none of these, mirth's my witness, an I had twice so many cares as you have, I'd drown them all in a cup of sack. Come, come, let's try it: I muse your parcel of a soldier returns not all this while.   [Exeunt.]

ACT IV

SCENE I—*A room in* KITELY'S *house.*

[*Enter* DOWNRIGHT *and* DAME KITELY.]

DOWNRIGHT. Well, sister, I tell you true; and you'll find it so in the end.

DAME KITELY. Alas, brother, what would you have me to do? I cannot help it; you see my brother brings them in here; they are his friends.

DOWNRIGHT. His friends! his fiends. 'Slud! they do nothing but haunt him up and down like a sort of unlucky spirits, and tempt him to all manner of villainy that can be thought of. Well, by this light, a little thing would make me play the devil with some of them: an 'twere not more for your husband's sake than any thing else, I'd make the house too hot for the best on 'em; they should say, and swear, hell were broken loose, ere they went hence. But, by God's will, 'tis nobody's fault but yours; for an you had done as you might have done, they should have been parboiled, and baked too, every mother's son, ere they should have come in, e'er a one of them.

DAME KITELY. God's my life! did you ever hear the like? what a strange man is this! Could I keep out all them, think you? I should put myself against half a dozen men, should I? Good faith, you'd mad the patien'st body in the world, to hear you talk so, without any sense or reason.

[*Enter* MISTRESS BRIDGET, MASTER MATHEW, *and* BOBADILL; *followed, at a distance, by* WELLBRED, EDWARD KNOWELL, STEPHEN, *and* BRAINWORM.]

BRIDGET. Servant, in troth you are too prodigal
Of your wit's treasure, thus to pour it forth
Upon so mean a subject as my worth.

MATHEW. You say well, mistress, and I mean as well.

DOWNRIGHT. Hoy-day, here is stuff!

WELLBRED. O, now stand close; pray Heaven, she can get him to read! he should do it of his own natural impudency.

BRIDGET. Servant, what is this same, I pray you?

MATHEW. Marry, an elegy, an elegy, an odd toy—

DOWNRIGHT. To mock an ape withal! O, I could sew up his mouth, now.

DAME KITELY. Sister, I pray you let's hear it.

DOWNRIGHT. Are you rhyme-given too?

MATHEW. Mistress, I'll read it if you please.

BRIDGET. Pray you do, servant.

DOWNRIGHT. O, here's no foppery! Death! I can endure the stocks better.

[*Exit.*]

EDWARD KNOWELL. What ails thy brother? can he not hold his water at reading of a ballad?

WELLBRED. O, no; a rhyme to him is worse than cheese, or a bag-pipe; but mark; you lose the protestation.

MATHEW. Faith, I did it in a humour; I know not how it is; but please you come near, sir. This gentleman has judgment, he knows how to censure of a—pray you, sir, you can judge?

STEPHEN. Not I, sir; upon my reputation, and by the foot of Pharaoh!

WELLBRED. O, chide your cousin for swearing.

EDWARD KNOWELL. Not I, so long as he does not forswear himself.

BOBADILL. Master Mathew, you abuse the expectation of your dear mistress, and her fair sister: fie! while you live avoid this prolixity.

MATHEW. I shall, sir, well; *incipere dulce.*

EDWARD KNOWELL. How, *insipere dulce!* a sweet thing to be a fool, indeed!

WELLBRED. What, do you take *incipere* in that sense?

EDWARD KNOWELL. You do not, you! This was your villainy, to gull him with a motte.

WELLBRED. O, the benchers' phrase: *pauca verba, pauca verba!*

MATHEW. Rare creature, let me speak without offence,
Would God my rude words had the influence
To rule thy thoughts, as thy fair looks do mine,
Then shouldst thou be his prisoner, who is thine.

EDWARD KNOWELL. This is Hero and Leander.

WELLBRED. O, ay: peace, we shall have more of this.

MATHEW. Be not unkind and fair: misshapen stuff
Is of behaviour boisterous and rough.

WELLBRED. How like you that, sir?

[MASTER STEPHEN *shakes his head.*]

EDWARD KNOWELL. 'Slight, he shakes

his head like a bottle, to feel an there be any brain in it.

MATHEW. But observe the catastrophe, now:

And I in duty will exceed all other,
As you in beauty do excel Love's mother.

EDWARD KNOWELL. Well, I'll have him free of the wit-brokers, for he utters nothing but stolen remnants.

WELLBRED. O, forgive it him.

EDWARD KNOWELL. A filching rogue, hang him!—and from the dead! it's worse than sacrilege.

[WELLBRED, EDWARD KNOWELL, and MASTER STEPHEN, come forward.]

WELLBRED. Sister, what have you here, verses? pray you let's see: who made these verses? they are excellent good.

MATHEW. O, Master Wellbred, 'tis your disposition to say so, sir. They were good in the morning: I made them ex tempore this morning.

WELLBRED. How! ex tempore?

MATHEW. Ay, would I might be hanged else; ask Captain Bobadill: he saw me write them, at the—pox on it!—the Star, yonder.

BRAINWORM. Can he find in his heart to curse the stars so?

EDWARD KNOWELL. Faith, his are even with him; they have curst him enough already.

STEPHEN. Cousin, how do you like this gentleman's verses?

EDWARD KNOWELL. O, admirable! the best that ever I heard, coz.

STEPHEN. Body o' Cæsar, they are admirable! the best that I ever heard, as I am a soldier!

[Reënter DOWNRIGHT.]

DOWNRIGHT. I am vext, I can hold ne'er a bone of me still: 'Heart, I think they mean to build and breed here.

WELLBRED. Sister, you have a simple servant here, that crowns your beauty with such encomiums and devices; you may see what it is to be the mistress of a wit, that can make your perfections so transparent, that every blear eye may look through them, and see him drowned over head and ears in the deep well of desire: Sister Kitely, I marvel you get you not a servant that can rhyme, and do tricks too.

DOWNRIGHT. O monster! impudence itself! tricks!

DAME KITELY. Tricks, brother! what tricks?

BRIDGET. Nay, speak, I pray you what tricks?

DAME KITELY. Ay, never spare any body here; but say, what tricks?

BRIDGET. Passion of my heart, do tricks!

WELLBRED. 'Slight, here's a trick vied and revied! Why, you monkeys, you, what a cater-wauling do you keep! has he not given you rhymes and verses and tricks?

DOWNRIGHT. O, the fiend!

WELLBRED. Nay, you lamp of virginity, that take it in snuff so, come, and cherish this tame poetical fury in your servant; you'll be begg'd else shortly for a concealment: go to, reward his muse. You cannot give him less than a shilling in conscience, for the book he had it out of cost him a teston at least. How now, gallants! Master Mathew! Captain! what, all sons of silence, no spirit?

DOWNRIGHT. Come, you might practise your ruffian tricks somewhere else, and not here, I wuss; this is no tavern or drinking-school, to vent your exploits in.

WELLBRED. How now; whose cow has calved?

DOWNRIGHT. Marry, that has mine, sir. Nay, boy, never look askance at me for the matter; I'll tell you of it, I, sir; you and your companions mend yourselves when I have done.

WELLBRED. My companions!

DOWNRIGHT. Yes, sir, your companions, so I say; I am not afraid of you, nor them neither; your hang-byes here. You must have your poets and your potlings, your soldados and foolados to follow you up and down the city; and here they must come to domineer and swagger. Sirrah, you ballad-singer, and slops your fellow there, get you out, get you home;

or by this steel, I'll cut off your ears, and that presently.

WELLBRED. 'Slight, stay, let's see what he dare do; cut off his ears! cut a whetstone. You are an ass, do you see; touch any man here, and by this hand I'll run my rapier to the hilts in you.

DOWNRIGHT. Yea, that would I fain see, boy. [*They all draw.*]

DAME KITELY. O Jesu! murder! Thomas!—Gasper!

BRIDGET. Help, help! Thomas!

[*Enter* CASH *and some of the house to part them.*]

EDWARD KNOWELL. Gentlemen, forbear, I pray you.

BOBADILL. Well, sirrah, you Holofernes; by my hand, I will pink your flesh full of holes with my rapier for this; I will, by this good heaven! nay, let him come, let him come, gentlemen; by the body of St. George, I'll not kill him.

[*Offer to fight again, and are parted.*]

CASH. Hold, hold, good gentlemen.

DOWNRIGHT. You whoreson, bragging coystril!

[*Enter* KITELY.]

KITELY. Why, how now! what's the matter, what's the stir here?
Whence springs the quarrel? Thomas! where is he?
Put up your weapons, and put off this rage:
My wife and sister, they are the cause of this.
What, Thomas! where is the knave?

CASH. Here, sir.

WELLBRED. Come, let's go: this is one of my brother's ancient humours, this.

STEPHEN. I am glad nobody was hurt by his ancient humour.

[*Exeunt* WELLBRED, STEPHEN, EDWARD KNOWELL, BOBADILL, *and* BRAINWORM.]

KITELY. Why, how now, brother, who enforced this brawl?

DOWNRIGHT. A sort of lewd rake-hells, that care neither for God nor the devil.

And they must come here to read ballads, and roguery, and trash! I'll mar the knot of 'em ere I sleep, perhaps; especially Bob there, he that's all manner of shapes: and songs and sonnets, his fellow.

BRIDGET. Brother, indeed you are too violent,
Too sudden in your humour: and you know
My brother Wellbred's temper will not bear
Any reproof, chiefly in such a presence,
Where every slight disgrace he should receive
Might wound him in opinion and respect.

DOWNRIGHT. Respect! what talk you of respect among such, as have no spark of manhood, nor good manners? 'Sdeins, I am ashamed to hear you! respect! [*Exit.*]

BRIDGET. Yes, there was one a civil gentleman,
And very worthily demeaned himself.

KITELY. O, that was some love of yours, sister.

BRIDGET. A love of mine! I would it were no worse, brother;
You'd pay my portion sooner than you think for.

DAME KITELY. Indeed he seem'd to be a gentleman of a very exceeding fair disposition, and of excellent good parts.

[*Exeunt* DAME KITELY *and* BRIDGET.]

KITELY. Her love, by heaven! my wife's minion.
Fair disposition! excellent good parts!
Death! these phrases are intolerable.
Good parts! how should she know his parts?
His parts! Well, well, well, well, well, well;
It is too plain, too clear: Thomas, come hither.
What, are they gone?

CASH.   Ay, sir, they went in.
My mistress and your sister—

KITELY. Are any of the gallants within?

CASH. No, sir, they are all gone.

KITELY.   Art thou sure of it?

CASH. I can assure you, sir.

KITELY. What gentleman was that they praised so, Thomas?

CASH. One, they call him Master Knowell, a handsome young gentleman, sir.

KITELY. Ay, I thought so; my mind gave me as much:

I'll die, but they have hid him in the house,

Somewhere, I'll go and search; go with me, Thomas:

Be true to me, and thou shalt find me a master. [*Exeunt.*]

SCENE II—*The lane before* COB'S *house.*

[*Enter* COB.]

COBS [*knocks at the door*]. What, Tib! Tib, I say!

TIB [*within*]. How now, what cuckold is that knocks so hard?

[*Enter* TIB.]

O, husband! is it you? What's the news?

COB. Nay, you have stunn'd me, i'faith; you have given me a knock o' the forehead will stick by me. Cuckold! 'Slid, cuckold!

TIB. Away, you fool! did I know it was you that knocked? Come, come, you may call me as bad when you list.

COB. May I? Tib, you are a whore.

TIB. You lie in your throat, husband.

COB. How, the lie! and in my throat too! do you long to be stabb'd, ha?

TIB. Why, you are no soldier, I hope.

COB. O, must you be stabbed by a soldier? Mass, that's true! when was Bobadill here, your captain? 'that rogue, that foist, that fencing Burgullion? I'll tickle him, i'faith.

TIB. Why, what's the matter, trow?

COB. O, he has basted me rarely, sumptuously! but I have it here in black and white, [*pulls out the warrant.*] for his black and blue shall pay him. O, the justice, the honestest old brave Trojan in London: I do honour the very flea of his dog. A plague on him, though, he put me once in a villanous filthy fear; marry, it vanished away like the smoke of tobacco; but I was smoked soundly first. I thank

the devil, and his good angel, my guest. Well, wife, or Tib, which you will, get you in, and lock the door; I charge you let nobody in to you, wife; nobody in to you; those are my words: not Captain Bob himself, nor the fiend in his likeness. You are a woman, you have flesh and blood enough in you to be tempted; therefore keep the door shut upon all comers.

TIB. I warrant you, there shall nobody enter here without my consent.

COB. Nor with your consent, sweet Tib; and so I leave you.

TIB. It's more than you know, whether you leave me so.

COB. How?

TIB. Why, *sweet.*

COB. Tut, sweet or sour, thou art a flower.

Keep close thy door, I ask no more.

[*Exeunt.*]

SCENE III—*A room in the Windmill Tavern.*

[*Enter* EDWARD KNOWELL, WELLBRED, STEPHEN, *and* BRAINWORM, *disguised as before.*]

EDWARD KNOWELL. Well, Brainworm, perform this business happily, and thou makest a purchase of my love for ever.

WELLBRED. I'faith, now let thy spirits use their best faculties: but, at any hand, remember the message to my brother; for there's no other means to start him.

BRAINWORM. I warrant you, sir; fear nothing; I have a nimble soul has waked all forces of my phant'sie by this time, and put them in true motion. What you have possest me withal, I'll discharge it amply, sir; make it no question. [*Exit.*]

WELLBRED. Forth, and prosper, Brainworm. Faith, Ned, how dost thou approve of my abilities in this device?

EDWARD KNOWELL. Troth, well, howsoever; but it will come excellent if it take.

WELLBRED. Take, man! why it cannot choose but take, if the circumstances miscarry not: but, tell me ingenuously, dost thou affect my sister Bridget as thou pretend'st?

EDWARD KNOWELL. Friend, am I worth belief?

WELLBRED. Come, do not protest. In faith, she is a maid of good ornament, and much modesty; and, except I conceived very worthily of her, thou should'st not have her.

EDWARD KNOWELL. Nay, that I am afraid, will be a question yet, whether I shall have her, or no.

WELLBRED. 'Slid, thou shalt have her; by this light thou shalt.

EDWARD KNOWELL. Nay, do not swear.

WELLBRED. By this hand thou shalt have her; I'll go fetch her presently. 'Point but where to meet, and as I am an honest man I'll bring her.

EDWARD KNOWELL. Hold, hold, be temperate.

WELLBRED. Why, by——what shall I swear by? thou shalt have her, as I am—

EDWARD KNOWELL. Praythee, be at peace, I am satisfied; and do believe thou wilt omit no offered occasion to make my desires complete.

WELLBRED. Thou shalt see, and know, I will not.   [*Exeunt.*]

SCENE IV—*The Old Jewry.*

[*Enter* FORMAL *and* KNOWELL.]

FORMAL. Was your man a soldier, sir?

KNOWELL.   Ay, a knave;
I took him begging o' the way, this morning,
As I came over Moorfields.

[*Enter* BRAINWORM, *disguised as before.*]
O, here he is!—you've made fair speed, believe me,
Where, in the name of sloth, could you be thus?

BRAINWORM. Marry, peace be my comfort, where I thought I should have had little comfort of your worship's service.

KNOWELL. How so?

BRAINWORM. O, sir, your coming to the city, your entertainment of me, and your sending me to watch—indeed all the circumstances either of your charge, or my employment, are as open to your son, as to yourself.

KNOWELL. How should that be, unless that villain, Brainworm,
Have told him of the letter, and discover'd
All that I strictly charg'd him to conceal?
'Tis so.

BRAINWORM. I am partly o' the faith, 'tis so, indeed.

KNOWELL. But, how should he know thee to be my man?

BRAINWORM. Nay, sir, I cannot tell; unless it be by the black art. Is not your son a scholar, sir?

KNOWELL. Yes, but I hope his soul is not allied
Unto such hellish practice: if it were,
I had just cause to weep my part in him,
And curse the time of his creation.
But, where didst thou find them, Fitz-Sword?

BRAINWORM. You should rather ask where they found me, sir; for I'll be sworn, I was going along in the street, thinking nothing, when, of a sudden, a voice calls, *Mr. Knowell's man!* another cries, *Soldier!* and thus half a dozen of them, till they had call'd me within a house, where I no sooner came, but they seem'd men, and out flew all their rapiers at my bosom, with some three or four score oaths to accompany them; and all to tell me, I was but a dead man, if I did not confess where you were, and how I was employed, and about what; which when they could not get out of me (as, I protest, they must have dissected, and made an anatomy of me first, and so I told them), they lock'd me up into a room in the top of a high house, whence by great miracle (having a light heart) I slid down by a bottom of packthread into the street, and so 'scaped. But, sir, thus much I can assure you, for I heard it while I was lock'd up, there were a great many rich merchants and brave citizens' wives with them at a feast; and your son, master Edward, withdrew with one of them, and has 'pointed to meet her anon at one Cob's house a water-bearer that dwells by the Wall. Now, there your worship shall be sure to take him, for there he preys, and fail he will not.

KNOWELL. Nor will I fail to break his match, I doubt not.

Go thou along with justice Clement's man,
And stay there for me. At one Cob's house, say'st thou?

BRAINWORM. Ay, sir, there you shall have him. [*Exit* KNOWELL.] Yes—invisible! Much wench, or much son! 'Slight, when he has staid there three or four hours, travailing with the expectation of wonders, and at length be deliver'd of air! O the sport that I should then take to look on him, if I durst! But now, I mean to appear no more afore him in this shape: I have another trick to act yet. O that I were so happy as to light on a nupson now of this justice's novice!—Sir, I make you stay somewhat long.

FORMAL. Not a whit, sir. Pray you what do you mean, sir?

BRAINWORM. I was putting up some papers.

FORMAL. You have been lately in the wars, sir, it seems.

BRAINWORM. Marry have I, sir, to my loss, and expense of all, almost.

FORMAL. Troth, sir, I would be glad to bestow a bottle of wine on you, if it please you to accept it—

BRAINWORM. O, sir—

FORMAL. But to hear the manner of your services, and your devices in the wars; they say they be very strange, and not like those a man reads in the Roman histories, or sees at Mile-end.

BRAINWORM. No, I assure you, sir; why at any time when it please you, I shall be ready to discourse to you all I know;—and more too somewhat. [*Aside.*]

FORMAL. No better time than now, sir; we'll go to the Windmill: there we shall have a cup of neat grist, we call it. I pray you, sir, let me request you to the Windmill.

BRAINWORM. I'll follow you, sir;—and make grist of you, if I have good luck. [*Aside.*] [*Exeunt.*]

SCENE V—*Moorfields.*

[*Enter* MATHEW, EDWARD KNOWELL, BOBADILL, *and* STEPHEN.]

MATHEW. Sir, did your eyes ever taste the like clown of him where we were today, Mr. Wellbred's half-brother? I think the whole earth cannot shew his parallel, by this daylight.

EDWARD KNOWELL. We were now speaking of him: captain Bobadill tells me he is fallen foul of you too.

MATHEW. O, ay, sir, he threatened me with the bastinado.

BOBADILL. Ay, but I think, I taught you prevention this morning, for that: You shall kill him beyond question; if you be so generously minded.

MATHEW. Indeed, it is a most excellent trick. [*Fences.*]

BOBADILL. O, you do not give spirit enough to your motion, you are too tardy, too heavy! O, it must be done like lightning, hay!
[*Practises at a post with his cudgel.*]

MATHEW. Rare, captain!

BOBADILL. Tut! 'tis nothing, an't be not done in a—punto.

EDWARD KNOWELL. Captain, did you ever prove yourself upon any of our masters of defence here?

MATHEW. O good sir! yes, I hope he has.

BOBADILL. I will tell you, sir. Upon my first coming to the city, after my long travel for knowledge, in that mystery only, there came three or four of them to me, at a gentleman's house, where it was my chance to be resident at that time, to intreat my presence at their schools: and withal so much importuned me, that I protest to you, as I am a gentleman, I was ashamed of their rude demeanour out of all measure: Well, I told them that to come to a public school, they should pardon me, it was opposite, in diameter, to my humour; but if so be they would give their attendance at my lodging, I protested to do them what right or favour I could, as I was a gentleman, and so forth.

EDWARD KNOWELL. So, sir! then you tried their skill?

BOBADILL. Alas, soon tried: you shall hear, sir. Within two or three days after, they came; and, by honesty, fair sir, believe me, I graced them exceedingly, shewed them some two or three tricks of prevention have purchased them since a credit to admiration: they cannot deny this; and yet now they hate me, and why? because I am excellent; and for no other vile reason on the earth.

EDWARD KNOWELL. This is strange and barbarous, as ever I heard.

BOBADILL. Nay, for a more instance of their preposterous natures; but note, sir. They have assaulted me some three, four, five, six of them together, as I have walked alone in divers skirts i' the town, as Turnbull, Whitechapel, Shoreditch, which were then my quarters; and since, upon the Exchange, at my lodging, and at my ordinary: where I have driven them afore me the whole length of a street, in the open view of all our gallants, pitying to hurt them, believe me. Yet all this lenity will not overcome their spleen; they will be doing with the pismire, raising a hill a man may spurn abroad with his foot at pleasure. By myself, I could have slain them all, but I delight not in murder. I am loth to bear any other than this bastinado for them: yet I hold it good polity not to go disarmed, for though I be skilful, I may be oppressed with multitudes.

EDWARD KNOWELL. Ay, believe me, may you, sir: and in my conceit, our whole nation should sustain the loss by it, if it were so.

BOBADILL. Alas, no? what's a peculiar man to a nation? not seen.

EDWARD KNOWELL. O, but your skill, sir.

BOBADILL. Indeed, that might be some loss; but who respects it? I will tell you, sir, by the way of private, and under seal; I am a gentleman, and live here obscure, and to myself; but were I known to her majesty and the lords,—observe me, —I would undertake, upon this poor head

and life, for the public benefit of the state, not only to spare the entire lives of her subjects in general; but to save the one half, nay, three parts of her yearly charge in holding war, and against what enemy soever. And how would I do it, think you?

EDWARD KNOWELL. Nay, I know not, nor can I conceive.

BOBADILL. Why thus, sir. I would select nineteen more, to myself, throughout the land; gentlemen they should be of good spirit, strong and able constitution; I would choose them by an instinct, a character that I have: and I would teach these nineteen the special rules, as your punto, your reverso, your stoccata, your imbroccato, your passada, your montanto; till they could all play very near, or altogether as well as myself. This done, say the enemy were forty thousand strong, we twenty would come into the field the tenth of March, or thereabouts; and we would challenge twenty of the enemy; they could not in their honour refuse us: Well, we would kill them; challenge twenty more, kill them; twenty more, kill them; twenty more, kill them too; and thus would we kill every man his twenty a day, that's twenty score; twenty score that's two hundred; two hundred a day, five days a thousand: forty thousand; forty times five, five times forty, two hundred days kills them all up by computation. And this will I venture my poor gentlemanlike carcase to perform, provided there be no treason practised upon us, by fair and discreet manhood; that is, civilly by the sword.

EDWARD KNOWELL. Why, are you so sure of your hand, captain, at all times?

BOBADILL. Tut! never miss thrust, upon my reputation with you.

EDWARD KNOWELL. I would not stand in Downright's state then, an you meet him, for the wealth of any one street in London.

BOBADILL. Why, sir, you mistake me: if he were here now, by this welkin, I would not draw my weapon on him. Let this gentleman do his mind: but I will bastinado him, by the bright sun, wherever I meet him.

MATHEW. Faith, and I'll have a fling at him, at my distance.

EDWARD KNOWELL. 'Ods, so, look where he is! yonder he goes.

[DOWNRIGHT *crosses the stage.*]

DOWNRIGHT. What peevish luck have I, I cannot meet with these bragging rascals?

BOBADILL. It is not he, is it?

EDWARD KNOWELL. Yes, faith, it is he.

MATHEW. I'll be hang'd then if that were he.

EDWARD KNOWELL. Sir, keep your hanging good for some greater matter, for I assure you that were he.

STEPHEN. Upon my reputation, it was he.

BOBADILL. Had I thought it had been he, he must not have gone so: but I can hardly be induced to believe it was he yet.

EDWARD KNOWELL. That I think, sir.

[*Reënter* DOWNRIGHT.]

But see, he is come again.

DOWNRIGHT. O, Pharaoh's foot, have I found you? Come, draw to your tools; draw, gipsy, or I'll thrash you.

BOBADILL. Gentleman of valour, I do believe in thee; hear me—

DOWNRIGHT. Draw your weapon then.

BOBADILL. Tall man, I never thought on it till now—— Body of me, I had a warrant of the peace served on me, even now as I came along, by a water-bearer; this gentleman saw it, Master Mathew.

DOWNRIGHT. 'Sdeath! you will not draw then? [*Disarms and beats him.* MATHEW *runs away.*]

BOBADILL. Hold, hold! under thy favour forbear!

DOWNRIGHT. Prate again, as you like this, you whoreson foist you! You'll control the point, you! Your consort is gone; had he staid he had shared with you, sir. [*Exit.*]

BOBADILL. Well, gentlemen, bear witness, I was bound to the peace, by this good day.

EDWARD KNOWELL. No, faith, it's an ill day, captain, never reckon it other: but, say you were bound to the peace, the law allows you to defend yourself: that will prove but a poor excuse.

BOBADILL. I cannot tell, sir; I desire good construction in fair sort. I never sustain'd the like disgrace, by heaven! sure I was struck with a planet thence, for I had no power to touch my weapon.

EDWARD KNOWELL. Ay, like enough; I have heard of many that have been beaten under a planet: go, get you to a surgeon. 'Slid! an these be your tricks, your passadoes, and your montantos, I'll none of them. [*Exit* BOBADILL.] O, manners! that this age should bring forth such creatures! that nature should be at leisure to make them! Come, coz.

STEPHEN. Mass, I'll have this cloak.

EDWARD KNOWELL. 'Od's will, 'tis Downright's.

STEPHEN. Nay, it's mine now, another might have ta'en it up as well as I: I'll wear it, so I will.

EDWARD KNOWELL. How an he see it? he'll challenge it, assure yourself.

STEPHEN. Ay, but he shall not have it: I'll say I bought it.

EDWARD KNOWELL. Take heed you buy it not too dear, coz. [*Exeunt.*]

SCENE IV—*A room in* KITELY'S *house.*

[*Enter* KITELY, WELLBRED, DAME KITELY, *and* BRIDGET.]

KITELY. Now, trust me, brother, you were much to blame,
T' incense his anger, and disturb the peace
Of my poor house, where there are sentinels
That every minute watch to give alarms
Of civil war, without adjection
Of your assistance or occasion.

WELLBRED. No harm done, brother, I warrant you: since there is no harm done, anger costs a man nothing; and a tall man is never his own man till he be angry. To keep his valour in obscurity, is to keep himself as it were in a cloak-bag. What's a musician, unless he play? What's a tall man unless he fight? For, indeed, all this my wise brother stands upon absolutely; and that made me fall in with him so resolutely.

DAME KITELY. Ay, but what harm might have come of it, brother?

WELLBRED. Might, sister? so might the good warm clothes your husband wears be poisoned, for any thing he knows: or the wholesome wine he drank, even now at the table.

KITELY. Now, God forbid! O me! now I remember
My wife drank to me last, and changed the cup,
And bade me wear this cursed suit to-day.
See, if Heaven suffer murder undiscover'd!
I feel me ill; give me some mithridate,
Some mithridate and oil, good sister, fetch me:
O, I am sick at heart, I burn, I burn.
If you will save my life, go fetch it me.

WELLBRED. O strange humour! my very breath has poison'd him.

BRIDGET. Good brother, be content, what do you mean?
The strength of these extreme conceits will kill you.

DAME KITELY. Beshrew your heart-blood, brother Wellbred, now,
For putting such a toy into his head!

WELLBRED. Is a fit simile a toy? will he be poison'd with a simile? Brother Kitely, what a strange and idle imagination is this! For shame, be wiser. O' my soul there's no such matter.

KITELY. Am I not sick? how am I then not poison'd? Am I not poison'd? how am I then so sick?

DAME KITELY. If you be sick, your own thoughts make you sick.

WELLBRED. His jealousy is the poison he has taken.

[Enter BRAINWORM, disguised in FORMAL'S clothes.]

BRAINWORM. Master Kitely, my master, justice Clement, salutes you; and desires to speak with you with all possible speed.

KITELY. No time but now, when I think

I am sick, very sick! well, I will wait upon his worship. Thomas!—Cob!—I must seek them out, and set them sentinels till I return. Thomas!—Cob!—Thomas!
[Exit.]

WELLBRED. This is perfectly rare, Brainworm; [takes him aside.] but how got'st thou this apparel of the justice's man?

BRAINWORM. Marry, sir, my proper fine pen-man would needs bestow the grist on me, at the Windmill, to hear some martial discourse; where I so marshall'd him, that I made him drunk with admiration: and, because too much heat was the cause of his distemper, I stript him stark naked as he lay along asleep, and borrowed his suit to deliver this counterfeit message in, leaving a rusty armour, and an old brown bill to watch him till my return; which shall be, when I have pawn'd his apparel, and spent the better part o' the money, perhaps.

WELLBRED. Well, thou art a successful merry knave, Brainworm: his absence will be a good subject for more mirth. I pray thee return to thy young master, and will him to meet me and my sister Bridget at the Tower instantly; for, here, tell him the house is so stored with jealousy, there is no room for love to stand upright in. We must get our fortunes committed to some larger prison, say; and than the Tower, I know no better air, nor where the liberty of the house may do us more present service. Away.
[Exit BRAINWORM.]

[Reënter KITELY, talking aside to CASH.]

KITELY. Come hither, Thomas. Now my secret's ripe,
And thou shalt have it: lay to both thine ears.
Hark what I say to thee. I must go forth, Thomas;
Be careful of thy promise, keep good watch,
Note every gallant, and observe him well,
That enters in my absence to thy mistress:
If she would shew him rooms, the jest is stale,

Follow them, Thomas, or else hang on
    him,
And let him not go after; mark their
    looks;
Note if she offer but to see his band,
Or any other amorous toy about him;
But praise his leg, or foot: or if she say
The day is hot, and bid him feel her hand,
How hot it is; O, that's a monstrous
    thing!
Note me all this, good Thomas, mark their
    sighs,
And if they do but whisper, break 'em off:
I'll bear thee out in it. Wilt thou do
    this?
Wilt thou be true, my Thomas?
    CASH.   As truth's self, sir.
    KITELY. Why, I believe thee: Where
is Cob, now? Cob!   [*Exit.*]
    DAME KITELY. He's ever calling for
Cob: I wonder how he employs Cob so.
    WELLBRED. Indeed, sister, to ask how
he employs Cob, is a necessary question
for you that are his wife, and a thing
not very easy for you to be satisfied in;
but this I'll assure you, Cob's wife is an
excellent bawd, sister, and oftentimes your
husband haunts her house; marry, to what
end? I cannot altogether accuse him; im-
agine you what you think convenient: but
I have known fair hides have foul hearts
ere now, sister.
    DAME KITELY. Never said you truer
than that, brother, so much I can tell
you for your learning. Thomas, fetch
your cloak and go with me. [*Exit* CASH.]
I'll after him presently: I would to for-
tune I could take him there, i'faith, I'd
return him his own, I warrant him!
                                [*Exit.*]
    WELLBRED. So, let 'em go; this may
make sport anon. Now, my fair sister-
in-law, that you knew but how happy a
thing it were to be fair and beautiful.
    BRIDGET. That touches not me, brother.
    WELLBRED. That's true; that's even
the fault of it; for indeed, beauty stands
a woman in no stead, unless it procure
her touching.—But, sister, whether it
touch you or no, it touches your beauties;
and I am sure they will abide the touch;

an they do not, a plague of all ceruse,
say I! and it touches me too in part,
though not in the—— Well, there's a
dear and respected friend of mine, sister,
stands very strongly and worthily affected
toward you, and hath vowed to inflame
whole bonfires of zeal at his heart, in
honour of your perfections. I have al-
ready engaged my promise to bring you
where you shall hear him confirm much
more. Ned Knowell is the man, sister:
there's no exception against the party.
You are ripe for a husband; and a min-
ute's loss to such an occasion, is a great
trespass in a wise beauty. What say you,
sister? On my soul he loves you; will you
give him the meeting?
    BRIDGET. Faith, I had very little confi-
dence in mine own constancy, brother, if
I durst not meet a man: but this motion
of yours savours of an old knight adven-
turer's servant a little too much, me-
thinks.
    WELLBRED. What's that, sister?
    BRIDGET. Marry, of the squire.
    WELLBRED. No matter if it did, I
would be such an one for my friend. But
see, who is return'd to hinder us!

                [*Reënter* KITELY.]
    KITELY. What villany is this? call'd
        out on a false message!
This was some plot; I was not sent for.—
        Bridget,
Where is your sister?
    BRIDGET. I think she be gone forth, sir.
    KITELY. How! is my wife gone forth?
whither, for God's sake?
    BRIDGET. She's gone abroad with
Thomas.
    KITELY. Abroad with Thomas! oh,
        that villain dors me:
Beast that I was, to trust him! whither,
        I pray you,
Went she?
    BRIDGET. I know not, sir.
    WELLBRED.   I'll tell you, brother,
Whither I suspect she's gone.
    KITELY.   Whither, good brother?
    WELLBRED. To Cob's house, I believe:
but, keep my counsel.

KITELY. I will, I will: to Cob's house!
doth she haunt Cob's?
She's gone a purpose now to cuckold me,
With that lewd rascal, who, to win her
favour,
Hath told her all.   [*Exit.*]
WELLBRED. Come, he is once more gone,
Sister, let's lose no time; the affair is
worth it.   [*Exeunt.*]

SCENE VII—*A street.*

[*Enter* MATHEW *and* BOBADILL.]
MATHEW. I wonder, captain, what they
will say of my going away, ha?
BOBADILL. Why, what should they say,
but as of a discreet gentleman; quick,
wary, respectful of nature's fair linea-
ments? and that's all.
MATHEW. Why so! but what can they
say of your beating?
BOBADILL. A rude part, a touch with
soft wood, a kind of gross battery used,
laid on strongly, borne most patiently;
and that's all.
MATHEW. Ay, but would any man have
offered it in Venice, as you say?
BOBADILL. Tut! I assure you, no: you
shall have there your nobilis, your gen-
tilezza, come in bravely upon your reverse,
stand you close, stand you firm, stand you
fair, save your retricato with his left leg,
come to the assalto with the right, thrust
with brave steel, defy your base wood!
But wherefore do I awake this remem-
brance? I was fascinated, by Jupiter;
fascinated, but I will be unwitch'd and
revenged by law.
MATHEW. Do you hear? is it not best
to get a warrant, and have him arrested
and brought before justice Clement?
BOBADILL. It were not amiss; would
we had it!

[*Enter* BRAINWORM *disguised as* FORMAL.]
MATHEW. Why, here comes his man;
let's speak to him.
BOBADILL. Agreed, do you speak.
MATHEW. Save you, sir.
BRAINWORM. With all my heart, sir.

MATHEW. Sir, there is one Downright
hath abused this gentleman and myself,
and we determine to make our amends by
law: now, if you would do us the favour
to procure a warrant to bring him afore
your master, you shall be well considered,
I assure you, sir.
BRAINWORM. Sir, you know my service
is my living; such favours as these gotten
of my master is his only preferment, and
therefore you must consider me as I may
make benefit of my place.
MATHEW. How is that, sir?
BRAINWORM. Faith, sir, the thing is
extraordinary, and the gentleman may be
of great account; yet, be he what he will,
if you will lay me down a brace of angels
in my hand you shall have it, otherwise
not.
MATHEW. How shall we do, captain?
he asks a brace of angels, you have no
money?
BOBADILL. Not a cross, by fortune.
MATHEW. Nor I, as I am a gentleman,
but twopence left of my two shillings in
the morning for wine and radish: let's
find him some pawn.
BOBADILL. Pawn! we have none to the
value of his demand.
MATHEW. O, yes; I'll pawn this jewel
in my ear, and you may pawn your silk
stockings, and pull up your boots, they
will ne'er be mist: it must be done now.
BOBADILL. Well, an there be no remedy,
I'll step aside and pull them off.
                              [*Withdraws.*]
MATHEW. Do you hear, sir? we have no
store of money at this time, but you shall
have good pawns; look you, sir, this jewel,
and that gentleman's silk stockings; be-
cause we would have it dispatch'd ere we
went to our chambers.
BRAINWORM. I am content, sir; I will
get you the warrant presently. What's
his name, say you? Downright?
MATHEW. Ay, ay, George Downright.
BRAINWORM. What manner of man is
he?
MATHEW. A tall big man, sir; he goes
in a cloak most commonly of silk-russet,
laid about with russet lace.

BRAINWORM. 'Tis very good, sir.

MATHEW. Here, sir, here's my jewel.

BOBADILL [*returning*]. And here are my stockings.

BRAINWORM. Well, gentlemen, I'll procure you this warrant presently; but who will you have to serve it?

MATHEW. That's true, captain: that must be considered.

BOBADILL. Body o' me, I know not; 'tis service of danger.

BRAINWORM. Why, you were best get one o' the varlets of the city, a serjeant: I'll appoint you one, if you please.

MATHEW. Will you, sir? why, we can wish no better.

BOBADILL. We'll leave it to you, sir.

[*Exeunt* BOBADILL *and* MATHEW.]

BRAINWORM. This is rare! Now will I go and pawn this cloak of the justice's man's at the broker's, for a varlet's suit, and be the varlet myself; and get either more pawns, or more money of Downright, for the arrest. [*Exit.*]

SCENE VIII—*The lane before* COB'S *house.*

[*Enter* KNOWELL.]

KNOWELL. Oh, here it is; I am glad I have found it now;

Ho! who is within here?

TIB [*within*]. I am within, sir; what's your pleasure?

KNOWELL. To know who is within beside yourself.

TIB. Why, sir, you are no constable, I hope?

KNOWELL. O, fear you the constable? then I doubt not,

You have some guests within deserve that fear;

I'll fetch him straight.

[*Enter* TIB.]

TIB. O' God's name, sir!

KNOWELL. Go to: come tell me, is not young Knowell here?

TIB. Young Knowell! I know none such, sir, o' mine honesty.

KNOWELL. Your honesty, dame! it flies too lightly from you.

There is no way but fetch the constable.

TIB. The constable! the man is mad, I think. [*Exit, and claps to the door.*]

[*Enter* DAME KITELY *and* CASH.]

CASH. Ho! who keeps house here?

KNOWELL. O, this is the female copesmate of my son:

Now shall I meet him straight.

DAME KITELY. Knock, Thomas, hard.

CASH. Ho, goodwife!

[*Reënter* TIB.]

TIB. Why, what's the matter with you?

DAME KITELY. Why, woman, grieves it you to ope your door?

Belike you get something to keep it shut.

TIB. What mean these questions, pray ye?

DAME KITELY. So strange you make it! is not my husband here?

KNOWELL. Her husband!

DAME KITELY. My tried husband, master Kitely?

TIB. I hope he needs not to be tried here.

DAME KITELY. No, dame, he does it not for need, but pleasure.

TIB. Neither for need nor pleasure is he here.

KNOWELL. This is but a device to balk me withal:

[*Enter* KITELY, *muffled in his cloak.*]

Soft, who is this? 'tis not my son disguised?

DAME KITELY [*spies her husband, and runs to him*]. O, sir, have I forestall'd your honest market,

Found your close walks? You stand amazed now, do you?

I'faith, I am glad I have smok'd you yet at last.

What is your jewel, trow? In, come, let's see her;

Fetch forth your housewife, dame; if she be fairer,

In any honest judgment, than myself,

I'll be content with it: but she is change,

She feeds you fat, she soothes your appetite,
And you are well! Your wife, an honest woman,
Is meat twice sod to you, sir! O, you treachour!
KNOWELL. She cannot counterfeit thus palpably.
KITELY. Out on thy more than strumpet impudence!
Steal'st thou thus to thy haunts? and have I taken
Thy bawd and thee, and thy companion,
This hoary-headed letcher, this old goat,
Close at your villainy, and would'st thou 'scuse it
With this stale harlot's jest, accusing me?
O, old incontinent [to KNOWELL] dost thou not shame,
When all thy powers in chastity are spent,
To have a mind so hot? and to entice,
And feed the enticements of a lustful woman?
DAME KITELY. Out, I defy thee, I, dissembling wretch!
KITELY. Defy me, strumpet! Ask thy pander here,
Can he deny it; or that wicked elder?
KNOWELL. Why, hear you, sir.
KITELY. Tut, tut, tut; never speak:
Thy guilty conscience will discover thee.
KNOWELL. What lunacy is this, that haunts this man?
KITELY. Well, good wife bawd, Cob's wife, and you,
That make your husband such a hoddy-doddy;
And you, young apple-squire, and old cuckold-maker;
I'll have you every one before a justice:
Nay, you shall answer it, I charge you go.
KNOWELL. Marry, with all my heart, sir, I go willingly;
Though I do taste this as a trick put on me,
To punish my impertinent search, and justly,
And half forgive my son for the device.
KITELY. Come, will you go?

DAME KITELY. Go! to thy shame believe it.

[Enter COB.]
COB. Why, what's the matter here, what's here to do?
KITELY. O, Cob, art thou come? I have been abused,
And in thy house; was never man so wrong'd!
COB. 'Slid, in my house, my master Kitely! who wrongs you in my house?
KITELY. Marry, young lust in old, and old in young here:
Thy wife's their bawd, here have I taken them.
COB. How, bawd! is my house come to that? Am I preferr'd thither? Did I not charge you to keep your doors shut, Isbel? and—you let them lie open for all comers! [Beats his wife.]
KNOWELL. Friend, know some cause, before thou beat'st thy wife.
This is madness in thee.
COB. Why, is there no cause?
KITELY. Yes, I'll shew cause before the justice, Cob:
Come, let her go with me.
COB. Nay, she shall go.
TIB. Nay, I will go. I'll see an you may be allowed to make a bundle of hemp of your right and lawful wife thus, at every cuckoldy knave's pleasure. Why do you not go?
KITELY. A bitter quean! Come, we will have you tamed. [Exeunt.]

SCENE IX—A street.

[Enter BRAINWORM, disguised as a city serjeant.]
BRAINWORM. Well, of all my disguises yet, now am I most like myself, being in this serjeant's gown. A man of my present profession never counterfeits, till he lays hold upon a debtor, and says, he rests him; for then he brings him to all manner of unrest. A kind of little kings we are, bearing the diminutive of a mace, made like a young artichoke, that always car-

ries pepper and salt in itself. Well, I know not what danger I undergo by this exploit; pray Heaven I come well off!

[*Enter* MATHEW *and* BOBADILL.]

MATHEW. See, I think, yonder is the varlet, by his gown.

BOBADILL. Let's go in quest of him.

MATHEW. 'Save you, friend! are not you here by appointment of justice Clement's man?

BRAINWORM. Yes, an't please you, sir; he told me, two gentlemen had will'd him to procure a warrant from his master, which I have about me, to be served on one Downright.

MATHEW. It is honestly done of you both; and see where the party comes you must arrest; serve it upon him quickly, afore he be aware.

BOBADILL. Bear back, master Mathew.

[*Enter* STEPHEN *in* DOWNRIGHT'S *cloak.*]

BRAINWORM. Master Downright, I arrest you in the queen's name, and must carry you afore a justice by virtue of this warrant.

STEPHEN. Me, friend! I am no Downright, I; I am master Stephen: You do not well to arrest me, I tell you, truly; I am in nobody's bonds nor books, I would you should know it. A plague on you heartily, for making me thus afraid afore my time!

BRAINWORM. Why, now you are deceived, gentlemen.

BOBADILL. He wears such a cloak, and that deceived us: but see, here a' comes indeed; this is he, officer.

[*Enter* DOWNRIGHT.]

DOWNRIGHT. Why how now, signior gull! are you turn'd filcher of late! Come, deliver my cloak.

STEPHEN. Your cloak, sir! I bought it even now, in open market.

BRAINWORM. Master Downright, I have a warrant I must serve upon you, procured by these two gentlemen.

DOWNRIGHT. These gentlemen! these rascals! [*Offers to beat them.*]

BRAINWORM. Keep the peace, I charge you in her majesty's name.

DOWNRIGHT. I obey thee. What must I do, officer?

BRAINWORM. Go before master justice Clement, to answer that they can object against you, sir: I will use you kindly, sir.

MATHEW. Come, let's before, and make the justice, captain.

BOBADILL. The varlet's a tall man, afore heaven!

[*Exeunt* BOBADILL *and* MATHEW.]

DOWNRIGHT. Gull, you'll give me my cloak.

STEPHEN. Sir, I bought it, and I'll keep it.

DOWNRIGHT. You will?

STEPHEN. Ay, that I will.

DOWNRIGHT. Officer, there's thy fee, arrest him.

BRAINWORM. Master Stephen, I must arrest you.

STEPHEN. Arrest me! I scorn it. There, take your cloak, I'll none on't.

DOWNRIGHT. Nay, that shall not serve your turn now, sir. Officer, I'll go with thee to the justice's; bring him along.

STEPHEN. Why, is not here your cloak? what would you have?

DOWNRIGHT. I'll have you answer it, sir.

BRAINWORM. Sir, I'll take your word, and this gentleman's too, for his appearance.

DOWNRIGHT. I'll have no words taken: bring him along.

BRAINWORM. Sir, I may choose to do that, I may take bail.

DOWNRIGHT. 'Tis true, you may take bail, and choose at another time; but you shall not now, varlet: bring him along, or I'll swinge you.

BRAINWORM. Sir, I pity the gentleman's case: here's your money again.

DOWNRIGHT. 'Sdeins, tell not me of my money; bring him away, I say.

BRAINWORM. I warrant you he will go with you of himself, sir.

DOWNRIGHT. Yet more ado?

BRAINWORM. I have made a fair mash on't.

STEPHEN. Must I go?

BRAINWORM. I know no remedy, master Stephen.

DOWNRIGHT. Come along afore me here; I do not love your hanging look behind.

STEPHEN. Why, sir, I hope you cannot hang me for it: can he, fellow?

BRAINWORM. I think not, sir; it is but a whipping matter, sure.

STEPHEN. Why then let him do his worst, I am resolute.   [*Exeunt.*]

ACT V

SCENE I—*Coleman-street. A hall in* JUS-TICE CLEMENT'S *house.*

[*Enter* CLEMENT, KNOWELL, KITELY, DAME KITELY, TIB, CASH, COB, *and* SERVANTS.]

CLEMENT. Nay, but stay, stay, give me leave: my chair, sirrah. You, master Knowell, say you went thither to meet your son?

KNOWELL. Ay, sir.

CLEMENT. But who directed you thither?

KNOWELL. That did mine own man, sir.

CLEMENT. Where is he?

KNOWELL. Nay, I know not now; I left him with your clerk, and appointed him to stay here for me.

CLEMENT. My clerk! about what time was this?

KNOWELL. Marry, between one and two, as I take it.

CLEMENT. And what time came my man with the false message to you, master Kitely?

KITELY. After two, sir.

CLEMENT. Very good: but, mistress Kitely, how chance that you were at Cob's, ha?

DAME KITELY. An't please you, sir, I'll tell you: my brother Wellbred told me, that Cob's house was a suspected place—

CLEMENT. So it appears, methinks: but on.

DAME KITELY. And that my husband used thither daily.

CLEMENT. No matter, so he used himself well, mistress.

DAME KITELY. True, sir: but you know what grows by such haunts oftentimes.

CLEMENT. I see rank fruits of a jealous brain, mistress Kitely: but did you find your husband there, in that case as you suspected?

KITELY. I found her there, sir.

CLEMENT. Did you, so! that alters the case. Who gave you knowledge of your wife's being there?

KITELY. Marry, that did my brother Wellbred.

CLEMENT. How, Wellbred first tell her; then tell you after! Where is Wellbred?

KITELY. Gone with my sister, sir, I know not whither.

CLEMENT. Why this is a mere trick, a device; you are gull'd in this most grossly all. Alas, poor wench! wert thou beaten for this?

TIB. Yes, most pitifully, an't please you.

COB. And worthily, I hope, if it shall prove so.

CLEMENT. Ay, that's like, and a piece of a sentence.—

[*Enter a* SERVANT.]

How now, sir! what's the matter?

SERVANT. Sir, there's a gentleman in the court without, desires to speak with your worship.

CLEMENT. A gentleman! what is he?

SERVANT. A soldier, sir, he says.

CLEMENT. A soldier! take down my armour, my sword quickly. A soldier speak with me! Why, when, knaves? Come on, come on [*arms himself*]; hold my cap there, so; give me my gorget, my sword: stand by, I will end your matters anon.—Let the soldier enter.

[*Exit* SERVANT.]

[*Enter* BOBADILL, *followed by* MATHEW.]

Now, sir, what have you to say to me?

BOBADILL. By your worship's favour—

CLEMENT. Nay, keep out, sir; I know not your pretence. You send me word, sir, you are a soldier: why, sir, you shall be answer'd here: here be them that have been amongst soldiers. Sir, your pleasure.

BOBADILL. Faith, sir, so it is, this gentleman and myself have been most uncivilly wrong'd and beaten by one Downright, a coarse fellow, about the town here; and for mine own part, I protest, being a man in no sort given to this filthy humour of quarrelling, he hath assaulted me in the way of my peace, despoiled me of mine honour, disarmed me of my weapons, and rudely laid me along in the open streets, when I not so much as once offered to resist him.

CLEMENT. O, God's precious! is this the soldier? Here, take my armour off quickly, 'twill make him swoon, I fear; he is not fit to look on't, that will put up a blow.

MATHEW. An't please your worship, he was bound to the peace.

CLEMENT. Why, an he were, sir, his hands were not bound, were they?

[*Reënter* SERVANT.]

SERVANT. There's one of the varlets of the city, sir, has brought two gentlemen here; one, upon your worship's warrant.

CLEMENT. My warrant!

SERVANT. Yes, sir; the officer says, procured by these two.

CLEMENT. Bid him come in. [*Exit* SERVANT.] Set by this picture.

[*Enter* DOWNRIGHT, STEPHEN, *and* BRAINWORM, *disguised as before.*]

What, Master Downright! are you brought in at Mr. Freshwater's suit here?

DOWNRIGHT. I'faith, sir, and here's another brought at my suit.

CLEMENT. What are you, sir?

STEPHEN. A gentleman, sir. O, uncle!

CLEMENT. Uncle! who, Master Knowell?

KNOWELL. Ay, sir; this is a wise kinsman of mine.

STEPHEN. God's my witness, uncle, I am wrong'd here monstrously, he charges me with stealing of his cloak, and would I might never stir, if I did not find it in the street by chance.

DOWNRIGHT. O, did you find it now? You said you bought it erewhile.

STEPHEN. And you said, I stole it: nay, now my uncle is here, I'll do well enough with you.

CLEMENT. Well, let this breathe awhile. You that have cause to complain there, stand forth: Had you my warrant for this gentleman's apprehension?

BOBADILL. Ay, an't please your worship.

CLEMENT. Nay, do not speak in passion so: where had you it?

BOBADILL. Of your clerk, sir.

CLEMENT. That's well! an my clerk can make warrants, and my hand not at them! Where is the warrant—officer, have you it?

BRAINWORM. No, sir; your worship's man, Master Formal, bid me do it for these gentlemen, and he would be my discharge.

CLEMENT. Why, Master Downright, are you such a novice, to be served and never see the warrant?

DOWNRIGHT. Sir, he did not serve it on me.

CLEMENT. No! how then?

DOWNRIGHT. Marry, sir, he came to me, and said he must serve it, and he would use me kindly, and so—

CLEMENT. O, God's pity, was it so, sir? *He must serve it!* Give me my long sword there, and help me off. So, come on, sir varlet, I *must* cut off your legs, sirrah; [BRAINWORM *kneels.*] nay, stand up. *I'll use you kindly;* I *must* cut off your legs, I say.

[*Flourishes over him with his long sword.*]

BRAINWORM. O, good sir, I beseech you; nay, good master justice!

CLEMENT. I must do it, there is no remedy; I *must* cut off your legs, sirrah, I *must* cut off your ears, you rascal, I must do it: I *must* cut off your nose, I *must* cut off your head.

BRAINWORM. O, good your worship!

CLEMENT. Well, rise; how dost thou do now? dost thou feel thyself well? hast thou no harm?

BRAINWORM. No, I thank your good worship, sir.

CLEMENT. Why so! I said I must cut off thy legs, and I must cut off thy arms, and I must cut off thy head; but I did not do it: so you said you must serve this gentleman with my warrant, but you did not serve him. You knave, you slave, you rogue, do you say you *must*, sirrah! away with him to the jail; I'll teach you a trick for your *must*, sir.

BRAINWORM. Good sir, I beseech you, be good to me.

CLEMENT. Tell him he shall to the jail; away with him, I say.

BRAINWORM. Nay, sir, if you will commit me, it shall be for committing more than this: I will not lose by my travail any grain of my fame, certain.

[*Throws off his serjeant's gown.*]

CLEMENT. How is this?

KNOWELL. My man Brainworm!

STEPHEN. O, yes, uncle; Brainworm has been with my cousin Edward and I all this day.

CLEMENT. I told you all there was some device.

BRAINWORM. Nay, excellent justice, since I have laid myself thus open to you, now stand strong for me; both with your sword and your balance.

CLEMENT. Body o' me, a merry knave! give me a bowl of sack: if he belong to you, Master Knowell, I bespeak your patience.

BRAINWORM. That is it I have most need of; Sir, if you'll pardon me, only, I'll glory in all the rest of my exploits.

KNOWELL. Sir, you know I love not to have my favours come hard from me. You have your pardon, though I suspect you shrewdly for being of counsel with my son against me.

BRAINWORM. Yes, faith, I have, sir, though you retain'd me doubly this morning for yourself: first as Brainworm; after, as Fitz-Sword. I was your reform'd soldier, sir. 'Twas I sent you to Cob's upon the errand without end.

KNOWELL. Is it possible? or that thou should'st disguise thy language so as I should not know thee?

BRAINWORM. O, sir, this has been the day of my metamorphosis. It is not that shape alone that I have run through to-day. I brought this gentleman, master Kitely, a message too, in the form of master Justice's man here, to draw him out o' the way, as well as your worship, while master Wellbred might make a conveyance of mistress Bridget to my young master.

KITELY. How! my sister stolen away?

KNOWELL. My son is not married, I hope.

BRAINWORM. Faith, sir, they are both as sure as love, a priest, and three thousand pound, which is her portion, can make them; and by this time are ready to bespeak their wedding-supper at the Windmill, except some friend here prevent them, and invite them home.

CLEMENT. Marry, that will I; I thank thee for putting me in mind on't. Sirrah, go you and fetch them hither upon my warrant. [*Exit* SERVANT.] Neither's friends have cause to be sorry, if I know the young couple aright. Here, I drink to thee for thy good news. But I pray thee, what hast thou done with my man, Formal?

BRAINWORM. Faith, sir, after some ceremony past, as making him drunk, first with story, and then with wine, (but all in kindness,) and stripping him to his shirt, I left him in that cool vein; departed, sold your worship's warrant to these two, pawn'd his livery for that varlet's gown, to serve it in; and thus have brought myself by my activity to your worship's consideration.

CLEMENT. And I will consider thee in another cup of sack. Here's to thee, which having drunk off this my sentence: Pledge me. Thou hast done, or assisted to nothing, in my judgment, but deserves to be pardon'd for the wit of the offence. If thy master, or any man here, be angry with thee, I shall suspect his ingine, while

I know him, for't. How now, what noise is that?

[*Enter* SERVANT.]

SERVANT. Sir, it is Roger is come home.

CLEMENT. Bring him in, bring him in.

[*Enter* FORMAL *in a suit of armour.*] What! drunk? in arms against me? your reason, your reason for this?

FORMAL. I beseech your worship to pardon me; I happened into ill company by chance, that cast me into a sleep, and stript me of all my clothes.

CLEMENT. Well, tell him I am Justice Clement, and do pardon him: but what is this to your armour? what may that signify?

FORMAL. An't please you, sir, it hung up in the room where I was stript; and I borrow'd it of one of the drawers to come home in, because I was loth to do penance through the street in my shirt.

CLEMENT. Well, stand by a while.

[*Enter* EDWARD KNOWELL, WELLBRED, *and* BRIDGET.]

Who be these? O, the young company; welcome, welcome! Give you joy. Nay, mistress Bridget, blush not; you are not so fresh a bride, but the news of it is come hither afore you. Master bridegroom, I have made your peace, give me your hand: so will I for all the rest ere you forsake my roof.

EDWARD KNOWELL. We are the more bound to your humanity, sir.

CLEMENT. Only these two have so little of man in them, they are no part of my care.

WELLBRED. Yes, sir, let me pray you for this gentleman, he belongs to my sister the bride.

CLEMENT. In what place, sir?

WELLBRED. Of her delight, sir, below the stairs, and in public: her poet, sir.

CLEMENT. A poet! I will challenge him myself presently at extempore,

Mount up thy Phlegon, Muse, and testify,
How Saturn, sitting in an ebon cloud,
Disrobed his podex, white as ivory,

And through the welkin thunder'd all aloud.

WELLBRED. He is not for extempore, sir: he is all for the pocket muse; please you command a sight of it.

CLEMENT. Yes, yes, search him for a taste of his vein.

[*They search* MATHEW'S *pockets.*]

WELLBRED. You must not deny the queen's justice, sir, under a writ of rebellion.

CLEMENT. What! all this verse? body o' me, he carries a whole realm, a commonwealth of paper in his hose: let us see some of his subjects. [*Reads.*]

Unto the boundless ocean of thy face,
Runs this poor river, charg'd with streams
of eyes.

How! this is stolen.

EDWARD KNOWELL. A parody! a parody! with a kind of miraculous gift, to make it absurder than it was.

CLEMENT. Is all the rest of this batch? bring me a torch; lay it together, and give fire. Cleanse the air. [*Sets the papers on fire.*] Here was enough to have infected the whole city, if it had not been taken in time. See, see, how our poet's glory shines! brighter and brighter! still it increases! O, now it is at the highest; and now it declines as fast. You may see, *sic transit gloria mundi!*

KNOWELL. There's an emblem for you, son, and your studies.

CLEMENT. Nay, no speech or act of mine be drawn against such as profess it worthily. They are not born every year, as an alderman. There goes more to the making of a good poet, than a sheriff. Master Kitely, you look upon me! —though I live in the city here, amongst you, I will do more reverence to him, when I meet him, than I will to the mayor out of his year. But these paper-pedlars! these ink-dabblers! they cannot expect reprehension or reproach; they have it with the fact.

EDWARD KNOWELL. Sir, you have saved me the labour of a defence.

CLEMENT. It shall be discourse for supper between your father and me, if he dare undertake me. But to dispatch away these, you sign o' the soldier, and picture of the poet, (but both so false, I will not have you hanged out at my door till midnight,) while we are at supper, you two shall penitently fast it out in my court without; and, if you will, you may pray there that we may be so merry within as to forgive or forget you when we come out. Here's a third, because we tender your safety, shall watch you, he is provided for the purpose. Look to your charge, sir.

STEPHEN. And what shall I do?

CLEMENT. O! I had lost a sheep an he had not bleated: why, sir, you shall give master Downright his cloak; and I will intreat him to take it. A trencher and a napkin you shall have in the buttery, and keep Cob and his wife company here; whom I will intreat first to be reconciled; and you to endeavour with your wit to keep them so.

STEPHEN. I'll do my best.

COB. Why, now I see thou art honest, Tib, I receive thee as my dear and mortal wife again.

TIB. And I you, as my loving and obedient husband.

CLEMENT. Good compliment! It will be their bridal night too. They are married anew. Come, I conjure the rest to put off all discontent. You, master Downright, your anger; you, master Knowell, your cares; Master Kitely and his wife, their jealousy.

For, I must tell you both, while that is fed,
Horns in the mind are worse than on the head.

KITELY. Sir, thus they go from me; kiss me, sweetheart.

See what a drove of horns fly in the air,
Wing'd with my cleansed and my credulous breath!
Watch 'em suspicious eyes, watch where they fall.
See, see! on heads that think they have none at all!
O, what a plenteous world of this will come!
When air rains horns, all may be sure of some.

I have learn'd so much verse out of a jealous man's part in a play.

CLEMENT. 'Tis well, 'tis well! This night we'll dedicate to friendship, love, and laughter. Master bridegroom, take your bride and lead; every one a fellow. Here is my mistress, Brainworm! to whom all my addresses of courtship shall have their reference: whose adventures this day, when our grandchildren shall hear to be made a fable, I doubt not but it shall find both spectators and applause.

[*Exeunt.*]

A WOMAN KILLED WITH KINDNESS

By THOMAS HEYWOOD

Produced at London, 1603

CHARACTERS

SIR FRANCIS ACTON, *brother of* MISTRESS FRANKFORD
SIR CHARLES MOUNTFORD
MASTER FRANKFORD
MASTER WENDOLL, *friend to* FRANKFORD
MASTER MALBY, *friend to* SIR FRANCIS
MASTER CRANWELL
SHAFTON, *a false friend to* SIR CHARLES
OLD MOUNTFORD, *uncle to* SIR CHARLES
TIDY, *cousin to* SIR CHARLES
SANDY,
RODER,
NICHOLAS,
JENKIN,
ROGER BRICKBAT, *servants to* FRANKFORD
JACK SLIME,
SPIGOT, *a butler,*
SHERIFF
A SERJEANT, A KEEPER, OFFICERS, FALCONERS, HUNTS-
MEN, A COACHMAN, CARTERS, SERVANTS, MUSICIANS
MISTRESS FRANKFORD
SUSAN, *sister of* SIR CHARLES
CICELY, *maid to* MISTRESS FRANKFORD
WOMEN SERVANTS

SCENE—*The North of England.*

448

ACT I

SCENE I—*A room in* FRANKFORD'S *house.*

[*Enter* MASTER FRANKFORD, MISTRESS FRANKFORD, SIR FRANCIS ACTON, SIR CHARLES MOUNTFORD, MASTER MALBY, MASTER WENDOLL, *and* MASTER CRANWELL.]

SIR FRANCIS. Some music there: none lead the bride a dance?

SIR CHARLES. Yes, would she dance "The Shaking of the Sheets";
But that's the dance her husband means to lead her.

WENDOLL. That's not the dance that every man must dance,
According to the ballad.

SIR FRANCIS. Music, ho!
By your leave, sister;—by your husband's leave,
I should have said: the hand that but this day
Was given you in the church I'll borrow: sound!
This marriage music hoists me from the ground.

FRANKFORD. Ay, you may caper, you are light and free:
Marriage hath yoked my heels; pray then pardon me.

SIR FRANCIS. I'll have you dance too, brother.

SIR CHARLES. Master Frankford,
You are a happy man, sir; and much joy
Succeed your marriage mirth! you have a wife
So qualified, and with such ornaments
Both of the mind and body. First, her birth
Is noble, and her education such
As might become the daughter of a prince:
Her own tongue speaks all tongues, and her own hand
Can teach all strings to speak in their best grace,
From the shrillest treble to the hoarsest base.
To end her many praises in one word,
She's beauty and perfection's eldest daughter,
Only found by yours, though many a heart hath sought her.

FRANKFORD. But that I know your virtues and chaste thoughts,
I should be jealous of your praise, Sir Charles.

CRANWELL. He speaks no more than you approve.

MALBY. Nor flatters he that gives to her her due.

MISTRESS FRANKFORD. I would your praise could find a fitter theme
Than my imperfect beauties to speak on:
Such as they be, if they my husband please,
They suffice me now I am marrièd:
His sweet content is like a flattering glass,
To make my face seem fairer to mine eye;
But the least wrinkle from his stormy brow
Will blast the roses in my cheeks that grow.

SIR FRANCIS. A perfect wife already, meek and patient:
How strangely the word "husband" fits your mouth,
Not married three hours since! Sister, 'tis good;
You, that begin betimes thus, must needs prove
Pliant and duteous in your husband's love.—
Gramercies, brother, wrought her to't already;
Sweet husband, and a curtsey, the first day!
Mark this, mark this, you that are bachelors,
And never took the grace of honest man;
Mark this, against you marry, this one phrase:
"In a good time that man both wins and woos,
That takes his wife down in her wedding shoes."

FRANKFORD. Your sister takes not after you, Sir Francis;
All his wild blood your father spent on you:
He got her in his age, when he grew civil:

All his mad tricks were to his land entailed,
And you are heir to all; your sister, she
Hath to her dower her mother's modesty.

SIR CHARLES. Lord, sir, in what a happy state live you!
This morning, which to many seems a burden
Too heavy to bear, is unto you a pleasure.
This lady is no clog, as many are:
She doth become you like a well-made suit,
In which the tailor hath used all his art;
Not like a thick coat of unseasoned frieze,
Forced on your back in summer. She's no chain
To tie your neck, and curb you to the yoke;
But she's a chain of gold to adorn your neck.
You both adorn each other, and your hands,
Methinks, are matches: there's equality
In this fair combination; you are both
Scholars, both young, both being descended nobly.
There's music in this sympathy; it carries
Consort, and expectation of much joy,
Which God bestow on you, from this first day
Until your dissolution; that's for aye.

SIR FRANCIS. We keep you here too long, good brother Frankford.
Into the hall; away! go cheer your guests.
What, bride and bridegroom both withdrawn at once?
If you be missed, the guests will doubt their welcome,
And charge you with unkindness.

FRANKFORD. To prevent it,
I'll leave you here, to see the dance within.

MISTRESS FRANKFORD. And so will I.
[*Exeunt* FRANKFORD and MISTRESS FRANKFORD.]

SIR FRANCIS. To part you, it were sin.
Now, gallants, while the town-musicians
Finger their frets within; and the mad lads
And country-lasses, every mother's child,
With nosegays and bridelaces in their hats,
Dance all their country measures, rounds, and jigs,
What shall we do? Hark, they are all on the hoigh;
They toil like mill-horses, and turn as round,—
Marry, not on the toe. Ay, and they caper,
Not without cutting; you shall see, tomorrow,
The hall-floor pecked and dinted like a mill-stone,
Made with their high shoes; though their skill be small,
Yet they tread heavy where their hobnails fall.

SIR CHARLES. Well, leave them to their sports. Sir Francis Acton,
I'll make a match with you; meet tomorrow
At Chevy-chase, I'll fly my hawk with yours.

SIR FRANCIS. For what? For what?

SIR CHARLES. Why, for a hundred pound.

SIR FRANCIS. Pawn me some gold of that.

SIR CHARLES. Here are ten angels;
I'll make them good a hundred pound tomorrow
Upon my hawk's wing.

SIR FRANCIS. 'Tis a match, 'tis done.
Another hundred pound upon your dogs;
Dare ye, Sir Charles?

SIR CHARLES. I dare: were I sure to lose,
I durst do more than that: here is my hand,
The first course for a hundred pound.

SIR FRANCIS. A match.

WENDOLL. Ten angels on Sir Francis Acton's hawk;
As much upon his dogs.

CRANWELL. I am for Sir Charles Mountford; I have seen
His hawk and dog both tried. What, clap you hands?
Or is't no bargain?

WENDOLL. Yes, and stake them down:
Were they five hundred, they were all my own.

Sir Francis. Be stirring early with
the lark to-morrow;
I'll rise into my saddle ere the sun
Rise from his bed.
Sir Charles. If there you miss me,
say
I am no gentleman: I'll hold my day.
Sir Francis. It holds on all sides.
Come, to-night let's dance,
Early to-morrow let's prepare to ride;
We had need be three hours up before
the bride.   [*Exeunt.*]

Scene II—*A yard.*

[*Enter* Nicholas, Jenkin, Jack Slime,
and Roger Brickbat, *with* Country
Wenches, *and two or three* Musicians.]

Jenkin. Come, Nick, take you Joan
Miniver to trace withal; Jack Slime,
traverse you with Cicely Milk-pail: I
will take Jane Trubkin, and Roger Brick-
bat shall have Isbel Motley; and now
that they are busy in the parlour, come,
strike up; we'll have a crash here in the
yard.

Nicholas. My humour is not com-
pendious; dancing I possess not, though I
can foot it; yet, since I am fallen into the
hands of Cicely Milk-pail, I consent.

Slime. Truly Nick, though we were
never brought up like serving courtiers,
yet we have been brought up with serving
creatures, ay, and God's creatures too; for
we have been brought up to serve sheep,
oxen, horses, hogs, and such like: and,
though we be but country fellows, it may
be in the way of dancing we can do the
horse-trick as well as serving-men.

Brickbat. Ay, and the cross-point too.

Jenkin. O Slime, O Brickbat, do not
you know that comparisons are odious?
now we are odious ourselves too, there-
fore there are no comparisons to be made
betwixt us.

Nicholas. I am sudden, and not super-
fluous;
I am quarrelsome, and not seditious;
I am peaceable, and not contentious;
I am brief, and not compendious.

Slime. Foot it quickly: if the music
overcome not my melancholy, I shall quar-
rel; and if they do not suddenly strike up,
I shall presently strike them down.

Jenkin. No quarrelling, for God's
sake: truly, if you do, I shall set a knave
between ye.

Slime. I come to dance, not to quarrel.
Come, what shall it be? "Rogero?"

Jenkin. "Rogero!" no; we will dance
"The Beginning of the World."

Cicely. I love no dance so well as
"John come kiss me now."

Nicholas. I, that have ere now de-
served a cushion, call for the "Cushion-
dance."

Brickbat. For my part, I like nothing
so well as "Tom Tyler."

Jenkin. No; we'll have "The Hunting
of the Fox."

Slime. "The Hay," "The Hay"; there's
nothing like "The Hay."

Nicholas. I have said, I do say, and
I will say again—

Jenkin. Every man agree to have it
as Nick says.

All. Content.

Nicholas. It hath been, it now is, and
it shall be—

Cicely. What, Master Nicholas, what?

Nicholas. "Put on your smock a'
Monday."

Jenkin. So the dance will come cleanly
off. Come, for God's sake agree of some-
thing: if you like not that, put it to the
musicians; or let me speak for all, and
we'll have "Sellenger's round."

All. That, that, that.

Nicholas. No, I am resolved, thus it
shall be:
First take hands, then take ye to your
heels.

Jenkin. Why, would ye have us run
away?

Nicholas. No; but I would have you
shake your heels.
Music, strike up!
          [*They dance.* Nicholas *whilst
          dancing speaks stately and
          scurvily, the rest after the
          country fashion.*]

JENKIN. Hey! lively, my lasses! here's a turn for thee! [*Exeunt.*]

SCENE III—*The open country.*

[*Horns wind. Enter* SIR CHARLES MOUNTFORD, SIR FRANCIS ACTON, MALBY, CRANWELL, WENDOLL, FALCONERS, *and* HUNTSMEN.]

SIR CHARLES. So; well cast off: aloft, aloft! well flown!
Oh, now she takes her at the souwse, and strikes her
Down to the earth, like a swift thunderclap.

WENDOLL. She hath struck ten angels out of my way.

SIR FRANCIS. A hundred pound from me.

SIR CHARLES. What, falconer!

FALCONER. At hand, sir.

SIR CHARLES. Now she hath seized the fowl, and 'gins to plume her,
Rebeck her not: rather stand still and check her.
So, seize her gets, her jesses, and her bells: Away!

SIR FRANCIS. My hawk killed too.

SIR CHARLES. Ay, but 'twas at the querre,
Not at the mount, like mine.

SIR FRANCIS. Judgment, my masters.

CRANWELL. Yours missed her at the ferre.

WENDOLL. Ay, but our merlin first had plumed the fowl,
And twice renewed her from the river too;
Her bells, Sir Francis, had not both one weight,
Nor was one semi-tune above the other:
Methinks these Milan bells do sound too full,
And spoil the mounting of your hawk.

SIR CHARLES. 'Tis lost.

SIR FRANCIS. I grant it not. Mine likewise seized a fowl
Within her talons; and you saw her paws
Full of the feathers: both her petty singles,

And her long singles gripped her more than other;
The terrials of her legs were stained with blood:
Not of the fowl only, she did discomfit
Some of her feathers; but she brake away.
Come, come, your hawk is but a rifler.

SIR CHARLES. How!

SIR FRANCIS. Ay, and your dogs are trindle-tails and curs.

SIR CHARLES. You stir my blood.
You keep not one good hound in all your kennel,
Nor one good hawk upon your perch.

SIR FRANCIS. How, knight!

SIR CHARLES. So, knight: you will not swagger, sir?

SIR FRANCIS. Why, say I did?

SIR CHARLES. Why, sir,
I say you would gain as much by swaggering,
As you have got by wagers on your dogs:
You will come short in all things.

SIR FRANCIS. Not in this:
Now I'll strike home.

SIR CHARLES. Thou shalt to thy long home,
Or I will want my will.

SIR FRANCIS. All they that love Sir Francis, follow me.

SIR CHARLES. All that affect Sir Charles, draw on my part.

CRANWELL. On this side heaves my hand.

WENDOLL. Here goes my heart.
[*They divide themselves.* SIR CHARLES MOUNTFORD, CRANWELL, FALCONER, *and* HUNTSMAN, *fight against* SIR FRANCIS ACTON, WENDOLL, *his* FALCONER, *and* HUNTSMAN; *and* SIR CHARLES'S *side gets the better, beating the others away, and killing both of* SIR FRANCIS'S *men. Exeunt all except* SIR CHARLES.]

SIR CHARLES. My God! what have I done? what have I done?
My rage hath plunged into a sea of blood,
In which my soul lies drowned. Poor innocents,

For whom we are to answer! Well, 'tis done,
And I remain the victor. A great conquest,
When I would give this right hand, nay, this head,
To breathe in them new life whom I have slain!
Forgive me, God! 'twas in the heat of blood,
And anger quite removes me from myself:
It was not I, but rage, did this vile murder;
Yet I, and not my rage, must answer it.
Sir Francis Acton he is fled the field;
With him all those that did partake his quarrel,
And I am left alone with sorrow dumb,
And in my height of conquest overcome.

[*Enter* SUSAN.]

SUSAN. O God! my brother wounded 'mong the dead!
Unhappy jest, that in such earnest ends:
The rumour of this fear stretched to my ears,
And I am come to know if you be wounded.
SIR CHARLES. Oh! sister, sister, wounded at the heart.
SUSAN. My God forbid!
SIR CHARLES. In doing that thing which He forbad,
I am wounded, sister.
SUSAN. I hope not at the heart.
SIR CHARLES. Yes, at the heart.
SUSAN. O God! a surgeon there!
SIR CHARLES. Call me a surgeon, sister, for my soul;
The sin of murder it hath pierced my heart,
And made a wide wound there: but for these scratches,
They are nothing, nothing.
SUSAN. Charles, what have you done?
Sir Francis hath great friends, and will pursue you
Unto the utmost danger of the law.
SIR CHARLES. My conscience is become mine enemy,
And will pursue me more than Acton can.

SUSAN. Oh, fly, sweet brother.
SIR CHARLES. Shall I fly from thee?
Why, Sue, art weary of my company?
SUSAN. Fly from your foe.
SIR CHARLES. You, sister, are my friend;
And, flying you, I shall pursue my end.
SUSAN. Your company is as my eyeball dear;
Being far from you, no comfort can be near;
Yet fly to save your life: what would I care
To spend my future age in black despair,
So you were safe? and yet to live one week
Without my brother Charles, through every cheek
My streaming tears would downwards run so rank,
Till they could set on either side a bank,
And in the midst a channel; so my face
For two salt-water brooks shall still find place.
SIR CHARLES. Thou shalt not weep so much, for I will stay
In spite of danger's teeth; I'll live with thee,
Or I'll not live at all. I will not sell
My country and my father's patrimony,
Nor thy sweet sight, for a vain hope of life.

[*Enter* SHERIFF, *with* OFFICERS.]

SHERIFF. Sir Charles, I am made the unwilling instrument
Of your attach and apprehension:
I'm sorry that the blood of innocent men
Should be of you exacted. It was told me
That you were guarded with a troop of friends,
And therefore I come thus armed.
SIR CHARLES. O, Master Sheriff,
I came into the field with many friends,
But see, they all have left me: only one
Clings to my sad misfortune, my dear sister.
I know you for an honest gentleman;
I yield my weapons, and submit to you;

Convey me where you please.

SHERIFF. To prison then,
To answer for the lives of these dead men.

SUSAN. O God! O God!

SIR CHARLES. Sweet sister, every strain
Of sorrow from your heart augments my pain;
Your grief abounds, and hits against my breast.

SHERIFF. Sir, will you go?

SIR CHARLES. Even where it likes you best. [*Exeunt.*]

ACT II

SCENE I—FRANKFORD'S *study.*

[*Enter* FRANKFORD.]

FRANKFORD. How happy am I amongst other men,
That in my mean estate embrace content!
I am a gentleman, and by my birth,
Companion with a king; a king's no more.
I am possessed of many fair revenues,
Sufficient to maintain a gentleman.
Touching my mind, I am studied in all arts;
The riches of my thoughts, and of my time,
Have been a good proficient; but the chief
Of all the sweet felicities on earth,
I have a fair, a chaste, and loving wife;
Perfection all, all truth, all ornament.
If man on earth may truly happy be,
Of these at once possessed, sure I am he.

[*Enter* NICHOLAS.]

NICHOLAS. Sir, there's a gentleman attends without
To speak with you.

FRANKFORD. On horseback?

NICHOLAS. Yes, on horseback.

FRANKFORD. Entreat him to alight, I will attend him.
Know'st thou him, Nick?

NICHOLAS. Know him! yes, his name's Wendoll:
It seems he comes in haste: his horse is booted
Up to the flank in mire, himself all spotted
And stained with plashing. Sure he rid in fear,
Or for a wager: horse and man both sweat;
I ne'er saw two in such a smoking heat.

FRANKFORD. Entreat him in: about it instantly. [*Exit* NICHOLAS.]
This Wendoll I have noted, and his carriage
Hath pleased me much: by observation
I have noted many good deserts in him:
He's affable, and seen in many things,
Discourses well, a good companion;
And though of small means, yet a gentleman
Of a good house, though somewhat pressed by want:
I have preferred him to a second place
In my opinion, and my best regard.

[*Enter* WENDOLL, MISTRESS FRANKFORD, *and* NICHOLAS.]

MISTRESS FRANKFORD. O Master Frankford, Master Wendoll here
Brings you the strangest news that e'er you heard.

FRANKFORD. What news, sweet wife? What news, good Master Wendoll?

WENDOLL. You knew the match made 'twixt Sir Francis Acton
And Sir Charles Mountford.

FRANKFORD. True, with their hounds and hawks.

WENDOLL. The matches were both played.

FRANKFORD. Ha! and which won?

WENDOLL. Sir Francis, your wife's brother, had the worst.
And lost the wager.

FRANKFORD. Why, the worse his chance:
Perhaps the fortune of some other day
Will change his luck.

MISTRESS FRANKFORD. Oh, but you hear not all.

Sir Francis lost, and yet was loth to
    yield:
At length the two knights grew to dif-
    ference,
From words to blows, and so to banding
    sides;
Where valorous Sir Charles slew in his
    spleen
Two of your brother's men; his falconer,
And his good huntsman, whom he loved
    so well:
More men were wounded, no more slain
    outright.
  FRANKFORD. Now, trust me, I am sorry
    for the knight;
But is my brother safe?
  WENDOLL. All whole and sound,
His body not being blemished with one
    wound:
But poor Sir Charles is to the prison led,
To answer at the assize for them that's
    dead.
  FRANKFORD. I thank your pains, sir;
    had the news been better
Your will was to have brought it, Master
    Wendoll.
Sir Charles will find hard friends; his
    case is heinous,
And will be most severely censured on:
I'm sorry for him. Sir, a word with
    you
I know you, sir, to be a gentleman
In all things; your possibilities but mean:
Please you to use my table and my purse,
They are yours.
  WENDOLL. O Lord, sir, I shall never
    deserve it.
  FRANKFORD. O sir, disparage not your
    worth too much:
You are full of quality and fair desert:
Choose of my men which shall attend on
    you,
And he is yours. I will allow you, sir,
Your man, your gelding, and your table,
    all
At my own charge; be my companion.
  WENDOLL. Master Frankford, I have
    oft been bound to you
By many favours; this exceeds them all,
That I shall never merit your least fa-
    vour:

But, when your last remembrance I for-
    get,
Heaven at my soul exact that weighty
    debt!
  FRANKFORD. There needs no protesta-
    tion; for I know you
Virtuous, and therefore grateful. Pr'ythee,
    Nan,
Use him with all thy loving'st courtesy.
  MISTRESS FRANKFORD. As far as mod-
    esty may well extend,
It is my duty to receive your friend.
  FRANKFORD. To dinner, come, sir; from
    this present day,
Welcome to me for ever; come, away.
    [*Exeunt* FRANKFORD, MISTRESS
      FRANKFORD, *and* WENDOLL.]
  NICHOLAS. I do not like this fellow by
    no means:
I never see him but my heart still yearns:
Zounds! I could fight with him, yet
    know not why:
The devil and he are all one in my eye.

    [*Enter* JENKIN.]
  JENKIN. O Nick, what gentleman is
that comes to lie at our house? my mas-
ter allows him one to wait on him, and
I believe it will fall to thy lot.
  NICHOLAS. I love my master; by these
    hilts I do!
But rather than I'll ever come to serve
    him,
I'll turn away my master.

    [*Enter* CICELY.]
  CICELY. Nich'las, where are you,
Nich'las? you must come in, Nich'las, and
help the young gentleman off with his
boots.
  NICHOLAS. If I pluck off his boots, I'll
    eat the spurs,
And they shall stick fast in my throat
    like burs.
  CICELY. Then, Jenkin, come you.
  JENKIN. Nay, 'tis no boot for me to
deny it. My master hath given me a coat
here, but he takes pains himself to brush
it once or twice a day with a holly-
wand.
  CICELY. Come, come, make haste, that

you may wash your hands again, and help to serve in dinner.

JENKIN. You may see, my masters, though it be afternoon with you, 'tis but early days with us, for we have not dined yet: stay a little, I'll but go in and help to bear up the first course, and come to you again presently.   [*Exeunt.*]

SCENE II—*A room in the gaol.*

[*Enter* MALBY *and* CRANWELL.]
MALBY. This is the sessions-day; pray can you tell me
How young Sir Charles hath sped? Is he acquit,
Or must he try the law's strict penalty?
    CRANWELL. He's cleared of all, spite of his enemies,
Whose earnest labour was to take his life:
But in this suit of pardon he hath spent
All the revenues that his father left him;
And he is now turned a plain countryman,
Reformed in all things. See, sir, here he comes.

[*Enter* SIR CHARLES *and* KEEPER.]
KEEPER. Discharge your fees, and you are then at freedom.
    SIR CHARLES. Here, Master Keeper, take the poor remainder
Of all the wealth I have: my heavy foes
Have made my purse light; but, alas! to me
'Tis wealth enough that you have set me free.
    MALBY. God give you joy of your delivery!
I am glad to see you abroad, Sir Charles.
    SIR CHARLES. The poorest knight in England, Master Malby:
My life hath cost me all my patrimony
My father left his son: well, God forgive them
That are the authors of my penury.

[*Enter* SHAFTON.]
SHAFTON. Sir Charles! a hand, a hand! at liberty?

Now, by the faith I owe, I am glad to see it.
What want you? wherein may I pleasure you?
    SIR CHARLES. O me! O most unhappy gentleman!
I am not worthy to have friends stirred up,
Whose hands may help me in this plunge of want.
I would I were in Heaven, to inherit there
The immortal birth-right which my Saviour keeps,
And by no unthrift can be bought and sold;
For here on earth what pleasures should we trust?
    SHAFTON. To rid you from these contemplations,
Three hundred pounds you shall receive of me;
Nay, five for fail. Come, sir; the sight of gold
Is the most sweet receipt for melancholy,
And will revive your spirits: you shall hold law
With your proud adversaries. Tush, let Frank Acton
Wage with his knighthood like expense with me,
And he will sink, he will. Nay, good Sir Charles,
Applaud your fortune, and your fair escape
From all these perils.
    SIR CHARLES. O sir, they have undone me.
Two thousand and five hundred pound a year
My father, at his death, possessed me of;
All which the envious Acton made me spend.
And, notwithstanding all this large expense,
I had much ado to gain my liberty:
And I have only now a house of pleasure,
With some five hundred pounds, reserved
Both to maintain me and my loving sister.
    SHAFTON [*aside*]. That must I have, it lies convenient for me:

If I can fasten but one finger on him,
With my full hand I'll gripe him to the
    heart.
'Tis not for love I proffered him this coin,
But for my gain and pleasure. [*Aloud.*]
    Come, Sir Charles,
I know you have need of money; take
    my offer.
SIR CHARLES.   Sir, I accept it, and
    remain indebted
Even to the best of my unable power.
Come, gentlemen, and see it tendered
    down.   [*Exeunt.*]

SCENE III—*A room in* FRANKFORD'S *house.*

[*Enter* WENDOLL *melancholy.*]
WENDOLL. I am a villain if I appre-
    hend
But such a thought: then, to attempt the
    deed,—
Slave, thou art damned without redemp-
    tion.
I'll drive away this passion with a song.
A song! ha, ha: a song! as if, fond man,
Thy eyes could swim in laughter, when
    thy soul
Lies drenched and drownèd in red tears
    of blood.
I'll pray, and see if God within my heart
Plant better thoughts. Why, prayers are
    meditations;
And when I meditate (O God, forgive
    me!)
It is on her divine perfections.
I will forget her; I will arm myself
Not to entertain a thought of love to her:
And, when I come by chance into her
    presence,
I'll hale these balls until my eye-strings
    crack,
From being pulled and drawn to look that
    way.

[*Enter over the stage,* FRANKFORD, MIS-
    TRESS FRANKFORD, *and* NICHOLAS.]
O God! O God! with what a violence
I'm hurried to mine own destruction.
There goest thou, the most perfectest man
That ever England bred a gentleman;

And shall I wrong his bed? Thou God
    of thunder!
Stay in thy thoughts of vengeance and of
    wrath,
Thy great, almighty, and all-judging hand
From speedy execution on a villain:
A villain, and a traitor to his friend.

[*Enter* JENKIN.]
JENKIN. Did your worship call?
WENDOLL. He doth maintain me, he
    allows me largely
Money to spend——
JENKIN. By my faith, so do not you
me; I cannot get a cross of you.
WENDOLL. My gelding, and my man——
JENKIN. That's Sorrell and I.
WENDOLL. This kindness grows of no
alliance 'twixt us——
JENKIN. Nor is my service of any
great acquaintance.
WENDOLL. I never bound him to me by
    desert:
Of a mere stranger, a poor gentleman,
A man by whom in no kind he could gain,
He hath placed me in the height of all
    his thoughts,
Made me companion with the best and
    chiefest
In Yorkshire. He cannot eat without me,
Nor laugh without me: I am to his body
As necessary as his digestion,
And equally do make him whole or sick:
And shall I wrong this man? Base man!
    ingrate
Hast thou the power straight with thy
    gory hands
To rip thy image from his bleeding heart?
To scratch thy name from out the holy
    book
Of his remembrance; and to wound his
    name
That holds thy name so dear? or rend his
    heart
To whom thy heart was knit and joined
    together?
And yet I must: then, Wendoll, be con-
    tent;
Thus villains, when they would, cannot
    repent.
JENKIN. What a strange humour is

my new master in! pray God he be not mad: if he should be so, I should never have any mind to serve him in Bedlam. It may be he's mad for missing of me.

WENDOLL [*seeing* JENKIN]. What, Jenkin, where's your mistress?

JENKIN. Is your worship married?

WENDOLL. Why dost thou ask?

JENKIN. Because you are my master; and if I have a mistress, I would be glad, like a good servant, to do my duty to her.

WENDOLL. I mean Mistress Frankford.

JENKIN. Marry, sir, her husband is riding out of town, and she went very lovingly to bring him on his way to horse. Do you see, sir? here she comes, and here I go.

WENDOLL. Vanish. [*Exit* JENKIN.]

[*Reënter* MISTRESS FRANKFORD.]

MISTRESS FRANKFORD. You are well met, sir; now, in troth, my husband, Before he took horse, had a great desire To speak with you: we sought about the house, Hollaed into the fields, sent every way, But could not meet you: therefore he enjoined me To do unto you his most kind commends. Nay, more; he wills you, as you prize his love, Or hold in estimation his kind friendship, To make bold in his absence, and command Even as himself were present in the house: For you must keep his table, use his servants, And be a present Frankford in his absence.

WENDOLL. I thank him for his love.— Give me a name, you whose infectious tongues Are tipped with gall and poison: as you would Think on a man that had your father slain, Murdered your children, made your wives base strumpets, So call me, call me so: print in my face

The most stigmatic title of a villain, For hatching treason to so true a friend.

[*Aside.*]

MISTRESS FRANKFORD. Sir, you are much beholding to my husband; You are a man most dear in his regard.

WENDOLL [*aside*]. I am bound unto your husband, and you too. I will not speak to wrong a gentleman Of that good estimation, my kind friend: I will not; zounds! I will not. I may choose, And I will choose. Shall I be so misled? Or shall I purchase to my father's crest The motto of a villain? If I say I will not do it, what thing can enforce me? What can compel me? What sad destiny Hath such command upon my yielding thoughts? I will not—Ha! some fury pricks me on, The swift Fates drag me at their chariot-wheel, And hurry me to mischief. Speak I must; Injure myself, wrong her, deceive his trust.

MISTRESS FRANKFORD. Are you not well, sir, that you seem thus troubled? There is sedition in your countenance.

WENDOLL. And in my heart, fair angel, chaste and wise. I love you: start not, speak not, answer not. I love you: nay, let me speak the rest: Bid me to swear, and I will call to record The host of Heaven.

MISTRESS FRANKFORD. The host of Heaven forbid Wendoll should hatch such a disloyal thought!

WENDOLL. Such is my fate; to this suit I was born, To wear rich pleasure's crown, or fortune's scorn.

MISTRESS FRANKFORD. My husband loves you.

WENDOLL. I know it.

MISTRESS FRANKFORD. He esteems you Even as his brain, his eye-ball, or his heart.

WENDOLL. I have tried it.

MISTRESS FRANKFORD. His purse is your exchequer, and his table

Doth freely serve you.

WENDOLL. So I have found it.

MISTRESS FRANKFORD. O! with what face of brass, what brow of steel,

Can you, unblushing, speak this to the face

Of the espoused wife of so dear a friend?

It is my husband that maintains your state;

Will you dishonour him that in your power

Hath left his whole affairs? I am his wife,

It is to me you speak.

WENDOLL. O speak no more!

For more than this I know, and have recorded

Within the red-leaved table of my heart.

Fair, and of all beloved, I was not fearful

Bluntly to give my life into your hand,

And at one hazard all my earthly means.

Go, tell your husband; he will turn me off,

And I am then undone. I care not, I;

'Twas for your sake. Perchance in rage he'll kill me:

I care not, 'twas for you. Say I incur

The general name of villain through the world,

Of traitor to my friend; I care not, I.

Beggary, shame, death, scandal, and reproach,

For you I'll hazard all: why, what care I?

For you I'll live, and in your love I'll die.

MISTRESS FRANKFORD. You move me, sir, to passion and to pity.

The love I bear my husband is as precious

As my soul's health.

WENDOLL. I love your husband too,

And for his love I will engage my life:

Mistake me not, the augmentation

Of my sincere affection borne to you

Doth no whit lessen my regard of him.

I will be secret, lady, close as night;

And not the light of one small glorious star

Shall shine here in my forehead, to bewray

That act of night.

MISTRESS FRANKFORD. What shall I say?

My soul is wandering, and ha*th lost her way.

Oh, Master Wendoll! Oh!

WENDOLL. Sigh not, sweet saint;

For every sigh you breathe draws frcm my heart

A drop of blood.

MISTRESS FRANKFORD. I ne'er offended yet:

My fault, I fear, will in my brow be writ.

Women that fall, not quite bereft of grace,

Have their offences noted in their face.

I blush and am ashamed. Oh, Master Wendoll,

Pray God I be not born to curse your tongue,

That hath enchanted me! This maze I am in

I fear will prove the labyrinth of sin.

[*Reënter* NICHOLAS *behind.*]

WENDOLL. The path of pleasure, and the gate to bliss,

Which on your lips I knock at with a kiss.

NICHOLAS [*aside*]. I'll kill the rogue.

WENDOLL. Your husband is from home, your bed's no blab.

Nay, look not down and blush.

[*Exeunt* WENDOLL *and* MISTRESS FRANKFORD.]

NICHOLAS. Zounds! I'll stab.

Ay, Nick, was it thy chance to come just in the nick?

I love my master, and I hate that slave:

I love my mistress, but these tricks I like not.

My master shall not pocket up this wrong;

I'll eat my fingers first. What say'st thou, metal?

Does not the rascal Wendoll go on legs

That thou must cut off? Hath he not ham strings

That thou must hough? Nay, metal, thou shalt stand

To all I say. I'll henceforth turn a spy,

And watch them in their close convey-
ances.
I never looked for better of that rascal,
Since he came miching first into our
house:
It is that Satan hath corrupted her,
For she was fair and chaste. I'll have an
eye
In all their gestures. Thus I think of
them,
If they proceed as they have done before:
Wendoll's a knave, my mistress is a ——
　　　　　　　　　　　　　　[*Exit.*]

ACT III

SCENE I—*A room in* SIR CHARLES
MOUNTFORD'S *house.*

[*Enter* SIR CHARLES MOUNTFORD *and*
SUSAN.]
　SIR CHARLES.　Sister, you see we are
　driven to hard shift
To keep this poor house we have left
unsold;
I am now enforced to follow husbandry,
And you to milk; and do we not live
well?
Well, I thank God.
　SUSAN.　O brother, here's a change.
Since old Sir Charles died, in our father's
house!
　SIR CHARLES.　All things on earth thus
　change, some up, some down;
Content's a kingdom. and I wear that
crown.

[*Enter* SHAFTON *with a* SERJEANT.]
　SHAFTON.　Good morrow, morrow, Sir
　Charles: what, with your sister,
Plying your husbandry?—Serjeant, stand
off.—
You have a pretty house here, and a
garden,
And goodly ground about it. Since it lies
So near a lordship that I lately bought,
I would fain buy it of you. I will give
you——
　SIR CHARLES.　O, pardon me: this house
　successively

Hath 'longed to me and my progenitors
Three hundred years. My great-great-
grandfather,
He in whom first our gentle style began,
Dwelt here; and in this ground, increased
this mole-hill
Unto that mountain which my father left
me.
Where he the first of all our house began,
I now the last will end, and keep this
house,
This virgin title, never yet deflowered
By any unthrift of the Mountfords'
line.
In brief, I will not sell it for more gold
Than you could hide or pave the ground
withal.
　SHAFTON.　Ha, ha! a proud mind and
　a beggar's purse!
Where's my three hundred pounds, be-
sides the use?
I have brought it to an execution
By course of law: what, is my moneys
ready?
　SIR CHARLES.　An execution, sir, and
　never tell me
You put my bond in suit! you deal ex-
tremely.
　SHAFTON.　Sell me the land, and I'll
　acquit you straight.
　SIR CHARLES.　Alas, alas! 'tis all trou-
　ble hath left me
To cherish me and my poor sister's life.
If this were sold, our names should then
be quite
Razed from the bed-roll of gentility.
You see what hard shift we have made to
keep it
Allied still to our own name. This palm,
you see,
Labour hath glowed within: her silver
brow,
That never tasted a rough winter's blast
Without a mask or fan, doth with a grace
Defy cold winter, and his storms out-
face.
　SUSAN.　Sir, we feed sparing, and we
　labour hard,
We lie uneasy, to reserve to us
And our succession this small plot of
ground.

SIR CHARLES. I have so bent my thoughts to husbandry,
That I protest I scarcely can remember
What a new fashion is; how silk or satin
Feels in my hand: why, pride is grown to us
A mere, mere stranger. I have quite forgot
The names of all that ever waited on me;
I cannot name ye any of my hounds,
Once from whose echoing mouths I heard all music
That e'er my heart desired. What should I say?
To keep this place I have changed myself away.

SHAFTON [to the SERJEANT]. Arrest him at my suit. Actions and actions
Shall keep thee in perpetual bondage fast:
Nay, more, I'll sue thee by a late appeal,
And call thy former life in question.
The keeper is my friend, thou shalt have irons,
And usage such as I'll deny to dogs:
Away with him!

SIR CHARLES [to SUSAN]. You are too timorous:
But trouble is my master,
And I will serve him truly.—My kind sister,
Thy tears are of no force to mollify
This flinty man. Go to my father's brother,
My kinsmen and allies; entreat them for me,
To ransom me from this injurious man,
That seeks my ruin.

SHAFTON. Come, irons, irons! come away;
I'll see thee lodged far from the sight of day.

[Exeunt SHAFTON and SERJEANT with SIR CHARLES.]

SUSAN. My heart's so hardened with the frost of grief,
Death cannot pierce it through. Tyrant too fell!
So lead the fiends condemnèd souls to hell.

[Enter SIR FRANCIS ACTON and MALBY.]

SIR FRANCIS. Again to prison! Malby, hast thou seen
A poor slave better tortured? Shall we hear
The music of his voice cry from the grate,
"Meat for the Lord's sake"? No, no, yet I am not
Throughly revenged. They say he hath a pretty wench
Unto his sister: shall I, in mercy-sake
To him and to his kindred, bribe the fool
To shame herself by lewd dishonest lust?
I'll proffer largely; but, the deed being done,
I'll smile to see her base confusion.

MALBY. Methinks, Sir Francis, you are full revenged
For greater wrongs than he can proffer you.
See where the poor sad gentlewoman stands.

SIR FRANCIS. Ha, ha! now will I flout her poverty,
Deride her fortunes, scoff her base estate;
My very soul the name of Mountford hates.
But stay, my heart! oh, what a look did fly
To strike my soul through with thy piercing eye!
I am enchanted; all my spirits are fled,
And with one glance my envious spleen struck dead.

SUSAN. Acton! that seeks our blood.
[Runs away.]

SIR FRANCIS. O chaste and fair!

MALBY. Sir Francis, why, Sir Francis, zounds! in a trance?
Sir Francis, what cheer, man? Come, come, how is't?

SIR FRANCIS. Was she not fair? Or else this judging eye
Cannot distinguish beauty.

MALBY. She was fair.

SIR FRANCIS. She was an angel in a mortal's shape,
And ne'er descended from old Mountford's line.
But soft, soft, let me call my wits together.

A poor, poor wench, to my great adversary
Sister, whose very souls denounce stern war,
One against other. How now, Frank, turned fool
Or madman, whether? But no; master of
My perfect senses and directest wits.
Then why should I be in this violent humour
Of passion and of love; and with a person
So different every way, and so opposed
In all contractions, and still-warring actions?
Fie, fie; how I dispute against my soul!
Come, come; I'll gain her, or in her fair quest
Purchase my soul free and immortal rest.
                                [*Exeunt.*]

SCENE II—*A sitting-room in* FRANKFORD'S *house.*

[*Enter* SERVING-MEN, *one with a voider and a wooden knife to take away; another with the salt and bread; another with the table-cloth and napkins; another with the carpet:* JENKIN *follows them with two lights.*]
JENKIN. So, march in order, and retire in battle array. My master and the guests have supped already, all's taken away: here, now spread for the serving-men in the hall. Butler, it belongs to your office.
BUTLER. I know it, Jenkin. What d'ye call the gentleman that supped there to-night?
JENKIN. Who, my master?
BUTLER. No, no; Master Wendoll, he's a daily guest: I mean the gentleman that came but this afternoon.
JENKIN. His name's Master Cranwell. God's light, hark, within there, my master calls to lay more billets upon the fire. Come, come! Lord, how we that are in office here in the house are troubled! One spread the carpet in the parlour, and stand ready to snuff the lights; the rest

be ready to prepare their stomachs. More lights in the hall there. Come, Nich'las.
                    [*Exeunt all but* NICHOLAS.]
NICHOLAS. I cannot eat, but had I Wendoll's heart
I would eat that; the rogue grows impudent.
Oh, I have seen such vile notorious tricks,
Ready to make my eyes dart from my head.
I'll tell my master, by this air I will!
Fall what may fall, I'll tell him. Here he comes.

[*Enter* FRANKFORD, *brushing the crumbs from his clothes with a napkin, as newly risen from supper.*]
FRANKFORD. Nicholas, what make you here? why are not you
At supper in the hall among your fellows?
NICHOLAS. Master, I stayed your rising from the board,
To speak with you.
FRANKFORD. Be brief, then, gentle Nicholas;
My wife and guests attend me in the parlour.
Why dost thou pause? Now, Nicholas, you want money,
And, unthrift-like, would eat into your wages
Ere you have earned it: here, sir, 's half a crown;
Play the good husband, and away to supper.
NICHOLAS. By this hand, an honourable gentleman! I will not see him wronged.
—Sir, I have served you long; you entertained me seven years before your beard. You knew me, sir, before you knew my mistress.
FRANKFORD. What of this, good Nicholas?
NICHOLAS. I never was a make-bate or a knave;
I have no fault but one: I'm given to quarrel,
But not with women. I will tell you, master,
That which will make your heart leap from your breast,

Your hair to startle from your head, your
    ears to tingle.

FRANKFORD.   What preparation's this
    to dismal news?

NICHOLAS.   'Sblood, sir!   I love you
    better than your wife;

I'll make it good.

FRANKFORD.   You are a knave, and I
    have much ado

With wonted patience to contain my rage,

And not to break thy pate.   Thou art a
    knave:

I'll turn you, with your base comparisons,

Out of my doors.

NICHOLAS.   Do, do: there is not room

For Wendoll and for me both in one
    house.

O master, master, that Wendoll is a
    villain.

FRANKFORD.   Ay, saucy!

NICHOLAS.   Strike, strike; do, strike;
    yet hear me: I am no fool,

I know a villain, when I see him act

Deeds of a villain.   Master, master, that
    base slave

Enjoys my mistress, and dishonours you.

FRANKFORD.   Thou hast killed me with
    a weapon whose sharp point

Hath pricked quite through and through
    my shivering heart:

Drops of cold sweat sit dangling on my
    hairs,

Like morning's dew upon the golden
    flowers,

And I am plunged into strange agonies.

What didst thou say?   If any word that
    touched

His credit or her reputation,

It is as hard to enter my belief

As Dives into heaven.

NICHOLAS.   I can gain nothing;

They are two that never wronged me.   I
    knew before

'Twas but a thankless office, and perhaps

As much as is my service, or my life

Is worth.   All this I know; but this and
    more,

More by a thousand dangers, could not
    hire me

To smother such a heinous wrong from you.

I saw, and I have said.

FRANKFORD [aside].   'Tis probable;
    though blunt, yet he is honest:

Though I durst pawn my life, and on their
    faith

Hazard the dear salvation of my soul,

Yet in my trust I may be too secure.

May this be true?   O, may it, can it be?

Is it by any wonder possible?

Man, woman, what thing mortal may we
    trust,

When friends and bosom wives prove so
    unjust?—

[To NICHOLAS.]   What instance hast thou
    of this strange report?

NICHOLAS.   Eyes, eyes.

FRANKFORD.   Thy eyes may be deceived,
    I tell thee:

For, should an angel from the heavens
    drop down,

And preach this to me that thyself hast
    told,

He should have much ado to win belief;

In both their loves I am so confident.

NICHOLAS.   Shall I discourse the same
    by circumstance?

FRANKFORD.   No more! to supper, and
    command your fellows

To attend us and the strangers.   Not a
    word,

I charge thee on thy life: be secret then,

For I know nothing.

NICHOLAS.   I am dumb; and, now that
    I have eased my stomach,

I will go fill my stomach.

FRANKFORD.   Away; be gone.   [Exit
                                    NICHOLAS.]

She is well born, descended nobly;

Virtuous her education, her repute

Is in the general voice of all the country

Honest and fair; her carriage, her de-
    meanour,

In all her actions that concern the love

To me her husband, modest, chaste, and
    godly.

Is all this seeming gold plain copper?

But he, that Judas that hath borne my
    purse,

And sold me for a sin!—O God! O God!

Shall I put up these wrongs?   No.   Shall
    I trust

The bare report of this suspicious groom,

Before the double-gilt, the well-hatched
　　ore
Of their two hearts? No, I will lose these
　　thoughts:
Distraction I will banish from my brow,
And from my looks exile sad discontent,
Their wonted favours in my tongue shall
　　flow;
Till I know all, I'll nothing seem to
　　know.
Lights and a table there! Wife, Master
　　Wendoll,
And gentle Master Cranwell.

[*Enter* MISTRESS FRANKFORD, WENDOLL,
CRANWELL, NICHOLAS, *and* JENKIN, *with
cards, carpets, stools, and other neces-
saries.*]

FRANKFORD. O Master Cranwell, you
　　are a stranger here,
And often baulk my house: faith, y'are
　　a churl:
Now we have supped, a table, and to
　　cards.

JENKIN. A pair of cards, Nicholas,
and a carpet to cover the table. Where's
Cicely with her counters and her box?
Candles and candlesticks there! Fie, we
have such a household of serving crea-
tures! unless it be Nick and I, there's not
one amongst them all can say bo to a
goose. Well said, Nick. [*They spread
a carpet, set down lights and cards.*]

MISTRESS FRANKFORD. Come, Master
Frankford, who shall take my part?

FRANKFORD. Marry, that will I, sweet
wife.

WENDOLL. No, by my faith, sir; when
you are together I sit out: it must be
Mistress Frankford and I, or else it is no
match.

FRANKFORD. I do not like that match.

NICHOLAS [*aside*]. You have no reason,
marry, knowing all.

FRANKFORD. 'Tis no great matter
neither. Come, Master Cranwell, shall
you and I take them up?

CRANWELL. At your pleasure, sir.

FRANKFORD. I must look to you, Mas-
ter Wendoll, for you will be playing false;
nay, so will my wife too.

NICHOLAS [*aside*]. Ay, I will be sworn
she will.

MISTRESS FRANKFORD. Let them that
are taken playing false, forfeit the set.

FRANKFORD. Content; it shall go hard
but I'll take you.

CRANWELL. Gentlemen, what shall our
game be?

WENDOLL. Master Frankford, you play
best at noddy.

FRANKFORD. You shall not find it so;
indeed you shall not.

MISTRESS FRANKFORD. I can play at
nothing so well as double ruff.

FRANKFORD. If Master Wendoll and
my wife be together, there's no playing
against them at double hand.

NICHOLAS. I can tell you, sir, the game
that Master Wendoll is best at.

WENDOLL. What game is that, Nick?

NICHOLAS. Marry, sir, knave out of
doors.

WENDOLL. She and I will take you at
lodam.

MISTRESS FRANKFORD. Husband, shall
we play at saint?

FRANKFORD. My saint's turned devil.
No, we'll none of saint:
You are best at new-cut, wife; you'll play
　　at that.

WENDOLL. If you play at new-cut, I
am soonest hitter of any here, for a wager.

FRANKFORD. 'Tis me they play on.
Well, you may draw out.
For all your cunning, 'twill be to your
　　shame;
I'll teach you, at your new-cut, a new
　　game.
Come, come.

CRANWELL. If you cannot agree upon
the game, to post and pair.

WENDOLL. We shall be soonest pairs;
　　and my good host,
When he comes late home, he must kiss
　　the post.

FRANKFORD. Whoever wins, it shall be
　　thy cost.

CRANWELL. Faith, let it be vide-ruff,
and let's make honours.

FRANKFORD. If you make honours, one
　　thing let me crave:

Honour the king and queen; except the knave.

WENDOLL. Well, as you please for that. Lift who shall deal.

MISTRESS FRANKFORD. The least in sight: what are you, Master Wendoll?

WENDOLL. I am a knave.

NICHOLAS [aside]. I'll swear it.

MISTRESS FRANKFORD. I a queen.

FRANKFORD [aside]. A quean thou shouldst say. [Aloud.] Well, the cards are mine;
They are the grossest pair that e'er I felt.

MISTRESS FRANKFORD. Shuffle, I'll cut: would I had never dealt.

FRANKFORD. I have lost my dealing.

WENDOLL. Sir, the fault's in me:
This queen I have more than mine own, you see.
Give me the stock.

FRANKFORD. My mind's not on my game.
Many a deal I have lost; the more's your shame.
You have served me a bad trick, Master Wendoll.

WENDOLL. Sir, you must take your lot. To end this strife,
I know I have dealt better with your wife.

FRANKFORD. Thou hast dealt falsely, then.

MISTRESS FRANKFORD. What's trumps?

WENDOLL. Hearts: partner, I rub.

FRANKFORD [aside]. Thou robb'st me of my soul, of her chaste love;
In thy false dealing thou hast robbed my heart.
[Aloud.] Booty you play; I like a loser stand,
Having no heart, or here or in my hand.
I will give o'er the set; I am not well.
Come, who will hold my cards?

MISTRESS FRANKFORD. Not well, sweet Master Frankford!
Alas, what ail you? 'Tis some sudden qualm.

WENDOLL. How long have you been so, Master Frankford?

FRANKFORD. Sir, I was lusty, and I had my health,
But I grew ill when you began to deal.
Take hence this table. Gentle Master Cranwell,
You are welcome; see your chamber at your pleasure.
I'm sorry that this meagrim takes me so,
I cannot sit and bear you company.
Jenkin, some lights, and show him to his chamber. [Exeunt CRANWELL and JENKIN.]

MISTRESS FRANKFORD. A night-gown for my husband; quickly there:
It is some rheum or cold.

WENDOLL. Now, in good faith, this illness you have got
By sitting late without your gown.

FRANKFORD. I know it, Master Wendoll.
Go, go to bed, lest you complain like me.
Wife, prithee, wife, into my bed-chamber;
The night is raw and cold, and rheumatic:
Leave me my gown and light; I'll walk away my fit.

WENDOLL. Sweet sir, good night.

FRANKFORD. Myself, good night.
[Exit WENDOLL.]

MISTRESS FRANKFORD. Shall I attend you, husband?

FRANKFORD. No, gentle wife, thou'lt catch cold in thy head;
Prythee, be gone, sweet; I'll make haste to bed.

MISTRESS FRANKFORD. No sleep will fasten on mine eyes, you know,
Until you come.

FRANKFORD. Sweet Nan, I prithee go.— [Exit MISTRESS FRANKFORD.]
I have bethought me: get me, by degrees,
The keys of all my doors, which I will mould
In wax, and take their fair impression,
To have by them new keys. This being compassed,
At a set hour a letter shall be brought me,
And, when they think they may securely play,
They nearest are to danger. Nick, I must rely
Upon thy trust and faithful secrecy.

NICHOLAS. Build on my faith.

FRANKFORD. To bed then, not to rest:
Care lodges in my brain, grief in my
    breast.   [*Exeunt.*]

ACT IV

SCENE I—*A room in old* MOUNTFORD'S
house.

[*Enter* SUSAN, OLD MOUNTFORD, SANDY,
    RODER, *and* TIDY.]

OLD MOUNTFORD. You say my nephew
    is in great distress:

Who brought it to him, but his own lewd
    life?

I cannot spare a cross. I must confess

He was my brother's son: why, niece,
    what then?

This is no world in which to pity men.

SUSAN. I was not born a beggar,
    though his extremes

Enforce this language from me: I protest

No fortune of mine own could lead my
    tongue

To this base key. I do beseech you, uncle,

For the name's sake, for Christianity,

Nay, for God's sake, to pity his distress:

He is denied the freedom of the prison,

And in the hole is laid with men con-
    demned;

Plenty he hath of nothing but of irons,

And it remains in you to free him thence.

OLD MOUNTFORD. Money I cannot spare;
    men should take heed;

He lost my kindred when he fell to need.
               [*Exit.*]

SUSAN. Gold is but earth, thou earth
    enough shalt have,

When thou hast once took measure of thy
    grave.

You know me, Master Sandy, and my suit.

SANDY. I knew you, lady, when the old
    man lived;

I knew you ere your brother sold his land;

Then you sung well, played sweetly on
    the lute;

But now I neither know you nor your
    suit.   [*Exit.*]

SUSAN. You, Master Roder, was my
    brother's tenant,

Rent-free he placed you in that wealthy
    farm,

Of which you are possessed.

RODER. True, he did;

And have I not there dwelt still for his
    sake?

I have some business now; but, without
    doubt,

They that have hurled him in will help
    him out.   [*Exit.*]

SUSAN. Cold comfort still: what say
    you, cousin Tidy?

TIDY. I say this comes of roysting,
    swaggering.

Call me not cousin: each man for himself.

Some men are born to mirth, and some to
    sorrow.

I am no cousin unto them that borrow.
               [*Exit.*]

SUSAN. O charity! why art thou fled
    to heaven,

And left all things upon this earth un-
    even?

Their scoffing answers I will ne'er return;

But to myself his grief in silence mourn.

[*Enter* SIR FRANCIS ACTON *and* MALBY.]

SIR FRANCIS. She is poor, I'll therefore
    tempt her with this gold.

Go, Malby, in my name deliver it,

And I will stay thy answer.

MALBY. Fair mistress, as I understand,
    your grief

Doth grow from want, so I have here in
    store

A means to furnish you, a bag of gold,

Which to your hands I freely tender
    you.

SUSAN. I thank you, Heavens! I thank
    you, gentle sir:

God make me able to requite this favour!

MALBY. This gold Sir Francis Acton
    sends by me,

And prays you——

SUSAN. Acton! O God! that name I am
    born to curse:

Hence, bawd! hence, broker! see, I spurn
    his gold;

My honour never shall for gain be sold.

SIR FRANCIS. Stay, lady, stay.

SUSAN. From you I'll posting hie,

Even as the doves from feathered eagles
   fly.   [*Exit.*]
SIR FRANCIS.   She hates my name, my
   face: how should I woo?
I am disgraced in every thing I do.
The more she hates me, and disdains my
   love,
The more I am rapt in admiration
Of her divine and chaste perfections.
Woo her with gifts I cannot, for all gifts
Sent in my name she spurns: with looks
   I cannot,
For she abhors my sight; nor yet with
   letters,
For none she will receive.   How then,
   how then?
Well, I will fasten such a kindness on her
As shall o'ercome her hate and conquer it.
Sir Charles, her brother, lies in execution
For a great sum of money; and, besides,
The appeal is sued still for my hunts-
   man's death,
Which only I have power to reverse:
In her I'll bury all my hate of him.
Go seek the keeper, Malby, bring him to
   me:
To save his body, I his debts will pay;
To save his life, I his appeal will stay.
                    [*Exeunt.*]

SCENE II—*A prison cell.*

[*Enter* SIR CHARLES MOUNTFORD, *with
irons, his feet bare, his garments all
ragged and torn.*]
SIR CHARLES.   Of all on the earth's face
   most miserable,
Breathe in this hellish dungeon thy
   laments,
Thus like a slave ragged, like a felon
   gyved.
What hurls thee headlong to this base
   estate?
O unkind uncle! O my friends ingrate!
Unthankful kinsmen! Mountford's all too
   base,
To let thy name be fettered in disgrace!
A thousand deaths here in this grave I
   die;
Fear, hunger, sorrow, cold, all threat my
   death,

And join together to deprive my breath.
But that which most torments me, my
   dear sister
Hath left to visit me, and from my friends
Hath brought no hopeful answer: there-
   fore I
Divine they will not help my misery.
If it be so, shame, scandal, and contempt
Attend their covetous thoughts; need
   make their graves!
Usurers they live, and may they die like
   slaves!

           [*Enter* KEEPER.]
KEEPER.   Knight, be of comfort, for I
   bring thee freedom
From all thy troubles.
SIR CHARLES.   Then I am doomed to
   die;
Death is the end of all calamity.
KEEPER.   Live: your appeal is stayed;
   the execution
Of all your debts discharged; your cred-
   itors
Even to the utmost penny satisfied.
In sign whereof, your shackles I knock off;
You are not left so much indebted to us
As for your fees; all is discharged, all
   paid.
Go freely to your house, or where you
   please,
After long miseries, embrace your ease.
SIR CHARLES.   Thou grumblest out the
   sweetest music to me
That ever organ played.   Is this a dream
Or do my waking senses apprehend
The pleasing taste of these applausive
   news?
Slave that I was, to wrong such honest
   friends,
My loving kinsmen, and my near allies.
Tongue, I will bite thee for the scandal
   breathed
Against such faithful kinsmen: they are
   all
Composed of pity and compassion,
Of melting charity, and of moving ruth.
That which I spake before was in my
   rage;
They are my friends, the mirrors of this
   age,

Bounteous and free. The noble Mount-
ford's race,
Ne'er bred a covetous thought, or humour
base.

[*Enter* SUSAN.]
SUSAN.   I can no longer stay from
visiting
My woful brother: while I could, I kept
My hapless tidings from his hopeful
ear.
SIR CHARLES. Sister, how much am I
indebted to thee,
And to thy travel!
SUSAN. What, at liberty?
SIR CHARLES. Thou seest I am, thanks
to thy industry:
Oh! unto which of all my courteous
friends
Am I thus bound? My uncle Mountford,
he
Even of an infant loved me: was it he?
So did my cousin Tidy; was it he?
So Master Roder, Master Sandy too:
Which of all these did this high kindness
do?
SUSAN. Charles, can you mock me in
your poverty,
Knowing your friends deride your misery?
Now, I protest I stand so much amazed
To see your bonds free, and your irons
knocked off,
That I am rapt into a maze of wonder:
The rather for I know not by what means
This happiness hath chanced.
SIR CHARLES. Why, by my uncle,
My cousins, and my friends: who else, I
pray,
Would take upon them all my debts to
pay?
SUSAN. O brother, they are men all of
flint,
Pictures of marble, and as void of pity
As chased bears. I begged, I sued, I
kneeled,
Laid open all your griefs and miseries,
Which they derided; more than that,
denied us
A part in their alliance; but, in pride,
Said that our kindred with our plenty
died.

SIR CHARLES. Drudges too much—what
did they? oh, known evil!
Rich fly the poor, as good men shun the
devil.
Whence should my freedom come? of
whom alive,
Saving of those, have I deserved so well?
Guess, sister, call to mind, remember me:
These I have raised; they follow the
world's guise;
Whom rich in honour, they in woe de-
spise.
SUSAN. My wits have lost themselves,
let's ask the keeper.
SIR CHARLES. Gaoler!
KEEPER. At hand, sir.
SIR CHARLES. Of courtesy resolve me
one demand.
What was he took the burthen of my
debts
From off my back, stayed my appeal to
death,
Discharged my fees, and brought me lib-
erty?
KEEPER. A courteous knight, one called
Sir Francis Acton.
SIR CHARLES. Ha! Acton! O me, more
distressed in this
Than all my troubles! hale me back,
Double my irons, and my sparing meals
Put into halves, and lodge me in a dun-
geon
More deep, more dark, more cold, more
comfortless.
By Acton freed! not all thy manacles
Could fetter so my heels as this one word
Hath thralled my heart; and it must now
lie bound
In more strict prison than thy stony gaol.
I am not free; I go but under bail.
KEEPER. My charge is done, sir, now I
have my fees;
As we get little, we will nothing leese.
[*Exit.*]
SIR CHARLES. By Acton freed, my dan-
gerous opposite!
Why, to what end? on what occasion? ha!
Let me forget the name of enemy,
And with indifference balance this high
favour:
Ha!

SUSAN [*aside*]. His love to me? upon my soul 'tis so:
That is the root from whence these strange things grow.
SIR CHARLES. Had this proceeded from my father, he
That by the law of nature is most bound
In offices of love, it had deserved
My best employment to requite that grace:
Had it proceeded from my friends or him,
From them this action had deserved my life:
And from a stranger more; because from such
There is less expectation of good deeds.
But he, nor father, nor ally, nor friend,
More than a stranger, both remote in blood
And in his heart opposed my enemy,—
That this high bounty should proceed from him,—
Oh, there I lose myself! What should I say,
What think, what do, his bounty to repay?
SUSAN. You wonder, I am sure, whence this strange kindness
Proceeds in Acton. I will tell you, brother:
He dotes on me, and oft hath sent me gifts,
Letters and tokens: I refused them all.
SIR CHARLES. I have enough, though poor; my heart is set,
In one rich gift to pay back all my debt.
[*Exeunt.*]

SCENE III—*A room in* FRANKFORD'S *house.*

[*Enter* FRANKFORD, *and* NICHOLAS *with keys.*]
FRANKFORD. This is the night that I must play my part
To try two seeming angels. Where's my keys?
NICHOLAS. They are made according to your mould in wax:
I bade the smith be secret, gave him money,
And here they are. The letter, sir.

FRANKFORD. True, take it, there it is;
[*Gives him letter.*]
And when thou seest me in my pleasant'st vein,
Ready to sit to supper, bring it me.
NICHOLAS. I'll do't, make no more question but I'll do't. [*Exit.*]

[*Enter* MISTRESS FRANKFORD, CRANWELL, WENDOLL, *and* JENKIN.]
MISTRESS FRANKFORD. Sirrah, 'tis six o'clock already struck!
Go bid them spread the cloth and serve in supper.
JENKIN. It shall be done, forsooth, mistress. Where's
Spigot, the butler, to give us our salt and trenchers? [*Exit.*]
WENDOLL. We that have been a-hunting all the day
Come with preparèd stomachs. Master Frankford,
We wished you at our sport.
FRANKFORD. My heart was with you, and my mind was on you.
Fie, Master Cranwell! you are still thus sad?
A stool, a stool. Where's Jenkin, and where's Nick?
'Tis supper-time at least an hour ago.
What's the best news abroad?
WENDOLL. I know none good.
FRANKFORD. But I know too much bad.
[*Aside.*]

[*Enter* JENKIN *and* BUTLER *with a table-cloth, bread, trenchers, and salt.*]
CRANWELL. Methinks, sir, you might have that interest
In your wife's brother, to be more remiss
In his hard dealing against poor Sir Charles,
Who, as I hear, lies in York Castle, needy,
And in great want.
[*Exeunt* JENKIN *and* BUTLER.]
FRANKFORD. Did not more weighty business of my own
Hold me away, I would have laboured peace
Betwixt them, with all care; indeed I would, sir.

MISTRESS FRANKFORD. I'll write unto
  my brother earnestly
In that behalf.
WENDOLL. A charitable deed,
And will beget the good opinion
Of all your friends that love you, Mistress
  Frankford.
FRANKFORD. That's you for one; I know
  you love Sir Charles,
And my wife too, well.
WENDOLL. He deserves the love
Of all true gentlemen; be yourselves
  judge.
FRANKFORD. But supper, ho! Now as
  thou lov'st me, Wendoll,
Which I am sure thou dost, be merry,
  pleasant,
And frolic it to-night. Sweet Master
  Cranwell,
Do you the like. Wife, I protest my heart
Was ne'er more bent on sweet alacrity.
Where be those lazy knaves to serve in
  supper?

[*Reënter* NICHOLAS.]
NICHOLAS. Here's a letter, sir.
FRANKFORD. Whence comes it? and who
  brought it?
NICHOLAS. A stripling that below at-
  tends your answer,
And, as he tells me, it is sent from York.
FRANKFORD. Have him into the cellar;
  let him taste
A cup of our March beer: go, make him
  drink.   [*Reads the letter.*]
NICHOLAS. I'll make him drunk, if he
  be a Trojan.
FRANKFORD. My boots and spurs!
  where' Jenkin? God forgive me,
How I neglect my business! Wife, look
  here;
I have a matter to be tried to-morrow
By eight o'clock, and my attorney writes
  me,
I must be there betimes with evidence,
Or it will go against me. Where's my
  boots?

[*Reënter* JENKIN *with boots and spurs.*]
MISTRESS FRANKFORD. I hope your
  business craves no such despatch
That you must ride to-night.

WENDOLL [*aside*]. I hope it doth.
FRANKFORD. God's me! no such de-
  spatch!
Jenkin, my boots. Where's Nick? Saddle
  my roan,
And the grey dapple for himself. Content
  ye,
It much concerns me. Gentle Master
  Cranwell,
And Master Wendoll, in my absence use
The very ripest pleasures of my house.
WENDOLL. Lord! Master Frankford,
  will you ride to-night?
The ways are dangerous.
FRANKFORD. Therefore will I ride
Appointed well; and so shall Nick my
  man.
MISTRESS FRANKFORD. I'll call you up
  by five o'clock to-morrow.
FRANKFORD. No, by my faith, wife, I'll
  not trust to that;
'Tis not such easy rising in a morning
From one I love so dearly: no, by my
  faith,
I shall not leave so sweet a bedfellow,
But with much pain. You have made me
  a sluggard
Since I first knew you.
MISTRESS FRANKFORD. Then, if you
  needs will go
This dangerous evening, Master Wendoll,
Let me entreat you bear him company.
WENDOLL. With all my heart, sweet
  mistress. My boots there!
FRANKFORD. Fie, fie, that for my pri-
  vate business
I should disease my friend, and be a
  trouble
To the whole house! Nick!
NICHOLAS. Anon, sir.
FRANKFORD. Bring forth my gelding.
            [*Exit* NICHOLAS.]
As you love me, sir,
Use no more words: a hand, good Master
  Cranwell.
CRANWELL. Sir, God be your good
  speed!
FRANKFORD. Good night, sweet Nan;
  nay, nay, a kiss and part.
[*Aside.*] Dissembling lips, you suit not
  with my heart.   [*Exit.*]

WENDOLL. How business, time, and hours, all gracious prove,
And are the furtherers to my new-born love!
I am husband now in Master Frankford's place,
And must command the house. My pleasure is
We will not sup abroad so publicly,
But in your private chamber, Mistress Frankford.
MISTRESS FRANKFORD. O, sir, you are too public in your love,
And Master Frankford's wife——
CRANWELL. Might I crave favour,
I would entreat you I might see my chamber;
am on the sudden grown exceeding ill,
And would be spared from supper.
WENDOLL. Light there, ho!
See you want nothing, sir; for, if you do,
You injure that good man, and wrong me too.
CRANWELL. I will make bold: good night. [*Exit.*]
WENDOLL. How all conspire
To make our bosom sweet, and full entire!
Come, Nan, I pr'ythee let us sup within.
MISTRESS FRANKFORD. Oh, what a clog unto the soul is sin!
We pale offenders are still full of fear;
Every suspicious eye brings danger near,
When they whose clear hearts from offence are free
Despise report, base scandals do outface,
And stand at mere defiance with disgrace.
WENDOLL. Fie, fie! you talk too like a puritan.
MISTRESS FRANKFORD. You have tempted me to mischief, Master Wendoll:
I have done I know not what. Well, you plead custom;
That which for want of wit I granted erst,
I now must yield through fear. Come, come, let's in;
Once o'er shoes, we are straight o'er head in sin.

WENDOLL. My jocund soul is joyful above measure;
I'll be profuse in Frankford's richest treasure. [*Exeunt.*]

SCENE IV—*Another part of the house.*

[*Enter* CICELY, JENKIN, *and* BUTLER.]
JENKIN. My mistress and Master Wendoll, my master, sup in her chamber tonight. Cicely, you are preferred from being the cook to be chambermaid: of all the loves betwixt thee and me, tell me what thou thinkest of this?
CICELY. Mum; there's an old proverb,—"when the cat's away, the mouse may play."
JENKIN. Now you talk of a cat, Cicely, I smell a rat.
CICELY. Good words, Jenkin, lest you be called to answer them.
JENKIN. Why, God make my mistress an honest woman! are not these good words? Pray God my new master play not the knave with my old master! is there any hurt in this? God send no villainy intended! and, if they do sup together, pray God they do not lie together! God make my mistress chaste, and make us all His servants! what harm is there in all this? Nay, more; here is my hand, thou shalt never have my heart unless thou say Amen.
CICELY. Amen, I pray God, I say.

[*Enter* SERVING-MAN.]
SERVING-MAN. My mistress sends that you should make less noise, to lock up the doors, and see the household all got to bed: you, Jenkin, for this night are made the porter to see the gates shut in.
JENKIN. Thus, by little and little, I creep into office. Come, to kennel, my masters, to kennel; 'tis eleven o'clock, already.
SERVING-MAN. When you have locked the gates in, you must send up the keys to my mistress.
CICELY. Quickly, for God's sake, Jenkin, for I must carry them. I am neither pil-

low nor bolster, but I know more than both.

JENKIN. To bed, good Spigot; to bed, good honest serving-creatures; and let us sleep as snug as pigs in pease-straw.

[*Exeunt.*]

SCENE V—*Outside* FRANKFORD'S *house.*

[*Enter* FRANKFORD *and* NICHOLAS.]

FRANKFORD. Soft, soft; we have tied our geldings to a tree,
Two flight-shot off, lest by their thundering hoofs
They blab our coming back. Hear'st thou no noise?

NICHOLAS. Hear! I hear nothing but the owl and you.

FRANKFORD. So; now my watch's hand points upon twelve,
And it is dead midnight. Where are my keys?

NICHOLAS. Here, sir.

FRANKFORD. This is the key that opes my outward gate;
This is the hall-door; this the withdrawing chamber;
But this, that door that's bawd unto my shame,
Fountain and spring of all my bleeding thoughts,
Where the most hallowed order and true knot
Of nuptial sanctity hath been profaned;
It leads to my polluted bed-chamber,
Once my terrestrial heaven, now my earth's hell,
The place where sins in all their ripeness dwell.
But I forget myself: now to my gate.

NICHOLAS. It must ope with far less noise than Cripple-gate, or your plot's dashed.

FRANKFORD. So, reach me my dark lanthorn to the rest;
Tread softly, softly.

NICHOLAS. I will walk on eggs this pace.

FRANKFORD. A general silence hath surprised the house,
And this is the last door. Astonishment,

Fear, and amazement play against my heart,
Even as a madman beats upon a drum.
Oh, keep my eyes, you Heavens, before I enter,
From any sight that may transfix my soul;
Or, if there be so black a spectacle,
Oh, strike mine eyes stark blind; or, if not so,
Lend me such patience to digest my grief
That I may keep this white and virgin hand
From any violent outrage or red murder!
And with that prayer I enter. [*Exeunt.*]

SCENE VI—*The hall of* FRANKFORD'S *house.*

[NICHOLAS *discovered.*]

NICHOLAS. Here's a circumstance.
A man be made cuckold in the time
That he's about it. An the case were mine,
As 'tis my master's,—'sblood that he makes me swear!—
I would have placed his action, entered there;
I would, I would.

[*Enter* FRANKFORD.]

FRANKFORD. Oh! oh!

NICHOLAS. Master, 'sblood! master! master!

FRANKFORD. O me unhappy! I have found them lying
Close in each other's arms, and fast asleep.
But that I would not damn two precious souls,
Bought with my Saviour's blood, and send them, laden
With all their scarlet sins upon their backs,
Unto a fearful judgment, their two lives
Had met upon my rapier.

NICHOLAS. 'Sblood, master, what, have you left them sleeping still? let me go wake them.

FRANKFORD. Stay, let me pause a while.
O God! O God! that it were possible

To undo things done; to call back yesterday!
That Time could turn up his swift sandy glass,
To untell the days, and to redeem these hours!
Or that the sun
Could, rising from the west, draw his coach backward,
Take from the account of time so many minutes,
Till he had all these seasons called again,
Those minutes, and those actions done in them,
Even from her first offence; that I might take her
As spotless as an angel in my arms!
But, oh! I talk of things impossible,
And cast beyond the moon. God give me patience!
For I will in and wake them.   [*Exit.*]
    NICHOLAS. Here's patience perforce;
He needs must trot afoot that tires his horse.

[*Enter* WENDOLL, *running over the stage in a night-gown,* FRANKFORD *after him with a sword drawn; a* MAID-SERVANT *in her smock stays his hand, and clasps hold on him.* FRANKFORD *pauses for a while.*]
    FRANKFORD. I thank thee, maid; thou, like the angel's hand,
Hast stayed me from a bloody sacrifice.
                    [*Exit* MAID-SERVANT.]
Go, villain, and my wrongs sit on thy soul
As heavy as this grief doth upon mine!
When thou record'st my many courtesies,
And shalt compare them with thy treacherous heart,
Lay them together, weigh them equally,
'Twill be revenge enough. Go, to thy friend
A Judas: pray, pray, lest I live to see
Thee, Judas-like, hanged on an elder-tree.

[*Enter* MISTRESS FRANKFORD *in her night attire.*]
    MISTRESS FRANKFORD.   Oh, by what word, what title, or what name,
Shall I entreat your pardon? Pardon! oh!

I am as far from hoping such sweet grace
As Lucifer from heaven. To call you husband—
O me, most wretched! I have lost that name,
I am no more your wife.
    NICHOLAS. 'Sblood, sir, she swoons.
    FRANKFORD. Spare thou thy tears, for I will weep for thee:
And keep thy countenance, for I'll blush for thee.
Now, I protest, I think 'tis I am tainted,
For I am most ashamed; and 'tis more hard
For me to look upon thy guilty face,
Than on the sun's clear brow. What wouldst thou speak?
    MISTRESS FRANKFORD.   I would I had no tongue, no ears, no eyes,
No apprehension, no capacity.
When do you spurn me like a dog? when tread me
Under your feet? when drag me by the hair?
Though I deserve a thousand thousand fold
More than you can inflict: yet, once my husband,
For womanhood, to which I am a shame,
Though once an ornament—even for His sake
That hath redeemed our souls, mark not my face
Nor hack me with your sword; but let me go
Perfect and undeformèd to my tomb.
I am not worthy that I should prevail
In the least suit; no, not to speak to you,
Nor look on you, nor to be in your presence.
Yet, as an abject, this one suit I crave;
This granted, I am ready for my grave.
                    [*Kneels.*]
    FRANKFORD. My God, with patience arm me! Rise, nay, rise,
And I'll debate with thee. Was it for want
Thou playedst the strumpet? Wast thou not supplied
With every pleasure, fashion, and new toy
Nay, even beyond my calling?

MISTRESS FRANKFORD. I was.

FRANKFORD. Was it then disability in me;

Or in thine eye seemed he a properer man?

MISTRESS FRANKFORD. Oh, no.

FRANKFORD. Did not I lodge thee in my bosom?

Wear thee here in my heart?

MISTRESS FRANKFORD. You did.

FRANKFORD. I did, indeed; witness my tears I did.

Go, bring my infants hither.

[*Enter* SERVANT *with two* CHILDREN.]
                    O Nan! O Nan!

If neither fear of shame, regard of honour,

The blemish of my house, nor my dear love

Could have withheld thee from so lewd a fact,

Yet for these infants, these young harmless souls,

On whose white brows thy shame is charactered,

And grows in greatness as they wax in years,—

Look but on them, and melt away in tears.

Away with them! lest, as her spotted body

Hath stained their names with stripe of bastardy,

So her adulterous breath may blast their spirits

With her infectious thoughts. Away with them.

            [*Exeunt* SERVANT *and* CHILDREN.]

MISTRESS FRANKFORD. In this one life I die ten thousand deaths.

FRANKFORD. Stand up, stand up; I will do nothing rashly;

I will retire a while into my study,

And thou shalt hear thy sentence presently.   [*Exit.*]

MISTRESS FRANKFORD. 'Tis welcome, be it death. O me, base strumpet,

That, having such a husband, such sweet children,

Must enjoy neither! Oh, to redeem my honour,

I would have this hand cut off, these my breasts seared,

Be racked, strappadoed, put to any torment:

Nay, to whip but this scandal out, I would hazard

The rich and dear redemption of my soul,

He cannot be so base as to forgive me;

Nor I so shameless to accept his pardon.

O women, women, you that yet have kept

Your holy matrimonial vow unstained,

Make me your instance: when you tread awry,

Your sins, like mine, will on your conscience lie.

[*Enter* CICELY, JENKIN, *and all the* SERVING-MEN *as newly come out of bed.*]

ALL. O mistress, mistress, what have you done, mistress?

NICHOLAS. 'Sblood, what a caterwauling keep you here!

JENKIN. O Lord, mistress, how comes this to pass? My master is run away in his shirt, and never so much as called me to bring his clothes after him.

MISTRESS FRANKFORD. See what guilt is! here stand I in this place,

Ashamed to look my servants in the face.

[*Enter* FRANKFORD *and* CRANWELL, *whom seeing she falls on her knees.*]

FRANKFORD. My words are registered in Heaven already,

With patience hear me. I'll not martyr thee,

Nor mark thee for a strumpet; but with usage

Of more humility torment thy soul,

And kill thee even with kindness.

CRANWELL. Master Frankford——

FRANKFORD. Good Master Cranwell. Woman, hear thy judgment.

Go make thee ready in thy best attire;

Take with thee all thy gowns, all thy apparel;

Leave nothing that did ever call thee mistress.

Or by whose sight, being left here in the house,

I may remember such a woman by.

Choose thee a bed and hangings for thy chamber;

Take with thee every thing that hath thy
mark,
And get thee to my manor seven mile off,
Where live; 'tis thine; I freely give it
thee.
My tenants by shall furnish thee with
wains
To carry all thy stuff, within two hours,—
No longer will I limit thee my sight.
Choose which of all my servants thou
likest best,
And they are thine to attend thee.
MISTRESS FRANKFORD. A mild sentence.
FRANKFORD. But, as thou hopest for
Heaven, as thou believest
Thy name's recorded in the book of life,
I charge thee never, after this sad day,
To see me, or to meet me, or to send
By word or writing, gift, or otherwise,
To move me, by thyself, or by thy friends;
Nor challenge any part in my two chil-
dren.
So, farewell, Nan! for we will henceforth
be
As we had never seen, ne'er more shall see.
MISTRESS FRANKFORD. How full my
heart is, in mine eyes appears;
What wants in words, I will supply in
tears.
FRANKFORD. Come, take your coach,
your stuff; all must along;
Servants and all, make ready; all be gone.
It was thy hand cut two hearts out of one.
[*Exeunt.*]

ACT V

SCENE I—*The entrance to* SIR FRANCIS
ACTON'S *house.*

[*Enter* SIR CHARLES MOUNTFORD, *and*
SUSAN, *both well dressed.*]
SUSAN. Brother, why have you tricked
me like a bride,
Bought me this gay attire, these orna-
ments?
Forget you our estate, our poverty?
SIR CHARLES. Call me not brother, but
imagine me
Some barbarous outlaw, or uncivil kern;
For if thou shutt'st thy eye, and only
hearest

The words that I shall utter, thou shalt
judge me
Some staring ruffian, not thy brother
Charles.
O sister!——
SUSAN. O brother, what doth this
strange language mean?
SIR CHARLES. Dost love me, sister?
wouldst thou see me live
A bankrupt beggar in the world's disgrace,
And die indebted to my enemies?
Wouldst thou behold me stand like a
huge beam
In the world's eye, a bye-word and a
scorn?
It lies in thee of these to acquit me free,
And all my debt I may out-strip by thee.
SUSAN. By me! why, I have nothing,
nothing left;
I owe even for the clothes upon my back;
I am not worth——
SIR CHARLES. O sister, say not so;
It lies in you my downcast state to raise,
To make me stand on even points with
the world.
Come, sister, you are rich; indeed you are;
And in your power you have, without
delay,
Acton's five hundred pound back to repay.
SUSAN. Till now I had thought you had
loved me. By my honour
(Which I have kept as spotless as the
moon),
I ne'er was mistress of that single doit
Which I reserved not to supply your
wants;
And do you think that I would hoard from
you?
Now, by my hopes in Heaven, knew I the
means
To buy you from the slavery of your debts
(Especially from Acton, whom I hate),
I would redeem it with my life or blood.
SIR CHARLES. I challenge it; and,
kindred set apart,
Thus, ruffian-like, I lay siege to your
heart.
What do I owe to Acton?
SUSAN. Why some five hundred pounds;
towards which, I swear,
In all the world I have not one denier.

SIR CHARLES. It will not prove so.
Sister, now resolve me:
What do you think (and speak your conscience)
Would Acton give, might he enjoy your bed?

SUSAN. He would not shrink to spend a thousand pound,
To give the Mountfords' name so deep a wound.

SIR CHARLES. A thousand pound! I but five hundred owe;
Grant him your bed, he's paid with interest so.

SUSAN. O brother!

SIR CHARLES. O sister! only this one way,
With that rich jewel you my debts may pay.
In speaking this my cold heart shakes with shame;
Nor do I woo you in a brother's name,
But in a stranger's. Shall I die in debt
To Acton, my grand foe, and you still wear
The precious jewel that he holds so dear?

SUSAN. My honour I esteem as dear and precious
As my redemption.

SIR CHARLES. I esteem you, sister,
As dear, for so dear prizing it.

SUSAN. Will Charles
Have me cut off my hands, and send them Acton?
Rip up my breast, and with my bleeding heart
Present him as a token?

SIR CHARLES. Neither, sister:
But hear me in my strange assertion.
Thy honour and my soul are equal in my regard;
Nor will thy brother Charles survive thy shame.
His kindness, like a burthen hath surcharged me,
And under his good deeds I stooping go,
Not with an upright soul. Had I remained
In prison still, there doubtless I had died:
Then, unto him that freed me from that prison,

Still do I owe this life. What moved my foe
To enfranchise me? 'Twas, sister, for your love,
With full five hundred pounds he bought your love,
And shall he not enjoy it? Shall the weight
Of all this heavy burthen lean on me,
And will not you bear part? You did partake
The joy of my release; will you not stand
In joint-bond bound to satisfy the debt?
Shall I be only charged?

SUSAN. But that I know
These arguments come from an honoured mind.
As in your most extremity of need
Scorning to stand in debt to one your hate,—
Nay, rather would engage your unstained honour
Than to be held ingrate,—I should condemn you.
I see your resolution, and assent;
So Charles will have me, and I am content.

SIR CHARLES. For this I tricked you up.

SUSAN. But here's a knife,
To save mine honour, shall slice out my life.

SIR CHARLES. Ay! know thou pleasest me a thousand times
More in that resolution than thy grant.—
Observe her love; to soothe it to my suit,
Her honour she will hazard, though not lose:
To bring me out of debt, her rigorous hand
Will pierce her heart. O wonder! that will choose,
Rather than stain her blood, her life to lose.—
Come, you sad sister to a woful brother,
This is the gate: I'll bear him such a present,
Such an acquittance for the knight to seal,
As will amaze his senses, and surprise
With admiration all his fantasies.

SUSAN. Before his unchaste thoughts shall seize on me,

'Tis here shall my imprisoned soul set free.

[*Enter* SIR FRANCIS ACTON *and* MALBY.]

SIR FRANCIS. How! Mountford with his sister, hand in hand!
What miracle's afoot?

MALBY. It is a sight
Begets in me much admiration.

SIR CHARLES. Stand not amazed to see me thus attended:
Acton, I owe thee money, and being unable
To bring thee the full sum in ready coin,
Lo! for thy more assurance, here's a pawn,—
My sister, my dear sister, whose chaste honour
I prize above a million: here, nay, take her;
She's worth your money, man; do not forsake her.

SIR FRANCIS. I would he were in earnest!

SUSAN. Impute it not to my immodesty:
My brother being rich in nothing else
But in his interest that he hath in me,
According to his poverty hath brought you
Me, all his store; whom howsoe'er you prize
As forfeit to your hand, he values highly,
And would not sell, but to acquit your debt,
For any emperor's ransom.

SIR FRANCIS. Stern heart, relent;
Thy former cruelty at length repent.
Was ever known, in any former age,
Such honourable wrested courtesy?
Lands, honours, life, and all the world forego,
Rather than stand engaged to such a foe.
[*Aside.*]

SIR CHARLES. Acton, she is too poor to be thy bride,
And I too much opposed to be thy brother.
There, take her to thee: if thou hast the heart
To seize her as a rape, or lustful prey;
To blur our house, that never yet was stained;

To murder her that never meant thee harm;
To kill me now, whom once thou savedst from death,
Do them at once: on her all these rely,
And perish with her spotted chastity.

SIR FRANCIS. You overcome me in your love, Sir Charles;
I cannot be so cruel to a lady
I love so dearly. Since you have not spared
To engage your reputation to the world,
Your sister's honour, which you prize so dear,
Nay, all the comforts which you hold on earth,
To grow out of my debt, being your foe,
Your honoured thoughts, lo! thus I recompense:
Your metamorphosed foe receives your gift
In satisfaction of all former wrongs.
This jewel I will wear here in my heart;
And, where before I thought her for her wants
Too base to be my bride, to end all strife,
I seal you my dear brother, her my wife.

SUSAN. You still exceed us: I will yield to fate,
And learn to love, where I till now did hate.

SIR CHARLES. With that enchantment you have charmed my soul,
And made me rich even in those very words:
I pay no debt, but am indebted more;
Rich in your love, I never can be poor.

SIR FRANCIS. All's mine is yours; we are alike in state,
Let's knit in love 'what was opposed in hate.
Come! for our nuptials we will straight provide,
Blest only in our brother and fair bride.
[*Exeunt.*]

SCENE II—*A room in* FRANKFORD'S *house.*

[*Enter* CRANWELL, FRANKFORD, *and* NICHOLAS.]

CRANWELL. Why do you search each room about your house.

Now that you have despatched your wife
  away?

FRANKFORD. O sir, to see that nothing
  may be left
That ever was my wife's. I loved her
  dearly,
And when I do but think of her unkind-
  ness,
My thoughts are all in hell; to avoid
  which torment,
I would not have a bodkin or a cuff,
A bracelet, necklace, or rebato wire;
Nor any thing that ever was called hers,
Left me, by which I might remember her.
Seek round about.

  NICHOLAS. 'Sblood, master! here's her
    lute flung in a corner.
  FRANKFORD. Her lute! O God! upon
    this instrument
Her fingers have run quick division,
Sweeter than that which now divides our
  hearts.
These frets have made me pleasant, that
  have now
Frets of my heart-strings made. O Master
  Cranwell,
Oft hath she made this melancholy
  wood,
Now mute and dumb for her disastrous
  chance,
Speak sweetly many a note, sound many
  a strain
To her own ravishing voice, which being
  well strung,
What pleasant strange airs have they
  jointly rung!
Post with it after her. Now nothing's
  left;
Of her and hers, I am at once bereft.

  NICHOLAS. I'll ride and overtake her;
    do my message,
And come back again.   [Exit.]
  CRANWELL.   Mean time, sir, if you
    please,
I'll to Sir Francis Acton, and inform him
Of what hath passed betwixt you and his
  sister.
  FRANKFORD. Do as you please. How ill
    am I bested,
To be a widower ere my wife be dead!
                            [Exeunt.]

SCENE III—*A country road.*

[*Enter* MISTRESS FRANKFOLD, *with*
JENKIN, CICELY, *a* COACHMAN, *and three*
CARTERS.]

  MISTRESS FRANKFORD. Bid my coach
    stay: why should I ride in state,
Being hurled so low down by the hand of
  fate?
A seat like to my fortunes let me have;
Earth for my chair, and for my bed a
  grave.

  JENKIN. Comfort, good mistress; you
have watered your coach with tears al-
ready: you have but two mile now to go
to your manor. A man cannot say by my
old master Frankford as he may say by
me, that he wants manors; for he hath
three or four, of which this is one that we
are going to now.

  CICELY. Good mistress, be of good
cheer; sorrow, you see, hurts you, but
helps you not: we all mourn to see you so
sad.

  CARTER. Mistress, I spy one of my
    landlord's men
Come riding post: 'tis like he brings some
  news.

  MISTRESS FRANKFORD. Comes he from
    Master Frankford, he is welcome;
So are his news because they come from
  him.

[*Enter* NICHOLAS.]

  NICHOLAS [*presenting lute*]. There.

  MISTRESS FRANKFORD. I know the lute;
    oft have I sung to thee:
We both are out of tune, both out of
  time.

  NICHOLAS. Would that had been the
worst instrument that e'er you played on.
My master commends him to ye; there's
all he can find that was ever yours: he
hath nothing left that ever you could lay
claim to but his own heart, and he could
afford you that. All that I have to deliver
you is this: he prays you to forget him,
and so he bids you farewell.

  MISTRESS FRANKFORD. I thank him:
    he is kind, and ever was.
All you that have true feeling of my grief,

That know my loss, and have relenting
  hearts,
Gird me about, and help me with your
  tears
To wash my spotted sins: my lute shall
  groan;
It cannot weep, but shall lament my moan.

[*Enter* WENDOLL.]

WENDOLL. Pursued with horror of a
  guilty soul,
And with the sharp scourge of repentance
  lashed
I fly from my own shadow. O my stars!
What have my parents in their lives de-
  served,
That you should lay this penance on their
  son?
When I but think of Master Frankford's
  love,
And lay it to my treason, or compare
My murdering him for his relieving me,
It strikes a terror like a lightning's flash
To scorch my blood up. Thus I, like the
  owl,
Ashamed of day, live in these shadowy
  woods,
Afraid of every leaf or murmuring blast,
Yet longing to receive some perfect
  knowledge
How he hath dealt with her. [*Sees* MIS-
  TRESS FRANKFORD.] O my sad fate!
Here, and so far from home, and thus
  attended!
O God! I have divorced the truest turtles
That ever lived together; and, being di-
  vided
In several places, make their several
  moan;
She in the fields laments, and he at home.
So poets write that Orpheus made the
  trees
And stones to dance to his melodious
  harp,
Meaning the rustic and the barbarous
  hinds,
That had no understanding part in them:
So she from these rude carters tears ex-
  tracts,
Making their flinty hearts with grief to
  rise,

And draw down rivers from their rocky
  eyes.

MISTRESS FRANKFORD [*to* NICHOLAS].
  If you return unto your master, say
(Though not from me; for I am all un-
  worthy
To blast his name so with a strumpet's
  tongue)
That you have seen me weep, wish myself
  dead:
Nay, you may say too, for my vow is
  passed,
Last night you saw me eat and drink my
  last.
This to your master you may say and
  swear;
For it is writ in Heaven, and decreed here.
  NICHOLAS. I'll say you wept: I'll swear
  you made me sad.
Why how now, eyes? what now? what's
  here to do?
I'm gone, or I shall straight turn baby
  too.
  WENDOLL. I cannot weep, my heart is
  all on fire:
Curst be the fruits of my unchaste desire!
  MISTRESS FRANKFORD. Go, break this
  lute upon my coach's wheel,
As the last music that I e'er shall make;
Not as my husband's gift, but my farewell
To all earth's joy; and so your master
  tell.
  NICHOLAS. If I can for crying.
  WENDOLL. Grief, have done,
Or like a madman I shall frantic run.
  MISTRESS FRANKFORD. You have beheld
  the wofullest wretch on earth;
A woman made of tears: would you had
  words
To express but what you see! My inward
  grief
No tongue can utter; yet unto your power
You may describe my sorrow, and disclose
To thy sad master my abundant woes.
  NICHOLAS. I'll do your commendations.
  MISTRESS FRANKFORD. O no:
I dare not so presume; nor to my chil-
  dren:
I am disclaimed in both; alas, I am.
Oh, never teach them, when they come to
  speak,

To name the name of mother; chide their
tongue,
If they by chance light on that hated
word;
Tell them 'tis naught; for, when that
word they name,
Poor pretty souls! they harp on their own
shame.

WENDOLL. To recompense her wrongs,
what canst thou do?
Thou hast made her husbandless and
childless too.

MISTRESS FRANKFORD. I have no more
to say. Speak not for me;
Yet you may tell your master what you
see.

NICHOLAS. I'll do't. [*Exit.*]

WENDOLL. I'll speak to her, and comfort her in grief.
Oh! but her wound cannot be cured with
words.
No matter though, I'll do my best goodwill
To work a cure on her whom I did kill.

MISTRESS FRANKFORD. So, now unto my
coach, then to my home,
So to my death-bed; for from this sad
hour
I never will nor eat, nor drink, nor taste
Of any cates that may preserve my life:
I never will nor smile, nor sleep, nor rest;
But when my tears have washed my black
soul white,
Sweet Saviour, to Thy hands I yield my
sprite.

WENDOLL. O Mistress Frankford—

MISTRESS FRANKFORD. Oh, for God's
sake fly!
The devil doth come to tempt me ere I die.
My coach! this fiend, that with an angel's
face
Conjured mine honour, till he sought my
wrack,
In my repentant eyes seems ugly black.
[*Exeunt all, except* WENDOLL *and*
JENKIN; *the* CARTERS *whistling.*]

JENKIN. What, my young master that
fled in his shirt! How come you by your
clothes again? You have made our house
in a sweet pickle, ha' ye not, think you?

What, shall I serve you still, or cleave to
the old house?

WENDOLL. Hence, slave! away with thy
unseasoned mirth!
Unless thou canst shed tears, and sigh,
and howl,
Curse thy sad fortunes, and exclaim on
fate,
Thou art not for my turn.

JENKIN. Marry, an you will not, another will: farewell, and be hanged!
Would you had never come to have kept
this coil within our doors; we shall ha'
you run away like a sprite again.
[*Exit.*]

WENDOLL. She's gone to death; I live
to want and woe;
Her life, her sins, and all upon my head.
And I must now go wander, like a Cain,
In foreign countries and remoted climes,
Where the report of my ingratitude
Cannot be heard. I'll over first to France,
And so to Germany and Italy;
Where when I have recovered, and by
travel
Gotten those perfect tongues, and that
these rumours
May in their height abate, I will return:
And I divine (however now dejected)
My worth and parts being by some great
man praised,
At my return I may in court be raised.
[*Exit.*]

SCENE IV—*Before the manor.*

[*Enter* SIR FRANCIS ACTON, SUSAN, SIR
CHARLES MOUNTFORD, CRANWELL,
and MALBY.]

SIR FRANCIS. Brother, and now my
wife, I think these troubles
Fall on my head by justice of the Heavens,
For being so strict to you in your extremities:
But we are now atoned. I would my
sister
Could with like happiness o'ercome her
griefs,
As we have ours.

SUSAN. You tell us, Master Cranwell,
wondrous things,

Touching the patience of that gentleman,
With what strange virtue he demeans his
  grief.
CRANWELL. I told you what I was a
  witness of;
It was my fortune to lodge there that
  night.
SIR FRANCIS. O that same villain Wen-
doll! 'twas his tongue
That did corrupt her; she was of herself
Chaste, and devoted well. Is this the
  house?
CRANWELL. Yes, sir, I take it here your
sister lies.
SIR FRANCIS. My brother Frankford
  showed too mild a spirit
In the revenge of such a loathèd crime;
Less than he did, no man of spirit could
  do:
I am so far from blaming his revenge,
That I commend it. Had it been my case,
Their souls at once had from their breasts
  been freed:
Death to such deeds of shame is the due
  meed.
        [*They enter the house.*]

SCENE V—*A room in the manor.*

[*Enter* SIR FRANCIS ACTON, SUSAN, SIR
  CHARLES MOUNTFORD, CRANWELL, *and*
  MALBY; JENKIN *and* CICELY *follow-
  ing them.*]
JENKIN. O my mistress, my mistress,
my poor mistress.
CICELY. Alas that ever I was born!
what shall I do for my poor mistress?
SIR CHARLES. Why, what of her?
JENKIN. O Lord, sir, she no sooner
heard that her brother and his friends
were come to see how she did, but she,
for very shame of her guilty conscience,
fell into such a swoon, that we had much
ado to get life into her.
SUSAN. Alas that she should bear so
hard a fate!
Pity it is repentance comes too late.
SIR FRANCIS. Is she so weak in body?
JENKIN. O sir, I can assure you there's
no hope of life in her, for she will take no

sustenance: she hath plainly starved her-
self, and now she is as lean as a lath.
She ever looks for the good hour. Many
gentlemen and gentlewomen of the coun-
try are come to comfort her.   [*Exeunt.*]

SCENE VI—MISTRESS FRANKFORD'S *bed-
chamber.*

[MISTRESS FRANKFORD *in bed; enter* SIR
  CHARLES MOUNTFORD, SIR FRANCIS
  ACTON, MALBY, CRANWELL, *and*
  SUSAN.]
MALBY. How fare you, Mistress Frank-
ford?
MISTRESS FRANKFORD. Sick, sick, oh,
sick. Give me some air, I pray you.
Tell me, oh, tell me where is Master
  Frankford?
Will not he deign to see me ere I die?
MALBY. Yes, Mistress Frankford:
  divers gentlemen,
Your loving neighbours, with that just
  request
Have moved, and told him of your weak
  estate:
Who, though with much ado to get belief,
Examining of the general circumstance,
Seeing your sorrow and your penitence,
And hearing therewithal the great desire
You have to see him ere you left the
  world,
He gave to us his faith to follow us,
And sure he will be here immediately.
MISTRESS FRANKFORD. You have half
  revived me with those pleasing news:
Raise me a little higher in my bed.
Blush I not, brother Acton? Blush I not,
  Sir Charles?
Can you not read my fault writ in my
  cheek?
Is not my crime there? tell me, gentle-
  men.
SIR CHARLES. Alas! good mistress,
  sickness hath not left you
Blood in your face enough to make you
  blush.
MISTRESS FRANKFORD. Then sickness,
  like a friend, my fault would hide.
Is my husband come? My soul but tarries
His arrive, then I am fit for Heaven.

SIR FRANCIS. I came to chide you; but my words of hate
Are turned to pity and compassionate grief.
I came to rate you; but my brawls, you see,
Melt into tears, and I must weep by thee.
Here's Master Frankford now.

[*Enter* FRANKFORD.]

FRANKFORD. Good-morrow, brother; morrow, gentlemen:
God, that hath laid this cross upon our heads,
Might (had He pleased) have made our cause of meeting
On a more fair and more contented ground;
But He that made us, made us to this woe.

MISTRESS FRANKFORD. And is he come? Methinks that voice I know.

FRANKFORD. How do you, woman?

MISTRESS FRANKFORD. Well, Master Frankford, well; but shall be better, I hope, within this hour. Will you vouchsafe,
Out of your grace and your humanity,
To take a spotted strumpet by the hand?

FRANKFORD. This hand once held my heart in faster bonds
Than now 'tis gripped by me. God pardon them
That made us first break hold!

MISTRESS FRANKFORD. Amen, amen.
Out of my zeal to Heaven, whither I'm now bound,
I was so impudent to wish you here;
And once more beg your pardon. O good man,
And father to my children, pardon me,
Pardon, oh, pardon me! My fault so heinous is,
That if you in this world forgive it not,
Heaven will not clear it in the world to come.
Faintness hath so usurped upon my knees
That kneel I cannot, but on my heart's knees
My prostrate soul lies thrown down at your feet

To beg your gracious pardon. Pardon, oh, pardon me!

FRANKFORD. As freely, from the low depth of my soul,
As my Redeemer hath forgiven His death,
I pardon thee. I will shed tears for thee, pray with thee;
And, in mere pity of thy weak estate,
I'll wish to die with thee.

ALL. So do we all.

NICHOLAS. So will not I;
I'll sigh and sob, but, by my faith, not die.

SIR FRANCIS. O Master Frankford, all the near alliance
I lose by her shall be supplied in thee:
You are my brother by the nearest way;
Her kindred hath fallen off, but yours doth stay.

FRANKFORD. Even as I hope for pardon at that day
When the great Judge of Heaven in scarlet sits,
So be thou pardoned. Though thy rash offence
Divorced our bodies, thy repentant tears
Unite our souls.

SIR CHARLES. Then comfort, Mistress Frankford;
You see your husband hath forgiven your fall;
Then rouse your spirits, and cheer your fainting soul.

SUSAN. How is it with you?

SIR FRANCIS. How do ye feel yourself?

MISTRESS FRANKFORD. Not of this world.

FRANKFORD. I see you are not, and I weep to see it.
My wife, the mother to my pretty babes!
Both those lost names I do restore thee back,
And with this kiss I wed thee once again:
Though thou art wounded in thy honoured name,
And with that grief upon thy death-bed liest,
Honest in heart, upon my soul, thou diest.

MISTRESS FRANKFORD. Pardoned on earth, soul, thou in Heaven art free
Once more: thy wife dies thus embracing thee. [*Dies.*]

FRANKFORD. New married, and new widowed. Oh! she's dead,
And a cold grave must be her nuptial bed.
SIR CHARLES. Sir, be of good comfort; and your heavy sorrow
Part equally amongst us: storms divided
Abate their force, and with less rage are guided.
CRANWELL. Do, Master Frankford: he that hath least part
Will find enough to drown one troubled heart.
SIR FRANCIS. Peace with thee, Nan.
Brothers, and gentlemen,
All we that can plead interest in her grief,
Bestow upon her body funeral tears.
Brother, had you with threats and usage bad
Punished her sin, the grief of her offence
Had not with such true sorrow touched her heart.
FRANKFORD. I see it had not: therefore on her grave
Will I bestow this funeral epitaph,
Which on her marble tomb shall be engraved.
In golden letters shall these words be filled,
"Here lies she whom her husband's kindness killed."

THE MAID'S TRAGEDY

By FRANCIS BEAUMONT AND JOHN FLETCHER

Produced at London, probably 1609

CHARACTERS

KING

LYSIPPUS, *brother to the* KING

AMINTOR, *a noble gentleman*

MELANTIUS,
DIPHILUS, } *brothers to* EVADNE

CALIANAX, *an old humorous lord, and father to* ASPATIA

CLEON,
STRATO, } *gentlemen*

DIAGORAS, *a servant to* CALIANAX

EVADNE, *sister to* MELANTIUS

ASPATIA, *troth-plight wife to* AMINTOR

ANTIPHILA,
OLYMPIAS, } *waiting-gentlewomen to* ASPATIA

DULA, *waiting-woman to* EVADNE

LADIES

NIGHT,
CYNTHIA,
NEPTUNE, } *masquers*
ÆOLUS,
SEA GODS,

SCENE—*The City of Rhodes.*

ACT I

SCENE I—*An apartment in the palace.*

[*Enter* CLEON, STRATO, LYSIPPUS, *and* DIPHILUS.]

CLEON. The rest are making ready, sir.

LYSIPPUS. So let them;
There's time enough.

DIPHILUS. You are the brother to the king, my lord;
We'll take your word.

LYSIPPUS. Strato, thou hast some skill in poetry:

What think'st thou of the masque? will
  it be well?
STRATO. As well as masque can be.
LYSIPPUS. As masque can be?
STRATO. Yes; they must commend their
  king, and speak in praise
Of the assembly; bless the bride and
  bridegroom
In person of some god. They are tied to
  rules
Of flattery.
CLEON. See, good my lord, who is re-
turn'd!

       [*Enter* MELANTIUS.]
LYSIPPUS. Noble Melantius! the land,
  by me,
Welcomes thy virtues home to Rhodes.
Thou, that with blood abroad buy'st us
  our peace!
The breath of kings is like the breath of
  gods;
My brother wish'd thee here, and thou
  art here.
He will be too kind, and weary thee
With often welcomes. But the time doth
  give thee
A welcome above his, or all the world's.
MELANTIUS. My lord, my thanks; but
  these scratch'd limbs of mine
Have spoke my love and truth unto my
  friends,
More than my tongue e'er could. My
  mind's the same
It ever was to you: Where I find worth,
I love the keeper till he let it go,
And then I follow it.
DIPHILUS. Hail, worthy brother!
He, that rejoices not at your return
In safety, is mine enemy for ever.
MELANTIUS. I thank thee, Diphilus.
  But thou art faulty;
I sent for thee to exercise thine arms
With me at Patria: Thou camest not,
  Diphilus;
'Twas ill.
DIPHILUS. My noble brother, my excuse
Is my king's strict command; which you,
  my lord,
Can witness with me.
LYSIPPUS. 'Tis true, Melantius;
He might not come, till the solemnity
Of this great match was past.

DIPHILUS. Have you heard of it?
MELANTIUS. Yes. I have given cause
  to those that envy
My deeds abroad, to call me gamesome:
I have no other business here at Rhodes.
LYSIPPUS. We have a masque to-night,
  and you must tread
A soldier's measure.
MELANTIUS. These soft and silken wars
  are not for me:
The music must be shrill, and all confused,
That stirs my blood; and then I dance
  with arms.
But is Amintor wed?
DIPHILUS. This day.
MELANTIUS. All joys upon him! for he
  is my friend.
Wonder not that I call a man so young
  my friend:
His worth is great; valiant he is, and
  temperate;
And one that never thinks his life his
  own,
If his friend need it. When he was a boy,
As oft as I returned (as, without boast,
I brought home conquests) he would gaze
  upon me,
And view me round, to find in what one
  limb
The virtue lay to do those things he heard.
Then would he wish to see my sword, and
  feel
The quickness of the edge, and in his
  hand
Weigh it: He oft would make me smile
  at this.
His youth did promise much, and his ripe
  years
Will see it all perform'd.

       [*Enter* ASPATIA.]
Hail, maid and wife!
Thou fair Aspatia, may the holy knot
That thou hast tied to-day, last till the
  hand
Of age undo it! may'st thou bring a race
Unto Amintor, that may fill the world
Successively with soldiers!
ASPATIA. My hard fortunes
Deserve not scorn; for I was never proud
When they were good.   [*Exit.*]
MELANTIUS. How's this?

LYSIPPUS. You are mistaken,
For she is not married.

MELANTIUS. You said Amintor was.

DIPHILUS. 'Tis true; but——

MELANTIUS. Pardon me, I did receive
Letters at Patria from my Amintor,
That he should marry her.

DIPHILUS. And so it stood
In all opinion long; but your arrival
Made me imagine you had heard the
change.

MELANTIUS. Who hath he taken then?

LYSIPPUS. A lady, sir,
That bears the light about her, and strikes
dead
With flashes of her eye: the fair Evadne,
Your virtuous sister.

MELANTIUS. Peace of heart betwixt
them!
But this is strange.

LYSIPPUS. The king my brother did it
To honour you; and these solemnities
Are at his charge.

MELANTIUS. 'Tis royal, like himself.
But I am sad
My speech bears so unfortunate a sound
To beautiful Aspatia. There is rage
Hid in her father's breast, Calianax,
Bent long against me; and he should not
think,
If I could call it back, that I would
take
So base revenges, as to scorn the state
Of his neglected daughter. Holds he still
His greatness with the king?

LYSIPPUS. Yes. But this lady
Walks discontented, with her watery eyes
Bent on the earth. The unfrequented
woods
Are her delight; and when she sees a bank
Stuck full of flowers, she with a sigh will
tell
Her servants what a pretty place it were
To bury lovers in; and make her maids
Pluck 'em, and strew her over like a
corse.
She carries with her an infectious grief,
That strikes all her beholders; she will
sing
The mournful'st things that ever ear
hath heard,

And sigh, and sing again; and when the
rest
Of our young ladies, in their wanton blood,
Tell mirthful tales in course, that fill the
room
With laughter, she will, with so sad a
look,
Bring forth a story of the silent death
Of some forsaken virgin, which her grief
Will put in such a phrase, that, ere she
end,
She'll send them weeping, one by one,
away.

MELANTIUS. She has a brother under
my command,
Like her; a face as womanish as hers;
But with a spirit that hath much out-
grown
The number of his years.

[Enter AMINTOR.]

CLEON. My lord, the bridegroom!

MELANTIUS. I might run fiercely, not
more hastily,
Upon my foe. I love thee well, Amintor;
My mouth is much too narrow for my
heart;
I joy to look upon those eyes of thine;
Thou art my friend, but my disorder'd
speech
Cuts off my love.

AMINTOR. Thou art Melantius;
All love is spoke in that. A sacrifice,
To thank the gods Melantius is return'd
In safety! Victory sits on his sword,
As she was wont: May she build there
and dwell;
And may thy armour be, as it hath been,
Only thy valour and thine innocence!
What endless treasures would our enemies
give,
That I might hold thee still thus!

MELANTIUS. I am but poor
In words; but credit me, young man, thy
mother
Could do no more but weep for joy to see
thee
After long absence: All the wounds I
have
Fetch'd not so much away, nor all the
cries

Of widowed mothers. But this is peace,
And that was war.

AMINTOR. Pardon, thou holy god
Of marriage bed, and frown not, I am
    forced,
In answer of such noble tears as those,
To weep upon my wedding-day.

MELANTIUS. I fear thou'rt grown too
fickle; for I hear
A lady mourns for thee; men say, to
    death;
Forsaken of thee; on what terms I know
    not.

AMINTOR. She had my promise; but the
king forbade it,
And made me make this worthy change,
    thy sister,
Accompanied with graces far above her;
With whom I long to lose my lusty youth,
And grow old in her arms.

MELANTIUS. Be prosperous!

[Enter MESSENGER.]

MESSENGER. My lord, the masquers
rage for you.

LYSIPPUS. We are gone. Cleon, Strato,
Diphilus—   [Exeunt LYSIPPUS, CLEON,
            STRATO, and DIPHILUS.]

AMINTOR. We'll all attend you.—We
shall trouble you
With our solemnities.

MELANTIUS. Not so, Amintor:
But if you laugh at my rude carriage
In peace, I'll do as much for you in war,
When you come thither. Yet I have a
    mistress
To bring to your delights; rough though
    I am,
I have a mistress, and she has a heart
She says; but, trust me, it is stone, no
    better;
There is no place that I can challenge in't.
But you stand still, and here my way lies.
            [Exeunt severally.]

SCENE II—A large hall in the same, with
    a gallery full of spectators.

[Enter CALIANAX, with DIAGORAS at the
            door.]

CALIANAX. Diagoras, look to the doors
better for shame; you let in all the world,
and anon the king will rail at me—why,
very well said—by Jove, the king will
have the show i' th' court.

DIAGORAS. Why do you swear so, my
lord? You know, he'll have it here.

CALIANAX. By this light, if he be wise,
he will not.

DIAGORAS. And if he will not be wise,
you are forsworn.

CALIANAX. One may wear out his heart
with swearing, and get thanks on no side.
I'll be gone—look to't who will.

DIAGORAS. My lord, I shall never keep
them out. Pray, stay; your looks will
terrify them.

CALIANAX. My looks terrify them, you
coxcombly ass, you! I'll be judged by
all the company whether thou hast not a
worse face than I.

DIAGORAS. I mean, because they know
you and your office.

CALIANAX. Office! I would I could put
it off; I am sure I sweat quite through
my office. I might have made room at
my daughter's wedding: they have near
kill'd her among them; and now I must
do service for him that hath forsaken her.
Serve that will.   [Exit.]

DIAGORAS. He's so humorous since his
daughter was forsaken— Hark, hark!
there, there! so, so! Codes, codes!
[Knock within.] What now?

MELANTIUS [within]. Open the door.

DIAGORAS. Who's there?

MELANTIUS [within]. Melantius.

DIAGORAS. I hope your lordship brings
no troop with you; for, if you do, I must
return them. [Opens the door. Persons
            endeavour to rush in.]

[Enter MELANTIUS and a LADY.]

MELANTIUS. None but this lady, sir.

DIAGORAS. The ladies are all placed
above, save those that come in the king's
troop: The best of Rhodes sit there, and
there's room.

MELANTIUS. I thank you, sir.—When I
have seen you placed, madam, I must at-
tend the king; but, the masque done, I'll
wait on you again.

[Exit with the LADY into the gallery.]

DIAGORAS. Stand back there!—Room for my lord Melantius!—pray, bear back —this is no place for such youths and their trulls—let the doors shut again.— No!—do your heads itch? I'll scratch them for you. [*Shuts the door.*]—So, now thrust and hang. [*Knocking.*] Again! who is't now—I cannot blame my lord Calianax for going away: 'Would he were here! he would run raging among them, and break a dozen wiser heads than his own, in the twinkling of an eye.— What's the news now?

[*Within.*] I pray you, can you help me to the speech of the master-cook?

DIAGORAS. If I open the door, I'll cook some of your calves-heads. Peace, rogues! [*Knocking.*]—Again! who is't?

MELANTIUS [*within*]. Melantius.

[*Enter* CALIANAX.]

CALIANAX. Let him not in.

DIAGORAS. O, my lord, I must.—Make room there for my lord.

[*Enter* MELANTIUS.]

Is your lady placed? [*To* MELANTIUS.]

MELANTIUS. Yes, sir.

I thank you.—My Lord Calianax, well met.

Your causeless hate to me, I hope, is buried.

CALIANAX. Yes, I do service for your sister here,

That brings my own poor child to timeless death;

She loves your friend Amintor; such another

False-hearted lord as you.

MELANTIUS. You do me wrong,

A most unmanly one, and I am slow

In taking vengeance! But be well advised.

CALIANAX. It may be so.—Who placed the lady there,

So near the presence of the king?

MELANTIUS. I did.

CALIANAX. My lord, she must not sit there.

MELANTIUS. Why?

CALIANAX. The place is kept for women of more worth.

MELANTIUS. More worth than she? It misbecomes your age,

And place, to be thus womanish. Forbear!

What you have spoke, I am content to think

The palsy shook your tongue to.

CALIANAX. Why, 'tis well

If I stand here to place men's wenches.

MELANTIUS. I shall forget this place, thy age, my safety,

And, thorough all, cut that poor sickly week,

Thou hast to live, away from thee.

CALIANAX. Nay, I know you can fight for your whore.

MELANTIUS. Bate the king, and be he flesh and blood,

He lies, that says it! Thy mother at fifteen

Was black and sinful to her.

DIAGORAS. Good my lord!

MELANTIUS. Some god pluck threescore years from that fond man,

That I may kill him and not stain mine honour.

It is the curse of soldiers, that in peace

They shall be braved by such ignoble men,

As, if the land were troubled, would with tears

And knees beg succour from 'em. 'Would, that blood,

That sea of blood, that I have lost in fight,

Were running in thy veins, that it might make thee

Apt to say less, or able to maintain,

Should'st thou say more! This Rhodes, I see, is nought

But a place privileged to do men wrong.

CALIANAX. Ay, you may say your pleasure.

[*Enter* AMINTOR.]

AMINTOR. What vile injury

Has stirr'd my worthy friend, who is as slow

To fight with words as he is quick of hand?

MELANTIUS. That heap of age, which I should reverence

If it were temperate: but testy years
Are most contemptible.
AMINTOR. Good sir, forbear.
CALIANAX. There is just such another
as yourself.
AMINTOR. He will wrong you, or me,
or any man,
And talk as if he had no life to lose,
Since this our match. The king is com-
ing in:
I would not for more wealth than I enjoy,
He should perceive you raging. He did
hear
You were at difference now, which has-
tened him.
CALIANAX. Make room there!
    [*Hautboys play within.*]

[*Enter* KING, EVADNE, ASPATIA, LORDS,
    and LADIES.]
KING. Melantius, thou art welcome,
    and my love
Is with thee still: But this is not a place
To brabble in. Calianax, join hands.
CALIANAX. He shall not have my hand.
KING. This is no time
To force you to it. I do love you both:
Calianax, you look well to your office;
And you, Melantius, are welcome home.—
Begin the masque!
MELANTIUS. Sister, I joy to see you,
    and your choice.
You look'd with my eyes when you took
    that man:
Be happy in him!   [*Recorders play.*]
EVADNE. O, my dearest brother!
Your presence is more joyful than this day
Can be unto me.

THE MASQUE.

[NIGHT *rises in mists.*]
NIGHT. Our reign is come; for in the
    raging sea
The sun is drown'd, and with him fell the
    Day.
Bright Cynthia, hear my voice; I am the
    Night,
For whom thou bear'st about thy borrow'd
    light.
Appear; no longer thy pale visage shroud,

But strike thy silver horns quite through
    a cloud
And send a beam upon my swarthy face;
By which I may discover all the place
And persons, and how many longing eyes
Are come to wait on our solemnities.

[*Enter* CYNTHIA.]
How dull and black am I! I could not
    find
This beauty without thee, I am so blind.
Methinks, they show like to those eastern
    streaks
That warn us hence, before the morning
    breaks!
Back, my pale servant, for these eyes
    know how
To shoot far more and quicker rays than
    thou.
CYNTHIA. Great queen, they be a troop
    for whom alone
One of my clearest moons I have put on;
A troop, that looks as if thyself and I
Had pluck'd our reins in, and our whips
    laid by,
To gaze upon these mortals, that appear
Brighter than we.
NIGHT. Then let us keep 'em here;
And never more our chariots drive away,
But hold our places and outshine the day.
CYNTHIA. Great queen of shadows, you
    are pleased to speak
Of more than may be done: We may not
    break
The gods' decrees; but, when our time is
    come,
Must drive away, and give the day our
    room.
Yet, while our reign lasts, let us stretch
    our power
To give our servants one contented hour,
With such unwonted solemn grace and
    state,
As may for ever after force them hate
Our brother's glorious beams; and wish
    the night
Crown'd with a thousand stars, and our
    cold light:
For almost all the world their service
    bend
To Phœbus, and in vain my light I lend;

Gazed on unto my setting from my rise
Almost of none, but of unquiet eyes.
 NIGHT. Then shine at full, fair queen,
  and by thy power
Produce a birth, to crown this happy hour,
Of nymphs and shepherds: Let their songs
  discover,
Easy and sweet, who is a happy lover.
Or, if thou woo't, then call thine own
  Endymion,
From the sweet flowery bed he lies upon,
On Latmus' top, thy pale beams drawn
  away,
And of this long night let him make a
  day.
 CYNTHIA. Thou dream'st, dark queen;
  that fair boy was not mine,
Nor went I down to kiss him. Ease and
  wine
Have bred these bold tales: Poets, when
  they rage,
Turn gods to men, and make an hour an
  age.
But I will give a greater state and glory,
And raise to time a noble memory
Of what these lovers are. Rise, rise, I say,
Thou power of deeps; thy surges laid
  away,
Neptune, great king of waters, and by me
Be proud to be commanded.

   [NEPTUNE *rises.*]
 NEPTUNE. Cynthia, see,
Thy word hath fetch'd me hither: Let
  me know
Why I ascend?
 CYNTHIA. Doth this majestic show
Give thee no knowledge yet?
 NEPTUNE. Yes, now I see
Something intended, Cynthia, worthy
  thee.
Go on: I'll be a helper.
 CYNTHIA. Hie thee then,
And charge the wind fly from his rocky
  den.
Let loose thy subjects; only Boreas,
Too foul for our intention, as he was,
Still keep him fast chain'd: we must have
  none here
But vernal blasts, and gentle winds ap-
  pear;

Such as blow flowers, and through the
  glad boughs sing
Many soft welcomes to the lusty spring:
These are our music. Next, thy watery
  race
Bring on in couples (we are pleased to
  grace
This noble night), each in their richest
  things
Your own deeps, or the broken vessel,
  brings.
Be prodigal, and I shall be as kind,
And shine at full upon you.
 NEPTUNE. Ho! the wind-
Commanding Æolus!

  [*Enter* ÆOLUS *out of a rock.*]
 ÆOLUS. Great Neptune?
 NEPTUNE. He.
 ÆOLUS. What is thy will?
 NEPTUNE. We do command thee free
Favonius, and thy milder winds, to wait
Upon our Cynthia; but tie Boreas
  straight;
He's too rebellious.
 ÆOLUS. I shall do it.
 NEPTUNE. Do.—— [*Exit* ÆOLUS *into
    the rock and reënters.*]
 ÆOLUS. Great master of the flood, and
  all below,
Thy full command has taken.—Ho! the
  Main!
Neptune!
 NEPTUNE. Here.
 ÆOLUS. Boreas has broke his chain,
And, struggling, with the rest has got
  away.
 NEPTUNE. Let him alone, I'll take him
  up at sea;
He will not long be thence. Go once again,
And call out of the bottoms of the main
Blue Proteus, and the rest; charge them
  put on
Their greatest pearls, and the most spar-
  kling stone
The beaten rock breeds; till this night is
  done
By me a solemn honour to the moon.
Fly, like a full sail.
 ÆOLUS. I am gone.
 CYNTHIA. Dark Night,

Strike a full silence; do a thorough right
To this great chorus; that our music may
Touch high as Heaven, and make the east
    break day
At mid-night.   [*Music.*]

SONG

Cynthia, to thy power and thee,
    We obey.
Joy to this great company!
    And no day
Come to steal this night away,
Till the rites of love are ended;
And the lusty bridegroom say,
Welcome, light, of all befriended.

Pace out, you watery powers below;
    Let your feet,
Like the gallies when they row,
    Even beat.
Let your unknown measures, set
To the still winds, tell to all,
That gods are come, immortal, great,
To honour this great nuptial.
    [*The Measure by the Sea-gods.*]

SECOND SONG

Hold back thy hours, dark Night, till we
    have done:
    The day will come too soon;
Young maids will curse thee if thou
    steal'st away,
And leav'st their losses open to the day;
    Stay, stay, and hide
    The blushes of the bride!
Stay, gentle Night, and with thy darkness
    cover
    The kisses of her lover.
Stay, and confound her tears, and her
    shrill cryings,
Her weak denials, vows, and often dyings;
    Stay, and hide all:
    But help not, though she call.

NEPTUNE.   Great queen of us and
    Heaven,
Hear what I bring to make this hour a
    full one,
If not o'ermeasure.

CYNTHIA.   Speak, sea's king.
NEPTUNE.   The tunes my Amphitrite
    joys to have,
When they will dance upon the rising
    wave,
And court me as she sails. My Tritons,
    play
Music to lead a storm; I'll lead the way.
               [*Measure.*]

SONG

To bed, to bed; come, Hymen, lead the
    bride,
    And lay her by her husband's side;
Bring in the virgins every one,
That grieve to lie alone;
That they may kiss while they may say,
    a maid;
To-morrow, 'twill be other, kiss'd, and
    said.
    Hesperus be long a-shining,
    Whilst these lovers are a-twining.

ÆOLUS.   Ho! Neptune!
NEPTUNE.   Æolus!
ÆOLUS.   The sea goes high,
Boreas hath raised a storm: Go and ap-
    ply
Thy trident; else, I prophesy, ere day
Many a tall ship will be cast away.
Descend with all the gods, and all their
    power,
To strike a calm.
    CYNTHIA.   A thanks to every one, and
    to gratulate
So great a service, done at my desire,
Ye shall have many floods, fuller and
    higher
Than you have wished for; no ebb shall
    dare
To let the day see where your dwellings
    are.
Now back unto your government in haste,
Lest your proud charge should swell above
    the waste,
And win upon the island.
    NEPTUNE.   We obey. [NEPTUNE *de-*
    scends, and the Sea-gods.]
    CYNTHIA.   Hold up thy head, dead
    Night; see'st thou not Day?

The east begins to lighten: I must down,
And give my brother place.
NIGHT. Oh, I could frown
To see the Day, the Day that flings his
    light
Upon my kingdom, and contemns old
    Night!
Let him go on and flame! I hope to see
Another wild-fire in his axletree;
And all fall drench'd. But I forgot;
    speak, queen.
The day grows on; I must no more be
    seen.
    CYNTHIA. Heave up thy drowsy head
    again, and see
A greater light, a greater majesty,
Between our set and us! Whip up thy
    team!
The day-break's here, and yon sun-flaring
    beam
Shot from the south. Say, which way
    wilt thou go?
    NIGHT. I'll vanish into mists.
    CYNTHIA. I into day.   [*Exeunt.*]

THE MASQUE ENDS.

KING. Take lights there!—Ladies, get
    the bride to bed.—
We will not see you laid. Good-night,
    Amintor;
We'll ease you of that tedious ceremony.
Were it my case, I should think time run
    slow.
If thou be'st noble, youth, get me a boy,
That may defend my kingdom from my
    foes.
    AMINTOR. All happiness to you.
    KING. Good night, Melantius.
                                [*Exeunt.*]

ACT II

SCENE I—*Antechamber to* EVADNE'S *bed-
    room in the palace.*

[*Enter* EVADNE, ASPATIA, DULA, *and other
    Ladies.*]

    DULA. Madam, shall we undress you
    for this fight?
The wars are nak'd that you must make
    to-night.

EVADNE. You are very merry, Dula.
DULA. I should be merrier far, if 'twere
With me as 'tis with you.
EVADNE. How's that?
DULA. That I might go to bed with him
With the credit that you do.
EVADNE. Why, how now, wench?
DULA. Come, ladies, will you help?
EVADNE. I am soon undone.
DULA. And as soon done:
Good store of clothes will trouble you at
    both.
EVADNE. Art thou drunk, Dula?
DULA. Why, here's none but we.
EVADNE. Thou think'st belike, there is
    no modesty.
When we're alone.
DULA. Ay, by my troth, you hit my
    thoughts aright.
EVADNE. You prick me, lady.
DULA. 'Tis against my will.
Anon you must endure more, and lie still;
You're best to practise.
EVADNE. Sure, this wench is mad.
DULA. No, 'faith, this is a trick that I
    have had
Since I was fourteen.
EVADNE. 'Tis high time to leave it.
DULA. Nay, now I'll keep it, till the
    trick leave me.
A dozen wanton words, put in your head,
Will make you livelier in your husband's
    bed.
EVADNE. Nay, 'faith, then take it.
DULA. Take it, madam? where?
We all, I hope, will take it, that are here.
EVADNE. Nay, then, I'll give you o'er.
DULA. So will I make
The ablest man in Rhodes, or his heart
    ache.
EVADNE. Wilt take my place to-night?
DULA. I'll hold your cards 'gainst any
    two I know.
EVADNE. What wilt thou do?
DULA. Madam, we'll do't, and make
    'em leave play too.
EVADNE. Aspatia, take her part.
DULA. I will refuse it.
She will pluck down a side; she does not
    use it.
EVADNE. Why, do.

DULA. You will find the play
Quickly, because your head lies well that
way.
EVADNE. I thank thee, Dula. 'Would
thou could'st instil
Some of thy mirth into Aspatia!
Nothing but sad thoughts in her breast
do dwell:
Methinks, a mean betwixt you would do
well.
DULA. She is in love: Hang me, if I
were so,
But I could run my country. I love, too,
To do those things that people in love do.
ASPATIA. It were a timeless smile
should prove my cheek:
It were a fitter hour for me to laugh,
When at the altar the religious priest
Were pacifying the offended powers
With sacrifice, than now. This should
have been
My night; and all your hands have been
employed
In giving me a spotless offering
To young Amintor's bed, as we are now
For you. Pardon, Evadne; 'would my
worth
Were great as yours, or that the king,
or he,
Or both, thought so! Perhaps he found
me worthless:
But, till he did so, in these ears of mine,
These credulous ears, he pour'd the sweet-
est words
That art or love could frame. If he were
false,
Pardon it, Heaven! and if I did want
Virtue, you safely may forgive that too;
For I have lost none that I had from you.
EVADNE. Nay, leave this sad talk,
madam.
ASPATIA. Would I could!
Then should I leave the cause.
EVADNE. See, if you have not spoil'd
all Dula's mirth.
ASPATIA. Thou think'st thy heart
hard; but if thou be'st caught,
Remember me; thou shalt perceive a fire
Shot suddenly into thee.
DULA. That's not so good; let 'em
shoot anything

But fire, I fear 'em not.
ASPATIA. Well, wench, thou may'st be
taken.
EVADNE. Ladies, good-night: I'll do
the rest myself.
DULA. Nay, let your lord do some.
ASPATIA [sings]. Lay a garland on my
hearse,
    Of the dismal yew.
EVADNE. That's one of your sad songs,
madam.
ASPATIA. Believe me, 'tis a very pretty
one.
EVADNE. How is it, madam?
ASPATIA [sings]. Lay a garland on my
hearse,
    Of the dismal yew;
Maidens, willow branches bear;
    Say I died true:
My love was false, but I was firm
    From my hour of birth.
Upon my buried body lie
    Lightly, gentle earth!
EVADNE. Fie on't, madam! The words
are so strange, they are able to make one
dream of hobgoblins. "I could never have
the power": Sing that, Dula.
DULA [sings]. I could never have the
power
To love one above an hour,
But my heart would prompt mine eye
On some other man to fly;
Venus, fix mine eyes fast,
Of if not, give me all that I shall see at
last.
EVADNE. So, leave me now.
DULA. Nay, we must see you laid.
ASPATIA. Madam, good-night. May all
the marriage joys
That longing maids imagine in their beds,
Prove so unto you! May no discontent
Grow 'twixt your love and you! But, if
there do,
Inquire of me, and I will guide your moan;
Teach you an artificial way to grieve,
To keep your sorrow waking. Love your
lord
No worse than I: but if you love so well,
Alas, you may displease him; so did I.
This is the last time you shall look on
me.—

Ladies, farewell. As soon as I am dead,
Come all, and watch one night about my
hearse;
Bring each a mournful story, and a
tear,
To offer at it when I go to earth.
With flatt'ring ivy clasp my coffin round;
Write on my brow my fortune; let my
bier
Be borne by virgins that shall sing, by
course,
The truth of maids, and perjuries of men.
[*Exit* EVADNE.]
EVADNE. Alas, I pity thee.
ALL. Madam, good-night.
1ST LADY. Come, we'll let in the bride-
groom.
DULA. Where's my lord?

[*Enter* AMINTOR.]
1ST LADY. Here, take this light.
DULA. You'll find her in the dark.
1ST LADY. Your lady's scarce a-bed yet;
you must help her.
ASPATIA. Go, and be happy in your
lady's love.
May all the wrongs, that you have done to
me,
Be utterly forgotten in my death!
I'll trouble you no more; yet I will take
A parting kiss, and will not be denied.
You'll come, my lord, and see the virgins
weep
When I am laid in earth, though you
yourself
Can know no pity. Thus I wind myself
Into this willow garland, and am prouder
That I was once your love, though now
refused,
Than to have had another true to me.
So with my prayers I leave you, and must
try
Some yet-unpractised way to grieve and
die. [*Exit.*]
DULA. Come, ladies, will you go?
ALL. Good-night, my lord.
AMINTOR. Much happiness unto you
all— [*Exeunt* LADIES.]
I did that lady wrong: Methinks, I feel
Her grief shoot suddenly through all my
veins.

Mine eyes run: This is strange at such a
time.
It was the king first moved me to't;—but
he
Has not my will in keeping.—Why do I
Perplex myself thus? Something whis-
pers me,
"Go not to bed." My guilt is not so great
As mine own conscience, too sensible,
Would make me think: I only break a
promise,
And 'twas the king that forced me.—
Timorous flesh,
Why shak'st thou so?—Away, my idle
fears!

[*Enter* EVADNE.]
Yonder she is, the lustre of whose eye
Can blot away the sad remembrance
Of all these things.—Oh, my Evadne,
spare
That tender body; let it not take cold.
The vapours of the night will not fall
here:
To bed, my love. Hymen will punish us
For being slack performers of his rites.
Cam'st thou to call me?
EVADNE. No.
AMINTOR. Come, come, my love,
And let us lose ourselves to one another.
Why art thou up so long?
EVADNE. I am not well.
AMINTOR. To bed, then; let me wind
thee in these arms,
Till I have banish'd sickness.
EVADNE. Good my lord,
I cannot sleep.
AMINTOR. Evadne, we will watch;
I mean no sleeping.
EVADNE. I'll not go to bed.
AMINTOR. I pr'ythee do.
EVADNE. I will not for the world.
AMINTOR. Why, my dear love?
EVADNE. Why? I have sworn I will
not.
AMINTOR. Sworn!
EVADNE. Ay.
AMINTOR. How! sworn, Evadne?
EVADNE. Yes, sworn, Amintor; and
will swear again,
If you will wish to hear me.

AMINTOR. To whom have you sworn this?

EVADNE. If I should name him, the matter were not great.

AMINTOR. Come, this is but the coyness of a bride.

EVADNE. The coyness of a bride?

AMINTOR. How prettily that frown becomes thee!

EVADNE. Do you like it so?

AMINTOR. Thou canst not dress thy face in such a look,
But I shall like it.

EVADNE. What look likes you best?

AMINTOR. Why do you ask?

EVADNE. That I may show you one less pleasing to you.

AMINTOR. How's that?

EVADNE. That I may show you one less pleasing to you.

AMINTOR. I pr'ythee, put thy jests in milder looks;
It shows as thou wert angry.

EVADNE. So, perhaps,
I am indeed.

AMINTOR. Why, who has done thee wrong?
Name me the man, and by thyself I swear,
Thy yet-unconquer'd self, I will revenge thee.

EVADNE. Now I shall try thy truth. If thou dost love me,
Thou weigh'st not anything compared with me:
Life, honour, joys eternal, all delights
This world can yield, or hopeful people feign,
Or in the life to come, are light as air
To a true lover when his lady frowns,
And bids him *do this*. Wilt thou kill this man?
Swear, my Amintor, and I'll kiss the sin
Off from thy lips.

AMINTOR. I will not swear, sweet love,
Till I do know the cause.

EVADNE. I would thou would'st.
Why, it is thou that wrong'st me; I hate thee;
Thou should'st have kill'd thyself.

AMINTOR. If I should know that, I should quickly kill
The man you hated.

EVADNE. Know it then, and do't.

AMINTOR. Oh, no; what look soe'er thou shalt put on
To try my faith, I shall not think thee false:
I cannot find one blemish in thy face,
Where falsehood should abide. Leave, and to bed.
If you have sworn to any of the virgins,
That were your old companions, to preserve
Your maidenhead a night, it may be done
Without this means.

EVADNE. A maidenhead, Amintor,
At my years?

AMINTOR. Sure, she raves!—This cannot be
Thy natural temper. Shall I call thy maids?
Either thy healthful sleep hath left thee long,
Or else some fever rages in thy blood.

EVADNE. Neither, Amintor: Think you I am mad,
Because I speak the truth?

AMINTOR. Will you not lie with me to-night?

EVADNE. To-night! you talk as if I would hereafter.

AMINTOR. Hereafter! yes, I do.

EVADNE. You are deceived.
Put off amazement, and with patience mark
What I shall utter; for the oracle
Knows nothing truer: 'tis not for a night,
Or two, that I forbear thy bed, but for ever.

AMINTOR. I dream! Awake, Amintor!

EVADNE. You hear right.
I sooner will find out the beds of snakes,
And with my youthful blood warm their cold flesh,
Letting them curl themselves about my limbs,
Than sleep one night with thee. This is not feign'd,
Nor sounds it like the coyness of a bride.

AMINTOR. Is flesh so earthly to endure all this?
Are these the joys of marriage? Hymen, keep

This story (that will make succeeding
    youth
Neglect thy ceremonies) from all ears;
Let it not rise up, for thy shame and
    mine,
To after-ages: We will scorn thy laws,
If thou no better bless them. Touch the
    heart
Of her that thou hast sent me, or the
    world
Shall know, there's not an altar that will
    smoke
In praise of thee; we will adopt us sons;
Then virtue shall inherit, and not blood.
If we do lust, we'll take the next we meet,
Serving ourselves as other creatures do;
And never take note of the female more,
Nor of her issue.—I do rage in vain;
She can but jest. O, pardon me, my love!
So dear the thoughts are that I hold of
    thee,
That I must break forth. Satisfy my
    fear;
It is a pain, beyond the hand of death,
To be in doubt: Confirm it with an oath,
If this be true.

EVADNE. Do you invent the form:
Let there be in it all the binding words
Devils and conjurers can put together,
And I will take it. I have sworn before,
And here, by all things holy, do again,
Never to be acquainted with thy bed.
Is your doubt over now?

AMINTOR. I know too much. Would I
    had doubted still!
Was ever such a marriage night as this!
Ye powers above, if you did ever mean
Man should be used thus, you have
    thought a way
How he may bear himself, and save his
    honour.
Instruct me in it; for to my dull eyes
There is no mean, no moderate course to
    run:
I must live scorn'd, or be a murderer.
Is there a third? Why is this night so
    calm?
Why does not Heaven speak in thunder
    to us,
And drown her voice?

EVADNE. This rage will do no good.

AMINTOR. Evadne, hear me: Thou hast
    ta'en an oath,
But such a rash one, that, to keep it, were
Worse than to swear it: Call it back to
    thee;
Such vows as those never ascend the
    Heaven;
A tear or two will wash it quite away.
Have mercy on my youth, my hopeful
    youth,
If thou be pitiful; for, without boast,
This land was proud of me. What lady
    was there,
That men call'd fair and virtuous in this
    isle,
That would have shunn'd my love? It is
    in thee
To make me hold this worth. Oh! we
    vain men,
That trust out all our reputation,
To rest upon the weak and yielding hand
Of feeble woman! But thou art not stone;
Thy flesh is soft, and in thine eyes doth
    dwell
The spirit of love; thy heart cannot be
    hard.
Come, lead me from the bottom of despair,
To all the joys thou hast; I know thou
    wilt;
And make me careful, lest the sudden
    change
O'ercome my spirits.

EVADNE. When I call back this oath,
The pains of hell environ me!

AMINTOR. I sleep, and am too temper-
    ate! Come to bed!
Or by those hairs, which, if thou hadst
    a soul
Like to thy locks, were threads for kings
    to wear
About their arms——

EVADNE. Why, so, perhaps, they are.

AMINTOR. I'll drag thee to my bed, and
    make thy tongue
Undo this wicked oath, or on thy flesh
I'll print a thousand wounds to let out
    life!

EVADNE. I fear thee not. Do what thou
    dar'st to me!
Every ill-sounding word, or threat'ning
    look,

Thou show'st to me, will be revenged at full.

AMINTOR. It will not, sure, Evadne?

EVADNE. Do not you hazard that.

AMINTOR. Have you your champions?

EVADNE. Alas, Amintor, think'st thou I forbear
To sleep with thee, because I have put on
A maiden's strictness? Look upon these cheeks,
And thou shalt find the hot and rising blood
Unapt for such a vow. No; in this heart
There dwells as much desire, and as much will
To put that wish'd act in practice, as ever yet
Was known to woman; and they have been shown,
Both. But it was the folly of thy youth
To think this beauty, to what land soe'er
It shall be call'd, shall stoop to any second.
I do enjoy the best, and in that height
Have sworn to stand or die: You guess the man.

AMINTOR. No: let me know the man that wrongs me so,
That I may cut his body into motes,
And scatter it before the northern wind.

EVADNE. You dare not strike him.

AMINTOR. Do not wrong me so.
Yes, if his body were a poisonous plant,
That it were death to touch, I have a soul
Will throw me on him.

EVADNE. Why, it is the king.

AMINTOR. The king!

EVADNE. What will you do now?

AMINTOR. 'Tis not the king!

EVADNE. What did he make this match for, dull Amintor?

AMINTOR. Oh, thou hast named a word, that wipes away
All thoughts revengeful! In that sacred name,
"The king," there lies a terror. What frail man
Dares lift his hand against it? Let the gods

Speak to him when they please: till when let us
Suffer, and wait.

EVADNE. Why should you fill yourself so full of heat,
And haste so to my bed? I am no virgin.

AMINTOR. What devil put it in thy fancy, then,
To marry me?

EVADNE. Alas, I must have one
To father children, and to bear the name
Of husband to me, that my sin may be
More honourable.

AMINTOR. What a strange thing am I!

EVADNE. A miserable one; one that myself
Am sorry for.

AMINTOR. Why, show it then in this:
If thou hast pity, though thy love be none,
Kill me; and all true lovers, that shall live
In after-ages cross'd in their desires,
Shall bless thy memory, and call thee good;
Because such mercy in thy heart was found,
To rid a ling'ring wretch.

EVADNE. I must have one
To fill thy room again, if thou wert dead;
Else, by this night, I would: I pity thee.

AMINTOR. These strange and sudden injuries have fallen
So thick upon me, that I lose all sense
Of what they are. Methinks I am not wrong'd:
Nor is it aught, if from the censuring world
I can but hide it. Reputation!
Thou art a word, no more.—But thou hast shown
An impudence so high, that to the world,
I fear, thou wilt betray or shame thyself.

EVADNE. To cover shame, I took thee; never fear
That I would blaze myself.

AMINTOR. Nor let the king
Know I conceive he wrongs me; then mine honour
Will thrust me into action, though my flesh

Could bear with patience. And it is some
    ease
To me in these extremes, that I knew
    this
Before I touch'd thee; else had all the
    sins
Of mankind stood betwixt me and the
    king,
I had gone through 'em to his heart and
    thine.
I have left one desire: 'tis not his crown
Shall buy me to thy bed, now I resolve,
He has dishonoured thee. Give me thy
    hand;
Be careful of thy credit, and sin close;
'Tis all I wish. Upon thy chamber-floor
I'll rest to-night, that morning-visitors
May think we did as married people use.
And, pr'ythee, smile upon me when they
    come,
And seem to toy, as if thou hadst been
    pleased
With what we did.
    EVADNE. Fear not; I will do this.
    AMINTOR. Come, let us practise: and
      as wantonly.
As ever loving bride and bridegroom met,
Let's laugh and enter here.
    EVADNE. I am content.
    AMINTOR. Down all the swellings of my
      troubled heart!
When we walk thus intwined, let all eyes
    see
If ever lovers better did agree. [*Exeunt.*]

SCENE II—*An apartment in the citadel.*

[*Enter* ASPATIA, ANTIPHILA, *and*
    OLYMPIAS.]
    ASPATIA. Away, you are not sad; force
it no further.
Good Gods, how well you look! Such a
    full colour
Young bashful brides put on. Sure, you
    are new married!
    ANTIPHILA. Yes, madam, to your grief.
    ASPATIA. Alas, poor wenches!
Go learn to love first; learn to lose your-
    selves;
Learn to be flatter'd, and believe, and bless

The double tongue that did it. Make a
    faith
Out of the miracles of ancient lovers,
Such as speak truth, and died in't; and,
    like me,
Believe all faithful, and be miserable.
Did you ne'er love yet, wenches? Speak,
    Olympias;
Thou hast an easy temper, fit for stamp.
    OLYMPIAS. Never.
    ASPATIA. Nor you, Antiphila?
    ANTIPHILA. Nor I.
    ASPATIA. Then, my good girls, be more
than women, wise:
At least be more than I was; and be
    sure
You credit anything the light gives light
    to,
Before a man. Rather believe the sea
Weeps for the ruin'd merchant, when he
    roars;
Rather, the wind courts but the preg-
    nant sails,
When the strong cordage cracks; rather,
    the sun
Comes but to kiss the fruit in wealthy
    autumn,
When all falls blasted. If you needs must
    love,
(Forced by ill fate) take to your maiden
    bosoms
Two dead-cold aspicks, and of them make
    lovers:
They cannot flatter, nor forswear; one kiss
Makes a long peace for all. But man,
Oh, that beast man! Come, let's be sad,
    my girls!
That down-cast of thine eye, Olympias,
Shows a fine sorrow. Mark, Antiphila;
Just such another was the nymph Œnone,
When Paris brought home Helen. Now, a
    tear;
And then thou art a piece expressing fully
The Carthage queen, when, from a cold
    sea-rock,
Full with her sorrow, she tied fast her
    eyes
To the fair Trojan ships; and, having lost
    them,
Just as thine eyes do, down stole a tear.
    Antiphila,

What would this wench do, if she were
Aspatia?
Here she would stand, till some more
pitying god
Turn'd her to marble! 'Tis enough, my
wench!
Show me the piece of needlework you
wrought.
ANTIPHILA. Of Ariadne, madam?
ASPATIA. Yes, that piece.—
This should be Theseus; he has a cozen-
ing face:
You meant him for a man?
ANTIPHILA. He was so, madam.
ASPATIA. Why, then, 'tis well enough.
Never look back:
You have a full wind, and a false heart,
Theseus!
Does not the story say, his keel was
split,
Or his masts spent, or some kind rock or
other
Met with his vessel?
ANTIPHILA. Not as I remember.
ASPATIA. It should have been so. Could
the gods know this,
And not, of all their number, raise a
storm?
But they are all as ill! This false smile
Was well express'd; just such another
caught me!
You shall not go [on] so, Antiphila:
In this place work a quicksand,
And over it a shallow smiling water,
And his ship ploughing it; and then a
Fear:
Do that Fear to the life, wench.
ANTIPHILA. 'Twill wrong the story.
ASPATIA. 'Twill make the story,
wrong'd by wanton poets,
Live long, and be believed. But where's
the lady?
ANTIPHILA. There, madam.
ASPATIA. Fie! you have miss'd it here,
Antiphila;
You are much mistaken, wench:
These colours are not dull and pale
enough
To show a soul so full of misery
As this sad lady's was. Do it by me;
Do it again, by me, the lost Aspatia,

And you shall find all true but the wild
island.
Suppose I stand upon the sea-beach now,
Mine arms thus, and mine hair blown
with the wind,
Wild as that desert; and let all about me
Be teachers of my story. Do my face
(If thou hadst ever feeling of a sorrow)
Thus, thus, Antiphila: Strive to make me
look
Like Sorrow's monument! And the trees
about me,
Let them be dry and leafless; let the
rocks
Groan with continual surges; and, be-
hind me,
Make all a desolation. Look, look,
wenches!
A miserable life of this poor picture!
OLYMPIAS. Dear madam!
ASPATIA. I have done. Sit down; and
let us
Upon that point fix all our eyes; that
point there.
Make a dull silence, till you feel a sud-
den sadness
Give us new souls.

[Enter CALIANAX.]
CALIANAX. The king may do this, and
he may not do it:
My child is wrong'd, disgraced.—Well,
how now, huswives!
What, at your ease? Is this a time to
sit still?
Up, you young lazy whores, up, or I'll
swinge you!
OLYMPIAS. Nay, good my lord.
CALIANAX. You'll lie down shortly.
Get you in, and work!
What, are you grown so resty you want
heats?
We shall have some of the court-boys heat
you shortly.
ANTIPHILA. My lord, we do no more
than we are charged.
It is the lady's pleasure we be thus
In grief: she is forsaken.
CALIANAX. There's a rogue too!
A young dissembling slave! Well, get
you in!

I'll have a bout with that boy. 'Tis high
   time
Now to be valiant; I confess my youth
Was never prone that way. What, made
   an ass?
A court-stale? Well, I will be valiant,
And beat some dozen of these whelps; I
   will!
And there's another of 'em, a trim cheat-
   ing soldier;
I'll maul that rascal; he has out-braved
   me twice:
But now, I thank the gods, I am valiant.—
Go, get you in! I'll take a course with
   all.   [*Exeunt.*]

ACT III

SCENE I—*Antechamber to* EVADNE'S *bed-
room in the palace.*

[*Enter* CLEON, STRATO, *and* DIPHILUS.]
   CLEON. Your sister is not up yet.
   DIPHILUS. Oh, brides must take their
morning's rest; the night is troublesome.
   STRATO. But not tedious.
   DIPHILUS. What odds, he has not my
sister's maidenhead to-night?
   STRATO. No; it's odds, against any
bridegroom living, he ne'er gets it while
he lives.
   DIPHILUS. You're merry with my sis-
ter; you'll please to allow me the same
freedom with your mother.
   STRATO. She's at your service.
   DIPHILUS. Then she's merry enough of
herself; she needs no tickling. Knock at
the door.
   STRATO. We shall interrupt them.
   DIPHILUS. No matter; they have the
year before them.—Good-morrow, sister!
Spare yourself to-day; the night will
come again.

[*Enter* AMINTOR.]
   AMINTOR. Who's there? my brother!
   I'm no readier yet.
Your sister is but now up.
   DIPHILUS. You look as you had lost
      your eyes to-night:
I think you have not slept.

   AMINTOR. I'faith I have not.
   DIPHILUS. You have done better, then.
   AMINTOR. We ventured for a boy:
      When he is twelve,
He shall command against the foes of
   Rhodes.
Shall we be merry?
   STRATO. You cannot; you want sleep.
   AMINTOR. 'Tis true.—But she, [*Aside.*]
As if she had drank Lethe, or had made
Even with Heaven, did fetch so still a
   sleep,
So sweet and sound——
   DIPHILUS. What's that?
   AMINTOR. Your sister frets
This morning; and does turn her eyes
   upon me,
As people on their headsman. She does
   chafe,
And kiss, and chafe again, and clap my
   cheeks;
She's in another world.
   DIPHILUS. Then I had lost: I was
      about to lay
You had not got her maidenhead to-
   night.
   AMINTOR. Ha! he does not mock me?
      [*Aside.*]—You had lost, indeed;
I do not use to bungle.
   CLEON. You do deserve her.
   AMINTOR. I laid my lips to hers, and
      that wild breath,
That was so rude and rough to me last
   night,
Was sweet as April.—I'll be guilty too,
If these be the effects.   [*Aside.*]

[*Enter* MELANTIUS.]
   MELANTIUS. Good day, Amintor! for,
      to me, the name
Of brother is too distant: We are friends.
And that is nearer.
   AMINTOR. Dear Melantius!
Let me behold thee. Is it possible?
   MELANTIUS. What sudden gaze is this?
   AMINTOR. 'Tis wond'rous strange!
   MELANTIUS. Why does thine eye de-
      sire so strict a view
Of that it knows so well? There's nothing
   here
That is not thine.

AMINTOR. I wonder, much, Melantius,
To see those noble looks, that make me
  think
How virtuous thou art; And, on the sud-
  den,
'Tis strange to me thou shouldst have
  worth and honour;
Or not be base, and false, and treacher-
  ous,
And every ill. But——
MELANTIUS. Stay, stay, my friend;
I fear this sound will not become our
  loves.
No more; embrace me.
AMINTOR. Oh, mistake me not:
I know thee to be full of all those
  deeds
That we frail men call good; but, by the
  course
Of nature, thou shouldst be as quickly
  changed
As are the winds; dissembling as the
  sea,
That now wears brows as smooth as vir-
  gins' be,
Tempting the merchant to invade his face,
And in an hour calls his billows up,
And shoots 'em at the sun, destroying
  all
He carries on him.—Oh, how near am I
To utter my sick thoughts!   [Aside.]
MELANTIUS. But why, my friend, should
  I be so by nature?
AMINTOR. I have wed thy sister, who
  hath virtuous thoughts
Enough for one whole family; and, 'tis
  strange
That you should feel no want.
MELANTIUS. Believe me, this compli-
  ment's too cunning for me.
DIPHILUS. What should I be then, by
  the course of nature,
They having both robb'd me of so much
  virtue?
STRATO. Oh, call the bride, my lord
  Amintor,
That we may see her blush, and turn her
  eyes down:
'Tis the prettiest sport!
AMINTOR. Evadne!
EVADNE [within]. My lord!

AMINTOR. Come forth, my love!
Your brothers do attend to wish you
  joy.
EVADNE. I am not ready yet.
AMINTOR. Enough, enough.
EVADNE. They'll mock me.
AMINTOR. 'Faith, thou shalt come in.

    [Enter EVADNE.]
MELANTIUS. Good morrow, sister! He
  that understands
Whom you have wed, need not to wish
  you joy;
You have enough: Take heed you be not
  proud.
DIPHILUS. Oh, sister, what have you
  done?
EVADNE. I done! why, what have I
  done?
STRATO. My lord Amintor swears you
  are no maid now.
EVADNE. Pish!
STRATO. I'faith, he does.
EVADNE. I knew I should be mock'd.
DIPHILUS. With a truth.
EVADNE. If 'twere to do again,
In faith, I would not marry.
AMINTOR. Nor I, by heaven! [Aside.]
DIPHILUS. Sister, Dula swears
She heard you cry two rooms off.
EVADNE. Fie, how you talk!
DIPHILUS. Let's see you walk, Evadne.
  By my troth,
You are spoil'd.
MELANTIUS. Amintor!
AMINTOR. Ha?
MELANTIUS. Thou art sad.
AMINTOR. Who, I? I thank you for
  that.
Shall Diphilus, thou, and I, sing a catch?
MELANTIUS. How!
AMINTOR. Pr'ythee, let's.
MELANTIUS. Nay, that's too much the
  other way.
AMINTOR. I am so lightened with my
  happiness!
How dost thou, love? kiss me.
EVADNE. I cannot love you, you tell
tales of me.
AMINTOR. Nothing but what becomes
  us.—Gentlemen,

'Would you had all such wives, and all
    the world,
That I might be no wonder! You are
    all sad:
What, do you envy me? I walk, me-
    thinks,
On water, and ne'er sink, I am so light.
MELANTIUS. 'Tis well you are so.
AMINTOR. Well? how can I be other,
When she looks thus?—Is there no music
    there?
Let's dance.
MELANTIUS. Why, this is strange,
Amintor!
AMINTOR. I do not know myself; yet
    I could wish
My joy were less.
DIPHILUS. I'll marry too, if it will
make one thus.
EVADNE. Amintor, hark.   [Aside.]
AMINTOR. What says my love?—I must
obey.
EVADNE. You do it scurvily, 'twill be
perceived.   [Apart to him.]
CLEON. My lord, the king is here.

    [Enter KING and LYSIPPUS.]
AMINTOR. Where?
STRATO. And his brother.
KING. Good morrow, all!—
Amintor, joy on joy fall thick upon
    thee!
And, madam, you are alter'd since I saw
    you;
I must salute you; you are now an-
    other's.
How liked you your night's rest?
EVADNE. Ill, sir.
AMINTOR. Ay, 'deed,
She took but little.
LYSIPPUS. You'll let her take more,
And thank her too, shortly.
KING. Amintor, wert
Thou truly honest till thou wert married.
AMINTOR. Yes, sir.
KING. Tell me, then, how shows the
    sport unto thee?
AMINTOR. Why, well.
KING. What did you do?
AMINTOR. No more, nor less, than other
    couples use;

You know what 'tis; it has but a coarse
    name.
KING. But pr'ythee, I should think, by
    her black eye,
And her red cheek, she should be quick
    and stirring
In this same business; ha?
AMINTOR. I cannot tell;
I ne'er try'd other, sir; but I perceive
She is as quick as you delivered.
KING. Well, you will trust me then,
    Amintor,
To chuse a wife for you again?
AMINTOR. No, never, sir.
KING. Why? like you this so ill?
AMINTOR. So well I like her.
For this I bow my knee in thanks to you,
And unto heaven will pay my grateful
    tribute
Hourly; and do hope we shall draw out
A long contented life together here,
And die both, full of grey hairs, in one
    day:
For which the thanks are yours. But if
    the powers
That rule us please to call her first away,
Without pride spoke, this world holds
    not a wife
Worthy to take her room.
KING. I do not like this.—All forbear
    the room,
But you, Amintor, and your lady.
    [Exeunt all but the KING, AMIN-
    TOR, and EVADNE.]
I have some speech with you, that may
    concern
Your after living well.
AMINTOR [aside]. He will not tell me
    that he lies with her?
If he do, something heavenly stay my
    heart,
For I shall be apt to thrust this arm of
    mine
To acts unlawful!
KING. You will suffer me to talk with
    her,
Amintor, and not have a jealous pang?
AMINTOR. Sir, I dare trust my wife
    with whom she dares
To talk, and not be jealous. [EVADNE
    and the KING speak apart.]

KING. How do you like
Amintor?

EVADNE. As I did, sir.

KING. How is that?

EVADNE. As one that, to fulfil your
will and pleasure,
I have given leave to call me wife and
love.

KING. I see there is no lasting faith
in sin;
They, that break word with heaven, will
break again
With all the world, and so dost thou with
me.

EVADNE. How, sir?

KING. This subtle woman's ignorance
Will not excuse you: thou hast taken
oaths,
So great, methought, they did not well
become
A woman's mouth, that thou wouldst ne'er
enjoy
A man but me.

EVADNE. I never did swear so;
You do me wrong.

KING. Day and night have heard it.

EVADNE. I swore indeed, that I would
never love
A man of lower place; but, if your for-
tune
Should throw you from this height, I
bade you trust
I would forsake you, and would bend to
him
That won your throne: I love with my
ambition,
Not with my eyes. But, if I ever yet
Touch'd any other, leprosy light here
Upon my face; which for your royalty
I would not stain!

KING. Why, thou dissemblest, and it
is
In me to punish thee.

EVADNE. Why, 'tis in me,
Then, not to love you, which will more
afflict
Your body than your punishment can
mine.

KING. But thou hast let Amintor lie
with thee.

EVADNE. I have not.

KING. Impudence! he says himself so.

EVADNE. He lies.

KING. He does not.

EVADNE. By this light he does,
Strangely and basely! and I'll prove it
so.
I did not shun him for a night; but told
him,
I would never close with him.

KING. Speak lower; 'tis false.

EVADNE. I am no man
To answer with a blow; or, if I were,
You are the king! But urge me not; 'tis
most true.

KING. Do not I know the uncon-
trolled thoughts
That youth brings with him, when his
blood is high
With expectation, and desire of that
He long hath waited for? Is not his
spirit,
Though he be temperate, of a valiant
strain
As this our age hath known? What could
he do,
If such a sudden speech had met his blood,
But ruin thee for ever, if he had not
kill'd thee?
He could not bear it thus. He is as we,
Or any other wrong'd man.

EVADNE. 'Tis dissembling.

KING. Take him! farewell! henceforth
I am thy foe;
And what disgraces I can blot thee with
look for.

EVADNE. Stay, sir!—Amintor!—You
shall hear.—Amintor!

AMINTOR [coming forward]. What, my
love?

EVADNE. Amintor, thou hast an in-
genuous look,
And shouldst be virtuous: It amazeth me,
That thou canst make such base malicious
lies!

AMINTOR. What, my dear wife!

EVADNE. Dear wife! I do despise thee.
Why, nothing can be baser than to sow
Dissension amongst lovers.

AMINTOR. Lovers! who?

EVADNE. The king and me.

AMINTOR. O, God!

EVADNE. Who should live long, and love without distaste.
Were it not for such pickthanks as thyself.
Did you lie with me? Swear now, and be punish'd
In hell for this!

AMINTOR. The faithless sin I made
To fair Aspatia, is not yet revenged;
It follows me.—I will not lose a word
To this vile woman: But to you, my king,
The anguish of my soul thrusts out this truth,
You are a tyrant! And not so much to wrong
An honest man thus, as to take a pride
In talking with him of it.

EVADNE. Now, sir, see
How loud this fellow lied.

AMINTOR. You that can know to wrong, should know how men
Must right themselves: What punishment is due
From me to him that shall abuse my bed?
Is it not death? Nor can that satisfy,
Unless I send your limbs through all the land,
To show how nobly I have freed myself.

KING. Draw not thy sword: thou know'st I cannot fear
A subject's hand; but thou shalt feel the weight
Of this, if thou dost rage.

AMINTOR. The weight of that!
If you have any worth, for Heaven's sake, think
I fear not swords; for as you are mere man,
I dare as easily kill you for this deed,
As you dare think to do it. But there is
Divinity about you, that strikes dead
My rising passions: As you are my king,
I fall before you, and present my sword
To cut mine own flesh, if it be your will.
Alas! I am nothing but a multitude
Of walking griefs! Yet, should I murder you,
I might before the world take the excuse
Of madness: For, compare my injuries,

And they will well appear too sad a weight
For reason to endure! But, fall I first
Amongst my sorrows, ere my treacherous hand
Touch holy things! But why (I know not what
I have to say) why did you chuse out me
To make thus wretched? There were thousand fools
Easy to work on, and of state enough,
Within the island.

EVADNE. I would not have a fool;
It were no credit for me.

AMINTOR. Worse and worse!
Thou, that dar'st talk unto thy husband thus,
Profess thyself a whore, and, more than so,
Resolve to be so still—It is my fate
To bear and bow beneath a thousand griefs,
To keep that little credit with the world!
But there were wise ones too; you might have ta'en
Another.

KING. No; for I believe thee honest,
As thou wert valiant.

AMINTOR. All the happiness
Bestowed upon me turns into disgrace.
Gods, take your honesty again, for I
Am loaden with it!—Good my lord the king,
Be private in it.

KING. Thou may'st live, Amintor.
Free as thy king, if thou wilt wink at this,
And be a means that we may meet in secret.

AMINTOR. A bawd! Hold, hold, my breast! A bitter curse
Seize me, if I forget not all respects
That are religious, on another word
Sounded like that; and, through a sea of sins,
Will wade to my revenge, though I should call
Pains here, and after life, upon my soul!

KING. Well, I am resolute you lay not with her;
And so I leave you.   [Exit KING.]

EVADNE. You must needs be prating; And see what follows.

AMINTOR. Pr'ythee, vex me not! Leave me: I am afraid some sudden start Will pull a murder on me.

EVADNE. I am gone; I love my life well. [*Exit* EVADNE.]

AMINTOR. I hate mine as much.— This 'tis to break a troth! I should be glad, If all this tide of grief would make me mad. [*Exit.*]

SCENE II—*A room in the palace.*

[*Enter* MELANTIUS.]

MELANTIUS. I'll know the cause of all Amintor's griefs, Or friendship shall be idle.

[*Enter* CALIANAX.]

CALIANAX. O Melantius, My daughter will die.

MELANTIUS. Trust me, I am sorry. Would thou hadst ta'en her room!

CALIANAX. Thou art a slave, A cut-throat slave, a bloody treacherous slave!

MELANTIUS. Take heed, old man; thou wilt be heard to rave, And lose thine offices.

CALIANAX. I am valiant grown, At all these years, and thou art but a slave!

MELANTIUS. Leave! Some company will come, and I respect Thy years, not thee, so much, that I could wish To laugh at thee alone.

CALIANAX. I'll spoil your mirth: I mean to fight with thee. There lie, my cloak! This was my father's sword, and he durst fight. Are you prepared?

MELANTIUS. Why wilt thou dote thy-self Out of thy life? Hence, get thee to bed! Have careful looking-to, and eat warm things,

And trouble not me: My head is full of thoughts, More weighty than thy life or death can be.

CALIANAX. You have a name in war, where you stand safe Amongst a multitude; but I will try What you dare do unto a weak old man In single fight. You will give ground, I fear. Come, draw.

MELANTIUS. I will not draw, unless thou pull'st thy death Upon thee with a stroke. There's no one blow, That thou canst give, hath strength enough to kill me. Tempt me not so far then: The power of earth Shall not redeem thee.

CALIANAX [*aside*]. I must let him alone: He's stout and able; and, to say the truth, However I may set a face, and talk, I am not valiant. When I was a youth, I kept my credit with a testy trick I had, 'mongst cowards, but durst never fight.

MELANTIUS. I will not promise to pre-serve your life, If you do stay.

CALIANAX. I would give half my land That I durst fight with that proud man a little. If I had men to hold him, I would beat him Till he ask'd me mercy.

MELANTIUS. Sir, will you be gone?

CALIANAX. I dare not stay; but I'll go home, and beat My servants all over for this. [*Exit* CALIANAX.]

MELANTIUS. This old fellow haunts me! But the distracted carriage of my Amintor Takes deeply on me: I will find the cause. I fear his conscience cries, he wrong'd Aspatia.

[Enter AMINTOR.]

AMINTOR.   Men's eyes are not so subtle to perceive
My inward misery: I bear my grief
Hid from the world.   How art thou wretched then?
For aught I know, all husbands are like me;
And every one I talk with of his wife,
Is but a well dissembler of his woes,
As I am.   'Would I knew it! for the rareness
Afflicts me now.
MELANTIUS.   Amintor, we have not enjoy'd our friendship of late,
For we were wont to change our souls in talk.
AMINTOR.   Melantius, I can tell thee a good jest
Of Strato and a lady the last day.
MELANTIUS.   How was't?
AMINTOR.   Why, such an odd one!
MELANTIUS.   I have long'd to speak with you;
Not of an idle jest, that's forced, but of matter
You are bound to utter to me.
AMINTOR.   What is that, my friend?
MELANTIUS.   I have observed your words
Fall from your tongue wildly; and all your carriage
Like one that strove to show his merry mood,
When he were ill disposed: You were not wont
To put such scorn into your speech, or wear
Upon your face ridiculous jollity.
Some sadness sits here, which your cunning would
Cover o'er with smiles, and 'twill not be.
What is it?
AMINTOR.   A sadness here! what cause
Can fate provide for me, to make me so?
Am I not loved through all this isle?   The king
Rains greatness on me.   Have I not received
A lady to my bed, that in her eye
Keeps mounting fire, and on her tender cheeks
Inevitable colour, in her heart
A prison for all virtue?   Are not you,
Which is above all joys, my constant friend?
What sadness can I have?   No; I am light,
And feel the courses of my blood more warm
And stirring than they were.   'Faith, marry too:
And you will feel so unexpress'd a joy
In chaste embraces, that you will indeed
Appear another.
MELANTIUS.   You may shape, Amintor,
Causes to cozen the whole world withal,
And yourself too: but 'tis not like a friend,
To hide your soul from me.   'Tis not your nature
To be thus idle: I have seen you stand
As you were blasted, 'midst of all your mirth;
Call thrice aloud, and then start, feigning joy
So coldly!—World, what do I hear? a friend
Is nothing.   Heaven, I would have told that man
My secret sins!   I'll search an unknown land,
And there plant friendship; all is wither'd here.
Come with a compliment!   I would have fought,
Or told my friend "he lied," ere sooth'd him so.
Out of my bosom!
AMINTOR.   But there is nothing——
MELANTIUS.   Worse and worse! farewell!
From this time have acquaintance, but no friend.
AMINTOR.   Melantius, stay: You shall know what it is.
MELANTIUS.   See, how you play'd with friendship!   Be advised
How you give cause unto yourself to say,
You have lost a friend.

AMINTOR. Forgive what I have done;
For I am so o'ergone with injuries
Unheard of, that I lose consideration
Of what I ought to do. Oh, oh!
MELANTIUS. Do not weep.
What is it? May I once but know the man
Hath turn'd my friend thus!
AMINTOR. I had spoke at first,
But that——
MELANTIUS. But what?
AMINTOR. I held it most unfit
For you to know. 'Faith, do not know it yet.
MELANTIUS. Thou see'st my love, that will keep company
With thee in tears! hide nothing, then, from me:
For when I know the cause of thy distemper,
With mine old armour I'll adorn myself,
My resolution, and cut through my foes,
Unto thy quiet; till I place thy heart
As peaceable as spotless innocence.
What is it?
AMINTOR. Why, 'tis this—It is too big
To get out—Let my tears make way awhile.
MELANTIUS. Punish me strangely, Heaven, if he 'scape
Of life or fame, that brought this youth to this!
AMINTOR. Your sister——
MELANTIUS. Well said.
AMINTOR. You will wish't unknown,
When you have heard it.
MELANTIUS. No.
AMINTOR. Is much to blame,
And to the king has given her honour up,
And lives in whoredom with him.
MELANTIUS. How is this?
Thou art run mad with injury, indeed;
Thou couldst not utter this else. Speak again;
For I forgive it freely; tell thy griefs.
AMINTOR. She's wanton: I am loth to say, "a whore,"
Though it be true.
MELANTIUS. Speak yet again, before mine anger grow

Up, beyond throwing down: What are thy griefs?
AMINTOR. By all our friendship, these.
MELANTIUS. What, am I tame?
After mine actions, shall the name of friend
Blot all our family, and stick the brand
Of whore upon my sister, unrevenged?
My shaking flesh, be thou a witness for me,
With what unwillingness I go to scourge
This railer, whom my folly hath called friend!——
I will not take thee basely; thy sword
Hangs near thy hand; draw it, that I may whip
Thy rashness to repentance. Draw thy sword!
AMINTOR. Not on thee, did thine anger swell as high
As the wild surges. Thou shouldst do me ease
Here, and eternally, if thy noble hand
Would cut me from my sorrows.
MELANTIUS. This is base
And fearful. They, that use to utter lies,
Provide not blows, but words, to qualify
The men they wrong'd. Thou hast a guilty cause.
AMINTOR. Thou pleasest me; for so much more like this
Will raise my anger up above my griefs,
(Which is a passion easier to be borne)
And I shall then be happy.
MELANTIUS. Take then more,
To raise thine anger: 'Tis mere cowardice
Makes thee not draw; and I will leave thee dead,
However. But if thou art so much press'd
With guilt and fear, as not to dare to fight,
I'll make thy memory loath'd, and fix a scandal
Upon thy name for ever.
AMINTOR. Then I draw,
As justly as our magistrates their swords
To cut offenders off. I knew before,
'Twould grate your ears; but it was base in you

To urge a weighty secret from your friend,
And then rage at it. I shall be at ease,
If I be kill'd; and if you fall by me,
I shall not long out-live you.
MELANTIUS. Stay awhile.—
The name of friend is more than family,
Or all the world besides: I was a fool!
Thou searching human nature, that didst wake
To do me wrong, thou art inquisitive,
And thrust'st me upon questions that will take
My sleep away! 'Would I had died, ere known
This sad dishonour!—Pardon me, my friend!
If thou wilt strike, here is a faithful heart;
Pierce it, for I will never heave my hand
To thine. Behold the power thou hast in me!
I do believe my sister is a whore,
A leprous one! Put up thy sword, young man.
　　AMINTOR. How shall I bear it then, she being so?
I fear, my friend, that you will lose me shortly;
And I shall do a foul act on myself,
Through these disgraces.
　　MELANTIUS. Better half the land
Were buried quick together. No, Amintor;
Thou shalt have ease. Oh, this adulterous king,
That drew her to it! Where got he the spirit
To wrong me so?
　　AMINTOR. What is it then to me,
If it be wrong to you?
　　MELANTIUS. Why, not so much:
The credit of our house is thrown away.
But from his iron den I'll waken Death,
And hurl him on this king! My honesty
Shall steel my sword; and on its horrid point
I'll wear my cause, that shall amaze the eyes
Of this proud man, and be too glittering
For him to look on.

　　AMINTOR. I have quite undone my fame.
　　MELANTIUS. Dry up thy watery eyes,
And cast a manly look upon my face;
For nothing is so wild as I, thy friend,
Till I have freed thee. Still this swelling breast!
I go thus from thee, and will never cease
My vengeance, till I find thy heart at peace.
　　AMINTOR. It must not be so. Stay!—Mine eyes would tell
How loth I am to this; but, love and tears,
Leave me awhile; for I have hazarded
All that this world calls happy.—Thou hast wrought
A secret from me, under name of friend,
Which art could ne'er have found, nor torture wrung
From out my bosom: Give it me again,
For I will find it, wheresoe'er it lies,
Hid in the mortal'st part! Invent a way
To give it back.
　　MELANTIUS. Why would you have it back?
I will to death pursue him with revenge.
　　AMINTOR. Therefore I call it back from thee; for I know
Thy blood so high, that thou wilt stir in this,
And shame me to posterity.
Take to thy weapon!
　　MELANTIUS. Hear thy friend, that bears
More years than thou.
　　AMINTOR. I will not hear! but draw,
Or I——
　　MELANTIUS. Amintor!
　　AMINTOR. Draw then; for I am full as resolute
As fame and honour can inforce me be!
I cannot linger. Draw!
　　MELANTIUS. I do. But is not
My share of credit equal with thine,
If I do stir?
　　AMINTOR. No; for it will be call'd
Honour in thee to spill thy sister's blood,
If she her birth abuse; and, on the king,
A brave revenge: But on me, that have walk'd

With patience in it, it will fix the name
Of fearful cuckold. Oh, that word! Be
  quick.
MELANTIUS. Then join with me.
AMINTOR. I dare not do a sin, or else
  I would.
Be speedy.
MELANTIUS. Then dare not fight with
  me; for that's a sin.—
His grief distracts him.—Call thy
  thoughts again,
And to thyself pronounce the name of
  friend,
And see what that will work. I will not
  fight.
AMINTOR. You must.
MELANTIUS. I will be kill'd first.
  Though my passions
Offer'd the like to you, 'tis not this earth
Shall buy my reason to it. Think awhile,
For you are (I must weep when I speak
  that)
Almost besides yourself.
AMINTOR. Oh, my soft temper!
So many sweet words from thy sister's
  mouth,
I am afraid, would make me take her
To embrace, and pardon her. I am mad
  indeed,
And know not what I do. Yet, have a
  care
Of me in what thou dost.
MELANTIUS. Why, thinks my friend
I will forget his honour? or, to save
The bravery of our house, will lose his
  fame,
And fear to touch the throne of maj-
  esty?
AMINTOR. A curse will follow that; but
  rather live
And suffer with me.
MELANTIUS. I'll do what worth shall
bid me, and no more.
AMINTOR. Faith, I am sick, and des-
  perately I hope;
Yet, leaning thus, I feel a kind of ease.
MELANTIUS. Come, take again your
mirth about you.
AMINTOR. I shall never do't.
MELANTIUS. I warrant you: look up;
  we'll walk together;

Put thine arm here; all shall be well
  again.
AMINTOR. Thy love (oh, wretched!) ay,
  thy love, Melantius!
Why, I have nothing else.
MELANTIUS. Be merry then. [*Exeunt.*]

[*Reënter* MELANTIUS.]
MELANTIUS. This worthy young man
  may do violence
Upon himself; but I have cherish'd him
To my best power, and sent him smiling
  from me,
To counterfeit again. Sword, hold thine
  edge;
My heart will never fail me.

[*Enter* DIPHILUS.]
Diphilus! Thou com'st as sent.
DIPHILUS. Yonder has been such laugh-
ing.
MELANTIUS. Betwixt whom?
DIPHILUS. Why, our sister and the
  king;
I thought their spleens would break; they
  laugh'd us all
Out of the room.
MELANTIUS. They must weep, Diphilus.
DIPHILUS. Must they?
MELANTIUS. They must.
Thou art my brother; and if I did be-
  lieve
Thou hadst a base thought, I would rip
  it out,
Lie where it durst.
DIPHILUS. You should not; I would
  first
Mangle myself and find it.
MELANTIUS. That was spoke
According to our strain. Come, join thy
  hands to mine,
And swear a firmness to what project I
Shall lay before thee.
DIPHILUS. You do wrong us both:
People hereafter shall not say, there
  pass'd
A bond, more than our loves, to tie our
  lives
And deaths together.
MELANTIUS. It is as nobly said as I
  would wish.

Anon I'll tell you wonders: We are wrong'd.

DIPHILUS. But I will tell you now, we'll right ourselves.

MELANTIUS. Stay not: Prepare the armour in my house;
And what friends you can draw unto our side,
Not knowing of the cause, make ready too.
Haste, Diphilus, the time requires it, haste!—   [*Exit* DIPHILUS.]
I hope my cause is just; I know my blood
Tells me it is; and I will credit it.
To take revenge, and lose myself withal,
Were idle; and to 'scape impossible,
Without I had the fort, which (misery!)
Remaining in the hands of my old enemy
Calianax—But I must have it. See,

[*Enter* CALIANAX.]

Where he comes shaking by me.—Good my lord,
Forget your spleen to me; I never wrong'd you,
But would have peace with every man.

CALIANAX. 'Tis well;
If I durst fight, your tongue would lie at quiet.

MELANTIUS. You are touchy without all cause.

CALIANAX. Do, mock me.

MELANTIUS. By mine honour I speak truth.

CALIANAX. Honour? where is it?

MELANTIUS. See, what starts
You make into your hatred, to my love
And freedom to you. I come with resolution
To obtain a suit of you.

CALIANAX. A suit of me!
'Tis very like it should be granted, sir.

MELANTIUS. Nay, go not hence:
'Tis this; you have the keeping of the fort,
And I would wish you, by the love you ought
To bear unto me, to deliver it
Into my hands.

CALIANAX. I am in hope thou'rt mad,
To talk to me thus.

MELANTIUS. But there is a reason
To move you to it: I would kill the king,
That wrong'd you and your daughter.

CALIANAX. Out, traitor!

MELANTIUS. Nay,
But stay: I cannot 'scape, the deed once done,
Without I have this fort.

CALIANAX. And should I help thee?
Now thy treacherous mind betrays itself.

MELANTIUS. Come, delay me not;
Give me a sudden answer, or already
Thy last is spoke! refuse not offer'd love,
When it comes clad in secrets.

CALIANAX. If I say   [*Aside.*]
I will not, he will kill me; I do see't
Writ in his looks; and should I say I will,
He'll run and tell the king.—I do not shun
Your friendship, dear Melantius, but this cause
Is weighty; give me but an hour to think.

MELANTIUS. Take it.—I know this goes unto the king;
But I am arm'd.   [*Exit* MELANTIUS.]

CALIANAX. Methinks I feel myself
But twenty now again! this fighting fool
Wants policy: I shall revenge my girl,
And make her red again. I pray, my legs
Will last that pace that I will carry them:
I shall want breath, before I find the king.   [*Exit.*]

ACT IV

SCENE I—*The apartment of* EVADNE *in the palace.*

[*Enter* MELANTIUS, EVADNE, *and* LADIES.]

MELANTIUS. Save you!

EVADNE. Save you, sweet brother!

MELANTIUS. In my blunt eye, methinks, you look, Evadne——

EVADNE. Come, you will make me blush.

MELANTIUS. I would, Evadne;
I shall displease my ends else.

EVADNE. You shall, if you commend me; I am bashful.

Come, sir, how do I look?

MELANTIUS. I would not have your women hear me
Break into commendation of you; 'tis not seemly.

EVADNE. Go, wait in the gallery.—
Now speak.   [*Exeunt* LADIES.]

MELANTIUS. I'll lock the door first.

EVADNE. Why?

MELANTIUS. I will not have your gilded things, that dance
In visitation with their Milan skins,
Choke up my business.

EVADNE. You are strangely disposed, sir.

MELANTIUS. Good madam, not to make you merry.

EVADNE. No; if you praise me it will make me sad.

MELANTIUS. Such a sad commendation
I have for you.

EVADNE. Brother, the court hath made you witty,
And learn to riddle.

MELANTIUS. I praise the court for't:
Has it learnt you nothing?

EVADNE. Me?

MELANTIUS. Ay, Evadne; thou art young and handsome,
A lady of a sweet complexion,
And such a flowing carriage, that it cannot
Chuse but inflame a kingdom.

EVADNE. Gentle brother!

MELANTIUS. 'Tis yet in thy repentance, foolish woman,
To make me gentle.

EVADNE. How is this?

MELANTIUS. 'Tis base
And I could blush, at these years, thorough all
My honour'd scars, to come to such a parley.

EVADNE. I understand you not.

MELANTIUS. You dare not, fool!
They, that commit thy faults, fly the remembrance.

EVADNE. My faults, sir! I would have you know, I care not

If they were written here, here in my forehead.

MELANTIUS. Thy body is too little for the story;
The lusts of which would fill another woman,
Though she had twins within her.

EVADNE. This is saucy:
Look you intrude no more! There lies your way.

MELANTIUS. Thou art my way, and I will tread upon thee,
Till I find truth out.

EVADNE. What truth is that you look for?

MELANTIUS. Thy long-lost honour.
'Would the gods had set me
Rather to grapple with the plague, or stand
One of their loudest bolts! Come, tell me quickly,
Do it without enforcement, and take heed
You swell me not above my temper.

EVADNE. How, sir.
Where got you this report?

MELANTIUS. Where there were people,
In every place.

EVADNE. They, and the seconds of it are base people:
Believe them not, they lied.

MELANTIUS. Do not play with mine anger, do not, wretch! [*Seizes her.*]
I come to know that desperate fool that drew
From thy fair life: Be wise and lay him open.

EVADNE. Unhand me, and learn manners! Such another
Forgetfulness forfeits your life.

MELANTIUS. Quench me this mighty humour, and then tell me
Whose whore you are; for you are one, I know it.
Let all mine honours perish, but I'll find him,
Though he lie lock'd up in thy blood! Be sudden;
There is no facing it, and be not flatter'd!
The burnt air, when the Dog reigns, is not fouler

Than thy contagious name, till thy re-
pentance
(If the gods grant thee any) purge thy
sickness.

EVADNE. Be gone! you are my brother;
that's your safety.

MELANTIUS. I'll be a wolf first! 'Tis,
to be thy brother,
An infamy below the sin of coward.
I am as far from being part of thee,
As thou art from thy virtue: Seek a
kindred
'Mongst sensual beasts, and make a goat
thy brother?
A goat is cooler. Will you tell me
yet?

EVADNE. If you stay here and rail thus,
I shall tell you,
I'll have you whipp'd! Get you to your
command,
And there preach to your sentinels, and
tell them
What a brave man you are: I shall laugh
at you.

MELANTIUS. You are grown a glorious
whore! Where be your fighters?
What mortal fool durst raise thee to this
daring,
And I alive! By my just sword, he had
safer
Bestride a billow, when the angry North
Plows up the sea, or made Heaven's fire
his food!
Work me no higher. Will you discover
yet?

EVADNE. The fellow's mad: Sleep and
speak sense.

MELANTIUS. Force my swoll'n heart no
further: I would save thee.
Your great maintainers are not here, they
dare not:
Would they were all, and arm'd! I would
speak loud;
Here's one should thunder to 'em! will
you tell me?
Thou hast no hope to 'scape: He that
dares most,
And damns away his soul to do thee
service,
Will sooner snatch meat from a hungry
lion,

Than come to rescue thee; thou hast death
about thee.
Who has undone thine honour, poison'd
thy virtue,
And, of a lovely rose, left thee a can-
ker?

EVADNE. Let me consider.

MELANTIUS. Do, whose child thou
wert,
Whose honour thou hast murder'd, whose
grave open'd,
And so pull'd on the gods, that in their
justice
They must restore him flesh again, and
life,
And raise his dry bones to revenge this
scandal.

EVADNE. The gods are not of my mind;
they had better
Let 'em lie sweet still in the earth; they'll
stink here.

MELANTIUS. Do you raise mirth out
of my casiness? [Draws.]
Forsake me, then, all weaknesses of na-
ture,
That make men women! Speak, you
whore, speak truth!
Or, by the dear soul of thy sleeping
father,
This sword shall be thy lover! Tell, or
I'll kill thee;
And, when thou hast told all, thou wilt
deserve it.

EVADNE. You will not murder me?

MELANTIUS. No; 'tis a justice, and a
noble one,
To put the light out of such base of-
fenders.

EVADNE. Help!

MELANTIUS. By thy foul self, no hu-
man help shall help thee,
If thou criest! When I have kill'd thee
as I
Have vow'd to do if thou confess not,
naked,
As thou has left thine honour, will I
leave thee;
That on thy branded flesh the world may
read
Thy black shame, and my justice. Wilt
thou bend yet?

EVADNE. Yes.

MELANTIUS. Up, and begin your story.

EVADNE. Oh, I am miserable!

MELANTIUS. 'Tis true, thou art. Speak truth still.

EVADNE. I have offended: Noble sir, forgive me.

MELANTIUS. With what secure slave?

EVADNE. Do not ask me, sir:
Mine own remembrance is a misery
Too mighty for me.

MELANTIUS. Do not fall back again:
My sword's unsheathed yet.

EVADNE. What shall I do?

MELANTIUS. Be true, and make your fault less.

EVADNE. I dare not tell.

MELANTIUS. Tell, or I'll be this day a-killing thee.

EVADNE. Will you forgive me then?

MELANTIUS. Stay; I must ask mine honour first.—
I have too much foolish nature in me:
Speak.

EVADNE. Is there none else here?

MELANTIUS. None but a fearful conscience; that's too many.
Who is't?

EVADNE. Oh, hear me gently. It was the king.

MELANTIUS. No more. My worthy father's and my services
Are liberally rewarded.—King, I thank thee!
For all my dangers and my wounds, thou hast paid me
In my own metal: These are soldiers' thanks!—
How long have you lived thus, Evadne?

EVADNE. Too long.

MELANTIUS. Too late you find it. Can you be sorry?

EVADNE. Would I were half as blameless.

MELANTIUS. Evadne, thou wilt to thy trade again!

EVADNE. First to my grave.

MELANTIUS. 'Would gods thou hadst been so blest.
Dost thou not hate this king now? pr'ythee hate him.

Couldst thou not curse him? I command thee, curse him.
Curse till the gods hear, and deliver him
To thy just wishes! Yet, I fear, Evadne,
You had rather play your game out.

EVADNE. No; I feel
Too many sad confusions here, to let in
Any loose flame hereafter.

MELANTIUS. Dost thou not feel, 'mongst all those, one brave anger
That breaks out nobly, and directs thine arm
To kill this base king?

EVADNE. All the gods forbid it!

MELANTIUS. No; all the gods require it:
They are dishonour'd in him.

EVADNE. 'Tis too fearful.

MELANTIUS. You are valiant in his bed, and bold enough
To be a stale whore, and have your madam's name
Discourse for grooms and pages; and, hereafter,
When his cool majesty hath laid you by,
To be at pension with some needy sir,
For meat and coarser clothes; Thus far you know
No fear. Come, you shall kill him.

EVADNE. Good sir!

MELANTIUS. An 'twere to kiss him dead, thou shouldst smother him.
Be wise, and kill him. Canst thou live, and know
What noble minds shall make thee, see thyself
Found out with every finger, made the shame
Of all successions, and in this great ruin
Thy brother and thy noble husband broken?
Thou shalt not live thus. Kneel, and swear to help me,
When I shall call thee to it; or, by all
Holy in Heaven and earth, thou shalt not live
To breathe a full hour longer; not a thought!
Come, 'tis a righteous oath. Give me thy hands,

And, both to Heaven held up, swear, by
that wealth
This lustful thief stole from thee, when
I say it,
To let his foul soul out.

EVADNE. Here I swear it;
And, all you spirits of abused ladies,
Help me in this performance!

MELANTIUS. Enough. This must be
known to none
But you and I, Evadne; not to your
 lord,
Though he be wise and noble, and a fel-
low
Dares step as far into a worthy action
As the most daring: ay, as far as justice.
Ask me not why. Farewell. [*Exit*
MELANTIUS.]

EVADNE. 'Would I could say so to my
black disgrace!
Oh, where have I been all this time? how
'friended,
That I should lose myself thus desper-
ately,
And none for pity show me how I wan-
dered?
There is not in the compass of the light
A more unhappy creature: Sure, I am
monstrous!
For I have done those follies, those mad
mischiefs,
Would dare a woman. Oh, my loaden soul,
Be not so cruel to me; choke not up
The way to my repentance! Oh, my
lord!

[*Enter* AMINTOR.]

AMINTOR. How now?

EVADNE. My much-abused lord!
[*Kneels.*]

AMINTOR. This cannot be!

EVADNE. I do not kneel to live; I dare
not hope it;
The wrongs I did are greater. Look
upon me,
Though I appear with all my faults.

AMINTOR. Stand up.
This is a new way to beget more sor-
row:
Heaven knows I have too many! Do not
mock me:

Though I am tame, and bred up with
my wrongs,
Which are my foster-brothers, I may
leap,
Like a hand-wolf, into my natural wild-
ness,
And do an outrage. Pr'ythee, do not mock
me.

EVADNE. My whole life is so leprous, it
infects
All my repentance. I would buy your
pardon,
Though at the highest set; even with my
life.
That slight contrition, that's no sacrifice
For what I have committed.

AMINTOR. Sure I dazzle:
There cannot be a faith in that foul
woman,
That knows no god more mighty than
her mischiefs.
Thou dost still worse, still number on thy
faults,
To press my poor heart thus. Can I
believe
There's any seed of virtue in that woman
Left to shoot up, that dares go on in
sin,
Known, and so known as thine is. Oh,
Evadne!
'Would there were any safety in thy sex,
That I might put a thousand sorrows off,
And credit thy repentance! But I must
not:
Thou hast brought me to that dull calam-
ity,
To that strange misbelief of all the world,
And all things that are in it, that I fear
I shall fall like a tree, and find my
grave,
Only remembering that I grieve.

EVADNE. My lord,
Give me your griefs: You are an inno-
cent,
A soul as white as heaven; let not my
sins
Perish your noble youth. I do not fall
here
To shadow, by dissembling with my tears,
(As, all say, women can), or to make
less,

What my hot will hath done, which
Heaven and you
Know to be tougher than the hand of
time
Can cut from man's remembrance. No,
I do not:
I do appear the same, the same Evadne,
Drest in the shames I lived in: the same
monster!
But these are names of honour, to what
I am:
I do present myself the foulest creature,
Most poisonous, dangerous, and despised
of men,
Lerna e'er bred, or Nilus! I am hell,
Till you, my dear lord, shoot your light
into me,
The beams of your forgiveness. I am soul-
sick,
And wither with the fear of one con-
demn'd,
Till I have got your pardon.

AMINTOR. Rise, Evadne.
Those heavenly powers that put this good
into thee,
Grant a continuance of it! I forgive
thee:
Make thyself worthy of it; and take
heed,
Take heed, Evadne, this be serious.
Mock not the powers above, that can and
dare
Give thee a great example of their justice
To all ensuing eyes, if thou playest
With thy repentance, the best sacrifice.

EVADNE. I have done nothing good to
win belief,
My life hath been so faithless. All the
creatures,
Made for Heaven's honours, have their
ends, and good ones,
All but the cozening crocodiles, false
women!
They reign here like those plagues, those
killing sores,
Men pray against; and when they die,
like tales
Ill told and unbelieved, they pass away
And go to dust forgotten! But, my lord,
Those short days I shall number to my
rest

(As many must not see me) shall, though
too late,
Though in my evening, yet perceive a
will;
Since I can do no good, because a woman,
Reach constantly at something that is
near it:
I will redeem one minute of my age,
Or, like another Niobe, I'll weep
Till I am water.

AMINTOR. I am now dissolved:
My frozen soul melts. May each sin thou
hast
Find a new mercy! Rise; I am at peace.
Hadst thou been thus, thus excellently
good,
Before that devil king tempted thy frailty,
Sure thou hadst made a star! Give me
thy hand.
From this time I will know thee; and, as
far
As honour gives me leave, be thy Amintor.
When we meet next, I will salute thee
fairly,
And pray the gods to give thee happy
days.
My charity shall go along with thee,
Though my embraces must be far from
thee.
I should have kill'd thee, but this sweet
repentance
Locks up my vengeance; for which thus I
kiss thee—
The last kiss we must take! And 'would
to Heaven
The holy priest, that gave our hands to-
gether,
Had given us equal virtues! Go, Evadne;
The Gods thus part our bodies. Have a
care
My honour falls no farther: I am well
then.

EVADNE. All the dear joys here, and,
above, hereafter,
Crown thy fair soul! Thus I take leave,
my lord;
And never shall you see the foul Evadne,
Till she have tried all honour'd means,
that may
Set her in rest, and wash her stains
away.   [Exeunt.]

SCENE II—*The presence chamber.*

[*Banquet—Enter* KING *and* CALIANAX—
      Hautboys play within.]

KING. I cannot tell how I should credit
    this
From you, that are his enemy.

CALIANAX. I am sure
He said it to me; and I'll justify it
What way he dares oppose—but with my
    sword.

KING. But did he break, without all
    circumstance,
To you, his foe, that he would have the
    fort,
To kill me, and then 'scape?

CALIANAX. If he deny it,
I'll make him blush.

KING. It sounds incredibly.

CALIANAX. Ay, so does everything I say
    of late.

KING. Not so, Calianax.

CALIANAX. Yes, I should sit
Mute, whilst a rogue with strong arms
    cuts your throat.

KING. Well, I will try him; and, if this
    be true,
I'll pawn my life I'll find it. If't be
    false,
And that you clothe your hate in such a
    lie,
You shall hereafter dote in your own
    house,
Not in the court.

CALIANAX. Why, if it be a lie,
Mine ears are false; for, I'll be sworn, I
    heard it.
Old men are good for nothing: You were
    best
Put me to death for hearing, and free
    him
For meaning it. You would have trusted
    me
Once, but the time is alter'd.

KING. And will still,
Where I may do with justice to the
    world:
You have no witness?

CALIANAX. Yes, myself.

KING. No more,
I mean, there were that heard it.

CALIANAX. How! no more?
Would you have more? why, am not I
    enough
To hang a thousand rogues?

KING. But, so, you may
Hang honest men too, if you please.

CALIANAX. I may!
'Tis like I will do so: There are a hun-
    dred
Will swear it for a need too, if I say
    it——

KING. Such witnesses we need not.

CALIANAX. And 'tis hard
If my word cannot hang a boisterous
    knave.

KING. Enough.—Where's Strato?

[*Enter* STRATO.]

STRATO. Sir!

KING. Why, where's all the company?
Call Amintor in;

Evadne. Where's my brother, and Melan-
    tius?
Bid him come too; and Diphilus. Call
    all
That are without there. [*Exit* STRATO.]
If he should desire
The combat of you, 'tis not in the power
Of all our laws to hinder it, unless
We mean to quit 'em.

CALIANAX. Why, if you do think
'Tis fit an old man, and a counsellor,
Do fight for what he says, then you may
    grant it.

[*Enter* AMINTOR, EVADNE, MELANTIUS,
DIPHILUS, LYSIPPUS, CLEON, STRATO,
      DIAGORAS.]

KING. Come, sirs!—Amintor, thou art
    yet a bridegroom,
And I will use thee so: Thou shalt sit
    down.—
Evadne, sit; and you, Amintor, too:
This banquet is for you, sir.—Who has
    brought
A merry tale about him, to raise laughter
Amongst our wine? Why, Strato, where
    art thou?
Thou wilt chop out with them unseason-
    ably,
When I desire them not.

STRATO. 'Tis my ill luck, sir, so to spend them then.

KING. Reach me a bowl of wine.—Melantius, thou
Art sad.

MELANTIUS. I should be, sir, the merriest here,
But I have ne'er a story of my own
Worth telling at this time.

KING. Give me the wine.
Melantius, I am now considering
How easy 'twere, for any man we trust,
To poison one of us in such a bowl.

MELANTIUS. I think it were not hard, sir, for a knave.

CALIANAX. Such as you are. [*Aside.*]

KING. I'faith, 'twere easy: It becomes us well
To get plain-dealing men about ourselves;
Such as you all are here.—Amintor, to thee;
And to thy fair Evadne.

MELANTIUS. Have you thought
Of this, Calianax? [*Apart to him.*]

CALIANAX. Yes, marry, have I.

MELANTIUS. And what's your resolution?

CALIANAX. You shall have it,—
Soundly, I warrant you.

KING. Reach to Amintor, Strato.

AMINTOR. Here, my love.
This wine will do thee wrong, for it will set
Blushes upon thy cheeks; and, till thou dost
A fault, 'twere pity.

KING. Yet, I wonder much
At the strange desperation of these men,
That attempt such acts here in our state:
He could not 'scape, that did it.

MELANTIUS. Were he known,
Impossible.

KING. It would be known, Melantius.

MELANTIUS. It ought to be: If he got then away,
He must wear all our lives upon his sword.
He need not fly the island; he must leave
No one alive.

KING. No; I should think no man
Could kill me, and 'scape clear, but that old man.

CALIANAX. But I! heaven bless me! I! should I, my liege?

KING. I do not think thou would'st;
but yet thou might'st;
For thou hast in thy hands the means to 'scape,
By keeping of the fort.—He has, Melantius,
And he has kept it well.

MELANTIUS. From cobwebs, sir,
'Tis clean swept: I can find no other art
In keeping of it now: 'Twas ne'er besieged
Since he commanded it.

CALIANAX. I shall be sure
Of your good word: But I have kept it safe
From such as you.

MELANTIUS. Keep your ill temper in:
I speak no malice. Had my brother kept it,
I should have said as much.

KING. You are not merry.
Brother, drink wine. Sit you all still:—
Calianax, [*Apart to him.*]
I cannot trust thus: I have thrown out words,
That would have fetch'd warm blood upon the cheeks
Of guilty men, and he is never moved:
He knows no such thing.

CALIANAX. Impudence may 'scape,
When feeble virtue is accused.

KING. He must,
If he were guilty, feel an alteration
At this our whisper, whilst we point at him:
You see he does not.

CALIANAX. Let him hang himself:
What care I what he does? This he did say.

KING. Melantius, you can easily conceive
What I have meant; for men that are in fault
Can subtly apprehend, when others aim
At what they do amiss: But I forgive

Freely, before this man. Heaven do so
too!
I will not touch thee, so much as with
shame
Of telling it. Let it be so no more.

CALIANAX. Why, this is very fine.

MELANTIUS. I cannot tell
What 'tis you mean; but I am apt enough
Rudely to thrust into an ignorant fault.
But let me know it: Happily, 'tis nought
But misconstruction; and, where I am
clear,
I will not take forgiveness of the gods,
Much less of you.

KING. Nay, if you stand so stiff,
I shall call back my mercy.

MELANTIUS. I want smoothness
To thank a man for pardoning of a crime
I never knew.

KING. Not to instruct your knowledge,
but to show you
My ears are everywhere, you meant to kill
me,
And get the fort to 'scape.

MELANTIUS. Pardon me, sir;
My bluntness will be pardoned: You pre-
serve
A race of idle people here about you,
Facers and talkers, to defame the worth
Of those that do things worthy. The man
that utter'd this
Had perish'd without food, be't who it
will,
But for this arm, that fenced him from
the foe.
And if I thought you gave a faith to this,
The plainness of my nature would speak
more.
Give me a pardon (for you ought to do't)
To kill him that spake this.

CALIANAX. Ay, that will be
The end of all: Then I am fairly paid
For all my care and service.

MELANTIUS. That old man,
Who calls me enemy, and of whom I
(Though I will never match my hate so
low)
Have no good thought, would yet, I think,
excuse me,
And swear he thought me wrong'd in
this.

CALIANAX. Who—I?
Thou shameless fellow! Didst thou not
speak to me
Of it thyself?

MELANTIUS. Oh, then it came from
him?

CALIANAX. From me! who should it
come from, but from me?

MELANTIUS. Nay, I believe your malice
is enough;
But I have lost my anger.—Sir, I hope
You are well satisfied.

KING. Lysippus, cheer
Amintor and his lady; there's no sound
Comes from you; I will come and do't
myself.

AMINTOR. You have done already, sir,
for me,
I thank you.   [Apart.]

KING. Melantius, I do credit this from
him,
How slight soe'er you make't.

MELANTIUS. 'Tis strange you should.

CALIANAX. 'Tis strange he should be-
lieve an old man's word
That never lied in's life.

MELANTIUS. I talk not to thee!—
Shall the wild words of this distemper'd
man,
Frantic with age and sorrow, make a
breach
Betwixt your majesty and me? 'Twas
wrong
To hearken to him; but to credit him,
As much, at least, as I have power to
bear.
But pardon me—whilst I speak only
truth
I may commend myself—I have bestow'd
My careless blood with you, and should be
loth
To think an action that would make me
lose
That, and my thanks too. When I was a
boy,
I thrust myself into my country's cause,
And did a deed that pluck'd five years
from time,
And styled me man then. And for you,
my king,
Your subjects all have fed by virtue of

My arm. This sword of mine hath plough'd the ground,
And reapt the fruit in peace;
And you yourself have lived at home in ease.
So terrible I grew, that, without swords,
My name hath fetch'd you conquest: And my heart
And limbs are still the same: my will as great
To do you service. Let me not be paid
With such a strange distrust.

KING. Melantius,
I held it great injustice to believe
Thine enemy, and did not; if I did,
I do not; let that satisfy.—What, struck
With sadness all? More wine!

CALIANAX. A few fine words
Have overthrown my truth. Ah, thou'rt a villain!

MELANTIUS. Why, thou wert better let me have the fort.   [*Apart to him.*]
Dotard! I will disgrace thee thus for ever:
There shall no credit lie upon thy words.
Think better, and deliver it.

CALIANAX. My liege,
He's at me now again to do it.—Speak;
Deny it, if thou canst.—Examine him
While he is hot; for if he cool again,
He will forswear it.

KING. This is lunacy,
I hope, Melantius.

MELANTIUS. He hath lost himself
Much, since his daughter miss'd the happiness
My sister gain'd; and, though he call me foe,
I pity him.

CALIANAX. Pity? a pox upon you!

MELANTIUS. Mark his disordered words! And, at the masque,
Diagoras knows, he raged, and rail'd at me,
And call'd a lady whore, so innocent
She understood him not. But it becomes
Both you and me too to forgive distraction:
Pardon him, as I do.

CALIANAX. I'll not speak for thee,
For all thy cunning.—If you will be safe,

Chop off his head! for there was never known
So impudent a rascal.

KING. Some, that love him,
Get him to bed. Why, pity should not let
Age make itself contemptible; we must be
All old; have him away.

MELANTIUS. Calianax, [*Apart to him.*]
The king believes you; come, you shall go home,
And rest; you have done well. You'll give it up
When I have used you thus a month, I hope.

CALIANAX. Now, now, 'tis plain, sir; he does move me still.
He says, he knows I'll give him up the fort,
When he has used me thus a month. I am mad,
Am I not, still?

ALL. Ha, ha, ha!

CALIANAX. I shall be mad indeed, if you do thus!
Why should you trust a sturdy fellow there
(That has no virtue in him; all's in his sword)
Before me? Do but take his weapons from him,
And he's an ass; and I'm a very fool,
Both with him, and without him, as you use me.

ALL. Ha, ha, ha!

KING. 'Tis well, Calianax. But if you use
This once again, I shall entreat some other
To see your offices be well discharged.
Be merry, gentlemen; it grows somewhat late.—
Amintor, thou wouldst be a-bed again.

AMINTOR. Yes, sir.

KING. And you, Evadne.—Let me take
Thee in my arms, Melantius, and believe
Thou art, as thou deserv'st to be, my friend
Still, and for ever.—Good Calianax,
Sleep soundly; it will bring thee to thyself.

[*Exeunt all but* MELANTIUS *and* CALIANAX.]

CALIANAX. Sleep soundly! I sleep soundly now, I hope;
I could not be thus else.—How darest thou stay
Alone with me, knowing how thou hast used me?
MELANTIUS. You cannot blast me with your tongue, and that's
The strongest part you have about you.
CALIANAX. I
Do look for some great punishment for this;
For I begin to forget all my hate,
And take't unkindly that mine enemy
Should use me so extraordinarily scurvily.
MELANTIUS. I shall melt too, if you begin to take
Unkindnesses: I never meant you hurt.
CALIANAX. Thou'lt anger me again.
Thou wretched rogue,
Meant me no hurt! Disgrace me, with the king;
Lose all my offices! This is no hurt,
Is it? I pr'ythee, what dost thou call hurt?
MELANTIUS. To poison men, because they love me not;
To call the credit of men's wives in question;
To murder children betwixt me and land;
This is all hurt.
CALIANAX. All this thou think'st is sport;
For mine is worse: But use thy will with me;
For, betwixt grief and anger, I could cry.
MELANTIUS. Be wise then, and be safe; thou may'st revenge.
CALIANAX. Ay, o' the king? I would revenge o' thee.
MELANTIUS. That you must plot yourself.
CALIANAX. I'm a fine plotter.
MELANTIUS. The short is, I will hold thee with the king
In this perplexity, till peevishness
And thy disgrace have laid thee in thy grave.
But if thou wilt deliver up the fort,
I'll take thy trembling body in my arms,
And bear thee over dangers: Thou shalt hold
Thy wonted state.
CALIANAX. If I should tell the king,
Canst thou deny't again?
MELANTIUS. Try, and believe.
CALIANAX. Nay, then, thou canst bring anything about.
Thou shalt have the fort.
MELANTIUS. Why, well;
Here let our hate be buried; and this hand
Shall right us both. Give me thy aged breast
To compass.
CALIANAX. Nay, I do not love thee yet;
I cannot well endure to look on thee:
And, if I thought it were a courtesy,
Thou shoulds't not have it. But I am disgraced;
My offices are to be ta'en away;
And, if I did but hold this fort a day,
I do believe, the king would take it from me,
And give it thee, things are so strangely carried.
Ne'er thank me for't; but yet the king shall know
There was some such thing in't I told him of;
And that I was an honest man.
MELANTIUS. He'll buy
That knowledge very dearly.—Diphilus,

[*Enter* DIPHILUS.]
What news with thee?
DIPHILUS. This were a night indeed
To do it in: The king hath sent for her.
MELANTIUS. She shall perform it then.
—Go, Diphilus,
And take from this good man, my worthy friend,
The fort; he'll give it thee.
DIPHILUS. Have you got that?
CALIANAX. Art thou of the same breed? Canst thou deny
This to the king too?
DIPHILUS. With a confidence
As great as his.
CALIANAX. Faith, like enough.
MELANTIUS. Away, and use him kindly.

CALIANAX. Touch not me;
I hate the whole strain. If thou follow me,
A great way off, I'll give thee up the fort;
And hang yourselves.
MELANTIUS. Be gone.
DIPHILUS. He's finely wrought.
    [*Exeunt* CALIANAX *and* DIPHILUS.]
MELANTIUS. This is a night, 'spite of astronomers,
To do the deed in. I will wash the stain,
That rests upon our house, off with his blood.

    [*Enter* AMINTOR.]
AMINTOR. Melantius, now assist me: If thou be'st
That which thou say'st, assist me. I have lost
All my distempers, and have found a rage
So pleasing! Help me.
MELANTIUS. Who can see him thus,
And not swear vengeance?—What's the matter, friend?
AMINTOR. Out with thy sword; and, hand in hand with me,
Rush to the chamber of this hated king:
And sink him, with the weight of all his sins,
To hell for ever.
MELANTIUS. 'Twere a rash attempt,
Not to be done with safety. Let your reason
Plot your revenge, and not your passion.
AMINTOR. If thou refusest me in these extremes,
Thou art no friend: He sent for her to me;
By Heaven, to me, myself! And, I must tell you,
I love her, as a stranger; there is worth
In that vile woman, worthy things, Melantius;
And she repents. I'll do't myself alone,
Though I be slain. Farewell.
MELANTIUS. He'll overthrow
My whole design with madness.—Amintor,
Think what thou dost: I dare as much as Valour;
But 'tis the king, the king, the king, Amintor,

With whom thou fightest!—I know he's honest,
And this will work with him.   [*Aside.*]
AMINTOR. I cannot tell
What thou hast said; but thou hast charm'd my sword
Out of my hand, and left me shaking here,
Defenceless.
MELANTIUS. I will take it up for thee.
AMINTOR. What a wild beast is uncollected man!
The thing, that we call honour, bears us all
Headlong to sin, and yet itself is nothing.
MELANTIUS. Alas, how variable are thy thoughts!
AMINTOR. Just like my fortunes: I was run to that
I purposed to have chid thee for. Some plot,
I did distrust, thou hadst against the king,
By that old fellow's carriage. But take heed;
There's not the least limb growing to a king,
But carries thunder in it.
MELANTIUS. I have none
Against him.
AMINTOR. Why, come then; and still remember,
We may not think revenge.
MELANTIUS. I will remember.   [*Exeunt.*]

ACT V

SCENE I—*A room in the palace.*

    [*Enter* EVADNE *and a* GENTLEMAN.]
EVADNE. Sir, is the king a-bed?
GENTLEMAN. Madam, an hour ago.
EVADNE. Give me the key then, and let none be near;
'Tis the king's pleasure.
GENTLEMAN. I understand you, madam; 'would 'twere mine.
I must not wish good rest unto your ladyship.
EVADNE. You talk, you talk.
GENTLEMAN. 'Tis all I dare do, madam; but the king

Will wake, and then——
EVADNE. Saving your imagination,
pray, good night, sir.
GENTLEMAN. A good night be it then,
and a long one, madam.
I am gone. [*Exeunt.*]

SCENE II—*The bedchamber.*

[*The* KING *discovered in bed, sleeping.
Enter* EVADNE.]
EVADNE. The night grows horrible;
and all about me
Like my black purpose. Oh, the conscience
Of a lost virgin! whither wilt thou pull
me?
To what things, dismal as the depth of
hell,
Wilt thou provoke me? Let no woman
dare
From this hour be disloyal, if her heart
be flesh,
If she have blood, and can fear: 'Tis a
daring
Above that desperate fool's that left his
peace,
And went to sea to fight. 'Tis so many
sins,
An age cannot repent 'em; and so great,
The gods want mercy for! Yet I must
through 'em.
I have begun a slaughter on my honour,
And I must end it there.—He sleeps.
Good Heavens!
Why give you peace to this untemperate
beast,
That hath so long transgress'd you; I
must kill him,
And I will do it bravely: The mere joy
Tells me, I merit in it. Yet I must not
Thus tamely do it, as he sleeps; that
were
To rock him to another world: My venge-
ance
Shall take him waking, and then lay be-
fore him
The number of his wrongs and punish-
ments.
I'll shake his sins like furies, till I waken
His evil angel, his sick conscience;

And then I'll strike him dead. King, by
your leave:
[*Ties his arms to the bed.*]
I dare not trust your strength. Your
grace and I
Must grapple upon even terms no more.
So. If he rail me not from my resolution,
I shall be strong enough.—My lord the
king!!
My lord!—He sleeps, as if he meant to
wake
No more.—My lord!—Is he not dead al-
ready?
Sir! My lord!
KING. Who's that?
EVADNE. Oh, you sleep soundly, sir!
KING. My dear Evadne,
I have been dreaming of thee. Come to
bed.
EVADNE. I am come at length, sir; but
how welcome?
KING. What pretty new device is this,
Evadne?
What, do you tie me to you? By my love,
This is a quaint one. Come, my dear, and
I'll be thy Mars; to bed, my queen of
love:
Let us be caught together, that the gods
May see, and envy our embraces.
EVADNE. Stay, sir, stay;
You are too hot, and I have brought you
physic
To temper your high veins.
KING. Pr'ythee, to bed then; let me
take it warm;
There thou shalt know the state of my
body better.
EVADNE. I know you have a surfeited
foul body;
And you must bleed.
KING. Bleed!
EVADNE. Ay, you shall bleed! Lie still;
and, if the devil,
Your lust, will give you leave, repent.
This steel
Comes to redeem the honour that you
stole,
King, my fair name; which nothing but
thy death
Can answer to the world.

KING. How's this, Evadne?

EVADNE. I am not she; nor bear I in this breast
So much cold spirit to be call'd a woman.
I am a tiger; I am anything
That knows not pity. Stir not! If thou dost,
I'll take thee unprepared; thy fears upon thee,
That make thy sins look double; and so send thee
(By my revenge, I will) to look those torments
Prepared for such black souls.

KING. Thou dost not mean this; 'tis impossible:
Thou art too sweet and gentle.

EVADNE. No, I am not.
I am as foul as thou art, and can number
As many such hells here. I was once fair,
Once I was lovely; not a blowing rose
More chastely sweet, till thou, thou, thou foul canker,
(Stir not) didst poison me. I was a world of virtue,
Till your curst court and you (Hell bless you for't!)
With your temptations on temptations,
Made me give up mine honour; for which, king,
I'm come to kill thee.

KING. No!

EVADNE. I am.

KING. Thou art not!
I pr'ythee speak not these things: Thou art gentle,
And wert not meant thus rugged.

EVADNE. Peace, and hear me.
Stir nothing but your tongue, and that for mercy
To those above us; by whose lights I vow,
Those blessed fires that shot to see our sin,
If thy hot soul had substance with thy blood,
I would kill that too; which, being past my steel,
My tongue shall reach. Thou art a shameless villain!
A thing out of the overcharge of nature;

Sent, like a thick cloud, to disperse a plague
Upon weak catching women! such a tyrant,
That for his lust would sell away his subjects!
Ay, all his Heaven hereafter!

KING. Hear, Evadne,
Thou soul of sweetness, hear! I am thy king.

EVADNE. Thou art my shame! Lie still, there's none about you,
Within your cries: All promises of safety
Are but deluding dreams. Thus, thus, thou foul man,
Thus I begin my vengeance! [Stabs him.]

KING. Hold, Evadne!
I do command thee, hold.

EVADNE. I do not mean, sir,
To part so fairly with you; we must change
More of these love-tricks yet.

KING. What bloody villain
Provoked thee to this murder?

EVADNE. Thou, thou monster.

KING. Oh!

EVADNE. Thou kept'st me brave at court, and whor'd'st me, king:
Then married me to a young noble gentleman,
And whor'd'st me still.

KING. Evadne, pity me.

EVADNE. He'll take me then! This for my lord Amintor!
This for my noble brother! and this stroke
For the most wrong'd of women!
[Kills him.]

KING. Oh! I die.

EVADNE. Die all our faults together!
I forgive thee. [Exit.]

[Enter two GENTLEMEN of the bed-chamber.]

1ST GENTLEMAN. Come, now she's gone, let's enter; the king expects it, and will be angry.

2ND GENTLEMAN. 'Tis a fine wench; we'll have a snap at her one of these nights, as she goes from him.

1ST GENTLEMAN. Content. How quickly he had done with her! I see, kings can do no more that way than other mortal people.

2ND GENTLEMAN. How fast he is! I cannot hear him breathe.

1ST GENTLEMAN. Either the tapers give a feeble light,
Or he looks very pale.

2ND GENTLEMAN. And so he does:
Pray Heaven he be well; let's look.—Alas! He's stiff, wounded and dead: Treason, treason!

1ST GENTLEMAN. Run forth and call.

2ND GENTLEMAN. Treason, treason!
[Exit.]

1ST GENTLEMAN. This will be laid on us:
Who can believe a woman could do this?

[Enter CLEON and LYSIPPUS.]

CLEON. How now! Where's the traitor?

1ST GENTLEMAN. Fled, fled, away; but there her woful act lies still.

CLEON. Her act! a woman!

LYSIPPUS. Where's the body?

1ST GENTLEMAN. There.

LYSIPPUS. Farewell, thou worthy man!
There were two bonds
That tied our loves, a brother and a king;
The least of which might fetch a flood of tears:
But such the misery of greatness is,
They have no time to mourn; then pardon me!—

[Enter STRATO.]
Sirs, which way went she?

STRATO. Never follow her;
For she, alas! was but the instrument.
News is now brought in, that Melantius
Has got the fort, and stands upon the wall;
And with a loud voice calls those few, that pass
At this dead time of night, delivering
The innocence of this act.

LYSIPPUS. Gentlemen,
I am your king.

STRATO. We do acknowledge it.

LYSIPPUS. I would I were not! Follow, all; for this
Must have a sudden stop. [Exeunt.]

SCENE III—*Before the citadel.*

[Enter MELANTIUS, DIPHILUS, and CALIANAX, *on the walls.*]

MELANTIUS. If the dull people can believe I am arm'd,
(Be constant, Diphilus!) now we have time,
Either to bring our banish'd honours home,
Or create new ones in our ends.

DIPHILUS. I fear not;
My spirit lies not that way.—Courage, Calianax.

CALIANAX. 'Would I had any! you should quickly know it.

MELANTIUS. Speak to the people: Thou art eloquent.

CALIANAX. 'Tis a fine eloquence to come to the gallows!
You were born to be my end. The devil take you!
Now must I hang for company. 'Tis strange,
I should be old, and neither wise nor valiant.

[Enter below, LYSIPPUS, DIAGORAS, CLEON, STRATO, and GUARD.]

LYSIPPUS. See where he stands, as boldly confident
As if he had his full command about him.

STRATO. He looks as if he had the better cause, sir;
Under your gracious pardon, let me speak it!
Though he be mighty-spirited, and forward
To all great things; to all things of that danger
Worse men shake at the telling of; yet, certainly,
I do believe him noble; and this action
Rather pull'd on, than sought: his mind was ever
As worthy as his hand.

LYSIPPUS. 'Tis my fear, too.
Heaven forgive all! Summon him, lord Cleon.

CLEON. Ho, from the walls there!

MELANTIUS. Worthy Cleon, welcome.
We could have wish'd you here, lord. You
    are honest.
CALIANAX. Well, thou art as flattering
    a knave, though
I dare not tell thee so——   [*Aside.*]
LYSIPPUS. Melantius!
MELANTIUS. Sir?
LYSIPPUS. I am sorry that we meet
    thus; our old love
Never required such distance. Pray
    Heaven,
You have not left yourself, and sought
    this safety
More out of fear than honour! You have
    lost
A noble master; which your faith, Melan-
    tius,
Some think, might have preserved: Yet
    you know best.
CALIANAX. When time was, I was mad;
    some, that dares fight,
I hope will pay this rascal.
MELANTIUS. Royal young man, whose
    tears look lovely on thee;
Had they been shed for a deserving one,
They had been lasting monuments! Thy
    brother,
While he was good, I call'd him king; and
    served him
With that strong faith, that most un-
    wearied valour,
Pull'd people from the farthest sun to
    seek him,
And beg his friendship. I was then his
    soldier.
But since his hot pride drew him to dis-
    grace me,
And brand my noble actions with his
    lust
(That never-cured dishonour of my sister,
Base stain of whore! and, which is
    worse,
The joy to make it still so) like myself,
Thus I have flung him off with my
    allegiance;
And stand here mine own justice, to re-
    venge
What I have suffered in him; and this old
    man,
Wronged almost to lunacy.

CALIANAX. Who—I?
You would draw me in. I have had no
    wrong,
I do disclaim ye all.
MELANTIUS. The short is this:
'Tis no ambition to lift up myself
Urgeth me thus; I do desire again
To be a subject, so I may be free.
If not, I know my strength, and will un-
    build
This goodly town. Be speedy and be wise,
In a reply.
STRATO. Be sudden, sir, to tie
All up again: What's done is past recall,
And past you to revenge: and there are
    thousands,
That wait for such a troubled hour as
    this.
Throw him the blank.
LYSIPPUS. Melantius, write in that
Thy choice: My seal is at it.
    [*Throws him a paper.*]
MELANTIUS. It was our honours drew
    us to this act,
Not gain; and we will only work our
    pardons.
CALIANAX. Put my name in too.
DIPHILUS. You disclaim'd us all
But now, Calianax.
CALIANAX. That is all one:
I'll not be hang'd hereafter by a trick:
I'll have it in.
MELANTIUS. You shall, you shall.—
Come to the back gate, and we'll call you
    king,
And give you up the fort.
LYSIPPUS. Away, away.   [*Exeunt.*]

SCENE IV—*Antechamber to* EVADNE'S
    apartments in the palace.

[*Enter* ASPATIA, *in man's apparel.*]
ASPATIA. This is my fatal hour. Heaven
    may forgive
My rash attempt, that causelessly hath
    laid
Griefs on me that will never let me rest;
And put a woman's heart into my breast.
It is more honour for you, that I die;
For she, that can endure the misery

That I have on me, and be patient too,
May live and laugh at all that you can do.

[*Enter* SERVANT.]

God save you, sir!

SERVANT. And you, sir. What's your
business?

ASPATIA. With you, sir, now; to do
me the fair office
To help me to your lord.

SERVANT. What, would you serve him?

ASPATIA. I'll do him any service; but
to haste,
For my affairs are earnest, I desire
To speak with him.

SERVANT. Sir, because you're in such
haste, I would be loth
Delay you any longer: You cannot.

ASPATIA. It shall become you, though,
to tell your lord.

SERVANT. Sir, he will speak with no-
body; but, in particular,
I have in charge, about no weighty mat-
ters.

ASPATIA. This is most strange. Art
thou gold-proof?
There's for thee; help me to him.

SERVANT. Pray be not angry, sir. I'll
do my best. [*Exit.*]

ASPATIA. How stubbornly this fellow
answered me!
There is a vile dishonest trick in man,
More than in woman: All the men I meet
Appear thus to me, are all harsh and
rude;
And have a subtilty in everything,
Which love could never know. But we
fond women
Harbour the easiest and the smoothest
thoughts,
And think, all shall go so! It is unjust,
That men and women should be match'd
together.

[*Enter* AMINTOR *and his man.*]

AMINTOR. Where is he?

SERVANT. There, my lord.

AMINTOR. What would you, sir?

ASPATIA. Please it your lordship to
command your man
Out of the room, I shall deliver things
Worthy your hearing.

AMINTOR. Leave us. [*Exit* SERVANT.]

ASPATIA. Oh, that that shape
Should bury falsehood in it! [*Aside.*]

AMINTOR. Now your will, sir.

ASPATIA. When you know me, my lord,
you needs must guess
My business; and I am not hard to know;
For till the chance of war mark'd this
smooth face
With these few blemishes, people would
call me
My sister's picture, and her mine. In
short,
I am the brother to the wrong'd Aspatia.

AMINTOR. The wrong'd Aspatia! 'Would
thou wert so too
Unto the wrong'd Amintor! Let me kiss
That hand of thine, in honour that I bear
Unto the wrong'd Aspatia. Here I stand,
That did it. 'Would he could not! Gentle
youth,
Leave me; for there is something in thy
looks,
That calls my sins, in a most hideous
form,
Into my mind; and I have grief enough
Without thy help.

ASPATIA. I would I could with credit.
Since I was twelve years old, I had not
seen
My sister till this hour; I now arrived:
She sent for me to see her marriage;
A woful one! But they, that are above,
Have ends in everything. She used few
words,
But yet enough to make me understand
The baseness of the injuries you did her.
That little training I have had, is war:
I may behave myself rudely in peace;
I would not, though. I shall not need to
tell you,
I am but young, and would be loth to lose
Honour, that is not easily gained again.
Fairly I mean to deal: The age is strict
For single combats; and we shall be
stopp'd,
If it be publish'd. If you like your sword,
Use it; if mine appear a better to you,
Change: for the ground is this, and this
the time,
To end our difference.

AMINTOR. Charitable youth,
(If thou be'st such) think not I will maintain
So strange a wrong: And, for thy sister's sake,
Know, that I could not think that desperate thing
I durst not do; yet, to enjoy this world,
I would not see her; for, beholding thee,
I am I know not what. If I have aught,
That may content thee, take it, and be-gone;
For death is not so terrible as thou.
Thine eyes shoot guilt into me.
ASPATIA. Thus, she swore,
Thou wouldst behave thyself; and give me words
That would fetch tears into mine eyes; and so
Thou dost indeed. But yet she bade me watch,
Lest I were cozen'd; and be sure to fight
Ere I return'd.
AMINTOR. That must not be with me.
For her I'll die directly; but against her
Will never hazard it.
ASPATIA. You must be urged.
I do not deal uncivilly with those
That dare to fight; but such a one as you
Must be used thus. [She strikes him.]
AMINTOR. I pr'ythee, youth, take heed.
Thy sister is a thing to me so much
Above mine honour, that I can endure
All this. Good gods! a blow I can en-dure!
But stay not, let thou draw a timeless death
Upon thyself.
ASPATIA. Thou art some prating fel-low;
One, that hath studied out a trick to talk,
And move soft-hearted people; to be kicked. [She kicks him.]
Thus, to be kick'd!—Why should he be so slow
In giving me my death? [Aside.]
AMINTOR. A man can bear
No more, and keep his flesh. Forgive me, then!
I would endure yet, if I could. Now show [Draws.]

The spirit thou pretend'st, and understand,
Thou hast no hour to live.——
[They fight; ASPATIA is wounded.]
What dost thou mean?
Thou canst not fight: the blows thou mak'st at me
Are quite besides; and those I offer at thee,
Thou spread'st thine arms, and tak'st upon thy breast,
Alas, defenceless!
ASPATIA. I have got enough,
And my desire. There is no place so fit
For me to die as here.

[Enter EVADNE, her hands bloody, with a knife.]
EVADNE. Amintor, I am loaden with events,
That fly to make thee happy. I have joys,
That in a moment can call back thy wrongs,
And settle thee in thy free state again.
It is Evadne still that follows thee,
But not her mischiefs.
AMINTOR. Thou canst not fool me to be-lieve again;
But thou hast looks and things so full of news,
That I am stay'd.
EVADNE. Noble Amintor, put off thy amaze,
Let thine eyes loose, and speak: Am I not fair?
Looks not Evadne beauteous, with these rites now
Were those hours half so lovely in thine eyes,
When our hands met before the holy man?
I was too foul within to look fair then:
Since I knew ill, I was not free till now.
AMINTOR. There is presage of some im-portant thing
About thee, which, it seems, thy tongue hath lost.
Thy hands are bloody, and thou hast a knife!
EVADNE. In this consists thy happiness and mine.
Joy to Amintor! for the king is dead.

AMINTOR. Those have most power to hurt us, that we love;
We lay our sleeping lives within their arms!
Why, thou hast raised up Mischief to his height,
And found out one, to out-name thy other faults.
Thou hast no intermission of thy sins,
But all thy life is a continued ill.
Black is thy colour now, disease thy nature.
Joy to Amintor! Thou hast touch'd a life,
The very name of which had power to chain
Up all my rage, and calm my wildest wrongs.
EVADNE. 'Tis done; and since I could not find a way
To meet thy love so clear as through his life,
I cannot now repent it.
AMINTOR. Couldst thou procure the gods to speak to me,
To bid me love this woman, and forgive,
I think I should fall out with them. Behold,
Here lies a youth whose wounds bleed in my breast,
Sent by his violent fate, to fetch his death
From my slow hand: And, to augment my woe,
You now are present, stain'd with a king's blood,
Violently shed. This keeps night here,
And throws an unknown wilderness about me.
ASPATIA. Oh, oh, oh!
AMINTOR. No more; pursue me not.
EVADNE. Forgive me then,
And take me to thy bed. We may not part.   [Kneels.]
AMINTOR. Forbear! Be wise, and let my rage go this way.
EVADNE. 'Tis you that I would stay, not it.
AMINTOR. Take heed;
It will return with me.
EVADNE. If it must be,
I shall not fear to meet it: take me home.

AMINTOR. Thou monster of cruelty, forbear!
EVADNE. For heaven's sake, look more calm: thine eyes are sharper
Than thou canst make thy sword.
AMINTOR. Away, away!
Thy knees are more to me than violence.
I am worse than sick to see knees follow me,
For that I must not grant. For heaven's sake stand.
EVADNE. Receive me, then.
AMINTOR. I dare not stay thy language;
In midst of all my anger and my grief
Thou dost awake something that troubles me,
And says, "I loved thee once." I dare not stay;
There is no end of woman's reasoning.
        [Leaves her.]
EVADNE. Amintor, thou shalt love me now again:
Go; I am calm. Farewell, and peace for ever!
Evadne, whom thou hat'st, will die for thee!   [Kills herself.]
AMINTOR. I have a little human nature yet,
That's left for thee, that bids me stay thy hand.   [Returns.]
EVADNE. Thy hand was welcome, but it came too late.
Oh, I am lost! the heavy sleep makes haste.   [She dies.]
ASPATIA. Oh, oh, oh!
AMINTOR. This earth of mine doth tremble, and I feel
A stark affrighted motion in my blood:
My soul grows weary of her house, and I
All over am a trouble to myself.
There is some hidden power in these dead things,
That calls my flesh unto 'em: I am cold!
Be resolute, and bear 'em company.
There's something, yet, which I am loth to leave.
There's man enough in me to meet the fears
That death can bring; and yet, 'would it were done!

I can find nothing in the whole discourse
Of death, I durst not meet the boldest
    way;
Yet still, betwixt the reason and the act,
The wrong I to Aspatia did stands up:
I have not such another fault to answer.
Though she may justly arm herself with
    scorn
And hate of me, my soul will part less
    troubled,
When I have paid to her in tears my sor-
    row.
I will not leave this act unsatisfied,
If all that's left in me can answer it.
    ASPATIA. Was it a dream? There
    stands Amintor still;
Or I dream still.
    AMINTOR. How dost thou? Speak! re-
    ceive my love and help.
Thy blood climbs up to his old place
    again:
There's hope of thy recovery.
    ASPATIA. Did you not name Aspatia?
    AMINTOR. I did.
    ASPATIA. And talk'd of tears and sor-
    row unto her?
    AMINTOR. 'Tis true; and till these
    happy signs in thee
Did stay my course, 'twas thither I was
    going.
    ASPATIA. Thou art there already, and
    these wounds are hers:
Those threats I brought with me sought
    not revenge;
But came to fetch this blessing from thy
    hand.
I am Aspatia yet.
    AMINTOR. Dare my soul ever look
    abroad again?
    ASPATIA. I shall surely live, Amintor;
    I am well:
A kind of healthful joy wanders within me.
    AMINTOR. The world wants lives to ex-
    cuse thy loss!
Come, let me bear thee to some place of
    help.
    ASPATIA. Amintor, thou must stay; I
    must rest here;
My strength begins to disobey my will.
How dost thou, my best soul? I would
    fain live

Now, if I could: Wouldst thou have loved
    me then?
    AMINTOR. Alas!
All that I am's not worth a hair from
    thee.
    ASPATIA. Give me thy hand; my hands
    grope up and down,
And cannot find thee: I am wondrous
    sick:
Have I thy hand, Amintor?
    AMINTOR. Thou greatest blessing of the
    world, thou hast.
    ASPATIA. I do believe thee better than
    my sense.
Oh! I must go. Farewell!   [*Dies.*]
    AMINTOR. She swoons! Aspatia!—
Help! for Heaven's sake, water!
Such as may chain life ever to this
    frame.—
Aspatia, speak!—What, no help yet? I
    fool!
I'll chafe her temples: Yet there's nothing
    stirs;
Some hidden power tell her, Amintor calls,
And let her answer me!—Aspatia, speak!
I have heard, if there be any life, but bow
The body thus, and it will show itself.
Oh, she is gone! I will not leave her yet.
Since out of justice we must challenge
    nothing,
I'll call it mercy, if you'll pity me,
Ye heavenly powers! and lend, for some
    few years,
The blessed soul to this fair seat again.
No comfort comes; the gods deny me too!
I'll bow the body once again.—Aspatia!—
The soul is fled for ever; and I wrong
Myself, so long to lose her company.
Must I talk now? Here's to be with thee,
    love!   [*Stabs himself.*]

      [*Enter* SERVANT.]
    SERVANT. This is a great grace to my
lord, to have the new king come to him:
I must tell him he is entering.—Oh, God!
Help! help!

[*Enter* LYSIPPUS, MELANTIUS, CALIANAX,
    CLEON, DIPHILUS, *and* STRATO.]
    LYSIPPUS. Where's Amintor?
    SERVANT. Oh, there, there.

LYSIPPUS. How strange is this!

CALIANAX. What should we do here?

MELANTIUS. These deaths are such acquainted things with me,
That yet my heart dissolves not. May I stand
Stiff here for ever! Eyes, call up your tears!
This is Amintor: Heart! he was my friend;
Melt; now it flows.—Amintor, give a word
To call me to thee.

AMINTOR. Oh!

MELANTIUS. Melantius calls his friend Amintor. Oh!
Thy arms are kinder to me than tny tongue!
Speak, speak!

AMINTOR. What?

MELANTIUS. That little word was worth all the sounds
That ever I shall hear again.

DIPHILUS. Oh, brother!
Here lies your sister slain; you lose yourself
In sorrow there.

MELANTIUS. Why, Diphilus, it is
A thing to laugh at, in respect of this:
Here was my sister, father, brother, son;
All that I had!—Speak once again: What youth
Lies slain there by thee?

AMINTOR. 'Tis Aspatia.
My last is said. Let me give up my soul
Into thy bosom.   [*Dies.*]

CALIANAX. What's that? what's that? Aspatia!

MELANTIUS. I never did

Repent the greatness of my heart till now;
It will not burst at need.

CALIANAX. My daughter dead here too!
And you have all fine new tricks to grieve; but I ne'er knew any but direct crying.

MELANTIUS. I am a prattler; but no more.   [*Offers to kill himself.*]

DIPHILUS. Hold, brother.

LYSIPPUS. Stop him.

DIPHILUS. Fie! how unmanly was this offer in you;
Does this become our strain?

CALIANAX. I know not what the matter is, but I am grown very kind, and am friends with you. You have given me that among you will kill me quickly; but I'll go home, and live as long as I can.

MELANTIUS. His spirit is but poor that can be kept
From death for want of weapons.
Is not my hand a weapon sharp enough
To stop my breath? or, if you tie down those,
I vow, Amintor, I will never eat,
Or drink, or sleep, or have to do with that
That may preserve life! This I swear to keep.

LYSIPPUS. Look to him though, and bear those bodies in.
May this a fair example be to me,
To rule with temper: For, on lustful kings,
Unlook'd-for, sudden deaths from heaven are sent;
But curst is he that is their instrument.
          [*Exeunt.*]

THE BEAUX-STRATAGEM

By GEORGE FARQUHAR

Produced at London, 1707

CHARACTERS

THOMAS AIMWELL,
FRANCIS ARCHER, } *two gentlemen of broken fortunes, the first as master, and the second as servant*

COUNT BELLAIR, *a French officer, prisoner at Lichfield*

SQUIRE SULLEN, *a country blockhead, brutal to his wife*

SIR CHARLES FREEMAN, *a gentleman from London, brother to Mrs. Sullen*

FOIGARD, *a priest, chaplain to the French officers*

GIBBET, *a highwayman*

HOUNSLOW,
BAGSHOT, } *his companions*

BONIFACE, *landlord of the inn*

SCRUB, *servant to Squire Sullen*

LADY BOUNTIFUL, *an old, civil, country gentlewoman, that cures all her neighbours of all distempers, and foolishly fond of her son, Squire Sullen*

MRS. SULLEN, *her daughter-in-law, wife to Squire Sullen*

DORINDA, *Lady Bountiful's daughter*

GIPSY, *maid to the ladies*

CHERRY, *the landlord's daughter in the inn*

TAPSTER, COACH-PASSENGERS, COUNTRYMAN, COUNTRYWOMAN, *and* SERVANTS

SCENE—*Lichfield.*

ACT I

SCENE I—*A room in* BONIFACE'S *inn.*

[*Enter* BONIFACE *running.*]

BONIFACE. Chamberlain! maid! Cherry! daughter Cherry! all asleep! all dead?

[*Enter* CHERRY *running.*]

CHERRY. Here, here! why d'ye bawl so, father? d'ye think we have no ears?

BONIFACE. You deserve to have none, you young minx! The company of the Warrington coach has stood in the hall

531

this hour, and nobody to show them to their chambers.

CHERRY. And let 'em wait farther; there's neither red-coat in the coach, nor footman behind it.

BONIFACE. But they threaten to go to another inn to-night.

CHERRY. That they dare not, for fear the coachman should overturn them to-morrow.—Coming! coming!—Here's the London coach arrived.

[Enter several people with trunks, band-boxes, and other luggage, and cross the stage.]

BONIFACE. Welcome, ladies!

CHERRY. Very welcome, gentlemen!—Chamberlain, show the Lion and the Rose.
[Exit with the company.]

[Enter AIMWELL in a riding-habit, and ARCHER as footman, carrying a portmantle.]

BONIFACE. This way, this way, gentlemen!

AIMWELL [to ARCHER]. Set down the things; go to the stable, and see my horses well rubbed

ARCHER. I shall, sir.			[Exit.]

AIMWELL. You're my landlord, I suppose?

BONIFACE. Yes, sir, I'm old Will Boniface, pretty well known upon this road, as the saying is.

AIMWELL. O Mr. Boniface, your servant!

BONIFACE. O sir!—What will your honour please to drink, as the saying is?

AIMWELL. I have heard your town of Lichfield much famed for ale; I think I'll taste that.

BONIFACE. Sir, I have now in my cellar ten tun of the best ale in Staffordshire; 'tis smooth as oil, sweet as milk, clear as amber, and strong as brandy; and will be just fourteen year old the fifth day of next March, old style.

AIMWELL. You're very exact, I find, in the age of your ale.

BONIFACE. As punctual, sir, as I am in the age of my children. I'll show you

such ale!—Here, tapster [enter TAPSTER], broach number 1706, as the saying is.—Sir, you shall taste my Anno Domini.—I have lived in Lichfield, man and boy, above eight-and-fifty years, and, I believe, have not consumed eight-and-fifty ounces of meat.

AIMWELL. At a meal, you mean, if one may guess your sense by your bulk.

BONIFACE. Not in my life, sir: I have fed purely upon ale; I have eat my ale, drank my ale, and I always sleep upon ale.

[Enter TAPSTER with a bottle and glass, and exit.]

Now, sir, you shall see!—[Filling out a glass.] Your worship's health.—[Drinks.] Ha! delicious, delicious! fancy it burgundy, only fancy it, and 'tis worth ten shillings a quart.

AIMWELL [drinks]. 'Tis confounded strong!

BONIFACE. Strong! it must be so, or how should we be strong that drink it?

AIMWELL. And have you lived so long upon this ale, landlord?

BONIFACE. Eight-and-fifty years, upon my credit, sir—but it killed my wife, poor woman, as the saying is.

AIMWELL. How came that to pass?

BONIFACE. I don't know how, sir; she would not let the ale take its natural course, sir; she was for qualifying it every now and then with a dram, as the saying is; and an honest gentleman that came this way from Ireland, made her a present of a dozen bottles of usquebaugh—but the poor woman was never well after: but, howe'er, I was obliged to the gentleman, you know.

AIMWELL. Why, was it the usquebaugh that killed her?

BONIFACE. My Lady Bountiful said so. She, good lady, did what could be done; she cured her of three tympanies, but the fourth carried her off. But she's happy, and I'm contented, as the saying is.

AIMWELL. Who's that Lady Bountiful you mentioned?

BONIFACE. Ods my life, sir, we'll drink her health.—[Drinks.] My Lady Bountiful is one of the best of women. Her last husband, Sir Charles Bountiful, left her worth a thousand pound a year; and, I believe, she lays out one-half on't in charitable uses for the good of her neighbours. She cures rheumatisms, ruptures, and broken shins in men; green-sickness, obstructions, and fits of the mother, in women; the king's evil, chincough, and chilblains, in children: in short, she has cured more people in and about Lichfield within ten years than the doctors have killed in twenty; and that's a bold word.

AIMWELL. Has the lady been any other way useful in her generation?

BONIFACE. Yes, sir; she has a daughter by Sir Charles, the finest woman in all our country, and the greatest fortune. She has a son too, by her first husband, Squire Sullen, who married a fine lady from London t'other day; if you please, sir, we'll drink his health.

AIMWELL. What sort of a man is he?

BONIFACE. Why, sir, the man's well enough; says little, thinks less, and does —nothing at all, faith. But he's a man of a great estate, and values nobody.

AIMWELL. A sportsman, I suppose?

BONIFACE. Yes, sir, he's a man of pleasure; he plays at whisk and smokes his pipe eight-and-forty hours together sometimes.

AIMWELL. And married, you say?

BONIFACE. Ay, and to a curious woman, sir. But he's a—he wants it here, sir. [Pointing to his forehead.]

AIMWELL. He has it there, you mean?

BONIFACE. That's none of my business; he's my landlord, and so a man, you know, would not—But—ecod, he's no better than—Sir, my humble service to you. —[Drinks.] Though I value not a farthing what he can do to me; I pay him his rent at quarterday; I have a good running-trade; I have but one daughter, and I can give her—but no matter for that.

AIMWELL. You're very happy, Mr. Boniface. Pray, what other company have you in town?

BONIFACE. A power of fine ladies; and then we have the French officers.

AIMWELL. Oh, that's right, you have a good many of those gentlemen: pray, how do you like their company?

BONIFACE. So well, as the saying is, that I could wish we had as many more of 'em: they're full of money, and pay double for everything they have. They know, sir, that we paid good round taxes for the taking of 'em, and so they are willing to reimburse us a little. One of 'em lodges in my house.

[Reënter ARCHER.]

ARCHER. Landlord, there are some French gentlemen below that ask for you.

BONIFACE. I'll wait on 'em.—[Aside to ARCHER.] Does your master stay long in town, as the saying is?

ARCHER. I can't tell, as the saying is.

BONIFACE. Come from London?

ARCHER. No.

BONIFACE. Going to London, mayhap?

ARCHER. No.

BONIFACE [aside]. An odd fellow this. —[To AIMWELL.] I beg your worship's pardon, I'll wait on you in half a minute. [Exit.]

AIMWELL. The coast's clear, I see.— Now, my dear Archer, welcome to Lichfield!

ARCHER. I thank thee, my dear brother in iniquity.

AIMWELL. Iniquity! prithee, leave canting; you need not change your style with your dress.

ARCHER. Don't mistake me, Aimwell, for 'tis still my maxim, that there is no scandal like rags, nor any crime so shameful as poverty.

AIMWELL. The world confesses it every day in its practice though men won't own it for their opinion. Who did that worthy lord, my brother, single out of the side-box to sup with him t'other night?

ARCHER. Jack Handicraft, a handsome, well-dressed, mannerly, sharping rogue, who keeps the best company in town.

AIMWELL. Right! And, pray, who

married my lady Manslaughter t'other day, the great fortune?

ARCHER. Why, Nick Marrabone, a professed pickpocket, and a good bowler; but he makes a handsome figure, and rides in his coach, that he formerly used to ride behind.

AIMWELL. But did you observe poor Jack Generous in the Park last week?

ARCHER. Yes, with his autumnal periwig, shading his melancholy face, his coat older than anything but its fashion, with one hand idle in his pocket, and with the other picking his useless teeth; and, though the Mall was crowded with company, yet was poor Jack as single and solitary as a lion in a desert.

AIMWELL. And as much avoided, for no crime upon earth but the want of money.

ARCHER. And that's enough. Men must not be poor; idleness is the root of all evil; the world's wide enough, let 'em bustle. Fortune has taken the weak under her protection, but men of sense are left to their industry.

AIMWELL. Upon which topic we proceed, and, I think, luckily hitherto. Would not any man swear now, that I am a man of quality, and you my servant, when if our intrinsic value were known——

ARCHER. Come, come, we are the men of intrinsic value who can strike our fortunes out of ourselves, whose worth is independent of accidents in life, or revolutions in government: we have heads to get money and hearts to spend it.

AIMWELL. As to our hearts, I grant ye, they are as willing tits as any within twenty degrees: but I can have no great opinion of our heads from the service they have done us hitherto, unless it be that they have brought us from London hither to Lichfield, made me a lord and you my servant.

ARCHER. That's more than you could expect already. But what money have we left?

AIMWELL. But two hundred pound.

ARCHER. And our horses, clothes, rings, etc.—Why, we have very good fortunes now for moderate people; and, let me tell you, that this two hundred pound, with the experience that we are now masters of, is a better estate than the ten we have spent.—Our friends, indeed, began to suspect that our pockets were low, but we came off with flying colours, showed no signs of want either in word or deed.

AIMWELL. Ay, and our going to Brussels was a good pretence enough for our sudden disappearing; and, I warrant you, our friends imagine that we are gone a-volunteering.

ARCHER. Why, faith, if this prospect fails, it must e'en come to that. I am for venturing one of the hundreds, if you will, upon this knight-errantry; but, in case it should fail, we'll reserve t'other to carry us to some counterscarp, where we may die, as we lived, in a blaze.

AIMWELL. With all my heart; and we have lived justly, Archer; we can't say that we have spent our fortunes, but that we have enjoyed 'em.

ARCHER. Right! so much pleasure for so much money. We have had our pennyworths; and, had I millions, I would go to the same market again.—O London! London!—Well, we have had our share, and let us be thankful: past pleasures, for aught I know, are best, such as we are sure of; those to come may disappoint us.

AIMWELL. It has often grieved the heart of me to see how some inhuman wretches murder their kind fortunes; those that, by sacrificing all to one appetite, shall starve all the rest. You shall have some that live only in their palates, and in their sense of tasting shall drown the other four: others are only epicures in appearances, such who shall starve their nights to make a figure a days, and famish their own to feed the eyes of others: a contrary sort confine their pleasures to the dark, and contract their specious acres to the circuit of a muff-string.

ARCHER. Right! But they find the Indies in that spot where they consume 'em, and I think your kind keepers have much the best on't: for they indulge the most senses by one expense, there's the seeing, hearing, and feeling, amply gratified; and, some philosophers will tell you, that from such a commerce there arises a sixth sense, that gives infinitely more pleasure than the other five put together.

AIMWELL. And to pass to the other extremity, of all keepers I think those the worst that keep their money.

ARCHER. Those are the most miserable wights in being, they destroy the rights of nature, and disappoint the blessings of Providence. Give me a man that keeps his five senses keen and bright as his sword, that has 'em always drawn out in their just order and strength, with his reason as commander at the head of 'em, that detaches 'em by turns upon whatever party of pleasure agreeably offers, and commands 'em to retreat upon the least appearance of disadvantage or danger! For my part, I can stick to my bottle while my wine, my company, and my reason, hold good; I can be charmed with Sappho's singing without falling in love with her face: I love hunting, but would not, like Actæon, be eaten up by my own dogs; I love a fine house, but let another keep it; and just so I love a fine woman.

AIMWELL. In that last particular you have the better of me.

ARCHER. Ay, you're such an amorous puppy, that I'm afraid you'll spoil our sport; you can't counterfeit the passion without feeling it.

AIMWELL. Though the whining part be out of doors in town, 'tis still in force with the country ladies: and let me tell you, Frank, the fool in that passion shall outdo the knave at any time.

ARCHER. Well, I won't dispute it now; you command for the day, and so I submit: at Nottingham, you know, I am to be master.

AIMWELL. And at Lincoln, I again.

ARCHER. Then, at Norwich I mount, which, I think, shall be our last stage; for, if we fail there, we'll embark for Holland, bid adieu to Venus, and welcome Mars.

AIMWELL. A match!—Mum!

[Reënter BONIFACE.]

BONIFACE. What will your worship please to have for supper?

AIMWELL. What have you got?

BONIFACE. Sir, we have a delicate piece of beef in the pot, and a pig at the fire.

AIMWELL. Good supper-meat, I must confess. I can't eat beef, landlord.

ARCHER. And I hate pig.

AIMWELL. Hold your prating, sirrah! do you know who you are?

BONIFACE. Please to bespeak something else; I have everything in the house.

AIMWELL. Have you any veal?

BONIFACE. Veal! sir, we had a delicate loin of veal on Wednesday last.

AIMWELL. Have you got any fish or wildfowl?

BONIFACE. As for fish, truly, sir, we are an inland town, and indifferently provided with fish, that's the truth on't; and then for wildfowl—we have a delicate couple of rabbits.

AIMWELL. Get me the rabbits fricasseed.

BONIFACE. Fricasseed! Lard, sir, they'll eat much better smothered with onions.

ARCHER. Psha! Damn your onions!

AIMWELL. Again, sirrah!—Well, landlord, what you please. But hold, I have a small charge of money, and your house is so full of strangers, that I believe it may be safer in your custody than mine; for when this fellow of mine gets drunk he minds nothing.—Here, sirrah, reach me the strong-box.

ARCHER. Yes, sir.—[Aside.] This will give us a reputation.

[Brings AIMWELL the box.]

AIMWELL. Here, landlord; the locks are sealed down both for your security and mine; it holds somewhat above two hundred pound: if you doubt it, I'll count it to you after supper; but be sure you lay it where I may have it at a minute's warning; for my affairs are a little dubious at present; perhaps I may be gone in half an hour, perhaps I may be your guest till the best part of that be spent;

and pray order your ostler to keep my horses always saddled. But one thing above the rest I must beg, that you would let this fellow have none of your *Anno Domini*, as you call it; for he's the most insufferable sot.—Here, sirrah, light me to my chamber.

[*Exit, lighted by* ARCHER.]

BONIFACE. Cherry! daughter Cherry!

[*Reënter* CHERRY.]

CHERRY. D'ye call, father?

BONIFACE. Ay, child, you must lay by this box for the gentleman: 'tis full of money.

CHERRY. Money! all that money! why, sure, father, the gentleman comes to be chosen parliament-man. Who is he?

BONIFACE. I don't know what to make of him; he talks of keeping his horses ready saddled, and of going perhaps at a minute's warning, or of staying perhaps till the best part of this be spent.

CHERRY. Ay, ten to one, father, he's a highwayman.

BONIFACE. A highwayman! upon my life, girl, you have hit it, and this box is some new-purchased booty. Now, could we find him out, the money were ours.

CHERRY. He don't belong to our gang.

BONIFACE. What horses have they?

CHERRY. The master rides upon a black.

BONIFACE. A black! ten to one the man upon the black mare; and since he don't belong to our fraternity, we may betray him with a safe conscience: I don't think it lawful to harbour any rogues but my own. Look'ee, child, as the saying is, we must go cunningly to work, proofs we must have; the gentleman's servant loves drink, I'll ply him that way, and ten to one loves a wench: you must work him t'other way.

CHERRY. Father, would you have me give my secret for his?

BONIFACE. Consider, child, there's two hundred pound to boot.—[*Ringing without.*] Coming! coming!—Child, mind your business. [*Exit.*]

CHERRY. What a rogue is my father! My father! I deny it. My mother was a good, generous, free-hearted woman, and I can't tell how far her good nature might have extended for the good of her children. This landlord of mine, for I think I can call him no more, would betray his guest, and debauch his daughter into the bargain—by a footman too!

[*Reënter* ARCHER.]

ARCHER. What footman, pray, mistress, is so happy as to be the subject of your contemplation?

CHERRY. Whoever he is, friend, he'll be but little the better for't.

ARCHER. I hope so, for, I'm sure, you did not think of me.

CHERRY. Suppose I had?

ARCHER. Why, then, you're but even with me; for the minute I came in, I was a-considering in what manner I should make love to you.

CHERRY. Love to me, friend!

ARCHER. Yes, child.

CHERRY. Child! manners!—If you kept a little more distance, friend, it would become you much better.

ARCHER. Distance! good-night, sauce-box. [*Going.*]

CHERRY [*aside*]. A pretty fellow! I like his pride.—[*Aloud.*] Sir, pray, sir, you see, sir [ARCHER *returns*], I have the credit to be entrusted with your master's fortune here, which sets me a degree above his footman; I hope, sir, you an't affronted?

ARCHER. Let me look you full in the face, and I'll tell you whether you can affront me or no. 'Sdeath, child, you have a pair of delicate eyes, and you don't know what to do with 'em!

CHERRY. Why, sir, don't I see everybody?

ARCHER. Ay, but if some women had 'em, they would kill everybody. Prithee, instruct me, I would fain make love to you, but I don't know what to say.

CHERRY. Why, did you never make love to anybody before?

ARCHER. Never to a person of your fig· ure, I can assure you, madam: my ad· dresses have been always confined to people within my own sphere, I never aspired so high before. [*Sings.*]

But you look so bright,
And are dress'd so tight,
That a man would swear you're right,
As arm was e'er laid over.
Such an air
You freely wear
To ensnare,
As makes each guest a lover!

Since then, my dear, I'm your guest,
Prithee give me of the best
Of what is ready drest:
Since then, my dear, etc.

CHERRY [*aside*]. What can I think of this man?—[*Aloud.*] Will you give me that song, sir?

ARCHER. Ay, my dear, take it while 'tis warm.—[*Kisses her.*] Death and fire! her lips are honeycombs.

CHERRY. And I wish there had been bees too, to have stung you for your impudence.

ARCHER. There's a swarm of Cupids, my little Venus, that has done the business much better.

CHERRY [*aside*]. This fellow is misbegotten as well as I.—[*Aloud.*] What's your name, sir?

ARCHER [*aside*]. Name! egad, I have 'orgot it.—[*Aloud.*] Oh! Martin.

CHERRY. Where were you born?

ARCHER. In St. Martin's parish.

CHERRY. What was your father?

ARCHER. St. Martin's parish.

CHERRY. Then, friend, good-night.

ARCHER. I hope not.

CHERRY. You may depend upon't.

ARCHER. Upon what?

CHERRY. That you're very impudent.

ARCHER. That you're very handsome.

CHERRY. That you're a footman.

ARCHER. That you're an angel.

CHERRY. I shall be rude.

ARCHER. So shall I.

CHERRY. Let go my hand.

ARCHER. Give me a kiss. [*Kisses her.*]
[*Call without.*] Cherry! Cherry!

CHERRY. I'm—my father calls; you plaguy devil, how durst you stop my breath so? Offer to follow me one step, if you dare. [*Exit.*]

ARCHER. A fair challenge, by this light! this is a pretty fair opening of an adventure; but we are knight-errants, and so Fortune be our guide. [*Exit.*]

ACT II

SCENE I—*A gallery in* LADY BOUNTIFUL'S *house.*

[*Enter* MRS. SULLEN *and* DORINDA, *meeting.*]

DORINDA. Morrow, my dear sister; are you for church this morning?

MRS. SULLEN. Anywhere to pray; for Heaven alone can help me. But I think, Dorinda, there's no form of prayer in the liturgy against bad husbands.

DORINDA. But there's a form of law in Doctors-Commons; and I swear, sister Sullen, rather than see you thus continually discontented, I would advise you to apply to that: for besides the part that I bear in your vexatious broils, as being sister to the husband, and friend to the wife, your example gives me such an impression of matrimony, that I shall be apt to condemn my person to a long vacation all its life. But supposing, madam, that you brought it to a case of separation, what can you urge against your husband? My brother is, first, the most constant man alive.

MRS. SULLEN. The most constant husband, I grant ye.

DORINDA. He never sleeps from you.

MRS. SULLEN. No, he always sleeps with me.

DORINDA. He allows you a maintenance suitable to your quality.

MRS. SULLEN. A maintenance! do you take me, madam, for an hospital child, that I must sit down, and bless my benefactors for meat, drink, and clothes? As I take it, madam, I brought your brother ten thousand pounds, out of which I might expect some pretty things, called pleasures.

DORINDA. You share in all the pleasures that the country affords.

MRS. SULLEN. Country pleasures! racks and torments! Dost think, child, that my limbs were made for leaping of ditches, and clambering over stiles? or that my parents, wisely forseeing my future happiness in country pleasures, had early instructed me in rural accomplishments of drinking fat ale, playing at whisk, and smoking tobacco with my husband? or of spreading of plasters, brewing of diet-drinks, and stilling rosemary-water, with the good old gentlewoman my mother-in-law?

DORINDA. I'm sorry, madam, that it is not more in our power to divert you; I could wish, indeed, that our entertainments were a little more polite, or your taste a little less refined. But, pray, madam, how came the poets and philosophers, that laboured so much in hunting after pleasure, to place it at last in a country life?

MRS. SULLEN. Because they wanted money, child, to find out the pleasures of the town. Did you ever see a poet or philosopher worth ten thousand pounds? if you can show me such a man, I'll lay you fifty pounds you'll find him somewhere within the weekly bills. Not that I disapprove rural pleasures, as the poets have painted them; in their landscape, every Phillis has her Corydon, every murmuring stream, and every flowery mead, gives fresh alarms to love. Besides, you'll find, that their couples were never married:—but yonder I see my Corydon, and a sweet swain it is, Heaven knows! Come, Dorinda, don't be angry, he's my husband, and your brother; and, between both, is he not a sad brute?

DORINDA. I have nothing to say to your part of him, you're the best judge.

MRS. SULLEN. O sister, sister! if ever you marry, beware of a sullen, silent sot, one that's always musing, but never thinks. There's some diversion in a talking blockhead; and since a woman must wear chains, I would have the pleasure of hearing 'em rattle a little. Now you shall see, but take this by the way. He came home this morning at his usual hour of four, wakened me out of a sweet dream of something else, by tumbling over the tea-table, which he broke all to pieces; after his man and he had rolled about the room, like sick passengers in a storm, he comes flounce into bed, dead as a salmon into a fishmonger's basket; his feet cold as ice, his breath hot as a furnace, and his hands and his face as greasy as his flannel night-cap. O matrimony! He tosses up the clothes with a barbarous swing over his shoulders, disorders the whole economy of my bed, leaves me half naked, and my whole night's comfort is the tuneable serenade of that wakeful nightingale, his nose! Oh, the pleasure of counting the melancholy clock by a snoring husband! But now, sister, you shall see how handsomely, being a well-bred man, he will beg my pardon.

[*Enter* SQUIRE SULLEN.]

SQUIRE SULLEN. My head aches consumedly.

MRS. SULLEN. Will you be pleased, my dear, to drink tea with us this morning? it may do your head good.

SQUIRE SULLEN. No.

DORINDA. Coffee, brother?

SQUIRE SULLEN. Psha!

MRS. SULLEN. Will you please to dress, and go to church with me? the air may help you.

SQUIRE SULLEN. Scrub!   [*Calls.*]

[*Enter* SCRUB.]

SCRUB. Sir!

SQUIRE SULLEN. What day o' th' week is this?

SCRUB. Sunday, an't please your worship.

SQUIRE SULLEN. Sunday! bring me a dram; and d'ye hear, set out the venison-pasty and a tankard of strong beer upon the hall-table, I'll go to breakfast.

[*Going.*]

DORINDA. Stay, stay, brother, you shan't get off so; you were very naughty last night, and must make your wife reparation; come, come, brother, won't you ask pardon?

SQUIRE SULLEN. For what?

DORINDA. For being drunk last night.

SQUIRE SULLEN. I can afford it, can't I?

MRS. SULLEN. But I can't, sir.

SQUIRE SULLEN. Then you may let it alone.

MRS. SULLEN. But I must tell you, sir, that this is not to be borne.

SQUIRE SULLEN. I'm glad on't.

MRS. SULLEN. What is the reason, sir, that you use me thus inhumanly?

SQUIRE SULLEN. Scrub!

SCRUB. Sir!

SQUIRE SULLEN. Get things ready to shave my head. [Exit.]

MRS. SULLEN. Have a care of coming near his temples, Scrub, for fear you meet something there that may turn the edge of your razor.—[Exit SCRUB.] Inveterate stupidity! did you ever know so hard, so obstinate a spleen as his? O sister, sister! I shall never ha' good of the beast till I get him to town; London, dear London, is the place for managing and breaking a husband.

DORINDA. And has not a husband the same opportunities there for humbling a wife?

MRS. SULLEN. No, no, child, 'tis a standing maxim in conjugal discipline, that when a man would enslave his wife, he hurries her into the country; and when a lady would be arbitrary with her husband, she wheedles her booby up to town. A man dare not play the tyrant in London, because there are so many examples to encourage the subject to rebel. O Dorinda! Dorinda! a fine woman may do anything in London: o' my conscience, she may raise an army of forty thousand men.

DORINDA. I fancy, sister, you have a mind to be trying your power that way here in Lichfield; you have drawn the French count to your colours already.

MRS. SULLEN. The French are a people that can't live without their gallantries.

DORINDA. And some English that I know, sister, are not averse to such amusements.

MRS. SULLEN. Well, sister, since the truth must out, it may do as well now as hereafter; I think, one way to rouse my lethargic, sottish husband, is to give him a rival: security begets negligence in all people, and men must be alarmed to make 'em alert in their duty. Women are like pictures, of no value in the hands of a fool, till he hears men of sense bid high for the purchase.

DORINDA. This might do, sister, if my brother's understanding were to be convinced into a passion for you; but, I fancy, there's a natural aversion on his side; and I fancy, sister, that you don't come much behind him, if you dealt fairly.

MRS. SULLEN. I own it, we are united contradictions, fire and water: but I could be contented, with a great many other wives, to humour the censorious mob, and give the world an appearance of living well with my husband, could I bring him but to dissemble a little kindness to keep me in countenance.

DORINDA. But how do you know, sister, but that, instead of rousing your husband by this artifice to a counterfeit kindness, he should awake in a real fury?

MRS. SULLEN. Let him: if I can't entice him to the one, I would provoke him to the other.

DORINDA. But how must I behave myself between ye?

MRS. SULLEN. You must assist me.

DORINDA. What, against my own brother?

MRS. SULLEN. He's but half a brother, and I'm your entire friend. If I go a step beyond the bounds of honour, leave me; till then, I expect you should go along with me in everything; while I trust my honour in your hands, you may trust your brother's in mine. The count is to dine here to-day.

DORINDA. 'Tis a strange thing, sister, that I can't like that man.

MRS. SULLEN. You like nothing; your time is not come; Love and Death have their fatalities, and strike home one time or other: you'll pay for all one day, I warrant ye. But come, my lady's tea is ready, and 'tis almost church time.

[*Exeunt.*]

SCENE II—*A room in* BONIFACE'S *inn.*

[*Enter* AIMWELL *dressed, and* ARCHER.]

AIMWELL. And was she the daughter of the house?

ARCHER. The landlord is so blind as to think so; but I dare swear she has better blood in her veins.

AIMWELL. Why dost think so?

ARCHER. Because the baggage has a pert *je ne sais quoi;* she reads plays, keeps a monkey, and is troubled with vapours.

AIMWELL. By which discoveries I guess that you know more of her.

ARCHER. Not yet, faith; the lady gives herself airs; forsooth, nothing under a gentleman!

AIMWELL. Let me take her in hand.

ARCHER. Say one word more o' that, and I'll declare myself, spoil your sport there, and everywhere else; look ye, Aimwell, every man in his own sphere.

AIMWELL. Right; and therefore you must pimp for your master.

ARCHER. In the usual forms, good sir, after I have served myself.—But to our business. You are so well dressed, Tom, and make so handsome a figure, that I fancy you may do execution in a country church; the exterior part strikes first, and you're in the right to make that impression favourable.

AIMWELL. There's something in that which may turn to advantage. The appearance of a stranger in a country church draws as many gazers as a blazing-star; no sooner he comes into the cathedral, but a train of whispers runs buzzing round the congregation in a moment: *Who is he? Whence comes he? Do you know him?* Then I, sir, tips me the verger with half-a-crown; he pockets the simony, and inducts me into the best pew in the church; I pull out my snuff-box, turn myself round, bow to the bishop, or the dean, if he be the commanding officer; single out a beauty, rivet both my eyes to hers, set my nose a-bleeding by the strength of imagination, and show the whole church my concern, by my endeavouring to hide it; after the sermon, the whole town gives me to her for a lover, and by persuading the lady that I am a-dying for her, the tables are turned, and she in good earnest falls in love with me.

ARCHER. There's nothing in this, Tom, without a precedent; but instead of riveting your eyes to a beauty, try to fix 'em upon a fortune; that's our business at present.

AIMWELL. Psha! no woman can be a beauty without a fortune. Let me alone, for I am a marksman.

ARCHER. Tom!

AIMWELL. Ay.

ARCHER. When were you at church before, pray?

AIMWELL. Um—I was there at the coronation.

ARCHER. And how can you expect a blessing by going to church now?

AIMWELL. Blessing! nay, Frank, I ask but for a wife. [*Exit.*]

ARCHER. Truly, the man is not very unreasonable in his demands.

[*Exit at the opposite door.*]

[*Enter* BONIFACE *and* CHERRY.]

BONIFACE. Well, daughter, as the saying is, have you brought Martin to confess?

CHERRY. Pray, father, don't put me upon getting anything out of a man; I'm but young, you know, father, and I don't understand wheedling.

BONIFACE. Young! why, you jade, as the saying is, can any woman wheedle that is not young? your mother was useless at five-and-twenty. Not wheedle! would you make your mother a whore, and me a cuckold, as the saying is? I tell you, his silence confesses it, and his master spends his money so freely, and is so much a gentleman every manner of way, that he must be a highwayman.

[*Enter* GIBBET, *in a cloak.*]

GIBBET. Landlord, landlord, is the coast clear?

BONIFACE. O Mr. Gibbet, what's the news?

GIBBET. No matter, ask no questions, all fair and honourable.—Here, my dear Cherry.—[*Gives her a bag.*] Two hundred sterling pounds, as good as any that ever hanged or saved a rogue; lay 'em by with the rest; and here—three wedding or mourning rings, 'tis much the same, you know—here, two silver-hilted swords; I took those from fellows that never show any part of their swords but the hilts—here is a diamond necklace which the lady hid in the privatest place in the coach, but I found it out—this gold watch I took from a pawnbroker's wife; it was left in her hands by a person of quality: there's the arms upon the case.

CHERRY. But who had you the money from?

GIBBET. Ah! poor woman! I pitied her;—from a poor lady just eloped from her husband. She had made up her cargo, and was bound for Ireland, as hard as she could drive; she told me of her husband's barbarous usage, and so I left her half-a-crown. But I had almost forgot, my dear Cherry, I have a present for you.

CHERRY. What is't?

GIBBET. A pot of ceruse, my child, that I took out of a lady's under-pocket.

CHERRY. What, Mr. Gibbet, do you think that I paint?

GIBBET. Why, you jade, your betters do; I'm sure the lady that I took it from had a coronet upon her handkerchief. Here, take my cloak, and go, secure the premises.

CHERRY. I will secure 'em. [*Exit.*]

BONIFACE. But, hark'ee, where's Hounslow and Bagshot?

GIBBET. They'll be here to-night.

BONIFACE. D'ye know of any other gentlemen o' the pad on this road?

GIBBET. No.

BONIFACE. I fancy that I have two that lodge in the house just now.

GIBBET. The devil! how d'ye smoke 'em?

BONIFACE. Why, the one is gone to church.

GIBBET. That's suspicious, I must confess.

BONIFACE. And the other is now in his master's chamber; he pretends to be servant to the other; we'll call him out and pump him a little.

GIBBET. With all my heart.

BONIFACE. Mr. Martin! Mr. Martin! [*Calls.*]

[*Enter* ARCHER, *combing a periwig and singing.*]

GIBBET. The roads are consumed deep, I'm as dirty as Old Brentford at Christmas.—A good pretty fellow that; whose servant are you, friend?

ARCHER. My master's.

GIBBET. Really!

ARCHER. Really.

GIBBET. That's much.—The fellow has been at the bar by his evasions.—But pray, sir, what is your master's name?

ARCHER. *Tall, all, dall!*—[*Sings and combs the periwig.*] This is the most obstinate curl——

GIBBET. I ask you his name?

ARCHER. Name, sir—*tall, all, dall!*—I never asked him his name in my life.— *Tall, all, dall!*

BONIFACE. What think you now? [*Aside to* GIBBET.]

GIBBET [*aside to* BONIFACE]. Plain, plain, he talks now as if he were before a judge.—[*To* ARCHER.] But pray, friend, which way does your master travel?

ARCHER. A-horseback.

GIBBET [*aside*]. Very well again, an old offender, right.—[*To* ARCHER.] But, I mean, does he go upwards or downwards?

ARCHER. Downwards, I fear, sir.— *Tall, all!*

GIBBET. I'm afraid my fate will be a contrary way.

BONIFACE. Ha! ha! ha! Mr. Martin, you're very arch. This gentleman is only travelling towards Chester, and would be glad of your company, that's all.—Come, captain, you'll stay to-night, I suppose? I'll show you a chamber—come, captain.

GIBBET. Farewell, friend!

ARCHER. Captain, your servant.— [*Exeunt* BONIFACE *and* GIBBET.] Captain! a pretty fellow! 'Sdeath, I wonder that the officers of the army don't conspire to beat all scoundrels in red but their own.

[*Reënter* CHERRY.]

CHERRY [*aside*]. Gone, and Martin here! I hope he did not listen; I would have the merit of the discovery all my own, because I would oblige him to love me.—[*Aloud.*] Mr. Martin, who was that man with my father?

ARCHER. Some recruiting serjeant, or whipped-out trooper, I suppose.

CHERRY. All's safe, I find.	[*Aside.*]

ARCHER. Come, my dear, have you conned over the catechise I taught you last night?

CHERRY. Come, question me.

ARCHER. What is love?

CHERRY. Love is I know not what, it comes I know not how, and goes I know not when.

ARCHER. Very well, an apt scholar.— [*Chucks her under the chin.*] Where does love enter?

CHERRY. Into the eyes.

ARCHER. And where go out?

CHERRY. I won't tell ye.

ARCHER. What are the objects of that passion?

CHERRY. Youth, beauty, and clean linen.

ARCHER. The reason?

CHERRY. The two first are fashionable in nature, and the third at court.

ARCHER. That's my dear.—What are the signs and tokens of that passion?

CHERRY. A stealing look, a stammering tongue, words improbable, designs impossible, and actions impracticable.

ARCHER. That's my good child, kiss me.—What must a lover do to obtain his mistress?

CHERRY. He must adore the person that disdains him, he must bribe the chambermaid that betrays him, and court the footman that laughs at him. He must— he must——

ARCHER. Nay, child, I must whip you if you don't mind your lesson; he must treat his——

CHERRY. Oh, ay!—he must treat his enemies with respect, his friends with indifference, and all the world with contempt; he must suffer much, and fear more; he must desire much, and hope little; in short, he must embrace his ruin, and throw himself away.

ARCHER. Had ever man so hopeful a pupil as mine!—Come, my dear, why is love called a riddle?

CHERRY. Because, being blind, he leads those that see, and, though a child, he governs a man.

ARCHER. Mighty well!—And why is Love pictured blind?

CHERRY. Because the painters out of the weakness or privilege of their art chose to hide those eyes that they could not draw.

ARCHER. That's my dear little scholar, kiss me again.—And why should Love, that's a child, govern a man?

CHERRY. Because that a child is the end of love.

ARCHER. And so ends Love's catechism. —And now, my dear, we'll go in and make my master's bed.

CHERRY. Hold, hold, Mr. Martin! You have taken a great deal of pains to instruct me, and what d'ye think I have learned by it?

ARCHER. What?

CHERRY. That your discourse and your habit are contradictions, and it would be nonsense in me to believe you a footman any longer.

ARCHER. 'Oons, what a witch it is!

CHERRY. Depend upon this, sir, nothing in this garb shall ever tempt me; for, though I was born to servitude, I hate it. Own your condition, swear you love me, and then——

ARCHER. And then we shall go make my master's bed?

CHERRY. Yes.

ARCHER. You must know, then, that I am born a gentleman, my education was liberal; but I went to London a younger brother, fell into the hands of sharpers, who stripped me of my money, my friends disowned me, and now my necessity brings me to what you see.

CHERRY. Then take my hand—promise to marry me before you sleep, and I'll make you master of two thousand pounds.

ARCHER. How?

CHERRY. Two thousand pounds that I have this minute in my own custody; so, throw off your livery this instant, and I'll go find a parson.

ARCHER. What said you? a parson!

CHERRY. What! do you scruple?

ARCHER. Scruple! no, no, but—Two thousand pounds, you say?

CHERRY. And better.

ARCHER [aside]. 'Sdeath, what shall I do?—[Aloud.] But hark'ee, child, what need you make me master of yourself and money, when you may have the same pleasure out of me, and still keep your fortune in your hands?

CHERRY. Then you won't marry me?

ARCHER. I would marry you, but——

CHERRY. O sweet sir, I'm your humble servant, you're fairly caught! Would you persuade me that any gentleman who could bear the scandal of wearing a livery would refuse two thousand pounds, let the condition be what it would? no, no, sir. But I hope you'll pardon the freedom I have taken, since it was only to inform myself of the respect that I ought to pay you. [Going.]

ARCHER [aside]. Fairly bit, by Jupiter!—[Aloud.] Hold! hold!—And have you actually two thousand pounds?

CHERRY. Sir, I have my secrets as well as you; when you please to be more open I shall be more free, and be assured that I have discoveries that will match yours, be what they will. In the meanwhile, be satisfied that no discovery I make shall ever hurt you, but beware of my father! [Exit.]

ARCHER. So! we're like to have as many adventures in our inn as Don Quixote had in his. Let me see—two thousand pounds —if the wench would promise to die when the money were spent, egad, one would marry her; but the fortune may go off in a year or two, and the wife may live —Lord knows how long. Then an innkeeper's daughter! ay, that's the devil— there my pride brings me off.

For whatso'er the sages charge on pride,
The angels' fall, and twenty faults beside,
On earth, I'm sure, 'mong us of mortal
    calling,
Pride saves man oft, and woman too, from
    falling. [Exit.]

ACT III

SCENE I—*The gallery in* LADY BOUNTI-
FUL'S *house.*

[*Enter* MRS. SULLEN *and* DORINDA.]

MRS. SULLEN. Ha! ha! ha! my dear sister, let me embrace thee! now we are friends indeed; for I shall have a secret of yours as a pledge for mine—now you'll be good for something, I shall have you conversable in the subjects of the sex.

DORINDA. But do you think that I am so weak as to fall in love with a fellow at first sight?

MRS. SULLEN. Psha! now you spoil all; why should not we be as free in our friendships as the men? I warrant you, the gentleman has got to his confidant already, has avowed his passion, toasted your health, called you ten thousand angels, has run over your lips, eyes, neck, shape, air, and everything, in a description that warms their mirth to a second enjoyment.

DORINDA. Your hand, sister, I an't well.

MRS. SULLEN. So—she's breeding already—come, child, up with it—hem a little—so—now tell me, don't you like the gentleman that we saw at church just now?

DORINDA. The man's well enough.

MRS. SULLEN. Well enough! is he not a demigod, a Narcissus, a star, the man i' the moon?

DORINDA. O sister, I'm extremely ill!

MRS. SULLEN. Shall I send to your mother, child, for a little of her cephalic plaster to put to the soles of your feet, or shall I send to the gentleman for something for you? Come, unlace your stays, unbosom yourself. The man is perfectly a pretty fellow; I saw him when he first came into church.

DORINDA. I saw him too, sister, and with an air that shone, methought, like rays about his person.

MRS. SULLEN. Well said, up with it!

DORINDA. No forward coquette behaviour, no airs to set him off, no studied looks nor artful posture—but Nature did it all——

MRS. SULLEN. Better and better!—one touch more—come!

DORINDA. But then his looks—did you observe his eyes?

MRS. SULLEN. Yes, yes, I did.—His eyes, well, what of his eyes?

DORINDA. Sprightly, but not wandering; they seemed to view, but never gazed on anything but me.—And then his looks so humble were, and yet so noble, that they aimed to tell me that he could with pride die at my feet, though he scorned slavery anywhere else.

MRS. SULLEN. The physic works purely! —How d'ye find yourself now, my dear?

DORINDA. Hem! much better, my dear. —Oh, here comes our Mercury!

[*Enter* SCRUB.]

Well, Scrub, what news of the gentleman?

SCRUB. Madam, I have brought you a packet of news.

DORINDA. Open it quickly, come.

SCRUB. In the first place I inquired who the gentleman was; they told me he was a stranger. Secondly, I asked what the gentleman was; they answered and said, that they never saw him before. Thirdly, I inquired what countryman he was; they replied, 'twas more than they knew. Fourthly, I demanded whence he came; their answer was, they could not tell. And, fifthly, I asked whither he went; and they replied, they knew nothing of the matter,—and this is all I could learn.

MRS. SULLEN. But what do the people say? can't they guess?

SCRUB. Why, some think he's a spy, some guess he's a mountebank, some say one thing, some another: but, for my own part, I believe he's a Jesuit.

DORINDA. A Jesuit! why a Jesuit?

SCRUB. Because he keeps his horses always ready saddled, and his footman talks French.

MRS. SULLEN. His footman!

SCRUB. Ay, he and the count's footman were jabbering French like two intriguing ducks in a mill-pond; and I believe they talked of me, for they laughed consumedly.

DORINDA. What sort of livery has the footman?

SCRUB. Livery! Lord, madam, I took him for a captain, he's so bedizzened with lace! And then he has tops to his shoes, up to his mid leg, a silver-headed cane dangling at his knuckles; he carries his hands in his pockets just so—[*Walks in the French air.*]—and has a fine long periwig tied up in a bag—Lord, madam, he's clear another sort of man than I!

MRS. SULLEN. That may easily be.— But what shall we do now, sister?

DORINDA. I have it—this fellow has a world of simplicity, and some cunning, the first hides the latter by abundance.— Scrub!

SCRUB. Madam!

DORINDA. We have a great mind to know who this gentleman is, only for our satisfaction.

SCRUB. Yes, madam, it would be a satisfaction, no doubt.

DORINDA. You must go and get acquainted with his footman, and invite him hither to drink a bottle of your ale because you're butler to-day.

SCRUB. Yes, madam, I am butler every Sunday.

MRS. SULLEN. O brave! sister, o' my conscience, you understand the mathematics already. 'Tis the best plot in the world: your mother, you know, will be gone to church, my spouse will be got to the ale-house with his scoundrels, and the house will be our own—so we drop in by accident, and ask the fellow some questions ourselves. In the country, you know, any stranger is company, and we're glad to take up with the butler in a country-dance, and happy if he'll do us the favour.

SCRUB. O madam, you wrong me! I never refused your ladyship the favour in my life.

[*Enter* GIPSY.]

GIPSY. Ladies, dinner's upon table.

DORINDA. Scrub, we'll excuse your waiting—go where we ordered you.

SCRUB. I shall. [*Exeunt.*]

SCENE II—*A room in* BONIFACE'S *inn*.

[*Enter* AIMWELL *and* ARCHER.]

ARCHER. Well, Tom, I find you're a marksman.

AIMWELL. A marksman! who so blind could be, as not discern a swan among the ravens?

ARCHER. Well, but hark'ee, Aimwell!

AIMWELL. Aimwell! call me Oroondates, Cesario, Amadis, all that romance can in a lover paint, and then I'll answer. O Archer! I read her thousands in her looks, she looked like Ceres in her harvest: corn, wine and oil, milk and honey, gardens, groves, and purling streams played on her plenteous face.

ARCHER. Her face! her pocket, you mean; the corn, wine, and oil lies there. In short, she has ten thousand pounds, that's the English on't.

AIMWELL. Her eyes——

ARCHER. Are demi-cannons, to be sure; so I won't stand their battery. [*Going.*]

AIMWELL. Pray excuse me, my passion must have vent.

ARCHER. Passion! what a plague, d'ye think these romantic airs will do our business? Were my temper as extravagant as yours, my adventures have something more romantic by half.

AIMWELL. Your adventures!

ARCHER. Yes,
The nymph that with her twice ten hundred pounds,
With brazen engine hot, and quoif clear-starched,
Can fire the guest in warming of the bed——
There's a touch of sublime Milton for you, and the subject but an innkeeper's daughter! I can play with a girl as an angler does with his fish; he keeps it at the end of his line, runs it up the stream, and down the stream, till at last he brings it to hand, tickles the trout, and so whips it into his basket.

[*Enter* BONIFACE.]

BONIFACE. Mr. Martin, as the saying is—yonder's an honest fellow below, my Lady Bountiful's butler, who begs the honour that you would go home with him and see his cellar.

ARCHER. Do my *baise-mains* to the gentleman, and tell him I will do myself the honour to wait on him immediately.

[*Exit* BONIFACE.]

AIMWELL. What do I hear?
Soft Orpheus play, and fair Toftida sing!

ARCHER. Psha! damn your raptures; I tell you, here's a pump going to be put into the vessel, and the ship will get into harbour, my life on't. You say, there's another lady very handsome there?

AIMWELL. Yes, faith.

ARCHER. I'm in love with her already.

AIMWELL. Can't you give me a bill upon Cherry in the meantime?

ARCHER. No, no, friend, all her corn, wine, and oil is ingrossed to my market. And once more I warn you, to keep your anchorage clear of mine; for if you fall foul of me, by this light you shall go to the bottom! What! make prize of my little frigate, while I am upon the cruise for you!——

AIMWELL. Well, well, I won't.

[*Exit* ARCHER.]

[*Reënter* BONIFACE.]

Landlord, have you any tolerable company in the house, I don't care for dining alone?

BONIFACE. Yes, sir, there's a captain below, as the saying is, that arrived about an hour ago.

AIMWELL. Gentlemen of his coat are welcome everywhere; will you make him a compliment from me and tell him I should be glad of his company?

BONIFACE. Who shall I tell him, sir, would——

AIMWELL [aside]. Ha! that stroke was well thrown in!—[Aloud.] I'm only a traveller, like himself, and would be glad of his company, that's all.

BONIFACE. I obey your commands, as the saying is.   [Exit.]

[Reënter ARCHER.]

ARCHER. 'Sdeath! I had forgot; what title will you give yourself?

AIMWELL. My brother's, to be sure; he would never give me anything else, so I'll make bold with his honour this bout: —you know the rest of your cue.

ARCHER. Ay, ay.   [Exit.]

[Enter GIBBET.]

GIBBET. Sir, I'm yours.

AIMWELL. 'Tis more than I deserve, sir, for I don't know you.

GIBBET. I don't wonder at that, sir, for you never saw me before—[Aside.] I hope.

AIMWELL. And pray, sir, how came I by the honour of seeing you now?

GIBBET. Sir, I scorn to intrude upon any gentleman—but my landlord——

AIMWELL. O sir, I ask your pardon, you're the captain he told me of?

GIBBET. At your service, sir.

AIMWELL. What regiment, may I be so bold?

GIBBET. A marching regiment, sir, an old corps.

AIMWELL [aside]. Very old, if your coat be regimental.—[Aloud.] You have served abroad, sir?

GIBBET. Yes, sir—in the plantations, 'twas my lot to be sent into the worst service; I would have quitted it indeed, but a man of honour, you know—Besides, 'twas for the good of my country that I should be abroad:—anything for the good of one's country—I'm a Roman for that.

AIMWELL [aside]. One of the first; I'll lay my life.—[Aloud.] You found the West Indies very hot, sir?

GIBBET. Ay, sir, too hot for me.

AIMWELL. Pray, sir, han't I seen your face at Will's coffee-house?

GIBBET. Yes, sir, and at White's too.

AIMWELL. And where is your company now, captain?

GIBBET. They an't come yet.

AIMWELL. Why, d'ye expect 'em here?

GIBBET. They'll be here to-night, sir.

AIMWELL. Which way do they march?

GIBBET. Across the country.—[Aside.] The devil's in't, if I han't said enough to encourage him to declare! But I'm afraid he's not right; I must tack about.

AIMWELL. Is your company to quarter in Lichfield?

GIBBET. In this house, sir.

AIMWELL. What! all?

GIBBET. My company's but thin, ha! ha! ha! we are but three, ha! ha! ha!

AIMWELL. You're merry, sir.

GIBBET. Ay, sir, you must excuse me, sir; I understand the world, especially the art of travelling: I don't care, sir, for answering questions directly upon the road—for I generally ride with a charge about me.

AIMWELL. Three or four, I believe.
                                   [Aside.]

GIBBET. I am credibly informed that there are highwaymen upon this quarter; not, sir, that I could suspect a gentleman of your figure—but truly, sir, I have got such a way of evasion upon the road, that I don't care for speaking truth to any man.

AIMWELL [aside]. Your caution may be necessary.—[Aloud.] Then I presume you're no captain?

GIBBET. Not I, sir; captain is a good travelling name, and so I take it; it stops a great many foolish inquiries that are generally made about gentlemen that travel, it gives a man an air of something, and makes the drawers obedient:

—and thus far I am a captain, and no farther.

AIMWELL. And pray, sir, what is your true profession?

GIBBET. O sir, you must excuse me!—upon my word, sir, I don't think it safe to tell ye.

AIMWELL. Ha! ha! ha! upon my word I commend you.

[*Reënter* BONIFACE.]

Well, Mr. Boniface, what's the news?

BONIFACE. There's another gentleman below, as the saying is, that hearing you were but two, would be glad to make the third man, if you would give him leave.

AIMWELL. What is he?

BONIFACE. A clergyman, as the saying is.

AIMWELL. A clergyman! is he really a clergyman? or is it only his travelling name, as my friend the captain has it?

BONIFACE. O sir, he's a priest, and chaplain to the French officers in town.

AIMWELL. Is he a Frenchman?

BONIFACE. Yes, sir, born at Brussels.

GIBBET. A Frenchman, and a priest! I won't be seen in his company, sir; I have a value for my reputation, sir.

AIMWELL. Nay, but, captain, since we are by ourselves—can he speak English, landlord?

BONIFACE. Very well, sir; you may know him, as the saying is, to be a foreigner by his accent, and that's all.

AIMWELL. Then he has been in England before?

BONIFACE. Never, sir; but he's a master of languages, as the saying is; he talks Latin—it does me good to hear him talk Latin.

AIMWELL. Then you understand Latin, Mr. Boniface?

BONIFACE. Not I, sir, as the saying is; but he talks it so very fast, that I'm sure it must be good.

AIMWELL. Pray, desire him to walk up.

BONIFACE. Here he is, as the saying is.

[*Enter* FOIGARD.]

FOIGARD. Save you, gentlemens, bote.

AIMWELL [*aside*]. A Frenchman!—[*To* FOIGARD.] Sir, your most humble servant.

FOIGARD. Och, dear joy, I am your most faithful shervant, and yours alsho.

GIBBET. Dóctor, you talk very good English, but you have a mighty twang of the foreigner.

FOIGARD. My English is very vell for the vords, but we foreigners, you know, cannot bring our tongues about the pronunciation so soon.

AIMWELL [*aside*]. A foreigner! a downright Teague, by this light!—[*Aloud.*] Were you born in France, doctor?

FOIGARD. I was educated in France, but I was borned at Brussels; I am a subject of the King of Spain, joy.

GIBBET. What King of Spain, sir? speak;

FOIGARD. Upon my shoul, joy, I cannot tell you as yet.

AIMWELL. Nay, captain, that was too hard upon the doctor; he's a stranger.

FOIGARD. Oh, let him alone, dear joy; I am of a nation that is not easily put out of countenance.

AIMWELL. Come, gentlemen, I'll end the dispute.—Here, landlord, is dinner ready?

BONIFACE. Upon the table, as the saying is.

AIMWELL. Gentlemen—pray—that door

FOIGARD. No, no, fait, the captain must lead.

AIMWELL. No, doctor, the church is our guide.

GIBBET. Ay, ay, so it is.

[*Exit* FOIGARD *foremost, the others following.*]

SCENE III—*The gallery in* LADY BOUNTIFUL'S *house.*

[*Enter* ARCHER *and* SCRUB *singing, and hugging one another, the latter with a tankard in his hand.* GIPSY *listening at a distance.*]

SCRUB. *Tall, all, dall!*—Come, my dear boy, let's have that song once more.

ARCHER. No, no, we shall disturb the family.—But will you be sure to keep the secret?

SCRUB. Pho! upon my honour, as I'm a gentleman.

ARCHER. 'Tis enough. You must know, then, that my master is the Lord Viscount Aimwell; he fought a duel t'other day in London, wounded his man so dangerously that he thinks fit to withdraw till he hears whether the gentleman's wounds be mortal or not. He never was in this part of England before, so he chose to retire to this place, that's all.

GIPSY. And that's enough for me. [*Exit.*]

SCRUB. And where were you when your master fought?

ARCHER. We never know of our masters' quarrels.

SCRUB. No! if our masters in the country here receive a challenge, the first thing they do is to tell their wives; the wife tells the servants, the servants alarm the tenants, and in half an hour you shall have the whole county in arms.

ARCHER. To hinder two men from doing what they have no mind for.—But if you should chance to talk now of my business?

SCRUB. Talk! ay, sir, had I not learned the knack of holding my tongue, I had never lived so long in a great family.

ARCHER. Ay, ay, to be sure there are secrets in all families.

SCRUB. Secrets! ay;—but I'll say no more. Come, sit down, we'll make an end of our tankard: here—— [*Gives* ARCHER *the tankard.*]

ARCHER. With all my heart; who knows but you and I may come to be better acquainted, eh? Here's your ladies' healths; you have three, I think, and to be sure there must be secrets among 'em. [*Drinks.*]

SCRUB. Secrets! ay, friend.—I wish I had a friend!

ARCHER. Am not I your friend? come, you and I will be sworn brothers.

SCRUB. Shall we?

ARCHER. From this minute. Give me a kiss:—and now, brother Scrub——

SCRUB. And now, brother Martin, I will tell you a secret that will make your hair stand on end. You must know that I am consumedly in love.

ARCHER. That's a terrible secret, that's the truth on't.

SCRUB. That jade, Gipsy, that was with us just now in the cellar, is the arrantest whore that ever wore a petticoat; and I'm dying for love of her.

ARCHER. Ha! ha! ha!—Are you in love with her person or her virtue, brother Scrub?

SCRUB. I should like virtue best, because it is more durable than beauty: for virtue holds good with some women long, and many a day after they have lost it.

ARCHER. In the country, I grant ye, where no woman's virtue is lost, till a bastard be found.

SCRUB. Ay, could I bring her to a bastard, I should have her all to myself; but I dare not put it upon that lay, for fear of being sent for a soldier. Pray, brother, how do you gentlemen in London like that same Pressing Act?

ARCHER. Very ill, brother Scrub; 'tis the worst that ever was made for us. Formerly I remember the good days, when we could dun our masters for our wages, and if they refused to pay us, we could have a warrant to carry 'em before a Justice: but now if we talk of eating, they have a warrant for us, and carry us before three Justices.

SCRUB. And to be sure we go, if we talk of eating; for the Justices won't give their own servants a bad example. Now this is my misfortune—I dare not speak in the house, while that jade Gipsy dings about like a fury.—Once I had the better end of the staff.

ARCHER. And how comes the change now?

SCRUB. Why, the mother of all this mischief is a priest.

ARCHER. A priest!

SCRUB. Ay, a damned son of a whore of Babylon, that came over hither to say grace to the French officers, and eat up our provisions. There's not a day goes over his head without a dinner or supper in this house.

ARCHER. How came he so familiar in the family?

SCRUB. Because he speaks English as if he had lived here all his life, and tells lies as if he had been a traveller from his cradle.

ARCHER. And this priest, I'm afraid, has converted the affections of your Gipsy?

SCRUB. Converted! ay, and perverted, my dear friend: for, I'm afraid, he has made her a whore and a papist! But this is not all; there's the French count and Mrs. Sullen, they're in the confederacy, and for some private ends of their own, to be sure.

ARCHER. A very hopeful family yours, brother Scrub! I suppose the maiden lady has her lover too?

SCRUB. Not that I know: she's the best on 'em, that's the truth on't: but they take care to prevent my curiosity, by giving me so much business, that I'm a perfect slave. What d'ye think is my place in this family?

ARCHER. Butler, I suppose.

SCRUB. Ah, Lord help you! I'll tell you. Of a Monday I drive the coach, of a Tuesday I drive the plough, on Wednesday I follow the hounds, a Thursday I dun the tenants, on Friday I go to market, on Saturday I draw warrants, and a Sunday I draw beer.

ARCHER. Ha! ha! ha! if variety be a pleasure in life, you have enough on't, my dear brother. But what ladies are those?

SCRUB. Ours, ours; that upon the right hand is Mrs. Sullen, and the other is Mrs. Dorinda. Don't mind 'em; sit still, man.

[*Enter* MRS. SULLEN *and* DORINDA.]

MRS. SULLEN. I have heard my brother talk of my Lord Aimwell; but they say that his brother is the finer gentleman.

DORINDA. That's impossible, sister.

MRS. SULLEN. He's vastly rich, but very close, they say.

DORINDA. No matter for that; if I can creep into his heart, I'll open his breast, I warrant him: I have heard say, that people may be guessed at by the behaviour of their servants; I could wish we might talk to that fellow.

MRS. SULLEN. So do I; for I think he's a very pretty fellow. Come this way, I'll throw out a lure for him presently.

[DORINDA *and* MRS. SULLEN *walk a turn towards the opposite side of the stage.*]

ARCHER [*aside*]. Corn, wine, and oil indeed!—But, I think, the wife has the greatest plenty of flesh and blood; she should be my choice.—Ay, ay, say you so!—[MRS. SULLEN *drops her glove,* ARCHER *runs, takes it up and gives to her.*] Madam—your ladyship's glove.

MRS. SULLEN. O sir, I thank you!— [*To* DORINDA.] What a handsome bow the fellow has!

DORINDA. Bow! why, I have known several footmen come down from London set up here for dancing-masters, and carry off the best fortunes in the country.

ARCHER [*aside*]. That project, for aught I know, had been better than ours. —[*To* SCRUB.] Brother Scrub, why don't you introduce me?

SCRUB. Ladies, this is the strange gentleman's servant that you saw at church to-day; I understood he came from London, and so I invited him to the cellar, that he might show me the newest flourish in whetting my knives.

DORINDA. And I hope you have made much of him?

ARCHER. Oh yes, madam, but the strength of your ladyship's liquor is a little too potent for the constitution of your humble servant.

MRS. SULLEN. What, then you don't usually drink ale?

ARCHER. No, madam; my constant drink is tea, or a little wine and water.

'Tis prescribed me by the physician for a remedy against the spleen.

SCRUB. Oh la! Oh la! a footman have the spleen!

MRS. SULLEN. I thought that distemper had been only proper to people of quality?

ARCHER. Madam, like all other fashions it wears out, and so descends to their servants; though in a great many of us, I believe, it proceeds from some melancholy particles in the blood, occasioned by the stagnation of wages.

DORINDA [aside to MRS. SULLEN]. How affectedly the fellow talks!—[To ARCHER.] How long, pray, have you served your present master?

ARCHER. Not long; my life has been mostly spent in the service of the ladies.

MRS. SULLEN. And pray, which service do you like best?

ARCHER. Madam, the ladies pay best; the honour of serving them is sufficient wages; there is a charm in their looks that delivers a pleasure with their commands, and gives our duty the wings of inclination.

MRS. SULLEN [aside]. That flight was above the pitch of a livery.—[Aloud.] And, sir, would not you be satisfied to serve a lady again?

ARCHER. As a groom of the chamber, madam, but not as a footman.

MRS. SULLEN. I suppose you served as footman before?

ARCHER. For that reason I would not serve in that post again; for my memory is too weak for the load of messages that the ladies lay upon their servants in London. My Lady Howd'ye, the last mistress I served, called me up one morning, and told me, "Martin, go to my Lady Allnight with my humble service; tell her I was to wait on her ladyship yesterday, and·left word with Mrs. Rebecca, that the preliminaries of the affair she knows of are stopped till we know the concurrence of the person that I know of, for which there are circumstances wanting which we shall accommodate at the old place; but that in the meantime there is a person about her ladyship, that from several hints and surmises, was accessory at a certain time to the disappointments that naturally attend things, that to her knowledge are of more importance——"

MRS. SULLEN. Dorinda. Ha! ha! ha! where are you going, sir?

ARCHER. Why, I han't half done!—The whole howd'ye was about half an hour long; so I happened to misplace two syllables, and was turned off, and rendered incapable.

DORINDA [aside to MRS. SULLEN]. The pleasantest fellow, sister, I ever saw!—[To ARCHER.] But, friend, if your master be married, I presume you still serve a lady?

ARCHER. No, madam, I take care never to come into a married family! the commands of the master and mistress are always so contrary, that 'tis impossible to please both.

DORINDA. There's a main point gained: my lord is not married, I find. [Aside.]

MRS. SULLEN. But I wonder, friend, that in so many good services, you had not a better provision made for you.

ARCHER. I don't know how, madam. I had a lieutenancy offered me three or four times; but that is not bread, madam —I live much better as I do.

SCRUB. Madam, he sings rarely! I was thought to do pretty well here in the country till he came; but alack a day, I'm nothing to my brother Martin!

DORINDA. Does he?—Pray, sir, will you oblige us with a song?

ARCHER. Are you for passion or humour?

SCRUB. Oh le! he has the purest ballad about a trifle——

MRS. SULLEN. A trifle! pray, sir, let's have it.

ARCHER. I'm ashamed to offer you a trifle, madam; but since you command me——

[Sings to the tune of "Sir Simon the King."]

A trifling song you shall hear, Begun with a trifle and ended:

All trifling people draw near,
And I shall be nobly attended.

Were it not for trifles, a few
That lately have come into play;
The men would want something to do,
And the women want something to say.

What makes men trifle in dressing?
Because the ladies (they know)
Admire, by often possessing,
That eminent trifle, a beau.

When the lover his moments has trifled,
The trifle of trifles to gain:
No sooner the virgin is rifled,
But a trifle shall part 'em again.

What mortal man would be able
At White's half an hour to sit?
Or who could bear a tea-table,
Without talking of trifles for wit?

The court is from trifles secure,
Gold keys are no trifles, we see:
White rods are no trifles, I'm sure,
Whatever their bearers may be.

But if you will go to the place,
Where trifles abundantly breed,
The levee will show you His Grace
Makes promises trifles indeed.

A coach with six footmen behind,
I count neither trifle nor sin:
But, ye gods! how oft do we find
A scandalous trifle within.

A flask of champagne, people think it
A trifle, or something as bad:
But if you'll contrive how to drink it,
You'll find it no trifle, egad!

A parson's a trifle at sea,
A widow's a trifle in sorrow:
A peace is a trifle to-day,
Who knows what may happen to-morrow?

A black coat a trifle may cloke,
Or to hide it, the red may endeavour:
But if once the army is broke,
We shall have more trifles than ever.

The stage is a trifle, they say,
The reason, pray carry along,
Because at every new play,
The house they with trifles so throng.

But with people's malice to trifle,
And to set us all on a foot:
The author of this is a trifle,
And his song is a trifle to boot.

MRS. SULLEN. Very well, sir, we're
obliged to you.—Something for a pair of
gloves.   [*Offering him money.*]
ARCHER. I humbly beg leave to be
excused: my master, madam, pays me;
nor dare I take money from any other
hand, without injuring his honour, and
disobeying his commands.   [*Exit
ARCHER and* SCRUB.]
DORINDA. This is surprising! Did you
ever see so pretty a well-bred fellow?
MRS. SULLEN. The devil take him for
wearing that livery!
DORINDA. I fancy, sister, he may be
some gentleman, a friend of my lord's,
that his lordship has pitched upon for his
courage, fidelity, and discretion, to bear
him company in this dress, and who ten
to one was his second too.
MRS. SULLEN. It is so, it must be so,
and it shall be so!—for I like him.
DORINDA. What! better than the
Count?
MRS. SULLEN. The Count happened to
be the most agreeable man upon the
place; and so I chose him to serve me in
my design upon my husband. But I
should like this fellow better in a design
upon myself.
DORINDA. But now, sister, for an inter-
view with this lord and this gentleman;
how shall we bring that about?
MRS. SULLEN. Patience! you country
ladies give no quarter if once you be
entered. Would you prevent their de-
sires, and give the fellows no wishing-
time? Look'ee, Dorinda, if my Lord
Aimwell loves you or deserves you, he'll
find a way to see you, and there we must
leave it. My business comes now upon the
tapis. Have you prepared your brother?

DORINDA. Yes, yes.

MRS. SULLEN. And how did he relish it?

DORINDA. He said little, mumbled something to himself, promised to be guided by me—but here he comes.

[*Enter* SQUIRE SULLEN.]

SQUIRE SULLEN. What singing was that I heard just now?

MRS. SULLEN. The singing in your head, my dear; you complained of it all day.

SQUIRE SULLEN. You're impertinent.

MRS. SULLEN. I was ever so, since I became one flesh with you.

SQUIRE SULLEN. One flesh! rather two carcasses joined unnaturally together.

MRS. SULLEN. Or rather a living soul coupled to a dead body.

DORINDA. So, this is fine encouragement for me!

SQUIRE SULLEN. Yes, my wife shows you what you must do.

MRS. SULLEN. And my husband shows you what you must suffer.

SQUIRE SULLEN. 'Sdeath, why can't you be silent?

MRS. SULLEN. 'Sdeath, why can't you talk?

SQUIRE SULLEN. Do you talk to any purpose?

MRS. SULLEN. Do you think to any purpose?

SQUIRE SULLEN. Sister, hark'ee!—[*Whispers.*] I shan't be home till it be late.   [*Exit.*]

MRS. SULLEN. What did he whisper to ye?

DORINDA. That he would go round the back way, come into the closet, and listen as I directed him. But let me beg you once more, dear sister, to drop this project; for as I told you before, instead of awaking him to kindness, you may provoke him to a rage; and then who knows how far his brutality may carry him?

MRS. SULLEN. I'm provided to receive him, I warrant you. But here comes the Count: vanish!   [*Exit* DORINDA.]

[*Enter* COUNT BELLAIR.]

Don't you wonder, Monsieur le Count, that I was not at church this afternoon?

COUNT BELLAIR. I more wonder, madam, that you go dere at all, or how you dare to lift those eyes to heaven that are guilty of so much killing.

MRS. SULLEN. If Heaven, sir, has given to my eyes with the power of killing the virtue of making a cure, I hope the one may atone for the other.

COUNT BELLAIR. Oh, largely, madam, would your ladyship be as ready to apply the remedy as to give the wound. Consider, madam, I am doubly a prisoner; first to the arms of your general, then to your more conquering eyes. My first chains are easy—there a ransom may redeem me; but from your fetters I never shall get free.

MRS. SULLEN. Alas, sir! why should you complain to me of your captivity, who am in chains myself? You know, sir, that I am bound, nay, must be tied up in that particular that might give you ease: I am like you, a prisoner of war—of war, indeed—I have given my parole of honour! would you break yours to gain your liberty?

COUNT BELLAIR. Most certainly I would, were I a prisoner among the Turks; dis is your case, you're a slave, madam, slave to the worst of Turks, a husband.

MRS. SULLEN. There lies my foible, I confess; no fortifications, no courage, conduct, nor vigilancy, can pretend to defend a place where the cruelty of the governor forces the garrison to mutiny.

COUNT BELLAIR. And where de besieger is resolved to die before de place. —Here will I fix [*Kneels.*];—with tears, vows, and prayers assault your heart and never rise till you surrender; or if I must storm—Love and St. Michael!—And so I begin the attack.

MRS. SULLEN. Stand off!—[*Aside.*] Sure he hears me not!—And I could almost wish he did not!—The fellow makes love very prettily.—[*Aloud.*] But, sir, why should you put such a value upon my person, when you see it despised by one that knows it so much better?

COUNT BELLAIR. He knows it not, though he possesses it; if he but knew the value of the jewel he is master of he would always wear it next his heart, and sleep with it in his arms.

MRS. SULLEN. But since he throws me unregarded from him——

COUNT BELLAIR. And one that knows your value well comes by and takes you up, is it not justice? [*Goes to lay hold of her.*]

[*Enter* SQUIRE SULLEN *with his sword drawn.*]

SQUIRE SULLEN. Hold, villain, hold!

MRS. SULLEN [*presenting a pistol*]. Do you hold!

SQUIRE SULLEN. What! murder your husband, to defend your bully!

MRS. SULLEN. Bully! for shame, Mr. Sullen, bullies wear long swords, the gentleman has none; he's a prisoner, you know. I was aware of your outrage, and prepared this to receive your violence; and, if occasion were, to preserve myself against the force of this other gentleman.

COUNT BELLAIR. O madam, your eyes be bettre firearms than your pistol; they nevre miss.

SQUIRE SULLEN. What! court my wife to my face!

MRS. SULLEN. Pray, Mr. Sullen, put up; suspend your fury for a minute.

SQUIRE SULLEN. To give you time to invent an excuse!

MRS. SULLEN. I need none.

SQUIRE SULLEN. No, for I heard every syllable of your discourse.

COUNT BELLAIR. Ah! and begar, I t'ink the dialogue was vera pretty.

MRS. SULLEN. Then I suppose, sir, you heard something of your own barbarity?

SQUIRE SULLEN. Barbarity! 'oons, what does the woman call barbarity? Do I ever meddle with you?

MRS. SULLEN. No.

SQUIRE SULLEN. As for you, sir, I shall take another time.

COUNT BELLAIR. Ah, begar, and so must I.

SQUIRE SULLEN. Look'ee, madam, don't think that my anger proceeds from any concern I have for your honour, but for my own, and if you can contrive any way of being a whore without making me a cuckold, do it and welcome.

MRS. SULLEN. Sir, I thank you kindly, you would allow me the sin but rob me of the pleasure. No, no, I'm resolved never to venture upon the crime without the satisfaction of seeing you punished for't.

SQUIRE SULLEN. Then will you grant me this, my dear? Let anybody else do you the favour but that Frenchman, for I mortally hate his whole generation. [*Exit.*]

COUNT BELLAIR. Ah, sir, that be ungrateful, for begar, I love some of yours. —Madam—— [*Approaching her.*]

MRS. SULLEN. No, sir.

COUNT BELLAIR. No, sir! garzoon, madam, I am not your husband.

MRS. SULLEN. 'Tis time to undeceive you, sir. I believed your addresses to me were no more than an amusement, and I hope you will think the same of my complaisance; and to convince you that you ought, you must know that I brought you hither only to make you instrumental in setting me right with my husband, for he was planted to listen by my appointment.

COUNT BELLAIR. By your appointment?

MRS. SULLEN. Certainly.

COUNT BELLAIR. And so, madam, while I was telling twenty stories to part you from your husband, begar, I was bringing you together all the while?

MRS. SULLEN. I ask your pardon, sir, but I hope this will give you a taste of the virtue of the English ladies.

COUNT BELLAIR. Begar, madam, your virtue be vera great, but garzoon, your honeste be vera little.

[*Reënter* DORINDA.]

MRS. SULLEN. Nay, now, you're angry, sir.

Count Bellair. Angry!—*Fair Dorinda* [*Sings "Fair Dorinda," the opera tune, and addresses* Dorinda.] Madam, when your ladyship want a fool, send for me. *Fair Dorinda, Revenge, etc.*
                    [*Exit singing.*]

Mrs. Sullen. There goes the true humour of his nation—resentment with good manners, and the height of anger in a song! Well, sister, you must be judge, for you have heard the trial.

Dorinda. And I bring in my brother guilty.

Mrs. Sullen. But I must bear the punishment. 'Tis hard, sister.

Dorinda. I own it; but you must have patience.

Mrs. Sullen. Patience! the cant of custom—Providence sends no evil without a remedy. Should I lie groaning under a yoke I can shake off, I were accessory to my ruin, and my patience were no better than self-murder.

Dorinda. But how can you shake off the yoke? your divisions don't come within the reach of the law for a divorce.

Mrs. Sullen. Law! what law can search into the remote abyss of nature? what evidence can prove the unaccountable disaffections of wedlock? Can a jury sum up the endless aversions that are rooted in our souls, or can a bench give judgment upon antipathies?

Dorinda. They never pretended, sister; they never meddle, but in case of uncleanness.

Mrs. Sullen. Uncleanness! O sister! casual violation is a transient injury, and may possibly be repaired, but can radical hatreds be ever reconciled? No, no, sister, nature is the first lawgiver, and when she has set tempers opposite, not all the golden links of wedlock nor iron manacles of law can keep 'em fast.

Wedlock we own ordain'd by Heaven's decree,
But such as Heaven ordain'd it first to be;—
Concurring tempers in the man and wife
As mutual helps to draw the load of life.

View all the works of Providence above,
The stars with harmony and concord move;
View all the works of Providence below,
The fire, the water, earth, and air, we know,
All in one plant agree to make it grow.
Must man, the chiefest work of art divine,
Be doom'd in endless discord to repine?
No, we should injure Heaven by that surmise,
Omnipotence is just, were man but wise.
                    [*Exeunt.*]

ACT IV

Scene I—*The gallery in* Lady Bountiful's *house.*

[Mrs. Sullen *discovered alone.*]

Mrs. Sullen. Were I born an humble Turk, where women have no soul nor property, there I must sit contented. But in England, a country whose women are its glory, must women be abused? where women rule, must women be enslaved? Nay, cheated into slavery, mocked by a promise of comfortable society into a wilderness of solitude! I dare not keep the thought about me. Oh, here comes something to divert me.

[*Enter a* Countrywoman.]

Woman. I come, an't please your ladyship—you're my Lady Bountiful, an't ye?

Mrs. Sullen. Well, good woman, go on.

Woman. I have come seventeen long mail to have a cure for my husband's sore leg.

Mrs. Sullen. Your husband! what, woman, cure your husband!

Woman. Ay, poor man, for his sore leg won't let him stir from home.

Mrs. Sullen. There, I confess, you have given me a reason. Well, good woman, I'll tell you what you must do. You must lay your husband's leg upon a table, and with a chopping-knife you must lay it open as broad as you can, then you must take out the bone, and beat the flesh soundly with a rolling-pin, then take salt, pepper, cloves, mace, and ginger, some sweet-herbs, and season it very well, then roll it up like brawn, and put it into the oven for two hours.

WOMAN. Heavens reward your ladyship!—I have two little babies too that are piteous bad with the graips, an't please ye.

MRS. SULLEN. Put a little pepper and salt in their bellies, good woman.

[*Enter* LADY BOUNTIFUL.]
I beg your ladyship's pardon for taking your business out of your hands; I have been a-tampering here a little with one of your patients.

LADY BOUNTIFUL. Come, good woman, don't mind this mad creature; I am the person that you want, I suppose. What would you have, woman?

MRS. SULLEN. She wants something for her husband's sore leg.

LADY BOUNTIFUL. What's the matter with his leg, goody?

WOMAN. It come first, as one might say, with a sort of dizziness in his foot, then he had a kind of laziness in his joints, and then his leg broke out, and then it swelled, and then it closed again, and then it broke out again, and then it festered, and then it grew better, and then it grew worse again.

MRS. SULLEN. Ha! ha! ha!

LADY BOUNTIFUL. How can you be merry with the misfortunes of other people?

MRS. SULLEN. Because my own make me sad, madam.

LADY BOUNTIFUL. The worst reason in the world, daughter; your own misfortunes should teach you to pity others.

MRS. SULLEN. But the woman's misfortunes and mine are nothing alike; her husband is sick, and mine, alas! is in health.

LADY BOUNTIFUL. What! would you wish your husband sick?

MRS. SULLEN. Not of a sore leg, of all things.

LADY BOUNTIFUL. Well, good woman, go to the pantry, get your bellyful of victuals, then I'll give you a receipt of diet-drink for your husband. But d'ye hear, goody, you must not let your husband move too much?

WOMAN. No, no, madam, the poor man's inclinable enough to lie still. [*Exit.*]

LADY BOUNTIFUL. Well, daughter Sullen, though you laugh, I have done miracles about the country here with my receipts.

MRS. SULLEN. Miracles indeed, if they have cured anybody; but I believe, madam, the patient's faith goes farther toward the miracle than your prescription.

LADY BOUNTIFUL. Fancy helps in some cases; but there's your husband, who has as little fancy as anybody, I brought him from death's door.

MRS. SULLEN. I suppose, madam, you made him drink plentifully of ass's milk.

[*Enter* DORINDA, *who runs to* MRS. SULLEN.]
DORINDA. News, dear sister! news! news!

[*Enter* ARCHER, *running.*]
ARCHER. Where, where is my Lady Bountiful?—Pray, which is the old lady of you three?

LADY BOUNTIFUL. I am.

ARCHER. O madam, the fame of your ladyship's charity, goodness, benevolence, skill and ability, have drawn me hither to implore your ladyship's help in behalf of my unfortunate master, who is this moment breathing his last.

LADY BOUNTIFUL. Your master! where is he?

ARCHER. At your gate, madam. Drawn by the appearance of your handsome house to view it nearer, and walking up the avenue within five paces of the court-yard, he was taken ill of a sudden with a sort of I know not what, but down he fell, and there he lies.

LADY BOUNTIFUL. Here, Scrub! Gipsy! all run, get my easy-chair down stairs, put the gentleman in it, and bring him in quickly! quickly!

ARCHER. Heaven will reward your ladyship for this charitable act.

LADY BOUNTIFUL. Is your master used to these fits?

ARCHER. O yes, madam, frequently: I have known him have five or six of a night.

LADY BOUNTIFUL. What's his name?

ARCHER. Lord, madam, he's a-dying! a minute's care or neglect may save or destroy his life.

LADY BOUNTIFUL. Ah, poor gentleman! —Come, friend, show me the way; I'll see him brought in myself. [*Exit with* ARCHER.]

DORINDA. O sister, my heart flutters about strangely! I can hardly forbear running to his assistance.

MRS. SULLEN. And I'll lay my life he deserves your assistance more than he wants it. Did not I tell you that my lord would find a way to come at you? Love's his distemper, and you must be the physician; put on all your charms, summon all your fire into your eyes, plant the whole artillery of your looks against his breast, and down with him.

DORINDA. O sister! I'm but a young gunner; I shall be afraid to shoot, for fear the piece should recoil, and hurt myself.

MRS. SULLEN. Never fear, you shall see me shoot before you, if you will.

DORINDA. No, no, dear sister; you have missed your mark so unfortunately, that I shan't care for being instructed by you.

[*Enter* AIMWELL *in a chair carried by* ARCHER *and* SCRUB, *and counterfeiting a swoon;* LADY BOUNTIFUL *and* GIPSY *following.*]

LADY BOUNTIFUL. Here, here, let's see the hartshorn drops.—Gipsy, a glass of fair water! His fit's very strong.—Bless me, how his hands are clinched!

ARCHER. For shame, ladies, what d'ye do? why don't you help us?—[*To* DOR-INDA.] Pray, madam, take his hand, and open it, if you can, whilst I hold his head. [DORINDA *takes his hand.*]

DORINDA. Poor gentleman!—Oh!—he has got my hand within his, and squeezes it unmercifully——

LADY BOUNTIFUL. 'Tis the violence of his convulsion, child.

ARCHER. Oh, madam, he's perfectly possessed in these cases—he'll bite if you don't have a care.

DORINDA. Oh, my hand! my hand!

LADY BOUNTIFUL. What's the matter with the foolish girl? I have got his hand open, you see, with a great deal of ease.

ARCHER. Ay, but, madam, your daughter's hand is somewhat warmer than your ladyship's, and the heat of it draws the force of the spirits that way.

MRS. SULLEN. I find, friend, you're very learned in these sorts of fits.

ARCHER. 'Tis no wonder, madam, for I'm often troubled with them myself; I find myself extremely ill at this minute.

[*Looking hard at* MRS. SULLEN.]

MRS. SULLEN. I fancy I could find a way to cure you. [*Aside.*]

LADY BOUNTIFUL. His fit holds him very long.

ARCHER. Longer than usual, madam.— Pray, young lady, open his breast and give him air.

LADY BOUNTIFUL. Where did his illness take him first, pray?

ARCHER. To-day at church, madam.

LADY BOUNTIFUL. In what manner was he taken?

ARCHER. Very strangely, my lady. He was of a sudden touched with something in his eyes, which, at the first, he only felt, but could not tell whether 'twas pain or pleasure.

LADY BOUNTIFUL. Wind, nothing but wind!

ARCHER. By soft degrees it grew and mounted to his brain, there his fancy caught it; there formed it so beautiful, and dressed it up in such gay, pleasing colours, that his transported appetite seized the fair idea, and straight conveyed it to his heart. That hospitable seat of life sent all its sanguine spirits forth to meet, and opened all its sluicy gates to take the stranger in.

LADY BOUNTIFUL. Your master should never go without a bottle to smell to.—Oh—he recovers! The lavender-water—some feathers to burn under his nose—Hungary water to rub his temples.—Oh, he comes to himself!—Hem a little, sir, hem.—Gipsy! bring the cordial-water.

[AIMWELL *seems to awake in amaze.*]

DORINDA. How d'ye, sir?

AIMWELL. Where am I? [*Rising.*]
Sure I have pass'd the gulf of silent death,
And now I land on the Elysian shore!—
Behold the goddess of those happy plains,
Fair Proserpine—let me adore thy bright divinity.

[*Kneels to* DORINDA, *and kisses her hand.*]

MRS. SULLEN. So, so, so! I knew where the fit would end!

AIMWELL. Eurydice perhaps—
How could thy Orpheus keep his word,
And not look back upon thee?
No treasure but thyself could sure have bribed him
To look one minute off thee.

LADY BOUNTIFUL. Delirious, poor gentleman!

ARCHER. Very delirious, madam, very delirious.

AIMWELL. Martin's voice, I think.

ARCHER. Yes, my lord.—How does your lordship?

LADY BOUNTIFUL. Lord! did you mind that, girls? [*Aside to* MRS. SULLEN *and* DORINDA.]

AIMWELL. Where am I?

ARCHER. In very good hands, sir. You were taken just now with one of your old fits, under the trees, just by this good lady's house; her ladyship had you taken in, and has miraculously brought you to yourself, as you see.

AIMWELL. I am so confounded with shame, madam, that I can now only beg pardon; and refer my acknowledgments for your ladyship's care till an opportunity offers of making some amends. I dare

be no longer troublesome.—Martin! give two guineas to the servants. [*Going.*]

DORINDA. Sir, you may catch cold by going so soon into the air; you don't look, sir, as if you were perfectly recovered.

[*Here* ARCHER *talks to* LADY BOUNTIFUL *in dumb show.*]

AIMWELL. That I shall never be, madam; my present illness is so rooted that I must expect to carry it to my grave.

MRS. SULLEN. Don't despair, sir; I have known several in your distemper shake it off with a fortnight's physic.

LADY BOUNTIFUL. Come, sir, your servant has been telling me that you're apt to relapse if you go into the air: your good manners shan't get the better of ours—you shall sit down again, sir. Come, sir, we don't mind ceremonies in the country—here, sir, my service t'ye.—You shall taste my water; 'tis a cordial I can assure you, and of my own making—drink it off, sir.—[AIMWELL *drinks.*] And how d'ye find yourself now, sir?

AIMWELL. Somewhat better —though very faint still.

LADY BOUNTIFUL. Ay, ay, people are always faint after these fits.—Come, girls, you shall show the gentleman the house. —'Tis but an old family building, sir; but you had better walk about, and cool by degrees, than venture immediately into the air. You'll find some tolerable pictures.—Dorinda, show the gentleman way. I must go to the poor woman below. [*Exit.*]

DORINDA. This way, sir.

AIMWELL. Ladies, shall I beg leave for my servant to wait on you, for he understands pictures very well?

MRS. SULLEN. Sir, we understand originals as well as he does pictures, so he may come along. [*Exeunt all but* SCRUB, AIMWELL *leading* DORINDA.]

[*Enter* FOIGARD.]

FOIGARD. Save you, Master Scrub!

SCRUB. Sir, I won't be saved your way —I hate a priest, I abhor the French, and I defy the devil. Sir, I'm a bold Briton, and will spill the last drop of my blood to keep out popery and slavery.

FOIGARD. Master Scrub, you would put me down in politics, and so I would be speaking with Mrs. Shipsy.

SCRUB. Good Mr. Priest, you can't speak with her; she's sick, sir, she's gone abroad, sir, she's—dead two months ago, sir.

[*Reënter* GIPSY.]

GIPSY. How now, impudence! how dare you talk so saucily to the doctor?—Pray, sir, don't take it ill; for the common people of England are not so civil to strangers, as——

SCRUB. You lie! you lie! 'tis the common people that are civilest to strangers.

GIPSY. Sirrah, I have a good mind to —get you out, I say!

SCRUB. I won't.

GIPSY. You won't, sauce-box!—Pray, doctor, what is the captain's name that came to your inn last night?

SCRUB [*aside*]. The captain! ah, the devil, there she hampers me again; the captain has me on one side and the priest on t'other: so between the gown and the sword, I have a fine time on't.—But, *Cedunt arma togæ.* [*Going.*]

GIPSY. What, sirrah, won't you march?

SCRUB. No, my dear, I won't march— but I'll walk.—[*Aside.*] And I'll make bold to listen a little too. [*Goes behind the side-scene and listens.*]

GIPSY. Indeed, doctor, the Count has been barbarously treated, that's the truth on't.

FOIGARD. Ah, Mrs. Gipsy, upon my shoul, now, gra, his complainings would mollify the marrow in your bones, and move the bowels of your commiseration! He veeps, and he dances, and he fistles, and he swears, and he laughs, and he stamps, and he sings; in conclusion, joy, he's afflicted *à-la-Française*, and a stranger would not know whider to cry or to laugh with him.

GIPSY. What would you have me do, doctor?

FOIGARD. Not'ing, joy, but only hide the Count in Mrs. Sullen's closet when it is dark.

GIPSY. Nothing! is that nothing? it would be both a sin and a shame, doctor.

FOIGARD. Here is twenty louis-d'ors, joy, for your shame; and I will give you an absolution for the shin.

GIPSY. But won't that money look like a bribe?

FOIGARD. Dat is according as you shall tauk it. If you receive the money beforehand, 'twill be *logicè*, a bribe; but if you stay till afterwards, 'twill be only a gratification.

GIPSY. Well, doctor, I'll take it *logicè*. But what must I do with my conscience, sir?

FOIGARD. Leave dat wid me, joy; I am your priest, gra; and your conscience is under my hands.

GIPSY. But should I put the Count into the closet——

FOIGARD. Vel, is dere any shin for a man's being in a closhet? one may go to prayers in a closhet.

GIPSY. But if the lady should come into her chamber, and go to bed?

FOIGARD. Vel, and is dere any shin in going to bed, joy?

GIPSY. Ay, but if the parties should meet, doctor?

FOIGARD. Vel den—the parties must be responsible. Do you be gone after putting the Count into the closhet; and leave the shins wid themselves. I will come with the Count to instruct you in your chamber.

GIPSY. Well, doctor, your religion is so pure! Methinks I'm so easy after an absolution, and can sin afresh with so much security, that I'm resolved to die a martyr to't. Here's the key of the garden door, come in the back way when 'tis late, I'll be ready to receive you; but don't so much as whisper, only take hold of my hand; I'll lead you, and do you lead the Count, and follow me. [*Exeunt.*]

SCRUB [*coming forward*]. What witchcraft now have these two imps of the devil been a-hatching here? "There's twenty louis-d'ors"; I heard that, and saw the purse.—But I must give room to my betters.   [*Exit.*]

[*Reënter* AIMWELL, *leading* DORINDA, *and making love in dumb show;* MRS. SULLEN *and* ARCHER *following.*]

MRS. SULLEN [*to* ARCHER]. Pray, sir, how d'ye like that piece?

ARCHER. Oh, 'tis Leda! You find, madam, how Jupiter comes disguised to make love——

MRS. SULLEN. But what think you there of Alexander's battles?

ARCHER. We only want a Le Brun, madam, to draw greater battles, and a greater general of our own. The Danube, madam, would make a greater figure in a picture than the Granicus; and we have our Ramillies to match their Arbela.

MRS. SULLEN. Pray, sir, what head is that in the corner there?

ARCHER. O madam, 'tis poor Ovid in his exile.

MRS. SULLEN. What was he banished for?

ARCHER. His ambitious love, madam. —[*Bowing.*] His misfortune touches me.

MRS. SULLEN. Was he successful in his amours?

ARCHER. There he has left us in the dark. He was too much a gentleman to tell.

MRS. SULLEN. If he were secret, I pity him.

ARCHER. And if he were successful, I envy him.

MRS. SULLEN. How d'ye like that Venus over the chimney?

ARCHER. Venus! I protest, madam, I took it for your picture; but now I look again, 'tis not handsome enough.

MRS. SULLEN. Oh, what a charm is flattery! If you would see my picture, there it is over that cabinet. How d'ye like it?

ARCHER. I must admire anything, madam, that has the least resemblance of you. But, methinks, madam—[*He looks at the picture and* MRS. SULLEN *three or four times, by turns.*] Pray, madam, who drew it?

MRS. SULLEN. A famous hand, sir.
          [*Here* AIMWELL *and* DORINDA *go off.*]

ARCHER. A famous hand, madam!— Your eyes, indeed, are featured there; but where's the sparking moisture, shining fluid, in which they swim? The picture, indeed, has your dimples; but where's the swarm of killing Cupids that should ambush there? The lips too are figured out; but where's the carnation dew, the pouting ripeness that tempts the taste in the original?

MRS. SULLEN. Had it been my lot to have matched with such a man! [*Aside.*]

ARCHER. Your breasts too—presumptuous man! what, paint Heaven!—Apropos, madam, in the very next picture is Salmoneus, that was struck dead with lightning, for offering to imitate Jove's thunder; I hope you served the painter so, madam?

MRS. SULLEN. Had my eyes the power of thunder, they should employ their lightning better.

ARCHER. There's the finest bed in that room, madam! I suppose 'tis your ladyship's bedchamber.

MRS. SULLEN. And what then,-sir?

ARCHER. I think the quilt is the richest that ever I saw. I can't at this distance, madam, distinguish the figures of the embroidery; will you give me leave, madam?

MRS. SULLEN [*aside*]. The devil take his impudence!—Sure, if I gave him an opportunity, he durst not offer it?—I have a great mind to try.—[*Going: returns.*] 'Sdeath, what am I doing?—And alone, too!—Sister! sister!   [*Runs out.*]

ARCHER. I'll follow her close—
For where a Frenchman durst attempt to storm,
A Briton sure may well the work perform.   [*Going.*]

[*Reënter* SCRUB.]

SCRUB. Martin! brother Martin!

ARCHER. O brother Scrub, I beg your

pardon, I was not a-going: here's a guinea my master ordered you.

SCRUB. A guinea! hi! hi! hi! a guinea! eh—by this light it is a guinea! But I suppose you expect one-and-twenty shillings in change?

ARCHER. Not at all; I have another for Gipsy.

SCRUB. A guinea for her! faggot and fire for the witch? Sir, give me that guinea, and I'll discover a plot.

ARCHER. A plot!

SCRUB. Ay, sir, a plot, and a horrid plot! First, it must be a plot, because there's a woman in't: secondly, it must be a plot, because there's a priest in't: thirdly, it must be a plot, because there's French gold in't: and fourthly, it must be a plot, because I don't know what to make on't.

ARCHER. Nor anybody else, I'm afraid, brother Scrub.

SCRUB. Truly, I'm afraid so too; for where there's a priest and a woman, there's always a mystery and a riddle. This I know, that here has been the doctor with a temptation in one hand and an absolution in the other, and Gipsy has sold herself to the devil; I saw the price paid down, my eyes shall take their oath on't.

ARCHER. And is all this bustle about Gipsy?

SCRUB. That's not all; I could hear but a word here and there; but I remember they mentioned a Count, a closet, a back-door, and a key.

ARCHER. The Count!—Did you hear nothing of Mrs. Sullen?

SCRUB. I did hear some word that sounded that way; but whether it was Sullen or Dorinda, I could not distinguish.

ARCHER. You have told this matter to nobody, brother?

SCRUB. Told! no, sir, I thank you for that; I'm resolved never to speak one word *pro* nor *con*, till we have a peace.

ARCHER. You're i' the right, brother Scrub. Here's a treaty afoot between the Count and the lady: the priest and the chambermaid are the plenipotentiaries. It shall go hard but I find a way to be included in the treaty.—Where's the doctor now?

SCRUB. He and Gipsy are this moment devouring my lady's marmalade in the closet.

AIMWELL [*from without*]. Martin! Martin!

ARCHER. I come, sir, I come.

SCRUB. But you forget the other guinea, brother Martin.

ARCHER. Here, I give it with all my heart.

SCRUB. And I take it with all my soul.—[*Exit* ARCHER.] Ecod, I'll spoil your plotting, Mrs. Gipsy! and if you should set the captain upon me, these two guineas will buy me off. [*Exit.*]

[*Reënter* MRS. SULLEN *and* DORINDA, *meeting.*]

MRS. SULLEN. Well, sister!

DORINDA. And well, sister!

MRS. SULLEN. What's become of my lord?

DORINDA. What's become of his servant?

MRS. SULLEN. Servant! he's a prettier fellow, and a finer gentleman by fifty degrees, than his master.

DORINDA. O' my conscience, I fancy you could beg that fellow at the gallows-foot!

MRS. SULLEN. O' my conscience I could, provided I could put a friend of yours in his room.

DORINDA. You desired me, sister, to leave you, when you transgressed the bounds of honour.

MRS. SULLEN. Thou dear censorious country girl! what dost mean? You can't think of the man without the bedfellow, I find.

DORINDA. I don't find anything unnatural in that thought: while the mind is conversant with flesh and blood, it must conform to the humours of the company.

MRS. SULLEN. How a little love and good company improves a woman! Why, child, you begin to live—you never spoke before.

DORINDA. Because I was never spoke to.—My lord has told me that I have more wit and beauty than any of my sex; and truly I begin to think the man is sincere.

MRS. SULLEN. You're in the right, Dorinda; pride is the life of a woman, and flattery is our daily bread; and she's a fool that won't believe a man there, as much as she that believes him in anything else. But I'll lay you a guinea that I had finer things said to me than you had.

DORINDA. Done! What did your fellow say to ye?

MRS. SULLEN. My fellow took the picture of Venus for mine.

DORINDA. But my lover took me for Venus herself.

MRS. SULLEN. Common cant! Had my spark called me a Venus directly, I should have believed him a footman in good earnest.

DORINDA. But my lover was upon his knees to me.

MRS. SULLEN. And mine was upon his tiptoes to me.

DORINDA. Mine vowed to die for me.

MRS. SULLEN. Mine swore to die with me.

DORINDA. Mine spoke the softest moving things.

MRS. SULLEN. Mine had his moving things too.

DORINDA. Mine kissed my hand ten thousand times.

MRS. SULLEN. Mine has all that pleasure to come.

DORINDA. Mine offered marriage.

MRS. SULLEN. O Lard! d'ye call that a moving thing?

DORINDA. The sharpest arrow in his quiver, my dear sister! Why, my ten thousand pounds may lie brooding here this seven years, and hatch nothing at last but some ill-natured clown like yours. Whereas, if I marry my Lord Aimwell, there will be title, place, and precedence, the Park, the play, and the drawing-room, splendour, equipage, noise, and flam-beaux.—*Hey, my Lady Aimwell's servants there!—Lights, lights to the stairs!—My*

*Lady Aimwell's coach put forward!—Stand by, make room for her ladyship!—*Are not these things moving?—What! melancholy of a sudden?

MRS. SULLEN. Happy, happy sister! your angel has been watchful for your happiness, whilst mine has slept regardless of his charge. Long smiling years of circling joys for you, but not one hour for me! [*Weeps.*]

DORINDA. Come, my dear, we'll talk of something else.

MRS. SULLEN. O Dorinda! I own myself a woman, full of my sex, a gentle, generous soul, easy and yielding to soft desires; a spacious heart, where love and all his train might lodge. And must the fair apartment of my breast be made a stable for a brute to lie in?

DORINDA. Meaning your husband, I suppose?

MRS. SULLEN. Husband! no; even husband is too soft a name for him.—But, come, I expect my brother here to-night or to-morrow; he was abroad when my father married me; perhaps he'll find a way to make me easy.

DORINDA. Will you promise not to make yourself easy in the meantime with my lord's friend?

MRS. SULLEN. You mistake me, sister. It happens with us as among the men, the greatest talkers are the greatest cowards? and there's a reason for it; those spirits evaporate in prattle, which might do more mischief if they took another course.—Though, to confess the truth, I do love that fellow;—and if I met him dressed as he should be, and I undressed as I should be—look'ee, sister, I have no supernatural gifts—I can't swear I could resist the temptation; though I can safely promise to avoid it; and that's as much as the best of us can do. [*Exeunt.*]

SCENE II—*A room in* BONIFACE'S *inn.*

[*Enter* AIMWELL *and* ARCHER *laughing.*]

ARCHER. And the awkward kindness of the good motherly old gentlewoman——

AIMWELL. And the coming easiness of the young one—'Sdeath, 'tis pity to deceive her!

ARCHER. Nay, if you adhere to these principles, stop where you are.

AIMWELL. I can't stop; for I love her to distraction.

ARCHER. 'Sdeath, if you love her a hair's-breadth beyond discretion, you must go no further.

AIMWELL. Well, well, anything to deliver us from sauntering away our idle evenings at White's, Tom's, or Will's, and be stinted to bare looking at our old acquaintance, the cards; because our impotent pockets can't afford us a guinea for the mercenary drabs.

ARCHER. Or be obliged to some purse-proud coxcomb for a scandalous bottle, where we must not pretend to our share of the discourse, because we can't pay our club o' th' reckoning.—Damn it, I had rather sponge upon Morris, and sup upon a dish of bohea scored behind the door!

AIMWELL. And there expose our want of sense by talking criticisms, as we should our want of money by railing at the government.

ARCHER. Or be obliged to sneak into the side-box, and between both houses steal two acts of a play, and because we han't money to see the other three, we come away discontented, and damn the whole five.

AIMWELL. And ten thousand such rascally tricks—had we outlived our fortunes among our acquaintance.—But now——

ARCHER. Ay, now is the time to prevent all this:—strike while the iron is hot.—This priest is the luckiest part of our adventure; he shall marry you, and pimp for me.

AIMWELL. But I should not like a woman that can be so fond of a Frenchman.

ARCHER. Alas, sir! Necessity has no law. The lady may be in distress; perhaps she has a confounded husband, and her revenge may carry her farther than her love. Egad, I have so good an opinion of her, and of myself, that I begin to fancy strange things: and we must say this for the honour of our women, and indeed of ourselves, that they do stick to their men as they do to their *Magna Charta*. If the plot lies as I suspect, I must put on the gentleman.—But here comes the doctor—I shall be ready. [*Exit.*]

[*Enter* FOIGARD.]

FOIGARD. Sauve you, noble friend.

AIMWELL. O sir, your servant! Pray, doctor, may I crave your name?

FOIGARD. Fat naam is upon me? My naam is Foigard, joy.

AIMWELL. Foigard! a very good name for a clergyman. Pray, Doctor Foigard, were you ever in Ireland?

FOIGARD. Ireland! no, joy. Fat sort of plaace is dat saam Ireland? Dey say de people are catched dere when dey are young.

AIMWELL. And some of 'em when they are old:—as for example.—[*Takes* FOIGARD *by the shoulder.*] Sir, I arrest you as a traitor against the government; you're a subject of England, and this morning showed me a commission, by which you served as chaplain in the French army. This is death by our law, and your reverence must hang for it.

FOIGARD. Upon my shoul, noble friend, dis is strange news you tell me! Fader Foigard a subject of England! de son of a burgomaster of Brussels, a subject of England! ubooboo——

AIMWELL. The son of a bog-trotter in Ireland! Sir, your tongue will condemn you before any bench in the kingdom.

FOIGARD. And is my tongue all your evidensh, joy?

AIMWELL. That's enough.

FOIGARD. No, no, joy, for I vill never spake English no more.

AIMWELL. Sir, I have other evidence.—Here, Martin!

[*Reënter* ARCHER.]

You know this fellow?

ARCHER [*in a brogue*]. Saave you, my dear cussen, how does your health?

FOIGARD [*aside*]. Ah! upon my shoul dere is my countryman, and his brogue will hang mine.—[*To* ARCHER.] Mynheer, *Ick wet neat watt hey zacht, Ick universton ewe neat, sacramant!*

AIMWELL. Altering your language won't do, sir; this fellow knows your person, and will swear to your face.

FOIGARD. Faash! fey, is dere a brogue upon my faash too?

ARCHER. Upon my soulvation dere ish, joy!—But cussen Mackshane, vil you not put a remembrance upon me?

FOIGARD. Mackshane! by St. Paatrick, dat ish my naam shure enough! [*Aside.*]

AIMWELL. I fancy, Archer, you have it. [*Aside to* ARCHER.]

FOIGARD. The devil hang you, joy! by fat acquaintance are you my cussen?

ARCHER. Oh, de devil hang yourshelf, joy! you know we were little boys togeder upon de school, and your fostermoder's son was married upon my nurse's chister, joy, and so we are Irish cussens.

FOIGARD. De devil taake de relation! vel, joy, and fat school was it?

ARCHER. I tinks it vas—aay—'twas Tipperary.

FOIGARD. No, no, joy; it vas Kilkenny.

AIMWELL. That's enough for us—self-confession,—come, sir, we must deliver you into the hands of the next magistrate.

ARCHER. He sends you to jail, you're tried next assizes, and away you go swing into purgatory.

FOIGARD. And is it so wid you, cussen?

ARCHER. It vil be sho wid you, cussen, if you don't immediately confess the secret between you and Mrs. Gipsy. Look'ee, sir, the gallows or the secret, take your choice.

FOIGARD. The gallows! upon my shoul I hate that saam gallow, for it is a diseash dat is fatal to our family. Vel, den, dere is nothing, shentlemens, but Mrs. Shullen would spaak wid the Count in her chamber at midnight, and dere is no haarm, joy, for I am to conduct the Count to the plash, myshelf.

ARCHER. As I guessed.—Have you communicated the matter to the Count?

FOIGARD. I have not sheen him since.

ARCHER. Right again! Why then, doctor—you shall conduct me to the lady instead of the Count.

FOIGARD. Fat, my cussen to the lady! upon my shoul, gra, dat is too much upon the brogue.

ARCHER. Come, come, doctor; consider we have got a rope about your neck, and if you offer to squeak, we'll stop your windpipe, most certainly: we shall have another job for you in a day or two, I hope.

AIMWELL. Here's company coming this way; let's into my chamber and there concert our affairs farther.

ARCHER. Come, my dear cussen, come along. [*Exeunt.*]

[*Enter* BONIFACE, HOUNSLOW, *and* BAGSHOT *at one door,* GIBBET *at the opposite.*]

GIBBET. Well, gentlemen, 'tis a fine night for our enterprise.

HOUNSLOW. Dark as hell.

BAGSHOT. And blows like the devil; our landlord here has showed us the window where we must break in, and tells us the plate stands in the wainscot cupboard in the parlour.

BONIFACE. Ay, ay, Mr. Bagshot, as the saying is, knives and forks, and cups and cans, and tumblers and tankards. There's one tankard, as the saying is, that's near upon as big as me; it was a present to the squire from his godmother, and smells of nutmeg and toast like an East-India ship.

HOUNSLOW. Then you say we must divide at the stairhead?

BONIFACE. Yes, Mr. Hounslow, as the saying is. At one end of that gallery lies my Lady Bountiful and her daughter, and at the other Mrs. Sullen. As for the squire——

GIBBET. He's safe enough, I have fairly entered him, and he's more than half seas over already. But such a parcel of scoundrels are got about him now, that, egad, I was ashamed to be seen in their company.

BONIFACE. 'Tis now twelve, as the

saying is—gentlemen, you must set out at one.

GIBBET. Hounslow, do you and Bagshot see our arms fixed, and I'll come to you presently.

HOUNSLOW. We will.

BAGSHOT. We will. [*Exeunt.*]

GIBBET. Well, my dear Bonny, you assure me that Scrub is a coward?

BONIFACE. A chicken, as the saying is. You'll have no creature to deal with but the ladies.

GIBBET. And I can assure you, friend, there's a great deal of address and good manners in robbing a lady; I am the most a gentleman that way that ever travelled the road.—But, my dear Bonny, this prize will be a galleon, a Vigo business.—I warrant you we shall bring off three or four thousand pounds.

BONIFACE. In plate, jewels, and money, as the saying is, you may.

GIBBET. Why then, Tyburn, I defy thee! I'll get up to town, sell off my horse and arms, buy myself some pretty employment in the household, and be as snug and as honest as any courtier of 'em all.

BONIFACE. And what think you then of my daughter Cherry for a wife?

GIBBET. Look'ee, my dear Bonny—Cherry *is the Goddess I adore*, as the song goes; but it is a maxim, that man and wife should never have it in their power to hang one another; for if they should, the Lord have mercy on 'em both!

[*Exeunt.*]

ACT V

SCENE I—*A room in* BONIFACE'S *inn.*

[*Knocking without, enter* BONIFACE.]

BONIFACE. Coming! Coming!—A coach and six foaming horses at this time o' night! some great man, as the saying is, for he scorns to travel with other people.

[*Enter* SIR CHARLES FREEMAN.]

SIR CHARLES. What, fellow! a public house, and abed when other people sleep?

BONIFACE. Sir, I an't abed, as the saying is.

SIR CHARLES. Is Mr. Sullen's family abed, think'ee?

BONIFACE. All but the squire himself, sir, as the saying is; he's in the house.

SIR CHARLES. What company has he?

BONIFACE. Why, sir, there's the constable, Mr. Gage the exciseman, the hunch-backed barber, and two or three other gentlemen.

SIR CHARLES. I find my sister's letters gave me the true picture of her spouse.

[*Aside.*]

[*Enter* SQUIRE SULLEN, *drunk.*]

BONIFACE. Sir, here's' the squire.

SQUIRE SULLEN. The puppies left me asleep—Sir!

SIR CHARLES. Well, sir.

SQUIRE SULLEN. Sir, I am an unfortunate man—I have three thousand pounds a year, and I can't get a man to drink a cup of ale with me.

SIR CHARLES. That's very hard.

SQUIRE SULLEN. Ay, sir; and unless you have pity upon me, and smoke one pipe with me, I must e'en go home to my wife, and I had rather go to the devil by half.

SIR CHARLES. But I presume, sir, you won't see your wife to-night; she'll be gone to bed. You don't use to lie with your wife in that pickle?

SQUIRE SULLEN. What! not lie with my wife! why, sir, do you take me for an atheist or a rake?

SIR CHARLES. If you hate her, sir, I think you had better lie from her.

SQUIRE SULLEN. I think so too, friend. But I'm a justice of peace, and must do nothing against the law.

SIR CHARLES. Law! as I take it, Mr. Justice, nobody observes law for law's sake, only for the good of those for whom it was made.

SQUIRE SULLEN. But, if the law orders me to send you to jail, you must lie there, my friend.

SIR CHARLES. Not unless I commit a crime to deserve it.

SQUIRE SULLEN. A crime? 'oons, an't I married?

SIR CHARLES. Nay, sir, if you call a marriage a crime, you must disown it for a law.

SQUIRE SULLEN. Eh! I must be acquainted with you, sir.—But, sir, I should be very glad to know the truth of this matter.

SIR CHARLES. Truth, sir, is a profound sea, and few there be that dare wade deep enough to find out the bottom on't. Besides, sir, I'm afraid the line of your understanding mayn't be long enough.

SQUIRE SULLEN. Look'ee, sir, I have nothing to say to your sea of truth, but, if a good parcel of land can entitle a man to a little truth, I have as much as any He in the country.

BONIFACE. I never heard your worship, as the saying is, talk so much before.

SQUIRE SULLEN. Because I never met with a man that I liked before.

BONIFACE. Pray, sir, as the saying is, let me ask you one question: are not man and wife one flesh?

SIR CHARLES. You and your wife, Mr. Guts, may be one flesh, because ye are nothing else; but rational creatures have minds that must be united.

SQUIRE SULLEN. Minds!

SIR CHARLES. Ay, minds, sir; don't you think that the mind takes place of the body?

SQUIRE SULLEN. In some people.

SIR CHARLES. Then the interest of the master must be consulted before that of his servant.

SQUIRE SULLEN. Sir, you shall dine with me to-morrow!—'Oons, I always thought that we were naturally one.

SIR CHARLES. Sir, I know that my two hands are naturally one, because they love one another, kiss one another, help one another in all the actions of life; but I could not say so much if they were always at cuffs.

SQUIRE SULLEN. Then 'tis plain that we are two.

SIR CHARLES. Why don't you part with her, sir?

SQUIRE SULLEN. Will you take her, sir?

SIR CHARLES. With all my heart.

SQUIRE SULLEN. You shall have her to-morrow morning, and a venison-pasty into the bargain.

SIR CHARLES. You'll let me have her fortune too?

SQUIRE SULLEN. Fortune! why, sir, I have no quarrel at her fortune: I only hate the woman, sir, and none but the woman shall go.

SIR CHARLES. But her fortune, sir——

SQUIRE SULLEN. Can you play at whisk, sir?

SIR CHARLES. No, truly, sir.

SQUIRE SULLEN. Nor at all-fours?

SIR CHARLES. Neither.

SQUIRE SULLEN [aside]. 'Oons! where was this man bred?—[Aloud.] Burn me, sir! I can't go home, 'tis but two o'clock.

SIR CHARLES. For half an hour, sir, if you please; but you must consider 'tis late.

SQUIRE SULLEN. Late! that's the reason I can't go to bed.—Come, sir!

[Exeunt.]

[Enter CHERRY, runs across the stage, and knocks at AIMWELL's chamber door. Enter AIMWELL in his nightcap and gown.]

AIMWELL. What's the matter? you tremble, child; you're frighted.

CHERRY. No wonder, sir—But, in short, sir, this very minute a gang of rogues are gone to rob my Lady Bountiful's house.

AIMWELL. How!

CHERRY. I dogged 'em to the very door, and left 'em breaking in.

AIMWELL. Have you alarmed anybody else with the news?

CHERRY. No, no, sir, I wanted to have discovered the whole plot, and twenty other things, to your man Martin; but I have searched the whole house, and can't find him: where is he?

AIMWELL. No matter, child; will you guide me immediately to the house?

CHERRY. With all my heart, sir; my Lady Bountiful is my godmother, and I love Mrs. Dorinda so well——

AIMWELL. Dorinda! the name inspires me, the glory and the danger shall be all my own.—Come, my life, let me but get my sword. [*Exeunt.*]

SCENE II—*A bedchamber in* LADY BOUNTIFUL'S *house.*

[MRS. SULLEN *and* DORINDA *discovered undressed; a table and lights.*]

DORINDA. 'Tis very late, sister, no news of your spouse yet?

MRS. SULLEN. No, I'm condemned to be alone till towards four, and then perhaps I may be executed with his company.

DORINDA. Well, my dear, I'll leave you to your rest; you'll go directly to bed, I suppose?

MRS. SULLEN. I don't know what to do. —Heigh-ho!

DORINDA. That's a desiring sigh, sister.

MRS. SULLEN. This is a languishing hour, sister.

DORINDA. And might prove a critical minute if the pretty fellow were here.

MRS. SULLEN. Here! what, in my bedchamber at two o'clock o' th' morning, I undressed, the family asleep, my hated husband abroad, and my lovely fellow at my feet!—O 'gad, sister!

DORINDA. Thoughts are free, sister, and them I allow you.—So, my dear, good night.

MRS. SULLEN. A good rest to my dear Dorinda!—[*Exit* DORINDA.] Thoughts free! are they so? Why, then suppose him here, dressed like a youthful, gay, and burning bridegroom, [*Here* ARCHER *steals out of a closet behind.*] with tongue enchanting, eyes bewitching, knees imploring.—[*Turns a little on one side and sees* ARCHER *in the posture she describes.*]— Ah!—[*Shrieks, and runs to the other side of the stage.*] Have my thoughts raised a spirit?—What are you, sir, a man or a devil?

ARCHER. A man, a man, madam. [*Rising.*]

MRS. SULLEN. How shall I be sure of it?

ARCHER. Madam, I'll give you demonstration this minute. [*Takes her hand.*]

MRS. SULLEN. What, sir! do you intend to be rude?

ARCHER. Yes, madam, if you please.

MRS. SULLEN. In the name of wonder, whence came ye?

ARCHER. From the skies, madam—I'm a Jupiter in love, and you shall be my Alcmena.

MRS. SULLEN. How came you in?

ARCHER. I flew in at the window, madam; your cousin Cupid lent me his wings, and your sister Venus opened the casement.

MRS. SULLEN. I'm struck dumb with wonder!

ARCHER. And I—with admiration! [*Looks passionately at her.*]

MRS. SULLEN. What will become of me?

ARCHER. How beautiful she looks!— The teeming jolly Spring smiles in her blooming face, and, when she was conceived, her mother smelt to roses, looked on lilies—

Lilies unfold their white, their fragrant charms,
When the warm sun thus darts into their arms. [*Runs to her.*]

MRS. SULLEN. Ah! [*Shrieks.*]

ARCHER. 'Oons, madam, what d'ye mean? you'll raise the house.

MRS. SULLEN. Sir, I'll wake the dead before I bear this!—What! approach me with the freedom of a keeper! I'm glad on't, your impudence has cured me.

ARCHER. If this be impudence— [*Kneels.*] I leave to your partial self; no panting pilgrim, after a tedious, painful voyage, e'er bowed before his saint with more devotion.

MRS. SULLEN [*aside*]. Now, now, I'm ruined if he kneels!—[*Aloud.*] Rise, thou prostrate engineer, not all thy undermining skill shall reach my heart.—Rise, and know I am a woman without my sex; I can love to all the tenderness of wishes, sighs, and tears—but go no farther.—Still, to convince you that I'm more than woman, I can speak my frailty, confess my weakness even for you, but——

ARCHER. For me!
[*Going to lay hold on her.*]
MRS. SULLEN. Hold, sir! build not upon that; for my most mortal hatred follows if you disobey what I command you now.—Leave me this minute.— [*Aside.*] If he denies I'm lost.
ARCHER. Then you'll promise——
MRS. SULLEN. Anything another time.
ARCHER. When shall I come?
MRS. SULLEN. To-morrow—when you will.
ARCHER. Your lips must seal the promise.
MRS. SULLEN. Psha!
ARCHER. They must! they must!— [*Kisses her.*] Raptures and paradise!— And why not now, my angel? the time, the place, silence, and secrecy, all conspire. And the now conscious stars have preordained this moment for my happiness.   [*Takes her in his arms.*]
MRS. SULLEN. You will not! cannot, sure!
ARCHER. If the sun rides fast, and disappoints not mortals of to-morrow's dawn, this night shall crown my joys.
MRS. SULLEN. My sex's pride assist me!
ARCHER. My sex's strength help me!
MRS. SULLEN. You shall kill me first!
ARCHER. I'll die with you.
[*Carrying her off.*]
MRS. SULLEN. Thieves! thieves! murder!

[*Enter* SCRUB *in his breeches, and one shoe.*]
SCRUB. Thieves! thieves! murder! popery!
ARCHER. Ha! the very timorous stag will kill in rutting time.
[*Draws, and offers to stab* SCRUB.]
SCRUB [*kneeling*]. O pray, sir, spare all I have, and take my life!
MRS. SULLEN [*holding* ARCHER'S *hand*]. What does the fellow mean?
SCRUB. O madam, down upon your knees, your marrow-bones!—he's one of 'em.
ARCHER. Of whom?

SCRUB. One of the rogues—I beg your pardon, one of the honest gentlemen that just now are broke into the house.
ARCHER. How!
MRS. SULLEN. I hope you did not come to rob me?
ARCHER. Indeed I did, madam, but I would have taken nothing but what you might ha' spared; but your crying "Thieves" has waked this dreaming fool, and so he takes 'em for granted.
SCRUB. Granted! 'tis granted, sir; take all we have.
MRS. SULLEN. The fellow looks as if he were broke out of Bedlam.
SCRUB. 'Oons, madam, they're broke into the house with fire and sword! I saw them, heard them; they'll be here this minute.
ARCHER. What, thieves!
SCRUB. Under favour, sir, I think so.
MRS. SULLEN. What shall we do, sir?
ARCHER. Madam, I wish your ladyship a good night.
MRS. SULLEN. Will you leave me?
ARCHER. Leave you! Lord, madam, did not you command me to be gone just now, upon pain of your immortal hatred?
MRS. SULLEN. Nay, but pray, sir——
[*Takes hold of him.*]
ARCHER. Ha! ha! ha! now comes my turn to be ravished.—You see now, madam, you must use men one way or other; but take this by the way, good madam, that none but a fool will give you the benefit of his courage, unless you'll take his love along with it.—How are they armed, friend?
SCRUB. With sword and pistol, sir.
ARCHER. Hush!—I see a dark lantern coming through the gallery.—Madam, be assured I will protect you, or lose my life.
MRS. SULLEN. Your life! no, sir, they can rob me of nothing that I value half so much; therefore now, sir, let me entreat you to be gone.
ARCHER. No, madam, I'll consult my own safety for the sake of yours; I'll work by stratagem. Have you courage enough to stand the appearance of 'em?

MRS. SULLEN. Yes, yes, since I have 'scaped your hands, I can face anything.

ARCHER. Come hither, brother Scrub! don't you know me?

SCRUB. Eh, my dear brother, let me kiss thee. [*Kisses* ARCHER.]

ARCHER. This way—here—

[ARCHER *and* SCRUB *hide behind the bed.*]

[*Enter* GIBBET, *with a dark lantern in one hand, and a pistol in the other.*]

GIBBET. Ay, ay, this is the chamber, and the lady alone.

MRS. SULLEN. Who are you, sir? what would you have? d'ye come to rob me?

GIBBET. Rob you! alack a day, madam, I'm only a younger brother, madam; and so, madam, if you make a noise, I'll shoot you through the head; but don't be afraid, madam.—[*Laying his lantern and pistol upon the table.*] These rings, madam; don't be concerned, madam, I have a profound respect for you, madam; your keys, madam; don't be frighted, madam, I'm the most of a gentleman.—[*Searching her pockets.*] This necklace, madam; I never was rude to any lady;—I have a veneration—for this necklace——

[*Here* ARCHER *having come round, and seized the pistol, takes* GIBBET *by the collar, trips up his heels, and claps the pistol to his breast.*]

ARCHER. Hold, profane villain, and take the reward of thy sacrilege!

GIBBET. Oh! pray, sir, don't kill me; I an't prepared.

ARCHER. How many is there of 'em, Scrub?

SCRUB. Five-and-forty, sir.

ARCHER. Then I must kill the villain, to have him out of the way.

GIBBET. Hold, hold, sir, we are but three, upon my honour.

ARCHER. Scrub, will you undertake to secure him?

SCRUB. Not I, sir; kill him, kill him!

ARCHER. Run to Gipsy's chamber, there you'll find the doctor; bring him hither presently.—[*Exit* SCRUB, *running.*] Come, rogue, if you have a short prayer, say it.

GIBBET. Sir, I have no prayer at all; the government has provided a chaplain to say prayers for us on these occasions.

MRS. SULLEN. Pray, sir, don't kill him: you fright me as much as him.

ARCHER. The dog shall die, madam, for being the occasion of my disappointment. —Sirrah, this moment is your last.

GIBBET. Sir, I'll give you two hundred pounds to spare my life.

ARCHER. Have you no more, rascal?

GIBBET. Yes, sir, I can command four hundred, but I must reserve two of 'em to save my life at the sessions.

[*Reënter* SCRUB *and* FOIGARD.]

ARCHER. Here, doctor, I suppose Scrub and you between you may manage him. Lay hold of him, doctor.

[FOIGARD *lays hold of* GIBBET.]

GIBBET. What! turned over to the priest already!—Look'ee, doctor, you come before your time; I an't condemned yet, I thank ye.

FOIGARD. Come, my dear joy, I vill secure your body and your shoul too; I vill make you a good Catholic, and give you an absolution.

GIBBET. Absolution! can you procure me a pardon, doctor?

FOIGARD. No, joy.

GIBBET. Then you and your absolution may go to the devil.

ARCHER. Convey him into the cellar, there bind him:—take the pistol, and if he offers to resist, shoot him through the head—and come back to us with all the speed you can.

SCRUB. Ay, ay, come, doctor, do you hold him fast, and I'll guard him.

[*Exit* FOIGARD *with* GIBBET, SCRUB *following.*]

MRS. SULLEN. But how came the doctor——

ARCHER. In short, madam—[*Shrieking without.*] 'Sdeath! the rogues are at work with the other ladies—I'm vexed I parted with the pistol; but I must fly to their assistance.—Will you stay here, madam, or venture yourself with me?

MRS. SULLEN [*taking him by the arm*]. Oh, with you, dear sir, with you.

[*Exeunt.*]

SCENE III—*Another bedchamber in the same.*

[*Enter* HOUNSLOW *and* BAGSHOT, *with swords drawn, haling in* LADY BOUNTIFUL *and* DORINDA.]

HOUNSLOW. Come, come, your jewels, mistress!

BAGSHOT. Your keys, your keys, old gentlewoman!

[*Enter* AIMWELL *and* CHERRY.]

AIMWELL. Turn this way, villains! I durst engage an army in such a cause.

[*He engages them both.*]

DORINDA. O madam, had I but a sword to help the brave man!

LADY BOUNTIFUL. There's three or four hanging up in the hall; but they won't draw. I'll go fetch one, however. [*Exit.*]

[*Enter* ARCHER *and* MRS. SULLEN.]

ARCHER. Hold, hold, my lord! every man his bird, pray.

[*They engage man to man;* HOUNSLOW *and* BAGSHOT *are thrown and disarmed.*]

CHERRY [*aside*]. What! the rogues taken! then they'll impeach my father: I must give him timely notice. [*Runs out.*]

ARCHER. Shall we kill the rogues?

AIMWELL. No, no, we'll bind them.

ARCHER. Ay, ay.—[*To* MRS. SULLEN, *who stands by him.*] Here, madam, lend me your garter.

MRS. SULLEN [*aside*]. The devil's in this fellow! he fights, loves, and banters, all in a breath.—[*Aloud.*] Here's a cord that the rogues brought with 'em, I suppose.

ARCHER. Right, right, the rogue's destiny, a rope to hang himself.—Come, my lord—this is but a scandalous sort of an office [*binding the highwaymen together*], if our adventures should end in this sort

of hangman-work; but I hope there is something in prospect, that——

[*Enter* SCRUB.]

ARCHER. Well, Scrub, have you secured your Tartar?

SCRUB. Yes, sir, I left the priest and him disputing about religion.

AIMWELL. And pray carry these gentlemen to read the benefit of the controversy.

[*Delivers the prisoners to* SCRUB, *who leads them out.*]

MRS. SULLEN. Pray, sister, how came my lord here?

DORINDA. And pray, how came the gentleman here?

MRS. SULLEN. I'll tell you the greatest piece of villainy——

[*They talk in dumb show.*]

AIMWELL. I fancy, Archer, you have been more successful in your adventures than the housebreakers.

ARCHER. No matter for my adventure, yours is the principal.—Press her this minute to marry you—now while she's hurried between the palpitation of her fear and the joy of her deliverance, now while the tide of her spirits is at high-flood—throw yourself at her feet, speak some romantic nonsense or other—address her, like Alexander in the height of his victory, confound her senses, bear down her reason, and away with her.—The priest is now in the cellar, and dare not refuse to do the work.

[*Reënter* LADY BOUNTIFUL.]

AIMWELL. But how shall I get off without being observed?

ARCHER. You a lover, and not find a way to get off!—Let me see——

AIMWELL. You bleed, Archer.

ARCHER. 'Sdeath, I'm glad on't; this wound will do the business. I'll amuse the old lady and Mrs. Sullen about dressing my wound, while you carry off Dorinda.

LADY BOUNTIFUL. Gentlemen, could we understand how you would be gratified for the services——

ARCHER. Come, come, my lady, this is no time for compliments; I'm wounded, madam.

LADY BOUNTIFUL, MRS. SULLEN. How! wounded!

DORINDA. I hope, sir, you have received no hurt?

AIMWELL. None but what you may cure—— [*Makes love in dumb show.*]

LADY BOUNTIFUL. Let me see your arm, sir—I must have some powder-sugar to stop the blood.—O me! an ugly gash; upon my word, sir, you must go into bed.

ARCHER. Ay, my lady, a bed would do very well.—[*To* MRS. SULLEN.] Madam, will you do me the favour to conduct me to a chamber.

LADY BOUNTIFUL. Do, do, daughter—while I get the lint and the probe and the plaster ready.

[*Runs out one way,* AIMWELL *carries off* DORINDA *another.*]

ARCHER. Come, madam, why don't you obey your mother's commands?

MRS. SULLEN. How can you, after what is passed, have the confidence to ask me?

ARCHER. And if you go to that, how can you, after what is passed, have the confidence to deny me? Was not this blood shed in your defence, and my life exposed for your protection. Look'ee, madam, I'm none of your romantic fools, that fight giants and monsters for nothing; my valour is downright Swiss; I'm a soldier of fortune, and must be paid.

MRS. SULLEN. 'Tis ungenerous in you, sir, to upbraid me with your services!

ARCHER. 'Tis ungenerous in you, madam, not to reward 'em.

MRS. SULLEN. How! at the expense of my honour?

ARCHER. Honour! can honour consist with ingratitude? If you would deal like a woman of honour, do like a man of honour. D'ye think I would deny you in such a case?

[*Enter a* SERVANT.]

SERVANT. Madam, my lady ordered me to tell you, that your brother is below at the gate. [*Exit.*]

MRS. SULLEN. My brother! Heavens be praised!—Sir, he shall thank you for your services; he has it in his power.

ARCHER. Who is your brother, madam?

MRS. SULLEN. Sir Charles Freeman.—You'll excuse me, sir; I must go and receive him. [*Exit.*]

ARCHER. Sir Charles Freeman! 'sdeath and hell! my old acquaintance. Now unless Aimwell has made good use of his time, all our fair machine goes souse into the sea like the Eddystone. [*Exit.*]

SCENE IV—*The gallery in the same house.*

[*Enter* AIMWELL *and* DORINDA.]

DORINDA. Well, well, my lord, you have conquered; your late generous action will, I hope, plead for my easy yielding; though I must own, your lordship had a friend in the fort before.

AIMWELL. The sweets of Hybla dwell upon her tongue!—Here, doctor——

[*Enter* FOIGARD, *with a book.*]

FOIGARD. Are you prepared boat?

DORINDA. I'm ready. But first, my lord, one word.—I have a frightful example of a hasty marriage in my own family; when I reflect upon't it shocks me. Pray, my lord, consider a little——

AIMWELL. Consider! do you doubt my honour or my love?

DORINDA. Neither: I do believe you equally just as brave: and were your whole sex drawn out for me to choose, I should not cast a look upon the multitude if you were absent. But, my lord, I'm a woman; colours, concealments may hide a thousand faults in me, therefore know me better first; I hardly dare affirm I know myself in anything except my love.

AIMWELL [*aside*]. Such goodness who could injure! I find myself unequal to the task of villain; she has gained my soul, and made it honest like her own.—I cannot, cannot hurt her.—[*Aloud.*] Doctor, retire.—[*Exit* FOIGARD.] Madam, behold your lover and your proselyte, and

judge of my passion by my conversion!—
I'm all a lie, nor dare I give a fiction to
your arms; I'm all counterfeit, except my
passion.

DORINDA.   Forbid it, Heaven! a coun-
terfeit!

AIMWELL.   I am no lord, but a poor
needy man, come with a mean, a scandal-
ous design to prey upon your fortune; but
the beauties of your mind and person
have so won me from myself that, like a
trusty servant, I prefer the interest of
my mistress to my own.

DORINDA.   Sure I have had the dream
of some poor mariner, a sleepy image of
a welcome port, and wake involved in
storms!—Pray, sir, who are you?

AIMWELL.   Brother to the man whose
title I usurped, but stranger to his hon-
our or his fortune.

DORINDA.   Matchless honesty!—Once I
was proud, sir, of your wealth and title,
but now am prouder that you want it:
now I can show my love was justly lev-
elled, and had no aim but love.—Doctor,
come in.

[*Enter* FOIGARD *at one door*, GIPSY *at
another, who whispers* DORINDA.]
[*To* FOIGARD.] Your pardon, sir, we shan't
want you now.—[*To* AIMWELL.] Sir, you
must excuse me—I'll wait on you pres-
ently.   [*Exit with* GIPSY.]

FOIGARD.   Upon my shoul, now, dis is
foolish.   [*Exit.*]

AIMWELL.   Gone! and bid the priest de-
part!—It has an ominous look.

[*Enter* ARCHER.]

ARCHER.   Courage, Tom!—Shall I wish
you joy?

AIMWELL.   No.

ARCHER.   'Oons, man, what ha' you been
doing?

AIMWELL.   O Archer! my honesty, I
fear, has ruined me.

ARCHER.   How?

AIMWELL.   I have discovered myself.

ARCHER.   Discovered! and without my
consent?   What! have I embarked my
small remains in the same bottom with

yours, and you dispose of all without my
partnership?

AIMWELL.   O Archer! I own my fault.

ARCHER.   After conviction—'tis then too
late for pardon.—You may remember, Mr.
Aimwell, that you proposed this folly: as
you begun, so end it.   Henceforth I'll hunt
my fortune single—so farewell!

AIMWELL.   Stay, my dear Archer, but
a minute.

ARCHER.   Stay! what, to be despised,
exposed, and laughed at!   No, I would
sooner change conditions with the worst
of the rogues we just now bound, than
bear one scornful smile from the proud
knight that once I treated as my equal.

AIMWELL.   What knight?

ARCHER.   Sir Charles Freeman, brother
to the lady that I had almost—but no
matter for that, 'tis a cursed night's work,
and so I leave you to make the best on't.
                                   [*Going.*]

AIMWELL.   Freeman! — One   word,
Archer.   Still I have hopes; methought
she received my confession with pleas-
ure.

ARCHER.   'Sdeath, who doubts it?

AIMWELL.   She consented after to the
match; and still I dare believe she will
be just.

ARCHER.   To herself, I warrant her, as
you should have been.

AIMWELL.   By all my hopes she comes,
and smiling comes!

[*Reënter* DORINDA, *mighty gay.*]

DORINDA.   Come, my dear lord—I fly
with impatience to your arms—the min-
utes of my absence were a tedious year.
Where's this priest?

[*Reënter* FOIGARD.]

ARCHER.   'Oons, a brave girl!

DORINDA.   I suppose, my lord, this gen-
tleman is privy to our affairs?

ARCHER.   Yes, yes, madam, I'm to be
your father.

DORINDA.   Come, priest, do your office.

ARCHER.   Make haste, make haste,
couple 'em any way.—[*Takes* AIMWELL'*s
hand.*] Come, madam, I'm to give you——

DORINDA. My mind's altered; I won't.

ARCHER. Eh!

AIMWELL. I'm confounded!

FOIGARD. Upon my shoul, and sho is myshelf.

ARCHER. What's the matter now, madam?

DORINDA. Look'ee, sir, one generous action deserves another.—This gentleman's honour obliged him to hide nothing from me; my justice engages me to conceal nothing from him. In short, sir, you are the person that you thought you counterfeited; you are the true Lord Viscount Aimwell, and I wish your Lordship joy.—Now, priest, you may be gone; if my Lord is pleased now with the match, let his Lordship marry me in the face of the world.

AIMWELL, ARCHER. What does she mean?

DORINDA. Here's a witness for my truth.

[*Enter* SIR CHARLES FREEMAN *and* MRS. SULLEN.]

SIR CHARLES. My dear Lord Aimwell, I wish you joy.

AIMWELL. Of what?

SIR CHARLES. Of your honour and estate. Your brother died the day before I left London; and all your friends have writ after you to Brussels;—among the rest I did myself the honour.

ARCHER. Hark'ee, sir knight, don't you banter now?

SIR CHARLES. 'Tis truth, upon my honour.

AIMWELL. Thanks to the pregnant stars that formed this accident.

ARCHER. Thanks to the womb of time that brought it forth!—away with it!

AIMWELL. Thanks to my guardian angel that led me to the prize!

[*Taking* DORINDA'S *hand*.]

ARCHER. And double thanks to the noble Sir Charles Freeman.—My Lord, I wish you joy.—My Lady, I wish you joy. —Egad, Sir Freeman, you're the honestest fellow living!—'Sdeath, I'm grown strange airy upon this matter!—My Lord, how

d'ye?—A word, my Lord; don't you remember something of a previous agreement, that entitles me to the moiety of this lady's fortune, which I think will amount to five thousand pounds?

AIMWELL. Not a penny, Archer; you would ha' cut my throat just now, because I would not deceive this lady.

ARCHER. Ay, and I'll cut your throat again, if you should deceive her now.

AIMWELL. That's what I expected; and to end the dispute, the lady's fortune is ten thousand pounds, we'll divide stakes: take the ten thousand pounds or the lady.

DORINDA. How! is your Lordship so indifferent?

ARCHER. No, no, no, madam! his Lordship knows very well that I'll take the money; I leave you to his Lordship, and so we're both provided for.

[*Enter* COUNT BELLAIR.]

COUNT BELLAIR. *Mesdames et Messieurs*, I am your servant trice humble! I hear you be rob here.

AIMWELL. The ladies have been in some danger, sir.

COUNT BELLAIR. And, begar, our inn be rob too!

AIMWELL. Our inn! by whom?

COUNT BELLAIR. By the landlord, begar!—Garzoon, he has rob himself, and run away!

ARCHER. Robbed himself!

COUNT BELLAIR. Ay, begar, and me too of a hundre pound.

ARCHER. A hundred pounds?

COUNT BELLAIR. Yes, that I owed him.

AIMWELL. Our money's gone, Frank.

ARCHER. Rot the money! my wench is gone.—[*To* COUNT BELLAIR.] *Savez-vous quelquechose de Mademoiselle Cherry?*

[*Enter a* COUNTRYMAN *with a strong-box and a letter*.]

COUNTRYMAN. Is there one Martin here?

ARCHER. Ay, ay—who wants him?

COUNTRYMAN. I have a box here, and letter for him.

ARCHER [*taking the box*]. Ha! ha! ha!

what's here? Legerdemain!—By this light, my lord, our money again!—But this unfolds the riddle.—[*Opening the letter.*] Hum, hum, hum!—Oh, 'tis for th‐ public good, and must be communicated to the company.   [*Reads.*]

"Mr. Martin.—My father being afraid of an impeachment by the rogues that are taken to-night, is gone off; but if you can procure him a pardon, he'll make great discoveries that may be useful to the country. Could I have met you instead of your master to-night, I would have delivered myself into your hands, with a sum that much exceeds that in your strong-box, which I have sent you, with an assurance to my dear Martin that I shall ever be his most faithful friend till death.—Cherry Boniface."

There's a *billet-doux* for you! As for the father, I think he ought to be encouraged; and for the daughter—pray, my Lord, persuade your bride to take her into her service instead of Gipsy.

Aimwell. I can assure you, madam, your deliverance was owing to her discovery.

Dorinda. Your command, my Lord, will do without the obligation. I'll take care of her.

Sir Charles. This good company meets opportunely in favour of a design I have in behalf of my unfortunate sister. I intend to part her from her husband—gentlemen, will you assist me?

Archer. Assist you! 'sdeath, who would not?

Count Bellair. Assist! garzoon, we all assist!

[*Enter* Squire Sullen.]

Squire Sullen. What's all this? They tell me, spouse, that you had like to have been robbed.

Mrs. Sullen. Truly, spouse, I was pretty near it, had not these two gentlemen interposed.

Squire Sullen. How came these gentlemen here?

Mrs. Sullen. That's his way of returning thanks, you must know.

Count Bellair. Garzoon, the question be apropos for all dat.

Sir Charles. You promised last night, sir, that you would deliver your lady to me this morning.

Squire Sullen. Humph!

Archer. Humph! what do you mean by humph? Sir, you shall deliver her—in short, sir, we have saved you and your family; and if you are not civil, we'll unbind the rogues, join with 'em, and set fire to your house. What does the man mean? not part with his wife!

Count Bellair. Ay, garzoon, de man no understan common justice.

Mrs. Sullen. Hold, gentlemen, all things here must move by consent, compulsion would spoil us; let my dear and I talk the matter over, and you shall judge it between us.

Squire Sullen. Let me know first who are to be our judges. Pray, sir, who are you?

Sir Charles. I am Sir Charles Freeman, come to take away your wife.

Squire Sullen. And you, good sir?

Aimwell. Thomas, Viscount Aimwell, come to take away your sister.

Squire Sullen. And you, pray, sir?

Archer. Francis Archer, esquire, come——

Squire Sullen. To take away my mother, I hope. Gentlemen, you're heartily welcome; I never met with three more obliging people since I was born!—And now, my dear, if you please, you shall have the first word.

Archer. And the last, for five pounds!

Mrs. Sullen. Spouse!

Squire Sullen. Rib!

Mrs. Sullen. How long have we been married?

Squire Sullen. By the almanac, fourteen months; but by my account, fourteen years.

Mrs. Sullen. 'Tis thereabout by my reckoning.

Count Bellair. Garzoon,. their account will agree.

MRS. SULLEN. Pray, spouse, what did you marry for?

SQUIRE SULLEN. To get an heir to my estate.

SIR CHARLES. And have you succeeded?

SQUIRE SULLEN. No.

ARCHER. The condition fails of his side.—Pray, madam, what did you marry for?

MRS. SULLEN. To support the weakness of my sex by the strength of his, and to enjoy the pleasures of an agreeable society.

SIR CHARLES. Are your expectations answered?

MRS. SULLEN. No.

COUNT BELLAIR. A clear case! a clear case!

SIR CHARLES. What are the bars to your mutual contentment?

MRS. SULLEN. In the first place, I can't drink ale with him.

SQUIRE SULLEN. Nor can I drink tea with her.

MRS. SULLEN. I can't hunt with you.

SQUIRE SULLEN. Nor can I dance with you.

MRS. SULLEN. I hate cocking and racing.

SQUIRE SULLEN. And I abhor ombre and piquet.

MRS. SULLEN. Your silence is intolerable.

SQUIRE SULLEN. Your prating is worse.

MRS. SULLEN. Have we not been a perpetual offence to each other? a gnawing vulture at the heart?

SQUIRE SULLEN. A frightful goblin to the sight?

MRS. SULLEN. A porcupine to the feeling?

SQUIRE SULLEN. Perpetual wormwood to the taste?

MRS. SULLEN. Is there on earth a thing we could agree in.

SQUIRE SULLEN. Yes—to part.

MRS. SULLEN. With all my heart.

SQUIRE SULLEN. Your hand.

MRS. SULLEN. Here.

SQUIRE SULLEN. These hands joined us, these shall part us.—Away!

MRS. SULLEN. North.

SQUIRE SULLEN. South.

MRS. SULLEN. East.

SQUIRE SULLEN. West—far as the poles asunder.

COUNT BELLAIR. Begar, the ceremony be vera pretty!

SIR CHARLES. Now, Mr. Sullen, there wants only my sister's fortune to make us easy.

SQUIRE SULLEN. Sir Charles, you love your sister, and I love her fortune; every one to his fancy.

ARCHER. Then you won't refund?

SQUIRE SULLEN. Not a stiver.

ARCHER. Then I find, madam, you must e'en go to your prison again.

COUNT BELLAIR. What is the portion?

SIR CHARLES. Ten thousand pounds, sir.

COUNT BELLAIR. Garzoon, I'll pay it, and she shall go home wid me.

ARCHER. Ha! ha! ha! French all over.—Do you know, sir, what ten thousand pounds English is?

COUNT BELLAIR. No, begar, not justement.

ARCHER. Why, sir, 'tis a hundred thousand livres.

COUNT BELLAIR. A hundre tousand livres! Ah! garzoon, me canno' do't, your beauties and their fortunes are both too much for me.

ARCHER. Then I will.—This night's adventure has proved strangely lucky to us all—for Captain Gibbet in his walk had made bold, Mr. Sullen, with your study and escritoir, and had taken out all the writings of your estate, all the articles of marriage with this lady, bills, bonds, leases, receipts to an infinite value: I took 'em from him, and I deliver 'em to Sir Charles.

[*Gives* SIR CHARLES FREEMAN *a parcel of papers and parchments.*]

SQUIRE SULLEN. How, my writings!—my head aches consumedly.—Well, gentlemen, you shall have her fortune, but I can't talk. If you have a mind, Sir Charles, to be merry, and celebrate my sister's wedding and my divorce, you may command my house—but my head aches consumedly.—Scrub, bring me a dram.

ARCHER [to MRS. SULLEN]. Madam, there's a country dance to the trifle that I sung to-day; your hand, and we'll lead it up.

[*Here a dance.*]

'Twould be hard to guess which of these parties is the better pleased, the couple joined, or the couple parted; the one rejoicing in hopes of an untasted happiness, and the other in their deliverance from an experienced misery.

Both happy in their several states we find,
Those parted by consent, and those conjoined.
Consent, if mutual, saves the lawyer's fee.
Consent is law enough to set you free.

[*Exeunt omnes.*]

SHE STOOPS TO CONQUER

By OLIVER GOLDSMITH

Produced at London, 1773

CHARACTERS

MEN

SIR CHARLES MARLOW
YOUNG MARLOW *(his son)*
HARDCASTLE
HASTINGS
TONY LUMPKIN
DIGGORY

WOMEN

MRS. HARDCASTLE
MISS HARDCASTLE
MISS NEVILLE
MAID
LANDLORD, SERVANTS, *etc.*

PROLOGUE

BY DAVID GARRICK, ESQ.

[*Enter* MR. WOODWARD, *dressed in black and holding a handkerchief to his eyes.*]

PROLOGUE. Excuse me, sirs, I pray—I can't yet speak—
I'm crying now—and have been all the week.
" 'Tis not alone this mourning suit," good masters;
"I've that within," for which there are no plasters!
Pray, would you know the reason why I'm crying?
The Comic Muse, long sick, is now a-dying!
And if she goes, my tears will never stop;
For, as a player, I can't squeeze out one drop:
I am undone, that's all—shall lose my bread—
I'd rather, but that's nothing—lose my head.
When the sweet maid is laid upon the bier,
Shuter and I shall be chief mourners here.
To her a mawkish drab of spurious breed,

Who deals in sentimentals, will succeed!
Poor Ned and I are dead to all intents;
We can as soon speak Greek as senti-
    ments!
Both nervous grown, to keep our spirits
    up,
We now and then take down a hearty cup.
What shall we do? If Comedy forsake us,
They'll turn us out, and no one else will
    take us.
But why can't I be moral?—Let me try—
My heart thus pressing—fix'd my face
    and eye—
With a sententious look, that nothing
    means
(Faces are blocks in sentimental scenes),
Thus I begin: "All is not gold that
    glitters,
Pleasures seem sweet, but prove a glass
    of bitters.
When ign'rance enters, folly is at hand:
Learning is better far than house and
    land.
Let not your virtue trip; who trips may
    stumble,
And virtue is not virtue, if she tumble."
I give it up—morals won't do for me;
To make you laugh, I must play tragedy.
One hope remains—hearing the maid was
    ill,
A Doctor comes this night to show his
    skill;
To cheer her heart, and give your mus-
    cles motion,
He, in Five Draughts prepar'd, presents
    a potion:
A kind of magic charm—for, be assur'd,
If you will swallow it, the maid is cur'd:
But desperate the Doctor. and her case
    is.
If you reject the dose, and make wry
    faces!
This truth he boasts, will boast it while
    he lives,
No pois'nous drugs are mix'd in what he
    gives,
Should he succeed, you'll give him his
    degree;
If not, within he will receive no fee!
The College *you*, must his pretensions
    back,
Pronounce him Regular, or dub him
    Quack.

ACT I

SCENE I—*A chamber in an old-fashioned
    house.*

[*Enter* MRS. HARDCASTLE *and* MR. HARD-
    CASTLE.]

MRS. HARDCASTLE. I vow, Mr. Hard-
castle, you're very particular. Is there
a creature in the whole country but our-
selves, that does not take a trip to town
now and then, to rub off the rust a little?
There's the two Miss Hoggs, and our
neighbour Mrs. Grigsby, go to take a
month's polishing every winter.

HARDCASTLE. Ay, and bring back van-
ity and affectation to last them the whole
year. I wonder why London cannot keep
its own fools at home. In my time, the
follies of the town crept slowly among
us, but now they travel faster than a
stage coach. Its fopperies come down not
only as inside passengers, but in the very
basket.

MRS. HARDCASTLE. Ay, your times were
fine times indeed; you have been telling
us of them for many a long year. Here
we live in an old rumbling mansion, that
looks for all the world like an inn, but
that we never see company. Our best
visitors are old Mrs. Oddfish, the curate's
wife, and little Cripplegate, the lame
dancing master; and all our entertainment
your old stories of Prince Eugene and the
Duke of Marlborough. I hate such old-
fashioned trumpery.

HARDCASTLE. And I love it. I love
everything that's old: old friends, old
times, old manners, old books, old wine;
and, I believe, Dorothy [*Taking her
hand*], you'll own, I've been pretty fond
of an old wife.

MRS. HARDCASTLE. Lord, Mr. Hardcas-
tle, you're for ever at your Dorothys, and
your old wives. You may be a Darby,
but I'll be no Joan, I promise you. I'm
not so old as you'd make me, by more

than one good year. Add twenty to twenty, and make money of that.

HARDCASTLE. Let me see; twenty added to twenty—makes just fifty and seven.

MRS. HARDCASTLE. It's false, Mr. Hardcastle; I was but twenty when I was brought to bed of Tony, that I had by Mr. Lumpkin, my first husband; and he's not come to years of discretion yet.

HARDCASTLE. Nor ever will, I dare answer for him. Ay, you have taught him finely.

MRS. HARDCASTLE. No matter. Tony Lumpkin has a good fortune. My son is not to live by his learning. I don't think a boy wants much learning to spend fifteen hundred a year.

HARDCASTLE. Learning, quotha! a mere composition of tricks and mischief.

MRS. HARDCASTLE. Humour, my dear; nothing but humour. Come, Mr. Hardcastle, you must allow the boy a little humour.

HARDCASTLE. I'd sooner allow him a horsepond. If burning the footmen's shoes, frightening the maids, and worrying the kittens, be humour, he has it. It was but yesterday he fastened my wig to the back of my chair, and when I went to make a bow, I popt my bald head in Mrs. Frizzle's face.

MRS. HARDCASTLE. And am I to blame? The poor boy was always too sickly to do any good. A school would be his death. When he comes to be a little stronger, who knows what a year or two's Latin may do for him?

HARDCASTLE. Latin for him! A cat and fiddle. No, no; the alehouse and the stable are the only schools he'll ever go to.

MRS. HARDCASTLE. Well, we must not snub the poor boy now, for I believe we shan't have him long among us. Anybody that looks in his face may see he's consumptive.

HARDCASTLE. Ay, if growing too fat be one of the symptoms.

MRS. HARDCASTLE. He coughs sometimes.

HARDCASTLE. Yes, when his liquor goes the wrong way.

MRS. HARDCASTLE. I'm actually afraid of his lungs.

HARDCASTLE. And truly, so am I; for he sometimes whoops like a speaking trumpet—[TONY *hallooing behind the scenes.*]—Oh, there he goes—a very consumptive figure, truly!

[*Enter* TONY *crossing the stage.*]

MRS. HARDCASTLE. Tony, where are you going, my charmer? Won't you give papa and I a little of your company, lovee?

TONY. I'm in haste, mother; I cannot stay.

MRS. HARDCASTLE. You shan't venture out this raw evening, my dear; you look most shockingly.

TONY. I can't stay, I tell you. The Three Pigeons expects me down every moment. There's some fun going forward.

HARDCASTLE. Ay; the alehouse, the old place; I thought so.

MRS. HARDCASTLE. A low, paltry set of fellows.

TONY. Not so low, neither. There's Dick Muggins, the exciseman; Jack Slang, the horse-doctor; little Aminadab, that grinds the music-box; and Tom Twist, that spins the pewter platter.

MRS. HARDCASTLE. Pray, my dear, disappoint them for one night, at least.

TONY. As for disappointing them, I should not so much mind; but I can't abide to disappoint myself.

MRS. HARDCASTLE [*detaining him*]. You shan't go.

TONY. I will, I tell you.

MRS. HARDCASTLE. I say you shan't.

TONY. We'll see which is strongest, you or I. [*Exit, hauling her out.*]

HARDCASTLE [*alone*]. Ay, there goes a pair that only spoil each other. But is not the whole age in combination to drive sense and discretion out of doors? There's my pretty darling, Kate! the fashions of the times have almost infected her too. By living a year or two in town, she is as fond of gauze and French frippery as the best of them.

[*Enter* MISS HARDCASTLE.]

HARDCASTLE. Blessings on my pretty innocence! drest out as usual, my Kate. Goodness! What a quantity of superfluous silk hast thou got about thee, girl! I could never teach the fools of this age, that the indigent world could be clothed out of the trimmings of the vain.

MISS HARDCASTLE. You know our agreement, sir. You allow me the morning to receive and pay visits, and to dress in my own manner; and in the evening, I put on my housewife's dress, to please you.

HARDCASTLE. Well, remember, I insist on the terms of our agreement; and, by the bye, I believe I shall have occasion to try your obedience this very evening.

MISS HARDCASTLE. I protest, sir, I don't comprehend your meaning.

HARDCASTLE. Then, to be plain with you, Kate, I expect the young gentleman I have chosen to be your husband from town this very day. I have his father's letter, in which he informs me his son is set out, and that he intends to follow himself shortly after.

MISS HARDCASTLE. Indeed! I wish I had known something of this before. Bless me, how shall I behave? It's a thousand to one I shan't like him; our meeting will be so formal, and so like a thing of business, that I shall find no room for friendship or esteem.

HARDCASTLE. Depend upon it, child, I'll never control your choice; but Mr. Marlow, whom I have pitched upon, is the son of my old friend, Sir Charles Marlow, of whom you have heard me talk so often. The young gentleman has been bred a scholar, and is designed for an employment in the service of his country. I am told he's a man of an excellent understanding.

MISS HARDCASTLE. Is he?

HARDCASTLE. Very generous.

MISS HARDCASTLE. I believe I shall like him.

HARDCASTLE. Young and brave.

MISS HARDCASTLE. I'm sure I shall like him.

HARDCASTLE. And very handsome.

MISS HARDCASTLE. My dear papa, say no more [*kissing his hand*], he's mine— I'll have him.

HARDCASTLE. And, to crown all, Kate, he's one of the most bashful and reserved young fellows in all the world.

MISS HARDCASTLE. Eh! You have frozen me to death again. That word *reserved* has undone all the rest of his accomplishments. A reserved lover, it is said, always makes a suspicious husband.

HARDCASTLE. On the contrary, modesty seldom resides in a breast that is not enriched with nobler virtues. It was the very feature in his character that first struck me.

MISS HARDCASTLE. He must have more striking features to catch me, I promise you. However, if he be so young, so handsome, and so everything, as you mention, I believe he'll do still. I think I'll have him.

HARDCASTLE. Ay, Kate, but there is still an obstacle. It's more than an even wager he may not have you.

MISS HARDCASTLE. My dear papa, why will you mortify one so?—Well, if he refuses, instead of breaking my heart at his indifference, I'll only break my glass for its flattery, set my cap to some newer fashion, and look out for some less difficult admirer.

HARDCASTLE. Bravely resolved! In the mean time, I'll go prepare the servants for his reception: as we seldom see company, they want as much training as a company of recruits the first day's muster. [*Exit.*]

MISS HARDCASTLE [*alone*]. Lud, this news of papa's puts me all in a flutter. Young, handsome; these he put last; but I put them foremost. Sensible, good-natured; I like all that. But then, reserved and sheepish; that's much against him. Yet, can't he be cured of his timidity by being taught to be proud of his wife? Yes, and can't I—But I vow I'm disposing of the husband before I have secured the lover.

[*Enter* MISS NEVILLE.]

MISS HARDCASTLE. I'm glad you're come, Neville, my dear. Tell me, Constance, how do I look this evening? Is there anything whimsical about me? Is it one of my well-looking days, child? Am I in face to-day?

MISS NEVILLE. Perfectly, my dear. Yet now I look again—bless me!—surely no accident has happened among the canary birds or the gold fishes? Has your brother or the cat been meddling? Or has the last novel been too moving?

MISS HARDCASTLE. No; nothing of all this. I have been threatened—I can scarce get it out—I have been threatened with a lover.

MISS NEVILLE. And his name—

MISS HARDCASTLE. Is Marlow.

MISS NEVILLE. Indeed!

MISS HARDCASTLE. The son of Sir Charles Marlow.

MISS NEVILLE. As I live, the most intimate friend of Mr. Hastings, my admirer. They are never asunder. I believe you must have seen him when we lived in town.

MISS HARDCASTLE. Never.

MISS NEVILLE. He's a very singular character, I assure you. Among women of reputation and virtue, he is the modestest man alive; but his acquaintance gives him a very different character among creatures of another stamp: you understand me.

MISS HARDCASTLE. An odd character, indeed. I shall never be able to manage him. What shall I do? Pshaw, think no more of him, but trust to occurrences for success. But how goes on your own affair, my dear? Has my mother been courting you for my brother Tony, as usual?

MISS NEVILLE. I have just come from one of our agreeable *tête-à-têtes*. She has been saying a hundred tender things, and setting off her pretty monster as the very pink of perfection.

MISS HARDCASTLE. And her partiality is such, that she actually thinks him so. A fortune like yours is no small tempta-

tion. Besides, as she has the sole management of it, I'm not surprised to see her unwilling to let it go out of the family.

MISS NEVILLE. A fortune like mine, which chiefly consists in jewels, is no such mighty temptation. But, at any rate, if my dear Hastings be but constant, I make no doubt to be too hard for her at last. However, I let her suppose that I am in love with her son; and she never once dreams that my affections are fixed upon another.

MISS HARDCASTLE. My good brother holds out stoutly. I could almost love him for hating you so.

MISS NEVILLE. It is a good-natured creature at bottom, and I'm sure would wish to see me married to anybody but himself. But my aunt's bell rings for our afternoon's walk round the improvements. *Allons!* Courage is necessary, as our affairs are critical.

MISS HARDCASTLE. Would it were bed-time, and all were well.   [*Exeunt.*]

SCENE II—*An alehouse room.*

[*Several shabby fellows with punch and tobacco.* TONY, *at the head of the table, a little higher than the rest, a mallet in his hand.*]

OMNES. Hurrea! hurrea! hurrea! bravo!

1ST FELLOW. Now, gentlemen, silence for a song. The 'Squire is going to knock himself down for a song.

OMNES. Ay, a song, a song!

TONY. Then I'll sing you, gentlemen, a song I made upon this alehouse, The Three Pigeons.

SONG

Let schoolmasters puzzle their brain
    With grammar, and nonsense, and learning;
Good liquor, I stoutly maintain,
    Gives *genus* a better discerning.
Let them brag of their heathenish gods,
    Their Lethes, their Styxes, and Stygians,

Their *Quis*, and their *Quæs*, and their
   Quods,
They're all but a parcel of Pigeons.
       Toroddle, toroddle, toroll.

When methodist preachers come down,
  A-preaching that drinking is sinful,
I'll wager the rascals a crown,
  They always preach best with a skin-
     ful.
But when you come down with your pence,
  For a slice of their scurvy religion,
I'll leave it to all men of sense,
  But you, my good friend, are the
     Pigeon.
      Toroddle, toroddle, toroll.

Then come, put the jorum about,
  And let us be merry and clever,
Our hearts and our liquors are stout,
  Here's the Three Jolly Pigeons for
     ever.
Let some cry up woodcock or hare,
  Your bustards, your ducks, and your
     widgeons;
But of all the birds in the air,
  Here's a health to the Three Jolly
     Pigeons.
      Toroddle, toroddle, toroll.

OMNES. Bravo, bravo!

1ST FELLOW. The 'Squire has got some
spunk in him.

2ND FELLOW. I loves to hear him sing,
bekeays he never gives us nothing that's
low.

3RD FELLOW. O! damn anything that's
low, I cannot bear it.

4TH FELLOW. The genteel thing is the
genteel thing any time: if so be that a
gentleman bees in a concatenation accord-
ingly.

3RD FELLOW. I like the maxum of it,
Master Muggins. What, though I am
obligated to dance a bear, a man may be
a gentleman for all that. May this be my
poison, if my bear ever dances but to the
very genteelest of tunes; "Water Parted,"
or "The minuet in Ariadne."

2ND FELLOW. What a pity it is the
'Squire is not come to his own. It would
be well for all the publicans within ten
miles round of him.

TONY. Ecod, and so it would, Master
Slang. I'd then show what it was to keep
choice of company.

2ND FELLOW. O, he takes after his own
father for that. To be sure, old 'Squire
Lumpkin was the finest gentleman I ever
set my eyes on. For winding the straight
horn, or beating a thicket for a hare, or
a wench, he never had his fellow. It was
a saying in the place, that he kept the
best horses, dogs, and girls, in the whole
county.

TONY. Ecod, and when I'm of age I'll
be no bastard, I promise you. I have been
thinking of Bet Bouncer and the miller's
gray mare to begin with. But come, my
boys, drink about and be merry, for you
pay no reckoning. Well, Stingo, what's
the matter?

[Enter LANDLORD.]

LANDLORD. There be two gentlemen in
a post-chaise at the door. They have lost
their way upo' the forest; and they are
talking something about Mr. Hardcastle.

TONY. As sure as can be, one of them
must be the gentleman that's coming down
to court my sister. Do they seem to be
Londoners?

LANDLORD. I believe they may. They
look woundily like Frenchmen.

TONY. Then desire them to step this
way, and I'll set them right in a twin-
kling. *[Exit* LANDLORD.] Gentlemen, as
they mayn't be good enough company for
you, step down for a moment, and I'll be
with you in the squeezing of a lemon.
              [Exeunt MOB.]

TONY *[alone]*. Father-in-law has been
calling me whelp and hound this half
year. Now, if I pleased, I could be so
revenged upon the old grumbletonian.
But then I'm afraid,—afraid of what?
I shall soon be worth fifteen hundred a
year, and let him frighten me out of *that*
if he can.

[Enter LANDLORD, *conducting* MARLOW *and*
      HASTINGS.]

MARLOW. What a tedious, uncomfort-
able day have we had of it! We were

told it was but forty miles across the country, and we have come above three-score!

HASTINGS. And all, Marlow, from that unaccountable reserve of yours, that would not let us inquire more frequently on the way.

MARLOW. I own, Hastings, I am unwilling to lay myself under an obligation to every one I meet; and often stand the chance of an unmannerly answer.

HASTINGS. At present, however, we are not likely to receive any answer.

TONY. No offence, gentlemen. But I'm told you have been inquiring for one Mr. Hardcastle, in these parts. Do you know what part of the country you are in?

HASTINGS. Not in the least, sir, but should thank you for information.

TONY. Nor the way you came?

HASTINGS. No, sir; but if you can inform us—

TONY. Why, gentlemen, if you know neither the road you are going, nor where you are, nor the road you came, the first thing I have to inform you is, that—you have lost your way.

MARLOW. We wanted no ghost to tell us that.

TONY. Pray, gentlemen, may I be so bold as to ask the place from whence you came?

MARLOW. That's not necessary towards directing us where we are to go.

TONY. No offence; but question for question is all fair, you know. Pray, gentlemen, is not this same Hardcastle a cross-grained, old-fashioned, whimsical fellow, with an ugly face: a daughter, and a pretty son?

HASTINGS. We have not seen the gentleman; but he has the family you mention.

TONY. The daughter, a tall, trapesing, trolloping, talkative maypole; the son, a pretty, well-bred, agreeable youth, that every body is fond of!

MARLOW. Our information differs in this. The daughter is said to be well-bred, and beautiful; the son, an awkward booby, reared up and spoiled at his mother's apron-string.

TONY. He-he-hem!—Then, gentlemen, all I have to tell you is, that you won't reach Mr. Hardcastle's house this night, I believe.

HASTINGS. Unfortunate!

TONY. It's a damn'd long, dark, boggy, dirty, dangerous way. Stingo, tell the gentlemen the way to Mr. Hardcastle's;—[Winking upon the LANDLORD.], Mr. Hardcastle's of Quagmire Marsh, you understand me?

LANDLORD. Master Hardcastle's! Lack-a-daisy, my masters, you're come a deadly deal wrong. When you came to the bottom of the hill, you should have crossed down Squash Lane.

MARLOW. Cross down Squash Lane!

LANDLORD. Then you were to keep straight forward, till you came to four roads.

MARLOW. Come to where four roads meet?

TONY. Ay; but you must be sure to take only one of them

MARLOW. O, sir, you're facetious.

TONY. Then, keeping to the right, you are to go sideways till you come upon Crack-skull Common; there you must look sharp for the track of the wheel, and go forward till you come to Farmer Murrain's barn. Coming to the farmer's barn, you are to turn to the right, and then to the left, and then to the right about again, till you find out the old mill—

MARLOW. Zounds, man! we could as soon find out the longitude.

HASTINGS. What's to be done, Marlow?

MARLOW. This house promises but a poor reception; though, perhaps, the landlord can accommodate us.

LANDLORD. Alack, master, we have but one spare bed in the whole house.

TONY. And to my knowledge, that's taken up by three lodgers already. [After a pause in which the rest seem disconcerted.] I have hit it. Don't you think, Stingo, our landlady could accommodate the gentlemen by the fireside, with —three chairs and a bolster?

HASTINGS. I hate sleeping by the fireside.

MARLOW. And I detest your three chairs and a bolster.

TONY. You do, do you?—then, let me see—what if you go on a mile further, to the Buck's Head; the old Buck's Head on the hill, one of the best inns in the whole country?

HASTINGS. O ho! so we have escaped an adventure for this night, however.

LANDLORD [apart to TONY]. Sure, you ben't sending them to your father's as an inn, be you?

TONY. Mum, you fool, you. Let them find that out. [To them.] You have only to keep on straight forward, till you come to a large old house by the road side. You'll see a pair of large horns over the door. That's the sign. Drive up the yard, and call stoutly about you.

HASTINGS. Sir, we are obliged to you. The servants can't miss the way?

TONY. No, no; but I tell you, though, the landlord is rich, and going to leave off business; so he wants to be thought a gentleman, saving your presence,—he! he! he! He'll be for giving you his company; and, ecod, if you mind him, he'll persuade you that his mother was an alderman, and his aunt a justice of peace.

LANDLORD. A troublesome old blade, to be sure; but a keeps as good wines and beds as any in the whole country.

MARLOW. Well, if he supplies us with these, we shall want no further connexion. We are to turn to the right, did you say?

TONY. No, no, straight forward. I'll just step myself, and show you a piece of the way. [To the LANDLORD.] Mum!

LANDLORD. Ah, bless your heart, for a sweet, pleasant, mischievous son.

[Exeunt.]

ACT II

SCENE I—*An old-fashioned house.*

[*Enter* HARDCASTLE, *followed by three or four awkward* SERVANTS.]

HARDCASTLE. Well, I hope you are perfect in the table exercise I have been teaching you these three days. You all know your posts and your places, and can show that you have been used to good company, without ever stirring from home.

OMNES. Ay, ay.

HARDCASTLE. When company comes, you are not to pop out and stare, and then run in again, like frighted rabbits in a warren.

OMNES. No, no.

HARDCASTLE. You, Diggory, whom I have taken from the barn, are to make a show at the side table; and you, Roger, whom I have advanced from the plough, are to place yourself behind my chair. But you're not to stand so, with your hands in your pockets. Take your hands from your pockets, Roger; and from your head, you blockhead, you. See how Diggory carries his hands. They're a little too stiff, indeed, but that's no great matter.

DIGGORY. Ay, mind how I hold them. I learned to hold my hands this way, when I was upon drill for the militia. And so being upon drill—

HARDCASTLE. You must not be so talkative, Diggory. You must be all attention to the guests. You must hear us talk, and not think of talking; you must see us drink, and not think of drinking; you must see us eat, and not think of eating.

DIGGORY. By the laws, your worship, that's perfectly unpossible. Whenever Diggory sees yeating going forward, ecod, he's always wishing for a mouthful himself.

HARDCASTLE. Blockhead! Is not a belly-full in the kitchen as good as a belly-full in the parlour? Stay your stomach with that reflection.

DIGGORY. Ecod, I thank your worship, I'll make a shift to stay my stomach with a slice of cold beef in the pantry.

HARDCASTLE. Diggory, you are too talkative. Then, if I happen to say a good thing, or tell a good story at table, you must not all burst out a-laughing, as if you made part of the company.

DIGGORY. Then, ecod, your worship must not tell the story of the Ould Grouse in the gun-room: I can't help laughing at that—he! he! he!—for the soul of me! We have laughed at that these twenty years—ha! ha! ha!

HARDCASTLE. Ha! ha! ha! The story is a good one. Well, honest Diggory, you may laugh at that—but still remember to be attentive. Suppose one of the company should call for a glass of wine, how will you behave? A glass of wine, sir, if you please, [*To* DIGGORY.]—Eh, why don't you move?

DIGGORY. Ecod, your worship, I never have courage till I see the eatables and drinkables brought upo' the table, and then I'm as bauld as a lion.

HARDCASTLE. What, will nobody move?

1ST SERVANT. I'm not to leave this pleace.

2ND SERVANT. I'm sure it's no pleace of mine.

3RD SERVANT. Nor mine, for sartain.

DIGGORY. Wauns, and I'm sure it canna mine.

HARDCASTLE. You numskulls! and so, while, like your betters, you are quarrelling for places, the guests must be starved. O you dunces! I find I must begin all over again—But don't I hear a coach drive into the yard? To your posts, you blockheads! I'll go in the meantime and give my old friend's son a hearty reception at the gate. [*Exit* HARDCASTLE.]

DIGGORY. By the elevens, my pleace is quite gone out of my head.

ROGER. I know that my pleace is to be every where.

1ST SERVANT. Where the devil is mine?

2ND SERVANT. My pleace is to be no where at all; and so Ize go about my business.

[*Exeunt* SERVANTS, *running about as if frightened, several ways.*]

[*Enter* SERVANT, *with candles, showing in* MARLOW *and* HASTINGS.]

SERVANT. Welcome, gentlemen, very welcome! This way.

HASTINGS. After the disappointments of the day, welcome once more, Charles, to the comforts of a clean room and a good fire. Upon my word, a very well-looking house; antique but creditable.

MARLOW. The usual fate of a large mansion. Having first ruined the master by good house-keeping, it at last comes to levy contributions as an inn.

HASTINGS. As you say, we passengers are to be taxed to pay all these fineries. I have often seen a good side-board, or a marble chimney-piece, though not actually put in the bill, inflame a reckoning confoundedly.

MARLOW. Travellers, George, must pay in all places; the only difference is, that in good inns you pay dearly for luxuries; in bad inns you are fleeced and starved.

HASTINGS. You have lived pretty much among them. In truth, I have been often surprised, that you who have seen so much of the world, with your natural good sense, and your many opportunities, could never yet acquire a requisite share of assurance.

MARLOW. The Englishman's malady. But tell me, George, where could I have learned that assurance you talk of? My life has been chiefly spent in a college, or an inn, in seclusion from that lovely part of the creation that chiefly teach men confidence. I don't know that I was ever familiarly acquainted with a single modest woman—except my mother—But among females of another class, you know—

HASTINGS. Ay, among them you are impudent enough, of all conscience!

MARLOW. They are of *us*, you know.

HASTINGS. But in the company of women of reputation I never saw such an idiot, such a trembler; you look for all the world as if you wanted an opportunity of stealing out of the room.

MARLOW. Why, man, that's because I do want to steal out of the room. Faith, I have often formed a resolution to break the ice, and rattle away at any rate. But I don't know how, a single glance from a pair of fine eyes has totally overset my resolution. An impudent fellow may counterfeit modesty, but I'll be hanged if a modest man can ever counterfeit impudence.

HASTINGS. If you could but say half the fine things to them that I have heard you lavish upon the barmaid of an inn, or even a college bed-maker—

MARLOW. Why, George, I can't say fine things to them; they freeze, they petrify me. They may talk of a comet, or a burning mountain, or some such bagatelle; but to me a modest woman, drest out in all her finery, is the most tremendous object of the whole creation.

HASTINGS. Ha! ha! ha! At this rate, man, how can you ever expect to marry?

MARLOW. Never; unless, as among kings and princes, my bride were to be courted by proxy. If, indeed, like an Eastern bridegroom, one were to be introduced to a wife he never saw before, it might be endured. But to go through all the terrors of a formal courtship, together with the episode of aunts, grandmothers, and cousins, and at last to blurt out the broad staring question of, "Madam, will you marry me?" No, no, that's a strain much above me, I assure you.

HASTINGS. I pity you. But how do you intend behaving to the lady you are come down to visit at the request of your father?

MARLOW. As I behave to all other ladies. Bow very low, answer yes or no to all her demands—But for the rest, I don't think I shall venture to look in her face till I see my father's again.

HASTINGS. I'm surprised that one who is so warm a friend can be so cool a lover.

MARLOW. To be explicit, my dear Hastings, my chief inducement down was to be instrumental in forwarding your happiness, not my own. Miss Neville loves you, the family don't know you; as my friend you are sure of a reception, and let honour do the rest.

HASTINGS. My dear Marlow! But I'll suppress the emotion. Were I a wretch, meanly seeking to carry off a fortune,

you should be the last man in the world I would apply to for assistance. But Miss Neville's person is all I ask, and that is mine, both from her deceased father's consent, and her own inclination.

MARLOW. Happy man! You have talents and art to captivate any woman. I'm doomed to adore the sex, and yet to converse with the only part of it I despise. This stammer in my address, and this awkward, prepossessing visage of mine can never permit me to soar above the reach of a milliner's 'prentice, or one of the duchesses of Drury Lane. Pshaw! this fellow here to interrupt us.

[*Enter* HARDCASTLE.]

HARDCASTLE. Gentlemen, once more you are heartily welcome. Which is Mr. Marlow? Sir, you are heartily welcome. It's not my way, you see, to receive my friends with my back to the fire. I like to give them a hearty reception in the old style at my gate. I like to see their horses and trunks taken care of.

MARLOW [*aside*]. He has got our names from the servants already. [*To him.*] We approve your caution and hospitality, sir. [*To* HASTINGS.] I have been thinking, George, of changing our travelling dresses in the morning. I am grown confoundedly ashamed of mine.

HARDCASTLE. I beg, Mr. Marlow, you'll use no ceremony in this house.

HASTINGS. I fancy, George, you're right; the first blow is half the battle. I intend opening the campaign with the white and gold.

HARDCASTLE. Mr. Marlow—Mr. Hastings—gentlemen—pray be under no restraint in this house. This is Liberty-hall, gentlemen. You may do just as you please here.

MARLOW. Yet, George, if we open the campaign too fiercely at first, we may want ammunition before it is over. I think to reserve the embroidery to secure a retreat.

HARDCASTLE. Your talking of a retreat, Mr. Marlow, puts me in mind of the Duke of Marlborough, when we went to besiege

Denain. He first summoned the garrison—

MARLOW. Don't you think the *ventre d'or* waistcoat will do with the plain brown?

HARDCASTLE. He first summoned the garrison, which might consist of about five thousand men—

HASTINGS. I think not: brown and yellow mix but very poorly.

HARDCASTLE. I say, gentlemen, as I was telling you, he summoned the garrison, which might consist of about five thousand men—

MARLOW. The girls like finery.

HARDCASTLE. Which might consist of about five thousand men, well appointed with stores, ammunition, and other implements of war. "Now," says the Duke of Marlborough to George Brooks, that stood next to him—you must have heard of George Brooks—"I'll pawn my dukedom," says he, "but I take that garrison without spilling a drop of blood." So—

MARLOW. What, my good friend, if you gave us a glass of punch in the meantime; it would help us to carry on the siege with vigour.

HARDCASTLE. Punch, sir! [*Aside.*] This is the most unaccountable kind of modesty I ever met with.

MARLOW. Yes, sir, punch! A glass of warm punch, after our journey, will be comfortable. This is Liberty-hall, you know.

HARDCASTLE. Here's a cup, sir.

MARLOW [*aside*]. So this fellow, in his Liberty-hall, will only let us have just what he pleases.

HARDCASTLE [*taking the cup*]. I hope you'll find it to your mind. I have prepared it with my own hands, and I believe you'll own the ingredients are tolerable. Will you be so good as to pledge me, sir? Here, Mr. Marlow, here is to our better acquaintance! [*Drinks.*]

MARLOW [*aside*]. A very impudent fellow this. But he's a character, and I'll humour him a little. Sir, my service to you. [*Drinks.*]

HASTINGS [*aside*]. I see this fellow wants to give us his company, and forgets that he's an innkeeper, before he has learned to be a gentleman.

MARLOW. From the excellence of your cup, my old friend, I suppose you have a good deal of business in this part of the country. Warm work, now and then, at elections, I suppose?

HARDCASTLE. No, sir, I have long given that work over. Since our betters have hit upon the expedient of electing each other, there is no business "for us that sell ale."

HASTINGS. So, then, you have no turn for politics, I find.

HARDCASTLE. Not in the least. There was a time, indeed, I fretted myself about the mistakes of government, like other people; but, finding myself every day grow more angry, and the government growing no better, I left it to mend itself. Since that, I no more trouble my head about Hyder Ally, or Ally Cawn, than about Ally Croaker. Sir, my service to you.

HASTINGS. So that, with eating above stairs, and drinking below, with receiving your friends within, and amusing them without, you lead a good, pleasant, bustling life of it.

HARDCASTLE. I do stir about a great deal, that's certain. Half the differences of the parish are adjusted in this very parlour.

MARLOW [*after drinking*]. And you have an argument in your cup, old gentleman, better than any in Westminster-hall.

HARDCASTLE. Ay, young gentleman, that, and a little philosophy.

MARLOW [*aside*]. Well, this is the first time I ever heard of an innkeeper's philosophy.

HASTINGS. So then, like an experienced general, you attack them on every quarter. If you find their reason manageable, you attack it with your philosophy; if you find they have no reason, you attack them with this. Here's your health, my philosopher. [*Drinks.*]

HARDCASTLE. Good, very good, thank you; ha! ha! Your generalship puts me in mind of Prince Eugene, when he fought the Turks at the battle of Belgrade. You shall hear.

MARLOW. Instead of the battle of Belgrade, I believe it's almost time to talk about supper. What has your philosophy got in the house for supper?

HARDCASTLE. For supper, sir!—[Aside]. Was ever such a request to a man in his own house!

MARLOW. Yes, sir, supper, sir; I begin to feel an appetite. I shall make devilish work to-night in the larder, I promise you.

HARDCASTLE [aside]. Such a brazen dog, sure, never my eyes beheld. [To him.] Why, really, sir, as for supper I can't well tell. My Dorothy and the cook-maid settle these things between them. I leave these kind of things entirely to them.

MARLOW. You do, do you?

HARDCASTLE. Entirely. By the bye, I believe they are in actual consultation upon what's for supper this moment in the kitchen.

MARLOW. Then I beg they'll admit me as one of their privy-council. It's a way I have got. When I travel I always choose to regulate my own supper. Let the cook be called. No offence, I hope, sir.

HARDCASTLE. O, no, sir, none in the least; yet I don't know how: our Bridget, the cook-maid, is not very communicative upon these occasions. Should we send for her, she might scold us all out of the house.

HASTINGS. Let's see your list of the larder, then. I ask it as a favour. I always match my appetite to my bill of fare.

MARLOW [to HARDCASTLE, who looks at them with surprise]. Sir, he's very right, and it's my way, too.

HARDCASTLE. Sir, you have a right to command here. Here, Roger, bring us the bill of fare for to-night's supper: I believe it's drawn out. [Exit ROGER.] Your manner, Mr. Hastings, puts me in mind of my uncle, Colonel Wallop. It was a saying of his, that no man was sure of his supper till he had eaten it.

HASTINGS [aside]. All upon the high ropes! His uncle a colonel! We shall soon hear of his mother being a justice of the peace. [Reënter ROGER.] But let's hear the bill of fare.

MARLOW [perusing]. What's here? For the first course; for the second course; for the dessert. The devil, sir, do you think we have brought down the whole Joiners' Company, or the Corporation of Bedford, to eat up such a supper? Two or three little things, clean and comfortable, will do.

HASTINGS. But let's hear it.

MARLOW [reading]. For the first course, at the top, a pig, and pruin sauce.

HASTINGS. Damn your pig, I say!

MARLOW. And damn your pruin sauce, say I!

HARDCASTLE. And yet, gentlemen, to men that are hungry, pig with pruin sauce is very good eating.

MARLOW. At the bottom, a calf's tongue and brains.

HASTINGS. Let your brains be knocked out, my good sir, I don't like them.

MARLOW. Or you may clap them on a plate by themselves. I do.

HARDCASTLE [aside]. Their impudence confounds me. [To them.] Gentlemen, you are my guests, make what alterations you please. Is there anything else you wish to retrench or alter, gentlemen?

MARLOW. Item: A pork pie, a boiled rabbit and sausages, a Florentine, a shaking pudding, and a dish of tiff—taff—taffety cream!

HASTINGS. Confound your made dishes! I shall be as much at a loss in this house as at a green and yellow dinner at the French ambassador's table. I'm for plain eating.

HARDCASTLE. I'm sorry, gentlemen, that I have nothing you like, but if there be any thing you have a particular fancy to—

MARLOW. Why, really, sir, your bill of fare is so exquisite, that any one part of it is full as good as another. Send us what you please. So much for supper.

And now to see that our beds are aired, and properly taken care of.

HARDCASTLE. I entreat you'll leave all that to me. You shall not stir a step.

MARLOW. Leave that to you! I protest, sir, you must excuse me, I always look to these things myself.

HARDCASTLE. I must insist, sir, you'll make yourself easy on that head.

MARLOW. You see I'm resolved on it.— [*Aside.*] A very troublesome fellow this, as ever I met with.

HARDCASTLE. Well, sir, I'm resolved at least to attend you. [*Aside.*] This may be modern modesty, but I never saw any thing look so like old-fashioned impudence.

[*Exeunt* MARLOW *and* HARDCASTLE.]

HASTINGS [*alone*]. So I find this fellow's civilities begin to grow troublesome. But who can be angry at those assiduities which are meant to please him? Ha! what do I see? Miss Neville, by all that's happy!

[*Enter* MISS NEVILLE.]

MISS NEVILLE. My dear Hastings! To what unexpected good fortune, to what accident, am I to ascribe this happy meeting?

HASTINGS. Rather·let me ask the same question, as I could never have hoped to meet my dearest Constance at an inn.

MISS NEVILLE. An inn! sure you mistake: my aunt, my guardian, lives here. What could induce you to think this house an inn.

HASTINGS. My friend, Mr. Marlow, with whom I came down, and I, have been sent here as to an inn, I assure you. A young fellow, whom we accidentally met at a house hard by, directed us hither.

MISS NEVILLE. Certainly it must be one of my hopeful cousin's tricks, of whom you have heard me talk so often; ha! ha! ha!

HASTINGS. He whom your aunt intends for you? he of whom I have such just apprehensions?

MISS NEVILLE. You have nothing to fear from him, I assure you. You'd adore him if you knew how heartily he despises me. My aunt knows it too, and has undertaken to court me for him, and actually begins to think she has made a conquest.

HASTINGS. Thou dear dissembler! You must know, my Constance, I have just seized this happy opportunity of my friend's visit here to get admittance into the family. The horses that carried us down are now fatigued with their journey, but they'll soon be refreshed; and, then, if my dearest girl will trust in her faithful Hastings, we shall soon be landed in France, where even among the slaves the laws of marriage are respected.

MISS NEVILLE. I have often told you, that though ready to obey you, I yet should leave my little fortune behind with reluctance. The greatest part of it was left me by my uncle, the India director, and chiefly consists in jewels. I have been for some time persuading my aunt to let me wear them. I fancy I'm very near succeeding. The instant they are put into ·my possession, you shall find me ready to make them and myself yours.

HASTINGS. Perish the baubles! Your person is all I desire. In the meantime, my friend Marlow must not be let into his mistake. I know the strange reserve of his temper is such, that if abruptly informed of it, he would instantly quit the house before our plan was ripe for execution.

MISS NEVILLE. But how shall we keep him in the deception? Miss Hardcastle is just returned from walking; what if we still continue to deceive him?—This, this way— [*They confer.*]

[*Enter* MARLOW.]

MARLOW. The assiduities of these good people tease me beyond bearing. My host seems to think it ill manners to leave me alone, and so he claps not only himself but his old-fashioned wife on my back. They talk of coming to sup with us, too; and then, I suppose, we are to run the gauntlet through all the rest of the family.—What have we got here?

HASTINGS. My dear Charles! Let me congratulate you!—The most fortunate accident!—Who do you think is just alighted?

MARLOW. Cannot guess.

HASTINGS. Our mistresses, boy, Miss Hardcastle and Miss Neville. Give me leave to introduce Miss Constance Neville to your acquaintance. Happening to dine in the neighborhood, they called on their return to take fresh horses here. Miss Hardcastle has just stept into the next room, and will be back in an instant. Wasn't it lucky? eh!

MARLOW [aside]. I have just been mortified enough of all conscience, and here comes something to complete my embarrassment.

HASTINGS. Well, but wasn't it the most fortunate thing in the world?

MARLOW. Oh, yes! Very fortunate—a most joyful encounter—But our dresses, George, you know, are in disorder—What if we should postpone the happiness till to-morrow?—To-morrow, at her own house —It will be every bit as convenient—and rather more respectful—To-morrow let it be. [Offering to go.]

MISS NEVILLE. By no means, sir. Your ceremony will displease her. The disorder of your dress will show the ardour of your impatience. Besides, she knows you are in the house, and will permit you to see her.

MARLOW. Oh, the devil! How shall I support it? Hem! hem! Hastings, you must not go. You are to assist me, you know. I shall be confoundedly ridiculous. Yet, hang it! I'll take courage. Hem!

HASTINGS. Pshaw, man! it's but the first plunge, and all's over. She's but a woman, you know.

MARLOW. And, of all women, she that I dread most to encounter.

[Enter MISS HARDCASTLE, as returned from walking, a bonnet, etc.]

HASTINGS [introducing them]. Miss Hardcastle, Mr. Marlow; I'm proud of bringing two persons of such merit together, that only want to know, to esteem each other.

MISS HARDCASTLE [aside]. Now for meeting my modest gentleman with a demure face, and quite in his own manner. [After a pause, in which he appears very uneasy and disconcerted.] I'm glad of your safe arrival, sir—I'm told you had some accidents by the way.

MARLOW. Only a few, madam. Yes, we had some. Yes, madam, a good many accidents, but should be sorry—madam—or rather glad of any accidents—that are so agreeably concluded. Hem!

HASTINGS [to him]. You never spoke better in your whole life. Keep it up, and I'll insure you the victory.

MISS HARDCASTLE. I'm afraid you flatter, sir. You that have seen so much of the finest company can find little entertainment in an obscure corner of the country.

MARLOW [gathering courage]. I have lived, indeed, in the world, madam; but I have kept very little company. I have been but an observer upon life, madam, while others were enjoying it.

MISS NEVILLE. But that, I am told, is the way to enjoy it at last.

HASTINGS [to him]. Cicero never spoke better. Once more, and you are confirmed in assurance for ever.

MARLOW [to him]. Hem! Stand by me then, and when I'm down, throw in a word or two to set me up again.

MISS HARDCASTLE. An observer, like you, upon life, were, I fear, disagreeably employed, since you must have had much more to censure than to approve.

MARLOW. Pardon me, madam. I was always willing to be amused. The folly of most people is rather an object of mirth than uneasiness.

HASTINGS [to him]. Bravo, bravo. Never spoke so well in your whole life. Well, Miss Hardcastle, I see that you and Mr. Marlow are going to be very good company. I believe our being here will but embarrass the interview.

MARLOW. Not in the least, Mr. Hastings. We like your company of all things.

[*To him.*] Zounds, George, sure you won't go? how can you leave us?

HASTINGS. Our presence will but spoil conversation, so we'll retire to the next room. [*To him.*] You don't consider, man, that we are to manage a little *tête-à-tête* of our own. [*Exeunt.*]

MISS HARDCASTLE [*after a pause*]. But you have not been wholly an observer, I presume, sir: the ladies, I should hope, have employed some part of your addresses.

MARLOW [*relapsing into timidity*]. Pardon me, madam, I—I—I—as yet have studied—only—to—deserve them.

MISS HARDCASTLE. And that, some say, is the very worst way to obtain them.

MARLOW. Perhaps so, madam. But I love to converse only with the more grave and sensible part of the sex.—But I'm afraid I grow tiresome.

MISS HARDCASTLE. Not at all, sir; there is nothing I like so much as grave conversation myself; I could hear it for ever. Indeed, I have often been surprised how a man of sentiment could ever admire those light, airy pleasures, where nothing reaches the heart.

MARLOW. It's—a disease—of the mind, madam. In the variety of tastes there must be some who, wanting a relish—for um—a—um—

MISS HARDCASTLE. I understand you, sir. There must be some, who, wanting a relish for refined pleasures, pretend to despise what they are incapable of tasting.

MARLOW. My meaning, madam, but infinitely better expressed. And I can't help observing—a—

MISS HARDCASTLE [*aside*]. Who could ever suppose this fellow impudent upon some occasions! [*To him.*] You were going to observe, sir—

MARLOW. I was observing, madam—I protest, madam, I forget what I was going to observe.

MISS HARDCASTLE [*aside*]. I vow and so do I. [*To him.*] You were observing, sir, that in this age of hypocrisy—something about hypocrisy, sir.

MARLOW. Yes, madam. In this age of hypocrisy there are few who upon strict inquiry do not—a—a—a—

MISS HARDCASTLE. I understand you perfectly, sir.

MARLOW [*aside*]. Egad! and that's more than I do myself.

MISS HARDCASTLE. You mean that, in this hypocritical age, there are a few who do not condemn in public what they practise in private, and think they pay every debt to virtue when they praise it.

MARLOW. True, madam; those who have most virtue in their mouths have least of it in their bosoms. But I'm sure I tire you, madam.

MISS HARDCASTLE. Not in the least, sir; there's something so agreeable and spirited in your manner, such life and force—pray, sir, go on.

MARLOW. Yes, madam, I was saying—that there are some occasions—when a total want of courage, madam, destroys all the—and puts us—upon—a—a—a—

MISS HARDCASTLE. I agree with you entirely; a want of courage upon some occasions assumes the appearance of ignorance, and betrays us when we most want to excel. I beg you'll proceed.

MARLOW. Yes, madam. Morally speaking, madam—but I see Miss Neville expecting us in the next room. I would not intrude for the world.

MISS HARDCASTLE. I protest, sir, I never was more agreeably entertained in all my life. Pray, go on.

MARLOW. Yes, madam, I was—But she beckons us to join her. Madam, shall I do myself the honour to attend you?

MISS HARDCASTLE. Well, then, I'll follow.

MARLOW [*aside*]. This pretty smooth dialogue has done for me. [*Exit.*]

MISS HARDCASTLE [*alone*]. Ha! ha! ha! Was there ever such a sober, sentimental interview? I'm certain he scarce looked in my face the whole time. Yet the fellow, but for his unaccountable bashfulness, is pretty well too. He has good sense, but then so buried in his fears, that it fatigues one more than ignorance.

If I could teach him a little confidence, it would be doing somebody that I know of a piece of service. But who is that somebody?—That, faith, is a question I can scarce answer.   [*Exit.*]

[*Enter* TONY *and* MISS NEVILLE, *followed by* MRS. HARDCASTLE *and* HASTINGS.]

TONY. What do you follow me for, cousin Con? I wonder you're not ashamed to be so very engaging.

MISS NEVILLE. I hope, cousin, one may speak to one's own relations, and not be to blame.

TONY. Ay, but I know what sort of a relation you want to make me, though; but it won't do. I tell you, cousin Con, it won't do; so I beg you'll keep your distance. I want no nearer relationship. [*She follows, coquetting him, to the back scene.*]

MRS. HARDCASTLE. Well! I vow, Mr. Hastings, you are very entertaining. There's nothing in the world I love to talk of so much as London, and the fashions, though I was never there myself.

HASTINGS. Never there! You amaze me! From your air and manner, I concluded you had been bred all your life either at Ranelagh, St. James's, or Tower Wharf.

MRS. HARDCASTLE. O, sir! you're only pleased to say so. We country persons can have no manner at all. I'm in love with the town, and that serves to raise me above some of our neighbouring rustics; but who can have a manner that has never seen the Pantheon, the Grotto Gardens, the Borough, and such places where the nobility chiefly resort? All I can do is to enjoy London at second-hand. I take care to know every *tête-à-tête* from the Scandalous Magazine, and have all the fashions, as they come out, in a letter from the two Miss Rickets of Crooked Lane. Pray, how do you like this head, Mr. Hastings?

HASTINGS. Extremely elegant and *degagée*, upon my word, madam. Your friseur is a Frenchman, I suppose?

MRS. HARDCASTLE. I protest, I dressed it myself from a print in the Ladies' Memorandum-book for the last year.

HASTINGS. Indeed! Such a head in a side-box, at the play-house, would draw as many gazers as my Lady Mayoress at a City Ball.

MRS. HARDCASTLE. I vow, since inoculation began, there is no such thing to be seen as a plain woman; so one must dress a little particular, or one may escape in the crowd.

HASTINGS. But that can never be your case, madam, in any dress.   [*Bowing.*]

MRS. HARDCASTLE. Yet, what signifies my dressing, when I have such a piece of antiquity by my side as Mr. Hardcastle: all I can say will never argue down a single button from his clothes. I have often wanted him to throw off his great flaxen wig, and where he was bald, to plaster it over, like my Lord Pately, with powder.

HASTINGS. You are right, madam; for, as among the ladies there are none ugly, so among the men there are none old.

MRS. HARDCASTLE. But what do you think his answer was? Why, with his usual Gothic vivacity, he said I only wanted him to throw off his wig to convert it into a *tête* for my own wearing!

HASTINGS. Intolerable! At your age you may wear what you please, and it must become you.

MRS. HARDCASTLE. Pray, Mr. Hastings, what do you take to be the most fashionable age about town?

HASTINGS. Some time ago, forty was all the mode; but I'm told the ladies intend to bring up fifty for the ensuing winter.

MRS. HARDCASTLE. Seriously? Then I shall be too young for the fashion!

HASTINGS. No lady begins now to put on jewels till she's past forty. For instance, miss there, in a polite circle, would be considered as a child, a mere maker of samplers.

MRS. HARDCASTLE. And yet Mrs. Niece thinks herself as much a woman, and is as fond of jewels, as the oldest of us all.

HASTINGS. Your niece, is she? And that young gentleman,—a brother of yours, I should presume?

MRS. HARDCASTLE. My son, sir. They are contracted to each other. Observe their little sports. They fall in and out ten times a-day, as if they were man and wife already. [*To them.*] Well, Tony, child, what soft things are you saying to your cousin Constance, this evening?

TONY. I have been saying no soft things; but that it's very hard to be followed about so. Ecod! I've not a place in the house now that's left to myself, but the stable.

MRS. HARDCASTLE. Never mind him, Con, my dear. He's in another story behind your back.

MISS NEVILLE. There's something generous in my cousin's manner. He falls out before faces to be forgiven in private.

TONY. That's a damned confounded —crack.

MRS. HARDCASTLE. Ah! he's a sly one. Don't you think they're like each other about the mouth, Mr. Hastings? The Blenkinsop mouth to a T. They're of a size too. Back to back, my pretties, that Mr. Hastings may see you. Come, Tony.

TONY. You had as good not make me, I tell you. [*Measuring.*]

MISS NEVILLE. O lud! he has almost cracked my head.

MRS. HARDCASTLE. O, the monster! For shame, Tony. You a man, and behave so!

TONY. If I'm a man, let me have my fortin. Ecod! I'll not be made a fool of no longer.

MRS. HARDCASTLE. Is this, ungrateful boy, all that I'm to get for the pains I have taken in your education? I that have rocked you in your cradle, and fed that pretty mouth with a spoon! Did not I work that waistcoat to make you genteel? Did not I prescribe for you every day, and weep while the receipt was operating?

TONY. Ecod! you had reason to weep, for you have been dosing me ever since I was born. I have gone through every receipt in the Complete Huswife ten times over; and you have thoughts of coursing me through Quincy next spring. But, ecod! I tell you, I'll not be made a fool of no longer.

MRS. HARDCASTLE. Wasn't it all for your good, viper? Wasn't it all for your good?

TONY. I wish you'd let me and my good alone, then. Snubbing this way when I'm in spirits! If I'm to have any good, let it come of itself; not to keep dinging it, dinging it into one so.

MRS. HARDCASTLE. That's false; I never see you when you're in spirits. No, Tony, you then go to the ale-house or kennel. I'm never to be delighted with your agreeable wild notes, unfeeling monster!

TONY. Ecod! mamma, your own notes are the wildest of the two.

MRS. HARDCASTLE. Was ever the like? But I see he wants to break my heart, I see he does.

HASTINGS. Dear madam, permit me to lecture the young gentleman a little. I'm certain I can persuade him to his duty.

MRS. HARDCASTLE. Well! I must retire. Come, Constance, my love. You see, Mr. Hastings, the wretchedness of my situation: was ever poor woman so plagued with a dear, sweet, pretty, provoking, undutiful boy.

[*Exeunt* MRS. HARDCASTLE *and* MISS NEVILLE.]

[HASTINGS, TONY.]

TONY [*singing*]. "There was a young man riding by, and fain would have his will. Rang do didlo dee." Don't mind her. Let her cry. It's the comfort of her heart. I have seen her and sister cry over a book for an hour together, and they said they liked the book the better the more it made them cry.

HASTINGS. Then you're no friend to the ladies, I find, my pretty young gentleman?

TONY. That's as I find 'um.

HASTINGS. Not to her of your mother's choosing, I dare answer? And yet she appears to me a pretty well-tempered girl.

TONY. That's because you don't know her as well as I. Ecod! I know every inch about her; and there's not a more bitter cantankerous toad in all Christendom!

HASTINGS [aside]. Pretty encouragement this for a lover!

TONY. I have seen her since the height of that. She has as many tricks as a hare in a thicket, or a colt the first day's breaking.

HASTINGS. To me she appears sensible and silent!

TONY. Ay, before company. But when she's with her playmates, she's as loud as a hog in a gate.

HASTINGS. But there is a meek modesty about her that charms me.

TONY. Yes, but curb her never so little, she kicks up, and you're flung in a ditch.

HASTINGS. Well, but you must allow her a little beauty.—Yes, you must allow her some beauty.

TONY. Bandbox! She's all a made-up thing, mun. Ah! could you but see Bet Bouncer of these parts, you might then talk of beauty. Ecod! she has two eyes as black as sloes, and cheeks as broad and red as a pulpit cushion. She'd make two of she.

HASTINGS. Well, what say you to a friend that would take this bitter bargain off your hands?

TONY. Anon!

HASTINGS. Would you thank him that would take Miss Neville, and leave you to happiness and your dear Betsy?

TONY. Ay; but where is there such a friend, for who would take her?

HASTINGS. I am he. If you but assist me, I'll engage to whip her off to France, and you shall never hear more of her.

TONY. Assist you! Ecod, I will, to the last drop of my blood. I'll clap a pair of horses to your chaise that shall trundle you off in a twinkling, and may be get you a part of her fortin besides, in jewels, that you little dream of.

HASTINGS. My dear 'Squire, this looks like a lad of spirit.

TONY. Come along, then, and you shall see more of my spirit before you have done with me.   [Singing.]
"We are the boys
     That fears no noise,
Where the thundering cannons roar."
                              [Exeunt.]

ACT III

SCENE I—The house.

[Enter HARDCASTLE, alone.]

HARDCASTLE. What could my old friend Sir Charles mean by recommending his son as the modestest young man in town? To me he appears the most impudent piece of brass that ever spoke with a tongue. He has taken possession of the easy chair by the fire-side already. He took his boots off in the parlour, and desired me to see them taken care of. I'm desirous to know how his impudence affects my daughter.— She will certainly be shocked at it.

[Enter MISS HARDCASTLE, plainly dressed.]

HARDCASTLE. Well, my Kate, I see you have changed your dress, as I bid you; and yet, I believe, there was no great occasion.

MISS HARDCASTLE. I find such a pleasure, sir, in obeying your commands, that I take care to observe them without ever debating their propriety.

HARDCASTLE. And yet, Kate, I sometimes give you some cause, particularly when I recommended my modest gentleman to you as a lover to-day.

MISS HARDCASTLE. You taught me to expect something extraordinary, and I find the original exceeds the description.

HARDCASTLE. I was never so surprised in my life! He has quite confounded all my faculties!

MISS HARDCASTLE. I never saw anything like it; and a man of the world, too!

HARDCASTLE. Ay, he learned it all abroad,—what a fool was I, to think a young man could learn modesty by traveling. He might as soon learn wit at a masquerade.

MISS HARDCASTLE. It seems all natural to him.

HARDCASTLE. A good deal assisted by bad company and a French dancing-master.

MISS HARDCASTLE. Sure, you mistake, papa! A French dancing-master could never have taught him that timid look,—that awkward address,—that bashful manner—

HARDCASTLE. Whose look? whose manner, child?

MISS HARDCASTLE. Mr. Marlow's: his *mauvaise honte*, his timidity, struck me at the first sight.

HARDCASTLE. Then your first sight deceived you; for I think him one of the most brazen first sights that ever astonished my senses.

MISS HARDCASTLE. Sure, sir, you rally! I never saw any one so modest.

HARDCASTLE. And can you be serious! I never saw such a bouncing, swaggering puppy since I was born. Bully Dawson was but a fool to him.

MISS HARDCASTLE. Surprising! He met me with a respectful bow, a stammering voice, and a look fixed on the ground.

HARDCASTLE. He met me with a loud voice, a lordly air, and a familiarity that made my blood freeze again.

MISS HARDCASTLE. He treated me with diffidence and respect; censured the manners of the age; admired the prudence of girls that never laughed; tired me with apologies for being tiresome; then left the room with a bow, and "Madam, I would not for the world detain you."

HARDCASTLE. He spoke to me as if he knew me all his life before; asked twenty questions, and never waited for an answer; interrupted my best remarks with some silly pun; and when I was in my best story of the Duke of Marlborough and Prince Eugene, he asked if I had not a good hand at making punch. Yes, Kate, he asked your father if he was a maker of punch.

MISS HARDCASTLE. One of us must certainly be mistaken.

HARDCASTLE. If he be what he has shown himself, I'm determined he shall never have my consent.

MISS HARDCASTLE. And if he be the sullen thing I take him, he shall never have mine.

HARDCASTLE. In one thing, then, we are agreed—to reject him.

MISS HARDCASTLE. Yes—but upon conditions. For if you should find him less impudent, and I more presuming; if you find him more respectful, and I more importunate—I don't know—the fellow is well enough for a man—Certainly we don't meet many such at a horse-race in the country.

HARDCASTLE. If we should find him so —But that's impossible. The first appearance has done my business. I'm seldom deceived in that.

MISS HARDCASTLE. And yet there may be many good qualities under that first appearance.

HARDCASTLE. Ay, when a girl finds a fellow's outside to her taste, she then sets about guessing the rest of his furniture. With her, a smooth face stands for good sense, and a genteel figure for every virtue.

MISS HARDCASTLE. I hope, sir, a conversation begun with a compliment to my good sense won't end with a sneer at my understanding?

HARDCASTLE. Pardon me, Kate. But if young Mr. Brazen can find the art of reconciling contradictions, he may please us both, perhaps.

MISS HARDCASTLE. And as one of us must be mistaken, what if we go to make further discoveries?

HARDCASTLE. Agreed. But depend on't, I'm in the right.

MISS HARDCASTLE. And, depend on't, I'm not much in the wrong. [*Exeunt.*]

[*Enter* TONY, *running in with a casket.*]

TONY. Ecod! I have got them. Here they are. My cousin Con's necklaces, bobs and all. My mother shan't cheat the poor souls out of their fortin neither. O, my genus! is that you?

[*Enter* HASTINGS.]

HASTINGS. My dear friend, how have you managed with your mother? I hope you have amused her with pretending love for your cousin, and that you are willing to be reconciled at last? Our horses will be refreshed in a short time, and we shall soon be ready to set off.

TONY. And here's something to bear your charges by the way,—[*giving the casket*] your sweetheart's jewels. Keep them; and hang those, I say, that would rob you of one of them!

HASTINGS. But how have you procured them from your mother?

TONY. Ask me no questions, and I'll tell you no fibs. I procured them by the rule of thumb. If I had not a key to every drawer in mother's bureau, how could I go to the alehouse so often as I do? An honest man may rob himself of his own at any time.

HASTINGS. Thousands do it every day. But to be plain with you; Miss Neville is endeavouring to procure them from her aunt this very instant. If she succeeds, it will be the most delicate way at least of obtaining them.

TONY. Well, keep them, until you know how it will be. But I know how it will be well enough; she'd as soon part with the only sound tooth in her head.

HASTINGS. But I dread the effects of her resentment when she finds she has lost them.

TONY. Never you mind her resentment, leave *me* to manage that. I don't value her resentment the bounce of a cracker. Zounds! here they are! Morrice! Prance!

[*Exit* HASTINGS.]

[TONY, MRS. HARDCASTLE, MISS NEVILLE.]

MRS. HARDCASTLE. Indeed, Constance, you amaze me. Such a girl as you want jewels? It will be time enough for jewels, my dear, twenty years hence, when your beauty begins to want repairs.

MISS NEVILLE. But what will repair beauty at forty will certainly improve it at twenty, madam.

MRS. HARDCASTLE. Yours, my dear, can admit of none. That natural blush is beyond a thousand ornaments. Besides, child, jewels are quite out at present. Don't you see half the ladies of our acquaintance, my Lady Kill-day-light, and Mrs. Crump, and the rest of them, carry their jewels to town, and bring nothing but paste and marcasites back?

MISS NEVILLE. But who knows, madam, but somebody that shall be nameless would like me best with all my little finery about me?

MRS. HARDCASTLE. Consult your glass, my dear, and then see if, with such a pair of eyes, you want any better sparklers. What do you think, Tony, my dear? Does your cousin Con want any jewels, in your eyes, to set off her beauty?

TONY. That's as thereafter may be.

MISS NEVILLE. My dear aunt, if you knew how it would oblige me.

MRS. HARDCASTLE. A parcel of old-fashioned rose and table-cut things. They would make you look like the court of King Solomon at a puppet-show. Besides, I believe I can't readily come at them. They may be missing, for aught I know to the contrary.

TONY [*apart to* MRS. HARDCASTLE]. Then why don't you tell her so at once, as she's so longing for them? Tell her they're lost. It's the only way to quiet her. Say they're lost, and call me to bear witness.

MRS. HARDCASTLE [*apart to* TONY]. You know, my dear, I'm only keeping them for you. So if I say they're gone, you'll bear me witness, will you? He! he! he!

TONY [*apart to* MRS. HARDCASTLE]. Never fear me. Ecod! I'll say I saw them taken out with my own eyes.

MISS NEVILLE. I desire them but for a day, madam. Just to be permitted to show them as relics, and then they may be locked up again.

MRS. HARDCASTLE. To be plain with you, my dear Constance, if I could find them, you should have them. They're missing, I assure you. Lost, for aught I know; but we must have patience wherever they are.

MISS NEVILLE. I'll not believe it; this is but a shallow pretence to deny me. I know they are too valuable to be so slightly kept, and as you are to answer for the loss—

MRS. HARDCASTLE. Don't be alarmed, Constance. If they be lost, I must restore an equivalent. But my son knows they are missing, and not to be found.

TONY. That I can bear witness to. They are missing, and not to be found; I'll take my oath on't.

MRS. HARDCASTLE. You must learn resignation, my dear; for though we lose our fortune, yet we should not lose our patience. See me, how calm I am.

MISS NEVILLE. Ay, people are generally calm at the misfortunes of others.

MRS. HARDCASTLE. Now, I wonder a girl of your good sense should waste a thought upon such trumpery. We shall soon find them; and, in the mean time, you shall make use of my garnets till your jewels be found.

MISS NEVILLE. I detest garnets!

MRS. HARDCASTLE. The most becoming things in the world to set off a clear complexion. You have often seen how well they look upon me. You *shall* have them. [*Exit.*]

MISS NEVILLE. I dislike them of all things. You shan't stir.—Was ever any thing so provoking, to mislay my own jewels, and force me to wear her trumpery?

TONY. Don't be a fool. If she gives you the garnets, take what you can get. The jewels are your own already. I have stolen them out of her bureau, and she does not know it. Fly to your spark; he'll tell you more of the matter. Leave me to manage her.

MISS NEVILLE. My dear cousin!

TONY. Vanish. She's here, and has missed them already. [*Exit* MISS NEVILLE.] Zounds! how she fidgets and spits about like a Catherine wheel.

[*Enter* MRS. HARDCASTLE.]

MRS. HARDCASTLE. Confusion! thieves! robbers! we are cheated, plundered, broke open, undone.

TONY. What's the matter, what's the matter, mamma? I hope nothing has happened to any of the good family!

MRS. HARDCASTLE. We are robbed. My bureau has been broke open, the jewels taken out, and I'm undone.

TONY. Oh! is that all? Ha! ha! ha! By the laws I never saw it better acted in my life. Ecod, I thought you was ruined in earnest, ha! ha! ha!

MRS. HARDCASTLE. Why, boy, I *am* ruined in earnest. My bureau has been broke open, and all taken away.

TONY. Stick to that; ha! ha! ha! stick to that. I'll bear witness, you know; call me to bear witness.

MRS. HARDCASTLE. I tell you, Tony, by all that's precious, the jewels are gone, and I shall be ruined forever.

TONY. Sure I know they're gone, and I am to say so.

MRS. HARDCASTLE. My dearest Tony, but hear me. They're gone, I say.

TONY. By the laws, mamma, you make me for to laugh, ha! ha! I know who took them well enough, ha! ha! ha!

MRS. HARDCASTLE. Was there ever such a blockhead, that can't tell the difference between jest and earnest! I can tell you I'm not in jest, booby!

TONY. That's right, that's right; you must be in a bitter passion, and then nobody will suspect either of us. I'll bear witness that they are gone.

MRS. HARDCASTLE. Was there ever such a cross-grained brute, that won't hear me! Can you bear witness that you're no better than a fool? Was ever poor woman so beset with fools on one hand, and thieves on the other!

TONY. I can bear witness to that.

MRS. HARDCASTLE. Bear witness again, you blockhead, you, and I'll turn you out of the room directly. My poor niece, what will become of her? Do you laugh, you unfeeling brute, as if you enjoyed my distress?

TONY. I can bear witness to that.

MRS. HARDCASTLE. Do you insult me, monster? I'll teach you to vex your mother, I will!

TONY. I can bear witness to that.

[*He runs off; she follows him.*]

[*Enter* MISS HARDCASTLE *and* MAID.]

MISS HARDCASTLE. What an unaccountable creature is that brother of mine, to send them to the house as an inn, ha! ha! I don't wonder at his impudence.

MAID. But what is more, madam, the young gentleman, as you passed by in your present dress, asked me if you were the bar-maid. He mistook you for the bar-maid, madam!

MISS HARDCASTLE. Did he? Then, as I live, I'm resolved to keep up the delusion. Tell me, Pimple, how do you like my present dress? Don't you think I look something like Cherry in the *Beaux' Stratagem?*

MAID. It's the dress, madam, that every lady wears in the country, but when she visits or receives company.

MISS HARDCASTLE. And are you sure he does not remember my face or person?

MAID. Certain of it!

MISS HARDCASTLE. I vow, I thought so; for though we spoke for some time together, yet his fears were such that he never once looked up during the interview. Indeed, if he had, my bonnet would have kept him from seeing me.

MAID. But what do you hope from keeping him in his mistake?

MISS HARDCASTLE. In the first place, I shall be seen, and that is no small advantage to a girl who brings her face to market. Then I shall perhaps make an acquaintance, and that's no small victory gained over one who ,never addresses any but the wildest of her sex. But my chief aim is to take my gentleman off his guard, and, like an invisible champion of romance, examine the giant's force before I offer to combat.

MAID. But are you sure you can act your part, and disguise your voice, so that he may mistake that, as he has already mistaken your person?

MISS HARDCASTLE. Never fear me. I think I have got the true bar cant.—Did your honour call?—Attend the Lion there. —Pipes and tobacco for the Angel.—The Lamb has been outrageous this half hour.

MAID. It will do, madam. But he's here. [*Exit* MAID.]

[*Enter* MARLOW.]

MARLOW. What a bawling in every part of the house; I have scarce a moment's repose. If I go to the best room, there I find my host and his story; if I fly to the gallery, there we have my hostess with her curtesy down to the ground. I have at last got a moment to myself, and now for recollection. [*Walks and muses.*]

MISS HARDCASTLE. Did you call, sir? Did your honour call?

MARLOW [*musing*]. As for Miss Hardcastle, she's too grave and sentimental for me.

MISS HARDCASTLE. Did your honour call? [*She still places herself before him, he turning away.*]

MARLOW No, child! [*Musing.*] Besides, from the glimpse I had of her, I think she squints.

MISS HARDCASTLE. I'm sure, sir, I heard the bell ring.

MARLOW. No, no! [*Musing.*] I have pleased my father, however, by coming down, and I'll to-morrow please myself by returning.

[*Taking out his tablets and perusing.*]

MISS HARDCASTLE. Perhaps the other gentleman called, sir?

MARLOW. I tell you no.

MISS HARDCASTLE. I should be glad to know, sir. We have such a parcel of servants.

MARLOW. No, no, I tell you. [*Looks full in her face.*] Yes, child, I think I did call. I wanted—I wanted—I vow, child, you are vastly handsome!

MISS HARDCASTLE. O la, sir, you'll make one ashamed.

MARLOW. Never saw a more sprightly, malicious eye. Yes, yes, my dear, I did call. Have you got any of your—a—what d'ye call it in the house?

MISS HARDCASTLE. No, sir, we have been out of that these ten days.

MARLOW. One may call in this house, I find, to very little purpose. Suppose I should call for a taste, just by way of trial, of the nectar of your lips; perhaps I might be disappointed in that too?

MISS HARDCASTLE. Nectar? nectar? That's a liquor there's no call for in these parts. French, I suppose. We keep no French wines here, sir.

MARLOW. Of true English growth, I assure you.

MISS HARDCASTLE. Then it's odd I should not know it. We brew all sorts of wines in this house, and I have lived here these eighteen years.

MARLOW. Eighteen years! Why, one would think, child, you kept the bar before you were born. How old are you?

MISS HARDCASTLE. O! sir, I must not tell my age. They say women and music should never be dated.

MARLOW. To guess at this distance, you can't be much above forty. [Approaching.] Yet nearer, I don't think so much. [Approaching.] By coming close to some women, they look younger still; but when we come very close indeed—[Attempting to kiss her.]

MISS HARDCASTLE. Pray, sir, keep your distance. One would think you wanted to know one's age as they do horses, by mark of mouth.

MARLOW. I protest, child, you use me extremely ill. If you keep me at this distance, how is it possible you and I can be ever acquainted?

MISS HARDCASTLE. And who wants to be acquainted with you? I want no such acquaintance, not I. I'm sure you did not treat Miss Hardcastle, that was here a while ago, in this obstropalous manner. I'll warrant me, before her you looked dashed, and kept bowing to the ground, and talked, for all the world, as if you were before a justice of peace.

MARLOW [aside]. Egad, she has hit it, sure enough! [To her.] In awe of her, child? Ha! ha! ha! A mere awkward squinting thing! No, no! I find you don't know me. I laughed and rallied her a little; but I was unwilling to be too severe. No, I could not be too severe, curse me!

MISS HARDCASTLE. Oh, then, sir, you are a favourite, I find, among the ladies?

MARLOW. Yes, my dear, a great favourite. And yet, hang me, I don't see what they find in me to follow. At the Ladies' Club in town I'm called their agreeable Rattle. Rattle, child, is not my real name, but one I'm known by. My name is Solomons; Mr. Solomons, my dear, at your service. [Offering to salute her.]

MISS HARDCASTLE. Hold, sir; you are introducing me to your club, not to yourself. And you're so great a favourite there, you say?

MARLOW. Yes, my dear. There's Mrs. Mantrap, Lady Betty Blackleg, the Countess of Sligo, Mrs. Longhorns, old Miss Biddy Buckskin, and your humble servant, keep up the spirit of the place.

MISS HARDCASTLE. Then it's a very merry place, I suppose?

MARLOW. Yes, as merry as cards, suppers, wine, and old women can make us.

MISS HARDCASTLE. And their agreeable Rattle, ha! ha! ha!

MARLOW [aside]. Egad! I don't quite like this chit. She looks knowing, methinks. You laugh, child?

MISS HARDCASTLE. I can't but laugh to think what time they all have for minding their work or their family.

MARLOW [aside]. All's well; she don't laugh at me. [To her.] Do you ever work, child?

MISS HARDCASTLE. Ay, sure. There's not a screen or a quilt in the whole house but what can bear witness to that.

MARLOW. Odso! Then you must show me your embroidery. I embroider and draw patterns myself a little. If you want a judge of your work, you must apply to me. [Seizing her hand.]

[*Enter* HARDCASTLE, *who stands in surprise.*]

MISS HARDCASTLE. Ay, but the colours don't look well by candlelight. You shall see all in the morning. [*Struggling.*]

MARLOW. And why not now, my angel? Such beauty fires beyond the power of resistance.—Pshaw! the father here! My old luck: I never nicked seven that I did not throw ames-ace three times following. [*Exit* MARLOW.]

HARDCASTLE. So, madam! So I find *this* is your *modest* lover. This is your humble admirer, that kept his eyes fixed on the ground, and only adored at humble distance. Kate, Kate, art thou not ashamed to deceive your father so?

MISS HARDCASTLE. Never trust me, dear papa, but he's still the modest man I first took him for; you'll be convinced of it as well as I.

HARDCASTLE. By the hand of my body, I believe his impudence is infectious! Didn't I see him seize your hand? Didn't I see him haul you about like a milkmaid? And now you talk of his respect and his modesty, forsooth!

MISS HARDCASTLE. But if I shortly convince you of his modesty, that he has only the faults that will pass off with time, and the virtues that will improve with age, I hope you'll forgive him.

HARDCASTLE. The girl would actually make one run mad! I tell you I'll not be convinced. I am convinced. He has scarcely been three hours in the house, and he has already encroached on all my prerogatives. You may like his impudence, and call it modesty; but my son-in-law, madam, must have very different qualifications.

MISS HARDCASTLE. Sir, I ask but this night to convince you.

HARDCASTLE. You shall not have half the time, for I have thoughts of turning him out this very hour.

MISS HARDCASTLE. Give me that hour, then, and I hope to satisfy you.

HARDCASTLE. Well, an hour let it be then. But I'll have no trifling with your father. All fair and open, do you mind me?

MISS HARDCASTLE. I hope, sir, you have ever found that I considered your commands as my pride; for your kindness is such that my duty as yet has been inclination. [*Exeunt.*]

ACT IV

SCENE I—*The house.*

[*Enter* HASTINGS *and* MISS NEVILLE.]

HASTINGS. You surprise me; Sir Charles Marlow expected here this night! Where have you had your information?

MISS NEVILLE. You may depend upon it. I just saw his letter to Mr. Hardcastle, in which he tells him he intends setting out in a few hours after his son.

HASTINGS. Then, my Constance, all must be complete before he arrives. He knows me; and should he find me here, would discover my name, and perhaps, my designs, to the rest of the family.

MISS NEVILLE. The jewels, I hope, are safe?

HASTINGS. Yes, yes. I have sent them to Marlow, who keeps the keys of our baggage. In the mean time, I'll go to prepare matters for our elopement. I have had the 'Squire's promise of a fresh pair of horses; and, if I should not see him again, will write him further directions. [*Exit.*]

MISS NEVILLE. Well, success attend you! In the mean time, I'll go amuse my aunt with the old pretence of a violent passion for my cousin. [*Exit.*]

[*Enter* MARLOW, *followed by a* SERVANT.]

MARLOW. I wonder what Hastings could mean by sending me so valuable a thing as a casket to keep for him, when he knows the only place I have is the seat of a post-coach at an inn-door. Have you deposited the casket with the landlady, as I ordered you? Have you put it into her own hands?

SERVANT. Yes, your honour,

MARLOW. She said she'd keep it safe, did she?

SERVANT. Yes; she said she'd keep it safe enough; she asked me how I came by it; and she said she had a great mind to make me give an account of myself.

[*Exit* SERVANT.]

MARLOW. Ha! ha! ha! They're safe, however. What an unaccountable set of beings have we got amongst! This little bar-maid, though, runs in my head most strangely, and drives out the absurdities of all the rest of the family. She's mine, she must be mine, or I'm greatly mistaken.

[*Enter* HASTINGS.]

HASTINGS. Bless me! I quite forgot to tell her that I intended to prepare at the bottom of the garden. Marlow here, and in spirits too!

MARLOW. Give me joy, George! Crown me, shadow me with laurels! Well, George, after all, we modest fellows don't want for success among the women.

HASTINGS. Some women, you mean. But what success has your honour's modesty been crowned with now that it grows so insolent upon us?

MARLOW. Didn't you see the tempting, brisk, lovely, little thing, that runs about the house with a bunch of keys to its girdle?

HASTINGS. Well, and what then?

MARLOW. She's mine, you rogue, you. Such fire, such motion, such eyes, such lips —but, egad! she would not let me kiss them though.

HASTINGS. But are you sure, so very sure of her?

MARLOW. Why, man, she talked of showing me her work above stairs, and I am to approve the pattern.

HASTINGS. But how can you, Charles, go about to rob a woman of her honour?

MARLOW. Pshaw! pshaw! We all know the honour of the bar-maid of an inn. I don't intend to rob her, take my word for it.

HASTINGS. I believe the girl has virtue.

MARLOW. And if she has, I should be the last man in the world that would attempt to corrupt it.

HASTINGS. You have taken care, I hope, of the casket I sent you to lock up? It's in safety?

MARLOW. Yes, yes. It's safe enough. I have taken care of it. But how could you think the seat of a post-coach at an inn-door a place of safety? Ah! numskull! I have taken better precautions for you than you did for yourself—I have—

HASTINGS. What?

MARLOW. I have sent it to the landlady to keep for you.

HASTINGS. To the landlady!

MARLOW. The landlady.

HASTINGS. You did!

MARLOW. I did. She's to be answerable for its forthcoming, you know.

HASTINGS. Yes, she'll bring it forth with a witness.

MARLOW. Wasn't I right? I believe you'll allow that I acted prudently upon this occasion.

HASTINGS [*aside*]. He must not see my uneasiness.

MARLOW. You seem a little disconcerted though, methinks. Sure, nothing has happened?

HASTINGS. No, nothing. Never was in better spirits in all my life. And so you left it with the landlady, who, no doubt, very readily undertook the charge?

MARLOW. Rather too readily. For she not only kept the casket, but, through her great precaution, was going to keep the messenger too. Ha! ha! ha!

HASTINGS. He! he! he! They're safe, however.

MARLOW. As a guinea in a miser's purse.

HASTINGS [*aside*]. So now all hopes of fortune are at an end, and we must set off without it. [*To him.*] Well, Charles, I'll leave you to your meditations on the pretty bar-maid, and, he! he! he! may you be as successful for yourself as you have been for me. [*Exit.*]

MARLOW. Thank ye, George: I ask no more. Ha! ha! ha!

[*Enter* HARDCASTLE.]

HARDCASTLE. I no longer know my own house. It's turned all topsey-turvey. His servants have got drunk already. I'll bear it no longer; and yet, from my respect for his father, I'll be calm. [*To him.*] Mr. Marlow, your servant. I'm your very humble servant. [*Bowing low.*]

MARLOW. Sir, your humble servant. [*Aside.*] What is to be the wonder now?

HARDCASTLE. I believe, sir, you must be sensible, sir, that no man alive ought to be more welcome than your father's son, sir. I hope you think so?

MARLOW. I do from my soul, sir. I don't want much entreaty. I generally make my father's son welcome wherever he goes.

HARDCASTLE. I believe you do, from my soul, sir. But though I say nothing to your own conduct, that of your servants is insufferable. Their manner of drinking is setting a very bad example in this house, I assure you.

MARLOW. I protest, my very good sir, that is no fault of mine. If they don't drink as they ought, they are to blame. I ordered them not to spare the cellar. I did, I assure you. [*To the side-scene.*] Here, let one of my servants come up. [*To him.*] My positive directions were, that as I did not drink myself, they should make up for my deficiencies below.

HARDCASTLE. Then they had your orders for what they do? I'm satisfied!

MARLOW. They had, I assure you. You shall hear it from one of themselves.

[*Enter* SERVANT, *drunk.*]

MARLOW. You, Jeremy! Come forward, sirrah! What were my orders? Were you not told to drink freely, and call for what you thought fit, for the good of the house?

HARDCASTLE [*aside*]. I begin to lose my patience.

JEREMY. Please your honour, liberty and Fleet Street forever! Though I'm but a servant, I'm as good as another man. I'll drink for no man before sup-

per, sir, damme! Good liquor will sit upon a good supper, but a good supper will not sit upon—hiccup—upon my conscience, sir. [*Exit.*]

MARLOW. You see, my old friend, the fellow is as drunk as he can possibly be. I don't know what you'd have more, unless you'd have the poor devil soused in a beer-barrel.

HARDCASTLE. Zounds! he'll drive me distracted, if I contain myself any longer. Mr. Marlow. Sir, I have submitted to your insolence for more than four hours, and I see no likelihood of its coming to an end. I'm now resolved to be master here, sir, and I desire that you and your drunken pack may leave my house directly.

MARLOW. Leave your house!—Sure, you jest, my good friend! What, when I am doing what I can to please you!

HARDCASTLE. I tell you, sir, you don't please me; so I desire you'll leave my house.

MARLOW. Sure, you cannot be serious? At this time of night, and such a night? You only mean to banter me.

HARDCASTLE. I tell you, sir, I'm serious! and, now that my passions are roused, I say this house is mine, sir; this house is mine, and I command you to leave it directly.

MARLOW. Ha! ha! ha! A puddle in a storm. I shan't stir a step, I assure you. [*In a serious tone.*] This your house, fellow! It's my house. This is my house. Mine, while I choose to stay. What right have you to bid me leave this house, sir? I never met with such impudence, curse me; never in my whole life before.

HARDCASTLE. Nor I, confound me if ever I did! To come to my house, to call for what he likes, to turn me out of my own chair, to insult the family, to order his servants to get drunk, and then to tell me, "This house is mine, sir." By all that's impudent, it makes me laugh. Ha! ha! ha! Pray, sir, [*bantering*] as you take the house, what think you to taking the rest of the furniture? There's a pair of silver candlesticks, and there's a fire-screen, and here's a pair of brazen-nosed bellows; perhaps you may take a fancy to them?

MARLOW. Bring me your bill, sir; bring me your bill, and let's make no more words about it.

HARDCASTLE. There are a set of prints, too. What think you of the Rake's Progress for your own apartment?

MARLOW. Bring me your bill, I say; and I'll leave you and your infernal house directly.

HARDCASTLE. Then there's a mahogany table that you may see your face in.

MARLOW. My bill, I say.

HARDCASTLE. I had forgot the great chair for your own particular slumbers, after a hearty meal.

MARLOW. Zounds! bring me my bill, I say, and let's hear no more on't.

HARDCASTLE. Young man, young man, from your father's letter to me, I was taught to expect a well-bred, modest man as a visitor here, but now I find him no better than a coxcomb and a bully; but he will be down here presently, and shall hear more of it. [Exit.]

MARLOW. How's this! Sure, I have not mistaken the house? Everything looks like an inn. The servants cry "Coming." The attendance is awkward; the bar-maid, too, to attend us. But she's here, and will further inform me. Whither so fast, child? A word with you.

[Enter MISS HARDCASTLE.]

MISS HARDCASTLE. Let it be short, then. I'm in a hurry.—[Aside.] I believe he begins to find out his mistake. But it's too soon quite to undeceive him.

MARLOW. Pray, child, answer me one question. What are you, and what may your business in this house be?

MISS HARDCASTLE. A relation of the family, sir.

MARLOW. What, a poor relation?

MISS HARDCASTLE. Yes, sir. A poor relation, appointed to keep the keys and to see that the guests want nothing in my power to give them.

MARLOW. That is, you act as the bar-maid of this inn.

MISS HARDCASTLE. Inn! O law— What brought that into your head? One of the first families in the county keep an inn!—Ha! ha! ha! old Mr. Hardcastle's house an inn!

MARLOW. Mr. Hardcastle's house! Is this Mr. Hardcastle's house, child?

MISS HARDCASTLE. Ay, sure. Whose else should it be?

MARLOW. So, then, all's out, and I have been damnably imposed on. O, confound my stupid head, I shall be laughed at over the whole town. I shall be stuck up in caricature in all the print-shops. The Dullissimo Macaroni. To mistake this house of all others for an inn, and my father's old friend for an innkeeper! What a swaggering puppy must he take me for! What a silly puppy do I find myself! There again, may I be hanged, my dear, but I mistook you for the bar-maid.

MISS HARDCASTLE. Dear me! dear me! I'm sure there's nothing in my *behaviour* to put me upon a level with one of that stamp.

MARLOW. Nothing, my dear, nothing. But I was in for a list of blunders, and could not help making you a subscriber. My stupidity saw everything the wrong way. I mistook your assiduity for assurance, and your simplicity for allurement. But it's over—this house I no more show *my* face in.

MISS HARDCASTLE. I hope, sir, I have done nothing to disoblige you. I'm sure I should be sorry to affront any gentleman who has been so polite, and said so many civil things to me. I'm sure I should be sorry [*pretending to cry*] if he left the family on my account. I'm sure I should be sorry people said anything amiss, since I have no fortune but my character.

MARLOW [*aside*]. By Heaven! she weeps. This is the first mark of tenderness I ever had from a modest woman, and it touches me. [*To her.*] Excuse me, my lovely girl; you are the only part of the family I leave with reluctance. But to be plain with you, the difference of our birth, fortune, and education, make an honourable connexion impossible; and I can never harbour a thought of seducing simplicity that trusted in my honour, or bringing ruin upon one whose only fault was being too lovely.

MISS HARDCASTLE [aside]. Generous man! I now begin to admire him. [To him.] But I am sure my family is as good as Miss Hardcastle's; and though I'm poor, that's no great misfortune to a contented mind; and, until this moment, I never thought that it was bad to want fortune.

MARLOW. And why now, my pretty simplicity?

MISS HARDCASTLE. Because it puts me at a distance from one that if I had a thousand pounds I would give it all to.

MARLOW [aside]. This simplicity bewitches me so that if I stay I'm undone. I must make one bold effort, and leave her. [To her.] Your partiality in my favour, my dear, touches me most sensibly, and were I to live for myself alone, I could easily fix my choice. But I owe too much to the opinion of the world, too much to the authority of a father; so that—I can scarcely speak it—it affects me. Farewell! [Exit.]

MISS HARDCASTLE. I never knew half his merit till now. He shall not go if I have power or art to detain him. I'll still preserve the character in which I *stooped to conquer*, but I will undeceive my papa, who, perhaps, may laugh him out of his resolution. [Exit.]

[Enter TONY and MISS NEVILLE.]

TONY. Ay, you may steal for yourselves the next time. I have done my duty. She has got the jewels again, that's a sure thing; but she believes it was all a mistake of the servants.

MISS NEVILLE. But, my dear cousin, sure you won't forsake us in this distress? If she in the least suspects that I am going off, I shall certainly be locked up, or sent to my aunt Pedigree's, which is ten times worse.

TONY. To be sure, aunts of all kinds are damned bad things. But what can I do? I have got you a pair of horses that will fly like Whistle-jacket; and I'm sure you can't say but I have courted you nicely before her face. Here she comes; we must court a bit or two more, for fear she should suspect us. [They retire and seem to fondle.]

[Enter MRS. HARDCASTLE.]

MRS. HARDCASTLE. Well, I was greatly fluttered, to be sure. But my son tells me it was all a mistake of the servants. I shan't be easy, however, till they are fairly married, and then let her keep her own fortune. But what do I see? fondling together, as I'm alive. I never saw Tony so sprightly before. Ah! have I caught you, my pretty doves? What, billing, exchanging glances, and broken murmurs? Ah!

TONY. As for murmurs, mother, we grumble a little now and then, to be sure. But there's no love lost between us.

MRS. HARDCASTLE. A mere sprinkling, Tony, upon the flame, only to make it burn brighter.

MISS NEVILLE. Cousin Tony promises to give us more of his company at home. Indeed, he shan't leave us any more. It won't leave us, cousin Tony, will it?

TONY. O, it's a pretty creature! No, I'd sooner leave my horse in a pound, than leave you when you smile upon one so. Your laugh makes you so becoming.

MISS NEVILLE. Agreeable cousin! Who can help admiring that natural humour, that pleasant, broad, red, thoughtless [Patting his cheek.]—ah! it's a bold face!

MRS. HARDCASTLE. Pretty innocence!

TONY. I'm sure I always loved cousin Con's hazel eyes, and her pretty long fingers, that she twists this way and that over haspicholls, like a parcel of bobbins.

MRS. HARDCASTLE. Ah! he would charm the bird from the tree. I was never so happy before. My boy takes after his father, poor Mr. Lumpkin, exactly. The jewels, my dear Con, shall be yours incontinently. You shall have them. Isn't he a sweet boy, my dear? You shall be married to-morrow, and we'll put off the rest of his education, like Dr. Drowsy's sermons, to a fitter opportunity.

[*Enter* DIGGORY.]

DIGGORY. Where's the 'Squire? I have got a letter for your worship.

TONY. Give it to my mamma. She reads all my letters first.

DIGGORY. I had orders to deliver it into your own hands.

TONY. Who does it come from?

DIGGORY. Your worship mun ask that o' the letter itself. [*Exit* DIGGORY.]

TONY. I could wish to know, though. [*Turning the letter, and gazing on it.*]

MISS NEVILLE [*aside*]. Undone! undone! A letter to him from Hastings. I know the hand. If my aunt sees it, we are ruined forever. I'll keep her employed a little, if I can. [*To* MRS. HARDCASTLE.] But I have not told you, madam, of my cousin's smart answer just now to Mr. Marlow. We so laughed—You must know, madam.—This way a little, for he must not hear us. [*They confer.*]

TONY [*still gazing.*] A damned cramp piece of penmanship as ever I saw in my life. I can read your print-hand very well. But here there are such handles, and shanks, and dashes that one can scarce tell the head from the tail. "To Anthony Lumpkin, Esquire." It's very odd, I can read the outside of my letters where my own name is, well enough. But when I come to open it, it's all—buzz. That's hard—very hard; for the inside of the letter is always the cream of the correspondence.

MRS. HARDCASTLE. Ha! ha! ha! Very well, very well. And so my son was too hard for the philosopher.

MISS NEVILLE. Yes, madam; but you must hear the rest, madam. A little more this way, or he may hear us. You'll hear how he puzzled him again.

MRS. HARDCASTLE. He seems strangely puzzled now himself, methinks.

TONY [*still gazing*]. A damned up and down hand, as if it was disguised in liquor. [*Reading.*] "Dear Sir,"—Ay, that's that. Then there's an M, and a T, and an S, but whether the next be an izzard or an R, confound me, I cannot tell!

MRS. HARDCASTLE. What's that, my dear? Can I give you any assistance?

MISS NEVILLE. Pray, aunt, let me read it. Nobody reads a cramp hand better than I. [*Twitching the letter from her.*] Do you know who it is from?

TONY. Can't tell, except from Dick Ginger, the feeder.

MISS NEVILLE. Ay, so it is. [*Pretending to read.*] Dear 'Squire, hoping that you're in health, as I am at this present. The gentlemen of the Shakebag club has cut the gentlemen of the Goose-green quite out of feather. The odds—um—odd battle—um—long fighting—um—here, here, it's all about cocks and fighting; it's of no consequence; here, put it up, put it up. [*Thrusting the crumpled letter upon him.*]

TONY. But I tell you, miss, it's of all the consequence in the world! I would not lose the rest of it for a guinea! Here, mother, do you make it out. Of no consequence! [*Giving* MRS. HARDCASTLE *the letter.*]

MRS. HARDCASTLE. How's this? [*Reads.*] "Dear 'Squire, I'm now waiting for Miss Neville, with a post-chaise and pair, at the bottom of the garden, but I find my horses yet unable to perform the journey. I expect you'll assist us with a pair of fresh horses, as you promised. Dispatch is necessary, as the *hag* (ay, the hag) your mother, will otherwise suspect us. Yours, Hastings." Grant me patience. I shall run distracted! My rage chokes me!

MISS NEVILLE. I hope, madam, you'll suspend your resentment for a few moments, and not impute to me any impertinence, or sinister design, that belongs to another.

MRS. HARDCASTLE [*curtesying very low*]. Fine spoken, madam; you are most miraculously polite and engaging, and quite the very pink of curtesy and circumspection, madam. [*Changing her tone.*] And you, you great ill-fashioned oaf, with scarce sense enough to keep your mouth shut: were you, too, joined against me? But I'll defeat all your plots in a moment. As for you, madam, since you have got a pair of fresh horses ready, it would be cruel to disappoint them. So, if you please, instead of running away with your spark, prepare this very moment to run off with *me*. Your old aunt Pedigree will keep you secure, I'll warrant me. You too, sir, may mount your horse, and guard us upon the way. Here, Thomas, Roger, Diggory! I'll show you that I wish you better than you do yourselves. [*Exit.*]

MISS NEVILLE. So, now I'm completely ruined.

TONY. Ay, that's a sure thing.

MISS NEVILLE. What better could be expected from being connected with such a stupid fool,—and after all the nods and signs I made him!

TONY. By the laws, miss, it was your own cleverness, and not my stupidity, that did your business. You were so nice and so busy with your Shake-bags and Goose-greens that I thought you could never be making believe.

[*Enter HASTINGS.*]

HASTINGS. So, sir, I find by my servant that you have shown my letter, and betrayed us. Was this well done, young gentleman?

TONY. Here's another. Ask miss, there, who betrayed you. Ecod, it was her doing, not mine.

[*Enter MARLOW.*]

MARLOW. So I have been finely used here among you. Rendered contemptible, driven into ill-manners, despised, insulted, laughed at.

TONY. Here's another. We shall have old Bedlam broke loose presently.

MISS NEVILLE. And there, sir, is the gentleman to whom we all owe every obligation.

MARLOW. What can I say to him, a mere boy, an idiot, whose ignorance and age are a protection.

HASTINGS. A poor, contemptible booby, that would but disgrace correction.

MISS NEVILLE. Yet with cunning and malice enough to make himself merry with all our embarrassments.

HASTINGS. An insensible cub.

MARLOW. Replete with tricks and mischief.

TONY. Baw! damme, but I'll fight you both, one after the other—with baskets.

MARLOW. As for him, he's below resentment. But your conduct, Mr. Hastings, requires an explanation. You knew of my mistakes, yet would not undeceive me.

HASTINGS. Tortured as I am with my own disappointments, is this a time for explanations? It is not friendly, Mr. Marlow.

MARLOW. But sir—

MISS NEVILLE. Mr. Marlow, we never kept on your mistake, till it was too late to undeceive you. Be pacified.

[*Enter SERVANT.*]

SERVANT. My mistress desires you'll get ready immediately, madam. The horses are putting to. Your hat and things are in the next room. We are to go thirty miles before morning. [*Exit SERVANT.*]

MISS NEVILLE. Well, well; I'll come presently.

MARLOW [*to HASTINGS*]. Was it well done, sir, to assist in rendering me ridiculous? To hang me out for the scorn of all my acquaintance? Depend upon it, sir, I shall expect an explanation.

HASTINGS. Was it well done, sir, if you're upon that subject, to deliver what I entrusted to yourself, to the care of another, sir?

MISS NEVILLE. Mr. Hastings! Mr. Marlow! Why will you increase my distress by this groundless dispute? I implore, I entreat you—

[*Enter* SERVANT.]

SERVANT. Your cloak, madam. My mistress is impatient.

MISS NEVILLE. I come. [*Exit* SERVANT.] Pray, be pacified. If I leave you thus, I shall die with apprehension!

[*Enter* SERVANT.]

SERVANT. Your fan, muff, and gloves, madam. The horses are waiting.

MISS NEVILLE. O, Mr. Marlow! if you knew what a scene of constraint and ill-nature lies before me. I'm sure it would convert your resentment into pity.

MARLOW. I'm so distracted with a variety of passions that I don't know what I do. Forgive me, madam. George, forgive me. You know my hasty temper, and should not exasperate it.

HASTINGS. The torture of my situation is my only excuse.

MISS NEVILLE. Well, my dear Hastings, if you have that esteem for me that I think, that I am sure you have, your constancy for three years will but increase the happiness of our future connexion. If—

MRS. HARDCASTLE [*within*]. Miss Neville. Constance, why, Constance, I say.

MISS NEVILLE. I'm coming. Well, constancy, remember, constancy is the word. [*Exit followed by the* SERVANT.]

HASTINGS. My heart! how can I support this! To be so near happiness, and such happiness!

MARLOW [*to* TONY]. You see now, young gentleman, the effects of your folly. What might be amusement to you is here disappointment, and even distress.

TONY [*from a reverie*]. Ecod, I have hit it. It's here. Your hands. Yours, and yours, my poor Sulky. My boots there, ho!—Meet me, two hours hence at the bottom of the garden; and if you don't find Tony Lumpkin a more good-natured fellow than you thought for, I'll give you leave to take my best horse, and Bet Bouncer into the bargain. Come along. My boots, ho! [*Exeunt*.]

ACT V

SCENE I—*Continues*.

[*Enter* HASTINGS *and* SERVANT.]

HASTINGS. You saw the old lady and Miss Neville drive off, you say?

SERVANT. Yes, your honour. They went off in a post-coach, and the young 'Squire went on horseback. They're thirty miles off by this time.

HASTINGS. Then all my hopes are over.

SERVANT. Yes, sir. Old Sir Charles is arrived. He and the old gentleman of the house have been laughing at Mr. Marlow's mistake this half hour. They are coming this way.

HASTINGS. Then I must not be seen. So now to my fruitless appointment at the bottom of the garden. This is about the time. [*Exit*.]

[*Enter* SIR CHARLES *and* HARDCASTLE.]

HARDCASTLE. Ha! ha! ha! The peremptory tone in which he sent forth his sublime commands!

SIR CHARLES. And the reserve with which I suppose he treated all your advances.

HARDCASTLE. And yet he might have seen something in me above a common innkeeper, too.

SIR CHARLES. Yes, Dick, but he mistook you for an uncommon innkeeper; ha! ha! ha!

HARDCASTLE. Well, I'm in too good spirits to think of anything but joy. Yes, my dear friend, this union of our families will make our personal friendships hereditary; and though my daughter's fortune is but small—

SIR CHARLES. Why, Dick, will you talk of fortune to *me*? My son is possessed of more than a competence already, and can want nothing but a good and virtuous girl to share his happiness and increase it. If they like each other, as you say they do—

HARDCASTLE. *If*, man! I tell you they *do* like each other. My daughter as good as told me so.

SIR CHARLES. But girls are apt to flatter themselves, you know.

HARDCASTLE. I saw him grasp her hand in the warmest manner myself; and here he comes to put you out of your *ifs*, I warrant him.

[*Enter* MARLOW.]

MARLOW. I come, sir, once more, to ask pardon for my strange conduct. I can scarce reflect on my insolence without confusion.

HARDCASTLE. Tut, boy, a trifle. You take it too gravely. An hour or two's laughing with my daughter will set all to rights again. She'll never like you the worse for it.

MARLOW. Sir, I shall be always proud of her approbation.

HARDCASTLE. Approbation is but a cold word, Mr. Marlow; if I am not deceived, you have something more than approbation thereabouts. You take me!

MARLOW. Really, sir, I have not that happiness.

HARDCASTLE. Come, boy, I'm an old fellow, and know what's what as well as you that are younger. I know what has past between you; but mum.

MARLOW. Sure, sir, nothing has past between us but the most profound respect on my side, and the most distant reserve on hers. You don't think, sir, that my impudence has been past upon all the rest of the family?

HARDCASTLE. Impudence! No, I don't say that—not quite impudence—though girls like to be played with, and rumpled a little, too, sometimes. But she has told no tales, I assure you.

MARLOW. I never gave her the slightest cause.

HARDCASTLE. Well, well, I like modesty in its place well enough. But this is over-acting, young gentleman. You *may* be open. Your father and I will like you the better for it.

MARLOW. May I die, sir, if I ever—

HARDCASTLE. I tell you she don't dislike you; and as I'm sure you like her—

MARLOW. Dear sir—I protest, sir—

HARDCASTLE. I see no reason why you should not be joined as fast as the parson can tie you.

MARLOW. But hear me, sir—

HARDCASTLE. Your father approves the match, I admire it; every moment's delay will be doing mischief, so—

MARLOW. But why won't you hear me? By all that's just and true, I never gave Miss Hardcastle the slightest mark of my attachment, or even the most distant hint to suspect me of affection. We had but one interview, and that was formal, modest, and uninteresting.

HARDCASTLE [*aside*]. This fellow's formal, modest impudence is beyond bearing.

SIR CHARLES. And you never grasped her hand, or made any protestations?

MARLOW. As Heaven is my witness, I came down in obedience to your commands. I saw the lady without emotion, and parted without reluctance. I hope you'll exact no further proofs of my duty, nor prevent me from leaving a house in which I suffer so many mortifications.

[*Exit.*]

SIR CHARLES. I'm astonished at the air of sincerity with which he parted.

HARDCASTLE. And I'm astonished at the deliberate intrepidity of his assurance.

SIR CHARLES. I dare pledge my life and honour upon his truth.

HARDCASTLE. Here comes my daughter, and I would stake my happiness upon her veracity.

[*Enter* MISS HARDCASTLE.]

HARDCASTLE. Kate, come hither, child. Answer us sincerely, and without reserve: has Mr. Marlow made you any professions of love and affection?

MISS HARDCASTLE. The question is very abrupt, sir! But since you require unreserved sincerity, I think he has.

HARDCASTLE [*to* SIR CHARLES]. You see.

SIR CHARLES. And pray, madam, have you and my son had more than one interview?

MISS HARDCASTLE. Yes, sir, several.

HARDCASTLE [to SIR CHARLES]. You see.

SIR CHARLES. But did he profess any attachment?

MISS HARDCASTLE. A lasting one.

SIR CHARLES. Did he talk of love?

MISS HARDCASTLE. Much, sir.

SIR CHARLES. Amazing! And all this formally?

MISS HARDCASTLE. Formally.

HARDCASTLE. Now, my friend, I hope you are satisfied.

SIR CHARLES. And how did he behave, madam?

MISS HARDCASTLE. As most professed admirers do: said some civil things of my face, talked much of his want of merit, and the greatness of mine; mentioned his heart, gave a short tragedy speech, and ended with pretended rapture.

SIR CHARLES. Now I'm perfectly convinced, indeed. I know his conversation among women to be modest and submissive. This forward, canting, ranting manner by no means describes him; and, I am confident, he never sat for the picture.

MISS HARDCASTLE. Then what, sir, if I should convince you to your face of my sincerity? If you and my papa, in about half an hour, will place yourselves behind that screen, you shall hear him declare his passion to me in person.

SIR CHARLES. Agreed. And if I find him what you describe, all my happiness in him must have an end. [Exit.]

MISS HARDCASTLE. And if you don't find him what I describe—I fear my happiness must never have a beginning.
[Exeunt.]

SCENE II—The back of the garden.

[Enter HASTINGS.]

HASTINGS. What an idiot am I, to wait here for a fellow who probably takes a delight in mortifying me. He never intended to be punctual, and I'll wait no longer. What do I see? It is he! and perhaps with news of my Constance.

[Enter TONY, booted and spattered.]

HASTINGS. My honest 'Squire! I now find you a man of your word. This looks like friendship.

TONY. Ay, I'm your friend, and the best friend you have in the world, if you knew but all. This riding by night, by the bye, is cursedly tiresome. It has shook me worse than the basket of a stage-coach.

HASTINGS. But how? Where did you leave your fellow-travellers? Are they in safety? Are they housed?

TONY. Five-and-twenty miles in two hours and a half is no such bad driving. The poor beasts have smoked for it: rabbet me, but I'd rather ride forty miles after a fox, than ten with such varment.

HASTINGS. Well, but where have you left the ladies? I die with impatience.

TONY. Left them? Why, where should I leave them but where I found them?

HASTINGS. This is a riddle.

TONY. Riddle me this, then. What's that goes round the house, and round the house, and never touches the house?

HASTINGS. I'm still astray.

TONY. Why, that's it, mon. I have led them astray. By jingo, there's not a pond or a slough within five miles of the place but they can tell the taste of.

HASTINGS. Ha! ha! ha! I understand: you took them in a round while they supposed themselves going forward, and so you have at last brought them home again.

TONY. You shall hear. I first took them down Feather-bed Lane, where we stuck fast in the mud. I then rattled them crack over the stones of Up-and-down Hill. I then introduced them to the gibbet on Heavy-tree Heath; and from that, with a circumbendibus, I fairly lodged them in the horse-pond at the bottom of the garden.

HASTINGS. But no accident, I hope?

Tony. No, no. Only mother is confoundedly frightened. She thinks herself forty miles off. She's sick of the journey; and the cattle can scarce crawl. So, if your own horses be ready, you may whip off with cousin, and I'll be bound that no soul here can budge a foot to follow you.

Hastings. My dear friend, how can I be grateful?

Tony. Ay, now it's "dear friend," "noble 'Squire." Just now, it was all "idiot," "cub," and run me through the guts. Damn *your* way of fighting, I say. After we take a knock in this part of the country, we kiss and be friends. But if you had run me through the guts, then I should be dead, and you might go kiss the hangman.

Hastings. The rebuke is just. But I must hasten to relieve Miss Neville: if you keep the old lady employed, I promise to take care of the young one.

Tony. Never fear me. Here she comes; vanish. [*Exit* Hastings.] She's got from the pond, and draggled up to the waist like a mermaid.

[*Enter* Mrs. Hardcastle.]

Mrs. Hardcastle. Oh, Tony, I'm killed. Shook! Battered to death! I shall never survive it. That last jolt, that laid us against the quickset-hedge, has done my business.

Tony. Alack, mamma, it was all your own fault. You would be for running away by night, without knowing one inch of the way.

Mrs. Hardcastle. I wish we were at home again. I never met so many accidents in so short a journey. Drenched in the mud, overturned in a ditch, stuck fast in a slough, jolted to a jelly, and at last to lose our way! Whereabouts do you think we are, Tony?

Tony. By my guess, we should be upon Crack-skull Common, about forty miles from home.

Mrs. Hardcastle. O lud! O lud! The most notorious spot in all the country. We only want a robbery to make a complete night on't.

Tony. Don't be afraid, mamma, don't be afraid. Two of the five that kept here are hanged, and the other three may not find us. Don't be afraid.—Is that a man that's galloping behind us? No; it's only a tree.—Don't be afraid.

Mrs. Hardcastle. The fright will certainly kill me.

Tony. Do you see anything like a black hat moving behind the thicket?

Mrs. Hardcastle. Oh, death!

Tony. No; it's only a cow. Don't be afraid, mamma, don't be afraid.

Mrs. Hardcastle. As I'm alive, Tony, I see a man coming toward us. Ah, I am sure on't. If he perceives us, we are undone.

Tony [*aside*]. Father-in-law, by all that's unlucky, come to take one of his night walks. [*To her.*] Ah, it's a highwayman, with pistols as long as my arm. A damned ill-looking fellow!

Mrs. Hardcastle. Good Heaven, defend us! He approaches.

Tony. Do you hide yourself in that thicket, and leave me to manage him. If there be any danger, I'll cough, and cry hem. When I cough, be sure to keep close. [Mrs. Hardcastle *hides behind a tree in the back scene.*]

[*Enter* Hardcastle.]

Hardcastle. I'm mistaken, or I heard voices of people in want of help. Oh, Tony, is that you? I did not expect you so soon back. Are your mother and her charge in safety?

Tony. Very safe, sir, at my aunt Pedigree's. Hem.

Mrs. Hardcastle [*from behind*]. Ah, death! I find there's danger.

Hardcastle. Forty miles in three hours; sure that's too much, my youngster.

Tony. Stout horses and willing minds make short journeys, as they say. Hem.

Mrs. Hardcastle [*from behind*]. Sure, he'll do the dear boy no harm.

Hardcastle. But I heard a voice here; I should be glad to know from whence it came.

TONY. It was I, sir, talking to myself, sir. I was saying that forty miles in four hours was very good going. Hem. As to be sure it was. Hem. I have got a sort of cold by being out in the air. We'll go in, if you please. Hem.

HARDCASTLE. But if you talked to yourself, you did not answer yourself. I'm certain I heard two voices, and am resolved [*Raising his voice.*] to find the other out.

MRS. HARDCASTLE [*from behind*]. Oh! he's coming to find me out. Oh!

TONY. What need you go, sir, if I tell you? Hem. I'll lay down my life for the truth—hem—I'll tell you all, sir. [*Detaining him.*]

HARDCASTLE. I tell you I will not be detained. I insist on seeing. It's in vain to expect I'll believe you.

MRS. HARDCASTLE [*running forward from behind*]. O lud! he'll murder my poor boy, my darling! Here, good gentleman, whet your rage upon me. Take my money, my life, but spare that young gentleman; spare my child, if you have any mercy.

HARDCASTLE. My wife, as I'm a Christian. From whence can she come? or what does she mean?

MRS. HARDCASTLE [*kneeling*]. Take compassion on us, good Mr. Highwayman. Take our money, our watches, all we have, but spare our lives. We will never bring you to justice; indeed we won't, good Mr. Highwayman.

HARDCASTLE. I believe the woman's out of her senses. What, Dorothy, don't you know *me?*

MRS. HARDCASTLE. Mr. Hardcastle, as I'm alive! My fears blinded me. But who, my dear, could have expected to meet you here, in this frightful place, so far from home? What has brought you to follow us?

HARDCASTLE. Sure, Dorothy, you have not lost your wits? So far from home, when you are within forty yards of your own door! [*To him.*] This is one of your old tricks, you graceless rogue, you! [*To her.*] Don't you know the gate and the mulberry tree; and don't you remember the horse-pond, my dear?

MRS. HARDCASTLE. Yes, I shall remember the horse-pond as long as I live; I have caught my death in it. [*To* TONY.] And is it to you, you graceless varlet, I owe all this? I'll teach you to abuse your mother, I will.

TONY. Ecod, mother, all the parish says you have spoiled me, and so you may take the fruits on't.

MRS. HARDCASTLE. I'll spoil you, I will. [*Follows him off the stage.*]

HARDCASTLE. There's morality, however, in his reply. [*Exit.*]

[*Enter* HASTINGS *and* MISS NEVILLE.]

HASTINGS. My dear Constance, why will you deliberate thus? If we delay a moment, all is lost forever. Pluck up a little resolution, and we shall soon be out of the reach of her malignity.

MISS NEVILLE. I find it impossible. My spirits are so sunk with the agitations I have suffered, that I am unable to face any new danger. Two or three years' patience will at last crown us with happiness.

HASTINGS. Such a tedious delay is worse than inconstancy. Let us fly, my charmer. Let us date our happiness from this very moment. Perish fortune. Love and content will increase what we possess beyond a monarch's revenue. Let me prevail!

MISS NEVILLE. No, Mr. Hastings, no. Prudence once more comes to my relief, and I will obey its dictates. In the moment of passion, fortune may be despised, but it ever produces a lasting repentance. I'm resolved to apply to Mr. Hardcastle's compassion and justice for redress.

HASTINGS. But though he had the will, he has not the power to relieve you.

MISS NEVILLE. But he has influence, and upon that I am resolved to rely.

HASTINGS. I have no hopes. But, since you persist, I must reluctantly obey you. [*Exeunt.*]

SCENE III—*Room at* MR. HARDCASTLE'S.

[*Enter* SIR CHARLES MARLOW *and* MISS HARDCASTLE.]

SIR CHARLES. What a situation am I in! If what you say appears, I shall then find a guilty son. If what he says be true, I shall then lose one that, of all others, I most wished for a daughter.

MISS HARDCASTLE. I am proud of your approbation; and to show I merit it, if you place yourselves as I directed, you shall hear his explicit declaration. But he comes.

SIR CHARLES. I'll to your father, and keep him to the appointment. [*Exit* SIR CHARLES.]

[*Enter* MARLOW.]

MARLOW. Though prepared for setting out, I come once more to take leave; nor did I, till this moment, know the pain I feel in the separation.

MISS HARDCASTLE [*in her own natural manner*]. I believe these sufferings cannot be very great, sir, which you can so easily remove. A day or two longer, perhaps, might lessen your uneasiness, by showing the little value of what you now think proper to regret.

MARLOW [*aside*]. This girl every moment improves upon me. [*To her.*] It must not be, madam; I have already trifled too long with my heart. My very pride begins to submit to my passion. The disparity of education and fortune, the anger of a parent, and the contempt of my equals begin to lose their weight; and nothing can restore me to myself but this painful effort of resolution.

MISS HARDCASTLE. Then go, sir: I'll urge nothing more to detain you. Though my family be as good as hers you came down to visit, and my education, I hope, not inferior, what are these advantages without equal affluence? I must remain contented with the slight approbation of imputed merit; I must have only the mockery of your addresses, while all your serious aims are fixed on fortune.

[*Enter* HARDCASTLE *and* SIR CHARLES MARLOW *from behind.*]

SIR CHARLES. Here, behind this screen.

HARDCASTLE. Ay, ay; make no noise. I'll engage my Kate covers him with confusion at last.

MARLOW. By heavens, madam, fortune was ever my smallest consideration. Your beauty at first caught my eye; for who could see that without emotion? But every moment that I converse with you steals in some new grace, heightens the picture, and gives it stronger expression. What at first seemed rustic plainness, now appears refined simplicity. What seemed forward assurance, now strikes me as the result of courageous innocence and conscious virtue.

SIR CHARLES. What can it mean? He amazes me!

HARDCASTLE. I told you how it would be. Hush!

MARLOW. I am now determined to stay, madam, and I have too good an opinion of my father's discernment, when he sees you, to doubt his approbation.

MISS HARDCASTLE. No, Mr. Marlow, I will not, cannot detain you. Do you think I could suffer a connexion in which there is the smallest room for repentance? Do you think I would take the mean advantage of a transient passion to load you with confusion? Do you think I could ever relish that happiness which was acquired by lessening yours?

MARLOW. By all that's good, I can have no happiness but what's in your power to grant me! Nor shall I ever feel repentance but in not having seen your merits before. I will stay even contrary to your wishes; and though you should persist to shun me, I will make my respectful assiduities atone for the levity of my past conduct.

MISS HARDCASTLE. Sir, I must entreat you'll desist. As our acquaintance began, so let it end, in indifference. I might have given an hour or two to levity; but seriously, Mr. Marlow, do you think I could ever submit to a connexion where I must appear mercenary, and *you* imprudent.

Do you think I could ever catch at the confident addresses of a secure admirer?

MARLOW [kneeling]. Does this look like security! Does this look like confidence? No, madam, every moment that shows me your merit, only serves to increase my diffidence and confusion. Here let me continue—

SIR CHARLES. I can hold it no longer. Charles, Charles, how hast thou deceived me! Is this your indifference, your uninteresting conversation?

HARDCASTLE. Your cold contempt: your formal interview! What have you to say now?

MARLOW. That I'm all amazement! What can it mean?

HARDCASTLE. It means that you can say and unsay things at pleasure; that you can address a lady in private, and deny it in public; that you have one story for us, and another for my daughter.

MARLOW. Daughter!—This lady your daughter?

HARDCASTLE. Yes, sir, my only daughter; my Kate; whose else should she be?

MARLOW. Oh, the devil!

MISS HARDCASTLE. Yes, sir, that very identical tall, squinting lady you were pleased to take me for [curtesying]; she that you addressed as the mild, modest, sentimental man of gravity, and the bold, forward, agreeable Rattle of the Ladies Club. Ha! ha! ha!

MARLOW. Zounds, there's no bearing this; it's worse than death!

MISS HARDCASTLE. In which of your characters, sir, will you give us leave to address you? As the faltering gentleman, with looks on the ground, that speaks just to be heard, and hates hypocrisy; or the loud, confident creature, that keeps it up with Mrs. Mantrap, and old Miss Biddy Buckskin, till three in the morning!—Ha! ha! ha!

MARLOW. O, curse on my noisy head. I never attempted to be impudent yet that I was not taken down. I must be gone.

HARDCASTLE. By the hand of my body, but you shall not. I see it was all a mistake, and I am rejoiced to find it. You shall not, sir, I tell you. I know she'll forgive you. Won't you forgive him, Kate? We'll all forgive you. Take courage, man. [They retire, she tormenting him, to the back scene.]

[Enter MRS. HARDCASTLE and TONY.]

MRS. HARDCASTLE. So, so they're gone off. Let them go, I care not.

HARDCASTLE. Who gone?

MRS. HARDCASTLE. My dutiful niece and her gentleman, Mr. Hastings, from town. He who came down with our modest visitor here.

SIR CHARLES. Who, my honest George Hastings? As worthy a fellow as lives, and the girl could not have made a more prudent choice.

HARDCASTLE. Then, by the hand of my body, I'm proud of the connexion.

MRS. HARDCASTLE. Well, if he has taken away the lady, he has not taken her fortune; that remains in this family to console us for her loss.

HARDCASTLE. Sure, Dorothy, you would not be so mercenary?

MRS. HARDCASTLE. Ay, that's my affair, not yours.

HARDCASTLE. But, you know, if your son, when of age, refuses to marry his cousin, her whole fortune is then at her own disposal.

MRS. HARDCASTLE. Ay, but he's not of age, and she has not thought proper to wait for his refusal.

[Enter HASTINGS and MISS NEVILLE.]

MRS. HARDCASTLE [aside]. What, returned so soon! I begin not to like it.

HASTINGS [to HARDCASTLE]. For my late attempt to fly off with your niece, let my present confusion be my punishment. We are now come back, to appeal from your justice to your humanity. By her father's consent, I first paid her my addresses, and our passions were first founded in duty.

MISS NEVILLE. Since his death, I have been obliged to stoop to dissimulation to avoid oppression. In an hour of levity, I was ready even to give up my fortune to secure my choice. But I am now recovered from the delusion, and hope from your tenderness what is denied me from a nearer connexion.

MRS. HARDCASTLE. Pshaw, pshaw, this is all but the whining end of a modern novel!

HARDCASTLE. Be it what it will, I'm glad they're come back to reclaim their due. Come hither, Tony, boy. Do you refuse this lady's hand whom I now offer you?

TONY. What signifies my refusing? You know I can't refuse her till I'm of age, father.

HARDCASTLE. While I thought concealing your age, boy, was likely to conduce to your improvement, I concurred with your mother's desire to keep it secret. But since I find she turns it to a wrong use, I must now declare you have been of age these three months.

TONY. Of age! Am I of age, father?

HARDCASTLE. Above three months.

TONY. Then you'll see the first use I'll make of my liberty. [*Taking* MISS NEVILLE'S *hand.*] Witness all men, by these presents, that I, Anthony Lumpkin, Esquire, of BLANK place, refuse you, Constantia Neville, spinster, of no place at all, for my true and lawful wife. So Constance Neville may marry whom she pleases, and Tony Lumpkin is his own man again.

SIR CHARLES. O brave 'Squire!

HASTINGS. My worthy friend!

MRS. HARDCASTLE. My undutiful offspring!

MARLOW. Joy, my dear George, I give you joy sincerely. And could I prevail upon my little tyrant here to be less arbitrary, I should be the happiest man alive, if you would return me the favour.

HASTINGS [*to* MISS HARDCASTLE]. Come, madam, you are now driven to the very last scene of all your contrivances.

I know you like him, I'm sure he loves you, and you must and shall have him.

HARDCASTLE [*joining their hands*]. And I say so too. And, Mr. Marlow, if she makes as good a wife as she has a daughter, I don't believe you'll ever repent your bargain. So now to supper. To-morrow we shall gather all the poor of the parish about us, and the mistakes of the night shall be crowned with a merry morning. So, boy, take her; and as you have been mistaken in the mistress, my wish is, that you may never be mistaken in the wife. [*Exeunt* OMNES.]

EPILOGUE

BY DR. GOLDSMITH, SPOKEN BY MRS. BULKLEY IN THE CHARACTER OF MISS HARDCASTLE.

Well, having stoop'd to conquer with success,
And gain'd a husband without aid from dress,
Still as a bar-maid, I could wish it too,
As I have conquer'd him to conquer you:
And let me say, for all your resolution,
That pretty bar-maids have done execution.
Our life is all a play, composed to please;
"We have our exits and our entrances."
The first act shows the simple country maid,
Harmless and young, of everything afraid;
Blushes when hired, and with unmeaning action,
"I hopes as how to give you satisfaction."
Her second act displays a livelier scene,—
Th' unblushing bar-maid of a country inn,
Who whisks about the house, at market caters,
Talks loud, coquets the guests, and scolds the waiters.
Next the scene shifts to town, and there she soars,
The chop-house toast of ogling *connoisseurs;*

On 'squires and cits she there displays her arts,
And on the gridiron broils her lovers' hearts;
And, as she smiles, her triumphs to complete,
E'en common-councilmen forget to eat.
The fourth act shows her wedded to the 'squire,
And madam now begins to hold it higher;
Pretends to taste, at operas cries *caro*,
And quits her Nancy Dawson for Che Faro:
Doats upon dancing, and in all her pride,
Swims round the room, the Heinel of Cheapside:
Ogles and leers with artificial skill,
Till having lost in age the power to kill,
She sits all night at cards, and ogles at spadille.
Such, through our lives, th' eventful history—
The fifth and last act still remains for me.
The bar-maid now for your protection prays,
Turns female barrister, and pleads for Bayes.

THE SCHOOL FOR SCANDAL

By RICHARD BRINSLEY SHERIDAN

Produced at London, 1777

CHARACTERS

SIR PETER TEAZLE

SIR OLIVER SURFACE

JOSEPH SURFACE

CHARLES SURFACE

CRABTREE

SIR BENJAMIN BACKBITE

ROWLEY

MOSES

TRIP

SNAKE

CARELESS

SIR HARRY BUMPER

LADY TEAZLE

MARIA

LADY SNEERWELL

MRS. CANDOUR

GENTLEMEN, MAID, AND SERVANTS

SCENE—*London.*

ACT I

SCENE I—LADY SNEERWELL'S *dressing-room.*

[LADY SNEERWELL *discovered at her toilet;* SNAKE *drinking chocolate.*]

LADY SNEERWELL. The paragraphs, you say, Mr. Snake, were all inserted?

SNAKE. They were, madam; and, as I copied them myself in a feigned hand, there can be no suspicion whence they came.

LADY SNEERWELL. Did you circulate the report of Lady Brittle's intrigue with Captain Boastall?

SNAKE. That's in as fine a train as your ladyship could wish. In the common course of things, I think it must reach Mrs. Clackitt's ears within four-and-twenty hours; and then, you know, the business is as good as done.

LADY SNEERWELL. Why, truly, Mrs. Clackitt has a very pretty talent, and a great deal of industry.

SNAKE. True, madam, and has been tolerably successful in her day. To my knowledge, she has been the cause of six matches being broken off, and three sons being disinherited; of four forced elopements, nine separate maintenances, and two divorces. Nay, I have more than once traced her causing a *tête-à-tête* in the "Town and Country Magazine," when the parties, perhaps, had never seen each other's face before in the course of their lives.

LADY SNEERWELL. She certainly has talents, but her manner is gross.

SNAKE. 'Tis very true. She generally designs well, has a free tongue and a bold invention; but her colouring is too dark, and her outlines often extravagant. She wants that delicacy of tint, and mellowness of sneer, which distinguish your ladyship's scandal.

LADY SNEERWELL. You are partial, Snake.

SNAKE. Not in the least; every body allows that Lady Sneerwell can do more with a word or look than many can with the most laboured detail, even when they happen to have a little truth on their side to support it.

LADY SNEERWELL. Yes, my dear Snake; and I am no hypocrite to deny the satisfaction I reap from the success of my efforts. Wounded myself, in the early part of my life, by the envenomed tongue of slander, I confess I have since known no pleasure equal to the reducing others to the level of my own reputation.

SNAKE. Nothing can be more natural. But, Lady Sneerwell, there is one affair in which you have lately employed me, wherein, I confess, I am at a loss to guess your motives.

LADY SNEERWELL. I conceive you mean with respect to my neighbour, Sir Peter Teazle, and his family?

SNAKE. I do. Here are two young men, to whom Sir Peter has acted as a kind of guardian since their father's death; the eldest possessing the most amiable character, and universally well spoken of;—the youngest, the most dissipated and extravagant young fellow in the kingdom, without friends or character: the former an avowed admirer of your ladyship, and apparently your favourite; the latter attached to Maria, Sir Peter's ward, and confessedly beloved by her. Now, on the face of these circumstances, it is utterly unaccountable to me, why you, the widow of a city knight, with a good jointure, should not close with the passion of a man of such character and expectations as Mr. Surface; and more so why you should be so uncommonly earnest to destroy the mutual attachment subsisting between his brother Charles and Maria.

LADY SNEERWELL. Then, at once to unravel this mystery I must inform you that love has no share whatever in the intercourse between Mr. Surface and me.

SNAKE. No!

LADY SNEERWELL. His real attachment is to Maria, or her fortune; but, finding in his brother a favoured rival, he has been obliged to mask his pretensions, and profit by my assistance.

SNAKE. Yet still I am more puzzled why you should interest yourself in his success.

LADY SNEERWELL. Heavens! how dull you are! Cannot you surmise the weakness which I hitherto, through shame, have concealed even from you? Must I confess that Charles—that extravagant, that bankrupt in fortune and reputation—that he it is for whom I am thus anxious and malicious, and to gain whom I would sacrifice every thing?

SNAKE. Now, indeed, your conduct appears consistent: but how came you and Mr. Surface so confidential?

LADY SNEERWELL. For our mutual interest, I have found him out a long time since. I know him to be artful, selfish, and malicious—in short, a sentimental knave; while with Sir Peter, and indeed with all his acquaintance, he passes for a youthful miracle of prudence, good sense, and benevolence.

SNAKE. Yes; yet Sir Peter vows he has not his equal in England; and, above all, he praises him as a man of sentiment.

LADY SNEERWELL. True; and with the assistance of his sentiment and hypocrisy he has brought Sir Peter entirely into his interest with regard to Maria; while poor Charles has no friend in the house— though, I fear, he has a powerful one in Maria's heart, against whom we must direct our schemes.

[Enter SERVANT.]

SERVANT. Mr. Surface.

LADY SNEERWELL. Show him up. *[Exit SERVANT.]* He generally calls about this time. I don't wonder at people giving him to me for a lover.

[Enter JOSEPH SURFACE.]

JOSEPH SURFACE. My dear Lady Sneerwell, how do you do to-day? Mr. Snake, your most obedient.

LADY SNEERWELL. Snake has just been rallying me on our mutual attachment, but I have informed him of our real views. You know how useful he has been to us; and, believe me, the confidence is not ill-placed.

JOSEPH SURFACE. Madam, it is impossible for me to suspect a man of Mr. Snake's sensibility and discernment.

LADY SNEERWELL. Well, well, no compliments now; but tell me when you saw your mistress, Maria—or, what is more material to me, your brother.

JOSEPH SURFACE. I have not seen either since I left you; but I can inform you that they never meet. Some of your stories have taken a good effect on Maria.

LADY SNEERWELL. Ah, my dear Snake! the merit of this belongs to you. But do your brother's distresses increase?

JOSEPH SURFACE. Every hour. I am told he has had another execution in the house yesterday. In short, his dissipation and extravagance exceed any thing I have ever heard of.

LADY SNEERWELL. Poor Charles!

JOSEPH SURFACE. True, madam; notwithstanding his vices, one can't help feeling for him. Poor Charles! I'm sure I wish it were in my power to be of any essential service to him; for the man who does not share in the distresses of a brother, even though merited by his own misconduct, deserves——

LADY SNEERWELL. O Lud! you are going to be moral, and forget that you are among friends.

JOSEPH SURFACE. Egad, that's true! I'll keep that sentiment till I see Sir Peter. However, it is certainly a charity to rescue Maria from such a libertine, who if he is to be reclaimed, can be so only by a person of your ladyship's superior accomplishments and understanding.

SNAKE. I believe, Lady Sneerwell, here's company coming: I'll go and copy the letter I mentioned to you. Mr. Surface, your most obedient.

JOSEPH SURFACE. Sir, your very devoted.—*[Exit SNAKE.]* Lady Sneerwell, I am very sorry you have put any farther confidence in that fellow.

LADY SNEERWELL. Why so?

JOSEPH SURFACE. I have lately detected him in frequent conference with old Rowley, who was formerly my father's steward, and has never, you know, been a friend of mine.

LADY SNEERWELL. And do you think he would betray us?

JOSEPH SURFACE. Nothing more likely: take my word for't, Lady Sneerwell, that fellow hasn't virtue enough to be faithful even to his own villany. Ah, Maria!

[Enter MARIA.]

LADY SNEERWELL. Maria, my dear, how do you do? What's the matter?

MARIA. Oh! there's that disagreeable lover of mine, Sir Benjamin Backbite, has just called at my guardian's, with his odious uncle, Crabtree; so I slipped out, and ran hither to avoid them.

LADY SNEERWELL. Is that all?

JOSEPH SURFACE. If my brother Charles had been of the party, madam, perhaps you would not have been so much alarmed.

LADY SNEERWELL. Nay, now you are severe; for I dare swear the truth of the matter is, Maria heard you were here. But, my dear, what has Sir Benjamin done, that you should avoid him so?

MARIA. Oh, he has done nothing—but 'tis for what he has said: his conversation is a perpetual libel on all his acquaintance.

JOSEPH SURFACE. Ay, and the worst of it is, there is no advantage in not knowing him; for he'll abuse a stranger just as soon as his best friend: and his uncle's as bad.

LADY SNEERWELL. Nay, but we should make allowance; Sir Benjamin is a wit and a poet.

MARIA. For my part, I own, madam, wit loses its respect with me, when I see it in company with malice. What do you think, Mr. Surface?

JOSEPH SURFACE. Certainly, madam; to smile at the jest which plants a thorn in another's breast is to become a principal in the mischief.

LADY SNEERWELL. Pshaw! there's no possibility of being witty without a little ill nature: the malice of a good thing is the barb that makes it stick. What's your opinion, Mr. Surface?

JOSEPH SURFACE. To be sure, madam; that conversation, where the spirit of raillery is suppressed, will ever appear tedious and insipid.

MARIA. Well, I'll not debate how far scandal may be allowable; but in a man, I am sure, it is always contemptible. We have pride, envy, rivalship, and a thousand motives to depreciate each other; but the male slanderer must have the cowardice of a woman before he can traduce one.

[*Reënter* SERVANT.]

SERVANT. Madam, Mrs. Candour is below, and, if your ladyship's at leisure, will leave her carriage.

LADY SNEERWELL. Beg her to walk in.— [*Exit* SERVANT.] Now, Maria, here is a character to your taste; for, though Mrs. Candour is a little talkative, every body allows her to be the best natured and best sort of woman.

MARIA. Yes, with a very gross affectation of good nature and benevolence, she does more mischief than the direct malice of old Crabtree.

JOSEPH SURFACE. I' faith that's true, Lady Sneerwell: whenever I hear the current running against the characters of my friends, I never think them in such danger as when Candour undertakes their defence.

LADY SNEERWELL. Hush—here she is!

[*Enter* MRS. CANDOUR.]

MRS. CANDOUR. My dear Lady Sneerwell, how have you been this century?— Mr. Surface, what news do you hear?— though indeed it is no matter, for I think one hears nothing else but scandal.

JOSEPH SURFACE. Just so, indeed, ma'am.

MRS. CANDOUR. Oh, Maria! child,— what, is the whole affair off between you and Charles? His extravagance, I presume—the town talks of nothing else.

MARIA. I am very sorry, ma'am, the town has so little to do.

MRS. CANDOUR. True, true, child: but there's no stopping people's tongues. I own I was hurt to hear it, as I indeed was to learn, from the same quarter, that your guardian, Sir Peter, and Lady Teazle have not agreed lately as well as could be wished.

MARIA. 'Tis strangely impertinent for people to busy themselves so.

MRS. CANDOUR. Very true, child: but what's to be done? People will talk— there's no preventing it. Why, it was but yesterday I was told that Miss Gadabout had eloped with Sir Filigree Flirt. But, Lord! there's no minding what one hears; though, to be sure, I had this from very good authority.

MARIA. Such reports are highly scandalous.

MRS. CANDOUR. So they are, child—shameful, shameful! But the world is so censorious, no character escapes. Lord, now who would have suspected your friend, Miss Prim, of an indiscretion? Yet such is the ill nature of people, that they say her uncle stopped her last week, just as she was stepping into the York Mail with her dancing-master.

MARIA. I'll answer for't there are no grounds for that report.

MRS. CANDOUR. Ah, no foundation in the world, I dare swear; no more, probably, than for the story circulated last month, of Mrs. Festino's affair with Colonel Cassino—though, to be sure, that matter was never rightly cleared up.

JOSEPH SURFACE. The licence of invention some people take is monstrous indeed.

MARIA. 'Tis so; but, in my opinion, those who report such things are equally culpable.

MRS. CANDOUR. To be sure they are; tale-bearers are as bad as the tale-makers—'tis an old observation, and a very true one: but what's to be done, as I said before? how will you prevent people from talking? To-day, Mrs. Clackitt assured me, Mr. and Mrs. Honeymoon were at last become mere man and wife, like the rest of their acquaintance. And at the same time Miss Tattle, who was by, affirmed that Lord Buffalo had discovered his lady at a house of no extraordinary fame; and that Sir Harry Bouquet and Tom Saunter were to measure swords on a similar provocation. But, Lord, do you think I would report these things! No, no! tale-bearers, as I said before, are just as bad as the tale-makers.

JOSEPH SURFACE. Ah! Mrs. Candour, if every body had your forbearance and good nature!

MRS. CANDOUR. I confess, Mr. Surface, I cannot bear to hear people attacked behind their backs; and when ugly circumstances come out against our acquaintance, I own I always love to think the best. By the by, I hope 'tis not true that your brother is absolutely ruined?

JOSEPH SURFACE. I am afraid his circumstances are very bad indeed, ma'am.

MRS. CANDOUR. Ah! I heard so—but you must tell him to keep up his spirits; every body almost is in the same way: Lord Spindle, Sir Thomas Splint, Captain Quinze, and Mr. Nickit—all up, I hear, within this week; so, if Charles is undone, he'll find half his acquaintance ruined too, and that, you know, is a consolation.

JOSEPH SURFACE. Doubtless, ma'am—a very great one.

[*Reënter* SERVANT.]

SERVANT. Mr. Crabtree and Sir Benjamin Backbite. [*Exit.*]

LADY SNEERWELL. So, Maria, you see your lover pursues you; positively you sha'n't escape.

[*Enter* CRABTREE *and* SIR BENJAMIN BACKBITE.]

CRABTREE. Lady Sneerwell, I kiss your hand. Mrs. Candour, I don't believe you are acquainted with my nephew, Sir Benjamin Backbite? Egad, ma'am, he has a pretty wit, and is a pretty poet too. Isn't he, Lady Sneerwell?

SIR BENJAMIN. Oh, fie, uncle!

CRABTREE. Nay, egad it's true; I back him at a rebus or a charade against the best rhymer in the kingdom. Has your ladyship heard the epigram he wrote last week on Lady Frizzle's feather catching fire?—Do, Benjamin, repeat it, or the charade you made last night extempore at Mrs. Drowzie's conversazione. Come now; your first is the name of a fish, your second a great naval commander, and——

SIR BENJAMIN. Uncle, now—pr'thee——

CRABTREE. I' faith, ma'am, 'twould surprise you to hear how ready he is at all these sort of things.

LADY SNEERWELL. I wonder, Sir Benjamin, you never publish any thing.

SIR BENJAMIN. To say truth, ma'am, 'tis very vulgar to print; and as my little productions are mostly satires and lampoons on particular people, I find they circulate more by giving copies in confidence to the friends of the parties. However, I have some love elegies, which, when favoured with this lady's smiles, I mean to give the public.

[*Pointing to* MARIA.]

CRABTREE [*to* MARIA]. 'Fore heaven, ma'am, they'll immortalize you!—you will be handed down to posterity, like Petrarch's Laura, or Waller's Sacharissa.

SIR BENJAMIN [*to* MARIA]. Yes, madam, I think you will like them, when you shall see them on a beautiful quarto page, where a neat rivulet of text shall meander through a meadow of margin. 'Fore Gad, they will be the most elegant things of their kind!

CRABTREE. But, ladies, that's true—have you heard the news?

MRS. CANDOUR. What, sir, do you mean the report of——

CRABTREE. No, ma'am, that's not it.—Miss Nicely is going to be married to her own footman.

MRS. CANDOUR. Impossible!

CRABTREE. Ask Sir Benjamin.

SIR BENJAMIN. 'Tis very true, ma'am: every thing is fixed, and the wedding liveries bespoke.

CRABTREE. Yes—and they do say there were pressing reasons for it.

LADY SNEERWELL. Why, I have heard something of this before.

MRS. CANDOUR. It can't be—and I wonder any one should believe such a story of so prudent a lady as Miss Nicely.

SIR BENJAMIN. O Lud! ma'am, that's the very reason 'twas believed at once. She has always been so cautious and so reserved, that every body was sure there was some reason for it at bottom.

MRS. CANDOUR. Why, to be sure, a tale of scandal is as fatal to the credit of a prudent lady of her stamp as a fever is generally to those of the strongest constitutions. But there is a sort of puny sickly reputation, that is always ailing, yet will outlive the robuster characters of a hundred prudes.

SIR BENJAMIN. True, madam, there are valetudinarians in reputation as well as constitution, who, being conscious of their weak part, avoid the least breath of air,

and supply their want of stamina by care and circumspection.

MRS. CANDOUR. Well, but this may be all a mistake. You know, Sir Benjamin, very trifling circumstances often give rise to the most injurious tales.

CRABTREE. That they do, I'll be sworn, ma'am. O Lud! Mr. Surface, pray is it true that your uncle, Sir Oliver, is coming home?

JOSEPH SURFACE. Not that I know of, indeed, sir.

CRABTREE. He has been in the East Indies a long time. You can scarcely remember him, I believe? Sad comfort, whenever he returns, to hear how your brother has gone on!

JOSEPH SURFACE. Charles has been imprudent, sir, to be sure; but I hope no busy people have already prejudiced Sir Oliver against him. He may reform.

SIR BENJAMIN. To be sure he may: for my part, I never believed him to be so utterly void of principle as people say; and, though he has lost all his friends, I am told nobody is better spoken of by the Jews.

CRABTREE. That's true, egad, nephew. If the Old Jewry was a ward, I believe Charles would be an alderman: no man more popular there, 'fore Gad! I hear he pays as many annuities as the Irish tontine; and that, whenever he is sick, they have prayers for the recovery of his health in all the synagogues.

SIR BENJAMIN. Yet no man lives in greater splendour. They tell me, when he entertains his friends he will sit down to dinner with a dozen of his own securities; have a score of tradesmen waiting in the antechamber, and an officer behind every guest's chair.

JOSEPH SURFACE. This may be entertainment to you, gentlemen, but you pay very little regard to the feelings of a brother.

MARIA [*aside*]. Their malice is intolerable!—[*Aloud.*] Lady Sneerwell, I must wish you a good morning: I'm not very well. [*Exit.*]

MRS. CANDOUR. O dear! she changes colour very much.

LADY SNEERWELL. Do, Mrs. Candour, follow her: she may want your assistance.

MRS. CANDOUR. That I will, with all my soul, ma'am.—Poor dear girl, who knows what her situation may be! [*Exit.*]

LADY SNEERWELL. 'Twas nothing but that she could not bear to hear Charles reflected on, notwithstanding their difference.

SIR BENJAMIN. The young lady's *penchant* is obvious.

CRABTREE. But, Benjamin, you must not give up the pursuit for that: follow her, and put her into good humour. Repeat her some of your own verses. Come, I'll assist you.

SIR BENJAMIN. Mr. Surface, I did not mean to hurt you; but depend on't your brother is utterly undone.

CRABTREE. O Lud, ay! undone as ever man was—can't raise a guinea!

SIR BENJAMIN. And every thing sold, I'm told, that was movable.

CRABTREE. I have seen one that was at his house. Not a thing left but some empty bottles that were overlooked, and the family pictures, which I believe are framed in the wainscots.

SIR BENJAMIN. And I'm very sorry also to hear some bad stories against him. [*Going.*]

CRABTREE. Oh, he has done many mean things, that's certain.

SIR BENJAMIN. But, however, as he's your brother—— [*Going.*]

CRABTREE. We'll tell you all another opportunity.

[*Exeunt CRABTREE and SIR BENJAMIN.*]

LADY SNEERWELL. Ha! ha! 'tis very hard for them to leave a subject they have not quite run down.

JOSEPH SURFACE. And I believe the abuse was no more acceptable to your ladyship than Maria.

LADY SNEERWELL. I doubt her affections are farther engaged than we imagine. But the family are to be here this evening, so you may as well dine where you are, and

we shall have an opportunity of observing farther; in the meantime, I'll go and plot mischief, and you shall study sentiment. [*Exeunt.*]

SCENE II—*A room in* SIR PETER TEAZLE'S *house.*

[*Enter* SIR PETER TEAZLE.]

SIR PETER. When an old bachelor marries a young wife, what is he to expect? 'Tis now six months since Lady Teazle made me the happiest of men—and I have been the most miserable dog ever since! We tiffed a little going to church, and fairly quarrelled before the bells had done ringing. I was more than once nearly choked with gall during the honeymoon, and had lost all comfort in life before my friends had done wishing me joy. Yet I chose with caution—a girl bred wholly in the country, who never knew luxury beyond one silk gown, nor dissipation above the annual gala of a race ball. Yet she now plays her part in all the extravagant fopperies of fashion and the town, with as ready a grace as if she never had seen a bush or a grass-plot out of Grosvenor Square! I am sneered at by all my acquaintance, and paragraphed in the newspapers. She dissipates my fortune, and contradicts all my humours; yet the worst of it is, I doubt I love her, or I should never bear all this. However, I'll never be weak enough to own it.

[*Enter* ROWLEY.]

ROWLEY. Oh! Sir Peter, your servant: how is it with you, sir?

SIR PETER. Very bad, Master Rowley, very bad. I meet with nothing but crosses and vexations.

ROWLEY. What can have happened since yesterday?

SIR PETER. A good question to a married man!

ROWLEY. Nay, I'm sure, Sir Peter, your lady can't be the cause of your uneasiness.

SIR PETER. Why, has any body told you she was dead?

ROWLEY. Come, come, Sir Peter, you love her, notwithstanding your tempers don't exactly agree.

SIR PETER. But the fault is entirely hers, Master Rowley. I am, myself, the sweetest-tempered man alive, and hate a teasing temper; and so I tell her a hundred times a day.

ROWLEY. Indeed!

SIR PETER. Ay; and what is very extraordinary, in all our disputes she is always in the wrong! But Lady Sneerwell, and the set she meets at her house, encourage the perverseness of her disposition. Then, to complete my vexation, Maria, my ward, whom I ought to have the power of a father over, is determined to turn rebel too, and absolutely refuses the man whom I have long resolved on for her husband; meaning, I suppose, to bestow herself on his profligate brother.

ROWLEY. You know, Sir Peter, I have always taken the liberty to differ with you on the subject of these two young gentlemen. I only wish you may not be deceived in your opinion of the elder. For Charles, my life on't! he will retrieve his errors yet. Their worthy father, once my honoured master, was, at his years, nearly as wild a spark; yet, when he died, he did not leave a more benevolent heart to lament his loss.

SIR PETER. You are wrong, Master Rowley. On their father's death, you know, I acted as a kind of guardian to them both, till their uncle Sir Oliver's liberality gave them an early independence: of course, no person could have more opportunities of judging of their hearts, and I was never mistaken in my life. Joseph is indeed a model for the young men of his age. He is a man of sentiment, and acts up to the sentiments he professes; but, for the other, take my word for't, if he had any grain of virtue by descent, he has dissipated it with the rest of his inheritance. Ah! my old friend, Sir Oliver, will be deeply mortified when he finds how part of his bounty has been misapplied.

ROWLEY. I am sorry to find you so violent against the young man, because this may be the most critical period of his fortune. I came hither with news that will surprise you.

SIR PETER. What! let me hear.

ROWLEY. Sir Oliver is arrived, and at this moment in town.

SIR PETER. How! you astonish me! I thought you did not expect him this month.

ROWLEY. I did not: but his passage has been remarkably quick.

SIR PETER. Egad, I shall rejoice to see my old friend. 'Tis sixteen years since we met. We have had many a day together:—but does he still enjoin us not to inform his nephews of his arrival?

ROWLEY. Most strictly. He means, before it is known, to make some trial of their dispositions.

SIR PETER. Ah! there needs no art to discover their merits—however, he shall have his way; but, pray, does he know I am married?

ROWLEY. Yes, and will soon wish you joy.

SIR PETER. What, as we drink health to a friend in a consumption! Ah! Oliver will laugh at me. We used to rail at matrimony together, but he has been steady to his text. Well, he must be soon at my house, though—I'll instantly give orders for his reception. But, Master Rowley, don't drop a word that Lady Teazle and I ever disagree.

ROWLEY. By no means.

SIR PETER. For I should never be able to stand Noll's jokes; so I'll have him think, Lord forgive me! that we are a very happy couple.

ROWLEY. I understand you:—but then you must be very careful not to differ while he is in the house with you.

SIR PETER. Egad, and so we must—and that's impossible. Ah! Master Rowley, when an old bachelor marries a young wife, he deserves—no—the crime carries its punishment along with it.

[*Exeunt.*]

ACT II

SCENE I—*A room in* SIR PETER TEAZLE'S *house.*

[*Enter* SIR PETER *and* LADY TEAZLE.]

SIR PETER. Lady Teazle, Lady Teazle, I'll not bear it!

LADY TEAZLE. Sir Peter, Sir Peter, you may bear it or not, as you please; but I ought to have my own way in every thing, and, what's more, I will too. What! though I was educated in the country, I know very well that women of fashion in London are accountable to nobody after they are married.

SIR PETER. Very well, ma'am, very well; so a husband is to have no influence, no authority?

LADY TEAZLE. Authority! No, to be sure: if you wanted authority over me, you should have adopted me, and not married me: I am sure you were old enough.

SIR PETER. Old enough!—ay, there it is. Well, well, Lady Teazle, though my life may be made unhappy by your temper, I'll not be ruined by your extravagance!

LADY TEAZLE. My extravagance! I'm sure I'm not more extravagant than a woman of fashion ought to be.

SIR PETER. No, no, madam, you shall throw away no more sums on such unmeaning luxury. 'Slife! to spend as much to furnish your dressing-room with flowers in winter as would suffice to turn the Pantheon into a greenhouse, and give a *fête champêtre* at Christmas.

LADY TEAZLE. And am I to blame, Sir Peter, because flowers are dear in cold weather? You should find fault with the climate, and not with me. For my part, I'm sure I wish it was spring all the year round, and that roses grew under our feet!

SIR PETER. 'Oons! madam—if you had been born to this, I shouldn't wonder at you talking thus; but you forget what your situation was when I married you.

LADY TEAZLE. No, no, I don't; 'twas a very disagreeable one, or I should never have married you.

SIR PETER. Yes, yes, madam, you were then in somewhat a humbler style—the daughter of a plain country squire. Recollect, Lady Teazle, when I saw you first sitting at your tambour, in a pretty figured linen gown, with a bunch of keys at your side, your hair combed smooth over a roll, and your apartment hung round with fruits in worsted, of your own working.

LADY TEAZLE. Oh, yes! I remember it very well, and a curious life I led. My daily occupation to inspect the dairy, superintend the poultry, make extracts from the family receipt-book, and comb my aunt Deborah's lap-dog.

SIR PETER. Yes, yes, ma'am, 'twas so indeed.

LADY TEAZLE. And then you know, my evening amusements! To draw patterns for ruffles, which I had not materials to make up; to play Pope Joan with the curate; to read a sermon to my aunt; or to be stuck down to an old spinet to strum my father to sleep after a fox-chase.

SIR PETER. I am glad you have so good a memory. Yes, madam, these were the recreations I took you from; but now you must have your coach—*vis-à-vis*—and three powdered footmen before your chair; and, in the summer, a pair of white cats to draw you to Kensington Gardens. No recollection, I suppose, when you were content to ride double, behind the butler, on a docked coach-horse.

LADY TEAZLE. No—I swear I never did that: I deny the butler and the coach-horse.

SIR PETER. This, madam, was your situation; and what have I done for you? I have made you a woman of fashion, of fortune, of rank—in short, I have made you my wife.

LADY TEAZLE. Well, then, and there is but one thing more you can make me to add to the obligations, that is——

SIR PETER. My widow, I suppose?

LADY TEAZLE. Hem! hem!

SIR PETER. I thank you, madam—but don't flatter yourself, for, though your ill conduct may disturb my peace of mind, it shall never break my heart, I promise you: however, I am equally obliged to you for the hint.

LADY TEAZLE. Then why will you endeavour to make yourself so disagreeable to me, and thwart me in every little elegant expense?

SIR PETER. 'Slife, madam, I say, had you any of these little elegant expenses when you married me?

LADY TEAZLE. Lud, Sir Peter! would you have me be out of the fashion?

SIR PETER. The fashion, indeed! what had you to do with the fashion before you married me?

LADY TEAZLE. For my part, I should think you would like to have your wife thought a woman of taste.

SIR PETER. Ay—there again—taste! Zounds! madam, you had no taste when you married me!

LADY TEAZLE. That's very true, indeed, Sir Peter! and after having married you, I should never pretend to taste again, I allow. But now, Sir Peter, since we have finished our daily jangle, I presume I may go to my engagement at Lady Sneerwell's.

SIR PETER. Ay, there's another precious circumstance—a charming set of acquaintance you have made there!

LADY TEAZLE. Nay, Sir Peter, they are all people of rank and fortune, and remarkably tenacious of reputation.

SIR PETER. Yes, egad, they are tenacious of reputation with a vengeance; for they don't choose any body should have a character but themselves! Such a crew! Ah! many a wretch has rid on a hurdle who has done less mischief than these utterers of forged tales, coiners of scandal, and clippers of reputation.

LADY TEAZLE. What, would you restrain the freedom of speech?

SIR PETER. Ah! they have made you just as bad as any one of the society.

LADY TEAZLE. Why, I believe I do bear a part with a tolerable grace.

SIR PETER. Grace indeed!

LADY TEAZLE. But I vow I bear no malice against the people I abuse: when I say an ill-natured thing, 'tis out of pure good humour; and I take it for granted they deal exactly in the same manner with me. But, Sir Peter, you know you promised to come to Lady Sneerwell's too.

SIR PETER. Well, well, I'll call in, just to look after my own character.

LADY TEAZLE. Then, indeed, you must make haste after me, or you'll be too late. So good-bye to ye.   [*Exit.*]

SIR PETER. So—I have gained much by my intended expostulation! Yet with what a charming air she contradicts every thing I say, and how pleasantly she shows her contempt for my authority! Well, though I can't make her love me, there is great satisfaction in quarrelling with her; and I think she never appears to such advantage as when she is doing every thing in her power to plague me. [*Exit.*]

SCENE II—*A room in* LADY SNEERWELL'S *house.*

[LADY SNEERWELL, MRS. CANDOUR, CRABTREE, SIR BENJAMIN BACKBITE, *and* JOSEPH SURFACE, *discovered.*]

LADY SNEERWELL. Nay, positively, we will hear it.

JOSEPH SURFACE. Yes, yes, the epigram, by all means.

SIR BENJAMIN. O plague on't, uncle! 'tis mere nonsense.

CRABTREE. No, no; 'fore Gad, very clever for an extempore!

SIR BENJAMIN. But, ladies, you should be acquainted with the circumstance. You must know, that one day last week, as Lady Betty Curricle was taking the dust in Hyde Park, in a sort of duodecimo phaeton she desired me to write some verses on her ponies; upon which, I took out my pocket-book, and in one moment produced the following:—

THE SCHOOL FOR SCANDAL

625

Sure never were seen two such beautiful
  ponies:
Other horses are clowns, but these maca-
  ronies:
To give them this title I'm sure can't be
  wrong,
Their legs are so slim, and their tails are
  so long.

CRABTREE. There, ladies, done in the
smack of a whip, and on horseback too.

JOSEPH SURFACE. A very Phœbus,
mounted—indeed, Sir Benjamin!

SIR BENJAMIN. Oh dear, sir! trifles—
trifles.

[*Enter* LADY TEAZLE *and* MARIA.]

MRS. CANDOUR. I must have a copy.

LADY SNEERWELL. Lady Teazle, I hope
we shall see Sir Peter?

LADY TEAZLE. I believe he'll wait on
your ladyship presently.

LADY SNEERWELL. Maria, my love, you
look grave. Come, you shall sit down to
piquet with Mr. Surface.

MARIA. I take very little pleasure in
cards—however, I'll do as your ladyship
pleases.

LADY TEAZLE [*aside*]. I am surprised
Mr. Surface should sit down with her; I
thought he would have embraced this
opportunity of speaking to me before Sir
Peter came.

MRS. CANDOUR. Now, I'll die, but you
are so scandalous, I'll forswear your so-
ciety.

LADY TEAZLE. What's the matter, Mrs.
Candour?

MRS. CANDOUR. They'll not allow our
friend Miss Vermilion to be handsome.

LADY SNEERWELL. Oh, surely she is a
pretty woman.

CRABTREE. I am very glad you think so,
ma'am.

MRS. CANDOUR. She has a charming
fresh colour.

LADY TEAZLE. Yes, when it is fresh put
on.

MRS. CANDOUR. Oh, fie! I'll swear her
colour is natural: I have seen it come and
go!

LADY TEAZLE. I dare swear you have,
ma'am: it goes off at night, and comes
again in the morning.

SIR BENJAMIN. True, ma'am, it not
only comes and goes; but, what's more,
egad, her maid can fetch and carry it!

MRS. CANDOUR. Ha! ha! ha! how I
hate to hear you talk so! But surely,
now, her sister is, or was, very handsome.

CRABTREE. Who? Mrs. Evergreen? O
Lord! she's six-and-fifty if she's an hour!

MRS. CANDOUR. Now positively you
wrong her; fifty-two or fifty-three is the
utmost—and I don't think she looks
more.

SIR BENJAMIN. Ah! there's no judging
by her looks, unless one could see her
face.

LADY SNEERWELL. Well, well, if Mrs.
Evergreen does take some pains to repair
the ravages of time, you must allow she
effects it with great ingenuity; and surely
that's better than the careless manner in
which the widow Ochre caulks her
wrinkles.

SIR BENJAMIN. Nay, now, Lady Sneer-
well, you are severe upon the widow.
Come, come, 'tis not that she paints so ill
—but, when she has finished her face, she
joins it on so badly to her neck, that she
looks like a mended statue, in which the
connoisseur may see at once that the head
is modern, though the trunk's antique.

CRABTREE. Ha! ha! ha! Well said,
nephew!

MRS. CANDOUR. Ha! ha! ha! Well, you
make me laugh; but I vow I hate you for
it. What do you think of Miss Simper?

SIR BENJAMIN. Why, she has very
pretty teeth.

LADY TEAZLE. Yea; and on that ac-
count, when she is neither speaking nor
laughing (which very seldom happens),
she never absolutely shuts her mouth, but
leaves it always a-jar, as it were—thus.
[*Shows her teeth.*]

MRS. CANDOUR. How can you be so ill-
natured?

LADY TEAZLE. Nay, I allow even that's
better than the pains Mrs. Prim takes to
conceal her losses in front. She draws her

mouth till it positively resembles the aperture of a poor's-box, and all her words appear to slide out edgewise, as it were— thus: [*Mimics.*] *How do you do, madam? Yes, madam.*

LADY SNEERWELL. Very well, Lady Teazle; I see you can be a little severe.

LADY TEAZLE. In defence of a friend it is but justice. But here comes Sir Peter to spoil our pleasantry.

[*Enter* SIR PETER TEAZLE.]

SIR PETER. Ladies, your most obedient. —[*Aside.*] Mercy on me, here is the whole set! a character dead at every word, I suppose.

MRS. CANDOUR. I am rejoiced you are come, Sir Peter. They have been so censorious—and Lady Teazle as bad as any one.

SIR PETER. That must be very distressing to you, indeed, Mrs. Candour.

MRS. CANDOUR. Oh, they will allow good qualities to nobody; not even good nature to our friend Mrs. Pursy.

LADY TEAZLE. What, the fat dowager who was at Mrs. Quadrille's last night?

MRS. CANDOUR. Nay, her bulk is her misfortune; and, when she takes so much pains to get rid of it, you ought not to reflect on her.

LADY SNEERWELL. That's very true, indeed.

LADY TEAZLE. Yes, I know she almost lives on acids and small whey; laces herself by pulleys; and, often, in the hottest noon in summer, you may see her on a little squat pony, with her hair plaited up behind like a drummer's and puffing round the Ring on a full trot.

MRS. CANDOUR. I thank you, Lady Teazle, for defending her.

SIR PETER. Yes, a good defence, truly.

MRS. CANDOUR. Truly, Lady Teazle is as censorious as Miss Sallow.

CRABTREE. Yes, and she is a curious being to pretend to be censorious—an awkward gawky, without any one good point under heaven.

MRS. CANDOUR. Positively you shall not be so very severe. Miss Sallow is a near relation of mine by marriage, and, as for her person, great allowance is to be made; for, let me tell you, a woman labours under many disadvantages who tries to pass for a girl of six-and-thirty.

LADY SNEERWELL. Though, surely, she is handsome still—and for the weakness in her eyes, considering how much she reads by candlelight, it is not to be wondered at.

MRS. CANDOUR. True, and then as to her manner; upon my word I think it is particularly graceful, considering she never had the least education: for you know her mother was a Welsh milliner, and her father a sugar-baker at Bristol.

SIR BENJAMIN. Ah! you are both of you too good-natured!

SIR PETER [*aside*]. Yes, damned good-natured! This their own relation! mercy on me!

MRS. CANDOUR. For my part, I own I cannot bear to hear a friend ill-spoken of.

SIR PETER. No, to be sure!

SIR BENJAMIN. Oh! you are of a moral turn. Mrs. Candour and I can sit for an hour and hear Lady Stucco talk sentiment.

LADY TEAZLE. Nay, I vow Lady Stucco is very well with the dessert after dinner; for she's just like the French fruit one cracks for mottoes—made up of paint and proverb.

MRS. CANDOUR. Well, I will never join in ridiculing a friend; and so I constantly tell my cousin Ogle, and you all know what pretensions she has to be critical on beauty.

CRABTREE. Oh, to be sure! she has herself the oddest countenance that ever was seen; 'tis a collection of features from all the different countries of the globe.

SIR BENJAMIN. So she has, indeed—an Irish front——

CRABTREE. Caledonian locks——

SIR BENJAMIN. Dutch nose——

CRABTREE. Austrian lips——

SIR BENJAMIN. Complexion of a Spaniard——

CRABTREE. And teeth *à la Chinoise*——

SIR BENJAMIN. In short, her face resembles a *table d'hôte* at Spa—where no two guests are of a nation——

CRABTREE. Or a congress at the close of a general war—wherein all the members, even to her eyes, appear to have a different interest, and her nose and chin are the only parties likely to join issue.

MRS. CANDOUR. Ha! ha! ha!

SIR PETER [*aside*]. Mercy on my life! —a person they dine with twice a week!

MRS. CANDOUR. Nay, but I vow you shall not carry the laugh off so—for give me leave to say, that Mrs. Ogle——

SIR PETER. Madam, madam, I beg your pardon—there's no stopping these good gentlemen's tongues. But when I tell you, Mrs. Candour, that the lady they are abusing is a particular friend of mine, I hope you'll not take her part.

LADY SNEERWELL. Ha! ha! ha! well said, Sir Peter! but you are a cruel creature—too phlegmatic yourself for a jest, and too peevish to allow wit in others.

SIR PETER. Ah, madam, true wit is more nearly allied to good nature than your ladyship is aware of.

LADY TEAZLE. True, Sir Peter: I believe they are so near akin that they can never be united.

SIR BENJAMIN. Or rather, suppose them man and wife, because one seldom sees them together.

LADY TEAZLE. But Sir Peter is such an enemy to scandal, I believe he would have it put down by parliament.

SIR PETER. 'Fore heaven, madam, if they were to consider the sporting with reputation of as much importance as poaching on manors, and pass an act for the preservation of fame, as well as game, I believe many would thank them for the bill.

LADY SNEERWELL. O Lud! Sir Peter; would you deprive us of our privileges?

SIR PETER. Ay, madam; and then no person should be permitted to kill characters and run down reputations, but qualified old maids and disappointed widows.

LADY SNEERWELL. Go, you monster!

MRS. CANDOUR. But, surely, you would not be quite so severe on those who only report what they hear?

SIR PETER. Yes, madam, I would have law merchant for them too; and in all cases of slander currency, whenever the drawer of the lie was not to be found, the injured parties should have a right to come on any of the indorsers.

CRABTREE. Well, for my part, I believe there never was a scandalous tale without some foundation.

LADY SNEERWELL. Come, ladies, shall we sit down to cards in the next room?

[*Enter* SERVANT, *who whispers* SIR PETER.]

SIR PETER. I'll be with them directly. —[*Exit* SERVANT.] [*Aside.*] I'll get away unperceived.

LADY SNEERWELL. Sir Peter, you are not going to leave us?

SIR PETER. Your ladyship must excuse me; I'm called away by particular business. But I leave my character behind me. [*Exit.*]

SIR BENJAMIN. Well—certainly, Lady Teazle, that lord of yours is a strange being: I could tell you some stories of him would make you laugh heartily if he were not your husband.

LADY TEAZLE. Oh, pray don't mind that; come, do let's hear them.

[*Exeunt all but* JOSEPH SURFACE *and* MARIA.]

JOSEPH SURFACE. Maria, I see you have no satisfaction in this society.

MARIA. How is it possible I should? If to raise malicious smiles at the infirmities or misfortunes of those who have never injured us be the province of wit or humour, Heaven grant me a double portion of dulness!

JOSEPH SURFACE. Yet they appear more ill-natured than they are; they have no malice at heart.

MARIA. Then is their conduct still more contemptible; for, in my opinion, nothing could excuse the intemperance of their tongues but a natural and uncontrollable bitterness of mind.

JOSEPH SURFACE. Undoubtedly, madam; and it has always been a sentiment of mine, that to propagate a malicious truth wantonly is more despicable than to falsify from revenge. But can you, Maria, feel thus for others, and be unkind to me alone? Is hope to be denied the tenderest passion?

MARIA. Why will you distress me by renewing this subject?

JOSEPH SURFACE. Ah, Maria! you would not treat me thus, and oppose your guardian, Sir Peter's will, but that I see that profligate Charles is still a favoured rival.

MARIA. Ungenerously urged! But, whatever my sentiments are for that unfortunate young man, be assured I shall not feel more bound to give him up, because his distresses have lost him the regard even of a brother.

JOSEPH SURFACE. Nay, but, Maria, do not leave me with a frown: by all that's honest, I swear. [Kneels.]

[Reënter LADY TEAZLE behind.]
[Aside.] Gad's life, here's Lady Teazle.—[Aloud to MARIA.] You must not—no, you shall not—for, though I have the greatest regard for Lady Teazle——

MARIA. Lady Teazle!

JOSEPH SURFACE. Yet were Sir Peter to suspect——

LADY TEAZLE [coming forward]. What is this, pray? Does he take her for me?—Child, you are wanted in the next room.—[Exit MARIA.] What is all this, pray?

JOSEPH SURFACE. Oh, the most unlucky circumstance in nature! Maria has somehow suspected the tender concern I have for your happiness, and threatened to acquaint Sir Peter with her suspicions, and I was just endeavouring to reason with her when you came in.

LADY TEAZLE. Indeed! but you seemed to adopt a very tender mode of reasoning—do you usually argue on your knees?

JOSEPH SURFACE. Oh, she's a child, and I thought a little bombast——But, Lady Teazle, when are you to give me your judgment on my library, as you promised?

LADY TEAZLE. No, no; I begin to think it would be imprudent, and you know I admit you as a lover no farther than fashion requires.

JOSEPH SURFACE. True—a mere Platonic cicisbeo, what every wife is entitled to.

LADY TEAZLE. Certainly, one must not be out of the fashion. However, I have so many of my country prejudices left, that, though Sir Peter's ill humour may vex me ever so, it never shall provoke me to——

JOSEPH SURFACE. The only revenge in your power. Well, I applaud your moderation.

LADY TEAZLE. Go—you are an insinuating wretch! But we shall be missed—let us join the company.

JOSEPH SURFACE. But we had best not return together.

LADY TEAZLE. Well, don't stay; for Maria sha'n't come to hear any more of your reasoning, I promise you. [Exit.]

JOSEPH SURFACE. A curious dilemma, truly, my politics have run me into! I wanted, at first, only to ingratiate myself with Lady Teazle, that she might not be my enemy with Maria; and I have, I don't know how, become her serious lover. Sincerely I begin to wish I had never made such a point of gaining so very good a character, for it has led me into so many cursed rogueries that I doubt I shall be exposed at last. [Exit.]

SCENE III—A room in SIR PETER TEAZLE'S house.

[Enter SIR OLIVER SURFACE and ROWLEY.]

SIR OLIVER. Ha! ha! ha! so my old friend is married, hey?—a young wife out of the country. Ha! ha! ha! that he should have stood bluff to old bachelor so long, and sink into a husband at last!

ROWLEY. But you must not rally him on the subject, Sir Oliver; 'tis a tender point, I assure you, though he has been married only seven months.

SIR OLIVER. Then he has been just half a year on the stool of repentance!—Poor

Peter! But you say he has entirely given up Charles—never sees him, hey?

ROWLEY. His prejudice against him is astonishing, and I am sure greatly increased by a jealousy of him with Lady Teazle, which he has industriously been led into by a scandalous society in the neighbourhood, who have contributed not a little to Charles's ill name. Whereas the truth is, I believe, if the lady is partial to either of them, his brother is the favourite.

SIR OLIVER. Ay, I know there are a set of malicious, prating, prudent gossips, both male and female, who murder characters to kill time, and will rob a young fellow of his good name before he has years to know the value of it. But I am not to be prejudiced against my nephew by such, I promise you! No, no: if Charles has done nothing false or mean, I shall compound for his extravagance.

ROWLEY. Then, my life on't, you will reclaim him. Ah, sir, it gives me new life to find that your heart is not turned against him, and that the son of my good old master has one friend, however, left.

SIR OLIVER. What! shall I forget, Master Rowley, when I was at his years myself? Egad, my brother and I were neither of us very prudent youths; and yet, I believe, you have not seen many better men than your old master was?

ROWLEY. Sir, 'tis this reflection gives me assurance that Charles may yet be a credit to his family. But here comes Sir Peter.

SIR OLIVER. Egad, so he does! Mercy on me! he's greatly altered, and seems to have a settled married look! One may read husband in his face at this distance.

[Enter SIR PETER TEAZLE.]

SIR PETER. Ha! Sir Oliver—my old friend! Welcome to England a thousand times!

SIR OLIVER. Thank you, thank you, Sir Peter! and i' faith I am glad to find you well, believe me!

SIR PETER. Oh! 'tis a long time since we met—fifteen years, I doubt, Sir Oliver, and many a cross accident in the time.

SIR OLIVER. Ay, I have had my share But, what! I find you are married, hey, my old boy? Well, well, it can't be helped; and so—I wish you joy with all my heart?

SIR PETER. Thank you, thank you, Sir Oliver.—Yes, I have entered into—the happy state; but we'll not talk of that now.

SIR OLIVER. True, true, Sir Peter; old friends should not begin on grievances at first meeting. No, no, no.

ROWLEY [aside to SIR OLIVER]. Take care, pray, sir.

SIR OLIVER. Well, so one of my nephews is a wild rogue, hey?

SIR PETER. Wild! Ah! my old friend, I grieve for your disappointment there; he's a lost young man, indeed. However, his brother will make you amends; Joseph is, indeed, what a youth should be—every body in the world speaks well of him.

SIR OLIVER. I am sorry to hear it; he has too good a character to be an honest fellow. Every body speaks well of him! Pshaw! then he has bowed as low to knaves and fools as to the honest dignity of genius and virtue.

SIR PETER. What, Sir Oliver! do you blame him for not making enemies?

SIR OLIVER. Yes, if he has merit enough to deserve them.

SIR PETER. Well, well—you'll be convinced when you know him. 'Tis edification to hear him converse; he professes the noblest sentiments.

SIR OLIVER. Oh, plague of his sentiments! If he salutes me with a scrap of morality in his mouth, I shall be sick directly. But, however, don't mistake me, Sir Peter; I don't mean to defend Charles's errors: but, before I form my judgment of either of them, I intend to make a trial of their hearts; and my friend Rowley and I have planned something for the purpose.

ROWLEY. And Sir Peter shall own for once he has been mistaken.

SIR PETER. Oh, my life on Joseph's honour!

SIR OLIVER. Well—come, give us a bottle of good wine, and we'll drink the lads' health, and tell you our scheme.

SIR PETER. *Allons*, then!

SIR OLIVER. And don't, Sir Peter, be so severe against your old friend's son. Odds my life! I am not sorry that he has run out of the course a little: for my part, I hate to see prudence clinging to the green suckers of youth; 'tis like ivy round a sapling, and spoils the growth of the tree. [*Exeunt.*]

ACT III

SCENE I—*A room in* SIR PETER TEAZLE'S *house.*

[*Enter* SIR PETER TEAZLE, SIR OLIVER SURFACE, *and* ROWLEY.]

SIR PETER. Well, then, we will see this fellow first, and have our wine afterwards. But how is this, Master Rowley? I don't see the jest of your scheme.

ROWLEY. Why, sir, this Mr. Stanley, whom I was speaking of, is nearly related to them by their mother. He was once a merchant in Dublin, but has been ruined by a series of undeserved misfortunes. He has applied, by letter, since his confinement, both to Mr. Surface and Charles: from the former he has received nothing but evasive promises of future service, while Charles has done all that his extravagance has left him power to do; and he is, at this time, endeavouring to raise a sum of money, part of which, in the midst of his own distresses, I know he intends for the service of poor Stanley.

SIR OLIVER. Ah! he is my brother's son.

SIR PETER. Well, but how is Sir Oliver personally to——

ROWLEY. Why, sir, I will inform Charles and his brother that Stanley has obtained permission to apply personally to his friends; and, as they have neither of them ever seen him, let Sir Oliver assume his character, and he will have a fair opportunity of judging, at least, of the benevolence of their dispositions: and be-

lieve me, sir, you will find in the youngest brother one who, in the midst of folly and dissipation, has still, as our immortal bard expresses it,—

"a heart to pity, and a hand,
Open as day, for melting charity."

SIR PETER. Pshaw! What signifies his having an open hand or purse either, when he has nothing left to give? Well, well, make the trial, if you please. But where is the fellow whom you brought for Sir Oliver to examine, relative to Charles's affairs?

ROWLEY. Below, waiting his commands and no one can give him better intelligence.—This, Sir Oliver, is a friendly Jew, who, to do him justice, has done every thing in his power to bring your nephew to a proper sense of his extravagance.

SIR PETER. Pray let us have him in.

ROWLEY [*calls to* SERVANT]. Desire Mr. Moses to walk upstairs.

SIR PETER. But, pray, why should you suppose he will speak the truth?

ROWLEY. Oh, I have convinced him that he has no chance of recovering certain sums advanced to Charles but through the bounty of Sir Oliver, who he knows is arrived; so that you may depend on his fidelity to his own interests. I have also another evidence in my power, one Snake, whom I have detected in a matter little short of forgery, and shall shortly produce to remove some of your prejudices, Sir Peter, relative to Charles and Lady Teazle.

SIR PETER. I have heard too much on that subject.

ROWLEY. Here comes the honest Israelite.

[*Enter* MOSES.]

—This is Sir Oliver.

SIR OLIVER. Sir, I understand you have lately had great dealings with my nephew Charles.

MOSES. Yes, Sir Oliver, I have done all I could for him; but he was ruined before he came to me for assistance.

SIR OLIVER. That was unlucky, truly; for you have had no opportunity of showing your talents.

MOSES. None at all; I hadn't the pleasure of knowing his distresses till he was some thousands worse than nothing.

SIR OLIVER. Unfortunate, indeed! But I suppose you have done all in your power for him, honest Moses?

MOSES. Yes, he knows that. This very evening I was to have brought him a gentleman from the city, who does not know him, and will, I believe, advance him some money.

SIR PETER. What, one Charles has never had money from before?

MOSES. Yes, Mr. Premium, of Crutched Friars, formerly a broker.

SIR PETER. Egad, Sir Oliver, a thought strikes me!—Charles, you say, does not know Mr. Premium?

MOSES. Not at all.

SIR PETER. Now then, Sir Oliver, you may have a better opportunity of satisfying yourself than by an old romancing tale of a poor relation; go with my friend Moses, and represent Premium, and then, I'll answer for it, you'll see your nephew in all his glory.

SIR OLIVER. Egad, I like this idea better than the other, and I may visit Joseph afterwards as old Stanley.

SIR PETER. True—so you may.

ROWLEY. Well, this is taking Charles rather at a disadvantage, to be sure. However, Moses, you understand Sir Peter, and will be faithful?

MOSES. You may depend upon me.— [Looks at his watch.] This is near the time I was to have gone.

SIR OLIVER. I'll accompany you as soon as you please, Moses——But hold! I have forgot one thing—how the plague shall I be able to pass for a Jew?

MOSES. There's no need—the principal is Christian.

SIR OLIVER. Is he? I'm very sorry to hear it. But, then again, an't I rather too smartly dressed to look like a money lender?

SIR PETER. Not at all; 'twould not be out of character, if you went in your own carriage—would it, Moses?

MOSES. Not in the least.

SIR OLIVER. Well, but how must I talk; there's certainly some cant of usury and mode of treating that I ought to know.

SIR PETER. Oh, there's not much to learn. The great point, as I take it, is to be exorbitant enough in your demands. Hey, Moses?

MOSES. Yes, that's a very great point.

SIR OLIVER. I'll answer for't I'll not be wanting in that. I'll ask him eight or ten per cent. on the loan, at least.

MOSES. If you ask him no more than that, you'll be discovered immediately.

SIR OLIVER. Hey! what, the plague! how much then?

MOSES. That depends upon the circumstances. If he appears not very anxious for the supply, you should require only forty or fifty per cent.; but if you find him in great distress, and want the moneys very bad, you may ask double.

SIR PETER. A good honest trade you're learning, Sir Oliver.

SIR OLIVER. Truly, I think so—and not unprofitable.

MOSES. Then, you know, you haven't the moneys yourself, but are forced to borrow them for him of a friend.

SIR OLIVER. Oh! I borrow it of a friend, do I?

MOSES. And your friend is an unconscionable dog: but you can't help that.

SIR OLIVER. My friend an unconscionable dog, is he?

MOSES. Yes, and he himself has not the moneys by him, but is forced to sell stock at a great loss.

SIR OLIVER. He is forced to sell stock at a great loss, is he? Well, that's very kind of him.

SIR PETER. I' faith, Sir Oliver—Mr. Premium, I mean—you'll soon be master of the trade. But, Moses! would not you have him run out a little against the Annuity Bill? That would be in character, I should think.

MOSES. Very much.

ROWLEY. And lament that a young man now must be at years of discretion before he is suffered to ruin himself?

MOSES. Ay, great pity!

SIR PETER. And abuse the public for allowing merit to an act whose only object is to snatch misfortune and imprudence from the rapacious gripe of usury, and give the minor a chance of inheriting his estate without being undone by coming into possession.

SIR OLIVER. So, so—Moses shall give me farther instructions as we go together.

SIR PETER. You will not have much time, for your nephew lives hard by.

SIR OLIVER. Oh, never fear! my tutor appears so able, that though Charles lived in the next street, it must be my own fault if I am not a complete rogue before I turn the corner.

[*Exit with* MOSES.]

SIR PETER. So, now, I think Sir Oliver will be convinced: you are partial, Rowley, and would have prepared Charles for the other plot.

ROWLEY. No, upon my word, Sir Peter.

SIR PETER. Well, go bring me this Snake, and I'll hear what he has to say presently. I see Maria, and want to speak with her.—[*Exit* ROWLEY.] I should be glad to be convinced my suspicions of Lady Teazle and Charles were unjust. I have never yet opened my mind on this subject to my friend Joseph—I am determined I will do it—he will give me his opinion sincerely.

[*Enter* MARIA.]

So, child, has Mr. Surface returned with you?

MARIA. No, sir; he was engaged.

SIR PETER. Well, Maria, do you not reflect, the more you converse with that amiable young man, what return his partiality for you deserves?

MARIA. Indeed, Sir Peter, your frequent importunity on this subject distresses me extremely—you compel me to declare, that I know no man who has ever paid me a particular attention whom I would not prefer to Mr. Surface.

SIR PETER. So—here's perverseness! No, no, Maria, 'tis Charles only whom you would prefer. 'Tis evident his vices and follies have won your heart.

MARIA. This is unkind, sir. You know I have obeyed you in neither seeing nor corresponding with him: I have heard enough to convince me that he is unworthy my regard. Yet I cannot think it culpable, if, while my understanding severely condemns his vices, my heart suggests some pity for his distresses.

SIR PETER. Well, well, pity him as much as you please; but give your heart and hand to a worthier object.

MARIA. Never to his brother!

SIR PETER. Go, perverse and obstinate! But take care, madam; you have never yet known what the authority of a guardian is: don't compel me to inform you of it.

MARIA. I can only say, you shall not have just reason. 'Tis true, by my father's will, I am for a short period bound to regard you as his substitute; but must cease to think you so, when you would compel me to be miserable. [*Exit.*]

SIR PETER. Was ever man so crossed as I am, every thing conspiring to fret me! I had not been involved in matrimony a fortnight, before her father, a hale and hearty man, died, on purpose, I believe, for the pleasure of plaguing me with the care of his daughter.—[LADY TEAZLE *sings without.*] But here comes my helpmate! She appears in great good humour. How happy I should be if I could tease her into loving me, though but a little!

[*Enter* LADY TEAZLE.]

LADY TEAZLE. Lud! Sir Peter, I hope you haven't been quarrelling with Maria? It is not using me well to be ill-humoured when I am not by.

SIR PETER. Ah, Lady Teazle, you might have the power to make me good-humoured at all times.

LADY TEAZLE. I am sure I wish I had; for I want you to be in a charming sweet temper at this moment. Do be good-humoured now, and let me have two hundred pounds, will you?

SIR PETER. Two hundred pounds; what, an't I to be in a good humour without paying for it! But speak to me thus, and i' faith there's nothing I could refuse you. You shall have it; but seal me a bond for the repayment.

LADY TEAZLE. Oh, no—there—my note of hand will do as well. [*Offering her hand.*]

SIR PETER. And you shall no longer reproach me with not giving you an independent settlement. I mean shortly to surprise you: but shall we always live thus, hey?

LADY TEAZLE. If you please. I'm sure I don't care how soon we leave off quarrelling, provided you'll own you were tired first.

SIR PETER. Well—then let our future contest be, who shall be most obliging.

LADY TEAZLE. I assure you, Sir Peter, good nature becomes you. You look now as you did before we were married, when you used to walk with me under the elms, and tell me stories of what a gallant you were in your youth, and chuck me under the chin, you would; and asked me if I thought I could love an old fellow, who would deny me nothing—didn't you?

SIR PETER. Yes, yes, and you were as kind and attentive——

LADY TEAZLE. Ay, so I was, and would always take your part, when my acquaintance used to abuse you, and turn you into ridicule.

SIR PETER. Indeed!

LADY TEAZLE. Ay, and when my cousin Sophy has called you a stiff, peevish old bachelor, and laughed at me for thinking of marrying one who might be my father, I have always defended you, and said, I didn't think you so ugly by any means.

SIR PETER. Thank you.

LADY TEAZLE. And I dared say you'd make a very good sort of a husband.

SIR PETER. And you prophesied right; and we shall now be the happiest couple——

LADY TEAZLE. And never differ again?

SIR PETER. No, never!—though at the same time, indeed, my dear Lady Teazle, you must watch your temper very seriously; for in all our little quarrels, my dear, if you recollect, my love, you always began first.

LADY TEAZLE. I beg your pardon, my dear Sir Peter: indeed, you always gave the provocation.

SIR PETER. Now see, my angel! take care—contradicting isn't the way to keep friends.

LADY TEAZLE. Then don't you begin it, my love!

SIR PETER. There, now! you—you are going on. You don't perceive, my life, that you are just doing the very thing which you know always makes me angry.

LADY TEAZLE. Nay, you know, if you will be angry without any reason, my dear——

SIR PETER. There! now you want to quarrel again.

LADY TEAZLE. No, I'm sure I don't: but, if you will be so peevish——

SIR PETER. There now! who begins first?

LADY TEAZLE. Why, you, to be sure. I said nothing—but there's no bearing your temper.

SIR PETER. No, no, madam: the fault's in your own temper.

LADY TEAZLE. Ay, you are just what my cousin Sophy said you would be.

SIR PETER. Your cousin Sophy is a forward, impertinent gipsy.

LADY TEAZLE. You are a great bear, I'm sure, to abuse my relations.

SIR PETER. Now may all the plagues of marriage be doubled on me, if ever I try to be friends with you any more!

LADY TEAZLE. So much the better.

SIR PETER. No, no, madam: 'tis evident you never cared a pin for me, and I was a madman to marry you—a pert, rural coquette, that had refused half the honest squires in the neighbourhood!

LADY TEAZLE. And I am sure I was a fool to marry you—an old dangling bachelor, who was single at fifty, only because he never could meet with any one who would have him.

SIR PETER. Ay, ay, madam; but you were pleased enough to listen to me: you never had such an offer before.

LADY TEAZLE. No! didn't I refuse Sir Tivy Terrier, who every body said would have been a better match? for his estate is just as good as yours, and he has broke his neck since we have been married.

SIR PETER. I have done with you, madam! You are an unfeeling, ungrateful—but there's an end of everything. I believe you capable of everything that is bad. Yes, madam, I now believe the reports relative to you and Charles, madam. Yes, madam, you and Charles are, not without grounds——

LADY TEAZLE. Take care, Sir Peter! you had better not insinuate any such thing! I'll not be suspected without cause, I promise you.

SIR PETER. Very well, madam! very well! A separate maintenance as soon as you please. Yes, madam, or a divorce! I'll make an example of myself for the benefit of all old bachelors. Let us separate, madam.

LADY TEAZLE. Agreed! agreed! And now, my dear Sir Peter, we are of a mind once more, we may be the happiest couple, and never differ again, you know: ha! ha! ha! Well, you are going to be in a passion, I see, and I shall only interrupt you—so, bye! bye! [*Exit.*]

SIR PETER. Plagues and tortures! can't I make her angry either! Oh, I am the most miserable fellow! But I'll not bear her presuming to keep her temper: no! she may break my heart, but she sha'n't keep her temper. [*Exit.*]

SCENE II—*A room in* CHARLES SURFACE'S *house.*

[*Enter* TRIP, MOSES, *and* SIR OLIVER SURFACE.]

TRIP. Here, Master Moses! if you'll stay a moment I'll try whether—what's the gentleman's name?

SIR OLIVER [*aside to* MOSES]. Mr. Moses, what is my name?

MOSES. Mr. Premium.

TRIP. Premium—very well. [*Exit, taking snuff.*]

SIR OLIVER. To judge by the servants, one wouldn't believe the master was ruined. But what!—sure, this was my brother's house?

MOSES. Yes, sir; Mr. Charles bought it of Mr. Joseph, with the furniture, pictures, etc., just as the old gentleman left it. Sir Peter thought it a piece of extravagance in him.

SIR OLIVER. In my mind, the other's economy in selling it to him was more reprehensible by half.

[*Reënter* TRIP.]

TRIP. My master says you must wait, gentlemen: he has company, and can't speak with you yet.

SIR OLIVER. If he knew who it was wanted to see him, perhaps he would not send such a message.

TRIP. Yes, yes, sir; he knows you are here—I did not forget little Premium: no, no, no.

SIR OLIVER. Very well; and I pray, sir, what may be your name?

TRIP. Trip, sir; my name is Trip, at your service.

SIR OLIVER. Well, then, Mr. Trip, you have a pleasant sort of place here, I guess?

TRIP. Why, yes—here are three or four of us pass our time agreeably enough; but then our wages are sometimes a little in arrear—and not very great either—but fifty pounds a year, and find our own bags and bouquets.

SIR OLIVER [*aside*]. Bags and bouquets! halters and bastinadoes!

TRIP. And à propos, Moses, have you been able to get me that little bill discounted?

SIR OLIVER [*aside*]. Wants to raise money too!—mercy on me! Has his distresses too, I warrant, like a lord, and affects creditors and duns.

MOSES. 'Twas not to be done, indeed, Mr. Trip.

TRIP. Good lack, you surprise me! My friend Brush has indorsed it, and I thought when he put his name at the back of a bill 'twas the same as cash.

MOSES. No, 'twouldn't do.

TRIP. A small sum—but twenty pounds. Hark'ee, Moses, do you think you couldn't get it me by way of annuity?

SIR OLIVER [aside]. An annuity! ha! ha! a footman raise money by way of annuity! Well done, luxury, egad!

MOSES. Well, but you must insure your place.

TRIP. Oh, with all my heart! I'll insure my place, and my life too, if you please.

SIR OLIVER [aside]. It's more than I would your neck.

MOSES. But is there nothing you could deposit?

TRIP. Why, nothing capital of my master's wardrobe has dropped lately; but I could give you a mortgage on some of his winter clothes, with equity of redemption before November—or you shall have the reversion of the French velvet, or a post-obit on the blue and silver;—these, I should think, Moses, with a few pair of point ruffles, as a collateral security—hey, my little fellow?

MOSES. Well, well.

[Bell rings.]

TRIP. Egad, I heard the bell! I believe, gentlemen, I can now introduce you. Don't forget the annuity, little Moses! This way, gentlemen, I'll insure my place, you know.

SIR OLIVER [aside]. If the man be a shadow of the master, this is the temple of dissipation indeed! [Exeunt.]

SCENE III—*Another room in the same.*

[CHARLES SURFACE, SIR HARRY BUMPER, CARELESS, and GENTLEMEN, discovered drinking.]

CHARLES SURFACE. 'Fore heaven, 'tis true!—there's the great degeneracy of the age. Many of our acquaintance have taste, spirit, and politeness; but, plague on't, they won't drink.

CARELESS. It is so, indeed, Charles! they give in to all the substantial luxuries of the table, and abstain from nothing but wine and wit. Oh, certainly society suffers by it intolerably! for now, instead of the social spirit of raillery that used to mantle over a ·glass of bright Burgundy, their conversation is become just like the Spa-water they drink, which has all the pertness and flatulency of champagne, without its spirit or flavour.

1ST GENTLEMAN. But what are they to do who love play better than wine?

CARELESS. True! there's Sir Harry diets himself for gaming, and is now under a hazard regimen.

CHARLES SURFACE. Then he'll have the worst of it. What! you wouldn't train a horse for the course by keeping him from corn? For my part, egad, I am never so successful as when I am a little merry: let me throw on a bottle of champagne, and I never lose.

ALL. Hey, what?

CHARLES SURFACE. At least I never feel my losses, which is exactly the same thing.

2ND GENTLEMAN. Ay, that I believe.

CHARLES SURFACE. And then, what man can pretend to be a believer in love, who is an abjurer of wine? 'Tis the test by which the lover knows his own heart. Fill a dozen bumpers to a dozen beauties, and she that floats at the top is the maid that has bewitched you.

CARELESS. Now then, Charles, be honest, and give us your real favourite.

CHARLES SURFACE. Why, I have withheld her only in compassion to you. If I toast her, you must give a round of her peers, which is impossible—on earth.

CARELESS. Oh! then we'll find some canonised vestals or heathen goddesses that will do, I warrant!

CHARLES SURFACE. Here then, bumpers, you rogues! bumpers! Maria! Maria!——

SIR HARRY. Maria who?

CHARLES SURFACE. Oh, damn the surname!—'tis too formal to be registered in Love's calendar—Maria!

ALL. Maria!

CHARLES SURFACE. But now, Sir Harry, beware, we must have beauty superlative.

CARELESS. Nay, never study, Sir Harry: we'll stand to the toast, though your mistress should want an eye, and you know you have a song will excuse you.

SIR HARRY. Egad, so I have! and I'll give him the song instead of the lady. [*Sings.*]

Here's to the maiden of bashful fifteen;
　Here's to the widow of fifty;
Here's to the flaunting extravagant quean,
And here's to the housewife that's thrifty

CHORUS. Let the toast pass,—
　　　　Drink to the lass,
I'll warrant she'll prove an excuse for the glass.

Here's to the charmer whose dimples we prize;
Now to the maid who has none, sir:
Here's to the girl with a pair of blue eyes,
And here's to the nymph with but one, sir.

CHORUS. Let the toast pass, etc.

Here's to the maid with a bosom of snow:
Now to her that's as brown as a berry:
Here's to the wife with a face full of woe,
And now to the damsel that's merry.

CHORUS. Let the toast pass, etc.

For let 'em be clumsy, or let 'em be slim,
　Young or ancient, I care not a feather;
So fill a pint bumper quite up to the brim,
　So fill up your glasses, nay, fill to the brim,
And let us e'en toast them together.

CHORUS. Let the toast pass, etc.

ALL. Bravo! bravo!

[*Enter* TRIP, *and whispers* CHARLES SURFACE.]

CHARLES SURFACE. Gentlemen, you must excuse me a little.—Careless, take the chair, will you?

CARELESS. Nay, pr'ythee, Charles, what now? This is one of your peerless beauties, I suppose, has dropped in by chance?

CHARLES SURFACE. No, faith! To tell you the truth, 'tis a Jew and a broker, who are come by appointment.

CARELESS. Oh! let's have the Jew in.

1ST GENTLEMAN. Ay, and the broker too, by all means.

2ND GENTLEMAN. Yes, yes, the Jew and the broker.

CHARLES SURFACE. Egad, with all my heart!—Trip, bid the gentlemen walk in. —[*Exit* TRIP.] Though there's one of them a stranger, I can tell you.

CARELESS. Charles, let us give them some generous Burgundy, and perhaps they'll grow conscientious.

CHARLES SURFACE. Oh, hang 'em, no! wine does but draw forth a man's natural qualities; and to make them drink would only be to whet their knavery.

[*Reënter* TRIP, *with* SIR OLIVER SURFACE *and* MOSES.]

CHARLES SURFACE. So, honest Moses; walk in, pray, Mr. Premium—that's the gentleman's name, isn't it, Moses?

MOSES. Yes, sir.

CHARLES SURFACE. Set chairs, Trip.— Sit down, Mr. Premium.—Glasses, Trip.— [TRIP *gives chairs and glasses, and exits.*] Sit down, Moses.—Come, Mr. Premium, I'll give you a sentiment; here's *Success to usury!*—Moses, fill the gentleman a bumper.

MOSES. Success to usury! [*Drinks.*]

CARELESS. Right, Moses—usury is prudence and industry, and deserves to succeed.

SIR OLIVER. Then here's—All the success it deserves! [*Drinks.*]

CARELESS. No, no, that won't do! Mr. Premium, you have demurred at the toast, and must drink it in a pint bumper.

1ST GENTLEMAN. A pint bumper, at least.

MOSES. Oh, pray, sir, consider—Mr. Premium's a gentleman.

CARELESS. And therefore loves good wine.

2ND GENTLEMAN. Give Moses a quart glass—this is mutiny, and a high contempt for the chair.

CARELESS. Here, now for't! I'll see justice done to the last drop of my bottle.

SIR OLIVER. Nay, pray, gentlemen—I did not expect this usage.

CHARLES SURFACE. No, hang it, you shan't; Mr. Premium's a stranger.

SIR OLIVER [aside]. Odd! I wish I was well out of their company.

CARELESS. Plague on 'em then! if they won't drink, we'll not sit down with them. Come, Harry, the dice are in the next room.—Charles, you'll join us when you have finished your business with the gentlemen?

CHARLES SURFACE. I will! I will!—[Exeunt SIR HARRY BUMPER and GENTLEMEN; CARELESS following.] Careless!

CARELESS [returning]. Well!

CHARLES SURFACE. Perhaps I may want you.

CARELESS. Oh, you know I am always ready: word, note, or bond, 'tis all the same to me. [Exit.]

MOSES. Sir, this is Mr. Premium, a gentleman of the strictest honour and secrecy; and always performs what he undertakes. Mr. Premium, this is—

CHARLES SURFACE. Pshaw! have done. Sir, my friend Moses is a very honest fellow, but a little slow at expression: he'll be an hour giving us our titles. Mr. Premium, the plain state of the matter is this: I am an extravagant young fellow who wants to borrow money; you I take to be a prudent old fellow, who have got money to lend. I am blockhead enough to give fifty per cent sooner than not have it; and you, I presume, are rogue enough to take a hundred if you can get it. Now, sir, you see we are acquainted at once, and may proceed to business without farther ceremony.

SIR OLIVER. Exceeding frank, upon my word. I see, sir, you are not a man of many compliments.

CHARLES SURFACE. Oh, no, sir! plain dealing in business I always think best.

SIR OLIVER. Sir, I like you the better for it. However, you are mistaken in one thing; I have no money to lend, but I believe I could procure some of a friend; but then he's an unconscionable dog. Isn't he, Moses? And must sell stock to accommodate you. Mustn't he, Moses?

MOSES. Yes, indeed! You know I always speak the truth, and scorn to tell a lie!

CHARLES SURFACE. Right. People that speak truth generally do. But these are trifles, Mr. Premium. What! I know money isn't to be bought without paying for't!

SIR OLIVER. Well, but what security could you give? You have no land, I suppose?

CHARLES SURFACE. Not a mole-hill, nor a twig, but what's in the bough-pots out of the window!

SIR OLIVER. Nor any stock, I presume?

CHARLES SURFACE. Nothing but live stock—and that's only a few pointers and ponies. But pray, Mr. Premium, are you acquainted at all with any of my connections?

SIR OLIVER. Why, to say truth, I am.

CHARLES SURFACE. Then you must know that I have a devilish rich uncle in the East Indies, Sir Oliver Surface, from whom I have the greatest expectations?

SIR OLIVER. That you have a wealthy uncle, I have heard; but how your expectations will turn out is more, I believe, than you can tell.

CHARLES SURFACE. Oh, no!—there can be no doubt. They tell me I'm a prodigious favourite, and that he talks of leaving me every thing.

SIR OLIVER. Indeed! this is the first I've heard of it.

CHARLES SURFACE. Yes, yes, 'tis just so. Moses knows 'tis true; don't you, Moses?

MOSES. Oh, yes! I'll swear to't.

SIR OLIVER [aside]. Egad, they'll persuade me presently I'm at Bengal.

CHARLES SURFACE. Now I propose, Mr. Premium, if it's agreeable to you, a post-obit on Sir Oliver's life: though at the same time the old fellow has been so liberal to me, that I give you my word, I should be very sorry to hear that anything had happened to him.

SIR OLIVER. Not more than I should, I assure you. But the bond you mention happens to be just the worst security you could offer me—for I might live to a hundred and never see the principal.

CHARLES SURFACE. Oh, yes, you would! the moment Sir Oliver dies, you know, you would come on me for the money.

SIR OLIVER. Then I believe I should be the most unwelcome dun you ever had in your life.

CHARLES SURFACE. What! I suppose you're afraid that Sir Oliver is too good a life?

SIR OLIVER. No, indeed I am not; though I have heard he is as hale and healthy as any man of his years in Christendom.

CHARLES SURFACE. There again, now, you are misinformed. No, no, the climate has hurt him considerably, poor uncle Oliver. Yes, yes, he breaks apace, I'm told—and is so much altered lately that his nearest relations would not know him.

SIR OLIVER. No! Ha! ha! ha! so much altered lately that his nearest relations would not know him! Ha! ha! ha! egad—ha! ha! ha!

CHARLES SURFACE. Ha! ha!—you're glad to hear that, little Premium?

SIR OLIVER. No, no, I'm not.

CHARLES SURFACE. Yes, yes, you are—ha! ha! ha!—you know that mends your chance.

SIR OLIVER. But I'm told Sir Oliver is coming over; nay, some say he is actually arrived.

CHARLES SURFACE. Pshaw! sure I must know better than you whether he's come or not. No, no, rely on't he's at this moment at Calcutta. Isn't he, Moses?

MOSES. Oh, yes, certainly.

SIR OLIVER. Very true, as you say, you must know better than I, though I have it from pretty good authority. Haven't I, Moses?

MOSES. Yes, most undoubted!

SIR OLIVER. But, sir, as I understand you want a few hundreds immediately, is there nothing you could dispose of?

CHARLES SURFACE. How do you mean?

SIR OLIVER. For instance, now, I have heard that your father left behind him a great quantity of massy old plate.

CHARLES SURFACE. O Lud! that's gone long ago. Moses can tell you how better than I can.

SIR OLIVER [aside]. Good lack! all the family race-cups and corporation-bowls! —[Aloud.] Then it was also supposed that his library was one of the most valuable and compact.

CHARLES SURFACE. Yes, yes, so it was —vastly too much so for a private gentleman. For my part, I was always of a communicative disposition, so I thought it a shame to keep so much knowledge to myself.

SIR OLIVER [aside]. Mercy upon me! learning that had run in the family like an heir-loom!—[Aloud.] Pray, what are become of the books?

CHARLES SURFACE. You must inquire of the auctioneer, Master Premium, for I don't believe even Moses can direct you.

MOSES. I know nothing of books.

SIR OLIVER. So, so, nothing of the family property left, I suppose?

CHARLES SURFACE. Not much, indeed; unless you have a mind to the family pictures. I have got a room full of ancestors above; and if you have a taste for old paintings, egad, you shall have 'em a bargain!

SIR OLIVER. Hey! what the devil! sure, you wouldn't sell your forefathers, would you?

CHARLES SURFACE. Every man of them, to the best bidder.

SIR OLIVER. What! your great-uncles and aunts?

CHARLES SURFACE. Ay, and my great-grandfathers and grandmothers too.

SIR OLIVER [aside]. Now I give him up!—[Aloud.] What the plague, have you no bowels for your own kindred? Odds life! do you take me for Shylock in the play, that you would raise money of me on your own flesh and blood?

CHARLES SURFACE. Nay, my little broker, don't be angry: what need you care, if you have your money's worth?

SIR OLIVER. Well, I'll be the purchaser: I think I can dispose of the family canvas.—[*Aside.*] Oh, I'll never forgive him this! never!

[*Reënter* CARELESS.]

CARELESS. Come, Charles, what keeps you?

CHARLES SURFACE. I can't come yet. I' faith, we are going to have a sale above stairs; here's little Premium will buy all my ancestors!

CARELESS. Oh, burn your ancestors!

CHARLES SURFACE. No, he may do that afterwards, if he pleases. Stay, Careless, we want you: egad, you shall be auctioneer—so come along with us.

CARELESS. Oh, have with you, if that's the case. I can handle a hammer as well as a dice-box! Going! going!

SIR OLIVER [*aside*]. Oh, the profligates!

CHARLES SURFACE. Come, Moses, you shall be appraiser, if we want one. Gad's life, little Premium, you don't seem to like the business?

SIR OLIVER. Oh, yes, I do, vastly! Ha! ha! ha! yes, yes, I think it a rare joke to sell one's family by auction—ha! ha! —[*Aside.*] Oh, the prodigal!

CHARLES SURFACE. To be sure! when a man wants money, where the plague should he get assistance, if he can't make free with his own relations! [*Exeunt.*]

SIR OLIVER. I'll never forgive him; never! never!

ACT IV

SCENE I—*A picture room in* CHARLES SURFACE'S *house.*

[*Enter* CHARLES SURFACE, SIR OLIVER SURFACE, MOSES, *and* CARELESS.]

CHARLES SURFACE. Walk in, gentlemen, pray walk in;—here they are, the family of the Surfaces, up to the Conquest.

SIR OLIVER. And, in my opinion, a goodly collection.

CHARLES SURFACE. Ay, ay, these are done in the true spirit of portrait-painting; no *volontière grace* or expression. Not like the works of your modern Raphaels, who give you the strongest resemblance, yet contrive to make your portrait independent of you; so that you may sink the original and not hurt the picture. No, no; the merit of these is the inveterate likeness—all stiff and awkward as the originals, and like nothing in human nature besides.

SIR OLIVER. Ah! we shall never see such figures of men again.

CHARLES SURFACE. I hope not. Well, you see, Master Premium, what a domestic character I am; here I sit of an evening surrounded by my family. But come, get to your pulpit, Mr. Auctioneer; here's an old gouty chair of my grandfather's will answer the purpose.

CARELESS. Ay, ay, this will do. But, Charles, I haven't a hammer; and what's an auctioneer without his hammer?

CHARLES SURFACE. Egad, that's true. What parchment have we here? Oh, our genealogy in full. [*Taking pedigree down.*] Here, Careless, you shall have no common bit of mahogany, here's the family tree for you, you rogue! This shall be your hammer, and now you may knock down my ancestors with their own pedigree.

SIR OLIVER [*aside*]. What an unnatural rogue!—an *ex post facto* parricide!

CARELESS. Yes, yes, here's a list of your generation indeed;—faith, Charles, this is the most convenient thing you could have found for the business, for 'twill not only serve as a hammer, but a catalogue into the bargain. Come, begin —A-going, a-going, a-going!

CHARLES SURFACE. Bravo, Careless! Well, here's my great-uncle, Sir Richard Raveline, a marvellous good general in his day, I assure you. He served in all the Duke of Marlborough's wars, and got that cut over his eye at the battle of Malplaquet. What say you, Mr. Premium? look at him—there's a hero! not cut out of his feathers, as your modern clipped captains are, but enveloped in wig and regimentals, as a general should be. What do you bid?

SIR OLIVER [aside to MOSES]. Bid him speak.

MOSES. Mr. Premium would have you speak.

CHARLES SURFACE. Why, then, he shall have him for ten pounds, and I'm sure that's not dear for a staff-officer.

SIR OLIVER [aside]. Heaven deliver me! his famous uncle Richard for ten pounds! —[Aloud.] Very well, sir, I take him at that.

CHARLES SURFACE. Careless, knock down my uncle Richard.—Here, now, is a maiden sister of his, my great-aunt Deborah, done by Kneller, in his best manner, and esteemed a very formidable likeness. There she is, you see, a shepherdess feeding her flock. You shall have her for five pounds ten—the sheep are worth the money.

SIR OLIVER [aside]. Ah! poor Deborah! a woman who set such a value on herself! —[Aloud.] Five pounds ten—she's mine.

CHARLES SURFACE. Knock down my aunt Deborah! Here, now, are two that were a sort of cousins of theirs.—You see, Moses, these pictures were done some time ago, when beaux wore wigs, and the ladies their own hair.

SIR OLIVER. Yes, truly, head-dresses appear to have been a little lower in those days.

CHARLES SURFACE. Well, take that couple for the same.

MOSES. 'Tis a good bargain.

CHARLES SURFACE. Careless!—This, now, is a grandfather of my mother's, a learned judge, well known on the western circuit. —What do you rate him at, Moses?

MOSES. Four guineas.

CHARLES SURFACE. Four guineas! Gad's life, you don't bid me the price of his wig.—Mr. Premium, you have more respect for the woolsack; do let us knock his lordship down at fifteen.

SIR OLIVER. By all means.

CARELESS. Gone!

CHARLES SURFACE. And there are two brothers of his, William and Walter Blunt, Esquires, both members of parliament, and noted speakers; and, what's very extraordinary, I believe, this is the first time they were ever bought or sold.

SIR OLIVER. That is very extraordinary, indeed! I'll take them at your own price, for the honour of parliament.

CARELESS. Well said, little Premium! I'll knock them down at forty.

CHARLES SURFACE. Here's a jolly fellow—I don't know what relation, but he was mayor of Norwich: take him at eight pounds.

SIR OLIVER. No, no; six will do for the mayor.

CHARLES SURFACE. Come, make it guineas, and I'll throw you the two aldermen there into the bargain.

SIR OLIVER. They're mine.

CHARLES SURFACE. Careless, knock down the mayor and aldermen. But, plague on't! we shall be all day retailing in this manner; do let us deal wholesale: what say you, little Premium? Give me three hundred pounds for the rest of the family in the lump.

CARELESS. Ay, ay, that will be the best way.

SIR OLIVER. Well, well, any thing to accommodate you; they are mine. But there is one portrait which you have always passed over.

CARELESS. What, that ill-looking little fellow over the settee.

SIR OLIVER. Yes, sir, I mean that; though I don't think him so ill-looking a little fellow, by any means.

CHARLES SURFACE. What, that? Oh; that's my uncle Oliver! 'twas done before he went to India.

CARELESS. Your uncle Oliver! Gad, then you'll never be friends, Charles. That, now, to me, is as stern a looking rogue as ever I saw; an unforgiving eye, and a disinheriting countenance! an inveterate knave, depend on't. Don't you think so, little Premium?

SIR OLIVER. Upon my soul, sir, I do not; I think it is as honest a looking face as any in the room, dead or alive. But I suppose uncle Oliver goes with the rest of the lumber?

CHARLES SURFACE. No; hang it! I'll not part with poor Noll. The old fellow has been very good to me, and, egad, I'll keep his picture while I've a room to put it in.

SIR OLIVER [aside]. The rogue's my nephew after all!—[Aloud.] But, sir, I have somehow taken a fancy to that picture.

CHARLES SURFACE. I'm sorry for't, for you certainly will not have it. Oons, haven't you got enough of them?

SIR OLIVER [aside]. I forgive him every thing!—[Aloud.] But, sir, when I take a whim in my head, I don't value money. I'll give you as much for that as for all the rest.

CHARLES SURFACE. Don't tease me, master broker; I tell you I'll not part with it, and there's an end of it.

SIR OLIVER [aside]. How like his father the dog is!—[Aloud.] Well, well, I have done.—[Aside.] I did not perceive it before, but I think I never saw such a striking resemblance.—[Aloud.] Here is a draft for your sum.

CHARLES SURFACE. Why, 'tis for eight hundred pounds!

SIR OLIVER. You will not let Sir Oliver go?

CHARLES SURFACE. Zounds! no! I tell you, once more.

SIR OLIVER. Then never mind the difference, we'll balance that another time. But give me your hand on the bargain; you are an honest fellow, Charles—I beg pardon, sir, for being so free.—Come, Moses.

CHARLES SURFACE. Egad, this is a whimsical old fellow!—But hark'ee, Premium, you'll prepare lodgings for these gentlemen.

SIR OLIVER. Yes, yes, I'll send for them in a day or two.

CHARLES SURFACE. But hold; do now send a genteel conveyance for them, for, I assure you, they were most of them used to ride in their own carriages.

SIR OLIVER. I will, I will—for all but Oliver.

CHARLES SURFACE. Ay, all but the little nabob.

SIR OLIVER. You're fixed on that?

CHARLES SURFACE. Peremptorily.

SIR OLIVER [aside]. A dear extravagant rogue!—[Aloud.] Good day!—Come, Moses.—[Aside.] Let me hear now who dares call him profligate.

[Exit with MOSES.]

CARELESS. Why, this is the oddest genius of the sort I ever met with!

CHARLES SURFACE. Egad, he's the prince of brokers, I think. I wonder how the devil Moses got acquainted with so honest a fellow.—Ha! here's Rowley.—Do, Careless, say I'll join the company in a few moments.

CARELESS. I will—but don't let that old blockhead persuade you to squander any of that money on old musty debts, or any such nonsense; for tradesmen, Charles, are the most exorbitant fellows.

CHARLES SURFACE. Very true, and paying them is only encouraging them.

CARELESS. Nothing else.

CHARLES SURFACE. Ay, ay, never fear. —[Exit CARELESS.] So! this was an odd old fellow, indeed. Let me see, two-thirds of these five hundred and thirty odd pounds are mine by right. 'Fore heaven! I find one's ancestors are more valuable relations than I took them for!—Ladies and gentlemen, your most obedient and very grateful servant. [Bows ceremoniously to the pictures.]

[Enter ROWLEY.]

Ha! old Rowley! egad, you are just come in time to take leave of your old acquaintance.

ROWLEY. Yes, I heard they were a-going. But I wonder you can have such spirits under so many distresses.

CHARLES SURFACE. Why, there's the point! my distresses are so many, that I can't afford to part with my spirits; but I shall be rich and splenetic, all in good time. However, I suppose you are surprised that I am not more sorrowful at parting with so many near relations; to be sure, 'tis very affecting, but you see they never move a muscle, so why should I?

ROWLEY. There's no making you serious a moment.

CHARLES SURFACE. Yes, faith, I am so now. Here, my honest Rowley, here, get me this changed directly, and take a hundred pounds of it immediately to old Stanley.

ROWLEY. A hundred pounds! Consider only——

CHARLES SURFACE. Gad's life, don't talk about it! poor Stanley's wants are pressing, and, if you don't make haste, we shall have some one call that has a better right to the money.

ROWLEY. Ah! there's the point! I never will cease dunning you with the old proverb——

CHARLES SURFACE. *Be just before you're generous.*—Why, so I would if I could; but Justice is an old hobbling beldame, and I can't get her to keep pace with Generosity, for the soul of me.

ROWLEY. Yet, Charles, believe me, one hour's reflection——

CHARLES SURFACE. Ay, ay, it's very true; but, hark'ee Rowley, while I have, by Heaven I'll give; and now for hazard. [*Exeunt.*]

SCENE II—*Another room in the same.*

[*Enter* SIR OLIVER SURFACE *and* MOSES.]

MOSES. Well, sir, I think, as Sir Peter said, you have seen Mr. Charles in high glory; 'tis great pity he's so extravagant.

SIR OLIVER. True, but he would not sell my picture.

MOSES. And loves wine and women so much.

SIR OLIVER. But he would not sell my picture.

MOSES. And games so deep.

SIR OLIVER. But he would not sell my picture. Oh, here's Rowley.

[*Enter* ROWLEY.]

ROWLEY. So, Sir Oliver, I find you have made a purchase——

SIR OLIVER. Yes, yes, our young rake has parted with his ancestors like old tapestry.

ROWLEY. And here has he commissioned me to redeliver you part of the purchase money—I mean, though, in your necessitous character of old Stanley.

MOSES. Ah! there is the pity of all; he is so charitable.

ROWLEY. And I left a hosier and two tailors in the hall, who, I'm sure, won't be paid, and this hundred would satisfy them.

SIR OLIVER. Well, well, I'll pay his debts, and his benevolence too. But now I am no more a broker, and you shall introduce me to the elder brother as old Stanley.

ROWLEY. Not yet awhile; Sir Peter, I know, means to call there about this time.

[*Enter* TRIP.]

TRIP. Oh, gentlemen, I beg pardon for not showing you out; this way—Moses, a word. [*Exit with* MOSES.]

SIR OLIVER. There's a fellow for you! Would you believe it, that puppy intercepted the Jew on our coming, and wanted to raise money before he got to his master?

ROWLEY. Indeed!

SIR OLIVER. Yes, they are now planning an annuity business. Ah, Master Rowley, in my days servants were content with the follies of their masters, when they were worn a little threadbare; but now they have their vices, like their birthday clothes, with the gloss on.
[*Exeunt.*]

SCENE III—*A library in* JOSEPH SURFACE'S *house.*

[*Enter* JOSEPH SURFACE *and* SERVANT.]

JOSEPH SURFACE. No letter from Lady Teazle?

SERVANT. No, sir.

JOSEPH SURFACE [*aside*]. I am surprised she has not sent, if she is prevented from coming. Sir Peter certainly does not suspect me. Yet I wish I may not lose the heiress, through the scrape I have drawn myself into with the wife; however, Charles's imprudence and bad character are great points in my favour.

[*Knocking without.*]

SERVANT. Sir, I believe that must be Lady Teazle.

JOSEPH SURFACE. Hold! See whether it is or not, before you go to the door: I have a particular message for you if it should be my brother.

SERVANT. 'Tis her ladyship, sir; she always leaves her chair at the milliner's in the next street.

JOSEPH SURFACE. Stay, stay; draw that screen before the window—that *will do;—my opposite neighbour is a maiden lady of so curious a temper.—[SERVANT *draws the screen, and exits.*] I have a difficult hand to play in this affair. Lady Teazle has lately suspected my views on Maria; but she must by no means be let into that secret,—at least, till I have her more in my power.

[*Enter* LADY TEAZLE.]

LADY TEAZLE. What, sentiment in soliloquy now? Have you been very impatient? O Lud! don't pretend to look grave. I vow I couldn't come before.

JOSEPH SURFACE. O madam, punctuality is a species of constancy very unfashionable in a lady of quality. [*Places chairs, and sits after* LADY TEAZLE *is seated.*]

LADY TEAZLE. Upon my word, you ought to pity me. Do you know Sir Peter is grown so ill-natured to me of late, and so jealous of Charles too—that's the best of the story, isn't it?

JOSEPH SURFACE [*aside*]. I am glad my scandalous friends keep that up.

LADY TEAZLE. I am sure I wish he would let Maria marry him, and then perhaps he would be convinced; don't you, Mr. Surface?

JOSEPH SURFACE [*aside*]. Indeed I do not.—[*Aloud.*] Oh, certainly I do! for then my dear Lady Teazle would also be convinced how wrong her suspicions were of my having any design on the silly girl.

LADY TEAZLE. Well, well, I'm inclined to believe you. But isn't it provoking, to have the most ill-natured things said of one? And there's my friend Lady Sneerwell has circulated I don't know how many scandalous tales of me, and all without any foundation too; that's what vexes me.

JOSEPH SURFACE. Ay, madam, to be sure, that is the provoking circumstance—without foundation; yes, yes, there's the mortification, indeed; for when a scandalous story is believed against one, there certainly is no comfort like the consciousness of having deserved it.

LADY TEAZLE. No, to be sure, then I'd forgive their malice; but to attack me, who am really so innocent, and who never say an ill-natured thing of any body—that is, of any friend; and then Sir Peter, too, to have him so peevish, and so suspicious, when I know the integrity of my own heart—indeed 'tis monstrous!

JOSEPH SURFACE. But, my dear Lady Teazle, 'tis your own fault if you suffer it. When a husband entertains a groundless suspicion of his wife, and withdraws his confidence from her, the original compact is broken, and she owes it to the honour of her sex to endeavour to outwit him.

LADY TEAZLE. Indeed! So that, if he suspects me without cause, it follows, that the best way of curing his jealousy is to give him reason for't?

JOSEPH SURFACE. Undoubtedly—for your husband should never be deceived in you: and in that case it becomes you to be frail in compliment to his discernment.

LADY TEAZLE. To be sure, what you say is very reasonable, and when the consciousness of my innocence——

JOSEPH SURFACE. Ah, my dear madam, there is the great mistake! 'tis this very conscious innocence that is of the greatest prejudice to you. What is it makes you negligent of forms, and careless of the world's opinion? why, the consciousness of your own innocence. What makes you thoughtless in your conduct, and apt to run into a thousand little imprudences? Why, the consciousness of your own innocence. What makes you impatient of Sir Peter's temper, and outrageous at his suspicions? why, the consciousness of your innocence.

LADY TEAZLE. 'Tis very true!

JOSEPH SURFACE. Now, my dear Lady Teazle, if you would but once make a trifling *faux pas*, you can't conceive how cautious you would grow, and how ready to humour and agree with your husband.

LADY TEAZLE. Do you think so?

JOSEPH SURFACE. Oh, I am sure on't; and then you would find all scandal would cease at once, for—in short, your character at present is like a person in a plethora, absolutely dying from too much health.

LADY TEAZLE. So, so; then I perceive your prescription is, that I must sin in my own defence, and part with my virtue to preserve my reputation?

JOSEPH SURFACE. Exactly so, upon my credit, ma'am.

LADY TEAZLE. Well, certainly this is the oddest doctrine, and the newest receipt for avoiding calumny!

JOSEPH SURFACE. An infallible one, believe me. Prudence, like experience, must be paid for.

LADY TEAZLE. Why, if my understanding were once convinced——

JOSEPH SURFACE. Oh, certainly, madam, your understanding should be convinced. Yes, yes—Heaven forbid I should persuade you to do any thing you thought wrong. No, no, I have too much honour to desire it.

LADY TEAZLE. Don't you think we may as well leave honour out of the argument?
[*Rises.*]

JOSEPH SURFACE. Ah, the ill effects of your country education, I see, still remain with you.

LADY TEAZLE. I doubt they do indeed; and I will fairly own to you, that if I could be persuaded to do wrong, it would be by Sir Peter's ill usage sooner than your honourable logic, after all.

JOSEPH SURFACE. Then, by this hand, which he is unworthy of——[*Taking her hand.*]

[*Reënter SERVANT.*]

'Sdeath, you blockhead—what do you want?

SERVANT. I beg your pardon, sir, but I thought you would not choose Sir Peter to come up without announcing him.

JOSEPH SURFACE. Sir Peter!—Oons—the devil!

LADY TEAZLE. Sir Peter! O Lud! I'm ruined! I'm ruined!

SERVANT. Sir, 'twasn't I let him in.

LADY TEAZLE. Oh! I'm quite undone! What will become of me? Now, Mr. Logic—Oh! mercy, sir, he's on the stairs —I'll get behind here—and if ever I'm so imprudent again——
[*Goes behind the screen.*]

JOSEPH SURFACE. Give me that book. [*Sits down. SERVANT pretends to adjust his chair.*]

[*Enter SIR PETER TEAZLE.*]

SIR PETER. Ay, ever improving himself—Mr. Surface, Mr. Surface——
[*Pats JOSEPH on the shoulder.*]

JOSEPH SURFACE. Oh, my dear Sir Peter, I beg your pardon.—[*Gaping, throws away the book.*] I have been dozing over a stupid book. Well, I am much obliged to you for this call. You haven't been here, I believe, since I fitted up this room. Books, you know, are the only things I am a coxcomb in.

SIR PETER. 'Tis very neat indeed. Well, well, that's proper; and you can make even your screen a source of knowledge. —hung, I perceive, with maps.

JOSEPH SURFACE. Oh, yes, I find great use in that screen.

SIR PETER. I dare say you must, certainly, when you want to find anything in a hurry.

JOSEPH SURFACE [*aside*]. Ay, or to hide any thing in a hurry either.

SIR PETER. Well, I have a little private business——

JOSEPH SURFACE [*to SERVANT.*] You need not stay.

SERVANT. No, sir. [*Exit.*]

JOSEPH SURFACE. Here's a chair, Sir Peter—I beg——

SIR PETER. Well, now we are alone, there is a subject, my dear friend, on which I wish to unburden my mind to you—a point of the greatest moment to my peace; in short, my good friend, Lady Teazle's conduct of late has made me very unhappy.

JOSEPH SURFACE. Indeed! I am very sorry to hear it.

SIR PETER. 'Tis but too plain she has not the least regard for me; but, what's worse, I have pretty good authority to suppose she has formed an attachment to another.

JOSEPH SURFACE. Indeed! you astonish me!

SIR PETER. Yes! and, between ourselves, I think I've discovered the person.

JOSEPH SURFACE. How! you alarm me exceedingly.

SIR PETER. Ay, my dear friend, I knew you would sympathise with me!

JOSEPH SURFACE. Yes, believe me, Sir Peter, such a discovery would hurt me just as much as it would you.

SIR PETER. I am convinced of it. Ah! it is a happiness to have a friend whom we can trust even with one's family secrets. But have you no guess who I mean?

JOSEPH SURFACE. I haven't the most distant idea. It can't be Sir Benjamin Backbite!

SIR PETER. Oh, no! What say you to Charles?

JOSEPH SURFACE. My brother! impossible!

SIR PETER. Oh, my dear friend, the goodness of your own heart misleads you. You judge of others by yourself.

JOSEPH SURFACE. Certainly, Sir Peter, the heart that is conscious of its own integrity is ever slow to credit another's treachery.

SIR PETER. True; but your brother has no sentiment—you never hear him talk so.

JOSEPH SURFACE. Yet I can't but think Lady Teazle herself has too much principle.

SIR PETER. Ay; but what is principle against the flattery of a handsome, lively young fellow?

JOSEPH SURFACE. That's very true.

SIR PETER. And then, you know, the difference of our ages makes it very improbable that she should have any great affection for me; and if she were to be frail, and I were to make it public, why the town would only laugh at me, the foolish old bachelor, who had married a girl.

JOSEPH SURFACE. That's true, to be sure—they would laugh.

SIR PETER. Laugh! ay, and make ballads, and paragraphs, and the devil knows what of me.

JOSEPH SURFACE. No, you must never make it public.

SIR PETER. But then again—that the nephew of my old friend, Sir Oliver, should be the person to attempt such a wrong, hurts me more nearly.

JOSEPH SURFACE. Ay, there's the point. When ingratitude barbs the dart of injury, the wound has double danger in it.

SIR PETER. Ay—I, that was, in a manner, left his guardian; in whose house he had been so often entertained; who never in my life denied him—my advice!

JOSEPH SURFACE. Oh, 'tis not to be credited! There may be a man capable of such baseness, to be sure; but, for my part, till you can give me positive proofs, I cannot but doubt it. However, if it should be proved on him, he is no longer a brother of mine—I disclaim kindred with him: for the man who can break the laws of hospitality, and tempt the wife of his friend, deserves to be branded as the pest of society.

SIR PETER. What a difference there is between you! What noble sentiments!

JOSEPH SURFACE. Yet I cannot suspect Lady Teazle's honour.

SIR PETER. I am sure I wish to think well of her, and to remove all ground quarrel between us. She has lately reproached me more than once with having made no settlement on her; and in our last quarrel, she almost hinted that she should not break her heart if I was dead. Now, as we seem to differ in our ideas of expense, I have resolved she shall have her own way, and be her own mistress in that respect for the future; and, if I were to die, she will find I have not been inattentive to her interest while living. Here, my friend, are the drafts of two deeds, which I wish to have your opinion on. By one, she will enjoy eight hundred a year independent while I live and, by the other, the bulk of my fortune at my death.

JOSEPH SURFACE. This conduct, Sir Peter, is indeed truly generous.—[Aside.] I wish it may not corrupt my pupil.

SIR PETER. Yes, I am determined she shall have no cause to complain, though I would not have her acquainted with the latter instance of my affection yet awhile.

JOSEPH SURFACE [aside]. Nor I, if I could help it.

SIR PETER. And now, my dear friend, if you please, we will talk over the situation of your hopes with Maria.

JOSEPH SURFACE [softly]. Oh, no, Sir Peter; another time, if you please.

SIR PETER. I am sensibly chagrined at the little progress you seem to make in her affections.

JOSEPH SURFACE [softly]. I beg you will not mention it. What are my disappointments when your happiness is in debate!—[Aside.] 'Sdeath, I shall be ruined every way!

SIR PETER. And though you are averse to my acquainting Lady Teazle with your passion, I'm sure she's not your enemy in the affair.

JOSEPH SURFACE. Pray, Sir Peter, now ʻʻe me. I am really too much affected ̠ subject we have been speaking of ̠ ̠ a thought on my own con- ̠ ̠ man who is entrusted with ̠resses can never——

[Reënter SERVANT.]

Well, sir?

SERVANT. Your brother, sir, is speaking to a gentleman in the street, and says he knows you are within.

JOSEPH SURFACE. 'Sdeath, blockhead, I'm not within—I'm out for the day.

SIR PETER. Stay—hold—a thought has struck me:—you shall be at home.

JOSEPH SURFACE. Well, well, let him come up.—[Exit SERVANT.] [Aside.] He'll interrupt Sir Peter, however.

SIR PETER. Now, my good friend, oblige me, I entreat you. Before Charles comes let me conceal myself somewhere, then do you tax him on the point we have been talking, and his answer may satisfy me at once.

JOSEPH SURFACE. Oh, fie, Sir Peter! would you have me join in so mean a trick?—to trepan my brother too?

SIR PETER. Nay, you tell me you are sure he is innocent; if so, you do him the greatest service by giving him an opportunity to clear himself, and you will set my heart at rest. Come, you shall not refuse me: [Going up.] here, behind the screen will be—Hey! what the devil! there seems to be one listener here already—I'll swear I saw a petticoat!

JOSEPH SURFACE. Ha! ha! ha! Well, this is ridiculous enough. I'll tell you, Sir Peter, though I hold a man of intrigue to be a most despicable character, yet, you know, it does not follow that one is to be an absolute Joseph either! Hark'ee, 'tis a little French milliner, a silly rogue that plagues me; and having some character to lose, on your coming, sir, she ran behind the screen.

SIR PETER. Ah, Joseph! Joseph! Did I ever think that you——But, egad, she has overheard all I have been saying of my wife.

JOSEPH SURFACE. Oh, 'twill never go any farther, you may depend upon it!

SIR PETER. No! then, faith, let her hear it out.—Here's a closet will do as well.

JOSEPH SURFACE. Well, go in there.

SIR PETER. Sly rogue! sly rogue!

[Goes into the closet.]

JOSEPH SURFACE. A narrow escape, indeed! and a curious situation I'm in, to part man and wife in this manner.

LADY TEAZLE [*peeping*]. Couldn't I steal off?

JOSEPH SURFACE. Keep close, my angel!

SIR PETER [*peeping*]. Joseph, tax him home.

JOSEPH SURFACE. Back, my dear friend!

LADY TEAZLE [*peeping*]. Couldn't you lock Sir Peter in?

JOSEPH SURFACE. Be still, my life!

SIR PETER [*peeping*]. You're sure the little milliner won't blab?

JOSEPH SURFACE. In, in, my dear Sir Peter!—'Fore Gad, I wish I had a key to the door.

[*Enter* CHARLES SURFACE.]

CHARLES SURFACE. Holla! brother, what has been the matter? Your fellow would not let me up at first. What! have you had a Jew with you?

JOSEPH SURFACE. No, brother, I assure you.

CHARLES SURFACE. But what has made Sir Peter steal off? I thought he had been with you.

JOSEPH SURFACE. He was, brother; but, hearing you were coming, he did not choose to stay.

CHARLES SURFACE. What! was the old gentleman afraid I wanted to borrow money of him?

JOSEPH SURFACE. No, sir: but I am sorry to find, Charles, you have lately given that worthy man grounds for great uneasiness.

CHARLES SURFACE. Yes, they tell me I do that to a great many worthy men. But how so, pray?

JOSEPH SURFACE. To be plain with you, brother, he thinks you are endeavouring to gain Lady Teazle's affections from him.

CHARLES SURFACE. Who, I? O Lud! not I, upon my word.—Ha! ha! ha! ha! so the old fellow has found out that he has got a young wife, has he?—or, what

is worse, Lady Teazle has found out she has an old husband?

JOSEPH SURFACE. This is no subject to jest on, brother. He who can laugh——

CHARLES SURFACE. True, true, as you were going to say—then, seriously, I never had the least idea of what you charge me with, upon my honour.

JOSEPH SURFACE [*raising his voice*]. Well, it will give Sir Peter great satisfaction to hear this.

CHARLES SURFACE. To be sure, I once thought the lady seemed to have taken a fancy to me; but, upon my soul, I never gave her the least encouragement. Besides, you know my attachment to Maria.

JOSEPH SURFACE. But sure, brother, even if Lady Teazle had betrayed the fondest partiality for you——

CHARLES SURFACE. Why, look'ee, Joseph, I hope I shall never deliberately do a dishonourable action; but if a pretty woman was purposely to throw herself in my way—and that pretty woman married to a man old enough to be her father——

JOSEPH SURFACE. Well!

CHARLES SURFACE. Why, I believe I should be obliged to——

JOSEPH SURFACE. What?

CHARLES SURFACE. To borrow a little of your morality, that's all. But, brother, do you know now that you surprise me exceedingly, by naming me with Lady Teazle; for, i' faith, I always understood you were her favourite.

JOSEPH SURFACE. Oh, for shame, Charles! This retort is foolish.

CHARLES SURFACE. Nay, I swear I have seen you exchange such significant glances——

JOSEPH SURFACE. Nay, nay, sir, this is no jest.

CHARLES SURFACE. Egad, I'm serious! Don't you remember one day, when I called here——

JOSEPH SURFACE. Nay, pr'ythee, Charles——

CHARLES SURFACE. And found you together——

JOSEPH SURFACE. Zounds, sir, I insist——

CHARLES SURFACE. And another time when your servant——

JOSEPH SURFACE. Brother, brother, a word with you!—[Aside.] Gad, I must stop him.

CHARLES SURFACE. Informed, I say that——

JOSEPH SURFACE. Hush! I beg your pardon, but Sir Peter has overheard all we have been saying. I knew you would clear yourself, or I should not have consented.

CHARLES SURFACE. How, Sir Peter! Where is he?

JOSEPH SURFACE. Softly, there! [Points to the closet.]

CHARLES SURFACE. Oh, 'fore Heaven, I'll have him out. Sir Peter, come forth!

JOSEPH SURFACE. No, no——

CHARLES SURFACE. I say, Sir Peter, come into court.—[Pulls in SIR PETER.] What! my old guardian!—What! turn inquisitor, and take evidence incog? Oh, fie! Oh, fie!

SIR PETER. Give me your hand, Charles —I believe I have suspected you wrongfully; but you mustn't be angry with Joseph—'twas my plan!

CHARLES SURFACE. Indeed!

SIR PETER. But I acquit you. I promise you I don't think near so ill of you as I did; what I have heard has given me great satisfaction.

CHARLES SURFACE. Egad, then, 'twas lucky you didn't hear any more. Wasn't it, Joseph?

SIR PETER. Ah! you would have retorted on him.

CHARLES SURFACE. Ah, ay, that was a joke.

SIR PETER. Yes, yes, I know his honour too well.

CHARLES SURFACE. But you might as have suspected him as me in this for all that. Mightn't he, Joseph?

~R. Well, well, I believe you.

~FACE [aside]. Would they
~ the room!

SIR PETER. And in future, perhaps, we may not be such strangers.

[Reënter SERVANT, and whispers JOSEPH SURFACE.]

SERVANT. Lady Sneerwell is below, and says she will come up.

JOSEPH SURFACE. Lady Sneerwell! Gad's life! she must not come here. [Exit SERVANT.] Gentlemen, I beg pardon—I must wait on you down stairs: here is a person come on particular business.

CHARLES SURFACE. Well, you can see him in another room. Sir Peter and I have not met in a long time, and I have something to say to him.

JOSEPH SURFACE [aside]. They must not be left together.—[Aloud.] I'll send Lady Sneerwell away, and return directly. —[Aside to SIR PETER.] Sir Peter, not a word of the French milliner.

SIR PETER [aside to JOSEPH SURFACE]. I! not for the world!—[Exit JOSEPH SURFACE.] Ah, Charles, if you associated more with your brother, one might indeed hope for your reformation. He is a man of sentiment. Well, there is nothing in the world so noble as a man of sentiment.

CHARLES SURFACE. Pshaw! he is too moral by half; and so apprehensive of his good name, as he calls it.

SIR PETER. No, no,—come, come,—you wrong him. No, no! Joseph is no rake, but he is no such saint either, in that respect.—[Aside.] I have a great mind to tell him—we should have such a laugh at Joseph.

CHARLES SURFACE. Oh, hang him! he's a very anchorite, a young hermit!

SIR PETER. Hark'ee—you must not abuse him: he may chance to hear of it again, I promise you.

CHARLES SURFACE. Why, you won't tell him?

SIR PETER. No—but—this way.—[Aside.] Egad, I'll tell him.—[Aloud.] Hark'ee—have you a mind to have a good laugh at Joseph?

CHARLES SURFACE. I should like it of all things.

SIR PETER. Then, i' faith, we will!

I'll be quit with him for discovering me. [*Whispers.*] He had a girl with him when I called.

CHARLES SURFACE. What! Joseph! you jest.

SIR PETER. Hush!—a little French milliner—and the best of the jest is— she's in the room now.

CHARLES SURFACE. The devil she is!

SIR PETER. Hush! I tell you. [*Points to the screen.*]

CHARLES SURFACE. Behind the screen! 'Slife, let's unveil her!

SIR PETER. No, no, he's coming:— you sha'n't, indeed!

CHARLES SURFACE. Oh, egad, we'll have a peep at the little milliner!

SIR PETER. Not for the world!— Joseph will never forgive me.

CHARLES SURFACE. I'll stand by you——

SIR PETER. Odds, here he is!

[CHARLES SURFACE *throws down the screen.*]

[*Reënter* JOSEPH SURFACE.]

CHARLES SURFACE. Lady Teazle, by all that's wonderful.

SIR PETER. Lady Teazle, by all that's damnable!

CHARLES SURFACE. Sir Peter, this is one of the smartest French milliners I ever saw. Egad, you seem all to have been diverting yourselves here at hide and seek, and I don't see who is out of the secret. Shall I beg your ladyship to inform me? Not a word!—Brother, will you be pleased to explain this matter? What! is Morality dumb too?—Sir Peter, though I found you in the dark, perhaps you are not so now! All mute!—Well —though I can make nothing of the affair, I suppose you perfectly understand one another; so I'll leave you to yourselves.—[*Going.*] Brother, I'm sorry to find you have given that worthy man grounds for so much uneasiness.—Sir Peter! there's nothing in the world so noble as a man of sentiment! [*Exit.*]

JOSEPH SURFACE. Sir Peter—notwithstanding—I confess—that appearances are against me—if you will afford me your patience—I make no doubt—but I shall explain every thing to your satisfaction.

SIR PETER. If you please, sir.

JOSEPH SURFACE. The fact is, sir, that Lady Teazle, knowing my pretensions to your ward Maria—I say, sir, Lady Teazle, being apprehensive of the jealousy of your temper—and knowing my friendship to the family—she, sir, I say—called here —in order that—I might explain these pretensions—but on your coming—being apprehensive—as I said—of your jealousy —she withdrew—and this, you may depend on it, is the whole truth of the matter.

SIR PETER. A very clear account, upon my word; and I dare swear the lady will vouch for every article of it.

LADY TEAZLE. For not one word of it, Sir Peter!

SIR PETER. How! don't you think it worth while to agree in the lie?

LADY TEAZLE. There is not one syllable of truth in what that gentleman has told you.

SIR PETER. I believe you, upon my soul, ma'am!

JOSEPH SURFACE [*aside to* LADY TEAZLE]. 'Sdeath, madam, will you betray me?

LADY TEAZLE. Good Mr. Hypocrite, by your leave, I'll speak for myself.

SIR PETER. Ay, let her alone, sir; you'll find she'll make out a better story than you, without prompting.

LADY TEAZLE. Hear me, Sir Peter!— I came here on no matter relating to your ward, and even ignorant of this gentleman's pretensions to her. But I came, seduced by his insidious arguments, at least to listen to his pretended passion, if not to sacrifice your honour to his baseness.

SIR PETER. Now, I believe, the truth is coming, indeed!

JOSEPH SURFACE. The woman's mad!

LADY TEAZLE. No, sir; she has recovered her senses, and your own arts have furnished her with the means.—Sir Pet

I do not expect you to credit me—but the tenderness you expressed for me, when I am sure you could not think I was a witness to it, has so penetrated to my heart, that had I left the place without the shame of this discovery, my future life should have spoken the sincerity of my gratitude. As for that smooth-tongued hypocrite, who would have seduced the wife of his too credulous friend, while he affected honourable addresses to his ward—I behold him now in a light so truly despicable, that I shall never again respect myself for having listened to him. [*Exit.*]

JOSEPH SURFACE. Notwithstanding all this, Sir Peter, Heaven knows——

SIR PETER. That you are a villain! and so I leave you to your conscience.

JOSEPH SURFACE. You are too rash, Sir Peter; you shall hear me. The man who shuts out conviction by refusing to——

SIR PETER. Oh, damn your sentiments! [*Exeunt* SIR PETER *and* JOSEPH SURFACE, *talking.*]

ACT V

SCENE I—*The library in* JOSEPH SUR-FACE'S *house.*

[*Enter* JOSEPH SURFACE *and* SERVANT.]
JOSEPH SURFACE. Mr. Stanley! and why should you think I would see him? you must know he comes to ask something.

SERVANT. Sir, I should not have let him in, but that Mr. Rowley came to the door with him.

JOSEPH SURFACE. Pshaw! blockhead! to suppose that I should now be in a temper to receive visits from poor relations!—Well, why don't you show the ʼow up?

ʼANT. I will, sir.—Why, sir, it ʼmy fault that Sir Peter discov-

ʼFACE. Go, fool!—[*Exit
Fortune never played a

man of my policy such a trick before! My character with Sir Peter, my hopes with Maria, destroyed in a moment! I'm in a rare humour to listen to other people's distresses! I sha'n't be able to bestow even a benevolent sentiment on Stanley.—So! here he comes, and Rowley with him. I must try to recover myself, and put a little charity into my face, however. [*Exit.*]

[*Enter* SIR OLIVER SURFACE *and* ROWLEY.]
SIR OLIVER. What! does he avoid us? That was he, was it not?

ROWLEY. It was, sir. But I doubt you are come a little too abruptly. His nerves are so weak, that the sight of a poor relation may be too much for him. I should have gone first to break it to him.

SIR OLIVER. Oh, plague of his nerves! Yet this is he whom Sir Peter extols as a man of the most benevolent way of thinking!

ROWLEY. As to his way of thinking, I cannot pretend to decide; for, to do him justice, he appears to have as much speculative benevolence as any private gentleman in the kingdom, though he is seldom so sensual as to indulge himself in the exercise of it.

SIR OLIVER. Yet he has a string of charitable sentiments at his fingers' ends.

ROWLEY. Or, rather, at his tongue's end, Sir Oliver; for I believe there is no sentiment he has such faith in as that *Charity begins at home.*

SIR OLIVER. And his, I presume, is of that domestic sort which never stirs abroad at all.

ROWLEY. I doubt you'll find it so; but he's coming. I mustn't seem to interrupt you; and you know, immediately as you leave him, I come in to announce your arrival in your real character.

SIR OLIVER. True; and afterwards you'll meet me at Sir Peter's.

ROWLEY. Without losing a moment. [*Exit.*]

SIR OLIVER. I don't like the complaisance of his features.

[*Reënter* JOSEPH SURFACE.]

JOSEPH SURFACE. Sir, I beg you ten thousand pardons for keeping you a moment waiting.—Mr. Stanley, I presume.

SIR OLIVER. At your service.

JOSEPH SURFACE. Sir, I beg you will do me the honour to sit down—I entreat you, sir.

SIR OLIVER. Dear sir—there's no occasion.—[*Aside.*] Too civil by half!

JOSEPH SURFACE. I have not the pleasure of knowing you, Mr. Stanley; but I am extremely happy to see you look so well. You were nearly related to my mother, I think, Mr. Stanley?

SIR OLIVER. I was, sir; so nearly that my present poverty, I fear, may do discredit to her wealthy children, else I should not have presumed to trouble you.

JOSEPH SURFACE. Dear sir, there needs no apology;—he that is in distress, though a stranger, has a right to claim kindred with the wealthy. I am sure I wish I was one of that class, and had it in my power to offer you even a small relief.

SIR OLIVER. If your uncle, Sir Oliver, were here, I should have a friend.

JOSEPH SURFACE. I wish he was, sir, with all my heart: you should not want an advocate with him, believe me, sir.

SIR OLIVER. I should not need one—my distresses would recommend me. But I imagined his bounty would enable you to become the agent of his charity.

JOSEPH SURFACE. My dear sir, you were strangely misinformed. Sir Oliver is a worthy man, a very worthy man; but avarice, Mr. Stanley, is the vice of age. I will tell you, my good sir, in confidence, what he has done for me has been a mere nothing; though people, I know, have thought otherwise, and for my part, I never chose to contradict the report.

SIR OLIVER. What! has he never transmitted you bullion—rupees—pagodas?

JOSEPH SURFACE. Oh, dear sir, nothing of the kind. No, no; a few presents now and then—china, shawls, congo tea, avadavats and Indian crackers—little more, believe me.

SIR OLIVER [*aside*]. Here's gratitude for twelve thousand pounds!—Avadavats and Indian crackers!

JOSEPH SURFACE. Then, my dear sir, you have heard, I doubt not, of the extravagance of my brother: there are very few would credit what I have done for that unfortunate young man.

SIR OLIVER [*aside*]. Not I, for one!

JOSEPH SURFACE. The sums I have lent him! Indeed I have been exceedingly to blame; it was an amiable weakness; however, I don't pretend to defend it—and now I feel it doubly culpable, since it has deprived me of the pleasure of serving you, Mr. Stanley, as my heart dictates.

SIR OLIVER [*aside*]. Dissembler—[*Aloud.*] Then, sir, you can't assist me?

JOSEPH SURFACE. At present, it grieves me to say, I cannot; but, whenever I have the ability, you may depend upon hearing from me.

SIR OLIVER. I am extremely sorry——

JOSEPH SURFACE. Not more than I, believe me; to pity, without the power to relieve, is still more painful than to ask and be denied.

SIR OLIVER. Kind sir, your most obedient humble servant.

JOSEPH SURFACE. You leave me deeply affected, Mr. Stanley.—[*Calls to* SERVANT.] William, be ready to open the door.

SIR OLIVER. Oh, dear sir, no ceremony.

JOSEPH SURFACE. Your very obedient.

SIR OLIVER. Your most obsequious.

JOSEPH SURFACE. You may depend upon hearing from me whenever I can be of service.

SIR OLIVER. Sweet sir, you are too good!

JOSEPH SURFACE. In the meantime I wish you health and spirits.

SIR OLIVER. Your ever grateful and perpetual humble servant.

JOSEPH SURFACE. Sir, yours as sincerely.

SIR OLIVER [*aside*]. Now I am satisfied. [*Exit.*]

JOSEPH SURFACE. This is one bad effect of a good character; it invites application from the unfortunate, and there needs no small degree of address to gain the reputation of benevolence without incurring the expense. The silver ore of pure charity is an expensive article in the catalogue of a man's good qualities; whereas the sentimental French plate I use instead of it makes just as good a show, and pays no tax.

[*Reënter* ROWLEY.]

ROWLEY. Mr. Surface, your servant: I was apprehensive of interrupting you, though my business demands immediate attention, as this note will inform you.

JOSEPH SURFACE. Always happy to see Mr. Rowley,—[*Aside.*] a rascal.—[*Reads the letter.*] Sir Oliver Surface!—My uncle arrived!

ROWLEY. He is, indeed: we have just parted—quite well, after a speedy voyage, and impatient to embrace his worthy nephew.

JOSEPH SURFACE. I am astonished!—[*Calls to* SERVANT.] William! stop Mr. Stanley, if he's not gone.

ROWLEY. Oh! he's out of reach, I believe.

JOSEPH SURFACE. Why did you not let me know this when you came in together?

ROWLEY. I thought you had particular business. But I must be gone to inform your brother, and appoint him here to meet your uncle. He will be with you in a quarter of an hour.

JOSEPH SURFACE. So he says. Well, I am strangely overjoyed at his coming.—[*Aside.*] Never, to be sure, was any thing so unlucky!

ROWLEY. You will be delighted to see how well he looks.

JOSEPH SURFACE. Oh! I'm overjoyed to hear it.—[*Aside.*] Just at this time!

ROWLEY. I'll tell him how impatiently you expect him.

JOSEPH SURFACE. Do, do; pray give my best duty and affection. Indeed, I cannot express the sensations I feel at the thought of seeing him.—[*Exit* ROWLEY.] Certainly his coming just at this time is the cruellest piece of ill fortune. [*Exit.*]

SCENE II—*A room in* SIR PETER TEAZLE'S *house.*

[*Enter* MRS. CANDOUR *and* MAID.]

MAID. Indeed, ma'am, my lady will see nobody at present.

MRS. CANDOUR. Did you tell her it was her friend Mrs. Candour?

MAID. Yes, ma'am; but she begs you will excuse her.

MRS. CANDOUR. Do go again; I shall be glad to see her, if it be only for a moment, for I am sure she must be in great distress.—[*Exit* MAID.] Dear heart, how provoking! I'm not mistress of half the circumstances! We shall have the whole affair in the newspapers, with the names of the parties at length, before I have dropped the story at a dozen houses.

[*Enter* SIR BENJAMIN BACKBITE.]
Oh, dear Sir Benjamin! you have heard, I suppose——

SIR BENJAMIN. Of Lady Teazle and Mr. Surface——

MRS. CANDOUR. And Sir Peter's discovery——

SIR BENJAMIN. Oh, the strangest piece of business, to be sure!

MRS. CANDOUR. Well, I never was so surprised in my life. I am so sorry for all parties, indeed.

SIR BENJAMIN. Now, I don't pity Sir Peter at all: he was so extravagantly partial to Mr. Surface.

MRS. CANDOUR. Mr. Surface! Why, 'twas with Charles Lady Teazle was detected.

SIR BENJAMIN. No, no, I tell you: Mr. Surface is the gallant.

MRS. CANDOUR. No such thing! Charles is the man. 'Twas Mr. Surface brought Sir Peter on purpose to discover them.

SIR BENJAMIN. I tell you I had it from one——

MRS. CANDOUR. And I have it from one——

SIR BENJAMIN. Who had it from one, who had it——

MRS. CANDOUR. From one immediately.

But here comes Lady Sneerwell; perhaps she knows the whole affair.

[*Enter* LADY SNEERWELL.]

LADY SNEERWELL. So, my dear Mrs. Candour, here's a sad affair of our friend Lady Teazle!

MRS. CANDOUR. Ay, my dear friend, who would have thought——

LADY SNEERWELL. Well, there is no trusting appearances; though, indeed, she was always too lively for me.

MRS. CANDOUR. To be sure, her manners were a little too free; but then she was so young!

LADY SNEERWELL. And had, indeed, some good qualities.

MRS. CANDOUR. So she had, indeed. But have you heard the particulars?

LADY SNEERWELL. No; but everybody says that Mr. Surface——

SIR BENJAMIN. Ay, there; I told you Mr. Surface was the man.

MRS. CANDOUR. No, no: indeed it was Charles.

LADY SNEERWELL. Charles! You alarm me, Mrs. Candour!

MRS. CANDOUR. Yes, yes; he was the lover. Mr. Surface, to do him justice, was only the informer.

SIR BENJAMIN. Well, I'll not dispute with you, Mrs. Candour; but, be it which it may, I hope that Sir Peter's wound will not——

MRS. CANDOUR. Sir Peter's wound! Oh, mercy! I didn't hear a word of their fighting.

LADY SNEERWELL. Nor I, a syllable.

SIR BENJAMIN. No! what, no mention of the duel?

MRS. CANDOUR. Not a word.

SIR BENJAMIN. Oh, yes: they fought before they left the room.

LADY SNEERWELL. Pray, let us hear.

MRS. CANDOUR. Ay, do oblige us with the duel.

SIR BENJAMIN. *Sir*, says Sir Peter, immediately after the discovery, *you are a most ungrateful fellow.*

MRS. CANDOUR. Ay, to Charles——

SIR BENJAMIN. No, no—to Mr. Sur-face—*a most ungrateful fellow; and old as I am, sir*, says he, *I insist on immediate satisfaction.*

MRS. CANDOUR. Ay, that must have been to Charles; for 'tis very unlikely Mr. Surface should fight in his own house.

SIR BENJAMIN. Gad's life, ma'am, not at all—*giving me immediate satisfaction.* —On this, ma'am, Lady Teazle, seeing Sir Peter in such danger, ran out of the room in strong hysterics, and Charles after her, calling out for hartshorn and water; then, madam, they began to fight with swords——

[*Enter* CRABTREE.]

CRABTREE. With pistols, nephew, pistols! I have it from undoubted authority.

MRS. CANDOUR. Oh, Mr. Crabtree, then it is all true!

CRABTREE. Too true, indeed, madam, and Sir Peter is dangerously wounded——

SIR BENJAMIN. By a thrust in segoon quite through his left side——

CRABTREE. By a bullet lodged in the thorax.

MRS. CANDOUR. Mercy on me! Poor Sir Peter!

CRABTREE. Yes, madam; though Charles would have avoided the matter, if he could.

MRS. CANDOUR. I told you who it was; I knew Charles was the person.

SIR BENJAMIN. My uncle, I see, knows nothing of the matter.

CRABTREE. But Sir Peter taxed him with the basest ingratitude——

SIR BENJAMIN. That I told you, you know——

CRABTREE. Do, nephew, let me speak! —and insisted on immediate——

SIR BENJAMIN. Just as I said——

CRABTREE. Odds life, nephew, allow others to know something too! A pair of pistols lay on the bureau (for Mr. Surface, it seems, had come home the night before late from Salthill, where he had been to see the Montem with a friend, who has a son at Eton), so, unluckily, the pistols were left charged.

SIR BENJAMIN. I heard nothing of this.

CRABTREE. Sir Peter forced Charles to take one, and they fired, it seems, pretty nearly together. Charles's shot took effect, as I tell you, and Sir Peter's missed; but, what is very extraordinary, the ball struck against a little bronze Shakespeare that stood over the fireplace, grazed out of the window at a right angle, and wounded the postman, who was just coming to the door with a double letter from Northamptonshire.

SIR BENJAMIN. My uncle's account is more circumstantial, I confess; but I believe mine is the true one, for all that.

LADY SNEERWELL [aside]. I am more interested in this affair than they imagine, and must have better information. [Exit.]

SIR BENJAMIN. Ah! Lady Sneerwell's alarm is very easily accounted for.

CRABTREE. Yes, yes, they certainly do say—but that's neither here nor there.

MRS. CANDOUR. But, pray, where is Sir Peter at present?

CRABTREE. Oh! they brought him home, and he is now in the house, though the servants are ordered to deny him.

MRS. CANDOUR. I believe so, and Lady Teazle, I suppose, attending him.

CRABTREE. Yes, yes; and I saw one of the faculty enter just before me.

SIR BENJAMIN. Hey! who comes here?

CRABTREE. Oh, this is he: the physician, depend on't.

MRS. CANDOUR. Oh, certainly! it must be the physician; and now we shall know.

[Enter SIR OLIVER SURFACE.]

CRABTREE. Well, doctor, what hopes?

MRS. CANDOUR. Ay, doctor, how's your patient?

SIR BENJAMIN. Now, doctor, isn't it a wound with a small sword?

CRABTREE. A bullet lodged in the thorax, for a hundred!

SIR OLIVER. Doctor! a wound with a small sword and a bullet in the thorax! —Oons! are you mad, good people?

SIR BENJAMIN. Perhaps, sir, you are not a doctor?

SIR OLIVER. Truly, I am to thank you for my degree if I am.

CRABTREE. Only a friend of Sir Peter's, then, I presume. But, sir, you must have heard of his accident?

SIR OLIVER. Not a word!

CRABTREE. Not of his being dangerously wounded?

SIR OLIVER. The devil he is!

SIR BENJAMIN. Run through the body——

CRABTREE. Shot in the breast——

SIR BENJAMIN. By one Mr. Surface——

CRABTREE. Ay, the younger.

SIR OLIVER. Hey! what the plague! you seem to differ strangely in your accounts: however, you agree that Sir Peter is dangerously wounded.

SIR BENJAMIN. Oh, yes, we agree in that.

CRABTREE. Yes, yes, I believe there can be no doubt of that.

SIR OLIVER. Then, upon my word, for a person in that situation, he is the most imprudent man alive; for here he comes, walking as if nothing at all was the matter.

[Enter SIR PETER TEAZLE.]

Odds heart, Sir Peter! you are come in good time, I promise you; for we had just given you over!

SIR BENJAMIN [aside to CRABTREE]. Egad, uncle, this is the most sudden recovery!

SIR OLIVER. Why, man! what do you out of bed with a small sword through your body, and a bullet lodged in your thorax?

SIR PETER. A small sword and a bullet!

SIR OLIVER. Ay; these gentlemen would have killed you without law or physic, and wanted to dub me a doctor, to make me an accomplice.

SIR PETER. Why, what is all this?

SIR BENJAMIN. We rejoice, Sir Peter, that the story of the duel is not true, and are sincerely sorry for your other misfortune.

SIR PETER [*aside*]. So, so; all over the town already!

CRABTREE. Though, Sir Peter, you were certainly vastly to blame to marry at your years.

SIR PETER. Sir, what business is that of yours?

MRS. CANDOUR. Though, indeed, as Sir Peter made so good a husband, he's very much to be pitied.

SIR PETER. Plague on your pity, ma'am! I desire none of it.

SIR BENJAMIN. However, Sir Peter, you must not mind the laughing and jests you will meet with on the occasion.

SIR PETER. Sir, sir! I desire to be master in my own house.

CRABTREE. 'Tis no uncommon case, that's one comfort.

SIR PETER. I insist on being left to myself: without ceremony, I insist on your leaving my house directly!

MRS. CANDOUR. Well, well, we are going; and depend on't, we'll make the best report of it we can. [*Exit.*]

SIR PETER. Leave my house!

CRABTREE. And tell how hardly you've been treated. [*Exit.*]

SIR PETER. Leave my house!

SIR BENJAMIN. And how patiently you bear it. [*Exit.*]

SIR PETER. Fiends! vipers! furies! Oh! that their own venom would choke them.

SIR OLIVER. They are very provoking indeed, Sir Peter.

[*Enter* ROWLEY.]

ROWLEY. I heard high words: what has ruffled you, sir?

SIR PETER. Pshaw! what signifies asking? Do I ever pass a day without my vexations?

ROWLEY. Well, I'm not inquisitive.

SIR OLIVER. Well, Sir Peter, I have seen both my nephews in the manner we proposed.

SIR PETER. A precious couple they are!

ROWLEY. Yes, and Sir Oliver is convinced that your judgment was right, Sir Peter.

SIR OLIVER. Yes, I find Joseph is indeed the man, after all.

ROWLEY. Ay, as Sir Peter says, he is a man of sentiment.

SIR OLIVER. And acts up to the sentiments he professes.

ROWLEY. It certainly is edification to hear him talk.

SIR OLIVER. Oh, he's a model for the young men of the age!—but how's this, Sir Peter? you don't join us in your friend Joseph's praise, as I expected.

SIR PETER. Sir Oliver, we live in a wicked world, and the fewer we praise the better.

ROWLEY. What! do you say so, Sir Peter, who were never mistaken in your life?

SIR PETER. Pshaw! plague on you both! I see by your sneering you have heard the whole affair. I shall go mad among you!

ROWLEY. Then, to fret you no longer, Sir Peter, we are indeed acquainted with it all. I met Lady Teazle coming from Mr. Surface's so humbled that she deigned to request me to be her advocate with you.

SIR PETER. And does Sir Oliver know all this?

SIR OLIVER. Every circumstance.

SIR PETER. What, of the closet and the screen, hey?

SIR OLIVER. Yes, yes, and the little French milliner. Oh, I have been vastly diverted with the story! ha! ha! ha!

SIR PETER. 'Twas very pleasant.

SIR OLIVER. I never laughed more in my life, I assure you: ah! ah! ah!

SIR PETER. Oh, vastly diverting! ha! ha! ha!

ROWLEY. To be sure, Joseph with his sentiments! ha! ha! ha!

SIR PETER. Yes, yes, his sentiments! ha! ha! ha! Hypocritical villain!

SIR OLIVER. Ay, and that rogue Charles to pull Sir Peter out of the closet: ha! ha! ha!

SIR PETER. Ha! ha! 'twas devilish entertaining, to be sure!

SIR OLIVER. Ha! ha! ha! Egad, Sir Peter, I should like to have seen your face when the screen was thrown down: ha! ha!

SIR PETER. Yes, yes, my face when the screen was thrown down: ha! ha! ha! Oh, I must never show my head again!

SIR OLIVER. But come, come, it isn't fair to laugh at you neither, my old friend; though, upon my soul, I can't help it.

SIR PETER. Oh, pray don't restrain your mirth on my account: it does not hurt me at all! I laugh at the whole affair myself. Yes, yes, I think being a standing jest for all one's acquaintance a very happy situation. Oh, yes, and then of a morning to read the paragraphs about Mr. S——, Lady T——, and Sir P——, will be so entertaining!

ROWLEY. Without affectation, Sir Peter, you may despise the ridicule of fools. But I see Lady Teazle going towards the next room; I am sure you must desire a reconciliation as earnestly as she does.

SIR OLIVER. Perhaps my being here prevents her coming to you. Well, I'll leave honest Rowley to mediate between you; but he must bring you all presently to Mr. Surface's, where I am now returning, if not to reclaim a libertine, at least to expose hypocrisy.

SIR PETER. Ah, I'll be present at your discovering yourself there with all my heart; though 'tis a vile unlucky place for discoveries.

ROWLEY. We'll follow.

[*Exit* SIR OLIVER SURFACE.]

SIR PETER. She is not coming here, you see, Rowley.

ROWLEY. No, but she has left the door of that room open, you perceive. See, she is in tears.

SIR PETER. Certainly a little mortification appears very becoming in a wife. Don't you think it will do her good to let her pine a little?

ROWLEY. Oh, this is ungenerous in you!

SIR PETER. Well, I know not what to think. You remember the letter I found of hers evidently intended for Charles?

ROWLEY. A mere forgery, Sir Peter! laid in your way on purpose. This is one of the points which I intend Snake shall give you conviction of.

SIR PETER. I wish I were once satisfied of that. She looks this way. What a remarkably elegant turn of the head she has! Rowley, I'll go to her.

ROWLEY. Certainly.

SIR PETER. Though, when it is known that we are reconciled, people will laugh at me ten times more.

ROWLEY. Let them laugh, and retort their malice only by showing them you are happy in spite of it.

SIR PETER. I' faith, so I will! and, if I'm not mistaken, we may yet be the happiest couple in the country.

ROWLEY. Nay, Sir Peter, he who once lays aside suspicion——

SIR PETER. Hold, Master Rowley! if you have any regard for me, never let me hear you utter anything like a sentiment: I have had enough of them to serve me the rest of my life. [*Exeunt.*]

SCENE III—*The library in* JOSEPH SURFACE'S *house.*

[*Enter* JOSEPH SURFACE *and* LADY SNEERWELL.]

LADY SNEERWELL. Impossible! Will not Sir Peter immediately be reconciled to Charles, and of course no longer oppose his union with Maria? The thought is distraction to me.

JOSEPH SURFACE. Can passion furnish a remedy?

LADY SNEERWELL. No, nor cunning either. Oh, I was a fool, an idiot, to league with such a blunderer!

JOSEPH SURFACE. Sure, Lady Sneerwell, I am the greatest sufferer; yet you see I bear the accident with calmness.

LADY SNEERWELL. Because the disappointment doesn't reach your heart; your interest only attached you to Maria. Had you felt for her what I have for that ungrateful libertine, neither your temper nor hypocrisy could prevent your showing the sharpness of your vexation.

JOSEPH SURFACE. But why should your reproaches fall on me for this disappointment?

LADY SNEERWELL. Are you not the cause of it? Had you not a sufficient field for your roguery in imposing upon Sir Peter, and supplanting your brother, but you must endeavour to seduce his wife? I hate such an avarice of crimes; 'tis an unfair monopoly and never prospers.

JOSEPH SURFACE. Well, I admit I have been to blame. I confess I deviated from the direct road of wrong, but I don't think we're so totally defeated neither.

LADY SNEERWELL. No!

JOSEPH SURFACE. You tell me you have made a trial of Snake since we met, and that you still believe him faithful to us?

LADY SNEERWELL. I do believe so.

JOSEPH SURFACE. And that he has undertaken, should it be necessary, to swear and prove, that Charles is at this time contracted by vows and honour to your ladyship, which some of his former letters to you will serve to support?

LADY SNEERWELL. This, indeed, might have assisted.

JOSEPH SURFACE. Come, come; it is not too late yet.—[Knocking at the door.] But hark! this is probably my uncle, Sir Oliver: retire to that room; we'll consult farther when he is gone.

LADY SNEERWELL. Well, but if he should find you out too?

JOSEPH SURFACE. Oh, I have no fear of that. Sir Peter will hold his tongue for his own credit's sake—and you may depend on it I shall soon discover Sir Oliver's weak side!

LADY SNEERWELL. I have no diffidence of your abilities: only be constant to one roguery at a time.

JOSEPH SURFACE. I will, I will!—[Exit LADY SNEERWELL.] So! 'tis confounded hard, after such bad fortune, to be baited by one's confederate in evil. Well, at all events, my character is so much better than Charles's, that I certainly—hey!—what—this is not Sir Oliver, but old Stanley again. Plague on't that he should return to tease me just now! I shall have Sir Oliver come and find him here—and——

[Enter SIR OLIVER SURFACE.]

Gad's life, Mr. Stanley, why have you come back to plague me at this time? You must not stay now, upon my word.

SIR OLIVER. Sir, I hear your uncle Oliver is expected here, and though he has been so penurious to you, I'll try what he'll do for me.

JOSEPH SURFACE. Sir, 'tis impossible for you to stay now, so I must beg—— Come any other time, and I promise you, you shall be assisted.

SIR OLIVER. No: Sir Oliver and I must be acquainted.

JOSEPH SURFACE. Zounds, sir! then I insist on your quitting the room directly.

SIR OLIVER. Nay, sir——

JOSEPH SURFACE. Sir, I insist on't! —Here, William! show this gentleman out. Since you compel me, sir, not one moment—this is such insolence. [Going to push him out.]

[Enter CHARLES SURFACE.]

CHARLES SURFACE. Heyday! what's the matter now? What the devil, have you got hold of my little broker here? Zounds, brother, don't hurt little Premium. What's the matter, my little fellow?

JOSEPH SURFACE. So! he has been with you too, has he?

CHARLES SURFACE. To be sure, he has. Why, he's as honest a little——But sure, Joseph, you have not been borrowing money too, have you?

JOSEPH SURFACE. Borrowing! no! But, brother, you know we expect Sir Oliver here every——

CHARLES SURFACE. O Gad, that's true! Noll mustn't find the little broker here, to be sure.

JOSEPH SURFACE. Yet Mr. Stanley insists——

CHARLES SURFACE. Stanley! why his name's Premium.

JOSEPH SURFACE. No, sir, Stanley.

CHARLES SURFACE. No, no, Premium.

JOSEPH SURFACE. Well, no matter which—but——

CHARLES SURFACE. Ay, ay, Stanley or Premium, 'tis the same thing, as you say; for I suppose he goes by half a hundred names, besides A. B. at the coffee-house. [Knocking.]

JOSEPH SURFACE. 'Sdeath! here's Sir Oliver at the door.—Now I beg, Mr. Stanley——

CHARLES SURFACE. Ay, ay, and I beg, Mr. Premium——

SIR OLIVER. Gentlemen——

JOSEPH SURFACE. Sir, by Heaven you shall go.

CHARLES SURFACE. Ay, out with him, certainly!

SIR OLIVER. This violence——

JOSEPH SURFACE. Sir, 'tis your own fault.

CHARLES SURFACE. Out with him, to be sure. [Both forcing SIR OLIVER out.]

[Enter SIR PETER and LADY TEAZLE, MARIA, and ROWLEY.]

SIR PETER. My old friend, Sir Oliver—hey! What in the name of wonder—here are dutiful nephews—assault their uncle at a first visit!

LADY TEAZLE. Indeed, Sir Oliver, 'twas well we came in to rescue you.

ROWLEY. Truly it was; for I perceive, Sir Oliver, the character of old Stanley was no protection to you.

SIR OLIVER. Nor of Premium either: the necessities of the former could not extort a shilling from that benevolent gentleman; and with the other I stood a chance of faring worse than my ancestors, and being knocked down without being bid for.

JOSEPH SURFACE. Charles!

CHARLES SURFACE. Joseph!

JOSEPH SURFACE. 'Tis now complete!

CHARLES SURFACE. Very.

SIR OLIVER. Sir Peter, my friend, and Rowley too—look on that elder nephew of mine. You know what he has already received from my bounty; and you also know how gladly I would have regarded half my fortune as held in trust for him: judge then my disappointment in discovering him to be destitute of truth, charity, and gratitude!

SIR PETER. Sir Oliver, I should be more surprised at this declaration, if I had not myself found him to be mean, treacherous, and hypocritical.

LADY TEAZLE. And if the gentleman pleads not guilty to these, pray let him call me to his character.

SIR PETER. Then, I believe, we need add no more: if he knows himself, he will consider it as the most perfect punishment, that he is known to the world.

CHARLES SURFACE [aside]. If they talk this way to Honesty, what will they say to me, by and by?

[SIR PETER, LADY TEAZLE, and MARIA retire.]

SIR OLIVER. As for that prodigal, his brother, there——

CHARLES SURFACE [aside]. Ay, now comes my turn: the family pictures will ruin me!

JOSEPH SURFACE. Sir Oliver—uncle, will you honour me with a hearing?

CHARLES SURFACE [aside]. Now, if Joseph would make one of his long speeches, I might recollect myself a little.

SIR OLIVER [to JOSEPH SURFACE]. I suppose you would undertake to justify yourself?

JOSEPH SURFACE. I trust I could.

SIR OLIVER [to CHARLES SURFACE]. Well, sir!—and you could justify yourself too, I suppose?

CHARLES SURFACE. Not that I know of, Sir Oliver.

SIR OLIVER. What!—Little Premium has been let too much into the secret, I suppose?

CHARLES SURFACE. True, sir; but they were family secrets, and should not be mentioned again, you know.

ROWLEY. Come, Sir Oliver, I know you

cannot speak of Charles's follies with anger.

SIR OLIVER. Odds heart, no more I can; nor with gravity either. Sir Peter, do you know the rogue bargained with me for all, his ancestors; sold me judges and generals by the foot, and maiden aunts as cheap as broken china.

CHARLES SURFACE. To be sure, Sir Oliver, I did make a little free with the family canvas, that's the truth on't. My ancestors may rise in judgment against me, there's no denying it; but believe me sincere when I tell you—and upon my soul I would not say so if I was not—that if I do not appear mortified at the exposure of my follies, it is because I feel at this moment the warmest satisfaction in seeing you, my liberal benefactor.

SIR OLIVER. Charles, I believe you. Give me your hand again: the ill-looking little fellow over the settee has made your peace.

CHARLES SURFACE. Then, sir, my gratitude to the original is still increased.

LADY TEAZLE [advancing]. Yet, I believe, Sir Oliver, here is one whom Charles is still more anxious to be reconciled to. [Pointing to MARIA.]

SIR OLIVER. Oh, I have heard of his attachment there; and, with the young lady's pardon, if I construe right—that blush——

SIR PETER. Well, child, speak your sentiments!

MARIA. Sir, I have little to say, but that I shall rejoice to hear that he is happy; for me, whatever claim I had to his attention, I willingly resign to one who has a better title.

CHARLES SURFACE. How, Maria!

SIR PETER. Heyday! what's the mystery now? While he appeared an incorrigible rake, you would give your hand to no one else; and now that he is likely to reform I'll warrant you won't have him!

MARIA. His own heart and Lady Sneerwell know the cause.

CHARLES SURFACE. Lady Sneerwell!

JOSEPH SURFACE. Brother, it is with great concern I am obliged to speak on this point, but my regard to justice compels me, and Lady Sneerwell's injuries can no longer be concealed. [Opens the door.]

[Enter LADY SNEERWELL.]

SIR PETER. So! another French milliner! Egad, he has one in every room in the house, I suppose!

LADY SNEERWELL. Ungrateful Charles! Well may you be surprised, and feel for the indelicate situation your perfidy has forced me into.

CHARLES SURFACE. Pray, uncle, is this another plot of yours? For, as I have life, I don't understand it.

JOSEPH SURFACE. I believe, sir, there is but the evidence of one person more necessary to make it extremely clear.

SIR PETER. And that person, I imagine, is Mr. Snake.—Rowley, you were perfectly right to bring him with us, and pray let him appear.

ROWLEY. Walk in, Mr. Snake.

[Enter SNAKE.]

I thought his testimony might be wanted: however, it happens unluckily, that he comes to confront Lady Sneerwell, not to support her.

LADY SNEERWELL. A villain! Treacherous to me at last! Speak, fellow, have you too conspired against me!

SNAKE. I beg your ladyship ten thousand pardons: you paid me extremely liberally for the lie in question; but I unfortunately have been offered double to speak the truth.

SIR PETER. Plot and counter-plot, egad!

LADY SNEERWELL. The torments of shame and disappointment on you all! [Going.]

LADY TEAZLE. Hold, Lady Sneerwell—before you go, let me thank you for the trouble you and that gentleman have taken, in writing letters from me to Charles, and answering them yourself; and let me also request you to make my respects to the scandalous college, of which you are president, and inform them, that Lady Teazle, licentiate, begs leave to return the diploma they granted her, as she leaves off practice, and kills characters no longer.

LADY SNEERWELL. You too, madam!—provoking—insolent! May your husband live these fifty years! [Exit.]

SIR PETER. Oons! what a fury!

LADY TEAZLE. A malicious creature, indeed!

SIR PETER. What! not for her last wish?

LADY TEAZLE. Oh, no!

SIR OLIVER. Well, sir, and what have you to say now?

JOSEPH SURFACE. Sir, I am so confounded, to find that Lady Sneerwell could be guilty of suborning Mr. Snake in this manner, to impose on us all, that I know not what to say: however, lest her revengeful spirit should prompt her to injure my brother, I had certainly better follow her directly. For the man who attempts to—— [Exit.]

SIR PETER. Moral to the last!

SIR OLIVER. Ay, and marry her, Joseph, if you can. Oil and vinegar!—egad you'll do very well together.

ROWLEY. I believe we have no more occasion for Mr. Snake at present?

SNAKE. Before I go, I beg pardon once for all, for whatever uneasiness I have been the humble instrument of causing to the parties present.

SIR PETER. Well, well, you have made atonement by a good deed at last.

SNAKE. But I must request of the company, that it shall never be known.

SIR PETER. Hey! what the plague! are you ashamed of having done a right thing once in your life?

SNAKE. Ah, sir, consider—I live by the badness of my character; and, if it were once known that I had been betrayed into an honest action, I should lose every friend I have in the world.

SIR OLIVER. Well, well—we'll not traduce you by saying any thing in your praise, never fear. [Exit SNAKE.]

SIR PETER. There's a precious rogue!

LADY TEAZLE. See, Sir Oliver, there needs no persuasion now to reconcile your nephew and Maria.

SIR OLIVER. Ay, ay, that's as it should be, and, egad, we'll have the wedding tomorrow morning.

CHARLES SURFACE. Thank you, dear uncle.

SIR PETER. What, you rogue! don't you ask the girl's consent first?

CHARLES SURFACE. Oh, I have done that a long time—a minute ago—and she has looked yes.

MARIA. For shame, Charles!—I protest, Sir Peter, there has not been a word——

SIR OLIVER. Well, then, the fewer the better; may your love for each other never know abatement.

SIR PETER. And may you live as happily together as Lady Teazle and I intend to do!

CHARLES SURFACE. Rowley, my old friend, I am sure you congratulate me; and I suspect that I owe you much.

SIR PETER. You do, indeed, Charles.

SIR PETER. Ay, honest Rowley always said you would reform.

CHARLES SURFACE. Why, as to reforming, Sir Peter, I'll make no promises, and that I take to be a proof that I intend to set about it. But here shall be my monitor—my gentle guide.—Ah! can I leave the virtuous path those eyes illumine?

Though thou, dear maid, shouldst waive
thy beauty's sway,
Thou still must rule, because I will obey:
An humble fugitive from Folly view,
No sanctuary near but Love and you:
                    [To the audience.]
You can, indeed, each anxious fear re-
move,
For even Scandal dies, if you approve.
          [Exeunt omnes.]

READING LIST

GENERAL

There is nothing in English on the whole subject of drama as full and authentic as the monumental works of Klein, Proelss, and Creizenach. However, the latest edition of the *Encyclopædia Britannica* is useful and dependable, so far as it goes. See the article on *Drama*.

Readable outlines are:

Sheldon Cheney, *The Theater* (New York, 1929)
Ashley Dukes, *Drama* (New York, 1926)
Glenn Hughes, *The Story of the Theater* (New York, 1928)
Karl Mantzius, *A History of Theatrical Art* (6 vols., London, 1903ff.)
Brander Matthews, *The Development of the Drama* (New York, 1903)
Allardyce Nicoll, *The Development of the Theater* (New York, 1927)
Thomas Wood Stevens, *The Theater: From Athens to Broadway* (New York, 1932)
Donald Clive Stuart, *The Development of Dramatic Art* (New York, 1928)

The drama and theater, according to countries and peoples, are treated more or less fully in the following works:

ANCIENT GREECE

Lewis Campbell, *A Guide to Greek Tragedy, etc.* (London, 1891)
Roy C. Flickinger, *The Greek Theater and Its Drama* (Chicago, 1918)
A. E. Haigh, *The Attic Theater* (Oxford, 1907)
A. E. Haigh, *The Tragic Drama of the Greeks* (Oxford, 1925)
R. G. Moulton, *The Ancient Classical Drama* (Oxford, 1898)
Gilbert Norwood, *Greek Tragedy* (Boston, 1920)
Gilbert Norwood, *Greek Comedy* (Boston, 1930)

ANCIENT ROME

M. S. Dimsdale, *A History of Latin Literature* (New York, 1915)
Gilbert Norwood, *The Art of Terence* (Oxford, 1923)

ANCIENT INDIA

A. Berriedale Keith, *The Sanskrit Drama* (Oxford, 1924)
Arthur A. Macdonell, *A History of Sanskrit Literature* (New York, 1925)

CHINA AND JAPAN

Kate Buss, *Studies in the Chinese Drama* (New York, 1930)
Herbert A. Giles, *A History of Chinese Literature* (New York, 1924)
Zoe Kincaid, *Kabuki, The Popular Stage of Japan* (London, 1925)
Frank A. Lombard, *An Outline History of the Japanese Drama* (Boston, 1929)
A. E. Zucker, *The Chinese Theater* (Boston, 1925)

MEDIEVAL EUROPE

E. K. Chambers, *The Medieval Stage* (2 vols., Oxford, 1903)

ENGLAND

E. K. Chambers, *The Elizabethan Stage* (4 vols., New York, 1923)
Allardyce Nicoll, *British Drama* (New York, 1925)
Felix E. Schelling, *English Drama* (New York, 1914)
A. W. Ward, *A History of English Dramatic Literature, etc.* (3 vols., New York, 1899)

READING LIST OF PLAYS

SUPPLEMENTING THE TEXTS PRINTED IN THE TWO VOLUMES OF *World Drama*

ANCIENT GREECE

Æschylus, *Agamemnon* (Everyman's Library)
Aristophanes, *The Birds* (Everyman's Library)
Euripides, *Electra* (Everyman's Library)
Sophocles, *Oedipus the King* (Everyman's Library)

ANCIENT ROME

Plautus, *The Twins* (Bohn Library; Loeb Library)
Seneca, *Thyestes* (Loeb Library)
Terence, *The Brothers* (Bohn Library; Loeb Library)

ANCIENT INDIA

Anonymous, *The Little Clay Cart* (Harvard University Press)

CHINA

Besides *The Chalk Circle* there is no other full-length Chinese play in English.

JAPAN

Anonymous, *Busu*
Chikamatsu, *The Soga Revenge*
Seami, *Ohara Goko*
These plays are included in F. A. Lombard, *An Outline History of the Japanese Drama* (Houghton Mifflin).

MEDIEVAL EUROPE

Anonymous, *Abraham and Isaac* [Brome Play] (Everyman's Library)
Anonymous, *The Castle of Perseverance* (Everyman's Library)
Hrosvitha, *Camillus* (J. M. Dent)

ENGLAND

Beaumont and Fletcher, *The Faithful Shepherdess* (Everyman's Library)
Richard Brinsley Sheridan, *The Rivals* (Everyman's Library)
William Congreve, *The Way of the World* (Everyman's Library)
Ben Jonson, *Catiline* (Everyman's Library)
Christopher Marlowe, *Tamburlaine* (Everyman's Library)

(1)

A CATALOG OF SELECTED DOVER
BOOKS IN ALL FIELDS OF INTEREST

CONCERNING THE SPIRITUAL IN ART, Wassily Kandinsky. Pioneering work by father of abstract art. Thoughts on color theory, nature of art. Analysis of earlier masters. 12 illustrations. 80pp. of text. 5⅜ × 8½.　　23411-8 Pa. $3.95

ANIMALS: 1,419 Copyright-Free Illustrations of Mammals, Birds, Fish, Insects, etc., Jim Harter (ed.). Clear wood engravings present, in extremely lifelike poses, over 1,000 species of animals. One of the most extensive pictorial sourcebooks of its kind. Captions. Index. 284pp. 9 × 12.　　23766-4 Pa. $11.95

CELTIC ART: The Methods of Construction, George Bain. Simple geometric techniques for making Celtic interlacements, spirals, Kells-type initials, animals, humans, etc. Over 500 illustrations. 160pp. 9 × 12. (USO)　　22923-8 Pa. $8.95

AN ATLAS OF ANATOMY FOR ARTISTS, Fritz Schider. Most thorough reference work on art anatomy in the world. Hundreds of illustrations, including selections from works by Vesalius, Leonardo, Goya, Ingres, Michelangelo, others. 593 illustrations. 192pp. 7⅛ × 10¼.　　20241-0 Pa. $8.95

CELTIC HAND STROKE-BY-STROKE (Irish Half-Uncial from "The Book of Kells"): An Arthur Baker Calligraphy Manual, Arthur Baker. Complete guide to creating each letter of the alphabet in distinctive Celtic manner. Covers hand position, strokes, pens, inks, paper, more. Illustrated. 48pp. 8¼ × 11.
24336-2 Pa. $3.95

EASY ORIGAMI, John Montroll. Charming collection of 32 projects (hat, cup, pelican, piano, swan, many more) specially designed for the novice origami hobbyist. Clearly illustrated easy-to-follow instructions insure that even beginning papercrafters will achieve successful results. 48pp. 8¼ × 11.　　27298-2 Pa. $2.95

THE COMPLETE BOOK OF BIRDHOUSE CONSTRUCTION FOR WOOD-WORKERS, Scott D. Campbell. Detailed instructions, illustrations, tables. Also data on bird habitat and instinct patterns. Bibliography. 3 tables. 63 illustrations in 15 figures. 48pp. 5¼ × 8½.　　24407-5 Pa. $1.95

BLOOMINGDALE'S ILLUSTRATED 1886 CATALOG: Fashions, Dry Goods and Housewares, Bloomingdale Brothers. Famed merchants' extremely rare catalog depicting about 1,700 products: clothing, housewares, firearms, dry goods, jewelry, more. Invaluable for dating, identifying vintage items. Also, copyright-free graphics for artists, designers. Co-published with Henry Ford Museum & Green-field Village. 160pp. 8¼ × 11.　　25780-0 Pa. $9.95

HISTORIC COSTUME IN PICTURES, Braun & Schneider. Over 1,450 costumed figures in clearly detailed engravings—from dawn of civilization to end of 19th century. Captions. Many folk costumes. 256pp. 8⅜ × 11¾.　　23150-X Pa. $10.95

STICKLEY CRAFTSMAN FURNITURE CATALOGS, Gustav Stickley and L. & J. G. Stickley. Beautiful, functional furniture in two authentic catalogs from 1910. 594 illustrations, including 277 photos, show settles, rockers, armchairs, reclining chairs, bookcases, desks, tables. 183pp. 6½ × 9¼.   23838-5 Pa. $8.95

AMERICAN LOCOMOTIVES IN HISTORIC PHOTOGRAPHS: 1858 to 1949, Ron Ziel (ed.). A rare collection of 126 meticulously detailed official photographs, called "builder portraits," of American locomotives that majestically chronicle the rise of steam locomotive power in America. Introduction. Detailed captions. xi + 129pp. 9 × 12.   27393-8 Pa. $12.95

AMERICA'S LIGHTHOUSES: An Illustrated History, Francis Ross Holland, Jr. Delightfully written, profusely illustrated fact-filled survey of over 200 American lighthouses since 1716. History, anecdotes, technological advances, more. 240pp. 8 × 10¾.   25576-X Pa. $11.95

TOWARDS A NEW ARCHITECTURE, Le Corbusier. Pioneering manifesto by founder of "International School." Technical and aesthetic theories, views of industry, economics, relation of form to function, "mass-production split" and much more. Profusely illustrated. 320pp. 6⅛ × 9¼. (USO)   25023-7 Pa. $8.95

HOW THE OTHER HALF LIVES, Jacob Riis. Famous journalistic record, exposing poverty and degradation of New York slums around 1900, by major social reformer. 100 striking and influential photographs. 233pp. 10 × 7⅞.
22012-5 Pa $10.95

FRUIT KEY AND TWIG KEY TO TREES AND SHRUBS, William M. Harlow. One of the handiest and most widely used identification aids. Fruit key covers 120 deciduous and evergreen species; twig key 160 deciduous species. Easily used. Over 300 photographs. 126pp. 5⅜ × 8½.   20511-8 Pa. $3.95

COMMON BIRD SONGS, Dr. Donald J. Borror. Songs of 60 most common U.S. birds: robins, sparrows, cardinals, bluejays, finches, more—arranged in order of increasing complexity. Up to 9 variations of songs of each species.
Cassette and manual 99911-4 $8.95

ORCHIDS AS HOUSE PLANTS, Rebecca Tyson Northen. Grow cattleyas and many other kinds of orchids—in a window, in a case, or under artificial light. 63 illustrations. 148pp. 5⅜ × 8½.   23261-1 Pa. $3.95

MONSTER MAZES, Dave Phillips. Masterful mazes at four levels of difficulty. Avoid deadly perils and evil creatures to find magical treasures. Solutions for all 32 exciting illustrated puzzles. 48pp. 8¼ × 11.   26005-4 Pa. $2.95

MOZART'S DON GIOVANNI (DOVER OPERA LIBRETTO SERIES), Wolfgang Amadeus Mozart. Introduced and translated by Ellen H. Bleiler. Standard Italian libretto, with complete English translation. Convenient and thoroughly portable—an ideal companion for reading along with a recording or the performance itself. Introduction. List of characters. Plot summary. 121pp. 5¼ × 8½.
24944-1 Pa. $2.95

TECHNICAL MANUAL AND DICTIONARY OF CLASSICAL BALLET, Gail Grant. Defines, explains, comments on steps, movements, poses and concepts. 15-page pictorial section. Basic book for student, viewer. 127pp. 5⅜ × 8½.
21843-0 Pa. $3.95

BRASS INSTRUMENTS: Their History and Development, Anthony Baines. Authoritative, updated survey of the evolution of trumpets, trombones, bugles, cornets, French horns, tubas and other brass wind instruments. Over 140 illustrations and 48 music examples. Corrected and updated by author. New preface. Bibliography. 320pp. 5⅜ × 8½. 27574-4 Pa. $9.95

HOLLYWOOD GLAMOR PORTRAITS, John Kobal (ed.). 145 photos from 1926–49. Harlow, Gable, Bogart, Bacall; 94 stars in all. Full background on photographers, technical aspects. 160pp. 8⅜ × 11¼. 23352-9 Pa. $9.95

MAX AND MORITZ, Wilhelm Busch. Great humor classic in both German and English. Also 10 other works: "Cat and Mouse," "Plisch and Plumm," etc. 216pp. 5⅜ × 8½. 20181-3 Pa. $5.95

THE RAVEN AND OTHER FAVORITE POEMS, Edgar Allan Poe. Over 40 of the author's most memorable poems: "The Bells," "Ulalume," "Israfel," "To Helen," "The Conqueror Worm," "Eldorado," "Annabel Lee," many more. Alphabetic lists of titles and first lines. 64pp. 5³⁄₁₆ × 8¼. 26685-0 Pa. $1.00

SEVEN SCIENCE FICTION NOVELS, H. G. Wells. The standard collection of the great novels. Complete, unabridged. First Men in the Moon, Island of Dr. Moreau, War of the Worlds, Food of the Gods, Invisible Man, Time Machine, In the Days of the Comet. Total of 1,015pp. 5⅜ × 8½. (USO) 20264-X Clothbd. $29.95

AMULETS AND SUPERSTITIONS, E. A. Wallis Budge. Comprehensive discourse on origin, powers of amulets in many ancient cultures: Arab, Persian, Babylonian, Assyrian, Egyptian, Gnostic, Hebrew, Phoenician, Syriac, etc. Covers cross, swastika, crucifix, seals, rings, stones, etc. 584pp. 5⅜ × 8½. 23573-4 Pa. $12.95

RUSSIAN STORIES/PYCCKNE PACCKA3bI: A Dual-Language Book, edited by Gleb Struve. Twelve tales by such masters as Chekhov, Tolstoy, Dostoevsky, Pushkin, others. Excellent word-for-word English translations on facing pages, plus teaching and study aids, Russian/English vocabulary, biographical/critical introductions, more. 416pp. 5⅜ × 8½. 26244-8 Pa. $8.95

PHILADELPHIA THEN AND NOW: 60 Sites Photographed in the Past and Present, Kenneth Finkel and Susan Oyama. Rare photographs of City Hall, Logan Square, Independence Hall, Betsy Ross House, other landmarks juxtaposed with contemporary views. Captures changing face of historic city. Introduction. Captions. 128pp. 8¼ × 11. 25790-8 Pa. $9.95

AIA ARCHITECTURAL GUIDE TO NASSAU AND SUFFOLK COUNTIES, LONG ISLAND, The American Institute of Architects, Long Island Chapter, and the Society for the Preservation of Long Island Antiquities. Comprehensive, well-researched and generously illustrated volume brings to life over three centuries of Long Island's great architectural heritage. More than 240 photographs with authoritative, extensively detailed captions. 176pp. 8¼ × 11. 26946-9 Pa. $14.95

NORTH AMERICAN INDIAN LIFE: Customs and Traditions of 23 Tribes, Elsie Clews Parsons (ed.). 27 fictionalized essays by noted anthropologists examine religion, customs, government, additional facets of life among the Winnebago, Crow, Zuni, Eskimo, other tribes. 480pp. 6⅛ × 9¼. 27377-6 Pa. $10.95

FRANK LLOYD WRIGHT'S HOLLYHOCK HOUSE, Donald Hoffmann. Lavishly illustrated, carefully documented study of one of Wright's most controversial residential designs. Over 120 photographs, floor plans, elevations, etc. Detailed perceptive text by noted Wright scholar. Index. 128pp. 9¼ × 10¾. 27133-1 Pa. $11.95

THE MALE AND FEMALE FIGURE IN MOTION: 60 Classic Photographic Sequences, Eadweard Muybridge. 60 true-action photographs of men and women walking, running, climbing, bending, turning, etc., reproduced from rare 19th-century masterpiece. vi + 121pp. 9 × 12. 24745-7 Pa. $10.95

1001 QUESTIONS ANSWERED ABOUT THE SEASHORE, N. J. Berrill and Jacquelyn Berrill. Queries answered about dolphins, sea snails, sponges, starfish, fishes, shore birds, many others. Covers appearance, breeding, growth, feeding, much more. 305pp. 5¼ × 8¼. 23366-9 Pa. $7.95

GUIDE TO OWL WATCHING IN NORTH AMERICA, Donald S. Heintzelman. Superb guide offers complete data and descriptions of 19 species: barn owl, screech owl, snowy owl, many more. Expert coverage of owl-watching equipment, conservation, migrations and invasions, etc. Guide to observing sites. 84 illustrations. xiii + 193pp. 5⅜ × 8½. 27344-X Pa. $7.95

MEDICINAL AND OTHER USES OF NORTH AMERICAN PLANTS: A Historical Survey with Special Reference to the Eastern Indian Tribes, Charlotte Erichsen-Brown. Chronological historical citations document 500 years of usage of plants, trees, shrubs native to eastern Canada, northeastern U.S. Also complete identifying information. 343 illustrations. 544pp. 6½ × 9¼. 25951-X Pa. $12.95

STORYBOOK MAZES, Dave Phillips. 23 stories and mazes on two-page spreads: Wizard of Oz, Treasure Island, Robin Hood, etc. Solutions. 64pp. 8¼ × 11. 23628-5 Pa. $2.95

NEGRO FOLK MUSIC, U.S.A., Harold Courlander. Noted folklorist's scholarly yet readable analysis of rich and varied musical tradition. Includes authentic versions of over 40 folk songs. Valuable bibliography and discography. xi + 324pp. 5⅜ × 8½. 27350-4 Pa. $7.95

MOVIE-STAR PORTRAITS OF THE FORTIES, John Kobal (ed.). 163 glamor, studio photos of 106 stars of the 1940s: Rita Hayworth, Ava Gardner, Marlon Brando, Clark Gable, many more. 176pp. 8⅜ × 11¼. 23546-7 Pa. $10.95

BENCHLEY LOST AND FOUND, Robert Benchley. Finest humor from early 30s, about pet peeves, child psychologists, post office and others. Mostly unavailable elsewhere. 73 illustrations by Peter Arno and others. 183pp. 5⅜ × 8½. 22410-4 Pa. $5.95

YEKL and THE IMPORTED BRIDEGROOM AND OTHER STORIES OF YIDDISH NEW YORK, Abraham Cahan. Film Hester Street based on Yekl (1896). Novel, other stories among first about Jewish immigrants on N.Y.'s East Side. 240pp. 5⅜ × 8½. 22427-9 Pa. $5.95

SELECTED POEMS, Walt Whitman. Generous sampling from *Leaves of Grass*. Twenty-four poems include "I Hear America Singing," "Song of the Open Road," "I Sing the Body Electric," "When Lilacs Last in the Dooryard Bloom'd," "O Captain! My Captain!"—all reprinted from an authoritative edition. Lists of titles and first lines. 128pp. 5³⁄₁₆ × 8¼. 26878-0 Pa. $1.00

THE BEST TALES OF HOFFMANN, E. T. A. Hoffmann. 10 of Hoffmann's most important stories: "Nutcracker and the King of Mice," "The Golden Flowerpot," etc. 458pp. 5⅜ × 8½. 21793-0 Pa. $8.95

FROM FETISH TO GOD IN ANCIENT EGYPT, E. A. Wallis Budge. Rich detailed survey of Egyptian conception of "God" and gods, magic, cult of animals, Osiris, more. Also, superb English translations of hymns and legends. 240 illustrations. 545pp. 5⅜ × 8½. 25803-3 Pa. $11.95

FRENCH STORIES/CONTES FRANÇAIS: A Dual-Language Book, Wallace Fowlie. Ten stories by French masters, Voltaire to Camus: "Micromegas" by Voltaire; "The Atheist's Mass" by Balzac; "Minuet" by de Maupassant; "The Guest" by Camus, six more. Excellent English translations on facing pages. Also French-English vocabulary list, exercises, more. 352pp. 5⅜ × 8½. 26443-2 Pa. $8.95

CHICAGO AT THE TURN OF THE CENTURY IN PHOTOGRAPHS: 122 Historic Views from the Collections of the Chicago Historical Society, Larry A. Viskochil. Rare large-format prints offer detailed views of City Hall, State Street, the Loop, Hull House, Union Station, many other landmarks, circa 1904–1913. Introduction. Captions. Maps. 144pp. 9⅜ × 12¼. 24656-6 Pa. $12.95

OLD BROOKLYN IN EARLY PHOTOGRAPHS, 1865–1929, William Lee Younger. Luna Park, Gravesend race track, construction of Grand Army Plaza, moving of Hotel Brighton, etc. 157 previously unpublished photographs. 165pp. 8⅞ × 11¾. 23587-4 Pa. $12.95

THE MYTHS OF THE NORTH AMERICAN INDIANS, Lewis Spence. Rich anthology of the myths and legends of the Algonquins, Iroquois, Pawnees and Sioux, prefaced by an extensive historical and ethnological commentary. 36 illustrations. 480pp. 5⅜ × 8½. 25967-6 Pa. $8.95

AN ENCYCLOPEDIA OF BATTLES: Accounts of Over 1,560 Battles from 1479 B.C. to the Present, David Eggenberger. Essential details of every major battle in recorded history from the first battle of Megiddo in 1479 B.C. to Grenada in 1984. List of Battle Maps. New Appendix covering the years 1967–1984. Index. 99 illustrations. 544pp. 6½ × 9¼. 24913-1 Pa. $14.95

SAILING ALONE AROUND THE WORLD, Captain Joshua Slocum. First man to sail around the world, alone, in small boat. One of great feats of seamanship told in delightful manner. 67 illustrations. 294pp. 5⅜ × 8½. 20326-3 Pa. $5.95

ANARCHISM AND OTHER ESSAYS, Emma Goldman. Powerful, penetrating, prophetic essays on direct action, role of minorities, prison reform, puritan hypocrisy, violence, etc. 271pp. 5⅜ × 8½. 22484-8 Pa. $5.95

MYTHS OF THE HINDUS AND BUDDHISTS, Ananda K. Coomaraswamy and Sister Nivedita. Great stories of the epics; deeds of Krishna, Shiva, taken from puranas, Vedas, folk tales; etc. 32 illustrations. 400pp. 5⅜ × 8½. 21759-0 Pa. $9.95

BEYOND PSYCHOLOGY, Otto Rank. Fear of death, desire of immortality, nature of sexuality, social organization, creativity, according to Rankian system. 291pp. 5⅜ × 8½. 20485-5 Pa. $7.95

A THEOLOGICO-POLITICAL TREATISE, Benedict Spinoza. Also contains unfinished Political Treatise. Great classic on religious liberty, theory of government on common consent. R. Elwes translation. Total of 421pp. 5⅜ × 8½. 20249-6 Pa. $7.95

CATALOG OF DOVER BOOKS

MY BONDAGE AND MY FREEDOM, Frederick Douglass. Born a slave, Douglass became outspoken force in antislavery movement. The best of Douglass' autobiographies. Graphic description of slave life. 464pp. 5⅜ × 8½.   22457-0 Pa. $8.95

FOLLOWING THE EQUATOR: A Journey Around the World, Mark Twain. Fascinating humorous account of 1897 voyage to Hawaii, Australia, India, New Zealand, etc. Ironic, bemused reports on peoples, customs, climate, flora and fauna, politics, much more. 197 illustrations. 720pp. 5⅜ × 8½.   26113-1 Pa. $15.95

THE PEOPLE CALLED SHAKERS, Edward D. Andrews. Definitive study of Shakers: origins, beliefs, practices, dances, social organization, furniture and crafts, etc. 33 illustrations. 351pp. 5⅜ × 8½.   21081-2 Pa. $7.95

THE MYTHS OF GREECE AND ROME, H. A. Guerber. A classic of mythology, generously illustrated, long prized for its simple, graphic, accurate retelling of the principal myths of Greece and Rome, and for its commentary on their origins and significance. With 64 illustrations by Michelangelo, Raphael, Titian, Rubens, Canova, Bernini and others. 480pp. 5⅜ × 8½.   27584-1 Pa. $9.95

PSYCHOLOGY OF MUSIC, Carl E. Seashore. Classic work discusses music as a medium from psychological viewpoint. Clear treatment of physical acoustics, auditory apparatus, sound perception, development of musical skills, nature of musical feeling, host of other topics. 88 figures. 408pp. 5⅜ × 8½. 21851-1 Pa. $9.95

THE PHILOSOPHY OF HISTORY, Georg W. Hegel. Great classic of Western thought develops concept that history is not chance but rational process, the evolution of freedom. 457pp. 5⅜ × 8½.   20112-0 Pa. $8.95

THE BOOK OF TEA, Kakuzo Okakura. Minor classic of the Orient: entertaining, charming explanation, interpretation of traditional Japanese culture in terms of tea ceremony. 94pp. 5⅜ × 8½.   20070-1 Pa. $2.95

LIFE IN ANCIENT EGYPT, Adolf Erman. Fullest, most thorough, detailed older account with much not in more recent books, domestic life, religion, magic, medicine, commerce, much more. Many illustrations reproduce tomb paintings, carvings, hieroglyphs, etc. 597pp. 5⅜ × 8½.   22632-8 Pa. $9.95

SUNDIALS, Their Theory and Construction, Albert Waugh. Far and away the best, most thorough coverage of ideas, mathematics concerned, types, construction, adjusting anywhere. Simple, nontechnical treatment allows even children to build several of these dials. Over 100 illustrations. 230pp. 5⅜ × 8½.   22947-5 Pa. $5.95

DYNAMICS OF FLUIDS IN POROUS MEDIA, Jacob Bear. For advanced students of ground water hydrology, soil mechanics and physics, drainage and irrigation engineering, and more. 335 illustrations. Exercises, with answers. 784pp. 6⅛ × 9¼.   65675-6 Pa. $19.95

SONGS OF EXPERIENCE: Facsimile Reproduction with 26 Plates in Full Color, William Blake. 26 full-color plates from a rare 1826 edition. Includes "The Tyger," "London," "Holy Thursday," and other poems. Printed text of poems. 48pp. 5¼ × 7.   24636-1 Pa. $3.95

OLD-TIME VIGNETTES IN FULL COLOR, Carol Belanger Grafton (ed.). Over 390 charming, often sentimental illustrations, selected from archives of Victorian graphics—pretty women posing, children playing, food, flowers, kittens and puppies, smiling cherubs, birds and butterflies, much more. All copyright-free. 48pp. 9¼ × 12¼.   27269-9 Pa. $5.95

PERSPECTIVE FOR ARTISTS, Rex Vicat Cole. Depth, perspective of sky and sea, shadows, much more, not usually covered. 391 diagrams, 81 reproductions of drawings and paintings. 279pp. 5⅜ × 8½. 22487-2 Pa. $6.95

DRAWING THE LIVING FIGURE, Joseph Sheppard. Innovative approach to artistic anatomy focuses on specifics of surface anatomy, rather than muscles and bones. Over 170 drawings of live models in front, back and side views, and in widely varying poses. Accompanying diagrams. 177 illustrations. Introduction. Index. 144pp. 8⅜ × 11¼. 26723-7 Pa. $7.95

GOTHIC AND OLD ENGLISH ALPHABETS: 100 Complete Fonts, Dan X. Solo. Add power, elegance to posters, signs, other graphics with 100 stunning copyright-free alphabets: Blackstone, Dolbey, Germania, 97 more—including many lower-case, numerals, punctuation marks. 104pp. 8⅛ × 11. 24695-7 Pa. $7.95

HOW TO DO BEADWORK, Mary White. Fundamental book on craft from simple projects to five-bead chains and woven works. 106 illustrations. 142pp. 5⅜ × 8. 20697-1 Pa. $4.95

THE BOOK OF WOOD CARVING, Charles Marshall Sayers. Finest book for beginners discusses fundamentals and offers 34 designs. "Absolutely first rate . . . well thought out and well executed."—E. J. Tangerman. 118pp. 7¾ × 10⅝. 23654-4 Pa. $5.95

ILLUSTRATED CATALOG OF CIVIL WAR MILITARY GOODS: Union Army Weapons, Insignia, Uniform Accessories, and Other Equipment, Schuyler, Hartley, and Graham. Rare, profusely illustrated 1846 catalog includes Union Army uniform and dress regulations, arms and ammunition, coats, insignia, flags, swords, rifles, etc. 226 illustrations. 160pp. 9 × 12. 24939-5 Pa. $10.95

WOMEN'S FASHIONS OF THE EARLY 1900s: An Unabridged Republication of "New York Fashions, 1909," National Cloak & Suit Co. Rare catalog of mail-order fashions documents women's and children's clothing styles shortly after the turn of the century. Captions offer full descriptions, prices. Invaluable resource for fashion, costume historians. Approximately 725 illustrations. 128pp. 8⅜ × 11¼. 27276-1 Pa. $10.95

THE 1912 AND 1915 GUSTAV STICKLEY FURNITURE CATALOGS, Gustav Stickley. With over 200 detailed illustrations and descriptions, these two catalogs are essential reading and reference materials and identification guides for Stickley furniture. Captions cite materials, dimensions and prices. 112pp. 6½ × 9¼. 26676-1 Pa. $9.95

EARLY AMERICAN LOCOMOTIVES, John H. White, Jr. Finest locomotive engravings from early 19th century: historical (1804–74), main-line (after 1870), special, foreign, etc. 147 plates. 142pp. 11⅜ × 8¼. 22772-3 Pa. $8.95

THE TALL SHIPS OF TODAY IN PHOTOGRAPHS, Frank O. Braynard. Lavishly illustrated tribute to nearly 100 majestic contemporary sailing vessels: Amerigo Vespucci, Clearwater, Constitution, Eagle, Mayflower, Sea Cloud, Victory, many more. Authoritative captions provide statistics, background on each ship. 190 black-and-white photographs and illustrations. Introduction. 128pp. 8⅞ × 11¾. 27163-3 Pa. $12.95

EARLY NINETEENTH-CENTURY CRAFTS AND TRADES, Peter Stockham (ed.). Extremely rare 1807 volume describes to youngsters the crafts and trades of the day: brickmaker, weaver, dressmaker, bookbinder, ropemaker, saddler, many more. Quaint prose, charming illustrations for each craft. 20 black-and-white line illustrations. 192pp. 4⅝ × 6. 27293-1 Pa. $4.95

VICTORIAN FASHIONS AND COSTUMES FROM HARPER'S BAZAR, 1867–1898, Stella Blum (ed.). Day costumes, evening wear, sports clothes, shoes, hats, other accessories in over 1,000 detailed engravings. 320pp. 9⅜ × 12¼. 22990-4 Pa. $13.95

GUSTAV STICKLEY, THE CRAFTSMAN, Mary Ann Smith. Superb study surveys broad scope of Stickley's achievement, especially in architecture. Design philosophy, rise and fall of the Craftsman empire, descriptions and floor plans for many Craftsman houses, more. 86 black-and-white halftones. 31 line illustrations. Introduction. 208pp. 6½ × 9¼. 27210-9 Pa. $9.95

THE LONG ISLAND RAIL ROAD IN EARLY PHOTOGRAPHS, Ron Ziel. Over 220 rare photos, informative text document origin (1844) and development of rail service on Long Island. Vintage views of early trains, locomotives, stations, passengers, crews, much more. Captions. 8⅞ × 11¾. 26301-0 Pa. $13.95

THE BOOK OF OLD SHIPS: From Egyptian Galleys to Clipper Ships, Henry B. Culver. Superb, authoritative history of sailing vessels, with 80 magnificent line illustrations. Galley, bark, caravel, longship, whaler, many more. Detailed, informative text on each vessel by noted naval historian. Introduction. 256pp. 5⅜ × 8½. 27332-6 Pa. $6.95

TEN BOOKS ON ARCHITECTURE, Vitruvius. The most important book ever written on architecture. Early Roman aesthetics, technology, classical orders, site selection, all other aspects. Morgan translation. 331pp. 5⅜ × 8½. 20645-9 Pa. $8.95

THE HUMAN FIGURE IN MOTION, Eadweard Muybridge. More than 4,500 stopped-action photos, in action series, showing undraped men, women, children jumping, lying down, throwing, sitting, wrestling, carrying, etc. 390pp. 7⅞ × 10⅝. 20204-6 Clothbd. $24.95

TREES OF THE EASTERN AND CENTRAL UNITED STATES AND CANADA, William M. Harlow. Best one-volume guide to 140 trees. Full descriptions, woodlore, range, etc. Over 600 illustrations. Handy size. 288pp. 4½ × 6⅜. 20395-6 Pa. $5.95

SONGS OF WESTERN BIRDS, Dr. Donald J. Borror. Complete song and call repertoire of 60 western species, including flycatchers, juncoes, cactus wrens, many more—includes fully illustrated booklet. Cassette and manual 99913-0 $8.95

GROWING AND USING HERBS AND SPICES, Milo Miloradovich. Versatile handbook provides all the information needed for cultivation and use of all the herbs and spices available in North America. 4 illustrations. Index. Glossary. 236pp. 5⅜ × 8½. 25058-X Pa. $5.95

BIG BOOK OF MAZES AND LABYRINTHS, Walter Shepherd. 50 mazes and labyrinths in all—classical, solid, ripple, and more—in one great volume. Perfect inexpensive puzzler for clever youngsters. Full solutions. 112pp. 8⅛ × 11. 22951-3 Pa. $3.95

PIANO TUNING, J. Cree Fischer. Clearest, best book for beginner, amateur. Simple repairs, raising dropped notes, tuning by easy method of flattened fifths. No previous skills needed. 4 illustrations. 201pp. 5⅜ × 8½.   23267-0 Pa. $5.95

A SOURCE BOOK IN THEATRICAL HISTORY, A. M. Nagler. Contemporary observers on acting, directing, make-up, costuming, stage props, machinery, scene design, from Ancient Greece to Chekhov. 611pp. 5⅜ × 8½.   20515-0 Pa. $11.95

THE COMPLETE NONSENSE OF EDWARD LEAR, Edward Lear. All nonsense limericks, zany alphabets, Owl and Pussycat, songs, nonsense botany, etc., illustrated by Lear. Total of 320pp. 5⅜ × 8½. (USO)   20167-8 Pa. $5.95

VICTORIAN PARLOUR POETRY: An Annotated Anthology, Michael R. Turner. 117 gems by Longfellow, Tennyson, Browning, many lesser-known poets. "The Village Blacksmith," "Curfew Must Not Ring Tonight," "Only a Baby Small," dozens more, often difficult to find elsewhere. Index of poets, titles, first lines. xxiii + 325pp. 5⅜ × 8¼.   27044-0 Pa. $8.95

DUBLINERS, James Joyce. Fifteen stories offer vivid, tightly focused observations of the lives of Dublin's poorer classes. At least one, "The Dead," is considered a masterpiece. Reprinted complete and unabridged from standard edition. 160pp. 5³⁄₁₆ × 8¼.   26870-5 Pa. $1.00

THE HAUNTED MONASTERY and THE CHINESE MAZE MURDERS, Robert van Gulik. Two full novels by van Gulik, set in 7th-century China, continue adventures of Judge Dee and his companions. An evil Taoist monastery, seemingly supernatural events; overgrown topiary maze hides strange crimes. 27 illustrations. 328pp. 5⅜ × 8½.   23502-5 Pa. $7.95

THE BOOK OF THE SACRED MAGIC OF ABRAMELIN THE MAGE, translated by S. MacGregor Mathers. Medieval manuscript of ceremonial magic. Basic document in Aleister Crowley, Golden Dawn groups. 268pp. 5⅜ × 8½.
23211-5 Pa. $7.95

NEW RUSSIAN-ENGLISH AND ENGLISH-RUSSIAN DICTIONARY, M. A. O'Brien. This is a remarkably handy Russian dictionary, containing a surprising amount of information, including over 70,000 entries. 366pp. 4½ × 6⅛.
20208-9 Pa. $8.95

HISTORIC HOMES OF THE AMERICAN PRESIDENTS, Second, Revised Edition, Irvin Haas. A traveler's guide to American Presidential homes, most open to the public, depicting and describing homes occupied by every American President from George Washington to George Bush. With visiting hours, admission charges, travel routes. 175 photographs. Index. 160pp. 8¼ × 11. 26751-2 Pa. $10.95

NEW YORK IN THE FORTIES, Andreas Feininger. 162 brilliant photographs by the well-known photographer, formerly with *Life* magazine. Commuters, shoppers, Times Square at night, much else from city at its peak. Captions by John von Hartz. 181pp. 9¼ × 10¾.   23585-8 Pa. $12.95

INDIAN SIGN LANGUAGE, William Tomkins. Over 525 signs developed by Sioux and other tribes. Written instructions and diagrams. Also 290 pictographs. 111pp. 6⅛ × 9¼.   22029-X Pa. $3.50

CATALOG OF DOVER BOOKS

ANATOMY: A Complete Guide for Artists, Joseph Sheppard. A master of figure drawing shows artists how to render human anatomy convincingly. Over 460 illustrations. 224pp. 8⅜ × 11¼. 27279-6 Pa. $9.95

MEDIEVAL CALLIGRAPHY: Its History and Technique, Marc Drogin. Spirited history, comprehensive instruction manual covers 13 styles (ca. 4th century thru 15th). Excellent photographs; directions for duplicating medieval techniques with modern tools. 224pp. 8⅜ × 11¼. 26142-5 Pa. $11.95

DRIED FLOWERS: How to Prepare Them, Sarah Whitlock and Martha Rankin. Complete instructions on how to use silica gel, meal and borax, perlite aggregate, sand and borax, glycerine and water to create attractive permanent flower arrangements. 12 illustrations. 32pp. 5⅜ × 8½. 21802-3 Pa. $1.00

EASY-TO-MAKE BIRD FEEDERS FOR WOODWORKERS, Scott D. Campbell. Detailed, simple-to-use guide for designing, constructing, caring for and using feeders. Text, illustrations for 12 classic and contemporary designs. 96pp. 5⅜ × 8½. 25847-5 Pa. $2.95

OLD-TIME CRAFTS AND TRADES, Peter Stockham. An 1807 book created to teach children about crafts and trades open to them as future careers. It describes in detailed, nontechnical terms 24 different occupations, among them coachmaker, gardener, hairdresser, lacemaker, shoemaker, wheelwright, copper-plate printer, milliner, trunkmaker, merchant and brewer. Finely detailed engravings illustrate each occupation. 192pp. 4⅝ × 6. 27398-9 Pa. $4.95

THE HISTORY OF UNDERCLOTHES, C. Willett Cunnington and Phyllis Cunnington. Fascinating, well-documented survey covering six centuries of English undergarments, enhanced with over 100 illustrations: 12th-century laced-up bodice, footed long drawers (1795), 19th-century bustles, 19th-century corsets for men, Victorian "bust improvers," much more. 272pp. 5⅜ × 8¼. 27124-2 Pa. $9.95

ARTS AND CRAFTS FURNITURE: The Complete Brooks Catalog of 1912, Brooks Manufacturing Co. Photos and detailed descriptions of more than 150 now very collectible furniture designs from the Arts and Crafts movement depict davenports, settees, buffets, desks, tables, chairs, bedsteads, dressers and more, all built of solid, quarter-sawed oak. Invaluable for students and enthusiasts of antiques, Americana and the decorative arts. 80pp. 6½ × 9¼. 27471-3 Pa. $7.95

HOW WE INVENTED THE AIRPLANE: An Illustrated History, Orville Wright. Fascinating firsthand account covers early experiments, construction of planes and motors, first flights, much more. Introduction and commentary by Fred C. Kelly. 76 photographs. 96pp. 8¼ × 11. 25662-6 Pa. $7.95

THE ARTS OF THE SAILOR: Knotting, Splicing and Ropework, Hervey Garrett Smith. Indispensable shipboard reference covers tools, basic knots and useful hitches; handsewing and canvas work, more. Over 100 illustrations. Delightful reading for sea lovers. 256pp. 5⅝ × 8½. 26440-8 Pa. $7.95

FRANK LLOYD WRIGHT'S FALLINGWATER: The House and Its History, Second, Revised Edition, Donald Hoffmann. A total revision—both in text and illustrations—of the standard document on Fallingwater, the boldest, most personal architectural statement of Wright's mature years, updated with valuable new material from the recently opened Frank Lloyd Wright Archives. "Fascinating"—*The New York Times.* 116 illustrations. 128pp. 9¼ × 10¾. 27430-6 Pa. $10.95

CATALOG OF DOVER BOOKS

PHOTOGRAPHIC SKETCHBOOK OF THE CIVIL WAR, Alexander Gardner. 100 photos taken on field during the Civil War. Famous shots of Manassas, Harper's Ferry, Lincoln, Richmond, slave pens, etc. 244pp. 10⅛ × 8¼.
22731-6 Pa. $9.95

FIVE ACRES AND INDEPENDENCE, Maurice G. Kains. Great back-to-the-land classic explains basics of self-sufficient farming. The one book to get. 95 illustrations. 397pp. 5⅜ × 8½.
20974-1 Pa. $6.95

SONGS OF EASTERN BIRDS, Dr. Donald J. Borror. Songs and calls of 60 species most common to eastern U.S.: warblers, woodpeckers, flycatchers, thrushes, larks, many more in high-quality recording.
Cassette and manual 99912-2 $8.95

A MODERN HERBAL, Margaret Grieve. Much the fullest, most exact, most useful compilation of herbal material. Gigantic alphabetical encyclopedia, from aconite to zedoary, gives botanical information, medical properties, folklore, economic uses, much else. Indispensable to serious reader. 161 illustrations. 888pp. 6½ × 9¼. 2-vol. set. (USO)
Vol. I: 22798-7 Pa. $9.95
Vol. II: 22799-5 Pa. $9.95

HIDDEN TREASURE MAZE BOOK, Dave Phillips. Solve 34 challenging mazes accompanied by heroic tales of adventure. Evil dragons, people-eating plants, bloodthirsty giants, many more dangerous adversaries lurk at every twist and turn. 34 mazes, stories, solutions. 48pp. 8¼ × 11.
24566-7 Pa. $2.95

LETTERS OF W. A. MOZART, Wolfgang A. Mozart. Remarkable letters show bawdy wit, humor, imagination, musical insights, contemporary musical world; includes some letters from Leopold Mozart. 276pp. 5⅜ × 8½.
22859-2 Pa. $6.95

BASIC PRINCIPLES OF CLASSICAL BALLET, Agrippina Vaganova. Great Russian theoretician, teacher explains methods for teaching classical ballet. 118 illustrations. 175pp. 5⅜ × 8½.
22036-2 Pa. $4.95

THE JUMPING FROG, Mark Twain. Revenge edition. The original story of The Celebrated Jumping Frog of Calaveras County, a hapless French translation, and Twain's hilarious "retranslation" from the French. 12 illustrations. 66pp. 5⅜ × 8½.
22686-7 Pa. $3.50

BEST REMEMBERED POEMS, Martin Gardner (ed.). The 126 poems in this superb collection of 19th- and 20th-century British and American verse range from Shelley's "To a Skylark" to the impassioned "Renascence" of Edna St. Vincent Millay and to Edward Lear's whimsical "The Owl and the Pussycat." 224pp. 5⅜ × 8½.
27165-X Pa. $4.95

COMPLETE SONNETS, William Shakespeare. Over 150 exquisite poems deal with love, friendship, the tyranny of time, beauty's evanescence, death and other themes in language of remarkable power, precision and beauty. Glossary of archaic terms. 80pp. 5³⁄₁₆ × 8¼.
26686-9 Pa. $1.00

BODIES IN A BOOKSHOP, R. T. Campbell. Challenging mystery of blackmail and murder with ingenious plot and superbly drawn characters. In the best tradition of British suspense fiction. 192pp. 5⅜ × 8½.
24720-1 Pa. $5.95

THE WIT AND HUMOR OF OSCAR WILDE, Alvin Redman (ed.). More than 1,000 ripostes, paradoxes, wisecracks: Work is the curse of the drinking classes; I can resist everything except temptation; etc. 258pp. 5⅜ × 8½.   20602-5 Pa. $4.95

SHAKESPEARE LEXICON AND QUOTATION DICTIONARY, Alexander Schmidt. Full definitions, locations, shades of meaning in every word in plays and poems. More than 50,000 exact quotations. 1,485pp. 6½ × 9¼. 2-vol. set.
Vol. 1: 22726-X Pa. $15.95
Vol. 2: 22727-8 Pa. $15.95

SELECTED POEMS, Emily Dickinson. Over 100 best-known, best-loved poems by one of America's foremost poets, reprinted from authoritative early editions. No comparable edition at this price. Index of first lines. 64pp. 5³⁄₁₆ × 8¼.
26466-1 Pa. $1.00

CELEBRATED CASES OF JUDGE DEE (DEE GOONG AN), translated by Robert van Gulik. Authentic 18th-century Chinese detective novel; Dee and associates solve three interlocked cases. Led to van Gulik's own stories with same characters. Extensive introduction. 9 illustrations. 237pp. 5⅜ × 8½.
23337-5 Pa. $5.95

THE MALLEUS MALEFICARUM OF KRAMER AND SPRENGER, translated by Montague Summers. Full text of most important witchhunter's "bible," used by both Catholics and Protestants. 278pp. 6⅝ × 10.   22802-9 Pa. $10.95

SPANISH STORIES/CUENTOS ESPAÑOLES: A Dual-Language Book, Angel Flores (ed.). Unique format offers 13 great stories in Spanish by Cervantes, Borges, others. Faithful English translations on facing pages. 352pp. 5⅜ × 8½.
25399-6 Pa. $8.95

THE CHICAGO WORLD'S FAIR OF 1893: A Photographic Record, Stanley Appelbaum (ed.). 128 rare photos show 200 buildings, Beaux-Arts architecture, Midway, original Ferris Wheel, Edison's kinetoscope, more. Architectural emphasis; full text. 116pp. 8¼ × 11.   23990-X Pa. $9.95

OLD QUEENS, N.Y., IN EARLY PHOTOGRAPHS, Vincent F. Seyfried and William Asadorian. Over 160 rare photographs of Maspeth, Jamaica, Jackson Heights, and other areas. Vintage views of DeWitt Clinton mansion, 1939 World's Fair and more. Captions. 192pp. 8⅞ × 11.   26358-4 Pa. $12.95

CAPTURED BY THE INDIANS: 15 Firsthand Accounts, 1750–1870, Frederick Drimmer. Astounding true historical accounts of grisly torture, bloody conflicts, relentless pursuits, miraculous escapes and more, by people who lived to tell the tale. 384pp. 5⅜ × 8½.   24901-8 Pa. $7.95

THE WORLD'S GREAT SPEECHES, Lewis Copeland and Lawrence W. Lamm (eds.). Vast collection of 278 speeches of Greeks to 1970. Powerful and effective models; unique look at history. 842pp. 5⅜ × 8½.   20468-5 Pa. $13.95

THE BOOK OF THE SWORD, Sir Richard F. Burton. Great Victorian scholar/adventurer's eloquent, erudite history of the "queen of weapons"—from prehistory to early Roman Empire. Evolution and development of early swords, variations (sabre, broadsword, cutlass, scimitar, etc.), much more. 336pp. 6⅛ × 9¼. 25434-8 Pa. $8.95

CATALOG OF DOVER BOOKS

AUTOBIOGRAPHY: The Story of My Experiments with Truth, Mohandas K. Gandhi. Boyhood, legal studies, purification, the growth of the Satyagraha (nonviolent protest) movement. Critical, inspiring work of the man responsible for the freedom of India. 480pp. 5⅜ × 8½. (USO) 24593-4 Pa. $7.95

CELTIC MYTHS AND LEGENDS, T. W. Rolleston. Masterful retelling of Irish and Welsh stories and tales. Cuchulain, King Arthur, Deirdre, the Grail, many more. First paperback edition. 58 full-page illustrations. 512pp. 5⅜ × 8½. 26507-2 Pa. $9.95

THE PRINCIPLES OF PSYCHOLOGY, William James. Famous long course complete, unabridged. Stream of thought, time perception, memory, experimental methods; great work decades ahead of its time. 94 figures. 1,391pp. 5⅜ × 8½. 2-vol. set.
Vol. I: 20381-6 Pa. $12.95
Vol. II: 20382-4 Pa. $12.95

THE WORLD AS WILL AND REPRESENTATION, Arthur Schopenhauer. Definitive English translation of Schopenhauer's life work, correcting more than 1,000 errors, omissions in earlier translations. Translated by E. F. J. Payne. Total of 1,269pp. 5⅜ × 8½. 2-vol. set.
Vol. 1: 21761-2 Pa. $10.95
Vol. 2: 21762-0 Pa. $11.95

MAGIC AND MYSTERY IN TIBET, Madame Alexandra David-Neel. Experiences among lamas, magicians, sages, sorcerers, Bonpa wizards. A true psychic discovery. 32 illustrations. 321pp. 5⅜ × 8½. (USO) 22682-4 Pa. $8.95

THE EGYPTIAN BOOK OF THE DEAD, E. A. Wallis Budge. Complete reproduction of Ani's papyrus, finest ever found. Full hieroglyphic text, interlinear transliteration, word-for-word translation, smooth translation. 533pp. 6½ × 9¼. 21866-X Pa. $9.95

MATHEMATICS FOR THE NONMATHEMATICIAN, Morris Kline. Detailed, college-level treatment of mathematics in cultural and historical context, with numerous exercises. Recommended Reading Lists. Tables. Numerous figures. 641pp. 5⅜ × 8½. 24823-2 Pa. $11.95

THEORY OF WING SECTIONS: Including a Summary of Airfoil Data, Ira H. Abbott and A. E. von Doenhoff. Concise compilation of subsonic aerodynamic characteristics of NACA wing sections, plus description of theory. 350pp. of tables. 693pp. 5⅜ × 8½. 60586-8 Pa. $13.95

THE RIME OF THE ANCIENT MARINER, Gustave Doré, S. T. Coleridge. Doré's finest work; 34 plates capture moods, subtleties of poem. Flawless full-size reproductions printed on facing pages with authoritative text of poem. "Beautiful. Simply beautiful."—*Publisher's Weekly*. 77pp. 9¼ × 12. 22305-1 Pa. $5.95

NORTH AMERICAN INDIAN DESIGNS FOR ARTISTS AND CRAFTSPEOPLE, Eva Wilson. Over 360 authentic copyright-free designs adapted from Navajo blankets, Hopi pottery, Sioux buffalo hides, more. Geometrics, symbolic figures, plant and animal motifs, etc. 128pp. 8⅜ × 11. (EUK) 25341-4 Pa. $7.95

SCULPTURE: Principles and Practice, Louis Slobodkin. Step-by-step approach to clay, plaster, metals, stone; classical and modern. 253 drawings, photos. 255pp. 8⅛ × 11. 22960-2 Pa. $9.95

THE INFLUENCE OF SEA POWER UPON HISTORY, 1660–1783, A. T. Mahan. Influential classic of naval history and tactics still used as text in war colleges. First paperback edition. 4 maps. 24 battle plans. 640pp. 5⅜ × 8½.
25509-3 Pa. $12.95

THE STORY OF THE TITANIC AS TOLD BY ITS SURVIVORS, Jack Winocour (ed.). What it was really like. Panic, despair, shocking inefficiency, and a little heroism. More thrilling than any fictional account. 26 illustrations. 320pp. 5⅜ × 8½. 20610-6 Pa. $7.95

FAIRY AND FOLK TALES OF THE IRISH PEASANTRY, William Butler Yeats (ed.). Treasury of 64 tales from the twilight world of Celtic myth and legend: "The Soul Cages," "The Kildare Pooka," "King O'Toole and his Goose," many more. Introduction and Notes by W. B. Yeats. 352pp. 5⅜ × 8½. 26941-8 Pa. $7.95

BUDDHIST MAHAYANA TEXTS, E. B. Cowell and Others (eds.). Superb, accurate translations of basic documents in Mahayana Buddhism, highly important in history of religions. The Buddha-karita of Asvaghosha, Larger Sukhavativyuha, more. 448pp. 5⅜ × 8½. 25552-2 Pa. $9.95

ONE TWO THREE . . . INFINITY: Facts and Speculations of Science, George Gamow. Great physicist's fascinating, readable overview of contemporary science: number theory, relativity, fourth dimension, entropy, genes, atomic structure, much more. 128 illustrations. Index. 352pp. 5⅜ × 8½. 25664-2 Pa. $8.95

ENGINEERING IN HISTORY, Richard Shelton Kirby, et al. Broad, nontechnical survey of history's major technological advances: birth of Greek science, industrial revolution, electricity and applied science, 20th-century automation, much more. 181 illustrations. ". . . excellent . . ."—Isis. Bibliography. vii + 530pp. 5⅜ × 8¼.
26412-2 Pa. $14.95

Prices subject to change without notice.

Available at your book dealer or write for free catalog to Dept. GI, Dover Publications, Inc., 31 East 2nd St., Mineola, N.Y. 11501. Dover publishes more than 500 books each year on science, elementary and advanced mathematics, biology, music, art, literary history, social sciences and other areas.